Lecture Notes in Computer Science 11598

More information about this series at http://www.springer.com/series/7410

Ian Goldberg · Tyler Moore (Eds.)

Financial Cryptography and Data Security

23rd International Conference, FC 2019
Frigate Bay, St. Kitts and Nevis, February 18–22, 2019
Revised Selected Papers

 Springer

Editors
Ian Goldberg
Cheriton School of Computer Science
University of Waterloo
Waterloo, ON, Canada

Tyler Moore ⓘ
Tandy School of Computer Science
University of Tulsa
Tulsa, USA

ISSN 0302-9743   ISSN 1611-3349   (electronic)
Lecture Notes in Computer Science
ISBN 978-3-030-32100-0   ISBN 978-3-030-32101-7   (eBook)
https://doi.org/10.1007/978-3-030-32101-7

LNCS Sublibrary: SL4 – Security and Cryptology

This Springer imprint is published by the registered company Springer Nature Switzerland AG
The registered company address is: Gewerbestrasse 11, 6330 Cham, Switzerland

Preface

FC 2019, the 23rd International Conference on Financial Cryptography and Data Security, was held February 18–22, 2019, at the St. Kitts Marriott Resort in Frigate Bay, St. Kitts and Nevis.

We received 178 paper submissions. Of these, 32 full papers and seven short papers were accepted, corresponding to a 21.9% acceptance rate. Revised papers appear in these proceedings.

The surge in interest in cryptocurrencies heralded by Bitcoin has been reflected in the composition of the program at FC for several years. Since 2014, a dedicated workshop, the Workshop on Bitcoin and Blockchain Research (BITCOIN), has been held in conjunction with FC. Given the quality and quantity of research appearing in this workshop, the International Financial Cryptography Association (IFCA) Steering Committee, in consultation with current and past program chairs of FC and the BIT-COIN workshop, decided to integrate the BITCOIN workshop into the main FC conference as a new blockchain track.

This decision resulted in a high-quality and balanced program, with 20 papers in the new blockchain track and 19 papers in the non-blockchain track. The two tracks were held on alternating days: The blockchain track was Monday and Wednesday, and the non-blockchain track was Tuesday and Thursday. By not holding the tracks in parallel, all FC attendees could enjoy the entirety of the program. Neha Narula, Director of the MIT Digital Currency Initiative, gave an inspiring keynote entitled "Preventing Catastrophic Cryptocurrency Attacks." Her talk highlighted some pressing and unique challenges of responsibly managing vulnerabilities affecting cryptocurrencies.

Overall, the program successfully realized the goal of creating a unified venue for blockchain papers, while keeping room for other topics that have long been part of FC. Feedback at the conference about the change was overwhelmingly positive. Therefore, we anticipate that this arrangement will continue in future editions of the conference.

We are grateful for the contributions of the 72 members of the Program Committee. Submissions had at least three reviews, or four in the case of a submission by a Program Committee member. An extensive online discussion phase was utilized to guide decisions. The Program Committee members provided thoughtful and constructive feedback to authors, which considerably strengthened the quality of the final papers appearing in this volume. Of the 39 accepted papers, 14 were shepherded by Program Committee members. We are especially thankful to the shepherds for their additional contributions. We also appreciate the reviews contributed by 59 external reviewers.

We would like to thank Rafael Hirschfeld for his unrivaled and continued dedication to FC, including his role serving as conference general chair. We also thank the IFCA directors and Steering Committee for their service.

Finally, we would like to thank the sponsors of the conference for their generous support: Research Institute, Blockstream, Chainanalysis, Kadena, Op Return, Quadrans Foundation, the Journal of Cybersecurity, and Worldpay.

We are excited to present the papers appearing in this volume. They represent some of the leading research in secure digital commerce, and we look forward to many more years of fruitful research presented at Financial Cryptography and Data Security.

July 2019

Ian Goldberg
Tyler Moore

Organization

Financial Cryptography and Data Security 2019
St. Kitts Marriott Resort, St. Kitts and Nevis
February 18–22, 2019

Organized by the
International Financial Cryptography Association

In cooperation with the
International Association for Cryptologic Research

General Chair

Rafael Hirschfeld   Unipay, The Netherlands

Program Committee Chairs

Ian Goldberg   University of Waterloo, Canada
Tyler Moore   The University of Tulsa, USA

Program Committee

Shashank Agrawal	Visa Research, USA
Ross Anderson	Cambridge University, UK
Elli Androulaki	IBM Research - Zurich, Switzerland
Diego F. Aranha	Aarhus University, Denmark/University of Campinas, Brazil
Frederik Armknecht	University of Mannheim, Germany
Foteini Baldimtsi	George Mason University, USA
Iddo Bentov	Cornell Tech, USA
Alex Biryukov	University of Luxembourg, Luxembourg
Jeremiah Blocki	Purdue University, USA
Rainer Böhme	Universität Innsbruck, Austria
Joseph Bonneau	New York University, USA
Alvaro A. Cardenas	University of Texas at Dallas, USA
Pern Hui Chia	Google, Switzerland
Sonia Chiasson	Carleton University, Canada
Nicolas Christin	Carnegie Mellon University, USA
Jeremy Clark	Concordia University, Canada
Gaby Dagher	Boise State University, USA
George Danezis	University College London, UK

Douglas Stebila   University of Waterloo, Canada
Luke Valenta   University of Pennsylvania, USA
Marie Vasek   University of New Mexico, USA
Marko Vukolic   IBM Research - Zurich, Switzerland
Eric Wustrow   University of Colorado Boulder, USA
Zhenfeng Zhang   Institute of Software, Chinese Academy of Sciences, China
Aviv Zohar   The Hebrew University, Israel

Additional Reviewers

Kamalesh Acharya
Sefa Akca
Miguel Ambrona
Dag Arne Osvik
Brian Arthur Shaft
Carsten Baum
Ritam Bhaumik
Chris Buckland
Matteo Campanelli
Panagiotis Chatzigiannis
Mo Chen
Gareth Davies
Angelo De Caro
Sergi Delgado Segura
Pooja Dhomse
Edward Eaton
Kasra EdalatNejad
Kaoutar Elkhiyaoui
Batnyam Enkhtaivan
Shayan Eskandari
Prastudy Fauzi
Daniel Feher
Michael Frwis
Benny Fuhry
Matthias Hamann
Ben Harsha
Haruna Higo
Toshiyuki Isshiki
Hkon Jacobsen
Benjamin Johnson

Keisuke Kajigaya
Dimitris Karakostas
Patrik Keller
Hamidreza Khoshakhlagh
Toomas Krips
Nikos Leonardos
Peiyuan Liu
Angelique Loe
Antonio Marcedone
Mohsen Minaei
Mahsa Moosavi
Pedro Geraldo Morelli Rodrigues Alves
Pratyay Mukherjee
Sanami Nakagawa
Alina Nesen
Bertram Poettering
Mastooreh Salajegheh
Sajin Sasy
Janno Siim
Claudio Soriente
Sergei Tikhomirov
Yiannis Tselekounis
Vesselin Velichkov
Dhinakaran Vinayagamurthy
Giuseppe Vitto
Tianhao Wang
Michal Zajac
Santiago Zanella
Samson Zhou

Contents

Payment Protocol Security

Multiparty Protocols

Fraud Detection and Game Theory

IoT Security, and Crypto Still Means Cryptography

Cryptocurrency Cryptanalysis

Biased Nonce Sense: Lattice Attacks Against Weak ECDSA Signatures in Cryptocurrencies

Joachim Breitner[1] and Nadia Heninger[2]

[1] DFINITY Foundation, Zug, Switzerland
joachim@dfinity.org
[2] University of California, San Diego, USA
nadiah@cs.ucsd.edu

Abstract. In this paper, we compute hundreds of Bitcoin private keys and dozens of Ethereum, Ripple, SSH, and HTTPS private keys by carrying out cryptanalytic attacks against digital signatures contained in public blockchains and Internet-wide scans. The ECDSA signature algorithm requires the generation of a per-message secret nonce. If this nonce is not generated uniformly at random, an attacker can potentially exploit this bias to compute the long-term signing key. We use a lattice-based algorithm for solving the hidden number problem to efficiently compute private ECDSA keys that were used with biased signature nonces due to multiple apparent implementation vulnerabilities.

Keywords: Hidden number problem · ECDSA · Lattices · Bitcoin · Crypto

1 Introduction

The security of the ECDSA signature algorithm relies crucially on the proper generation of a per-signature nonce value that is used as an ephemeral private key. It is well known that if an ECDSA private key is ever used to sign two messages with the same signature nonce, the long-term private key is trivial to compute [7, 8, 11, 13, 18, 37].

Repeated nonce values are not the only type of bias that can render an ECDSA key insecure, however. In fact, *many* types of nonuniformities in the ECDSA signature nonces can reveal the private key, given sufficiently many signatures. In this paper, we carry out lattice-based cryptanalytic attacks against ECDSA signatures collected from the Bitcoin, Ethereum, and Ripple blockchains as well as Internet-wide scans of HTTPS and SSH hosts, and efficiently compute hundreds of Bitcoin private keys and a handful of Ethereum and SSH private keys. As a side effect, we also find numerous Bitcoin, Ethereum, Ripple, SSH, and HTTPS private keys that were compromised through repeated signature nonces.

The lattice attacks we apply are based on algorithms for solving the hidden number problem. [6] While the hidden number problem is a popular tool in

© International Financial Cryptography Association 2019
I. Goldberg and T. Moore (Eds.): FC 2019, LNCS 11598, pp. 3–20, 2019.
https://doi.org/10.1007/978-3-030-32101-7_1

the cryptanalytic literature for recovering private keys based on side channel attacks [5,14], to our knowledge we are the first to apply these techniques to already-generated keys in the wild, and the first to observe that these techniques may apply to signatures in cryptocurrencies. In total, we computed around 300 Bitcoin keys with these techniques. As of this writing, 818,975 satoshis, or around $54, and 30.40 XRP, or about $14, remain in Bitcoin and Ripple accounts whose keys we were able to compute, suggesting that these flaws do not yet appear to be known, or else the funds would have already been stolen.

The attacks we use are significantly faster than naive brute force or the state of the art algorithms for the elliptic curve discrete log problem. Using a square root-time algorithm like Pollard rho [28], one could feasibly carry out a targeted attack against a small number of the 64-bit or 128-bit nonces we discovered; carrying out this attack against *all* of the approximately 2^{30} signatures in the Bitcoin blockchain would have required significantly more computational resources than we have access to. In contrast, we spent around 40 CPU-years total on our computations, implemented in Python, for all of the blockchains.

The nonce vulnerabilities fall into several classes that suggest that we have found several independent implementation vulnerabilities. We first use the hidden number problem algorithm to discover the long-term ECDSA signature key when used with nonces that are shorter than expected, and found keys used with nonces with lengths 64 bits, 110 bits, 128 bits, and 160 bits. We extend this technique to discover nonces with shared prefixes and suffixes, and found keys used with signature nonces that shared prefixes and varied in their 64 least significant bits, as well as keys used with signature nonces that shared suffixes and varied in their 128 and 224 most significant bits.

Ethics. We are unable to validate the existence of these vulnerabilities without actually computing the private keys for vulnerable addresses. In the case of cryptocurrencies, these keys give us, or any other attacker, the ability to claim the funds in the associated accounts. In the case of SSH or HTTPS, these keys would give us, or any other attacker, the ability to impersonate the end hosts. We did not do so, and in the course of our research we did not carry out any cryptocurrency transactions or active attacks ourselves; our research is entirely passive, and requires only observation of transactions or general-purpose network measurements. However, given that we find evidence that other attackers are already emptying the accounts of cryptocurrency users whose keys are revealed through known vulnerabilities (both repeated nonces and private keys posted online), we anticipate that users will be affected once knowledge of this flaw becomes public. We have attempted to disclose flaws to the small number of parties we were able to identify, but in most cases we were unable to identify any particular vendors, maintainers, or users to responsibly disclose to.

Countermeasures. All of the attacks we discuss in this paper can be prevented by using deterministic ECDSA nonce generation [29], which is already implemented in the default Bitcoin and Ethereum libraries.

2 Related Work

The Hidden Number Problem and ECDSA. The Hidden Number Problem and the lattice-based algorithm we used to solve it were formulated by Boneh and Venkatesan, who used it to prove the hardness of computing most significant bits for Diffie-Hellman [6]. Howgrave-Graham and Smart [19] and Nguyen and Shparlinski [26] applied the hidden number problem to show that the DSA and ECDSA signature schemes are insecure if an attacker can learn some most significant bits of the signature nonces. Since then, this technique has been applied in practice in the context of side-channel attacks [5,14].

Repeated DSA/ECDSA Signature Nonces. A number of works have examined vulnerabilities in DSA and ECDSA due to repeated signature nonces in the wild. Heninger, Durumeric, Wustrow, and Halderman [18] compromised SSH host keys for 1% of SSH hosts in 2012 by searching for repeated DSA signature nonces from SSH handshakes. They traced the problems primarily back to implementation vulnerabilities in random number generation on low-resource devices. Bos, Halderman, Heninger, Moore, Naehrig, and Wustrow [7] documented repeated nonces in the Bitcoin blockchain in 2013, as part of a broader study of elliptic curve cryptography use. Valsorda studied repeated Bitcoin nonces in 2014 [37]. Courtois, Emirdag, and Valsorda [13] studied repeated Bitcoin nonces in 2014 and noted that it would be possible to chain compromises across keys. Castellucci and Valsorda studied repeated nonces and variants of weak keys and nonces repeated across keys in Bitcoin in 2016 [11]. Brengel and Rosow examined repeated nonces within signatures from the same key and chained compromised nonces across signatures from different keys in the Bitcoin blockchain in 2018 [8].

Key Generation Issues in Cryptocurrencies. In 2013, a major bug in Android SecureRandom was blamed for the theft of Bitcoin from many users of Android wallets, due to the faulty random number generators generating repeated ECDSA signature nonces [20,22]. In 2015, the Blockchain.info Android application was discovered to be generating duplicate private keys because the application was seeding from random.org, which had started serving a 403 Redirect to their https URL several months prior [35].

Cryptocurrency Cryptanalysis. The Large Bitcoin Collider is a project that is searching for Bitcoin private keys using an apparently linear brute force search algorithm [30] that has searched up to a 54 bit key space. For public keys that are already revealed, it would be more efficient to use square root discrete log algorithms [28,34] to recover short private keys of this type, but we are unaware of any dedicated efforts in this direction.

3 The Elliptic Curve Digital Signature Algorithm (ECDSA)

The public domain parameters for an elliptic curve digital signature include an elliptic curve E over a finite field and a base point G of order n on E. The private signing key is an integer d modulo n, and the public signature verification key is a point $Q = dG$. Elliptic curve public keys can be represented in uncompressed form by providing both the x and y coordinates of the public point Q, or in compressed form by providing the x coordinate only and a single parity bit from the y value [9].

To sign a message hash h, the signer chooses a per-message random integer k modulo n, computes the point kG, and then computes the values $(x_r, y_r) = kG \bmod n$, and outputs $r = x_r$ and $s = k^{-1}(h + dr) \bmod n$. The signature is the pair (r, s). To verify a message hash using a public key Q, the verifier computes $(x'_r, y'_r) = hs^{-1}G + rs^{-1}Q$ and verifies that $x'_r \equiv r \bmod n$. If the bit length ℓ of the curve is shorter than the bit length of the hash function used to compute h, h is truncated to its ℓ most significant bits prior to the calculation [25].

3.1 ECDSA in Cryptocurrencies

Bitcoin [23], Ethereum [10], and Ripple [33] all use the elliptic curve secp256k1 [9]. A Bitcoin address is derived from a public key by repeatedly hashing the uncompressed or compressed ECDSA public key with SHA-256 and RIPEMD-160. An Ethereum address is the last 20 bytes of the Keccak-256 hash of the uncompressed ECDSA public key, where Keccak-256 is an early version of the SHA-3 standard. Ethereum public keys are not explicitly included along with the signature; instead, the signature includes an additional byte v that allows the public key to be derived from the signature. A Ripple address is derived from a compressed public key by repeatedly hashing with SHA-256 and RIPEMD-160, and concatenating portions of the hashes. For the purposes of the analysis in our paper, in all of these cryptocurrencies the ECDSA public key is only revealed after an address has been used to sign a transaction. Bitcoin and Ripple explicitly reveal the ECDSA public key in uncompressed or compressed format along with a signature; in Ethereum, clients must derive the public key from the signature itself using key recovery.

ECDSA signatures are used to authenticate the sending party of a transaction. Addresses can be single signature, corresponding to a single public key, or multisignature addresses, which require valid signatures from k out of a set of n public keys in order to spend money from a transaction. Users are typically recommended to use a fresh new address for every transaction [2].

Signature Normalization. ECDSA signatures have the property that both the signatures (r, s) and $(r, -s)$ will validate with the same public key. In October 2015, Bitcoin introduced a change in the signing procedure to use the smaller of s and $-s \bmod n$ in a signature in order to make signatures unique.[1] Ethereum and Ripple also do this type of signature normalization, which affects our attack.

---

[1] https://github.com/bitcoin-core/secp256k1/commit/0c6ab2ff.

3.2 ECDSA in Network Protocols.

ECDSA signatures can also be used in other network protocols. In TLS, every certificate is signed either by a certificate authority or is self-signed. Most of these signatures remain RSA signatures in practice. However, when ephemeral Diffie-Hellman key exchange is chosen as part of the cipher suite in TLS 1.2 and below, the server signs its portion of the the key exchange, and the client uses the public key in the certificate to validate this signature [16]. In SSH, every host has a host key that it uses to sign the entire handshake between client and server [38]. The client authenticates the server by verifying the signature with the host public key.

3.3 Elementary Attacks on ECDSA

If an attacker learns the per-message nonce k used to generate an ECDSA signature, the long-term secret key d is easy to compute as $d = (sk - h)r^{-1} \bmod n$.

It is also well known that if the same nonce k is used to sign two different messages h_1 and h_2 with the same secret key, then the secret key is revealed. Let (r_1, s_1) be the signature generated on message hash h_1, and (r_2, s_2) be the signature on message hash h_2. We have immediately that $r_1 = r_2$, since $r_1 = r_2 = x(kG)$. Then we can compute $k = (h_1 - h_2)(s_1 - s_2)^{-1} \bmod n$, and recover the secret key as above.

4 Lattice Attacks on ECDSA

The signature nonce k must also be generated uniformly at random modulo n. If only a subset of the possible values module n are produce as nonces, techniques for solving the hidden number problem can be used to solve for the secret key d.

4.1 The Hidden Number Problem

In the hidden number problem as formulated by Boneh and Venkatesan [6], there is a secret integer α modulo a public prime p, and one is given information about the most significant bits of multiples $t_i\alpha \bmod p$, where the t_i are generated at random and known to the attacker. In other words, one is given m pairs of integers $\{(t_i, a_i)\}_{i=1}^m$ such that $t_i\alpha - a_i \bmod p = b_i$ with $|b_i| < B$ for some $B < p$.

One can reformulate this problem as seeking a solution $x_1 = b_1, x_2 = b_2, \dots, x_m = b_m, y = \alpha$ to the underconstrained system of linear equations

$$x_1 - t_1y + a_1 \equiv 0 \bmod p$$

$$\vdots \tag{1}$$

$$x_m - t_my + a_m \equiv 0 \bmod p$$

There are two techniques used to solve this problem in the literature. The first uses lattice-based techniques [6,19,26] to solve this system in the case of

larger biases and fewer samples (up to
around 100 in practice, with B several bits
smaller than p), and the second uses Fourier
analysis [3,15] and is more suitable with
many samples (at least 2^{32}) and very small
bias. In this paper, we focus on the former
technique, which is better suited to the limited number of signatures we encounter in
the wild.

$$M = \begin{bmatrix} p & & & & \\ & p & & & \\ & & \ddots & & \\ & & & p & \\ t_1 & t_2 & \dots & t_m & B/p \\ a_1 & a_2 & \dots & a_m & & B \end{bmatrix} \quad (2)$$

To solve the hidden number problem using lattices, consider the lattice generated by the rows of matrix M in Eq. (2). The $m \times m$ upper left quadrant is
a slightly rescaled version of the lattice given by Boneh and Venkatesan, who
suggest using a CVP algorithm to find a vector that is close to the target, which
is the $(m + 1)$st row in our lattice basis. The most efficient implementations of
lattice algorithms are SVP approximation algorithms, so we follow [5] in embedding this lattice basis into a slightly larger one and using an SVP approximation
algorithm instead.

The vector $v_b = (b_1, b_2, \dots, b_m, B\alpha/p, B)$ is a short vector generated by the
rows of Eq. (2), and by construction $|v_b| < \sqrt{m + 2}B$. When $|v_b| \leq \det L^{1/\dim L}$,
we hope to recover v_b among the short vectors of a reduced basis for the lattice
generated by M. We have $\det M = B^2 p^{m-1}$ and $\dim M = m + 2$. The LLL [21] or
BKZ [31,32] lattice basis reduction algorithms can be used to find short vectors
in this lattice. In practice on random lattices, the LLL algorithm will find a vector
satisfying $|v| \leq 1.02^{\dim L}(\det L)^{1/\dim L}$ in polynomial time [27]. The performance
of BKZ depends on the block size, and will in time exponential in the block size
β find vectors $|v| \leq (1 + \epsilon)_\beta^{\dim L}(\det L)^{1/\dim L}$ where ϵ_β depends on the block
size, but $\epsilon_\beta = 0.01$ is achievable in practice [12].

In this paper, we focus on relatively small dimension lattices, so that the
approximation factor of LLL or BKZ is largely insignificant. In this case, we
expect to solve the problem when $\log B \leq \lfloor \log p(m - 1)/m - (\log m)/2 \rfloor$.

4.2   Optimizations

There are two further optimizations that should be applied to this attack. The
first is that in the case of most significant bits known, the value b_i is always
positive, and thus one can increase the bias by recentering the b_i by writing each
equation as $x_i' - t_i y + a_m + B \equiv 0 \bmod p$ which has a solution $x_i' = b_i - B$.
The second improvement is to decrease the dimension of the lattice by one by
eliminating the variable y from Eq. (1) so that one has $m - 1$ equations in m
unknowns, all bounded.

4.3   Implicit Prefixes

We are also interested in the case where the b_i share an identical prefix, or in
other words, that they share most significant bits when viewed as an integer
between 0 and p, but we do not know this prefix. That is, the input to the

problem is samples $\{t_i, a_i\}_{i=1}^m$ satisfying $b_i + c + a_i \equiv t_i\alpha \bmod p$, with $|b_i| < B$ and $0 \leq c < p$ is unknown. We can reduce this problem to the previous problem with $m - 1$ samples by using one of the samples to eliminate the unknown c. That is, we solve the hidden number problem with input $\{t_i' = t_i - t_m\}_{i=1}^{m-1}$, $a_i' = a_i - a_m$, and the desired solutions $b_i' = b_i - b_m$ satisfy $|b_i'| \leq 2B$.

4.4 Implicit Suffixes

The technique described in Sect. 4.3 can also be adapted to solve for b_i that share an identical suffix, that is, that they share least significant bits when viewed as an integer between 0 and p. More precisely, the input to our problem in this case is samples $\{t_i, a_i\}_{i=1}^m$ satisfying $2^\ell b_i + c + a_i \equiv t_i\alpha \bmod p$, with $0 \leq b_i < B$, $0 \leq c < p$ unknown, and $2^\ell B \leq p$. We can reduce this problem to the case of shared prefixes by multiplying each sample by $2^{-\ell} \bmod n$, so that our rescaled input is samples $\{2^{-\ell}t_i, 2^{-\ell}a_i\}_{i=1}^m$ satisfying $b_i + 2^{-\ell}c + 2^{-\ell}a_i \equiv (2^{-\ell}t_i)\alpha \bmod p$, where $|b_i| < B$ and $2^{-\ell}c$ is still unknown. At this point this is precisely the case of shared prefixes, so we may use the hidden number problem algorithm to solve the case of $m - 1$ samples generated as $\{t_i' = 2^{-\ell}(t_i - t_m) \bmod n\}_{i=1}^{m-1}$, $a_i' = 2^{-\ell}(a_i - a_m) \bmod n$, and the desired solutions $b_i' = b_i - b_m$ satisfy $|b_i'| \leq 2B$.

4.5 Breaking ECDSA with the Hidden Number Problem

To attack ECDSA with biased k values using the hidden number problem [19,26], note that each signature (r_i, s_i) on h_i satisfies

$$k_i - s_i^{-1}r_id - s_i^{-1}h_i \equiv 0 \bmod n \tag{3}$$

If the k_i are all small ($|k_i| < B$) or share a common prefix or suffix, then this is precisely our setting for the hidden number problem variants we describe above, with $k_i = b_i$, $\alpha = d$, $p = n$, and s_i, r_i, and h_i public per signature.

We construct the input to our problem by hypothesizing that a set of signatures contains one of the vulnerabilities necessary to carry out the attacks described in Sects. 4.1, 4.3, or 4.4, construct the corresponding lattice, and apply a lattice basis reduction algorithm. For each candidate solution for k_i, we compute the value $d_{k_i} = (s_ik_i - h_i)r_i^{-1} \bmod n$, and compare $d_{k_i}G$ to the public key or address.

Experimentally, we found that for a 256-bit n, our case of interest for secp256k1, we were able to recover the private key from two signatures with 128-bit nonces by reducing a 3-dimensional lattice with 75% probability, from three signatures with 170-bit nonces with a 4-dimensional lattice with 95% probability, from 4 samples with 190-bit nonces with 100% probability; from 20 samples with 242-bit nonces by reducing a 21-dimensional lattice with 100% probability, and from 40 samples with 248-bit nonces and 41-dimensional lattices.

One can keep continuing by increasing the dimension of the lattice, to a practical limit of a bias of three or four bits for this 256-bit curve order, at the cost of solving near-exact SVP, which runs in time exponential in the lattice dimension, in a high-dimensional lattice.

Unfortunately for the attacker applying these attacks to cryptocurrency signatures, the signature normalization described in Sect. 3.1 adds complexity. We expect half of the signatures to contain a negated s value, but we will not be able to tell which. From Eq. (3), negating s will negate the derived value of k_i. Thus an attack on *small* k_i would still be expected to succeed, since the lattice algorithm can recover both small positive or small negative values, but the normalizations required to solve for the case of shared prefixes in Sect. 4.3 or shared suffixes in Sect. 4.4 would produce outputs that do not have the desired properties. For these cases, we brute forced signs for the s_i.

The signature normalization also means that the relations defining ECDSA private key recovery from known or repeated nonces as described in Sect. 3.3 may not hold as described. For these cases we also brute forced sign values for s.

5 Bitcoin

5.1 Collecting Data

To collect Bitcoin signatures we modified the official client to output hash values and signatures as they are verified, and re-validated the entire blockchain.

We used a snapshot of the blockchain from September 13, 2018 (block height 541,244). At this point, the blockchain contained 975,560,082 signatures from 446,605,479 distinct keys. 40,497,752 of these keys had been used to generate more than one signature. 569,396,463, or 58% of the signatures in our snapshot had been generated by one of these keys.

5.2 Cryptanalytic Tests for Biased Nonces

We clustered signatures by public key and eliminated signatures that were fully identical, that is, that shared both the hash h and the signature (r, s). For keys associated with $m > 1$ distinct signatures, we ran the following randomized tests on subsamples of the signatures:

- Check if the set of distinct signatures generated by this key contains any duplicate r values. If so, we compute the private key and all signature nonces k using Sect. 3.3 and do not run any of the following.
- Select two signatures at random and check for nonces of length less than 128 bits. We repeated this test $2m$ times for each key.
- Select three signatures at random and check for nonces of length less than 170 bits. We repeated this test $2m$ times for each key.
- Select three signatures at random and check for nonces sharing 128 most significant bits, brute forcing signature normalizations. We repeated this test $2m$ times for each key.
- Select three signatures at random and check for nonces sharing 128 least significant bits, brute forcing signature normalizations. We repeated this test $2m$ times for each key.

– For $m \leq 40$, check for nonces of length less than $\lfloor 256(m-1)/m \rfloor - 1$ bits, using all m signatures without signature normalization.

– For $m > 40$, choose a random subset of 41 signatures and check for nonces of length less than 248 bits. We repeated this test $m/20$ times for each key, without signature normalization.

The parameters were chosen so that these tests would complete in a reasonable length of time even for the most common keys.

5.3 Running the Cryptanalysis

We implemented these tests in Sage [36], using the built-in BKZ implementation for lattice basis reduction. We ran the computation parallelized across 2000 cores of a heterogeneous cluster with mostly Intel Xeon E5 processors. We ended up running the computation twice, once without signature normalization on a snapshot of the blockchain from March 2018 and once with normalization in September 2018. For the low-dimensional lattice attacks, the bottleneck of the computation was the elliptic curve multiplications required to check whether we had found the correct private key. The total running time for both jobs was 38 CPU years, and the longest-running job (corresponding to a single key that had generated 1,021,572 signatures in March 2018) completed in 30 calendar days.

5.4 Results and Analysis

Biased Nonces. After running our attacks, we had computed the private keys for 302 distinct keys that were compromised via small nonces, nonces with shared prefixes, or nonces with shared suffixes. These keys had generated 6,026 signatures with these vulnerable nonces in the blockchain, and 7,328 signatures overall, including signatures that we did not classify as using vulnerable nonces.

For further analysis, we used the BlockSci library [4]. We classified keys by the signature nonce vulnerability that had compromised them and summarize the data in Table 1. Nearly all of the compromised keys had been used as part of multisignature addresses of type 1-out-of-1, 1-out-of-2, 1-out-of-3, 2-out-of-2, 2-out-of-3, 2-out-of-5, or 3-out-of-5.

On September 23, 2018, a total of 745,990 satoshis were in non-multisignature addresses whose keys were compromised by these biased nonces. An additional 72,985 satoshis were in a multisignature address where we possessed all of the necessary keys for the account. A further 6,480,000 satoshis were present in addresses for which we possessed one out of two necessary signatures.

We plot the signatures from biased nonces over time in Fig. 1. Nearly all of the compromised nonces fell into a few clear classes based on the length of the variable portion of the nonce. We found short nonces of length 160 bits, 128 bits, 110 bits, 64 bits, and a few sporadic nonces below 32 bits. We also found nonces that shared a fixed prefix followed by a variable 64-bit suffix, and nonces that varied in the 128 most significant bits and shared a fixed 128-bit suffix. Most of the affected keys were part of multisignature addresses.

Table 1. Biased signatures and keys. We classified the compromised keys and signatures by the type of nonce vulnerability that had compromised the private key. Nearly all of the compromised keys had been used as part of multisignature addresses.

Nonce type	Signatures	Distinct keys	Multisignature keys
Prefix + 64 bits	27	2	0
128 bits + Suffix	121	13	4
160 bits	3	1	0
128 bits	4	2	2
110 bits	2	1	0
64 bits	5,863	280	279
≤ 32 bits	6	3	0

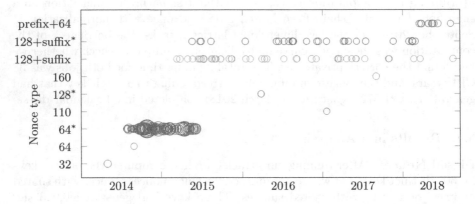

Fig. 1. Bitcoin signatures with small and biased nonces over time. We plot signatures with biased nonces over time, grouped by the class of bias we observed, and whether they are used with multisignature addresses (marked with *). Larger circles correspond to more signatures on a given date. We note that the different types of biases appear at different date ranges, suggesting that these vulnerabilities are specific to distinct implementations.

64-bit Nonces. We found 5,863 signatures from 280 distinct keys that used 64-bit nonces. All but one of these keys was used as part of multisignature addresses. All of these signatures appeared between July 26, 2014 and June 1, 2015.

Two accounts related to these keys have a non-zero balance: One 2-out-of-2 address, for which we have one private key, has a single satoshi. One 2-out-of-3 address, for which we have two private keys, has a balance of 72,985 satoshis.

After we posted a preprint of this paper online, Gregory Maxwell in personal communication identified the likely culprit: On July 12th, the bitcore library, a general purpose JavaScript bitcoin library provided by BitPay, was updated to use a different elliptic curve library. The changes introduced in this update included setting the length of the random nonces to eight bytes.[2] This matches the July 2014 appearance of the vulnerable 64-bit nonces we identified.

The bug was fixed on August 11, 2014.[3] Yet we observed these nonces for almost a full year; this indicates that not all products that build on top of bitcore upgrade their dependencies in a timely manner.

64-bit Nonces and Single-Signature Keys. Our lattice attack only applies when at least *two* signatures with a small nonce are created using the same secret key. A single 64-bit nonce requires only 2^{32} time to break using Shanks's baby-step-giant-step algorithm [34] or the Pollard rho algorithm [28], feasible with only modest computation resources. However, applying this attack to *all* of the 2^{30} Bitcoin signatures was beyond our resources, so we searched a random sample.

We precomputed a set of 2^{39} small powers, storing the low 64 bits of the x coordinate, and also computed a lookup table mapping 2^{32} small powers to their exponent. The bottleneck is the random accesses into the precomputed lookup tables, so we chose the parameters so that they fit into the RAM of our largest-memory machine (2.2TB). One signature takes approximately five minutes on one core to search.[4]

We spent 4 calendar days of computation time, or 4,000 core-hours, to check a random sample of 50,000 Bitcoin multisig signatures from the relevant period in 2014–2015. We found 169 small nonces this way, revealing 116 private keys. Of these, 108 were already compromised using the lattice attacks.

110-, 128-, and 160-bit Nonces. We found a few sporadic signatures that used larger nonce lengths that were broken by our lattice techniques. These may be individual programming errors, but do not appear to be part of common implementations. None of the affected accounts had a non-zero balance.

- Three 160-bit nonces, all of which were used with the same key, all on the same date in September 2017. This key did not produce any more signatures in our data. We hypothesized that a 160-bit nonce length might be explained by a user generating a nonce using a hash function with 160-bit output, as in deterministic ECDSA, but were unable to verify this.
- Four 128-bit nonces from two keys. Each key generated two signatures with 128-bit nonces on the same two days in March 2016, and no further signatures.
- One signed 110-bit nonce, used with one key in January 2017, which had also generated a normal-looking 256-bit nonce on the same day.

256-bit Nonces with Shared 128-bit Suffixes. 121 signatures were compromised by nonces that shared a 128-bit suffix with at least one other signature. 55 of these signatures were used with multisignature addresses and 66 were generated by non-multisignature addresses. 13 keys were compromised this way, which had generated a total of 224 signatures. There were 20 distinct suffixes that had

---

[2] https://github.com/bitpay/bitcore/pull/409/commits/ac4d318.
[3] https://github.com/bitpay/bitcore/commit/9f9e2f1d.
[4] The code can be found at: https://github.com/nomeata/secp265k1-lookup-table.

been used by these keys. The earliest signature of this type that we found was from March 2015, and the most recent was from August 2018. Some of the keys were used with nonces that all shared the same suffix, and some were used with nonces of varying and occasionally unique suffixes.

We found that a number of the addresses associated with these compromised signatures had been posted on the web along with their private keys for a variety of reasons: they corresponded to small integer private keys, private keys derived from easy-to-guess passwords such as "satoshi", or private keys used as examples in documentation. All of the affected accounts had a zero balance.

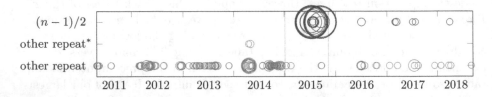

Fig. 2. Bitcoin signatures with repeated nonces over time. We plot repeated signature nonces over time, separating the value $(n-1)/2$, which seems to have been used intentionally, from other repeated nonces. Larger circles correspond to more signatures on a given date. Signatures involving multisignature addresses are marked with *. The vertical bars mark when the development (left) and release (right) versions of the official bitcoin client began to create nonces deterministically [29].

Interestingly, in 54 of the signatures, the 128-bit nonce suffix is identical to the 128 most significant bits of the private key. The vulnerable transactions emptied the relevant accounts. We hypothesize that the vulnerable nonce suffixes we observe may actually be due to a custom implementation used by an *attacker* who is emptying accounts from Bitcoin addresses that were already compromised online. The overlapping bits between the nonce and the private key might be an artifact from a bug in a program written in a memory-unsafe language like C.

256-bit Nonces with Shared 192-bit Prefixes. We computed 2 keys that had been used with 27 signatures with nonces sharing prefixes. Each key had some signatures with the shared prefix and some without. One of the two keys has a balance of 495,990 satoshis, and seems to be in current use at the time of writing.

Repeated Nonces. As a side effect of our analysis, we also calculated 1,296 private keys from repeated signature nonces. These keys had generated 4,295,141 signatures. Nearly all of the repeated nonces, in 2,456,870 signatures, used `0x7fffffffffffffffffffffffffffffff5d576e7357a4501ddfe92f46681b20a0`. As noted by [8], this is $(n-1)/2$ where n is the order of the `secp256k1` curve. The x-coordinate of $G \cdot (n-1)/2$ is 166 bits long, where one would expect a random point to have 256 bits. It appears to not be known why `secp256k1` has this property; Gregory Maxwell [1] notes that `secp224k1` shares the same 166-bit string doubled to produce the generator, and speculates that this value is the output of SHA-1. According to [1], this value is used to sweep "dust" transactions.

We note that even for a "final" transaction for a given key, an attacker could observe a proposed transaction, derive the secret key, and race the original transaction. This is not a concern if the key has already been compromised, however. Some of the transactions using $k = (n - 1)/2$ are withdrawing money from addresses derived from easily guessable brainwallet passwords.

Table 2 summarizes the distribution of compromised keys and signatures. There were no funds left in any of the addresses with repeated nonces at the time that we examined the results. Since this failure mode of ECDSA is well known, it appears that multiple entities regularly scan the blockchain for repeated nonces and remove any funds from vulnerable keys. However, there were two multisignature addresses with nonzero account balances for which repeated nonces revealed one of the necessary addresses:

- The website https://www.darkwallet.is/ asks for donations to be sent to a 3-out-of-5 multisignature address, which currently holds a balance of 1,722,498,619 satoshis (approx. 110 kUSD). One of the five keys was compromised by a repeated signature nonce. We contacted Amir Taaki, one of the founders, who told us that signatures from these addresses had been calculated manually, suggesting that the random number generator may not have been seeded.
- One 2-out-of-3 address had a balance of 179,400 satoshis.

In Fig. 2, we plot non-unique signature nonces over time. Clusters of repeated nonces in 2013 appear to correspond to one of the reported RNG vulnerabilities discussed in Sect. 2. The rate of repeats decreases after 2014.

Other Small Nonces. We brute forced all 32-bit nonce values, and found 275 signatures from 52 keys. The small number and the observed nonces (1, 2, 9, 100, 1337, 13337, 133337, 1333337, 12345678, and 2147491839) do not point to a flawed implementation, but rather hand-crafted transactions and signatures.

6   Ethereum

Collecting Data. We collected Ethereum signatures by querying a local Ethereum node via its RPC interface. We ran our analysis on a snapshot of the blockchain from September 17, 2018 (block 6,346,730). It contained 311,118,952 signatures from 34,754,686 distinct public keys. 19,558,608 (57%) keys had generated more than one signature, resulting in 295,922,874 (95%) signatures from such keys.

Running the Cryptanalysis. We clustered signatures by public key, and examined the keys that had generated more than one signature. We ran the same tests as for Bitcoin, and as with Bitcoin, we ran the computation twice, once with signature normalization on our September 2018 blockchain snapshot and once without on a snapshot from July 2018. The total computation took 9.5 CPU years, and the longest-running job (corresponding to a single key that had generated 1,321,734 signatures in July 2018) completed in 25 calendar days.

Table 2. Repeated signature nonces. Nearly all of the repeated signature nonces on the Bitcoin blockchain have the value $(n-1)/2$. These represented the majority of keys compromised through repeated nonces.

Nonce	Total signatures	Repeated nonce signatures	Distinct keys
$(n-1)/2$	4,275,639	2,456,870	918
Others	19,052	2,214	378

Results and Analysis

256-bit Nonce with 192-bit Prefix. One key was compromised via biased nonces. It had generated seven signatures in our dataset, of which five nonces shared the same nonzero, random-looking 192-bit prefix and differed only in the last 64 bits of the nonce. The remaining two signatures that had been generated by this key look random, and do not share this prefix. The key holds 0.00002 Ether.

Repeated Nonces. Three keys were compromised from repeated nonces, with 185 signatures between them. The repeated nonces include four occurrences of the nonce 1, two occurrences of a seemingly random 256-bit nonce, and `123456789abcdef`. No funds are held by these keys.

7   Ripple

Collecting Data. We downloaded a portion of the Ripple blockchain that included 218,101,343 signatures. There were 571,482 unique public keys, of which 379.575 had generated more than one signature, totaling 217,909,436 signatures (99%) that were generated by a key that had been used more than once.

Running the Cryptanalysis. We clustered signatures by public key, and examined the keys that had generated more than one signature. We ran the same tests as for Bitcoin. The total computation time took 1.1 CPU years, and the longest single computation took 5 calendar days for a single key that had generated 361,366 signatures.

Results and Analysis. We found one private key that had been compromised by a repeated signature nonce. This key had generated 21 signatures. It holds 30.40 XRP (approx. 14 USD) and 1.81 CNY. We deduce that attackers have not yet begun to systematically observe the Ripple blockchain for repeated nonces.

8 SSH

Collecting Data. We gathered DSA and ECDSA signatures from Internet-wide scans of SSH on port 22 that were performed by Censys [17] between April 3, 2018 and September 18, 2018. The scans contained between 7.9 million and 9.4 million DSA and ECDSA signatures each, for a total of 196,884,009 signatures from 20,103,764 distinct public keys. These included 191,855,472 NIST P-256 signatures, 2,634,869 DSA signatures, 2,095,181 NIST P-521 signatures, 164,919 NIST P-384 signatures, and 133,568 ed25519 signatures.

Running the Cryptanalysis. The SSH dataset included a wide variety of different DSA groups. We ran the tests described in Sect. 5.2, scaled to the relevant group size. The total computation time was 2.8 CPU-years, and the longest computation took 8 days to process the most common key, which had been used for 1,450,916 signatures from our scans.

Results and Analysis

256-bit Keys with 32-bit Shared Suffixes. Three private keys produced signatures whose nonces all shared the suffix f27871c6. The hosts have gone offline since, and we were unable to identify the implementation. This suffix is one of the "constant words" used in the calculation of a SHA-2 hash [24], with swapped byte order. We can speculate that the server is using SHA-2 to generate the nonce, but has a bug in the implementation.

224-bit Keys with 160-bit Nonces. One further key was compromised due to the use of small nonces. All 23 signatures by this key used a 160 bit nonce with a 2048-bit DSA public key with a 224-bit subgroup, and were observed at the same IP address. We speculate that this may be due to the use of a 160-bit hash function like SHA-1 or MD5 being used to generate the nonce in a 224-bit group.

Repeated Nonces. 681 signatures were compromised by repeated nonces. Of these, 612 used DSA, and 69 used ECDSA with NIST P-256. These came from 34 distinct public keys on 80 distinct IP addresses.

We compared this number to repeated nonces found in a March 25, 2012 scan of SSH that requested only DSA host keys provided by the authors of [18]. In the 2012 scan, 22,182 nonces had been used more than once, and 58 distinct keys were vulnerable on 24,893 distinct IP addresses. We conclude that many of these vulnerable implementations have been taken offline or patched since then.

9 HTTPS

Collecting Data. We gathered ECDSA signatures from weekly Internet-wide scans of HTTPS on port 443 performed by Censys [17] between April 3, 2018 and September 6, 2018. The number of ECDSA signatures per scan increased from 1.5 million to 1.9 million, resulting in 50,313,795 total ECDSA signatures from 182,843 distinct keys on 3,333,482 distinct IP address. 50,096,848 signatures were from NIST P-256, 212,523 were from NIST P-384, 4,400 were from NIST P-521, and 24 were from NIST P-224.

Running the Cryptanalysis. We ran the same sequence of tests as described in Sect. 5.2, scaling the number of bits to the curve order. The total computation time was 152 CPU-days, and the longest computation took 17 days to process a single key that had produced 4,093,917 signatures from our scan.

Results and Analysis. We did not find any small or biased signature nonces. We found three different sources of signatures with repeated nonces, which we hypothesize are due to flawed random number generators. These resulted in 462 vulnerable signatures that had been generated by 7 distinct private keys on 97 distinct IP addresses.

Acknowledgements. We thank Luke Valenta and Zakir Durumeric for help in updating ZGrab and Censys to collect HTTPS and SSH signature hashes, Tanja Lange for the reference on the surprisingly small binary representation of $k = 1/2$ in secp256k1, and Greg Maxwell and Dan Brown for insightful comments on the preprint. Much of the work for this paper was done while the authors were at the University of Pennsylvania. This work was supported by the National Science Foundation under grants no. CNS-1651344 and CNS-1513671. We are grateful to Cisco for donating much of the computing cluster used to carry out our computations.

References

1. The most repeated r value on the blockchain (2015). https://bitcointalk.org/index.php?topic=1118704.0
2. Bitcoin wiki: Address reuse (2018). https://en.bitcoin.it/wiki/Address_reuse
3. Akavia, A.: Solving hidden number problem with one bit oracle and advice. In: Halevi, S. (ed.) CRYPTO 2009. LNCS, vol. 5677, pp. 337–354. Springer, Heidelberg (2009). https://doi.org/10.1007/978-3-642-03356-8_20
4. Bartoletti, M., Lande, S., Pompianu, L., Bracciali, A.: A general framework for blockchain analytics. In: Proceedings of the 1st Workshop on Scalable and Resilient Infrastructures for Distributed Ledgers, SERIAL 2017, pp. 7:1–7:6. ACM, New York (2017). https://doi.org/10.1145/3152824.3152831. http://doi.acm.org/10.1145/3152824.3152831
5. Benger, N., van de Pol, J., Smart, N.P., Yarom, Y.: "Ooh aah... just a little bit": a small amount of side channel can go a long way. In: Batina, L., Robshaw, M. (eds.) CHES 2014. LNCS, vol. 8731, pp. 75–92. Springer, Heidelberg (2014). https://doi.org/10.1007/978-3-662-44709-3_5
6. Boneh, D., Venkatesan, R.: Hardness of computing the most significant bits of secret keys in Diffie-Hellman and related schemes. In: Koblitz, N. (ed.) CRYPTO 1996. LNCS, vol. 1109, pp. 129–142. Springer, Heidelberg (1996). https://doi.org/10.1007/3-540-68697-5_11

7. Bos, J.W., Halderman, J.A., Heninger, N., Moore, J., Naehrig, M., Wustrow, E.: Elliptic curve cryptography in practice. In: Christin, N., Safavi-Naini, R. (eds.) FC 2014. LNCS, vol. 8437, pp. 157–175. Springer, Heidelberg (2014). https://doi.org/10.1007/978-3-662-45472-5_11

8. Brengel, M., Rossow, C.: Identifying key leakage of bitcoin users. In: Bailey, M., Holz, T., Stamatogiannakis, M., Ioannidis, S. (eds.) RAID 2018. LNCS, vol. 11050, pp. 623–643. Springer, Cham (2018). https://doi.org/10.1007/978-3-030-00470-5_29

9. Brown, D.R.L.: SEC 2: Recommended elliptic curve domain parameters (2010). http://www.secg.org/sec2-v2.pdf

10. Buterin, V.: Ethereum: a next-generation smart contract and decentralized application platform (2013). https://github.com/ethereum/wiki/wiki/White-Paper

11. Castellucci, R., Valsorda, F.: Stealing bitcoin with math (2016). https://news.webamooz.com/wp-content/uploads/bot/offsecmag/151.pdf

12. Chen, Y., Nguyen, P.Q.: BKZ 2.0: better lattice security estimates. In: Lee, D.H., Wang, X. (eds.) ASIACRYPT 2011. LNCS, vol. 7073, pp. 1–20. Springer, Heidelberg (2011). https://doi.org/10.1007/978-3-642-25385-0_1

13. Courtois, N.T., Emirdag, P., Valsorda, F.: Private key recovery combination attacks: on extreme fragility of popular bitcoin key management, wallet and cold storage solutions in presence of poor RNG events. Cryptology ePrint Archive, Report 2014/848 (2014). https://eprint.iacr.org/2014/848

14. Dall, F., et al.: Cachequote: efficiently recovering long-term secrets of SGX EPID via cache attacks. IACR Trans. Cryptogr. Hardware Embed. Syst. 2018(2), 171–191 (2018). https://doi.org/10.13154/tches.v2018.i2.171-191. https://tches.iacr.org/index.php/TCHES/article/view/879

15. De Mulder, E., Hutter, M., Marson, M.E., Pearson, P.: Using bleichenbacher's solution to the hidden number problem to attack nonce leaks in 384-bit ECDSA. In: Bertoni, G., Coron, J.-S. (eds.) CHES 2013. LNCS, vol. 8086, pp. 435–452. Springer, Heidelberg (2013). https://doi.org/10.1007/978-3-642-40349-1_25

16. Dierks, T., Rescorla, E.: The Transport Layer Security (TLS) protocol. IETF RFC RFC5246 (2008)

17. Durumeric, Z., Adrian, D., Mirian, A., Bailey, M., Halderman, J.A.: A search engine backed by internet-wide scanning. In: 22nd ACM Conference on Computer and Communications Security, October 2015

18. Heninger, N., Durumeric, Z., Wustrow, E., Halderman, J.A.: Mining your Ps and Qs: detection of widespread weak keys in network devices. In: Proceedings of the 21st USENIX Security Symposium, August 2012

19. Howgrave-Graham, N.A., Smart, N.P.: Lattice attacks on digital signatureschemes. Des. Codes Crypt. 23(3), 283–290 (2001). https://doi.org/10.1023/A:1011214926272

20. Klyubin, A.: Some SecureRandom thoughts, August 2013. https://android-developers.googleblog.com/2013/08/some-securerandom-thoughts.html

21. Lenstra, A.K., Lenstra, H.W., Lovasz, L.: Factoring polynomials with rational coefficients. Math. Ann. 261, 515–534 (1982)

22. Michaelis, K., Meyer, C., Schwenk, J.: Randomly failed! The state of randomness in current Java implementations In: Dawson, E. (ed.) CT-RSA 2013. LNCS, vol. 7779, pp. 129–144. Springer, Heidelberg (2013). https://doi.org/10.1007/978-3-642-36095-4_9

23. Nakamoto, S.: Bitcoin: A peer-to-peer electronic cash system (2009). http://bitcoin.org/bitcoin.pdf

24. National Institute of Standards and Technology: FIPS PUB 180-2: Secure Hash Standard, August 2002
25. National Institute of Standards and Technology: FIPS PUB 186-4: Digital Signature Standard (DSS), July 2013
26. Nguyen, P.Q., Shparlinski, I.E.: The insecurity of the elliptic curve digital signature algorithm with partially known nonces. Des. Codes Crypt. **30**(2), 201–217 (2003). https://doi.org/10.1023/A:1025436905711
27. Nguyen, P.Q., Stehlé, D.: LLL on the average. In: Hess, F., Pauli, S., Pohst, M. (eds.) ANTS 2006. LNCS, vol. 4076, pp. 238–256. Springer, Heidelberg (2006). https://doi.org/10.1007/11792086_18
28. Pollard, J.M.: Monte Carlo methods for index computation (mod p). In: Mathematics of Computation, vol. 32 (1978)
29. Pornin, T.: Deterministic usage of the digital signature algorithm (DSA) and elliptic curve digital signature algorithm (ECDSA) (2013). https://tools.ietf.org/html/rfc6979
30. rico666: Large bitcoin collider. https://lbc.cryptoguru.org/
31. Schnorr, C.P.: A hierarchy of polynomial time lattice basis reductionalgorithms. Theor. Comput. Sci. **53**(2–3), 201–224 (1987). https://doi.org/10.1016/0304-3975(87)90064-8
32. Schnorr, C.P., Euchner, M.: Lattice basis reduction: improved practical algorithms and solving subset sum problems. Math. Program. **66**(2), 181–199 (1994). https://doi.org/10.1007/BF01581144
33. Schwartz, D., Youngs, N., Britto, A.: The Ripple protocol consensus algorithm (2014). https://ripple.com/files/ripple_consensus_whitepaper.pdf. Accessed 08 Aug 2016
34. Shanks, D.: Class number, a theory of factorization, and genera. In: Proceedings of Symposia in Pure Mathematics, vol. 20, pp. 41–440 (1971)
35. Blockchain Team: Android wallet security update. https://blog.blockchain.com/2015/05/28/android-wallet-security-update/
36. The Sage Developers: SageMath, the Sage Mathematics Software System (Version 8.1) (2017). http://www.sagemath.org
37. Valsorda, F.: Exploiting ECDSA failures in the bitcoin blockchain. Hack In The Box (HITB) (2014)
38. Ylonen, T., Lonvick, C.: The Secure Shell (SSH) transport layer protocol.IETF RFC 4253 (2006)

Proofs of Stake

Snow White: Robustly Reconfigurable Consensus and Applications to Provably Secure Proof of Stake

Phil Daian, Rafael Pass, and Elaine Shi[(✉)]

Cornell/CornellTech, New York, USA
elaine@cs.cornell.edu

Abstract. We present the a provably secure proof-of-stake protocol called Snow White. The primary application of Snow White is to be used as a "green" consensus alternative for a decentralized cryptocurrency system with open enrollment. We break down the task of designing Snow White into the following core challenges:

1. identify a core "permissioned" consensus protocol suitable for proof-of-stake; specifically the core consensus protocol should offer robustness in an Internet-scale, heterogeneous deployment;
2. propose a robust committee re-election mechanism such that as stake switches hands in the cryptocurrency system, the consensus committee can evolve in a timely manner and always reflect the most recent stake distribution; and
3. relying on the formal security of the underlying consensus protocol, prove the full end-to-end protocol to be secure—more specifically, we show that any consensus protocol satisfying the desired robustness properties can be used to construct proofs-of-stake consensus, *as long as money does not switch hands too quickly.*

Snow White was publicly released in September 2016. It provides the first formal, end-to-end proof of a proof-of-stake system in a truly decentralized, open-participation network, where nodes can join at any time (not necessarily at the creation of the system). We also give the first formal treatment of a well-known issue called "costless simulation" in our paper, proving both upper- and lower-bounds that characterize exactly what setup assumptions are needed to defend against costless simulation attacks. We refer the reader to our detailed chronological notes on a detailed comparison of Snow White and other prior and concurrent works, as well as how subsequent works (including Ethereum's proof-of-stake design) have since extended and improved our ideas.

1 Introduction

Although consensus protocols have been investigated by the distributed systems community for 30 years, in the past decade a new breakthrough called Bitcoin established a new, blockchain-based paradigm for reaching consensus in a distributed system. Relying on proof-of-work, Bitcoin's consensus protocol

ⓒ International Financial Cryptography Association 2019
I. Goldberg and T. Moore (Eds.): FC 2019, LNCS 11598, pp. 23–41, 2019.
https://doi.org/10.1007/978-3-030-32101-7_2

(often called Nakamoto consensus), for the first time, enabled consensus in an open, unauthenticated environment where nodes do not share any pre-established public keys [11,17,18,22]. One commonly known painpoint with this approach is the enormous energy waste. Motivated by the need for a green alternative, the community searched for a paradigm shift, and hoped to obtain a consensus paradigm, commonly called "proof-of-stake", that is based on the idea of "one vote per unit of stake" (as opposed to "one vote per unit of hash-power").

The design of proof-of-stake protocols was first initiated in online forums and blog-posts and subsequently considered by the academic community [2,3,7,14–16,24–26]. Prior to our work, we were not aware of any candidate protocol that offered provable guarantees.

Snow White is the first work to provide end-to-end, formal proofs of security of a full proof-of-stake protocol. Security is proven in a truly decentralized, open-participation environment where honest nodes can join the protocol late in time (and not necessarily at the system's creation). We give the first formal treatment of the well-known "costless simulation" problem (also called posterior corruption in this paper) pertaining to proof-of-stake, proving upper- and lower-bounds that precisely characterize under what assumptions it is possible to defend against costless simulation.

In the remainder of the introduction, we first present an informal technical overview of our results. We then provide detailed chronological notes that position our work in light of other concurrent and subsequent works, and summarize our work's contributions and impact.

1.1 Robustly Reconfigurable Consensus

We ask the question: what is a suitable consensus protocol for a proof-of-stake system? In a proof-of-stake system, at any point of time, we would like the *present* stake-holders to have voting rights that are weighed by their respective stake amount. Thus if we examine any single snapshot in the system, proof-of-stake in fact requires a "permissioned" core consensus protocol, since the set of public-keys owning stake is publicly known. However, proof-of-stake systems aim to support open participation—and this can be enabled through periodic committee reconfiguration. Suppose that the system starts with a well-known set of stake-holders who form the initial consensus committee. As stake switches hands in the system, the consensus committee should be updated in a timely manner to track the present (and not the past) stake distribution. This is important for the security of a proof-of-stake system, since users who no longer hold stake in the system may be incentivized to deviate, e.g., to launch a double-spending attack.

We formulate the task of designing "a consensus protocol suitable for proof-of-stake" as "robustly reconfigurable consensus". A robustly reconfiguration consensus protocol should have the following desirable properties.

Robustness in the Presence of Sporadic Participation. In a large-scale, decentralized environment, users tend to have *sporadic participation*, and it may be difficult to anticipate how many users will be online at any point of time. Almost all classical-style consensus protocols rely on tallying sufficiently many votes to make progress. If fewer than the anticipated number of users actually show up to vote, the consensus protocol may get stuck.

To address this challenge, Snow White employs the recently proposed "sleepy consensus" [21] paradigm as its core permissioned consensus building block. Sleepy consensus [21] is inspired by the beautiful "longest-chain" idea behind Nakamoto's consensus [17], but the idea is instead applied to a non-proof-of-work, permissioned setting with a public-key infrastructure (PKI). Pass and Shi prove that the resulting consensus protocol is robust in the presence of sporadic participation: concretely, the protocol need not be parametrized with an a-priori fixed number of players that are expected to show up. As long as the majority of *online* players are honest, the protocol guarantees consistency and liveness.

Robust Committee Reconfiguration. Roughly speaking, our system proceeds in epochs. In each epoch, a most recent set of stake-holders are elected as committee and may be randomly chosen to generate blocks. We argue that committee reconfiguration and random block-proposer selection are challenging and subtle due to the following two possible attacks.

1. *Adaptive key selection attacks.* Since proof-of-stake systems admit open participation, anyone can buy up stake in the system and participate. This also means anyone can (possibly maliciously) choose their public-keys through which they participate in the consensus. A possible attack, therefore, is to adaptively choose public-keys, after gathering partial information about the randomness seed used for block-proposer selection, such that corrupt nodes are elected more often as block-proposer than their fair chance.
2. *Randomness-biasing attacks* (commonly known as the "grinding attack"). Another important question is: how do we obtain the randomness needed for block proposer selection? A most straightforward idea is to use the hash of past blocks—but as several works have shown [4], the blocks' hashes can be subject to adversarial influence, and it is unclear what security can be guaranteed when we use such randomness sources with adversarial bias for block proposer selection. For example, the adversary can bias the randomness in a way that allows corrupt nodes to be selected more often.

In the worst case, if through possibly a combination of the attacks, the adversary can control the majority of the block-proposer slots, consistency of the underlying consensus (in our case, sleepy consensus) can be broken.

Snow White proposes a novel "two-lookback" mechanism that addresses the above two challenges simultaneously[1]. We determine each epoch's new consensus committee and randomness seed in a two-phase process, where each phase spans

---

[1] Subsequent works, including newer versions of Algorand [6] released *after* our publication, Ouroboros Praos [9], and the latest Ethereum's proof-of-stake proposal [1] incorporated elements of this design and suggested improvements, e.g., for concrete security. See Sect. 1.3 for more discussions.

roughly κ blocks of time for some appropriate security parameter[2] κ. This two-phase process is enabled by two look-back parameters as we describe informally below (a formal description is deferred to the technical sections)—henceforth suppose that *chain* is the current longest chain.

1. We look back 2κ blocks, and use the prefix $chain[: -2\kappa]$ (i.e., the prefix of *chain* removing the trailing 2κ blocks) to determine the new consensus committee.
2. We look back κ blocks, and extract the randomness contained in the blocks $chain[-2\kappa : -\kappa]$ (i.e., the part of *chain* from 2κ blocks ago to κ blocks ago) to form a randomness seed—this seed then seeds a random oracle used for block-proposer selection in the current epoch.

Roughly speaking, we defeat the adaptively chosen key attack by determining the consensus committee κ blocks earlier than the randomness seed, such that when corrupt nodes choose their public keys, they cannot predict the randomness seed, which will be generated much later in time and with sufficient entropy contributed by honest nodes as we explain below. We argue that due to chain quality of the underlying sleepy consensus, the blocks $chain[-2\kappa : -\kappa]$ must contain an honest block. Since honest nodes embed a sufficiently long uniform random seed in its block, we can extract sufficiently high-entropy randomness from $chain[-2\kappa : -\kappa]$ which is then used to seed the block-proposer-selection random oracle. Even though the extracted randomness is subject to adversarial bias, as long as it is high-entropy, and importantly, as long as *the same randomness is used to seed the block-proposer selection sufficiently many times*, we can achieve the desired measure concentration properties. More specifically, although indeed, the adversary can bias the random seed to allow corrupt nodes to be selected (as block-proposers) quite surely for a few number of slots; the adversary is not able to consistently gain advantage over a sufficiently large number of slots, i.e., corrupt nodes cannot own noticeably more block-proposer slots than its fair share.

We stress that turning the above intuitive argument into a formal proof requires significant and non-trivial effort which is part our main contributions. In our technical sections, we formally prove security of this approach under a mildly adaptive adversary, i.e., when the adversary is subject to a mild corruption delay and as long as nodes remain honest till shortly after they stop serving on a consensus committee, our robustly reconfigurable consensus protocol is secure. Subsequent works (including newer versions of the Algorand paper that are published *after* the release of Snow White, as well as the subsequent work Ourboros Praos [9]) have suggested approaches for achieving fully adaptive security, but relying on the fact that the majority of nodes will *erase* secret signing keys from memory after signing a block (and by introducing mild addi-

---

[2] Suppose that except with negligible in κ probability, the underlying sleepy consensus guarantees consistency by chopping off the trailing κ blocks, and guarantees the existence of an honest block in every consecutive window of κ blocks.

tional complexity in the cryptographic schemes employed)—see Sect. 1.3 for a more detailed comparison.

Understanding Posterior Corruption, i.e., "Costless Simulation" Attacks. A oft-cited attack for proof-of-stake systems is the so-called "costless simulation" attack (also referred to as a posterior corruption attack in this paper). The idea is that when stake-holders have sold their stake in the system, nothing prevents them from performing a history-rewrite attack. Specifically, suppose that a set of nodes denoted C control the majority stake in some past committee. These nodes can collude to fork the history from the point in the past when they control majority—and in this alternate history money can transfer in a way such that C continues to hold majority stake (possibly transferred to other pseudonyms of the corrupt nodes) such that the attack can be sustained.

In this paper, we formally prove that under a mild setup assumption—when nodes join the system they can access a set of online nodes the majority of whom are honest—we can provably defend against such a posterior corruption attack. This is achieved by having the newly joining user obtain a somewhat recent checkpoint from the set of nodes it can access upon joining.

We also prove a corresponding lower bound, that absent this setup assumption, defense against such posterior corruption attacks is *impossible*—to the best of our knowledge, ours is the first formal treatment of this well-known costless simulation attack in the context of proof-of-stake.

1.2   From Robustly Reconfigurable Consensus to Proof-of-Stake

Application to Proof-of-Stake and Achieving Incentive Compatibility. We show how to apply such a "robustly reconfigurable consensus" protocol to realize proof-of-stake (the resulting protocol called Snow White), such that nodes obtain voting power roughly proportional to their stake in the cryptocurrency system. As long as *money does not switch hands too fast* (which is enforceable by the cryptocurrency layer), we show that the resulting proof-of-stake protocol can attain security when the adversary controls only a minority of the stake in the system. Further, borrowing ideas from the recent Fruitchain work [19], we suggest *incentive compatible* mechanisms for distributing rewards and transaction fees, such that the resulting protocol achieves a coalition-resistant ϵ-Nash equilibrium, i.e., roughly speaking, as long as the adversary controls a minority of the stake, it cannot obtain more than ϵ fraction more than its fair share of payout, even when it has full control of network transmission and can deviate arbitrarily from the protocol specification.

Preventing Nothing-at-Stake Attacks. Later in Sect. 3, we will also discuss how to leverage guarantees provided by our core consensus protocol, and build additional mechanisms that not only discourage *nothing-at-stake* attackers, but in fact penalize them.

1.3 Chronological Notes, Closely Related, and Subsequent Works

Comparison with Algorand. The first manuscript of Algorand [6] was published prior to our work. Algorand also proposes a proof-of-stake system. Their core consensus protocol is a newly designed classical-style consensus protocol, and therefore they cannot guarantee progress under sporadic participation—instead, Algorand proposes a notion of "lazy participation", where users know when they are needed to vote in the consensus and they only need to be online when they are needed. However, if many users who are anticipated to show up failed to do so, progress will be hampered. Algorand employs a Verifiable Random Function (VRF) to perform random leader/committee election.

Algorand's algorithm has been improved for several iterations. The version of Algorand that existed before the publication of Snow White gave proofs of their core consensus protocol but did not provide end-to-end proofs for the full proof-of-stake system. In particular, the version of Algorand that existed prior to Snow White's publication did not discuss the well-known issue of costless simulation or clearly state the implicit assumptions they make to circumvent the lower bound we prove in this paper.

In their subsequent versions, they adopted the erasure model and rely on honest nodes' capability to safely erase secrets from memory to achieve *adaptive* security (and implicitly, by adopting erasures one could defend against the costless simulation). The newer versions of Algorand (released *after* the Snow White) also started to adopt a similar look-back idea (first described by Snow White) to secure against the adaptive chosen-key attack mentioned earlier. The recent versions also provided more thorough mathematical proofs of this approach.

Comparison with Ouroboros and Ouroboros Praos. Snow White was publicly released in September 2016. A closely related work (independent and concurrent from our effort) known as Ouroboros [13] was release about 10 days prior to Snow White. Ouroboros Praos is an improvement over Ouroboros published in 2017 [9].

The Ouroboros version that was released around the same time as Snow White focused on proving the underlying permissioned consensus building block secure, and there is only a short paragraph containing a proof sketch of their full proof-of-stake system (and this proof sketch has been somewhat expanded to a few paragraphs in later versions). In comparison, our Snow White paper adopts a permissioned consensus building block whose security was formally proven secure in a related paper [21]—the full-length of our technical sections are dedicated to a *thorough* treatment of the security of the end-to-end proof-of-stake system.

A notable difference between Snow White and Ouroboros seems to be that their formal treatment does not seem to capture a truly decentralized environment (necessary for decentralized cryptocurrency applications) where nodes may join the system late and not from the very start—had they done so, they would have encountered the well-known costless simulation issue, which, as we show, is impossible to defend against without extra setup assumptions (and indeed, we introduce a reasonable setup assumption to circumvent this lower bound).

A subsequently improved work, called Ouroboros Praos [9], extends the VRF approach described first by Algorand [6] and Dfinity [12] for random block-proposer election. Similar to the newer versions of Algorand, Ouroboros Praos [9] also started adopting an erasure model to achieve adaptive security (and implicitly, defend against costless simulation[3]).

Neither Ouroboros nor Ouroboros Praos adopts an underlying consensus mechanism that provably provides support for sporadic participation. Finally, the improved version Ouroboros Praos [9] started adopting a look-back mechanism that appears to be inspired by Snow White to for committee rotation and random block-proposer selection.

Comparison with Ethereum's Proof-of-Stake Design. Ethereum began proof-of-stake explorations several years ago. Their design has undergone several versions. At the time of the writing, Ethereum was aiming to do "hybrid proof-of-stake", i.e., use Casper as a finality gadget on top of their existing proof-of-work blockchain.

In the past year 2018, conversations with Ethereum core researchers suggest that Ethereum is considering replacing their proof-of-work blockchain with a proof-of-stake blockchain similar to Snow White. Their committee election and random block proposer selection algorithm seems to be improvement of Snow White. Specifically, they would like to adopt an economically secure coin toss protocol for randomness generation (commonly known as RANDAO). This specific protocol is also subject to adversarial bias much like our randomness seed generation (although biasing attacks may lead to economic loss). Thus they rely on exactly the same observation that was proposed in our paper: although the adversary can bias the randomness sufficiently to control a few block proposer slots, he cannot consistently get an advantage over a large number of slots. Interestingly, Ethereum has several practical optimizations that improve the concrete security parameters of the above analysis [1].

2   Snow White's Core Consensus Protocol

We focus on an intuitive exposition of our scheme in the main body. In the online full version [8], we present formal definitions, a formal description of the protocol, as well as the full proofs. We stress that formalizing the end-to-end security of a proof-of-stake system is a significant effort and this leads to our choice of presentation.

2.1   Background: Sleepy Consensus and Sleepy Execution Model

Sleepy Execution Model and Terminology. We would like to adopt an execution model that captures a decentralized environment where nodes can

---

[3] Snow White's approach of combining checkpointing and "bootstrapping through social consensus" to defend against costless simulation is simpler and more practical in real-world implementations (than relying on VRFs and erasure [6,9]). Notably, our usage of checkpointing and "bootstrapping through social consensus" already exists in real-world cryptocurrencies.

spawn late in time, and can go to sleep and later wake up. In such a model, the protocol may not have a way to anticipate the number of players at any time.

We thus adopt the sleepy model of execution proposed by Pass and Shi [21]. Nodes are either *sleepy* (i.e., offline) or *awake* (i.e., online and actively participating). For simplicity, we also refer to nodes that are awake and honest as *alert*; and all corrupt nodes are assumed to be awake by convention.

Messages delivered by an alert node is guaranteed to arrive at all other alert nodes within a maximum delay of Δ, where Δ is an input parameter to the protocol. A sleepy node captures any node that is either offline or suffering a slower than Δ network connection. A sleepy node can later wake up, and upon waking at time t, all pending messages sent by alert nodes before $t - \Delta$ will be immediately delivered to the waking node.

We allow the adversary to *dynamically spawn* new nodes, and newly spawned nodes can either be honest or corrupt. Further, as we discuss later, we allow the adversary to declare corruptions and put alert nodes to sleep in a mildly adaptive fashion.

For readability, we defer a detailed presentation of the formal model to our online full version [8].

The Sleepy Protocol as a Starting Point. Classical consensus protocols must count sufficiently many votes to make progress and thus the protocol must know a-priori roughly how many nodes will show up to vote. Since Pass and Shi's Sleepy consensus protocol is the only protocol known to provide consensus under sporadic participation, i.e., the protocol need not have a-priori knowledge of the number of players at any time. We thus consider Sleepy as a starting point for constructing our notion of robustly reconfigurable consensus. We now briefly review the Sleepy consensus protocol as necessary background.

Sleepy is a blockchain-style protocol but without proof-of-work. For practical considerations, below we describe the version of Sleepy instantiated with a random oracle (although Pass and Shi [21] also describe techniques for removing the random oracle). Sleepy relies on a random oracle to elect a leader in every time step. The elected leader is allowed to extend a blockchain with a new block, by signing a tuple that includes its own identity, the transactions to be confirm, the current time, and the previous block's hash. Like in the Nakamoto consensus, nodes always choose the longest chain if they receive multiple different ones. To make this protocol fully work, Sleepy [21] proposes new techniques to timestamp blocks to constrain the possible behaviors of an adversary. Specifically, there are two important blockchain timestamp rules:

1. a valid blockchain must have strictly increasing timestamps; and
2. honest nodes always reject a chain with future timestamps.

All aforementioned timestamps can be adjusted to account for possible clock offsets among nodes by applying a generic protocol transformation [21].

2.2   Handling Committee Reconfiguration

As mentioned, our starting point is the Sleepy consensus protocol, which assumes that all consensus nodes know each other's public keys; although it may not be known a-priori how many consensus nodes will show up and participate.

We now discuss how to perform committee reconfiguration such that the consensus committee tracks the latest stake distribution. To support a wide range of applications, our Snow White protocol does not stipulate how applications should select the committee over time. Roughly speaking, we wish to guarantee security as long as the application-specific committee selection algorithm respects the constraint that there is honest majority among all awake nodes. Therefore, we assume that there is some application-specific function elect_cmt($chain$) that examines the state of the blockchain and outputs a new committee over time. In a proof-of-stake context, for example, this function can roughly speaking, output one public key for each currency unit owned by the user. In Sect. 3, we discuss in a proof-of-stake context, how one might possibly translate assumptions on the distribution of stake to the formal requirements expected by the consensus protocol.

Strawman Scheme: Epoch-Based Committee Selection. Snow White provides an epoch-based protocol for committee reconfiguration. To aid understanding, we begin by describing a strawman solution. Each T_{epoch} time, a new epoch starts, and the beginning of each epoch provides a committee reconfiguration opportunity. Let start(e) and end(e) denote the beginning and ending times of the e-th committee. Every block in a valid blockchain whose time stamp is between [start(e), end(e)) is associated with the e-th committee.

It is important that all honest nodes agree on what the committee is for each epoch. To achieve this, our idea is for honest nodes to determine the new committee by looking at a *stabilized* part of the chain. Therefore, a straightforward idea is to make the following modifications to the basic Sleepy consensus protocol:

- Let 2ω be a look-back parameter.
- At any time $t \in$ [start(e), end(e)) that is in the e-th epoch, an alert node determines the e-th committee in the following manner: find the latest block in its local *chain* whose timestamp is no greater than start(e) $- 2\omega$, and suppose this block resides at index ℓ.
- Now, output extractpks($chain[: \ell]$) as the new committee.

In general, the look-back parameter 2ω must be sufficiently large such that all alert nodes have the same prefix $chain[: \ell]$ in their local chains by time start(e). On the other hand, from an application's perspective, 2ω should also be recent enough such that the committee composition does not lag significantly behind.

Preventing an Adaptive Key Selection Attack. Unfortunately, the above scheme is prone to an adaptive key selection attack where an adversary can break consistency with constant probability. Specifically, as the random oracle H is chosen prior to protocol start, the adversary can make arbitrary queries to H. Therefore, the adversary can spawn corrupt nodes and seed them with public keys that causes them to be elected leader at desirable points of time. For example, since the adversary can query H, it is able to infer exactly in which time steps honest nodes are elected leader. Now, the adversary can pick corrupt nodes' public keys, such that every time an honest node is leader, a corrupt node is leader too—and he can sustain this attack till he runs out of corrupt nodes. Since the adversary may control up to $\Theta(n)$ nodes, he can thus break consistency for $\Omega(n)$ number of blocks.

Our idea is to have nodes determine the next epoch's committee first, and then select the next epoch's hash—in this way, the adversary will be unaware of next epoch's hash until well after the next committee is determined. More specifically, we can make the following changes to the Sleepy protocol:

- Let 2ω and ω be two look-back parameters, for determining the next committee and next hash respectively.
- At any time $t \in [\mathsf{start}(e), \mathsf{end}(e))$ that is in the e-th epoch, an alert node determines the e-th committee in the following manner: find the latest block its local *chain* whose timestamp is no greater than $\mathsf{start}(e) - 2\omega$, and suppose this block resides at index ℓ_0. Now, output $\mathsf{extractpks}(chain[: \ell_0])$ as the new committee.
- At any time $t \in [\mathsf{start}(e), \mathsf{end}(e))$ an alert node determines the e-th hash in the following manner: find the latest block its local *chain* whose timestamp is no greater than $\mathsf{start}(e) - \omega$, and suppose this block resides at index ℓ_1. Now, output $\mathsf{extractnonce}(chain[: \ell_1])$ as a nonce to seed the new hash.
- We augment the protocol such that alert nodes always embed a random seed in any block they mine, and $\mathsf{extractnonce}(chain[: \ell_1])$ can simply use the seeds in the prefix of the chain as a nonce to seed the random oracle H.

For security, we require that

1. The two look-back parameters 2ω and ω are both sufficiently long ago, such that all alert nodes will have agreement on $chain[: \ell_0]$ and $chain[: \ell_1]$ by the time $\mathsf{start}(e)$; and
2. The two look-back parameters 2ω and ω must be sufficiently far part, such that the adversary cannot predict $\mathsf{extractnonce}(chain[: \ell_1])$ until well after the next committee is determined.

Achieving Security Under Adversarially Biased Hashes. It is not hard to see that the adversary can bias the nonce used to seed the hash, since the adversary can place arbitrary seeds in the blocks it contributes. In particular, suppose that the nonce is extracted from the prefix $chain[: \ell_1]$. Obviously, with at least constant probability, the adversary may control the ending block in this prefix. By querying H polynomially many times, the adversary can influence the seed in the last block $chain[\ell_1]$ of the prefix, until it finds one that it likes.

Indeed, if each nonce is used only to select the leader in a small number of time steps (say, $O(1)$ time steps), such adversarial bias would indeed have been detrimental—in particular, by enumerating polynomially many possibilities, the adversary can cause itself to be elected with probability almost 1 (assuming that the adversary controls the last block of the prefix).

However, we observe that as long as the same nonce is used sufficiently many times, the adversary cannot consistently cause corrupt nodes to be elected in many time steps. Specifically, suppose each nonce is used to elect at least $\Omega(\kappa)$ leaders, then except with $\mathsf{negl}(\kappa)$ probability, the adversary cannot increase its share by more than an ϵ fraction—for an arbitrarily small constant $\epsilon > 0$. Therefore, to prove our scheme secure, it is important that each epoch's length (henceforth denoted T_{epoch}) be sufficiently long, such that once a new nonce is determined, it is used to elect sufficiently many leaders.

Reasoning About Security Under Adversarially Biased Hashes. Formalizing this above intuition is somewhat more involved. Specifically, our proof needs to reason about the probability of bad events (related to chain growth, chain quality, and consistency) over *medium-sized* windows such that the bad events depend only on $O(1)$ number of hashes (determined by the nonces used to seed them). This way, we can apply a union bound that results in polynomial security loss. If the window size is too small, it would not be enough to make the failure probability negligible; on the other hand, if the window were too big, the blowup of the union bound would be exponential. Finally, we argue if no bad events occur for every medium-sized window, then no bad events happen for every window (as long as the window is not too small). We defer the detailed discussions and formal proofs to our online full version [8].

2.3   Handling Mildly Adaptive and Posterior Corruptions

We now consider how to defend against an adversary that can adaptively corrupt nodes after they are spawned. In this paper, we will aim to achieve security against a *mildly adaptive adversary*. Specifically, a mildly adaptive adversary is allowed to dynamically corrupt nodes or make them sleep, but such corrupt or sleep instructions take a while to be effective. For example, in practice, it may take some time to infect a machine with malware. Such a "mildly adaptive" corruption model has been formally defined in earlier works [20], where they call it the τ-agile corruption model, where τ denotes the delay parameter till corrupt or sleep instructions take effect. Intuitively, as long as τ is sufficiently large, it will be too late for an adversary to corrupt a node or make the node sleep upon seeing the next epoch's hash. By the time the corrupt or sleep instruction takes effect, it will already be well past the epoch.

The main challenge in handling mildly adaptive corruptions is the threat of a *history rewriting* attack when *posterior corruption* is possible: members of past committees may, at some point, have sold their stake in the system, and thus they have nothing to lose to create an alternative version of history.

We rely on a *checkpointing* idea to provide resilience to such posterior corruption—as long as there is no late joining or rejoining (we will discuss how to handle late joining or rejoining later). Checkpointing is a technique that has been explored in the classical distributed systems literature [5] but typically for different purposes, e.g., in the case of PBFT [5] it was used as an efficiency mechanism. Suppose that we can already prove the consistency property as long as there is no majority posterior corruption. Now, to additionally handle majority posterior corruption, we can have alert nodes always reject any chain that diverges from its current longest chain at a point sufficiently far back in the past (say, at least W time steps ago). In this way, old committee members that have since become corrupt cannot convince alert nodes to revise history that is too far back—in other words, the confirmed transaction log stabilizes and becomes immutable after a while.

2.4   Late Joining in the Presence of Posterior Corruption

Indeed, the above approach almost would work, if there are no late spawning nodes, and if there are no nodes who wake up after sleeping for a long time. However, as mentioned earlier, handling late joining is important for a decentralized network.

Recall that we described a history revision attack earlier, where if the majority of an old committee become corrupt at a later point of time, they can simulate an alternate past, and convince a newly joining node believe in the alternate past. Therefore, it seems that the crux is the following question:

> How can a node joining the protocol correctly identify the true version of history?

Unfortunately, it turns out that this is impossible without additional trust—in fact, we can formalize the aforementioned attack and prove a lower bound (see our online full version [8]) which essentially shows that in the presence of majority posterior corruption, a newly joining node has no means of discerning a real history from a simulated one:

> [Lower bound for posterior corruption]: Absent any additional trust, it is impossible to achieve consensus under sporadic participation, if the majority of an old committee can become corrupt later in time.

We therefore ask the following question: what minimal, additional trust assumptions can we make such that we can defend against majority posterior corruption? Informally speaking, we show that all we need is a secure bootstrapping process for newly joining nodes as described below. We assume that a newly joining node is provided with a list of nodes L the majority of whom must be alert—if so, the new node can ask the list of nodes in L to vote on the current state of the system, and thus it will not be mislead to choose a "simulated" version of the history.

2.5   Putting It Altogether: Informal Overview of Snow White

In summary, our protocol, roughly speaking, works as follows. A formal description of the protocol, the parameter choices and their relations, and proofs of security are deferred to our online full version [8].

- First, there is a random oracle H that determines if a member of the present committee is a leader in each time step. If a node is leader in a time step t, he can extend the blockchain with a block of the format $(h_{-1}, \mathsf{txs}, \mathsf{time}, \mathsf{nonce}, \mathsf{pk}, \sigma)$, where h_{-1} is the previous block's hash, txs is a set of transactions to be confirmed, nonce is a random seed that will be useful later, pk is the node's public key, and σ is a signature under pk on the entire contents of the block. A node can verify the validity of the block by checking that (1) $\mathsf{H}^{\mathsf{nonce}_e}(\mathsf{pk}, \mathsf{time}) < D_p$ where D_p is a difficulty parameter[4] such that the hash outcome is smaller than D_p with probability p, and nonce_e is a nonce that is reselected every epoch (we will describe how the nonce is selected later); (2) the signature σ verifies under pk; and (3) pk is a member of the present committee as defined by the prefix of the blockchain.
- A valid blockchain's timestamps must respect two constraints: (1) all timestamps must strictly increase; and (2) any timestamp in the future will cause a chain to be rejected.
- Next, to defend against old committees that have since become corrupt from rewriting history, whenever an alert node receives a valid chain that is longer than his own, he only accepts the incoming chain if the incoming chain does not modify blocks too far in the past, where "too far back" is defined by the parameter κ_0.
- Next, a newly joining node or a node waking up from long sleep must invoke a secure bootstrapping mechanism such that it can identify the correct version of the history to believe in. One mechanism to achieve this is for the (re)spawning node to contact a list of nodes the majority of whom are alert.
- Finally, our protocol defines each contiguous T_{epoch} time steps to be an epoch. At the beginning of each epoch, committee reconfiguration is performed in the following manner. First, nodes find the latest prefix (henceforth denoted $chain_{-2\omega}$) in their local chain whose timestamp is at least 2ω steps ago. This prefix $chain_{-2\omega}$ will be used to determine the next committee—and Snow White defers to the application-layer to define how specifically to extract the next committee from the state defined by $chain_{-2\omega}$. Next, nodes find the latest prefix (denoted $chain_{-\omega}$) in their local chain whose timestamp is at least ω steps ago. Given this prefix $chain_{-\omega}$, we extract the nonces contained in all blocks, the resulting concatenated nonce will be used to seed the hash function H for the next epoch.

---

[4] As we discuss in our online full version [8], in practice, the next committee is read from a stabilized prefix of the blockchain and we know its total size a-priori. Therefore, assuming that an upper bound on the fraction of awake nodes (out of each committee) is known a-priori, we can set the difficulty parameter D_p accordingly to ensure that the expected block interval is sufficiently large w.r.t. to the maximum network delay (and if the upper bound is loose, then the confirmation time is proportionally slower). Although on the surface our analysis assumes a fixed expected block interval throughout, it easily generalizes to the case when the expected block interval varies by a known constant factor throughout (and is sufficiently large w.r.t. to the maximum network delay).

Resilience Condition. In the online full version [8], we will give a formal presentation of our protocol and prove it secure under the following resilience condition. We require that the majority of the committee remain honest not only during the time it is active, but also for a short duration (e.g., a handoff period) afterwards. In particular, even if the entire committee becomes corrupt after this handoff period, it should not matter to security.

In other words, we require that *for any committee, the number of alert committee members that remain honest for a window of W outnumber the number of committee members that become corrupt during the same window.* In particular, we will parametrize the window W such that it incorporates this short handoff period after the committee becomes inactive. Somewhat more formally, we require that there exists a constant $\psi > 0$ such that for every possible execution trace view, for every $t \leq |\text{view}|$, let $r = \min(t + W, |\text{view}|)$,

$$\frac{\text{alert}^t(\text{cmt}^t(\text{view}), \text{view}) \cap \text{honest}^r(\text{cmt}^t(\text{view}), \text{view})}{\text{corrupt}^r(\text{cmt}^t(\text{view}), \text{view})} \geq 1 + \psi \tag{1}$$

where $\text{alert}^t(\text{cmt}^s(\text{view}), \text{view})$, $\text{honest}^t(\text{cmt}^s(\text{view}), \text{view})$, and $\text{corrupt}^t(\text{cmt}^s(\text{view}), \text{view})$ output the number of nodes in the committee of time s that are alert (or honest, corrupt, resp.) at time t.

3   From Robustly Reconfigurable Consensus to PoS

We now discuss how to apply our core consensus protocol in a proof-of-stake (PoS) application. There are two challenges: (1) in a system where money can switch hands, how to make the committee composition closely track the stake distribution over time; and (2) how to distribute fees and rewards to ensure incentive compatibility.

3.1   Base Security on Distribution of Stake

Roughly speaking, our core consensus protocol expects the following assumption for security: at any point of time, there are more alert committee members that will remain honest sufficiently long than there are corrupt committee members. In a proof-of-stake setting, we would like to articulate assumptions regarding the distribution of stake among stake-holders, and state the protocol's security in terms of such assumptions.

Since our core consensus protocol allows a committee reelection opportunity once every epoch, it is possible that the distribution of the stake in the system lags behind the committee election. However, suppose that this is not the case, e.g., pretend for now that there is no money transfer, then it is simple to translate the assumptions to distribution on stake. Imagine that the application-defined elect_cmt(*chain*) function will output one public key for each unit of currency as expressed by the state of *chain*. If a public key has many units of coin, one could simply output the public key pk along with its multiplicity m—and the strings pk$||1, \ldots,$ pk$||m$ may be used in the hash query for determining the leader. Snow White's core consensus protocol does not care about the implementation details of elect_cmt($chain$), and in fact that is an advantage of our modular composition approach. In this way, our Snow White protocol retains security as long as the at any point of time, more stake is alert and will remain honest sufficiently long than the stake that is corrupt. Here when we say "a unit of stake is alert (or honest, corrupt, resp.)", we mean that the node that owns this unit of stake is alert (or honest, corrupt, resp.).

In the real world, however, there is money transfer—after all that is the entire point of having cryptocurrencies—therefore the committee election lags behind the redistribution of stake. This may give rise to the following attack: once a next committee is elected, the majority of the stake in the committee can now sell their currency units and perform an attack on the cryptocurrency (since they now no longer have stake). For example, the corrupt coalition can perform a double-spending attack where they spend their stake but attempt to fork a history where they did not spend the money.

The Limited Liquidity Assumption. One approach to thwart such an attack is to limit the liquidity in the system—in fact, Snow White expects that the cryptocurrency layer enforces that money will not switch hands too quickly. For example, imagine that at any point of time, $a = 30\%$ of the stake is alert and will remain honest sufficiently long, $c = 20\%$ is corrupt, and the rest are sleepy. We can have the cryptocurrency layer enforce the following rule: only $\frac{a-c}{2} - \epsilon = 5\% - \epsilon$ of the stake can switch hands during every window of size $2\omega + T_{\mathrm{epoch}} + W$. In other words, if in any appropriately long window, only l fraction of money in the system can move, it holds that as long as at any time, $2l + \epsilon$ more stake is alert and remain honest sufficiently long than the stake that is corrupt, we can guarantee that the conditions expected by the consensus protocol, that is, at any time, more committee members are alert and remain honest sufficiently long, than the committee members that are corrupt.

4 Achieving Incentive Compatibility

4.1 Fair Reward Scheme

In a practical deployment, an important desideratum is incentive compatibility. Roughly speaking, we hope that each node will earn a "fair share" of rewards and transaction fees—and in a proof-of-stake system, fairness is defined as being proportional to the amount of stake a node has. In particular, any minority coalition of nodes should not be able to obtain an unfair share of the rewards by deviating from the protocol—in this way, rational nodes should not be incentivized to deviate.

Since Snow White is a blockchain-style protocol, we also inherit the well-known selfish mining attack [10,18] where a minority coalition can increase its rewards by a factor of nearly 2 in the worst case. Fortunately, inspired by the recent work Fruitchains [19] we provide a solution to *provably* defend against any form of selfish mining attacks, and ensure that the honest protocol is a coalition-safe ϵ-Nash equilibrium. At a high level, Fruitchains provides a mechanism to *transform any (possibly unfair) blockchain that achieves consistency and liveness into an approximately fair blockchain in a blackbox manner.* Our key observation is that this transformation is also applicable to our non-proof-of-work blockchain—since we realize the same abstraction as a proof-of-work blockchain. Since we apply the essentially same techniques below as Fruitchains, we give an overview of the mechanisms below for completeness and refer the reader to Fruitchains [19] for full details.

Two Mining Processes. Like in Fruitchains [19], we propose to have two "mining" processes piggybacked atop each other. Recall that earlier each node invokes the hash function H in every time step to determine whether it is a leader in this time step. Now, we will use the first half of H to determine leadership, and use the second half to determine if the user mines a "fruit" in this time step. Additionally, we will add to the input of H the digest of a recently stablized block such that any fruit mined will "hang" from a recently stablized block—which block a fruit hangs from indicates the roughly when the fruit was "mined", i.e., the *freshness* of the fruit. Whenever an honest node finds a fruit, it broadcasts the fruit to all peers, and honest nodes will incorporate all outstanding and fresh fruits in any block that it "mines". Note that fruits incorporated in blocks are only considered valid if they are sufficiently fresh. Finally, all valid fruits contained in the blockchain can be linearized, resulting in an ordered "fruit chain".

The formal analysis conducted in Fruitchains [19] can be adapted to our setting in a straightforward manner, giving rise to the following informal claim:

Claim (Approximate fairness [19]). Assume appropriate parameters. Then for any (arbitrarily small) constant ϵ, in any $\frac{\kappa}{\epsilon}$ number of consecutive fruits, the fraction of fruits belonging to an adversarial coalition is at most ϵ fraction more than its fair share, as long as, informally speaking, in any committee, alert committee members that remain honest by the posterior corruption window outnumber members that become corrupt by the same window.

We refer the reader to Fruitchains [19] for a formal proof of this claim. Intuitively, this claim holds because the underlying blockchain's liveness property ensures that no honest fruits will ever be lost (i.e., the adversary cannot "erase" honest nodes' work in mining fruits like what happens in a selfish mining attack); and moreover, in any sufficiently long window, the adversary can incorporate only legitimate fruits belonging to this window (and not any fruits ϵ-far into the past or future).

Payout Distribution. Based on the above claim of approximate fairness, we devise the following payout mechanism following the approach of Fruitchain [19]. We will distribute all forms of payout, including mining rewards and transaction fees to fruits rather than blocks. Furthermore, every time payout is issued, it will be distributed equally among a recent segment of roughly $\Omega(\frac{\kappa}{\epsilon})$ fruits. Like in Fruitchains, this guarantees that as long as at any time, there are more alert committee members that remain honest sufficiently long than corrupt committee members, the corrupt coalition cannot increase its share by more than ϵ no matter how it deviates from the prescribed protocol—in other words, the honest protocol is a coalition-safe ϵ-Nash equilibrium.

4.2 Thwarting Nothing-at-Stake Attacks

Nothing-at-stake refers to a class of well-known attacks in the proof-of-stake context [23], where participants have nothing to lose for signing multiple forked histories. We describe how Snow White defends against such attacks. Nothing-at-stake attacks apply to both signing forked chains in the past and in the present—since the former refers to posterior corruption style attacks which we already addressed earlier, in the discussion below, we focus on signing forked chains in the present.

First, as long as the adversary does not control the majority, our core consensus protocol formally guarantees that signing forked chains does not break consistency. In fact, we incentivize honest behavior by proving that the adversary cannot increase its rewards by an arbitrarily small ϵ fraction, no matter how it deviates from honest behavior which includes signing forked chains.

With ϵ-Nash equilibrium, one limitation is that players can still do a small ϵ fraction better by deviating, and it would be desirable to enforce a stronger notion where players do strictly worse by deviating. We can make sure that nothing-at-stake attackers do strictly worse by introducing a penalty mechanism in the cryptocurrency layer: by having players that sign multiple blocks with the same timestamp lose an appropriate amount of collateral—to achieve this we need that the underlying core consensus protocol achieves consistency, when roughly speaking, the adversary controls only the minority. Even absent such a penalty mechanism, players currently serving on a committee likely care about the overall health of the cryptocurrency system where they still hold stake due to the limited liquidity assumption—this also provides disincentives for deviating.

The holy grail, of course, is to design a provably secure protocol where *any* deviation, not just nothing-at-stake attacks, cause the player to do strictly worse. We leave this as an exciting open question. It would also be interesting to consider security when the attack controls the majority—however, if such a majority attacker can behave arbitrarily, consistency was shown to be impossible [21]. Therefore, it thus remains an open question even what meaningful notions of security one can hope for under possibly majority corruption.

Additional Materials in Online Full Version

In our online full version [8], we present full formalism including definitions, proofs, and lower bound results. We also present simulation and experimental results, and discuss concrete parameters in the online full version.

Acknowledgments. We gratefully acknowledge Siqiu Yao and Yuncong Hu for lending critical help in building the simulator. We thank Lorenzo Alvisi for suggesting the name Snow White. We also thank Rachit Agarwal, Kai-Min Chung, and Ittay Eyal for helpful and supportive discussions.

References

1. Personal communication with Vitalik Buterin, and public talks on sharding by Vitalik Buterin (2018)
2. Bentov, I., Gabizon, A., Mizrahi, A.: Cryptocurrencies without proof of work. In: Clark, J., Meiklejohn, S., Ryan, P.Y.A., Wallach, D., Brenner, M., Rohloff, K. (eds.) FC 2016. LNCS, vol. 9604, pp. 142–157. Springer, Heidelberg (2016). https://doi.org/10.1007/978-3-662-53357-4_10
3. Bentov, I., Lee, C., Mizrahi, A., Rosenfeld, M.: Proof of activity: extending bitcoin's proof of work via proof of stake. In: Proceedings of the ACM SIGMETRICS 2014 Workshop on Economics of Networked Systems, NetEcon (2014)
4. Bonneau, J., Clark, J., Goldfeder, S.: On bitcoin as a public randomness source. IACR Cryptology ePrint Archive 2015:1015 (2015)
5. Castro, M., Liskov, B.: Practical byzantine fault tolerance. In: OSDI (1999)
6. Chen, J., Micali, S.: Algorand: the efficient and democratic ledger (2016). https://arxiv.org/abs/1607.01341
7. User "cunicula" and Meni Rosenfeld. Proof of stake brainstorming, August 2011. https://bitcointalk.org/index.php?topic=37194.0
8. Daian, P., Pass, R., Shi, E.: Snow white: provably secure proofs of stake. Cryptology ePrint Archive, Report 2016/919, online full version of this paper (2016)
9. David, B., Gaži, P., Kiayias, A., Russell, A.: Ouroboros praos: an adaptively-secure, semi-synchronous proof-of-stake protocol. Cryptology ePrint Archive, Report 2017/573 (2017). http://eprint.iacr.org/2017/573
10. Eyal, I., Sirer, E.G.: Majority is not enough: bitcoin mining is vulnerable. In: FC (2014)
11. Garay, J., Kiayias, A., Leonardos, N.: The bitcoin backbone protocol: analysis and applications. In: Oswald, E., Fischlin, M. (eds.) EUROCRYPT 2015. LNCS, vol. 9057, pp. 281–310. Springer, Heidelberg (2015). https://doi.org/10.1007/978-3-662-46803-6_10
12. Hanke, T., Movahedi, M., Williams, D.: Dfinity technology overview series: Consensus system. https://dfinity.org/tech
13. Kiayias, A., Russell, A., David, B., Oliynykov, R.: Ouroboros: a provably secure proof-of-stake blockchain protocol. In: Katz, J., Shacham, H. (eds.) CRYPTO 2017. LNCS, vol. 10401, pp. 357–388. Springer, Cham (2017). https://doi.org/10.1007/978-3-319-63688-7_12
14. King, S., Nadal, S.: Ppcoin: peer-to-peer crypto-currency with proof-of-stake (2012). https://peercoin.net/assets/paper/peercoin-paper.pdf
15. Kwon, J.: Tendermint: consensus without mining (2014). http://tendermint.com/docs/tendermint.pdf
16. Maxwell, G., Poelstra, A.: Distributed consensus from proof of stake is impossible (2014). https://download.wpsoftware.net/bitcoin/pos.pdf
17. Nakamoto, S.: Bitcoin: a peer-to-peer electronic cash system (2008)

18. Pass, R., Seeman, L., Shelat, A.: Analysis of the blockchain protocol in asynchronous networks. In: Coron, J.-S., Nielsen, J.B. (eds.) EUROCRYPT 2017. LNCS, vol. 10211, pp. 643–673. Springer, Cham (2017). https://doi.org/10.1007/978-3-319-56614-6_22
19. Pass, R., Shi, E.: Fruitchains: a fair blockchain (2016, manuscript)
20. Pass, R., Shi, E.: Hybrid consensus: efficient consensus in the permissionless model (2016, manuscript)
21. Pass, R., Shi, E.: The sleepy model of consensus (2016). http://eprint.iacr.org/2016/918
22. Pass, R., Shi, E.: Rethinking large-scale consensus. In: CSF (2017)
23. Poelstra, A.: Distributed consensus from proof of stake is impossible. https://download.wpsoftware.net/bitcoin/alts.pdf
24. User "QuantumMechanic". Proof of stake instead of proof of work, July 2011. https://bitcointalk.org/index.php?topic=27787.0
25. User "tacotime". Netcoin proof-of-work and proof-of-stake hybrid design (2013). http://web.archive.org/web/20131213085759/www.netcoin.io/wiki/Netcoin_Proof-of-Work_and_Proof-of-Stake_Hybrid_Design
26. Griffith, V., Buterin, V.: Casper the friendly finality gadget. https://arxiv.org/abs/1710.09437

Compounding of Wealth in Proof-of-Stake Cryptocurrencies

Giulia Fanti[1]([⊠]), Leonid Kogan[2], Sewoong Oh[3], Kathleen Ruan[1], Pramod Viswanath[4], and Gerui Wang[4]

[1] Carnegie Mellon University, Pittsburgh, USA
{gfanti,kruan}@andrew.cmu.edu
[2] Massachusetts Institute of Technology, Cambridge, USA
lkogan2@mit.edu
[3] University of Washington, Seattle, USA
sewoong@cs.washington.edu
[4] University of Illinois Urbana-Champaign, Urbana, USA
{pramodv,geruiw2}@illinois.edu

Abstract. Proof-of-stake (PoS) is a promising approach for designing efficient blockchains, where block proposers are randomly chosen with probability proportional to their stake. A primary concern in PoS systems is the "rich getting richer" effect, whereby wealthier nodes are more likely to get elected, and hence reap the block reward, making them even wealthier. In this paper, we introduce the notion of equitability, which quantifies how much a proposer can amplify her stake compared to her initial investment. Even with everyone following protocol (i.e., honest behavior), we show that existing methods of allocating block rewards lead to poor equitability, as does initializing systems with small stake pools and/or large rewards relative to the stake pool. We identify a *geometric* reward function, which we prove is maximally equitable over all choices of reward functions under honest behavior and bound the deviation for strategic actions; the proofs involve the study of optimization problems and stochastic dominances of Pólya urn processes. These results allow us to provide a systematic framework to choose the parameters of a practical incentive system for PoS cryptocurrencies.

Keywords: Proof-of-stake · Cryptocurrencies · Random processes

1 Introduction

A central problem in blockchain systems is that of block proposal: how to choose which block should be appended to the global blockchain next. Many blockchains use a proposal mechanism by which one node is randomly selected as leader (or *block proposer*). This leader gets to propose the next block in exchange for a token reward—typically a combination of transaction fees and a freshly-minted *block reward*, which is chosen by the system designers. Early cryptocurrencies,

I. Goldberg and T. Moore (Eds.): FC 2019, LNCS 11598, pp. 42–61, 2019.
https://doi.org/10.1007/978-3-030-32101-7_3

including Bitcoin, mainly used a leader election mechanism called *proof of work* (PoW). Under PoW, all nodes execute a computational puzzle. The node who solves the puzzle first is elected leader. PoW is quite robust to security threats, but also energy-inefficient, consuming more energy than developed nations [1].

An appealing alternative to PoW is called *proof-of-stake* (PoS). In PoS, proposers are not chosen according to their computational power, but according to the stake they hold in the cryptocurrency. For example, if Alice has 30% of the tokens, she is selected as the next proposer with probability 0.3. Although the idea of PoS is both natural and energy-efficient, the research community is still grappling with how to design a PoS system that provides security while also incentivizing nodes to act as network validators. Part of incentivizing validators is simply providing enough reward (in expectation) to compensate their resource usage. However, it is also important to ensure that validators are treated fairly compared to their peers. In other words, they cannot only be compensated adequately on average; the variance also matters.

This observation is complicated in PoS systems by a key issue that does not arise in PoW systems: *compounding*. Compounding means that whenever a node (Alice) earns a proposal reward, that reward is added to her account, which increases her chances of being elected leader in the future, and increases her chances of reaping even more rewards. This leads to a rich-get-richer effect, causing dramatic concentration of wealth.

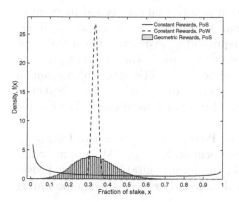

Fig. 1. Fractional stake distribution of a party that starts with 1/3 of the stake in a system initialized with Bitcoin's financial parameters. Results of geometric reward PoS and constant reward PoW are shown after $T = 1,000$ blocks.

To see this, consider what would happen if Bitcoin were a PoS system. Bitcoin started with an initial stake pool of 50 BTC, and the block reward was fixed at 50 BTC/block for several years. Under these conditions, suppose a party A starts with $\frac{1}{3}$ of the stake. Using a basic PoS model described in Sect. 2, A's stake would evolve according to a standard Pólya urn process [14], converging almost surely to a random variable with distribution Beta($\frac{1}{3}, \frac{2}{3}$) [16], (black solid line in Fig. 1). In this example, compounding gives A a high probability of accumulating a stake fraction near 0 or 1. This is highly undesirable because the proposal incentive mechanism should not unduly amplify or shrink one party's fraction of stake.

Notice that this is not caused by an adversarial or strategic behavior, but by the *randomness* in the PoS protocol, combined with compounding.

In PoW, on the other hand, the analogue would be for party A to hold 1/3 of the computational power. In that case, A's stake after T blocks would be instead binomially distributed with mean $50T/3$ (black dashed line in Fig. 1). Notice that the binomial (PoW) stake distribution concentrates around $1/3$ as $T \to \infty$, so if A contributes $1/3$ of stake at the beginning, she also reaps $1/3$ of the rewards in the long term.[1] Among randomized protocols that choose proposers independently at each time slot, the binomial distribution is the best we can hope for; it represents the setting where party A wins each block with probability equal to its initial stake. A natural question is whether we can achieve this PoW baseline distribution in a PoS system with compounding.

We study this question from the perspective of the block reward function. Most cryptocurrencies today use a *constant block reward* function like Bitcoin's, which remains fixed over a long timespan (e.g., years). We ask how a PoS system's choice of block reward function can affect concentration of wealth, and whether one can achieve the PoW baseline stake distribution simply by changing the block reward function. This paper has five main contributions:

(1) We define the *equitability* of a block reward function, which intuitively captures how much the fraction of total stake belonging to a node can grow or shrink (under that block reward function), compared to the node's initial investment.

(2) We introduce an alternative block reward function called the *geometric reward function*, whose rewards increase geometrically over time. We show that it is the most equitable PoS block reward function, by showing that it is the unique solution to an optimization problem on the second moment of a time-varying urn process; this optimization may be of independent interest. We note that despite optimizing equitability, geometric rewards do not achieve the PoW baseline stake distribution—this is the *inherent* price we pay for the efficiency of PoS compared to PoW. The green histogram in Fig. 1 illustrates the empirical, simulated stake distribution when geometric rewards are used for 1 000 blocks, with total rewards as in the PoW example ($50 \times 1\,000$ units).

(3) Borrowing ideas from mining pools in PoW systems, a natural strategy is for participants in a PoS system to form stake pools. We quantify the exact gains of stake pool formation in terms of equitability, which proves that participating in a stake pool can significantly reduce the compounding effect of a PoS system.

(4) We study the effects of strategic behavior (e.g. selfish mining) on the rich-get-richer phenomenon. We find that in general, compounding can exacerbate the efficacy of strategic behavior compared to PoW systems. However, these effects can be partially mitigated by carefully choosing the amount of block reward dispensed over some time period relative to the initial stake pool size.

(5) Our analyses of the equitability of various reward functions provide guidelines for choosing system parameters—including the initial token pool size

---

[1] Compounding can also happen in PoW if miners use their profits to purchase more mining equipment. However, this feedback loop is much slower and less direct than PoS compounding, so we approximate PoW by a system with no compounding.

and the total rewards to dispense in a given time interval—to ensure equitability. We show that cryptocurrencies that start with large initial stake pools (relative to the block rewards being disseminated) can mitigate the concentration of wealth, both for constant and geometric reward schemes.

The remainder of this paper is organized as follows. In Sect. 2, we present our model. In Sect. 3, we study equitability under honest behavior. We use Sect. 4 to study the effects of strategic behavior on equitability.

1.1   Related Work

The compounding of wealth in PoS systems has been widely discussed in forum and blog posts [17,22,27], with recent work on *stake-bleeding attacks* exploiting exactly this property [11]. In this work, we quantify concentration of wealth through a new metric called equitability, which enables us to mathematically compare PoS to PoW, and different block reward schemes. As we discuss in Sect. 2, equitability is closely tied to the variance of a block reward scheme. Thus far, researchers and practitioners have reduced variance in block rewards through two main approaches: pooling resources (e.g., mining or stake pools) and proposing new protocols for disseminating block rewards.

Resource pooling is common in cryptocurrencies, e.g. in mining pools [9,25]. In PoS systems, the analogous concept is stake pooling, where nodes aggregate their stake under a single node; block rewards are shared across the pool. In Sect. 3, we show that the proposed geometric reward function is still the most equitable even if some parties are forming stake pools. Recent work by Brunjes *et al.* also studies stake pools and how to incentivize their formation through the design of reward mechanisms [6]. Our work differs in that we aim to optimize equitability, whereas [6] aims to incentivize the formation of a target number of mining pools. Also, [6] does not consider the effects of compounding in PoS.

A second variance reduction approach changes the block reward allocation protocol; our work falls in this category. Two examples are Fruitchains [20], which spread block rewards evenly across a sequence of block proposers, and Ouroboros [15], which rewards nodes for being part of a block formation committee, even if they do not contribute to block proposal. Both of these approaches were proposed in order to provide incentive-compatibility for block proposers; they do not explicitly aim to reduce the variance of rewards. However, they implicitly reduce variance by spreading rewards across multiple nodes, thereby preventing the randomized accumulation of wealth. In our work, instead of changing how block rewards are disseminated, we change the block reward function itself.

2   Models and Notation

We provide a probabilistic model for the evolution of the stakes under a PoS system, and introduce a measure of fairness, we call *equitability*. We begin with a model of a chain-based proof-of-stake system with m parties: $\mathcal{A} = \{A_1, \ldots, A_m\}$.

We assume that all parties keep all of their stake in the *proposal stake pool*, which is a pool of tokens that is used to choose the next proposer. We consider a discrete-time system, $n = 1, 2, \ldots, T$, where each time slot corresponds to the addition of one block to the blockchain. In reality, new blocks may not arrive at perfectly-synchronized time intervals, but we index the system by block arrivals. For any integer x, we use the notation $[x] := \{1, 2, \ldots, x\}$. For all $i \in [m]$, let $S_{A_i}(n)$ denote the total stake held by party A_i in the proposal stake pool at time n. We let $S(n) = \sum_{i=1}^{m} S_{A_i}(n)$ denote the total stake in the proposer stake pool at time n, and $v_{A_i}(n)$ denotes the *fractional stake* of node A_i at time n:

$$v_{A_i}(n) = \frac{S_{A_i}(n)}{S(n)}.$$

For simplicity, we normalize the initial stake pool size to $S(0) = 1$; this is without loss of generality as the random process is homogeneous in scaling both the rewards and the initial stake by a constant. Each party starts with $S_{A_i}(0) = v_{A_i}(0)$ fraction of the original stake. At each time $n \in [T]$, the system chooses a proposer node $W(n) \in \mathcal{A}$ so that

$$W(n) = \begin{cases} A_1 & w.p. \quad v_{A_1}(n) \\ \ldots \\ A_m & w.p. \quad v_{A_m}(n). \end{cases} \tag{1}$$

Upon being selected as a proposer, $W(n)$ appends a *block*, or set of transactions, to the *blockchain*, which is a sequential list of blocks held by all nodes in the system. As compensation for this service, $W(n)$ receives a *block reward* of $r(n)$ stake, which is immediately added to its allocation in the proposer pool. I.e.,

$$S_{W(n)}(n + 1) = S_{W(n)}(n) + r(n).$$

The reward $r(n)$ is freshly-minted, so it increases the total token pool size. We assume the total reward dispensed in time period T is fixed, such that $\sum_{n=1}^{T} r(n) = R$.

Modeling Assumptions. Our model implicitly makes several assumptions, such as a single proposer per time slot. Many cryptocurrencies have proposer election protocols that allow more than one proposer to be chosen per time slot (Bitcoin [18], PoSv3 [8], Snow White [5]). If two proposers are elected at time n, for example, then each can append its block to one block at height $n - 1$; here the *height* of a block is its index in the blockchain. However, in these systems, only one leader can win the block reward since only one fork of the blockchain is ultimately adopted. Assuming the winner is chosen uniformly at random from the set of selected proposers, the dynamics of our Markov process remain unchanged.

Some cryptocurrencies (e.g., Qtum, Particl) choose proposer(s) as a function of the time slot *and* the preceding block. This does not affect our results in the honest setting (for the same reason as above), but it does increase the efficacy of strategic behavior like grinding [29] and selfish mining [9]. We discuss these implications in Sect. 4. Although we do not consider BFT-based PoS protocols in this paper [12,28], such protocols provide robustness to strategic behavior by forcing consensus on each block. Such protocols may also provide robustness to compounding, since block rewards can be shared among many nodes.

We have also assumed in this work that users instantly re-invest rewards into the proposer stake pool, for two reasons. (1) In PoS systems where users explicitly deposit stake, existing implementations automatically deposit rewards back into the stake pool. For example, the reference implementation of Casper the Friendly Finality Gadget (a PoS finalization mechanism proposed for Ethereum) automatically re-allocates all rewards back into the deposited stake pool [23]. (2) In other PoS systems, the stake pool is simply the set of all stake in the system, and is not separate from the pool of tokens used for transactions [8]. Hence as soon as a proposer earns a reward, that reward is used to calculate the next proposer (modulo some maturity period); the user is not actively re-investing block rewards—it just happens naturally. In practice, there may be a delay (maturity period) before the reward is counted; we do not model this effect.

Block Reward Choices. Many cryptocurrencies use Bitcoin's block reward schedule, which fixes the total supply of coins at about 21 million coins, and halves the reward every 210,000 blocks (≈ 4 years) [2]. Figure 2 illustrates this; if we let T_i and R_i denote the ith block interval and total reward, respectively, we can take $T_i = 210,000$ blocks, and $R_i = 50 \cdot \frac{1}{2^{i-1}} \cdot 210,000$. Several systems have adopted similar block rewards that are constant over long periods of time (e.g., Ethereum [3], ZCash [13], Dash [7], Particl).

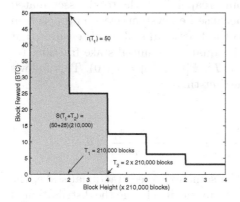
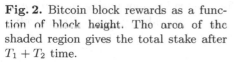
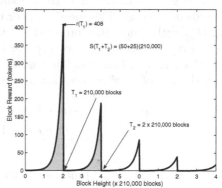

Fig. 2. Bitcoin block rewards as a function of block height. The area of the shaded region gives the total stake after $T_1 + T_2$ time.

Fig. 3. Geometric block rewards as a function of block height, using Bitcoin-based T_i and R_i values from Fig. 2.

In this paper, we revisit the question of how to choose $r(n)$. A key observation is that $r(n)$ must compensate nodes for the cost of proposing blocks. Many cryptocurrencies implicitly adopt the following maxim:

On short timescales, each block should yield the same block reward.

Notice that this maxim does not specify whether the value of a block reward is measured in tokens or in fiat. As illustrated earlier, most cryptocurrencies today measure value in tokens. We call this approach the *constant block reward*:

$$r_c(n) := \frac{R}{T}. \tag{2}$$

A natural alternative is to measure the block reward's value in fiat currency. This depends on the cryptocurrency's valuation over time interval $[T]$; if we assume it to be constant, then the resulting reward function should give a constant fraction of the *total* stake at each time slot. We call this the *geometric reward*:

$$r_g(n) := (1 + R)^{\frac{n}{T}} - (1 + R)^{\frac{n-1}{T}}. \tag{3}$$

Figure 3 shows geometric block rewards as a function of time if we use the same T_i's and R_i's as in Fig. 2, reflecting Bitcoin's block reward schedule.

Equitability. To compare reward functions, we define a metric called equitability. Consider the stochastic dynamic of the fractional stake of a party A that starts with $v_A(0)$ fraction of the initial total stake of $S(0) = 1$. We denote the fractional stake at time n by $v_{A,r}(n)$, to make the dependence on the reward function explicit. A straw-man metric for measuring fairness is the expected fractional stake at time T: i.e., if A contributes 10% of the proposal stake pool at the beginning of the time, then A should reap 10% of the total disseminated rewards on average. This metric is poor because PoS systems elect a proposer (in Eq. (1)) with probability proportional to the fractional stake; this ensures that each party's expected fractional reward is equal to its initial stake fraction, for any block reward function. That is, $\forall n \in [T]$, $\mathbb{E}[v_{A,r}(n)] = v_A(0)$. This follows from the law of total expectation and the fact that

$$\mathbb{E}[v_{A,r}(n) \,|\, v_{A,r}(n-1) = v]$$
$$= v\frac{v\,S(n-1) + r(n-1)}{S(n)} + \left(1 - v\right)\frac{v\,S(n-1)}{S(n)} = v.$$

Although all reward functions yield the same expected fractional stake, the choice of reward function can nonetheless dramatically change the distribution of the final stake, as seen in Fig. 1. We therefore instead propose using the *variance* of the final fractional stake, $\text{Var}(v_{A,r}(T))$, as an equitability metric. Intuitively, smaller variance implies less uncertainty and higher equitability:

Definition 1. *For a positive vector $\varepsilon \in \mathbb{R}^m$, we say a reward function $r : [T] \to \mathbb{R}^+$ over T time steps is ε-equitable for $\varepsilon = [\varepsilon_1, \ldots, \varepsilon_m]$ where $\varepsilon_i > 0$, if*

$$\frac{\mathrm{Var}(v_{A_i,r}(T))}{v_{A_i}(0)(1 - v_{A_i}(0))} \leq \varepsilon_i \tag{4}$$

for all $i \in [m]$. For two reward functions $r_1 : [T] \to \mathbb{R}^+$ and $r_2 : [T] \to \mathbb{R}^+$ with the same total reward, $\sum_{n=1}^{T} r_1(n) = \sum_{n=1}^{T} r_2(n)$, we say r_1 is more equitable than r_2 for player $i \in [m]$ if

$$\mathrm{Var}\big(v_{A_i,r_1}(T)\big) \leq \mathrm{Var}\big(v_{A_i,r_2}(T)\big), \tag{5}$$

when both random processes start with the same initial fraction of $v_{A_i}(0)$.

The normalization in Eq. (4) ensures the left-hand side is at most one, as we show in Remark 1. It also cancels out the dependence on the initial fraction $v_A(0)$ such that the left-hand side only depends on the reward function r and the time T, as shown in Lemma 1.

Remark 1. When starting with an initial fractional stake $v_A(0)$, the maximum achievable variance is

$$\sup_{T \in \mathbb{Z}^+} \sup_r \mathrm{Var}(v_{A,r}(T)) = v_A(0)(1 - v_A(0)), \tag{6}$$

where the supremum is taken over all positive integers T and reward function $r : [T] \to \mathbb{R}^+$ (a proof is provided in a longer version of this paper [10]).

From the analysis of a time-dependent Pólya's urn model, we know the variance satisfies the following formula (a proof is provided in a longer version of this paper [10] and also [21]).

Lemma 1. *Let $e^{\theta_n} \triangleq S(n)/S(n-1)$, then*

$$\mathrm{Var}(v_{A,r}(T)) = \big(v_{A,r}(0) - v_{A,r}(0)^2\big)\Big(1 - \frac{S(0)^2}{S(T)^2} \prod_{n=1}^{T} (2e^{\theta_n} - 1)\Big). \tag{7}$$

(a proof is provided in a longer version of this paper [10])

Although Definition 1 applies to an arbitrary number of parties, Lemma 1 implies that it is sufficient to consider a single party's stake. More precisely:

Remark 2. If reward function $r : [T] \to \mathbb{R}^+$ over T time steps is ε-*equitable* for vector $\varepsilon = [\varepsilon_1, \ldots, \varepsilon_m]$ where $\varepsilon_i > 0$, then r is also $\tilde{\varepsilon}$-equitable, where

$$\tilde{\varepsilon} \triangleq \mathbf{1} \cdot \min_{i \in [m]} \varepsilon_i,$$

with $\mathbf{1}$ denoting the vector of all ones.

As such, the remainder of this paper will study equitability from the perspective of a single (arbitrary) party A. We will also describe reward functions as ε-equitable as shorthand for $\boldsymbol{\varepsilon}$-equitable, where $\boldsymbol{\varepsilon} = \mathbf{1} \cdot \varepsilon$. Note that even if the total reward R is fixed, equitability can differ dramatically across reward functions. In the example of Fig. 1, the constant reward function is 0.5-equitable. On the other hand, the geometric rewards of (3) have a smaller chance of losing all its fractional stake (i.e. $v_{A,r_g}(T) \approx 0$) or taking over the whole stake (i.e. $v_{A,r_g}(T) \approx 1$). It is 0.05-equitable in this example.

3   Equitability Under Honest Behavior

In this section, we analyze the equitability of different block reward functions, assuming that every party is honest, i.e. follows protocol, and the PoS system is *closed*, so no stake is removed or added to the proposal stake pool over a fixed time period T. Each party's stake changes only because of the block rewards it earns and compounding effects. We discuss the effects of strategic behavior in Sect. 4, and open systems in a longer version of this paper [10].

The metric of equitability leads to a core optimization problem for PoS system designers: given a fixed total reward R to be dispensed, how do we distribute it over the time T to achieve the highest equitability? Perhaps surprisingly, we show that this optimization has a simple, closed-form solution.

Theorem 1. *For all $R \in \mathbb{R}^+$ and $T \in \mathbb{Z}^+$, the geometric reward r_g defined in (3) is the most equitable among functions that dispense R tokens over time T, jointly over all parties A_i, for $i \in [m]$.*

A proof is provided in a longer version of this paper [10]. Intuitively, geometric rewards optimize equitability because they dispense small rewards in the beginning when the stake pool is small, so a single block reward cannot substantially change the stake distribution. The rewards subsequently grow proportionally to the size of the total stake pool, so the effect of a single block remains bounded throughout the time period. We emphasize that the geometric reward function does not depend on the initial stake of the party A, and hence is universally most equitable for all parties in the system simultaneously.

Composition. The geometric reward function does not only optimize equitability for a single time interval. Consider a sequence $(T_1, R_1), \ldots, (T_k, R_k)$ of checkpoints, where T_i is increasing in i, and R_i denotes the amount of reward to be disbursed between time $T_{i-1} + 1$ and T_i (inclusive). These checkpoints could represent target inflation rates on a monthly or yearly basis, for instance. A natural question is how to choose a block reward function that optimizes equitability over all the checkpoints jointly. The solution is to iteratively and independently apply geometric rewards over each time interval, giving a block reward function like the one shown in Fig. 3.

Theorem 2. *Consider a sequence of checkpoints* $\{(T_i, R_i)\}_{i \in [k]}$. *Let* $\tilde{R}_j :=$ $\sum_{i=1}^{j} R_i$. *The most equitable reward function is*

$$r(n) = (1 + \tilde{R}_{i-1}) \left(\left(\frac{1 + \tilde{R}_i}{1 + \tilde{R}_{i-1}} \right)^{\frac{n - T_{i-1}}{T_i - T_{i-1}}} - \left(\frac{1 + \tilde{R}_i}{1 + \tilde{R}_{i-1}} \right)^{\frac{n - 1 - T_{i-1}}{T_i - T_{i-1}}} \right) \tag{8}$$

for $n \in [T_{i-1} + 1, T_i]$.

A proof is provided in a longer version of this paper [10]. When there is only one checkpoint, Theorem 2 simplifies to Theorem 1. This implies that checkpoints can be chosen *adaptively*, i.e., they do not need to be fixed upfront to optimize equitability. Because of composition, we assume a single checkpoint for the remainder of this paper. In practice, the abrupt change in geometric block rewards at a checkpoint (Fig. 3) may lead to miner/validator attrition [4]. Liquidity limits may slow down this attrition, but cannot stop it [5]. One option is that a PoS system need not choose its block reward function based on equitability alone; it could also consider smoothness and/or monotonicity constraints. Another is that PoS blockchains could use geometric rewards only for the first epoch (when compounding poses the greatest risk), and then transition to a smoother block reward schedule of their choosing. We leave such exploration to future work.

Stake Pools. Participants also have the freedom to form stake pools, as explored in [6,9,25]. We show that stake pools reduce the variances of the fractional stake of all pool members, and quantify this gain. Consider a single party that owns $v_A(0)$ fraction of the stake at time $t = 0$. We know from Lemma 1 that the variance at time T is $\mathrm{Var}(v_{A,r}(T)) = \left(v_A(0) - v_A(0)^2 \right) \left(1 - \frac{S(0)^2}{S(T)^2} \prod_{n=1}^{T} (2e^{\theta_n} - 1) \right)$. Consider a case where the same party now participates in a stake pool, where the pool P has $v_P(0)$ of the initial stake (including the contribution from party A), and every time the stake pool is awarded a reward for block proposal, the reward is evenly shared among the participants of the pool according to their stakes. The stake of party A under this pooling is denoted by $v_{\tilde{A}}(T)$, and it follows from Lemma 1 immediately that

$$\mathrm{Var}(v_{\tilde{A},r}(T)) = \left(\frac{v_A(0)}{v_P(0)} \right)^2 \left(v_P(0) - v_P(0)^2 \right) \left(1 - \frac{S(0)^2}{S(T)^2} \prod_{n=1}^{T} (2e^{\theta_n} - 1) \right)$$

$$= \frac{1 - v_P(0)}{v_P(0)} \frac{v_A(0)}{1 - v_A(0)} \mathrm{Var}(v_{A,r}(T)) . \tag{9}$$

Thus party A's variance reduces by a factor of $(v_P(0)/v_A(0))((1 - v_A(0))/(1 - v_P(0)))$ by joining a stake pool of size $v_P(0)$. Note that the variance is monotonically decreasing under stake pooling. In practice, stake pools can organically form as long as this gain in equitability exceeds the cost of pool formation. Applying the Definition 1 to a single party A, an ε-equitable party A will achieve $\varepsilon \frac{v_A(0)(1-v_P(0))}{v_P(0)(1-v_A(0))}$-equitability by forming a stake pool. Further, geometric rewards are still the most equitable reward function in the presence of stake pools. This follows from the fact that the effect of pooling is isolated from the effect of the choice of the reward function in Eq. (9),

Practical Parameter Selection. The equitability of a system is determined by four factors: the number of block proposals T, choice of reward function r, initial stake of a party $v_A(0)$, and the total reward R. We saw that geometric rewards optimize equitability; in this section, we study its dependence on T, $S(0)$, and R. Recall that without loss of generality, we normalized the initial stake $S(0)$ to be one. For general choices of $S(0)$, the total reward R should be rescaled by $1/S(0)$. The evolution of the fractional stakes is exactly the same for one system with $S(0) = 2$ and $R = 200$ and another with $S(0) = 1$ and $R = 100$. We assume here that the system designer can choose the total reward R, either by setting the initial stake size $S(0)$ and/or the total reward during T. We study how equitability trades off with the total reward R for different choices of the reward function.

Geometric Rewards. For $r_g(n)$, we have $e^{\theta_n} = (1 + R)^{1/T}$. It follows from Lemma 1 that

$$\frac{\text{Var}(v_{A,r_g}(T))}{v_A(0) - v_A(0)^2} = 1 - \frac{(2(1 + R)^{1/T} - 1)^T}{(1 + R)^2}, \tag{10}$$

When R is fixed and we increase T, we can distribute small amounts of rewards across T and achieve vanishing variance. On the other hand, if R increases much faster than T, then we are giving out increasing amounts of rewards per time slot and the uncertainty grows. This follows from the above variance formula, which we make precise in the following.

Remark 3. For a closed PoS system with a total reward $R(T)$ chosen as a function of T and a geometric reward function $r_g(n) = (1 + R(T))^{n/T} - (1 + R(T))^{(n-1)/T}$, it is sufficient and necessary to set

$$R(T) = \left(\left(\frac{1}{1 - \sqrt{\frac{\log(1/(1-\varepsilon))}{T}}} \right)^T - 1 \right) (1 + o(1)), \tag{11}$$

in order to ensure ε-equitability asymptotically, i.e. $\lim_{T \to \infty} \frac{Var(v_{A,r_g}(T))}{v_A(0)(1-v_A(0))} = \varepsilon$.

Remark 3 follows from substituting the choice of $R(T)$ in the variance in Eq. (10), which gives

$$\lim_{T \to \infty} \frac{\text{Var}(v_{A,r_g}(T))}{v_A(0) - v_A(0)^2} = \lim_{T \to \infty} 1 - \left(1 - \frac{\log(1/(1-\varepsilon))}{T} \right)^T (1 + o(1)).$$
$$= \varepsilon , \tag{12}$$

The limiting variance is monotonically non-decreasing in R and non-increasing in T, as expected from our intuition. For example, if R is fixed, one can have the initial stake $S(0)$ as small as $\exp(-\sqrt{T}/(\log T))$ and still achieve a vanishing variance. As the geometric reward function achieves the smallest variance (Theorem 1), the above $R(T)$ is the largest reward that can be dispensed while achieving a desired normalized variance of ε in time T (with initial stake of one). This scales as $R(T) \simeq (1 + 1/\sqrt{T})^T \simeq e^{\sqrt{T}}$. We need more initial stake or less total reward, if we choose to use other reward functions.

Constant Rewards. In comparison, consider the constant reward function of Eq. (2). As $e^{\theta_n} = (1 + nR/T)/(1 + (n-1)R/T)$, it follows from Lemma 1 that

$$\frac{\mathrm{Var}(v_{A,r_c}(T))}{v_A(0) - v_A(0)^2} = 1 - \frac{1 + R + \frac{R}{T}}{1 + R + \frac{R}{T} + \frac{R^2}{T}}$$

$$= \frac{R^2}{(T+R)(1+R)} . \tag{13}$$

Again, this is monotonically non-decreasing in R and non-increasing in T, as expected. The following condition immediately follows from Eq. (13).

Remark 4. For a closed PoS system with a total reward $R(T)$ chosen as a function of T and a constant reward function $r_c(n) = R(T)/T$, it is sufficient and necessary to set

$$R(T) = \frac{\varepsilon T}{1 - \varepsilon} (1 + o(1)) , \tag{14}$$

in order to ensure ε-equitability asymptotically as T grows.

By choosing a constant reward function, the cost we pay is in the size of the total reward, which can now only increase as $O(T)$. Compared to $R(T) \simeq e^{\sqrt{T}}$ of the geometric reward, there is a significant gap. Similarly, in terms of how small initial stake can be with fixed total reward R, constant reward requires at least $S(0) \simeq R/T$. This trend gets even more extreme for a decreasing reward function, which we discuss in a longer version of this paper [10].

Comparison of Rewards. For $S(0) = 1$ and $R = 10$, Fig. 4 illustrates the normalized variance of the three reward functions as a function of T, the total number of blocks. As expected, variance decays with T and geometric rewards exhibit the lowest normalized variance. Similarly, for a fixed desired (normalized) variance level of $\varepsilon = 0.1$, Fig. 5 shows how the total reward grows as a function of time T. Notice that under constant rewards, the reward allocation grows linearly in T, whereas geometric rewards grow subexponentially while still satisfying the same equitability constraint. These observations add nuance to the ongoing conversation about how to initialize PoS cryptocurrencies. A recent lawsuit against Ripple highlighted that the large initial stake pool could put disproportionate power in the hands of the system designers [26]. While Ripple itself is not PoS, our results suggest that in standard PoS systems, a large initial stake pool can actually help to ensure equitability.

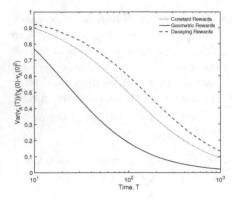
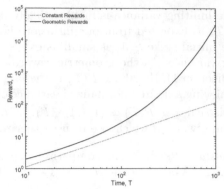

Fig. 4. Normalized variance after dispensing $R = 10$ tokens over T blocks, under different reward schemes.

Fig. 5. Amount of reward that can be dispensed over T blocks while guaranteeing a normalized variance of at most $\varepsilon = 0.1$.

4   Strategic Behavior

In practice, proposers can behave strategically to maximize their rewards (e.g., *selfish mining* [9,19,24]). In selfish mining, miners who discover blocks do not immediately publish them, but build a private *withheld fork* of blocks. By eventually releasing a private chain that is longer than the main chain, the adversary can invalidate honest blocks. This gives the adversary a greater fraction of main chain blocks and wastes honest parties' effort. In this section, we show that such strategic attacks are exacerbated by the compounding effects of PoS, and geometric rewards do not provide adequate protection.

Modeling the space of strategic behaviors in PoS requires more nuance than the corresponding problem in PoW [24]. We include a full model in Appendix A, which includes all the notation required to prove the theorems in this section. Due to space limitations, we summarize the model here. We consider two parties: A, which is adversarial, and H, which is honest. At any time, both parties can see the main chain, which is built upon by the honest party. We denote the length of this chain at time t by ℓ_t. In parallel, A can maintain as many private withheld forks as it wants, as long as the sequence of block proposers in each side chain respects the global leader election sequence. Since each block is associated with a time slot, A must have been the elected leader for each block in a withheld fork. I.e., if a withheld fork block is associated with time slot n, then $W(n) = A$.

At each time slot, the adversary has three options: (1) It can *wait*, or continue to build upon its withheld forks without releasing them. (2) It can *match* the main chain by releasing enough blocks from a single withheld fork to equal the height of the main chain, ℓ_t. After a match, there will be two publicly-visible chains of length ℓ_t in the system; we assume the honest party adopts the adversarial fork with probability γ, a parameter that captures the adversary's connectivity. (3) The adversary can *override* the main chain by releasing a withheld fork up of length $\ell_t + 1$. If the withheld fork is longer than $\ell_t + 1$, it only releases the first $\ell_t + 1$ blocks. Since the released fork is longer than the main chain, it is always adopted by the honest party. Given this action space, the adversary's goal is to maximize the fraction of main chain blocks that belong to the adversary.

4.1   Strategic Selfish Mining

We show that adversarial gains from strategic behavior are exacerbated by compounding. In practice, the adversary needs a strategy that balances the gains of keeping a long side chain to potentially overtake a long main chain, with the loss in intermediate leader elections due to withheld rewards. We propose a family of schemes called *Match-Override-k* (MO-*k*). Under MO-*k*, the adversary only keeps side chains whose tip is at most *k* blocks ahead of the main chain. The strategy is as follows: Every time a new honest block is generated, it is appended to the main chain. Next, if there is a side chain that (a) is longer than ℓ_t, and (b) does not already include the entire honest chain, the adversary *matches* the main chain. Now there are two chains of equal length in the system; with probability γ, the newly-released side chain becomes the new main chain. Otherwise, the previous honest main chain continues to be the main chain, and the failed side chain is discarded. If there is no such side chain to match, then the adversary *waits*. Any side chains shorter than ℓ_t are discarded.

Every time a new adversarial block is generated, the adversary appends it to every side chain she is managing currently. She also starts a new side chain branching from the tip of the main chain, if there is not a side chain there already. The adversary now checks every side chain. If there is a side chain that branches at the tip of the main chain and is at least *k* blocks ahead of the main chain, the adversary *overrides* with this side chain, thereby incrementing the main chain length by one. Otherwise, the main chain remains as is, and the adversary *waits*.

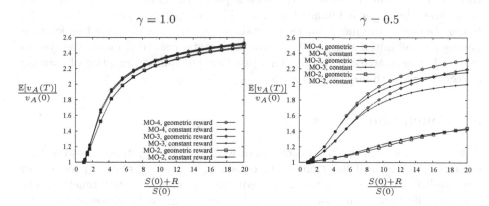

Fig. 6. Average fractional stake of an adversary can increase significantly as the total reward R increases. We fix initial fraction $v_A(0) = 1/3$, $S(0) = 1$, and $T = 10,000$ time steps, and show for two values of network connectivity of the adversary $\gamma \in \{0.5, 1.0\}$ and varying total reward R.

Figure 6 simulates how much the adversary can gain in average fractional stake by using MO-k strategies. As the total reward R increases, the relative fractional stake approaches 3, which is the maximum achievable value, since the expected fractional stake is normalized by $v_A(0) = 1/3$. The simulations were run for $T = 10,000$ time steps, with $S(0) = 1$. When the adversary is well-connected, i.e., $\gamma = 1.0$, such attacks are effective even with short side chains, such as $k = 3$ or 4. Further, there is no distinguishable difference in the reward function used. On the other hand, when the adversary has 0.5 probability of matching honest chains, $\gamma = 0.5$, it is more effective to keep longer side chains. Figure 6 demonstrates dramatic gains in fractional stake due to strategic behavior. A natural question is how large these gains can be. The following theorem gives an upper bound on stake amplification due to strategic behavior. Given the time-varying nature of the underlying random process and the optimization over a large space of strategic actions, the proof is mathematically sophisticated. This proof, discussed in a longer version of this paper [10], involves stochastic dominance results of time-varying Pólya urn processes, and may be of independent interest.

Theorem 3. *Let $v_A(t)$ denote the fractional stake of the adversary under selfish mining (mathematically defined in Appendix A), when the total initial stake is $S(0)$, initial fractional stake of the adversary is $v_A(0)$, and the total reward dispensed over time T is $R = cT$. If $R \leq S(0)(1 - v_A(0))$, then*

$$\mathbb{E}[v_A(T)] \;=\; (1 + \eta)\, v_A(0)\,, \tag{15}$$

where $\eta \triangleq R/(S(0) + c)$.

A proof is provided in a longer version of this paper [10]. We find empirically in [10] that this upper bound is tight when $\frac{S(0)+R}{S(0)}$ is small. Under the assumption that R is less than the stake of the honest party, the gain of strategic behavior over honest behavior is bounded by $\mathbb{E}[v_A(T)] - \mathbb{E}[v_A(0)] \leq \eta\, v_A(0)$, since under honest behavior the mean fractional stake is $v_A(0)$ for all t. This implies that having a small initial stake $S(0)$ relative to the total reward R makes the system vulnerable to strategic behavior. This justifies the common practice of starting a PoS system with large initial stake.

5   Conclusion

This work measures the concentration of wealth in PoS systems, showing that existing block reward functions (e.g., constant, decreasing rewards) have poor equitability. We introduce a maximally-equitable geometric reward function. The negative effects of compounding can be further mitigated by choosing the total block rewards for each epoch to be small compared to the initial stake pool size.

Several open questions remain. First, our results do not account for proposers add or removing stake during an epoch. Another challenge, discussed in [10], is that geometric rewards may not be desirable in practice because of the sharp changes in block rewards between epochs. A natural solution is to impose smoothness constraints on the class of reward functions—an interesting direction for future work. Finally, although strategic players are not specific to PoS systems, we show that geometric rewards alone do not protect against them. Designing incentive-compatible consensus protocols is a major open question.

Appendix

A   Strategic Behavior

We restrict ourselves in this section to two parties: A, which is adversarial, and H, which is honest. Note that this is without loss of generality, as H represent the collective set of multiple honest parties as their behavior is independent of how many parties are involved in H. The adversarial party A can also represent the collective set of multiple adversarial parties, as having a single adversary A is the worst case when all adversaries are colluding. Throughout this section, we use the terms *adversarial* and *strategic* interchangeably.

Since A does not always publish its blocks on schedule, we distinguish the notion of a block slot (indexed by $n \in [T]$) and wall-clock time (indexed by $t \in [T]$). It will still be the case that each *block slot* n has a single leader $W(n)$—in practice, this is determined by a distributed protocol—and a new block slot leader is elected at every tick of the wall clock (i.e., at a given time t, $W(n)$ is only defined for $n \leq t$). However, due to strategic behavior (i.e., the adversary can withhold its own blocks and override honest ones), it can happen that no block occupies slot n, even at time $t \geq n$; moreover, the occupancy of block slot n can change over time. Thus, unlike our previous setting, if we wait T time slots, the resulting chain may have fewer than T blocks. This is consistent with the adversarial model considered in PoS systems (e.g., Ouroboros [15]) that elect a single leader per block slot. Other PoS systems, like PoSv3 [8], choose an independent leader to succeed each block; such a PoS model can lead to even worse attacks, which we do not consider in this work.

The honest party and the adversary have two different views of the blockchain, illustrated in Fig. 7. Both honest and adversarial parties see the *main chain* B_t; we let $B_t(n)$ denote the block (i.e., leader) of the nth slot, as perceived by the honest nodes at time t. If a block slot n does not have an associated block at time t (either because the nth block was withheld or overridden, or because $n > t$), we say that $B_t(n) = \emptyset$. Notice that due to adversarial manipulations, it is possible for $B_t(n) = \emptyset$ and $B_{t-1}(n) \neq \emptyset$, and vice versa.

In addition to the main chain, the adversary maintains arbitrarily many private *side chains*, $\tilde{B}_t^1, \ldots, \tilde{B}_t^s$, where s denotes the number of side chains. The blocks in each side chain must respect the global leader sequence $W(n)$. An adversary can choose at any time to publish a side chain, but we also assume that the adversary's attacks are *covert*: it never publishes a side chain that conclusively proves that it is keeping side chains. For example, if the main chain contains a block B created by the adversary for block slot n, the adversary will never publish a side chain containing block $\tilde{B} \neq B$, where $\tilde{B}$ is also associated with block slot n.

Each side chain $\tilde{B}_t^i$ with $i \in [s]$ overlaps with the honest chain in at least one block (the genesis block), and may diverge from the main chain after some $f_t^i \in \mathbb{N}_+$ (Fig. 7). That is,

$$f_t^i := \max\{n \in \mathbb{N}_+ \ : \ B_t(n) = \tilde{B}_t^i(n)\}.$$

Different side chains can also share blocks; in reality, the union of side chains is a tree. However, for simplicity of notation, we consider each path from the genesis block to a leaf of this forest as a separate side chain, instead of considering side trees. We use ℓ_t and $\tilde{\ell}_t^i$ to denote the chain length of B_t and $\tilde{B}_t^i$, respectively, at time t:

$$\ell_t = |\{n \in [T] \ : \ B_t(n) \neq \emptyset\}| \ , \quad \text{and} \quad \tilde{\ell}_t^i = |\{n \in [T] \ : \ \tilde{B}_t^i(n) \neq \emptyset\}|,$$

and we use the heights h_t and $\tilde{h}_t^i$ to denote the block indices of the ℓ_tth and $\tilde{\ell}_t^i$th blocks, respectively:

$$h_t = \max\{n \in [T] \ : \ B_t(n) \neq \emptyset\} \ , \quad \text{and} \quad \tilde{h}_t^i = \max\{n \in [T] \ : \ \tilde{B}_t^i(n) \neq \emptyset\}.$$

If $f_t^i = h_t$, then the adversary is building its ith side chain from the tip of the current main chain.

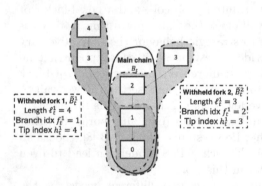

Fig. 7. In PoS, the adversary can keep arbitrarily many side chains at negligible cost, and release (part of) a side chain whenever it chooses.

State Space. The state space for the system consists of three pieces of data: (1) The current time $t \in [T]$; (2) The main chain B_t; and (3) The set of all side chains $\{\tilde{B}_t^i\}_{i \in [s]}$. Notice in particular that the set of side chains grows exponentially in t. In practice, most systems prevent the main chain from being overtaken by a longer side chain that branches more than Δ blocks prior to h_t; this is called a *long-range attack*. Hence we can upper bound the size of the side chain set by imposing the condition that for all $i \in [s]$, $h_t - f_t^i \leq \Delta$. Regardless, the size of the state space is considerably larger than it is in prior work on selfish mining in PoW [24], where the computational cost of creating a block forces the adversary to keep a single side chain.

Objective. The adversary A's goal is to maximize its fraction of the total stake in the main chain by the end of the experiment,

$$v_A(t) \ = \ \frac{|\{n \in [T] \ : \ (W(n) = A) \wedge (B_T(n) \neq \emptyset)\}|}{\ell_T}.$$

This objective is closely related to the metric of prior work [24], except for the finite time duration.

Strategy Space. The adversary has two primary mechanisms for achieving its objective: choosing where to append its blocks, and choosing when to release a side chain. If the honest party H is elected at time t, by the protocol, it always builds on the longest chain visible to it; since we assume small enough network latency, H appends to block $B_{t-1}(h_{t-1})$. However, if A is elected at time t, A can append to *any* known block in $B_{t-1} \cup \{\tilde{B}^i_{t-1}\}_{i \in [s]}$. The system must allow such a behavior for robustness reasons: even an honest proposer may not have received a block $B_{t-1}(h_{t-1})$ or its predecessors due to network latency.

The adversary can also choose when to release blocks. In our model, H always releases its block immediately when elected. However, an adversarial proposer elected at time t can choose to release its block at any time $\geq t$; it can also choose not to release a given block. Late block announcements are also tolerated because of network latency; it is impossible to distinguish between a node that releases their blocks late and a node whose blocks arrive late because of a poor network connection.

Notice that if A is elected at time t and chooses to withhold its block, the system advances to time $t + 1$ without appending A's block to the main chain. This means that the next proposer $W(t+1)$ is selected based on the stake ratios at time $t - 1$. So the adversary may have incurred a selfish mining gain from withholding its block, but it lost the opportunity to compound the tth block reward. This tradeoff is the main difference between our analysis and prior work on selfish mining attacks in PoW systems.

Drawing from [9,24], at each time slot t, the adversary has three classes of actions available to it: match, override, and wait.

(1) The adversary **matches** by choosing a side chain $\tilde{B}^i_t$ and releasing the first h_t blocks. This means the released chain has the same height as the honest chain. In accordance with [9,24], we assume that after a match, the honest chain will choose to build on the adversarial chain with probability γ, which captures how connected the adversarial party is to the rest of the nodes.
(2) The adversary **overrides** by choosing a side chain $\tilde{B}^i_t$ and releasing the first $h = h_t + 1$ blocks. The released chain becomes the new honest chain.
(3) If the adversary chooses to **wait**, it does not publish anything, and continues to build on all of its side chains.

Unlike [9,24], we do not explicitly include an action wherein the adversary adopts the main chain. Because our model allows the adversary to keep an unbounded number of side chains, adopting the main chain is always a suboptimal strategy; it forces the adversary to throw away chains that could eventually overtake the main chain. The primary nuance in the adversary's strategy is choosing *when* to match or override (rather than waiting), and *which* side chain to choose. Identifying an optimal mining strategy through MDP solvers as in [24] is computationally intractable due to the substantially larger state space in this PoS problem.

References

1. Bitcoin energy consumption index (2018). https://digiconomist.net/BITCOIN-ENERGY-CONSUMPTION
2. Controlled supply. bitcoinwiki (2018). https://en.bitcoin.it/wiki/Controlled_supply#cite_note-2
3. Mining. Ethereum Wiki (2018). https://github.com/ethereum/wiki/wiki/Mining
4. Bambrough, B.: A bitcoin halvening is two years away – here's what'll happen to the bitcoin price. Forbes, May 2018
5. Bentov, I., Pass, R., Shi, E.: Snow white: provably secure proofs of stake. IACR Cryptology ePrint Archive 2016, p. 919 (2016)
6. Brünjes, L., Kiayias, A., Koutsoupias, E., Stouka, A.-P.: Reward sharing schemes for stake pools. arXiv preprint arXiv:1807.11218 (2018)
7. Duffield, E., Diaz, D.: Dash: a privacycentric cryptocurrency (2015, self-published)
8. Earls, J.: The missing explanation of proof of stake version 3 (2017). http://earlz.net/view/2017/07/27/1904/the-missing-explanation-of-proof-of-stake-version
9. Eyal, I., Sirer, E.G.: Majority is not enough: bitcoin mining is vulnerable. Commun. ACM **61**(7), 95–102 (2018)
10. Fanti, G., Kogan, L., Oh, S., Ruan, K., Viswanath, P., Wang, G.: Compounding of wealth in proof-of-stake cryptocurrencies. arXiv preprint arXiv:1809.07468 (2018)
11. Gaži, P., Kiayias, A., Russell, A.: Stake-bleeding attacks on proof-of-stake blockchains. In: 2018 Crypto Valley Conference on Blockchain Technology (CVCBT), pp. 85–92. IEEE (2018)
12. Gilad, Y., Hemo, R., Micali, S., Vlachos, G., Zeldovich, N.: Algorand: scaling byzantine agreements for cryptocurrencies. In: Proceedings of the 26th Symposium on Operating Systems Principles, pp. 51–68. ACM (2017)
13. Hopwood, D., Bowe, S., Hornby, T., Wilcox, N.: Zcash protocol specification. Technical report, 2016–1.10. Zerocoin Electric Coin Company (2016)
14. Johnson, N.L., Kotz, S.: Urn Models and Their Application: An Approach to Modern Discrete Probability Theory, vol. 77. Wiley, New York (1977)
15. Kiayias, A., Russell, A., David, B., Oliynykov, R.: Ouroboros: a provably secure proof-of-stake blockchain protocol. In: Katz, J., Shacham, H. (eds.) CRYPTO 2017. LNCS, vol. 10401, pp. 357–388. Springer, Cham (2017). https://doi.org/10.1007/978-3-319-63688-7_12
16. Mahmoud, H.: Pólya Urn Models. Chapman and Hall/CRC, Boca Raton (2008)
17. moh_man. How does pos stake concept deal with rich becoming richer issue? Reddit (2017). https://www.reddit.com/r/ethereum/comments/6x0xv8/how_does_pos_stake_concept_deal_with_rich/
18. Nakamoto, S.: Bitcoin: a peer-to-peer electronic cash system (2008)
19. Nayak, K., Kumar, S., Miller, A., Shi, E.: Stubborn mining: generalizing selfish mining and combining with an eclipse attack. In: 2016 IEEE European Symposium on Security and Privacy (EuroS&P), pp. 305–320. IEEE (2016)
20. Pass, R., Shi, E.: Fruitchains: a fair blockchain. In: Proceedings of the ACM Symposium on Principles of Distributed Computing, pp. 315–324. ACM (2017)
21. Pemantle, R.: A time-dependent version of pólya's urn. J. Theor. Probab. **3**(4), 627–637 (1990)
22. Rammeloo, G.: The economics of the proof of stake consensus algorithm. Medium (2017). https://medium.com/@gertrammeloo/the-economics-of-the-proof-of-stake-consensus-algorithm-e28adf63e9db

23. Ryan, D., Liang, C.-C.: Hybrid Casper FFG (2017). https://github.com/ethereum/EIPs/blob/master/EIPS/eip-1011.md
24. Sapirshtein, A., Sompolinsky, Y., Zohar, A.: Optimal selfish mining strategies in bitcoin. In: Grossklags, J., Preneel, B. (eds.) FC 2016. LNCS, vol. 9603, pp. 515–532. Springer, Heidelberg (2017). https://doi.org/10.1007/978-3-662-54970-4_30
25. Schrijvers, O., Bonneau, J., Boneh, D., Roughgarden, T.: Incentive compatibility of bitcoin mining pool reward functions. In: Grossklags, J., Preneel, B. (eds.) FC 2016. LNCS, vol. 9603, pp. 477–498. Springer, Heidelberg (2017). https://doi.org/10.1007/978-3-662-54970-4_28
26. Taylor-Copeland, J.: Coffey vs. Ripple class action complaint (2018)
27. Trustnodes.com. "proof of work is the rich get richer square" says vitalik buterin. Trustnodes (2018). https://www.trustnodes.com/2018/07/10/proof-work-rich-get-richer-squared-says-vitalik-buterin
28. Vukolić, M.: The quest for scalable blockchain fabric: proof-of-work vs. BFT replication. In: Camenisch, J., Kesdoğan, D. (eds.) iNetSec 2015. LNCS, vol. 9591, pp. 112–125. Springer, Cham (2016). https://doi.org/10.1007/978-3-319-39028-4_9
29. Wiki, E.: Proof of stake FAQs. https://github.com/ethereum/wiki/wiki/Proof-of-Stake-FAQs

Short Paper: I Can't Believe It's Not Stake! Resource Exhaustion Attacks on PoS

Sanket Kanjalkar(✉), Joseph Kuo(✉), Yunqi Li(✉), and Andrew Miller(✉)

University of Illinois Urbana Champaign (UIUC), Urbana, USA
{smk7,josephk4,yunqil3,soc1024}@illinois.edu

Abstract. We present a new resource exhaustion attack affecting several chain-based proof-of-stake cryptocurrencies, and in particular Qtum, a top 30 cryptocurrency by market capitalization ($300M as of Sep '18). In brief, these cryptocurrencies do not adequately validate the proof-of-stake before allocating resources to data received from peers. An attacker can exploit this vulnerability, even without any stake at all, simply by connecting to a victim and sending malformed blocks, which the victim stores on disk or in RAM, eventually leading to a crash. We demonstrate and benchmark the attack through experiments attacking our own node on the Qtum main network; in our experiment we are able to fill the victim's RAM at a rate of 2MB per second, or the disk at a rate of 6MB per second. We have begun a responsible disclosure of this vulnerability to appropriate development teams. Our disclosure includes a Docker-based reproducibility kit using the Python-based test framework. This problem has gone unnoticed for several years. Although the attack can be mitigated, this appears to require giving up optimizations enjoyed by proof-of-work cryptocurrencies, underscoring the difficulty in implementing and deploying chain-based proof-of-stake.

1 Introduction

Bitcoin mining is expensive, with power consumption estimates ranging from hundreds of megawatts [3,8] to gigawatts [9]. Naturally, there has been significant interest in reducing this cost. The main idea behind Proof-of-stake (PoS) is to move the mining competition from the physical realm to the financial realm, replacing computational mining with a random lottery based on held coins. Chain-based PoS is a minimal modification of the Bitcoin protocol with this insight. Instead of computing hash functions over an arbitrary space, we compute hash functions of each of the transaction outputs, and compare it against a difficulty threshold, weighted by the coin amount. This approach is employed by Peercoin, the first PoS currency, as well as scores of others currently in production, and is also the basis for several protocols from the research community [2,4,6,11]. Because of the similarities to Bitcoin, chain-based PoS cryptocurrencies typically fork the Bitcoin codebase or some descendent thereof.

© International Financial Cryptography Association 2019
I. Goldberg and T. Moore (Eds.): FC 2019, LNCS 11598, pp. 62–69, 2019.
https://doi.org/10.1007/978-3-030-32101-7_4

Most analysis of chain-based PoS has focused on consensus, aiming to show that properties like chain quality and chain growth are ensured in the same way as in Bitcoin (i.e., they hold when 51% of the stakeholders follow the protocol). However, proof-of-work in Bitcoin serves a second purpose, which is to guard access to limited resources, such as its disk, bandwidth, memory, CPU. Proof-of-work is easy to check, but expensive to create, and so Bitcoin uses this as the first line of defense against junk data sent from untrusted network peers: First check the proof of work, then check everything else. This is similar to earlier (pre-Bitcoin) uses of proof-of-work, such as preventing spam and guarding access to server resources [5,7,10]. Recent versions of Bitcoin build further on this approach, transmitting separate data structures containing just the proofs-of-work ("headers") ahead of the actual payload ("blocks").

Unfortunately this idea from Bitcoin does not carry over properly into Proof-of-Stake. In particular, since the stake in a PoS block is found in the second transaction (the "coinstake" transaction) rather than in the header, headers-first processing is prone to attack. To explore the consequences of this insight, we examined the leading chain-based proof-of-stake cryptocurrencies, and found that five are vulnerable to a resource exhaustion attack. Roughly the attack involves sending malformed chains of invalid blocks or headers that are stored in RAM or on disk without being properly validated. We implemented and benchmarked these attacks and have begun a responsible disclosure of this issue.

2   Background

2.1   Proof of Stake

Chain-based proof-of-stake protocols can be defined in terms of two functions, a mining function M and a validation function V [4]. The validation function V takes as input a chain of blocks, and outputs 1 if and only if the chain is valid according to the application-specific rules of the cryptocurrency (i.e., all of the transaction semantics and valid proofs-of-stake). The mining function M takes as input a previous block B to build on, a coin C, and timestamp t and outputs a new block B' if it is indeed possible to mine a block, otherwise it outputs nothing. Similar to Bitcoin, nodes following the protocol attempt to extend the longest valid chain they know of.

As in Proof of Work, the mining function M involves comparing a hash of block data to a difficulty target. Instead of hashing the entire block, PoS introduces the notion of kernel hash, which depends mainly on the first transaction in the block, called the coinstake transaction. In more detail, the coin C spent by the coinstake transaction is hashed alongside the block's timestamp, the kernel hash of the previous block, and a few other metadata. Finally, the difficulty is weighted against the quantity of coins in C. Roughly speaking, those with more coins are proportionally more likely to be eligible to mine the next block.

2.2   Validating PoS Blockchains

To mine on the largest valid block chain, as described above, a node must determine whether blocks received from peers are valid according to V. This can be expensive—in particular, it requires checking every transaction comes with correct signatures and does not double-spend any coins. Bitcoin, as well as Qtum and other PoS cryptocurrencies derived from it, have fairly complex machinery to perform this task efficiently. We give a bit more detail on how this works, focusing on the details relevant to our attack.

First of all, the node keeps track of the state of the current best chain, as well as a lookup table **pcoinsTip** of the Unspent Transaction Outputs (UTXOs) available in this chain. The **ConnectBlock()** method appends a block to the current main chain, validating each new transaction with the help of pcoinsTip.

The node maintains an in-RAM data structure **mapBlockIndex**, which represents a tree of every (valid) block header received, including the current longest chain as well as any forks. The **AcceptBlockHeader()** method performs simple checks before storing an entry in mapBlockIndex. We note here that in Bitcoin, this method checks the Proof-of-Work contained in the header, but since the coinstake transaction is not contained in the header, the analogous checking of Proof-of-Stake does not occur.

Blocks are stored on disk in append-only **block files**. Before storing on disk, the **AcceptBlock()** method first invokes AcceptBlockHeader(), and then hashes the transactions to check they match the *hashMerkleRoot* of the header. However, the transactions themselves are not checked until later.

If a chain of accepted blocks grows longer than the current main chain, then it is necessary to perform a "reorg" (Fig. 1A). This method unwinds the *pcoinsTip*, disconnecting the blocks one at a time down to the fork point, and finally connecting (and validating) the blocks in the new chain one at a time.

3   Explanation of the Attack

We describe our attack scenarios from the viewpoint of an attacker node that has already formed a connection to the victim node.

Attack on RAM. We first describe the variation of our attack targeting RAM. The goal is to create fake block headers that pass *AcceptBlockHeaders()* so that the victim stores them in *mapBlockIndex*. The attack begins by picking an arbitrary fork point in the blockchain, and constructing a header that extends this block, as illustrated in Fig. 1B. Each header's *nTime* field must be strictly greater than its parent. The *hashMerkleRoot*, which ordinarily would commit to a batch of new transactions, is instead set to a garbage value. To optimize the attack, a single headers message contains a chain of the maximum number of 500 headers. To avoid being disconnected, the attacker ensures that the chain of bogus headers is strictly shorter than the current main chain; otherwise, the victim would request the corresponding blocks, disconnecting the peer after a timeout if they are not received. Detailed pseudocode is given in Algorithm 1.

Attack on Disk. Next we describe a variation of the attack that targets disk. The goal is to create a chain of fake blocks that pass *AcceptBlock()* so that the victim stores them in *mapBlockIndex* and in the blocks database. The attacker first creates a chain of blocks, starting from an arbitrary fork point in history, and reaching exactly up to the length of the main chain. Each block is filled to the maximum size with dummy transactions. The transactions have arbitrary values for their signatures and references to input transactions, as neither of these are checked during *AcceptBlock()*. Before broadcasting the blocks, the attacker first broadcasts just the headers. The reason for this is that *AcceptBlock()* discards a block unless it has been explicitly requested; by sending the headers first, once the headers chain in *mapBlockIndex* reaches the same height as the main chain, the victim requests all the blocks. Notice that full block validation is only triggered in case of reorg as shown in Fig. 1. Since the attacker only sends blocks that do not exceed the length of the current chain, the victim never reorgs or validates the block. The pseudo-code for attack on disk is described in Algorithm 2.

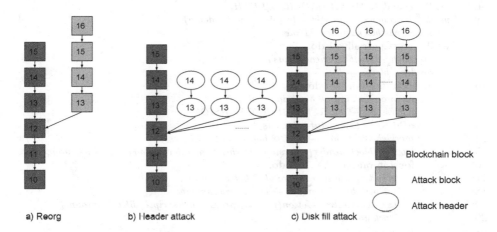

Fig. 1. Resource exhaustion attack

4 Evaluating the Attack

4.1 Analysis of Affected Cryptocurrencies

To determine the impact of this vulnerability on the ecosystem, we collected a list of known cryptocurrencies from coinmarketcap.com (on Aug. 9th 2018), sorted by market cap, and filtered by chain-based PoS consensus type. We only looked at cryptocurrencies whose codebase was forked from (a descendent of) Bitcoin, i.e. in C++. We also omitted cryptocurrencies with smaller than $10M market-cap. In total we examined 26 cryptocurrencies. Next we inspected the source code and determined whether each had support for headers-based block downloads

---

Algorithm 1. RAM attack nothing at stake

```
1: procedure RAM ATTACK(target_peer)
2:     block ← empty
3:     blockcount ← getblockcount()
4:     depth ← rand(1, MAX_HEADERS_DEPTH)
5:     pastblock_header ← getblockheader(blockcount - depth)
6:     nTime ← pastblock_header.nTime
7:     while target_peers.alive() do:
8:         prevhash ← pastblock_header.hash
9:         for d in depth do:
10:            nTime ← nTime + block_interval*d
11:            nVersion ← CURRENT_BLOCK_VERSION
12:            nBits ← get_next_difficulty_bits()
13:            merklehash, nonce ← rand32_bytes(), rand4_bytes()
14:            block_header ← block_header(nVersion, prevhash, merkleroot, nTime, nBits, nonce)
15:            send_msg_header(target_peer, block_header)
16:            prevhash ← block_header.hash
```

Algorithm 2. Disk attack nothing at stake

```
1: procedure DISK ATTACK(target_peer)
2:     block ← empty
3:     blockcount ← getblockcount()
4:     depth ← rand(1, MAX_HEADERS_DEPTH)
5:     pastblock_header ← getblockheader(blockcount - depth)
6:     nTime ← pastblock_header.nTime
7:     while target_peer.alive() do:
8:         prevhash ← pastblock_header.hash
9:         headers, blocks ← [],[]
10:        for d in range(depth) do:
11:            nTime ← nTime + block_interval*d
12:            nVersion ← CURRENT_BLOCK_VERSION
13:            nBits ← get_next_difficulty_bits()
14:            merklehash, nonce ← rand32_bytes(), rand4_bytes()
15:            block ← block_header(nVersion, prevhash, merkleroot, nTime, nBits, nonce)
16:            for j in range(MAX_TX) do:
17:                prev_tx, prev_index ← rand32_bytes(), 0
18:                scriptPubKey, amount ← b" ", rand_amount
19:                tx ← create_transaction(prev_tx, prev_index, scriptPubKey, amount)
20:                block.append(tx)
21:            block.rehash()
22:            prevhash ← block.hash
23:            headers.append(block.header)
24:            blocks.append(block)
25:            send_msg_headers(target_peer, headers)        ▷ Wait for peer to request blocks
26:            send_msg_blocks(target_peer, blocks[-1])
```

(i.e., if the AcceptBlockHeaders() method was present). By inspection, we estimated that the first 5 coins in Table 1 would be vulnerable to these attacks.

The second-from-bottom row of Table 1 is an aggregate (combined market cap) of 7 cryptocurrencies that include AcceptBlockHeader() but have disabled its functionality (i.e., do not process "headers" network messages). Likewise the bottom row is an aggregate of 14 cryptocurrencies that do not implement AcceptBlockHeader() at all.

Table 1. Vulnerability analysis of chain-based PoS cryptocurrencies

Name	Market cap (USD)	Vulnerable to RAM attack	Vulnerable to disk attack	Check TxDB for coinstake	Coordinated disclosure	Security process
Qtum (QTUM)	952,265,768	✓	✓	✗	✓	✗
Emercoin (EMC)	110,386,208	✓	✓	✗	✓	✗
Particl (PART)	47,065,433	✓	✓	✗	✓	✗
NavCoin (NAV)	39,029,633	✓	✓	✗	✓	✓
HTMLCOIN (HTML)	25,447,981	✓	✓	✗	✓	✗
Header disabled (PIVX etc.)	239,172,527	✗	✗	✓	N/A	N/A
No header (PPC etc.)	736,472,358	✗	✗	✓	N/A	N/A

To confirm the vulnerability, we next implemented the attacks in each of the codebases. We made use of existing test suites in Bitcoin software, specifically the "regtest" mode, which enables simulated timestamps and easy-to-create blocks, and a Python-based test node that can be extended with attacker behavior. We used Docker containers to package these tests, their dependencies, and the specific commit hash affected, into a reproducibility kit that we could easily share with developer teams as part of a vulnerability disclosure.

4.2   Benchmarking the Attack

To verify that the attack works in a live network setting (and not only in the regtest mode), we conducted an attack against our own node running on Qtum's live network. We optimized our attack to benchmark how effectively it could be carried out in practice, including forming up to 10 multiple connections to the victim, and by generating the block/header payloads in a pipelined fashion while transmitting them over the connections. Our victim node had a download speed of 1825.35 Mbit/s while our attacker node had an upload speed of 49.27 Mbit/s. We were able to fill the victim's disk at a rate of 6.05 MB/s, or the victim's RAM at 2.52 MB/s. For the disk attack, the main bottleneck in our testing was the amount of bandwidth between the attacker and victim. However for the headers attack, we reached a bottleneck of computational overhead as the victim processes the headers message.

5 Coordinated Vulnerability Disclosure

Resource exhaustion attacks in cryptocurrencies are considered critical vulnerabilities.[1] Because of the ease of exploiting this, we initiated a coordinated disclosure process to give developers of all the affected codebases an opportunity to deploy mitigations.

As highlighted by a recent vulnerability affecting Bitcoin and their rival Bitcoin Cash,[2] there are not yet clearly established guidelines for disclosures involving multiple cryptocurrencies. Cryptocurrencies are decentralized, and in principle may have no one officially recognized development team [1]. However, in this instance, all five of the affected projects are clearly associated with an official website and have publicly listed contact information. We note that only one of the projects (NavCoin) has a published vulnerability disclosure process and dedicated security contact.

Cryptocurrency communities have at times been embroiled in bitter disputes. We considered that disclosing the vulnerability too widely could increase the risk that one may leak it or attack another. We note that Qtum's market cap is around 5x larger than the rest combined. However, as all five responded to our initial email, and all codebases had active development (commits on GitHub within the past week), we decided to communicate simultaneously to them all.

6 Mitigations

We propose some easy to implement mitigations for the affected currencies. We can Checkpoint every K blocks so that the node does not accept forking blocks more than K blocks deep. Another such mitigation might include Disabling headers support and use TxDb check to determine if they have seen the coinstake transaction. This mitigation, although not perfect atleast requires the adversary to have some stake in the past. Lastly, we propose to UTXO snapshot every K blocks and perform validation of all blocks by rolling the pcoinsTip struct from the closest snaphot to the fork point.

7 Discussion and Conclusion

We show a resource exhaustion attack that can be carried out by a malicious peer without any stake in the currency and without any privileged network position. We found only a small number of the seventy chain-based PoS cryptocurrencies we considered to be vulnerable; however, weighted by market cap, this is more than half. The affected projects were all forked from a relatively recent Bitcoin version (version 0.10.0 or later, released February 2015) that incorporates the "headers first" feature, while those based on earlier versions of Bitcoin code are

---

[1] https://en.bitcoin.it/wiki/Common_Vulnerabilities_and_Exposures.
[2] https://bitcoincore.org/en/2018/09/20/notice/.

not vulnerable. We suspect the most likely outcome of our report is that the affected cryptocurrencies will downgrade to adopt behavior like the others.

However, we observe that even the non-vulnerable cryptocurrencies do not correctly implement the idealized protocol described in the research literature [2, 4, 6, 11]. In particular, the coinstake transactions in accepted blocks are validated against the coins database associated with the current main chain—even if the new block in question is on a fork from the main chain. In other words, the validation function V_p is not applied deterministically, but instead approximated. We plan to explore the consequences of this in future work.

The insights behind our attack are related to, but distinct from, the "nothing-at-stake" problem. This refers to the observation that in chain-based PoS, stakeholders are not penalized for mining on blocks on a conflicting fork. Our resource exhaustion attack is different in that the attacker need not have ever been a stakeholder at all. However, both cases highlight the difficulties in adapting designs ideas from proof-of-work into the proof-of-stake setting.

References

1. Azouvi, S., Maller, M., Meiklejohn, S.: Egalitarian society or benevolent dictatorship: the state of cryptocurrency governance. In: Zohar, A., et al. (eds.) FC 2018. LNCS, vol. 10958, pp. 127–143. Springer, Heidelberg (2019). https://doi.org/10.1007/978-3-662-58820-8_10
2. Bentov, I., Gabizon, A., Mizrahi, A.: Cryptocurrencies without proof of work. In: Clark, J., Meiklejohn, S., Ryan, P.Y.A., Wallach, D., Brenner, M., Rohloff, K. (eds.) FC 2016. LNCS, vol. 9604, pp. 142–157. Springer, Heidelberg (2016). https://doi.org/10.1007/978-3-662-53357-4_10
3. Böhme, R., Christin, N., Edelman, B., Moore, T.: Bitcoin: economics, technology, and governance. J. Econ. Perspect. **29**(2), 213–38 (2015)
4. Brown-Cohen, J., Narayanan, A., Psomas, C.A., Weinberg, S.M.: Formal barriers to longest-chain proof-of-stake protocols. arXiv preprint arXiv:1809.06528 (2018)
5. Dwork, C., Naor, M.: Pricing via processing or combatting junk mail. In: Brickell, E.F. (ed.) CRYPTO 1992. LNCS, vol. 740, pp. 139–147. Springer, Heidelberg (1993). https://doi.org/10.1007/3-540-48071-4_10
6. Fan, L., Zhou, H.S.: A scalable proof-of-stake blockchain in the open setting (or, how to mimic nakamoto's design via proof-of-stake). Cryptology ePrint Archive, Report 2017/656 (2017). https://eprint.iacr.org/2017/656
7. Juels, A., Brainard, J.G.: Client puzzles: a cryptographic countermeasure against connection depletion attacks. In: NDSS, vol. 99, pp. 151–165 (1999)
8. Narayanan, A., Bonneau, J., Felten, E., Miller, A., Goldfeder, S.: Bitcoin and Cryptocurrency Technologies: A Comprehensive Introduction. Princeton University Press, Princeton (2016)
9. O'Dwyer, K., Malone, D.: Bitcoin mining and its energy footprint. In: IET Conference Proceedings. The Institution of Engineering & Technology (2014)
10. Parno, B., Wendlandt, D., Shi, E., Perrig, A., Maggs, B., Hu, Y.C.: Portcullis: protecting connection setup from denial-of-capability attacks. ACM SIGCOMM Comput. Commun. Rev. **37**(4), 289–300 (2007)
11. Pass, R., Shi, E.: Fruitchains: a fair blockchain. In: Proceedings of the ACM Symposium on Principles of Distributed Computing, pp. 315–324. ACM (2017)

Measurement

Short Paper: An Exploration of Code Diversity in the Cryptocurrency Landscape

Pierre Reibel, Haaroon Yousaf, and Sarah Meiklejohn[(⊠)]

University College London, London, UK
{pierre.reibel.16,h.yousaf,s.meiklejohn}@ucl.ac.uk

Abstract. Interest in cryptocurrencies has skyrocketed since their introduction a decade ago, with hundreds of billions of dollars now invested across a landscape of thousands of different cryptocurrencies. While there is significant diversity, there is also a significant number of scams as people seek to exploit the current popularity. In this paper, we seek to identify the extent of innovation in the cryptocurrency landscape using the open-source repositories associated with each one. Among other findings, we observe that while many cryptocurrencies are largely unchanged copies of Bitcoin, the use of Ethereum as a platform has enabled the deployment of cryptocurrencies with more diverse functionalities.

1   Introduction

Since the introduction of Bitcoin in 2008 [23] and its deployment in January 2009, cryptocurrencies have become increasingly popular and subject to increasing amounts of hype and speculation. Initially, the promise behind cryptocurrencies like Bitcoin was the ability to send frictionless global ʼpayments: anyone in the world could act as a peer in Bitcoin's peer-to-peer network and broadcast a transaction that—without having to pay exorbitant fees—would send money to anyone else in the world, regardless of their location, citizenship, or what bank they used. This is achieved by the decentralization inherent in the open consensus protocol, known as proof-of-work, that allows any peer to not only broadcast transactions but also act to seal them into the official ledger.

While the realities of Bitcoin have shifted in the ensuing years, the landscape of cryptocurrencies has also shifted considerably. There are now thousands of alternative cryptocurrencies, supporting more exotic functionalities than the simple atomic transfer of money supported by Bitcoin. Ethereum, for example, promises to act as a distributed consensus computer (the Ethereum Virtual Machine, or EVM for short) by enabling arbitrary stateful programs to be executed by transactions, while Monero and Zcash promise to improve on the anonymity achieved by Bitcoin transactions. Others don't promise new functionalities but instead aim to support the same functionality as Bitcoin in more cost-effective ways; e.g., Zilliqa [9, 16, 17, 19, 28] and Cardano [7, 15] incorporate

ⓒ International Financial Cryptography Association 2019
I. Goldberg and T. Moore (Eds.): FC 2019, LNCS 11598, pp. 73–83, 2019.
https://doi.org/10.1007/978-3-030-32101-7_5

respective ideas from the academic literature about achieving consensus without relying entirely on proof-of-work.

Alongside this rapid expansion in the functionality of cryptocurrencies (or indeed the general applicability of the underlying concept of a blockchain), there has also been a genuine explosion of investment into these technologies. In July 2013, for example, there were 42 cryptocurrencies listed on the popular data tracker CoinMarketCap,[1] and the collective market capitalization was just over 1 billion USD. In July 2018, in contrast, there were 1664 cryptocurrencies, and the collective market capitalization was close to 1 trillion USD. While comprehensive in terms of deployed cryptocurrencies, this list does not even include many of the recent "initial coin offerings" (ICOs) that have similarly attracted millions in investment despite there having been many documented scams.[2,3] Against this backdrop of hype and investment, it is thus crucial to gain some insight into the different types of functionalities offered by these many different cryptocurrencies, to understand which coins offer truly novel features and are backed by genuine development efforts, and which ones are merely hoping to cash in on the hype.

This paper takes a first step in this direction, by examining the entire landscape of cryptocurrencies in terms of the publicly available source code used to support each one. While source code may not be the most accurate representation of a cryptocurrency (as, for example, the actual client may use a different codebase), it does reflect the best practices of the open-source software community, so we believe it to be a reasonable proxy for how a cryptocurrency does (or should) represent itself.

2   Related Work

We treat as related research that measures either general properties of open-source software, or research that measures properties of cryptocurrencies. In terms of the former, there have been numerous papers measuring GitHub repositories. For example, Hu et al. [12] and Thung et al. [29] measured the influence of software projects according to their position of their repositories and developers in the GitHub social graph, and others have taken advantage of the volume of source code available on GitHub to analyze common coding practices [34] or how bugs vary across different programming languages [24].

In terms of the latter, there are by now many papers that have focused on measuring properties of both the peer-to-peer networks [1,4,8,18] and the blockchain data associated with cryptocurrencies [3,5,6,14,20,22,25–27,30], as well as their broader ecosystem of participants [21,31–33]. Given the volume of research, we focus only on those papers most related to our own, in that they analyze properties across multiple cryptocurrencies, rather than within a single one like Bitcoin. In terms of comparing Bitcoin and Ethereum, Gencer et al. [10] compared

---

[1] https://coinmarketcap.com/historical/20130721/.
[2] https://deadcoins.com/.
[3] https://magoo.github.io/Blockchain-Graveyard/.

the level of decentralization in their peer-to-peer networks and found, for example, that Ethereum mining was more centralized than it was in Bitcoin, but that Bitcoin nodes formed more geographic clusters. Azouvi et al. [2] also compared their level of decentralization, in terms of the discussions on and contributions to their GitHub repositories, and found that Ethereum was more centralized in terms of code contribution and both were fairly centralized in terms of the discussions. Gervais et al. [11] introduced a framework for identifying the tradeoff between security and performance in any cryptocurrency based on proof-of-work, and found that the same level of resilience to double-spending attacks was achieved by 37 blocks in Ethereum as by 6 blocks in Bitcoin. Finally, Huang et al. [13] compared the effectiveness of different mining and speculation activities for 18 cryptocurrencies, and found that the profitability of both was affected by when a cryptocurrency was listed on an exchange.

3   Data Collection

In order to collect the source code associated with each cryptocurrency, we started with the list maintained at CoinMarketCap, which is generally regarded as one of the most comprehensive resources for cryptocurrency market data. The site maintains not only market data for each cryptocurrency (its market capitalization, price, circulating supply, etc.), however, but also links to any websites, blockchain explorers, or—crucially for us—source code repositories. We last scraped the site on July 24 2018, at which point there were 1664 cryptocurrencies listed, with a cumulative market capitalization of 293B USD.

3.1   Source Code Repositories

Of the listed cryptocurrencies, 1123 had a link available on CoinMarketCap to some source code repository. We examined a random sample of 10% of these links (and all the links for the top 20 cryptocurrencies) to ensure that they were legitimate, and in some cases replaced links where the information was inaccurate (for Bitcoin Cash, for example, the provided link was for the repositories backing bitcoincash.org rather than the actual software code). Of these links, 1108 (98.7%) pointed to GitHub.

As should be expected, many of the cryptocurrencies had multiple software repositories available; indeed, the links provided on CoinMarketCap were to the lists of repositories for a given GitHub organization, and in total there were 13,694 individual repositories available. The vast majority of these repositories had been created after October 2014, with a notable rise in frequency starting in April 2017. These repositories typically fell into one of three categories: (1) integral to the cryptocurrency itself, such as implementations of the reference client or supporting libraries; (2) irrelevant, such as a different project by the same organization; or (3) unchanged forks or mirrors of popular software projects, such as llvm. Given our goal of differentiating between the various cryptocurrencies, we did not want to clone every available repository but instead sought to isolate the first category of "meaningful" code.

To do this we assigned a rating to each repository for a given cryptocurrency according to: (1) the gap between its last update and the current date, to capture activity (where this was subtracted from the rating, as a longer gap indicates less activity); (2) its number of forks, to capture popularity and reuse; and (3) information about the name of the repository, to capture relevance. (For example, repositories with names including 'website' were excluded and ones with names including 'core' or 'token' were given a higher rating.) For each cryptocurrency, we then cloned the top 20% of the list of repositories, sorted from high to low by these ratings (or cloned one repository, whichever was larger). We then manually examined the repositories (both selected and unselected) for a random sample of 10% of the cryptocurrencies in order to ensure that we had selected the "right" repositories, although without ground truth data it was of course impossible to guarantee this for all cryptocurrencies. A full list of the 13,694 available repositories, along with our ratings and our decision of whether to clone them or not, is available online.[4] We cloned 2354 repositories in total, which comprised roughly 100 GB of data.

3.2 Deployed Source Code

As evidenced by the 866 (52%) listed cryptocurrencies that were categorized as tokens (and the fact that 74 of these even had 'token' in their name), it is popular to launch new cryptocurrencies not as standalone coins, but as tokens that are supported by existing cryptocurrencies. Of these, by far the most popular type is an ERC20 token, supported by Ethereum. Of these listed tokens, 406 did not have any source code link available. For ERC20 tokens that have been deployed, however, it is often possible to obtain the contract code from another source: the version deployed on the Ethereum blockchain itself is compiled bytecode, but it is common practice to provide the Solidity code and display it on blockchain explorers such as Etherscan.[5]

For these tokens, we thus chose to use Etherscan as a data source (in addition to any provided repositories), in order to aid our Ethereum-based analysis in Sect. 5. At the time that we scraped Etherscan, there were 612 ERC20 tokens listed, identified by a name and a currency symbol (e.g., OmiseGO and OMG). Of these, we found 438 with a match on CoinMarketCap, where we defined a match as having (1) identical currency symbols, and (2) closely matching names. (We couldn't also require the name to be identical because in some cases the name of the contract was somewhat altered from the name of the cryptocurrency; e.g., SPANK instead of SpankChain.) We scraped the available contract code for each of these tokens, which in all but 9 cases was Solidity code rather than just on-chain bytecode. We thus ended up with 429 deployed ERC20 contracts.

---

[4] https://github.com/manganese/alteramentum-repo-data.
[5] https://etherscan.io/.

4   Bitcoin Code Reuse

In this section, we attempt to identify the extent to which cryptocurrencies reuse the codebases of others, and in particular of Bitcoin. We do this by looking, very simply, at taking files from other repositories and using them without any modification. To identify this, we computed and stored the hash of every source code file in our cloned repositories; we identified source code file extensions using the CLOC library.[6] We then computed a similarity score S_{hash} between a repository A and another one B by counting the number of files in A with an identical file in B (meaning the hash was the same), and then dividing by the total number of files in A. To elevate this to the level of cryptocurrencies C_1 and C_2, we then computed $S_{\mathsf{hash}}(C_1, C_2)$ as

$$S_{\mathsf{hash}}(C_1, C_2) = \frac{\sum_{A \in C_1} S_{\mathsf{hash}}(A, \cup_{B \in C_2} B)}{\sum_{A \in C_1} \# \text{ files in } A};$$

i.e., for each repository A contributing to C_1 we counted the number of files that were identical to a file in any repository contributing to C_2, and then divided this by the total number of files across all repositories contributing to C_1.

We ran this for every pair of cryptocurrencies A and B (for both $S_{\mathsf{hash}}(A, B)$ and $S_{\mathsf{hash}}(B, A)$, since they are not symmetric), and used the results to create a graph in which nodes represent cryptocurrencies and there is a directed edge from A to B if $S_{\mathsf{hash}}(A, B) > 0.7$. This resulted in a graph with 445 nodes and 1854 edges, the largest connected component of which can be seen in Fig. 1 (consisting of 302 nodes and 1599 edges).

Most of this component consists of Bitcoin forks. The exception is cluster 9, which consists of one cryptocurrency (Zeepin) that is 100% similar to 16 other cryptocurrencies. The reason is simple: its repository consisted solely of an LGPL-3.0 license, so it matched other repositories with the same version of this license. At the time we scraped CoinMarketCap, Zeepin had a market capitalization of 23 million USD. We can briefly explain clusters 1–8 as follows:

- **1.** The node at the center of this cluster, Akuya Coin, has a directory structure similar (63%) to a version of the Bitcoin codebase from 2013, but many (32%) of its files are empty and thus have the same hash, which makes it appear similar to 76 other Bitcoin forks.
- **2 and 3.** Both of these clusters also have a directory structure similar to older versions of the Bitcoin codebase (the average directory similarity was 89% for cluster 2 and 82% for cluster 3), and are similar to the same cryptocurrency (BumbaCoin). Many also incorporate the Zerocoin code:[7] 84% of the nodes in cluster 2 and 65% of the nodes in cluster 3. This is notable given that this code comes with the emphatic warning "THIS CODE IS UNMAINTAINED AND HAS KNOWN EXPLOITS. DO NOT USE IT." In total it is included in repositories for 97 different cryptocurrencies.

---

[6] https://github.com/AlDanial/cloc.
[7] https://github.com/Zerocoin/libzerocoin.

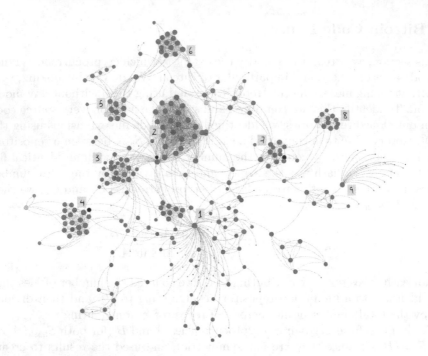

Fig. 1. The largest connected component of the graph formed by creating an edge from A to B if $S_{\mathsf{hash}}(A, B) > 0.7$, along with labels for the most prominent clusters.

- **4 and 5.** These clusters were the ones most similar to Bitcoin: on average we had $S_{\mathsf{hash}} = 0.51$ and $S_{\mathsf{dir}} = 0.80$ for cluster 4 and $S_{\mathsf{hash}} = 0.37$ and $S_{\mathsf{dir}} = 0.96$ for cluster 5. For cluster 4, the matching versions were also in quite a tight range from September 2013 to September 2014 (our versions 9 to 11), whereas most other clusters ranged more evenly across all 18 versions.
- **6 and 7.** These clusters consisted largely of forks from Litecoin: 100% of cluster 6 had the file `scrypt.c`, which is unique to Litecoin. 64% of cluster 7 had files with `scrypt` in the name, although only 21% identified as copyright derivatives of anything other than Bitcoin.
- **8.** The nodes in this cluster were on average newer than the others (with the first repository created in June 2015), and indeed their directory structure is more consistent with newer versions of the Bitcoin codebase.

5   Ethereum as a Platform

As discussed in Sect. 3.2, it is increasingly popular to deploy cryptocurrencies as tokens on the Ethereum blockchain; indeed, over half of the cryptocurrencies listed on CoinMarketCap fell into this category. This section thus explores this type of cryptocurrency deployment, focusing again on the extent to which ERC20 tokens are similar to or different from each other. As an ERC20 token consists of just a single file, our methods from the previous sections do not apply here so we develop new methods for identifying similarities.

The basic functionality of an ERC20 token—allowing the transfer of tokens from one holder to another—defines a contract type called `Basic` (or `BasicToken`) or—with one slight functional difference—`ERC20`. There are, however, many additional types that ERC20 tokens can have. For example, if they want to allow for the creation of new tokens they can be `Mintable` and if they want to allow for the destruction of existing tokens they can be `Destructible` or `Burnable`. These types are not standardized, and in fact new types can be defined and used within the Solidity code for a contract.

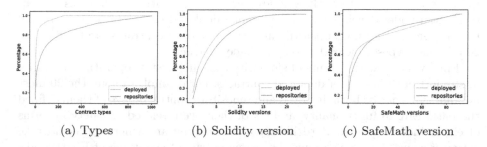

(a) Types   (b) Solidity version   (c) SafeMath version

Fig. 2. When ranked from most to least popular, the cumulative percentage of contracts matching three different features, for both the set of deployed contracts and the ones found in repositories.

To identify the types of a given token, we identified all lines in its contract of the form `contract X is Y {` , where `X` is the name of the contract and `Y` is its type. Some intermediate types themselves appear as names (e.g., `contract Mintable is Ownable`), which we exclude from our final results but carry over transitively to the higher-level contract names; e.g., if `X` is `Mintable` and `Mintable` is `Ownable` then `X` is both `Mintable` and `Ownable`. This resulted in a map from the higher-level token names to a list of all of their types.

Beyond these types, we also looked at the version the contract used of Solidity and of the SafeMath library, which provides safe arithmetic operations.For the version of Solidity, we looked for lines starting with `pragma solidity` and extracted the version from what followed (typically of the form `0.4.X`). To determine the version of SafeMath, we first used CLOC to strip the comments from the `.sol` file. We then identified the lines of code that defined the SafeMath library (starting with either `contract SafeMath {` or `library SafeMath {` and ending with `}`), and hashed this substring to form a succinct representation.

We extracted this information from all Solidity files, whether deployed on the Ethereum blockchain (and thus scraped from Etherscan, as described in Sect. 3.2) or contained in a repository.[8] For the types, Solidity and SafeMath versions, we

---

[8] Interestingly, these sets were non-intersecting; i.e., there was no contract in a repository that was identical to a deployed one.

ordered them from most to least popular and plotted this as a CDF, as seen in Fig. 2; i.e., we plotted the percentage y of all contracts that had one of the top x attributes.

The relatively long tails in all of the figures indicate a relatively high level of diversity among these features in both deployed contracts and those still under development. For example, the Solidity version most popular among deployed contracts (version 18) was still used in only 23% of them. Whereas Fig. 2b and c show similar curves for both sets of contracts, Fig. 2a shows a much longer tail for contracts contained in repositories, with 246 distinct types in deployed contracts and 1002 in ones in repositories. This indicates—as should perhaps be expected—that (1) there are just many more possibilities for contract types than for versions, and (2) there is greater experimentation with types in contracts still under development. Even among deployed contracts, 129 out of 429 had a type that did not appear in any other deployed contracts, and 148 of the 246 distinct types appeared in only a single contract.

Finally, we view the points of similarity that did exist as operating primarily in support of the safety of deployed contracts. For example, among the 20 most popular types across both deployed and repository contracts, five of them defined the basic ERC20 functionality, and six of them were related to safety in terms of either including a standard library or in defining an owner who could take action if something went wrong. The same is true of the usage of FirstBlood's `StandardToken`, which was the first safe implementation of this type, or of the `SafeMath` library. We thus view these similarities as a sign of good development practices, rather than the copying of ideas.

6   Conclusions

This paper considered diversity in the cryptocurrency landscape, according to the source code available for each one, in order to identify the extent to which new cryptocurrencies provide meaningful innovation. This was done by examining the source code for over a thousand cryptocurrencies, and—in the case of ERC20 tokens—the deployed code of hundreds more. While more sophisticated static analysis of the source code would likely yield further insights, even our relatively coarse methods clearly indicated the dominance of Bitcoin and Ethereum, as well as the extent to which creating a standalone platform is a significantly greater undertaking (leading to the reuse of much of the Bitcoin codebase) than defining just the transaction semantics of an Ethereum-based token.

Acknowledgements. The authors were supported in part by EPSRC Grant EP/N028104/1 and in part by the EU H2020 TITANIUM project under grant agreement number 740558.

References

1. Apostolaki, M., Zohar, A., Vanbever, L.: Hijacking Bitcoin: routing attacks on cryptocurrencies. In: 2017 IEEE Symposium on Security and Privacy, San Jose, CA, USA, 22–26 May 2017, pp. 375–392. IEEE Computer Society Press (2017)

2. Azouvi, S., Maller, M., Meiklejohn, S.: Egalitarian society or benevolent dictatorship: the state of cryptocurrency governance. In: Proceedings of the 5th Workshop on Bitcoin and Blockchain Research (2018)
3. Bartoletti, M., Carta, S., Cimoli, T., Saia, R.: Dissecting Ponzi schemes on Ethereum: identification, analysis, and impact (2017)
4. Biryukov, A., Khovratovich, D., Pustogarov, I.: Deanonymisation of clients in Bitcoin P2P network. In: Ahn, G.-J., Yung, M., Li, N. (eds.) ACM CCS 2014, Scottsdale, AZ, USA, 3–7 November 2014, pp. 15–29. ACM Press (2014)
5. Bos, J.W., Halderman, J.A., Heninger, N., Moore, J., Naehrig, M., Wustrow, E.: Elliptic curve cryptography in practice. In: Christin, N., Safavi-Naini, R. (eds.) FC 2014. LNCS, vol. 8437, pp. 157–175. Springer, Heidelberg (2014). https://doi.org/10.1007/978-3-662-45472-5_11
6. Chen, W., Zheng, Z., Cui, J., Ngai, E., Zheng, P., Zhou, Y.: Detecting Ponzi schemes on Ethereum: towards healthier blockchain technology. In: Proceedings of the 2018 World Wide Web Conference (WWW) (2018)
7. David, B., Gaži, P., Kiayias, A., Russell, A.: Ouroboros praos: an adaptively-secure, semi-synchronous proof-of-stake blockchain. In: Nielsen, J.B., Rijmen, V. (eds.) EUROCRYPT 2018, Part II. LNCS, vol. 10821, pp. 66–98. Springer, Cham (2018). https://doi.org/10.1007/978-3-319-78375-8_3
8. Donet, J.A.D., Pérez-Solà, C., Herrera-Joancomartí, J.: The Bitcoin P2P network. In: Böhme, R., Brenner, M., Moore, T., Smith, M. (eds.) FC 2014. LNCS, vol. 8438, pp. 87–102. Springer, Heidelberg (2014). https://doi.org/10.1007/978-3-662-44774-1_7
9. Eyal, I., Gencer, A.E., Sirer, E.G., van Renesse, R.: Bitcoin-ng: a scalable blockchain protocol. In: Proceedings of NSDI 2016 (2016)
10. Gencer, A.E., Basu, S., Eyal, I., Renesse, R.V., Sirer, E.G.: Decentralization in Bitcoin and Ethereum networks. In: Proceedings of the 22nd International Conference on Financial Cryptography and Data Security (FC) (2018)
11. Gervais, A., Karame, G.O., Wüst, K., Glykantzis, V., Ritzdorf, H., Capkun, S.: On the security and performance of proof of work blockchains. In: Weippl, E.R., Katzenbeisser, S., Kruegel, C., Myers, A.C., Halevi, S. (eds.) ACM CCS 2016, Vienna, Austria, 24–28 October 2016, pp. 3–16. ACM Press (2016)
12. Hu, Y., Zhang, J., Bai, X., Yu, S., Yang, Z.: Influence analysis of GitHub repositories. SpringerPlus 5(1), 1268 (2016)
13. Huang, D.Y., Levchenko, K., Snoeren, A.C.: Measuring profitability of alternative crypto-currencies. In: Proceedings of the 22nd International Conference on Financial Cryptography and Data Security (FC) (2018)
14. Kappos, G., Yousaf, H., Maller, M., Meiklejohn, S.: An empirical analysis of anonymity in Zcash. In: Proceedings of the USENIX Security Symposium (2018)
15. Kiayias, A., Russell, A., David, B., Oliynykov, R.: Ouroboros: a provably secure proof-of-stake blockchain protocol. In: Katz, J., Shacham, H. (eds.) CRYPTO 2017, Part I. LNCS, vol. 10401, pp. 357–388. Springer, Cham (2017). https://doi.org/10.1007/978-3-319-63688-7_12
16. Kogias, E.K., Jovanovic, P., Gailly, N., Khoffi, I., Gasser, L., Ford, B.: Enhancing Bitcoin security and performance with strong consistency via collective signing. In: Proceedings of USENIX Security 2016 (2016)
17. Kokoris-Kogias, E., Jovanovic, P., Gasser, L., Gailly, N., Ford, B.: Omniledger: a secure, scale-out, decentralized ledger. In: Proceedings of the 39th IEEE Symposium on Security & Privacy (2018)

18. Koshy, P., Koshy, D., McDaniel, P.: An analysis of anonymity in Bitcoin using P2P network traffic. In: Christin, N., Safavi-Naini, R. (eds.) FC 2014. LNCS, vol. 8437, pp. 469–485. Springer, Heidelberg (2014). https://doi.org/10.1007/978-3-662-45472-5_30

19. Luu, L., Narayanan, V., Zheng, C., Baweja, K., Gilbert, S., Saxena, P.: A secure sharding protocol for open blockchains. In: Weippl, E.R., Katzenbeisser, S., Kruegel, C., Myers, A.C., Halevi, S. (eds.) ACM CCS 2016, Vienna, Austria, 24–28 October 2016, pp. 17–30. ACM Press (2016)

20. Meiklejohn, S., et al.: A fistful of bitcoins: characterizing payments among men with no names. In: Proceedings of the 2013 Internet Measurement Conference (IMC), pp. 127–140 (2013)

21. Moore, T., Christin, N.: Beware the middleman: empirical analysis of Bitcoin-exchange risk. In: Sadeghi, A.-R. (ed.) FC 2013. LNCS, vol. 7859, pp. 25–33. Springer, Heidelberg (2013). https://doi.org/10.1007/978-3-642-39884-1_3

22. Möser, M., et al.: An empirical analysis of linkability in the Monero blockchain. Proc. Privacy Enhancing Technol. **2016**(3), 143–163 (2018)

23. Nakamoto, S.: Bitcoin: a peer-to-peer electronic cash system (2008). bitcoin.org/bitcoin.pdf

24. Ray, B., Posnett, D., Filkov, V., Devanbu, P.: A large scale study of programming languages and code quality in GitHub. In: Proceedings of the 22nd ACM SIGSOFT International Symposium on Foundations of Software Engineering (FSE), pp. 155–165 (2014)

25. Reid, F., Harrigan, M.: An analysis of anonymity in the Bitcoin system. In: Altshuler, Y., Elovici, Y., Cremers, A., Aharony, N., Pentland, A. (eds.) Security and Privacy in Social Networks, pp. 197–223. Springer, New York (2013). https://doi.org/10.1007/978-1-4614-4139-7_10

26. Ron, D., Shamir, A.: Quantitative analysis of the full Bitcoin transaction graph. In: Sadeghi, A.-R. (ed.) FC 2013. LNCS, vol. 7859, pp. 6–24. Springer, Heidelberg (2013). https://doi.org/10.1007/978-3-642-39884-1_2

27. Spagnuolo, M., Maggi, F., Zanero, S.: BitIodine: extracting intelligence from the Bitcoin network. In: Christin, N., Safavi-Naini, R. (eds.) FC 2014. LNCS, vol. 8437, pp. 457–468. Springer, Heidelberg (2014). https://doi.org/10.1007/978-3-662-45472-5_29

28. Syta, E., et al.: Keeping authorities "honest or bust" with decentralized witness cosigning. In: 2016 IEEE Symposium on Security and Privacy, San Jose, CA, USA, 22–26 May 2016, pp. 526–545. IEEE Computer Society Press (2016)

29. Thung, F., Bissyandé, T.F., Lo, D., Jiang, L.: Network structure of social coding in GitHub. In: Proceedings of the 17th European Conference on Software Maintenance and Reengineering (2013)

30. Vasek, M., Bonneau, J., Castellucci, R., Keith, C., Moore, T.: The Bitcoin brain drain: examining the use and abuse of Bitcoin brain wallets. In: Grossklags, J., Preneel, B. (eds.) FC 2016. LNCS, vol. 9603, pp. 609–618. Springer, Heidelberg (2017). https://doi.org/10.1007/978-3-662-54970-4_36

31. Vasek, M., Moore, T.: There's no free lunch, even using Bitcoin: tracking the popularity and profits of virtual currency scams. In: Böhme, R., Okamoto, T. (eds.) FC 2015. LNCS, vol. 8975, pp. 44–61. Springer, Heidelberg (2015). https://doi.org/10.1007/978-3-662-47854-7_4

32. Vasek, M., Moore, T.: Analyzing the Bitcoin Ponzi scheme ecosystem. In: Proceedings of the 5th Workshop on Bitcoin and Blockchain Research (2018)

33. Vasek, M., Thornton, M., Moore, T.: Empirical analysis of denial-of-service attacks in the Bitcoin ecosystem. In: Böhme, R., Brenner, M., Moore, T., Smith, M. (eds.) FC 2014. LNCS, vol. 8438, pp. 57–71. Springer, Heidelberg (2014). https://doi.org/10.1007/978-3-662-44774-1_5
34. Zhu, J., Zhou, M., Mockus, A.: Patterns of folder use and project popularity: a case study of Github repositories. In: Proceedings of the 8th ACM/IEEE International Symposium on Empirical Software Engineering and Measurement (2014)

Short Paper: An Empirical Analysis of Blockchain Forks in Bitcoin

Till Neudecker[✉] and Hannes Hartenstein

Institute of Telematics, Karlsruhe Institute of Technology, Karlsruhe, Germany
{till.neudecker,hannes.hartenstein}@kit.edu

Abstract. Temporary blockchain forks are part of the regular consensus process in permissionless blockchains such as Bitcoin. As forks can be caused by numerous factors such as latency and miner behavior, their analysis provides insights into these factors, which are otherwise unknown. In this paper we provide an empirical analysis of the announcement and propagation of blocks that led to forks of the Bitcoin blockchain. By analyzing the time differences in the publication of competing blocks, we show that the block propagation delay between miners can be of similar order as the block propagation delay of the average Bitcoin peer. Furthermore, we show that the probability of a block to become part of the main chain increases roughly linearly in the time the block has been published before the competing block. Additionally, we show that the observed frequency of short block intervals between two consecutive blocks mined by the same miner after a fork is conspicuously large. While selfish mining can be a cause for this observation, other causes are also possible. Finally, we show that not only the time difference of the publication of competing blocks but also their propagation speeds vary greatly.

1 Introduction

Blockchain forks, which occur when two miners independently find and publish a new block referencing the same previous block, occur regularly in permissionless blockchains such as Bitcoin [7]. As subsequent blocks resolve the temporary inconsistency, forks are part of a blockchain's normal operation. While the existence of delay between miners inevitably leads to blockchain forks, deviating mining strategies such as selfish mining [3] can also lead to forks. Recent discussions on block size, the feasibility of selfish mining (*negative gamma*), and speculations on the network topology between miners are all related to factors affecting the security of permissionless blockchains [5]. As forks are affected by many of these factors, the analysis of forks that actually took place may help to improve the understanding of these factors.

Based on measurements of the Bitcoin peer-to-peer (P2P) network since 2015 we analyze the announcement and propagation of blocks that led to blockchain forks. Specifically, we compare the time differences between the first announcement of competing blocks to the average block propagation delay. Furthermore,

© International Financial Cryptography Association 2019
I. Goldberg and T. Moore (Eds.): FC 2019, LNCS 11598, pp. 84–92, 2019.
https://doi.org/10.1007/978-3-030-32101-7_6

we analyze the effect of a *headstart* of one block over competing blocks (i.e., how much earlier a block was published) on the block's probability to become part of the main chain. In order to assess whether deviating mining strategies were performed, we analyze the block intervals immediately after blockchain forks. Finally, we study the differences in the propagation of blocks of four selected forks through the Bitcoin P2P network.

2   Fundamentals and Related Work

We will now briefly sketch the relevant aspects of mining and block propagation in Bitcoin. A thorough introduction can be found in, e.g., [8]. Bitcoin blocks are generated in the process of mining by aggregating a set of previously published transactions into a block and solving a proof-of-work puzzle for that block. Each block contains the hash value of the previous block, which creates a chain of blocks. Miners are expected to work on top of the longest valid blockchain known to them, i.e., when a miner receives a new block extending the current blockchain, the miner should update the block she is working on by changing the reference to the newly received block.

A *blockchain fork* occurs if two new blocks that reference the same previous block are independently found at the same time by different miners. Because solving the proof-of-work puzzle is a random process and block propagation between miners is subject to network and processing delays, such forks occur regularly. However, forks can also be the result of selfish mining [3], a mining strategy in which a miner withholds new blocks instead of immediately publishing them in order to gain an advantage in finding the next block. Another strategy that can create blockchain forks is the *fork after withholding* attack [6].

Propagation of new blocks and transactions is performed by flooding via the Bitcoin peer-to-peer network, and by transmission via additional, possibly private networks (e.g., the *Fibre* network) [2]. Several characterizations of the Bitcoin P2P network have been published in the past [1,4]. Furthermore, there are several websites that publish statistics such as block propagation delays, i.e., the time it takes blocks to propagate through a certain share of the network.[1]

3   Measurement and Analysis Method

Since 2015 we have operated two monitor nodes that establish connections to all reachable peers of the Bitcoin P2P network. The number of connections varied between around 6,000 and 14,000 in the considered period. The monitor nodes stay mostly passive (except for establishing connections and sending and answering PING messages) and log the announcement of new transactions and blocks via *inventory messages* (*INV*) by remote peers. Therefore, our dataset contains tuples consisting of (time, hash value, IP address). From this data the

---

[1] E.g., https://blockchain.info, https://bitnodes.earn.com, http://bitcoinstats.com/network/propagation, https://dsn.tm.kit.edu/bitcoin.

timestamp of the first announcement of a block can be derived. Furthermore, the propagation speed of a block (i.e., how many announcements were received within a certain time) can be derived.

As our monitor nodes do not actually request blocks from remote peers, our dataset does not contain the block headers and does not indicate whether forks happened. Therefore, we combine our data with data published by *blockchain.info* that contains further information on each block hash, such as the reference to the previous block, whether the block became part of the main chain, and the miner as indicated in the coinbase transaction (set by the miner). All data used in this paper can be accessed at https://dsn.tm.kit.edu/bitcoin/forks.

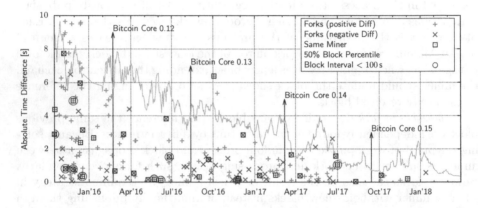

Fig. 1. Time difference between the first announcement of forking blocks. A green cross (*positive Diff*) indicates that the block that was announced first became part of the main chain, a red cross (*negative Diff*) indicates that the later announced block became part of the main chain. Boxes around blocks indicate that the subsequent block has been mined by the same miner; additional circles around blocks indicate that the subsequent block has been mined by the same miner within less than 100 s. Finally, the average 50% block propagation percentile is shown. (Color figure online)

4   Analysis of Bitcoin Blockchain Forks

As a first step, we analyze the time differences between the first announcements of the competing blocks that cause a fork. If all miners follow the protocol and immediately start working on top of any new valid block they receive, these time differences should not be larger than the block propagation delay between miners. Figure 1 shows all forks between October 2015 and March 2018 that we have data on, and the time difference between the first announcements of both blocks of each fork: every cross indicates one fork, i.e., one blockchain height at which two blocks have been announced. A green cross indicates that the block that has been announced first became part of the main chain, a red cross indicates that the later announced block became part of the main chain.

The data confirms that the fork rate decreased substantially in the past years. Additionally, the observed announcement time differences decreased from several seconds in late 2015 to less then two seconds since mid 2017. Figure 1 also shows the measured average 50% block propagation percentile, i.e., the time difference between the first announcement of a block and the time the block has been announced by 50% of all peers. While we expect mining pools to be better connected to the Bitcoin P2P network than *the average peer*, the 50% block propagation percentile gives an idea of the latency between peers. The decreased block propagation delay also reflects the improvements made to the block propagation mechanism of Bitcoin. The comparison of the announcement time difference to the block propagation delay shows that the announcement time difference of almost all forks is smaller than the 50% block propagation percentile. However, some announcement time differences are still strikingly large, and a few are even larger than the 50% block propagation percentile.

Assuming that all miners always mine on top of the longest blockchain they received, the data indicates that the block propagation delay between miners that caused forks was not substantially lower than the block propagation delay of average Bitcoin peers. While this might be surprising, we emphasize that the observed announcement delays might be caused by single miners that temporarily suffer from a high link latency, i.e., they represent worst cases, whereas the shown 50% block propagation percentile represents an average case.

Several questions arise from the discussion of the data shown in Fig. 1. First, while the block that is announced first is regularly included in the main chain, the effect of the *headstart* of one block over another block on the probability to become included in the main chain is unclear. Secondly, the data is not sufficient to assess whether miners deviate from the mining strategy, e.g., by selfish mining. Finally, the effect of the P2P propagation speed of forking blocks remains unclear. We will address all three questions in the remainder of this section.

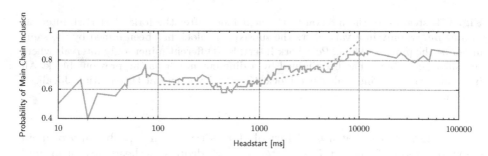

Fig. 2. Probability (moving average, binsize = 50 ms) of a forking block becoming part of the main chain depending on the headstart over the competing block.

4.1   Effect of Headstart on Probability of Main Chain Inclusion

In order to analyze the relationship between the headstart of a block (i.e., the time difference the block has been announced before the competing block) and the probability that this block becomes part of the main chain, we look at the block that was announced first and check whether this block became part of the main chain. Hence, each fork can be represented by a tuple (headstart, $i \in \{1, 0\}$). By sorting all tuples by the headstart, a moving average of the probability of main chain inclusion can be calculated. Figure 2 shows the moving average of the probability of a block becoming part of the main chain depending on the headstart over the competing block. At the borders of the plot, the moving average window is reduced symmetrically, hence, the variance of the plot increases in these areas. Although the sample size of the data is small, a general trend can be seen, especially between 100 ms and 10 s. For this interval, Fig. 2 also shows a linear trend line ($y = 3.07 \cdot 10^{-5}x + 0.63$).

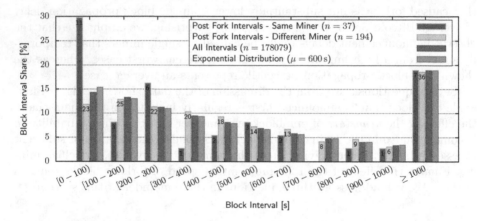

Fig. 3. Histogram of the interval to the next block after the fork. Post Fork Intervals - Same miner: only intervals where the subsequent block has been mined by the same miner as the previous block. Post Fork Intervals - Different miner: only intervals where the subsequent block has been mined by a different miner as the previous block. All Intervals: All block intervals since block 350,000. Exponential Distribution: Idealized block interval.

The data shows that a headstart of 100 ms results in a probability of main chain inclusion of around 70%. After a short drop at a headstart of around 500 ms, the probability increases to more than 80% for a headstart of 10 s. We emphasize that the data is dominated by the large number of forks until around mid 2017. It is likely that due to the reduced block propagation delay, today a smaller headstart leads to a much larger probability of main chain inclusion.

4.2 Deviating Mining Strategy

Consider a miner following the selfish mining strategy that withholds two blocks and receives a competing block for her first block withheld. In that case the selfish miner would publish both withheld blocks within a short period of time in order to prevent the competing block from becoming included in the main chain, rendering the withheld blocks useless. Hence, very small block intervals after the occurrence of a fork can be caused by selfish mining. We will now analyze the block intervals after forks.

For all forks, we calculate the block interval between the first announcement of the block that got included in the main chain and the first announcement of the subsequent block (i.e., the block at the next height). We split all forks we have data about into two groups: Group *Same Miner* contains all 37 forks where the block that got included in the main chain and the subsequent block has both been mined by the same miner (also shown in Fig. 1 as rectangles). Group *Different Miner* contains all 194 forks where both blocks were mined by different miners. Please note that the miner attribution is done based on information embedded by the miner in the block, which can be freely set by the miner. For comparison, we also calculate all block intervals since block 350,000.

Figure 3 shows histograms of the block interval for the groups *Same Miner* and *Different Miner* along with all block intervals and an idealized block interval distribution modeled by an exponential distribution. While the relative frequencies of all groups correspond well for larger block intervals, major differences can be observed for the smallest interval (<100 s): Out of the 37 forks with the same miner, 11 forks (30%) had a block interval of less than 100 s between the fork and the subsequent block. Contrary, only 23 forks of the 194 forks with different miners had a block interval of less than 100 s (12%). The expected relative frequency is in the order of 14% (measured) or 15% (idealized).

We will now discuss possible reasons for the observed deviation. First, although a validation of our measurements with other data shows a high correspondence, we cannot completely rule out measurement errors. Secondly, the probability that 11 or more samples out of 37 samples of the idealized block interval distribution are smaller than 100 s is around 2%. Therefore, while the observation seems unlikely, there is a substantial probability that the observation is simply the result of the random mining process and the small sample size.

Thirdly, the presence of block propagation delays makes the considered events statistically dependent. For instance, if a block interval is smaller than the block propagation delay, the subsequent block is definitely mined by the same miner, as other miners did not receive the previous block yet. However, the peculiar relative frequency shown in Fig. 3 corresponds to the conditional probability of observing a small block interval *given that* a fork occurred and both blocks were mined by the same miner. The existence of a fork is independent of the next block interval, as the mining power remains constant (although split). However, the block propagation delay gives the miner of the last block an advantage in finding the subsequent block, until other miners have received the block. Therefore, during block propagation, the overall mining power is reduced to the mining power of the miners that have already received the block. Hence, the overall block interval should actually increase (minimally) compared to the idealized block interval as modeled by an exponential distribution. Furthermore, all observed block intervals in the *Same Miner* group are at least 40 s, hence block propagation delay should not affect the interval, as the advantage of the miner vanishes as soon as other miners receive a block.

Finally, selfish mining could be the cause for the observed block intervals. Blocks of 9 of the 11 forks with block intervals below 100 s were mined by only two different mining pools, which had a share of the network hash rate of around 20% and 10%, respectively, at the time. Hence a single mining pool following the selfish mining strategy could have caused the observed deviations. However, the fact that all observed block intervals were at least 40 s raises doubts that selfish mining was actually performed, because one would expect miners to immediately publish the subsequent block. Furthermore, one would not expect a selfish miner to voluntarily include information about its identity in a mined block. Finally, the mining power shares of the pools render selfish mining only lucrative when assuming a significant network advantage γ [3].

Although all discussed possible causes for the observed block intervals seem unlikely, the presented data provides insights into a specific aspect of the mining process and can serve as a starting point for further research.

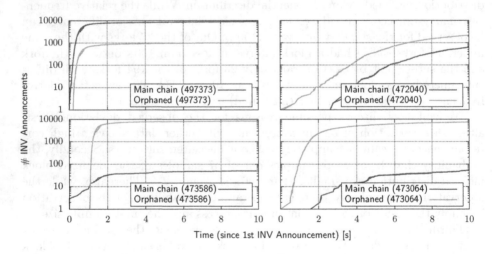

Fig. 4. Block propagation for both blocks (*Main chain*, *Orphaned*) for selected forks.

4.3   Peer-to-Peer Propagation Comparison

The differences in the time a block has been announced shown in Fig. 1 only show that a block has not been received by a miner within this time difference, but do not give reasons for why the block has not reached the other miner. Figure 4 shows the P2P propagation of the blocks that caused four different selected forks.

The fork at height 497373 (top left) shows the *standard* case: The main chain block is propagated slightly before the orphaned block, which is announced only by those peers that have not already received the main chain block. In contrast, in the fork at height 472040 (top right) the orphaned block is propagated first, however, it propagates very slowly. More than one second later, the included block is propagated at a similar propagation speed. In the fork at height 473586 (bottom left) the main chain block is propagated first, but is only announced by less than 100 peers within 10 s. Contrary, the orphaned block is published one second later, but propagates very fast through the network. Finally, the main chain block at height 473064 (bottom right) is published more than a second after the well propagated orphaned block, but still it became part of the main chain.

The examples show that not only the first announcement of a block plays a role in which block becomes part of the main chain, but also the propagation speed of each block. However, as all combinations of headstart (positive vs. negative) and propagation speed (slow vs. fast) could be observed, P2P propagation of blocks does not seem to be the main decisive factor in which block becomes part of the main chain. A possible reason for slow propagation speeds could be extremely long validation times for these blocks. For instance, if a block contains a transaction on which other transactions that are contained in a peer's mempool depend, the peer also has to validate and order these transactions. Additionally, the examples show that the propagation of each block can differ drastically, hence a purely statistical model of block propagation can be insufficient.

5 Conclusions and Future Work

We provided an empirical analysis of the announcement and propagation of Bitcoin blocks that caused blockchain forks. The large differences in the first announcements of competing blocks indicate that the block propagation delay between miners can be of similar order as the observed 50% block propagation percentile. The probability of a block to become part of the main chain increases linearly in the headstart (i.e., the time the block has been published before the competing block) between 100 ms and 10 s (from less than 70% to more than 80%). The observed frequency of block intervals between two consecutive blocks mined by the same miner to be less than 100 s is conspicuously large. While selfish mining can be a cause for this observation, other causes are also possible.

A better understanding of the factors influencing the propagation speed of specific blocks might be gained by an in-depth analysis of (orphaned) blocks and client implementations. Furthermore, our analysis might profit from more data, especially on recent forks. While the reduced frequency of forks is generally good for the system, it is unfortunate for empirical research.

Acknowledgments. This work was supported by the German Federal Ministry of Education and Research within the projects *KASTEL_IoE* and *KASTEL_ISE* in the Competence Center for Applied Security Technology (*KASTEL*) and by the state of

Baden-Württemberg through bwHPC, bwFileStorage, and LSDF. The authors would like to thank Tim Ruffing and the anonymous reviewers for their valuable comments and suggestions.

References

1. Decker, C., Wattenhofer, R.: Information propagation in the bitcoin network. In: Peer-to-Peer 2013 IEEE Thirteenth International Conference on Computing (P2P), pp. 1–10. IEEE (2013)
2. Delgado-Segura, S., Pérez-Solà, C., Herrera-Joancomartí, J., Navarro-Arribas, G., Borrell, J.: Cryptocurrency networks: a new p2p paradigm. Mobile Inf. Syst. **2018**, 1–16 (2018)
3. Eyal, I., Sirer, E.G.: Majority is not enough: bitcoin mining is vulnerable. In: Christin, N., Safavi-Naini, R. (eds.) FC 2014. LNCS, vol. 8437, pp. 436–454. Springer, Heidelberg (2014). https://doi.org/10.1007/978-3-662-45472-5_28
4. Gencer, A.E., Basu, S., Eyal, I., van Renesse, R., Sirer, E.G.: Decentralization in bitcoin and ethereum networks. arXiv preprint arXiv:1801.03998 (2018)
5. Gervais, A., Karame, G.O., Wüst, K., Glykantzis, V., Ritzdorf, H., Capkun, S.: On the security and performance of proof of work blockchains. In: Proceedings of the 2016 ACM SIGSAC Conference on Computer and Communications Security (2016)
6. Kwon, Y., Kim, D., Son, Y., Vasserman, E., Kim, Y.: Be selfish and avoid dilemmas: fork after withholding (faw) attacks on bitcoin. In: Proceedings of the 2017 ACM SIGSAC Conference on Computer and Communications Security. ACM (2017)
7. Nakamoto, S.: Bitcoin: A peer-to-peer electronic cash system (2008)
8. Narayanan, A., Bonneau, J., Felten, E., Miller, A., Goldfeder, S.: Bitcoin and Cryptocurrency Technologies: A Comprehensive Introduction. Princeton University Press, Princeton (2016). http://bitcoinbook.cs.princeton.edu/

Detecting Token Systems on Ethereum

Michael Fröwis[1]($\boxtimes$), Andreas Fuchs[2], and Rainer Böhme[1,2]

[1] Department of Computer Science, Universität Innsbruck, Innsbruck, Austria
michael.froewis@uibk.ac.at
[2] Department of Information Systems, University of Münster, Münster, Germany

Abstract. We propose and compare two approaches to identify smart contracts as token systems by analyzing their public bytecode. The first approach symbolically executes the code in order to detect token systems by their characteristic behavior of updating internal accounts. The second approach serves as a comparison base and exploits the common interface of ERC-20 , the most popular token standard. We present quantitative results for the Ethereum blockchain, and validate the effectiveness of both approaches using a set of curated token systems as ground truth. We observe 100% recall for the second approach. Recall rates of 89% (with well explainable missed detections) indicate that the first approach may also be able to identify "hidden" or undocumented token systems that intentionally do not implement the standard. One possible application of the proposed methods is to facilitate regulators' tasks of monitoring and policing the use of token systems and their underlying platforms.

Keywords: Smart contract · Symbolic execution · ERC-20 · Token systems · Ethereum

1 Introduction

Arguably, it has been easier to create a virtual asset on Ethereum in 2017 than a website on the Internet in 1997. In September 2018, the market valuation of the well observable virtual assets ("tokens") on the Ethereum platform amounts to US\$ 35 billion, not counting the US\$ 17.6 billion of ether, the platform's hardwired cryptocurrency.[1] These figures are the result of the 2017 boom of *initial coin offerings* (ICOs), enabled by a combination of a hype around blockchain technology, lack of attractive conventional investment alternatives, and greed.

The sheer amount of money involved calls for regulators to take note and, where necessary, step in. While governments' concerns with cryptocurrencies, such as Bitcoin, were mainly focused on tracking payment flows of criminal origin (o. g., from trade with illegal goods, ransomware, money laundering, terrorism financing), the vast growth of an investment universe in virtual assets poses new

---

[1] Sources: Etherscan.io and Coinmarketcap.com on 12 September 2018, own calculations.

© International Financial Cryptography Association 2019
I. Goldberg and T. Moore (Eds.): FC 2019, LNCS 11598, pp. 93–112, 2019.
https://doi.org/10.1007/978-3-030-32101-7_7

challenges. These include enforcement of security laws [10], consumer protection [28], and prudential monitoring in the interest of financial stability [11]. These tasks require proven methods and adequate tools to detect, classify, and monitor virtual assets on platforms that can in principle host any kind of decentralized application. Therefore, in this work we set out to offer a scientific approach for the relevant case of token detection on Ethereum.

In jargon, *token* is a shorthand for a transferable virtual good. The community distinguishes fungible from non-fungible tokens. Although the notion of fungibility is not precisely defined for all corner cases, a token is said to be fungible if all units are alike, i. e., each unit is interchangeable with every other unit. By contrast, a non-fungible token has an identifying feature, such as a serial number, color, etc.

Typical token systems on Ethereum are computer programs that allow its users to exchange tokens with each other in a decentralized, secure, and atomic way, up to the extent enforceable by the underlying blockchain-based system. Such tokens can be useful in many scenarios. For instance, fungible tokens can serve as means of payment (e. g., sub-currencies), securitized rights (e. g., to vote or claim profit), or store of value. Non-fungible tokens are virtual collectibles.

Our approach is novel in that we detect fungible token systems by the characteristic program behavior, which is related to the secure exchange functionality. The behavior is detected by combining symbolic execution and taint analysis, two established static code analysis techniques, which were adapted to the application. As a comparison base, we also propose a signature-based detection method that searches for instances of standard interfaces for token systems . We compare the effectiveness of both methods on a curated ground truth dataset before we generalize and present results for the entire Ethereum blockchain.

The paper is organized as follows. The next Sect. 2 introduces necessary background. Sections 3 and 4 present our behavior-based and signature-based methods, respectively. Performance measurements are reported and discussed in Sect. 5. Section 6 connects to relevant related work, before Sect. 7 concludes with a discussion and an outlook to future applications and research directions.

2   Background and Principles

This section recalls relevant properties of the Ethereum platform, specifically its virtual machine and calling conventions. It further sets up the static analysis techniques: symbolic execution, taint analysis, and the Ethereum call graph.

2.1   Ethereum Virtual Machine (EVM)

Ethereum is a decentralized system that updates a global state in a public, append-only data structure called *blockchain* [29]. At every point in time, the global state is an injective mapping from addresses to account states. Account states include the balance in ether, permanent storage, and optionally code controlling the account. By convention, accounts with code are called *smart contracts*, whereas accounts without code are called *externally owned accounts*. *Transactions* sent to the Ethereum network update the global state. A transaction can (1) transfer ether between accounts, (2) create new accounts, (3) invoke code of any smart contract of the current state, or combinations thereof. Arguments can be passed to code by supplying *input data* in the transaction.

The Ethereum Virtual Machine (EVM) is a stack-based virtual machine that executes the bytecode in account states. Single-byte opcodes are followed by an optional immediate argument of length between 1 and 32 bytes. To prevent long-running or infinite computations, Ethereum charges a fee for every instruction executed, accounted in units of *gas*. Most developers program the EVM in *Solidity*, a high-level imperative programming language.

2.2 Ethereum Application Binary Interface (ABI)

The Application Binary Interface (ABI) specifies the calling conventions between smart contracts. Since the EVM has no native concept of functions, every transaction sent to a contract starts the execution at the same entry point. Function-like behavior is implemented by a *function dispatching* mechanism, which evaluates the leading 4 bytes of the input data. Specifically, every function is identified by a 4-byte *function selector*, which is deterministically derived from the hash value of the *function signature*. A function signature is a concatenation of the function name and a list of argument types as defined in Solidity. For example, `transfer(address,uint256)` is a signature for a function called "transfer" accepting two arguments of type "address" and unsigned 32-byte integer, respectively.

Listing 1 illustrates the function dispatching mechanism in EVM bytecode as generated by the Solidity compiler. The full ABI definition can be found at [1].

```
 4 : PUSH1 0x4          // Push constant 4 on stack
 5 : CALLDATALOAD       // Load first 4 bytes from input data
 6 : PUSH4 0xa9059cbb   // Function selector transfer(address,uint256)
 7 : EQ                 // Check equality
 8 : PUSH1 0x20         // Push jump target 0x20 = 32
 9 : JUMPI              // Jump if true (cf. line 7)
10: PUSH1 0x4           // If not equal, continue with this instruction
...
32: JUMPDEST            // Implementation of transfer(address,uint256)
33: ...
```

Listing 1. EVM bytecode illustrating the ABI function dispatching.

The ABI specification is not part of the Ethereum protocol. Anyone is free to define their own calling conventions. However, to our knowledge, all popular compilers targeting the EVM produce ABI-compliant bytecode.

2.3 Symbolic Execution and Taint Analysis

Symbolic execution is a program analysis technique [17]. In contrast to concrete execution, symbolic execution does not only explore one execution path through a program by using concrete inputs, but tries to explore *all* paths in a systematic manner. Program inputs are therefore represented as symbols. The symbolic execution engine executes instructions akin the actual runtime environment as long as no symbolic values are involved. When an instruction depends on at least one symbolic value, the symbolic execution engine cannot execute the instruction directly, but builds a symbolic expression that describes the execution result.

Special consideration is needed when it comes to control flow. Whenever a conditional branch is reached that depends on a symbolic branch condition c within path π_n, the engine cannot decide which path to follow. Consequently, it follows both ($\pi_{n|true} \leftarrow \pi_n \wedge c$, $\pi_{n|false} \leftarrow \pi_n \wedge \bar{c}$) execution paths using backtracking. To avoid the exploration of impossible paths, typical engines use an SMT solver to find a satisfying assignment for the path condition in question. If a suitable assignment is found the path is further explored.

For example, when the code in Listing 1 is symbolically executed with initial path constraint $\pi \leftarrow true$, the symbolic execution engine generates a path constraint $\pi_{true} \leftarrow \delta = \texttt{0xa9059cbb}$ for the path $\langle ..., 4, 5, 6, 7, 8, 9, 32, ...\rangle$, where δ is a symbolic variable representing the first four bytes of the input data. When the symbolic execution of the path corresponding to π_{true} completes, the symbolic execution engine performs backtracking, generates a constraint $\pi_{false} \leftarrow \delta \neq \texttt{0xa9059cbb}$, and continues on the path $\langle ..., 4, 5, 6, 7, 8, 9, 10, ...\rangle$.

In this work we mainly exploit two properties of symbolic execution. First, we use the explored paths as input to *static taint analysis* [25]. Taint analysis is a technique to trace data flows of interest through a program execution. More concretely, we label user inputs with markers ("taint") and track which storage locations are affected by it. Our second use of symbolic execution is to access the structure of symbolic expressions generated by the engine.

Symbolic execution faces many limitations in practice [12]: path explosion, unbounded loops, and the NP-hardness of the SMT problem all require tradeoffs, such as imposing timeouts and skipping paths. The success of symbolic execution can be measured in terms of code coverage. Gladly, most smart contracts on Ethereum are very short programs, gas makes unbounded loops expensive, and therefore Ethereum is more amenable to symbolic execution than other platforms.

2.4   Ethereum Call Graph

Both detection methods introduced in this work operate locally. This means we only analyze code of one address at a time. Consequently, the methods are blind to behavior or signatures located outside the smart contract under analysis. Recall from Sect. 2.1 that transactions can invoke code of any smart contract active in the current state. Smart contracts can create transactions using the call family[2] of instructions. Such calls are used in smart contracts to (1) interact with other parties (smart contracts), and (2) reuse code already deployed.

A useful tool to look beyond the local address is the Ethereum call graph [16]. It holds information on relationships between contracts obtained by parsing

---

[2] *CALL*, *DELEGATECALL*, *CALLCODE*, *STATICCALL*.

all bytecode on the Ethereum blockchain and extracting all statically encoded addresses used in instructions of the call family. Nodes in the graph are addresses with code. Directed edges denote static calls from caller to callee.

The so-constructed call graph captures only statically encoded references. References to other contracts set on construction, calculated at runtime, or provided as user input are missed. The only practical way to work around this limitation is dynamic analysis, which makes a different trade-off as it limits the analysis to actually executed rather than all possible paths.

3   Behavior-Based Token Detection

Now we describe our behavior-based heuristic detection method for fungible token systems on the Ethereum platform. We first justify the behavioral pattern, then present our detection method, and finally discuss known limitations.

3.1   Pattern

Fungiblity means that all tokens in a given token system are alike. As a result, token systems do not need to store which specific token belongs to which party. The only relevant information is who owns how many tokens. A straightforward (and gas-efficient) way to implement the state of a token system is storing a mapping of owners (identified by addresses) to a non-negative number of tokens.

An important property of token systems is the ability to transfer tokens. We assume that a token system wants to preserve the total amount of tokens in circulation as they are transferred. In order to detect smart contracts that behave like token systems we define:

Definition 1. *A token system according to its behavior, is a smart contract that (1) stores users' balances as integers in permanent storage, and (2) provides a function to transfer tokens between users while keeping the total balance constant, where (3) the transferred value is controlled by user input.*

Fixing the data type to integers in (1) is reasonable as the EVM does not natively support floating point or rational numbers.

```
1  contract FungibleTokenPattern {
2      mapping(address => uint) balance;
3
4      function sendToken(address to, uint value) public {
5          require(balance[msg.sender] >= value);
6          balance[msg.sender] = balance[msg.sender] - value;
7          balance[to] = balance[to] + value;
8      }
9  }
```

Listing 2. Transfer pattern in Solidity, typical for fungible tokens.

Listing 2 shows a Solidity implementation of a minimalistic token system that complies with Definition 1.

3.2 Detection Method

We propose an approach that analyzes the behavior of potential token systems based on symbolic execution and static taint analysis.

Our approach works as follows. We look for a possible execution path that updates two integers in storage, one for the sender and recipient, by a value defined as parameter. For (1) and (3) of Definition 1, we use taint analysis to find storage write states (sws), where the value stored can be influenced by user input. For each of those stores of input data sws_0, we try to find a matching store sws_1 that follows our tainted store on some possible execution path. Furthermore, we look for constraints in the path condition that check if the value in some storage field is larger than or equal to some user input field (c_{ge}). This captures the check that the sender's balance cannot be negative. We organize our stores and path constraint in triplets of the form (sws_0, sws_1, c_{ge}), meaning we found a storage write sws_0 with its value influenced by user input. sws_0 is followed by sws_1 on some viable execution path. Additionally, we have a constraint c_{ge} on this path that checks if some storage field is larger than a user input field. We call such a triplet *transfer candidate*. What remains to verify is (2), i. e., whether the operations on sws_0 and sws_1 are really transferring value and if c_{ge} is a constraint on one of the fields written to. Here we apply a heuristic that looks at the term structure of transfer candidates.

Algorithm 1 shows the analysis done for every possible transfer candidate triplet. We use $\lhd$ and $\unlhd$ to denote the proper subterm and subterm relation.

Algorithm 1. Analyzing transfer candidates.

---
function $\text{ISTOKEN}_{sym}(S)$ $\diamond$ a set S of triplets (sws_0, sws_1, c_{ge})
$\quad s_{ops} \leftarrow \{+, -\}$
$\quad$**for** (sws_0, sws_1, c_{ge}) $\in S$ **do**
$\quad\quad b_{rss}, s_{opsLeft}, b_{usedC} \leftarrow \text{CHECKSTORETERM}(sws_0, s_{ops}, true)$
$\quad\quad$**if** $b_{rss} \wedge |s_{opsLeft}| = |s_{ops}| - 1$ **then**
$\quad\quad\quad b_{rss}, s_{opsLeft}, b_{usedC} \leftarrow \text{CHECKSTORETERM}(sws_1, s_{opsLeft}, \neg b_{usedC})$
$\quad\quad\quad$**if** $b_{rss} \wedge s_{opsLeft} = \emptyset \wedge b_{useC}$ **then**
$\quad\quad\quad\quad$**return** $true$ $\diamond$ Found a token-like behavior.
$\quad$**return** $false$ $\diamond$ None of the candidates indicates a tokens system.
function $\text{CHECKSTORETERM}(sws_n, c_{ge}, s_{ops}, b_{cToEqC})$
$\quad b_{selfRef}, b_{callData}, b_{toEqC} \leftarrow false$
$\quad t_{to}, t_{val} \leftarrow sws_n.to, sws_n.value$ $\diamond$ Store has an address and a value.
$\quad s_{opFirst} \leftarrow \text{FINDFIRSTOPBFS}(t_{val}, s_{ops})$ $\diamond$ Get first matching function symbol.
$\quad b_{selfRef} \leftarrow t_{to} \lhd t_{val}$ $\diamond$ Store updates itself?
$\quad b_{callData} \leftarrow c_{ge}.smallerTerm \lhd t_{val}$ $\diamond$ Term contains input from constraint?
$\quad b_{toEqC} \leftarrow t_{to} \unlhd c_{ge}.largerTerm$ $\diamond$ Is constraint on assignment?
$\quad$**return** ($t_{selfRef} \wedge t_{calldata}, s_{ops} \setminus s_{opFirst}, (b_{cToEqC} \wedge b_{toEqC}) \vee \neg b_{cToEqC}$)

Example: We use the example contract in Listing 2 to illustrate how the algorithm works. We refer to source code when possible, although the actual analysis is done on bytecode. First we perform taint analysis to find storage writes influenced by user input. We find stores in lines 6 and 7. Then we look for followup stores along a viable execution path. Only for the store in line 6 we find a following store, namely in line 7. Furthermore, we look at path conditions at the program state of the first store in line 6. We find one suitable condition that matches our restrictions that the condition checks if a storage field is larger than (or equal to) some user input in line 5. This means we found one transfer candidate to check (*line* 6, *line* 7, *line* 5). First we execute CHECKSTORETERM on `balance[msg.sender]` = `balance[msg.sender]` - `value` with `balance[msg.sender]` >= `value` as a constraint and $\{+, -\}$ as possible operations, and $b_{cToEqC} = true$. Then we check if the *right hand side* (RHS) of the store term contains itself, which it does. It follows a check if the RHS of the constraint `value` is a subterm of our store term, meaning that the constraint and store refer to the same user input. If that is the case, we check if we can either find an addition or subtraction in our term. FINDFIRSTOPBFS checks all function applications in the term against a list of operations (starting with $\{+, -\}$) and returns a set with the first operation to occur, or an empty set if the operations are not found. Finally, we check if the storage field used in the constraint is the target of the store, which is true in our case. The function then returns a tuple with $(true, \{+\}, true)$, since the terms of our transfer candidate fulfill all conditions. We found that minus is the root operation on the term and already found the constraint value to be written on. We then continue with calling CHECKSTORETERM again for the second term, with a reduced list of operations, only looking for plus and no longer looking for writes on our constraint values. This call returns $(true, \emptyset, true)$, thus we found token-like behavior according to our definition.

3.3 Known Limitations

We inherit the limitations from symbolic execution (cf. Sect. 2.3). We use `mythril` [6], a tool designed for security analyses that is known to reach high accuracy [22] despite using heuristics. For our experiments, we run `mythril` with a timeout of 60 s and a maximum path length of 58. Furthermore, `mythril` is under active development and has a couple of limitations that may influence our results and their replicability. For example in taint analysis, the current version of `mythril` (0.18.11) cannot spread taint over storage or memory fields. This can cause problems when function parameters are passed by reference.

The locality is dealt with in the following way: whenever the symbolic execution reaches a call, we consider it as communication with the unknown environment. Hence, the engine introduces a fresh unrestricted symbol for the return value and carries on. That means the analysis is blind to everything that happens outside of the code of the current address. We evaluate the impact of this limitation empirically with the call graph in Sect. 5.3.

Another limitation lies in the definition of the pattern. It is not straightforward to find the best approximation for the behavior we search for, since the same behavior can be implemented in various ways that may result in vastly different bytecode. What eases this problem somewhat is that much of the byte-code currently deployed on Ethereum is produced by a pretty homogeneous toolchain (Solidity and `solc`). Moreover, gas favors simple programs, often rendering abstractions that would complicate the underlying bytecode uneconomic.

4   Signature-Based Token Detection

Now we present a simple signature-based heuristic to detect token systems . It evaluates if the bytecode implements the ABI standard for the ERC-20 interface. We need this method as a benchmark to evaluate the behavior-based approach.

4.1   Pattern

To improve the interoperability of tokens in the Ethereum ecosystem, the community has established a set of standards for token systems . ERC-20 [3] is the most popular standard for fungible tokens. It also serves as basis for extensions, such as ERC-223 and ERC-621. Even ERC-777, while still at draft stage at the time of writing, is backward compatible: a token can implement both standards to interact with older systems that require the ERC-20 interface [2]. Given the vast dominance of ERC-20 today, we restrict our analysis to this standard.

The standard defines six functions and two events that must be implemented to be fully compliant. (Listing 3 in Appendix B shows the ERC-20 interface skeleton in Solidity.) Since the applications of tradable tokens are diverse, the standard does not define how tokens are created, initially distributed, or how data storage should be organized. It only defines that ERC-20 tokens must have functions to securely transfer tokens, and some helper functions to check balances.

4.2   Detection Method

A naïve way to detect tokens is to check if the code implements the methods defined by the ERC-20 standard. From the ABI definition (see Sect. 2.2) we know how function calls are encoded and how functions are dispatched.

In order to detect token systems based on a signature we define:

Definition 2. *A token system according to its signature is a smart contract that introduces at least 5 of the 6 function selectors defined by the ERC-20 standard.*

We used five as a threshold to account for incomplete implementations of ERC-20 .

We use Definition 2 and the fact that the only way to introduce constants in the EVM are *PUSH* instructions. Since function selectors are 4 bytes long according to the ABI, the detection method looks for *PUSH4* instructions. Algorithm 2 takes as input a list of EVM instructions, inspects all 4-byte constants introduced, and checks membership in the pre-determined set of ERC-20 function selectors (variable $s_{signatures}$).

Algorithm 2. Detection method based on disassembly and signatures.

$s_{signatures} \leftarrow \{18160ddd, 70a08231, dd62ed3e, a9059cbb, 095ea7b3, 23b872dd\}$
function IsToken$_{\text{Sig}}(I)$ $\diamond$ I is a list of instruction tuples $t \in (opcode \times arg)$
   $s_{constants} \leftarrow \emptyset$
   for $(i_{opcode}, i_{argument}) \in I$ **do**
      if $i_{opcode} = PUSH4$ **then**
         $s_{constants} \leftarrow s_{constants} \cup \{i_{argument}\}$
   return $|s_{constants} \cap s_{signatures}| \geq 5$

4.3 Known Limitations

This method is obviously prone to false positives if a contract pushes all required constants to the stack but never uses them. This may even happen in dead code. Hence, we also get false positives if we analyze so-called *factory contracts* that create new token systems when called [4]. The code of the factory includes the code of the token system to create, and thus contains push instructions of the required constants.[3] The common cause for these weaknesses is that the method considers neither data nor control flow.

Similar to the behavior-based method, the signature-based method is a local heuristic. This can result in false negatives. For example, if the smart contract does not implement the ERC-20 interface, but delegates calls to a suitable implementation. This form of delegation is common practice on the Ethereum platform because it makes deployments cheaper. Furthermore, it enables code updates by swapping the reference to the actual implementation [7,8].

5 Measurements

5.1 Data and Procedure

To evaluate our two detection methods we study the Ethereum main chain from the day of its inception until 30 May 2018.[4] We extract all *unique runtime byte-code instances* and the addresses they are deployed on. With *runtime bytecode* we denote code that is executed when a transaction is sent to the contract after its deployment. This means we do not analyze initialization code.

In total we found 6 684 316 addresses that hosted bytecode at one point in time. From these addresses we extract 111 882 *unique runtime bytecode instances*, henceforth referred to as *bytecode instances* for brevity, unless stated otherwise. Observe that we do not double-count bytecode instances unlike it is often the case in headline statistics on smart contracts. We do not exclude contracts that were disabled by selfdestruct, i. e., we analyze all code ever deployed. Consequently, we also analyze bytecode instances that are barely used.

To evaluate that our detection results are not biased towards barely used or test code, we also define a subset of *active* instances. We define a bytecode

---

[3] One such instance can be found at `0xbf209cd9f641363931f65c0e8ef44c79ca379301`.
[4] Block number: 5 700 000.

Table 1. Recall of signature- and behavior-based detection methods against our GTD.

	Detected by Sig	Not Detected by Sig	
Detected by Behav	87.89% (508)	0.87% (5)	88.75% (513)
Not Detected by Behav	11.25% (65)	0.00% (0)	11.25% (65)
	99.13% (573)	0.87% (5)	100.00% (578)

instance as *active* if all hosting addresses combined handled a volume of at least 1000 transactions until 30 May 2018.

To build a *ground truth dataset* (GTD) for the evaluation, we downloaded 612 Top ERC-20 tokens[5] from Etherscan. Etherscan, a popular Ethereum block explorer, curates its top list of ERC-20 tokens by only including systems that are popular, supported by at least one major exchange, compliant with ERC-20 , and have a visible website. We exclude all token systems that were created after 30 May 2018, leaving us with a curated list of 595 ground truth token systems , of which we extract 578 bytecode instances.

We run both of detection methods over all bytecode instances and evaluate the results. The signature-based method (Sig) is able to process all of the input contracts. The behavior-based method (Behav) fails to analyze 1373 (1.23% of the total) instances. Failures occur if, for example, the bytecode contains syntactic errors not handled in the engine. We consider those 1373 instances as negative detection results. On the remaining 110509 instances, our behavior-based method reaches a mean (median) code coverage of 71,9% (82,2%). Over 70% of the instances reach a coverage above 50%, supporting the claim that smart contracts are a very suitable for symbolic execution techniques.[6]

To confirm our restriction to the ERC-20 interface in the signature-based method, we adapted our method to count the number of ERC-777 tokens. We encounter only four systems implementing at least 4 of the 13 functions required by ERC-777. All of them also implement ERC-20 for backward compatibility.

5.2 Validation on Ground Truth Data and Error Analysis

Table 1 presents the detection results of both methods evaluated against our curated GTD. Observe that the signature-based method alone is pretty good at detecting tokens, reaching 99.13% recall. The behavior-based method performs visibly worse with a recall of 88.75% on our curated GTD. Since no token systems remained undetected by both methods, the combination of both (Behav ∨ Sig) gives us perfect 100% recall. Our GTD does not allow us to calculate the precision.

---

[5] Ranked by market cap, retrieved on 23 Aug. 18 from https://etherscan.io/tokens.
[6] 100% - #16056, ≤ 75% - #50874, ≤ 50% - #31298, ≤ 25% - #5165, ≤ 10% - #1031.

The behavior-based method is able to detect the exact five contracts that are missed by the signature-based approach (Behav ∧ $\overline{\text{Sig}}$). Further manual investigation of these contracts shows that all of them do not implement ERC-20 up to our threshold. Fortunately, all of the five contracts published Solidity source code. Thus, we could confirm that they are missed by the signature-method because they implement only three of the six ERC-20 functions, namely `totalSupply()`, `balanceOf(address)`, and `transfer(address,uint256)`. This suggests that our initial threshold is too high, or in other words that even major token systems handle standards laxer than expected. Table 8 in Appendix C lists those five contracts.

The signature-based method identified 65 token systems that were not found by the behavior-based method ($\overline{\text{Behav}}$ ∧ Sig). We conjecture that either those tokens implement their internal state differently or they use libraries that implement the bookkeeping of storage values, thereby escaping our local behavior-based analysis. We try to answer why those tokens are not detected by manually inspecting a random sample of 20 (out of 65) bytecode instances (listed in Table 9 in Appendix C). We find that all of them are large and reasonably complex contracts.[7] We encountered three main causes for missed detection:

Delegation of Bookkeeping (6): We found 6 bytecode instances in our sample that do not implement any asset management logic in the contract itself. It is delegated to another contract. The front-end contract implements the ERC-20 interface, but many back-end bookkeeping contracts do not, e. g., the *Digix Gold Token*. Delegation patterns (or "hooks") like this one are often used to allow updates (by reference substitution) of the asset management logic.

Violation of Definition 1 (10): The second reason concerns mainly tokens that are derived from the popular MiniMeToken [5]. We found 9 of those in our sample. MiniMe uses a different storage layout. Instead of a plain integer that is updated over time, it writes a new checkpoint for every transfer into an array. This violates our detection assumption (1) in Definition 1, or, more specifically, fails our check that the field gets updated (self reference). Even though this already defeats our detection method, we find that `mythril` was not able to inspect the relevant paths in the transfer function. The average code coverage is as low as 34.8% on the 9 MiniMe-based tokens in our sample.

Also the *MakerDAO* instance is not detected for a violation of Definition 1, although it is not derived from MiniMe and reached high coverage (94.3%). It does not implement a balance check before the actual transfer as required in Definition 1. This can be fixed with an ad-hoc adjustment of the method, but we are concerned about the (not observable) false positive risk of a relaxed behavioral pattern.

Litations of Symbolic Execution and Taint Analysis (4): Four contracts in our sample neither delegate the bookkeeping work nor are derived from the MiniMeToken. All of them use a simple integer value to store the balance of the participants. *Storiqua* (42.9%), *LocalCoinSwap* (34.82%), and *LOCIcoin* (18.5%)

---

[7] Mean (median) code size: all instances 3315.0 (2541), $\overline{\text{Behav}}$ ∧ Sig 8153.86 (7828)
   Code coverage: 41.75% (40.25%).

suffer from low coverage. In the *Storiqua* instance, our method finds the relevant paths in the transfer function but does not find a matching store. In the case of *LocalCoinSwap*, we do not find a suitable constraint although the symbolic execution engine explores the relevant paths in transfer. *LOCIcoin* has the lowest coverage. The engine does not discover the relevant paths in the transfer method. Finally, *TrueUSD* reaches high coverage (72.9%), but the behavior-based method did not find a suitable constraint in the transfer function. All of those cases are examples for known limitations of symbolic execution (reaching low coverage, missing relevant paths), taint analysis (failing to find matching stores), as well as our detection approach (missed constraints).

5.3   Generalization to All Smart Contracts on Ethereum

Table 2 reports detection statistics over all bytecode instances. We find that 33.17% of the bytecode instances on the Ethereum platform can be said to be token systems with high confidence because they are detected by both methods (Sig $\land$ Behav). The interesting part is where both methods disagree.

Recall from our manual ground truth analysis that all instances missed by the signature-based method but detected by the behavior-based method (Behav $\land$ $\overline{\text{Sig}}$) are caused by our high threshold. So we re-run the analysis with a lower threshold of 3, as our manual inspection suggested. Tables 4 and 5 (both in Appendix A) show the updated results of Tables 1 and 2, respectively. With the lower threshold, the signature-based method detects 7193 more bytecode instances as tokens. 3232 of those newly detected token systems were already identified by the behavior-based method. The remaining tokens would have been missed otherwise. We conjecture that the 1772 bytecode instances only detected by the behavior-based method (Behav $\land \overline{\text{Sig}}$) are either non-ERC-20 bookkeeping contracts, as found in the *Digix Gold Token*, or token systems that do not implement ERC-20 for other reasons, such as obscuring their nature.

In the case of token systems detected by the signature-based but not by the behavior-based method ($\overline{\text{Behav}} \land$ Sig), we found mixed reasons in our GTD. First, we saw systems that implement the ERC-20 interface but delegate all bookkeeping tasks to other contracts. In order to study if this pattern generalizes to the whole dataset, we extract bytecode metrics, such as the number of call instructions. We find that contracts that are detected by the signature-based method contain an above-average number of call instructions. Table 7 (in Appendix A) presents the mean and median values of call-family instructions for different subsets of bytecode instances. The highlighted row stands out: $\overline{\text{Behav}} \land$ Sig instances have on average 2.2 times as many calls as the average bytecode instance. This indicates the use of delegation patterns as found in the *Digix Gold Token*. To further strengthen this interpretation, we us the Ethereum call graph (cf. Sect. 2.4) to find out if those instances have calls to other instances that are otherwise classified as token systems. For 920 of 10472 instances ($\overline{\text{Behav}} \land$ Sig) we find static references. 563 have direct hardcoded calls to another instance classified as token system, suggesting that the detectable behavior is implemented in the callee. The second and third reason for missing tokens were inherent limitations of symbolic execution, which we could not further evaluate on the entire dataset.

Table 3 shows detection results for all *active* bytecode instances. The results are pretty comparable to Table 5. Note that the behavior-based method misses relatively more instances detected via signature than on the complete dataset. One interpretation is that high-profile tokens implement more complex logic, therefore evading detection by symbolic execution. This conjecture is supported by the observed bytecode sizes as well as code coverage reached: active bytecode instances are on average around 1.6 times as large as the average bytecode instance. Average code coverage also drops from 71.9 (82.2%) to 66.2 (69.6%).

Table 2. Comparison of signature- and behavior-based detection methods on *all* bytecode instances. (Note that this is not a performance measurement. We cannot expect 100%.)

	Detected by Sig	Not Detected by Sig	
Detected by Behav	33.17% (37 114)	4.47% (5004)	37.65% (42 118)
Not Detected by Behav	5.82% (6512)	56.53% (63 252)	62.35% (69 764)
	38.99% (43 626)	61.01% (68 256)	100.00% (111 882)

Table 3. Comparison of signature- and behavior-based detection methods on all *active* bytecode instances (with signature threshold ≥ 3).

	Detected by Sig	Not Detected by Sig	
Detected by Behav	32.56% (2052)	0.73% (46)	33.29% (2098)
Not Detected by Behav	18.15% (1144)	48.56% (3060)	48.56% (4204)
	50.71% (3196)	49.29% (3106)	100.00% (6302)

5.4   Insights into the Token Ecosystem

The automatic detection of token systems allows us to shed more light into the token ecosystem. Looking at bytecode reuse, for instance, puts the headline numbers into perspective and informs us about the actual amount of innovation happening in the ICO community. To this end, Fig. 1 connects our technical level of analysis (bytecode instances) to the publicly visible level of addresses hosting token systems. The most frequently deployed bytecode instance of a token system is a standard template by *ConsenSys*.[8] It has been deployed 8729 times to the

---

[8] https://github.com/ConsenSys/Token-Factory/blob/master/contracts/ HumanStandardToken.sol.

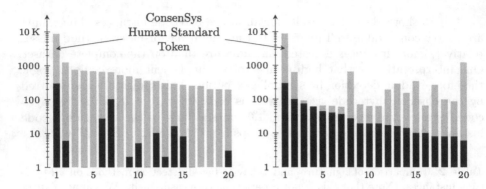

Fig. 1. Bytecode reuse of Ethereum token systems: number of addresses hosting a unique bytecode instance detected as token system. Top-20 ranked by total addresses (left) and "busy" addresses handling more than 100 transactions (right). Note the log scale.

Ethereum blockchain. 298 of these deployments have processed more than 100 transactions. Altogether 49 bytecode instances have been deployed more than 100 times, and 16 bytecode instances have 10 or more "busy" deployments.[9] These figures give some early intuition, but likely underestimate the extent of code reuse as trivial modifications of template code (or the output of token factories that deploy polymorphic code) are not consolidated.

6 Related Work

As we are not the first to systematically analyze smart contracts on Ethereum or to study tokens on the Ethereum platform, we summarize prior art by topic area.

Mapping the Smart Contract Ecosystem: Using source code provided by Etherscan, Bartoletti and Pompianu [13] manually classify 811 smart contracts by application domain (e. g., financial, gaming, notary) and identify typical design patterns. Norvill et al. [21] propose unsupervised clustering to group 936 smart contracts on the Ethereum blockchain. Zhou et al. [30] develop Erays a Ethereum reverse engineering tool that lifts EVM bytecode to a human readable pseudocode representation, for futher inspection. They conduct four case studies to show the effectiveness of the approach.

Vulnerability Detection in Smart Contracts: Luu et al. [19] execute 19366 smart contracts symbolically with the intention to uncover security vulnerabilities, which they find in 8833 cases. Tsankov et al. [27] build SECURIFY, a symbolic execution framework to uncover security problems in smart contracts. Security patterns are specified in a domain-specific language based on Datalog. Nikolic et al. [20] study so-called trace vulnerabilities that manifest after multiple runs

---

[9] Note that "busy" is similar to our notion of *active*, however on the level of addresses rather than bytecode instances.

of a program. Introducing MAIAN, a symbolic execution framework to reason about trace properties, they identify 3686 vulnerable smart contracts. Brent et al. [14] present VANDAL, a smart contract security analysis framework. It uses a Datalog-based language tailored to describe static analysis checks.

Token Systems: Somin et al. [26] study network properties of token trades and show that the degree distribution has power-law properties. They use a simple token detection method based on ERC-20 events generated at runtime, therefore relying on the standard compliance of the contracts. Etherscan identifies token systems using a signature-based approach [9]. However, the details of the method are proprietary and thus not available for replicable science. Etherscan's headline numbers count addresses with code, not bytecode instances.

Symbolic Execution: Symbolic execution is a very mature discipline as witnessed by the number of literature surveys published. For instance, Baloni et al. [12] provide an overview of the main ideas and challenges in symbolic execution. Păsăreanu et al. [23] offer a survey of trends in symbolic execution research and applications with special focus on test generation and program analysis. Person et al. [24] introduce differential symbolic execution to calculate behavioral differences between versions of programs or methods.

Malware Detection: The prime application of symbolic execution in systems security is malware analysis. Luo et al. [18] use symbolic execution compare code based on behavior. Christodorescu et al. [15] have developed a semantics-aware malware detection framework that uses templates to specify malicious patterns.

Financial Regulation: We are not aware of symbolic execution in tools that support financial authorities in their monitoring and supervision tasks, although some applications stand to reason given the prevalence of algorithmic trading.

In contrast to the above-mentioned work on smart contracts and symbolic execution, we do not aim at generating test cases or show the absence of certain conditions in programs, e.g., integer overflows. We apply symbolic execution to explore all paths through a program and analyze whether that program can be classified based on a given structure, or the presence of certain behavior.

7   Conclusion and Future Work

The idea of this work is to detect Ethereum token systems based on behavioral patterns. We have presented a method and evaluated it as effective using curated ground truth data and a reference method based on signatures.

Both methods have specific advantages. The signature-based approach is simple, but limited to standard-compliant token systems. It is easy to defeat detection by slightly deviating from the standard. The method bears a false positive risk in case of factory contracts or dead code. Quantifying this risk is left as future work. The method can be improved by taking data flow into account.

The behavior-based method does not depend on standard-compliance. It is robust against reordering of parameters or renaming of functions. To which extent it can deal with sophisticated obfuscation is left for future work. The effectiveness of this method demonstrates that symbolic execution is practical on Ethereum.

Both methods fail if the detectable pattern spans over more than one address. If this limitation becomes problematic in practice, the use of concolic execution [12] in conjunction with the current blockchain state is a way to overcome the locality.

In particular the behavior-based method is hand-crafted to the application of token detection. A direction of future work is to generalize the approach by building a domain-specific language in which behavioral patterns can be specified on a high level of abstraction. This would facilitate extensions of our approach to detect other kinds of behavior, such as smart contracts implementing non-fungible tokens, decentralized exchanges, or gambling services. Evaluating the transactions between the so-identified services would provide the necessary information to draw a map of the Ethereum ecosystem.

Acknowledgments. We like to thank ConsenSys for the work on mythril. This work has received funding from the European Union's Horizon 2020 research and innovation programme under grant agreement No. 740558.

A   Supplemental Result Tables

Table 6 presents the same detection results as Table 5 but unitl block 7000000.

Table 4. Recall of signature- and behavior-based detection methods against our GTD with lower signature threshold (≥ 3).

	Detected by Sig	Not Detected by Sig	
Detected by Behav	88.75% (513)	0.00% (0)	88.75% (513)
Not Detected by Behav	11.25% (65)	0.00% (0)	11.25% (65)
	100.00% (578)	0.00% (0)	100.00% (578)

Table 5. Comparison of signature- and behavior-based detection methods on all bytecode instances with lower signature threshold (≥ 3).

	Detected by Sig	Not Detected by Sig	
Detected by Behav	36.06% (40 346)	1.58% (1772)	37.65% (42 118)
Not Detected by Behav	9.36% (10 473)	52.99% (59 291)	62.35% (69 764)
	45.42% (50 819)	54.58% (61 063)	100.00% (111 882)

Table 6. Comparison of signature- and behavior-based detection methods on all byte-code instances with lower signature threshold (≥ 3). Update until block 7000000.

	Detected by Sig	Not Detected by Sig	
Detected by Behav	35.44% (64 223)	1.28% (2319)	37.72% (66 542)
Not Detected by Behav	13.41% (24 296)	49.87% (90 369)	62.28% (114 665)
	48.85% (88 519)	51.15% (92 688)	100.00% (181 207)

Table 7. Call instructions statistics for different bytecode subsets (mean/median).

Subset	CALLCODE	CALL	DELEGATECALL
-	(0.05 / 0)	(4.08 / 1)	(0.56 / 0)
Behav ∨ Sig	(0.05 / 0)	(2.91 / 1)	(0.10 / 0)
Behav ∧ Sig	(0.05 / 0)	(1.34 / 1)	(0.70 / 0)
$\overline{\text{Behav}}$ ∧ Sig	(0.05 / 0)	(9.06 / 6)	(0.20 / 0)
Behav ∧ $\overline{\text{Sig}}$	(0.01 / 0)	(2.20 / 0)	(0.04 / 0)

B   ERC-20 Interface Specification

```
1  contract ERC20Interface {
2      // Function Signatures
3      function totalSupply() public constant returns (uint);
4      function balanceOf(address tokenOwner)
5          public constant returns (uint balance);
6      function allowance(address tokenOwner, address spender)
7          public constant returns (uint remaining);
8      function transfer(address to, uint tokens)
9          public returns (bool success);
10     function approve(address spender, uint tokens)
11         public returns (bool success);
12     function transferFrom(address from, address to, uint tokens)
13         public returns (bool success);
14     // Events
15     event Transfer(address indexed from,
16                    address indexed to,
17                    uint tokens);
18     event Approval(address indexed tokenOwner,
19                    address indexed spender,
20                    uint tokens);
21 }
```

Listing 3. ERC-20 interface in Solidity.

C   Documentation of Manual Inspections

Table 8. Five smart contracts of the GTD missed by the signature-based but found by the behavior-based method.

Name	Address	Code Hash	# ERC-20 Functions
LatiumX	0x2f85e502a98af76f7ee6d...	0xf30b6028435e...	3
Pylon	0x7703c35cffdc5cda8d27aa...	0x96858625adfa...	3
Minereum	0x1a95b271b0535d15fa499...	0x65d59c447f7c...	3
All Sports Coin	0x2d0e95bd4795d7ace0da...	0x1c57e11bbd6e7...	3
Golem	0xa74476443119a942de498...	0x35e72568bdaa...	3

Table 9. Random sample of 20 smart contracts in the GTD missed by the behavior-based but found by signature-based method.

	Address	Code Hash
Delegation of Bookkeeping		
EmphyCoin	0x50ee674689d75c0f88e8f...	0x19780d1f0151fc...
Digix Gold Token	0x4f3afec4e5a3f2a6a1a411d...	0x941fab0f7c206...
FunFair	0x419d0d8bdd9af5e606ae2...	0xe29653f94e73...
Education	0x5b26c5d0772e5bbac8b31...	0xe359bf40848d...
Devery.io	0x923108a439c4e8c2315c4...	0x6b8bff0af6051...
UniBright	0x8400d94a5cb0fa0d041a3...	0x3058c20470fb...
Violation of Definition 1		
Ethbits	0x1b9743f556d65e757c4c6...	0xd3f516225294...
Aston X	0x1a0f2ab46ec630f9fd6380...	0xc2b817789336...
Sharpe Platform Token	0xef2463099360a085f1f10b...	0xe0e29e2655db...
FundRequest	0x4df47b4969b2911c96650...	0x519dc5c0384b...
SwarmCity	0xb9e7f8568e08d5659f5d2...	0x88b20869ae32...
Mothership	0x68aa3f232dabdc23434...	0x63e44909ce93...
Ethfinex Nectar Token	0xcc80c051057b774cd7506...	0x5c7c39e24430...
DaTa eXchange Token	0x765f0c16d1ddc279295c1a...	0xc4bdfc9026f14...
Swarm Fund	0x9e88613418cf03dca54d6...	0x56dd7cb818b4...
MakerDAO	0x9f8f72aa9304c8b593d55...	0xe69355035f77...
Limitations of Symbolic Execution and Taint Analysis		
Storiqa	0x5c3a228510d246b78a37...	0x93be59026507...
LocalCoinSwap Cr.	0xaa19961b6b858d9f18a115...	0x8/8b9c793a727...
LOCIcoin	0x9c23d67aea7b95d80942e...	0x9488b89a5ee6...
TrueUSD	0x8dd5fbce2f6a956c3022b...	0xf447f893b44fd...

References

1. Contract ABI Specification. https://solidity.readthedocs.io/en/develop/abi-spec.html. Accessed 5 Sept 2018
2. EIP 777: A New Advanced Token Standard. https://eips.ethereum.org/EIPS/eip-777. Accessed 18 Sept 2018
3. ERC-20 Token Standard. https://github.com/ethereum/EIPs/blob/master/EIPS/eip-20.md. Accessed 5 Sept 2018
4. Manage several contracts with factories. https://ethereumdev.io/manage-several-contracts-with-factories/. Accessed 5 Sept 2018
5. Minime Token. ERC20 compatible clonable token. https://github.com/Giveth/minime. Accessed 5 Sept 2018
6. Mythril: Security analysis tool for Ethereum smart contracts. https://github.com/ConsenSys/mythril. Accessed 31 July 2017
7. Proxy Patterns. https://blog.zeppelinos.org/proxy-patterns/. Accessed 13 Sept 2018
8. The Parity Wallet Hack Explained. https://blog.zeppelin.solutions/on-the-parity-wallet-multisig-hack-405a8c12e8f7. Accessed 13 Sept 2018
9. What is an ERC20 token and how to identify them on Etherscan? https://etherscancom.freshdesk.com/support/solutions/articles/35000081107-what-is-an-erc20-token-and-how-to-identify-them-on-etherscan-. Accessed 18 Sept 2018
10. Report of Investigation Pursuant to Section 21(a) of the Securities Exchange Act of 1934: The DAO. No. 81207, Securities and Exchange Commission, July 2017
11. Crypto-assets: Report to the G20 on work by the FSB and standard-setting bodies. Financial Stability Board, July 2018
12. Baldoni, R., Coppa, E., D'elia, D.C., Demetrescu, C., Finocchi, I.: A survey of symbolic execution techniques. ACM Comput. Surv. (CSUR) 51(3), 50 (2018)
13. Bartoletti, M., Pompianu, L.: An empirical analysis of smart contracts: platforms, applications, and design patterns. arXiv preprint arXiv:1703.06322 (2017)
14. Brent, L., et al.: Vandal: A Scalable Security Analysis Framework for Smart Contracts. arXiv preprint arXiv:1809.03981 (2018)
15. Christodorescu, M., Jha, S., Seshia, S.A., Song, D., Bryant, R.E.: Semantics-aware malware detection. In: 2005 IEEE Symposium on Security and Privacy (SP 2005), pp. 32–46, May 2005. https://doi.org/10.1109/SP.2005.20
16. Fröwis, M., Böhme, R.: In code we trust? In: Garcia-Alfaro, J., Navarro-Arribas, G., Hartenstein, H., Herrera-Joancomartí, J. (eds.) ESORICS/DPM/CBT -2017. LNCS, vol. 10436, pp. 357–372. Springer, Cham (2017). https://doi.org/10.1007/978-3-319-67816-0_20
17. King, J.C.: Symbolic execution and program testing. Commun. ACM 19(7), 385–394 (1976)
18. Luo, L., Ming, J., Wu, D., Liu, P., Zhu, S.: Semantics-based obfuscation-resilient binary code similarity comparison with applications to software and algorithm plagiarism detection. IEEE Trans. Softw. Eng. 43(12), 1157–1177 (2017). https://doi.org/10.1109/TSE.2017.2655046
19. Luu, L., Chu, D.H., Olickel, H., Saxena, P., Hobor, A.: Making smart contracts smarter. In: Proceedings of the 2016 ACM SIGSAC Conference on Computer and Communications Security, pp. 254–269. ACM (2016)
20. Nikolic, I., Kolluri, A., Sergey, I., Saxena, P., Hobor, A.: Finding the greedy, prodigal, and suicidal contracts at scale. arXiv preprint arXiv:1802.06038 (2018)

21. Norvill, R., Awan, I.U., Pontiveros, B., Cullen, A.J., et al.: Automated labeling of unknown contracts in Ethereum (2017)
22. Parizi, R.M., Dehghantanha, A., Choo, K.K.R., Singh, A.: Empirical Vulnerability Analysis of Automated Smart Contracts Security Testing on Blockchains. arXiv preprint arXiv:1809.02702 (2018)
23. Păsăreanu, C.S., Visser, W.: A survey of new trends in symbolic execution for software testing and analysis. Int. J. Softw. Tools Technol. Transf. **11**(4), 339 (2009)
24. Person, S., Dwyer, M.B., Elbaum, S., Păsăreanu, C.S.: Differential symbolic execution. In: Proceedings of the 16th ACM SIGSOFT International Symposium on Foundations of software engineering, pp. 226–237. ACM (2008)
25. Schwartz, E.J., Avgerinos, T., Brumley, D.: All you ever wanted to know about dynamic taint analysis and forward symbolic execution (but might have been afraid to ask). In: 2010 IEEE symposium on Security and privacy (SP), pp. 317–331. IEEE (2010)
26. Somin, S., Gordon, G., Altshuler, Y.: Social Signals in the Ethereum Trading Network. arXiv preprint arXiv:1805.12097 (2018)
27. Tsankov, P., Dan, A., Cohen, D.D., Gervais, A., Buenzli, F., Vechev, M.: Securify: Practical Security Analysis of Smart Contracts, August 2018. https://arxiv.org/pdf/1806.01143.pdf. Accessed 5 Sept 2018
28. Underwood, B.: Virtual Markets Integrity Initiative. Office of the New York State Attorney General, September 2018
29. Wood, G.: Ethereum: A secure decentralised generalised transaction ledger (EIP-150 revision) (2017). http://gavwood.com/paper.pdf. Accessed 18 June 2017
30. Zhou, Y., Kumar, D., Bakshi, S., Mason, J., Miller, A., Bailey, M.: Erays: reverse engineering ethereum's opaque smart contracts. In: USENIX Security

Measuring Ethereum-Based ERC20 Token Networks

Friedhelm Victor$^{(\boxtimes)}$ (iD) and Bianca Katharina Lüders (iD)

Technical University of Berlin, Straße des 17. Juni 135, 10623 Berlin, Germany
{friedhelm.victor,bianca.lueders}@tu-berlin.de

Abstract. The blockchain and cryptocurrency space has experienced tremendous growth in the past few years. Covered by popular media, the phenomenon of startups launching Initial Coin Offerings (ICOs) to raise funds led to hundreds of virtual tokens being distributed and traded on blockchains and exchanges. The trade of tokens among participants of the network yields *token networks*, whose structure provides valuable insights into the current state and usage of blockchain-based decentralized trading systems. In this paper, we present a descriptive measurement study to quantitatively characterize those networks. Based on the first 6.3 million blocks of the Ethereum blockchain, we provide an overview on more than 64,000 ERC20 token networks and analyze the top 1,000 from a graph perspective. Our results show that even though the entire network of token transfers has been claimed to follow a power-law in its degree distribution, many individual token networks do not: they are frequently dominated by a single hub and spoke pattern. Furthermore, we generally observe very small clustering coefficients and mostly disassortative networks. When considering initial token recipients and path distances to exchanges, we see that a large part of the activity is directed towards these central instances, but many owners never transfer their tokens at all. In conclusion, we believe that our findings about the structure of token distributions on the Ethereum platform may benefit the design of future decentralized asset trade systems and can support and influence regulatory measures.

Keywords: Blockchain · Ethereum · Tokens · Network analysis

1 Introduction

In the past years, blockchains and in particular ICOs have seen increased attention, with startups frequently selling *tokens* to obtain seed funding. Such tokens may represent both digital and physical assets or utilities as entries on the distributed ledger, similar to native digital currencies such as Bitcoin or Ether. They are commonly enabled by ERC20-compliant smart contracts implemented on the Ethereum blockchain. To date, their sale and trade are unregulated in most countries. A lot of research was already dedicated to the analysis of content and communication graphs on different blockchains. In contrast to these,

© International Financial Cryptography Association 2019
I. Goldberg and T. Moore (Eds.): FC 2019, LNCS 11598, pp. 113–129, 2019.
https://doi.org/10.1007/978-3-030-32101-7_8

which focused on the trade of native currencies, we investigate the trade of tokens. We define the network between addresses that reflects the distribution and trade of each token as its *token network*, in which each edge represents the transfer of a specified amount of the respective token between two addresses. To the best of our knowledge, no large-scale study of individual token networks on the Ethereum blockchain has been provided to date. We advance approaches developed in the area of network analysis to this new domain and analyze token networks quantitatively from a graph perspective to capture their structure and topology. This allows us to obtain a sound overview of the token landscape. An in-depth understanding of graph structures and usage patterns in the decentralized and unsupervised domain of cryptocurrencies and tokens is necessary to evaluate current token trading systems and serves as a basis for further research.

The remainder of this paper is structured as follows: In Sects. 2 and 3, we provide an overview of the theoretical background, current research results and related work on cryptocurrencies, blockchains and smart contracts. In Sect. 4, we describe our data collection methodology and provide a set of high-level statistics of our data set, followed by an analysis of the token networks based on graph theoretic measures in Sect. 5. Finally, we summarize our paper and provide approaches for future work in Sect. 6.

2 Background

In recent years, the popularity of blockchain-based cryptocurrencies has grown significantly. As of 2018, hundreds of different coins are in circulation, with a large portion of them developed on top of the Ethereum blockchain in the form of tokens, that have recently been the basis for many crowdfunded ventures. A new type of token can be created by implementing a smart contract. While their implementation often follows a standard, their behavior can be implemented arbitrarily. With regulation currently still under development, questions have been raised whether a certain token constitutes a security or a utility, and how they should be treated.

2.1 Ethereum, the EVM and Smart Contracts

Similar to Bitcoin, Ethereum is an open-source, public, distributed, blockchain-based platform with a Proof of Work-based consensus algorithm coupled with rewards, which absolves the need for trusted intermediaries [6]. If popularity were measured by market capitalization, it would be the second most popular blockchain as of September 2018. Ethereum's most significant feature is the Ethereum Virtual Machine (EVM) - a stack-based runtime environment that can execute programs known as *smart contracts*. They can be developed in high-level languages such as Solidity and deployed on the blockchain as bytecode by any participant of the network. The immutable code is reachable through the address of the smart contract account and stored on the ledger, along with all historic state changes. By sending transactions from externally owned accounts (EOA), users can interact with smart contracts and call their functions [27].

2.2   Tokens

The resilience of smart contracts to tampering makes them appealing for many application scenarios - *financial, notary, game, wallet,* and *library* contracts were identified by Bartoletti and Pompianu [4]. The authors further analyzed smart contract design patterns and showed that many of the contracts in the financial category use the token pattern for the representation of fungible assets. In contrast to the native *coins* that typically represent a digital currency, tokens may represent a variety of transferable and countable goods such as digital and physical assets, shares, votes, memberships, or loyalty points. Any third party can create smart contracts and develop, define and distribute their own named asset. A frequent approach to distribute tokens and raise funds is an *initial coin offering* (ICO). The term leans on *Initial Public Offering*, the stock market launch in the traditional economy. Another distribution mode, the so-called *Airdrop*, is designed to distribute tokens without requiring prior investment. Once they have value, the founders can sell additional tokens.

2.3   The ERC20 Token Standard

To establish a common interface for fungible tokens, the ERC20[1] standard was proposed in late 2015. To be compatible, a smart contract needs to implement a set of functions, of which only the signatures, but not the implementations are specified. Within a smart contract's bytecode, these signatures can be identified by their entrypoints, marked by the first 4-bytes of the Keccak hashes of the high level function signature (Table 1). Thus, ERC20-compatible contracts can be identified by means of the corresponding entrypoint hashes in the deployed contract bytecodes.

Table 1. ERC20 signatures and hashes

Classification			Signature	First 4-byte Keccak hash
ERC20	Required	Method	totalSupply()	18160ddd
			balanceOf(address)	70a08231
			transfer(address,uint256)	a9059cbb
			transferFrom(address,address,uint256)	23b872dd
			approve(address,uint256)	095ea7b3
			allowance(address,address)	dd62ed3e
		Event	Transfer(address,address,uint256)	ddf252ad
			Approval(address,address,uint256)	8c5be1e5
	Optional	Method	name()	06fdde03
			symbol()	95d89b41
			decimals()	313ce567

---

[1] https://github.com/ethereum/EIPs/blob/master/EIPS/eip-20-token-standard.md.

Pos.	Sender	Receiver	Function call
1	A	X	transfer(B, 3)
2	A	X	transfer(C, 7)
3	B	X	transfer(C, 2)
4	C	X	transfer(D, 4)

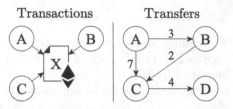

Fig. 1. Transactions to a token contract and corresponding graph perspectives

To send tokens from address A to address B, the owner of address A sends a transaction to a token contract X, calling its `transfer` function. If successful, the balance of both addresses will be updated within the contract, constituting a state change. As balances may also be affected by other functions included by the smart contract developer, the ERC20 standard recommends to emit a `Transfer` event whenever a token transfer has occurred. Figure 1 illustrates the relationship between transactions that call functions and the emitted transfers.

These token transfers yield a graph, in which the nodes are addresses connected by transfers. This graph may also contain addresses that never interacted with the token contract: during deployment or with a specific function, a common way to associate tokens with particular addresses are *initial balances*, which the contract creator allocates to certain addresses upon creating the contract. Some developers have chosen to emit these allocations as transfer events, where the source address is for example set to `0x0`, but mostly, these balance allocations are not emitted as transfer events. Later standard proposals such as ERC621 additionally introduced `Mint` and `Burn` events to increase or decrease balances without requiring a transfer at all. These events change the total supply of the respective token. Although not used widely yet, shortcomings of the ERC20 design that are beyond the scope of this paper are tackled with proposals ERC223, ERC667 and ERC777.

3   Related Work

Several seminal works and studies in the area of graph theory and network analysis, also including the analysis of social networks, as well as in digital currencies and Ethereum smart contracts form the basis of our research.

3.1   Cryptocurrencies and Smart Contracts

The literature on Bitcoin and other cryptocurrencies covers not only the underlying distributed ledger and consensus technologies and protocols, but also the publicly available transactional data, which provides a unique opportunity to analyze real, large-scale financial networks. Various aspects of Bitcoin have been discussed, such as by Barber et al. [3], who investigated the design, success factors, history, strengths and weaknesses. Tschorsch and Scheuermann [24] provided a comprehensive survey on the technical aspects of decentralized digital currencies. Furthermore, Akcora et al. [1] presented a holistic view on distributed ledgers with a focus on graph theoretical aspects.

Going beyond Bitcoin, Bonneau et al. [6] provided the first systematic exposition of the second generation of cryptocurrencies and analyzed *altcoins* that have been implemented as alternate protocols. Similarly, Anderson et al. [2] explored three representative blockchains - Ethereum, Namecoin and Peercoin - which have extended Bitcoin's original mechanism and focused on the features that distinguish them from the pure currency use case. Research on smart contracts frequently focuses on design patterns, applications and security issues [23]. In the first methodic survey and quantitative investigation on their usage and programming, Bartoletti and Pompianu [4] proposed a taxonomy of smart contract application domain categories and identified common programming and design patterns. With a focus on security, Nikolic et al. [20] presented a novel characterization of trace vulnerabilities, which allow to identify contracts as *greedy*, *prodigal* or *suicidal*.

3.2 Blockchain Graph Analysis

Each blockchain can be analyzed from a graph-centric perspective on two layers: as *communication graphs*, which reflect the underlying peer-to-peer communication on the network layer, and as *content graphs*, which reflect transfers of assets on the application layer [1]. For example, Miller et al. [17] investigated the public topology of the Bitcoin peer-to-peer network in a quantitative measurement and analyzed how nodes participate and collaborate in mining pools.

In the analysis of content graphs, techniques from the area of social network analysis are commonly used. For a general overview of social network analysis, the reader is referred to fundamental works such as Newman [19]. Mislove et al. [18] proposed a detailed comparison of the characteristics of multiple online social network graphs at large scale and confirmed the power-law, small-world and scale-free properties of these social networks. A commonly used methodology to detect and validate power laws was presented by Clauset et al. [8].

Content graphs can be modelled on different levels. First, in *transaction graphs*, the nodes represent transactions that happen on the distributed ledger and the edges represent the flow of transferred assets. These graphs start from the genesis block, each transaction can have incoming edges only and a DAG (*directed acyclic graph*) emerges [1,12,21]. In *address graphs*, the nodes denote addresses, and each edge represents a particular transaction between two of them. Address graphs provide a useful abstraction for exploring and tracing flows through the system and identifying recurrent patterns in transactions [12]. A recent approach to investigate the whole address graph spanned up by the trade of all ERC20-compliant tokens on the Ethereum blockchain was presented by Somin, Gordon and Altshuler [23]. The authors consider all trading wallets as the nodes of the network, construct the edges based on buy-sell trades and demonstrate that the degree distribution of the resulting network displays strong power-law properties. Finally, *user* or *entity graphs* reflect the flow of value between real-world entities. In these graphs, each node represents a user or an entity, and each edge represents a transaction between source and target entity [1]. Building these graphs requires to identify and associate public addresses that possibly belong to the same real-world entity. Many approaches to cluster addresses on the Bitcoin blockchain have been presented to date, along with discussions of connected anonymity issues [10,16,21,22]. To the best of our knowledge, no such heuristics exist for Ethereum's account model yet.

Many of the approaches to analyze content graphs arising through the usage of cryptocurrencies rely on methods and assumptions known from the area of social network analysis. Yet, the network generation mechanisms are different. Since the Ethereum network combines aspects of social and financial transaction networks, we also consider analysis approaches that focus on the latter. In this area, Inaoka et al. [13] investigated the network structure of financial transactions on the basis of the logged data of the BOJ-Net. Similarly, Kyriakopoulos et al. [15] analyzed the network of financial transactions of major financial players within Austria and reported the characteristic network parameters. Some of their many empirical findings include the dependency of the network topology on the time scales of observation and the existence of power laws in the cumulative degree distributions.

3.3   Contribution

In summary, these different graph-theoretical approaches provide an intuition for the flow and spread of assets on different blockchains. While previous analyses took either the entire blockchain or the whole network of token trades into consideration, we center our attention on a new type of address graphs: *token networks*, which we define as the network of addresses (nodes) that have owned a specific type of token at any point in time, connected by the transfers of the respective token. Since the tokens are not comparable, neither in their value, which heavily fluctuates over time, nor in their respective total supply, which may further be influenced by Mint and Burn events, we omit the weight of the transfers, such that we obtain a directed, unweighted graph. Further, due to a lack of approaches for address clustering on Ethereum, we define nodes as addresses in these token networks and assume that they represent different entities, which may be either a user, an exchange, a miner, or another smart contract. A new token network emerges for each newly published ERC20-compliant token contract. Each address may be part of several token networks, and each analyzed token network is essentially an overlay graph of the entire network of Ethereum addresses. To the best of our knowledge, these individual token networks have not been studied yet, and we hope that our measurement and evaluation inspires further research in this area.

4   Data

In this chapter, we describe how we identified ERC20-compatible smart contracts, how we extracted and filtered the transfer events, and provide an overview of the token network landscape in the form of summary statistics.

4.1   Data Collection

The basis for generating token networks are token transfers emitted by ERC20-compatible smart contracts. We used the Parity client[2] for the set-up of a fully synchronized Ethereum node and extracted all transactions, contract addresses and the corresponding smart contract bytecodes from the first 6,300,000 blocks, covering the period from July 30th, 2015 until September 9th, 2018. We identified 7,323,377 smart contract creations, including those that were created by other contracts, of which 75,514 fulfill the criteria introduced in Sect. 2.3 and are thus labeled as ERC20-compatible.

Next, we retrieved the token transfer events emitted by those ERC20-compatible smart contracts. These events can be identified by the corresponding event type and contain information about the source, the target and the amount of tokens that were passed in the respective transfer. In total, we extracted 97,671,089 transfer events. It is noteworthy that the transfer events are only related to 46,970 of the ERC20-compatible smart contracts (62.2%), such that 28,544 of the token contracts have never emitted any transfer events. This does not necessarily imply that the tokens have never been traded on the Ethereum blockchain, but there are no events that document their transfers.

Since it is up to the developer of the smart contract to decide when a transfer event is emitted, not all actual token transfers are logged as such. To account for initial balance allocations, which are only rarely emitted as transfer events (Sect. 2), we added the initial balances as synthetic transfers to our dataset, where the source address is the artificial address 0x0 and the target address corresponds to the address mentioned in the contract bytecode. We could identify the allocation of initial balances in 52,554 ERC20-compatible smart contracts, where each smart contract that uses this method distributes the assets to 2.96 entities on average (median 1). These numbers are comprehensible, since the smart contract developer has an interest so assign a certain amount of tokens to himself and/or his team, which is usually a rather small set of users. These initial balances add 142,673 new token transfers to our dataset, such that we capture a total of 97,813,762 token transfers related to 64,393 ERC20 token contracts.

Figure 2 compares the amount of transactions that were initiated by externally owned accounts (EOAs) to ERC20-compatible smart contracts (white) with the corresponding amount of transactions to all other, non-ERC20-compatible contracts (gray) and the resulting token transfers (black dots) emitted by the ERC20-compatible contracts. All three numbers exhibit a significant increase starting in the beginning of 2017, and the growth indicates an increasing popularity of ERC20-compatible token contracts in terms of contract interactions initiated by EOAs. Since a single interaction with a token contract may yield multiple transfer events, we observe in total more transfer events than ERC20 contract transactions.

---

[2] https://www.parity.io/.

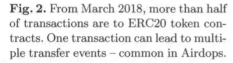

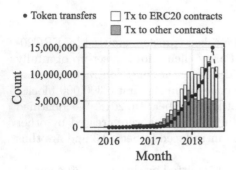

Fig. 2. From March 2018, more than half of transactions are to ERC20 token contracts. One transaction can lead to multiple transfer events – common in Airdops.

Fig. 3. CDF of transfers and unique edges related to token contracts. Almost 90% of all transfers/edges belong to the top 1,000 token contracts.

4.2   Summary Statistics

The entire set of 64,393 ERC20 token networks captures 19,45 million unique addresses, which corresponds to nearly 45, 9% of all addresses on the Ethereum blockchain as of September 9, 2018.

The smallest 599 networks consist of only one node, which may have up to 5 self-edges associated to itself. In general, the size distribution is skewed towards smaller values - while the median is 3 (mean 890), some of the networks capture up to 1.52 million nodes (*Tronix* and *An Etheal Promo*). Other popular token networks which stand out due to their size are *VIU*, *Bitcoin EOS*, and the *Basic Attention Token*. On the other hand, 80.38% of the token networks consist of only 10 nodes or less.

In terms of *edges* per token network, we differentiate between simple, multiple and self-edges, such that $n_{simple} + n_{multi} + n_{self} = n_{edges}$. Besides the networks that consist of only one node, there are five others that have only self-edges – the largest of them (*Explore Coin*) has 46 nodes which are only connected to themselves. Similar to the size in terms of the amount of nodes, 80.33% of the networks have 10 unique edges or less. On average, the networks contain 1519 edges (median 2), the largest network has 3,17 million edges in total (*EOS Token Contract*). The five networks with the largest amount of edges further include *Tronix*, *OMG Token*, *An Etheal Promo*, *BeautyChain*, and these are also the networks with most unique edges, i.e. those with the most connections between different addresses. Still, even in these networks, each node has on average two adjacent edges, which might correspond to obtaining tokens from the contract and then transferring them to an exchange.

In total, the ratio of total edges per node varies from 0.5 to 2631, where the highest ratio is in the *Ether Token*. Removing self-edges and multiple edges, this value drops to at most 8.69 (*Consumer Activity Token*), with a mean of 0.7315, such that we have relatively sparse networks.

5 Analysis

In this section, we present our data selection steps and analyze the structure of the token networks with respect to distributions of degree, density, components, clustering coefficients and assortativity. We then focus on how tokens are received and transferred, with an emphasis on the role of exchanges – providing insight into the activity within token trading networks.

5.1 Data Selection

As discussed in Sect. 4, the majority of token networks consists of only a few transfers and nodes. To remove those from the analysis, since they may not exhibit a concise graph structure comparable to the larger networks and might bias the results, we assess the amount of transfers per token network. Figure 3 shows the cumulative distribution function (CDF) of all transfers, respectively connections between nodes, that the networks add to the total amount. We observe that the top 1000 token networks capture more than 85% of both measures, such that we limit our analysis to these, which account for 86,54 million transfers in total (88.48% of the original amount).

5.2 Degree Distributions

A fundamental property of nodes in a directed graph are their *in-* and *out-*degrees. The frequency distribution of degrees, where p_k is the fraction of nodes with degree k, can provide an insight into the network's structure. Many real-world networks exhibit highly right-skewed degree distributions with a *heavy tail*, which indicates that a significant portion of observations is in the tail and demonstrates the existence of high-degree hubs. Several real-world networks have been confirmed to follow *power laws* in their degree distribution [7,14,18,19]. Power laws are distributions of the form $p_k = Ck^{-\alpha}$, in which the dependent variable, the probability that a node has degree k, varies inversely as a power of the independent variable, the degree k. p_k decreases monotonically [18,19] and decays significantly slower than exponential decays in normal distributions. While the non-negative constant C is fixed by normalization, the parameter α is called the *coefficient* of the power law [9,19] and typically is in the range $2 \le \alpha \le 3$.

Using the poweRlaw package in R [11], we estimate parameters for each token network, using maximum likelihood estimation and the *Kolmogorov-Smirnov* statistic to quantify the distance between the observed degree distribution and the estimated power law. We perform goodness-of-fit tests via a bootstrapping to obtain a p value, following the approach of Clauset et al. [8].

Whereas Somin et al. [23] have shown that the full transfer graph consisting of all token networks combined appears to follow a power-law in both in- and outdegree, Figs. 4 and 5 illustrate a different result for the individual token networks. While we can fit a power law model to all of the networks, most of the

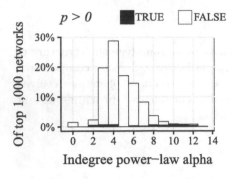 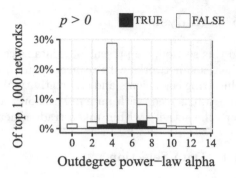

Fig. 4. Estimated indegree power-law coefficients. In most cases, the hypothesis can be rejected.

Fig. 5. Estimated outdegree power-law coefficients. The hypothesis can be rejected in fewer cases than for the indegree.

p values obtained via bootstrapping have returned a value of 0, indicating that they likely do not follow a power law.

For those where we cannot reject the power law hypothesis, we suppose that if a network contains multiple exchanges, multiple high indegree addresses are likely to be present. These same addresses frequently also have a high outdegree. Considering that many networks additionally contain a large initial distribution in the form of a star-shaped subgraph, one further address with high outdegree is likely to exist. This may explain why about 10% of token networks appear to follow a power law in their outdegree distribution.

Generally, the fitted power law exponents are very high, indicating quickly decaying degree distributions. This is contraindicative to the power law hypothesis, but adequate for the use case: in token networks, as opposed to social networks, the amount of hubs, i.e. exchanges, is limited institutionally. While social networks allow for an organic growth of "popular" nodes, only a limited number of exchanges are known for securely handling token trades. This reflects an issue of trust - while any user can open an exchange on the basis of pre-defined protocols, most users only trust and trade their tokens on a few well-known ones.

Another aspect that might differentiate the full transfer graph from the individual token networks in terms of power laws in their degree distributions, is that initial token distributions, especially airdrops, frequently choose existing, active addresses. This process, which follows the logic of preferential attachment, leads to these nodes becoming connectors between individual token networks, which adds smaller hubs to the full transfer graph.

5.3 Density and Components

The density d represents the fraction of existent to theoretically possible edges in a network. In general, we observe that a larger number of nodes in a token network leads to a lower graph density (Fig. 6). The network with the highest density, also related to the number of nodes, is the *NPXS Smart Token Relay*.

Further, we investigate the number of weakly connected *components*, disconnected portions of the token networks. Given common token distribution modes (Sect. 2.2), we expect the tokens to be distributed starting from the addresses with the initial balances, and assume that each network consists of a single, large, weakly connected component. We observe that this holds for 75% of the observed token networks when we take the initial balances into account (Sect. 4). Several components indicate that the tokens were not distributed in an ICO, but based on another logic, such as minting, which credits an arbitrary amount of tokens to a specified address and typically emits a `Mint` event (Sect. 2.3). We also find that 29 token networks have more than 100 components, and three consist of more than 3,000 components (*blockwell.ai KYC Casper Token, SanDianZhong* and *VGAMES*). This might indicate that many of the nodes in the network received their tokens in a non-standard process, yielding an anomalous graph structure.

5.4 Clustering Coefficients

To measure the clustering coefficient, which indicates the strength of local community structure, two measures are common: (1) the *global* clustering coefficient C_g, which measures the fraction of paths of length two in the network that are closed, and (2) the average of the *local* clustering coefficients, C_{avg_l}, which define for each individual node the share of possible connections among the node's neighbors that actually exist in the network. In either case, the clustering coefficient indicates how much more likely it is to connect to a neighbor's neighbor than to a randomly chosen node [19], and a large clustering coefficient is regarded as an indicator for small-world networks. Values of $C_g = 0.20$ (film actor collaborations), $C_g = 0.09$ (biologist collaborations) and $C_g = 0.16$ (university email communication) are high compared to estimates based on random connections, but typical values for social networks [19]. Similarly, Baumann et al. [5] found that the average local clustering coefficient (C_{avg_l}) in the Bitcoin address graph is fluctuating around 0.1 and thus rather high over time, also indicating a small world network.

For the token networks, we need to take into account that there is, as discussed in Sect. 4.2, a large fraction of nodes with degree one, for which the local clustering coefficient should be set to $C_i = 0$ [19]. If there is a significant number of such nodes, C_{avg_l} would be dominated by these minimum-degree nodes, yielding a poor picture of the overall network properties. Additionally, vertices with a low degree of which 2 or 3 neighbors are connected raises C_{avg_l} disproportionately high. Thus, we rely on C_g, which measures the global cliquishness of the network and provides evidence for a small-world network [26]. For the entire network of token transfers, we observe $C_g = 0.00001062$ and $C_{avg_l} = 0.3042$, which is higher than the known measure for the entire network of Bitcoin addresses [5].

This might indicate that the network of token trades has a higher tendency to form communities, maybe based on users who recommend or send tokens to each other. Similarly, airdrops tend to focus on existing active users, which could further lead to the forming of communities.

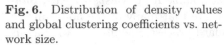

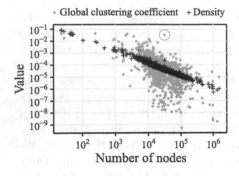

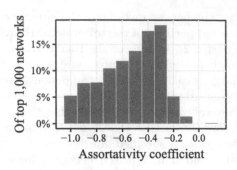

Fig. 6. Distribution of density values and global clustering coefficients vs. network size.

Fig. 7. Distribution of degree assortativity coefficients. All but one token network are disassortative.

For the individual token networks, we observe a mean global clustering coefficient of 0.0008831 and a maximum value of 0.0941 for the *NPXS Smart Token Relay*. This network is rather small, with only 24 nodes. Figure 6 illustrates C_g related to the size of the network, showing a general decrease, and exhibits another outstanding token: *TEST POGO 1* (circled), which has the highest C_g (0.0324) relative to its size. Further, we observe that 707 of the networks in the sample have a higher C_g than the network that connects them. Thus, related to their size, it is more likely that two neighboring nodes are connected to the same third node. On the opposite side, we identify 7 networks with $C_g = 0$, among them the *Funkey Coin* and the *NucleusVisionCore*. Their ratio of simple edges to nodes indicates that they are either very similar or correspond exactly to star schemas - for example, the *FunkeyCoin* has 18106 nodes and 18105 simple edges.

5.5 Degree Assortativity

The assortativity indicates how nodes are connected with respect to a given property, such as the degree. If the degree correlation r_{deg} [25] of a network is positive, nodes tend to connect to other nodes with a similar degree - a network is said to be disassortative if this relationship is inverted, such that high degree nodes tend to be connected to low degree nodes. We calculate the degree assortativity for the simplified, undirected token networks (Fig. 7) and find that almost all of them are disassortative. Those networks that exhibit a degree assortativity of close to $r_{deg} = -1$ resemble star shapes, where most nodes have a connection to only one or a few high degree nodes. The only network with $r_{deg} > 0$ is the *blockwell.ai KYC Casper Token*, potentially due to its high number of small components.

5.6 Network Activity

To further quantify the activity inside a token network, we examine the initial token recipients and determine whether they send their tokens onward. As many tokens are listed on exchanges, and speculating with tokens is a common use case, we also examine whether a token network contains an address that is known to belong to an exchange. For this purpose we manually collected 113 exchange addresses from discussion forums and blockchain explorers such as Etherscan[3].

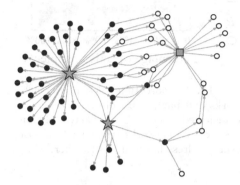

Fig. 8. SoftChainCoin Token Network with distributors (stars), initial recipients (black) and exchange (square).

Fig. 9. SoftChainCoin Token Network with distribution and exchange addresses removed.

To illustrate our approach, Fig. 8 shows the small network of a token named *SoftChainCoin*[4]. The star-shaped nodes on the left distributed tokens to the black nodes - the initial recipients (R_i). Some of these, the active initial recipients (R_{ai}), have transferred tokens to other addresses. The active recipients (R_a), including both initial and secondary recipients, then transferred them to an exchange (square-shaped) or to other nodes. We define for each token network:

(a) The fraction of R_i (colored black in Fig. 8) relative to all addresses (R)
(b) The fraction of R_{ai} (that have sent tokens) relative to R_i
(c) The fraction of R_{ai} where there exists a path to an exchange
(d) The fraction of edges remaining, if distribution and exchange addresses are removed (Fig. 9), relative to the number of edges in the original network
(e) The mean minimum path length of those in c to an exchange.

We obtain the set of initial distributing nodes by determining the two nodes with the highest outdegree within the first 10% of transfers seen. We choose two, because manual inspection shows that sometimes tokens are not distributed from the first address itself, as can be seen in Fig. 8. We find that in about 25% of the token networks, the R_i account for 90–100% of all addresses (Fig. 10). These are likely airdrops that did not attract further users. On the other end, also in about 25% of the networks, the R_i account for less than 10% of all addresses, indicating that there are many addresses that joined the network after

---

[3] https://etherscan.io/.
[4] Token address: 0x86696431d6aca9bae5ce6536ecf5d437f2e6dba2.

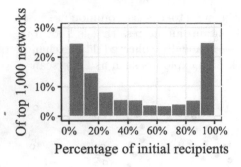

Percentage of initial recipients

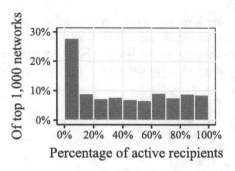

Percentage of active recipients

Fig. 10. In ≈25% of the networks (right bar), almost 100% of all nodes are initial recipients. Similarly, in ≈25% of the networks (left bar), nearly all addresses received tokens by other means.

Fig. 11. In more than 25% of the networks (left bar), ≤10% of token recipients transferred their tokens. Conversely, in ≈8% of the networks (right bar), almost every address has issued a transfer.

the initial distribution, or that there has never been a large initial distribution at all. Figure 11 illustrates how many of these R_i have ever sent tokens onward – showed signs of activity (R_{ai}). Here we observe that in more than 25% of the networks, less than 10% of the initial recipients ever transferred their tokens. While it could be argued that these are users simply holding their tokens, another possibility is that these tokens are not wanted, and can be seen as a type of spam. In ≈8% of the networks, this activity percentage is near 100%, indicating that there exist strong incentives to transfer the corresponding token, such as the opportunity to sell the tokens at an exchange.

Figure 12 displays a scatter plot, where each cross represents one token network, positioned by the fraction of R_{ai} (b)), and the fraction of how many of these have an outgoing path to an identified exchange (c)). This fraction is not constant: as more initial recipients are active, more of them tend to send their tokens to an exchange. However, it is worth noting that the mere fact that an exchange offers to trade a certain token may also lead to increased activity directed towards exchanges. Nevertheless, very few token networks show active initial recipients without paths to exchanges, indicating that the main utility of most tokens is their trade on exchanges. If we remove distributing and exchange addresses from the graph, the median fraction of edges remaining (d)) is 42%, indicating that large parts of the networks only exist for that purpose.

For those R_{ai} with paths to exchanges, we determine for each network the shortest path to any identified exchange and compute the average shortest path length between active initial recipients and exchanges. Figure 13 shows that about half of the networks have a mean distance of two transfers. Given that exchanges often create artificial addresses for each customer, this implies that tokens are often sent directly to an exchange, indicating that trading is a main use case.

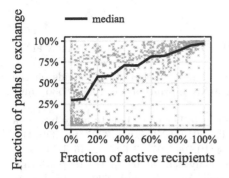

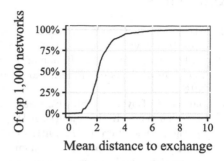

Fig. 12. When more initial recipients are active, more of them have a path to an exchange.

Fig. 13. In more than 50% of networks, those addresses that have a path to an exchange, their mean shortest path is ≤ 2.

6   Conclusion and Future Work

In this paper, we present a measurement study to analyze token networks, enabled through smart contracts on the Ethereum blockchain, from a graph perspective. We find that many follow either a star or a hub-and-spoke pattern. The heavy tails in the degree distributions are not as pronounced as in social networks - the networks tend to contain less and smaller hubs, such that they are mostly dominated by emitting addresses with a large out-degree and exchanges with a large in-degree. The number of exchanges is limited, only a few succeeded to gain the trust of the users. Small values for density and clustering coefficient embody the anonymity prevalent in these networks, as users mostly don't know each other and it's not very common yet to transfer tokens to acquaintances. A main use case of many tokens appears to be their sale, rather than their circulation, and some token networks barely show any activity after the initial distribution. The presented approach is part of our ongoing work on blockchain graph analysis, and our results help to understand current usage patterns and to design future systems.

Further research may refine the common understanding of token networks. While the presented approach observes the token network at the moment of data collection, observing the development of the networks over time might be even more insightful. Similarly, the presented approach is based on the assumption that each Ethereum address represents a single entity - we have not yet taken into consideration that an entity might be represented by several addresses. Furthermore, the forming of communities in the graph could be investigated, and not yet quantitatively available features such as the completeness and trustworthiness of ICO whitepapers could be included. Bitcoin and other cryptocurrencies offer a large field for criminals, while users show a large trust in ICOs even though faced with a total lack of a central contact address in case of a loss - knowledge about typical structures might lead to a differentiation between normal structures and anomalies, which may help to identify potentially fraudulent systems.

References

1. Akcora, C.G., Gel, Y.R., Kantarcioglu, M.: Blockchain: A Graph Primer. arXiv e-prints arXiv:1708.08749, August 2017
2. Anderson, L., Holz, R., Ponomarev, A., Rimba, P., Weber, I.: New kids on the block: an analysis of modern blockchains. arXiv e-prints arXiv:1606.06530, June 2016
3. Barber, S., Boyen, X., Shi, E., Uzun, E.: Bitter to better — how to make bitcoin a better currency. In: Keromytis, A.D. (ed.) FC 2012. LNCS, vol. 7397, pp. 399–414. Springer, Heidelberg (2012). https://doi.org/10.1007/978-3-642-32946-3_29
4. Bartoletti, M., Pompianu, L.: An empirical analysis of smart contracts: platforms, applications, and design patterns. In: Brenner, M., et al. (eds.) FC 2017. LNCS, vol. 10323, pp. 494–509. Springer, Cham (2017). https://doi.org/10.1007/978-3-319-70278-0_31
5. Baumann, A., Fabian, B., Lischke, M.: Exploring the bitcoin network. In: WebDB 04: Proceedings of the 10th International Conference on Web Information Systems and Technologies (2014)
6. Bonneau, J., Miller, A., Clark, J., Narayanan, A., Kroll, J.A., Felten, E.W.: SoK: research perspectives and challenges for bitcoin and cryptocurrencies. In: 2015 IEEE Symposium on Security and Privacy, pp. 104–121, May 2015. https://doi.org/10.1109/SP.2015.14
7. Broder, A., et al.: Graph structure in the web. Comput. Netw. **33**(1), 309–320 (2000). https://doi.org/10.1016/S1389-1286(00)00083-9
8. Clauset, A., Shalizi, C., Newman, M.: Power-law distributions in empirical data. SIAM Rev. **51**(4), 661–703 (2009). https://doi.org/10.1137/070710111
9. Donato, D., Leonardi, S., Millozzi, S., Tsaparas, P.: Mining the inner structure of the web graph. J. Phys. A: Math. Theoret. **41**(22), 224017 (2008)
10. Filtz, E., Polleres, A., Karl, R., Haslhofer, B.: Evolution of the bitcoin address graph. Data Science – Analytics and Applications, pp. 77–82. Springer, Wiesbaden (2017). https://doi.org/10.1007/978-3-658-19287-7_11
11. Gillespie, C.S.: Fitting heavy tailed distributions: the poweRlaw package. J. Stat. Softw. **64**(2), 1–16 (2015). http://www.jstatsoft.org/v64/i02/
12. Haslhofer, B., Karl, R., Filtz, E.: O bitcoin where art thou? insight into large-scale transaction graphs. In: SEMANTICS (Posters, Demos), vol. 1695 (2016)
13. Inaoka, H., Ninomiya, T., Tanigushi, K., Shimizu, T., Takayasu, H.: Fractal network derived from banking transaction. An analysis of network structures formed by financial institutions. Bank of Japan Working Paper Series (04) (2004)
14. Kleinberg, J.M., Kumar, R., Raghavan, P., Rajagopalan, S., Tomkins, A.S.: The web as a graph: measurements, models, and methods. In: Asano, T., Imai, H., Lee, D.T., Nakano, S., Tokuyama, T. (eds.) COCOON 1999. LNCS, vol. 1627, pp. 1–17. Springer, Heidelberg (1999). https://doi.org/10.1007/3-540-48686-0_1
15. Kyriakopoulos, F., Thurner, S., Puhr, C., Schmitz, S.W.: Network and eigenvalue analysis of financial transaction networks. Eur. Phys. J. B **71**(4), 523 (2009). https://doi.org/10.1140/epjb/e2009-00255-7
16. Meiklejohn, S., et al.: A fistful of bitcoins: characterizing payments among men with no names. In: Proceedings of the 2013 Conference on Internet Measurement Conference IMC 2013, pp. 127–140. ACM, New York (2013). https://doi.org/10.1145/2504730.2504747
17. Miller, A., et al.: Discovering Bitcoin's Public Topology and Influential Nodes (2015)

18. Mislove, A., Marcon, M., Gummadi, K.P., Druschel, P., Bhattacharjee, B.: Measurement and analysis of online social networks. In: Proceedings of the 7th ACM SIGCOMM Conference on Internet Measurement IMC 2007, pp. 29–42. ACM, New York (2007). https://doi.org/10.1145/1298306.1298311, http://doi.acm.org/10.1145/1298306.1298311

19. Newman, M.: Networks: An Introduction. Oxford University Press, Oxford (2010)

20. Nikolic, I., Kolluri, A., Sergey, I., Saxena, P., Hobor, A.: Finding The Greedy, Prodigal, and Suicidal Contracts at Scale. arXiv e-prints arXiv:1802.06038, February 2018

21. Reid, F., Harrigan, M.: An analysis of anonymity in the bitcoin system. In: Altshuler, Y., Elovici, Y., Cremers, A., Aharony, N., Pentland, A. (eds.) Security and Privacy in Social Networks, pp. 197–223. Springer, New York (2013). https://doi.org/10.1007/978-1-4614-4139-7_10

22. Ron, D., Shamir, A.: Quantitative analysis of the full bitcoin transaction graph. In: Sadeghi, A.-R. (ed.) FC 2013. LNCS, vol. 7859, pp. 6–24. Springer, Heidelberg (2013). https://doi.org/10.1007/978-3-642-39884-1_2

23. Somin, S., Gordon, G., Altshuler, Y.: Network analysis of ERC20 tokens trading on ethereum blockchain. In: Morales, A.J., Gershenson, C., Braha, D., Minai, A.A., Bar-Yam, Y. (eds.) ICCS 2018. SPC, pp. 439–450. Springer, Cham (2018). https://doi.org/10.1007/978-3-319-96661-8_45

24. Tschorsch, F., Scheuermann, B.: Bitcoin and beyond: a technical survey on decentralized digital currencies. IEEE Commun. Surv. Tutorials **18**(3), 2084–2123 (2016). https://doi.org/10.1109/COMST.2016.2535718

25. Van Steen, M.: Graph theory and complex networks. An Introduction, vol. 144 (2010)

26. Watts, D.J., Strogatz, S.H.: Collective dynamics of small-world networks. Nature **393**(6684), 440 (1998)

27. Wood, G.: Ethereum: A secure decentralised generalised transaction ledger. https://github.com/ethereum/yellowpaper

Traceability and How to Stop It

New Empirical Traceability Analysis
of CryptoNote-Style Blockchains

Zuoxia Yu[1], Man Ho Au[1(✉)], Jiangshan Yu[2], Rupeng Yang[1,3], Qiuliang Xu[4],
and Wang Fat Lau[1]

[1] Department of Computing, The Hong Kong Polytechnic University,
Hung Hom, Hong Kong SAR
csallen@comp.polyu.edu.hk
[2] Monash University, Melbourne, Australia
[3] School of Computer Science and Technology, Shandong University, Jinan, China
[4] School of Software, Shandong University, Jinan, China

Abstract. The cascade effect attacks (PETS' 18) on the untraceability of Monero are circumvented by two approaches. The first one is to increase the minimum ring size of each input, from 3 (version 0.9.0) to 7 in the latest update (version 0.12.0). The second approach is introducing the ring confidential transactions with enhanced privacy guarantee. However, so far, no formal analysis has been conducted on the level of anonymity provided by the new countermeasures in Monero. In addition, since Monero is only an example of leading CryptoNote-style blockchains, the actual privacy guarantee provided by other similar blockchains in the wild remains unknown.

In this paper, we propose a more sophisticated statistical analysis on CryptoNote-style cryptocurrencies. In particular, we introduce a new attack on the transaction untraceability called *closed set* attack. We prove that our attack is optimal assuming that no additional information is given. In other words, in terms of the result, *closed set* attack is equivalent to brute force attack, which exhausts all possible input choices and removes those that are impossible given the constraints imposed by the mixins of each transaction.

To verify the impact of our attack in reality, we conduct experiments on the top 3 CryptoNote-style cryptocurrencies, namely, Monero, Bytecoin and DigitalNote, according to their market capitalization. Since the computational cost of performing *closed set* attack is prohibitively expensive, we propose an efficient algorithm, called clustering algorithm, to (approximately) implement our attack. By combining our clustering method with the cascade attack, we are able to identify the real coin being spent in 70.52% Monero inputs, 74.25% Bytecoin inputs, and in 91.56% DigitalNote inputs.

In addition, we provide a theoretical analysis on the identified *closed set* attack, i.e., if every input in a CryptoNote-style blockchain has 3 mixins, and all mixins are sampled uniformly from all existing coins, the success rate of this attack is very small (about 2^{-19}). Given that *closed set* attack is equivalent to the best possible statistical attack, our findings provide two key insights. First, the current system

© International Financial Cryptography Association 2019
I. Goldberg and T. Moore (Eds.): FC 2019, LNCS 11598, pp. 133–149, 2019.
https://doi.org/10.1007/978-3-030-32101-7_9

configuration of Monero is secure against statistical attacks, as the minimum number of mixin is 6. Second, we identify a new factor in improving anonymity, that is, the number of unspent keys. Our analysis indicates that the number of mixins in an input does not need to be very large, if the percentage of unspent keys is high.

1   Introduction

Since the introduction of Bitcoin in 2009 [10], numerous distributed cryptocurrencies have been proposed. Nonetheless, most of existing cryptocurrencies are not designed to provide strong privacy protection. For instance, several works [7,11,13] showed Bitcoin, currently the most popular and largest cryptocurrency, is vulnerable to de-anonymization attacks.

To address this problem, privacy-preserving cryptocurrencies with stronger privacy guarantees are attracting increasing attentions. Among them, CryptoNote-style cryptocurrencies are one of the noteworthy efforts. The CryptoNote protocol was first introduced in [14], with a focus on protecting the privacy and anonymity of the electronic cash. Since its introduction, many variations utilizing this protocol have been proposed, including Bytecoin, Boolberry, Dashcoin, DigitalNote, Monero, etc. Similar to many other distributed cryptocurrencies, CryptoNote also adopts the notion of transaction to represent the process of spending coins. Each transaction contains several inputs and outputs, where inputs consume coins from the sender, outputs transfer coins to the receiver. The total amount of coins consumed in the inputs and the total amount of coins transferred to the outputs should be equal. Besides, each transaction should be signed by the sender to authorize the transfer, by using the private key associated to the public-key (address)[1] of a to-be-spent coin. Moreover, a ring signature [6,12] scheme is adopted to guarantee the privacy of the real-spend of each input, which is a cryptographic primitive that allows a user to anonymously sign a message on behalf of a group of users. Therefore, the identity of the real-spend is hidden. All other decoy coins in the input are called mixins.

However, in practice, CryptoNote-style cryptocurrencies fall short from realizing their claimed anonymity. Recently, two independent and concurrent works [5,8][2] demonstrate that Monero transactions may be de-anonymized via statistical analysis. Specifically, they found that most inputs in Monero have very small number of mixins and more than half inputs are paid without having any mixin. Those inputs without mixins can be trivially de-anonymized. Even worse, once a coin payed without mixin is chosen as a mixin in another transaction, the input of this transaction also faces a danger of being de-anonymized. Based on this simple yet vital observation, these two works adopt similar strategies to

---

[1] Throughout this paper, we interchangeably use the term coin, output and the public-key.

[2] An updated version [9] of [8] also appears recently, but both the method and the result for the traceability analysis are similar in these two works, thus we focus on the initial version.

conduct empirical evaluations, which are based on the so-called "chain-reaction" analysis [8] or cascade effect [5]. Roughly speaking, the attacker first identifies all inputs with zero-mixin. As each located input is payed by merely one public-key, the public-key must be the real payer of the input. Since each public-key can only be used once in Monero, it is safe to delete these de-anonymized public-keys in mixins of the remaining inputs. This will lead to new zero-mixin inputs and the attack could be conducted repeatedly. According to the experiment results of [5,8], by Feb 2017, nearly 65% of transaction inputs are with zero-mixin, and the cascade effect can render another 22% of inputs traceable, i.e., nearly 87% of all Monero inputs are insecure when considering users' anonymity.

Having witnessed (and predicted) this type of attacks, Monero has proposed a few countermeasures. First, at version 0.9.0 (January 1, 2016), it releases a mandatory requirement that each transaction input should include at least 2 mixins. Subsequently, at version 0.10.0 (September 19, 2016), ring confidential transaction (RingCT), which aims at further enhancing privacy of users via hiding the transaction amount, is introduced. An added advantage of employing RingCTs is that all RingCT input must use outputs of RingCTs as its mixins, i.e., no public-key used before version 0.10.0 will be chosen as mixin for a RingCT input. Therefore, neither the chain-reaction attack nor the cascade attack works for RingCTs. Besides, after realizing the effect of the number of mixins, the minimum number of mixins is further increased from 2 to 6 in version 0.12.0 (March 29, 2018).

There is no doubt that known attacks are circumvented by Monero, but more fundamental problem remains, and it still threatens all CryptoNote-style currencies. That is, can anonymity of users be well-protected with the current ring size, i.e., the countermeasures for known attacks? A related question is how to theoretically analyze the security level achieved by those cryptocurrencies adopting ring signature for untraceability. Besides, how about the anonymity achieved in practice by other CryptoNote-style currencies?

Our Contributions. In this paper, we give answers to the above questions. First, we show that the current countermeasures to resist known attacks make Monero a good system to provide anonymity. However, on the negative side, we show other CryptoNote-style protocols are still suffering from the same type of attacks. In fact, our combined attacks are much more effective on Bytecoin and DigitalNote, as we can de-anonymize up to 91.56% transactions in the chain of DigitalNote.

We introduce a new attack on the untraceability of CryptoNote-style currencies called *closed set* attack. This attack is based on the fact that n transaction inputs will and must use n distinct public-keys as real-spend, since each public-key can only be redeemed once. A set of inputs is called a *closed set* if the number of inputs equals to the number of distinct public-keys included. Hence, we can deduce that all public-keys included in a *closed set* must be mixins in other inputs outside of this *closed set*. In this way, the searching for *closed sets* will be helpful to trace the real-spend of some other inputs. Different from cascade effect attack which relies on the "chain-reaction analysis" due to zero-mixin inputs, *closed set* attack conducts further traceability without relying on any previous traceable inputs.

The contributions of this work can be divided into the following aspects:

1. We introduce *closed set* attack on the untraceability of CryptoNote-style blockchains, and prove that *closed set* attack is *optimal*. In particular, it could get the minimal mixin for every input, i.e., it deletes all public-keys payed elsewhere in a mixin, identical to the results of brute-force attack.
2. We verify the impact of our attack via performing experiments on actual blockchain data, where we pick the top 3 CryptoNote-style currencies by market capitalization, i.e., Monero, Bytecoin and DigitalNote. As the proposed attack is too expensive to run due to its high complexity, we propose an efficient algorithm, namely, clustering algorithm, to (approximately) implement *closed set* attack. We give a lower bound of our clustering algorithm in implementing the *closed set* attack. Specifically, we prove that our algorithm can find all *closed set* of size less than or equal to 5. The experiment results of these three currencies are given in Table 1.

Table 1. Experiment Results. All inputs considered in this paper are non-coinbase transaction unless specific stated. The items under column "Cas." (resp. "Clu.") denote the total number and percentage of inputs traced by cascade attack (resp. clustering attack). "No. of C.S." denotes the total number of *closed sets* found by the clustering algorithm.

Coin	Total blocks	Total inputs	Deducible (%)	Cas. (%)	Clu. (%)	No. of C.S.
Monero	1541236 (30 March 2018)	23164745	16334967 (70.516%)	16329215 (99.96%)	5752 (0.04%)	3017
Bytecoin	1586652 (3 August 2018)	45663011	33902808 (74.25 %)	33822593 (99.763%)	80215 (0.237%)	5912
DigitalNote	699748 (13 August 2018)	8110602	7426036 (91.56%)	7425987 (99.9993%)	49 (0.0007%)	38

3. In addition, we also provide a theoretical analysis on the existence of *closed set*. We find that if all inputs have 3 mixins and all mixins are uniformly distributed, with all but a very small probability (about 2^{-19}), there will not exist any *closed set*. Our analysis suggests that the usage rate of outputs is closely related to the anonymity of Monero. Moreover, if we can guarantee that the probability of choosing an unspent key as mixin is 25%, then the number of mixins of each input could be as small as 3 to render brute-force attack ineffective.

Related Works. Yu et al. [15] first identified that transaction untraceability could be compromised by merely observing how mix-ins are selected. They called this new class of attacks by "inference attacks". They initiated a theoretical study on inference attacks, and develop models to formally capture attacks of this class. However, no concrete attack algorithm nor experimental analysis is given. Cascade effect attacks [5,8] can be seen as special cases of the passive "inference attacks". The *closed set* attack proposed in this work provides the first algorithm to implement an efficient and generic passive inference attacks with experimental analysis.

Communication with the Community. We have fully disclosed our results to the related research communities, including CryptoNote, Monero, Bytecoin, and DigitalNote. We learnt that Monero researchers have concurrently and independently observed similar attacks [3], and the blackball tool developed by Monero is able to identify a part of the closed sets we identified in this work. Considering Monero, no RingCT transactions are affected under their blackball tool and our current analysis. We will release our code as an open-source repository, and work with Monero to help improving its tool set to enhance user privacy.

2 Preliminary

CryptoNote Protocol. CryptoNote protocol [14] aims at providing a privacy enhanced cryptocurrency, with the following two properties:

- Untraceability: for any transaction, the real-spend should be anonymous among all the sets of outputs in an input;
- Unlinkability: for any two transactions, it is impossible to prove that they were sent to a same user.

To guarantee unlinkability, for each output in a transaction, CryptoNote uses a one-time random public-key as the destination, which is derived from receiver's public-key and sender's random data. In this way, only the receiver who holds the permanent secret key can redeem that output. For the untraceability, CryptoNote adopts ring signature, which is a primitive that allows a user to anonymously sign a transaction on behalf of a group of users, which is usually referred as a ring. Therefore, the real-spend will be hidden via the help of other outputs, which are called mixins. Obviously, for an input with n public-keys, the number of mixin is n-1.

Notation. We use $[m]$ to denote the integer set $\{1, 2, \ldots, m\}$. For any set S, we use $|S|$ to denote its size. For a transaction tx, we use $tx.in$ to denote an input of this transaction, which is a set of public-keys $\{pk_1, pk_2, \ldots, pk_\ell\}$ used to create a ring signature. We also interchangeably call each input $tx.in$ of a transaction as a ring R throughout this paper. Specifically, we use $R = \{pk_1, pk_2, \ldots, pk_n\}$ to denote the transaction input including public-keys $pk_1, pk_2, \ldots, pk_n$.

We also need the Chernoff bound in our analysis. There are various forms of the Chernoff bound, here we use the one from [4].

Lemma 1 (Chernoff Bounds). *Let* $X = \sum_{i=1}^{n} X_i$*, where* $X_i = 1$ *with probability* p_i *and* $X_i = 0$ *with probability* $1 - p_i$*, and all* X_i *are independent. Let* $\mu = \mathbb{E}(X) = \sum_{i=1}^{n} p_i$*. Then*

$$\Pr[X \geq (1 + \delta)\mu] \leq e^{-\frac{\delta^2}{2+\delta}\mu} \text{ for all } \delta > 0;$$

$$\Pr[X \leq (1 - \delta)\mu] \leq e^{-\frac{\delta^2}{2}\mu} \text{ for all } 0 < \delta < 1.$$

3   Closed Set Attack

In this section, we introduce our *closed set* attack. All attacks considered in this section only assume access to the transactions in the blockchain of a CryptoNote-style currency, without any further active ability. This assumption is valid since all transactions on the blockchains are publicly accessible.

We prove that our proposed *closed set* attack is optimal, i.e., brute-force attack. Looking ahead, brute-force attack will traverse all possible assignments of payers of all inputs and delete those with conflict data. Both our attack and brute-force attack return the minimum set of candidates for the real payer of each input.

3.1   Brute-Force Attack

Brute-force attack is an attack that tries all possible sequence of distinct public-keys to test whether it is valid for the assignments of the real-spends for all transaction inputs. While a sequence of public-keys is valid if it satisfies requirements: (1) the size of the sequence equals to the number of total transaction inputs in the dataset; (2) all public-keys included in the sequence are distinct; (3) for all index i of that sequence, the i-th public-key in the sequence belongs to the corresponding i-th input in the dataset. In other words, brute-force attack is the process of searching for all valid sequences among the permutations of all public-keys with specific length according to the above requirements. We call all elements included in index i ($i \leq$ no. of all inputs) of all valid sequences as the candidates for the real-spend of the i-th transaction input. Therefore, the resulting valid sequences are the combinations of the possible real-spend of each transaction input. Besides, if a transaction input only has one candidate for the real payer, then the candidate must be its payer.

It is not hard to see that brute-force attack is a perfect attack which can find out all possible real-spends for each transaction input. Assume that there are n distinct keys and m transaction inputs in our dataset, and without loss of generality, n is larger than m. Let $\mathbb{A}_n^m$ denote the number of permutations of m elements among n elements. The number of valid sequences after the execution of brute-force attack is ($\mathbb{A}_n^m - |\mathsf{Conflicts}|$), where $\mathsf{Conflicts}$ denotes the set of deleted permutations which fail to the above requirements.

3.2   Our Attack

Although the aforementioned brute-force attack is perfect, the complexity is prohibitively high in practice, which is $\mathcal{O}(n!)$. Considering the inefficiency and impracticability of brute-force attack, we propose a new attack called *closed set*, which is more efficient while providing the same result.

The proposed *closed set* attack is based on the observation that if the number of distinct public-keys included in a set of transaction inputs equals to the number of the inputs of the set, then we can deduce that each public-key included must be a real-spend of a certain input in this set, and be mixin in other outside inputs. In this way, the finding of a *closed set* has at least two significant impacts. Firstly, it will render other inputs become traceable after removing public-keys of a *closed set*. Secondly, the average size of the inputs will decrease, which is helpful for further operation.

The *closed set* attack is an iteration process that finds out all possible *closed sets* from the transaction inputs, removes public-keys included, and finds those traceable inputs. Compared with the previous cascade effect attack presented by [5] or "chain-reaction" analysis by [8], the *closed set* attack can render more inputs traceable. More precisely, cascade effect attack utilizes the fact that the zero-mixins inputs will affect the traceability of other inputs who pick those public-keys of them as mixins. In other words, this attack bases on the set of previous traceable inputs to track the remaining anonymous ones, while our attack can start from any anonymous input.

To better explain our attack, we give a brief example below. Here we consider four inputs included in transactions $\{tx_i\}_{i\in[4]}$ and assume that there are four distinct public-keys $\{pk_j\}_{j\in[4]}$ included in the input sets of them, i.e.,

$$tx_1.in = \{pk_1, pk_2, pk_3\};$$
$$tx_2.in = \{pk_2, pk_3\};$$
$$tx_3.in = \{pk_1, pk_3\};$$
$$tx_4.in = \{pk_1, pk_2, pk_3, pk_4\}.$$

Note that, there must exist no other transaction input who is only composed of public-keys among $\{pk_j\}_{j\in[4]}$. Otherwise, the design principle of Monero that one output can only be redeemed once will be broken. While the original cascade attack [5,8] does not work here, since there exists no 0-mixin input.

Although we can not make all aforementioned inputs traceable, but we can trace the real-spend of one of them. Specifically, consider the set $S = \{tx_i.in\}_{i\in[3]}$. Among that, the union set of all distinct public-keys included is $\{pk_1, pk_2, pk_3\}$. Clearly, the size of S equals to the number of distinct public-keys included in it such that it is a *closed set*. Since each output can be spent once only, then the output pk_j ($j \in [3]$) must be a real-spend in a certain $tx_j (j \subset [3])$. In this way, we can deduce that the real-spend of tx_4 must be pk_4.

A Naive Implementation. A naive method to find all *closed sets* is to visit all possible subsets of transaction inputs. For each visited subset, we check whether it is a *closed set* by comparing the number of inputs and the number of distinct public-keys included in it. If yes, we further conduct the removing and tracing operations triggered by this *closed set*. Otherwise, continue the process until all subsets have been visited. Due to space limitation, we give this algorithm in Appendix A.

Theoretically, this algorithm can find all *closed set* included in all transaction inputs. However, it is expensive to implement in reality, since the complexity of traversing all subsets of inputs is $\theta(2^m)$, where m is the total number of all transaction inputs included in the blockchain. For instance, up to block 1541236 of Monero, the number of untraceable inputs remained is 6835530 after the execution of the cascade attack. Starting from these inputs, at the step of searching subsets of size 5, the complexity of the algorithm will become $\mathcal{O}(2^{100})$.

Analysis of Closed Set Attack. We prove that our *closed set* attack is optimal. In other words, our *closed set* attack is equivalent to brute-force attack. Specifically, we prove that after the execution of our *closed set* attack, each transaction input is the set of candidates of the real-spend of it found by brute-force attack. The analysis is concluded by the following theorem.

Theorem 1. *The aforementioned closed set attack is equivalent to brute-force attack. In other words, for any set of transactions, the impact of our attack on it is identical to the impact of brute-force attack.*

Due to space limitation, we refer readers to the full version of this paper for the proof of this theorem.

3.3   On the Existence of Closed Set: A Theoretical Perspective

As mentioned before, the *closed set* attack is optimal. This is to say, we can conclude that anonymity of inputs cannot be reduced if no *closed set* exists. In this section, we estimate the probability that there exists at least one *closed set* in an ideal scenario, namely, all inputs have a (small) constant number of mixins and all mixins are selected uniformly from all keys.

More concretely, we consider a scenario that

- There are $6 \cdot 2^{20}$ inputs, with $6 \cdot 2^{20}$ real-spend public-keys;
- There are also additional 25% (i.e. $2 \cdot 2^{20}$) unspent public-keys;
- Each input has 3 mixins;
- Each mixin is sampled uniformly from all $8 \cdot 2^{20}$ keys;

where the first two conditions come from the real data of Monero after cascade attack, and the third condition is based on the fact that the average ring size after the cascade attack is 4.62.

Lemma 2. *With all but a small probability 2^{-19}, there does not exist any closed set in the above dataset if all inputs have 3 mixins and all mixins are sampled uniformly from all keys.*

The proof of this lemma is given in the full version of this paper.

4   Our Clustering Algorithm

Considering the impracticability of subset-based algorithm mentioned above, here we introduce an approximate but efficient algorithm for searching *closed sets*, which is named as clustering algorithm. Looking ahead, although the clustering algorithm is just an approximate algorithm, we show that the lower bound of the size of *closed set* found by it is 5. In other words, all *closed set* with size less than or equal to 5 can be found. Besides, we conduct experiments and find that our clustering algorithm achieves a better result during the actual execution.

Intuition of Our Clustering Algorithm. Recall that, the main feature of a *closed set* is that it embraces the same number of transaction inputs and distinct public-keys. Hence, our target should be finding a set of inputs with the above characteristics. To do so, one intuitive way is forming a set from a certain input, then absorb other input which is helpful to achieve a *closed set*. A key challenge is how to select other rings?

We observe that since the ultimate target is to make two numbers about this set equal, it is possible to select rings based on the consequence of adding an input into a set. For instance, assuming the set being considered now is called S, which is initialized by input R. Whenever an input R' is added into S, the possible consequences can be divided into the following three cases:

- Case 1. If all public-keys included in R' are a subset of all public-keys contained in S, then for set S, the number of included transaction inputs is increased by one, and the number of distinct public-keys remains the same. Thus, the insertion of R' will certainly increase the possibility of S becoming a *closed set*. We call such kind of input as useful input.
- Case 2. If the insertion of R' will only introduce one distinct public-key to S, then the insertion of this input will not change the current relationship between the number of distinct public-keys and the number of inputs included in S. This kind of input extends the public-key set of S, which maybe helpful for absorbing other inputs. We call such kind of input as uncertain input.
- Case 3. If the insertion of R' will introduce two or more distinct public-keys to S, then the number of inputs will only be increased by one, but the number of public-keys will be increased by 2 or more. As this does not help our analysis at all, we call such kind of input as bad input.

Above all, if we only pick the relatively useful and uncertain inputs to a set, then we can find a *closed set* faster with high probability.

Definition of Cluster. A cluster $Clus$ is defined as a set of inputs, namely, $Clus = \{R_1, R_2, ..., R_n\}$. Each cluster represents a set PK_Clus, which is defined as $PK\_Clus = \bigcup_{R \in Clus} R$. In other words, PK_Clus is the set used to collect all distinct public-keys included in the inputs of $Clus$.

The *distance* from an input to a cluster is defined as the number of public-keys included in the input but not in the cluster. The formal definition of it is given below:

$$Dist(R, Clus) = Dist(R, PK\_Clus) = |R| - |PK\_Clus \cap R|,$$

where R is the input considered to be added, and $Clus$ is a cluster with public-keys set PK_Clus. Notably, this definition is not symmetric. According to our definition, the distance from an input to a cluster, i.e., $Dist(R, Clus)$, is different with the distance from a cluster to an input, i.e., $Dist(Clus, R)$.

For instance, consider the cluster $Clus$ and the input R composed as follows:

$$Clus = \{\{pk_1, pk_2\}, \{pk_1, pk_3\}, \{pk_2, pk_4\}\},$$
$$R = \{pk_1, pk_3, pk_5\}.$$

Obviously, the public-key set of $Clus$ is $PK\_Clus = \{pk_1, pk_2, pk_3, pk_4\}$. The size of R is 3, and number of common public-keys are 2. Hence, according to our definition, the distance from R to $Clus$ is $Dist(R, Clus) = Dist(R, PK\_Clus) = 3 - 2 = 1$. So, if we add R into $Clus$, then only one new public-key, i.e., pk_5, will be introduced in $Clus$.

Starting from a specific input, the construction of a cluster is a dynamic process of searching for other qualified inputs. To clarify which kind of inputs can be absorbed into a cluster, we associate each cluster with a distance. More precisely, we say a cluster $Clus$ with distance 1, if only those inputs satisfying $Dist(R, Clus) \leq 1$ can be added into it. As the insertion operation may cause changes to a cluster, we should always adopt the present cluster to calculate the distance from an input to it. The construction algorithm of a cluster from a certain input is given in Algorithm 1.

Algorithm 1. $Cluster\_Form$(R)

1: Start with an input R, and define the cluster as $Clus = \{R\}$
2: Let $DataSet$ be all transaction inputs in the blockchain
3: **for** each $R'(\neq R) \in DataSet$ **do**
4:     **if** $Dist(R', Clus) \leq 1$ **then**
5:         $Clus = Clus \cup \{R'\}$
6: **return** $Clus$

For each cluster, we use two additional parameters to check whether it is a *closed set*. One is the number of inputs included in it, the other one is the number of distinct public-keys included. Formally, if the number of inputs equals to the number of distinct public-keys included in a cluster, we say that this cluster is a *closed set*. Besides, in some cases, a *closed set* may contain other sub-*closed set*. To find all *closed sets*, whenever we get a *closed set* via this algorithm, we further conduct a sub-*closed set* searching operation. An important observation is that if a public-key only appears once in a *closed set*, then it must be the real spend of the input including it. For simplicity, we utilize this method to test whether there exists sub-*closed set* inside a *closed set*, since the complexity of brute-forcing all subsets of this *closed set* is quite large.

Next we introduce the clustering algorithm for all clusters with distance 1.

The main idea is that we repeatedly pass over all the transaction inputs via numerous iterations. In each iteration, the algorithm picks an input and uses it to initialize a cluster *Clus*. Then we run the constructing cluster algorithm (Algorithm 1) to add proper inputs into *Clus*. We continue the next iteration if the resulted cluster is not a *closed set*. Otherwise, before starting with the next iteration, the algorithm should finish the following operations. Remove all public-keys contained in this cluster from the remaining inputs, and find the traceable ones. Afterwards, we check whether the current *closed set* includes a public-key such that it only appears in one input. If yes, we further de-anonymize inputs inside a *closed set*.

The algorithm of searching for all clusters with distance 1 from all transaction inputs in the blockchain is given in Algorithm 2. Notably, all rings considered in our algorithm are anonymous. Once finding the real-spend of an input, we will not do any operation on that input. Besides, our algorithm concentrates on resulting data after the execution of cascade effect attack. Hence, in Algorithm 2, we abuse the concept, where a cascade effect algorithm is first invoked.

Algorithm 2. Clustering Algorithm

1: Let *DataSet* be all transaction inputs in the blockchain.
2: Cascade-Effect(Dataset)
3: Flag = true
4: **while** Flag == true **do**
5:      Flag = false
6:      **for** each $R \in DataSet$ **do**
7:          $Clus\_Form(R) \to Clus$
8:          **if** *Clus* is a *closed set* **then**
9:              Remove(*Clus*) $\to Flag$
10:             **if** Flag == true **then**
11:                 find traceable inputs
12:                 check whether rings inside *Clus* are traceable

---

Analysis of Accuracy. The accuracy of the clustering algorithm is analyzed through the following theorem, which gives a lower bound of the clustering algorithm. This is to say that all *closed sets* with size less than or equal to 5 can be found after the execution of the clustering algorithm.

Theorem 2. *After the execution of our clustering algorithm with searching distance 1, all indivisible closed sets with size less than or equal to 5 can be returned by our algorithm.*

We refer readers to the full version of this paper for the proof of this theorem.

Analysis of Complexity. Assume the total number of transaction inputs included in the blockchain is N. The number of iterations in our algorithm is $\theta(N)$. Suppose the average length of an input is ℓ. While in each iteration, in the worst case, we calculate $\mathcal{O}(\ell N)$ times distance between all inputs and the current clusters. Therefore, in the worst case, the complexity is $\theta(\ell N^2)$.

5   Experiment Result

To evaluate the level of anonymity achieved by the CryptoNote-style currencies, as well as the estimation of the probability of the existence of *closed sets* in reality, we implement our clustering algorithm in C++, and the program is executed on a computer with 3.1 GHz Intel Core i5 Processor, 16 GB RAM and 256 GB SSD storage disk. Notably, here we only analyze the top three CryptoNote-style currencies according to their market capitalizations [1], i.e., Monero, Bytecoin and DigitalNote. For all these three currencies, we export all related data directly from the corresponding blockchain database via modifying its source codes.

5.1   Analysis of Monero

As there are two pioneering works [5,8] considering cascade effect attacks on the untraceability of Monero transactions, we mainly concentrate on the analysis of the anonymity of those data after the known attacks.

Dataset Collection. We collect all blocks in the Monero blockchain from the first block (18th April 2014) up to block 1541236 (30th March 2018). Additionally, all related data is directly exported from the blockchain database via modifying the source code of Monero [2]. Our dataset in total contains 4153307 transactions. Among them, 2612070 are non-coinbase transactions, which are composed of 23164745 transaction inputs in total, and 25126033 distinct public-keys are involved. Notably, throughout this paper, we only consider those non-coinbase transactions unless otherwise stated.

Experiment Results. In Table 2, we give the result of the clustering algorithm on the aforementioned dataset. As it turns out, a total of 16334967 inputs become traceable. Specifically, 16329215 inputs are traceable due to the cascade effect attack, and the remaining inputs, i.e., 5752 in total, are traced by the finding of *closed set*. Total of 70.52% of Monero transaction inputs are traceable. While for the dataset after the cascade effect attack, only 0.084% inputs can be further traced.

Besides, a total of 6829778 transaction inputs are still untraceable. For all these remaining inputs, we give the frequency of number of mixins before and after the execution of clustering algorithm in Fig. 1.

The clustering algorithm also finds 3017 distinct *closed sets*, whose size vary from 2 to 55, and include a total of 7478 distinct public-keys. As we mentioned before, these 7478 public-keys must be the real-spend of a certain input contained

Table 2. The traceability of Monero.

No. of mixins	Total	Deducible	Cascade effect	Clustering algorithm	(%)
0	12209675	12209675	12209675	0	100
1	707786	625641	625264	377	88.39
2	4496490	1779134	1776192	2942	39.57
3	1486593	952855	951984	871	64.10
4	3242625	451959	451230	729	13.94
5	319352	74186	73980	206	23.23
6	432875	202360	202100	260	46.75
7	21528	4296	4282	14	19.96
8	30067	3506	3490	16	11.66
9	17724	2178	2162	16	12.29
$\geq$10	200030	29177	28856	321	14.59
Total	23164745	16334967	16329215	5752	70.52

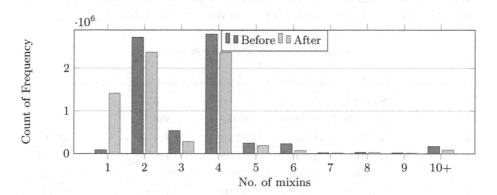

Fig. 1. Frequency of number of mixins of those anonymous inputs before and after the execution of clustering algorithm.

in these *closed set*. In other words, we can deduce that they are spent although we do not know which concrete transaction they are used. However, it is useless for the anonymity if any other new input picking public-keys from them.

One may wonder there is a discrepancy between probability of 2^{-19} for finding *closed set* and the existence of 3017 *closed sets* found during the experiment. This is due to the fact that our analysis assumes mixins are chosen uniformly and that each input has 3 mixins. However, in practice, sampling distributions and number of mixins of all inputs are not uniform. This will increase slightly the probability of finding *closed set*.

5.2 Analysis of Bytecoin

We provide analysis on the untraceability of Bytecoin via cascade effect attack and clustering attack.

Dataset Collection. We collect all blocks in the Bytecoin blockchain from block 1 (4 July 2012) to block 1586652 (3 August 2018). A total of 3782566 non-coin based transactions is contained in this dataset, and there are altogether 45663011 transaction inputs included. Additionally, a total of 48613764 distinct public-keys are involved.

Experiment Results. The experiment result on Bytecoin dataset is summarized in Table 3. More specifically, a total of 33902808 Bytecoin transaction inputs become traceable, counting for 74.25% of all inputs considered in our dataset. Among them, 28591486 inputs are zero-mixin inputs, and the cascade effect caused by them further makes 5231107 inputs become traceable, which covers 99.763% of the total traceable inputs. Besides, our clustering algorithm traces another 80215 transaction inputs from the remaining ones, which count to 0.68% of those untraceable inputs after the cascade effect attacks. There are a total of 5912 *closed sets* found, whose size vary from 2 to 55.

Table 3. The traceability of Bytecoin.

No. of mixins	Total	Deducible	Cascade effect	Clustering algorithm	(%)
0	28591486	28591486	28591486	0	100
1	5751268	3281500	3240142	41358	57.06
2	2840745	1133602	1112648	20954	39.91
3	1442133	261197	260298	899	18.11
4	2516851	276237	275172	1065	10.98
5	617041	59922	59493	429	9.71
6	3145092	270355	255156	15199	8.60
7	388759	26434	26160	274	6.80
8	81504	1231	1220	11	1.51
9	65379	397	389	8	0.61
≥10	222753	447	429	18	0.2
Total	45663011	33902808	33822593	80215	74.25

5.3 Analysis of DigitalNote

We also provide the first work on analyzing the untraceability of DigitalNote.

Dataset Collection. We collect all 633548 non-coin based transactions included in the block 1 (31 May 2014) up to block 699748 (13 August 2018) in the Digital-Note blockchain. A total of 8110602 inputs are included in the aforementioned transactions, and 8396472 distinct public-keys are involved.

Experiment Results. The experiment result of DigitalNote is given in Table 4. Specifically, 91.56% of all transaction inputs in our dataset is traceable, while 60.39% of them is without any mixin. Besides, the cascade attack further contributes 39.60% of those traceable inputs. Our clustering algorithm makes 49 additional inputs traceable, which covers 0.007% of the untraceable inputs after the cascade effect attacks, with the help of 38 *closed sets*.

Table 4. The traceability of DigitalNote.

No. of mixins	Total	Deducible	Cascade effect	Clustering algorithm	(%)
0	4484726	4484726	4484726	0	100
1	2087295	1847151	1847132	19	88.49
2	1194410	895480	895472	8	74.97
3	129700	101872	101872	0	78.54
4	6225	4362	4358	4	70.07
5	193669	85941	85939	2	44.38
6	3071	1840	1837	3	59.92
7	844	442	440	2	52.38
8	1686	856	853	3	50.77
9	1288	682	681	1	52.95
≥ 10	7688	2684	2677	7	34.91
Total	8110602	7426036	7425987	49	91.56

6   Observations and Recommendations

In this section, we give our observations and recommendations according to the experiment results.

- **Observation 1**: *The usage rate of outputs is an important factor for the anonymity of CryptoNote-style currencies.* The usage rate of outputs refers to the percentage of public-keys that have been spent, which can be easily calculated by using the total amount of inputs in the dataset over the total number of distinct outputs (i.e., public-keys), as each output can only be redeemed once. As mentioned in Sect. 3.3, those unspent public-keys play an important role in preventing the formation of a *closed set*. Hence, it is fair to say that, to some degree, decreasing the usage rate will improve anonymity.
- **Observation 2**: *Closed sets are closely related to the anonymity of inputs.* In this work, we have shown that finding *closed sets* could help identify real-spends or decrease the ring size (so the level of anonymity) of those inputs. Although the probability of the existence of a *closed set* is not high, but *closed sets* do exist and threaten the anonymity of inputs.

- **Recommendation 1:** *Decreasing the usage rate of outputs by generating more outputs.* Recall that a lower usage rate of outputs is beneficial to the anonymity of Monero inputs. Hence, to decrease the usage rate of outputs, we recommend users to additionally generate some outputs with 0 amount, which can make the unspent output set larger.
- **Recommendation 2:** *Do not pick the useless mixin.* Take the Monero as an example, our clustering algorithm has found 3017 distinct *closed sets*, which contain 7478 distinct public-keys. These 7478 public-keys must be the real-spend of a certain input contained in these *closed sets*. Hence, for any newly generated input, picking these keys as mixin will not improve anonymity. So, we recommend users not to pick these useless mixins. However, for an ordinary user, it is difficult to determine whether an output is contained in *closed sets* or not. Thus, we will release our code that implements the attack.

Acknowledgement. We appreciate the anonymous reviewers for their valuable suggestions. Part of this work was supported by the National Natural Science Foundation of China (Grant No. 61602396, U1636205, 61572294, 61632020), the MonashU-PolyU-Collinstar Capital Joint Lab on Blockchain and Cryptocurrency Technologies, from the Research Grants Council of Hong Kong (Grant No. 25206317), and the Fonds National de la Recherche Luxembourg (FNR) through PEARL grant FNR/P14/8149128.

A   Subset-Based Algorithm

Here we give a naive algorithm to search for all *closed sets* through finding all subsets of transaction inputs. Looking head, we use Cascade-Effect(inputs) to denote the function which implements the cascade effect attack. Assume Remove (*closed set CS*) $\rightarrow flag$ is a function will remove all public-keys contained *closed set CS* from other inputs outside CS, and outputs a variable $flag = true$ if any removing operation happens. The algorithm is given in Algorithm 3 below.

Algorithm 3. Subset-Searching Algorithm

1: Let DataSet be the set of all transaction inputs in the blockchain.
2: Let ℓ be the size of current subset, and $\ell \geq 2$.
3: Cascade-Effect(Dataset).
4: **while** $\ell \leq |DataSet|$ **do**
5:     Let $Set_\ell \subseteq DataSet$ be the set of all inputs, s.t., the size of each input is equal or smaller than ℓ.
6:     Let $\{Subset_{\ell,j}\}$ be all subsets of Set_ℓ with size ℓ, where $j \in \mathcal{C}^\ell_{|Set_\ell|}$, and each $Subset_{\ell,j} = \{R_1, R_2, \ldots, R_\ell|\ \forall i \in [\ell], R_i \in Set_\ell\}$
7:         **for** $j = 1$ to $\mathcal{C}^\ell_{|Set_\ell|}$ **do**
8:             **if** $Subset_{\ell,j}$ is a *closed set* **then**
9:                 Remove($Subset_{\ell,j}$) $\rightarrow flag$
10:                **if** flag $==$ true **then**
11:                    find traceable inputs
12:                    **goto while** with $\ell++$

References

1. Cryptocurrencies market capacity. https://coinmarketcap.com/all/views/all/. Accessed 16 Apr 2018
2. Monero source code. https://github.com/monero-project/monero. Accessed 30 Mar 2018
3. Sets of spent outputs. https://ww.getmonero.org/resources/research-lab/pubs/MRL-0007.pdf. Accessed 26 Nov 2018
4. Goemans, M.: Lecture notes in chernoff bounds, and some applications, February 2015. http://math.mit.edu/~goemans/18310S15/chernoff-notes.pdf
5. Kumar, A., Fischer, C., Töple, S., Saxena, P.: A traceability analysis of monero's blockchain. In: Foley, S.N., Gollmann, D., Snekkenes, E. (eds.) ESORICS 2017. LNCS, vol. 10493, pp. 153–173. Springer, Cham (2017). https://doi.org/10.1007/978-3-319-66399-9_9
6. Liu, J.K., Susilo, W., Wong, D.S.: Ring signature with designated linkability. In: Yoshiura, H., Sakurai, K., Rannenberg, K., Murayama, Y., Kawamura, S. (eds.) IWSEC 2006. LNCS, vol. 4266, pp. 104–119. Springer, Heidelberg (2006). https://doi.org/10.1007/11908739_8
7. Meiklejohn, S., et al.: A fistful of bitcoins: characterizing payments among men with no names. In: Proceedings of the 2013 Conference on Internet Measurement Conference, pp. 127–140. ACM (2013)
8. Miller, A., Möser, M., Lee, K., Narayanan, A.: An empirical analysis of linkability in the monero blockchain. arXiv preprint arXiv:1704.04299 (2017)
9. Möser, M., et al.: An empirical analysis of traceability in the monero blockchain. Proc. Priv. Enhancing Technol. 3, 143–163 (2018)
10. Nakamoto, S.: Bitcoin: A peer-to-peer electronic cash system (2008)
11. Reid, F., Harrigan, M.: An analysis of anonymity in the bitcoin system. In: 2011 IEEE Third International Conference on Privacy, Security, Risk and Trust (PASSAT) and 2011 IEEE Third International Conference on Social Computing (Social-Com), pp. 1318–1326. IEEE (2011)
12. Rivest, R.L., Shamir, A., Tauman, Y.: How to leak a secret. In: Boyd, C. (ed.) ASIACRYPT 2001. LNCS, vol. 2248, pp. 552–565. Springer, Heidelberg (2001). https://doi.org/10.1007/3-540-45682-1_32
13. Ron, D., Shamir, A.: Quantitative analysis of the full bitcoin transaction graph. In: Sadeghi, A.-R. (ed.) FC 2013. LNCS, vol. 7859, pp. 6–24. Springer, Heidelberg (2013). https://doi.org/10.1007/978-3-642-39884-1_2
14. Van Saberhagen, N.: Cryptonote v 2.0 (2013)
15. Yu, J., Au, M.H., Esteves-Verissimo, P.: Re-thinking untraceability in the cryptonote-style blockchain. In: IEEE Computer Security Foundations Symposium (CSF) (2019). The sun tzu survival problem

Short Paper: An Empirical Analysis of Monero Cross-chain Traceability

Abraham Hinteregger[1,2(✉)] and Bernhard Haslhofer[1]

[1] Austrian Institute of Technology, Seibersdorf, Austria
a.hinteregger@outlook.at
[2] Vienna University of Technology, Vienna, Austria

Abstract. Monero is a privacy-centric cryptocurrency that makes payments untraceable by adding decoys to every real input spent in a transaction. Two studies from 2017 found methods to distinguish decoys from real inputs, which enabled traceability for a majority of transactions. Since then, a number protocol changes have been introduced, but their effectiveness has not yet been reassessed. Furthermore, little is known about traceability of Monero transactions across hard fork chains. We formalize a new method for tracing Monero transactions, which is based on analyzing currency hard forks. We use that method to perform a (passive) traceability analysis on data from the Monero, MoneroV and Monero Original blockchains and find that only a small amount of inputs are traceable. We then use the results to estimate the effectiveness of known heuristics for recent transactions and find that they do not significantly outperform random guessing. Our findings suggest that Monero is currently mostly immune to known passive attack vectors and resistant to tracking and tracing methods applied to other cryptocurrencies.

1 Introduction

Monero is a privacy-enhancing cryptocurrency that exceeds others (Zcash, Dash) in terms of market capitalization and promises privacy and anonymity through *unlinkable* and *untraceable* transactions. It thereby addresses a central shortcoming of well-established currencies such as Bitcoin, which cannot offer a meaningful level of anonymity because transactions sent to addresses are linkable and payments among pseudonymous addresses are traceable. There are now a number of commercial (e.g., Chainalysis) and non-commercial tools [1,2] that implement well-known analytics techniques (c.f., [4]) and provide cryptocurrency analytics features, including tracking and tracing of payments made in cryptocurrencies.

Technically, Monero is based on the CryptoNote protocol and aims to address Bitcoin's privacy issues using three central methods: *Stealth addresses*, which are one-time keys that are generated from the recipient's address and a random value, should prevent the identification of transactions sent to a given address and provide *unlinkability*. The use of *Ring Signatures* in Monero transactions, which mixes an output that is spent (real input) with other decoy outputs

© International Financial Cryptography Association 2019
I. Goldberg and T. Moore (Eds.): FC 2019, LNCS 11598, pp. 150–157, 2019.
https://doi.org/10.1007/978-3-030-32101-7_10

(mixin input), obscures the path of a given coin and provide *untraceability* of payments. Finally, *Confidential Transactions* hide the value of non-mining transactions and should prevent tracing by value and guessing of change addresses, which are used to send excess input funds back to the issuer of the transaction, based on values.

Nevertheless, in 2017, two concurrent studies [3,5] have shown that *untraceability* can be compromised by applying heuristics that can identify mixins. They were able to trace the majority of transactions up to the introduction of RingCTs (confidential transactions) in Jan. 2017. In the following releases (Sep. 2017 and Mar. 2018), additional improvements such as a higher mandatory minimal ringsize and an improved sampling technique for decoys were rolled out. The 2017 studies already showed that the share of traceable transactions plummeted after the introduction of RingCTs, but a more up-to-date picture on the effectiveness of those improvements is still missing.

Furthermore, another traceability method that exploits information leaked by currency hard forks (a split of the currency with a shared history; unspent pre-fork TXOs can be spent on both post-fork branches) has been discussed in the community for some time. The general idea of the attack vector is to exploit differences between rings spending the same output on the two post-fork branches. However, we are not aware of a formal description, nor of an evaluation of its effectiveness.

The contributions of this work are twofold: first, in Sect. 3, we propose and formalize a new Monero cross-chain analysis method, which exploits information leaked by currency hard forks. Second, in Sect. 4, we empirically analyze Monero cross-chain traceability by combining known heuristics with our new method. Our analysis, which considers Monero blocks 0 to 1 651 346 (2018-08-31), also provides an up-to-date assessment on the effectiveness of the previously mentioned countermeasures by evaluating the accuracy of known heuristics on recent transactions.

Our findings suggest that Monero is currently mostly immune to known passive attack vectors and resistant to established tracking and tracing methods applied to other cryptocurrencies. They also confirm that the changes to the protocol, which were introduced as countermeasures to the heuristics proposed by Kumar et al. [3] and Möser et al. [5], were effective. Consequently, this implies that currently available cryptocurrency analytics tools that work for Bitcoin and its derivatives cannot be applied for tracking and tracing of Monero payments.

All the analysis done in this work can be reproduced by using the MONitERO toolchain, which can be found on GitHub[1].

2   Known Monero Traceability Methods

Currently we are not aware of any known method to compromise confidential transactions and stealth addresses. Untraceability has been successfully diminished by Kumar et al. and Möser et al. with the following approaches:

---

[1] https://github.com/oerpli/MONitERO

Zero Mixin Removal (ZMR) [3,5]. As each ring has exactly one real member, all rings with only one (non-mixin) member can be traced, just like in Bitcoin. As the referenced outputs can only be spent once, occurrences of these outputs in other rings can be marked as *mixins*. Repeated applications of this rule is called *Zero Mixin Removal (ZMR)*. If the average ringsize is small enough, repeated applications of this rule can result in a chain reaction. To prevent this, the mandatory minimum ringsize has been increased several times ($0 \rightarrow 3$ in 2016, $3 \rightarrow 5$ in 2017 and $5 \rightarrow 7$ in 2018). In October 2018 (after the cutoff of our dataset) the ringsize has been increased (from $7 \rightarrow 11$) and removed as parameter, i.e. all transactions issued since v0.13 have a fixed ringsize of 11. This removes a possible attack vector, based on the assumption that transaction with certain nonstandard ringsizes are issued by the same (set of) users. In our analysis we did not find a method to exploit this.

Intersection Removal (IR) [5]. This heuristic is a generalization of ZMR: If N rings contain the same N (non-mixin) members, it is (usually) impossible to determine, which output has been spent in which ring, but as all of them are spent in one of the rings, we mark them as *spent* and other references to these outputs as mixin. If $N = 1$, this method is identical to ZMR. This can be generalized even further: Instead of N identical rings with N members we look for sets S of rings (where each ring is a set of transaction outputs, abbreviated as TXOs) with the property: $|S| = |\bigcup_{r \in S} r|$ (if there are n sets in S, the union of those sets contain n elements). This maps to the matching problem for bipartite graphs $G = (V_1, V_2, E)$, where the property $|S| \leq |N(S)|$ (where $N(x)$ is the set of neighbors of x) holds $\forall S : S \subseteq V_1$ iff there is a perfect matching.

Guess Newest Heuristic [3,5]. While the outputs spent in a transaction are (mostly) fixed, the choice of decoys is somewhat arbitrary. Most Monero TXOs are spent a few days after they've been received (resulting in an age distribution of the real inputs that is heavily left-skewed). The mixins on the other hand were initially (until v0.9 in 2016) sampled uniformly from all eligible existing outputs. Starting from January 2016, a triangular distribution was used (according to Möser et al. [5], which still wasn't sufficiently left-skewed and did not match real spending behavior), from December 2016 on, $\approx 25\%$ of the inputs where sampled from the *recent zone* (outputs less than 5 days old). In September 2017, two changes have been made to the sampling from the recent zone. The recent zone has been reduced to outputs less than 1.8 days old and the number of decoys sampled from the recent zone has been increased to 50%[2]. The two publications from April 2017 (shortly after the introduction of the recent zone sampling), proposed a simple yet highly effective heuristic, which guessed that the real input is the most recent one.

Output Merging Heuristic [3]. If multiple inputs of a transaction reference distinct outputs from the same transaction, this heuristic assumes that these outputs are the real inputs. Before the introduction of confidential transactions this arose naturally, as outputs where split up into denominations (e.g. an output of 8XMR

---

[2]   https://github.com/monero-project/monero/pull/1996/files.

would have been split up into three outputs with denominations 1,2 and 5 XMR). If the recipient wants to spend his funds, he would have to merge these outputs. While this heuristic also works for confidential transactions, these TXs tend to have fewer outputs (mostly 2 outputs, one of which is the change output), which results in fewer "merging-transactions".

3   Hard Forks and Cross Chain Analysis

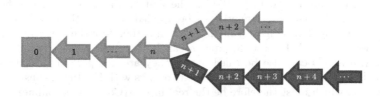

Fig. 1. Illustration of a currency hard fork. The blocks between the genesis block (0) and the fork height (n) are shared. Unspent outputs from pre-fork TXs can be spent on both branches.

Like software projects, cryptocurrencies and their blockchains can be forked, resulting in two currencies with a partly shared transaction history. There are different forking mechanisms, though for this work only hard forks (see Fig. 1) are relevant. The important aspect for our method is that unspent pre-fork TXOs can be spent on both branches. To prevent double spending, each (input) ring is published with a *key image*, which is uniquely determined by the spent output (the ring signature is used to verify that this is the case). If a coin is spent in multiple (one per branch) rings after a fork, the real input has to be in the intersection of the rings and the remaining members, i.e. the pairwise symmetric differences, can be marked as mixins, as illustrated in Fig. 2.

4   Results

We used the methods from Kumar et al. and Möser et al. that do not produce false positives (Zero Mixin Removal & Intersection Removal) as well as our new method (Cross Chain Analysis) to deduce mixins and real inputs for Monero transactions. We focus on *nontrivial rings*, i.e. rings that have at least one mixin (ringsize > 1). If some of the ring members are identified as mixin, we refer to the remaining number of possible real inputs as *effective ringsize*. A ring with an effective ringsize of 1 is *traced*. Statistics from our dataset can be found in Table 1.

Overall, were able to trace 4 212 422 nontrivial rings. As can be seen in Fig. 3, in the first years of Monero's existence most nontrivial rings where traceable (as most mixins were spent in trivial rings). To prevent this, mandatory minimum ringsizes have been introduced, though the sampling of older, provably spent

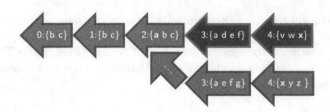

Fig. 2. An illustration of the Monero blockchain (XMR) and a fork of it (XMO), two blocks before and the first two blocks after a fork. Each block contains one ring (format: "$\langle$KeyImg (0–9)$\rangle${$\langle$ring members (a–z)$\rangle$}"). The first two rings (0, 1) have the same two members, i.e. intersection removal can be applied to mark these inputs (b, c) as mixin (black) in ring 2, leaving only input a, which is therefore the real (green) input. From the two rings with KeyImg 3, input a can be therefore removed as it is spent. Additionally, d and g can also be ruled out as they are not part of the intersection $\{a, d, e, f\} \cap \{a, e, f, g\}$. The intersection of the two rings with KeyImg 4 consists of only one element, x, which must therefore be the real input. (Color figure online)

outputs as mixins remained a problem. Starting from 2017, the introduction of RingCT mostly eliminates this threat, as RingCT transactions only sample outputs from other RingCT transactions, all of which were issued after the introduction of mandatory minimum ringsizes.

In the weeks following the MoneroV and Monero Original hard forks, the fraction of traceable rings increases. This is due to our newly proposed method, which allows us to identify the real spent output of 73 321 (improved from 25 256) out of 1 565 858 transaction inputs in the 685 608 (non-coinbase) transactions that have been issued between 2018-04-01 and 2018-08-31. The number of identified mixins in this time span has also more than doubled, from 203 251 to 544 131. Taken together, the status (real or mixin) of 617 452 out of 11 826 525 ring members in this time frame has been identified, which amounts to 5.22% (compared to 228 507 and 1.93% without cross-chain analysis). Results from our traceability analysis can be found in Table 2.

Using the results from our traceability analysis, we also investigated the accuracy of the guess newest heuristic (GNH) and the output merging heuristic (OMH) for recent transactions (see Table 3). We find that the performance of the GNH (see Fig. 4) is not better than random guessing for recent transactions. For the OMH (see Fig. 5) we used two different methods to aggregate the data by months, once considering the time where the outputs were created ("Out") and when they where spent ("In"). Overall, the number of true and false positives is identical, though the distributions over time differ somewhat. A problem of the OMH is the fact that RingCT transactions have fewer inputs and outputs, resulting in less transactions that merge outputs from previous transactions and thus less possible applications of the OMH.

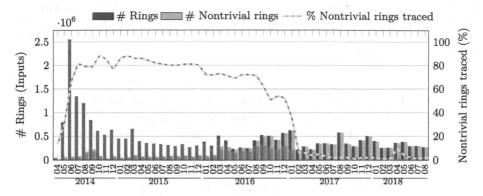

Fig. 3. Bar chart of monthly number of nontrivial rings (NTR, >1 member). Shaded bars represent traced rings. Traceability plummets after introduction of RingCT, small peak after hard forks in Spring 2018 due to cross-chain analysis.

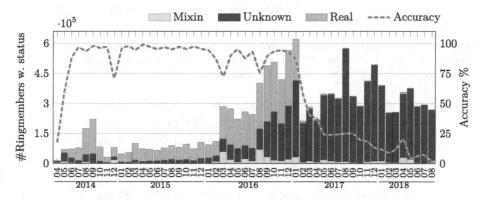

Fig. 4. Performance of GNH over time: After January 2017 the number of identified mixins and real inputs plummet and the accuracy is estimated based on a small sample. (Estimated) accuracy plummets for recent transactions.

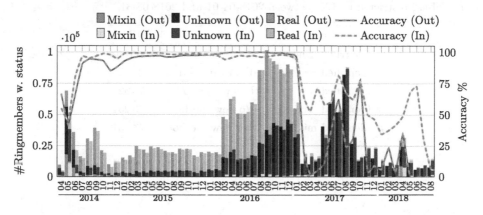

Fig. 5. Performance of OMH over time: Outputs are created at time *out* and spent at time *in*. Left bar for each month uses *out*-time for aggregation, right bar uses *in*.

Table 1. Dataset statistics: As the Monero (XMR), MoneroV (XMV) and Monero Original (XMO) blockchains share some parts, the values from the two forks (XMV & XMO) only refer to data unique to their blockchain. "Last block" refers to the last block used for the analysis in this work.

	XMR	XMO	XMV
First TX date	2014-04-18	2018-04-06	2018-05-03
Last TX date	2018-08-31	2018-08-31	2018-08-31
First block	1	1 546 600	1 564 966
Last block	1 651 346	1 651 728	1 647 778
# Transactions	4 955 908	146 475	146 215
# Coinbase TXs	1 651 347	105 729	82 814
# TX outputs	28 878 846	198 618	450 773
# Rings (TX inputs)	24 760 168	244 965	212 919
# Nontrivial rings	12 538 632	241 464	212 919
# Ring members	70 767 723	1 243 479	1 701 036

Table 2. Traceability results: Overall results for Monero and its two forks as well as results for recent Monero TXs. Ringmembers are *spent* if they have been found in an intersection set (i.e. spent but it is not known in which TX)

	XMR	XMO	XMV
# Nontrivial rings	12 538 632	241 464	212 919
# Ring members	70 767 723	1 243 479	1 701 036
# Traced nontrivial rings	4 212 422	50 861	7 671
# Identified mixin ringmembers	16 270 257	230 128	49 035
# Identified real ringmembers	16 433 958	54 362	7 671
# Identified spent ringmembers	13 240	0	0

Table 3. XMR Traceability results for recent TXs: Subset of the XMR dataset from Table 2 restricted to TXs between 2018-04-01 and 2018-08-31.

	XMR
# Nontrivial rings	1 565 858
# Identified real rm. w/o new method	25 256
# Identified real rm. with new method	73 321
# Identified mixin rm. w/o new method	203 251
# Identified mixin rm. with new method	544 131

5   Discussion

Before mandatory minimum ringsizes were introduced, most rings were traceable. With increasing mandatory minimum ringsizes (2016/09) the percentage of traceable NTR dropped and since the introduction of RingCT (2017) only a small fraction of all transactions can be traced with blockchain analysis techniques. While our newly proposed method enables the tracing of some additional transaction inputs, the overall impact from this attack vector seems to be small so far. This could change when a Monero fork with considerably higher traction is launched, which would presumably result in more redeemed outputs. Using the traced rings we looked at the accuracy of the GNH & OMH and found that their performance suffered from the recent changes to the transaction protocol. Though it may be the case that our analysis underestimates the accuracy of the GNH, as most of the traced rings in recent months were traced with our new method, which identifies the real spent pre-fork output in post-fork transactions. This skews the age of the spent outputs compared to regular usage. Overall, the fraction of traceable rings remains low and we believe that unless additional attack vectors emerge, Monero remains resistant to analysis methods which have been applied to other cryptocurrencies.

Acknowledgments. This work was partly funded by the European Commission through the project TITANIUM (Project ID: 740558) and by Austrian Research Promotion Agency (FFG) through the project VIRTCRIME (Project ID: 860672)

References

1. Haslhofer, B., Karl, R., Filtz, E.: O bitcoin where art thou? insight into large-scale transaction graphs. In: SEMANTiCS (Posters, Demos, SuCCESS) (2016)
2. Kalodner, H., Goldfeder, S., Chator, A., Möser, M., Narayanan, A.: BlockSci: design and applications of a blockchain analysis platform. arXiv:1709.02489 [cs], September 2017. arXiv: 1709.02489
3. Kumar, A., Fischer, C., Tople, S., Saxena, P.: A traceability analysis of monero's blockchain. In: Foley, S.N., Gollmann, D., Snekkenes, E. (eds.) ESORICS 2017. LNCS, vol. 10493, pp. 153–173. Springer, Cham (2017). https://doi.org/10.1007/978-3-319-66399-9_9
4. Meiklejohn, S., et al.: A fistful of bitcoins: characterizing payments among men with no names. In: Proceedings of the 2013 Conference on Internet Measurement Conference, pp. 127–140. ACM (2013)
5. Möser, M., et al.: An empirical analysis of traceability in the monero blockchain. Proc. Priv. Enhancing Technol. **2018**(3), 143–163 (2018)

PRCash: Fast, Private and Regulated Transactions for Digital Currencies

Karl Wüst[1]([✉]), Kari Kostiainen[1], Vedran Čapkun[2], and Srdjan Čapkun[1]

[1] Department of Computer Science, ETH Zurich, Zürich, Switzerland
{karl.wuest,kari.kostiainen,srdjan.capkun}@inf.ethz.ch
[2] HEC Paris, Jouy-en-Josas, France
capkun@hec.fr

Abstract. Fiat currency implemented as a blockchain can enable multiple benefits such as reduced cost compared to expensive handling of cash and better transparency for increased public trust. However, such deployments have conflicting requirements including fast payments, strong user privacy and regulatory oversight. None of the existing blockchain transaction techniques supports all of these three requirements. In this paper we design a new blockchain currency, called PRCash, that addresses the above challenge. The primary technical contribution of our work is a novel regulation mechanism for transactions that use cryptographic commitments. We enable regulation of spending limits using zero-knowledge proofs. PRCash is the first blockchain currency that provides fast payments, good level of user privacy and regulatory control at the same time.

1 Introduction

Over the last years, decentralized cryptocurrencies based on blockchains have gained significant attention. The primary technical primitives of blockchains are consensus and transactions. Currencies like Bitcoin [1] leverage permissionless consensus schemes and therefore operate without any trusted authority. The main drawback of permissionless consensus is low performance. Permissioned blockchains, e.g. based on Byzantine agreement, achieve better performance, but require pre-assigned validators. Regardless of the chosen consensus model, most blockchains use transactions that offer some level of anonymity. Additionally, blockchains provide transparency of money creation and transaction correctness.

While blockchains were originally envisioned to operate without any trusted parties, recently the idea of central banks issuing a fiat currency on a blockchain has gained popularity [2–9]. A fiat currency on a blockchain could provide multiple benefits to the society, including reduced cost compared to expensive handling of cash, improved privacy over current non-anonymous digital payments like credit card payments, and transparency for increased public trust.

Fiat currencies have critical requirements. The first is high performance, as the such systems must be able to handle high transactions loads fast (e.g., process

I. Goldberg and T. Moore (Eds.): FC 2019, LNCS 11598, pp. 158–178, 2019.
https://doi.org/10.1007/978-3-030-32101-7_11

thousands of payment transactions per second overall and confirm individual payments within seconds). The second requirement is user privacy. The third is regulation, as without any regulatory oversight, criminal activities such as money laundering are difficult to prevent. The lack of regulatory support is a major obstacle for the adoption of cryptocurrencies as fiat money.

High performance, strong anonymity and regulatory oversight are conflicting requirements and current blockchain transaction techniques provide only some of them. For example, transactions that use plaintext identities and amounts are fast to process and easy to regulate but provide no privacy. Usage of pseudonyms, similar to Bitcoin transactions, improves user privacy, but makes regulation ineffective. Novel transaction techniques like Confidential Transactions [10] and Mimblewimble [11] leverage cryptographic commitments for increased privacy protection. Such transaction enable hidden payment identities and values and easy transaction mixing but no regulation. More sophisticated cryptographic schemes like Zerocash [12] provide full transaction unlinkability which is often considered the strongest notion of privacy for blockchain currencies. Recent research has also shown how regulatory oversight can be added to such payments [13]. However, such techniques suffer from poor performance. For example, creation of Zerocash transactions takes up to minutes and requires downloading the entire ledger which may be infeasible on resource-constrained mobile devices. Therefore, such solutions cannot easily replace cash or card payments.

In this paper, we design a new blockchain currency, called PRCash, that addresses the above conflict between performance, privacy and regulation. The main use case for our solution is to enable deployment of fiat money on a blockchain by a trusted authority like a central bank. We focus on the permissioned blockchain model where transactions are confirmed by a set of appointed validators, because permissioned consensus provides significantly better performance. We assume that money is issued by a central authority. However, we emphasize that our solution is orthogonal to how consensus is achieved or how money is issued.

The primary technical contribution of our work is a novel regulation mechanism. We use commitment-based Mimblewimble transactions [11] as a starting point for our solution, because such transactions provide attractive hiding properties and sufficient performance. We add regulatory support to such transactions using a novel zero-knowledge proof construction and improve the privacy of Mimblewimble with small modifications to the transaction creation protocol.

In our regulation scheme, we limit the total amount of money that any user can receive anonymously within an epoch. Such limits are implemented using verifiable pseudorandom identifiers and range proofs. We choose to control receiving of money, to mimic existing laws in many countries (e.g., in the US, received cash transactions exceeding $10,000 must be reported to the IRS), but our solution can be easily modified to limit spending as well. The user can choose for each payment if it should be made anonymous as long as he stays within the allowed limit, chosen by a regulatory authority. Anonymous transactions preserve the privacy properties of Mimblewimble, i.e. they hide payer identity, recipient identity and the transaction value. While validators of the blockchain system have limited ability to link transactions with the same recipient issued within a short period of time, privacy towards third parties is even improved compared to Mimblewimble due to validators mixing transactions which removes the link between transaction inputs and outputs.

We implemented a prototype of PRCash and evaluated its performance. Transaction creation and verification is fast. For example, creation of a typical transaction and associated proofs takes less than 0.1 s and verification of 1000 transactions per second is possible with modest computing infrastructure (e.g., 4 validators with 25 quad-core servers each). When standard Byzantine agreement is used for consensus, transactions can also be confirmed quickly (e.g. within a second), which makes PRCash suitable for real-time payments.

Our regulation mechanism maintains the core privacy properties of Mimblewimble transactions, namely hidden sender and recipient identities and transaction amounts and easy mixing. Similar to Mimblewimble, our solution does provide full unlinkability of transactions. To the best of our knowledge, PRCash is the first blockchain currency that provides high performance, significantly improved privacy and regulation support at the same time.

Regulation based on zero-knowledge proofs has been previously proposed for coin-based currencies by Camenisch et al. [14]. In contrast to our solution, coin-based currencies used in [14] do not hide the recipient identity or provide transparency. Regulation extensions have also been designed for Zerocash [13]. While such schemes provide stronger anonymity guarantees and more expressive regulatory policies than our solution, their performance is significantly inferior which prevents usage in many practical scenarios. Finally, centrally-issued cryptocurrencies, like RSCoin [7], have been proposed prior to us. The main focus of such works is on consensus performance while our work focuses on transaction privacy and regulation.

To summarize, in this paper we make the following contributions:

- *Novel regulation mechanism.* We propose PRCash, a new blockchain currency. The primary technical contribution of this solution is a novel regulation mechanism that leverages zero-knowledge proofs for commitment-based transactions.
- *Implementation and evaluation.* We show that our transactions and regulation mechanism enable fast, fault-tolerant, large-scale deployments.

The rest of this paper is organized as follows. Section 2 gives an overview of our solution. Section 3 describes our currency in detail. We analyze the security in Sect. 4 and explain our implementation and evaluation in Sect. 5. Section 6 reviews related work and Sect. 7 concludes the paper.

2 PRCash Overview

Our goal in this paper is to design a new blockchain currency that enables fast payments at large scale, strong user privacy and regulatory support. The primary deployment model we consider is one where our solution is used by a central bank to implement fiat money on a blockchain. In this section we give an overview of our solution, PRCash.

2.1 System and Trust Model

Figure 1 shows our system model. We consider a standard permissioned blockchain model that is complemented with a regulatory authority and a central issuer of money. Here, we describe the involved entities:

Issuer. In our currency new money is created by a central entity called the *issuer*. For simplicity the primary model we consider in this paper is one where the issuer is a single entity like a central bank. In Appendix A.4 we explain how this role can be distributed if needed.

Users. Users in our system can act in two roles: as *payers* and as payment *recipients*. Users of the currency can be private individuals or organizations.

Validators. We assume a set of permissioned *validators* that maintain the ledger. The role of the validators could be taken, e.g., by commercial banks or other institutions appointed by the central bank.

Regulator. The flow of money is regulated by a central entity called the *regulator*. For simplicity, we assume that the role of the regulator is taken by a single entity, e.g., by a public authority like the IRS. In Appendix A.5 we explain how this role can be distributed among multiple parties.

If PRCash is used for a privately-issued currency, these roles can be assigned differently.

We consider an adversary that controls all networking between the users and from users to validators. The validators and the regulator are connected with secure links. Users are in possession of the public keys of the validators and the regulator and can establish secure connections to them. We otherwise rely on the standard assumptions of permissioned consensus (i.e., honest two-thirds majority of validators).

2.2 High-Level Operation and Regulation Main Idea

In many countries, the law requires reporting of large financial transactions. For example, in the US companies and individuals are mandated to report any received cash transaction that exceeds $10,000 [15]. To enable enforcement of such laws, we design a regulation mechanism that limits the *total amount* of anonymous payments any user can *receive* within a time period (epoch). By adjusting the amount and the period, authorities can control the flow of anonymous money, e.g., reception of anonymous payments up to $10,000 could be allowed within a month. With small changes, limits can also be put on spending instead of receiving.

Figure 1 illustrates the high-level operation of PRCash. To supply new money, the issuer creates signed issuance transactions that it sends to the validators, who

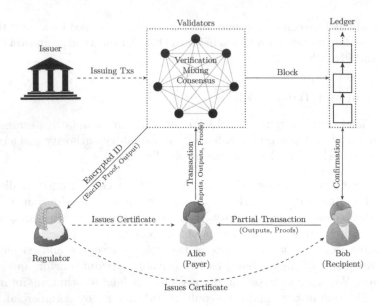

Fig. 1. System model and operation. In PRCash, new money is created centrally by the issuer. Users enroll in the system by obtaining certificates from the regulator. In each payment, the payer (Alice) and the recipient (Bob) prepare a transaction that is sent to permissioned validators who verify its correctness and add it to the next block in the public ledger. If the transaction exceeds the allowed amount of anonymous payments for Bob, he has to reveal his identity to the regulator by encrypting it with the regulator's public key.

verify them and publish them to the ledger. Each user enrolls in the system by obtaining a payment credential (certificate) from the regulator. As the user may lose his certificate, or the corresponding private key, we limit their validity to I_Δ epochs.

Payments involve two parties: the payer (Alice) and the recipient (Bob). To initiate a payment, Alice and Bob first agree on the transaction value. Each payment transaction consists of inputs and outputs (where the inputs are outputs from previous transactions) that are cryptographic commitments that hide payer and recipient identities and transferred amounts, similar to Mimblewimble [11]. The blinding factors for the output commitments are chosen such that the sum of the input commitments is equal to the sum of the output commitments, if the sum of the input values is equal to the sum of the output values. This allows verifying the correctness of a transaction without knowledge of the transferred values. One of the outputs is a special non-spendable output to which no value is attached. This allows the recipient of a transaction to create output commitments without the payer knowing the blinding factor, i.e., the blinding factor of the commitment is only known to the recipient of a payment, and can thus be used to authenticate a following payment.

To realize regulation for such transactions, for each payment the user has two choices. First, if the user wants that the transaction remains anonymous, he must prove without disclosing his identity that he does not exceed the limit v_a in the current epoch e. Second, if the user wants to exceed his anonymous receiving limit, he must connect his identity encrypted with the regulator's public key to the transaction.

For anonymous transactions within the limit, each user computes a pseudo-random ID per epoch (PID_e) that he attaches to his transaction outputs. He additionally attaches a zero-knowledge proof that the ID was computed correctly and a range proof over the sum of all transaction outputs from this PID. These values are sent together with the transaction outputs to the validators. The proofs are checked by the validators and after verifying their correctness, the PIDs and the corresponding proofs are not published with the transactions for efficiency and to preserve unlinkability towards third parties.

Note that, if they choose to use non-anonymous outputs, the attached proof contains their identity encrypted with the regulator's public key, i.e. towards any other entity, they remain anonymous. Bob prepares his part of the transaction (that includes value outputs and proofs) and sends it to Alice, who completes the transaction (by adding inputs, change outputs, proofs, and an encrypted identifier in case of a non-anonymous transaction). Alice sends the complete transaction to the validators.

The validators work in rounds. In each round, the validators collect incoming transactions, verify their correctness, mix the order of transaction inputs and outputs for increased privacy, and agree on the set of transaction that should be published. Consensus among validators is achieved through standard (Byzantine fault tolerant) protocols. At the end of the round, the validators publish a set of verified transactions as a new block on the ledger. Once the recipient (Bob) verifies the presence of the transaction in the ledger, he considers the payment confirmed. Bob can then use the value outputs from this transaction as inputs in the next payment.

If a transaction does not pass the verification (e.g., Alice or Bob attempts to create a transaction that exceeds the allowed anonymity limit, transaction inputs and outputs do not match, or one of the attached proofs is invalid), the transaction is rejected by the validators and not included in the next block. If the transaction contains any non-anonymous outputs, the validators first verify its correctness, and then forward the encrypted identifier to the regulator, who can recover the identity of Alice or Bob, depending on which transaction output was made non-anonymous.

Since anonymous change outputs are indistinguishable from anonymous value transferring outputs, they count towards the receiving limit. However, as users are in control of the size of the outputs they receive, they can mitigate this issue by using smaller received outputs, by splitting larger outputs in non-anonymous transactions, or by creating large change outputs non-anonymously.

3 PRCash Details

In this section, we describe PRCash in further detail. Our solution uses a number of cryptographic techniques as building blocks. We provide background on them in the Appendix in the full online version of the paper.

3.1 System Initialization

Our system uses two groups $G = \langle g \rangle$ and $\mathbf{G} = \langle \mathbf{g_1} \rangle = \langle \mathbf{g_2} \rangle = \langle \mathbf{h} \rangle$ of the same order, where the discrete logarithms of $\mathbf{g_1}$, $\mathbf{g_2}$, and $\mathbf{h}$ with respect to each other are unknown. The involved entities perform the following initialization steps:

Regulator. The regulator generates a keypair $(pk_{R,S}, sk_{R,S})$ for randomizable signatures (cf. full online version of the paper), an encryption keypair $(pk_{R,E}, sk_{R,E})$ for Elgamal encryption, and publishes the public keys as part of the setup.

Validators. Each validator creates a keypair and publishes the public key as part of the system setup. Validators can use the private keys for signing new blocks. Users use the validator public keys to send transactions securely to the validators. We assume the typical permissioned blockchain model where a trusted authority dynamically assigns a set of validators, i.e. the set of validators can be updated.

Issuer. The issuer also creates a keypair that he uses for transactions that create and delete money. The issuer publishes his public key as part of the system setup.

3.2 User Enrollment

Every new user obtains the system setup that includes the public keys of the regulator, issuer, and validators. To enroll in the system, the user generates a keypair $(pk_U, sk_U) = (\mathbf{g_1}^{sk_U}, sk_U)$ for regulation proofs and sends the public key to the regulator while proving knowledge of the secret key. To ensure that a user cannot enroll multiple identities, and thus circumvent the regulation, the regulator has to verify the identity of the user. If a PKI is already in place, this can be used for identification, otherwise users could, e.g., be required to visit a registration office in person.

The regulator then creates a certificate consisting of a randomizable signature σ on (sk_U, I_V) based on the user's public key pk_U and I_V, the index of the first epoch in which the certificate is valid, and sends the signature σ to the user. Recall that a randomizable signature is a signature on a list of committed values. Using values pk_U and I_V, the regulator creates and signs the commitment $pk_U \cdot \mathbf{g_2}^{I_V} \mathbf{h}^r = \mathbf{g_1}^{sk_U} \mathbf{g_2}^{I_V} \mathbf{h}^r$ where r is chosen at random.

3.3 Transaction Creation

Blockchain transactions based on cryptographic commitments, such as Confidential Transactions [10] and MimbleWimble [11], have attractive features. They hide payer and recipient identities and transaction amounts, provide public verifiability and easy mixing. However, such transaction have also the undesirable property that the payment recipient necessarily sees the change outputs created by the payer. This means that, e.g., a merchant can link two independent sales if a client uses a change output from a previous transaction with the same merchant. For these reasons, we use MimbleWimble as our starting point, but modify transaction creation slightly for improved privacy.

Similar to [10,11], our transactions are based on a group G in which the discrete logarithm problem is hard, with generators g and h for which the discrete logarithm to each others base is unknown. These generators are used to represent transaction inputs and outputs as homomorphic commitments to the associated value (we use Pedersen commitments [16]), thereby hiding their values from other parties. The homomorphic commitments have the property that one can easily add and subtract committed values without opening the commitments, e.g. for two output commitments $\mathsf{Out}_1 = g^{r_1} h^{v_1}$ and $\mathsf{Out}_2 = g^{r_2} h^{v_2}$ to the values v_1 and v_2, one can easily compute a commitment to their sum $v_1 + v_2$ by multiplying the commitments: $g^{r_1} h^{v_1} \cdot g^{r_2} h^{v_2} = g^{r_1+r_2} h^{v_1+v_2}$. If the blinding factors are chosen such that the sum of the blinding factors of the inputs is equal to the sum of the blinding factors of the outputs, this property can be used to check that the sum of the input values of a transaction is equal to the sum of the output values, and the knowledge of the blinding factors can be used to authenticate and authorize payments [11] by creating an additional *excess output* $\mathsf{Ex}_0 = g^{r_0}$ such that the product of the output commitments (including Ex_0) is equal to the product of all input commitments.

In our modified version, the exponent in Ex_0 is simply another random value, but we add an additional output value r_Δ which facilitates mixing transactions and which has to be chosen such that the product of all output commitments and g^{r_Δ} is equal to the product of the inputs. We provide the details of our modified Mimblewimble construction in Appendix A and show in the Appendix in the full online version of the paper that the knowledge of the blinding factor of an output is a secure method for payment authorization.

3.4 Regulation Proof Creation

In each epoch e, the user computes a pseudorandom ID as $\mathsf{PID}_e = f_{sk_U}(e)$ (cf. Appendix in the full online version of the paper) and initializes the value of anonymously spent transaction outputs to $v_e = 0$. Regulation proofs are created either when Bob creates value outputs during transaction preparation or when Alice creates change outputs during transaction completion. For each output, the user can choose if it should be made anonymous or non-anonymous. For each new output, the user creates a *regulation proof*. Depending on whether the output should be anonymous or not, he does one of the following to construct the proof:

Anonymous Output. If the user wants to create an output anonymously and the value v_o of the transaction output plus the previously (in epoch e) received amount v_e is below the limit v_a, the user adds PID_e and a zero-knowledge proof of knowledge of (sk_U, I_V, σ) to the transaction such that:

(i) The certificate is valid in the current epoch, i.e., a range proof that $I_{current} - I_\Delta < I_V \leq I_{current}$.
(ii) The value PID_e is equal to the output of the pseudorandom function based on the secret key sk_U on input e, i.e., $\mathsf{PID}_e = f_{sk_U}(e)$.
(iii) The certificate is valid, i.e. $\mathsf{verify}(pk_{R,S}, (sk_U, I_V), \sigma) = \mathsf{true}$

In detail, the regulation proof consists of the following steps:

(i) The user creates two commitments $\mathbf{A} = \mathbf{g_1}^{sk_u} \mathbf{h}^{r_1}$ and $\mathbf{B} = \mathbf{g_2}^{I_V} \mathbf{h}^{r_2}$ with two fresh random values r_1 and r_2 and proves knowledge of a signature on the openings of these commitments.
(ii) Prove that $\mathbf{B}$ is a commitment to an integer in the range $[I_{current} - I_\Delta + 1, I_{current}]$.
(iii) Given the commitment $\mathbf{A}$ to the value sk_U, prove that

$$\mathsf{PID}_e = f_{sk_U}(e) = g^{1/(e+sk_U)}$$

i.e., this is the following proof of knowledge:

$$PK\{(\alpha, \gamma) : \mathbf{A} = \mathbf{g_1}^\alpha \mathbf{h}^\gamma \wedge g \cdot \mathsf{PID}_e^{-e} = \mathsf{PID}_e^\alpha\}$$

We use the common notation where greek letters correspond to values of which knowledge is being proven. In the proof above, α corresponds to sk_U and γ corresponds to the blinding value of the commitment. The second term proves that the ID was computed correctly since

$$g \cdot \mathsf{PID}_e^{-e} = \mathsf{PID}_e^\alpha$$
$$\Rightarrow \quad g = \mathsf{PID}_e^{e+\alpha}$$
$$\Rightarrow \quad g^{\frac{1}{e+sk_U}} = \left(\mathsf{PID}_e^{e+\alpha}\right)^{\frac{1}{e+\alpha}} = \mathsf{PID}_e$$

The interactive protocol can be easily converted to a non-interactive signature on the message $M = H(o)$ using the Fiat-Shamir heuristic [17], where o is the transaction output. Including this message in the zero-knowledge proof binds the proof to the transaction output.

(iv) The user additionally creates a range proof over the product of all anonymous outputs that share the same identifier PID_e, proving that their combined value $v_e + v_0$ is below the allowed limit v_a.

The user then updates $v_e := v_e + v_o$ after completing the transaction.

Non-anonymous Output. If the user does not want to create the output anonymously or the value v_o of the output plus v_e is above the transaction amount limit v_a, the user adds his public key encrypted with the public key of the regulator to the transaction, together with a proof that the encryption was created correctly. The user completes the following steps to create the regulation proof:

(i) The user creates two commitments $\mathbf{A} = \mathbf{g_1}^{sk_u}\mathbf{h}^{r_1}$ and $\mathbf{B} = \mathbf{g_2}^{I_V}\mathbf{h}^{r_2}$ with two fresh random values r_1 and r_2 and proves knowledge of a signature on the openings of these commitments.

(ii) Prove that $\mathbf{B}$ is a commitment to an integer in the range $[I_{current} - I_\Delta + 1, I_{current}]$.

(iii) Compute $C = \mathsf{ENC}(pk_U, pk_{R,E}) = \left(g^{y_1}, pk_{R,E}^{y_1} \cdot pk_U\right)$

(iv) Given the commitment $\mathbf{A}$ to the value sk_U, prove that

$$C = \mathsf{ENC}(pk_U, pk_{R,E}) = \left(g^{y_1}, pk_{R,E}^{y_1} \cdot pk_U\right)$$

i.e., this is the following proof of knowledge:

$$PK\{(\alpha, \gamma_1, \gamma_2) : \mathbf{A} = \mathbf{g_1}^\alpha\mathbf{h}^{\gamma_1} \wedge C[0] = g^{\gamma_2} \wedge C[1] = pk_{R,E}^{\gamma_2}g^\alpha\}$$

Here, α again corresponds to sk_U and γ_1 corresponds to the blinding value of the commitment, while γ_2 corresponds to the random value used for the Elgamal encryption of the users public key. The interactive protocol can again be converted to a non-interactive signature on the message $M = H(o)$ using the Fiat-Shamir heuristic [17], where o is the transaction output, to bind the proof to the transaction output.

3.5 Transaction Verification

The validators work in rounds and verify every received transaction. A transaction is correct, if

(i) all inputs are unspent outputs of previous transactions,
(ii) the range proofs for all outputs are correct,
(iii) the zero-knowledge proof for excess outputs is correct, and
(iv) the total amount of transaction inputs matches the outputs: $\Pi_{i=1}^n \mathsf{In}_i = g^{r_\Delta} \cdot \mathsf{Ex}_0 \cdot \Pi_{i=1}^{k+m}\mathsf{Out}_i$

In addition to verifying the correctness of the transaction itself, the validators verify the regulation proofs. First, the validators verify the randomized certificate, i.e., they verify the signature on the provided commitments and check if the range proof for I_V is correct. If the verification fails, the transaction is discarded.

Otherwise, for anonymous transaction outputs, the validators verify that PID_e has been computed correctly and that the proof is bound to the associated output. If this check succeeds, they compute the product of all outputs from epoch e that share the pseudorandom identifier PID_e and check if the provided range proof holds for this product. If this is the case, the total associated value is below the allowed limit and the transaction can be included in the next block. Otherwise, the transaction is discarded.

For non-anonymous transaction outputs, the validators verify the corresponding regulation proof, i.e., that the public key of the user has been encrypted correctly with the public encryption key of the regulator and that this proof is bound to the associated transaction output. If these verifications are successful, the validators include the transaction in the next block and forward the output and the proof to the regulator, otherwise the transaction is discarded.

When the regulator receives transaction outputs with their corresponding proofs, he can decrypt the encrypted public key which serves as identifier for the user. The regulator also checks the proofs to ensure that the output was indeed created by the owner of the corresponding public key. Since the regulator knows the real-world identities associated with each public key, he can then take action as required.

In Appendix A, we provide details on how transactions in a block can be mixed by the validators, how blocks can be structured and on how the issuer can create and destroy currency.

4   Security Analysis

In this section, we provide an informal security analysis of PRCash. We first discuss the integrity guarantees of the system. Then we discuss the provided privacy properties, in particular, how our modifications of Mimblewimble [11] (which provides value and identity hiding, but not full unlinkability) and the added regulation impact privacy.

Payment Authorization. We first consider an attacker that tries to spend an output belonging to another user without the knowledge of the corresponding blinding factor. If an adversary capable of such an attack exists, our assumptions are violated, namely either the discrete logarithm problem can be solved efficiently in the used group or the adversary knows the discrete logarithm of h to base g, where g and h are the generators used for the commitments (see full online version of the paper). The intuition behind this is that, to create a valid transaction, the outputs require range proofs for which knowledge of the blinding factor is needed and the outputs have to be chosen such that their product is equal to that of the inputs.

Double-Spending Protection. During each round, each non-compromised validator discards transactions with previously used or otherwise invalid inputs (cf. Sect. 3.5), and then all validators run a Byzantine fault tolerant consensus protocol. Thus, compromised validators cannot produce a block that would contain conflicting transactions and will be accepted by the network.

Creation of Money. Only the issuer can create new money. Creation of money using normal transactions is prevented as the validators verify (i) the range proofs of all outputs for overflow and (ii) that the sum of inputs values matches the sum of output values, and only include compliant transactions in the next block. The underlying consensus protocol guarantees that each block contains only compliant transactions.

Regulation Enforcement. The security of our regulation system relies on the security of the underlying zero-knowledge proofs and the pseudorandom function. The pseudorandom function is secure under the decisional Diffie-Hellman inversion assumption (DDHI). The zero-knowledge proofs rely on the hardness of the discrete logarithm problem (which is implied by DDHI) and they are secure as non-interactive proofs in the random oracle model using the Fiat-Shamir heuristic [17, 18].

Privacy Towards Third Parties. Transaction values are completely hidden and can therefore not leak any information about a transaction. Additionally, all transactions are mixed by the validators, and since the delta outputs of all transactions are summed up (cf. Sect. 3.3) and not published individually, it becomes impossible for third parties examining the ledger to determine which outputs belong to which inputs, even for a merchant receiving a transaction. PRCash therefore provides k-anonymity [19] against third parties, where k is the number of transactions in a block. For example, even if an adversary knows that Alice payed Bob in a transaction with output Out_1 contained in a block with 500 transaction inputs, he can only guess Alice' input with probability of at most $\frac{1}{500}$. If more privacy is desired, blocks can be made larger and validators could even add dummy transactions (with a tradeoff in efficiency).

Privacy Between Users. As the payer finalizes the transaction, the recipient only sees his own outputs, i.e. he is in the same position as the third party entity with partial information as described above. The payer additionally sees output commitments from the recipient which allows him to see when the output is spent. However, once the output has been used, no more information is leaked to the user.

Privacy Towards Validators. Recall that we assume the standard trust model for permissioned consensus where up to one third of the validators may be malicious or get compromised by the adversary. Malicious validators do not learn transaction amounts or user identities, as our transactions are based on cryptographic commitments. Malicious validators can link transaction inputs to the corresponding outputs for all the transactions that they receive, but they cannot link inputs to their outputs for transactions that are mixed by other validators. Additionally, malicious validators are able to link multiple outputs from the same epoch that share the same pseudorandom ID. Therefore our solution does not provide full unlinkability towards validators. If combined with additional out-of-band information, this could potentially lead to some loss of privacy towards validators. The expected number of outputs sharing the same PID can be controlled by adjusting the length of the epoch (shorter epochs means fewer transactions with the same PID). Transaction linking can be addressed by using third party mixing services.

5   Evaluation

We implemented a prototype of PRCash to evaluate its performance. In this section, we describe our implementation, transaction verification models, verification overhead, and overall performance in terms of throughput and latency. We concentrate on performance in terms of verification time as opposed to proof generation time here, since verification is the limiting factor in our system. Note, however, that proof generations times are similar to verification times for all proofs, i.e. transactions can be created efficiently, even on devices with restricted performance such as mobile phones. On a standard PC, creation of a typical transaction takes less than 0.1 s.

5.1   Implementation

We implemented a prototype that covers the generation and verification of transactions, including regulation proofs. Our implementation uses the randomizable signature from Pointcheval and Sanders [20] for the generation of certificates. Other signatures with efficient protocols, such as CL-Signatures [21,22], could be used as well. We use the RELIC toolkit [23] for the elliptic curve and bilinear map operations. Our implementation makes use of the 256-bit elliptic curve BN-P256 as the base curve of a type-3 pairing that we use for the randomizable signatures. Our range proofs use commitments to digits in base 4 as this is in practice the most efficient base for the size and computation of bit-commitment based proofs. Size and computation required for the proofs could be optimized using bulletproofs from Bünz et al. [24].

5.2   Verification Models

The throughput and latency of PRCash depends on the used transaction verification model. For our evaluation, we consider the following two verification models, to give examples of performance under different assumptions and requirements.

VM1: Full replication. In this model, all validators verify all transactions, including the regulation proofs, and consensus is needed on the validity of all transactions and proofs. This model guarantees transaction correctness, double-spending protection, and enforcement regulation at all times, assuming our standard permissioned consensus trust model (at most one third malicious or compromised validators).

VM2: Partitioned regulation, replicated verification. In this model, all validators verify correctness of all transactions including their range proofs, but excluding the regulation proofs. Verification of regulation proofs is instead partitioned evenly among the validators. If one validator attests to the validity of a regulation proof, it is accepted by the other validators. If a validator gets compromised, users can transact anonymously above the regulatory limit. This model may be used, if it is acceptable to lose the ability to enforce regulation momentarily. Transaction correctness (i.e., no new money is created and no double-spending occurs) is guaranteed regardless of the compromise. This model may be suitable, if e.g. regulation is delegated to commercial banks that act as validators and check the regulation proofs for their customers.

5.3   Transaction Verification Overhead

We measured the verification overhead (shown in Table 1), averaged over 1000 runs on a single core of an Intel Core i7-4770 CPU, for the following proof types:

ZKPoK of discrete log. This is a zero-knowledge proof of knowledge (ZKPoK) of the discrete logarithm and is required to verify that an excess output has no value attached.

PIDProof. This is the proof that the pseudo-random ID was constructed correctly, i.e., the user who created the proof is in possession of a valid certificate on his key and that the PID was derived correctly from this key. Depending on the number of epochs for which the signature is valid, the computation time differs, due to the included range proof. In Table 1, the measurements for epoch ranges between 2^6 and 2^{10} are shown.

EncIDProof. This is the proof that the user who created the proof is in possession of a valid certificate on his key and that his corresponding public key was correctly encrypted with the public key of the regulator. Again, the verification time differs depending on the number of epochs for which the certificate is valid.

RangeProof. The range proof by itself is used to show that an output is in the correct range, which is necessary to show that no overflow occurs, and to prove that the sum of anonymous outputs with the same PID are below the allowed threshold. The size and verification time of the range proof depend on the size of the range. For example, with a granularity of cents, a range of 2^{32} would allow transaction outputs of up to 43 million dollars.

Most commonly, transactions will have one value-transferring output, one change output, one or more inputs, plus an excess and a delta output. Since inputs do not require range proofs, and the time required to compute the commitment to the sum of their values is negligible compared to the proof verification time, we can estimate the time required to validate a standard transaction independently of the number of inputs. In the case of a transaction with two anonymous outputs (different PIDs each), a full verification of the transaction requires verifying one ZKPoK of a discrete logarithm, two PID proofs, and four range proofs (one for each individual output and one per PID).

Since the maximum amount for anonymous transactions is limited, one can use a smaller range proof than for non-anonymous transactions. For example, the US requires reporting for transactions above \$10,000 [15]. An equivalent regulatory rule with a granularity of cents would approximately correspond to a

Table 1. The average time for proof verification for different proof types and their sizes.

Proof type	Time [s]	Size [bytes]
ZKPoK of discrete log (DLProof)	0.00038	64
PIDProof (epoch range = 2^6)	0.01067	1033
PIDProof (epoch range = 2^8)	0.01235	1226
PIDProof (epoch range = 2^{10})	0.01404	1419
EncIDProof (epoch range = 2^6)	0.01115	968
EncIDProof (epoch range = 2^8)	0.01284	1161
EncIDProof (epoch range = 2^{10})	0.01452	1354
RangeProof (range = 2^8)	0.00665	722
RangeProof (range = 2^{16})	0.01345	1544
RangeProof (range = 2^{20})	0.01678	1930
RangeProof (range = 2^{32})	0.02722	3088

range of 2^{20}. Assuming a certificate validity of 2^{10} epochs, this leads to a total verification time of 0.096 s.

For transactions with non-anonymous outputs, we can allow a much larger range (e.g., 2^{32}), since in this case the goal is not to limit transaction size but to prevent overflows. Such a transaction requires two range proofs, giving, in the same setting as before, a verification time of 0.084 s. Combinations, where one output is anonymous and one is not, are, of course, also possible. Given this transaction verification overhead, within one second, roughly ten transactions can be fully verified on a single core. From this value we can in turn estimate the required computing resources to handle the expected transaction load.

In verification model **VM1**, each validator checks all transactions and proofs. To verify 1000 tps, each validator would require approximately 25 quad-core servers. In **VM2**, transactions and range proofs are verified by all validators to protect against overflows in outputs, but verification of regulation proofs can be partitioned across the validators. Assuming 16 validators, each of them would require 15 quad-core servers to process 1000 tps.

Based on measurements from Croman et al. [26], we can estimate figures for latency and throughput (see full online version of the paper) given a standard consensus protocol (PBFT [25]) showing that using 16 validators, a throughput of 480 transactions per second can be achieved. Since the nodes in the experiment by Croman et al. were globally distributed and only had limited bandwidth, it is reasonable to assume that higher throughputs can be achieved in the setting we consider, if validators are geographically close and may even be connected through dedicated lines.

6   Related Work

Regulation in Coin-Based Currencies. Camenisch et al. introduced an e-cash system where a trusted authority can control the total amount of anonymously spent money [14]. We use similar zero-knowledge proof techniques for PRCash. However, these two solutions have noteworthy differences. In their scheme, it suffices to limit the number of transactions, since the system is coin-based, i.e., the number of spent coins is equal to the amount. In our solution, we also need to take into account the values of the transactions, while keeping them secret. In a coin-based scheme, the size of the transaction and the computation required to verify the proofs grows with the transaction value. Additionally, such a system is not transferable and thus leaks the total amount received by the merchant to the bank once it is deposited. Partial value secrecy is possible when offline payments are allowed, but this option ensures only double-spending detection (no prevention). In comparison, PRCash provides better privacy, constant payment overhead, and more transparency.

Regulation in Blockchain Currencies. Zerocash [12] is a sophisticated decentralized anonymous payment scheme that leverages a blockchain. Zerocash provides what is commonly considered the strongest level of anonymity, i.e., it hides transaction identities and values and makes transactions unlinkable. Garman et al. [13] have proposed a solution for regulation for Zerocash payments. However, as with regular Zerocash transactions, while verification is efficient, transaction creation is prohibitively expensive in terms of computation, which makes it unusable for replacement of cash or card payments, where transaction should be finalized within seconds. Additionally, Zerocash-style transactions requires full nodes, as a client has to download the entire ledger and decrypt every transaction to determine whether it is the recipient of the transaction. These requirements make anonymous transactions unpractical for resource constrained devices and causes most participants to use unshielded transactions in practice (i.e. in Zcash [27]), which decreases anonymity overall [28].

Centrally-Issued Currencies. RSCoin [7] is a centrally-issued cryptocurrency solution. The main technical contribution of their work is scalability of consensus, while the primary contribution of our work is a novel regulation mechanism that address the conflict between performance, privacy and regulation.

7   Conclusion

Despite more than three decades of research on digital currencies, their adoption as fiat money issued by a central bank has not become a reality. While the reasons for this may be numerous, and not always purely technical, a major obstacle for their adoption is the fact that such deployments have conflicting technical requirements. In this paper, we have presented PRCash that is the first blockchain currency with transactions that are fast, private and regulated at the same time.

A   Transaction Details and Block Creation

In this Appendix, we provide the details of the modifications made to Mimblewimble [11] transactions, prove that knowledge of the blinding factors can be used for payment authorization, and we give an overview of how transactions can be mixed and blocks can be created.

A.1   Transaction Creation

To prevent the transaction tracking of Mimblewimble [11] transactions, mentioned in Sect. 3, we modify the transaction creation such that the payer finalizes the transaction. To increase payment anonymity further, we also include another output (r_Δ) that does not have a value attached. This additional output is submitted to the validators as a scalar such that multiple transactions can be merged. Inclusion of such additional output makes it impossible to later match transaction inputs to corresponding outputs.[1]

Our transaction creation protocol, that includes the regulation proofs explained above, works as follows:

(i) The recipient, Bob, creates k *value outputs* $\mathsf{Out}_i = g^{r'_i} h^{v'_i}$ $(1 \leq i \leq k)$, for the payment value $v_T = \sum_{i=1}^{k} v'_i$. For each of the value outputs, he also creates a range proof to prove that the value is in a valid range (i.e., that no overflow occurs where money is created out of nothing). He additionally attaches a regulation proof to each output as described above in Sect. 3.4. He then creates an *excess output* $\mathsf{Ex}_0 = g^{r'_0}$ that has no value attached, proves knowledge of r'_0 by proving knowledge of the discrete log of Ex_0 to base g (DLProof(Ex_0)) and sends his outputs (including range proofs, proof of knowledge of r'_0 and regulation proofs), v_T and $r' = r'_0 + \sum_{i=1}^{k} r'_i$ to Alice. The additional excess output Ex_0 is required to ensure that only Bob can spend his newly created outputs. Otherwise Alice would know the sum of the blinding factors of his outputs and could thus spend them.

(ii) If Alice agrees with the transaction value v_T, with her inputs $\mathsf{In}_i = g^{r_i} h^{v_i}$ $(1 \leq i \leq n)$, s.t. $v = \sum_{i=1}^{n} v_i$ and $r = \sum_{i=1}^{n} r_i$, she creates m *change outputs* $\mathsf{Out}_i = g^{r'_i} h^{v_i}$ $(k < i \leq k+m)$, s.t. $v - \sum_{i=k+1}^{k+m} v'_i = v_T$ and range proofs and regulation proofs for these outputs. She then computes a *delta output* $r_\Delta = r - \sum_{i=k+1}^{k+m} r'_i - r'$ and combines all of her inputs, Bob's and her outputs (including all proofs) and r_Δ into a *complete transaction*. Alice' inputs are outputs of previous transactions that can be money issuing transactions as described in Appendix A.4.

(iii) Finally, Alice sends the complete transaction to one or more validators, encrypted under their public keys. The number of validators depends on the used transaction validation strategy (see Sect. 5).

---

[1] Matching transaction inputs to outputs after reordering is in general already an NP-complete problem (subset sum). However, most transactions will only have few inputs and outputs, which can make linking feasible in practice without this additional measure.

The validators then verify the transaction as described in Sect. 3.5.

A.2 Mixing and Consensus

The validators collect a set of verified transactions and in the end of the round mix them by using two merging properties of our transactions. The first merging option is to *combine* two valid transactions together which creates another valid transaction. Combining several transactions into one large transaction breaks the direct correlation between inputs and outputs in the original transactions. The more transactions are combined in one round, the harder it is for third parties to link inputs and outputs based on published, combined transactions. Since the order of inputs and outputs is irrelevant for the correctness of a transaction, they can be reordered arbitrarily (e.g. ordered in binary order). Additionally, by only publishing the sum of the delta outputs instead of the individual values, deciding which set of transaction outputs belong to which set of inputs becomes impossible.

The second merging option is *compacting*. If an output of one transaction appears as an input in another transaction, the matching input-output pair can be simply be removed, resulting in a smaller but still valid transaction. Compacting makes transaction linking more difficult and improves storage efficiency. Once the validator has verified and merged (mixed) all received transactions in the current round, the remaining inputs and outputs can be simply sorted as a list for publishing.

The validators then need to achieve consensus over the content of the next block depending and we assume that they run a Byzantine fault tolerant consensus protocol to protect against double spending. Validators can cache unspent transaction outputs from all previous blocks to speed up verification of new transactions (needed for double-spending protection). After achieving consensus over a block, validators can remove all inputs of the block from their cached set and add all new outputs to it.

A.3 Block Structure

Each block consists of a first part signed by the validators and a second part containing auxiliary information. The first signed part contains the sum of all delta outputs, all excess outputs including the zero-knowledge proofs of their exponents, and the hash of the previous block. Additionally, if the block contains an issuance or a deletion transaction, the signed part also contains the explicit amounts of money that are added or removed. As auxiliary information, the block contains a list of inputs and a list of outputs including their range proofs.

The signed part of the block only contains the excess outputs and the sum of the delta outputs of all transactions (Ex_0, Ex_1 and r_Δ | r'_Δ in the example). The transaction inputs and transaction outputs with a value do not need to be included in the signed part, but they still need to be published including the range proofs of the outputs, so that other parties can verify the correctness of the blockchain.

This block structure allows compression of the blockchain by compacting transactions across blocks. Outputs of previous transactions that are used as inputs in the new block can be removed from storage without losing the ability to verify the complete chain. All that is required for the verification is the set of unspent transaction outputs, excess and delta outputs of all blocks, and the values of issuance and deletion transactions. All of this combined can be interpreted as one large transaction that, if valid, implies the validity of the whole blockchain. This makes the storage required to verify the full chain very small and slowly growing for third parties that do not want to store all transactions.

A.4   Issuance

Our currency provides an explicit mechanism for the issuer to increase, or decrease, the amount of currency in circulation. This can be done with a special transaction type that requires a signature from the issuer.

Specifically, the issuer can publish an *issuance transaction* with an explicitly stated amount v. The issuer creates k transaction outputs $\mathsf{Out}_i = g^{r_i'} h^{v_i'}$ ($1 \leq i \leq k$), such that $v = \sum_{i=1}^{k} v_i'$, and which all have a range proof attached. The issuer then additionally creates an excess output $\mathsf{Ex}_0 = g^{r_0'}$, s.t. $r_0' + \sum_{i=1}^{k} r_i' = 0$ and proves knowledge of r_0'. The transaction is valid, if h^v is equal to the sum of the outputs. The outputs created by such an issuing transaction could, e.g., be transferred to commercial banks who can then further distribute the newly created money. The issued amount v is published in plaintext to the next block with the issuance transaction.

The role of the issuer can easily be distributed among multiple parties by requiring signatures from multiple parties for issuance transactions. This may be particularly interesting for private deployments, where there is no central bank that can be assumed to be trusted.

A.5   Distributing Regulation

The role of the regulator can be distributed between multiple parties without changes to the rest of the system by using a threshold cryptosystem. In such a scheme, a set of n parties would be responsible for regulation, of which at least a threshold number k must cooperate to decrypt an encrypted identity. To set up the system, the regulator parties would run a key generation protocol that creates a public key and distributes shares of the corresponding secret key to the parties. The created public key is then used as the regulator public key in our system.

Since we use Elgamal encryption in our system, which can be used for threshold encryption (e.g. [29]), the process of encrypting identities and creating proofs does not differ from the system described in Sect. 3.4. In order to decrypt the ciphertexts without reconstructing the shared secret key, the regulator parties then again need to run a decryption protocol (e.g. [30]).

References

1. Nakamoto, S.: Bitcoin: A peer-to-peer electronic cash system (2008)
2. Bech, M.L., Garratt, R.: Central bank cryptocurrencies (2017)
3. Mills, D., et al.: Distributed ledger technology in payments, clearing, and settlement. Board of Governors of the Federal Reserve System, Washington (2016). https://doi.org/10.17016/FEDS.2016.095
4. Wilkins, C.A.: Fintech and the financial ecosystem: Evolution or revolution? (2016). http://www.bankofcanada.ca/wp-content/uploads/2016/06/remarks-170616.pdf
5. Mas working with industry to apply distributed ledger technology in securities settlement and cross border payments (2017). http://www.mas.gov.sg/News-and-Publications/Media-Releases/2017/MAS-working-with-industry-to-apply-Distributed-Ledger-Technology.aspx
6. Koning, J.P.: Fedcoin: a central bank-issued cryptocurrency. R3 Report, 15 (2016)
7. Danezis, G., Meiklejohn, S.: Centrally banked cryptocurrencies. In: 23nd Annual Network and Distributed System Security Symposium, NDSS 2016, San Diego, California, USA, 21–24 February 2016
8. Ingves, S.: The e-krona and the payments of the future (2018). https://www.riksbank.se/globalassets/media/tal/engelska/ingves/2018/the-e-krona-and-the-payments-of-the-future.pdf
9. Billner, A.: Now there are plans for 'e-krona' in cash-shy sweden (2018). https://www.bloomberg.com/news/articles/2018-10-26/riksbank-to-develop-pilot-electronic-currency-amid-cash-decline
10. Maxwell, G.: Confidential transactions (2015). https://people.xiph.org/~greg/confidential_values.txt
11. Jedusor, T.E.: Mimblewimble. http://mimblewimble.org/mimblewimble.txt
12. Ben-Sasson, E., et al.: Zerocash: decentralized anonymous payments from bitcoin. In: 2014 IEEE Symposium on Security and Privacy (SP), pp. 459–474. IEEE (2014)
13. Garman, C., Green, M., Miers, I.: Accountable privacy for decentralized anonymous payments. In: Grossklags, J., Preneel, B. (eds.) FC 2016. LNCS, vol. 9603, pp. 81–98. Springer, Heidelberg (2017). https://doi.org/10.1007/978-3-662-54970-4_5
14. Camenisch, J., Hohenberger, S., Lysyanskaya, A.: Balancing accountability and privacy using E-cash (extended abstract). In: De Prisco, R., Yung, M. (eds.) SCN 2006. LNCS, vol. 4116, pp. 141–155. Springer, Heidelberg (2006). https://doi.org/10.1007/11832072_10
15. 31 CFR 1010.330 - Reports relating to currency in excess of $10,000 received in a trade or business (2012). https://www.law.cornell.edu/cfr/text/31/1010.330
16. Pedersen, T.P.: Non-interactive and information-theoretic secure verifiable secret sharing. In: Feigenbaum, J. (ed.) CRYPTO 1991. LNCS, vol. 576, pp. 129–140. Springer, Heidelberg (1992). https://doi.org/10.1007/3-540-46766-1_9
17. Fiat, A., Shamir, A.: How to prove yourself: practical solutions to identification and signature problems. In: Odlyzko, A.M. (ed.) CRYPTO 1986. LNCS, vol. 263, pp. 186–194. Springer, Heidelberg (1987). https://doi.org/10.1007/3-540-47721-7_12
18. Pointcheval, D., Stern, J.: Security proofs for signature schemes. In: Maurer, U. (ed.) EUROCRYPT 1990. LNCS, vol. 1070, pp. 387–398. Springer, Heidelberg (1996). https://doi.org/10.1007/3-540-68339-9_33
19. Samarati, P., Sweeney, L.: Protecting privacy when disclosing information: k-anonymity and its enforcement through generalization and suppression. Technical report, SRI International (1998)

20. Pointcheval, D., Sanders, O.: Short randomizable signatures. In: Sako, K. (ed.) CT-RSA 2016. LNCS, vol. 9610, pp. 111–126. Springer, Cham (2016). https://doi.org/10.1007/978-3-319-29485-8_7

21. Camenisch, J., Lysyanskaya, A.: A signature scheme with efficient protocols. In: Cimato, S., Persiano, G., Galdi, C. (eds.) SCN 2002. LNCS, vol. 2576, pp. 268–289. Springer, Heidelberg (2003). https://doi.org/10.1007/3-540-36413-7_20

22. Camenisch, J., Lysyanskaya, A.: Signature schemes and anonymous credentials from bilinear maps. In: Franklin, M. (ed.) CRYPTO 2004. LNCS, vol. 3152, pp. 56–72. Springer, Heidelberg (2004). https://doi.org/10.1007/978-3-540-28628-8_4

23. Aranha, D.F., Gouvêa, C.P.L.: RELIC is an Efficient LIbrary for Cryptography. https://github.com/relic-toolkit/relic

24. Bünz, B., Bootle, J., Boneh, D., Poelstra, A., Wuille, P., Maxwell, G.: Bulletproofs: Efficient range proofs for confidential transactions. Technical report, Cryptology ePrint Archive, Report 2017/1066 (2017). https://eprint.iacr.org/2017/1066

25. Castro, M., Liskov, B.: Practical byzantine fault tolerance. In: Proceedings of the Third Symposium on Operating Systems Design and Implementation, OSDI 1999, pp. 173–186. USENIX Association, Berkeley, CA, USA (1999)

26. Croman, K., et al.: On scaling decentralized blockchains. In: Clark, J., Meiklejohn, S., Ryan, P.Y.A., Wallach, D., Brenner, M., Rohloff, K. (eds.) FC 2016. LNCS, vol. 9604, pp. 106–125. Springer, Heidelberg (2016). https://doi.org/10.1007/978-3-662-53357-4_8

27. Zcash. https://z.cash/

28. Kappos, G., Yousaf, H., Maller, M., Meiklejohn, S.: An empirical analysis of anonymity in zcash. In: 27th USENIX Security Symposium (USENIX Security 18), pp. 463–477. USENIX Association, Baltimore, MD (2018)

29. Pedersen, T.P.: A threshold cryptosystem without a trusted party. In: Davies, D.W. (ed.) EUROCRYPT 1991. LNCS, vol. 547, pp. 522–526. Springer, Heidelberg (1991). https://doi.org/10.1007/3-540-46416-6_47

30. Desmedt, Y., Frankel, Y.: Threshold cryptosystems. In: Brassard, G. (ed.) CRYPTO 1989. LNCS, vol. 435, pp. 307–315. Springer, New York (1990). https://doi.org/10.1007/0-387-34805-0_28

ZLiTE: Lightweight Clients for Shielded Zcash Transactions Using Trusted Execution

Karl Wüst[1]([✉]), Sinisa Matetic[1], Moritz Schneider[1], Ian Miers[2],
Kari Kostiainen[1], and Srdjan Čapkun[1]

[1] Department of Computer Science, ETH Zurich, Zürich, Switzerland
{karl.wuest,sinisa.matetic,moritz.schneider,
kari.kostiainen,srdjan.capkun}@inf.ethz.ch
[2] Cornell Tech, New York, USA
imiers@cornell.edu

Abstract. Cryptocurrencies record transactions between parties in a blockchain maintained by a peer-to-peer network. In most cryptocurrencies, transactions explicitly identify the previous transaction providing the funds they are spending, revealing the amount and sender/recipient pseudonyms. This is a considerable privacy issue. Zerocash resolves this by using zero-knowledge proofs to hide both the source, destination and amount of the transacted funds. To receive payments in Zerocash, however, the recipient must scan the blockchain, testing if each transaction is destined for them. This is not practical for mobile and other bandwidth constrained devices. In this paper, we build ZLiTE, a system that can support the so called "light clients", which can receive transactions aided by a server equipped with a Trusted Execution Environment. Even with the use of a TEE, this is not a trivial problem. First, we must ensure that server processing the blockchain does not leak sensitive information via side channels. Second, we need to design a bandwidth efficient mechanism for the client to keep an up-to-date version of the witness needed in order to spend the funds they previously received.

1 Introduction

Decentralized cryptocurrencies offer the potential to revolutionize payments. By providing transparent means to audit transactions, they reduce the need to rely on trusted incumbents and allow new innovation on financial applications. But this same transparency renders nearly all cryptocurrencies completely unsuited for wide-scale adoption: all transaction are broadcast publicly in a manner that can be readily linked to real world identities [4,26], raising issues with government surveillance, harassment and stalking, and the viability of business competition when competitors can see all cash flow.

K. Wüst and S. Matetic—Equally contributing authors.

A variety of protocols have been proposed, such as Solidus [2,9], Cryptonote [37], Zerocoin [27] and Zerocash [5], that, with varying effectiveness [21,22,29], alleviate these issues. For example, in Cryptonote the destination address is always a newly generated one-time public key derived from the receiver's public key and some randomness from the sender. Zerocoin functions as an overlay on Bitcoin, where users mint a zerocoin and issue a transaction to transfer the funds to its commitment. The coin can be further spent by using zero-knowledge proofs. The most promising of these protocols, Zerocash, removes all information, such as sender/recipient identity, value, and linkability through the use of a zero-knowledge proof that there exists some past transaction which gave the user the funds they are spending. Zerocash is deployed in the cryptocurrency Zcash.

Payment Notification. Unlike in traditional means of payment, like credit cards and cash payments, in nearly all cryptocurrencies, including Bitcoin, Ethereum, and Zcash, it is possible to send money to a recipient's address without direct interaction or communication with the recipient. The recipient is paid, but only learns this next time when she is online. This raises the problem of *payment notification*, that is, the recipient must find out they were paid. Some cryptocurrencies, like Ethereum, use an account model where there is a single, well-defined location for payments. As a result, the recipient and, more significantly, anyone else, can see when and for how much someone is paid. Other cryptocurrencies, including Bitcoin and Zerocash, eschew this approach for improved privacy, storing payments individually as unspent transaction outputs (UTXOs) in unpredictable locations. In such systems, there must be some mechanism for users to discover a UTXO belongs to them. The simplest way to do this is to scan the blockchain and check each transaction.

Payment notification is a particular problem for privacy-preserving systems like Zcash. Transactions in Zcash, consist of an opaque commitment, a ciphertext, a serial number to prevent double spending, and a zero-knowledge proof of the transaction's correctness and the existence of funds to spend. In particular, there is no metadata to identify the sender or recipient. The only way for a client to identify if a payment is directed to them is by trial decryption of the ciphertext associated with a transaction: each transaction contains a ciphertext under the recipient's public key. To monitor for payments, clients must, therefore, conduct a trial decryption for *every* transaction on the blockchain. While this is completely feasible for well-resourced clients, running on platforms like standard desktop PCs, it is not desirable, nor often feasible, for resource-constrained clients like mobile devices where both power and bandwidth are major constraints. In this paper, we focus on such resource-constrained clients.

Light Client Model. Several cryptocurrencies address this problem with a model, exemplified by Bitcoin's Simplified Payment Verification (SPV) scheme [30], where "light clients" entrust a server (*full node*) to respond to queries about payments to a given address. The SPV protocol reveals to the server which (pseudonymous) addresses belong to a client and thus links multiple addresses together and potentially to real world identities, reducing user privacy. Directly applying the same model to Zcash is not possible without revealing the client's decryption key to the server so that it can perform the trial decryption for transactions, and thus completely breaking the privacy properties of Zcash.

Another challenge for resource-constrained clients is that simply notifying users that they received funds is not sufficient to use them for new payments in Zcash. To spend funds sent to them in a previous transaction tx in block n, users must prove that there exists a path (called *witness*) w from the root of a Merkle tree (called *note commitment tree*) to tx. Moreover, this information is not static and it needs to be updated as new transactions are added to the tree.

Our Contribution. In this paper, we introduce ZLiTE, a system that enables efficient *privacy-preserving light clients for Zcash*. Our approach follows the common "light client and server" model, thus minimizing the client bandwidth and computation requirements by offloading processing to the server. To tackle the privacy problem of client queries, we leverage trusted execution, namely Intel SGX [19], on the server. This approach allows the server to perform the trial decryption for transactions without learning the client's key.

Although this approach is conceptually simple, realizing it securely requires overcoming technical challenges. First, *external* reads and writes from the SGX enclave to the blocks stored on the server or to response buffers can leak which transactions belong to the client. Second, SGX enclaves are susceptible to side-channel attacks [7,8,15,28,34,39] that can leak their *internal* memory access patterns. Secret-dependent code and data accesses can enable a malicious server to infer the used client's key. Third, our system also needs to ensure that the residing platform cannot mount a combination of eclipse attacks [18,38] on the blockchain and replay client messages to identify queried transactions. And fourth, we need to efficiently provide the client with up-to-date Merkle tree witnesses needed to spend funds from a given transaction without leaking any private information.

To address these challenges, ZLiTE combines, in a novel way, a number of known techniques from private information retrieval and side-channel resilient trusted execution, making the processing of client queries oblivious towards a powerful adversary controlling the supporting server. We also design a new commitment tree update mechanism that allows the client to obtain efficiently from the server all the needed information to spend the received funds.

Parallel Work. Finally, we note that, in parallel work, a similar solution has been suggested for privacy protection in Bitcoin [25]. While our overall approach is similar, the technical challenges that we address are specific to Zcash, and thus different. We review such parallel work in more detail in Sect. 7.

2   Background

Transactions in Cryptocurrencies. Many cryptocurrencies operate in the so called Unspent Transaction Output (UTXO) model. In this model, a transaction consists of a set of outputs, each with a numerical amount of money and an *address*, and a set of inputs each of which references the output of a previous transaction. For a transaction to be valid, the following conditions have to be met: (1) referenced outputs must exist, (2) inputs must be signed by the key specified in the referenced output address, (3) the $\sum$(output amounts) must be $\leq$ to the $\sum$(input amounts), and (4) referenced outputs must not be spent by a previous transaction.

In Bitcoin, this is accomplished by directly identifying the referenced outputs, checking that they are not referenced by any other transactions, and then checking the sum inputs and outputs. If a transaction validates, then the outputs it references are removed from the UTXO set and the outputs it generates added. Transactions in Bitcoin and most cryptocurrencies are validated via a peer-to-peer network and assembled into blocks (e.g., every 10 min), that are broadcast to the network.

In Zcash there are two types of transactions: transparent and shielded transactions. The transparent kind is directly derived from Bitcoin and will not be considered for the rest of this paper.

Shielded transactions also take some inputs and create new outputs, but the similarities end there. Outputs, also called notes, are created by so called *joinsplits* and are a commitment to an amount and the address it belongs to. A *joinsplit* takes a transparent input and up to two notes as input and creates one transparent output and up to two notes as output. However this information is encrypted and can only be inspected by the receiver. Additionally a Merkle tree is constructed over all notes on the blockchain forming the *note commitment tree*. A zero-knowledge proof forms the second part of the transaction and shows that conditions (1)–(3) hold with respect to that Merkle tree root. Because the "outputs" that a shielded transaction spends are not revealed, they cannot be removed from the UTXO set. Instead, a unique serial number, sometimes called a *nullifier*, is produced by the transaction that ensures the referenced outputs cannot be used again. This prevents double spending.

To perform operations in Zcash, each user has two keys associated to his shielded address. First, the *spending key* that is used during the creation of a zero-knowledge proof allowing the users to prove ownership of the received funds. Second, the *viewing key* that is used to decrypt the shielded transaction in the blocks and verify if each transaction belongs to the user.

Full Nodes and Light Clients. To interact with a cryptocurrency, one must have a client. In both Bitcoin and Zcash, the default client is a *full node*, which receives and validates every block, and contains the full state of the blockchain. Full nodes do not need to trust other entities, provided the system functions as assumed, e.g., for Proof-of-Work systems the majority of the network's computational power is honest and messages disseminate without problems. While full nodes offer the best security and privacy, they entail considerable resource usage. The computation and network resources necessary to maintain a full node are a major impediment and in some cases, e.g. mobile devices, simply prohibitive.

In contrast, *lightweight clients* are nodes that have smaller resource footprint. They were originally proposed for Bitcoin [30] as the *Simplified Payment*

Verifications (SPV) scheme. In this proposal, clients store only the header of each block instead of the entire blockchain. This is sufficient to check the Proof-of-Work on each block and verify the presence of transactions by checking their inclusion in the Merkle tree whose root is contained in the block header: clients must merely request both a transaction and the witness to its inclusion in the Merkle tree from a full node.

The reduced resource usage of SPV clients comes at a major cost: privacy. As the light client must request individual transactions from a full node, it reveals which transactions and addresses belong to the requesting client. In Bitcoin, this allows multiple addresses to be linked together. In Zcash, this effect is far more pronounced since the client completely loses privacy: without such queries, no shielded transaction can be linked together, i.e., an adversary learns nothing.

ORAM. Encryption provides data confidentiality but access patterns can leak information possibly leading to reconstruction of the content itself. Oblivious RAM (ORAM) [14] is a popular scheme that hides access patterns and achieves fully oblivious data accesses. Most ORAM algorithms use randomized encryption and shuffling techniques to build a fully oblivious database. Intuitively ORAM hides the address, access patterns, whether the same data access is repeated and the type of operation, i.e. read or write. Note that ORAM operations still leak timing information related to the frequency of access operations themselves.

3 Our Approach

3.1 Requirements

The main goal of this paper is to design a solution that enables privacy-preserving light clients assisted by full-node servers for Zcash. More precisely, we specify the following requirements for our solution:

R1 Privacy. ZCash light clients should be able to privately retrieve all transaction related data without revealing sensitive information (e.g., viewing key, transaction count, blocks containing transactions) to the server.

R2 Integrity. The server that is assisting the light client should not be able to steal funds or make a client falsely accept a payment.

R3 Completeness. The retrieval of transactions should guarantee that the light client receives *all* data necessary for spending the funds they received.

R4 Performance. The solution should have minimal bandwidth and processing requirement for the client. The server's processing should be in the same order of magnitude as the normal full node operation.

3.2 Main Idea

Our main idea is to leverage commonly-available Trusted Execution Environments (TEEs) and apply them to full nodes (servers) to enable privacy-preserving light clients for Zcash. In particular, we use Intel's SGX [19] which provides isolated execution of security-critical application code, called *enclaves*, such that enclave data confidentiality and execution integrity remains protected from untrusted software such as other applications, the OS, hypervisor. In SGX, the CPU enforces that untrusted software cannot access enclave memory. For space reasons we omit details regarding Intel SGX. We refer readers unfamiliar with the technology to a more detailed SGX introduction [12, 20].

Similar to SPV in Bitcoin, we assume deployments where the light Zcash clients may be assisted by *any number of* servers (full nodes) that support TEEs. Some of the servers could be run by well-known companies as commercial services where light clients may have to pay a small fee for the service. Other servers could be run by private individuals, like members of the cryptocurrency community, as a free service. As in SPV, the light clients are free to choose which servers to use, if any. In this regard, our solution retains the decentralized nature of Zcash.

3.3 Controversy and Challenges

The use of TEEs is often controversial. TEEs rely on a trusted authority to design a secure processor and issue some form of certification for it. Attestations from the TEE can be forged either via exploiting design flaws or by corrupting the provider and falsely claiming that an attestation came from a genuine piece of hardware. The hardware and software are frequently closed source and the manufacturers opaque. These kind of trust assumptions are frequently an anathema, especially for cryptocurrencies. Moreover, usage of TEEs often seems like lazy systems design choice, since, if one assumes fully trusted TEEs (e.g., none of the enclaves can be compromised, no side-channel leakage, full resilience on physical attacks etc.), solving many problems becomes relatively easy.

However, current TEEs including SGX enclaves have noteworthy limitations such as side-channel attacks that leak information and no resilience to physical attacks. We argue that the real research challenge is to leverage TEEs such that one can enable improved performance and privacy, but at the same time address the limitations of TEEs such as side-channel leakage. In the (unlikely) case that TEEs are fully broken (e.g., a new severe processor vulnerability is discovered), the system should fail gracefully. One example of graceful failure is that the affected clients' privacy may be reduced, but integrity of the system is preserved, i.e., in a cryptocurrency, no money is lost or stolen.

3.4 Adversary Model

In this paper, we consider the standard SGX adversary model where the attacker controls the OS and all other system software in the supporting server. In practice, the adversary could be a malicious administrator in a company that provides the full node service, an external attacker that has compromised the OS on the full node server, or a malicious individual operating a free server.

The adversary is able to perform digital side-channel attacks [7, 8, 15]. We assume that he is able to *perfectly* observe the enclave's control flow with instruction-level granularity and its data accesses with byte-level granularity (best known attacks are cache-line granularity). We overestimate the attacker capabilities, as all current side-channel attacks suffer from significant noise and cannot extract perfect traces in pratcice. By assuming such an adversary, we design our solution for future attacks that may be able to mount more precise side-channels. Additionally, the adversary has full control over the communication and can thus read, modify, block or delay all messages sent by the enclave.

The adversary *cannot* break the hardware protections of SGX along with cryptographic primitives such as encryption schemes and signatures. More specifically, the adversary cannot access SGX's processor-specific keys and the enclave's encrypted runtime memory protected by the CPU.

Finally, even if full compromise of SGX is outside our adversary model, we consider this possibility in our system design and discuss how our solution handles such worst case scenario in Sect. 5.3.

3.5   Strawman Solutions

We propose to leverage TEEs to protect the privacy of Zcash light clients. If client privacy relies on TEEs, it becomes natural to ask if one needs a complicated solution like Zcash and if anonymous payments can be realized through a much simpler solution using TEEs. To answer this question, we consider the limitations of a few strawman solutions.

Our first strawman solution is that clients send all transactions in an encrypted format to a set of authorized TEEs that process them privately. Such a solution would protect user privacy, but in case the enclaves get broken, the adversary can perform unlimited double spending on all users. Additionally, such a solution would not be decentralized.

Our second strawman solution is to use pseudonymous transactions that are published to a permissionless ledger, similar to Bitcoin, and mix them in one or more TEEs for improved privacy. Such a solution would prevent double spending, ensuring security for all users, even in the event that TEEs are broken. However, such a solution does not provide the same strong privacy protection, namely *unlinkability*, as Zcash, since the anonymity set for a transaction output only consists of the inputs of the mixed transaction. An adversary controlling the OS on the mixing service can further reduce anonymity by blocking incoming transactions or injecting his own.

Our third strawman solution is to use the Zcash system, due to its strong privacy properties, but allow light clients to offload their complete wallets to TEEs that perform new payments and notification of received payments for them. The main drawback of this approach is that if the TEE would be compromised, it would incur direct monetary loss for a high number of clients.

Our goal is to design a solution that enables light clients for Zcash, and thus benefits from its sophisticated privacy protections, but avoids the above discussed limitations of simple TEE-based solutions.

3.6 Solution Overview

In our solution, when a light clients wants to be notified about received funds or make new payments, she connects to one of the TEE-enabled full node servers, performs remote attestation of the server's SGX enclave, and establishes a secure channel to it.

To enable payment notification, the client sends its *viewing keys* for the addresses that she owns to the enclave and indicates from which point on (e.g., the latest known block to the client) she wishes to update the light client's state. The enclave obtains the data and information from the locally stored blockchain and processes it in a *side-channel oblivious* manner based on the client request and sends back the response to the client.

To enable new payments by the client, the server also prepares a witness for each new transaction of the client, as well as the note commitment tree update and sends them to the client. Given this information, the client can efficiently create new transactions, and the associated zero-knowledge proofs, using the received funds, without revealing his *spending key* to the enclave.

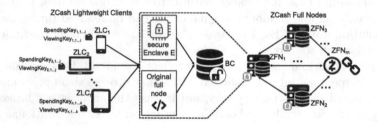

Fig. 1. System model. Lightweight clients request transaction verification and payment issuing service from enclaves hosted on full Zcash nodes.

4 ZLiTE System Design

4.1 System Model and Operation Overview

Figure 1 presents our system model. The main stakeholders in the system are Zcash Lightweight Clients $ZLC_1...ZLC_n$ and Zcash Full Nodes $ZFN_1...ZFN_m$. A lightweight client ZLC_a connects to any full node ZFN_b that supports our service by hosting an enclave E when she wants to acquire information regarding transactions and addresses that belong to the client or to issue new transactions towards another Zcash client. ZLC_a can own one or more addresses in her wallet that are also characterized by the $SpendingKey_{a,1...c}$ and the $ViewingKey_{a,1...c}$.

Full nodes maintain the local version of the blockchain (BC) as usual, appending each new confirmed block to the longest chain they have. The blockchain is maintained outside the secure environment, either on the disk or memory of the platform where the node resides. SGX enclave memory is limited (128 MB) and is only suitable for smaller storage related to the currently executed task.

A client that wants to retrieve transactions, performs remote attestation for the ZLiTE enclave and then establishes a secure connection (TLS), through which she sends her viewing key and the height h of the last known block B_h. The enclave then scans the blockchain for transactions for this viewing key starting from B_h and obliviously moves them to a temporary *response ORAM* (rORAM) to hide which transactions are of the client's interest. Additionally, the ORAM structure is obliviously serialized in the response buffer sent to the client.

Oblivious Scanning. All processes that rely on secret data, i.e. the clients viewing key, must be performed in an oblivious fashion to prohibit any leakage of sensitive information (see Sect. 5). Finding the transactions that match the clients viewing key clearly depends on the client's secrets. To make block scanning oblivious to a side-channel observer (see the adversary model in Sect. 3.4), processing of each transaction should produce the same side-channel trace. A naive way to solve this is to do a fake copy of each non-matching transaction (viewing key does not result in a valid decryption) to the response buffer as well. However, in that case the response buffer is as big as the scanned blocks (no performance improvement). To improve the performance we use a *response ORAM* to hold all relevant transactions of the current client. The rORAM allows us to perform one ORAM operation per transaction while still hiding if this operation is a write (relevant transaction) or a read (irrelevant transaction). This is achieved by constant-time branchless code using the cmov instruction [32]. In conclusion, the enclave performs the following operations for each transaction:

(1) check if the viewing key manages to decrypt the transaction
(2) calculate the Merkle tree
(3) perform an ORAM operation (write or read transaction into the rORAM depending on the outcome of (1))

Together with the transactions stored in the rORAM, ZLiTE delivers the corresponding Merkle paths, all block headers since B_h, and the note commitment tree update for the requested interval (see Sect. 4.3). Below we first describe the details of the ZLiTE operation and the retrieval of transactions and then describe how a lightweight client using our system can create new shielded transaction.

4.2   Transaction Retrieval

The operation of the synchronization protocol (see Fig. 2) works as follows:

Initialization and Continuous Operation.

(a) On initialization the Full Node ZFN_j connects to the P2P network (**a-1**) and downloads the full ZCash blockchain (**a-2**). This locally stored blockchain is continuously updated as new blocks are received from the network.

(b) When the lightweight client is installed, it contains a checkpoint block header (this can be from a recent date or the genesis block). The client then downloads all newer block headers from the P2P network and verifies them (i.e. the client checks the PoW and that their hash chain leads to the checkpoint). All but a small number of the most recent block headers (to handle shallow forks) can be deleted afterwards. This state is later updated during the synchronization process that the client performs with a ZLITE node in order to check for received transactions or before sending transactions (see below). This is similar to the operation of existing lightweight clients for other blockchains (e.g. Bitcoin).

Synchronization of Transactions. Clients synchronize with a ZLITE enclave as follows:

(1) The ZCash Lightweight Client ZLC_i performs attestation with the secure Enclave E_j residing on the full node ZFN_j.
(2) If the attestation was successful, the ZCash Lightweight Client ZLC_i establishes a secure communication channel to the Enclave E_j using TLS.
(3) The Lightweight Client ZLC_i sends a request containing its viewing key and the number of the latest known block.

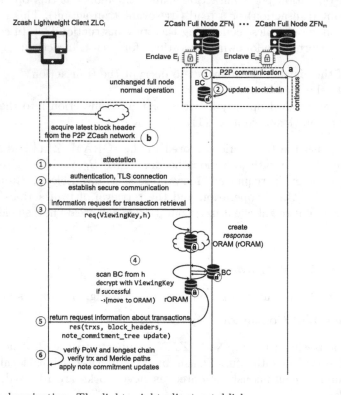

Fig. 2. Synchronization. The lightweight client establishes a secure connection to an enclave on a full node and sends a request that contains its viewing key and latest known block to perform the retrieval of all of her transaction information.

(4) The Enclave E_j creates a temporary in-memory *response ORAM* (rORAM) to store the transactions that will be sent to the client. E_j then *scans* its locally stored copy of the blockchain (BC) starting at the block number specified by the client and decrypts the transactions with the specified viewing key. The decryption will either result in garbage or in a valid plaintext transaction. If the decryption is successful, E_j moves the transaction and the corresponding Merkle paths (for the transaction and for the note commitments) to the response ORAM, and if it is not successful, E_j performs a read operation, thereby performing the move obliviously using the cmov technique mentioned in Sect. 4.1 to replace conditional statements.

(5) After the scanning operation has finished, the rORAM is serialized by moving the entries to a fixed-size (dependent on the request, i.e., number of requested blocks for update) response array that is then sent to the client. In addition, the response contains all of the block headers and the note commitment tree updates (see Sect. 4.3 for details).

(6) The ZCash Lightweight Client ZLC_i verifies that the received block headers have a valid proof of work, create a chain to its latest known header and that the chain is the heaviest chain advertised in the P2P network. For every received transaction, it checks whether the recomputed Merkle root, given the received path, matches the corresponding block header. The client then updates the witnesses for all transactions with the received note commitment tree update and finally deletes old block headers that no longer need to be stored.

4.3 Transaction Creation

The lightweight client receives all information necessary to create shielded Zcash transactions from our system. Namely, for every output he wants to spend, he requires the witness (at the time of creating the new transaction) of the corresponding note commitment (i.e., its Merkle path in the note commitment tree).

These witnesses could be retrieved from a ZLiTE node at the time of spending. However, this would require the node to retrieve the witness in an oblivious fashion on request, which becomes computationally expensive as the commitment tree gets larger. Instead, when scanning the chain for a client, we additionally supply the witness of a note at the block height where it was created (see Sect. 4.2). When synchronizing, the client then also receives *commitment tree updates*, which allow him to update witnesses for any previous note commitment. In this case, there is no need for oblivious computation since the update only depends on the block height and not on the transaction relevant to the client.

Given a note commitment tree at time t_1 and a note commitment tree at time t_2, to compute the commitment tree update, the enclave starts with an empty list U_{ct} to store the update. Let cm_i be the latest note commitment in the tree at time t_1, i.e., it is the rightmost non-empty leaf. Then, in the tree at time t_2, for every node on the path from cm_i to the root of the tree, add the right child to U_{ct}. A client in the possession of a witness at time t_1 for some note, can then apply the update by replacing any node on the witness with the corresponding node from U_{ct}, if these two nodes have the same location in the Merkle tree. We present a proof in Appendix A that this construction results in a correct witness for the note commitment tree at time t_2.

5 Security Analysis

In this Section, we provide an informal security analysis of ZLITE. We first discuss protection against information leakage, then discuss the completeness of responses, and finally consider the worst-case scenario, i.e. a full break of SGX.

5.1 Protection Against Information Leakage

Since ORAM reads and writes are indistinguishable, an adversary observing memory access patterns is not able to determine which transactions were written. For ORAM accesses, when accessing the stash, indexes or the position map, every location is accessed to hide memory access patterns.

To protect against side channels (e.g. [8,15,28,34]), conditional statements that depend on transactions (e.g. during the process of moving transactions to the response ORAM) are replaced using the cmov instruction. Since this results in the same control flow independent of the transaction, protection against leakage even against an adversary that can observe the control flow with instruction level granularity is guaranteed. The cmov instruction has been previously used to protect against side channels by Raccoon [32], Zerotrace [33] and also Obliviate [3] in the context of providing secure ORAM access using SGX. This prior research shows that cmov can effectively protect against digital side channels.

Finally, the response size only depends on the number of scanned blocks, i.e. it is independent of how many (or if any) transactions are in the response, and thus does not leak any information about a client's viewing key or transactions.

5.2 Integrity and Completeness

The ZLITE node delivers the requested information along with all block information needed for simple payment verification. The client herself then verifies the block headers using the Merkle paths for her transactions. Similar to SPV in Bitcoin lightweight clients [30], this ensures that the server cannot make a client falsely accept payments for which the transactions are not included in the chain. As the client can also check the proof of work and gossips with the P2P network to receive block headers, she can ensure that she receives information from the longest chain. Thus, the server does not have stronger capabilities to eclipse a lightweight client than against a full node.

In contrast to standard SPV (as e.g. in Bitcoin [30]), where the client cannot be sure to have received all of her transactions, the usage of a TEE makes sure that the received response contains all of her transactions for the scanned interval given the ZLITE node's view of the blockchain.

5.3 Impact of Full SGX Compromise

While our adversary model considers side-channel attacks, we do not consider a full compromise of SGX, i.e., forged attestations, arbitrary control flow change or enclave secrets reading. However, recent research has shown that secrets can be read even from the quoting enclave allowing an adversary to extract attestation keys [10,36] which makes it necessary to discuss such a worst-case scenario.

While it is obvious that the privacy provided by ZLiTE can no longer hold, if the adversary can read all secrets, or a client connects to a server that uses a forged attestation to impersonate an SGX enclave, such a breach cannot lead to loss of funds. In addition to the loss of privacy, a client also loses completeness, since a node may omit payments. However, because the client's spending key is never sent to a ZLiTE node and the client performs Simple Payment Verification for all of his transactions, a node is not able to steal coins from the client or make him falsely accept a payment.

5.4 Trust Assumptions Comparison

In terms of security properties like double-spending protection, Zcash relies on the following two trust assumptions: First, there must be an honest majority of mining power. Second, the dissemination of messages broadcast to the peer-to-peer network must be sufficiently good, i.e., no eclipse attacks. ZLiTE relies on the same trust assumptions as Zcash for its security properties.

For privacy, Zcash relies on securely-generated public parameters and hardness of numeric cryptographic assumptions. ZLiTE requires the same assumptions and additional trust in TEEs.

6 Performance Evaluation

6.1 Implementation Details

Our implementation of ZLiTE is based on the protocol specification of Zcash. It consists of a blockchain parser, an oblivious Path ORAM implementation [35] and it makes use of some bundled cryptographic libraries. We support the current Zcash protocol specification including the'overwinter' protocol update.

The Trusted Computing Base (TCB) of our implementation can be split up into a network part that is responsible for the communication with a client (around 1.5k LoC) and the blockchain relevant part (around 3.7k LoC). Additionally we use well reviewed crypto libraries like *mbedTLS* (53k LoC) and small libraries that provide crypto primitives: sha256, blake2b, ripemd160, ChaCha20Poly1305 and ed25519 totaling to around 2.2k LoC. All of the included crypto primitives come from well reviewed sources. We will not go into details on the TLS library *mbedTLS* [23] and refer the interested reader to [24,40] for implementation details and performance results.

6.2   Performance

ZLITE measurements were done on an i7-8700k processor with an SSD. Note that all the reported timing results are without the additional TLS latency. All measurements are according to the blockchain activity as of August 2018.

Lower Bound. Any node that wants to check for new transactions needs to parse the new blocks and test its viewing keys against all transaction in the blocks. This is part of the Zcash specification and implies a lower bound for any full node. Testing viewing keys is computationally intensive because it involves a key exchange based on an elliptic curve for each transaction and viewing key. Our implementation manages to parse blocks of an entire day and test a single viewing key against the transactions within 1.24s compared to fully oblivious operation of ZLITE which takes around 5s. We have to retrieve the Merkle paths and perform at least one ORAM operation per shielded transaction while non oblivious solutions can skip this for all non-relevant transactions.

Average Transaction Size. We measured the average number of *joinsplits* in a shielded transaction and show a histogram in Fig. 3a. Around 95% of all shielded transactions only contain one *joinsplit*, thus they have at most 2 shielded inputs and 2 shielded outputs. Every *joinsplit* occupies around 2KB of data. We also have to store the *commitment tree update* (see Appendix A) which is around 1KB in size. The average shielded transaction thus requires an ORAM operation for around 3KB of data. These measurements allow us to chose optimal ORAM block size for our response ORAM of 3KB.

Latency. We measured the time required to fetch various amounts of blocks and show a comparison between different expected client data per hour in Table 1. Note that the time per block rises when a client requests a longer time period because the response ORAM is chosen accordingly and a big ORAM database leads to slower accesses. Additionally, slower responses are observed when the client expects a lot of activity and requests a lot of client data.

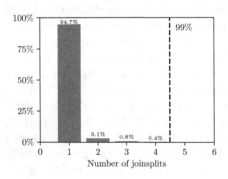

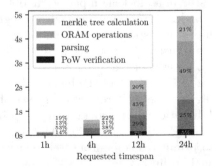

(a) Joinsplit distribution in all shielded transactions up until block 350000.

(b) Enclave latency for various request sizes (with 24576B of client data/hour).

Fig. 3. Performance measurements.

Table 1. Total time for various request and response sizes. (100 runs)

Time	Blocks	Client data per hour		
		6144B	12288B	24576B
24 h	576	4187 ms ± 504 ms	4382 ms ± 510 ms	4967 ms ± 617 ms
12 h	288	1875 ms ± 315 ms	2122 ms ± 364 ms	2317 ms ± 397 ms
4 h	96	541 ms ± 75 ms	583 ms ± 92 ms	631 ms ± 104 ms
1 h	24	123 ms ± 21 ms	129 ms ± 21 ms	130 ms ± 21 ms

Figure 3b shows the latency for a request with 24576B of client data per hour and various requested time spans. The latency is further divided in the four main contributors to the total: parsing the block, proof of work verification, ORAM operations and generating the merkle tree. Note that the ORAM operations start to take the lions share of the latency as soon as longer time spans are requested.

Bandwidth. The required bandwidth can be split into a static part (not dependent on the number of blocks requested) and a dynamic part. The dynamic part is composed of the blockheader (1487B) and the private data per block that is used to return transactions to the client. For reasonable usage we estimate a lightweight client to have (at most) one transaction every hour occupying 12kB. This results in 1024B of private data per block and the total dynamic bandwidth accumulates to 2511B per block. The static part only consists of the *commitment tree update* and is therefore $29 * 32B = 928B$ large. A client that requests one day of blocks from our system gets a response of 1.38MB.

Increased Blockchain Activity. As of August 2018 shielded transactions are not very common on the Zcash blockchain (only 1.5 shielded txs/block). With single steps measurements we estimated ZLiTE performance with increased future activity. For 100 shielded transactions per block, a daily request would take 112 s, while with an hourly one the latency would shrink to around 750 ms.

7 Related Work

Privacy for Lightweight Clients. Nakamoto introduced SPV in [30] in order to enable light clients for Bitcoin. The straight forward application of SPV trivially sacrifices client privacy, which is why BIP 37 [17] introduced Bloom filters [6] to somewhat hide the client's addresses in requests. Gervais et al. showed that this only marginally improves privacy [13]. Recently, Bitcoin protocol changes were proposed where full nodes publish a filter for all transactions in a block and clients download the block if the filter matches one of his addresses [31].

Most closely related to our work, Matetic et al. recently used SGX to provide privacy to Bitcoin lightweight clients in a system called BITE [25]. While the main challenge was to efficiently protect privacy in a system that already provides light clients, we tackle the problem of enabling light clients in a system that provides privacy, but until now does not support operation of light clients. One notable difference between [25] and our work is that in Zcash spending previously received funds requires the witness to the transaction's inclusion in the Merkle tree of all transactions, and therefore client must obtain, in efficient manner, an up-to-date version of this witness to spend the funds.

Zcash Scalable Clients. Several proposals aim to lower the resource requirements for clients in Zcash. While protocol upgrades [1] have reduced the computational resources required to generate a transaction, they have not substantially changed the bandwidth or verification requirements.

Bolt [16] proposes privacy preserving payment channels in which clients conduct most transactions off chain in a fully private manner. However, the current version requires clients to either monitor the blockchain for channel closure using a full-node, or entrust a third party to do so. While this does not violate privacy, failures by the third party can result in monetary loss. No such risk of theft exists with ZLiTE even if TEE integrity is violated. Moreover, Bolt requires payers to have an existing relationship with the recipient or an intermediate payment hub. While promising, Bolt is not a full solution for bandwidth limited clients.

In [11], Chiesa et al. explore the use of probabilistic micro-payments as a way of increasing throughput. In this setting, a sequence of, e.g., 100 micro-payments for one cent, is approximated by paying \$1 with probability $\frac{1}{100}$. Thus only $\frac{1}{100}$ of transactions are actually issued. However, this is only suitable for small and frequently repeated payments. Moreover, it is unclear if it will reduce the total volume of transactions or simple free up capacity for even more transactions.

8 Conclusion

Zcash provides strong privacy for its users. Shielded transactions, however, require clients to download and process every block which is impractical for devices like smartphones, and consequently no mobile client that supports shielded transactions exists in the market. In this paper we have developed a new solution that enables light clients to create and receive shielded payments by leveraging a supporting server and a commonly available TEE. Usage of trusted execution, obviously, changes the original trust model of Zcash, but we argue that such a solution strikes a balance between the best possible privacy and the range of scenarios where Zcash can be used in practice. Thanks to our solution, development of mobile clients that support shielded transactions becomes possible and more users can benefit from the sophisticated privacy protections of Zcash.

A Commitment Tree Updates

As described in Sect. 4.3, the commitment tree update U_{ct} for the interval between time t_1 and t_2 consists of the right child of the path from cm_i to the root at time t_2, where cm_i is the rightmost non-empty leaf at time t_1.

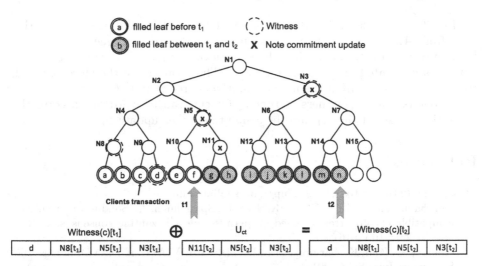

Fig. 4. At a time t_1 the note commitments Merkle tree is fully updated up to the latest block. A specific client holds a transaction with a note commitment c and knows the witness (i.e. the Merkle path) for it (d, N8, N5, and N3 nodes). After some time the blockchain is updated and new transactions added, thus, the Merkle Tree is updated accordingly (t_2). In order for the client to update the witness of her commitment c, she only needs the updated information from nodes (N11, N5, N3).

In Fig. 4, we show an example for the commitment tree update. In this example, the leaf f is the rightmost non-empty leaf at t_1, i.e. it corresponds to cm_i, which means that the commitment tree update consists of the values of the nodes N11, N5, N3 at time t_2. In the example, the update is applied to the witness of the leaf c (consisting of the nodes d, N8, N5, and N3). In this case, the values of the leaf d and node N8 do not change between time t_1 and t_2, the values of N5 and N3 do, however, and thus the values are contained in the commitment tree update and updated from there.

We now show that given a witness at time t_1 for a commitment cm_j (where $j < i$, i.e. cm_j was added to the tree before cm_i) and the commitment tree update U_{ct}, a client can compute the witness for cm_j at time t_2.

Let A_{ji} be the lowest common ancestor node of cm_j and cm_i in the commitment tree, i.e. cm_j is in the left subtree of A_{ji} and cm_i is in the right subtree. Any node in the left subtree of A_{ji} remains unchanged between t_1 and t_2, i.e. any node from that subtree which is part of the witness for cm_j also remains unchanged. Since none of these nodes changes through the update process, updating the witness with U_{ct} results in the correct values.

Similarly, any node of the witness for cm_j that is a left child of a node on the path from A_{ji} to the root remains unchanged in the Merkle tree at time t_2, since all leafs in any left subtree are already fixed at time t_1 and thus all node values are already final. Since our update process does not change any left children in the tree, it also leaves these values unchanged and thus results in the correct values.

Finally, any node of the witness for cm_j that is a left child of a node on the path from A_{ji} to the root may change in the Merkle tree at time t_2. Since A_{ji} is an ancestor of cm_i, any such node is included in U_{ct}, i.e. these nodes on the witness are updated in our update process. These values are therefore changed to the correct values from the note commitment tree at time t_2.

It follows that the witness at time t_2 for cm_j can be constructed correctly given the witness at time t_1 and the commitment tree update U_{ct}.

References

1. Sapling (2018). https://z.cash/upgrade/sapling.html
2. Abraham, I., Malkhi, D., Nayak, K., Ren, L., Spiegelman, A.: Solidus: an incentive-compatible cryptocurrency based on permissionless byzantine consensus. CoRR, abs/1612.02916 (2016)
3. Ahmad, A., Kim, K., Sarfaraz, M.I., Lee, B.: OBLIVIATE: A Data Oblivious File System for Intel SGX (2018)
4. Androulaki, E., Karame, G.O., Roeschlin, M., Scherer, T., Capkun, S.: Evaluating user privacy in bitcoin. In: Sadeghi, A.-R. (ed.) FC 2013. LNCS, vol. 7859, pp. 34–51. Springer, Heidelberg (2013). https://doi.org/10.1007/978-3-642-39884-1_4
5. Ben-Sasson, E., et al.: Zerocash: decentralized anonymous payments from bitcoin. In: IEEE Symposium on Security and Privacy, pp. 459–474. IEEE Computer Society (2014)
6. Bloom, B.H.: Space/time trade-offs in hash coding with allowable errors. Commun. ACM **13**(7), 422–426 (1970)
7. Brasser, F., et al.: DR.SGX: hardening SGX enclaves against cache attacks with data location randomization (2017). http://arxiv.org/abs/1709.09917
8. Brasser, F., Müller, U., Dmitrienko, A., Kostiainen, K., Capkun, S., Sadeghi, A.R.: Software grand exposure: SGX cache attacks are practical. In: 11th USENIX Workshop on Offensive Technologies, WOOT 2017. USENIX (2017)
9. Cecchetti, E., Zhang, F., Ji, Y., Kosba, A.E., Juels, A., Shi, E.: Solidus: confidential distributed ledger transactions via PVORM. In: Proceedings of the 2017 ACM SIGSAC Conference on Computer and Communications Security, CCS 2017, Dallas, TX, USA, 30 October–03 November 2017, pp. 701–717 (2017). https://doi.org/10.1145/3133956.3134010. http://doi.acm.org/10.1145/3133956.3134010
10. Chen, G., Chen, S., Xiao, Y., Zhang, Y., Lin, Z., Lai, T.H.: Sgxpectre attacks: leaking enclave secrets via speculative execution. arXiv preprint arXiv:1802.09085 (2018)
11. Chiesa, A., Green, M., Liu, J., Miao, P., Miers, I., Mishra, P.: Decentralized anonymous micropayments. In: Coron, J.-S., Nielsen, J.B. (eds.) EUROCRYPT 2017, Part II. LNCS, vol. 10211, pp. 609–642. Springer, Cham (2017). https://doi.org/10.1007/978-3-319-56614-6_21
12. Costan, V., Devadas, S.: Intel SGX explained. In: Cryptology ePrint Archive (2016)
13. Gervais, A., Capkun, S., Karame, G.O., Gruber, D.: On the privacy provisions of bloom filters in lightweight bitcoin clients. In: Proceedings of the 30th Annual Computer Security Applications Conference, pp. 326–335. ACM (2014)
14. Goldreich, O., Ostrovsky, R.: Software protection and simulation on oblivious rams. J. ACM (JACM) **43**(3), 431–473 (1996)

15. Götzfried, J., Eckert, M., Schinzel, S., Müller, T.: Cache attacks on Intel SGX. In: Proceedings of the 10th European Workshop on Systems Security, p. 2. ACM (2017)
16. Green, M., Miers, I.: Bolt: anonymous payment channels for decentralized currencies. In: Proceedings of the 2017 ACM SIGSAC Conference on Computer and Communications Security, CCS 2017, Dallas, TX, USA, 30 October–03 November 2017, pp. 473–489 (2017). https://doi.org/10.1145/3133956.3134093. http://doi.acm.org/10.1145/3133956.3134093
17. Hearn, M., Corallo, M.: Connection bloom filtering. Bitcoin Improvement Proposal 37 (2012). https://github.com/bitcoin/bips/blob/master/bip-0037.mediawiki
18. Heilman, E., Kendler, A., Zohar, A., Goldberg, S.: Eclipse attacks on bitcoin's peer-to-peer network. In: USENIX Security Symposium, pp. 129–144 (2015)
19. Intel: Intel Software Guard Extensions. https://software.intel.com/en-us/sgx
20. Intel: Software Guard Extensions Tutorial Series (2016). https://software.intel.com/en-us/articles/introducing-the-intel-software-guard-extensions-tutorial-series
21. Kappos, G., Yousaf, H., Maller, M., Meiklejohn, S.: An empirical analysis of anonymity in zcash. In: 27th USENIX Security Symposium, USENIX Security 2018, Baltimore, MD, USA, 15–17 August 2018, pp. 463–477 (2018). https://www.usenix.org/conference/usenixsecurity18/presentation/kappos
22. Kumar, A., Fischer, C., Tople, S., Saxena, P.: A traceability analysis of monero's blockchain. In: Foley, S.N., Gollmann, D., Snekkenes, E. (eds.) ESORICS 2017. LNCS, vol. 10493, pp. 153–173. Springer, Cham (2017). https://doi.org/10.1007/978-3-319-66399-9_9
23. Limited, A.: mbedTLS (formerly known as PolarSSL) (2015). https://tls.mbed.org/
24. Matetic, S., Schneider, M., Miller, A., Juels, A., Capkun, S.: Delegatee: brokered delegation using trusted execution environments. In: 27th USENIX Security Symposium (USENIX Security 2018). USENIX Association (2018)
25. Matetic, S., Wüst, K., Schneider, M., Kostiainen, K., Karame, G., Capkun, S.: BITE: bitcoin lightweight client privacy using trusted execution. IACR Cryptology ePrint Archive 2018, XXXX (2018)
26. Meiklejohn, S., et al.: A fistful of bitcoins: characterizing payments among men with no names. In: Proceedings of the 2013 Conference on Internet Measurement Conference, pp. 127–140. ACM (2013)
27. Miers, I., Garman, C., Green, M., Rubin, A.D.: Zerocoin: anonymous distributed e-cash from bitcoin. In: 2013 IEEE Symposium on Security and Privacy (SP), pp. 397–411. IEEE (2013)
28. Moghimi, A., Irazoqui, G., Eisenbarth, T.: CacheZoom: how SGX amplifies the power of cache attacks. In: Fischer, W., Homma, N. (eds.) CHES 2017. LNCS, vol. 10529, pp. 69–90. Springer, Cham (2017). https://doi.org/10.1007/978-3-319-66787-4_4
29. Möser, M., Soska, K., Heilman, E., Lee, K., Heffan, H., Srivastava, S., Hogan, K., Hennessey, J., Miller, A., Narayanan, A., Christin, N.: An empirical analysis of traceability in the monero blockchain. PoPETs 2018(3), 143–163 (2018)
30. Nakamoto, S.: Bitcoin: a peer-to-peer electronic cash system (2008)
31. Osuntokun, O., Akselrod, A., Posen, J.: Client side block filtering. Bitcoin Improvement Proposal 157 (2017). https://github.com/bitcoin/bips/blob/master/bip-0157.mediawiki
32. Rane, A., Lin, C., Tiwari, M.: Raccoon: closing digital side-channels through obfuscated execution. In: USENIX Security Symposium (2015)

33. Sasy, S., Gorbunov, S., Fletcher, C.: Zerotrace: Oblivious memory primitives from Intel SGX. In: Symposium on Network and Distributed System Security (NDSS) (2017)

34. Schwarz, M., Weiser, S., Gruss, D., Maurice, C., Mangard, S.: Malware Guard Extension: Using SGX to Conceal Cache Attacks (2017). http://arxiv.org/abs/1702.08719

35. Stefanov, E., et al.: Path ORAM: an extremely simple oblivious ram protocol. In: Proceedings of the 2013 ACM SIGSAC Conference on Computer & Communications Security, pp. 299–310. ACM (2013)

36. Van Bulck, J., et al.: Foreshadow: extracting the keys to the Intel SGX kingdom with transient out-of-order execution. In: Proceedings of the 27th USENIX Security Symposium. USENIX Association (2018)

37. Van Saberhagen, N.: Cryptonote v 2.0 (2013). https://cryptonote.org/whitepaper.pdf

38. Wüst, K., Gervais, A.: Ethereum eclipse attacks. Technical report, ETH Zurich (2016)

39. Xu, Y., Cui, W., Peinado, M.: Controlled-channel attacks: deterministic side channels for untrusted operating systems. In: 2015 IEEE Symposium on Security and Privacy (SP), pp. 640–656. IEEE (2015)

40. Zhang, F., Cecchetti, E., Croman, K., Juels, A., Shi, E.: Town crier: an authenticated data feed for smart contracts. In: CCS (2016)

Payment Protocol Security

Designed to Be Broken: A Reverse Engineering Study of the 3D Secure 2.0 Payment Protocol

Mohammed Aamir Ali and Aad van Moorsel[✉]

Newcastle University, Newcastle upon Tyne, UK
md.aamir.ncl@gmail.com, aad.vanmoorsel@newcastle.ac.uk

Abstract. 3 Domain Secure 2.0 (3DS 2.0) is the most prominent user authentication protocol for credit card based online payment. 3DS 2.0 relies on risk assessment to decide whether to challenge the payment initiator for second factor authentication information (e.g., through a passcode). The 3DS 2.0 standard itself does not specify how to implement transaction risk assessment. The research questions addressed in this paper therefore are: how is transaction risk assessment implemented for current credit cards and are there practical exploits against the 3DS 2.0 risk assessment approach? We conduct a detailed reverse engineering study of 3DS 2.0 for payment using a browser, the first study of this kind. Through experiments with different cards, from different countries and for varying amounts, we deduct the data and decision making process that card issuers use in transaction risk assessment. We will see that card issuers differ considerable in terms of their risk appetite. We also demonstrate a practical impersonation attack against 3DS 2.0 that avoids being challenged for second factor authentication information, requiring no more data than obtained with the reverse engineering approach presented in this paper.

Keywords: Payment systems · Credit card security · Reverse engineering · User authentication · Impersonation attack · EMV Protocol

1 Introduction

In 2001, payment networks (Visa, MasterCard and Amex) introduced the 3 Domain Secure 1.0 (3DS 1.0) protocol [35]. 3DS 1.0 introduced user authentication, requiring payment initiators (customers) to prove their identity with static passwords. For instance, 'Verified by Visa' asked three characters of a registered password. 3DS 1.0 received criticisms for both security and usability reasons. Security was impaired because registering the password could not be guaranteed to have been done by the card owner, and phishing attacks on card data and passwords could not be ruled out. However, the deciding drawback of 3DS 1.0

© International Financial Cryptography Association 2019
I. Goldberg and T. Moore (Eds.): FC 2019, LNCS 11598, pp. 201–221, 2019.
https://doi.org/10.1007/978-3-030-32101-7_13

for merchants was 'lost sales', that is, customers who failed to complete the purchase because they cannot recall or refuse to go through the trouble of finding and entering the password [3,16,20,23].

The European Commission proposed in 2015 the Payment Services Directive 2015/2366 (PSD II), a regulatory standard that asks card issuers within Europe to provide *Strong Customer Authentication* for *each* online payment transaction [13], very much like 3DS 1.0 would provide. The industry (card issuing banks, payment processors and online merchants) expressed concerns that the methods proposed in PSD II ignored the objectives of user-friendliness and argued that Strong Customer Authentication should be applied only to transactions deemed 'high risk' in a *Transaction Risk Assessment* (TRA). After a six-month negotiation including over 200 payment industry stakeholders, Strong Customer Authentication in PSD II was augmented with Transaction Risk Assessment.

In October 2016, EMVCo (a consortium of card payment networks), revised 3DS 1.0 to include TRA, resulting in the current 3D Secure 2.0 protocol suite [10]. 3DS 2.0 provides two options: *challenged* and *frictionless* authentication. Challenged authentication is for purchases with a high risk and prompts an authentication challenge to the payment initiator. Frictionless authentication requires no additional authentication information and is meant for low-risk transactions. TRA sacrifices strict security requirements for usability–from a security perspective, it is 'designed to be broken'.

The 3DS 2.0 protocol does not specify how TRA should be implemented, apart from some generic guidance. Therefore, we present in this paper an in-depth investigation in existing 3DS 2.0 implementations, the first of its kind. We show that transaction risk is determined from data collected at the payment initiator's browser, combined with transaction or network information (such as the transaction amount or IP address). The browser data acts as a 'fingerprint' of the user (see Sect. 2). In Sect. 4 we conduct an additional set of experiments with different transactions from different locations to learn when the authenticator allows frictionless authentication. We will see that different card issuers implement TRA differently, with different issuers exhibiting considerably different risk appetite as summarized in the flow diagrams of Figs. 3 and 4.

Our reverse engineering exercise uses five credit cards, from Visa as well as Mastercard, used at a number of different web sites. Experimental research with credit cards is challenging, for instance because of the possibility of blocked cards. It is therefore probably not surprising that the experimental research literature for online payment is relatively light, and that no studies on the scale of this paper exist. The five cards are representative for cards in general, in that the experiments generated similar fingerprint information. We note that all cards belonged to the authors, and ethics approval was obtained through regular processes of the authors' institution. Responsible disclosure through informing selected partners has taken place through our network of partners.

The design of 3DS 2.0 also suggests an obvious vulnerability, in that the authentication service may decide incorrectly not to challenge a payment. We will demonstrate an *impersonation attack*, in which a perpetrator impersonates

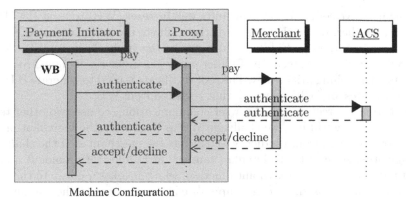

Machine Configuration

Fig. 1. Reverse engineering set-up, intercepting 3DS 2.0 transactions through a proxy.

a payment initiator, thus 'tricking' the authentication service into allowing a transaction to complete without being challenged for second factor authentication information, even for high transaction amounts. We will demonstrate two versions, one copying the fingerprint info to another machine that is configured arbitrarily, and one creating the same fingerprint on another machine with an identical configuration as the original machine. The impersonation exploit can be made into a practical attack if one manages to install malware that transports the fingerprint to the attacker, who can use it for a purchase impersonating the card holder (see Sect. 3 for details). This paper shows that such exploits can be conducted by anyone who reverse engineers TRA in the manner of this paper, without requiring any additional knowledge about TRA.

2   Reverse Engineering Transaction Risk Assessment: Fingerprinting

3DS 2.0 specifies very little about how card issuers should implement Transaction Risk Assessment. To understand how merchants and card issuers assess the risk of consumer payments we therefore reverse engineer existing implementations.

2.1   Reverse Engineering System Set-Up

Figure 1 shows the reverse engineering set-up. Within 3DS 2.0, a number of services and stakeholders are involved: the payment initiator using a browser, the merchant providing the check-out page at every purchase, and a set of services and servers for the authentication, termed the Access Control Server (ACS). The ACS maintains payment initiator's data which can be used to authenticate the cardholder during a purchase.

To intercept communication, we use the Fiddler proxy, which is available as open-source [32]. The proxy runs on the machine of the payment initiator (i.e., our own machine). We configure the machine's web browser (WB) to send HTTP(S) requests to Fiddler, which then forwards the traffic to the merchant or ACS. The responses are returned to Fiddler, which passes the traffic back to WB. When HTTPS decryption is enabled, the Fiddler proxy generates a self-signed root certificate and a matching private key. The root certificate is used to generate HTTPS server certificates for each secure site that is visited from WB.

Apart from intercepting the browser communication, we use two other techniques. First, using Fiddler, we challenge WB as if we were the merchant or the card issuer. Secondly, from Fiddler, we challenge the merchant as if the challenge was originating from WB. To handle ('tamper' in Fiddler terminology) a challenge, Fiddler provides a breakpoint function, which invokes a pause to the communication. Once paused, we can tamper or edit the changes to the communication data.

In total, we used five test cards for our experiments, three Visa cards (C1-C3) and two MasterCard cards (C4, C5). To make sure that 3DS 2.0 does not have any machine identifiers pre-installed on the machine, we had a fresh installation of Windows 10 operating system and Chrome 59.x web browser.

The merchant web sites we used were all enabled with 3DS 2.0 checkout and were selected from the Alexa list of merchant web sites [2]. The 'Verified by (payment-network)' icon on the merchant web site indicates that it is 3D Secure enabled. To ensure that we have a representative sample of merchant web sites, we kept track of the ACS URL's to which our transaction were redirected. All 'Verified by (payment-network)' websites redirected us to the same ACS URL indicating that the implementation of 3DS is issuer based. For each test card, we made several legitimate transactions and recorded the complete checkout session for each transaction with Fiddler. We decided to stop making further transactions once authenticated by ACS using frictionless authentication. This ensures that the ACS trusts WB enough for frictionless authentication. We decoded the 3DS 2.0 transaction data as necessary and analysed the outcomes in detail.

2.2 3DS 2.0 Authentication Protocol

Figure 2 shows the transaction sequence for frictionless authentication over 3DS 2.0, collating 3DS 2.0 specification with transaction information extracted from Fiddler. The box labelled 'Tunnel (Customer,ACS)' represents the reverse engineered part of transaction visible from WB, while the transaction sequence steps for the rest of the parties are derived from 3DS 2.0 specifications.

In Fig. 2 the customer initiates the payment in step 1 and in step 2 the merchant decides to trigger user authentication through 3DS 2.0. Step 3 and 4 set up the connection between payment initiator and ACS.

Message 5 through 11 detail the interaction between browser and ACS, where the ACS retrieves the data from the browser used to assess the transaction risk. In step 6, the ACS sends JavaScript dfp.js to the browser and posts the results back in step 8. Note that dfp stands for device finger print, it aims at identifying the device by fingerprinting it, so that subsequent payment can be traced back to the same machine (and, therefore, more likely to the same payment initiator).

If this is the first time the browser uploads the JavaScript, the ACS repeats the process in steps 9–11 to install persistent cookies (IDCookie) at the browser.

Hereafter, the transaction is processed according to the rules specified in EMV 3DS 2.0 specifications that states the 3DS Server to submit an Authentication Request (AReq) to the ACS. Transaction Risk Assessment is then completed in step 13, here resulting in frictionless authorization as indicated by No Challenge. The merchant can now submit an Authorization request (message 15).

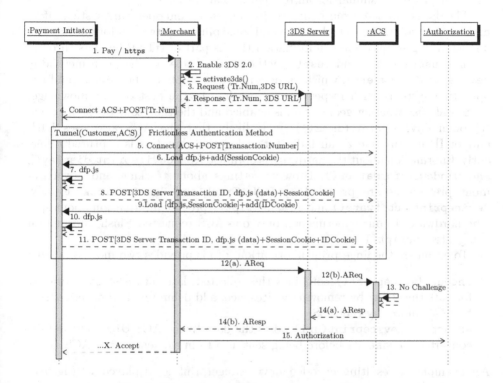

Fig. 2. Frictionless transaction sequence diagram.

2.3 3DS 2.0 Transaction Risk Assessment Data

The reverse engineering exercise shows how the ACS builds up a fingerprint of the payment initiator's machine. The ACS uses three pieces of information to establish a fingerprint, as discussed in this section:

1. the fingerprint information extracted from the browser using JavaScript
2. the 3DS 2.0 ID cookies fetched from the browser
3. the HTTP headers from payment initiator's browser forwarded by the merchant to the ACS

Fingerprint Data Using JavaScript. The JavaScript fingerprinting scripts that we analysed contain functions to (i) collect browser-supplied information from the end-user device, and (ii) forward the collected data to the 3DS 2.0 server as a single Base-64 encoded string (the 3DS 2.0 specifications [10] requires all the data messages to be in Base-64 format). Table 2 in Appendix A shows an exhaustive list of device attributes from card C1 to C5 that are passed from WB to the ACS. The loading and execution of dfp.js by the ACS as a part of the checkout process is similar for all test cards that we used.

The data obtained is quite diverse, from browser and operating system information, to display, time, geo-location and some plug-in software information. The fingerprinting script obtains information that is part of HTTP headers through the `nav.userAgent()` and `test()` methods (see Table 2). The main method is `deviceprint_browser()`, which gathers information about the browser and the operating system. With respect to geolocation, to the best of our knowledge, ACSs only use whether geolocation is enabled and the time zone of the machine (through `deviceprint_timez()`). It is likely that the ACS also uses URL and/or IP information as an indicator of location, but this is captured differently. Information about the hardware is obtained from `deviceprint_display()` and `window_information()`. Browser settings about tracking and advertisement preferences are provided by `DoNotTrack` and `Useofadblock`. Finally, `deviceprint_ software()` and `flashscript()` provide information about specific hardware. In our experiments, only one ACS requested Flash information using `flashscript()`.

To exchange the fingerprint information, dfp.js provides two more methods:

- `encode_deviceprint()` combines the collected data into a single string. It formats the string by removing whitespace, add delimiters and other characters as requires by the ACS.
- `asyncpost_deviceprint(url)` posts the data to the ACS URL. The data is converted to `base-64` before being sent as a form element to the ACS.

An example of resulting encoded device fingerprint is displayed in Fig. 5 of Appendix A.

Cookies. We found three types of cookies installed by the ACS on our machines. These are also described in Table 2, bottom rows. Full cookies are displayed in Fig. 6 of Appendix A.

- `Session_cookie`. Session cookie. The cookie is deleted after a user closes the session.
- `Test_cookie`. A test cookie with a name TESTCOOKIE and a value of Y was observed in exchanges during the transaction. This is set by the ACS server to determine if the user browser settings allowed cookies to be set.
- `IDcookie`. When the cardholder first enrolls into the 3DS 2.0 system, a token in the form of ID Cookie(s) is placed on the cardholder browser. The number of cookies installed varied from one to three. In all instances we found

that these cookies have a validity of three years from the date of installation and also have an HTTP-only security tag. The HTTP-only tag on a cookie protects it from being accessed by cross-domain websites.

Data Passed from Merchant to ACS. Data passed by the merchant in AReq message (step 12 of Fig. 2) contains elements that identify payment initiator browser configuration. For instance, Table A.1 in the EMV 3DS 2.0 specifications [10], suggests merchants to pass browser accept headers, language, screen details and user agent in the AReq message. The browser configuration helps the ACS to render a correct iframe for the cardholder device and may be used by the ACS to compare the information passed with dfp.js. To inspect the methods by which the merchant collects data to frame the AReq message, we referred to the merchant developer guides from payment networks Visa [36] and MasterCard [22] and payment service providers like PayPal [26], which suggest to use the HTTP headers passed on by the merchants during checkout as a part of WB's authentication data.

2.4   Discussion of 3DS 2.0 Implementations

There exist a number of notable differences between different implementations of 3DS 2.0. These differences can be categorized as follows:

1. difference in the use of 3DS protocol version
2. difference in transporting the device fingerprint: obfuscated versus plain-text
3. difference in amount of data collected as a fingerprint: JavaScript based versus HTTP headers and cookies only.

Difference in the Use of 3DS Protocol Version. We observed that the ACS associated with card C2 adds a layer of frictionless authentication over the 3DS 1.0 protocol. As opposed to 3DS 2.0, the browser collects and submits the AReq message with the transaction identifier, following the 3DS 1.0 specification. The ACS installs and collects the fingerprint data from the browser. Similar to 3DS 2.0 frictionless authentication, if this is the first 3DS 1.0 transaction from the machine, the ACS repeats messages to install IDCookie. Hereafter the transaction is processed according to the 3DS 1.0 specification. The ACS decision (to not challenge) is added to the ARes which is then forwarded to the merchant via the browser. Comparing the frictionless authentication of 3DS 1.0 and 3DS 2.0, both of these protocols capture static fingerprint data in base-64 encoded format and use HTTP-only IDCookies for TRA.

Difference in Device Fingerprint Implementation. In two cases (C2 and C5) we noticed that code obfuscation techniques were applied to make the JavaScript difficult to read and analyse. However, obfuscated codes has certain general limitations, in that, it is an encoding technique (not encryption) and needs to make sure that the code does not loose its functionality when executed over the system. The 3DS 2.0 device fingerprint JavaScript can still be run to obtain base-64 device fingerprint values.

Additionally, code obfuscation is a technique that has long been used by malware writers to hide their malicious code. Therefore there are plethora of security tutorials and freely available security tools designed to de-obfuscate JavaScript. The most reliable de-obfuscater that we discovered for our research is available as open source from Intelligent Systems Lab, Zurich [18].

Difference in Amount of Machine Data Collected. Although Table 2 shows an exhaustive list of all the data elements collected by the fingerprinting scripts and HTTP headers, the amount of data collected by each implementation of the JavaScript varies substantially. Some of the card issuers have no device fingerprinting JavaScript implemented at all. For example the card issuer of C3 implements frictionless authentication over 3DS 1.0 and only relies on the data received in the AReq message.

As a final note, the 3DS 2.0 protocol also defines an enrolment phase during which the card issuer collects the fingerprints from the card issuer computer and signs the fingerprint data to create ID cookies. The card holder computer is then 'tagged' through the usual cookie mechanism with these ID cookies. This enrolment phase is imperfect, in that it cannot be determined if the payment initiator who enrols a certain card is a legitimate user of the card.

3   Impersonation Attack

In this section we device a realistic impersonation attack, where an attacker uses obtained data described in the previous section and avoids being challenged for a second factor of authentication information. We first describe the precise attack model in Sect. 3.1, and then explain in Sect. 3.2 how the attack can be implemented, particularly related to obtaining the data. We carried out a number of experiments with different machines to demonstrate that the impersonation attack indeed succeeds, as we will describe in Sect. 3.3.

3.1   Attack Model

The objective of the attack is to use the credit card of another party to successfully complete an online purchase, despite the fact that the merchant uses 3DS 2.0. We assume that the attacker has no manner in which it could respond successfully to a challenge for a second factor of authentication information. Therefore, the objective of the attacker is to avoid a challenge and be allowed to complete a frictionless transaction. We consider the attack successful if an attacker avoids being challenged in situations the ACS actually should challenge.

To succeed, the attacker needs to obtain the credit card details, the cookies and the fingerprint data used for Transaction Risk Assessment, as described in the previous section. We do not assume any insider administrative access privileges of the attacker, neither at the payment initiator's machine nor at any of the 3DS 2.0 services. The attack assumes a perpetrator manages to install malware or plug-in that collects the necessary data from the payment initiator's machine, which includes running the JavaScript fingerprinting scripts–we will argue in the next section that that is not far-fetched. Shipping this data to the attacker allows the attacker to impersonate the cardholder's identity by crafting its 3DS 2.0 authentication data to be identical to that of the payment initiator.

3.2   Attack Implementation

The attack implementation needs to complete two stages: (1) obtaining the card and transaction risk assessment data, and (2) using the card and transaction risk assessment data.

Obtaining Card and Transaction Risk Assessment Data. In this stage, the attacker needs to obtain credit card details and machine fingerprint data (including cookies). There is a variety of reasons why this can only be done through a Man in the Browser.

A challenge is that the ID cookies (see Sect. 2.3) are http-only protected, that is, they cannot be read by any cross-domain web pages or through JavaScript. Browsers allow access to http-only cookies to extensions (including malware) because extensions are considered "trusted" once installed, whereas regular JavaScript is not. Cross-site scripting (XSS) [4,5,33], in which a script from a web site different than the merchant or 3DS 2.0 server attempts to access information such as cookies, is therefore not possible.

The most basic approach to obtain the required data is a browser plug-in that can sniff the browser communication to steal http-only cookies, record keystrokes to steal user payment data and execute device fingerprint JavaScript to capture the device fingerprints. More advanced malwares have such features, and are commonly available at [21,38], see for instance the ZeUS, SpyEye, Dridex and Tinba malwares. Once such malware is installed, it has an ability to obtain card transaction data for a purchase, the associated transaction risk assessment data described in the previous section, as well as the http-only cookies [12,19,34]. Malware SpyEye, for example, gets into a browser by prompting them to install a pdf reader or a flash player plug-in. Once into the browser, it updates itself as needed to configure fake entity certificates into the browser storage, record keystrokes, sniff the browser communication, records browser sessions and even capture screen shots [15,31].

Using the Obtained Card and Transaction Risk Assessment Data. The task in exploiting the obtained data is to impersonate the card holder in the attacker's browser. The attacker copies the cookies to their own browser, and initiates a transaction with the merchant of choice, even if the merchant uses 3DS 2.0. It also receives credit card details and machine fingerprint data, per the above. At payment, the attacker creates or replays the correct responses in the protocol of Fig. 2. Since there is no randomness in the fingerprint data, the same string of dfp.js data and HTTP headers obtained from the payment initiator's machine can be replayed on the attacker's machine using Fiddler (if required).

To tamper the data, fiddler breakpoints are added whenever the merchant and the ACS connect to the attacker's browser.

3.3   Attack Demonstration

The demonstration of the attack aims to identify if it indeed is possible to impersonate from a different machine a legitimate payment initiator. In this demonstration we use the data obtained from machine M1, using the experiment set-up from Fig. 1. We randomly selected a merchant with 3DS 2.0 enabled checkout and repeated transactions using all test cards C1 to C5 until M1 was trusted enough for frictionless authentication. The payment sessions made from M1 were recorded by the Fiddler proxy and were reused on a differently configured machine M2. We also show how a different machine M3 that is identically configured generates the same fingerprint. We note that M2 and M3 were on networks different from M1, so that the IP source address is different.

The approach behind our experiments is as follows. We conduct the experiment for the five credit cards mentioned. First, we ran an experiment to verify that transactions from the differently configured machine M2 are indeed challenged if one only enters card information (and does not impersonate the card holder with the risk assessment data). This verification was successful in all of the cases except for card C1 where lower value transactions below £10 were approved (we will get back to this in the next section). Then, we ran an experiment in which we used the obtained transaction risk assessment data to impersonate the card holder, to see if we were allowed to complete the purchase unchallenged, i.e., in frictionless mode. We initiated transactions where we selected products with values ranging between a £1 to £300, on an online merchant that uses 3D Secure 2.0 at checkout.

We were successfully able to execute the attack for all our test cards (C1–C5), in that the transactions were approved without any challenge by the card issuing bank's ACS. Interestingly, only for test card C5, the card issuer ACS issued challenges when the value of transaction reached above £200 (a typical transaction threshold set for frictionless authentication).

We ran a second experiment, using a different but identically configured machine M3, with the same hardware and software as M1. In so doing, we wanted to see if different machines that are configured identically generate identical Fingerprint data. This is to simulate a scenario where an attacker is unable to obtain the device fingerprint data but was able to get the ID cookies. In all cases, the transactions were allowed to go on without being challenged. Close inspection of the data that M3 sent to the merchant and ACS revealed that the transaction risk data was essentially identical for M1 and M3.

Reflection. For consumers it would be important to know how merchants and card issuers respond if the above attack took place. To that end, we communicated with the card issuing banks to understand how it would react if we were to report the fraudulent transactions that were made from the attacker machine. The card issuer for C3 asks cardholders to identify some previous transactions made from the victim's machine and would not register the transactions made from attacker machine as fraud. The card issuer for C3 also blocks and re-issues a new payment card to the card holder. However, in two cases (C4 and C5), the card issuer argued that the transactions must have originated from the actual card holder's machine. They argued the card holder is trying to perform a 'friendly fraud', and so is denied a refund of any reported losses. This paper shows that this conclusion is not necessarily correct.

4   Reverse Engineering Transaction Risk Assessment: Decision-Making

Section 2 established which data 3DS 2.0 implementations used in their transaction risk assessment, and we showed that with that data alone, one can execute an impersonation attack. However, this does not yet provide us with full understanding of the way risks are being assessed by the ACS. First, the ACS may use additional sources of data, for example, it may use header info from the protocol stack such as the IP source address or some other data about the card holder available from the card issuer. Secondly, the ACS will set certain rules about when to invoke a challenge. These rules will stipulate which fingerprint data to consider, and specifies bounds on data outside which the transaction will be challenged (e.g., a limit for the transaction amount).

There are number of questions of interest motivating further re-engineering of the risk assessment approach. First, it provides information about which variants of the impersonation attack would succeed and thus allows us to assess the security and risks behind online payment. Secondly, it serves as a suggestion for a possible methodology to assess consumer implications of Transaction Risk Assessment. TRA shifts liability to the card issuer but nevertheless still exposes consumers to possible distress when an impersonation attack is carried out. Arguably, it would be in the interest of the public if there is visibility in the implementation of Transaction Risk Assessment. The re-engineering experiments in this section demonstrates how to provide such visibility.

The experiments in this section obtain responses from the ACS for transactions in 8 different scenarios. These scenarios provide all combinations of the following three features:

1. submitting the machine data and IDCookie or not (from Sects. 2.3)
2. submitting different transaction values
3. submitting transactions from different regions

Table 1 shows selected results from our experiments on two test cards C1 and C2. Our set-up was identical to Sect. 3, with data obtained from machine M1 used on an alternative machine M2. Payments were initiated on two merchant websites (W1 and W2) that enforce 3DS user authentication. W1 is a web merchant local to the country where the victim card is issued and W2 is an overseas merchant for a victim's card.

Table 1. Experiments with and results for cards C1 and C2

Transaction number	Scenario	Machine data	Cookie ID	Value (£)	Region	Website	Card	Challenged?	Transaction status	Blocked
T1	S1	✓	✓	10	✓	W1	C1	✗	Approved	✗
T2							C2	✗	Approved	✗
T3						W2	C1	✗	Approved	✗
T4							C2	✗	Approved	✗
T5	S2	✓	✓	309	✓	W1	C1	✗	Approved	✗
T6							C2	✗	Approved	✗
T7						W2	C1	✗	Approved	✗
T8							C2	✗	Approved	✗
T9	S3	✓	✓	10	✗	W1	C1	✗	Approved	✗
T10							C2	✓	Declined	✗
T11						W2	C1	✗	Approved	✗
T12							C2	✗	Approved	✗
T13	S4	✓	✓	309	✗	W1	C1	✗	Approved	✗
T14							C2	✓	Declined	✓
T15						W2	C1	✗	Declined	✗
T16							C2	✓	Declined	✓
T17	S5	✗	✗	10	✓	W1	C1	✗	Approved	✗
T18							C2	✗	Approved	✗
T19						W2	C1	✗	Approved	✗
T20							C2	✓	Declined	✗
T21	S6	✗	✗	309	✓	W1	C1	✓	Declined	✗
T22							C2	✓	Declined	✓
T23						W2	C1	✓	Declined	✗
T24							C2	✓	Declined	✓
T25	S7	✗	✗	10	✗	W1	C1	✗	Approved	✗
T26							C2	✓	Declined	✗
T27						W2	C1	✗	Approved	✗
T28							C2	✓	Declined	✗
T29	S8	✗	✗	309	✗	W1	C1	✓	Declined	✗
T30							C2	✓	Declined	✓
T31						W2	C1	✗	Declined	✓
T32							C2	✓	Declined	✓

The rows give the various scenarios. For instance, Scenario S1 copies the machine data and the ID Cookie, for a low value transaction, within the region. With respect to the region, experiments for C1 and C2 were made from UK and Germany. Region (✓) indicates the transaction attempts were made from same country.

We see from Table 1 that different card issuers make different risk trade-offs. In particular, the card issuer of C1 allows more frictionless authentication, whereas the card issuing bank for C2 challenges the payment initiator more often. Comparing transaction T4 and T10 for C2 we see that C2's card issuer challenges every transaction if the web merchant is in a different country. Table 1 also shows that cards are generally treated more harshly, when transactions are made from different regions. For instance, when transactions were made from different country and machine data is corrupted there is more likelihood of being challenged and transaction being declined (as opposed to transactions when initiated from the country local to the card issuer).

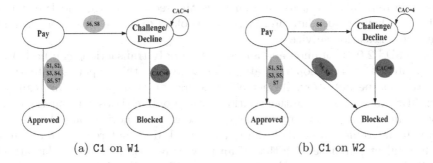

(a) C1 on W1   (b) C1 on W2

Fig. 3. Summarising C1's risk assessment outcomes over merchants W1 and W2

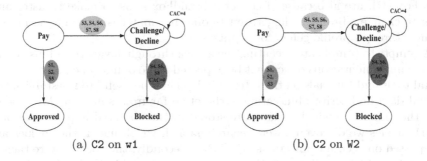

(a) C2 on w1   (b) C2 on W2

Fig. 4. Summarising C2's risk assessment outcomes over merchants W1 and W2

Figures 3 and 4 summarize the findings of Table 1. The 'states' are phases in the 3DS 2.0 transaction, where Pay indicates initiating payment, while the other refer to possible outcomes, either approved, challenged/declined or blocked. Note that for our purposes we do not have to differentiate between challenge and declined, they both imply that the transaction has not gone through as frictionless. The arcs are labelled with the scenario given in the second column of Table 1. CAC stands for challenge limit counter, which counts down from the limit to zero. Here, the limit is 4, and at the fifth attempt the card is blocked. For an impersonator, Figs. 3 and 4 serves as a reference map in case where more card details are stolen belonging to C1 and C2 card issuer.

5 Discussion of Card Payment Systems Security

The problem of authenticating cardholders in the online payment system is exacerbated by the desire to cause minimal friction during the checkout. The introduction of 3DS 2.0 addresses this security/usability challenge through the use of

Transaction Risk Assessment, and it is clear that the industry strongly favours such risk based approaches, given that in the US about 75% of the card issuers have adopted risk-based authentication [7]. However, as we have seen in this paper, the remaining security bottleneck is the secure storage and transfer of machine authentication data and http-only cookies from the customer machine to the authentication service.

Once 3DS 2.0 is common and authorization-only transactions can no longer be exploited, the impersonation attack presented in this paper is potentially attractive for perpetrators. Its net effect would be that perpetrators can use stolen 3DS 2.0 frictionless authentication data in online shops without the cardholder being negligent, exactly as was the case with authorization-only systems before the introduction of 3D Secure. The attack does not require to synchronize fraudulent purchase with that of an unwitting customer (as a relay attack would). Malware could easily be designed to sniff the 3DS 2.0 transaction data and later forward it to the attacker server. In fact, there are a number of such open source browser extension available and installed be thousands of browsers, e.g., HTTPWatch [17] and LiveHTTPHeaders [11]. Other developments, such as FraudFox [37], are also cause of concern. FraudFox aims to make it faster and easier to change a browser's fingerprint to one that matches that of a victim, for instance through profile generator scripts.

Attempts to complicate executing the attack through JavaScript obfuscation, as some implementations do, cannot be expected to be of much help. There exist several tools and tutorials on the Internet which can be useful to re-establish the original data and script obfuscation is therefore far from sufficient. More helpful is the manner in which cookies are stored in the observed implementations. All ID cookies we discovered were secure enabled, which means the cookies are only passed on secure connections (HTTPS). Secondly, the cookies were tagged http-only, which implies that the cookie is not readable to JavaScript. This prevents the cookies from being accessed by the cross-domain websites, i.e., prevents cross-site scripting attacks (XSS). Nevertheless, cookie storage in browsers remains non-secure unless the machine uses secure storage.

Technologically, an obvious solution for secure transfer would be to use private/public key approaches to encrypt and sign messages between the payment initiator and the 3DS Server. However, for such a solution to gain acceptance would require a separate trusted secure storage environment for cryptographic keys and certificates. The payment industry standards [27,28] require payment credentials, including keys and certificates to be stored in 'Tamper-Resistant Security Module,' which is defined as the set of hardware, software, firmware, or some combination thereof that implements cryptographic logic or process (including cryptographic algorithms and key generation) and is contained within the cryptographic boundary. Today's computer systems and their software systems are not provably secure enough. This issue has come up before, when Google first introduced Android pay with the concept of Host Card Emulation with Android KitKat 4.4 [14] in 2014. The key storage security model for Host Card Emulation was software controlled and contained the threat that an attacker may compromise the mobile OS to steal the credentials. This approach was therefore not found suitable to host EMV payment applications [1].

6   Related Work

This section details the comparison of card payment protocols and the security technologies they utilize. The section also highlights reported attacks on card payments that are made possible when any security feature is not included in the protocol. It would go too far to discuss the technologies and protocols in all detail, but we provide a summary discussion of the salient points.

Solutions for Card Present. This category corresponds to payments when the card is physically present. With magnetic stripe cards, data integrity and card authentication (confirming the identity of the card) features were not placed on the actual card itself. The data stored in a magnetic stripe is static and is kept in plain text which made magnetic stripe cards vulnerable to identity theft attacks [23], cardholder impersonation attacks [24] and card cloning attacks [6].

EMV extended the features of smart cards which provided a secure, "tamper proof", storage for the card's private cryptographic keys. The Chip and Pin protocol defined by EMV makes use of RSA public key infrastructure in three variants. The Static Data Authentication (SDA) card has a static signature which is generated by the issuer signed by using the issuer's private key, and written to the SDA card during manufacture. However, static signatures are used to approve every transaction, which makes SDA cards vulnerable to cloning attacks [6,25]. Dynamic Data Authentication (DDA) payments on the other hand generate a unique 'challenge-response' RSA signature (SDAD) for each transaction, including a nonce. Combined Data Authenitcation (CDA) improves upon DDA by encoding the Application Cryptogram into the signature rather than the transaction data. This makes DDA and especially CDA highly robust against any form of attack.

EMV contactless provides convenience to the customer by authenticating the card instead of actually prompting the cardholder to approve the transactions [9]. Fast DDA (fDDA) and CDA (fCDA) are enhanced versions of DDA and CDA of EMV chip and PIN, excluding the cardholder authentication methods from the protocol. Both DDA and SDA offer protection against known attacks on the payment system, however, each DDA and SDA enabled transactions would require the cardholders to prove their identity, thus adversely affecting usability. This was further addressed with an enhanced versions of fDDA and fCDA in EMV contactless [8].

Solutions for Card Not Present. If the card is not present, the situation is very challenging, as we have seen in this paper. As discussed in the introduction, the complications associated with the implementation of the 3DS 1.0 protocol made it possible for attackers to bypass its security features and perform identity theft attacks [16,23]. Chip Authentication Programme (CAP) and Transaction Authentication Numbers (TAN) [29,30] are two token generation technologies that consumers use to produce the answer to a challenge from the authorization system. Typically, this is done with a little machine that reads a credit card and/or uses a PIN to generate a response to a challenge. These are increasingly commonly provided by banks, but in many cases are limited to payments through banking transactions.

In conclusion, different payment protocols have been developed for different purposes. Satisfactory solutions find a successful combination of usability and security, and also manage the exposure to risk were something to go wrong. For instance, transaction limits on contactless cards as well as the frictionless 3DS 2.0 payment limit both manage the risk by limiting loss exposure of consumers. Not surprisingly, sound approaches challenge for a second factor information, through a PIN such as in Chip & PIN as well as Challenged Authentication in 3DS 2.0 or using token generators such as in CAP and TAN. However, these do not satisfy the usability wishes of merchants, leaving consumer with systems such as 3DS 2.0 that are designed to allow less secure payments and therefore inherently (and by design) expose consumers and card issuers to fraud.

7   Conclusion

This paper presents the first sizeable experimental study of real-life implementations of 3DS 2.0. Through a reverse engineering study, we map out the transaction sequences for frictionless transactions. In most implementations we encountered, the payment initiator's machine is fingerprinted through JavaScripts, except for the implementation based on 3DS 1.0. In our experiments we obtained further insights in the decision making of the authorization service, experimenting with transaction amounts and the region from which payment was initiated. We found that card issuers differ in terms of their risk appetite, with some issuers considerable more liberal in allowing transaction to proceed unchallenged.

We also demonstrated an impersonation attack against 3DS 2.0, using only data that is available from a reverse engineering exercise such as described in this paper. This impersonation attack is practically feasible and exploits that fingerprinting information from the payment initiator's machine can be recreated by malware or plug-ins, if installed on that machine. This exploit demonstrates the vulnerability of credit card based payment using browsers, compared to the more sophisticated security of mobile payment solutions.

A key question for the regulator is whether it was justified to allow risk assessment based approach to online payment security as result of the PSD II negotiations. A complete answer to that question would require insight in a variety of factors, including technological feasibility and acceptance, ease-of-use, liability, as well as vulnerabilities and threats. In addition, one would need deeper insight into the specifics of the risk assessment carried out by the card issuer. However, the reverse engineering approach introduced in this paper provides

```
encode_deviceprint()
```
version%3D2%26pm%5Ffpua%3Dmozilla%2F5%2E0%20%28windows%20nt%2010%2E0%3B%20win64%3B%20x64%29%20applewebkit/537%2E36%20%28kht
ml%2C%20like%20gecko%29%20chrome62%2E0%2E3202%2E94%20safari/537%2E36%7C5%2E0%20%28Windows%20NT%2010%2E0%3B%20Win64%3B%20x64
%29%20AppleWebKit/537%2E36%20%28KHTML%2C%20like%20Gecko%29%20Chrome/62%2E0%2E3202%2E94%20Safari/537%2E36%7CWin32%7Cen%2DUS%
26pm%5Ffpsc%3D24%7Ci280%7C720%7C680%26pm%5Ffpsw%3D%26pm%5Ffptz%3D5%2E5%26pm%5Ffpln%3D1ang%3Den%2DUS%7Csyslang%3D%7Cuserlang
%3D%26pm%5Ffpjv%3D0%26pm%5Ffpco%3D2

asyncpost_deviceprint(url)

dmVyc21vbiUzRDE1MjZwbSUiRmZwdWElMORtb3ppbGxhJTJGNSUyRTA1MjA1Mjh3aW5kb3dzJTIwbnQlMjAxMCUyRTA1MOI1MjB3aW42NCUzQiUyMHg2NCUyO
SUyMGFwcGxld2Via2l0JTJGNTM2JTIwJTI4a2h0bWwlMkM1MjBsaWt1JTIwZ2Vja281MjklMjBjaHJvbWUvNjU1MkUwJTJFMzMyNSUyRTE4MSUyMHNhZm
FyaS81Mzc1MkUzNiU3QzU1MkUwJTIwJTI4V21uZG93cyUyME5UJTIwMTA1MkUwJTNCJTIwV21uNjQlMOI1MjB4NjQ1Mjk1MjBBcHBsZVd1YktpdC81Mzc1MkU
zNiUyMCUyOEt1VE1MJTJDJTIwbGlrZSUyMEd1Y2tvJTI5JTIwQ2hyb211LzYxJTJFMCUyRTMzMjU1MkUxODE1MjBTYWZhcmkvNTM3JTJFMzYlNONXaW4zMiU3
Q2VuJTJEROI1MjZwbSUiRmZwc2M1MOQyNCU3QzEzODBjQ0NOM3NjglNOM3Mjg1MjZwbSUiRmZwc3c1MOQ1MjZwbSUiRmZwdHolMOQxJTI2cGOlNUZmcGxuJTNEb
GFuZyUzRGVuJTJEROI1NONzeXNsYW5nJTNEJTdDdXN1cmxhbmclMOQ1MjZwbSUiRmZwanYlMOQwJTI2cGOlNUZmcGNvJTNEMQ==

Fig. 5. Device fingerprint information encoded and sent to ACS.

```
3DS 2.0 Cookies
TESTCOOKIE=Y

ID Cookies
DMC=AiZVNMlzeO1ukqlXqlc7y%2BkM5Vi%2FGf%2Fa1D1CXYyox7%2F
XIr4kfbI1X04cU%2Bc%2BgWifX5WmJxQFY%2F18fH2ysgUzk3FUyhV
jlih3wcIx1G17uFJgBtWgMiZNjoRU6zut3NLLmlXPYLocrIlecsFsRW  w%2B6D6JRuya4fb
Hmsww1D0ogjzLL41tobs%3D
cy_track_user=C.28474910.1603347569
3DSSTBIP=yHWvyRz68jCQRAI7zSC3a5YqJJYDrgbtKRs50bDYIkJTU
Xik3MMi6BYEz5zbiX0awTcVFYARXRLY
```

Fig. 6. Device fingerprint information encoded and sent to ACS.

an interesting set of tools to find out how risk assessment is implemented and for the regulator to assess whether the resulting decisions are in the interest of customers.

A   Data Used for Transaction Risk Assessment

Table 2 shows an exhaustive list of device attributes from card C1 to C5 that are passed from WB to the ACS. The loading and execution of dfp.js by the ACS as a part of the checkout process is similar for all our test cards that we used. The 'Method' column indicates the functions implemented in the dfp.js that extract information from WB (for readability, in some cases we have simplified the method name). The details that are fetched in each function are shown in 'Attribute description' column of the table. The 'Source' column marks the origin of each attribute (JavaScript or HTTP). Finally, the rightmost column shows an example output value of each function.

Figures 5 and 6 show the encoded device fingerprint and the full cookie content, respectively.

Table 2. Data used for transaction risk assessment extracted by javascript file dfp.js.

Method	Attribute description	Source	Example values
nav.userAgent()	User agent(UA), OS	JavaScript	Mozilla/5.0 (Windows NT 10.0; Win64; x64) AppleWebKit/537.36 (KHTML, like Gecko) Chrome/60.0.3112.113 Safari/537.36
test()	Accepted MIME types/ Documents	HTTP header	text/html, application/xhtml+xml, application/xml; q = 0.9, image/webp, image/apng, */*q = 0.8
	Accepted charsets	HTTP header	utf-8, iso-8859-1; q = 0.5
	Accepted encodings	HTTP header	gzip deflate
	Accepted languages	HTTP header	en-US, en; q = 0.8
	ActiveX, GeckoActiveX	HTTP header	?1:0
	Adobe reader and components	HTTP header	?1:0
	XMLHttpReqest, Serializer, Parser support	HTTP header	Yes/No
deviceprint_browser()	UA(Version, cpuClass, language)	JavaScript	5.0 (Windows NT 10.0; Win64; x64) AppleWebKit/537.36 (KHTML, like Gecko) Chrome/60.0.3112.113 Safari/537.36; Win32; en-US
	navigator.appName	JavaScript	Netscape
	navigator.appCode Name	JavaScript	Mozilla
	navigator.appVersion	JavaScript	5.0 (Windows NT 10.0; Win64; x64) AppleWebKit/537.36 (KHTML, like Gecko) Chrome/61.0.3163.100 Safari/537.36
	navigator.appMinor Version	JavaScript	5.0
	navigator.vendor	JavaScript	GoogleInc
	navigator.userAgent	JavaScript	Mozilla/5.0 (Windows NT 10.0; Win64; x64) AppleWebKit/537.36 (KHTML, like Gecko) Chrome/65.0.3325.181 Safari/537.36
	navigator.oscpu	JavaScript	Windows NT 10.0
	navigator.platform	JavaScript	Win32
	navigator.security Policy	JavaScript	US & CA domestic policy or Export Policy
	navigator.onLine	JavaScript	True
	info_browser.name	JavaScript	Chrome
	info_browser.version	JavaScript	61.0.3163.100
	info_layout.name	JavaScript	Webkit
	info_layout.version	JavaScript	536.36
	info_os.name	JavaScript	win
	navigator.geoLocation	JavaScript	?1:0
deviceprint_display()	Screen's (colorDepth, width, height, availHeight, availWidth, HDPI, VDPI, Pixel Depth, ColorDepth, bufferDepth, FontSmoothing, Update interval)	JavaScript	2560*1440; 2560*1400; 24; 24

(*continued*)

Table 2. (*continued*)

Method	Attribute description	Source	Example values
window_ information()	innerWidth, innerHeight, outerWidth, outerHeight, length	JavaScript	675,473,1392,760,3
DoNotTrack	navigator.doNot Track	JavaScript	?1:0
Useofadblock	alert_test	javaScript	?1:0
deviceprint_ software()	Plugins installed	JavaScript	Adobe Acrobat, Macromedia Flash, Java, MS office, Cortana...
deviceprint_ time()	TimeZone	JavaScript	-60
deviceprint_ java()	Java enabled	JavaScript	?1:0
	Java Supported	JavaScript	?1:0
	Java Version	JavaScript	1.6. 1.8
	javaScript cookies support	JavaScript	?1:0
	Server cookies support	JavaScript	?1:0
	HTTP only support	JavaScript	?1:0
flashscript	Flash Version	FlashScript	WIN 28,0,0,126
	Flash Version	JavaScript	28,0,0
	Flash Details	FlashScript	Platform, Major Version, Minor Version, Capabilities (Audio, Accessibility, Audio support, MP3 support, Language, Manufacturer, OS, Pixel aspect, Color support, Dot per inch, Horizontal size, Vertical size, Video
	Number of Fonts	FlashScript	226
	List of Fonts	FlashScript	List of Fonts
deviceprint_ cookie()	Cookie enabled	JavaScript	?1:0
	Session cookie	HTTP header	!yEpKXp9eMDojNcc7zSC3a5YqJJYDrqVB23 H1Cy/yThmhX+omXVM933/...AIr8S7ldvbA==
	Test cookie	HTTP header	TESTCOOKIE=Y
	IDCookie	HTTP header	35BWzcxFkUu1aDdY%2B%2F%2FxvL3VrDuvgoXau%2FAgU %2BJqzYvZZoWiGPKKeYruvsGaPTeecduMcSLa%2FU lf1QGU07S89bddR3dVSFT2dwVeUOd%2FkXvaw7JknH xjFlk4...GY4I7drTK0nT CNJ%2BhHYW8Y5Wis%3D

References

1. Ahmad, Z., Francis, L., Ahmed, T., Lobodzinski, C., Audsin, D., Jiang, P.: Enhancing the security of mobile applications by using TEE and (U)SIM. In: 2013 IEEE 10th International Conference on Ubiquitous Intelligence and Computing and 2013 IEEE 10th International Conference on Autonomic and Trusted Computing, pp. 575–582, December 2013. https://doi.org/10.1109/UIC-ATC.2013.76
2. Alexa: Alexa - Top Sites by Category: Business/E-Commerce (2018). https://goo. gl/V52tcs
3. Ali, M.A., Arief, B., Emms, M., van Moorsel, A.: Does the online card payment landscape unwittingly facilitate fraud? IEEE Secur. Priv. **15**(2), 78–86 (2017)
4. AOWASP: Cross-site scripting (XSS) OWASP (2018). https://goo.gl/x54ner

5. Barth, A., Caballero, J., Song, D.: Secure content sniffing for web browsers, or how to stop papers from reviewing themselves. In: 2009 30th IEEE Symposium on Security and Privacy, pp. 360–371. IEEE (2009)

6. van den Breekel, J., Ortiz-Yepes, D.A., Poll, E., de Ruiter, J.: EMV in a nutshell. Technical report, Radboud Universiteit Nijmegen (2016)

7. CardinalCommerce: Use of consumer authentication in ecommerce, annual survey 2017: The fraud practice (2017). https://goo.gl/z2mByt

8. Emms, M., Arief, B., Freitas, L., Hannon, J., van Moorsel, A.: Harvesting high value foreign currency transactions from EMV contactless credit cards without the PIN. In: Proceedings of the 2014 ACM SIGSAC Conference on Computer and Communications Security, CCS 2014, pp. 716–726. ACM, New York (2014). https://doi.org/10.1145/2660267.2660312. http://doi.acm.org/10.1145/2660267.2660312

9. Emms, M., Arief, B., Little, N., van Moorsel, A.: Risks of offline verify PIN on contactless cards. In: Sadeghi, A.-R. (ed.) FC 2013. LNCS, vol. 7859, pp. 313–321. Springer, Heidelberg (2013). https://doi.org/10.1007/978-3-642-39884-1_26

10. EMVCo: 3D Secure 2.0 (2017). https://goo.gl/d1ksLf

11. E.solutions: Live HTTP Header (2018). https://www.esolutions.se/

12. Etaher, N., Weir, G.R., Alazab, M.: From ZeuS to ZitMo: trends in banking malware. In: 2015 IEEE Trustcom/BigDataSE/ISPA, vol. 1, pp. 1386–1391. IEEE (2015)

13. EU Council: Directive (EU) 2015/2366 (2015). https://goo.gl/psyvps

14. GoogleAndroid: Android pay (2014). https://www.android.com/pay/

15. Nayyar, H.: Clash of the Titans: ZeuS v SpyEye. SANS Institute InfoSec Reading Room (2010). https://www.sans.org/reading-room/whitepapers/malicious/clash-titans-zeus-spyeye-33393

16. Herley, C., van Oorschot, P.C., Patrick, A.S.: Passwords: if we're so smart, why are we still using them? In: Dingledine, R., Golle, P. (eds.) FC 2009. LNCS, vol. 5628, pp. 230–237. Springer, Heidelberg (2009). https://doi.org/10.1007/978-3-642-03549-4_14

17. HTTP Watch: HttpWatch 11: HTTP Sniffer for Chrome, IE, iPhone and iPad (2018). https://www.httpwatch.com/

18. Intelligent Systems Lab: JS NICE: Statistical renaming, Type inference and Deobfuscation (2018). http://jsnice.org/

19. Kim, D., Kwon, B.J., Dumitraş, T.: Certified malware: measuring breaches of trust in the windows code-signing PKI. In: Proceedings of the 2017 ACM SIGSAC Conference on Computer and Communications Security, CCS 2017, pp. 1435–1448. ACM, New York (2017). https://doi.org/10.1145/3133956.3133958. http://doi.acm.org/10.1145/3133956.3133958

20. King, R.: Verified by Visa: bad for security, worse for business - Richard's Kingdom (2009). https://goo.gl/NgUUvn

21. MalShare: Malware Repository for Researchers (2018). https://malshare.com/

22. Mastercard: Merchant SecureCode implementation guide (2014). https://goo.gl/DyQ7Jb

23. Murdoch, S.J., Anderson, R.: Verified by visa and mastercard securecode: or, how not to design authentication. In: Sion, R. (ed.) FC 2010. LNCS, vol. 6052, pp. 336–342. Springer, Heidelberg (2010). https://doi.org/10.1007/978-3-642-14577-3_27

24. Murdoch, S.J., Anderson, R.: Security protocols and evidence: where many payment systems fail. In: Christin, N., Safavi-Naini, R. (eds.) FC 2014. LNCS, vol. 8437, pp. 21–32. Springer, Heidelberg (2014). https://doi.org/10.1007/978-3-662-45472-5_2

25. Murdoch, S.J., Drimer, S., Anderson, R., Bond, M.: Chip and PIN is broken. In: 2010 IEEE Symposium on Security and Privacy, pp. 433–446. IEEE (2010). https://doi.org/10.1109/SP.2010.33
26. PayPal: PayPal Pro - 3D secure developer guide (2018). https://goo.gl/7mPWWt
27. PCIDSS: Payment card industry (PCI) data security standard requirements and security assessment procedures (2016). https://goo.gl/PNSEq3
28. PCISCC: Payment card industry (PCI) hardware security module (HSM) security requirements (2009). https://goo.gl/JQKH3T
29. RedTeam Pentesting: Man-in-the-Middle Attacks against the chipTAN comfort Online Banking System. Technical report, RedTeam Pentesting (2009). https://www.redteam-pentesting.de/publications/2009-11-23-MitM-chipTAN-comfort_RedTeam-Pentesting_EN.pdf
30. RedTeam Pentesting: New banking security system iTAN not as secure as claimed. Technical report, RedTeam Pentesting (2009). https://www.redteam-pentesting.de/en/advisories/rt-sa-2005-014/-new-banking-security-system-itan-not-as-secure-as-claimed
31. Sood, A.K., Zeadally, S., Enbody, R.J.: An empirical study of HTTP-based financial botnets. IEEE Trans. Dependable Secure Comput. 13(2), 236–251 (2016)
32. Telerik: Fiddler web debugging tool (2018). https://goo.gl/BURSaH
33. Ter Louw, M., Venkatakrishnan, V.: Blueprint: robust prevention of cross-site scripting attacks for existing browsers. In: 2009 30th IEEE Symposium on Security and Privacy, pp. 331–346. IEEE (2009)
34. Thomas, K., et al.: Data breaches, phishing, or malware?: understanding the risks of stolen credentials. In: Proceedings of the 2017 ACM SIGSAC Conference on Computer and Communications Security, CCS 2017, pp. 1421–1434. ACM, New York (2017). https://doi.org/10.1145/3133956.3134067. https://doi.acm.org/10.1145/3133956.3134067
35. Visa Inc: 3D Secure (2017). https://goo.gl/TZSTEc
36. Visa Inc: Visa Developer Centre (2018). https://goo.gl/8dDqWv
37. WickyBay: FRAUDFOX VM, WickyBay Store (2017). https://goo.gl/aAZY1K
38. Zeltser, L.: (2018). https://zeltser.com/malware-sample-sources/

Short Paper: Making Contactless EMV Robust Against Rogue Readers Colluding with Relay Attackers

Tom Chothia[1], Ioana Boureanu[2(✉)], and Liqun Chen[2]

[1] School of Computer Science, University of Birmingham, Birmingham, UK
[2] Department of Computer Science, University of Surrey, Guildford, UK
icboureanu@gmail.com

Abstract. It is possible to relay signals between a contactless EMV card and a shop's EMV reader and so make a fraudulent payment without the card-owner's knowledge. Existing countermeasures rely on *proximity checking*: the reader will measure round trip times in message-exchanges, and will reject replies that take longer than expected (which suggests they have been relayed). However, it is the reader that would receive the illicit payment from any relayed transaction, so a rogue reader has little incentive to enforce the required checks. Furthermore, cases of malware targeting point-of-sales systems are common. We propose three novel proximity-checking protocols that use a trusted platform module (TPM) to ensure that the reader performs the time-measurements correctly. After running one of our proposed protocols, the bank can be sure that the card and reader were in close proximity, even if the reader tries to subvert the protocol. Our first protocol makes changes to the cards and readers, our second modifies the readers and the banking backend, and our third allows the detection of relay attacks, after they have happened, with only changes to the readers.

1 Introduction

Wireless and particularly contactless systems, such as the EMV (Europay, Mastercard and Visa) contactless-payment protocols, are vulnerable to *relay attacks*. That is, an adversary can stand near a victim (e.g., a bankcard) and relay signals from that device to a second attacker found near the authentication-verifying party (e.g., a payment terminal). This type of attack has already been used to steal cars[1]. As relayed messages take longer to travel then direct messages, *proximity-checking* or *distance-bounding* (DB) protocols [1] measure the round trip time (RTT) it takes for some authenticating party, called *prover*, to answer challenges sent by an authentication-verifying party, called *verifier*. If the

---

[1] See e.g. http://www.bbc.com/news/av/uk-42132804/relay-crime-theft-caught-on-camera.

T. Chothia and I. Boureanu—Contributed equally to this work.

© International Financial Cryptography Association 2019
I. Goldberg and T. Moore (Eds.): FC 2019, LNCS 11598, pp. 222–233, 2019.
https://doi.org/10.1007/978-3-030-32101-7_14

RTT is within a given bound, then there is a low likelihood that a relay attack occurred. As such, the contactless version of the EMV protocol has recently been enhanced with such a relay-counteraction mechanism [5] (see Fig. 2), in the style of a previously proposed DB protocol [4]. As with other DB protocols, these newly proposed EMV protocols assume that the reader is honest. However, this threat-model conflicts with the setting of EMV. I.e, in the current EMV protocols, the entity tasked with enforcing the proximity checks is also the one that stands to benefit if these checks are ignored: an EMV reader has an incentive to be dishonest as it will receive the payments from any (relayed) transaction. EMV readers have also been the target of malware (see e.g. [7]), which could also override the RTT-measuring software.

	Prevents collusive relay attacks	Provides audit-able evidence	Reader may be offline	Changes to card	Changes to EMV reader	Changes to bank system backend	Checks carried out by
Protocol PayCCR	✓	✓	✓	Yes	Yes	No	card
Protocol PayBCR	✓	✓	×	No	Yes	Yes	bank
Protocol PayBCRv2	×	✓	✓	No	Yes	No	auditor

Fig. 1. A summary of the protocols presented in this paper

The above suggests that one should assume that the EMV reader could collude with relay attackers in mounting fraudulent payments. Moreover, the current relay-counteracting EMV protocols [4,5] do not provide any evidence that the protocols were run correctly. So even if a complaint by a card-holder is made, it would not be possible to audit the EMV reader and see whether the distance-bounding checks had been performed. In this paper, we address these shortcomings. Concretely, our contributions are as follows:

I. We define the notion of *collusive relay attacks* to mean relay attacks in which the authentication-verifying party (EMV reader) can collude with a MiM relayer to mount a relay attack against an authentication and payment scheme; we define an attacker model and security definition for this new type of attack.

II. We present three new EMV protocols that defend against such a malicious reader. A summary of these protocols is given in Fig. 1. A complicating factor is that bank cards have no accurate clock. Therefore, the card cannot distance-bound the reader. The complex EMV infrastructure also makes distance bounding between the bank and the card impractical. Our solutions show how adding a TPM as a hardware root of trust on-board the reader can solve these issues.

III. We discuss our design choices, and provide a high-level argument w.r.t. the resistance to collusive relaying of the EMV protocols we propose.

2   Background and Foundational Aspects

Contactless EMV. Past work [4] has showed an effective relay attack against contactless EMV protocols, and suggested a version of contactless EMV called *PaySafe* that deters relay attacks. Following this, the main idea of the PaySafe protocol was added to the MasterCard specification (EMV contactless specifications v3.1 [5]) and yielded MasterCard's Relay Resistant Protocol (RRP). Part of this protocol is shown in Fig. 2.

As with all EMV protocols, the card includes: (1) a private key Pv_C; (2) a symmetric key K_M that it shares with the bank; (3) a certificate chain $Cert_{Pv_{CA}}(Pub_C)$ for the card's public key Pub_C. The reader has the public key Pub_{CA} of the Certificate Authority, and so can extract and verify the card's public key. RRP starts with a setup phase (not shown in Fig. 2), in which the reader asks the card what protocols it supports and selects one to run. The card and reader then generate single-use random numbers N_C and UN, respectively. The reader then sends an "EXCHANGE RELAY RESISTANCE DATA" command to the card, which contains the nonce UN. The card immediately replies with its own nonce N_C, and the reader times this round trip time. The card also provides timing information, which tells the reader how long this exchange should take. The reader compares the time taken with the timing information on the card. If the time taken was too long, the reader stops the transaction as a suspected relay attack. Otherwise, the reader requests that the card generates a "cryptogram" (a.k.a. AC). The card uses the unique key K_M, which it shares with the bank, to encrypt its application transaction counter ATC (which equals the number of times the card has been used). This encryption equates to a session-key denoted K_S. The cryptogram AC is a MAC keyed with K_S of data including the ATC, the nonce UN, and the transaction information. As the reader cannot check the AC, the card generates the "Signed Dynamic Application Data ($SDAD$)": the card's signature on a message including UN, amount, currency, ATC, N_C. The reader checks the $SDAD$ before accepting the payment.

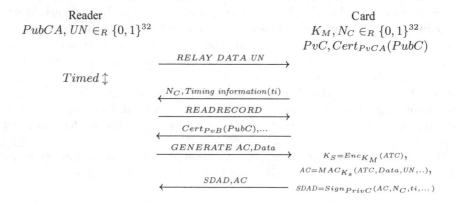

Fig. 2. MasterCard's relay-protected EMV

On TPMs. The Trusted Platform Module (TPM 2.0) is a hardware root of trust (see https://trustedcomputinggroup.org). It provides two measures of time: one is "Clock" (see page 205 of [8]) and the other is "Time" (see page 176 of [8]). Time is a 64-bit ms count from when the TPM was powered up. Clock shows the real time; this is set when the TPM is created and must be "accurate even if there is no reliable external clock" [8]. The TPM2_GetTime() command takes the handle for a signature scheme and some input, and it returns a signature over TPM-AttestedTime=(Clock, Time) and the input. As such, TPM2_GetTime() can produce a signed version of a timestamped nonce, with attested time-information.

Attacks onto TPM-AttestedTime are mainly relevant w.r.t. the TPM Clock (see 36.3 and 36.6 [8]), as this has a non-volatile dimension, unlike Time. Notably, if the TPM is powered down, the Clock value is correct when the TPM reboots. The threats w.r.t. Clock documented by TCG, are as follows: (a) if adversaries can manipulate external software and local clocks like the CMOS clock on PC platforms, but if the TPM is not physically attacked, then the Clock's accuracy (w.r.t. a small deviation from real time) is assumed to remain within "acceptable tolerance" (see page 206 of [8]); (b) the Clock value can only be deviated forward, i.e., it cannot be rewound.

3 System Setup, Threat Model and Security Requirements

Protocol Entities. Past distance-bounding work has involved a *"prover"* who demonstrates to a *"verifier"* that it is close (and possibly authenticates too). Our framework is different to this past work on DB. Rather than the two entities of the classic DB model, we have four entities in our setting: a *"card"* that interacts with an *"EMV reader"* in a DB-fashion, the EMV reader will have an onboard hardware root of trust (a *"TPM"*), and the reader will send evidence for the transaction to the *"bank system backend"*.

General Infrastructure and PKI. Our protocols use EMV's existing Public Key Infrastructure (PKI), augmented to support TPMs inside the readers. We assume that Certificate Authorities (CAs) have issued certificates on the TPMs' endorsement keys, that the banks, cards and EMV-related authorities have access to the right key-chains/certificate-chains to verify all certificates and, notably, first extract the TPMs endorsement keys. These endorsement keys are then use to verify other certificates sent by the TPM, e.g., certificating the public counterpart of a TPM's signing key. In this way, the bank and cards can, for instance, verify signatures issued by the TPM via a full chain-of-trust, up to the CAs.

Our Participants' and Communication Model. Between any card and any reader, we assume that all messages (irrespective of their bit-length) travel at an a-priori fixed constant speed, which is also the maximum speed of these radio interfaces. We assume that communication between the reader's software and the onboard TPM happens also at the maximum speed of the link between the two. We also assume that cards and readers can run several concurrent executions of the protocols. Such *honest* communication is possible if the card and the reader are no further than an a-priori fixed distance from one another.

Computation Model. Previous DB models have assumed a single, static RTT bound for all devices. However, our protocols (and MasterCard's RRP) use a card specific time bound. To help us formalise this we make the following two definitions:

Definition 1 (Proximity-Checking Phase). *The* proximity-checking phase *of a protocol is an exchange of challenges and responses, which is timed by the challenger.*

Definition 2 (Card Time-Bounding Functions t_d(cardID) and t(cardID)). *We call* t *(cardID) a time-bounding function; it maps a card identified by cardID to the time, in time units, taken for that card to perform the computational part of the timed phase.*

We call t_d *(cardID) a d-time-bounding function; it defines the duration of the proximity-checking phase when executed by a card identified by cardID and physically found at a distance no larger than d from the reader. We write just* t_d*, when cardID is implicit.*

Typically, t_d(cardID) = tcardID + "time for all messages of the proximity-checking phase to travel distance $(2 \times d)$". We now define DB protocols with variable time limits.

Definition 3 (Contactless EMV Protocol with Proximity-checking Phase of Distance-Bound d). *A contactless EMV protocol with proximity-checking phase of distance-bound d (or, for short, contactless EMV protocol with distance-bound d) is a protocol between the EMV entities card, EMV reader and bank system backend, that has a proximity-checking phase. The protocol has additional parameters defined by the time-bounding function t(cardID) and the d-time-bounding function t_d(cardID), for each cardID. The reader side of the protocol may make use of a TPM. One of the EMV entities checks that the time recorded for the proximity-checking phase is inline with t_d(cardID). If this is not the case, then the protocol finishes unsuccessfully.*

Definition 4 (Correct Execution). *Consider a contactless EMV protocol with proximity-checking phase of distance-bound d. If all entities in the system follow the protocol and the distance between the card and the EMVreader is no larger than d, then the protocol finishes successfully and a correct cryptogram AC for a payment will be issued by the card, and it will be eventually accepted by the bank.*

Our Attacker Model. Combining DB [3,6] and EMV models [2], we assume an attacker that also completely controls a number of cards, including all their key material. The attacker can act and use the corrupted card's keys at any location. Unlike in previous DB models [6], the attacker can know the readers' key/secret material and can control the software on the readers to make it perform arbitrary actions.

We assume that the TPM is as secure as is claimed in its specification, see page 3, Sect. 2. That is, 1. our attacker cannot tamper with the initial setup of the TPM's Clock; 2. our attacker cannot mount any physical attack on the TPM's time-reporting TPM-AttestedTime=(Clock, Time); 3. our attacker can deviate the TPM's Clock only by making it go forward w.r.t. to the real time by a negligible fraction.

We assume the attacker cannot make the messages travel faster between the card and the reader, nor on the link between the reader and the TPM; recall from the communication model that both these interfaces are respectively set at their the maximum communication speeds (which is also constant).

We assume all cryptographic primitives used in the EMV protocol are secure w.r.t. their respective threat-models, e.g., signatures are *unforgeable* etc.

Our Security Requirements. The main aim of our attacker is to trick the bank system backend to accept an AC generated by a card that was not in close proximity with a reader. We formalise this as:

Definition 5 (Resistance to Collusive Relaying). *A contactless EMV protocol of distance-bound d is resistant to collusive-relaying if, for any attacker in the threat and communication model above, for any payment AC that the bank system backend accepts from a card that is not controlled by the attacker, the card must have been within distance d of the reader for the time bounding phase that lead to the generation of the AC.*

4   EMV Protocols Resistant to Collusive-Relaying

4.1   PayCCR: A Protocol Compatible with the Current Banking Backend

Our first protocol, *PayCCR*, is shown in Fig. 3. It modifies the EMV protocol on the card and the EMV reader's side, yet the bank system backend remains unchanged from the current standard. As with MasterCard's RRP protocol, the time bound t_d(cardID) to be enforced for the proximity-checking phase is embedded in each card. Below, we write this bound as t_d. This time bound is chosen when the card is created, based on its processing speed, to ensure that the card and EMV reader are less than d distance from each other. The full protocol starts off with a standard EMV set up phase, in which the payment app is selected. The reader starts the proximity-checking stage of the protocol by sending the card a certificate chain for the TPM's public part of the signing key.

The EMV reader will then send a nonce N_R to the TPM to be timestamped. The TPM receives this bitstring N_R passed to the $TPM2\_GetTime$ command,

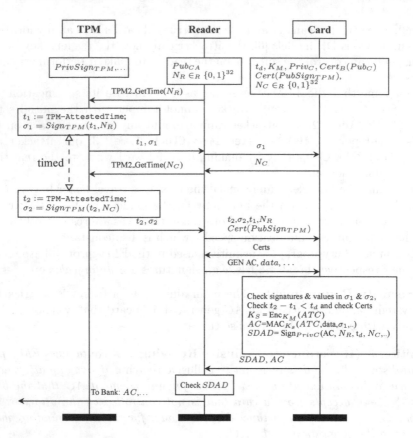

Fig. 3. PayCCR: protection against collusive-relay and no changes to the bank's backend

the TPM timestamps it with `TPM-AttestedTime`, and using the randomised signing algorithm ECDSA produces the signature σ_1. Then, the EMV reader forwards σ_1 to the card. This should be done by the reader at the maximum speed of the interface, i.e., as each bit is received from the TPM it should be forwarded to the NFC interface. We allow the nonces to be split into bytes and the time stamping and nonce exchange to be repeated four times, once per byte. The average of the four time differences would be compared with t_d.

The nonce N_C is pre-generated, thus making the reply time fast. The TPM timestamps N_C (producing σ_2), and the reader sends the signature σ_2 to the card. The card sends its certificates to the EMV reader, which then asks the card to generate the AC to complete a payment. Before generating the AC the card checks the TPM certificate provided by the EMV reader, verifies the signatures on the timestamps σ_1 & σ_2, and ascertains that the time bound is less than its allowed maximum value t_d. If these checks pass, then the card generates an AC and $SDAD$, which are sent to bank via the reader, and checked by the bank as normal. If any of the card's checks fail, then the card sends a declined message to the reader and aborts.

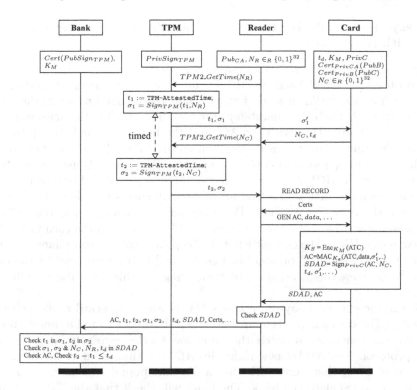

Fig. 4. PayBCR: Contactless EMV protection with no changes to the card

Discussion. This protocol, and the others herein, make two main assumptions:

1. that a time bound t_d for each card can be apriori set;
2. dishonest reader cannot receive and/or send proximity-checking-phase messages faster than an honest reader, except for an insignificant amount.

We detail on the second assumption above. The assumption, present in our threat model in the previous section, implies that the TPM and NFC APIs used must run at their maximum speeds. Even so, a dishonest reader may gain some advantage by running at a faster clock speed than an honest reader. However, as the only effective timed action undertaken by the reader is forwarding bits from the TPM interface to the NFC interface, an overclocked reader can only gain an advantage in the order of nanoseconds (referred to in assumption 2 as an "insignificant amount"). Such an advantage would translate into a theoretical relay attack (including w.r.t. our definition), however –in practice– it would be a relay over a distance larger than the bound only by a few centimetres. We could tighten Def. 5 to exclude such practically irrelevant attacks. Instead, we choose to just discard it out right, on grounds of it being insignificant. In the conclusions, we discuss other ways of deterring/detecting readers running in an overclocked mode in the proximity-checking phase.

4.2 PayBCR: A Collusive-Relay Resistant Protocol Compatible with RRP Cards

Our second protocol, *PayBCR*, does not modify the card's side w.r.t. the current RRP protocol [5]. PayBCR achieves this in three steps: (1) it uses a timestamped signature from the TPM instead of what is now the reader's nonce in the EMV protocol v3.1; (2) the TPM timestamps the card nonce; (3) both timestamps are passed to the bank along with the AC, and the bank can check the difference between the timestamps to ensure the card and EMV reader where close. Additionally, the timing information ti on the current RRP cards is used as our time bound t_d. As with RRP, storing the time bound on the card and signing it avoids the bank having to maintain a look up table of all card's time bounds. The full protocol is shown in Fig. 4. The EMV reader sends its nonce N_R to the TPM to be time stamped. The signature σ_1 from the TPM is sent to the card instead of the first nonce UN in the current RRP. To keep the protocol compliant with the current contactless EMV protocol in Fig. 2, this bitstring we send to the card should be shorter, this is achieved by truncating σ_1; this truncation we denote as σ_1'.

Like in the current relay-protecting EMV protocol, the card replies with its nonce N_C. The card's nonce is immediately sent to the TPM to be timestamped. The protocol continues in nearly the same way as the current relay-protecting EMV protocol. The *SDAD* now signs the AC, the timing information and σ_1' (in place of UN), this along with the card's time-bound t_d, σ_1, σ_2, t_1 and t_2 and the AC are sent to the bank. The bank will check that the TPM's signed timestamps match the nonce values used in the AC, the timing information is correctly signed, and the time difference between the nonces is less than this time bound. Other details, not in Fig. 4, are either as in protocol PayCCR or are self-explanatory.

PayBCRv2: As a variant of our PayBCR, we can have the EMV readers store the TPM's signed timestamps σ_1 & σ_2, and the time values t_1 & t_2, the *SDAD* and card certificates, and not send them to the bank system backend, i.e., the protocol would be backwards compatible with both the current standards for the bank system backend and cards; only changes to the EMV readers are required.

Such a variant would entail that a collusive-relay attack could not be stopped in real time. Rather this version of the protocol would be suited for when a card owner raises a complaint, or for the bank to detect possible fraud a-posteriori. At such a point, the EMV reader would be audited and all of the transactions would be checked.

Discussion. This protocol variant would be much easier to deploy than those discussed above, EMV reader manufacturers could add this protection unilaterally, without needing to make any changes to the current EMV specifications or the bank system backend. Making changes to the specifications for cards would be a slow process requiring input from many stakeholders, and making changes to the bank system backend would be expensive, due to the dedicated hardware banks generally use. Therefore, this protocol variant has a clear advantage over the others. The disadvantage of this protocol variant is that collusive-relay attacks could still be carried out and only detected during an audit. However, this is in keeping with much of the rest of the EMV security model that allows some fraud and aims to detect, roll back or refund it after the event. Our protocol would make any malicious interference by the EMV reader in the proximity-checking phase detectable, meaning that the bank could refuse payments to the reader, if the audit information was missing or did not check out, so removing all motivation for this attack. Therefore, while the protections provided by the PayBCRv2 protocol are the weakest, it is perhaps the most practical to introduce.

Lastly, whilst our protocols implicitly timestamp payments, in this work we do *not* investigate links between correct/secure payments and their associated transaction time.

5 High-Level Security Assessment

Our protocols do not alter any security property of the current contactless EMV; the authentication properties of our protocols follow from the basic EMV protocol. As in EMV, the freshness from the card and the reader stop replay attacks. The AC is generated based on a key shared only between the card and the bank, so the bank can be sure that this came from a card; the reader gets similar guarantees from the signed $SDAD$.

Assume protocol PayCCR is run in the presence of an arbitrary attacker in our model, and an AC is sent out by a card not controlled by the attacker. In PayCCR if the bank system backend accepted an AC then:

1. The backend checks the AC based on the card key. So, the AC must have come from that card (which is not controlled by the attacker), therefore this card will have executed its algorithm, i.e., performed the required checks.
2. The card checks the certificate for the TPM's signing key. Therefore, the card can be sure of the timestamps signed by the TPM.
3. Since the card checks that σ_1 includes the timestamp t_1, the card can be sure that the σ_1 message originated at the EMV reader's TPM at time t_1.
4. The card will only broadcast N_C after it has received σ_1.
5. The card checks that σ_2 includes its nonce N_C and the time t_2, therefore it can be sure that the reader received the nonce N_C before time t_2.
6. Together (3), (4) and (5) ensure that the RTT of the messages σ_1 and N_C was at least $t_2 - t_1$ and that these messages went between the card and the TPM.
7. The card knows its time-bound t_d. So, checking that $t_2 - t_1 < t_d$ ensures that the card was within distance d of the reader, which gives us resistance to collusive-relaying (Definition 5).

We now place ourselves in the setting where the protocol PayBCR is run in the presence of an arbitrary attacker in our model and an AC is sent out by a card not controlled by the attacker. For our second protocol, PayBCR, recall that the checks are carried out by the bank system backend, therefore the following reasoning applies:

1. Checking that σ_1' and N_C are in the $SDAD$ ensures that the reader/attacker sent σ_1' to the card, and that the card thereafter used the nonce N_C.
2. As σ_1 is a high-entropy, randomised signature, checking that σ_1 signs t_1 means that σ_1 was generated at time t_1 and cannot have been sent to the card before this.
3. By looking at the timestamps in σ_1 and in σ_2, and at the fact that σ_2 also signs N_C, the bank system backend will know that N_C was only broadcast by the card after t_1 (and in fact after σ_1 was received) and before t_2. The bank system backend also checks this against $SDAD$, which signs N_C, σ_1.
4. Together (2), (3) and (4) guarantee that the round trip time between the card and the EMV reader's TPM was less than $t_2 - t_1$.
5. Checking that t_d is in the $SDAD$ ensures that the correct time-bound for the specific card is used in the checks.
6. Checking that $t_2 - t_1 < t_d$ together with (5) and (6) ensures that the distance between the card and the reader was within distance d of each other.

6   Conclusions

In this paper, we presented three protocols that show how –by using a TPM– rogue readers can be stopped from subverting the relay-detecting checks in contactless EMV. The three protocols with different levels of compatibility with the current EMV framework. We also put forward an attacker model (in line with using TPMs as roots of trust, considering dishonest EMV readers, etc.) and a new security definition that protects against reader-assisted relaying in EMV protocols.

In one line of future work, we wish to develop a new, fully-fledged symbolic formalism and a provably-secure models that can be used to prove the correctness and security w.r.t. collusive relaying.

Moreover, we plan to implement our protocols to show that our proposed use of the TPM can lead to a workable EMV protocol with such protections against strong relaying. For PayCCR, we will measure the time it takes for ubiquitous smart-cards to verify different randomised signatures.

We will investigate the second assumption of our designs, i.e., that reader's computations in the proximity-checking phase being kept at a constant amount. A step further to investigate is to certify the read/write speed of the readers via a TPM (i.e., using TPM_GetQuote or other host-attestation methods); this type of method can add security guarantees but it would clearly require further checks by the bank.

Acknowledgments. The authors acknowledge the support of the NCSC-funded "TimeTrust" project. The authors also thank all anonymous reviewers, as well as Urs Hengartner for helpful comments. Also, Ioana Boureanu thanks Anda Anda for interesting discussions on this topic.

References

1. Brands, S., Chaum, D.: Distance-bounding protocols. In: Helleseth, T. (ed.) EURO-CRYPT 1993. LNCS, vol. 765, pp. 344–359. Springer, Heidelberg (1994). https://doi.org/10.1007/3-540-48285-7_30
2. Brzuska, C., Smart, N.P., Warinschi, B., Watson, G.J.: An analysis of the EMV channel establishment protocol. In: Conference on Computer & Communications Security (2013)
3. Chothia, T., de Ruiter, J., Smyth, B.: Modelling and analysis of a hierarchy of distance bounding attacks. In: 27th USENIX Security Symposium, USENIX Security 2018 (2018)
4. Chothia, T., Garcia, F.D., de Ruiter, J., van den Breekel, J., Thompson, M.: Relay cost bounding for contactless EMV payments. In: Böhme, R., Okamoto, T. (eds.) FC 2015. LNCS, vol. 8975, pp. 189–206. Springer, Heidelberg (2015). https://doi.org/10.1007/978-3-662-47854-7_11
5. EMVCo. Book C-2 kernel 2 specification v2.7. EMV contactless specifications for payment system, February 2018
6. Boureanu, I., Mitrokotsa, A., Vaudenay, S.: Practical and provably secure distance-bounding. J. Comput. Secur. 23(2), 229–257 (2015)
7. Shu, X., Tian, K., Ciambrone, A., Yao, D. Breaking the target: an analysis of target data breach and lessons learned. CoRR, abs/1701.04940 (2017)
8. Trusted Computing Group: Trusted Platform Module Library Family 2.0, Specification - Part 1: Architecture, Revision 1.38 and Part 3: Commands, Revision 1.38 (2016)

Short Paper: How to Attack PSD2 Internet Banking

Vincent Haupert$^{(\boxtimes)}$ and Stephan Gabert

Friedrich-Alexander University Erlangen-Nürnberg (FAU), Erlangen, Germany
`vincent.haupert@cs.fau.de`

Abstract. Internet banking security is set to take a major step forward: On September 14, 2019, the Regulatory Technical Standards of the Revised Payment Service Directive (PSD2) are going to be effective within the European Union and the European Economic Area. This regulation makes two widely demanded transaction security properties mandatory: two-factor authentication, and the dynamic linking of the authentication code to the transaction's beneficiary and amount (full transaction authentication). Even though the regulation is undoubtedly a positive development from a security perspective, it does not account for all the technical and human weak points involved in the transaction process. In this paper, we look at a series of attacks targeting online and mobile banking that are possible even in a post-PSD2 era. Despite the regulatory motivation of this work, the presented issues and suggestions to address them are likely to be universal for internet banking in general.

Keywords: Online banking · PSD2 · RTS · SCA · Attacks

1   Introduction

At FC 2013, Adham *et al.* presented a work entitled "How to Attack Two-Factor Authentication Internet Banking" [1]. They outlined the current state of online banking transaction security in the United Kingdom (UK) and pointed out how it might be attacked. Although they appreciated the increasing adoption of a second factor for transaction authentication, they argued that an additional one-time password (OTP) alone would not sufficiently protect a customer from falling prey to malware. Their primary concern was that the to date employed transaction authentication methods did not provide full transaction authentication. That means, that the resulting OTP as generated by the respective two-factor authentication (2FA) method did not allow for an independent verification of the transaction's integrity. As a consequence, 2FA did only stop adversaries from performing arbitrary transactions at any time, but did not prevent a real-time transaction manipulation attack.

In March 2018, the Regulatory Technical Standards (RTS) came into force and are going to apply from September 2019 [8]. The RTS are part of the Revised

ⓒ International Financial Cryptography Association 2019
I. Goldberg and T. Moore (Eds.): FC 2019, LNCS 11598, pp. 234–242, 2019.
https://doi.org/10.1007/978-3-030-32101-7_15

Payment Service Directive (PSD2) which replaced its predecessor PSD that initially introduced the Single European Payment Area (SEPA). A primary goal of the RTS is to make payment services more secure and to foster the population's trust in online banking as it is still on a steady rise [9]. To achieve this, the RTS stipulate strong customer authentication (SCA) that requires remote payments to make use of at least two independent and mutually exclusive elements of the categories knowledge, possession and inherence. Additionally, the payment service provider must issue a single-use authentication code that is dynamically linked to the transaction's beneficiary and amount, with both being displayed to the customer for verification. The latter makes full transaction authentication mandatory. This enables a customer to reliably detect fraud even if the transfer-issuing device is compromised by malware.

Even though undoubtedly a positive development, the RTS are not going to rule out all of the attack vectors. In the spirit of Adham et al., we aim at identifying weak points that neither full transaction authentication nor the new regulation addresses. To that end, we include attacks that leverage technical as well as social engineering aspects.

2   Background and Related Work

Carrying out a credit transfer consists of two steps: issuing and confirming. At first, customers need to log in to their online banking. This process is usually secured through a knowledge authentication element, i.e., a password. After successful login, the customer *issues* a transfer to a desired beneficiary by specifying the account number and the amount. To make the transfer effective, the bank additionally requires the transaction's *confirmation*, usually by asking for an OTP which is frequently referred to as TAN (transaction authentication number) in the context of online banking. The method that dynamically links the transaction and yields the TAN is hence called TAN method.

In the following, we outline related works for three popular TAN methods. All of these methods offer a 2FA as well as full transaction authentication and, hence, display the transfer details—i.e., the beneficiary's account number and the amount—on a second device. It is the responsibility of the customer to verify that the displayed transfer details match the desired ones [19]. If they do not match, the customer must abort the transaction ("What You See Is What You Sign", WYSIWYS).

SMS Authentication. The SMS-based authentication procedure (smsTAN) relies on the short message service (SMS) to transmit a text message with the transfer details and the TAN from the bank to the customer. In 2008 and 2014, Engel discovered several vulnerabilities in the Signalling System No. 7 (SS7) protocol that forms the foundation SMS messages are built on [21]. Also Long-Term Evolution (LTE)—the to date latest mobile communication standard—is prone to attacks [22]. Mulliner et al. also addressed the security of the SMS [18] and showed how to abuse flaws to attack the smsTAN method [17].

Smartcard Authentication. Particularly European banks rely on the Chip and PIN (EMV) standard to create a TAN using the customer's bank card. This method requires a dedicated reader device that also displays the transfer details to the customer. In 2009, Drimer *et al.* uncovered various design and protocol flaws in the respective implementation of banks in the UK. A year later, Murdoch *et al.* successfully launched an attack against the EMV protocol that allowed for using a stolen card without knowing the PIN [20]. In 2011, the attack of Murdoch *et al.* even appeared in the wild, when about 40 sophisticated card forgeries surfaced in France, causing an estimated net loss below €600,000 [12]. In 2014, Bond *et al.* discovered another flaw in the EMV protocol that enabled an adversary to de facto clone a card using a rogue point-of-sale terminal [3].

Smartphone Authentication. With the advent of smartphones, banks also started to leverage their high availability and cost effectiveness by implementing app-based TAN methods. These procedures work similar to the smsTAN method but deliver the data over the internet using a dedicated app developed by the bank. In 2014, Dmitrienko *et al.* identified various weaknesses in app-based 2FA solutions [5]. They successfully infected both authentication devices—personal computers and mobile phones—with a self-implemented cross-platform malware. Similarly, Konoth *et al.* presented an attack against smsTAN that only required the infection of the user's computer due to the high integration smartphones and PCs offer today [15]. Haupert *et al.* have contributed to the field of attacks that target one-device mobile banking, a transaction authentication scheme that is becoming increasingly popular [2]. They argue that core requirements of a secure 2FA are violated if both authentication elements are operated by the same multi-purpose device without providing a trusted path [13,14].

3   Threat Model

We suppose that a customer ordered a product online and pays by bank wire transfer through her online banking. This customer uses 2FA with a TAN method that provides full transaction authentication. To that end, the TAN method displays the transfer details on a second, independent device for verification.

An attacker targets at redirecting the customer's transfer order to another account. The adversary only replaces the beneficiary's account number and leaves the amount unchanged. This happens due to the following reason: when paying an invoice, the customer is usually aware of the amount but frequently unaware of the beneficiary's account number. For the purpose of manipulating a transaction, we assume that the adversary can completely compromise the transfer-issuing channel, which enables her to observe or tamper all the details the customer receives, sees, enters or sends. The attacker cannot, however, control the victim's TAN method. Instead, the attacker attempts to discourage the victim from performing a correct verification of the account number during confirmation.

The assumed threat model is rather weak as it does not require infection of both devices that are involved in the transaction authentication process. Owing to the success of banking malware families like *ZeuS* [7], it even became a best practice for banks to regard the customer's computer as malware-infected [10].

4   Attacks and Challenges

4.1   Clipboard Hijacking

On desktop and mobile operating systems, the clipboard is a shared resource that every application can read and write. This allows for stealing [11] and manipulating [26] the data by monitoring the contents of the system clipboard.

The international banking account number (IBAN)—the default within the SEPA—adheres to a well-defined ISO standard. According to that standard, an IBAN can consist of up to 34 alphanumeric characters. In the case that a customer receives a digital invoice, e.g., a PDF, a customer is likely going to use the copy and paste method to avoid entering the IBAN manually.

Attack. As the IBAN also contains two check digits, it is easy to validate the correctness of a given candidate. Consequently, an attacker monitoring the clipboard can also detect an IBAN in the system clipboard and replace it with the IBAN of an attacker-controlled account. As a customer pasted the IBAN, she might assume it must be correct—ignoring a potentially infected computer—and, hence, skips the account number verification. As the customer did not enter the IBAN manually, recalling the original IBAN is less likely.

Defense. To mitigate this attack, a bank should disable the possibility to paste clipboard data into a form element. Developers can prevent this within web and mobile applications by installing a custom listener for paste events.

4.2   SMS Autofill on iOS and MacOS

In 2016, Konoth *et al.* already criticized the synchronisation of SMS from iOS to macOS, as this allows for an attacker to only infect the transfer-issuing channel to control both authentication elements [15]. With the release of iOS 12 and macOS 10.14 (Mojave) in September 2018, this integration became even closer: if a customer visits a webpage that asks for an OTP sent by SMS, Safari on macOS 10.14 offers automatic insertion of the OTP in a predefined field [16]. This feature is also available for text fields in apps running on iOS 12.

Attack. Autofilling an OTP is only meaningful and without security implications if the authentication happens without context. This is true for user but not for transaction authentication: the essential security task during transaction confirmation is the verification of the transfer details contained within the SMS. Autofilling the TAN encourages the customer to omit this verification step. An attacker who compromised the device and manipulated a transfer could trigger the autofill. Consequently, the victim might not verify the transfer for integrity as the TAN gets filled in automatically. Instead, she might just proceed making the transfer effective.

Defense. Our tests show that the keyword "code" is necessary within the SMS to trigger this feature. As a consequence, banks should avoid this word within their SMS text message. In our tests, the words "OTP" or "TAN" did not trigger the autofill feature, but Apple might change this behavior at any time.

4.3   Stealthy Transaction Manipulation

In the course of our research, we noticed that many important and large German banks—for example, *Sparkassen* as well as *Volksbanken und Raiffeisenbanken*— also show a transaction's details on the confirmation webpage that asks the customer for a TAN. This behavior has a counter-productive effect, as it suggests that the transfer-issuing channel is trustworthy. To make things worse, it might even habituate a user to perform a faulty transaction verification: instead of comparing the details shown on the customer's TAN device to the original invoice, she might compare them to the details shown within the transfer-issuing channel, e.g., the web browser.

Attack. An adversary can leverage this potential habituation: a customer who compares the information within the TAN device to the details shown within the transfer-issuing channel, is not going to spot a deviation. One might argue that a customer might recall the account number she originally entered. This is, of course, possible. In the case of an IBAN, however, this scenario is at least debatable because of the cumbersome format with up to 34 digits.

Defense. This is an issue of usable security [24]. From a technical point of view, banks should stop displaying transaction details within the transfer-issuing channel, as this behavior is plain unconducive.

4.4   Digital Invoice Manipulation

After purchase, online shops send out an e-mail to their customers that contains a PDF invoice or a link that displays the invoice and payment details within the browser. Even if a customer pays on account, they frequently do no longer receive a paper invoice along with the ordered item.

Attack. Instead of tampering with the transfer order, a malware might as well directly modify the invoice. Due to the IBAN's well-defined format, it is easy to detect and replace occurrences within a PDF or HTML page. Hence, an attacker could manipulate the invoiced account number directly. Even in the case that a customer correctly verifies the transaction, she has no chance to spot the fraud.

Defense. Online shops could send out the payment details by postal mail only. Particularly for payments in advance, however, this is probably not an option. Signing PDF invoices is not going to help either as the majority of users would not deem an unsigned PDF suspicious.

4.5   Transfer Templates

To avoid having the customer enter the account number for recurring recipients, many banks offer explicit and implicit transfer templates. For explicit transfer templates, a customer has to actively create a new entry within the online banking that contains the beneficiary's name and account number. When a customer wants to perform a credit transfer to one of her contacts saved as transfer template, she can just select this contact from a list. Implicit transfer templates work similarly but do not require the customer to actively create entries: when a customer types the beneficiary's name into the transfer order form, the online banking automatically searches the past transactions and suggests filling in the corresponding account number.

Attack. Transfer templates operate on the client side. That means, that they help to fill in a form only but the data sent to the bank is the same as filling in that information manually. As a consequence, an attacker can fill in an arbitrary account number when a customer makes use of a transfer template. During transaction confirmation, the customer does likely not have an invoice or another channel to verify the displayed transaction details; that is likely the reason why the customer made use of a transfer template in the first place.

Defense. Transfer templates are difficult to reconcile with the principle of WYSIWYS. Therefore, it is hard to create a solution that offers the comfort of transfer templates on the one hand, but also encourages a customer to verify a transaction's account number on the other hand. Masking a small part of the account numbers for transfer templates and past transactions helps addressing this issue: it spares most typing but makes sure that the customer has the beneficiary's account number available through a source different from the online banking.

5   Conclusion

In this paper, we presented five different attacks which target the way online banking credit transfers work and how the customer uses them. Most of the attacks have in common that the customer is not aware of the payee's account number. Moreover, account number formats like the IBAN make transaction verification a cumbersome task. In addition, the currently used TAN methods only display the IBAN but not the name of the recipient.

This, however, could make transaction verification an easier task: Apart from the beneficiary's account number and the amount of the transfer, the TAN method should also display the beneficiary's name. For that purpose, a TAN method could perform a lookup in the customer's transaction history. If a customer never used the given account number before, a bank could at least use their global transaction history to show a confidence level for the that account number. A similar service was already introduced by Dutch banks in 2017, with a system which ensures that the beneficiary's name belongs to the specified IBAN [6].

As our threat model assumes full control over the transfer-issuing channel, our proposed defenses are not going to fully eliminate but rather complicate a successful attack. To mitigate attacks, it is essential that a customer is aware of the untrustworthiness of the transfer-issuing channel. The user, however, frequently lacks this awareness [4,23,25]. To eliminate this attack vector, banks need to come up with procedures that guarantee integrity as soon as the customer enters the payment details. This, however, remains a medium-term task. Nevertheless, the PSD2 is a step into the right direction and will make payments more secure.

References

1. Adham, M., Azodi, A., Desmedt, Y., Karaolis, I.: How to attack two-factor authentication internet banking. In: Sadeghi, A.-R. (ed.) FC 2013. LNCS, vol. 7859, pp. 322–328. Springer, Heidelberg (2013). https://doi.org/10.1007/978-3-642-39884-1_27
2. Bankenverband/GfK: Online-Banking in Deutschland (2018). http://go.bdb.de/UHbYz
3. Bond, M., Choudary, O., Murdoch, S.J., Skorobogatov, S.P., Anderson, R.J.: Chip and skim: cloning EMV cards with the pre-play attack. In: 2014 IEEE Symposium on Security and Privacy, SP 2014, Berkeley, CA, USA, pp. 49–64, 18–21 May 2014. https://doi.org/10.1109/SP.2014.11
4. Dhamija, R., Tygar, J.D., Hearst, M.A.: Why phishing works. In: Proceedings of the 2006 Conference on Human Factors in Computing Systems, CHI 2006, Montréal, Québec, Canada, pp. 581–590, 22–27 April 2006. https://doi.org/10.1145/1124772.1124861
5. Dmitrienko, A., Liebchen, C., Rossow, C., Sadeghi, A.-R.: On the (in)security of mobile two-factor authentication. In: Christin, N., Safavi-Naini, R. (eds.) FC 2014. LNCS, vol. 8437, pp. 365–383. Springer, Heidelberg (2014). https://doi.org/10.1007/978-3-662-45472-5_24
6. Dutch Payments Association: Dutch banks introduce innovative IBAN-Name Check (2017). https://www.betaalvereniging.nl/en/actueel/persberichten/dutch-banks-introduce-innovative-iban-name-check/
7. Etaher, N., Weir, G.R.S., Alazab, M.: From ZeuS to zitmo: Trends in banking malware. In: 2015 IEEE TrustCom/BigDataSE/ISPA, Helsinki, Finland, vol. 1, pp. 1386–1391, 20–22 August 2015. https://doi.org/10.1109/Trustcom.2015.535

8. European Commission: Commission delegated regulation (EU) 2018/389 supplementing directive (EU) 2015/2366 of the European parliament and of the council with regard to regulatory technical standards for strong customer authentication and common and secure open standards of communication (2018). https://eur-lex.europa.eu/legal-content/EN/TXT/PDF/?uri=CELEX:32018R0389

9. European Commission: Internet banking on the rise (2018). http://ec.europa.eu/eurostat/web/products-eurostat-news/-/DDN-20180115-1

10. European Union Agency for Network and Information Security: Flash note: EU cyber security agency ENISA; "high roller" online bank robberies reveal security gaps (2012). https://www.enisa.europa.eu/news/enisa-news/copy_of_eu-cyber-security-agency-enisa-201chigh-roller201d-online-bank-robberies-reveal-security-gaps

11. Fahl, S., Harbach, M., Oltrogge, M., Muders, T., Smith, M.: Hey, you, get off of my clipboard. In: Sadeghi, A.-R. (ed.) FC 2013. LNCS, vol. 7859, pp. 144–161. Springer, Heidelberg (2013). https://doi.org/10.1007/978-3-642-39884-1_12

12. Ferradi, H., Géraud, R., Naccache, D., Tria, A.: When organized crime applies academic results: a forensic analysis of an in-card listening device. J. Cryptogr. Eng. 6(1), 49–59 (2016). https://doi.org/10.1007/s13389-015-0112-3

13. Haupert, V., Maier, D., Müller, T.: Paying the price for disruption: how a fintech allowed account takeover. In: Proceedings of the 1st Reversing and Offensive-oriented Trends Symposium, pp. 7:1–7:10. ROOTS, ACM, New York (2017). https://doi.org/10.1145/3150376.3150383

14. Haupert, V., Maier, D., Schneider, N., Kirsch, J., Müller, T.: Honey, i shrunk your app security: the state of android app hardening. In: Giuffrida, C., Bardin, S., Blanc, G. (eds.) DIMVA 2018. LNCS, vol. 10885, pp. 69–91. Springer, Cham (2018). https://doi.org/10.1007/978-3-319-93411-2_4

15. Konoth, R.K., van der Veen, V., Bos, H.: How anywhere computing just killed your phone-based two-factor authentication. In: Grossklags, J., Preneel, B. (eds.) FC 2016. LNCS, vol. 9603, pp. 405–421. Springer, Heidelberg (2017). https://doi.org/10.1007/978-3-662-54970-4_24

16. Miller, C.: Here's how iOS 12's new security code auto-fill feature works (2018). https://9to5mac.com/2018/06/04/safari-security-code-auto-fill

17. Mulliner, C., Borgaonkar, R., Stewin, P., Scifert, J.-P.: SMS-based one-time passwords: attacks and defense. In: Rieck, K., Stewin, P., Seifert, J.-P. (eds.) DIMVA 2013. LNCS, vol. 7967, pp. 150–159. Springer, Heidelberg (2013). https://doi.org/10.1007/978-3-642-39235-1_9

18. Mulliner, C., Golde, N., Seifert, J.: SMS of death: from analyzing to attacking mobile phones on a large scale. In: Proceedings of the 20th USENIX Security Symposium, San Francisco, CA, USA, 8–12 August 2011. http://static.usenix.org/events/sec11/tech/full_papers/Mulliner.pdf

19. Murdoch, S.J., et al.: Are payment card contracts unfair? (short paper). In: Grossklags, J., Preneel, B. (eds.) FC 2016. LNCS, vol. 9603, pp. 600–608. Springer, Heidelberg (2017). https://doi.org/10.1007/978-3-662-54970-4_35

20. Murdoch, S.J., Drimer, S., Anderson, R.J., Bond, M.: Chip and PIN is broken. In: 31st IEEE Symposium on Security and Privacy, S&P 2010, Berleley/Oakland, California, USA, pp. 433–446, 16–19 May 2010. https://doi.org/10.1109/SP.2010.33

21. Rao, S.P., Kotte, B.T., Holtmanns, S.: Privacy in LTE networks. In: Proceedings of the 9th EAI International Conference on Mobile Multimedia Communications, MobiMedia 2016, Xi'an, China, pp. 176–183, 18–20 June 2016. http://dl.acm.org/citation.cfm?id=3021417

22. Rupprecht, D., Kohls, K., Holz, T., Pöpper, C.: Breaking LTE on layer two. In: IEEE Symposium on Security & Privacy (SP). IEEE, May 2019
23. Schechter, S.E., Dhamija, R., Ozment, A., Fischer, I.: The emperor's new security indicators. In: 2007 IEEE Symposium on Security and Privacy (S&P 2007), Oakland, California, USA, pp. 51–65, 20–23 May 2007. https://doi.org/10.1109/SP.2007.35
24. Schneier, B.: Stop trying to fix the user. IEEE Secur. Priv. **14**(5), 96 (2016)
25. Watson, B., Zheng, J.: On the user awareness of mobile security recommendations. In: Proceedings of the 2017 ACM Southeast Regional Conference, Kennesaw, GA, USA, pp. 120–127, 13–15 April 2017. https://doi.org/10.1145/3077286.3077563
26. Zhang, X., Du, W.: Attacks on android clipboard. In: Dietrich, S. (ed.) DIMVA 2014. LNCS, vol. 8550, pp. 72–91. Springer, Cham (2014). https://doi.org/10.1007/978-3-319-08509-8_5

Your Money or Your Life—Modeling and Analyzing the Security of Electronic Payment in the UC Framework

Dirk Achenbach[2], Roland Gröll[2], Timon Hackenjos[2], Alexander Koch[1], Bernhard Löwe[1], Jeremias Mechler[1], Jörn Müller-Quade[1], and Jochen Rill[2(✉)]

[1] Karlsruhe Institute of Technology (KIT), Karlsruhe, Germany
[2] FZI Research Center for Information Technology, Karlsruhe, Germany
rill@fzi.de

Abstract. EMV, also known as Chip and PIN, is the world-wide standard for card-based electronic payment. Its security wavers: over the past years, researchers have demonstrated various practical attacks, ranging from using stolen cards by disabling PIN verification to cloning cards by pre-computing transaction data. Most of these attacks rely on violating certain unjustified and not explicitly stated core assumptions upon which EMV is built, namely that the input device (e.g. the ATM) is trusted and all communication channels are non-interceptable. In addition, EMV lacks a comprehensive formal description of its security.

In this work we give a formal model for the security of electronic payment protocols in the Universal Composability (UC) framework. A particular challenge for electronic payment is that one participant of a transaction is a human who cannot perform cryptographic operations. Our goal is twofold. First, we want to enable a transition from the iterative engineering of such protocols to using cryptographic security models to argue about a protocol's security. Second, we establish a more realistic adversarial model for payment protocols in the presence of insecure devices and channels.

We prove a set of necessary requirements for secure electronic payment with regards to our model. We then discuss the security of current payment protocols based on these results and find that most are insecure or require unrealistically strong assumptions. Finally, we give a simple payment protocol inspired by chipTAN and photoTAN and prove its security.

Our model captures the security properties of electronic payment protocols with human interaction. We show how to use this to reason about necessary requirements for secure electronic payment and how to develop

R. Gröll and J. Rill—This work was supported by grants from the Federal Ministry for Economic Affairs and Energy of Germany (BMWi) for the EDV Project.
A. Koch and B. Löwe—This work was supported by the German Federal Ministry of Education and Research within the framework of the projects KASTEL_IoE, KASTEL_SVI and KASTEL_Base in the Competence Center for Applied Security Technology (KASTEL).

I. Goldberg and T. Moore (Eds.): FC 2019, LNCS 11598, pp. 243–261, 2019.
https://doi.org/10.1007/978-3-030-32101-7_16

a protocol based on the resulting guidelines. We hope that this will facilitate the development of new protocols with well-understood security properties.

Keywords: EMV · Universal Composability · Security models · Human-server-interaction · Electronic payment

1   Introduction

"Your money, or your life!"—surrender your belongings or face death. This threat was used by bandits in England until the 19th century [25]. As people often needed to carry all their valuables with them when traveling, banditry was a lucrative (albeit dangerous) endeavor. Today, electronic money transfer (EMT) systems alleviate the need to have one's valuables at hand, but introduce new threats as well. Instead of resorting to violence, modern thieves may compromise their victim's bank account. Once they are widely deployed, insecure EMT systems are notoriously difficult to transition away from—magnetic stripes are still in use today. The current state-of-the-art payment standard EMV (short for *Europay International, MasterCard and VISA*, also known as "Chip and PIN") improves on this, but falls short of providing a secure solution to payment (or money withdrawal), as shown by its many weaknesses described in literature.

Among these are practical attacks, such as (i) "cloning" chip cards by precomputing transaction messages (so-called "pre-play attacks") [4], (ii) disabling the personal identification number (PIN) verification of stolen cards by intercepting the communication between chip card and point of sale (POS) device [24], (iii) tricking an innocent customer into accepting fraudulent transactions by relaying transaction data from a different POS (so-called "relay attacks") [17].

Upon close examination of these attacks one finds that these issues mainly stem from *two major false assumptions* which are baked into the design of the EMV protocol: (i) that the communication between all protocol participants (e.g. between the chip card and the POS) cannot be intercepted and (ii) that the POS (or the automated teller machine (ATM)) itself is trustworthy. Even though these assumptions are critical for the security of EMV, they are not explicitly stated in the standardization documents [19–21]. We suggest that this is mainly because EMV has been created by a functionality-focused engineering process in which problems are fixed as they occur and features are added when necessary, rather than a design process that uses formal models and techniques. Modern cryptographic protocols in contrast are designed by first providing a formal description of the protocol, explicitly stating all necessary assumptions and then giving a proof of security. This does not make cryptographic protocols unbreakable, but it does make their potential breaking points explicit. Therefore, we argue that it is necessary to start developing electronic payment protocols by using the same methodology of rigorous formal modeling as has already been established in cryptography.

1.1   Our Contribution

In this work, we give a novel formal model for electronic payment based on the Universal Composability (UC) framework by Canetti [6], which incorporates a stronger, but also more realistic adversarial model than has been used for the design of EMV. We first give a *formal description* of electronic payment which works for both payment at a POS and for the withdrawal of cash at an ATM. Second, we provide an ideal functionality for electronic payment, which captures the desired security guarantees for such protocols. Our model can also be used in the case where one participant is human.

We then prove a set of *general requirements* for designing such protocols. These requirements can act as a guideline for future protocol designers. Based on these results, we argue that a number of current payment systems are insecure already on a conceptual level. Inspired by this analysis, we propose a simple electronic payment protocol which mainly requires secure communication between the bank and the initiator of a transaction. We propose to realize this with a smartphone, as is common in many modern payment protocols. However, unlike these protocols, our protocol can be proven secure if *either* the smartphone *or* the ATM/POS device behaves honestly, whereas all other protocols we analyzed need to trust at least one of them exclusively.

1.2   Related Work

Secure Human-Server Communication. Basin, Radomirovic, and Schläpfer [3] give an enumeration of minimal topologies of channels between a human (restricted in its abilities), a trusted server, a possibly corrupted intermediary and a trusted device, that realize an authenticated channel between the human and the server. Our work differs in two main aspects: Their model uses either fully secure or untrusted channels only and cannot account for just authenticated or just confidential communication, which is important in our setting due to the presence of CCTV cameras or shoulder-surfing. For example, we assume that everything displayed at the ATM or a user's smartphone is not confidential, while entering a PIN at the PIN pad can be done in a confidential way, by suitably covering the pad in the process. Second, our model is given in the UC framework, which gives stronger guarantees and composability, as well as security for concurrent and interleaved execution, compared to the stand-alone setting they consider.

Alternative Hardware Assumptions. As we will see later in Sect. 2.2, the *confirmation of payment information* by the user is an important sub-problem we aim to solve for achieving secure payment. A possible solution is "Display TAN" [5] providing a smartcard with a display to show the transaction data. Smart-Guard [15] uses such smartcards with a display together with an encrypting keyboard fixed to the card to achieve a functionality which may be used for payment. These strong hardware assumptions allow for flexible trust assumptions, accounting for several combinations of trusted/hacked status of the involved devices. Their protocol comes with a formally verified security proof, albeit not in the UC framework. For our construction we do not propose a new kind of hardware device, but rely on the user's smartphone.

Ecash and Cryptocurrencies. Besides human-server payment protocols, there is also electronic cash, first invented by [9], and modern decentralized cryptocurrencies, such as Bitcoin [22], which can be used to transfer money. In general, these have very different design goals, as they care to establish an electronic money system with certain anonymity/pseudonymity properties, without the possibility to double-spend and in particular, without a trusted bank. In contrast, we are concerned with the authenticated transmission of the transaction data from a human user to the bank. To the best of our knowledge, there is no UC-based model of electronic payment as presented in our work.

EMV. EMV is not only a single payment protocol, but a complete protocol suite for electronic payment (cf. [19–21]). Protocols that are EMV-compliant might just implement the EMV interface while using another secure protocol. This means that, while there are multiple attacks against the EMV *payment protocol*, not every protocol with EMV in its name is automatically insecure. In addition to the attacks mentioned previously, there are other attacks as described by Chothia et al. [10] and Emms et al. [18].

Anderson et al. [2] discuss whether EMV is a monolithic system reducing the possibilities for innovation. Since we use the UC framework for our model, we inherently support non-monolithic, modular systems. Sub-protocols that UC-realize each other can be exchanged for one another. Furthermore, [2] explore the possibility to use smartcards (as used by EMV) for other applications. Following a similar goal, we give a formalization of signature cards within our model in the full version [1] and show limits to using such cards.

Degabriele et al. [14] investigate the joint security of encryption and signatures in EMV using the same key-pair. A scheme based on elliptic curves (as it is used in EMV) is proven secure in their model. However, as they conclude, their proof does not eliminate certain kinds of protocol-level attacks. Cortier et al. [13] present an EMV-compliant protocol using trusted enclaves and prove the security of their protocol using TAMARIN [29]. Both approaches lack the modularity, composability and concurrent security provided by the UC framework.

1.3 The (Generalized) Universal Composability Framework

The Universal Composability (UC) framework, introduced by Canetti in 2001 [6], is a widely established tool for proving the security of cryptographic protocols based on the real-world–ideal-world paradigm. The desired security properties of a protocol are described in terms of a so-called *ideal functionality*, which can be seen as an incorruptible third party carrying out the desired task by definition. The ideal functionality *explicitly* captures the allowed influence an adversary can have and the knowledge he can gain during an execution of the protocol. Informally, a protocol π is said to UC-realize an ideal functionality $\mathcal{F}$ if there is no interactive distinguisher $\mathcal{Z}$ (the so-called *environment*) that can distinguish between the execution of π and the execution of (the ideal protocol of) $\mathcal{F}$.

The framework is specifically well-suited for our case, as it already incorporates an adversary that can control all communication between the protocol parties. If one wants to deviate from this (e.g. when secure communication is available) one must explicitly add new functionalities for communication to the model (so-called *hybrid functionalities*), making the security assumptions of the protocol explicit.

The UC framework's security definition does not capture shared state between several protocol instances. Canetti et al. [7] proposed an extension—the so-called Generalized Universal Composability (GUC) framework—which introduces globally shared functionalities. They can be used by multiple protocols, allowing to share state between different executions of protocols. This extension can be used to model smartcards as used in EMV, allowing us to capture e.g. pre-play attacks in our model. One of the main advantages of the (G)UC framework is that it, unlike stand-alone security models, brings a strong composition theorem. This allows for breaking protocols into smaller components and proving their security individually. A comprehensive description of the framework and its extension can be found in the full version [1].

2   A Formal Model for Electronic Payment

As a basis for our model, observe the process of withdrawing cash at an automated teller machine (ATM). First, there is the bank and its customer, Alice. Second, there is the money dispensing unit inside the ATM. Assuming authenticated communication from Alice to the bank and from the bank to the money dispensing unit, secure payment is easy: Alice communicates the amount of cash she needs and the identity of the money dispensing unit she expects to receive the cash from. The bank then instructs the money dispensing unit to dispense the money. However, Alice is a human and therefore cannot perform cryptographic operations required for a classical channel establishment protocol. Thus, Alice needs another party which offers a user interface to her and communicates with the bank, namely an ATM.

This does not only apply to cash withdrawal but can be extended to electronic money transfer (EMT) in general. To this end, think of Alice as the *initiator* of a transaction and the money dispensing unit as the *receiver*. The process of money withdrawal can now be framed as a payment of money from Alice's account to the account of the money dispensing unit (which, upon receiving money, promptly outputs cash) using the ATM as an (input) *device*. The same works for the point of sale: here, the device's owner (e.g. the supermarket) is the receiver.

Regarding our adversarial model, as discussed earlier, we make no assumption about the trustworthiness of the ATM whatsoever and do assume that the adversary has control over all communication. We do make certain assumptions regarding the trustworthiness of different protocol participants. First, we assume the money dispensing unit (or receiver in general) to be trusted. If it is under adversarial control, the adversary could simply dispense money at will. Second, since our work focuses on the challenges that arise from the interaction of humans with untrustworthy devices over insecure communication, we do not model the bank's book-keeping and therefore assume the bank to be incorruptible. Third, for reasons of simplicity, our model only considers a single bank, even though in practice most transactions involve at least two banks. This is justified, however, as banks in general can communicate securely with each other.

2.1   Modeling Electronic Payment in the UC Framework

In the following, to simplify the model, we consider the case of *static corruption*, where parties may only be corrupted prior to protocol execution. Extending our work to adaptive corruption is left for future work.

We denote the set of initiators as S_I, the set of receivers as S_R, the set of devices as S_D and the bank as B. We also define a mapping $D \colon S_R \to S_D$ of receivers to single devices ($D(R)$) to explicitly name which device belongs to which receiver.

In order to model the adversary's probability of successfully attacking credentials like PINs, we introduce a parametrized distribution $\mathcal{D}$. Let X denote the event of a successful attack. Then $\mathcal{D} : A \to F_X$ maps a value d (e.g. the amount) from a domain A (e.g. $\mathbb{Q}$) to a probability mass function $f_{d,X} \in F_X$ over $\{\texttt{confirm}, \texttt{reject}\}$. An adversary's success probability of correctly guessing a four-digit PIN chosen uniformly at random with one try could be modeled as follows: $\mathcal{D}(m_\$) = f_X$ for all $m_\$ \in \mathbb{Q}$ with $f_X(\texttt{confirm}) = \frac{1}{10000}$, $f_X(\texttt{reject}) = \frac{9999}{10000}$. $\mathcal{D}$ could also map different $d \in A$ to different $f_{X,d}$, modeling that transactions with small amounts require less protection than ones with bigger amounts. $\mathcal{F}_\mathcal{D}$ is the ideal functionality $\mathcal{F}$ parametrized with $\mathcal{D}$. Ideal functionalities may have additional parameters, either implicit or explicit ones passed as arguments, e.g. $\mathcal{F}_\mathcal{D}(A, B)$.

In the best possible scenario, ideal payment would work as follows: the initiator submits his desired transaction data to an ideal functionality, which then notifies the bank and the receiver about who paid which amount of money to whom without involvement of the adversary whatsoever. In our adversarial model, no payment protocol realizes this strong ideal functionality: an attacker who controls all communication will at least be able to observe that a transaction takes place, even if he cannot see or change its contents. What is more, such a strict security definition would ignore the fact that in all payment protocols which rely on the initiator being protected by a short secret (like a PIN), an attacker always has a small chance of success by guessing the secret correctly.

Our ideal functionality for electronic payment is thus designed with regards to the following principles: (i) The adversary always gains access to all transaction data. An electronic payment operation can be secure (that is all participants of the transaction get notified about the correct and non-manipulated transaction data) without the transaction data being secret. (ii) The adversary can always successfully change the transaction data at will with a small probability (e.g. if he guesses the PIN correctly). (iii) The payment operation occurs in three stages. In the first stage, the initiator inputs his intended transaction data which the adversary can change at will. This models that a corrupted input device will always be able to change the human initiator's transaction data, even if it will be detected at a later stage. In the second and third stage, the receiver and the bank are notified about the transaction data. The resulting functionality is depicted in Fig. 1.

2.2 Confirmation Is Key

Since the human initiator of a transaction cannot be sure that an untrusted input device correctly processes his transaction data, he needs a way of confirming the transaction data with the bank before the transaction is processed. We formalize this confirmation mechanism within the ideal functionality $\mathcal{F}_{\text{CONF}}$ (specified in Fig. 2). $\mathcal{F}_{\text{CONF}}$ is a two-party functionality which allows a sender to transmit a message and the receiver of the message to *confirm* or *reject* it. As with the ideal payment functionality, the adversary gets the chance to force a confirmation with a certain probability, modeling the insecurity inherent to real-world protocols which use short secrets. Note that he can always force the confirmation to be rejected.

The Ideal Functionality for Electronic Payment $\mathcal{F}_{\text{PAY},\mathcal{D}}(I, B, R)$.

Parametrized by a set of receivers S_R, a designated receiver $R \in S_R$, a set of initiators S_I, an initiator $I \in S_I$, the bank B and a parametrized distribution $\mathcal{D}$.

Initialize $I' = I$, $R' = R$, *attacked* = **no**.
Assertion: At any time, $I, I' \in S_I$ and $R, R' \in S_R$. If the assertion is violated, halt.

Phase 1: Collecting Information
1. Upon receipt of message (**transfer**, sid, R, $m_\$$) from I: Send (sid, I, R, $m_\$$) to the adversary, receive (sid, I', R', $m'_\$$) and output (**input-received**, sid, I', R', $m'_\$$) to B.

Phase 2: Confirmation and Execution
2. Resume upon instruction by the adversary.
3. If I' is honest, $(I', R', m'_\$) \neq (I, R, m_\$)$ and *attacked* = **no**, halt.
4. Make a public delayed output of (**received**, sid, I', $m'_\$$) to R'.

Phase 3: Ensuring Consistency
5. Resume upon instruction by the adversary and make a public delayed output of (**processed**, sid, I', R', $m'_\$$) to B. Halt upon confirmation by the adversary.

Attack
– Upon receiving an input (**attack**, sid) in Phase 2 from the adversary, sample an element $b \in \{\text{confirm}, \text{reject}\}$ according to $\mathcal{D}(m'_\$)$. If $b = \text{confirm}$, set *attacked* = **yes**, otherwise set *attacked* = **no**. Return (**attack**, sid, *attacked*) to the adversary. Ignore all further **attack** queries.

Fig. 1. The ideal functionality $\mathcal{F}_{\text{PAY}}$ for electronic payment.

To realize $\mathcal{F}_{\text{PAY}}$, we need authenticated communication from the bank to the receiver, so that the receiver can be notified of the transaction. For most real-world payment protocols, this authenticated communication is easy to establish, since receivers are electronic devices and not humans. In the case of cash withdrawal, the bank owns the money dispensing unit and can pre-distribute cryptographic keys to establish authenticated communication.

Using $\mathcal{F}_{\text{CONF}}$ and $\mathcal{F}_{\text{AUTH}}$ [6, Sect. 6.3], we propose a protocol π_{PAY} which realizes $\mathcal{F}_{\text{PAY}}$. This protocol is informally depicted in Fig. 3.

The comprehensive formal description of the protocol can be found in the full version [1].

Having defined all required protocols and functionalities, we are now ready to state our theorem.

Theorem 1. *Let I, B, R, and $D(R)$ ITMs, where I is human, and B and R are honest. Then, π_{PAY}, informally depicted in Fig. 3, UC-realizes $\mathcal{F}_{\text{PAY},\mathcal{D}}(I,B,R)$ in the $\mathcal{F}_{\text{AUTH}}(B,R), \mathcal{F}_{\text{AUTH}}(R,B), \mathcal{F}_{\text{CONF},\mathcal{D}}(B,I)$-hybrid model.*

For the proof, see the full version [1].

Even though this might seem unsurprising at first, this allows us to break down the complexity of realizing $\mathcal{F}_{\text{PAY}}$ into two easier problems: realizing a confirmation mechanism between the initiator and the bank and realizing authenticated communication between the receiver and the bank.

The Ideal Functionality for Confirmation $\mathcal{F}_{\text{CONF},\mathcal{D}}(S,C)$

Parameters: The message sender S, the respective confirmer C and a parametrized distribution $\mathcal{D}$.
Initialize $attacked = \text{no}$, $initiated = \text{no}$, $completed = \text{no}$.

- Upon receiving $(\text{initiate}, sid, C, m)$ from ITI S, make a public delayed output of $(\text{initiate}, sid, S, m)$ to C and set $initiated = \text{yes}$. Ignore all subsequent initiate messages.
- Upon receiving $(\text{reply}, sid, S, b)$ from ITI C when $initiated = \text{yes}$, $completed = \text{no}$ and $b \in \{\text{confirm}, \text{reject}\}$: Make a public delayed output of $(\text{answer}, sid, C, b)$ to S. Upon confirmation from the adversary, set $completed = \text{yes}$ and halt.
- Upon receiving $(\text{force-confirm}, sid)$ from the adversary, assert that C is honest, $initiated = \text{yes}$, $completed = \text{no}$ and $attacked = \text{no}$. If this holds, set $attacked = \text{yes}$ and sample an element $b \in \{\text{confirm}, \text{reject}\}$ according to $\mathcal{D}(m)$. If $b = \text{confirm}$, set $completed = \text{yes}$ and make a public delayed output of $(\text{answer}, sid, C, \text{confirm})$ to S and halt upon confirmation by the adversary. Otherwise, return (fail, sid) to the adversary.
- Upon receiving $(\text{force-reject}, sid)$ from the adversary, assert that C is honest, $initiated = \text{yes}$, $completed = \text{no}$ and $attacked = \text{no}$. If this holds, set $attacked = \text{yes}$ and $completed = \text{yes}$, make a public delayed output of $(\text{answer}, sid, C, \text{reject})$ to S and halt upon confirmation by the adversary. Otherwise, return (fail, sid) to the adversary.

Fig. 2. The ideal functionality for confirmation of messages.

2.3   How Our Model Captures Existing Attacks

One of our main motivations for establishing a new formal model for electronic payment is to make trust assumptions explicit in order to detect unrealistic ones which enable practical attacks like [4,24] and [17]. Thus, our model needs to be able to capture these kinds of attacks. Protocols analyzed within our framework must be insecure if they allow for these attacks. In the following, we explain how this is achieved.

Changing Transaction Data. An adversary controlling all communication or the input device can easily change transaction data. Protocols which allow this unconditionally are insecure in our model, since $\mathcal{F}_{\text{PAY}}$ only allows to change the transaction data successfully if the adversary mounts a successful attack (i.e. guesses the initiator's PIN in the real world) or the (possibly changed) initiator is corrupted.

Relay Attacks. The aim of a relay attack [17] is to get Alice to authorize an unintended transaction, which benefits the attacker, by relaying legitimate protocol messages between the point of sale (POS) device she uses to pay for goods to another POS device which Alice uses at the same time. If Alice's input device is corrupted, she cannot know with certainty which transaction data she authorizes. Depending on the point of view, this amounts to either changing the *receiver* of a transaction initiated by Alice or changing the *initiator* of a transaction initiated by a third party Carol. Thus, in our model, this attack is just a special case of *changing transaction data*.

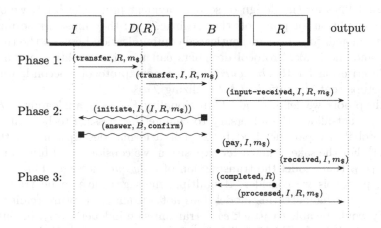

Fig. 3. The protocol π_{PAY} realizing $\mathcal{F}_{\text{PAY},\mathcal{D}}(I, B, R)$ using $\mathcal{F}_{\text{CONF},\mathcal{D}}(B, I)$, $\mathcal{F}_{\text{AUTH}}(B, R)$ and $\mathcal{F}_{\text{AUTH}}(R, B)$, the latter two depicted as ●→. The use of an imperfect $\mathcal{F}_{\text{CONF},\mathcal{D}}$ is depicted via ■→. The protocol is between the human initiator I, the ATM $D(R)$, the bank B and the money dispenser R. The protocol proceeds in three phases, namely (1) the information collection phase, (2) the confirmation and execution phase and (3) the phase which ensures a consistent view on what happened.

Pre-play Attacks. Pre-play attacks [4] basically rely on two facts: (i) once unlocked, smartcards, as used in the EMV protocol, can be coerced into generating message authentication codes (MACs) for arbitrary transaction messages and (ii) that even honest ATMs use predictable "unpredictable numbers". Cards interacting with a corrupted ATM can be used to easily generate additional MAC tags. This attack can be modeled by using a global smartcard functionality (which we present in the full version [1]) within the Generalized Universal Composability (GUC) extension of the basic Universal Composability (UC) framework. In the GUC framework, the environment (and thus indirectly the adversary) can even access the smartcard in the name of *honest* parties in protocol sessions different from the challenge session. Thus, a payment protocol that

GUC-realizes $\mathcal{F}_{\mathrm{PAY}}$ must in particular be secure against all kinds of attacks that result from injecting pre-calculated (sensitive) data into other sessions. Protocols which do not prevent these kinds of attacks (e.g. by enforcing some sort of freshness on the protocol messages) cannot be secure in our model.

3   Towards Realizing Secure Electronic Payment

The core challenge when realizing $\mathcal{F}_{\mathrm{PAY}}$ is the authenticated transmission of transaction data from the (human) initiator to the bank. This can also be captured formally: the functionality $\mathcal{F}_{\mathrm{PAY}}$ can be used to implement the ideal authenticated communication functionality $\mathcal{F}_{\mathrm{AUTH}}$ between initiator and bank (up to the attack success probability captured by the distribution $\mathcal{D}$) by encoding the message as an amount to be transmitted. We use this insight to establish several guidelines for the design of secure payment protocols: First, we state a *necessary* condition for protocols that realize $\mathcal{F}_{\mathrm{PAY}}$: they must use setups that are strong enough to realize authenticated communication between the (human) initiator and the bank. Protocol designers can use this condition as an easily checkable criterion for the *insecurity* of payment protocols. Second, we state several setups that are *sufficient* for realizing $\mathcal{F}_{\mathrm{PAY}}$.

For the proofs, we define an ideal functionality $\mathcal{F}_{\mathrm{AUTH},\mathcal{D}}$, analogous to $\mathcal{F}_{\mathrm{CONF}}$ and $\mathcal{F}_{\mathrm{PAY}}$, that allows the adversary to change the message to be sent with a certain probability parametrized by $\mathcal{D}$. For a formal description, see the full version [1]. For the sake of an easier exposition, we consider ideal functionalities like $\mathcal{F}_{\mathrm{AUTH},\mathcal{D}}$ that model the transmission of *only one* message. This is in line with the protocols we consider. If multiple messages have to be transmitted over the same "channel", this model does not adequately capture reality, as an adversary would be able to attack *each* transmission independently. In this case, ideal functionalities for channels like $\mathcal{F}_{\mathrm{SC}}$ (cf. [8]) can be adapted the same way.

3.1   Requirements for Secure Electronic Payment

In this section, we establish necessary and sufficient criteria for secure electronic payment. Let $\mathcal{F}_{\mathrm{AUTH},\mathcal{D}}(I, R)$ denote the imperfect ideal authenticated communication functionality between parties I and R, and $\mathcal{F}_{\mathrm{SMT},\mathcal{D}}(I, R)$ the corresponding ideal secure message transfer functionality (where successful attacks relative to $\mathcal{D}$ results in loss of secrecy and authenticity). For a formal description, see the full version [1]. Throughout this section, let I, B, R be ITMs, where I is human[1], B is honest and $\mathcal{D}$ a parametrized distribution. We obtain the following theorem:

Theorem 2. *There exists a protocol π that UC-realizes $\mathcal{F}_{\mathrm{AUTH},\mathcal{D}}(I, R)$ in the $\mathcal{F}_{\mathrm{PAY},\mathcal{D}}(I, \star, R)$-hybrid model, where $\star$ is an arbitrary protocol party.*

In particular, Theorem 2 implies that protocols without any authenticated communication or only between the bank and the receiver cannot realize $\mathcal{F}_{\mathrm{PAY}}$:

---

[1] Note that our results hold for arbitrary I.

Corollary 1. *Let π be a protocol that is in the $\mathcal{F}_{\text{AUTH}}(B, R)$, $\mathcal{F}_{\text{AUTH}}(R, B)$-hybrid model only (in particular, there is no authenticated communication between I and B). Then there is no protocol ρ in the bare model such that ρ^π UC-realizes $\mathcal{F}_{\text{PAY},\mathcal{D}}(I, B, R)$ if $\mathcal{D}$ admits the adversary at least a non-negligible successful attack probability.*

This insight can be generalized and gives a *necessary condition*: A protocol π that realizes $\mathcal{F}_{\text{PAY},\mathcal{D}}(I, B, R)$ must use setups that can be used to realize $\mathcal{F}_{\text{AUTH},\mathcal{D}}(I, B)$.

Theorem 3 (Necessary Requirements for Setups). *Let F be a set of ideal functionalities. Let Π be the set of all subroutine-respecting protocols with the set of protocol parties $P \subseteq \{I, R, B\}$ that use only ideal functionalities in F. If there is no protocol $\pi \in \Pi$ such that π^F realizes $\mathcal{F}_{\text{AUTH},\mathcal{D}}(I, B)$, then there is no protocol $\rho \in \Pi$ such that ρ^F realizes $\mathcal{F}_{\text{PAY},\mathcal{D}}(I, B, R)$.*

Conversely, it is easy to see that $\mathcal{F}_{\text{PAY},\mathcal{D}}$ can be realized by (also) using e.g. $\mathcal{F}_{\text{AUTH},\mathcal{D}}(I, B)$. Several sufficient requirements are stated in the following theorem:

Theorem 4 (Sufficient Requirements). *Let π be a protocol that UC-realizes (i) $\mathcal{F}_{\text{AUTH},\mathcal{D}}(I, B)$, or (ii) $\mathcal{F}_{\text{SMT},\mathcal{D}}(B, I)$, or (iii) $\mathcal{F}_{\text{CONF},\mathcal{D}}(B, I)$. Then, there exists a protocol ρ such that ρ^π UC-realizes $\mathcal{F}_{\text{PAY},\mathcal{D}}(I, B, R)$ in the $\mathcal{F}_{\text{AUTH}}(B, R)$, $\mathcal{F}_{\text{AUTH}}(R, B)$-hybrid model.*

The proofs of Theorems 2–4 and Corollary 1 are in the full version [1].

3.2 No Authentication Using Smartcards Without Additional Trust

By default, EMV uses smartcards containing shared secrets with the bank in order to authenticate transactions. However, this only works if the input device which accesses the smartcard (e.g. the automated teller machine (ATM)) can be trusted. Otherwise, after the initiator enters his personal identification number (PIN) to authorize a seemingly legitimate transaction, the input device can present false (transaction) data to the smartcard (cf. e.g. [4]). We can prove the intuition that smartcards are not sufficient for realizing $\mathcal{F}_{\text{PAY}}$. In the full version [1], we give a global signature card functionality $\overline{\mathcal{G}}_{\text{SigCard}}$, closely modeled after similar functionalities in the literature. We then prove that no protocol which uses only this functionality (and authenticated communication between the bank and the receiver) can realize (transferrable) authenticated communication between the initiator and the bank. Using Theorem 3, we can conclude that $\overline{\mathcal{G}}_{\text{SigCard}}$ is insufficient to realize $\mathcal{F}_{\text{PAY}}$ even in the presence of bidirectional authenticated communication between the bank and the receiver:

Theorem 5 (informal). *There exists no protocol π in the $\overline{\mathcal{G}}_{\text{SigCard}}$, $\mathcal{F}_{\text{AUTH}}(B, R)$, $\mathcal{F}_{\text{AUTH}}(R, B)$-hybrid model that GUC-realizes $\mathcal{F}_{\text{AUTH},\mathcal{D}}(I, B)$ if I is human and has no trusted interface to the card and $\mathcal{D}$ does not admit an overwhelming attack probability for all amounts.*

The proof of Theorem 5 is in the full version [1].

3.3   Realistic Assumptions

Protocols build on assumptions to achieve security. However, there often is a huge discrepancy regarding to how realistic these assumptions are. EMV relies on the security of the ATM which is often publicly accessible and offers a large attack surface. Unpatched operating systems and exposed Universal Serial Bus interfaces are only two examples for vulnerabilities that have been exploited successfully. As explained in Sect. 2.2, a secure protocol can be constructed by establishing a confirmation mechanism. However, if the input device is corrupted, an additional device is required.

Such additional devices could for example be transaction authentication number (TAN) generators or smartphones. In principle these allow for the creation of protocols that are secure in our model. However, smartphones, which are increasingly used to replace smartcards, regularly call attention because of vulnerabilities. They are complex systems connected to the Internet and are thus more vulnerable to attacks—especially if they are operated by people without expertise in IT security. However, this dilemma can be resolved by requiring trust in only *one of the two devices*. We call this property 1-of-2 (*one-out-of-two*) security (which is, in the case of authentication, also known as multi-factor authentication). This means that a protocol is still secure if one of the two devices is corrupted, no matter which one of them. We argue that, in addition to realizing $\mathcal{F}_{\mathrm{PAY}}$, payment protocols should support this property in order to further reduce the attack surface.

4   On the Security of Current Payment Protocols

In this chapter, we use our acquired insights to analyze current protocols for withdrawing cash, paying at the point of sale (POS), and online banking. Table 1 summarizes our findings. Our model allows for a structured and fast categorization of payment protocols on a conceptual level, even without a detailed protocol description. Even though EMV is the most widely used standard for payments, we do not elaborate on its security in this chapter. As mentioned before, its design incorporates at least two assumptions that do not hold, as several attacks have been demonstrated. Current payment protocols such as Google Pay, Apple Pay, Samsung Pay, Microsoft Pay and Garmin Pay provide an app that uses the EMV contactless standard to communicate with existing POS devices via nearfield communication [28,30]. Since they rely on Consumer Device Cardholder Verification Method, the user is authenticated by the mobile device exclusively. Currently, these apps use a personal identification number (PIN), a fingerprint or face recognition and thus do not incorporate a second device such as the POS device for authentication. Therefore the security of the protocol is solely based on the mobile device.

The protocols discussed in this section make additional implicit assumptions, which we believe to be plausible, but want to make explicit. These include the following: (i) An additional trusted device beside the input device. This is a plausible assumption if the device is simple, less so if it is a smartphone. However, using an additional device could enable protocols to be 1-of-2-secure. (ii) Authenticated communication between the initiator of a transaction and an additional personal device. This is a realistic assumption, since the initiator owns the device. Likewise the initiator can authenticate themselves to the device, e.g. by unlocking the screen of a mobile device. (iii) Confidential communication from the initiator to the automated teller machine (ATM), which can be realized by covering the PIN pad with one's hand if the ATM is not compromised. (iv) Confidential communication from the ATM to the bank. This can be realized using public-key cryptography.

In the following, we examine multiple protocols for cash withdrawal and online banking.

Cardless Cash. Cardless Cash [12] is an app-based protocol for cash withdrawal offered by numerous banks in Australia. In its most simple variant, it works as follows: After registration, the app can be used to create a "cash code" by entering the desired amount and a phone number. The phone number is used to send a PIN via SMS and allows to permit someone else to withdraw cash. To dispense the cash, the PIN has to be entered at the ATM alongside the cash code. The security of the protocol is solely based on the ATM, since all relevant information is entered there and no additional confirmation mechanism is established.

VR-mobileCash. VR-mobileCash [31] is another app-based protocol for cash withdrawal offered by Volks- und Raiffeisenbanken, a German association of banks. Upon registration, the user receives the mobile personal identification number (mPIN), which has to be entered on the ATM later on to confirm a transaction. To withdraw cash, the user has to enter the desired amount in the app. After selecting mobile payment at the ATM, the ATM shows a mobile transaction identification number (mTIN) which has to be entered in the app. The ATM then shows the requested amount and asks the user to enter the mPIN. If the mPIN is correct the ATM dispenses the requested amount of cash.

Although not stated explicitly in the public documentation, the mobile device has to be online during the transaction, as the ATM is informed about the transaction data. If the mobile device is corrupted but the ATM is honest, a user can detect an attack because he has to confirm the transaction by entering the mPIN at the ATM and thus verifies the location of the ATM. However, a *corrupted ATM* can employ a relay attack by displaying the mTIN of another corrupted ATM and forwarding the entered mPIN to it thus allowing the second corrupted ATM to dispense the cash. This could be fixed by adding a serial number imprinted on the ATM which is also displayed in the app after entering the mTIN. Thereby VR-mobileCash could potentially realize $\mathcal{F}_{PAY}$ and even be 1-of-2-secure.

chipTAN Comfort. ChipTAN comfort [26] is a protocol for online banking widely used in Germany. Here, the initiator uses a computer as an input device and possesses two additional personal devices: a transaction authentication number (TAN) generator and a smartcard. The TAN generator is used to confirm transactions and thus realizes a confirmation mechanism. This works as follows: First, a transaction has to be requested in the browser. Then, the banking website shows a flickering code. The user puts the smartcard into the TAN generator and scans the flickering code. After reviewing the transaction data presented on the personal device, he presses a button which reveals a TAN that has to be entered into the website.

This protocol satisfies all requirements for a secure realization of $\mathcal{F}_{\mathrm{PAY}}$ by establishing a confirmation channel that allows a user to detect tampering of the transaction data. What is more, the protocol potentially provides a form of 1-of-2 security, since as long as either the input device or alternatively the TAN generator together with the smartcard are uncorrupted, there exists a confirmation mechanism from the bank to the initiator. This is only true for single transactions, however (see [27] for details).

Table 1. Comparison of different payment protocols. A protocol is marked as offline, if the additional device does not require an Internet connection during the payment process. The security of a protocol is put in parentheses if it meets our requirements for a secure protocol but has not been proven secure.

Protocol	Offline	Secure	Applicable for
Cardless Cash	✓	×	Withdrawal
VR-mobileCash	×	×	Withdrawal
chipTAN comfort	✓	(✓: 1-of-2)	Online banking
photoTAN	✓	(✓: 1-of-2)	Online banking
L-Pay (our scheme)	✓	✓: 1-of-2	Withdrawal, PoS

photoTAN. photoTAN (or QR-TAN) is a variant of chipTAN comfort, where the code to transmit data to the TAN generator is encrypted by the bank. Furthermore, a smartphone can be used as an alternative to a special-purpose TAN generator. In our model, this encryption does not have an impact on security, since the transaction data is not confidential and is displayed on the smartphone nonetheless. However, some banking apps for photoTAN [11,16] show the TAN immediately after scanning the code and before the transaction data have been confirmed by the user. Thus, in the scenario of cash withdrawal, an attacker that corrupted an ATM and deploys a camera monitoring the ATM could change the submitted transaction data at the ATM, read the TAN from the victim's display and confirm the transaction without the initiator's consent.

5   Realizing Secure Electronic Payment

In Sect. 2.2, we gave a protocol π_{PAY} that realizes $\mathcal{F}_{\mathrm{PAY},\mathcal{D}}(I, R, B)$ in the $\mathcal{F}_{\mathrm{AUTH}}(B, R)$, $\mathcal{F}_{\mathrm{AUTH}}(R, B)$, $\mathcal{F}_{\mathrm{CONF},\mathcal{D}}(B, I)$-hybrid model. While realizing

$\mathcal{F}_{\text{AUTH}}$ between the bank and the receiver is simple, realizing $\mathcal{F}_{\text{CONF},\mathcal{D}}(B,I)$ in a way suitable for humans is a challenge under realistic trust assumptions.

The protocols in Sect. 4 use one or more additional devices, such as smartphones, smartcards or transaction authentication number (TAN) generator to give the initiator a confirmation capability. Yet all cash withdrawal protocols still need a trusted automated teller machine (ATM). In the following, we improve on this by presenting a simple offline protocol called L-Conf (informally described by $\pi_{\text{L-Conf}}$ in Fig. 4). It is inspired by chipTAN and photoTAN which use similar mechanisms. Our protocol is secure even if either the additional device A, such as the initiator's smartphone, or the input device is compromised. We call this property *one-out-of-two security*, formally defined as follows:

Definition 1 (One-out-of-two security). *Let X_1, X_2 be Boolean variables, π a protocol and $\mathcal{F}$ an ideal functionality. We say that π UC-realizes $\mathcal{F}$ with one-out-of-two security relative to X_1 and X_2, if $X_1 \vee X_2$ implies that π UC-realizes $\mathcal{F}$.*

$\pi_{\text{L-Conf}}$ can be used with π_{PAY} to realize $\mathcal{F}_{\text{PAY}}$. We call the resulting protocol L-Pay. The protocol starts with a setup phase: The bank B and the initiator I agree on a personal identification number (PIN) and the initiator's smartphone shares keys with the bank for an authenticated secret-key encryption scheme.

The main part, depicted in Fig. 4, consists of the execution of two protocols π_1 and π_2, each realizing $\mathcal{F}_{\text{CONF}}(B,I)$ under different assumptions. By combining their results, the composed protocol $\pi_{\text{L-Conf}}$ realizes $\mathcal{F}_{\text{CONF}}(B,I)$ even if either the input device or the additional device is compromised.

In π_1, the bank first encrypts the transaction data together with a fresh one-time TAN. The ciphertext is then transmitted to the initiator's input device, displayed appropriately, transferred to the smartphone (e.g. by scanning a QR code) and is decrypted. The TAN is only shown after the transaction data has been checked and *explicitly confirmed* by the initiator. Afterwards, the initiator enters the TAN into the input device.

In order to achieve security even if the initiator's smartphone is corrupted, π_2 requires the initiator to also check and confirm the transaction by entering his PIN into the input device (confidentially over $\mathcal{F}_{\text{Confid}}$), which is then sent to the bank confidentially. Only if the bank receives both the correct TAN and PIN, it considers the transaction to be confirmed. Now, if only the initiator's smartphone is corrupted, the adversary is able to present false transaction data to them or even to perform the confirmation himself. However, this would be noticed immediately, since the transaction data shown on the input device would be wrong and the initiator would not enter his PIN. Conversely, if only the input device is malicious and displays wrong transaction data, the initiator will notice this using their smartphone.

Theorem 6. *Let I, B, $D(R)$ and A be ITMs, where I is human. Let S be the domain of $\mathcal{D}_1, \mathcal{D}_2$, let π_1 UC-realize $\mathcal{F}_{\text{CONF},\mathcal{D}_1}(B,I)$ if A is honest and let π_2 UC-realize $\mathcal{F}_{\text{CONF},\mathcal{D}_2}(B,I)$ if $D(R)$ is honest. Then, $\pi_{\text{L-Conf}}$*

UC-realizes $\quad\mathcal{F}_{\mathrm{CONF},\mathcal{D}_3}(B,I)\quad$ *in* $\quad$ *the* $\quad\mathcal{F}_{\mathrm{AUTH}}(A,I),\quad\mathcal{F}_{\mathrm{AUTH}}(I,A),$
$\mathcal{F}_{\mathrm{AUTH}}(D(R),I),\,\mathcal{F}_{\mathrm{Confid}}(I,D(R)),\,\mathcal{F}_{\mathrm{Confid}}(D(R),B)$*-hybrid model*
   where for all $x \in S$:

$$\mathcal{D}_3(m_\$)(x) := \begin{cases} \max\left(\mathcal{D}_1(m_\$)(\mathtt{confirm}), \mathcal{D}_2(m_\$)(\mathtt{confirm})\right) & x = \mathtt{confirm} \\ 1 - \max(\mathcal{D}_1(m_\$)(\mathtt{confirm}), \mathcal{D}_2(m_\$)(\mathtt{confirm})) & x = \mathtt{reject} \end{cases}$$

Proof (Sketch). The protocol $\pi_{\mathrm{L\text{-}Conf}}$ (Fig. 4) can be interpreted as the composition of two confirmation protocols π_1 (Part 1) and π_2 (Part 2) UC-realizing $\mathcal{F}_{\mathrm{CONF},\mathcal{D}_1}(B,I)$ if A is honest resp. realizing $\mathcal{F}_{\mathrm{CONF},\mathcal{D}_2}(B,I)$ if $D(R)$ is honest (omitting the initial message from B to $D(R)$ to initiate Part 2). Let $b \in \{\mathtt{confirm}, \mathtt{reject}\}$ denote the initiator's input and let $b_1, b_2 \in \{\mathtt{confirm}, \mathtt{reject}\}$ denote the outputs of π_1 and π_2 as received by B, respectively. After having received b_1 and b_2, B outputs b', which is $\mathtt{confirm}$ if $b_1 = b_2 = \mathtt{confirm}$, and $\mathtt{reject}$ otherwise. By definition, $b' = \mathtt{confirm}$ while $b = \mathtt{reject}$ holds with probability upper-bounded by $\max\left(\mathcal{D}_1(m_\$)(\mathtt{confirm}), \mathcal{D}_2(m_\$)(\mathtt{confirm})\right)$.

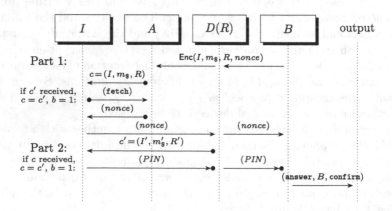

Fig. 4. Main phase of $\pi_{\mathrm{L\text{-}Conf}}$ realizing $\mathcal{F}_{\mathrm{CONF},\mathcal{D}}(B,I)$ using authenticated and confidential channels drawn as •→ and →•, resp. The protocol is between the human initiator I, his personal device A, the ATM $D(R)$ and the bank B. The bit $b \in \{0,1\}$ indicates, whether I wants to confirm, hence (*nonce*) and (*PIN*) are only sent in this case.

Thus, $\pi_{\mathrm{L\text{-}Conf}}$ UC-realizes $\mathcal{F}_{\mathrm{CONF},\mathcal{D}_3}(B,I)$ with one-out-of-two security relative to the assumptions that A or $D(R)$ is honest, respectively. $\qquad\square$

For the complete construction and proof, see the full version [1].

6   Conclusion and Future Work

Designing secure payment protocols poses a particular challenge. They typically involve a human user who is not capable of performing cryptographic operations and therefore needs an intermediate device (e.g. an automated teller machine (ATM)) to interface with the protocol, which cannot always be trusted. In this work we introduce a formal model for the security of such protocols. In particular, we do not assume all intermediate devices as trusted. We use the Universal Composability (UC) framework, guaranteeing strong security and composability even in concurrent and interleaved executions.

With our model, we develop a set of basic requirements for electronic payment protocols without which no protocol can be considered secure. Based on these results, we discuss different current payment protocols and find that most do not realize these requirements. We then specify a protocol called L-Pay (based upon chipTAN and photoTAN), which uses an additional smartphone and which is secure in our model even if either the ATM or the smartphone is malicious.

One important security mechanism missing in our model is time (e.g. for arguing about the security of timestamps), which is impossible to model in the standard (G)UC framework however. Extensions exist that model time [23] which could be incorporated in our model in the future. Since we assume the bank to be trusted, we limited our model to a single bank and disregarded the problem of book-keeping. Future work could expand our model to include these features.

References

1. Achenbach, D., et al.: Your Money or Your Life-Modeling and Analyzing the Security of Electronic Payment in the UC Framework, Full version of the paper (2019). https://crypto.iti.kit.edu/fileadmin/User/Mechler/AGHKLMMQR19.pdf
2. Anderson, R., Bond, M., Choudary, O., Murdoch, S.J., Stajano, F.: Might financial cryptography kill financial innovation? – the curious case of EMV. In: Danezis, G. (ed.) FC 2011. LNCS, vol. 7035, pp. 220–234. Springer, Heidelberg (2012). https://doi.org/10.1007/978-3-642-27576-0_18
3. Basin, D.A., Radomirovic, S., Schläpfer, M.: A complete characterization of secure human-server communication. In: Fournet, C., Hicks, M.W., Viganó, L. (eds.) IEEE 28th Computer Security Foundations Symposium, CSF 2015, pp. 199–213. IEEE Computer Society (2015)
4. Bond, M., Choudary, O., Murdoch, S.J., Skorobogatov, S.P., Anderson, R.J.: Chip and skim: cloning EMV cards with the pre-play attack. In: 2014 IEEE Symposium on Security and Privacy, SP 2014, pp. 49–64. IEEE Computer Society (2014)
5. Borchert IT-Sicherheit UG: Display-TAN Mobile Banking: Secure and Mobile (2018). http://www.display-tan.com/. Accessed 18 Sep 2018
6. Canetti, R.: Universally composable security: a new paradigm for cryptographic protocols. In: 42nd Annual Symposium on Foundations of Computer Science, FOCS 2001, pp. 136–145. IEEE Computer Society (2001)
7. Canetti, R., Dodis, Y., Pass, R., Walfish, S.: Universally composable security with global setup. In: Vadhan, S.P. (ed.) TCC 2007. LNCS, vol. 4392, pp. 61–85. Springer, Heidelberg (2007). https://doi.org/10.1007/978-3-540-70936-7_4
8. Canetti, R., Krawczyk, H.: Universally composable notions of key exchange and secure channels. In: Knudsen, L.R. (ed.) EUROCRYPT 2002. LNCS, vol. 2332, pp. 337–351. Springer, Heidelberg (2002). https://doi.org/10.1007/3-540-46035-7_22

9. Chaum, D., Fiat, A., Naor, M.: Untraceable electronic cash. In: Goldwasser, S. (ed.) CRYPTO 1988. LNCS, vol. 403, pp. 319–327. Springer, New York (1990). https://doi.org/10.1007/0-387-34799-2_25

10. Chothia, T., Garcia, F.D., de Ruiter, J., van den Breekel, J., Thompson, M.: Relay cost bounding for contactless EMV payments. In: Böhme, R., Okamoto, T. (eds.) FC 2015. LNCS, vol. 8975, pp. 189–206. Springer, Heidelberg (2015). https://doi.org/10.1007/978-3-662-47854-7_11

11. Commerzbank: Das photoTAN-Lesegerät. https://www.commerzbank.de/portal/media/a-30-sonstige-medien/pdf/themen/sicherheit-1/Flyer_Lesegeraet.pdf. Accessed 13 Dec 2018

12. Commonwealth Bank of Australia: Cardless Cash (2018). https://www.commbank.com.au/digital-banking/cardless-cash.html. Accessed 25 Sep 2018

13. Cortier, V., Filipiak, A., Florent, J., Gharout, S., Traoré, J.: Designing and proving an EMV-compliant payment protocol for mobile devices. In: 2017 IEEE European Symposium on Security and Privacy, EuroS&P 2017, pp. 467–480. IEEE (2017)

14. Degabriele, J.P., Lehmann, A., Paterson, K.G., Smart, N.P., Strefler, M.: On the joint security of encryption and signature in EMV. In: Dunkelman, O. (ed.) CT-RSA 2012. LNCS, vol. 7178, pp. 116–135. Springer, Heidelberg (2012). https://doi.org/10.1007/978-3-642-27954-6_8

15. Denzel, M., Bruni, A., Ryan, M.D.: Smart-guard: defending user input from malware. In: 2016 Intl IEEE Conferences on Ubiquitous Intelligence & Computing, Advanced and Trusted Computing, Scalable Computing and Communications, Cloud and Big Data Computing, Internet of People, and Smart World Congress (UIC/ATC/ScalCom/CBDCom/IoP/SmartWorld), pp. 502–509. IEEE Computer Society (2016)

16. Deutsche Bank: photoTAN - schnell und einfach aktiviert. https://www.deutschebank.de/pfb/data/docs/Photo_TAN_Smartphone_2.pdf. Accessed 13 Dec 2018

17. Drimer, S., Murdoch, S.J.: Keep your enemies close: distance bounding against smartcard relay attacks. In: Provos, N. (ed.) Proceedings of the 16th USENIX Security Symposium 2007. USENIX Association (2007)

18. Emms, M., Arief, B., Freitas, L., Hannon, J., van Moorsel, A.P.A.: Harvesting high value foreign currency transactions from EMV contactless credit cards without the PIN. In: Ahn, G., Yung, M., Li, N. (eds.) 2014 ACM SIGSAC Conference on Computer and Communications Security, pp. 716–726. ACM (2014)

19. EMV: Integrated Circuit Card Specifications for Payment Systems: Book 1. Application Independent ICC to Terminal Interface Requirements, Version 4.3 (2011)

20. EMV: Integrated Circuit Card Specifications for Payment Systems: Book 2. Security and Key Management, Version 4.3 (2011)

21. EMV: Integrated Circuit Card Specifications for Payment Systems: Book 3. Application Specification, Version 4.3 (2011)

22. Garay, J., Kiayias, A., Leonardos, N.: The bitcoin backbone protocol: analysis and applications. In: Oswald, E., Fischlin, M. (eds.) EUROCRYPT 2015. LNCS, vol. 9057, pp. 281–310. Springer, Heidelberg (2015). https://doi.org/10.1007/978-3-662-46803-6_10

23. Katz, J., Maurer, U., Tackmann, B., Zikas, V.: Universally composable synchronous computation. In: Sahai, A. (ed.) TCC 2013. LNCS, vol. 7785, pp. 477–498. Springer, Heidelberg (2013). https://doi.org/10.1007/978-3-642-36594-2_27

24. Murdoch, S.J., Drimer, S., Anderson, R.J., Bond, M.: Chip and PIN is broken. In: 31st IEEE Symposium on Security and Privacy, S&P 2010, pp. 433–446. IEEE Computer Society (2010)

25. Old Bailey Proceedings Online (ed.): Trial of J. Buckley, T. Shenton, version 8.0. (1781). https://www.oldbaileyonline.org/browse.jsp?div=t17810912-37. Accessed 22 Sep 2018

26. Postbank: Postbank chipTAN comfort (2018). https://www.postbank.de/privatkunden/chiptan-comfort.html. Accessed Sep 25 2018

27. RedTeam Pentesting GmbH: Man-in-the-Middle Attacks against the chipTAN comfort Online Banking System (2009). https://www.redteam-pentesting.de/publications/2009-11-23-MitM-chipTAN-comfort_RedTeam-Pentesting_EN.pdf. Accessed 25 Sep 2018

28. Smart Card Alliance: Contactless EMV Payments: Benefits for Consumers, Merchants and Issuers. http://www.emv-connection.com/downloads/2016/06/Contactless-2-0-WP-FINAL-June-2016.pdf. Accessed 17 Dec 2018

29. Tamarin: Tamarin prover (2018). https://tamarin-prover.github.io/. Accessed 19 Dec 2018

30. Visa: Visa Token Service. https://usa.visa.com/partner-with-us/paymenttechnology/visa-token-service.html. Accessed 17 Dec 2018

31. Volksbank Mittelhessen eG: VR-mobileCash: Geld abheben ohne Karte. https://www.vb-mittelhessen.de/privatkunden/girokonto-kreditkarten/infosbanking/geld-abheben-ohne-karte.html. Accessed 25 Sep 2018

Multiparty Protocols

Secure Trick-Taking Game Protocols

How to Play Online Spades with Cheaters

Xavier Bultel[1] and Pascal Lafourcade[2]([✉])

[1] Univ Rennes, CNRS, IRISA, Rennes, France
[2] University Clermont Auvergne, LIMOS, Clermont-Ferrand, France
pascal.lafourcade@uca.fr

Abstract. Trick-Taking Games (TTGs) are card games in which each player plays one of his cards in turn according to a given rule. The player with the highest card then wins the trick, *i.e.,* he gets all the cards that have been played during the round. For instance, Spades is a famous TTG proposed by online casinos, where each player must play a card that follows the leading suit when it is possible. Otherwise, he can play any of his cards. In such a game, a dishonest user can play a wrong card even if he has cards of the leading suit. Since his other cards are hidden, there is no way to detect the cheat. Hence, the other players realize the problem later, *i.e.,* when the cheater plays a card that he is not supposed to have. In this case, the game is biased and is canceled. Our goal is to design protocols that prevent such a cheat for TTGs. We give a security model for secure Spades protocols, and we design a scheme called SecureSpades. This scheme is secure under the Decisional Diffie-Hellman assumption in the random oracle model. Our model and our scheme can be extended to several other TTGs, such as Belotte, Whist, Bridge, etc.

1 Introduction

The first card games originate around the 9th century, during the Tang dynasty. Today, they are played all around the world, and a multitude of different games exist. For instance, Poker is probably the most famous gambling card game. Thanks to the Internet, many web sites implement online card game applications, where players meet other players. Cards games websites require some security guarantees, such as secure access for payment, robust software, trusted servers, and cheating detection protocols. These guarantees are crucial for the reputation of the web site in the card game community.

Spades is a famous online gambling card game. It is a *trick-taking game*: at each round, players take turns playing, then the player that plays the highest card wins the *trick*, *i.e.,* all cards that have been played this round. Moreover, if it is possible, then players must play a card that follows the suit of the first card played in the round, otherwise they can play any other card. However, if a player cheats by playing a card of another suit while he has some cards of the leading suit, there is no way to detect it immediately. The other players will

© International Financial Cryptography Association 2019
I. Goldberg and T. Moore (Eds.): FC 2019, LNCS 11598, pp. 265–281, 2019.
https://doi.org/10.1007/978-3-030-32101-7_17

detect the cheat later, if the cheater plays a card of the leading suit. As a result, the game is biased, because players revealed some of their cards, hence players cannot replay the game, which must be canceled. Cheaters often get a penalty, but Spades is a team game, hence the cheater's partner is also punished, even if he is not an accomplice. It is even more unfair if the partners do not know each other and/or do not trust each other, which is the case in online games, where teams are chosen by the server.

To avoid this problem, online Spades web sites use a trusted server that manages the game. This server deals the cards, and prevents players from cheating, which means it knows all the cards of each player. However, having a trusted server is a strong security hypothesis, because if some players corrupt the server, then the security properties do not longer hold.

Our motivation is to design a cryptographic scheme, called SecureSpades, that allows the players to check that the other players do not cheat, whithout revealing any information about the cards of each player, and without any trusted server.

Contributions: In this paper, we focus on Trick-Taking Games (TTGs), which are card games where each player plays one of his cards in turn, and where the player with the highest card wins the trick. For the sake of clarity, we focus our work on Spades, because it is the most played online TTG for real money, and its rules are simple. However, our protocol can be extended to other TTGs, such as Whist or Bridge.

We propose a scheme for Spades that has the following security properties:

– The game server is not trusted.
– The players are convinced that nobody cheats. It means that:
  1. *Theft-resistance*: a player cannot play a card that is not in his hand, nor can a player play cards from the hand of his partner.
  2. *Cheating-resistance*: a player cannot play a card that does not follow the rules of the game (in Spades, if a player has a card of the leading suit, he must play it).
– *Unpredictability*: the cards are dealt at random.
– *Hand-privacy*: the players do not know the hidden cards of the other players.
– *Game-privacy*: at each round, the protocol does not leak any information except for the played cards.

We propose a formal definition of a Spades scheme, then we give a formal definition of the security properties described above. We also design SecureSpades, a protocol based on the Decisional Diffie-Hellman (DDH) assumption, and zero-knowledge proofs. Finally, we prove the security of SecureSpades in the random oracle model.

Our protocol not only ensures all the security properties of the real card games, it also provides additional security features. In real card games, it is not possible to detect cheating exactly when the wrong card is played. In fact, our protocol also allows players to detect cheats that are undetectable with real cards, hence it can be used to create new TTGs, for instance a Spades variant where the game is stopped after 5 rounds. In this variant, if the players do not have to reveal the cards they did not play, then there is no way to prevent them from cheating. However, with our approach, such a game can be securely implemented.

Related Work: In 1982, Goldwasser and Micali introduced the *Mental Poker* problem [10]: it asks whether it is possible to play a fair game of poker without physical cards and without a trusted dealer, *i.e.,* by phone or over the Internet. Since then, several works have focused on this primitive, such as [1,13,15]. In [12], the author brings together references to scientific papers related to this problem.

Most of mental poker protocols are based on the following paradigm. The players encrypt the cards together and shuffle them, then ciphertexts are assigned to each player, and each player receives information from the other players in order to decrypt their own cards. At the end of the game, the players reveal their encryption keys, which reveals the hand of all the players. In trick-taking games, each time a player plays a card, he must prove that the card is in his hand and that he has no *high-priority* card that he should play instead of this card. To achieve this property, we model the deck in a different way: each card is associated to a commitment of the secret key of a player. The player plays a card by proving that the committed secret key matches one of its public keys. This allows the player to prove that he cannot play high-priority cards by proving that none of his public keys match possible high-priority cards.

David *et al.* [8] introduced protocols for secure multi-party computation with penalties and secure cash distribution, which can be used for online poker. Bentov *et al.* [2] give a poker protocol in a stronger security model, which is more efficient than [8]. More recently, David *et al.* [9] proposed *Royale*, a universally composable protocol for securely playing any card games with financial rewards/penalties enforcement.

All of these works focus on mental card game protocols with secure payment distributions, but they cannot prevent players from cheating by playing illegal cards. Indeed, these protocols allow the users to play cards digitally with the same security level as if they play with real cards. Our goal is not only to implement a secure trick-taking game, but also to increase its security, in comparison with its physical version.

Finally, an other line of research is to detect collusion frauds in online card games, as done for instance in [14]. Players may exchange information about their cards using some side channels. The goal of [14] is to detect such a collusion attack via the users' behavior. This work is complementary to ours, because these collusion detection processes can also be used with our protocol.

Outline: In Sect. 2, we describe the rules of *Spades*. In Sect. 3, we give an informal overview of our scheme. In Sect. 4, we present the cryptographic tools used in the paper. In Sect. 5, we model Spades schemes. In Sect. 6, we define the security properties. In Sect. 7, we describe SecureSpades before concluding in the last section.

2   Spades Rules

Spades was created in the United States in the 1930s. Since the mid-1990s it has become very popular thanks to its accessibility in online card gaming rooms on the Internet. This game uses a standard deck of 52 cards and allows between two and five players. The most famous version requires four players, which are splitted in two teams of two. As indicated by the name of the game, spades are always trump. We give the rules of Spades for the four players version:

1. All 52 cards are distributed one by one to each player, meaning each player has 13 cards at the beginning of the game.
2. There are 13 successive rounds. In the first round, the first player is chosen at random, and subsequently the player that won the previous round begins. Players then each play a card in turn.
3. At each round, the player who plays the highest card wins the trick (*i.e.,* he takes the four cards played this round, but he cannot replay these cards). The rank of the cards is the following, form highest to lowest: Ace, King, Queen, Jack, 10, 9, 8, 7, 6, 5, 4, 3, 2. Trumps are higher than cards of the suit of the first card of the round, which are higher than all other cards.
4. Each player has to follow the suit of the first card of the round. If a player has no card that follows the suit, then he can play any other cards.
5. The game is finished once all players have played all of their cards.

Before playing the cards, each player bids the number of tricks he expects to perform. The sum of all the propositions for all players should be different from the number of cards per player. At the end of the game, each player calculates his score according to his bid and the number of tricks he has won.

3   An Overview of Our Protocol

We now give an informal overview of our Spades protocol. The idea is that the players must prove that each card they play follows the rule of the game. More precisely, the player first proves that he has the played card. If this card does not follow the suit, then he proves that none of his other cards are of the leading suit.

1. **Dealing cards**: We need to model the cards in such a way that these proofs are feasible. Each player i generates 13 pairs of public/private keys $(\mathsf{pk}_{i,j}, \mathsf{sk}_{i,j})$ (for $1 \leq j \leq 13$). To deal the cards, the players run a protocol that privately assigns each key to each card with the following steps: (i) each player generates commitments on his 13 secret keys, (ii) the players group all the $13 \cdot 4 = 52$ commitments together, (iii) each player shuffles and randomizes the commitments in turn, (iv) the players jointly associate each commitment to each card of the deck at random. The hand of a player is the set of the 13 cards that match the commitments of his secret keys. Figure 1 illustrates our dealing cards protocol, where $c(\mathsf{sk})$ denotes the commitment of

a secret key sk, and $c'(sk)$ denotes the randomization of $c(sk)$. In this example, the 1st card of player 1 is A♣, his 2nd card is 2♡, and his 13th card is A♠. Note that the commitments and the public keys must be unlinkable for anyone who does not know the corresponding secret keys.

2. **Play a card**: To play a card, the player proves that this card matches the commitment of one of his secret keys. If the player does not follow the suit, then he proves that none of his other cards are of the leading suit. To do so, he proves that each commitment that matches a card of a non-leading suit commits one of his (not yet used) keys.

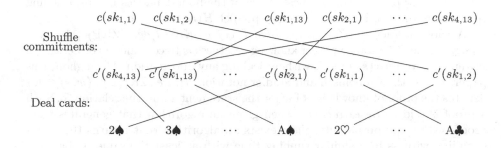

Fig. 1. Dealing cards in our Spades protocol.

4 Cryptographic Tools

We present the cryptographic tools used throughout this paper.

Definition 1 (DDH [4]). *Let* $\mathbb{G}$ *be a prime order group. The DDH assumption states that given* $(g, g^a, g^b, g^z) \in \mathbb{G}^4$, *it is hard to decide whether* $z = a \cdot b$ *or not.*

A *n-party random generator* is a protocol that allows n users to generate a random number, even if $n - 1$ users are dishonest.

Definition 2 (Multi-party random generator [3]). *A n-party $\mathcal{S}$-random generator* $\mathsf{RG}_{P_1,\ldots,P_n}$ *is a protocol where n parties* $(P_1, \ldots, P_n)$ *interact, and return* $s \in \mathcal{S}$. *Such a protocol is said to be secure when for any polynomial time distinguisher* $\mathcal{D}$, *any polynomial time adversary* $\mathcal{A}$, *there exists a negligible function* ϵ *such that:* $|\Pr[1 \leftarrow D(s) : s \xleftarrow{\$} \mathcal{S}] - \Pr[1 \leftarrow D(s) : s \leftarrow \mathsf{RG}_{\mathcal{C},\mathcal{A}}(k)]| \leq \epsilon(k)$ *where* $s \xleftarrow{\$} \mathsf{RG}_{\mathcal{C},\mathcal{A}}$ *denotes the output of* $\mathcal{C}$ *at the end of the protocol* RG *where* $\mathcal{C}$ *plays the role of a honest user, and* $\mathcal{A}$ *plays the role of the $n - 1$ other users.*

Inspired by [3], we propose the following multi-party random generator protocol based on the random oracle model (ROM).

Definition 3. *Let* S *be a set and* n *be an integer, and let* $H : \{0,1\}^* \to \{0,1\}^k$ *and* $H' : \{0,1\}^* \to S$ *be two hash functions simulated by random oracles. The protocol* $\mathsf{RandGen}^S_{P_1,\dots,P_n}(k)$ *is a* n*-party* S*-random generator defined as follows. Each player* P_i *(where* $1 \leq i \leq n$*) chooses* $r_i \xleftarrow{\$} \{0,1\}^k$ *at random, computes* $H(r_i)$*, and broadcasts it, then each player reveals* r_i*. Each player returns* $H'(r_0 \| \dots \| r_n)$.

Lemma 1. *For any set* S *and any integer* n*,* $\mathsf{RandGen}^S_{P_1,\dots,P_n}(k)$ *is secure in the random oracle model.*

The proof of this lemma is given in the full version of this paper [6]. The idea is that dishonest parties cannot guess the r_i of the honest parties before revealing their commitments, hence they cannot predict $H(r_0 \| \dots \| r_n)$.

A (non-interactive) *Zero-Knowledge Proof of Knowledge* (ZKP) [11] for a binary relation $\mathcal{R}$ allows a prover knowing a witness w to convince a verifier that a statement s verifies $(s, w) \in \mathcal{R}$ without leaking any information. Throughout this paper, we use the Camenisch and Stadler notation [7], *i.e.*, $\mathsf{ZK}\{(w) : (w, s) \in \mathcal{R}\}$ denotes the proof of knowledge of w for the statement s and the relation $\mathcal{R}$. Such a proof is said to be *extractable* when given an algorithm that generates valid proofs with some probability, there exists an algorithm that returns the corresponding witness in a similar running time with at least the same probability. Such a proof is said to be *zero-knowledge* when there exists a polynomial time simulator that follows the same probability distribution as an honest prover.

5   Formal Definitions

We formalize Spades schemes and the corresponding security requirements. We model a 52 cards deck by a tuple $D = (\mathsf{id}_1, \dots, \mathsf{id}_{52})$ such that $\forall\ i \in [\![1, 52]\!]$, $\mathsf{id}_i = (\mathsf{id}_i.\mathsf{suit}, \mathsf{id}_i.\mathsf{val}) \in \{\heartsuit, \spadesuit, \diamondsuit, \clubsuit\} \times \{1, \dots, 10, \mathsf{J}, \mathsf{Q}, \mathsf{K}\}$ is called *a card*, where $\forall\ (i,j) \in [\![1, 52]\!]^2$ such that $i \neq j$, $\mathsf{id}_i \neq \mathsf{id}_j$. The set of all possible decks is denoted by Decks.

We first define Spades schemes, which are tuples that contain all the algorithms that are used by the players. KeyGen allows each player to generate its public/secret key. $\mathsf{GKeyGen}$ allows the players to generate a public game key. $\mathsf{DeckGen}$ is a protocol that generates a random deck. $\mathsf{GetHand}$ determines the hand of a given player from his secret key and the game key. Play allows a player to play a card, and to prove that it is a *legal* play. Verif allows the other players to check this proof. Finally, $\mathsf{GetSuit}$ returns the leading suit of the current round (in Spades, the suit of the first card played during this round).

Definition 4. *A* Spade *scheme is a tuple of eight algorithms* $W = (\mathsf{Init}, \mathsf{KeyGen}, \mathsf{GKeyGen}, \mathsf{DeckGen}, \mathsf{GetHand}, \mathsf{Play}, \mathsf{Verif}, \mathsf{GetSuit})$ *defined as follows:*

$\mathsf{Init}(k)$: *It returns a setup* setup.
$\mathsf{KeyGen}(\mathsf{setup})$: *It returns a key pair* $(\mathsf{pk}, \mathsf{sk})$.

GKeyGen: *It is a 4-party protocol, where for all* $j \in [\![1,4]\!]$ *the* j^{th} *party is denoted* P_j *and takes as input* $(\mathsf{sk}_j, \{\mathsf{pk}_i\}_{1 \leq i \leq 4})$. *This protocol returns a game public key* PK, *or the bottom symbol* $\bot$.

DeckGen: *It is a 4-party* Decks-*random generator.*

GetHand$(\mathsf{sk}, \mathsf{pk}, \mathsf{PK}, D)$: *It returns a set of* 13 *different cards* H *called a hand (where* $D \in$ Decks*).*

Play$(n, \mathsf{id}, \mathsf{sk}, \mathsf{pk}, \mathsf{st}, \mathsf{PK}, D)$: *It takes as input a player index* $n \in [\![1,4]\!]$, *a card* id, *a pair of secret/public key, a global state* st *that stores the relevent information about the previous plays, the game public key* PK *and the deck* D, *and returns a proof* Π, *and the updated global state* st'.

Verif$(n, \mathsf{id}, \Pi, \mathsf{pk}, \mathsf{st}, \mathsf{st}', \mathsf{PK}, D)$: *It takes as input a player index* $n \in [\![1,4]\!]$, *a card identity* id, *a proof* Π *generated by the algorithm* Verif, *the global state* st *and the updated global state* st', *the game public key* PK *and the deck* D, *and returns a bit* b. *If* $b = 1$, *we say that* Π *is valid.*

GetSuit(st): *It returns a suit* $\mathsf{suit} \in \{\heartsuit, \spadesuit, \diamondsuit, \clubsuit\}$ *from the current global state of the game* st, *where* suit *is the leading suit for the current turn.*

We then define the *Spades protocol*, which allows four players to play Spades using the algorithms of the Spades scheme. It is divided in four phases:

Initialisation phase: One player generates and broadcasts the public setup.

Keys generation phase: After they have generated their public/private keys, the players run GKeyGen to generate the game key together.

Shuffle phase: The players choose a deck using DeckGen, then they compute their own hand using GetHand.

Game phase: Finally, they play in turn using the algorithms Play and Verif to prove the validity of the cards they play. If some verification fails, the player has to cancel only the last card he has played, and to simply play another card.

Definition 5. *Let* $W = ($Init, KeyGen, GKeyGen, DeckGen, GetHand, Play, Verif, GetSuit$)$ *be a Spades scheme and* $k \in \mathbb{N}$ *be a security parameter. Let* Player$_1$, Player$_2$, Player$_3$, Player$_4$ *be four polynomial time algorithms. The* Spades *protocol instantiated by* W *and the setup* setup *between* Player$_1$, Player$_2$, Player$_3$ *and* Player$_4$ *is the following protocol:*

Initialisation phase: Player$_1$ *runs* setup $\leftarrow$ Init(k) *and broadcasts* setup.

Keys generation phase: *The players set* st $= \bot$. *Each player* Player$_i$ *runs* $(\mathsf{pk}_i, \mathsf{sk}_i) \leftarrow$ KeyGen$(setup)$ *and broadcasts* pk_i, *then the players generate* PK *by running the protocol* GKeyGen *together.*

Shuffle phase: *The players generate a deck* $D \in$ Decks *by running* DeckGen *together. For all* $i \in [\![1,4]\!]$, Player$_i$ *runs* $H_i \leftarrow$ GetHand$(\mathsf{sk}_i, \mathsf{pk}_i, \mathsf{PK}, D)$.

Game phase: *This phase is composed of* 52 *(sequential) steps (corresponding to the* 52 *cards played in a game). The players initialize the current player index* $p = 1$. *At each turn,* Player$_p$ *designates the player who plays. Each step proceeds as follows:*

- Player$_p$ *chooses* id $\in H_p$, *then runs* $(\Pi, \mathsf{st}') \leftarrow$ Play$(p, \mathsf{id}, \mathsf{sk}_p, \mathsf{pk}_p, \mathsf{st}, \mathsf{PK}, D)$.

- *For all $i \in [\![1, 4]\!] \setminus \{p\}$, Player$_p$ sends* $(\mathrm{id}, \Pi, \mathrm{st}')$ *to* Player$_i$.
- *Each* Player$_i$ *then checks that* $\mathsf{Verif}(p, \mathrm{id}, \Pi, \mathsf{pk}_p, \mathrm{st}, \mathrm{st}', \mathsf{PK}, D) = 1$, *otherwise,* Player$_i$ *sends* error *to* Player$_p$, *who repeats this step and plays a valid card.*
- *If* $\mathsf{Verif}(p, \mathrm{id}, \Pi, \mathsf{pk}_p, \mathrm{st}, \mathrm{st}', \mathsf{PK}, D) = 1$, *all players update the state* $\mathrm{st} := \mathrm{st}'$, *and update the index* p *that points the next player according to the rule of the game.*

6   Security Properties

We first define *Spades strategies*. In a card game, each player chooses what card he wants to play depending on his hand and the previously played cards of the other players. In order to formalize the security of our protocol, we need to model honest players who choose the cards they play themselves. A Spades strategy is an algorithm that decides which card to play using all known information by a given player. We define security experiments where the choices of each honest player is simulated by a Spades strategy. The idea is that a Spades scheme is secure if for any polynomial time adversary, the probability of winning the experiment is negligible, whatever the Spades strategies used by the experiment.

Definition 6. *A* Spades strategy *is a polynomial time algorithm* Strat *that takes as input a tuple of cards* played *(which represents all cards played at some point in a Spades game) and a set of cards* hand *(which represents all cards of a player at the same point), a first player index* p_*, *a player index* p, *and that returns a card* $\mathrm{id} \in$ Hand *which is valid according to the rules of Spades (i.e., that follows the suit of the first card of the current round).*

We define an experiment where a challenger simulates the Spades protocol to an adversary. We use this experiment to define Spades' security properties. The adversary first chooses the index of the player he wants to corrupt. The challenger generates the public/secret keys of the three other users, then the adversary sends his public key together with the index of an *accomplice*. The accomplice allows the experiment to capture the attacks where a dishonest player and his game partner collude. The adversary has access to the private key of all players. The adversary and the challenger then run the game key and the deck generation protocol, such that the adversary plays the role of the corrupted player and the accomplice. The challenger generates the hand of each player. Note that the challenger cannot use the hand generation algorithm for the corrupted player, because he does not know his secret key; however, the challenger can deduce this hand because it contains the 13 cards that are not in the hand of the three other users. Finally, the challenger and the adversary run the game phase, such that the adversary plays the role of the corrupted user and his accomplice.

Definition 7. *Let* $W = ($Init, KeyGen, GKeyGen, DeckGen, GetHand, Play, Verif, GetSuit$)$ *be a Spades scheme,* $S = ($Strat$_1$, Strat$_2$, Strat$_3$, Strat$_4)$ *be a tuple of strategies, and* $k \in \mathbb{N}$ *be a security parameter. Let* $\mathcal{A}$ *and* $\mathcal{C}$ *be two polynomial time algorithms. The* Spades *experiment* $\mathsf{Exp}_{W,S,\mathcal{A}}^{\mathsf{Spades}}(k)$ *instantiated by* W *and* S *between the adversary* $\mathcal{A}$ *and the challenger* $\mathcal{C}$ *is defined as follows:*

Keys generation phase: $\mathcal{C}$ *runs* setup $\leftarrow$ Init(k), *sets* st $=\perp$, *and sends the pair* (setup, st) *to* $\mathcal{A}$, *who returns a corrupted user index* $i_c \in [\![1,4]\!]$. *For all* $i \in [\![1,4]\!] \setminus \{i_c\}$, $\mathcal{C}$ *runs* $(\mathsf{pk}_i, \mathsf{sk}_i) \leftarrow$ KeyGen(setup) *and sends* $(\mathsf{pk}_i, \mathsf{sk}_i)$ *to* $\mathcal{A}$, *who returns the public key* pk_{i_c} *and an accomplice index* i_a.

Game key generation phase: $\mathcal{C}$ *and* $\mathcal{A}$ *generate* PK *by running the algorithm* GKeyGen *together, such that* $\mathcal{A}$ *plays the role of the players* P_{i_c} *and* P_{i_a}, *and* $\mathcal{C}$ *plays the role of the other players. If* PK $=\perp$, *then* $\mathcal{C}$ *aborts and returns* 0.

Shuffle phase: $\mathcal{C}$ *and* $\mathcal{A}$ *generate* D *by running the algorithm* DeckGen *together, such that* $\mathcal{A}$ *plays the role of the players* P_{i_c} *and* P_{i_a}, *and* $\mathcal{C}$ *plays the role of the two other players.* $\mathcal{C}$ *sets* $p = 1$ *and parses* D *as* $(\mathsf{id}_1, \ldots, \mathsf{id}_{52})$. *For all* $i \in [\![1,4]\!] \setminus \{i_c\}$, $\mathcal{C}$ *runs* $H_i \leftarrow$ GetHand($\mathsf{sk}_i, \mathsf{pk}_i$, PK, D), *and sets* $H_{i_c} = \{\mathsf{id}_i\}_{1 \leq i \leq 52} \setminus (\cup_{i=1; i \neq i_c}^{4} H_i)$.

Game phase: $\mathcal{C}$ *initializes the current player index* $p = 1$ *and the corrupted play index* $\gamma = 0$, *and* played $=\perp$. *For* $i \in [\![1,52]\!]$:

If $p \neq i_c$ **and** $p \neq i_a$: $\mathcal{C}$ *runs* id $\leftarrow$ Strat$_p$(played, H_p, p_*, p), *then* $\mathcal{C}$ *runs* $(\Pi, \mathsf{st}') \leftarrow$ Play(p, id, $\mathsf{sk}_p, \mathsf{pk}_p$, st, PK, D). $\mathcal{C}$ *sends* (id, Π, st') *to* $\mathcal{A}$ *and updates* st $:=$ st$'$.

If $p = i_a$: $\mathcal{C}$ *receives* (id, Π, st') *from* $\mathcal{A}$. *If* Verif(i_a, id, Π, pk_{i_a}, st, st$'$, PK, D) $= 0$, *then* $\mathcal{C}$ *aborts and the experiment returns* 0. *Else,* $\mathcal{C}$ *updates* st $:=$ st$'$.

If $p = i_c$: $\mathcal{C}$ *increments* $\gamma := \gamma + 1$, *then receives* (id, Π, st') *from* $\mathcal{A}$ *and sets* $(\mathsf{id}_{i_c,\gamma}, \Pi_{i_c,\gamma}) = (\mathsf{id}, \Pi)$. $\mathcal{C}$ *sets* $\mathsf{st}_\gamma = \mathsf{st}$ *and* $\mathsf{st}'_\gamma = \mathsf{st}'$. $\mathcal{C}$ *sets* $\mathsf{suit}_{i_c,\gamma} =$ GetSuit(st). *If* Verif(i_c, $\mathsf{id}_{i_c,\gamma}$, $\Pi_{i_c,\gamma}$, pk_{i_c}, st_γ, st'_γ, PK, D) $= 0$, *then* $\mathcal{C}$ *aborts and the experiment returns* 0. *Else,* $\mathcal{C}$ *updates* st $:=$ st$'$.

$\mathcal{C}$ *then updates the index* p *that points to the next player according to the rule of Spades, parses* played *as* $(\mathsf{pl}_1, \ldots, \mathsf{pl}_n)$ *(where* $n = |\mathsf{played}|$*) and updates* played $:= (\mathsf{pl}_1, \ldots, \mathsf{pl}_n, \mathsf{id})$.

Final phase: *The experiment returns* 1.

The first security property of a Spades scheme is the *theft-resistance*, which ensures that no adversary is able to play a card that is not in his hand, even if the card is in the hand of his accomplice. On the other words, two partners are not able to exchange their cards.

Definition 8. *A Spades scheme* W *is said to be* theft-resistant *if for any tuple of strategies* $S = ($Strat$_1$, Strat$_2$, Strat$_3$, Strat$_4$*) and any polynomial time adversary* $\mathcal{A}$ *who plays the Spade experiment instantiated by* W *and* S, *the probability that there exists* $\gamma \in [\![1,13]\!]$ *such that:*

- Verif(i_c, $\mathsf{id}_{i_c,\gamma}$, $\Pi_{i_c,\gamma}$, pk_{i_c}, st_γ, st'_γ, PK, D) $= 1$, *i.e., the* γ^{th} *play of the adversary is accepted for the card* $\mathsf{id}_{i_c,\gamma}$; *and*
- $\forall$ id $\in H_{i_c}$, $\mathsf{id}_{i_c,\gamma} \neq$ id, *i.e., the card* $\mathsf{id}_{i_c,\gamma}$ *is not in the adversary hand;*

is negligible.

We then define the *cheating-resistance* property, which ensures that no adversary is able to play a card if he should play another valid one.

Definition 9. *A Spades scheme W is said to be* cheating-resistant *if for any tuple of strategies $S = (\mathsf{Strat}_1, \mathsf{Strat}_2, \mathsf{Strat}_3, \mathsf{Strat}_4)$ and any polynomial time adversary $\mathcal{A}$ who plays the Spade experiment instantiated by W and S, the probability that there exists $\gamma \in [\![1, 13]\!]$ such that:*

- *$\mathsf{Verif}(i_c \mathsf{id}_{i_c, \gamma}, \Pi_{i_c, \gamma}, \mathsf{pk}_{i_c}, \mathsf{st}_\gamma, \mathsf{st}'_\gamma, \mathsf{PK}, D) = 1$, i.e., the γth play of the adversary is accepted for the card $\mathsf{id}_{i_c, \gamma}$; and*
- *$\mathsf{id}_{i_c, \gamma}.\mathsf{suit} \neq \mathsf{suit}_{i_c, \gamma}$ and $\mathsf{suit}_{i_c, \gamma} \neq \perp$ i.e., the suit of the card $\mathsf{id}_{i_c, \gamma}$ is not the leading suit; and*
- *$\exists\ \bar{\mathsf{id}} \in H_{i_c}$ such that: $\forall\ l \leq \gamma, \mathsf{id}_{i_c, l} \neq \bar{\mathsf{id}}$ and $\bar{\mathsf{id}}.\mathsf{suit} = \mathsf{suit}_{i_c, \gamma}$. i.e., the adversary has a card of the leading suit in his hand that was not already played before the γth play;*

is negligible.

We define the *unpredictability*, which ensures that no adversary can influence the card dealing, *i.e.*, $\mathcal{A}$ cannot predict which card will be in which hand.

Definition 10. *A Spades scheme W is said to be* unpredictable *if for any tuple of strategies $S = (\mathsf{Strat}_1, \mathsf{Strat}_2, \mathsf{Strat}_3, \mathsf{Strat}_4)$, any polynomial time adversary $\mathcal{A}$ who plays the Spades experiment instantiated by W and S, for all $i \in [\![1, 52]\!]$ the probability that $\mathsf{id}_i \in H_{i_c}$ is negligibly close to $1/4$.*

We introduce a new experiment that is called the *hand Spades experiment*, where the challenger simulates the key generation phase of the Spades protocol (but not the game phase). In this experiment the adversary does not know the private keys of the other players and has no accomplice. This experiment will be used to model the attacks where an adversary tries to guess the cards of the other players, including his partner.

Definition 11. *Let $W = (\mathsf{Init}, \mathsf{KeyGen}, \mathsf{GKeyGen}, \mathsf{DeckGen}, \mathsf{GetHand}, \mathsf{Play}, \mathsf{Verif}, \mathsf{GetSuit})$ be a Spades scheme and $k \in \mathbb{N}$ be a security parameter. Let $\mathcal{A}$ and $\mathcal{C}$ be two polynomial time algorithms. The hand Spades experiment $\mathsf{Exp}^{\mathsf{HSpades}}_{W, \mathcal{A}}(k)$ instantiated by W between the adversary $\mathcal{A}$ and the challenger $\mathcal{C}$ is defined by:*

Key generation phase: *$\mathcal{C}$ runs setup $\leftarrow \mathsf{Init}(k)$. It sets $\mathsf{st} = \perp$. It sends the pair $(\mathsf{setup}, \mathsf{st})$ to $\mathcal{A}$, who returns $i_c \in [\![1, 4]\!]$. For all $i \in [\![1, 4]\!] \setminus \{i_c\}$, $\mathcal{C}$ runs $(\mathsf{pk}_i, \mathsf{sk}_i) \leftarrow \mathsf{KeyGen}(\mathsf{setup})$ and sends pk_i to $\mathcal{A}$, who returns pk_{i_c}.*

Game key generation phase: *$\mathcal{C}$ and $\mathcal{A}$ generate PK by running the algorithm $\mathsf{GKeyGen}$ together, such that $\mathcal{A}$ plays the role of P_{i_c}, and $\mathcal{C}$ plays the role of the three other players. If $\mathsf{PK} = \perp$, then $\mathcal{C}$ aborts and returns 0.*

Shuffle phase: *$\mathcal{A}$ sends a deck $D \in \mathsf{Decks}$ to $\mathcal{C}$. $\mathcal{C}$ parses D as $(\mathsf{id}_1, \ldots, \mathsf{id}_{52})$. For all $i \in [\![1, 4]\!] \setminus \{i_c\}$, $\mathcal{C}$ runs $H_i \leftarrow \mathsf{GetHand}(\mathsf{sk}_i, \mathsf{pk}_i, \mathsf{PK}, D)$, and sets $H_{i_c} = \{\mathsf{id}_i\}_{1 \leq i \leq 52} \setminus (\cup_{i=1; i \neq i_c}^4 H_i)$.*

Challenge phase: *$\mathcal{C}$ picks (θ_0, θ_1) in $([\![1, 4]\!] \setminus \{i_c\})^2$ such that $\theta_0 \neq \theta_1$. $\mathcal{C}$ picks $b \xleftarrow{\$} \{0, 1\}$ and $\bar{\mathsf{id}} \xleftarrow{\$} H_{\theta_b}$, and sends $(\bar{\mathsf{id}}, \theta_0, \theta_1)$ to $\mathcal{A}$, who returns b_*.*

Final phase: *If $b = b_*$, then $\mathcal{C}$ returns 1, else it returns 0.*

We then define the *hand-privacy*. This property ensures that an adversary has no information about the hand of the other players before the game phase is run.

Definition 12. *A Spades scheme W is said to be* hand-private *if for any tuple of strategies $S = (\mathsf{Strat}_1, \mathsf{Strat}_2, \mathsf{Strat}_3, \mathsf{Strat}_4)$ and any polynomial time adversary $\mathcal{A}$ who plays the hand-Spades experiment instantiated by W and S, the probability that the experiment returns 1 is negligibly closed to $1/2$.*

The last property is the *game-privacy*. The idea is that, at each step of the game phase, the players learn nothing else than the cards that have been previously played. We show that, after the game key is generated, each player is able to simulate all the protocol interactions knowing the players' strategies. More formally, there exists a simulator that takes as input values known by the player such that the player cannot distinguish whether he plays the real game experiment or he interacts with the simulator.

Definition 13. *For any $k \in \mathbb{N}$, any Spades scheme W, any quadruplet of strategies S, any adversary $\mathcal{D}$ and any $K = (\mathsf{setup}, \mathsf{pk}_{i_c}, \{(\mathsf{pk}_i, \mathsf{sk}_i)\}_{1 \leq i \leq 4; i \neq i_c}, \mathsf{PK})$, $Exp^{\mathsf{Spades}}_{W,S,K,\mathcal{D}}(k)$ denotes the same experiment as $Exp^{\mathsf{Spades}}_{W,S,\mathcal{D}}(k)$ except:*

1. *The challenger and the adversary use the setup and the keys in K instead of generating fresh setup and keys during the experiment.*
2. *The challenger does not send sk_i for all $1 \leq i \leq 4$ such that $i \neq i_c$ to $\mathcal{A}$, and $\mathcal{A}$ has no accomplice.*

A Spades scheme W is said to be game-private *if there exists a polynomial time simulator Sim such that for any tuple of strategies S and any polynomial time 5-party algorithm $\mathcal{D} = (\mathcal{D}_1, \mathcal{D}_2, \mathcal{D}_3, \mathcal{D}_4, \mathcal{D}_5)$, $|P_{\mathsf{real}}(\mathcal{D}, k) - P_{\mathsf{sim}}(\mathcal{D}, k)|$ is negligible, where*

$$P_{\mathsf{real}}(k) =$$

$$\Pr\left[1 \leftarrow \mathcal{D}_5(\mathsf{vw}) : \begin{array}{l} \mathsf{setup} \leftarrow \mathsf{Init}(k); i_c \leftarrow \mathcal{D}_1(\mathsf{setup}); \\ \forall i \in [\![1,4]\!], \\ \mathit{If}\ i \neq i_c, (\mathsf{pk}_i, \mathsf{sk}_i) \leftarrow \mathsf{KeyGen}(\mathsf{setup}); \\ \mathit{Else}\ \mathsf{pk}_{i_c} \leftarrow \mathcal{D}_2(\mathsf{setup}, \{\mathsf{pk}_i\}_{1 \leq j \leq i}, \mathsf{vw}); \\ \mathsf{PK} \leftarrow \mathsf{GKeyGen}_{P_1, P_2, P_3, P_4}\ \mathit{where}\ P_{i_c} = \mathcal{D}_3; \\ K := (\mathsf{setup}, \mathsf{pk}_{i_c}, \{(\mathsf{pk}_i, \mathsf{sk}_i)\}_{1 \leq i \leq 4; i \neq i_c}, \mathsf{PK}); \\ \mathit{If}\ \mathsf{PK} = \perp, \mathsf{vw}_r := \perp; \\ \mathit{Else}\ b \leftarrow Exp^{\mathsf{Spades}}_{W,S,K,\mathcal{D}_4(\mathsf{vw})}(k); \end{array} \right]$$

$$P_{\mathsf{sim}}(k) =$$

$$\Pr\left[1 \leftarrow \mathcal{D}_5(\mathsf{vw}) : \begin{array}{l} \mathsf{setup} \leftarrow \mathsf{Init}(k); i_c \leftarrow \mathcal{D}_1(\mathsf{setup}); \\ \forall i \in [\![1,4]\!], \\ \mathit{If}\ i \neq i_c, (\mathsf{pk}_i, \mathsf{sk}_i) \leftarrow \mathsf{KeyGen}(\mathsf{setup}); \\ \mathit{Else}\ \mathsf{pk}_{i_c} \leftarrow \mathcal{D}_2(\mathsf{setup}, \{\mathsf{pk}_i\}_{1 \leq j \leq i}, \mathsf{vw}); \\ \mathsf{PK} \leftarrow \mathsf{GKeyGen}_{P_1, P_2, P_3, P_4}\ \mathit{where}\ P_{i_c} = \mathcal{D}_3; \\ \mathit{If}\ \mathsf{PK} = \perp, \mathsf{vw}_r := \perp; \\ \mathit{Else}\ b \leftarrow \mathsf{Sim}^{\mathsf{Spades}}_{W,S,\mathcal{D}_4(\mathsf{vw})}(k, \mathsf{setup}, i_c, \{\mathsf{pk}_i\}_{1 \leq i \leq 4}, \mathsf{PK}, \mathsf{vw}); \end{array} \right]$$

and where vw *denotes the view of* $\mathcal{D}$*, i.e., all the values sent and received by each algorithm of* $\mathcal{D}$ *during his interaction with the experiment.*

Note that if a scheme is both hand-private and private-game, then players have no information about the other players' hands except for all the cards they have already played.

7   Schemes

We first informally show how our protocol, SecureSpades, works, then we give its formal definition.

Keys generation. Each player i generates 13 key pairs $(\mathsf{pk}_{i,j}, \mathsf{sk}_{i,j})$ for $1 \leq j \leq 13$ such that $\mathsf{pk}_{i,j} = g^{\mathsf{sk}_{i,j}}$. The players then generate a game key PK together, which is made of 52 pairs (h_l, PK_l) such that $h_l^{\mathsf{sk}_{i,j}} = \mathsf{PK}_l$. The keys PK_l are shuffled, meaning each player does not know which PK_l corresponds to which $\mathsf{pk}_{i,j}$, except for his own public keys. To build PK, for all $l \in [\![1, 52]\!]$ the players set $h_{0,l} = g$ and $\mathsf{PK}_{0,l} = \mathsf{pk}_{i,j}$ such that (i,j) is in $[\![1,4]\!] \times [\![1,13]\!]$ and is different for each l. Note that it holds that $h_{0,l}^{\mathsf{sk}_{i,j}} = \mathsf{PK}_{0,l}$. The first player then randomizes and shuffles all pairs $(h_{0,l}, \mathsf{PK}_{0,l})$, *i.e.*, he chooses a random vector r and a random permutation δ and computes $h_{1,l} = (h_{0,\delta(i)})^{r_i}$ and $\mathsf{PK}_{1,l} = (\mathsf{PK}_{0,\delta(i)})^{r_i}$. The three other players randomize and shuffle the pairs $(h_{n,l}, \mathsf{PK}_{n,l})$ in order to obtain the pairs $(h_{n+1,l}, \mathsf{PK}_{n+1,l})$ for $1 \leq n \leq 3$ in turn in the same way, then they set $(h_l, \mathsf{PK}_l) = (h_{4,l}, \mathsf{PK}_{4,l})$ for all l. If the shuffles are correctly built, then it holds that for each l there exists a different pair (i,j) such that $h_l^{\mathsf{sk}_{i,j}} = \mathsf{PK}_l$. After each shuffle, the player proves that each $(h_{i,l}, \mathsf{PK}_{i,l})$ is a correct randomization of one $(h_{i-1,l'}, \mathsf{PK}_{i-1,l'})$ where $1 \leq l' \leq 52$. Each player then checks that each of his secret keys match one PK_l, otherwise he aborts the protocol. Since each player shuffles the keys using a secret permutation, they do not know which PK_l matches which $\mathsf{pk}_{i,j}$, except for their own public keys.

Hand generation. Players generate a random deck $D = (\mathsf{id}_1, \ldots, \mathsf{id}_{52})$ using the $\mathsf{RandGen}^{\mathsf{Deck}}$ protocol, then for all $1 \leq l \leq 52$, the key PK_l corresponds to the card id_l. The hand of the player i is the set of all cards id_l such that there exists $1 \leq j \leq 13$ such that $h_l^{\mathsf{sk}_{i,j}} = \mathsf{PK}_l$. Since the player does not know the keys $\mathsf{sk}_{i',j}$ for $i' \neq i$, he does not know the cards of the other players.

Play a card. To play the card id_l, the player i proves that the card id_l matches one of his key $\mathsf{pk}_{i,j}$ by showing that $h_l^{\mathsf{sk}_{i,j}} = \mathsf{PK}_l$. Note that since the player does not reveal $\mathsf{sk}_{i,j}$, he can use the same set of public keys for different games. To prove that he cannot play any card of the leading suit, the player i sets L such that $l \in L$ if and only if id_l is not of the leading suit, then the player i proves in a zero-knowledge way that for all $\mathsf{pk}_{i,j}$ that correspond to cards that are not already played, there exists an (unrevealed) $l \in L$ such that $\log_{h_l}(\mathsf{PK}_l) = \log_g(\mathsf{pk}_{i,j})$. This implies that the player has no card of the leading suit, hence he is not cheating.

Definition 14. *SecureSpades is a Spades scheme defined as follows:*

Init(k): *It generates a group $\mathbb{G}$ of prime order q, a generator $g \in \mathbb{G}$ and returns $(\mathbb{G}, p, g)$.*

KeyGen(setup): *For all $i \in [\![1, 13]\!]$, it picks $\mathsf{sk}_i \xleftarrow{\$} \mathbb{Z}_q^*$ and computes $\mathsf{pk}_i = g^{\mathsf{sk}_i}$. It returns $\mathsf{pk} = (\mathsf{pk}_1, \ldots, \mathsf{pk}_{13})$ and $\mathsf{sk} = (\mathsf{sk}_1, \ldots, \mathsf{sk}_{13})$.*

GKeyGen: *It is a 4-party protocol, where for all $i \in [\![1, 4]\!]$ the ith party is denoted P_i, and takes as input $(\mathsf{sk}_i, \{\mathsf{pk}_j\}_{1 \leq j \leq 4})$. This protocol returns a game public key PK, or the bottom symbol $\perp$. If there exist (i_1, j_1) and (i_2, j_2) such that $(i_1, j_1) \neq (i_2, j_2)$ and $\mathsf{pk}_{i_1, j_1} = \mathsf{pk}_{i_2, j_2}$, then the players abort and return $\perp$.*

- *For all $i \in [\![1, 4]\!]$, each player parses pk_i as $(\mathsf{pk}_{i,1}, \ldots, \mathsf{pk}_{i,13})$. For all $j \in [\![1, 13]\!]$, each player sets $h_{0,(i-1)\cdot 13+j} = g$ and $\mathsf{PK}_{0,(i-1)\cdot 13+j} = \mathsf{pk}_{i,j}$.*
- *Each player P_i (for $i \in [\![1, 4]\!]$) does the following step in turn: P_i picks $r = (r_1, \ldots, r_{52}) \xleftarrow{\$} (\mathbb{Z}_q^*)^{52}$, and a permutation δ on the set $[\![1, 52]\!]$. P_i computes $h_{i,l} = h_{i-1,\delta(l)}^{r_l}$ and $\mathsf{PK}_{i,l} = (\mathsf{PK}_{i-1,\delta(l)})^{r_l}$ for all $l \in [\![1, 52]\!]$, then runs $\Pi_i = \mathsf{ZK}\left\{(r, \delta) : \bigwedge_{l=1}^{52} \left(h_{i,l} = h_{i-1,\delta(l)}^{r_l} \wedge \mathsf{PK}_{i,l} = \mathsf{PK}_{i-1,\delta(l)}^{r_l}\right)\right\}$. This proof ensures that each $(h_{i,l}, \mathsf{PK}_{i,l})$ is the randomization of one pair $(h_{i-1,l'}, \mathsf{PK}_{i-1,l'})$ for $l' \in [\![1, 52]\!]$. P_i broadcasts $\{(h_{i,l}, \mathsf{PK}_{i,l})\}_{1 \leq l \leq 52}$ and Π_i, then each player verifies the proof Π_i. If the verification fails, then the player aborts and returns $\perp$.*
- *If there exists j such that for all l, $h_{4,l}^{\mathsf{sk}_{i,j}} \neq \mathsf{PK}_{4,l}$, then P_i aborts the protocol and returns $\perp$. For each $i \in [\![1, 4]\!]$, P_i sets $\mathsf{PK}_i' = ((h_{4,1}, \mathsf{PK}_{4,1}), \ldots, (h_{4,52}, \mathsf{PK}_{4,52}))$ and broadcasts it. If there exists i_1 and i_2 such that $\mathsf{PK}_{i_1}' \neq \mathsf{PK}_{i_2}'$, then P_i aborts and returns $\perp$, else P_i returns $\mathsf{PK} = \mathsf{PK}_i'$.*

DeckGen: *It is the 4-party Deck-random generator $\mathsf{RandGen}^{\mathsf{Deck}}$ protocol.*

GetHand($\mathsf{sk}, \mathsf{pk}, \mathsf{PK}, D$): *It parses sk as $(\mathsf{sk}_1, \ldots, \mathsf{sk}_{13})$, PK as $((h_1, \mathsf{PK}_1), \ldots, (h_{52}, \mathsf{PK}_{52}))$ and D as $(\mathsf{id}_1, \ldots, \mathsf{id}_{52})$. It returns the set H such that $\mathsf{id}_i \in H$ iff there exists $j \in [\![1, 13]\!]$ such that $\mathsf{PK}_i = h_i^{\mathsf{sk}_j}$.*

Play($n, \mathsf{id}, \mathsf{sk}, \mathsf{pk}, \mathsf{st}, \mathsf{PK}, D$): *It parses D as $(\mathsf{id}_1, \ldots, \mathsf{id}_{52})$, sk as $(\mathsf{sk}_1, \ldots, \mathsf{sk}_{13})$, pk as $(\mathsf{pk}_1, \ldots, \mathsf{pk}_{13})$, PK as $((h_1, \mathsf{PK}_1), \ldots, (h_{52}, \mathsf{PK}_{52}))$, and st as $(\alpha, \mathsf{suit}, U_1, U_2, U_3, U_4)$. If $\mathsf{st} = \perp$ it sets four empty sets U_1, U_2, U_3 and U_4. Let $v \in [\![1, 52]\!]$ be the integer such that $\mathsf{id} = \mathsf{id}_v$ (i.e., v is the index of the played card id) and $t \in [\![1, 13]\!]$ be the integer such that $\log_g(\mathsf{pk}_t) = \log_{h_v}(\mathsf{PK}_v)$ (i.e., t is the index of the public key that corresponds to the played card id). It sets $U_n' = U_n \cup \{t\}$. Note that at each step of the game, the set U_n contains the indexes of all the public keys of the user n that have already been used to play a card. For all $i \in [\![1, 4]\!] \setminus \{n\}$, it sets $U_i' = U_i$.*
If $\alpha = 4$ or $\mathsf{st} = \perp$ then it sets $\alpha' = 1$ and $\mathsf{suit}' = \mathsf{id.suit}$. Else it sets $\alpha' = \alpha + 1$ and $\mathsf{suit}' = \mathsf{suit}$. The index α states how many players have already played this round, so if $\alpha = 4$, players start a new round. Moreover, suit states which suit is the leading suit of the round, given by the first card played in the round. This algorithm sets $\mathsf{st}' = (\alpha', \mathsf{suit}', U_1', U_2', U_3', U_4')$. It generates $\Pi_0 = \mathsf{ZK}\{(\mathsf{sk}_t) : \mathsf{pk}_t = g^{\mathsf{sk}_t} \wedge \mathsf{PK}_v = h_v^{\mathsf{sk}_t}\}$, which proves that the played card id_v matches one of the secret keys of the player. Let $L \in [\![1, 52]\!]$ be a set such

that for all $l \in L$, suit$' \neq$ id$_l$.suit, *i.e.,* L *is the set of the indexes of the cards that are not of the leading suit this round. For all* $j \in [\![1,13]\!]$

- *If* suit$' =$ id.suit, *it sets* $\Pi_j = \bot$ *(if the card* id *is of the leading suit, then the player can play it in any case, so no additional proof is required).*
- *If* $j \in U_n$, *it sets* $\Pi_j = \bot$ *(We omit the keys that have already been used in the previous rounds).*
- *If* $j \notin U_n$ *it generates* $\Pi_j = \mathsf{ZK}\left\{(\mathsf{sk}_j) : \bigvee_{l \in L}(\mathsf{pk}_j = g^{\mathsf{sk}_j} \wedge \mathsf{PK}_l = h_l^{\mathsf{sk}_j})\right\}$. *This proof ensures that the card that corresponds to each public key* pk_j *is not of the leading suit, which proves that the player* n *cannot play a card of the leading suit.*

Finally, it returns the proof $\Pi = (t, \Pi_0, \ldots, \Pi_{13})$, *and the updated value* st$'$.

Verif$(n, \mathsf{id}, \Pi, \mathsf{pk}, \mathsf{st}, \mathsf{st}', \mathsf{PK}, D)$: *It parses* st *as* $(\alpha, \mathsf{suit}, U_1, U_2, U_3, U_4)$, st$'$ *as* $(\alpha', \mathsf{suit}', U_1', U_2', U_3', U_4')$, pk *as* $(\mathsf{pk}_1, \ldots, \mathsf{pk}_{13})$, *the key* PK *as* $((h_1, \mathsf{PK}_1), \ldots, (h_{52}, \mathsf{PK}_{52}))$, D *as* $(\mathsf{id}_1, \ldots, \mathsf{id}_{52})$ *and* Π *as* $(t, \Pi_0, \ldots, \Pi_{13})$. *If* st $= \bot$, *it sets four empty sets* U_1, U_2, U_3 *and* U_4. *Let* v *be the integer such that* id$_v =$ id *(i.e.,* v *is the index of the played card* id*). Let* $L \in [\![1, 52]\!]$ *be a set such that for all* $l \in L$, suit$' \neq$ id$_l$.suit, *i.e.,* L *is the set of the indexes of the cards that are not of the leading suit. This algorithm first verifies that the state* st *is correctly updated in* st$'$ *according to the* Play *algorithm:*

- *If there exists* $i \in [\![1, 4]\!] \setminus \{n\}$ *such that* $U_i' \neq U_i$, *then it returns* 0.
- *If* $t \in U_n$ *or* $U_n \cup \{t\} \neq U_n'$, *then it returns* 0.
- *If* $\alpha = 4$ *or* st $= \bot$, *and* $\alpha' \neq 1$ *or* suit$' \neq$ id.suit, *then it returns* 0.
- *If* $\alpha \neq 4$ *and* suit $\neq \bot$, *and* $\alpha' \neq \alpha + 1$ *or* suit$' \neq$ suit, *then it returns* 0.

This algorithm then verifies the zero-knowledge proofs in order to check that the player does not cheat by playing a card he has not, or by playing a card that is not of the leading suit even though he could play a card of the leading suit.

- *If* Π_0 *is not valid then it returns* 0.
- *If* suit$' \neq$ id.suit *and there exists an integer* $j \in [\![1, n]\!]$ *such that* $j \notin U_n$ *and* Π_j *is not valid then it returns* 0.

If none of the previous checks fails, then this algorithm returns 1.

GetSuit(st): *It parses* st *as* $(\alpha, \mathsf{suit}, U_1, U_2, U_3, U_4)$ *and returns* suit.

Instantiation. We show how to instantiate the two zero-knowledge proofs of knowledge used in our protocol. The first one is a zero-knowledge OR-proof of the equality of two discrete logarithms denoted $\mathsf{ZK}\{(w) : \bigvee_{i=1}^{n} a_i{}^w = c_i \wedge b_i{}^w = d_i\}$. An efficient instantiation of such ZKPs in the random oracle model is given in [5]. Our protocol also uses a proof of correctness of a randomization of a set of shuffled commitments. This proof is denoted $\mathsf{ZK}\{((r_1, \ldots, r_n), \delta) : \bigwedge_{i=1}^{n} c_i = a_{\delta(i)}^{r_i} \wedge d_i = b_{\delta(i)}^{r_i}\}$, and can be instantiated using the previous one, since it consists in proving the equality of two discrete logarithms for the statement $\{(a_i, b_i, c_j, d_j)\}_{1 \leq j \leq n}$ for each j in $[\![1, 52]\!]$.

Security. We prove the security of our scheme in Theorem 1, then we give the intuition of the proof. The full proof is given in the full version of this paper [6].

Theorem 1. *If the two proofs of knowledge are sound, extractable and zero-knowledge, then SecureSpades is theft-resistant, cheating-resistant, hand-private, unpredictable, and game-private under the DDH assumption in the ROM.*

Theft-resistant. To play a card, the player i must prove that the discrete logarithm of one of his public keys $pk_{i,j}$ is equal to the discrete logarithm of the key PK_l that corresponds to the card. If the card is not in his hand, then none of the discrete logarithms of the public keys $pk_{i,j}$ is equal to the discrete logarithm of the key PK_l. Hence, to play a card that is not in his hand, the player should forge a proof of a false statement, which is not possible, since the proof system is sound.

Cheating-resistant. To play a card that is not of the leading suit, the player i must prove that the discrete logarithm of each public key $pk_{i,j}$ is equal to the discrete logarithm of one key PK_l that corresponds to a card that is not of the leading suit. Hence, assuming that the player has some cards of the leading suit, in order to play another card, he should forge a proof of a false statement. This is not possible, since the proof system is sound.

Unpredictable. Since the deck D is chosen at random thanks to the protocol RandGen, players have no way of guessing which card matches which public key during the keys generation phase.

Hand-private. Each player shuffles the keys PK_l using a secret permutation when he runs the GKeyRound algorithm. Moreover, the zero-knowledge proofs ensure that for each PK_l there exists a key $pk_{i,j}$ such that $\log_{h_l}(PK_l) = \log_g(pk_{i,j})$. Guessing the hand of a player i is equivalent to guessing pairs (j, l) such that the key PK_l has the same discrete logarithm in basis h_l as the key $pk_{i,j}$, which is equivalent to guessing whether PK_l is the Diffie-Hellman of h_l and $pk_{i,j}$.

Game-private. During the game, the players use nothing other than zero-knowledge proofs, which leak nothing about the secret values of the players.

Other TTGs. Our Spades security model and scheme can be generalized to several trick-taking games. It works for any number of cards, of players, and for any team configuration. Moreover, it can be generalized to any game where players must play some kinds of cards according to a priority order, as long as the players can establish the set of all the cards that should be played (when it is possible) instead of the played one. This includes (but is not restricted to) all variants of Spades, Whist, Bridge, Belotte, Napoleon or Boston. Moreover, physical cards limit trick-taking games to games where players reveal all their cards, because if they do not, cheating could not be detected, even later. Our protocol allows the creation of new fair TTGs where players do not play all the cards of their hand.

8 Conclusion

In this paper, we have designed a secure protocol for trick-taking games. We used Spades, a famous online gambling card game, to illustrate our approach. Until now, such games required a trusted sever that ensures that players are not cheating. Our protocol allows the players to manage the game and detect cheating by themselves, without leaking any information about the hidden cards. Hence, a player cannot play a card that he does not have or that does not follow the rule of the game. Our construction is based on the discrete logarithm assumption and zero knowledge proofs. We proposed a security model and prove the security of our protocol.

In the future, we would like to implement a prototype, in order to evaluate the practical efficiency of our solution. Moreover, we would like to add secure payment distributions mechanism to our protocol. Another perspective is to try to generalize this approach to other games.

Acknowledgement. We thank Wouter Lueks for his helpful comments and suggestions. We also thank the tarot players of *Le Checkpoint Café*.

References

1. Barnett, A., Smart, N.P.: Mental poker revisited. In: Paterson, K.G. (ed.) Cryptography and Coding 2003. LNCS, vol. 2898, pp. 370–383. Springer, Heidelberg (2003). https://doi.org/10.1007/978-3-540-40974-8_29
2. Bentov, I., Kumaresan, R., Miller, A.: Instantaneous decentralized poker. In: Takagi, T., Peyrin, T. (eds.) ASIACRYPT 2017. LNCS, vol. 10625, pp. 410–440. Springer, Cham (2017). https://doi.org/10.1007/978-3-319-70697-9_15
3. Blum, M.: Coin flipping by telephone a protocol for solving impossible problems. SIGACT News **15**(1), 23–27 (1983). https://doi.org/10.1145/1008908.1008911
4. Boneh, D.: The decision Diffie-Hellman problem. In: Buhler, J.P. (ed.) ANTS 1998. LNCS, vol. 1423, pp. 48–63. Springer, Heidelberg (1998). https://doi.org/10.1007/BFb0054851
5. Bultel, X., Lafourcade, P.: Unlinkable and strongly accountable sanitizable signatures from verifiable ring signatures. In: Capkun, S., Chow, S.S.M. (eds.) CANS 2017. LNCS, vol. 11261, pp. 203–226. Springer, Cham (2018). https://doi.org/10.1007/978-3-030-02641-7_10
6. Bultel, X., Lafourcade, P.: Secure trick-taking game protocols: how to play online spades with cheaters. Cryptology ePrint Archive, Report 2019/375 (2019). https://eprint.iacr.org/2019/375
7. Camenisch, J., Stadler, M.: Efficient group signature schemes for large groups. In: Kaliski, B.S. (ed.) CRYPTO 1997. LNCS, vol. 1294, pp. 410–424. Springer, Heidelberg (1997). https://doi.org/10.1007/BFb0052252
8. David, B., Dowsley, R., Larangeira, M.: Kaleidoscope: an efficient poker protocol with payment distribution and penalty enforcement. In: Meiklejohn, S., Sako, K. (eds.) FC 2018. Lecture Notes in Computer Science, vol. 10957, pp. 500–519. Springer, Heidelberg (2018). https://doi.org/10.1007/978-3-662-58387-6_27
9. David, B., Dowsley, R., Larangeira, M.: ROYALE: a framework for universally composable card games with financial rewards and penalties enforcement. IACR Cryptology ePrint Archive 2018, 157 (2018). http://eprint.iacr.org/2018/157

10. Goldwasser, S., Micali, S.: Probabilistic encryption & how to play mental poker keeping secret all partial information. In: Proceedings of the Fourteenth Annual ACM Symposium on Theory of Computing, STOC 1982, pp. 365–377. ACM, New York (1982). https://doi.org/10.1145/800070.802212
11. Goldwasser, S., Micali, S., Rackoff, C.: The knowledge complexity of interactive proof systems. SIAM J. Comput. **18**(1) (1989)
12. Stamer, H.: Bibliography on mental poker. https://www.nongnu.org/libtmcg/MentalPoker.pdf
13. Wei, T.J.: Secure and practical constant round mental poker. Inf. Sci. **273**, 352–386 (2014)
14. Yan, J.: Collusion detection in online bridge. In: Fox, M., Poole, D. (eds.) Proceedings of the Twenty-Fourth AAAI Conference on Artificial Intelligence, AAAI 2010, Atlanta, Georgia, USA, 11–15 July 2010. AAAI Press (2010). http://www.aaai.org/ocs/index.php/AAAI/AAAI10/paper/view/1942
15. Zhao, W., Varadharajan, V., Mu, Y.: A secure mental poker protocol over the internet. In: Johnson, C., Montague, P., Steketee, C. (eds.) ACSW Frontiers 2003, Conferences in Research and Practice in Information Technology, pp. 105–109. Australian Computer Society (2003)

ROYALE: A Framework for Universally Composable Card Games with Financial Rewards and Penalties Enforcement

Bernardo David[1], Rafael Dowsley[2,4], and Mario Larangeira[3,4(✉)]

[1] IT University of Copenhagen, Copenhagen, Denmark
bernardo@bmdavid.com
[2] Aarhus University, Aarhus, Denmark
rafael@cs.au.dk
[3] Tokyo Institute of Technology, Tokyo, Japan
mario@c.titech.ac.jp
[4] IOHK, Hong Kong, China

Abstract. While many tailor made card game protocols are known, the vast majority of those lack three important features: mechanisms for distributing financial rewards and punishing cheaters, composability guarantees and flexibility, focusing on the specific game of poker. Even though folklore holds that poker protocols can be used to play any card game, this conjecture remains unproven and, in fact, does not hold for a number of protocols (including recent results). We both tackle the problem of constructing protocols for general card games and initiate a treatment of such protocols in the Universal Composability (UC) framework, introducing an ideal functionality that captures card games that use a set of core card operations. Based on this formalism, we introduce Royale, the first UC-secure general card games which supports financial rewards/penalties enforcement. We remark that Royale also yields the first UC-secure poker protocol. Interestingly, Royale performs better than most previous works (that do not have composability guarantees), which we highlight through a detailed concrete complexity analysis and benchmarks from a prototype implementation.

1 Introduction

Online card games have become highly popular with the advent of online casinos, which act as trusted third parties performing the roles of both dealers and cashiers. However, a malicious casino (potentially compromised by an insider attacker) can easily subvert game outcomes [33]. Solving this issue has inspired

This project has received funding from the European research Council (ERC) under the European Unions's Horizon 2020 research and innovation programme (grant agreement No. 669255).

This work was supported by the Input Output Cryptocurrency Collaborative Research Chair funded by Input Output HK.

a long line of research on *mental poker*, *i.e.* playing poker among distrustful players without relying on a trusted third party [3,14,16,17,22,27,29–32,35,36]. Nevertheless, the aforementioned mental poker protocols did not provide formal security definitions or proofs. In fact, concrete flaws in the protocols of [35,36] (resp. [3,14]) have been identified in [29] (resp. [19]). Moreover, even if some of these protocols can be proven secure, they do not ensure that aborting adversaries cannot prevent the game to reach an outcome or that honest players receive the resulting financial rewards.

Techniques for ensuring that players receive their rewards according to game outcomes were only developed recently by Andrychowicz *et al.* [1,2,6,23], building on decentralized cryptocurrencies. Their techniques also prevent misbehavior (including aborts) by imposing financial penalties to adversaries who are caught deviating from the protocol. Basically, they ensure that honest players either receive the rewards determined by the game outcome or a share of the penalty imposed to the adversary in case an outcome is not reached. These techniques were subsequently improved by Kumaresan *et al.* [24], [7], who also applied them to constructing protocols for secure card games with financial rewards/penalties. However, neither of these works provided formal security definitions and proofs for their card game protocols.

The first security definition and provably secure protocol for secure poker with financial rewards/penalties enforcement were recently proposed by David *et al.* [19], which still only captures the specific game of poker. Moreover, the protocol of [19] lacks composability guarantees, meaning that it cannot be arbitrarily executed along with copies of itself and other protocols. In fact, none of the previous mental poker protocols are composable and, consequently, repurposing them for playing other games would void their security guarantees, contradicting the folklore belief that poker protocols yield protocols for any card game. While the recent work of [18] constructs composable card game protocols, it only captures games without secret state (*i.e.* it cannot be used to instantiate games where bluffing is a key element, such as poker). Our work closes this gap by proposing a protocol for playing general card games that use a set of core card operations with security proven in the Universal Composability (UC) [11] framework, also yielding the first UC-secure protocol for the specific case of poker.

1.1   Our Contributions

We initiate a composable treatment of card game protocols, introducing both the first ideal functionality for general card games and the first UC-secure tailormade protocol for *general* card games. Our functionality and matching protocol support core operations that can be used to construct a large number of different card games, as opposed to previous protocols, which focus specifically on the game of poker. Besides capturing a large number of card games, our protocol enforces financial rewards/penalties while achieving efficiency comparable to previous works without UC-security. In fact, for practical parameters, a DDH-based instantiation of our protocol is concretely more efficient than most previous works, most of which have no provable security guarantees. Our contributions are summarized as follows:

- The *first* ideal functionality for general card games that can be expressed in terms of a set of core card operations: $\mathcal{F}_{CG}$;
- Royale, the *first* provably secure protocol for *general* card games satisfying $\mathcal{F}_{CG}$;
- Royale is proven to UC-realize our functionality in the restricted programmable and observable global random oracle model [9], being the *first universally composable* card game protocol (also yielding the first UC-secure poker protocol);
- An efficient mechanism for financial rewards/penalties enforcement in Royale, and a detailed efficiency analysis showing it outperforms previous works for practical parameters and benchmarks obtained from a prototype implementation.

As a first step in providing a composable treatment, we introduce an ideal functionality that captures general card games. It is parameterized by a program describing the flow of the game being modeled, differently from the ideal functionality introduced in [19], which only captures the flow of a poker game. This program determines the order in which the functionality carries out a number of operations that are used throughout the game, as well as the conditions under which a player wins or loses the game. Namely, the game rules can request a number of core card operations: public shuffling of closed cards on the table, private opening of cards (towards only one player, used for drawing cards), public opening of cards and shuffling of cards in a player's private hand (which can be used to securely swap cards among players). Moreover we provide an interface for the game rules to request public actions from the players (allowing players to broadcast their course of action), such as placing a bet or choosing a card from the table. We achieve financial rewards/penalties enforcement by following the basic approach of [7] based on stateful contracts, which are modeled as a separate ideal functionality in our construction. Each player deposits a *collateral* that is forfeited (and distributed among the other players) in case he behaves maliciously during protocol execution. If a player suspects that another player is misbehaving (*e.g.* failing to send a message), a complaint is sent to the stateful contract functionality, which mediates the protocol execution until the conflict is resolved or a culprit is found, resulting in the termination of the protocol after collateral deposit distribution. As pointed out in [7], such a stateful contract functionality can be implemented based on smart contracts on blockchain-based systems such as Ethereum [8].

Finally, we construct Royale, a protocol for general card games that is proven to UC-realize our functionality with the help of a stateful contract. It is constructed in a modular fashion based on generic signature, threshold encryption and non-interactive zero-knowledge (NIZK) proofs that can be efficiently instantiated under standard computational assumptions (DDH) in the restricted programmable and observable global random oracle model of [9]. As the contract is ultimately implemented by a blockchain-based solution, one of the main bottlenecks in such a protocol is the amount of on-chain storage required for executing the stateful contract, which must analyze the protocol execution and determine whether a player has correctly executed the protocol or not when a complaint is issued. We achieve low on-chain storage complexity by providing compact *checkpoint witnesses* that allow the players to prove that the protocol has been correctly executed (or not), differently from [7], which requires large amounts of the protocol transcript to be sent to the contract.

The individual card operations in our protocol are inspired by Kaleidoscope [19], which achieves the desired efficiency for the specific case of poker. However, Kaleidoscope is based specifically on the DDH assumption and does not achieve UC-security, Kaleidoscope's security proof involves a simulator that makes heavy use of extraction of witnesses of NIZK proofs of knowledge based on the Fiat-Shamir heuristic, which require rewinding the adversary in the security proof, an operation that is not allowed in proofs in the UC framework. While substituting such Fiat-Shamir NIZKs for UC-secure ZK proofs would solve this issue, the efficiency of the resulting protocol would be greatly affected, since current UC-secure constructions [10] are significantly less efficient than the simple NIZKs used in Kaleidoscope. We overcome this obstacle without sacrificing efficiency through subtle modifications to the protocol itself, employing NIZK proofs of membership and a novel proof strategy that only requires the simulator to generate simulated proofs, eliminating the need for rewinding.

1.2 Related Works

Even though there is a large number of previous works on protocols for secure card games, the problem of aborting adversaries and reward distribution for poker games has only been (efficiently) addressed recently [7]. Moreover, as previously discussed, formal security definitions and proofs for secure card game protocols were only recently introduced in Kaleidoscope [19]. Since we aim at addressing both the issues of composability and financial penalties/rewards distribution, we center our discussion on the works of [7,19], which are more closely related to this goal. See [19] for a comprehensive discussion of efficiency and concrete security issues of previous works.

Enforcing Financial Rewards and Penalties: Most games of poker are played with money at stake, posing two central challenges that were overlooked in the first poker protocols but need to be solved in order to allow for practical deployment: (1) protecting against potentially aborting cheaters and (2) ensuring that winners receive their rewards. In the case of general secure computation, these challenges were only recently addressed in an efficient way by Bentov et ul. [7] with further optimizations of an approach previously developed and pursued in [1,2,6,23,24]. The central idea in the general purpose secure computation protocol of [7] is to execute an unfair protocol without any interaction with the cryptocurrency network, relying on a single stateful contract that handles funds distribution and financially punishes misbehaving parties. Before the unfair protocol is executed, the stateful contract receives deposits of funds that will be distributed according to the protocol output as well as of collateral funds that will be used to punish misbehaving parties and compensate honest parties. In case a party suspects cheating, it "complains" to the stateful contract, which will mediate the protocol execution until a cheater is found or the complaint is solved (so that execution can proceed off-chain). In case a party is found to be cheating, its collateral funds are distributed among the honest parties and the protocol execution ends. If the protocol reaches an output, the stateful contract distributes the funds deposited at the onset of execution according to the output. Bentov et al. [7] apply this general approach to tailor-made poker protocols [31,32], aiming at implementing a secure poker protocol with higher efficiency than their general purpose secure computation protocol. However, their tailor-made protocol is not formally proven secure and, even if found to be secure, has efficiency issues, as discussed in the remainder of this section.

Formal Security Guarantees: The vast majority of poker protocols [3,7,14, 16,17,22,24,27,29–32,35,36] claim different levels of security but do not provide formal securities. Besides making it hard to assess the exact security offered by such protocols, the lack of clear security definitions and proofs has led to concrete security flaws in many of these protocols [3,14,35,36], as pointed out in [19,29]. While Bentov et al. [7] argue that their framework can be directly applied to tailor-made poker protocols to provide financial rewards/penalties enforcement with high efficiency, they do not provide a security proof for such a direct application of their framework to tailor-made protocols nor describe the properties the underlying poker protocol should satisfy. Their work specifically mentions the protocols of [31,32] as potential building blocks. However, [31,32] are not formally proven secure. Using such protocols as building blocks in a black-box way without a clear security definition and proofs can lead to both security and composition issues. Moreover, even if proven secure, [31,32] face efficiency issues for practical parameters. In the poker case, the lack of formal security definitions and proofs was only recently remedied by Kaleidoscope [19], which introduced both the first security definition for poker functionalities and a matching protocol, considering financial rewards/penalties enforcement.

Efficiency Issues: As Royale is the first work to consider general card games, we compare the efficiency of each card operation provided by Royale to the similar operations provided in previous works on poker protocols. The most costly operation is the shuffling of cards. The protocol of Barnett and Smart [3] (that serves as the basis for many subsequent protocols) and the protocol of Wei and Wang [32] (cited as a potential building block in [7]) rely on a cut-and-choose based ZK proof of shuffle correctness, incurring high computational and communication overheads. A subsequent work by Wei [31] (also cited as a potential building block in [7]) improves on the complexity of the shuffle procedure by eliminating the need for cut-and-choose but still requires a large number of rounds (more than $4n$ rounds, where n is the number of players), which is also the case of [32]. The Kaleidoscope [19] protocol employs a novel shuffling phase based on efficient NIZK proofs of shuffle correctness, achieving better concrete efficiency both in terms of communication and computation than previous works for practical parameters, while only requiring n rounds (for n players). The shuffling procedure of a DDH-based instantiation of Royale (Sect. 3) inherits the same high efficiency of the Kaleidoscope shuffle while achieving UC-security. The computational, communication and round complexities of opening cards in Royale are very similar to those of previous works, which already achieved high efficiency for these operations. For a more detailed discussion, we refer to Sect. 4.

Composability Issues: The need for arbitrary composability naturally arises in poker and general card game protocols with financial rewards/penalties enforcement, since those protocols need to use other cryptographic protocols, *e.g.* secure channels and cryptocurrency protocols. This is specially critical in the case of general card game protocols, where card operations are arbitrarily mixed and matched in order to create different games, which can potentially cause serious security issues in protocols without arbitrary composability guarantees. However, none of the previous works on poker or card games protocols have considered this issue, and Kaleidoscope [19], the only poker protocol with provable security guarantees, only achieves sequential composability. The UC framework [11] is widely used to reason about arbitrary composability for cryptographic protocols. The main obstacle to providing a proof of security for Kaleidoscope as well as other previous poker protocols lies in their use of NIZK proofs of Knowledge obtained from applying the Fiat-Shamir transformation to Sigma protocols, heavily relying on rewinding for extracting witnesses in their security proofs. In Royale, this is solved by employing a proof strategy that only requires the simulator to generate simulated NIZKs without sacrificing efficiency.

2 Preliminaries

We denote the security parameter by κ and sampling an element x uniformly at random from a set $\mathcal{X}$ by $x \xleftarrow{\$} \mathcal{X}$. See the full version [20] for complete notation.

Re-Randomizable Threshold PKE: A re-randomizable threshold public key encryption (RTE [34]) scheme is a central in our protocols. Intuitively, we focus of the (n, n)-Threshold case, where the n parties need to cooperate in the decryption. We present formal definitions in the full version [20]. A summary of the main RTE algorithms used in our construction is given below:

- KeyGen(param) takes as input parameters param and outputs a public key pk_i and a secret key sk_i.
- CombinePK($\mathsf{pk}_1, \ldots, \mathsf{pk}_n$) is a deterministic algorithm that takes as input a set of public keys ($\mathsf{pk}_1, \ldots, \mathsf{pk}_n$) and outputs a combined public key pk.
- Enc(pk, m) takes as input a public key pk and a plaintext message m, and outputs a ciphertext ct.
- ReRand(pk, ct) is a re-randomization algorithm that takes as input a public key pk and a ciphertext ct, and outputs a re-randomized ciphertext ct'.

- ShareDec(sk_i, ct) is a deterministic algorithm that takes as input a secret key share sk_i and a ciphertext ct, and outputs a decryption share d_i.
- ShareCombine(ct, $d_1, \ldots, d_n$) is a deterministic decryption share combining algorithm that takes as input a ciphertext ct and a set of decryption shares $(d_1, \ldots, d_n)$, and outputs a plaintext message m.

NIZKs for Relations over RTE: We need a number of NIZKs for relations over the RTE scheme we employ. Basically, a NIZK scheme $NIZK_{\mathcal{R}}$ for relation $\mathcal{R}$ and algorithm Prov that takes as input $(x, w) \in \mathcal{R}$ and outputs a proof π and an algorithm Verify that takes as input (x, π) and outputs 1 if the proof is valid and 0 otherwise. For the sake of clarity, we define the following generic relations for which we need to prove statements in zero-knowledge and describe our protocols and simulators in terms of those: *(1) $\mathcal{R}_1$ - Correctness of public key share:* This relation shows that the prover knows the randomness used for generating a public/secret key pair (pk_i, sk_i) and the secret key sk_i; *(2) $\mathcal{R}_2$ - Correctness of decryption share:* This relation shows that the prover used the secret key sk_i corresponding to its public key pk_i for computing a decryption share d_i of a ciphertext ct; *(3) $\mathcal{R}_3$ - Correctness of shuffle:* This relation shows that the prover correctly shuffled a set of ciphertexts $(ct_1, \ldots, ct_m)$ by re-randomizing them with randomness $(r_1, \ldots, r_m)$ and permuting them with a permutation Π. Formal definitions for these NIZKs and an instantiation from sigma protocols in the Global Random Oracle model are presented inthe full version [20].

Security Model: We prove our protocols secure in the UC framework [11]. UC-secure protocols retain their security even when used in parallel with other cryptographic protocols or as building blocks of more complex applications. We consider static malicious adversaries, who can arbitrarily deviate from the protocol but only corrupt parties before execution starts. It is known that UC-secure two-party and multiparty protocols for non-trivial functionalities require a setup assumption [13]. The main setup assumption for our work is the global random oracle model [5] modelled as the $\mathcal{G}_{\mathsf{rpoRO}}$-hybrid model [9], a digital signature functionality $\mathcal{F}_{\mathsf{DSIG}}$ from [12], and a smart contract functionality (defined in Sect. 3). See the full version [20] for details.

The Stateful Smart Contract Functionality $\mathcal{F}_{\mathsf{SC}}$: We follow the approach of Bentov *et al.* [7] in describing a functionality $\mathcal{F}_{\mathsf{SC}}$ that models a *stateful contract*. Such a contract receives coins from the players in a check-in procedure and, after that, is only activated in case a player wishes to report misbehavior or wishes to leave the game, retrieving the coins that he owns at that point. While Bentov *et al.* describe a stateful contract functionality that models execution of general programs with secure cash distribution (*i.e.* the output of the computation determines how coins are distributed among honest players) and penalties for misbehavior, we focus on the specific case of card games. That means that our functionality only allows a program GR that specifies the game rules to execute specific card operations instead of general computation. The card operations supported by our protocol are the ones described in functionality $\mathcal{F}_{\mathsf{CG}}$. However, we can extend $\mathcal{F}_{\mathsf{CG}}$ by incorporating other functionalities for which UC protocols exist. In this case, GR is also allowed to specify the operations described in these functionalities and the stateful contract modelled by GR is also responsible for ensuring that the protocols realizing these functionalities are correctly executed. We describe $\mathcal{F}_{SC}$ in Fig. 1.

3   Secure Protocol for Playing Card Games

In this section we describe a protocol that realizes functionality $\mathcal{F}_{CG}$ (defined in the full version [20]). with the help of a smart contract. The role of the smart contract is to make sure that all players are executing the card operations (and other game actions) as specified by the game rules programmed in GR and punish (resp. compensate) malicious (resp. honest) players in case of dispute. The basic idea is to follow the secure computation with financial penalties framework initiated by [1,2] and have each player send to the contract an amount of coins that will be used for betting in the protocol and another amount of coins used as collateral. If a player suspects that another player is cheating in the game or misbehaving in protocol execution, it sends a request to the smart contract, which verifies protocol execution and, in case a player was actually found to be misbehaving, financially punishes the malicious player by distributing its collateral coins among the honest players.

Protocol π_{CG}: We construct a Protocol π_{CG} that realizes $\mathcal{F}_{CG}$ in a modular fashion. The main building block of this protocol is a re-randomizable threshold public key encryption (RTE) and associated non-interactive zero-knowledge proofs (NIZK). Moreover, we will rely on a global random oracle functionality $\mathcal{G}_{rpoRO}$ to apply the Fiat-Shamir heuristic to sigma protocols used for instantiating these NIZKs as described in the full version [20]. Additionally, a standard digital signature functionality $\mathcal{F}_{DSIG}$ will be used as building block in this protocol. Later on, we will describe a concrete instantiation of the protocol under the DDH assumption.

In this protocol, the players start by jointly generating a public key for the RTE scheme along with individual secret key shares. The main idea is to represent open cards as ciphertexts of the RTE scheme encrypting a card value $[1, \ldots, 52]$ without any randomness (or randomness 0) while closed cards are shuffled such that they are represented by a re-randomized ciphertext that is permuted in way that cannot be reversed by any proper subset of the players (so that no collusion of players can trace the shuffling back to the open cards). The shuffle operation is done by having each player act in sequence, taking turns in rerandomizing all ciphertexts representing cards and permuting the resulting rerandomized ciphertexts, while proving in zero-knowledge that these operations were executed correctly. When a closed (shuffled) card has to be revealed to a player, all other players send decryption shares of the ciphertext representing this card computed with their respective secret keys, along with proofs that these decryption shares have been correctly computed.

Throughout the protocol, after the players perform a card operation or answer an action request from GR, they jointly generate a checkpoint witness

---

Functionality $\mathcal{F}_{SC}$

$\mathcal{F}_{SC}$ is executed with players $\mathcal{P}_1, \ldots, \mathcal{P}_n$ and is parametrized by a timeout limit τ, and the values of the initial stake t, the compensation q and the security deposit $d \geq (n-1)q$. There is an embedded program GR that represents the game's rules and a protocol verification mechanism pv.

- **Players Check-in:** When execution starts, $\mathcal{F}_{SC}$ waits to receive from each player $\mathcal{P}_i$ the message (CHECKIN, $sid, \mathcal{P}_i, \text{coins}(d+t), \text{SIG}.vk_i, \text{pk}_i, \pi^i_{\mathcal{R}_1}$) containing the necessary coins, its signature verification key, its share of the threshold ElGamal public-key and the zero-knowledge proof of knowledge of the secret-key's share. Record the values and send (CHECKEDIN, $sid, \mathcal{P}_i, \text{SIG}.vk_i, \text{pk}_i, \pi^i_{\mathcal{R}_1}$) to all players. If some player fails to check-in within the timeout limit τ or if a message (CHECKIN-FAIL, sid) is received from any player, then send (COMPENSATION, $\text{coins}(d+t)$) to all players who have checked in and halt.

- **Player Check-out:** Upon receiving (CHECKOUT-INIT, $sid, \mathcal{P}_j$) from $\mathcal{P}_j$, send to all players (CHECKOUT-INIT, $sid, \mathcal{P}_j$). Upon receiving (CHECKOUT, $sid, \mathcal{P}_j, \text{payout}, \sigma_1, \ldots, \sigma_n$) from $\mathcal{P}_j$, verify that $\sigma_1, \ldots, \sigma_n$ are valid signatures by the players $\mathcal{P}_1, \ldots, \mathcal{P}_n$ on (CHECKOUT|payout) according to $\mathcal{F}_{DSIG}$. If all tests succeed, for $i = 1, \ldots, n$, send (PAYOUT, $sid, \mathcal{P}_i, \text{coins}(w)$) to $\mathcal{P}_i$, where $w = \text{payout}[i] + d$, and halt.

- **Recovery:** Upon receiving a recovery request (RECOVERY, sid) from a player $\mathcal{P}_i$, send the message (REQUEST, sid) to all players. Upon receiving (RESPONSE, $sid, \mathcal{P}_j$, Checkpoint$_j$, proc$_j$) from some player $\mathcal{P}_j$ with checkpoint witnesses (which are not necessarily relative to the same checkpoint as the ones received from other players) and witnesses for the current procedure; or an acknowledgement of the witnesses previous submitted by another player, forward this message to the other players. Upon receiving replies from all players or reaching the timeout limit τ, fix the current procedure by picking the most recent checkpoint that has valid witnesses (*i.e.* the most recent checkpoint witness signed by all players $\mathcal{P}_i$). Verify the last valid point of the protocol execution using the current procedure's witnesses, the rules of the game GR, and pv. If some player $\mathcal{P}_i$ misbehaved in the current phase (by sending an invalid message), then send (COMPENSATION, $\text{coins}(d + q + \text{balance}[j] + \text{bets}[j])$) to each $\mathcal{P}_j \neq \mathcal{P}_i$, send the leftover coins to $\mathcal{P}_i$ and halt. Otherwise, proceed with a mediated execution of the protocol until the next checkpoint using the rules of the game GR and pv to determine the course of the actions and check the validity of the answer. Messages (NXT-STP, $sid, \mathcal{P}_i$, proc, round) are used to request from player $\mathcal{P}_i$ the protocol message for round round of procedure proc according to the game's rules specified in GR, who answer with messages (NXT-STP-RSP, $sid, \mathcal{P}_i$, proc, round, msg), where msg is the requested protocol message. All messages (NXT-STP, $sid, \ldots$) and (NXT-STP-RSP, $sid, \ldots$) are delivered to all players. If during this mediated execution a player misbehaves or does not answer within the timeout limit τ, penalize him and compensate the others as above, and halt. Otherwise send (RECOVERED, sid, proc, Checkpoint), to the parties once the next checkpoint Checkpoint is reached, where proc is the procedure for which Checkpoint was generated.

Fig. 1. Functionality $\mathcal{F}_{SC}$

proving that the operation has been completed successfully. These checkpoint witnesses contain signatures by all users on the current state of the protocol, *i.e.* ciphertexts representing cards and each player's balance and current bets. If a player suspects that any other player is cheating (or has aborted) during an execution, it complains to the smart contract, providing its latest checkpoint.

The execution is then mediated by the smart contract, which receives (and broadcasts) all messages generated by the players. If the smart contract detects that a player is cheating in this execution (by examining the transcript), it punishes the misbehaving player by distributing its collateral coins among the honest players. We describe Protocol π_{CG} in Figs. 2, 3 and 4.

Security Analysis: Due to page limit the security analysis is given in the full version [20].

A DDH-Based Instantiation: We now describe an instantiation of the Protocol π_{CG} that is secure under the popular DDH assumption in the random oracle model (*i.e.* substituting $\mathcal{F}_{RO}$ for a cryptographic hash function). The main components we need to construct in order to instantiate our protocol are the re-randomizable threshold public-key encryption scheme RTE and the NIZKs Proof of Membership schemes $NIZK_{\mathcal{R}_1}, NIZK_{\mathcal{R}_2}, NIZK_{\mathcal{R}_3}$ for relations $\mathcal{R}_1, \mathcal{R}_2, \mathcal{R}_3$. It was shown in [34, Appendix C.2], that the threshold version of the ElGamal cryptosystem is a secure re-randomizable threshold public-key encryption scheme under the DDH assumption. Moreover, it was also shown in [34, Appendix C.2] that there exist NIZKs $NIZK_{\mathcal{R}_1}, NIZK_{\mathcal{R}_2}, NIZK_{\mathcal{R}_3}$ for relations $\mathcal{R}_1, \mathcal{R}_2, \mathcal{R}_3$ secure under the DDH assumption. $NIZK_{\mathcal{R}_1}$ can be implemented by the sigma protocol of Schnorr [28], $NIZK_{\mathcal{R}_2}$ can be implemented by the protocol of Chaum and Pedersen [15] and $NIZK_{\mathcal{R}_3}$ can be implemented by the protocol of Bayer and Groth [4]. Notice that the zero-knowledge argument of shuffle correctness of Bayer and Groth [4] requires a common reference string that consists of random group elements such that the discrete logarithm of these elements in a given base is unknown. We point out that such a common reference string can be trivially constructed before π_{CG} is run by coin tossing, which can be UC-realized based on UC-secure commitments [11,13]. UC-secure commitments can be efficiently constructed in the restricted programmable and observable global random oracle model as proven in [9]. Even though these protocols are interactive, they can be made non-interactive through the Fiat-Shamir heuristic [21,26]. Notice that their simulators are straight-line since they only need to program the random oracle. As for the digital signature functionality $\mathcal{F}_{DSIG}$, it is known that EUF-CMA signature schemes (*e.g.* DSA and ECDSA) realize $\mathcal{F}_{DSIG}$. If we use the resulting DDH-based instantiation to implement poker, we obtain a protocol very similar to the Kaleidoscope [19], thus obtaining a universally composable protocol for poker with rewards and penalties that matches the best current (but not UC-secure) protocol.

4   Efficiency Analysis

Royale is both the first cryptographic protocol to support general card games that use a set of core card operations and one of the very few based on generic primitives, making it hard to compare its efficiency with previous works that are based on specific computational assumptions and focused on poker. Therefore, we estimate and compare the computational, communication and round

---

Protocol π_{CG} (First Part)

Let RTE be a secure re-randomizable threshold public-key encryption For $i \in \{1, 2, 3\}$, let $\mathsf{NIZK}_{\mathcal{R}_i} = (\mathsf{Prov}, \mathsf{Verify}, \mathsf{Sim}, \mathsf{Ext})$ be a NIZK proof of membership scheme for the relation $\mathcal{R}_i$. Protocol π_{CG} is parametrized by a security parameter 1^κ, RTE parameters param $\leftarrow \mathsf{Setup}(1^\kappa)$, a timeout limit τ, the values of the initial stake t, the compensation q, the security deposit $d \geq (n-1)q$ and an embedded program GR that represents the rules of the game. In all queries (SIGN, sid, m) to $\mathcal{F}_{\mathsf{DSIG}}$, the message m is implicitly concatenated with NONCE and cnt, where NONCE $\xleftarrow{\$} \{0,1\}^\kappa$ is a fresh nonce (sampled individually for each query) and cnt is a counter that is increased after each query. Every player $\mathcal{P}_i$ rejecting signatures that reuse nonces and implicitly concatenates the corresponding NONCE and cnt values with message m in all queries (VERIFY, $sid, m, \sigma, \mathsf{SIG}.vk'$) to $\mathcal{F}_{\mathsf{DSIG}}$. Protocol π_{CG} is executed by players $\mathcal{P}_1, \ldots, \mathcal{P}_n$ interacting with functionalities $\mathcal{F}_{CG}$, $\mathcal{G}_{\mathsf{rpoRO}}$ and $\mathcal{F}_{\mathsf{DSIG}}$ as follows:

- **Checkpoint Witnesses:** After the execution of a procedure, the players store a checkpoint witness that consists of the lists $\mathcal{C}_O, \mathcal{C}_C, \mathcal{C}_1, \ldots, \mathcal{C}_n$, the vectors balance and bets as well as a signature by each of the other players on the concatenation of all these values. Each signature is generated using $\mathcal{F}_{\mathsf{DSIG}}$ and all players check all signatures using the relevant procedure of $\mathcal{F}_{\mathsf{DSIG}}$. Old checkpoint witnesses are deleted. If any check fails for $\mathcal{P}_i$, he goes to the recovery procedure.
- **Recovery Triggers:** All signatures and zero-knowledge proofs in received messages are verified by default. Players are assumed to have loosely synchronized clocks and, after each round of the protocol starts, players expect to receive all messages sent in that round before a timeout limit τ. If a player $\mathcal{P}_i$ does not receive an expected message from a player $\mathcal{P}_j$ in a given round before the timeout limit τ, $\mathcal{P}_i$ considers that $\mathcal{P}_j$ has aborted. After the check-in procedure, if any player receives an invalid message or considers that another player has aborted, it proceeds to the recovery procedure.
- **Tracking Balance and Bets:** Every player $\mathcal{P}_i$ keeps a local copy of the vectors balance and bets, such that balance[j] and bets[j] represent the balance and current bets of each player $\mathcal{P}_j$, respectively. To keep the copies up to date, every player performs:
  - At each point that GR specifies that a betting action from $\mathcal{P}_i$ takes place, player $\mathcal{P}_i$ broadcasts a message (BET, $sid, \mathcal{P}_i, bet_i$), where bet_i is the value of its bet. It updates balance[i] = balance[i] $- b_i$ and bets[i] = bets[i] $+ b_i$.
  - Upon receiving a message (BET, $sid, \mathcal{P}_j, bet_j$) from $\mathcal{P}_j$, player $\mathcal{P}_i$ sets balance[j] = balance[j] $- b_j$ and bets[j] = bets[j] $+ b_j$.
  - When GR determines that player $\mathcal{P}_j$ receives an amount pay_j and has its bet amount updated to b'_j, player $\mathcal{P}_i$ sets balance[j] = balance[j] $+ pay_j$ and bets[j] = b'_j.
- **Executing Actions:** Each $\mathcal{P}_i$ follows GR that represents the rules of the game, performing the necessary card operations, as well as updates on the list of card and balance and bet vectors, in the order specified by GR. If GR request an action with description $act - desc$ from $\mathcal{P}_i$, all the players output (ACT, $sid, \mathcal{P}_i, act - desc$) and $\mathcal{P}_i$ executes any necessary operations. $\mathcal{P}_i$ broadcasts (ACTION-RSP, $sid, \mathcal{P}_i, act - rsp, \sigma_i$), where $act - rsp$ is his answer and σ_i his signature on $act - rsp$, and outputs (ACTION-RSP, $sid, \mathcal{P}_i, act - rsp$). Upon receiving this message, all other players check the signature, and if it is valid output (ACTION-RSP, $sid, \mathcal{P}_i, act - rsp$). If a player $\mathcal{P}_j$ believes cheating happened, he proceeds to the recovery procedure.
- **Compensation:** Upon receiving from $\mathcal{F}_{\mathsf{SC}}$ (COMPENSATION, $sid, \mathcal{P}_i, \mathsf{coins}(w)$), output this message and halt.

Fig. 2. Protocol π_{CG} (first part).

Protocol π_{CG} (Second Part)

- **Check-in:** Every player $\mathcal{P}_i$ proceeds as follows:

1. Send (KEYGEN, sid) to $\mathcal{F}_{DSIG}$, receiving (VERIFICATION KEY, sid, SIG.vk_i).

2. Sample $r_i \xleftarrow{\$} \{0,1\}^{\kappa}$ and generate a key pair $(\mathsf{pk}_i, \mathsf{sk}_i) \leftarrow \mathsf{KeyGen}(\mathsf{param}, r_i)$ and a NIZK of public key correctness $\pi_{\mathcal{R}_1}^i$ by computing NIZK$_{\mathcal{R}_1}$.Prov with (r_i, sk_i) as witness.

3. Send (CHECKIN, sid, $\mathcal{P}_i$, coins($d+t$), SIG.vk_i, pk_i, $\pi_{\mathcal{R}_1}^i$) to $\mathcal{F}_{SC}$.

4. For $\mathcal{P}_j \neq p_i$, upon receiving (CHECKEDIN, sid, $\mathcal{P}_j$, SIG.vk_j, pk_j, $\pi_{\mathcal{R}_1}^j$) from $\mathcal{F}_{SC}$, check if $\pi_{\mathcal{R}_1}^j$ is valid. If valid, output (CHECKEDIN, sid, $\mathcal{P}_j$).

5. Upon receiving valid check-in from all parties, compute $\mathsf{pk} \leftarrow \mathsf{CombinePK}(\mathsf{pk}_1, \ldots, \mathsf{pk}_n)$. Initialize the internal lists of open cards $\mathcal{C}_O$, of closed cards $\mathcal{C}_C$ and of private cards of each player $\mathcal{P}_i$, $\mathcal{C}_i$, as empty sets. We assume parties have a sequence of unused card id values (*e.g.* a counter). Initialize vectors balance$[j] = t$ and bets$[j] = 0$ for $j = 1, \ldots, n$.

6. If $\mathcal{P}_i$ fails to receive a check-in of another party $\mathcal{P}_j$ within the timeout limit τ, it requests $\mathcal{F}_{SC}$ to dropout and receive its coins back.

- **Create Card:** To create a card with value v, every player $\mathcal{P}_i$ selects the next unused card id id, stores (id, v) in $\mathcal{C}_O$ and outputs (NEWCARD, sid, id, v).

- **Shuffle Cards:** To shuffle a set of cards with id values $\mathsf{id}_1, \ldots, \mathsf{id}_m$, $\mathcal{P}_i$ removes all the (eventual) cards $(\mathsf{id}_k, v_{\mathsf{id}_k})$, for $k \in \{1, \ldots, m\}$, that are in the list of opened cards $\mathcal{C}_O$ from that list and adds (id, $\mathsf{ct}_{\mathsf{id}_k}$), for $\mathsf{ct}_{\mathsf{id}_k} \leftarrow \mathsf{Enc}(\mathsf{pk}, v_{\mathsf{id}_k}, 0)$, in $\mathcal{C}_C$. Define $(\mathsf{ct}_{\mathsf{id}_1}^0, \ldots, \mathsf{ct}_{\mathsf{id}_m}^0) = (\mathsf{ct}_{\mathsf{id}_1}, \ldots, \mathsf{ct}_{\mathsf{id}_m})$, where the right-hand side cards are stored, together with the respective id values, in the internal list $\mathcal{C}_C$. For $j = 1, \ldots, n$:

1. If $j \neq i$, upon receiving the message (SHUFFLE, sid, $\mathcal{P}_j$, $\mathsf{id}_1, \ldots, \mathsf{id}_m$, $\mathsf{ct}_{\mathsf{id}_1}^j, \ldots, \mathsf{ct}_{\mathsf{id}_m}^j$, $\pi_{\mathcal{R}_3}^j$) from $\mathcal{P}_j$, $\mathcal{P}_i$ verifies if $\pi_{\mathcal{R}_3}^j$ is valid.

2. If $j = i$, sample a random permutation Π and, for $k = 1, \ldots, m$, let $r_k \xleftarrow{\$} \{0,1\}^{\kappa}$ and $\mathsf{ct}_{\mathsf{id}_k}^i \leftarrow \mathsf{ReRand}(\mathsf{pk}, \mathsf{ct}_{\Pi(\mathsf{id}_k)}^{i-1}, r_k)$. Broadcast (SHUFFLE, sid, $\mathcal{P}_i$, $\mathsf{id}_1, \ldots, \mathsf{id}_m$, $\mathsf{ct}_{\mathsf{id}_1}^i, \ldots, \mathsf{ct}_{\mathsf{id}_m}^i$, $\pi_{\mathcal{R}_3}^i$), where $\pi_{\mathcal{R}_3}^i$ is generated by computing NIZK$_{\mathcal{R}_3}$.Prov with $(\Pi, (r_1, \ldots, r_m))$ as witness.

Every player $\mathcal{P}_i$ sets its internal list of closed cards $\mathcal{C}_C$ to $((\mathsf{id}_1, \mathsf{ct}_{\mathsf{id}_1}^n), \ldots, (\mathsf{id}_m, \mathsf{ct}_{\mathsf{id}_m}^n))$ and outputs (SHUFFLED, sid, $\mathsf{id}_1, \ldots, \mathsf{id}_m$).

- **Shuffle Private Cards:** In order to shuffle a set of private cards with id values $\mathsf{id}_1, \ldots, \mathsf{id}_m$ belonging to player $\mathcal{P}_j$, player $\mathcal{P}_i$ proceed as follows:

  - If $i = j$, sample a random permutation Π and let $r_k \xleftarrow{\$} \{0,1\}^{\kappa}$, $\mathsf{ct}_{\mathsf{id}_k}' \leftarrow \mathsf{ReRand}(\mathsf{pk}, \mathsf{ct}_{\Pi(\mathsf{id}_k)}, r_k)$ for $k = 1, \ldots, m$. Broadcast (PRIVSHUFFLE, sid, $\mathcal{P}_j$, $\mathsf{id}_1, \ldots, \mathsf{id}_m$, $\mathsf{ct}_{\mathsf{id}_1}', \ldots, \mathsf{ct}_{\mathsf{id}_m}'$, $\pi_{\mathcal{R}_3}^j$), where $\pi_{\mathcal{R}_3}^j$ is generated by computing NIZK$_{\mathcal{R}_3}$.Prov with $(\Pi, (r_1, \ldots, r_m))$ as witness.

  - If $i \neq j$, upon receiving (PRIVSHUFFLE, sid, $\mathcal{P}_j$, $\mathsf{id}_1, \ldots, \mathsf{id}_m$, $\mathsf{ct}_{\mathsf{id}_1}', \ldots, \mathsf{ct}_{\mathsf{id}_m}'$, $\pi_{\mathcal{R}_3}^i$) from $\mathcal{P}_j$, verify if $\pi_{\mathcal{R}_3}^i$ is valid.

  $\mathcal{P}_j$ outputs (PRIVATE-SHUFFLED, sid, $(\mathsf{id}_1, v_1'), \ldots, (\mathsf{id}_m, v_m')$), where the new card values $v_1', \ldots, v_m'$ associated to each id value are known to him, and the other parties output (PRIVATE-SHUFFLED, sid, $\mathsf{id}_1, \ldots, \mathsf{id}_m$). All players update their local list $\mathcal{C}_C$.

Fig. 3. Protocol π_{CG} (second part).

Protocol π_{CG} (Third Part)

– **Open Public Card:** In order to open a public card ct_{id}, each $\mathcal{P}_i$ proceeds as follows:
  - Compute $d_i \leftarrow \mathsf{ShareDec}(sk_i, ct_{id})$ and generate a NIZK of decryption share correctness $\pi^i_{\mathcal{R}_2}$ by computing $\mathsf{NIZK}_{\mathcal{R}_2}.\mathsf{Prov}$ with (r_i, sk_i) as witness (where r_i was used in generating (pk_i, sk_i)) and broadcast $(\text{OPENCARD}, sid, \mathcal{P}_i, id, d_i, \pi^i_{\mathcal{R}_2})$.
  - Upon receiving $(\text{OPENCARD}, sid, \mathcal{P}_j, id, d_j, \pi^j_{\mathcal{R}_2})$ from $\mathcal{P}_j$, verify if $\pi^j_{\mathcal{R}_2}$ is valid. Upon receiving valid decryption shares from all players, retrieve the value of card ct_{id} by computing $v_{id} \leftarrow \mathsf{ShareCombine}(d_1, \ldots, d_n)$. Add (id, v_{id}) to $\mathcal{C}_O$ and output $(\text{CARD}, sid, id, v_{id})$.

– **Open Private Card:** To open a private card ct_{id} towards player $\mathcal{P}_j$, all players proceed as follows:
  - For $i \neq j$, $\mathcal{P}_i$ computes $d_i \leftarrow \mathsf{ShareDec}(sk_i, ct_{id})$ and generates a NIZK of decryption share correctness $\pi^i_{\mathcal{R}_2}$ by computing $\mathsf{NIZK}_{\mathcal{R}_2}.\mathsf{Prov}$ with (r_i, sk_i) as witness (r_i is the randomness used to generate (pk_i, sk_i)) and sends $(\text{OPENCARD}, sid, \mathcal{P}_i, id, d_i, \pi^i_{\mathcal{R}_2})$ to $\mathcal{P}_j$. Add id to $\mathcal{C}_j$.
  - Player $\mathcal{P}_j$, upon receiving $(\text{OPENCARD}, sid, \mathcal{P}_i, id, d_i, \pi^i_{\mathcal{R}_2})$ from $\mathcal{P}_i$, verifies if $\pi^i_{\mathcal{R}_2}$ is valid. Upon receiving valid decryption shares from all other players, $\mathcal{P}_j$ computes $d_j \leftarrow \mathsf{ShareDec}(sk_j, ct_{id})$ and retrieves the value of the card by computing $v_{id} \leftarrow \mathsf{ShareCombine}(d_1, \ldots, d_n)$. $\mathcal{P}_j$ adds id to $\mathcal{C}_j$ and outputs $(\text{CARD}, sid, id, v_{id})$.

– **Check-out:** A player $\mathcal{P}_j$ can initiate the check-out procedure and leave the protocol at any point that GR allows, in which case all players will receive the money that they currently own plus their collateral refund. The players proceed as follows:
  1. $\mathcal{P}_j$ sends $(\text{CHECKOUT-INIT}, sid, \mathcal{P}_j)$ to $\mathcal{F}_{SC}$.
  2. Upon receiving $(\text{CHECKOUT-INIT}, sid, \mathcal{P}_j)$ from $\mathcal{F}_{SC}$, each $\mathcal{P}_i$ (for $i = 1, \ldots, n$) sends $(\text{SIGN}, sid, (\text{CHECKOUT}|\text{payout}))$ to $\mathcal{F}_{DSIG}$ (where payout is a vector containing the amount of money that each player will receive according to GR), obtaining $(\text{SIGNATURE}, sid, (\text{CHECKOUT}|\text{payout}), \sigma_i)$ as answer. Player $\mathcal{P}_i$ sends σ_i to $\mathcal{P}_j$.
  3. For all $i \neq j$, $\mathcal{P}_j$ sends $(\text{VERIFY}, sid, (\text{CHECKOUT}|\text{payout}), \sigma_i, \text{SIG}.vk_i)$ to $\mathcal{F}_{DSIG}$, where payout is computed locally by $\mathcal{P}_j$. If $\mathcal{F}_{DSIG}$ answers all queries $(\text{VERIFY}, sid, (\text{CHECKOUT}|\text{payout}), \sigma_i, \text{SIG}.vk_i)$ with $(\text{VERIFIED}, sid, (\text{CHECKOUT}|\text{payout}), 1)$, $\mathcal{P}_j$ sends $(\text{CHECKOUT}, sid, \text{payout}, \sigma_1, \ldots, \sigma_n)$ to $\mathcal{F}_{SC}$. Otherwise, go to Recovery.
  4. Upon receiving $(\text{PAYOUT}, sid, \mathcal{P}_i, \text{coins}(w))$ from $\mathcal{F}_{SC}$, $\mathcal{P}_i$ outputs that and halts.

– **Recovery:** Player $\mathcal{P}_i$ proceeds as follows:
  - If player $\mathcal{P}_i$ activates the Recovery procedure, it sends $(\text{RECOVERY}, sid)$ to $\mathcal{F}_{SC}$.
  - Upon receiving $(\text{REQUEST}, sid)$ from $\mathcal{F}_{SC}$, every player $\mathcal{P}_i$ sends $(\text{RESPONSE}, sid, \mathcal{P}_i, \text{Checkpoint}_i, \text{proc}_i)$ to $\mathcal{F}_{SC}$, where Checkpoint_i is $\mathcal{P}_i$'s latest checkpoint witness and proc_i is $\mathcal{P}_i$'s witness for the protocol phase that started after the latest checkpoint; or acknowledges another player's witness if it matches Checkpoint_i.
  - Upon receiving $(\text{NXT-STP}, sid, \mathcal{P}_i, \text{proc}, \text{round})$ from $\mathcal{F}_{SC}$, $\mathcal{P}_i$ sends $(\text{NXT-STP-RSP}, sid, \mathcal{P}_i, \text{proc}, \text{round}, \text{msg})$ to $\mathcal{F}_{SC}$, where msg is the protocol message that should be sent at round round of procedure proc of the protocol according to GR.
  - Upon receiving a message $(\text{NXT-STP-RSP}, sid, \mathcal{P}_j, \text{proc}, \text{round}, \text{msg})$ from $\mathcal{F}_{SC}$, every player $\mathcal{P}_i$ considers msg as the protocol message sent by $\mathcal{P}_j$ in round of procedure proc and take it into consideration for future messages.
  - Upon receiving a message $(\text{RECOVERED}, sid, \text{proc}, \text{Checkpoint})$ from $\mathcal{F}_{SC}$, every player $\mathcal{P}_i$ records Checkpoint as the latest checkpoint and continues protocol execution according to the game rules GR.

Fig. 4. Protocol π_{CG} (third part).

complexities of each individual card operation in the works that introduce the previously most efficient (but unproven) poker protocols with the card operations in the DDH-based instantiation of Royale (described in Sect. 3). For the comparison, we consider the works of Barnett and Smart [3], and the protocols proposed as a building block for the (unproven) tailor-made poker protocol of Bentov et al. [7]: Wei and Wang [32] and Wei [31]. We remark that these previous works have not been formally proven secure. Moreover, differently from Royale, even if these previous works can be proven to implement a game of poker, using their card operations arbitrarily might cause security issues, as they are not composable.

Instantiating the Building Blocks: We consider the protocols of Barnett and Smart [3], Wei and Wang [32] and Wei [31] to be instantiated with the same random oracle-based commitments and NIZKs based on the Fiat-Shamir heuristic used in our DDH-based instantiation of Royale. For the protocols of [3] and [32] a cut-and-choose security parameter of $s = 40$ is considered, while for the protocol of [31], we consider the parameter $k = 4$. In the NIZK of shuffle correctness used by Royale (the construction of [4]), the total number of cards is represented as $m = m_1 m_2$ and the choice of m_1 and m_2 affects both the computational and communication complexities. Even though the choice of m_1 and m_2 can be optimized to obtain either shorter or faster proofs, in our general comparison we assume that $m_1 = m_2 = \lceil \sqrt{m} \rceil$.

Computational Complexity: The estimation is in terms of modular exponentiations executed for each card operation, since these operations tend to dominate the complexity. We present the amount of local computation performed on Table 1. As previously observed, the Open Public Card and Open Private Card of all protocols in our comparison have roughly the same concrete complexity, while the Shuffle Cards phase is the main bottleneck. Notice that the two most efficient protocols in our comparison are Royale and Wei's protocol [31] (and consequently the instantiation of Bentov et al. [7] based on it), which has better asymptotic efficiency than Royale. However, we remark Royale achieves *better concrete efficiency* for *practical* parameters. For example, in a 6-player game and a standard deck of 52 cards (*e.g.* Poker), the Shuffle Cards phase of [31] requires approximately 3 times more exponentiations than Royale. Further estimations for practical parameters are in the full version [20].

Communication Complexity: We estimate the communication complexity in terms of the number of elements of $\mathbb{G}$ and elements of $\mathbb{Z}_p$ exchanged in each phase of the protocols in Table 1. In contrast to the case of computational complexity, we consider the total amount of data exchanged over the network by all players during each phase of the analyzed protocols. As it is the case with computational complexity, the Shuffle Cards phase constitutes the main bottleneck and dominates complexity. Notice that the most efficient protocols in our comparison are Royale and the protocol of Wei [31] (and consequently the instantiation of Bentov et al. [7] based on it). However, in this case, Royale actually achieves both better asymptotic communication complexity and *better concrete efficiency* than [31]. For example, in a 6-player game and a standard deck of 52 cards (*e.g.* Poker), the Shuffle Cards phase of [31] exchanges approximately 8 times more elements of $\mathbb{G}$ and twice more elements of $\mathbb{Z}_p$. Further estimations for practical parameters are in given in the full version [20].

Round Complexity: As in the previous cases, the Shuffle Cards phase is the main bottleneck. Royale's Shuffle Card phase requires only n rounds (where n is the number of players) while [32] and [31] require respectively $4n + 1$ and $4n + 3$ rounds. Hence, Royale has a clear advantage in round complexity, which results in better performance in high latency networks such as the Internet.

Checkpoint and On-Chain Storage Complexity: When the smart contract functionality $\mathcal{F}_{SC}$ is implemented by a smart contract system running on top of a blockchain, the information sent by the players to $\mathcal{F}_{SC}$ has to be stored in space-constrained blocks, raising a concern about on-chain storage complexity. First, we remark that Royale is designed in such a way that only the Check-in, Check-out and Recovery phases cause any information to be sent to $\mathcal{F}_{SC}$ (and consequently stored in the blockchain), with the Recovery phase only being activated if a player misbehaves. In the Check-in phase, signature verification keys and public key shares (plus associated proofs of validity) for each players are registered with the smart contract, amounting to storing $(2 \ \mathbb{G} + 2 \ \mathbb{Z}_p)n$ bits, where n is the number of players. In the Check-out phase, the vector payout (of size |payout|) along with signatures by each player are sent to the smart contract, amounting to $|payout| + 2n \ \mathbb{Z}_p$ of storage. In the Recovery phase, the most up-to-date checkpoint witness is sent to the smart contract, which subsequently registers all other player's messages for the phase to be executed after this checkpoint witness was generated. The worst case for checkpoint witness size is that where all cards are still closed, resulting in size $2m \ \mathbb{G} + |id|m + |balance| + |bets| + 2n \ \mathbb{Z}_p$ bits, where n is the number of players, m is the number of cards and |id|, |balance| and |bets| are the sizes of card identification string id, vector balance and vector bets, respectively. The messages of the phase executed after the latest checkpoint amount to extra on-chain storage equal to the communication complexity of each phase (as estimated above). On the other hand, the protocol of Bentov *et al.* [7] (based on [31] or [32]), does not specify checkpoint witnesses (seemingly requiring the full transcript of the current poker game to be sent to the smart contract) nor offers any complexity estimates for Check-in and Check-out phases, making it hard to provide a meaningful comparison.

Benchmarks. We now present benchmarks of Royale obtained with a prototype implementation of the DDH-based instantiation, showcasing the efficiency of our protocol for practical parameters. Our prototype implementation was done in Haskell using NIST curve P-256. Experiments were conducted on a XPS 9370 with a i7 8550U CPU and 16 GB RAM running with Linux Fedora 28 (kernel 4.16). We analyze the network communication and execution time of Royale with different numbers of cards (denoted by m in the tables) and players (denoted by n in the tables). We focus on the following phases of Royale: Check-Out, Check-Out, Shuffle Cards, Shuffle Private Cards. Moreover, we analyse on-chain storage

Table 1. Complexities for each player in terms of modular exponentiations and group and ring elements $\mathbb{G}$ and $\mathbb{Z}_p$, for n players and m cards.

	Computational complexity			Communication complexity		
	Shuffle Cards	Open Private Card (drawer; others)	Open Public Card	Shuffle Cards	Open Private Card (drawer; others)	Open Public Card
[3]	$240m(n-1)$ $+161m$	$4n-3; 3$	$4n$	$164\,nm$ G, $122\,nm$ $\mathbb{Z}_p$	$45\,nm$ G, $(2n^2+$ $80n+2\,nm)$ $\mathbb{Z}_p$	$n(17m+5)$ G, $n(m+18)$ $\mathbb{Z}_p$
[7,32]	$(44n+1)m$	$4n-3; 3$	$4n$	$3(n-1)$ G, $2(n-1)$ $\mathbb{Z}_p$	$(n-1)$ G, $2(n-1)$ $\mathbb{Z}_p$	$(n-1)$ G, $2(n-1)$ $\mathbb{Z}_p$
[7,31]	$81m+2n+25$	$4n-3; 3$	$4n$	$3n$ G, $2n$ $\mathbb{Z}_p$	n G, $2n$ $\mathbb{Z}_p$	n G, $2n$ $\mathbb{Z}_p$
Royale	$(2\log(\lceil\sqrt{m}\rceil)$ $+4n-2)m$	$4n-3; 3$	$4n$	$n(2m+$ $\lceil\sqrt{m}\rceil)$ G, $5n\lceil\sqrt{m}\rceil$ $\mathbb{Z}_p$	$(n-1)$ G, $2(n-1)$ $\mathbb{Z}_p$	n G, $2n$ $\mathbb{Z}_p$

requirements for the Checkpoint Witnesses used in the Recovery Phase considering an implementation of the smart contract functionality $\mathcal{F}_{SC}$ based on a smart contract that verifies individual steps of Royale (*i.e.* checking NIZK, signature and encryption validity). We evaluate the execution time required by the aforementioned phases of Royale in milliseconds (ms) and consider network delays in terms of Round Trip Times (RTT). Our analysis shows that Royale achieves high computational efficiency, with network delays representing the main bottleneck. We analyze the on-chain storage required by Royale in terms of the size in kilobytes (KB) of the data stored by the smart contract in each phase, which is zero for all phases, except for Check-in, Check-out and Recovery. Our analysis shows that the on-chain footprints of these three latter phases is reasonably small for practical parameters. While the Recovery phase always requires storage of the must up-to-date checkpoint witness, it also requires players' messages for the current phase to be stored (*i.e.* the network communication required for each phase).

Table 2. On-chain storage size (in KB).

n	Check-In	Check-Out
2	0.25	0.38
4	0.51	0.75
6	0.76	1.13
8	1.02	1.5
10	1.27	1.88
12	1.52	2.25

Table 3. Execution time in ms and Round-trip time (RTT) for the Shuffle Card.

n	m		
	52	104	208
2	200.64 + 1 RTT	387.67 + 1 RTT	886.32 + 1 RTT
4	401.28 + 2 RTT	775.33 + 2 RTT	1772.64 + 2 RTT
6	601.93 + 3 RTT	1163 + 3 RTT	2658.96 + 3 RTT
8	802.57 + 4 RTT	1550.66 + 4 RTT	3545.28 + 4 RTT
10	1003.21 + 5 RTT	1938.33 + 5 RTT	4431.6 + 5 RTT
12	1203.85 + 6 RTT	2326 + 6 RTT	5317.92 + 6 RTT

The on-chain storage requirements of the Check-in and Check-Out Phases are presented in Table 2. Notice that all communication in these phases is done via the smart contract and does not depend on the number of cards. The execution time and network communication for the Shuffle Cards phase are presented in Tables 3 and 4, respectively. The execution time is presented as the sum of the local computation time required of each player and the network Round Trip Times necessary for delivering this phase's messages. Checkpoint witnesses size for our implementation is presented in Table 5. As previously discussed, we consider the size of checkpoint witnesses in the worst case, where all cards are closed (which results in the largest representation). For the setting of a poker game with 52 cards and 6 players, we obtain a worst case checkpoint witness of less than 4 KB. In case the Recovery Phase is activated, the smart contract receives (and stores on-chain) both the latest checkpoint witness and the next messages to be generated in the protocol, corresponding to the network communication of the current phase. Further benchmark data are presented in the full version [20].

Table 4. Network communication in the Shuffle Cards phase in (KB).

n	m		
	52	104	208
2	13.73	24.49	40.73
4	27.45	48.98	81.47
6	41.18	73.48	122.2
8	54.91	97.97	162.94
10	68.63	122.46	203.67
12	82.36	146.95	244.41

Table 5. Checkpoint witnesses on-chain storage size (KB).

n	m		
	52	104	208
2	3.61	7.06	13.97
4	3.77	7.22	14.13
6	3.92	7.38	14.28
8	4.08	7.53	14.44
10	4.23	7.69	14.59
12	4.39	7.84	14.75

References

1. Andrychowicz, M., Dziembowski, S., Malinowski, D., Mazurek, Ł.: Fair two-party computations via bitcoin deposits. In: Böhme, R., Brenner, M., Moore, T., Smith, M. (eds.) FC 2014. LNCS, vol. 8438, pp. 105–121. Springer, Heidelberg (2014). https://doi.org/10.1007/978-3-662-44774-1_8

2. Andrychowicz, M., Dziembowski, S., Malinowski, D., Mazurek, L.: Secure multiparty computations on bitcoin. In: 2014 IEEE Symposium on Security and Privacy, pp. 443–458. IEEE Computer Society Press, May 2014

3. Barnett, A., Smart, N.P.: Mental poker revisited. In: Paterson, K.G. (ed.) Cryptography and Coding 2003. LNCS, vol. 2898, pp. 370–383. Springer, Heidelberg (2003). https://doi.org/10.1007/978-3-540-40974-8_29

4. Bayer, S., Groth, J.: Efficient zero-knowledge argument for correctness of a shuffle. In: Pointcheval, D., Johansson, T. (eds.) EUROCRYPT 2012. LNCS, vol. 7237, pp. 263–280. Springer, Heidelberg (2012). https://doi.org/10.1007/978-3-642-29011-4_17

5. Bellare, M., Rogaway, P.: Random oracles are practical: a paradigm for designing efficient protocols. In: Ashby, V. (ed.) ACM CCS 93, pp. 62–73. ACM Press, November 1993

6. Bentov, I., Kumaresan, R.: How to use bitcoin to design fair protocols. In: Garay, J.A., Gennaro, R. (eds.) CRYPTO 2014. LNCS, vol. 8617, pp. 421–439. Springer, Heidelberg (2014). https://doi.org/10.1007/978-3-662-44381-1_24

7. Bentov, I., Kumaresan, R., Miller, A.: Instantaneous decentralized poker. In: Takagi, T., Peyrin, T. (eds.) ASIACRYPT 2017. LNCS, vol. 10625, pp. 410–440. Springer, Cham (2017). https://doi.org/10.1007/978-3-319-70697-9_15

8. Buterin, V.: White paper. https://github.com/ethereum/wiki/wiki/White-Paper (2013). Accessed 5 Dec 2017

9. Camenisch, J., Drijvers, M., Gagliardoni, T., Lehmann, A., Neven, G.: The wonderful world of global random Oracles. In: Nielsen, J.B., Rijmen, V. (eds.) EUROCRYPT 2018. LNCS, vol. 10820, pp. 280–312. Springer, Cham (2018). https://doi.org/10.1007/978-3-319-78381-9_11

10. Camenisch, J., Krenn, S., Shoup, V.: A framework for practical universally composable zero-knowledge protocols. In: Lee, D.H., Wang, X. (eds.) ASIACRYPT 2011. LNCS, vol. 7073, pp. 449–467. Springer, Heidelberg (2011). https://doi.org/10.1007/978-3-642-25385-0_24

11. Canetti, R.: Universally composable security: a new paradigm for cryptographic protocols. In: 42nd FOCS, pp. 136–145. IEEE Computer Society Press, October 2001

12. Canetti, R.: Universally composable signature, certification, and authentication. In: 17th IEEE Computer Security Foundations Workshop, (CSFW-17 2004), p. 219. IEEE Computer Society (2004)

13. Canetti, R., Fischlin, M.: Universally composable commitments. In: Kilian, J. (ed.) CRYPTO 2001. LNCS, vol. 2139, pp. 19–40. Springer, Heidelberg (2001). https://doi.org/10.1007/3-540-44647-8_2

14. Castellà-Roca, J., Sebé, F., Domingo-Ferrer, J.: Dropout-tolerant TTP-free mental poker. In: Katsikas, S., López, J., Pernul, G. (eds.) TrustBus 2005. LNCS, vol. 3592, pp. 30–40. Springer, Heidelberg (2005). https://doi.org/10.1007/11537878_4

15. Chaum, D., Pedersen, T.P.: Wallet databases with observers. In: Brickell, E.F. (ed.) CRYPTO 1992. LNCS, vol. 740, pp. 89–105. Springer, Heidelberg (1993). https://doi.org/10.1007/3-540-48071-4_7

16. Crépeau, C.: A secure poker protocol that minimizes the effect of player coalitions. In: Williams, H.C. (ed.) CRYPTO 1985. LNCS, vol. 218, pp. 73–86. Springer, Heidelberg (1986). https://doi.org/10.1007/3-540-39799-X_8

17. Crépeau, C.: A zero-knowledge poker protocol that achieves confidentiality of the players' strategy or how to achieve an electronic poker face. In: Odlyzko [25], pp. 239–247

18. David, B., Dowsley, R., Larangeira, M.: 21 - bringing down the complexity: fast composable protocols for card games without secret state. In: Susilo, W., Yang, G. (eds.) ACISP 2018. LNCS, vol. 10946, pp. 45–63. Springer, Cham (2018). https://doi.org/10.1007/978-3-319-93638-3_4

19. David, B., Dowsley, R., Larangeira, M.: Kaleidoscope: an efficient poker protocol with payment distribution and penalty enforcement. To appear on Financial Cryptography and Data Security (FC) 2018 (2018). http://eprint.iacr.org/2017/899

20. David, B., Dowsley, R., Larangeira, M.: Royale: a framework for universally composable card games with financial rewards and penalties enforcement. Cryptology ePrint Archive, Report 2018/157 (2018). https://eprint.iacr.org/2018/157

21. Fiat, A., Shamir, A.: How to prove yourself: practical solutions to identification and signature problems. In: Odlyzko [25], pp. 186–194

22. Golle, P.: Dealing cards in poker games. In: International Symposium on Information Technology: Coding and Computing (ITCC 2005), vol. 1, 4–6 April 2005, Las Vegas, Nevada, USA, pp. 506–511 (2005)

23. Kumaresan, R., Bentov, I.: How to use bitcoin to incentivize correct computations. In: Ahn, G.J., Yung, M., Li, N. (eds.) ACM CCS 2014, pp. 30–41. ACM Press, November 2014

24. Kumaresan, R., Moran, T., Bentov, I.: How to use bitcoin to play decentralized poker. In: Ray, I., Li, N., Kruegel: C. (eds.) ACM CCS 2015, pp. 195–206. ACM Press (Oct 2015)

25. Odlyzko, A.M. (ed.): CRYPTO 1986. LNCS, vol. 263. Springer, Heidelberg (1987). https://doi.org/10.1007/3-540-47721-7

26. Pointcheval, D., Stern, J.: Security proofs for signature schemes. In: Maurer, U. (ed.) EUROCRYPT 1996. LNCS, vol. 1070, pp. 387–398. Springer, Heidelberg (1996). https://doi.org/10.1007/3-540-68339-9_33

27. Schindelhauer, C.: A toolbox for mental card games. Technical report, University of Lübeck (1998)

28. Schnorr, C.P.: Efficient signature generation by smart cards. J. Cryptol. 4(3), 161–174 (1991)

29. Sebe, F., Domingo-Ferrer, J., Castella-Roca, J.: On the security of a repaired mental poker protocol. In: Third International Conference on Information Technology: New Generations, pp. 664–668 (2006)

30. Shamir, A., Rivest, R.L., Adleman, L.M.: Mental poker. In: Klarner, D.A. (ed.) The Mathematical Gardner, pp. 37–43. Springer, Boston (1981)

31. Wei, T.J.: Secure and practical constant round mental poker. Inf. Sci. 273, 352–386 (2014)

32. Wei, T.J., Wang, L.C.: A fast mental poker protocol. J. Math. Cryptol. 6(1), 39–68 (2012)

33. Wikipedia: Online Poker (2017). https://en.wikipedia.org/wiki/Online_poker. Accessed 29 Aug 2017

34. Zhang, B., Zhou, H.S.: Digital liquid democracy: How to vote your delegation statement. Cryptology ePrint Archive, Report 2017/616 (2017). http://eprint.iacr.org/2017/616

35. Zhao, W., Varadharajan, V.: Efficient TTP-free mental poker protocols. In: International Symposium on Information Technology: Coding and Computing (ITCC 2005), vol. 1, 4–6 April 2005, Las Vegas, Nevada, USA, pp. 745–750 (2005)

36. Zhao, W., Varadharajan, V., Mu, Y.: A secure mental poker protocol over the internet. In: Proceedings of the Australasian Information Security Workshop Conference on ACSW Frontiers 2003, ACSW Frontiers 2003, vol. 21, pp. 105–109. Australian Computer Society Inc., Darlinghurst (2003)

Universally Verifiable MPC and IRV Ballot Counting

Kim Ramchen[1,3(✉)], Chris Culnane[1], Olivier Pereira[1,2],
and Vanessa Teague[1(✉)]

[1] Department of Computing and Information Systems, The University of Melbourne,
Melbourne, Australia
kramchen@gmail.com, {christopher.culnane,vjteague}@unimelb.edu.au
[2] ICTEAM, UCLouvain, 1348 Louvain-la-Neuve, Belgium
olivier.pereira@uclouvain.be
[3] Faculty of Information Technology, Monash University, Clayton, Australia

Abstract. We present a very simple universally verifiable MPC protocol. The first component is a threshold somewhat homomorphic cryptosystem that permits an arbitrary number of additions (in the source group), followed by a single multiplication, followed by an arbitrary number of additions in the target group. The second component is a blackbox construction of universally verifiable distributed encryption switching between any public key encryption schemes supporting shared setup and key generation phases, as long as the schemes satisfy some natural additive-homomorphic properties. This allows us to switch back from the target group to the source group, and hence perform an arbitrary number of multiplications. The key generation algorithm of our prototypical cryptosystem, which is based upon concurrent verifiable secret sharing, permits robust re-construction of powers of a shared secret.

Keywords: Multiparty computation · Elections · Voting · Instant runoff voting · Verifiable computation · Verifiability

1 Introduction

We explore the design of efficient universally verifiable MPC protocols, motivated by applications to the counting of complex ballots in an election. *Universal verifiability* means that the computation should be verifiably correct, even to people who do not participate, and even if all parties involved in the computation are misbehaving. Apart from verifiability, we also require privacy to be guaranteed as long as the number of trustees behaving honestly is above a certain threshold. As trustees must be able to compute the result of the computation, and therefore jointly have access to the inputs, this appears to be the best we can hope for, at least in the absence of extra setup assumptions. (anonymous channel, tamper-proof devices, *etc.*).

Achieving these goals is particularly important in elections: we need the correctness of the tally to be guaranteed, even if all the people in charge of

© International Financial Cryptography Association 2019
I. Goldberg and T. Moore (Eds.): FC 2019, LNCS 11598, pp. 301–319, 2019.
https://doi.org/10.1007/978-3-030-32101-7_19

running the election are corrupted – or if all of their computing devices have been hacked – and ballots need to remain secret. Of course, this setting is meaninful in a lot of other contexts: secret bid auctions in which the winning bid is determined by the organisers and, more generally, any cloud application in which a group of users outsource their secret data to one or more cloud service providers, and expect correct computation while maintaining the confidentiality of their data.

Homomorphic encryption lends itself naturally to universally verifiable computation, because the computation itself can be performed by anyone. The private key can be shared among several trustees, who need only prove that they decrypted the final result correctly. For simple elections in which tallying consists only of addition, efficient solutions exist based on additive-homomorphic encryption [1,5,14]. We are interested in complex election schemes in which more than a simple sum is needed. Our particular application is *Instant runoff voting (IRV)*, also called alternative voting, which is used in verious places around the globe, either in general public elections (e.g., Australia, Ireland, San Francisco), or in internal consititutencies or political party elections (e.g., Canada, India, U.K.). In IRV, each voter lists some or all the candidates in their order of preference. At each iteration, each ballot is credited towards its highest uneliminated candidate. The candidate with the lowest tally is then eliminated (so each ballot is then credited to its next uneliminated candidate). This terminates when one candidate has a strict majority. This elimination process requires multiplications on top of addition, which cannot be homomorphically achived with traditional efficient schemes like ElGamal or Paillier. For this case, leveled homomorphic encryption [9] would work, but would need to be parameterized in advance for the maximum depth of multiplications that might possibly be needed, and pay an efficiency cost on that basis. In our setting, that depth would be the total number of candidates (minus 2), which might be a lot more than the actual number of eliminations.

1.1   Summary of Our Contribution

We build a simple universally verifiable MPC protocol from two components.

1. *A somewhat homomorphic encryption scheme with threshold key generation in the malicious static adversary setting.* It is similar to [11] in allowing arbitrary additions in a source space, then one multiplication. Our threshold key generation protocol allows efficient proofs of correct decryption.
2. *A multiparty encryption switching protocol that transforms a ciphertext from the target space, i.e., resulting from a homomorphic multiplication, into a ciphertext in the source space, hence making it possible to perform more multiplications.* This protocol is universally verifiable in the setting of [28].

Our scheme only requires computation in standard prime order groups and relies on standard computational assumptions (e.g., SXDH). The availability of addition and multiplication is sufficient to perform arbitrary computation (Fig. 1). It supports threshold key generation in the malicious setting with static corruption.

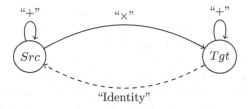

Fig. 1. Operations supported by our encryption scheme. Continuous (resp. dashed) arrows refer to non-interactive (resp. interactive) operations.

As a demonstration for our example application, we present a privacy-preserving universally verifiable implementation of the tallying phase of Instant Runoff Voting, based on our universally verifiable computation protocol. Our sample implementation was run on real-world data from public elections in Australia, which shows that our protocol is efficient enough for tallying real-world elections within a reasonable time frame, while leaving ample space for further optimization.

1.2   Comparison with Related Work on MPC

Our approach bears some resemblance to the encryption-switching approach of Couteau *et al.* [13], but has some significant differences. They switch between additively and multiplicatively homomorphic encryption schemes, while we switch between spaces in which we have additively homomorphic encryption, with the possibility to perform a multiplication as part of a switch. They have two switching protocols, between the additively and multiplicatively homomorphic ciphertext spaces, while we only need a protocol to switch from our target space back to our source space. Their protocols for secure computation are 2-party protocols and highly asymmetric (assigning specific roles to each party), while our protocols are multi-party, perfectly symmetric and universally verifiable.

Catalano and Fiore [11] describe boosting linearly homomorphic encryption to achieve server aided two-party secure function evaluation on parallel inputs in the semi-honest setting. We do not know if this approach can be generalised to the N-party setting. Like [8], their system allows evaluation of 2DNF formulae, that is, an addition, followed by one multiplication, followed by more additions. However, additions in the target space require ciphertext expansion, which is not the case in our scheme.

Three recent works address universally verifiable MPC. Their main bottleneck is key generation. Baum et al. [3] add universally verifiable proofs of correctness to SPDZ [15], which uses a somewhat homomorphic encryption scheme that has n-out-of-n key generation in the covert adversary model. The protocol therefore only offers confidentiality in that model. We have security in the traditional malicious adversary setting. This approach naturally scales to arbitrary multiplications, with cost proportional to the total number actually done.

However, the structure of the protocols, based on secret shared data, uses secure bidirectional channels between the input parties (e.g., the voters) and the computing parties (e.g., the election trustees), which is a challenging constraint for large scale applications. Our focus is on single pass protocols [7], in which voters can vote by submitting a single message built from a public election description, and have a computational work independent of the number of trustees.

Schoenmakers and Veeningen [28] rely on Damgaard-Jurik encryption, which supports efficient threshold key generation if an RSA modulus with unknown factorization is available bringing us back to key generation difficulties.

The most closely related work comes from Castagnos et al. [10], who propose new encryption schemes and switching protocols following [13], but working in prime order groups (like we do), hence also supporting threshold operations. They combine additively and multiplicatively homomorphic schemes (while we use a somewhat homomorphic approach). Their encryption scheme however relies on the hardness of DDH in very specific groups: subgroups of the class group of an order of a quadratic field of discriminant $-p^3$, which comes with efficiency penalties. They also need to work in subgroups of unknown order, which increases the cost of the ZK proofs needed for verifiability. Our protocol works in a standard computational setting (traditional asymmetric pairings), with efficiency and compatibility advantages (in particular, standard sigma protocols for prime order groups can be used). The tradeoff between the two would depend on the computation: in our IRV counting setting, we have many additions, followed by a single multiplication, followed by many more additions, repeatedly. For this kind of circuit our approach is more efficient than [10]. However, a computation with unbounded successive multiplications would eventually be faster with their method, despite the use of more expensive components.

In concurrent work, Attrapadung et al. [2] introduce a somewhat homomorphic encryption scheme that is a specific instance of our encryption scheme family. However, they do not offer a threshold (or distributed) variant, or a switching protocol, which are the key ingredients for our universally verifiable MPC protocol, nor do they consider general computation or voting.

1.3 Counting IRV Ballots

Plaintext IRV tallying raises coercion issues. The number of possible votes is more than $c!$ (where c is the number of candidates), which may be much larger than the number of votes actually cast. This introduces the possibility of an attack often called the *Italian attack:* a coercer demands a certain pattern of preferences, presumably with her favourite candidate first, and then checks to see whether that pattern appears in the final tally. To thwart this attack, many works describe universally verifiable IRV tallying without revealing individual ballots [6,19,20,25–27].

However, these all use mix-nets [23], which count among the most complex cryptographic protocols ever deployed. Besides, even when mixes use strong zero knowledge-proof based verification, if a single mix misbehaves then the entire mix-net halts until a replacement is found, leading to a protocol which is inherently non-robust. Ours is the first universally verifiable scheme for privacy-preserving IRV tallying without mixnets.

For our example application we implemented the single-authority version of our cryptosystem and switching protocol and used it to recount two real IRV elections, using public data from the Australian state of New South Wales. Each election included more than 40,000 ballots. The first, involving 5 candidates and a single elimination round, completed in 2 h. The second, with 6 candidates and 4 elimination rounds, took 15 h. This does not include the proofs of correct switching, which would add a constant multiplicative factor. The details are in Appendix J of the full version of this paper, at https://eprint.iacr.org/2018/246.

1.4   Structure of This Paper

The next section contains cryptographic background. In Sect. 2 we present a new candidate cryptosystem with which to instantiate source and destination encryption schemes for the N-party encryption switching primitive. Next, in Sect. 3, we tackle the problem of constructing a distributed key generation procedure for this protocol. Then in Sect. 4 we describe the universally verifiable protocol for switching from target back to source encryption schemes. Our prototype implementation for Instant Runoff Vote counting is in Sect. 5.

1.5   Background

We define a generic access structure for linear secret sharing schemes.

Definition 1 (Access Structure [22,30]). *Let S be a set of parties. A collection $\mathbb{A} \subset 2^S$ is monotone if $\forall\ B, C : if\ B \in \mathbb{A}$ and $B \subseteq C$ then $C \in \mathbb{A}$. An access structure, respectively monotone access structure, is a collection (respectively monotone collection) $\mathbb{A}$ of non-empty subsets of 2^S i.e., $\mathbb{A} \subseteq 2^S \setminus \{\emptyset\}$. The sets in $\mathbb{A}$ are called the authorised sets; the sets not in $\mathbb{A}$ are called unauthorised sets.*

Definition 2 (Linear Secret-Sharing Scheme [4,30]). *A secret-sharing scheme Π over a set of parties P is called linear over field $\mathbb{Z}_p$ if*

1. *The shares of the parties form a vector of dimension at most l over $\mathbb{Z}_p$.*
2. *There exists a matrix M with ℓ rows and d columns called the share-generating matrix for Π. There also exists a function ρ which maps each row of the matrix to an associated party. That is for $i = 1, \ldots, \ell$, the value $\rho(i)$ is the party associated with row i. When we consider the column vector $v = (s, r_2, \ldots, r_d)^T$, where $s \in \mathbb{Z}_p$ is the secret to be shared, and $r_2, \ldots, r_d \in \mathbb{Z}_p$ are randomly chosen, then Mv is the vector of ℓ shares of the secret s according to Π. The share $(Mv)_i$ belongs to the party $\rho(i)$.*

It is proven in [4] that every every linear secret-sharing scheme (LSSS) satisfies the following property, called *linear-reconstruction* in [30]. Suppose that Π is an LSSS for the access structure $\mathbb{A}$. Let $V \in \mathbb{A}$ be any authorised set, and let $I \subseteq \{1, \ldots, \ell\}$ be defined as $I = \{i : \rho(i) \in V\}$. Then there exist constants $\{\Lambda_{i,V} \in \mathbb{Z}_p : i \in I\}$ such that, if $\{s_i\}$ are valid shares of any secret s according to Π, then $\sum_{i \in I} \Lambda_{i,V} \cdot s_i = s$. Moreover these constants $\{\Lambda_{i,V}\}$ can be found in time polynomial in the dimensions of the share-generating matrix M.

Definition 3 (*T*-Threshold Access Structure). *Of specific interest for our purposes is the T-party threshold access structure, defined as* $\mathbb{A}_{T\text{-Th}} = \{S : S \in 2^{\{P_1, \ldots, P_n\}}, |S| \geq T\}$, *where* $T < n/2$. *Let* M *be the linear secret-sharing scheme matrix corresponding to* $\mathbb{A}_{T\text{-Th}}$. *In that case there exists* M *with row-dimension* $l = n$ *and column-dimension* $d = T$.

Pairings on Prime-Order Groups. To build our one-time homomorphic cryptosystem of Sect. 3, we require the notion of *projecting bilinear group generators* [17]. Our specific choice of generator will be a variant of the polynomial-induced projecting generator introduced by Herold et al. [21], tailored for the asymmetric pairing setting.

Definition 4 (Bilinear Group Generator [17]). *A bilinear group generator is an algorithm* $\mathcal{G}$ *that takes as input a security parameter* λ *and outputs a description of five abelian groups* G, G_1, H, H_1, G_t *with* $G_1 < G$ *and* $H_1 < H$. *Assume that this description permits polynomial-time group operations and random sampling in each group. The algorithm also outputs an efficiently computable map* $e : G \times H \to G_t$ *that satisfies:*

Bilinearity. *For all* $g_1, g_2 \in G$ *and* $h_1, h_2 \in H$,
   $e(g_1 g_2, h_1 h_2) = e(g_1, h_1) e(g_1, h_2) e(g_2, h_1) e(g_2, h_2).$
Non-degeneracy. $e(g, h) = 1 \ \forall h \in H \iff g = 1$
   and $e(g, h) = 1 \ \forall g \in G \iff h = 1.$

A bilinear group generator $\mathcal{G}$ is prime-order if G, G_1, H, H_1, G_t all have prime order p.

Definition 5 (Projecting Bilinear Group Generator [17]). *Let* $\mathcal{G}$ *be a bilinear group generator. Say that* $\mathcal{G}$ *is projecting if it also outputs a group* $G'_t < G_t$ *and three group homomorphisms* π_1, π_2, π_t *mapping* G, H, G_t *to themselves such that*

1. *Subgroups* G_1, H_1, G'_t *are contained in the kernels of* π_1, π_2, π_t *respectively.*
2. $e(\pi_1(g), \pi_2(h)) = \pi_t(e(g, h))$ *for all* $g \in G, h \in H$.

We propose a projecting bilinear group operator induced by tensor product, instead of relying on the polynomial product previously proposed [21]. The polynomial solution was designed for the symmetric pairing setting, but raises difficulties in the definition of the projecting operator when moving to the asymmetric setting. Our tensor product based solution offers an efficient alternative that makes it possible to have efficient ciphertext in the base groups, by relying on the sXDH assumption.

Definition 6 (*l*-Symmetric Cascade Assumption [16]). *Let $\{\mathbb{G}_\lambda\}_\lambda$ be an ensemble of cyclic groups with prime-orders $\{\mathbb{Z}_{p(\lambda)}\}_\lambda$ where $\exists c > 0 \;\forall \lambda \;|p(\lambda)| < \lambda^c$. For fixed λ, let $\mathbb{Z}_p = \mathbb{Z}_{p(\lambda)}$ and define the distribution of matrices over $\mathbb{Z}_p^{(l+1)\times l}$:*

$$SC_l =: \begin{pmatrix} -s & 0 & \dots & 0 & 0 \\ 1 & -s & \dots & 0 & 0 \\ 0 & 1 & & 0 & 0 \\ & \ddots & & \ddots & \\ 0 & 0 & \dots & 1 & -s \\ 0 & 0 & \dots & 0 & 1 \end{pmatrix} : s \in_R \mathbb{Z}_p.$$

Then $\forall$ PPT adversaries $\mathcal{A}$, the difference below is a negligible function of λ.

$$|\Pr[1 \leftarrow \mathcal{A}(\mathbb{G}, g, g^A, g^{Aw}) : g \in_R \mathbb{G}, A \in SC_l, w \in_R \mathbb{Z}_p^l] - $$
$$\Pr[1 \leftarrow \mathcal{A}(\mathbb{G}, g, g^A, g^u) : g \in_R \mathbb{G}, A \in SC_l, u \in_R \mathbb{Z}_p^{l+1}]|.$$

Definition 7 (External *l*-Symmetric Cascade Assumption). *Let $\mathcal{D}_1$, $\mathcal{D}_2$ and $\mathcal{D}_t$ be three ensembles of cyclic groups, such that for every $\lambda \in \mathbb{N}$, if $\mathbb{G}_1 = \mathbb{G}_{1\lambda} \in \mathcal{D}_1$, $\mathbb{G}_2 = \mathbb{G}_{2\lambda} \in \mathcal{D}_2$ and $\mathbb{G}_t = \mathbb{G}_{t\lambda} \in \mathcal{D}_t$, there exists an efficiently computable pairing $e(\cdot, \cdot)$, such that $e : \mathbb{G}_1 \times \mathbb{G}_2 \to \mathbb{G}_t$. The External l-Symmetric Cascade assumption is that the l-Symmetric Cascade assumption holds in each of the ensembles $\mathcal{D}_1$ and $\mathcal{D}_2$.*

Proposition 1. *The Symmetric External Diffie-Hellman Assumption [29] holds with respect to group ensembles $\mathcal{D}_1, \mathcal{D}_2$, iff the External 1-Symmetric Cascade Assumption holds with respect to $\mathcal{D}_1, \mathcal{D}_2$.*

CF Encryption. Recently Catalano and Fiore [11] showed how to generalise earlier work on 2DNF formulae [8] to transform virtually any linearly homomorphic cryptosystem into one permitting the computation of any degree-2 formula. Multiplication transforms two input ciphertexts from a "level-1" space into an encryption of the product in the "level-2" space. In this level-2 space, further homomorphic additions remain possible, at the cost of ciphertext expansion at each step. Still, it is not possible to perform any further multiplications.

For concreteness we will assume additive ElGamal encryption for the base public key encryption scheme. Let $(\overline{\text{Keygen}}, \overline{\text{Enc}}, \overline{\text{Dec}})$ be additive ElGamal on message space $(\mathcal{M}, +)$. The Catalano-Fiore cryptosystem is as follows.

Keygen(1^λ) Let $(\overline{\text{pk}}, \overline{\text{sk}}) \leftarrow \overline{\text{Keygen}}(1^\lambda)$.
    Set $(\text{pk}, \text{sk}) \leftarrow (\overline{\text{pk}}, \overline{\text{sk}})$.
Enc(pk, M) Choose $b \in_R \mathcal{M}$.
    Output $C = (M - b, \overline{\text{Enc}}(\text{pk}, b))$.
Multiply(pk, C, C') Let $C = (C_0, C_1)$ and $C' = (C_0', C_1')$ be inputs. Let $\alpha = \overline{\text{Enc}}(\overline{\text{pk}}, C_0 C_0') \cdot (C_1)^{C_0'} \cdot (C_1')^{C_0}$.
    Output (α, C_1, C_1').

$\mathsf{Dec}(\mathsf{sk}, C)$ Accept $C = (\alpha, C_1, C_1')$ as input.
  Let $M' \leftarrow \overline{\mathsf{Dec}}(\mathsf{sk}, \alpha)$, $b \leftarrow \overline{\mathsf{Dec}}(\mathsf{sk}, C_1)$ and
  $b' \leftarrow \overline{\mathsf{Dec}}(\mathsf{sk}, C_1')$ as input. Output $M = M' + bb'$.

Noninteractive Zero Knowledge Proofs. We use non-interactive zero knowledge proofs of the following NP relations. Efficient constructions of these can be found in Appendix D of the full version. Let $\Pi_{\mathsf{range}} = (G_{\mathsf{range}}, P_{\mathsf{range}}, V_{\mathsf{range}})$ be a non-interactive zero knowledge proof for the relation $\mathcal{R}_{\mathsf{range}} = \{(c, y) | \exists\, a, r :$ $c_i = \mathsf{Enc}(y, a; r) \wedge a \in [0, 2^\lambda - 1]\}$. Let $\mathcal{R}_{\mathsf{bit}} \subseteq \mathcal{R}_{\mathsf{range}}$ be the special case $\lambda = 1$ and Π_{bit} be the corresponding proof system. Let $\Pi_{\mathsf{eq}} = (G_{\mathsf{eq}}, P_{\mathsf{eq}}, V_{\mathsf{eq}})$ be a non-interactive zero knowledge proof system for the relation $\mathcal{R}_{\mathsf{eq}} = \{(c, c', \mathsf{pk}_1, \mathsf{pk}_2) | \exists m, r, r' : c = \mathsf{Enc}_1(\mathsf{pk}_1, m; r) \wedge c' = \mathsf{Enc}_2(\mathsf{pk}_2, m; r')\}$. For $1 \le j \le N$ let σ_j be the common reference string belonging to P_j.

2 One-Time Multiplicatively Homomorphic Cryptosystem

The basis of our universally verifiable MPC protocol is a homomorphic cryptosystem that supports arbitrarily many additions, followed by one multiplication, followed by arbitrarily many additions.

Many such encryption schemes have been already proposed, starting with the BGN pairing-based scheme [8]. However, threshold key generation for BGN and similar schemes is challenging, as it would require the generation of RSA-type moduli with unknown factorization, and computing in the resulting pairing groups of composite order is also quite demanding. Unverifiable trust assumptions would undermine the main purpose of this work.

This motivates our construction of a pairing based homomorphic cryptosystem on *prime-order* groups, for which a secure and robust key generation procedure can be derived. This has been explored by Freeman [17], who shows how to build such schemes from projecting pairings and, more recently by Herold et al. [21] who show how to build them from hidden matrix-rank based indistinguishability assumptions [16] on the source group of symmetric pairings.

As these symmetric pairings have also become extremely expensive from a computational point of view due to the recent attacks on the discrete logarithm in low characteristic, we aim for a more efficient scheme based an asymmetric pairings, by extending their work to that setting. This requires performing operations in parallel in the two source groups of the pairing, and designing a tensor product-based projecting pairing as a replacement for their polynomial product. The underlying indistinguishability problem induced by this pairing on both source groups is a generalisation of the well-known XDH problem [29].

This section contains only the simplest instance of our encryption scheme, based on the External 1-Symmetric Cascade Assumption. A general version based on the External l-Symmetric Cascade Assumption is presented in Appendix C of the full version. Here we construct a projecting bilinear group as a special case with $l = 1$.

Definition 8 (Projecting pairing construction). *Take as input a prime-order bilinear group* $(p, \mathbb{G}_1, \mathbb{G}_2, \mathbb{G}_t, \hat{e})$, *elements* $g \in \mathbb{G}_1$ *and* $h \in \mathbb{G}_2$, *and secret keys* s *and* s' *in* $\mathbb{Z}_p$.

Define $G = \mathbb{G}_1^2$, $H = \mathbb{G}_2^2$, $G_t = \mathbb{G}_t^4$, *and define the bilinear map* $e : G \times H \to G_t$ *as* $e((g_0, g_1), (h_0, h_1)) = (\hat{e}(g_0, h_0), \hat{e}(g_0, h_1), \hat{e}(g_1, h_0), \hat{e}(g_1, h_1))$.

Define G_1 *(resp.* H_1*) as the subgroup of* G *(resp.* H*) generated by* $g^{(-s,1)} = (g^{-s}, g)$ *(resp.* $h^{(-s',1)}$*).*

Define the following projecting maps:

- $\pi_1 : G \to \mathbb{G}_1$ *as* $\pi_1(g_1, g_2) = g_1 g_2^s$,
- $\pi_2 : H \to \mathbb{G}_2$ *as* $\pi_2(h_1, h_2) = h_1 h_2^{s'}$,
- $\pi_t : G_t \to \mathbb{G}_t$ *as* $\pi_t(g_1, g_2, g_3, g_4) = g_1 g_2^{s'} g_3^s g_4^{ss'}$.

Output secret key $\mathsf{sk} = (\pi_1, \pi_2, \pi_t)$ *and public key* $\mathsf{pk} = (G, G_1, H, H_1, G_t, e, g, h)$.

It is easy to see that G_1 and H_1 are the kernel of π_1 and π_2 and that these operators essentially offer a decryption operation for ElGamal-like encryption schemes that use s and s' as secret keys.

Notation: $v_1 \cdot v_2$ denotes elementwise multiplication; $v_2{}^n$ is elementwise exponentiation.

Our encryption scheme is then defined as follows.

$\mathsf{Setup}(1^\lambda)$: Let $\mathcal{P}$ be a prime-order bilinear group generator. Let $\mathcal{M} = \mathbb{Z}_p$. Output $\mathsf{pp} = (p, \mathbb{G}_1, \mathbb{G}_2, \mathbb{G}_t, \hat{e}) \leftarrow \mathcal{P}(1^\lambda)$.

$\mathsf{KeyGen}(\mathsf{pp})$: Select s and s' in $\mathbb{Z}_p$, set $\boldsymbol{x} = (-s, 1)$ and $\boldsymbol{x}' = (-s', 1)$. Choose $g \in_R \mathbb{G}_1$, $h \in_R \mathbb{G}_2$, and define $\mathbf{g} = g^{\boldsymbol{x}} = (g^{-s}, g)$ and $\mathbf{h} = h^{\boldsymbol{x}'} = (h^{-s'}, h)$. Run the Projecting Pairing construction on input pp, g, h, s, s'. Output the resulting secret key $\mathsf{sk} = (\pi_1, \pi_2, \pi_t)$ and the public key $\mathsf{pk} = (G, G_1, H, H_1, G_t, e, g, h)$. Note that G_1 and H_1 are described by their generators $\mathbf{g}$ and $\mathbf{h}$ respectively.

$\mathsf{Enc}_{\mathsf{src}}(\mathsf{pk}, M)$: Choose a, b at random in $\mathbb{Z}_p$. Let $\mathbf{g}_1 = (\mathbf{g})^a = (g^{-as}, g^a)$ and $\mathbf{h}_1 = (\mathbf{h})^b = (h^{-bs'}, h^b)$. Let $C_0 = \mathbf{g}^M \cdot \mathbf{g}_1$, $C_1 = \mathbf{h}^M \cdot \mathbf{h}_1$. Output the ciphertext (C_0, C_1) in $G \times H$.

$\mathsf{Enc}_{\mathsf{tgt}}(\mathsf{pk}, M)$: Choose a, b at random in $\mathbb{Z}_p$. Let $\mathbf{g}_1 = (\mathbf{g})^a = (g^{-as}, g^a)$ and $\mathbf{h}_1 = (\mathbf{h})^b = (h^{-bs'}, h^b)$. Output the ciphertext $C = e(\mathbf{g}, \mathbf{h})^M \cdot e(\mathbf{g}, \mathbf{h}_1) \cdot e(\mathbf{g}_1, \mathbf{h})$ in G_t.

$\mathsf{Multiply}_{\mathsf{src}}(\mathsf{pk}, C, C')$: Take as input two ciphertexts $C = (C_0, C_1)$ and $C' = (C_0', C_1')$. Choose $\mathbf{g}_1 \in_R G_1$ and $\mathbf{h}_1 \in_R H_1$, as in the above routine. Output $C = e(C_0, C_1') \cdot e(\mathbf{g}, \mathbf{h}_1) \cdot e(\mathbf{g}_1, \mathbf{h})$, an element of G_t.

$\mathsf{Add}_{\mathsf{src}}(\mathsf{pk}, C, C')$: Take as input two ciphertexts $C = (C_0, C_1)$ and $C' = (C_0', C_1')$. Choose $\mathbf{g}_1 \in_R G_1$ and $\mathbf{h}_1 \in_R H_1$. Let $C_0'' = C_0 \cdot C_0' \cdot \mathbf{g}_1$. Let $C_1'' = C_1 \cdot C_1' \cdot \mathbf{h}_1$. Output $C'' = (C_0'', C_1'')$.

$\mathsf{Add}_{\mathsf{tgt}}(\mathsf{pk}, C, C')$: Take as input two ciphertexts C and C' in G_t. Choose $\mathbf{g}_1 \in_R G_1$ and $\mathbf{h}_1 \in_R H_1$.

Let $C'' = C \cdot C' \cdot e(\mathbf{g}, \mathbf{h}_1) \cdot e(\mathbf{g}_1, \mathbf{h})$. Output C''.

$\mathsf{Dec}_{\mathsf{src}}(\mathsf{sk}, C)$: Take as input a ciphertext $C = (C_0, C_1)$ in $G \times H$. Compute $M \leftarrow \log_{\pi_1(\mathbf{g})}(\pi_1(C_0))$ and $M' \leftarrow \log_{\pi_2(\mathbf{h})}(\pi_2(C_1))$. Output M if $M = M'$ or $\perp$ otherwise.

$\mathsf{Dec}_{\mathsf{tgt}}(\mathsf{sk}, C)$: Take as input a ciphertext C in G_t. Output $M \leftarrow \log_{\pi_t(e(\mathbf{g},\mathbf{h}))}(\pi_t(C))$.

Lemma 1. *Suppose that the External 1-Symmetric Cascade assumption, i.e., Symmetric External Diffie Hellman assumption, holds with respect to the groups $\mathbb{G}_1$ and $\mathbb{G}_2$. Then the above cryptosystem is semantically secure.*

Proof. See Appendix C of the full version.

3   Distributed Key Generation Protocol for One-Time Multiplicative Homomorphic Cryptosystem

In this section we describe key generation for the one-time multiplicatively homomorphic cryptosystem of Sect. 2. Traditional protocols for threshold key generation [18,24] would be a natural choice, except that they fail for the $\mathsf{Dec}_{\mathsf{tgt}}$ algorithm, because the evaluation of π_t requires the sharing of a quadratic secret ss', while the traditional protocols are defined for linear terms only.

To overcome this difficulty, our protocol requires each party in the qualified set to split their individual secrets into chunks over a small interval. We construct a blinded version, i.e, $ss' + b$, in which the blinding factor b is distributed across parties, in such a way that it can be cancelled out from shares submitted by a qualified set. To perform the private construction of the blinded square, we use the Catalano-Fiore transformation [11], which enables depth-one multiplications on any linearly homomorphic cryptosystem. A problem arises with the natural choice of additive El Gamal as the base scheme with which to bootstrap the computation of the square. This cryptosystem mandates that only secrets from a small space can be safely decrypted, while the space over which s and s' are derived is much larger. We solve this problem by splitting the individual secrets of qualified players into chunks. Thus the private product of individual secrets becomes equivalent to a private product of polynomials, crucially ones for which the coefficient space is small and therefore amenable to the discrete log problem.

Another problem is how to construct the blinding factor so that no information is leaked on ss' in the construction of $ss' + b$. We show that this is possible via direct verifiable secret sharing of the chunks corresponding to b in polynomial form. As long as the chunk-size used to derive b is sufficiently larger than the chunk-size used to derive ss', we may treat them as distinct secrets to be jointly constructed by the qualified set. For this, and for constructing the Catalano-Fiore encryption key, we may simply employ the key-generation protocol of Pedersen [24] or the later protocol by Gennaro *et al.* [18].

Thus, after CF decryption, a blinding of the square of the secret is revealed in the clear, while the blinding factor is a distributed secret. The blinding factor can be cancelled out "on demand" by a threshold set of qualified players, leading to a fully contained key generation protocol for our multiplicative cryptosystem. Like the key generation protocols of [12,18,24], our protocol uses concurrent verifiable secret sharing to build a secret key but assumes as input shares of a transport key under which the main key generation protocol runs. For the latter purpose one may use any of those schemes.

Let $[\cdot]_y$ denote a CF encryption under key y. Let $g_1, g_2, g_{\mathsf{vss}}, g_{\mathsf{pke}} \in \mathbb{G}_1$ and $h_1, h_2, h_{\mathsf{pke}} \in \mathbb{G}_2$ be public. Let $c_A = 2^{\lambda_A}$ and $c_B = 2^{\lambda_B}$ be the chunk sizes of individual secrets and individual blinding factors. One may set $c_A = p^{\frac{1}{4l}} \cdot 2^{-\frac{\lambda}{2}}$ and $c_B = p^{\frac{1}{2l}}$ where l is chosen so that discrete logarithms are feasible in the range $[0, N \cdot p^{\frac{1}{2l}}]$. Appropriate sizes are given in Lemma 3, Appendix F of the full version.

Recall the security properites of a distributed key generation protocol [18].

Correctness: All subsets of T shares provided by honest players define the same unique secret key sk; all honest parties have the same value of the public key pk, which is correct wrt sk; sk is uniformly distributed among a range $\{0, 1\}^\lambda$, where λ is the security parameter.

Resilience: There is a procedure to reconstruct the secret key sk out of T or more shares, which is resilient in the presence of malicious parties.

Security: No information can be learned on sk except for what is implied by the public key pk.

The full protocol is given in Figs. 2 and 3. The NIZKs are described in Appendix D of the full version.

3.1 Protocol Description and Security Properties

Theorem 2. *Protocol 1 is a distributed key generation protocol for the cryptosystem of Sect. 3 and that is correct, resilient and secure against an active adversary corrupting fewer than T statically chosen players.*

Proof. Proofs of this theorem and the following two propositions are in Appendix K of the full version.

Proposition 3. *The values $x = \sum_{i \in Q} s_i$, $x' = \sum_{i \in Q} s'_i$ and $b = \sum_{i \in Q} t_i$ are distributed secrets according to the threshold access structure.*

Proposition 4. *The values γ, x, x' and b computed in Step 6 satisfy the relation $\gamma = xx' + b$.*

4 Distributed Encryption Switching

In this section we present universally verifiable switching between target and source encryption schemes using only the additive homomorphism on the ciphertext spaces. The protocol is in Fig. 4. The idea is for each party to contribute an equivalent encryption of a blinding factor under both cryptosystems together with a zero knowledge proof of plaintext equality. In the source space the blinding factors are homomorphically added to the input ciphertext and the result

---

Protocol 1: Key Generation for one-time homomorphic cryptosystem

Common Input : CF public key y. Generators $g_{\text{vss}}, g_{\text{pke}} \in \mathbb{G}_1$ and $h_{\text{pke}} \in \mathbb{G}_2$. Chunk sizes $c_A = 2^{\lambda_A}$ and $c_B = 2^{\lambda_B}$, of individual secrets and individual blinding factors respectively.

Private Input : P_i holds shares s_i, s_i' and t_i of secret keys s, s' and t respectively.

Public Output : Public key pk for the source and target encryption schemes.

Private Output : To each P_i, shares x_i and x_i' of the source and target encryption schemes, and shares b_i of $ss' + b$. Blinding factor γ.

1. *Each party P_i breaks its secret shares into chunks, commits publicly to the chunks, and shares individual chunks with other parties as follows.*
   Write s_i as $\sum_{k=0}^{\ell-1} \alpha_{ik} c_B^k$, s_i' as $\sum_{k=0}^{\ell-1} \alpha_{ik}' c_B^k$, and t_i as $\sum_{k=0}^{2\ell-2} \beta_{ik} c_B^k$, where $\alpha_{ik}, \alpha_{ij}' \in_R [0, 2^{\lambda_A} - 1]$ and $\beta_{ik} \in_R [0, 2^{\lambda_B} - 1]$. P_i creates vectors
   $\boldsymbol{v}_i = (s_i, r_{i2}, \ldots, r_{iT})^t$, $\boldsymbol{v}_i' = (s_i', r_{i2}', \ldots, r_{iT}')^t$, $\boldsymbol{w}_i = (t_i, r_{i2}'', \ldots, r_{iT}'')^t$. Recall
   secret-sharing matrix M from Definition 3. P_i computes the share vectors
   $\boldsymbol{s}_i = M\boldsymbol{v}_i, \boldsymbol{s}_i' = M\boldsymbol{v}_i'$ and $\boldsymbol{t}_i = M\boldsymbol{w}_i$. Let $V_i = g_{\text{vss}}^{\boldsymbol{v}_i}, V_i' = g_{\text{vss}}^{\boldsymbol{v}_i'}, W_i = g_{\text{vss}}^{\boldsymbol{w}_i}$. P_i
   broadcasts the values $\{V_i, V_i', W_i\}$. P_i sends $s_{ij} = \boldsymbol{s}_i[j], s_{ij}' = \boldsymbol{s}_i'[j], t_{ij} = \boldsymbol{t}_i[j]$
   to each P_j via a private channel, for $1 \leq j \leq N$. Note that

$$g_{\text{vss}}^{s_{ij}} = V_i^{M(j)}, g_{\text{vss}}^{s_{ij}'} = V_i'^{M(j)}, g_{\text{vss}}^{t_{ij}} = W_i^{M(j)} \tag{1}$$

2. P_i verifies that the shares received from P_j, i.e., s_{ji}, s_{ji}' and t_{ji} are correct, by verifying Equation 1. If any of these equations do not hold for the received values s_{ji}, s_{ji}' and t_{ji}, P_i broadcasts the message $(P_i, \text{complain}, P_j)$.

3. For each broadcast message $(P_{i_\alpha}, \text{complain}, P_j)$, player P_j is disqualified if $(s_{ji_\alpha}, s_{ji_\alpha}', t_{ji_\alpha})$ are sent that do not satisfy Equation 1. Let Q be the set of continuing (i.e. non-disqualified) players.

Fig. 2. Key gen protocol for one-time homomorphic cryptosystem.

decrypted under a threshold decryption scheme. From this plaintext, the blinding factors under the target encryption scheme are homomorphically subtracted, producing an encryption of the input message under the target cryptosystem.

To blind the ciphertexts without increasing the size of the messages (remember that it requires a DL extraction), we apply the blinding using an xor-sum. Specifically, we assume an ideal functionality for bit-wise sum, $\mathcal{F}_{\text{SUM}}$ with the following behaviour:

- On input $(\text{setup}, 1^\lambda)$ initialises $\mathcal{D} \leftarrow \emptyset, t \leftarrow 0$.
- On input (send, C), if $t < N$, sets $\mathcal{D} \leftarrow \mathcal{D} \cup \{C\}, t \leftarrow t+1$, if $t = N$, output C_s which is an encryption of the bit-wise sum of all decrypted ciphertexts contained in $\mathcal{D}$.

The details of the protocol realising this functionality are in Appendix E of the full version.

Protocol 1– Part 2

4) *Each party commits to its blinding factors and share vectors from Step 1, then proves that the chunks it shared in Step 1 are within the required range, and that the chunks sum correctly to the committed values, as follows.*

Let $A_i = g_{\mathsf{pke}}^{v_i}, B_i = g_{\mathsf{pke}}^{w_i}, A_i' = h_{\mathsf{pke}}^{v_i'}, B_i' = h_{\mathsf{pke}}^{w_i}, C_i = ([\alpha_{i0}]_y, \ldots, [\alpha_{i(\ell-1)}]_y)$, $C_i' = ([\alpha_{i0}']_y, \ldots, [\alpha_{i(\ell-1)}']_y), \quad D_i = ([\beta_{i0}]_y, \ldots, [\beta_{i(2(\ell-1))}]_y)$ where v_i, v_i', w_i are sampled as in Step 1. Let $\varepsilon_i \leftarrow (P_{\mathsf{range}}((C_{ik})_k, c_A)$, $P_{\mathsf{range}}((C_{ik}')_k, c_A), \qquad P_{\mathsf{range}}((D_{ik})_k, c_B), \qquad P_{\mathsf{eq}}(A_i[1], \prod_{k=0}^{\ell-1}[\alpha_{ik}]_y^{c_B^k})$, $P_{\mathsf{eq}}(A_i'[1], \prod_{k=0}^{\ell-1}[\alpha_{ik}']_y^{c_B^k}), \quad P_{\mathsf{eq}}(B_i[1], \prod_{k=0}^{2(\ell-1)}[\beta_{ik}]_y^{c_B^k}))$. P_i broadcasts the values $\{A_i, A_i', B_i, B_i', C_i, C_i', D_i, \varepsilon_i\}$. Note that

$$g_{\mathsf{pke}}^{s_{ij}} = A_i^{M(j)}, g_{\mathsf{pke}}^{t_{ij}} = B_i^{M(j)},$$
$$h_{\mathsf{pke}}^{s_{ij}'} = A_i'^{M(j)}, h_{\mathsf{pke}}^{t_{ij}} = B_i'^{M(j)} \tag{2}$$

5) P_i verifies that for the values sent by every other P_j in Q, Equation 2 holds. If any of these equations do not hold for the values s_{ji}, s_{ji}' and t_{ji}, P_i broadcasts the message $(P_i, \mathsf{complain}, P_j)$.

6) For each broadcast message $(P_{i_\alpha}, \mathsf{complain}, P_j)$ or proofs not satisfying $V_{\mathsf{range}}(\sigma_j, (C_j, C_j', D_j), \varepsilon_j) = 1 \wedge V_{\mathsf{eq}}(\sigma_j, (A_j, A_j', B_j), (C_j, C_j', D_j), \varepsilon_j) = 1$ the other players in Q reconstruct the values $s_j, t_j, v_j, w_j, A_j, A_j', B_j, B_j', C_j, C_j', D_j$.

7) For $0 \le k \le 2(\ell-1)$, P_i computes $\mathsf{ct}_k = \sum_{i,j \in Q} \sum_{f+g=k} C_{if} C_{jg}' + \sum_{i \in Q} D_{ik}$ and $\gamma_k \leftarrow \mathsf{Dec}(k_i, \mathsf{ct}_k)$. Outputs $\gamma = \sum_{k=0}^{2(\ell-1)} \gamma_k c_B^k$.

8) P_i computes their share of the secret as the sum of all shares received in Step 2 among continuing players, i.e., $x_i = \sum_{j \in Q} s_{ji}$ $x_i' = \sum_{j \in Q} s_{ji}'$ and $b_i = \sum_{j \in Q} t_{ji}$. P_i computes $\mathsf{vk}_i = (g_{\mathsf{vss}}^{x_i}, g_{\mathsf{vss}}^{x_i'}, g_{\mathsf{vss}}^{b_i})$ and $y_{\mathsf{pke}} = \prod_{i \in Q} A_i[1], z_{\mathsf{pke}} = \prod_{i \in Q} A_i'[1]$. P_i sets $\mathbf{g_1} = (y_{\mathsf{pke}}, g_{\mathsf{pke}})$ and $\mathbf{h_1} = (z_{\mathsf{pke}}, h_{\mathsf{pke}})$. The public key is $\mathsf{pk} = ((g_1, g_2), \mathbf{g_1}, (h_1, h_2), \mathbf{h_1}, \{[\gamma_k]_y\}_k, \{V_i, V_i', W_i\}_{i \in Q})$. The secret is (x, x', b, γ). Note that x, x' and b are distributed secrets while γ is held in entirety by each player in Q.

Fig. 3. Key gen protocol for one-time homomorphic cryptosystem, Part 2.

If the ciphertexts are known to be small, the xor-sum can be avoided and we can just homomorphically add a blinding factor, like we did for key generation. This blinding factor can be large enough to offer statistical blinding (e.g., 40 bits more than an upper-bound on the plaintext size) and small enough to support efficient decryption, possibly using a baby-step giant-step algorithm. This comes with the benefit of being a completely non interactive process, and works fine for our voting application.

Our definition of universally verifiable secure computation is derived from [28] and given in Appendix H of the full version. It formalises the idea that either a threshold of honest participants produces a true answer, or the output fails verification.

Theorem 5. *Protocol π_{SWITCH} securely computes universally verifiable encryption switching in the $\mathcal{F}_{\mathsf{SUM}}$-hybrid model against statically chosen adversaries if π_{COM} is a secure non-malleable commitment scheme and $\mathcal{P}_{\mathsf{eq}}$ is a secure NIZK proof system.*

Proof. See Appendix K of the full version.

Given that the switch is the only operation of our protocols that requires the use of secret information (i.e., decryption keys), and that this operation is verifiable, we obtain a universally verifiable MPC protocol: addition and multiplication are publicly performed using our encryption scheme, and the verifiable switch offers the possibility to repeat these operations as often as needed. In Appendix H.2 of the full version, we use this approach to evaluate any function class representable by an arithmetic circuit of polynomial size over $\mathcal{M}$.

Protocol π_{SWITCH} for Player P_i.
Common Input : $c = \mathsf{Enc}_1(\mathsf{pk}, m) : m \in \mathcal{M}$ and π_{COM} be a non-malleable commitment scheme with key ck. Threshold t.
Private Input : P_i holds a share of the secret key, sk_i

1. Choose $u_i \in_R \mathbb{Z}_p$ and publish $\delta_i = \mathsf{com}_{ck}(u_i)$ using randomiser r_i.
2. Publish $C'_i = \mathsf{Enc}_1(\mathsf{pk}, u_i)$ and $\overline{C}_i = \mathsf{Enc}_2(\mathsf{pk}, u_i)$ and $\varepsilon_i \leftarrow (\mathcal{P}_{\mathsf{eq}}(\delta_i, C'_i), \mathcal{P}_{\mathsf{eq}}(C'_i, \overline{C}_i))$.
3. If at least t of the ε_i pass verification, let $C' = \prod_{j=1}^{\lambda} c'_{ij} \otimes 2^{j-1}$ and $\overline{C} = \prod_{j=1}^{\lambda} \overline{c}_{ij} \otimes 2^{j-1}$ where $(c'_{ij})_{j=1}^{\lambda} \leftarrow \pi_{\mathsf{SUM}}(C'_1, \ldots, C'_N)$ and $(\overline{c}_{ij})_{j=1}^{\lambda} \leftarrow \pi_{\mathsf{SUM}}(\overline{C}_1, \ldots, \overline{C}_N)$. Otherwise output $\bot$.
4. Let $d \leftarrow c \cdot C', d_i \leftarrow d^{\mathsf{sk}_i}, \xi_i \leftarrow \Sigma_{\mathsf{CD}}(d, d_i, \mathsf{pk}, \mathsf{vk}_i)$.
5. If at least t pass verification for both ε_i and ξ_i, let $m' \leftarrow \prod_{i=1}^{T} d_i$ and output $\overline{c} = \mathsf{Enc}_2^*(m') \cdot \overline{C}^{-1}$. Otherwise output $\bot$.

Fig. 4. Protocol π_{SWITCH}.

5   Tallying Instant Runoff Voting (IRV)

In this section we describe how to use the primitives described earlier to construct a universally verifiable protocol for tallying encrypted ballots according to the IRV algorithm. Ballots are input to the tallying protocol in encrypted form. We reveal only the tallies of each candidate after each round of the IRV algorithm. The main challenge is to ensure that the privacy of ballots is maintained between tallying rounds. We use distributed encryption switching on the cryptosystems $\Pi_{\mathsf{src}} = (\mathsf{Setup}, \mathsf{KeyGen}, \mathsf{Enc}_{\mathsf{src}}, \mathsf{Dec}_{\mathsf{src}})$ and $\Pi_{\mathsf{tgt}} = (\mathsf{Setup}, \mathsf{KeyGen}, \mathsf{Enc}_{\mathsf{tgt}}, \mathsf{Dec}_{\mathsf{tgt}})$

of Sect. 2. Suppose that $\Pi_{\mathsf{tgt}} \to \Pi_{\mathsf{src}}$ is a distributed encryption switching protocol, where $\mathsf{Enc}_{\mathsf{src}}$ is used to encrypt votes. Recall that in an IRV election, after each phase of tallying, if a candidate is not elected, then the candidate with fewest votes is eliminated. Each ballot should count towards its most-preferred uneliminated candidate. We can use the one-time multiplicative homomorphism to compute the necessary product computations on ballots for the first two rounds of tallying. This takes ballots from the ciphertext space of Π_{src} to the ciphertext space of Π_{tgt}, for which addition, but not multiplication, is possible. To compute the product computations corresponding to further rounds of tallying, the election trustees will come together and perform a distributed switch on the ballots, will take them back to the ciphertext space of Π_{src}, and for which multiplications are again possible. In this way, for every round of tallying after the first, distributed encryption switching can be used to ensure that the trustees can compute the tally for each uneliminated candidate.

5.1 Protocol Details

Ballot Representation. Assume c candidates and M voters. An IRV ballot allows expression of up to k preferences, where $k \leq c$ is a constant specific to the election. For the purpose of homomorphic tallying, we will use a special "preference-order" ballot. Let $\mu_n : \{1, \dots, k\} \to \{1, \dots, c\}$ be an (injective) function representing the preferences of voter n. The ballot used for tallying, B_n, will be an encryption of the indicator vectors $\mathbf{e}_{\mu_n(1)}, \dots, \mathbf{e}_{\mu_n(k)}$. The indicator vector $\mathbf{e}_{\mu_n(j)}$ is encrypted as a tuple of c ciphertexts, $\mathbf{v}_j$. Thus B_n is simply a list of k encrypted c-tuples Fig. 5 (left) shows an example.

Updating of Ballots. This ballot representation permits a convenient method for eliminating candidates, by simply striking out the corresponding column in B_n's matrix of preferences. Since each elimination is a function of publicly verifiable totals, there is no ambiguity as to the representation of any ballot at any stage of tallying. An important feature of this is that the sequence of accesses made by Protocol 2 is derivable from the sequence of intermediate tallies it produces until termination. Input obliviousness follows. Figure 5 (right) shows a preference-order ballot after a candidate has been eliminated.

preference\ candidate	1 2 3 4 5 6		1 2 3 4 5 6
1	0 0 1 0 0 0		0 0 × 0 0 0
2	0 0 0 0 1 0		0 0 × 0 1 0
3	1 0 0 0 0 0		1 0 × 0 0 0

Fig. 5. Preference-order ballot for $c = 6$ and $k = 3$, in its initial form (left) and after elimination of candidate 3 (right), when it should count in candidate 5's tally.

Tallying Votes. Let $B_n = (\mathbf{v}_1, \ldots, \mathbf{v}_k)$ be a ballot, S_C be the set of uneliminated candidates, and $\Sigma_{S_C}(\mathbf{v}_i)$ be the homomorphic sum of the entries of the ith preference vector over uneliminated candidates. Clearly $\Sigma_{S_C}(\mathbf{v}_i)$ is an encryption of 1 iff the ith preference is for an uneliminated candidate, and an encryption of 0 otherwise. Let $C \boxtimes_{\mathsf{src}} C' = \mathsf{Enc}_{\mathsf{src}}(\mathsf{pk}, MM') : M = \mathsf{Dec}_{\mathsf{src}}(\mathsf{sk}, C)$ and $M' = \mathsf{Dec}_{\mathsf{src}}(\mathsf{sk}, C')$. After $l \le k$ rounds of tallying, the product

$$\boldsymbol{\pi}_j^{(l)} := {\boxtimes_{\mathsf{src}}^{1 \le j'' \le j}} \left(\mathsf{Enc}_1^*(1) - \Sigma_{S_C}(\mathbf{v}_{j'}) \right) : j \le l$$

is an encryption of 0 iff at least one of the first j preferences is for an uneliminated candidate, and an encryption of 1 otherwise. After $l - 1$ rounds of tallying, there is at least one $j \le l$ such that the jth preference is for a continuing candidate.[1] Therefore after l rounds of tallying, the homomorphic dot product $\sum_{j=1}^{l} \mathbf{v}_j \boxtimes_{\mathsf{src}} \boldsymbol{\pi}_j$ is an encryption of the indicator vector describing which candidate this vote should count for in round l. The protocol is shown in Fig. 14, Appendix J of the full version.

Implementation. We implemented the single-authority version of our system and tested it using elections data for the districts of Albury and Auburn for the 2015 New South Wales state election.[2] The implementation encrypted each of the entries in the ballot matrix prior to commencing the count, to simulate the receipt of encrypted ballots. Ballots were represented as per Fig. 5. The experiments were performed on an Intel i7-6770HQ with 4 cores (8 threads) and 32 GB RAM. The results are shown in Table 1.

We also ran experiments to time the main primitives, i.e. switching and multiplication. We ran the multiply and switch functions 1000 times and took the mean time. Multiplication in the source group averages 0.0671 s, while switching averages 0.0971 s. The code is available at https://github.com/vteague/PPAT/tree/chris-dev.

Table 1. Results for Sample IRV Counts. Timings in seconds.

	District	
	Albury (5 candidates)	Auburn (6 candidates)
No. ballots	46347	43738
Ballot encryption time	3069 s	3936 s
No. elimination rounds	1	4
Count time	6979 s	54637 s

---

[1] For example, the use of a "stop" candidate by [20] remedies the case that a ballot is exhausted prematurely.

[2] From http://pastvtr.elections.nsw.gov.au/SGE2015/la-home.htm.

6   Conclusion

We have devised a very simple universally verifiable MPC protocol based on combining an efficient distributed key generation, a somewhat homomorphic cryptosystem in which one multiplication comes almost for free, and a switching protocol that allows a return to the cryptosystem from which more multiplications can be performed.

Acknowledgement. Olivier Pereira is grateful to the Belgian Fund for Scientific Research (F.R.S.- FNRS) for its financial support provided through the SeVoTe project, to the European Union (EU) and the Walloon Region through the FEDER project USERMedia (convention number 501907-379156), and to the Melbourne School of Engineering for its fellowship.

A   Appendix

Appendices are in the full version of the paper on the IACR eprint archive at https://eprint.iacr.org/2018/246.

References

1. Adida, B., De Marneffe, O., Pereira, O., Quisquater, J.J.: Electing a university president using open-audit voting: analysis of real-world use of helios. In: Proceedings of the 2009 Conference on Electronic Voting Technology/Workshop on Trustworthy Elections, EVT/WOTE 2009, p. 10. USENIX Association, Berkeley (2009). http://dl.acm.org/citation.cfm?id=1855491.1855501
2. Attrapadung, N., Hanaoka, G., Mitsunari, S., Sakai, Y., Shimizu, K., Teruya, T.: Efficient two-level homomorphic encryption in prime-order bilinear groups and a fast implementation in webassembly. In: Proceedings of the 2018 on Asia Conference on Computer and Communications Security, pp. 685–697. ACM (2018)
3. Baum, C., Damgård, I., Orlandi, C.: Publicly auditable secure multi-party computation. In: Abdalla, M., De Prisco, R. (eds.) SCN 2014. LNCS, vol. 8642, pp. 175–196. Springer, Cham (2014). https://doi.org/10.1007/978-3-319-10879-7_11. Also Cryptology ePrint Archive, Report 2014/075: http://eprint.iacr.org/2014/075
4. Beimel, A.: Secure schemes for secret sharing and key distribution. Ph.D. thesis, Israel Institute of Technology (1996)
5. Benaloh, J., et al.: Star-vote: a secure, transparent, auditable, and reliable voting system. CoRR abs/1211.1904 (2012). http://arxiv.org/abs/1211.1904
6. Benaloh, J., Moran, T., Naish, L., Ramchen, K., Teague, V.: Shuffle-sum: coercion-resistant verifiable tallying for STV voting. Trans. Info. For. Sec. 4(4), 685–698 (2009). https://doi.org/10.1109/TIFS.2009.2033757
7. Bernhard, D., Cortier, V., Pereira, O., Smyth, B., Warinschi, B.: Adapting helios for provable ballot privacy. In: Atluri, V., Diaz, C. (eds.) ESORICS 2011. LNCS, vol. 6879, pp. 335–354. Springer, Heidelberg (2011). https://doi.org/10.1007/978-3-642-23822-2_19
8. Boneh, D., Goh, E.-J., Nissim, K.: Evaluating 2-DNF formulas on ciphertexts. In: Kilian, J. (ed.) TCC 2005. LNCS, vol. 3378, pp. 325–341. Springer, Heidelberg (2005). https://doi.org/10.1007/978-3-540-30576-7_18

9. Brakerski, Z., Gentry, C., Vaikuntanathan, V.: (Leveled) fully homomorphic encryption without bootstrapping. ACM Trans. Comput. Theory **6**(3), 13:1–13:36 (2014)
10. Castagnos, G., Imbert, L., Laguillaumie, F.: Encryption switching protocols revisited: switching modulo p. In: Katz, J., Shacham, H. (eds.) CRYPTO 2017. LNCS, vol. 10401, pp. 255–287. Springer, Cham (2017). https://doi.org/10.1007/978-3-319-63688-7_9
11. Catalano, D., Fiore, D.: Using linearly-homomorphic encryption to evaluate degree-2 functions on encrypted data. In: Proceedings of the 22nd ACM SIGSAC Conference on Computer and Communications Security, CCS 2015, pp. 1518–1529. ACM, New York (2015). https://doi.org/10.1145/2810103.2813624. http://doi.acm.org/10.1145/2810103.2813624
12. Cortier, V., Galindo, D., Glondu, S., Izabachène, M.: Distributed elgamal à la pedersen: application to helios. In: Proceedings of the 12th ACM Workshop on Workshop on Privacy in the Electronic Society, WPES 2013, pp. 131–142. ACM, New York (2013). https://doi.org/10.1145/2517840.2517852. http://doi.acm.org/10.1145/2517840.2517852
13. Couteau, G., Peters, T., Pointcheval, D.: Encryption switching protocols. In: Robshaw, M., Katz, J. (eds.) CRYPTO 2016, Part I. LNCS, vol. 9814, pp. 308–338. Springer, Heidelberg (2016). https://doi.org/10.1007/978-3-662-53018-4_12
14. Cramer, R., Gennaro, R., Schoenmakers, B.: A secure and optimally efficient multi-authority election scheme. In: Fumy, W. (ed.) EUROCRYPT 1997. LNCS, vol. 1233, pp. 103–118. Springer, Heidelberg (1997). https://doi.org/10.1007/3-540-69053-0_9
15. Damgård, I., Pastro, V., Smart, N., Zakarias, S.: Multiparty computation from somewhat homomorphic encryption. In: Safavi-Naini, R., Canetti, R. (eds.) CRYPTO 2012. LNCS, vol. 7417, pp. 643–662. Springer, Heidelberg (2012). https://doi.org/10.1007/978-3-642-32009-5_38
16. Escala, A., Herold, G., Kiltz, E., Ràfols, C., Villar, J.: An algebraic framework for diffie-hellman assumptions. In: Canetti, R., Garay, J.A. (eds.) CRYPTO 2013, Part II. LNCS, vol. 8043, pp. 129–147. Springer, Heidelberg (2013). https://doi.org/10.1007/978-3-642-40084-1_8
17. Freeman, D.M.: Converting pairing-based cryptosystems from composite-order groups to prime-order groups. In: Gilbert, H. (ed.) EUROCRYPT 2010. LNCS, vol. 6110, pp. 44–61. Springer, Heidelberg (2010). https://doi.org/10.1007/978-3-642-13190-5_3
18. Gennaro, R., Jarecki, S., Krawczyk, H., Rabin, T.: Secure distributed key generation for discrete-log based cryptosystems. J. Cryptol. **20**(1), 51–83 (2007). https://doi.org/10.1007/s00145-006-0347-3
19. Goh, E.-J., Golle, P.: Event driven private counters. In: Patrick, A.S., Yung, M. (eds.) FC 2005. LNCS, vol. 3570, pp. 313–327. Springer, Heidelberg (2005). https://doi.org/10.1007/11507840_27
20. Heather, J.: Implementing STV securely in prêt à voter. In: Proceedings of the 20th IEEE Computer Security Foundations Symposium, CSF 2007, pp. 157–169. IEEE Computer Society, Washington (2007). https://doi.org/10.1109/CSF.2007.22
21. Herold, G., Hesse, J., Hofheinz, D., Ràfols, C., Rupp, A.: Polynomial spaces: a new framework for composite-to-prime-order transformations. Cryptology ePrint Archive, Report 2014/445 (2014). http://eprint.iacr.org/2014/445

22. Ito, M., Saito, A., Nishizeki, T.: Secret sharing scheme realizing general access structure. Electron. Commun. Jpn (Part III: Fundam. Electron. Sci.) **72**(9), 56–64 (1989). https://doi.org/10.1002/ecjc.4430720906. https://onlinelibrary.wiley.com/doi/abs/10.1002/ecjc.4430720906

23. Park, C., Itoh, K., Kurosawa, K.: Efficient anonymous channel and all/nothing election scheme. In: Helleseth, T. (ed.) EUROCRYPT 1993. LNCS, vol. 765, pp. 248–259. Springer, Heidelberg (1994). https://doi.org/10.1007/3-540-48285-7_21. http://dl.acm.org/citation.cfm?id=188307.188351

24. Pedersen, T.P.: A threshold cryptosystem without a trusted party. In: Davies, D.W. (ed.) EUROCRYPT 1991. LNCS, vol. 547, pp. 522–526. Springer, Heidelberg (1991). https://doi.org/10.1007/3-540-46416-6_47. http://dl.acm.org/citation.cfm?id=1754868.1754929

25. Ryan, P.Y.A.: Prêt à voter with paillier encryption. Math. Comput. Model. **48**(9–10), 1646–1662 (2008). https://doi.org/10.1016/j.mcm.2008.05.015

26. Ryan, P.Y.A.: A variant of the chaum voter-verifiable scheme. In: Proceedings of the 2005 Workshop on Issues in the Theory of Security, WITS 2005, pp. 81–88. ACM, New York (2005). https://doi.org/10.1145/1045405.1045414. http://doi.acm.org/10.1145/1045405.1045414

27. Ryan, P.Y.A., Teague, V.: Ballot permutations in prêt à voter. In: Proceedings of the 2009 Conference on Electronic Voting Technology/Workshop on Trustworthy Elections, EVT/WOTE 2009, p. 13. USENIX Association, Berkeley (2009). http://dl.acm.org/citation.cfm?id=1855491.1855504

28. Schoenmakers, B., Veeningen, M.: Universally verifiable multiparty computation from threshold homomorphic cryptosystems. In: Malkin, T., Kolesnikov, V., Lewko, A.B., Polychronakis, M. (eds.) ACNS 2015. LNCS, vol. 9092, pp. 3–22. Springer, Cham (2015). https://doi.org/10.1007/978-3-319-28166-7_1. http://eprint.iacr.org/2015/058

29. Scott, M.: Authenticated id-based key exchange and remote log-in with simple token and pin number. Cryptology ePrint Archive, Report 2002/164 (2002). http://eprint.iacr.org/2002/164

30. Waters, B.: Ciphertext-policy attribute-based encryption: an expressive, efficient, and provably secure realization. In: Catalano, D., Fazio, N., Gennaro, R., Nicolosi, A. (eds.) PKC 2011. LNCS, vol. 6571, pp. 53–70. Springer, Heidelberg (2011). https://doi.org/10.1007/978-3-642-19379-8_4. http://dl.acm.org/citation.cfm?id=1964658.1964664

Synchronous Byzantine Agreement with Expected $O(1)$ Rounds, Expected $O(n^2)$ Communication, and Optimal Resilience

Ittai Abraham[1], Srinivas Devadas[2], Danny Dolev[3], Kartik Nayak[1,4], and Ling Ren[1,5(✉)]

[1] VMware Research, Palo Alto, USA
{iabraham,nkartik,lingren}@vmware.com
[2] MIT, Cambridge, USA
devadas@mit.edu
[3] Hebrew University of Jerusalem, Jerusalem, Israel
danny.dolev@mail.huji.ac.il
[4] Duke University, Durham, USA
[5] University of Illinois at Urbana-Champaign, Urbana, USA

Abstract. We present new protocols for Byzantine agreement in the synchronous and authenticated setting, tolerating the optimal number of f faults among $n = 2f + 1$ parties. Our protocols achieve an expected $O(1)$ round complexity and an expected $O(n^2)$ communication complexity. The exact round complexity in expectation is 10 for a static adversary and 16 for a strongly rushing adaptive adversary. For comparison, previous protocols in the same setting require expected 29 rounds.

1 Introduction

Byzantine agreement [24] is a fundamental problem in distributed computing and cryptography. It has been used to build fault tolerant distributed systems [5,9,22,33], secure multi-party computation [7,17], and more recently cryptocurrencies [4,21,28,29]. In Byzantine agreement, a group n parties, each holding an initial input value, hope to commit on a common value; up to f parties can have Byzantine faults and deviate from the protocol arbitrarily. In a closely related problem called Byzantine broadcast, instead of each party holding an input value, there is one designated *sender* who tries to broadcast a value. To rule out trivial solutions, both problems have additional validity requirements.

Byzantine agreement and Byzantine broadcast have been studied under various combinations of assumptions, most notably timing assumptions – synchrony, asynchrony or partial synchrony, and setup assumptions – cryptography and public-key infrastructure (PKI). It is now well understood that these assumptions drastically affect the fault tolerance bounds. In particular, Byzantine broadcast and Byzantine agreement both require $f < n/3$ under partial synchrony or

---

A preliminary draft of the paper appeard on ePrint in 2017 [2]. The current version improves and subsumes the Byzantine agreement part of the preliminary draft.

© International Financial Cryptography Association 2019
I. Goldberg and T. Moore (Eds.): FC 2019, LNCS 11598, pp. 320–334, 2019.
https://doi.org/10.1007/978-3-030-32101-7_20

asynchrony. But under synchrony with digital signatures and PKI, Byzantine agreement can be solved with $f < n/2$ while Byzantine broadcast can be solved with $f < n - 1$.

In this paper, we consider Byzantine agreement in the synchronous and authenticated (i.e., assuming digital signatures and PKI) setting. The efficiency metrics we consider are (1) round complexity, i.e., the number of rounds of communication before the protocol terminates, and (2) communication complexity, i.e., the amount of information exchanged between parties during the protocol. For convenience, we measure communication complexity using the number of signatures exchanged between parties. Assuming each signature has λ bits, multiplying our communication complexity by λ yields the asymptotic communication complexity in bits.

In the synchronous and authenticated setting, Dolev and Strong gave a deterministic Byzantine broadcast protocol for $f < n - 1$ [12]. Their protocol achieves $f + 1$ round complexity and $O(n^2 f)$ communication complexity. The $f + 1$ round complexity matches the lower bound for deterministic protocols [12,15]. To further improve round complexity, randomized protocols have been introduced [6,14,16,31]. The most efficient protocol to our knowledge is proposed by Katz and Koo [19], which solves Byzantine agreement for $f < n/2$ in expected 29 rounds.[1]

In this work, we improve communication complexity to expected $O(n^2)$ and round complexity to expected 16. Our protocols use threshold signatures [8,32] to reduce communication complexity and a random leader election subroutine to reduce round complexity. The random leader election subroutine can be constructed using common-coin protocols, and there exist constructions with a single round and $O(n^2)$ communication in the literature [8,27]. The protocol by Cachin et al. [8] is secure against a static adversary whereas the protocol by Loss and Moran [27] is secure against an adaptive adversary. With these, we achieve the following result.

Theorem 1. *Synchronous authenticated Byzantine agreement can be solved for $f < n/2$ with*

- *expected 10 rounds and expected $O(n^2)$ communication against a static adversary assuming a single-round common-coin protocol,*
- *expected 16 rounds and expected $O(n^2)$ communication against a strongly rushing adaptive adversary assuming an adaptively secure single-round common-coin protocol.*

It is worth noting that our protocols work even in the presence of a very powerful adversary, which we call a *strongly rushing adaptive adversary*. The adversary can adaptively decide which f parties to corrupt and when to corrupt

---

[1] Katz and Koo [19] did not analyze communication complexity in their paper. Based on our understanding, their unrolled protocol in the appendix can achieve $O(n^2)$ communication complexity by similarly incorporating threshold signatures and a quadratic common-coin protocol.

them. And by "strongly rushing", we mean that if the adversary decides to corrupt a party h after observing messages sent from h to any other party in round r, it can remove h's round-r messages from the network before they reach other honest parties. In comparison, a standard rushing adversary can decide its own round-r messages after learning honest parties' round-r messages, but if it corrupts h in round r, it cannot "take back" or alter h's round-r messages to other parties. The Dolev-Strong and Katz-Koo protocols also work against such a strongly rushing adaptive adversary.

The $O(1)$ expected round complexity is clearly asymptotically optimal. A natural question is whether or not the expected quadratic communication can be further improved. In a follow-up work [1], building on a work by Dolev and Reischuk [11], we show that $\Omega(f^2)$ expected messages are necessary against a *strongly rushing* adaptive adversary. King-Saia [20] and our follow-up work [1] solve Byzantine agreement using sub-quadratic communication. Not surprisingly, these protocols work against a standard rushing adaptive adversary but not a strongly rushing adaptive one.

1.1   Technical Overview

We first describe our core protocol, which ensures agreement (referred to as safety for the rest of the paper) and termination as required by Byzantine broadcast/agreement, but provides a weak notion of validity. Specifically, it achieves

- **Termination:** all honest parties eventually commit,
- **Agreement/safety:** all honest parties commit on the same value, and
- **Validity:** if all honest parties start with certificates for the same value v, and no Byzantine party starts with a certificate for a contradictory value, then all honest parties commit on v.

In Sect. 4 we will describe how to obtain these certificates to solve Byzantine broadcast or Byzantine agreement.

The core protocol runs in iterations. In each iteration, a unique leader is elected. Each new leader picks up the state left by previous leaders and proposes a value in its iteration. Parties then cast votes on the leader's value v. In more detail, each iteration consists of 4 rounds. The first three rounds are conceptually similar to Paxos and PBFT: (1) the leader learns the states of the system, (2) the leader proposes a value, and (3) parties vote on the value. If a party receives $f+1$ votes for the same value and does not detect leader equivocation, it commits on that value. We then add another round: (4) if a party commits, it notifies all other parties about the commit; upon receiving a notification, other parties *accept* the committed value and will vouch for that value to future leaders.

Ideally, if the leader is honest, all honest parties commit v upon receiving $f+1$ votes for v at the end of that iteration. A Byzantine leader can easily waste its iteration by not proposing. But it can also perform the following more subtle attacks: (1) send contradicting proposals to different honest parties, or (2) send a proposal to some but not all honest parties. We must ensure these Byzantine behaviors do not violate safety.

The Need for Equivocation Checks. To ensure safety in the first attack, parties engage in an all-to-all round of communication to forward the leader's proposal to each other for an equivocation check. If a party detects leader equivocation, i.e., sees two conflicting signed proposals from the leader, it does not commit even if it receives $f + 1$ votes.

The Need for a notify Round. Using the second attack, a Byzantine leader can make some, but not all, honest parties commit on a value v. If the other honest parties do not know that v has been committed, they may commit $v' \neq v$ in a subsequent iteration. Therefore, whenever an honest party h commits on a value v, h needs to *notify* all other honest parties of its commit. h can do this by broadcasting the $f + 1$ votes it received. When another party h' receives such a notification, it "accepts" the value v. If a party has accepted v and receives a proposal $v' \neq v$ in a later iteration, it will not vote for v' unless it is shown a proof that voting for v' is safe. The details can be found in Sect. 3.

Safety, Termination, and Validity. Safety is preserved because when an honest party commits, (1) no other party can commit a different value in the same iteration (due to equivocation checks), and (2) no other value can gather enough votes in subsequent iterations (due to notify by the honest party). Validity follows from a similar argument: if all honest parties start the protocol with the same certified (i.e., accepted) value v and Byzantine parties do not have a different certified value, only v can gather enough votes. Termination is achieved when some honest party h receives $f + 1$ notify messages. At this point, h sends these $f+1$ notifications to all other parties and terminates. The $f+1$ notifications h sends will ensure termination of all other parties in the next round. If an honest leader emerges, all parties terminate in its iteration.

Round Complexity and Communication Complexity. Since there are $f+1$ honest out of $2f + 1$ parties, by electing a random leader in every iteration, the protocol terminates in 2 iterations in expectation. Depending on the adversarial model, each iteration ranges from 4 to 7 rounds. Each round uses $O(n^2)$ messages (all-to-all) and each message is either a single signature or a single $(f + 1)$-out-of-n threshold signature. Thus, the protocol runs in expected $O(1)$ rounds and uses expected $O(n^2)$ communication.

Paxos, PBFT, XPaxos, and Our Protocol. Abstractly, this core protocol resembles the synod algorithm in Paxos [23] but is adapted to the synchronous and Byzantine setting. The main idea of the synod algorithm is to ensure *quorum* intersection [23] at one *honest* party. The core idea of Paxos is to form a quorum of size $f + 1$ before committing a value. With $n = 2f + 1$, two quorums always intersect at one party, which is honest in Paxos. This honest party in the intersection will force a future leader to respect the committed value. In order to tolerate f Byzantine faults, PBFT [9] uses quorums of size $2f + 1$ out of $n = 3f + 1$, so that two quorums intersect at $f + 1$ parties, among which one is guaranteed to be honest. Similar to PBFT, we also need to ensure quorum intersection at $f + 1$ parties. But this requires new techniques with $n = 2f + 1$ parties in total. On the one hand, an intersection of size $f + 1$ seems to require quorums of size $1.5f + 1$. (An subsequent work called Thunderella [30] uses this quorums size to improve the optimistic case.) On the other hand, a quorum size larger than $f + 1$ (the number of honest parties) seems to require participation from Byzantine parties and thus loses liveness. As described in the core protocol, our synchronous *notify* round forms a *post-commit quorum* of size $2f + 1$, which intersects with any *pre-commit quorum* of size $f + 1$ at $f + 1$ parties. This satisfies the requirement of one honest party in the intersection. Moreover, since parties in the post-commit quorum only receive messages, liveness is not affected.

Our protocol also shares some similarity to XPaxos [26]. In XPaxos, a view-change involves changing a set of $f + 1$ active replicas (instead of only changing the leader). So far as all the active replicas in the old view notify all the active replicas in the new view, there will be one honest replica in the new view that can carry state across views. However, XPaxos makes progress only if all $f + 1$ active replicas are honest. In comparison, our protocol only requires the leader to be honest to make progress.

Achieving Byzantine Broadcast and Byzantine Agreement. The core protocol already ensures safety and termination, so we only need some technique to boost its weaker validity to what Byzantine broadcast/agreement require. Our protocol achieves this using a single round of all-to-all communication before invoking the protocol. This allows us to avoid the standard transformation of composing n parallel Byzantine broadcasts to achieve Byzantine agreement. As a result, our Byzantine agreement protocol has the same asymptotic round/communication complexity as the core protocol.

2   Model

We assume synchrony. If an honest party i sends a message to another honest party j at the beginning of a round, the message is guaranteed to reach by the end of that round. We describe the protocol assuming lock-step execution, i.e., parties enter and exit each round simultaneously. Later in Sect. 5, we will present a clock synchronization protocol to bootstrap lock-step execution from bounded message delay.

We assume digital signatures and trusted setup. In the trusted setup phase, a trusted dealer generates public/private key pairs for digital signatures and other cryptographic primitives for each party, and certifies each party's public keys. We use $\langle x \rangle_i$ to denote a message x signed by party i, i.e., $\langle x \rangle_i = (x, \sigma)$ where σ is a signature of message x produced by party i using its private signing key. For efficiency, it is customary to sign the hash digest of a message. A message can be signed by multiple parties (or the same party) in layers, i.e., $\langle\langle x \rangle_i \rangle_j = \langle x, \sigma_i \rangle_j = (x, \sigma_i, \sigma_j)$ where σ_i is a signature of x and σ_j is a signature of $x \parallel \sigma_i$ ($\parallel$ denotes concatenation). When the context is clear, we omit the signer and simply write $\langle x \rangle$ or $\langle\langle x \rangle\rangle$.

We require a random leader election subroutine. As mentioned, this subroutine can be instantiated using common-coin protocols [8,27] or verifiable random functions [28]. It may also be left to higher level protocols. For example, a cryptocurrency may elect leaders based on proof of work.

We assume a strongly rushing adaptive adversary. After the trusted setup phase, the adversary can adaptively decide which f parties to corrupt and when to corrupt each of them as the protocol executes. Note, however, that the adversary is not *mobile*: it cannot un-corrupt a Byzantine party to restore its corruption budget. The adversary is also strongly rushing. In each round, the adversary observes any party i's message to any other party j. If the adversary decides to corrupt i at this point, it controls which other honest parties (if any) i sends messages to and what messages i sends them *in that round*.

3   A Synchronous Byzantine Synod Protocol

3.1   Core Protocol

Our core protocol is a synchronous Byzantine synod protocol with $n = 2f + 1$ parties. The goal of the core synod protocol is to guarantee that all honest parties eventually commit (termination) on the same value (agreement). In addition, it achieves the following notion of validity: if (1) all honest parties start with the same value and have a *certificate* for this value, and (2) the adversary does not start with a certificate for a contradictory value, then all honest parties commit on this value. In Sect. 4, we show how to obtain these certificates using a single pre-round to achieve Byzantine broadcast and Byzantine agreement. For ease of exposition, we will temporarily assume a static adversary in Sect. 3.1 while presenting the core protocol. A static adversary has to decide which parties to corrupt after the trusted setup phase and before the protocol starts.

We now describe the protocol in detail. When a leader proposes a value v in iteration k, we say the proposal has rank k and write them as a tuple (v, k). The first iteration has $k = 1$. Each party i internally maintains states $\mathsf{accepted}_i = (v_i, k_i, \mathcal{C}_i)$ across iterations to record its *accepted* proposal. Initially, each party i initializes $\mathsf{accepted}_i := (\bot, 0, \bot)$. If party i later accepts (v, k), it sets $\mathsf{accepted}_i := (v, k, \mathcal{C})$ such that $\mathcal{C}$ *certifies* that v is legally accepted in iteration k. $\mathcal{C}$ consists of $f+1$ commit requests for proposal (v, k) (see the protocol for details). We also say $\mathcal{C}$ certifies, or is a certificate for, (v, k). Proposals are ranked by the iteration number in which they are made. Namely, (v, k) is ranked higher than, lower than, or equal to (v', k') if $k > k'$, $k < k'$ and $k = k'$, respectively. Certificates are ranked by the proposals they certify. When we say a party "broadcasts" a message, we mean it sends the message to all parties including itself.

Round 0 (elect). All parties participate in the threshold coin-tossing scheme from [8]. Their scheme costs a single round and outputs a random string to all parties. The random string modulo n defines a random leader L_k for the current iteration k. We henceforth write L_k as L for simplicity.

Round 1 (status). Each party i sends a $\langle k, \mathsf{status}, v_i, k_i, \mathcal{C}_i \rangle_i$ message to L to report its current accepted value.

At the end of this round, if party i reports the highest certificate to L (i could be L itself), L sets $\mathsf{accepted}_L = (v_L, k_L, \mathcal{C}_L) := (v_i, k_i, \mathcal{C}_i)$. If no party reports a certificate, L chooses v_L freely and sets $k_L := 0$ and $\mathcal{C}_L := \bot$.

Round 2 (propose). L broadcasts a signed proposal $\langle\langle k, \mathsf{propose}, v_L\rangle_L, k_L, \mathcal{C}_L\rangle_L$.

At the end of this round, party i sets $v_{L\to i} := v_L$ if the certificate it receives in the above leader proposal is no lower than what i reported to the leader, i.e., if $k_L \geq k_i$. Otherwise (leader is faulty), it sets $v_{L\to i} := \bot$.

Round 3 (commit). If $v_{L\to i} \neq \bot$, then party i forwards the proposal $\langle k, \mathsf{propose}, v_{L\to i}\rangle_L$ to all other parties and broadcasts a $\langle k, \mathsf{commit}, v_{L\to i}\rangle_i$ request.

At the end of this round, if party i is forwarded a properly signed proposal $\langle k, \mathsf{propose}, v'\rangle_L$ in which $v' \neq v_{L\to i}$, it does not commit in this iteration (leader has equivocated). Else, if party i receives $f+1$ $\langle k, \mathsf{commit}, v\rangle_j$ requests in all of which $v = v_{L\to i}$, it commits on v and sets its internal state $\mathcal{C}_i$ to be these $f+1$ commit requests concatenated. In other words, party i commits if and only if it receives $f+1$ matching commit requests and does not detect leader equivocation.

Round 4 (notify). If party i has committed on v at the end of the previous round, it sends a notification $\langle\langle \mathsf{notify}, v\rangle_i, \mathcal{C}_i\rangle_i$ to every other party.

At the end of this round, if party i receives a $\langle\langle \mathsf{notify}, v\rangle_j, \mathcal{C}\rangle_j$ message, it accepts v by setting $\mathsf{accepted}_i = (v_i, k_i, \mathcal{C}_i) := (v, k, \mathcal{C})$. If party i receives multiple valid notify messages with different values (how this can happen is explained at the end of Sect. 3.2), it can accept an arbitrary one. Lastly, party i increments the iteration counter k and enters the next iteration.

Early and Non-simultaneous Termination. At any point during the protocol, if a party gathers *notification headers* (excluding certificates) $\langle \mathsf{notify}, v\rangle$ from $f+1$ distinct parties, it sends these $f+1$ notification headers to all other parties and terminates. This ensures that when the first honest party terminates, all other honest parties receive $f+1$ notification headers and terminate in the next round.

3.2   Safety, Termination, and Validity

In this section, we prove that the core protocol in Sect. 3.1 provides safety, termination and a weak notion of validity.

Safety. We first give some intuition to aid understanding. The scenario to consider for safety is when an honest party h commits on a value v^* in iteration k^*. We first show that Byzantine parties cannot hold a certificate for a value other than v^* in iteration k^*. Thus, all other honest parties accept v^* at the end of iteration k^* upon receiving notify from the honest party h. Thus, a value other than v^* cannot gather enough votes in iteration k^*+1, and hence cannot be committed or accepted in iteration k^*+1, and hence cannot gather enough votes in iteration k^*+2, and so on. Safety then holds by induction (Fig. 1).

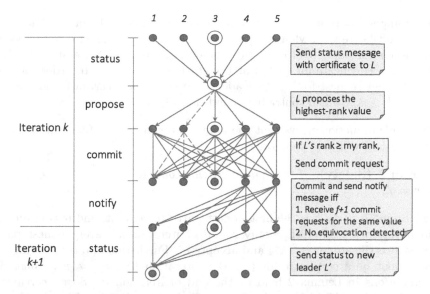

Fig. 1. An example iteration of the core protocol. In this example, $f = 2$, $n = 2f + 1 = 5$, parties 3 and 4 are Byzantine. **1.** (status) Each party sends its current states to $L = 3$. **2.** (propose) No party has committed or accepted any value, so L can propose any value of its choice. L equivocates and sends one proposal to party 4 (shown by dashed red arrow) and a different proposal to honest parties. **3.** (commit) Honest parties forward L's proposal and send commit requests to all parties. Party 4 only sends to parties $\{3, 4, 5\}$. Parties 1 and 2 receive $f + 1$ commit requests for the blue value and do not detect equivocation, so they commit. Party 5 detects leader equivocation and does not commit despite also receiving $f + 1$ commit requests for the blue value. **4.** (notify) Parties 1 and 2 notify all other parties. On receiving a valid notification, party 5 accepts the blue value. **5.** (status) The parties send status messages to the new leader $L' = 1$ for iteration $k + 1$. (Color figure online)

We now formalize the above intuition by proving the following lemma about certificates: once an honest party commits, all certificates in that iteration and future iterations can only certify its committed value.

Lemma 1. *Suppose party h is the first honest party to commit and it commits on v^* in iteration k^*. If a certificate C for (v, k^*) exists, then $v = v^*$.*

Proof. C must consist of $f + 1$ commit requests for v. At least one of these comes from an honest party (call it h_1). Thus, h_1 must have received a proposal for v from the leader, and must have forwarded the proposal to all other parties. If $v \neq v^*$, h would have detected leader equivocation, and would not have committed on v^* in this iteration. So we have $v = v^*$.

Lemma 2. *If at the start of iteration k, (1) every honest party i has a certificate for (v, k_i), and (2) all conflicting certificates are lower ranked, i.e, any certificate for (v', k') where $v \neq v'$ must have $k' < k_i$ for all honest i, then the above two conditions will hold at the end of iteration k.*

Proof. Suppose for contradiction that some party (honest or Byzantine) acquires a *higher* certificate than what it had previously for $v' \neq v$. Then it must receive from one honest party (call it h) a $\langle k, \mathsf{commit}, v' \rangle_h$ request in iteration k. Note that h has a certificate for (v, k_h) at the start of iteration k. In order for h to send a commit request for v', the leader L_k must show a certificate for (v', k') such that $k' \geq k_h$, which contradicts condition (2).

A simple induction shows that the above two conditions, if true at the start of an iteration, will hold true forever.

Theorem 2 (Safety). *If two honest parties commit on v and v' respectively, then $v = v'$.*

Proof. Suppose party h is the first honest party to commit, and it commits on v^* in iteration k^*. After the notify round of iteration k^*, every honest party receives a certificate for (v^*, k^*) and accepts v^*. Furthermore, due to Lemma 1, there cannot be a certificate for (v, k^*) in iteration k^* for $v \neq v^*$. Thus, the two conditions in Lemma 2 hold at the end of iteration k^*. So no certificate for a value other than v^* can be formed from this point on. In order for an honest party to commit on v, there must be a certificate for (v, k) where $k \geq k^*$. Therefore, $v = v^*$. Similarly, $v' = v^*$, and we have $v = v'$.

Termination. We now show that an honest leader will guarantee all honest parties terminate by the end of that iteration.

Theorem 3 (Termination). *If the leader L_k in iteration k is honest, then every honest party terminates one round after iteration k (or earlier).*

Proof. The honest leader L_k will send a proposal to all parties. It will propose a value reported by the highest certificate it collects in the status round. This certificate will be no lower than any certificate held by honest parties. Additionally, the unforgeability of digital signatures prevents Byzantine parties from falsely accusing L of equivocating. Therefore, all honest parties will send commit requests for v, receive $f + 1$ commit requests for v, commits on v, send notification headers for v, receive $f + 1$ notification headers for v (this is the end of iteration k), and terminate in the next round. (It is possible that they receive $f + 1$ notification headers and terminate at any earlier time.)

Validity. We now discuss the validity achieved by our core protocol. In the theorem, we assume the existence of initial certificates for $(v, 0)$ that are input to our core protocol. These initial certificates will be provided by higher-level protocols that invoke the core protocol (c.f. Sect. 4).

Theorem 4 (Validity). *All honest parties will commit on v if (1) every honest party starts with an initial certificate $\mathcal{C}$ certifying v, and (2) no Byzantine party has a certificate $\mathcal{C}'$ certifying $v' \neq v$.*

Proof. The proof is straightforward from Lemma 2 and Theorem 3. The input constraints satisfy the two conditions for Lemma 2 with each $k_i = 0$. Due to Lemma 2, for all subsequent iterations, only v can have certificates and thus, only v can be committed. By Theorem 3, when an honest leader emerges, all honest parties will commit on v.

Finally, we mention an interesting scenario that does not have to be explicitly addressed in the proofs. Before any honest party commits, Byzantine parties may obtain certificates for multiple values in the same iteration. In particular, the Byzantine leader proposes two values v and v' to all the f Byzantine parties. (An example with more than two values is similar.) Byzantine parties then exchange f commit requests for both values among them. Additionally, the Byzantine leader proposes v and v' to different honest parties. Now with one more commit request for each value from honest parties, Byzantine parties can obtain certificates for both v and v', and can make honest parties accept different values by showing them different certificates (notify messages). However, this will not lead to a safety violation because no honest party would have committed in this iteration: the leader has equivocated to honest parties, so all honest parties will detect equivocation from forwarded proposals and thus refuse to commit. This scenario showcases the necessity of both the synchrony assumption and the use of digital signatures for our protocol. Lacking either one, equivocation cannot be reliably detected and any protocol will be subject to the $f < n/3$ bound. For completeness, we note that the above scenario will not lead to a violation of the termination property, either. At the end of the iteration, honest parties may accept either value. But in the next iteration, they can still vote for either value despite having accepted the other, since the two values have the same rank.

3.3   Random Leader Election Against an Adaptive Adversary

The protocol presented so far does not achieve expected constant rounds against an adaptive adversary. The adversary learns who the leader L is after the elect round in an iteration. It can then immediately corrupt L and prevent it from sending any proposal. This way, the adversary forces the protocol to run for f iterations.

A first modification towards adaptive security is to move the elect round after the propose round and before the commit round. The hope is that, by the time L is corrupted, all honest parties have already received its proposal. This means every party should act as a potential leader before L_k is revealed, i.e., in status and propose rounds to collect status and make a proposal. From the commit round onward, only L's proposal is relevant.

However, this idea alone is not sufficient. At the end of the elect round, after learning the identity of L, the adversary corrupts L, signs an equivocating proposal using L's secret key and forwards it to all honest parties. Honest parties will detect equivocation from L and will not commit in this iteration. We are again forced to run the protocol for f iterations.

To this end, we need to add a step for each party to "prepare" its proposal before the leader is revealed. Afterwards, only "prepared" proposals are considered in equivocation checking. The prepare step should guarantee that, if a party h is honest throughout the prepare process but becomes corrupted afterwards, an adversary cannot construct a "prepared" equivocating proposal on h's behalf. We achieve the prepare step in two rounds as follows.

Round P1 ($\mathsf{prepare}_1$). Each party i broadcasts its proposal $\langle v_i, k \rangle_i$.

Round P2 ($\mathsf{prepare}_2$). If party j receives a proposal $\langle v_i, k \rangle_i$ from party i in the previous round, party j signs the proposal and sends $\langle v_i, k \rangle_j$ back to party i.

We say a proposal (v_i, k) is prepared if it carries $f + 1$ signatures from distinct parties. Each honest party will be able to prepare its proposal. If party i is honest in the two **prepare** rounds and becomes corrupted only afterwards, preparing a conflicting proposal on party i's behalf requires forging at least one honest party's signature, which a computationally bounded adversary cannot do.

The core protocol against a strongly rushing adaptive adversary now has 7 rounds: status, $\mathsf{prepare}_1$, $\mathsf{prepare}_2$, $\mathsf{propose}$, elect, commit, and notify. Proofs for safety and validity remain unchanged from the static case. Proof of termination and round complexity analysis also hold once we observe that (1) there is a $> 1/2$ chance that each leader L_k is honest up to the point at which it is revealed, (2) if L_k is still honest by the end of the $\mathsf{propose}$ round of iteration k, all honest parties will consider its proposal valid and terminate one round after iteration k.

We remark that leader election based on verifiable random function [28], when combined with our **prepare** rounds, achieves expected 2 iterations against a (normal) rushing adaptive adversary. But it will run into f iterations against a strongly rushing adaptive adversary, who can prevent a leader from announcing its rank after receiving it.

3.4   Round Complexity and Communication Complexity

The first honest leader will ensure termination. The random leader election subroutine ensures a $(f + 1)/(2f + 1) > 1/2$ probability that each leader is honest, so the core protocol terminates in expected 2 iterations, plus one extra round to forward $f + 1$ notify. Thus, if an iteration requires r rounds, our core protocol requires $2r + 1$ rounds to terminate in expectation. If the adversary is adaptive and strongly rushing, each iteration requires $r = 7$ rounds. If the adversary is adaptive and normal rushing, the elect round can happen in parallel to $\mathsf{propose}$, and each iteration has $r = 6$ rounds. If the adversary is static (rushing or otherwise), we do not need the two **prepare** rounds, and the elect round can happen in parallel to either status or $\mathsf{propose}$, giving $r = 4$ rounds per iteration.

Next, we analyze the communication complexity. We will show that each round consumes $O(n^2)$ communication. Hence, the core protocol requires expected $O(n^2)$ communication (whether the adversary is adaptive or static, rushing or not). First of all, note that although a certificate consists of $f + 1$

signatures, its size can be reduced to a single signature using threshold signatures [8, 18, 25, 32].

1. In the status round, every party is reporting its currently accepted certificate to every other party (every party can potentially be the leader since the leader identity has not been revealed).
2. In prepare$_1$, every party sends a signed proposal, which is $O(1)$ in size, to every other party.
3. In prepare$_2$, every party sends back a doubly signed proposal, which is $O(1)$ in size, to every other party.
4. In the propose round, every party sends a proposal, which carries a certificate, to every other party. (A proposal need not contain status messages, following the suggestion of the HotStuff protocol [3]).
5. In the elect round, the common-coin protocol by Loss and Moran [27] requires $O(n^2)$ communication.
6. In the commit round, every party sends an $O(1)$-sized commit message to every other party.
7. In the notify round, every party sends a notify message, which carries a certificate, to every other party.
8. Lastly, before termination, every party sends $f + 1$ notification headers $\langle \text{notify}, v \rangle$, which can be reduced to a single threshold signature, to every other party.

4   Byzantine Broadcast and Agreement

In this section, we describe how to use the core protocol to solve synchronous authenticated Byzantine broadcast and agreement for the $f < n/2$ case. For both problems, we design a "pre-round" to let honest parties obtain initial certificates and then invoke the core protocol.

Byzantine Broadcast. In Byzantine broadcast, a designated *sender* tries to broadcast a value to n parties. A solution needs to satisfy three requirements:

   (termination) all honest parties eventually commit,
   (agreement) all honest parties commit on the same value, and
   (validity) if the sender is honest, then all honest parties commit on the value it broadcasts.

Let L_s be the designated sender. In the pre-round, L_s broadcasts a signed value $\langle v_s \rangle_{L_s}$ to every party. Such a signed value by the sender is an initial certificate certifying $(v_s, 0)$. We then invoke the core protocol. Safety and termination are satisfied due to Theorems 2 and 3. If the designated sender is honest, each honest party has a certificate for $(v_s, 0)$ and no conflicting initial certificate can exist, satisfying the condition for Theorem 4. Thus, validity is satisfied.

Byzantine Agreement. In Byzantine agreement, every party holds an initial input value. A solution needs to satisfy the same termination and agreement requirements as in Byzantine broadcast. There exist a few different validity notions. We adopt a common one known as strong unanimity [13]:

(validity) if all honest parties hold the same input value v, then they all commit on v.

In the pre-round, every party i broadcasts its value $\langle v_i \rangle_i$. $f + 1$ signatures from distinct parties for the same value v form an initial certificate for $(v, 0)$. We then invoke the core protocol. Safety and termination are satisfied due to Theorems 2 and 3. If all honest parties have the same input value, then they will have an initial certificate for v and no conflicting initial certificate can exist, satisfying the condition for Theorem 4. Thus, validity is satisfied.

The efficiency of the protocols is straightforward given the analysis of the core protocol. Both protocols require one more round than the core protocol and the same $O(n^2)$ communication complexity as the core protocol.

5   Clock Synchronization

An important question is how practical the synchrony assumption is, which will be the topic of this section. The synchrony assumption essentially states that all honest replicas' messages arrive in time. This requires two properties: (i) a bounded message delay and (ii) locked step execution, i.e., honest replicas enter each round roughly at the same time. The second property is important because, if replica i enters a round much earlier than replica j, then i may end up finishing the round too soon without waiting for j's message to arrive. In our protocol, for example, this could prevent i from detecting leader equivocation and result in a safety violation.

The XFT paper provided some justification for the bounded message delay assumption in certain applications [26]. But we still need a mechanism to enforce locked step execution. To this end, we will use the following clock synchronization protocol, which may be interesting outside Byzantine agreement. It is a variation of the clock synchronization protocol by Dolev et al. [10]. The key change is to have parties sign independently in parallel (as opposed to sequentially) to facilitate the use of threshold signatures.

The protocol will be executed at known time intervals. We call each interval a "day".

Round 0 (sync). When party i's clock reaches the beginning of day X, it sends a $\langle \text{sync}, X \rangle_i$ message to all parties including itself.

Round 1 (new-day). The first time a party j receives $f + 1$ $\langle \text{sync}, X \rangle$ messages from distinct parties (either as $f + 1$ separate sync messages or within a single new-day message), it

- sets its clock to the beginning of day X, and
- sends all other parties a new-day message, which is the concatenation of $f + 1$ $\langle \text{sync}, X \rangle$ messages from distinct parties.

The above protocol bootstraps lock-step synchrony from the message delay bound Δ and a clock drift bound. Each sync message is triggered by a party's own local clock, independent of when day X would start for other parties. The $f + 1$ sync messages can be replaced with a threshold signature for better efficiency. The protocol refreshes honest parties' clock difference to at most the message delay bound Δ at the beginning of each day. The first honest party to start a new day will broadcast a new-day message, which makes all other honest parties start the new day within Δ time. Obtaining a new-day message also means at least one honest party has sent a valid sync message, ensuring that roughly one day has indeed passed since the previous day. We can then set the duration of each round to $2\Delta + \phi$ where ϕ is the maximum clock drift between two honest parties in a "day".

Acknowledgments. We thank Dahlia Malkhi and Benjamin Chan for many useful discussions.

References

1. Abraham, I., et al.: Communication complexity of byzantine agreement, revisited. arXiv preprint, arXiv:1805.03391 (2018)
2. Abraham, I., Devadas, S., Dolev, D., Nayak, K., Ren, L.: Synchronous byzantine agreement with expected $O(1)$ rounds, expected $O(n^2)$ communication, and optimal resilience. Cryptology ePrint Archive, Report 2018/1028 (2018). https://eprint.iacr.org/2018/1028
3. Abraham, I., Gueta, G., Malkhi, D.: Hot-stuff the linear, optimal-resilience, one-message BFT devil. arXiv preprint arXiv:1803.05069 (2018)
4. Abraham, I., Malkhi, D., Nayak, K., Ren, L., Spiegelman, A.: A blockchain protocol based on reconfigurable byzantine consensus. In: OPODIS, Solida (2017)
5. Adya, A., et al.: FARSITE: federated, available, and reliable storage for an incompletely trusted environment. ACM SIGOPS Oper. Syst. Rev. **36**(SI), 1–14 (2002)
6. Ben-Or, M.: Another advantage of free choice (extended abstract): completely asynchronous agreement protocols. In: Proceedings of the Second Annual ACM Symposium on Principles of Distributed Computing, pp. 27–30. ACM (1983)
7. Ben-Or, M., Goldwasser, S., Wigderson, A.: Completeness theorems for non-cryptographic fault-tolerant distributed computation. In: Proceedings of the 20th Annual ACM Symposium on Theory of Computing, pp. 1–10. ACM (1988)
8. Cachin, C., Kursawe, K., Shoup, V.: Random oracles in constantinople: practical asynchronous byzantine agreement using cryptography. J. Cryptol. **18**(3), 219–246 (2005)
9. Castro, M., Liskov, B.: Practical byzantine fault tolerance. In: OSDI, vol. 99, pp. 173–186 (1999)
10. Dolev, D., Halpern, J., Simons, B., Strong, R.: Dynamic fault-tolerant clock synchronization. J. ACM **42**(1), 143–185 (1995)
11. Dolev, D., Reischuk, R.: Bounds on information exchange for Byzantine agreement. J. ACM (JACM) **32**(1), 191–204 (1985)
12. Dolev, D., Raymond Strong, H.: Authenticated algorithms for Byzantine agreement. SIAM J. Comput. **12**(4), 656–666 (1983)

13. Dwork, C., Lynch, N., Stockmeyer, L.: Consensus in the presence of partial synchrony. J. ACM **35**(2), 288–323 (1988)
14. Feldman, P., Micali, S.: An optimal probabilistic protocol for synchronous byzantine agreement. SIAM J. Comput. **26**(4), 873–933 (1997)
15. Fischer, M.J., Lynch, N.A.: A lower bound for the time to assure interactive consistency. Inf. Process. Lett. **14**(4), 183–186 (1982)
16. Fitzi, M., Garay, J.A.: Efficient player-optimal protocols for strong and differential consensus. In: Proceedings of the Twenty-Second Annual Symposium on Principles of Distributed Computing, pp. 211–220. ACM (2003)
17. Goldwasser, S., Micali, S., Wigderson, A.: How to play any mental game, or a completeness theorem for protocols with an honest majority. In: Proceedings of the 19th Annual ACM STOC, vol. 87, pp. 218–229 (1987)
18. Gueta, G.G., et al.: SBFT: a scalable decentralized trust infrastructure for blockchains. arXiv preprint arXiv:1804.01626 (2018)
19. Katz, J., Koo, C.-Y.: On expected constant-round protocols for Byzantine agreement. In: Dwork, C. (ed.) CRYPTO 2006. LNCS, vol. 4117, pp. 445–462. Springer, Heidelberg (2006). https://doi.org/10.1007/11818175_27
20. King, V., Saia, J.: Breaking the $O(n^2)$ bit barrier: scalable Byzantine agreement with an adaptive adversary. J. ACM **58**(4), 18 (2011)
21. Kogias, E.K., Jovanovic, P., Gailly, N., Khoffi, I., Gasser, L., Ford, B.: Enhancing bitcoin security and performance with strong consistency via collective signing. In: 25th USENIX Security Symposium, pp. 279–296. USENIX Association (2016)
22. Kubiatowicz, J., et al.: OceanStore: an architecture for global-scale persistent storage. ACM Sigplan Not. **35**(11), 190–201 (2000)
23. Lamport, L.: The part-time parliament. ACM Trans. Comput. Syst. **16**(2), 133–169 (1998)
24. Lamport, L., Shostak, R., Pease, M.: The Byzantine generals problem. ACM Trans. Program. Lang. Syst. **4**(3), 382–401 (1982)
25. Libert, B., Joye, M., Yung, M.: Born and raised distributively: fully distributed non-interactive adaptively-secure threshold signatures with short shares. Theoret. Comput. Sci. **645**, 1–24 (2016)
26. Liu, S., Cachin, C., Quéma, V., Vukolic, M.: XFT: practical fault tolerance beyond crashes. In: 12th USENIX Symposium on Operating Systems Design and Implementation, pp. 485–500. USENIX Association (2016)
27. Loss, J., Moran, T.: Combining asynchronous and synchronous Byzantine agreement: the best of both worlds. Cryptology ePrint Archive 2018/235 (2018)
28. Micali, S.: ALGORAND: the efficient and democratic ledger. arXiv:1607.01341 (2016)
29. Pass, R., Shi, E.: Feasibilities and infeasibilities for achieving responsiveness in permissionless consensus. In: International Symposium on Distributed Computing. Springer (2017)
30. Pass, R., Shi, E.: Thunderella: blockchains with optimistic instant confirmation. In: Nielsen, J.B., Rijmen, V. (eds.) EUROCRYPT 2018. LNCS, vol. 10821, pp. 3–33. Springer, Cham (2018). https://doi.org/10.1007/978-3-319-78375-8_1
31. Rabin, M.O.: Randomized Byzantine generals. In: Proceedings of the 24th Annual Symposium on Foundations of Computer Science, pp. 403–409. IEEE (1983)
32. Shoup, V.: Practical threshold signatures. In: Preneel, B. (ed.) EUROCRYPT 2000. LNCS, vol. 1807, pp. 207–220. Springer, Heidelberg (2000). https://doi.org/10.1007/3-540-45539-6_15
33. Zhou, L., Schneider, F., van Renesse, R.: COCA: a secure distributed online certification authority. ACM Trans. Comput. Syst. **20**(4), 329–368 (2002)

Crypto Means Cryptography

Oblivious PRF on Committed Vector Inputs and Application to Deduplication of Encrypted Data

Jan Camenisch[1], Angelo De Caro[2], Esha Ghosh[3(✉)], and Alessandro Sorniotti[2]

[1] DFINITY Zurich Research Lab, Zürich, Switzerland
jan@dfinity.org
[2] IBM Research, Zurich, Rüschlikon, Switzerland
{ADC,aso}@zurich.ibm.com
[3] Microsoft Research, Redmond, USA
esha.ghosh@microsoft.com

Abstract. Ensuring secure deduplication of encrypted data is a very active topic of research because deduplication is effective at reducing storage costs. Schemes supporting deduplication of encrypted data that are not vulnerable to content guessing attacks (such as Message Locked Encryption) have been proposed recently [Bellare *et al.* 2013, Li *et al.* 2015]. However in all these schemes, there is a key derivation phase that solely depends on a short hash of the data and not the data itself. Therefore, a file specific key can be obtained by anyone possessing the hash. Since hash values are usually not meant to be secret, a desired solution will be a more robust oblivious key generation protocol where file hashes need not be kept private. Motivated by this use-case, we propose a new primitive for oblivious pseudorandom function (OPRF) on committed vector inputs in the universal composable (UC) framework. We formalize this functionality as $\mathcal{F}_{OOPRF}$, where OOPRF stands for *Ownership-based Oblivious PRF*. $\mathcal{F}_{OOPRF}$ produces a unique random key on input a vector digest provided the client proves knowledge of a (parametrisable) number of random positions of the input vector.

To construct an *efficient* OOPRF protocol, we carefully combine a hiding vector commitment scheme, a variant of the PRF scheme of Dodis-Yampolskiy [Dodis *et al.* 2005] and a homomorphic encryption scheme glued together with concrete, efficient instantiations of proofs of knowledge. To the best of our knowledge, our work shows for the first time how these primitives can be combined in a secure, efficient and useful way. We also propose a new vector commitment scheme with constant sized public parameters but $(\log n)$ size witnesses where n is the length of the committed vector. This can be of independent interest.

1 Introduction

Cloud storage systems are becoming increasingly popular as a way to reduce costs while increasing availability and flexibility of storage. A promising technology that keeps the cost of cloud storage systems down is data deduplication,

© International Financial Cryptography Association 2019
I. Goldberg and T. Moore (Eds.): FC 2019, LNCS 11598, pp. 337–356, 2019.
https://doi.org/10.1007/978-3-030-32101-7_21

which can reduce up to 68% storage needs in standard file systems [24]. Data deduplication avoids storing multiple copies of the same data at the cloud storage. For example, if two clients upload the same file, the cloud server detects that, stores a single copy of the file and gives access to it to both clients.

However, if two clients locally encrypt their files with their individual keys, completely independent ciphertexts would result even if the underlying plaintext file is the same, thereby making deduplication impossible. A fundamental challenge in deduplicating encrypted files is the following: how can two mistrusting users obtain a common encryption key that depends on the content of a file they both own, without revealing anything about this fact, or about the file's content? Schemes that address this problem *and* are not vulnerable to content guessing or offline brute-force attacks have been proposed recently [22,23]. But all these schemes rely on an oblivious key derivation phase, executed between a key server KS and a client C, whose input solely depends on a short hash of the file and not on the file itself. In these systems, a file-specific key will not only be revealed to the legitimate owners of the file but, crucially, to anyone knowing the hash of the file. This vulnerability will be particularly disastrous if a malicious party (modeling insider threat in cloud storage systems, like a malicious administrator) gets hold of a ciphertext and the hash of a file.

Hash values are usually not meant to be secret and are in fact openly used in multiple contexts, e.g. for checksumming, in standard deduplication protocols, in blockchain systems, and for authentication in Merkle trees. Note that the fundamental issue here is that the key generation solely depends on a *short hash* of the file, so getting this short hash is sufficient to get the key for the file through the oblivious protocol. This concern remains unaddressed even if domain separation [22] is used (i.e., domain specific salt is used for generating hash for the key server), since the oblivious key generation will still depend on the short hash. A desired solution will be a more robust oblivious key generation protocol where file hashes need not be kept private. In other words, any small leakage on a file, *should not be sufficient* to get the legitimate file specific key.

The obvious first attempt in achieving a robust oblivious key generation protocol is to add a proof of knowledge step in the key generation phase. The oblivious key generation phase is usually achieved using Oblivious Pseudorandom Function (OPRF). An OPRF [18] is a two-party protocol between Alice and Bob for securely computing a pseudorandom function $f_k(x)$ where Alice holds the key k and Bob wants to evaluate the function on input x. Despite its simplicity, OPRF has been shown to be a powerful primitive with application in multiple contexts [18,20,21] and in particular for secure-deduplication [22,23] in cloud storage systems. Security of OPRF requires that Bob learns only $f_k(x)$ while Alice learns nothing from the interaction. However, the OPRF protocols in the literature [20,21] can only handle large inputs with a considerable loss in efficiency when Bob is malicious. In particular, none of the OPRF functionalities in the literature can handle the following situation: Bob wants to evaluate the function on a short representation of his large input, while Alice wants Bob to prove knowledge of his large input, and not the short representation, *efficiently*, i.e., with communication complexity asymptotically smaller than the length of his input. We address this precise question here. Notice that this is exactly the question we are asking in the context of oblivious key generation for secure deduplication.

Is it possible to construct an OPRF protocol that can handle large input from a malicious party with communication complexity that is asymptotically strictly smaller than the size of the input?

In order to solve the conflict between the requirements expressed in the above question, we envision a protocol where the output of the OPRF still depends solely on the hash of the input, but that requires a user to prove knowledge of the pre-image of that hash in an *efficient way*, while retaining privacy. This implies that the system should enable efficient and compact proof of knowledge of the preimage of a hash without revealing anything about the hash or the preimage.

These multi-fold requirements naturally suggest combining a Proof-of-Ownership (PoW) [19] with an OPRF protocol. In a PoW protocol, ownership of a file is ascertained probabilistically by challenging the user to prove knowledge of certain blocks of the input file. However, by definition, a PoW scheme requires a deterministic hash of the file to be maintained at the server, and therefore, is stateful. Moreover, a PoW server, by definition, should be able to decide if two users possess the same file or not. Therefore, any PoW scheme falls short of our privacy goals where we do not want to reveal any information about the file in the proof-of-knowledge phase.

1.1 Our Result

We answer the question in the previous section in the affirmative by proposing a new OPRF primitive on committed vector inputs in the *universal composablilty* (UC) framework. We formalize this functionality as $\mathcal{F}_{OOPRF}$ where OOPRF stands for *Ownership-based Oblivious PRF*. $\mathcal{F}_{OOPRF}$ produces a unique random key on an input vector digest, only if the client proves knowledge of a (parametrisable) number of random positions of the input vector. By carefully tuning the number of positions to challenge the client on, bandwidth consumption can be reduced while ensuring that a malicious client can only cheat with negligible probability. We discuss how this tunable parameter should be set and how it affects the soundness error of the protocol. We further describe how to make our protocol more efficient in the weaker stand-alone security model.

Threat Model. The general setting of secure deduplication consists of three parties: a storage server (SS), a set of clients (C_i) who store their encrypted files on SS and a key server (KS) who aids the deduplication process by assisting the client to generate encryption keys that are unique for each file to be encrypted. In the first phase, the clients interact with the KS to get a key which is used to encrypt the input file such that the resulting ciphertext can be deduplicated. This is obtained as a result of the fact that a file encrypted with the same key will always produce the same ciphertext.

We will focus on the key generation phase that is executed between the KS and a client C_i. The clients are malicious and the KS is honest-but-curious in our threat model (we discuss how to tolerate a malicious KS in Sect. 4). This is a threat model that captures a wide range of realistic settings where a malicious client is in possession of ciphertexts (modeling an attacker hacking into the SS, or a malicious administrator of the SS with access to ciphertexts or an intelligence agency coercing the SS into releasing ciphertexts) and hashes of the files produced by an honest client. The malicious client can then try to obtain the decryption key for the file by fooling the KS. The KS typically models a cloud service provider that has no incentive in generating weak or incorrect keys for the files. A more realistic scenario is where the KS may stealthily deviate from the protocol to learn information about the client files. But we protect against any such information leakage. In other words, we protect the input privacy of the clients even against a malicious KS.

It is also easy to detect (with high probability) if KS is misbehaving in generating the key by sending the same file twice and observing if the same key is generated. Since KS generates the key obliviously, it will not be able to detect that it has received the same file. So, if KS is not faithfully generating the keys, with very high probability it will end up generating different keys and thus risk detection.

UC Security. With the increasing popularity of cloud platforms, significant effort went into developing customized solutions for various problems related to the security and privacy of outsourced data and computations. These protocols are not very modular by design and it is extremely challenging to compose them to achieve multiple security goals at once. In this work, we take an important step towards modular design by formalizing the security requirements in the *Universally Composable* (UC) framework which provides composable security guarantees.

Efficiency. Designing UC-secure protocols introduce some performance over-heads. However, it is often trivial to optimize a UC-secure protocol (making it only secure in weaker models), whereas it is often extremely complex (if not out-right infeasible) to demonstrate UC-security for a protocol that is only secure in weaker models. For achieving stand-alone security in our protocol, it is suffi-cient to instantiate all the zero-knowledge proofs of knowledge in our protocol with generalized Schnorr proofs using the Fiat-Shamir heuristic, which are very efficient in practice.

Ideal Functionality. A naive attempt to define the ideal functionality, $\mathcal{F}_{\mathsf{OOPRF}}$, is the following. A (possibly malicious) client C hands in its entire input file to the functionality. If $\mathcal{F}_{\mathsf{OOPRF}}$ has not seen this file before, it generates a fresh random key, stores it with the file, and returns that key to the client. Otherwise, $\mathcal{F}_{\mathsf{OOPRF}}$ just returns the key it has stored for that file. Any realization of such a functionality would require communication between C and KS to be linear in length of C's input. This is because the simulator will need to extract on-line, the entire file from a malicious client, to be able to input it to the functionality. This defeats the compactness requirement we are looking for. To avoid this, we could let $\mathcal{F}_{\text{OOPRF}}$ remember some *succinct representation* of each file and then allow the simulator to input just that representation and get the key from the functionality. However, this would let malicious clients get away safely with knowing the succinct representation only rather than the full file. This is precisely the security issue we are trying to overcome!

We envision a protocol where a client will just have to commit to the whole file (e.g., with a vector commitment) and then to prove that it knows sufficiently many blocks, it, can open sufficiently many random positions of the vector commitment. Vector commitments [13] allow a party to commit to a vector of messages in such a way that it can later provide a witness that proves that $x[i]$ is indeed the i-th value in the committed vector x.

To allow for such communication-efficient protocol realizations, we need to model inside the functionality, that a file is only provided partially. We do this by allowing the simulator to obtain keys from $\mathcal{F}_{\text{OOPRF}}$ on input a *succinct representation* of a file together with *sufficiently many blocks* of the file, where "sufficiently many" is defined in terms of a security parameter t. $\mathcal{F}_{\text{OOPRF}}$ will choose a fresh key for each representation of a file, store the key, the representation of the file and the provided blocks. When $\mathcal{F}_{\text{OOPRF}}$ sees the same representation again, it will check whether the blocks on file for that representation are consistent with the newly provided blocks. The representation and blocks provided by the simulator will also have to be consistent with the *full file input* to $\mathcal{F}_{\text{OOPRF}}$ by honest clients. So, $\mathcal{F}_{\text{OOPRF}}$ will have to compute its own representation for full file input (it cannot ask the simulator as then the input of the honest client would no longer remain secret as we require). Thus, we need to provide $\mathcal{F}_{\text{OOPRF}}$ with a function (vector commit) to compute this representation.

Notice that the guarantee that $\mathcal{F}_{\text{OOPRF}}$ provides is that, when the input files are same, the client will get the same key. But the client cannot get the key by knowing a short representation for a large file; it has to show that it knows "sufficiently many" blocks of the file. This is significantly different from *Proof-of-Retrievability* [26] schemes where the guarantee is that the *entire* outsourced file is saved at all times (at the server).

Protocol. To construct a protocol that securely realizes $\mathcal{F}_{\text{OOPRF}}$, we combine hiding vector commitments [13], a hiding and binding commitment scheme [25], a variant of the PRF scheme of Dodis-Yampolskiy [14, 17, 21], and a homomorphic encryption scheme [9, 16] together with *concrete, efficient instantiations of proofs of knowledge*. At a high level, the construction is designed as follows.

The PRF is obliviously evaluated on a succinct deterministic commitment to C's input $\boldsymbol{x}$, say s. We implement the oblivious PRF by leveraging the homomorphism of the encryption scheme. Now recall that C has to prove knowledge of random positions in the preimage of s *efficiently* and wants to preserve the confidentiality of its input. This can be addressed by using a randomized/hiding vector commitment. Still, the PRF needs to be evaluated on s, to ensure that the protocol always returns the same output given the same input. We provide an efficient proof of knowledge implementation that binds the randomized vector commitment with a commitment to s. Our protocol ensures that all these components can inter-operate efficiently. To the best of our knowledge, our work shows for the first time how these primitives can be combined in a secure, efficient and useful way.

As a subroutine of our protocol, we construct a new vector commitment (VC) scheme with *constant-sized public parameters* and $\log n$ size witnesses where n is the length of the committed vector. The scheme is based on the Merkle Hash Tree (MHT) based accumulator construction presented in [4]. Very recently [3] proposed a non-hiding MHT based VC with efficient batching of witnesses of position binding in groups of unknown order. Their batch openings only saves (asymptotically) when a few of the positions in the committed vector are set and all this positions are opened in a batch. This is incompatible with our requirement where a few positions are opened selectively. Moreover, their proofs require very expensive group operations in groups of unknown order.

1.2   Organization

The rest of the paper is organized as follows. In Sect. 2, we describe the cryptographic primitives. In Sect. 3 we describe the ideal functionality $\mathcal{F}_{\mathsf{OOPRF}}$ and in Sect. 4 we give a secure realization of $\mathcal{F}_{\mathsf{OOPRF}}$. One of the main building blocks of the protocol is vector commitment. In Sect. 5, we give an instantiation of VC and defer the second instantiation to the full version [6]. Throughout the protocol and the VC implementations we use abstract PoK notation for the proofs of knowledge. In Sect. 6, we give the concrete implementations of all the PoK's. Finally, we conclude in Sect. 7.

2   Preliminaries

In this section we discuss the cryptographic primitives used in our protocol.

2.1   Proof Systems (PK)

By $\mathsf{PoK}\{(w) : statement(w)\}$ we denote a generic interactive zero-knowledge proof protocol of knowledge of a witness w such that the $statement(w)$ is true. A PoK system must fulfil *completeness, zero-knowledge and simulation-sound extractability*. A PoK system consists of the two protocols: PK.Setup, PK.Prove. On input a security parameter 1^λ, PK.Setup(1^λ) outputs ($\mathsf{par}_{\mathsf{PK}}$). PK.Prove($\mathsf{par}_{\mathsf{PK}}, \cdot$) is an interactive protocol between prover and a verifier that $statement(w)$ is true. The additional input the prover holds is the witness w for the statement. Simulation-sound extractability for a PoK system requires the existence of an efficient algorithm $\mathcal{SE}$ that outputs ($\mathsf{par}_{\mathsf{PK}}, \mathsf{td}_s, \mathsf{td}_e$) such that $\mathsf{par}_{\mathsf{PK}}$ is identically distributed to the $\mathsf{par}_{\mathsf{PK}}$ generated by PK.Setup (td_e is the extraction trapdoor and td_s is the simulation trapdoor). When we need witnesses to be online-extractable, we make this explicit by writing $\mathsf{PoK}\{(\underline{w_1}, w_2) : statement(w_1, w_2)\}$ the proof of witnesses w_1 and w_2, where w_1 can be extracted.

For concrete realizations of PoK's, i.e., generalized Schnorr-signature proofs [8], we will use notation [10] such as $\mathsf{GSPK}\{(a, b, c) : y = g^a h^b \wedge \tilde{y} = \tilde{g}^a \tilde{h}^c\}$.

Whenever a witness needs to be on-line extractable, we will use verifiable encryption under a public key contained in the CRS. To allow for a proper assessment of our protocols, we will always spell these encryptions out (so there will not be any underlined witnesses in this notation). Finally, to make the 3-move generalized Schnorr-signature proofs concurrent zero-knowledge and simulations sound, one can use any of the standard generic techniques [15,27], typically resulting in a 4-move protocol.

2.2 Commitment Scheme (CS)

We will instantiate CS with Pedersen commitment which satisfies correctness, hiding and binding properties. In addition to that, Pedersen commitments are homomorphic. We instantiate the commitment scheme in a composite order group to be compatible with the other primitives that we will be using [4].

CS.Setup(1^λ): The setup algorithm picks two λ bit safe primes p, q such that $\gcd(p - 1, q - 1, 7) = 1$ and sets $N = pq$ and sets message space and randomness space respectively as: $\mathcal{M} = \mathbb{Z}_N^*, \mathcal{R} = \mathbb{Z}_N^*$.

Then, the algorithm picks a prime ρ such that $\rho = 2kN + 1$ where k is a small prime. Let $G = \langle \mathsf{G} \rangle = \langle \mathsf{H} \rangle$ be order-N subgroup of the group $\mathbb{Z}_\rho^*$ and G and H are two random generators of G, such that $\log_\mathsf{H} \mathsf{G}$ is unknown. Note that G is a cyclic subgroup of $\mathbb{Z}_\rho^*$ of order N and all the operations will happen modulo ρ (i.e., reduced mod N in the exponent). Finally, the algorithm outputs public parameters par := $(\rho, N, G, \mathsf{G}, \mathsf{H}, \mathcal{M}, \mathcal{R})$.

CS.Commit(par, m, r): Compute com $\leftarrow \mathsf{G}^m \mathsf{H}^r$ mod ρ. Output (com, open = r).

CS.Verify(par, com, m, open): Output 1 if com $\leftarrow \mathsf{G}^m \mathsf{H}^{\mathsf{open}}$ mod ρ, 0 otherwise.

Theorem 1 ([25]). *The commitment scheme CS is information-theoretically hiding and binding under the Discrete Log assumption.*

2.3 Pseudorandom Function (PRF)

We will use the PRF scheme proposed in [14,21] which is a variant of the PRF scheme of Dodis-Yampolskiy [17] based on the Boneh-Boyen unpredictable function [2], instantiated on a composite-order group instead of a prime-order group. This PRF was proven to be secure for a domain of arbitrary size based solely on subgroup hiding in [14]. The proof for the original PRF instantiated with prime-order groups only allows for a domain which is polynomial sized in the security parameter. Notice that, for our application, it is crucial to have arbitrary size domain in order to disallow offline brute-force attack by a honest-but-curious KS. Here we recall the PRF definition and its security [14].

PRF.Setup(1^λ): On input the security parameter λ, the setup algorithm picks two λ-bit safe primes p, q and sets $N = pq$. Then, it generates groups

$(N, \mathbb{G}, (\mathbb{G}_1, \mathbb{G}_2)) \leftarrow \mathcal{G}(1^\lambda)$, where $\mathbb{G}_1, \mathbb{G}_2$ are subgroups of $\mathbb{G}$.[1] Reasonable candidates for group $\mathbb{G}$ are composite-order elliptic curve groups *without* efficient pairings or the target group of a composite-order bilinear group. Finally, the setup algorithm picks $g \leftarrow \mathbb{G}$, sets the $\mathsf{D} = \mathsf{K} \leftarrow \mathbb{Z}_N^*, \mathsf{R} \leftarrow \mathbb{G}$, and output $\mathsf{par} = (N, \mathbb{G}, g, \mathsf{D}, \mathsf{K}, \mathsf{R})$.

PRF.KeyGen$(1^\lambda, \mathsf{par})$: On input the security and public parameters λ, par, the key generation algorithm picks $k \leftarrow \mathsf{K}$ and output k.

PRF.Evaluate(par, k, m): On input the public parameters par, key $k \in \mathsf{K}$ and input $m \in \mathsf{D}$, the evaluation algorithm does the following: If $\gcd((k+m), N) \neq 1$, then output $\perp$, else output $g^{\frac{1}{(k+m)} \mod N} \in \mathsf{R}$.

Theorem 2 ([14]). *For all $\lambda \in \mathbb{N}$, if subgroup hiding holds with respect to $\mathbb{G}$ for its subgroups $\mathbb{G}_1$ and $\mathbb{G}_2$, if $N = pq$ for distinct primes $p, q \in \Omega(2^{poly(\lambda)})$, and if $\mathbb{G}_1$ is a cyclic group of prime order, then the function family defined above is a pseudorandom function family.*

2.4 Homomorphic Encryption Scheme (HES)

Here we present the Projective Paillier Encryption scheme [9,16]. This scheme preserves the homomorphic properties of Paillier encryption; however, unlike the original Paillier scheme, the scheme has a dense set of public-keys.

HES.Setup(1^λ): On input the security parameter λ, the setup algorithm picks two λ bit safe primes p, q and sets $N = pq$.[2] Then, it generates a random element $g' \in (\mathbb{Z}_{N^2})$ and sets $\mathsf{g} := g'^{2N}$ and $\mathsf{h} := (1 + N \mod N^2) \in \mathbb{Z}_{N^2}^*$, a special element of order N. Finally, the algorithm outputs $\mathsf{par} := (N, \mathsf{g}, \mathsf{h})$.

HES.KeyGen(par): On input the public parameters par, the key generation algorithm picks a random $t \in [N/4]$ and computes $\mathsf{epk} \leftarrow \mathsf{g}^t \mod N^2$. Finally, the algorithm outputs $(\mathsf{epk}, \mathsf{esk} := t)$.

HES.Enc(epk, m): On input the public key epk and message m, the encryption algorithm picks a random $r \in [N/4]$ and computes $\mathsf{u} \leftarrow \mathsf{g}^r \mod N^2; \mathsf{v} \leftarrow \mathsf{epk}^r \mathsf{h}^m \mod N^2$. Finally, the algorithm outputs ciphertext $\mathsf{ct} := (\mathsf{u}, \mathsf{v})$. We will sometime use the notation $[[m]]$ to mean the encryption of m.

HES.Dec$(\mathsf{esk}, \mathsf{ct})$: On input the secret key esk and ciphertext ct, the decryption algorithm computes $m' \leftarrow \mathsf{v}/\mathsf{u}^{\mathsf{esk}} \mod N^2$. If m' is of the form $(1 + Nm \mod N^2)$ for some $n \in [N]$, output m. Else output $\perp$.

Theorem 3 ([16]). *Under the Decision Composite Residuosity assumption, the Projective Paillier encryption scheme is semantically secure.*

---

[1] Notice that $\mathbb{G}_1, \mathbb{G}_2$ are not explicitly used in the construction, but are required from the security proof.

[2] Algesheimer et al. describe how to generate such an N distributedly [1].

2.5   Vector Commitments (VC)

Vector commitments (VC) [13] allow one to commit to a vector of messages in such a way that it is later possible to open the commitment to one of the messages i.e, provide a witness that proves that x_i is indeed the ith value in the committed vector $\boldsymbol{x}$. The size of the commitment and the opening are independent of the length of the vector. We relax the efficiency requirement of VC in our definition. Let n be the length of the committed vector. We require the size of the commitment to be independent from n, but the size of the opening should be asymptotically smaller than n. A VC can either be *non-hiding/deterministic* (detVC) or *hiding/randomized* (randVC)[3]. For a detVC the only security requirement is *binding*. Informally, this property requires that once an adversary comes up with a VC, it should not be able to prove two different values with respect to the same position for that VC. For a randVC, the *hiding* is an additional security requirement. Informally, this requirement states that the VC should conceal the committed vector, i.e., an adversary should not be able to distinguish if a VC was created for a vector $\boldsymbol{x}$ or a vector $\boldsymbol{y}$, where $\boldsymbol{x} \neq \boldsymbol{y}$. For the formal definition of binding, refer to [13]. Hiding can be defined as for standard commitment.

Here we recall the primitives for a VC. Most of the inputs to the algorithms are common for a randVC and a detVC. The inputs that are needed exclusively for a randVC are highlighted.

VC.Setup($1^\lambda, n$): On input security parameter 1^λ and an upper bound n on the size of the vector, generate the parameters of commitment scheme par, which include a description of message space $\mathcal{M}$ and a description of randomness space $\mathcal{R}$.

VC.Commit(par, $\boldsymbol{x}, r$): On input public parameters par, a vector $\boldsymbol{x} \in \mathcal{M}^l$, ($l \leq n$) *and* $r \in \mathcal{R}$, the algorithm outputs a commitment com to $\boldsymbol{x}$.

VC.Prove(par, $i, \boldsymbol{x}, r$): On input public parameters par, position index i, vector $\boldsymbol{x}$, *and* $r \in \mathcal{R}$, the algorithm generates a witness w for x_i and outputs (w, x_i).

VC.Verify(par, i, com, w, x): On input public parameters par, position index i, commitment com and witness w for x, the algorithm outputs 1 if w is a valid witness for x being at position i and 0 otherwise.

Below we define two new algorithms (VC.RandCommitment, VC.RandWitness). Informally, VC.RandCommitment allows to update a detVC to a randVC and VC.RandWitness allows to update a detVC witness to a randVC witness.

VC.RandCommitment(par, com, r): On input public parameters par, a non-hiding commitment com and $r \in \mathcal{R}$, outputs a randVC com′.

VC.RandWitness(par, com, i, r, w): On input public parameters par, a detVC witness w, a non-hiding commitment com and $r \in \mathcal{R}$, outputs a randVC witness w'.

UC Security: In the full version [6] we give a brief overview of UC security and direct the readers to [7,11,12] for more details.

---

[3] We will use the following terms interchangeably in the context of VC: non-hiding and deterministic, hiding and randomized.

3   Ideal Functionality for Ownership-Based Oblivious PRF (OOPRF)

In this section we describe the ideal functionality $\mathcal{F}_{OOPRF}$. As a warm-up, we start from a *bandwidth inefficient* version of $\mathcal{F}_{OOPRF}$ denoted as $\mathcal{F}_{BI-OOPRF}$. The functionality is designed as follows:

1. $\mathcal{F}_{BI-OOPRF}$ receives input x from client C_i.
2. $\mathcal{F}_{BI-OOPRF}$ maintains a table to store the tuples (x, r_x) where x is the input from C_i and r_x is the *unique random key* that the functionality picks for x.
3. For input x from C_i, if x is in the table, the functionality returns the corresponding r_x to C_i. Otherwise, it picks a fresh random key r_x, stores (x, r_x) in its table and returns r_x to C_i.

Since the client has to hand in the entire set of blocks of a file[4] of length n to the functionality, any protocol that will achieve this functionality will be inefficient in terms of communication bandwidth. This is because the protocol will have to ensure that the entire file can be on-line extracted from a malicious client, which will amount to verifiably encrypting each file block. To overcome this, we are interested in a protocol where a client will just have to commit to the whole file (e.g., with a vector commitment) and then prove that it knows sufficiently many blocks, i.e., can open sufficiently many random positions of the vector commitment. To allow for such a construction, we need to model inside the functionality, that a file is only provided partially. To this end, we will have to allow the simulator to obtain keys from the functionality on input a representation of a file together with sufficiently many blocks of the file, where "sufficiently many" is defined in terms of a security parameter t. The functionality will then choose a fresh key for each representation of a file, store the key, the representation of the file and the provided blocks. Furthermore, when in the future, the functionality sees the same representation again, it will check whether the blocks on file for that representation are consistent with the newly provided blocks. Of course, the representation and blocks provided by the simulator will also have to be consistent with the full file input to the functionality by honest clients. To this end, the functionality will have to compute its own representation (it cannot ask the simulator as then the input of the client would no longer remain secret as we require). Thus, we need to provide the functionality with a function to compute this representation. This could either done by asking the simulator for this function in the setup phase or by parameterizing the functionality with this function. We chose the latter. Of course, the functionality will also have to enforce consistency between the blocks for the representations it computes itself and those it receives from the adversary/simulator.

Note that in $\mathcal{F}_{OOPRF}$, both honest and malicious clients invoke the functionality with file x. But, in case of malicious clients, the functionality generates the random key based on the input from the simulator and its internal state. The simulator's input is checked only against the stored internal state of the

---

[4] We use the word file and vector interchangeably.

functionality, and not with respect to the input x with which a malicious client invokes the functionality. Thus, $\mathcal{F}_{\mathsf{OOPRF}}$ does not require the entire file to be on-line extracted from a malicious client.

Functionality $\mathcal{F}_{\mathsf{OOPRF}}$ (Parameterized with detVC.Commit(par))

Setup: Upon receiving (Setup, sid) from KS:
1. Send (Setup, sid) to Sim and wait for (Setup, sid, ok) from Sim.
2. Initialize an empty table $\mathsf{T}_{\mathsf{sid}}$.
3. Store (sid, $\mathsf{T}_{\mathsf{sid}}$).
4. Output (Setup, sid) to KS.

Evaluate: Upon receiving input (Evaluate, sid, qid, x) from C_i:
1. Proceed only if (sid, $\mathsf{T}_{\mathsf{sid}}$) is stored.

   If C_i is honest: (a) Send (Evaluate, sid, qid, startEvaluate) to Sim and wait for (Evaluate, sid, qid, startEvaluateok) from Sim.

     (b) Compute $s \leftarrow$ detVC.Commit(x).

     (c) If $(s, x', r) \in \mathsf{T}_{\mathsf{sid}}$, for some x' and r, do the following:

       i. If the row corresponding to s contains $x' \neq x$, set variable out $\leftarrow \perp$. Otherwise, out $\leftarrow r$.

       ii. Output (Evaluate, sid, qid, out) to C_i.

     (d) Else, pick $r \leftarrow \mathcal{R}$, insert (s, x, r) in $\mathsf{T}_{\mathsf{sid}}$ and output (Evaluate, sid, qid, r) to C_i.

   If C_i is malicious: (a) Send (Evaluate, sid, qid, startEvaluate) to Sim and wait for (Evaluate, sid, qid, startEvaluateok, $s, x[i_1], \ldots, x[i_t]$) from Sim.

     (b) If $(s, x', r) \in \mathsf{T}_{\mathsf{sid}}$, for some x' and r, do the following:

       i. If x' contains $x'[i_1], \ldots, x'[i_t]$ for which the received $x[i_1], \ldots, x[i_t]$ are unequal at least in one position, set out $\leftarrow \perp$.

       ii. Else, update x' on positions $i_1 \ldots, i_t$ with values $x[i_1], \ldots, x[i_t]$, respectively, and set out $\leftarrow r$.

       iii. Output (Evaluate, sid, qid, out) to C_i.

     (c) Else, pick $r \leftarrow \mathcal{R}$, insert $(s, (x[i_1], \ldots, x[i_t]), r)$ in $\mathsf{T}_{\mathsf{sid}}$.

     (d) output (Evaluate, sid, qid, r) to C_i.

---

4 Secure Realization of $\mathcal{F}_{\mathsf{OOPRF}}$

In this section we describe a protocol Π_{OOPRF} that securely realizes functionality $\mathcal{F}_{\mathsf{OOPRF}}$. We present the construction here and defer the proof of security to the full version [6].

4.1 Protocol Π_{OOPRF}

First we give the high level intuition behind our construction. The protocol is designed in the CRS model, so each party receives the public parameters of the scheme from a trusted party. KS additionally picks a key for a PRF. The protocol has two major building blocks, namely VC and PRF. Recall that the requirements for the key that KS will generate for C_i's input file were (1) the key should be random (2) it should be unique for a file and (3) the key should not be publicly computable. All these properties are provided if the file key is a PRF evaluation on a succinct *deterministic and binding* vector commitment to its input file x. Let us denote this deterministic vector commitment as s.

The PRF evaluation has to be carried out obliviously as KS should learn no information about C_i's input. We implement the oblivious PRF evaluation protocol between KS (holding k) and C_i (holding s) for the PRF described in Sect. 2.3. To design this part of the protocol (Steps 7–13) we leverage the homomorphic encryption scheme that we described in Sect. 2.4. In order to tolerate malicious C_i's, we require that C_i commits to its input s, i.e., compute $\mathsf{com} = \mathsf{CS.Commit}(s, r)$ (where r is the randomness used to compute com using a standard commitment scheme as described in Sect. 2.2) and proves knowledge of its opening, r to KS before KS engages in computing the PRF ($\mathsf{PoK}\pi_{c2}$).

But committing to s is not sufficient; C_i has to prove knowledge of the preimage of s *efficiently*. This is where the properties of VC can be leveraged. A VC lets C_i prove knowledge of some random positions of the preimage. We utilize this property as follows: we let KS challenge C_i to prove knowledge of t random positions of its input, where t is much less than the length of x. C_i can do this efficiently. The question of how to decide on the parameter t depends on the soundness error the protocol is ready to accept. We discuss this in more detail following the construction.

Notice however that C_i does not want to reveal any information about x to KS. A hiding (or randomized) VC scheme tackles this issue but a hiding vector commitment cannot be used directly as the PRF input. This is because, for the same input x, if the PRF is computed on two randomized VC's for x, then it will generate different outputs. So we require that PRF is computed on a deterministic vector commitment to the input vector. Let s' be a randomized vector commitment to C_i's input x.

We solve problem above by having C_i send both com and s' and a proof that ensures that com and s' are appropriately related, namely that they both refer to the same deterministic vector commitment s.

Armed with this intuition, we are ready to give full construction of the protocol. In Sect. 6 we give the full implementations of the PoK's used here[5,6].

Setup: On input of $(\mathsf{Setup}, \mathsf{sid})$, the key server KS executes:
1. Receive (par) on the $\mathcal{F}_{\mathsf{CRS}}^{\mathsf{PRF.Setup}, \mathsf{VC.Setup}, \mathsf{CS.Setup}, \mathsf{PK.Setup}, \mathsf{HES.Setup}, \mathsf{sp}}$ interface.[5]
2. Run $k \leftarrow \mathsf{PRF.KeyGen}(1^\lambda, \mathsf{par})$ and store k.

---

[5] Note that $\mathsf{par} = (\mathsf{par}_{\mathsf{PRF}}, \mathsf{par}_{\mathsf{VC}}, \mathsf{par}_{\mathsf{CS}}, \mathsf{par}_{\mathsf{PK}}, \mathsf{par}_{\mathsf{HES}})$, but by the choice of our schemes, they all work in the same setting with shared parameters. To simplify notation, when the primitive used is clear from the context, we will just refer to par and not to the specific parameters of that primitive.

[6] It is clear that the randomness r_3 cancels out only with algebraic PRF's with appropriate codomains as the one chosen in our construction.

3. Output $(\mathsf{Setup}, \mathsf{sid})$

Evaluate: On input $(\mathsf{Evaluate}, \mathsf{sid}, \mathsf{qid}, \boldsymbol{x} = (x_1, \ldots, x_n) \in \mathsf{par}.\mathcal{M}^n)$ to client C_i, the following protocol is executed between C_i and KS:

1. Receive (par) on the $\mathcal{F}_{\mathsf{CRS}}^{\mathsf{PRF.Setup, VC.Setup, CS.Setup, PK.Setup, HES.Setup, sp}}$ interface.

2. C_i picks a random $r_1 \leftarrow \mathsf{par}.\mathcal{R}$ and computes $s \leftarrow \mathsf{VC.Commit}(\mathsf{par}, \boldsymbol{x})$ and $s' \leftarrow \mathsf{VC.RandCommitment}(\mathsf{par}, s, r_1)$.

   Additionally, C_i does the following:

   (a) Pick a random $r_2 \leftarrow \mathsf{par}.\mathcal{R}$

   (b) Compute $, \leftarrow \mathsf{CS.Commit}(\mathsf{par}, s, r_2)$

   (c) Then, C_i generates the following proof of knowledge

   $$\pi_{c00} := \mathsf{PoK}\{(\underline{s}, \underline{r_2}) :, = \mathsf{CS.Commit}(\mathsf{par}, s, r_2)\}$$

   (d) Additionally, C_i computes the following proof of knowledge

   $$\pi_{c01} := \mathsf{PoK} \left\{ \begin{array}{c} (s, r_1, r_2) :, = \mathsf{CS.Commit}(\mathsf{par}, s, r_2) \quad \wedge \\ s' = \mathsf{VC.RandCommitment}(\mathsf{par}, s, r_1) \end{array} \right\}$$

   and sends $(s', , , \pi_{c00}, \pi_{c01})$ to KS.

3. KS verifies π_{c00}, π_{c01} if the verifications pass through, then it proceeds to the next step.

4. KS picks a set of indices $I = \{j_1, \ldots, j_t\}$ from $[1, n]$ randomly and sends them to C_i

5. For each challenged index $j \in I$, C_i computes

   $$(w'_j, x_j) \leftarrow \mathsf{VC.Prove}(\mathsf{par}, j, \boldsymbol{x}) \ ,$$

   $$(w_j) \leftarrow \mathsf{VC.RandWitness}(\mathsf{par}, s, j, r_1, w'_j)$$

   and generates the following proof of knowledge

   $$\pi_j = \mathsf{PoK} \left\{ (\underline{w_j}, \underline{x_j}) : 1 = \mathsf{VC.Verify}(\mathsf{par}, j, s', w_j, x_j) \right\}$$

   Let $\pi_{c1} = \{\pi_j | j \in I\}$. C_i sends π_{c1} back to KS.

6. KS verifies π_{c1} and if the verification passes, KS proceeds to the next step.

7. KS picks $(\mathsf{epk}, \mathsf{esk}) \leftarrow \mathsf{HES.KeyGen}(\mathsf{par})$, computes $[k] \leftarrow \mathsf{HES.Enc}(\mathsf{epk}, k)$ and sends $\mathsf{epk}, [k]$ to C_i.

8. Then C_i picks $r_3 \in \mathsf{par}.\mathcal{R}$ and computes

   $$\mathsf{ct} \leftarrow ([k][s])^{r_3} \ ,$$

   where $[s] \leftarrow \mathsf{HES.Enc}(\mathsf{epk}, s)$

9. Next, C_i generates the following proof of knowledge

   $$\pi_{c2} = \mathsf{PoK} \left\{ \begin{array}{c} (s, r_2, \underline{r_3}) :, = \mathsf{CS.Commit}(\mathsf{par}, s, r_2) \quad \wedge \\ \mathsf{ct} = ([k][s])^{r_3} \end{array} \right\}$$

   C_i sends ct, π_{c2} to KS.

10. KS verifies π_{c2} and if the verifications succeed, KS continues.

11. KS computes $V \leftarrow \mathsf{HES.Dec}(\mathsf{esk}, \mathsf{ct})$

12. Then KS computes $K' \leftarrow \mathsf{PRF.Evaluate}(\mathsf{par}, k, V)$ and sends it to C_i.

13. If $K' = \perp$, output $\perp$. Otherwise compute $K \leftarrow K'^{(r_3 \bmod \mathsf{par}.N)}$ and output K.[6]

Choosing Parameter t: Parameter t is a tuning parameter that trades communication bandwidth for efficiency. In order to achieve high confidence that the prover (i.e., the client) owns the entire file, t has to be adjusted accordingly. Intuitively, for higher confidence that the prover possesses the entire file, the verifier can set t to a large value. To minimize soundness error, a file can be erasure coded first and then a VC commitment can be computed on the erasure coded file. If the erasure code is resilient to erasures of up to α fraction of the bits and ϵ is the desired soundness bound, then t should be picked as follows: t should be the smallest integer such that $(1 - \alpha)^t < \epsilon$. [19] discusses in detail how to tune t. Even though this scheme achieves a high level of soundness, good erasure codes for very large files are expensive to compute. In [19], the authors propose a pairwise hash function with public parameters that can be used to hash the input file down to a constant size and then run VC on it. This scheme achieves a weaker level of security than the erasure coded version.

Discussion on Tolerating Malicious KS. The functionality is independent of whether or not KS is honest-but-curious or not. This only matters for the implementation and to what extent it realizes the functionality, i.e., our protocol Π_{OOPRF} realizes the functionality under the assumption that KS is honest or honest-but-curious. Notice that, in the functionality, the key server KS does not learn any information about C_i's input by design. So the functionality protects the privacy of C_i's input even from a malicious KS.

The choice of making KS honest-but-curious merits further discussion. In Π_{OOPRF}, KS can be made to commit to its PRF key and to return a proof of knowledge that it has computed the OPRF correctly as Jarecki and Liu do [21]. However, this does not guarantee that KS will pick a strong key or keep that key secret both of which would defeat the purpose of the protocol. Thus, to address a fully malicious KS, we need to ensure that KS has chosen its PRF key by sampling randomly the desired key space. We notice that this is not addressed by Jarecki et al. [21] either, even though they claim to handle fully malicious KS (i.e., PRF evaluator). Handling this aspect is left as future work.

5   Merkle Tree-Based Vector Commitment

In this section we present a new VC construction scheme based on the Merkle Hash Tree (MHT) based accumulator construction presented in [4]. Unlike [4], we do not need to hide the index position of the leaf. This allows for some efficiency enhancement since the prover does not need to hide if a node is the left child or the right child of its parent. We first provide a detVC construction and then describe algorithms RandCommitment, RandWitness to convert it to randVC. Notice that in this VC construction, the public parameter is constant-sized as opposed to the CDH and RSA based VC schemes proposed in [13]. The drawback is that the proofs have length logarithmic in n as opposed to constant.

5.1 detVC and randVC Constructions

VC.Setup$(1^\lambda, n)$: On input security parameter 1^λ and an upper bound n, the algorithm invokes CS.Setup(1^λ). Let CS.Setup(1^λ) return $(\rho, N, G, \mathsf{G}, \mathsf{H}, \mathcal{M}, \mathcal{R})$. This algorithm appends the tuple with the collision-resistant hash function $H :$ $(\mathbb{Z}_N)^2 \rightarrow \mathbb{Z}_N$ defined as follows [4]: $H(x, y) = x^7 + 3y^7 \mod N$ and return it as par. For further details on the hash function, see [4].

VC.Commit$(\mathsf{par}, \boldsymbol{x})$: On input public parameters par and input $\boldsymbol{x} = x_1, \ldots, x_n$, the algorithm, using $H(\cdot, \cdot)$, recursively builds a Merkle Hash Tree on $\boldsymbol{x}$. (If n is not a power of two, insert "dummy" elements into $\boldsymbol{x}$ until n is a perfect power of 2.) Let MR be the root of the MHT. The algorithm outputs commitment com = MR.

VC.Prove$(\mathsf{par}, i, \boldsymbol{x})$: On input public parameters par, position i and input $\boldsymbol{x} =$ $x_1, \ldots, x_n$, the algorithm does the following: Let us denote the node values along the path from the root node with value MR, to the leaf node, with value $x[i]$, in the MHT as: $\mathcal{P} = (p_0, p_1, \ldots, p_d)$. Note that $p_0 = $ MR and $p_d = x[i]$. Let $\mathcal{P}_S = (p'_1, \ldots, p'_d)$ be the sibling path of $\mathcal{P}$ (note that p_0 has no sibling). Then, the algorithm computes $\mathcal{P}_S$ and outputs witness $(w = \mathcal{P}_S, x_i)$.

VC.Verify$(\mathsf{par}, i, \mathsf{com}, w, x)$: On input public parameters par, position i, commitment com = MR, witness (w, x), the algorithm parses w as $\mathcal{P}_S = (p'_1, \ldots, p'_d)$ and sets $p_d = x$. For each $j = d, \ldots 1$, the algorithm recursively computes the internal nodes by hashing the left and right child. Let $p_0 = H(p_1, p'_1)$ (if p_1 is the left sibling, $H(p'_1, p_1)$ otherwise.). This algorithm checks if MR $= p_0$. It outputs 1 if the equality holds, 0 otherwise.

VC.RandCommitment$(\mathsf{par}, \mathsf{com}, r)$: On input public parameters par, non-hiding vector commitment com = MR and randomness $r \in \mathcal{R}$, the algorithm invokes CS.Commit$(\mathsf{par}, \mathsf{MR}, r)$. Let CS.Commit$(\mathsf{par}, \mathsf{MR}, r)$ return $(\mathsf{com}_{\mathsf{MR}}, \mathsf{open}_{\mathsf{MR}})$. Output com$' = \mathsf{com}_{\mathsf{MR}}$.

VC.RandWitness$(\mathsf{par}, \mathsf{com}, i, r, w)$: On input public parameters par, non-hiding vector commitment com = MR, position i, randomness $r \in \mathcal{R}$ and a deterministic witness w, the algorithm does the following: (1) parses w as $\mathcal{P}_S = ((p'_1, \ldots, p'_d), v)$ (2) computes $(\mathsf{com}_{\mathsf{MR}}, \mathsf{open}_{\mathsf{MR}}) = $ CS.Commit$(\mathsf{par}, \mathsf{MR}, r)$ (3) computes $w' = (\mathcal{P}_S, v, \mathsf{com}_{\mathsf{MR}}, \mathsf{open}_{\mathsf{MR}})$ and outputs w'.

VC.Verify *for randomized witness: the only changes in the verification algorithm are the following: (1) parse w as $(\mathcal{P}_S = (p'_1, \ldots, p'_d), x_i, \mathsf{com}_{\mathsf{MR}}, \mathsf{open}_{\mathsf{MR}})$ (2) in the last step instead of checking if* MR $= p_0$, *check if* CS.Verify$(\mathsf{par}, \mathsf{com}_{\mathsf{MR}}, \mathsf{MR}, \mathsf{open}_{\mathsf{MR}}) = 1$. *The algorithm will output 1 if the equality holds, 0 otherwise.*

6 GSPK Proofs

In the following, we give the concrete implementations of our PoK protocols. To this end we require the CRS to contain the public key of the CPA version of the Camenisch-Shoup encryption scheme [9]. We already have the modulus N in the CRS which we can use. Recall that N is a product of two safe primes which can be generated distributedly [1]. Furthermore, let g' and y' and be a random elements of $\mathbb{Z}_{N^2}^*$ contained in the CRS and set $g = g'^{2N}$, $y = y'^{2N}$, and $h = 1 + N \bmod N^2$.

First we show how proof protocols π_{c00} and π_{c2} are realized. More specifically, the proof protocol

$$\pi_{c00} = \mathsf{PoK}\{(\underline{s}, \underline{r}) : \mathsf{com} = \mathsf{CS.Commit}(\mathsf{par}, s, r)\}$$

is realized by first computing $E_s = (g^{r_1} \bmod N^2, h^s y^{r_1} \bmod N^2)$, $E_r = (g^{r_2} \bmod N^2, h^r y^{r_2} \bmod N^2)$, and with r_1 and r_2 being randomly drawn from $[N/4]$, sending these values to the verifier, and the executing the following proof protocol with the verifier:

$$\mathsf{GSPK}\{(s, r, r_1, r_2) : \mathsf{com} = \mathsf{G}^s \mathsf{H}^r \wedge E_s = (g^{r_1}, h^s y^{r_1}) \wedge E_r = (g^{r_2}, h^r y^{r_2})\}$$

where we have dropped $\bmod \rho$ and $\bmod N^2$ from the terms for brevity.

Notice that, VC.RandCommitment is the same as CS.Commit algorithm, which computes a Pedersen commitment to the detVC, MR. So, π_{c01} will be just a standard proof of equality [9]. In fact, the following optimization can be done: use s' as com throughout the protocol and skip π_{c01}. The proof protocol

$$\pi_{c2} = \mathsf{PoK}\{(s, r_2, \underline{r_3}) : \mathsf{com} = \mathsf{CS.Commit}(\mathsf{par}, s; r_2) \wedge \mathsf{ct} = ([k][s])^{r_3}\}$$

is realized as follows: Let us denote $[k] = (e_1, e_2)$. The prover first computes $E_r = (g^{u_r} \bmod N^2, h^{r_3} y^{u_r} \bmod N^2)$, where u_r being randomly drawn from $[N/4]$, sends these values to the verifier, and executes the following proof protocol with the verifier:

$$\mathsf{GSPK}\{(s, r_2, r_3, w, r) : \mathsf{com} = \mathsf{G}^s \mathsf{H}^{r_2} \wedge 1 = \mathsf{com}^{-r_3} \mathsf{G}^w \mathsf{H}^{r'} \wedge$$
$$\mathsf{ct} = (e_1^{r_3} \mathsf{epk}^B \mathsf{h}^w, e_2^{r_3} \mathsf{g}^B) \wedge E_r = (g^{u_r}, h^{r_3} y^{u_r})\}$$

Here, the term $1 = \mathsf{com}^{-r_3} \mathsf{G}^w \mathsf{H}^{r'}$ shows that $w = sr_3$ and hence that $\mathsf{ct} = ([k][s])^{r_3}$ with B being the value that the prover used to randomize the encryption.

For the proofs π_j: $\mathsf{PoK}\{(\underline{w}, \underline{x}) : 1 = \mathsf{randVC.Verify}(\mathsf{par}, j, \mathsf{com}, w, x)\}$, proving these relations is a bit more involved and requires the following steps:

1. The algorithm parses w as $(\mathcal{P}_S = (p'_1, \ldots, p'_d), \mathsf{com}_{\mathsf{MR}}, \mathsf{open}_{\mathsf{MR}})$. Let us denote the node values along the path from the root node with value MR, to the leaf node, with value x_i, in the MHT as: $\mathcal{P} = (p_0, p_1, \ldots, p_d)$. The algorithm recovers this path recursively bottom up using $H(\cdot, \cdot)$ on $\mathcal{P}_S$. Note that the index position j uniquely decides the left and the right child at each step.
2. Then, the algorithm commits to every value p_j in this path and to the values of the left and right children of p_j in the MHT, i.e., if l_j is the left child and r_j is the right child of p_j, then the algorithm computes

$$(P_j, s_j) \leftarrow \mathsf{CS.Commit}(\mathsf{par}, p_j, s_j), (L_j, s'_j) \leftarrow \mathsf{CS.Commit}(\mathsf{par}, l_j, s'_j),$$
$$(R_j, s''_j) \leftarrow \mathsf{CS.Commit}(\mathsf{par}, r_j, s''_j)$$

3. Then, the algorithm generates a proof that P_0 is indeed a commitment to the root.[7]

$$\mathsf{PoK_{MR}}\{(\underline{\mathsf{MR}}, \underline{r}, \underline{s}) : \mathsf{com} = \mathsf{CS.Commit(par, MR}, r) \wedge P_0 = \mathsf{CS.Commit(par, MR}, s)\}$$

4. Next, for $j = 0, \ldots, d - 1$, the following proof of knowledge that each triplet (P_j, L_j, R_j) is well formed. Note that L_j (or R_j) is used as P_{j+1}.

$$\mathsf{PoK}_j\{(\underline{l}, \underline{r}, s, s', s'') : P_j = \mathsf{CS.Commit(par}, l^7 + 3r^7, s) \wedge$$
$$L_j = \mathsf{CS.Commit(par}, l, s') \wedge R_j = \mathsf{CS.Commit(par}, r, s'')\}$$

This proof requires some sub steps which are the following:

(a) This proof uses the homomorphic property of Pedersen commitment scheme and a subprotocol for $\mathsf{PoK_{mult}}$ for multiplication of two values. This protocol is instantiated using standard techniques [5,9].

$$\mathsf{PoK_{mult}}\{(\underline{x}, \underline{y}, \underline{z}, s_x, s_y, s_z) : C_x = \mathsf{CS.Commit(par}, x, s_x) \wedge$$
$$C_y = \mathsf{CS.Commit(par}, y, s_y) \wedge C_z = \mathsf{CS.Commit(par}, z, s_z) \wedge z = x \cdot y\}$$

(b) The prover computes $C_l, C_{l^2}, C_{l^4}, C_{l^6}, C_{l^7}$ and $C_r, C_{r^2}, C_{r^4}, C_{r^6}, C_{r^7}$ and invokes $\mathsf{PoK_{mult}}$ on each of the following triplets to prove the correctness of the commitments and sends them to the verifier.

$$(C_l, C_l, C_{l^2}) \quad (C_{l^2}, C_{l^2}, C_{l^4}) \quad (C_{l^2}, C_{l^4}, C_{l^6}) \quad (C_l, C_{l^6}, C_{l^7})$$
$$(C_r, C_r, C_{r^2}) \quad (C_{r^2}, C_{r^2}, C_{r^4}) \quad (C_r, C_{r^4}, C_{r^6}) \quad (C_r, C_{r^6}, C_{r^7})$$

Now we show how to realize proof protocols $\mathsf{PoK_{MR}}$ and $\mathsf{PoK_{mult}}$ for our MHT-VC. In details, the proof protocol

$$\mathsf{PoK_{MR}}\{(\underline{\mathsf{MR}}, \underline{r}, \underline{s}) : \mathsf{com} = \mathsf{CS.Commit(par, MR}, r) \wedge$$
$$P_0 = \mathsf{CS.Commit(par, MR}, s)\}$$

is done as first computing $\mathsf{E_{MR}} = (g^{r_1} \bmod N^2, h^{\mathsf{MR}} y^{r_1} \bmod N^2)$, $\mathsf{E}_r = (g^{r_2} \bmod N^2, h^r y^{r_2} \bmod N^2)$, and $\mathsf{E}_s = (g^{r_3} \bmod N^2, h^s y^{r_3} \bmod N^2)$, with $r_1, r_2,$ and r_3 being randomly drawn from $[N/4]$, sending these values to the verifier, and then executing the following proof protocol with the verifier

$$\mathsf{GSPK}\{(\mathsf{MR}, r, s, r_1, r_2, r_3) : \mathsf{com} = \mathsf{G^{MR} H}^r \wedge P_0 = \mathsf{G^{MR} H}^r \wedge$$
$$\mathsf{E_{MR}} = (g^{r_1}, h^{\mathsf{MR}} y^{r_1}) \wedge \mathsf{E}_r = (g^{r_2}, h^r y^{r_2}) \wedge \mathsf{E}_s = (g^{r_3}, h^s y^{r_3})\} ,$$

where we have dropped $\bmod \rho$ and $\bmod N^2$ from the terms for brevity.

---

[7] We are going to abuse the notation a little and ignore the **open** in the output of CS.Commit for notational convenience.

On the other hand, proof protocol

$$\mathsf{PoK}_{\mathsf{mult}}\{(\underline{x},\underline{y},\underline{z},s_x,s_y,s_z): C_x = \mathsf{CS.Commit}(\mathsf{par},x,s_x)\wedge$$
$$C_y = \mathsf{CS.Commit}(\mathsf{par},y,s_y)\wedge C_z = \mathsf{CS.Commit}(\mathsf{par},c_z,s_z)\wedge z = x\cdot y\}$$

is done by first computing $\mathsf{E}_x = (g^{u_1} \bmod N^2, h^x y^{u_1} \bmod N^2)$ and $\mathsf{E}_y = (g^{u_2} \bmod N^2, h^y y^{u_2} \bmod N^2)$, with r_1 and r_2 being randomly drawn from $[N/4]$, sending these values to the verifier, and then executing the following proof protocol with the verifier:

$$\mathsf{GSPK}\{(x,y,z,s_x,s_y,s_z,s',u_1,u_2): C_x = \mathsf{G}^x\mathsf{H}^{s_x} \wedge\ C_y = \mathsf{G}^y\mathsf{H}^{s_y}\wedge$$
$$C_z = \mathsf{G}^z\mathsf{H}^{s_z} \wedge\ C_z = C_y^x\mathsf{H}^{s'} \wedge\ \mathsf{E}_x = (g^{u_1},h^x y^{u_1}) \wedge\ \mathsf{E}_y = (g^{u_2},h^y y^{u_2})\}\ .$$

Notice that we do not need to verifiably encrypt the witness z as this one can be computed from x and y. Similarly, a number of encryptions can be dropped when combing these proofs into the bigger proof of the hash-tree path. We leave these optimizations to the reader.

7   Conclusion

In this paper, we identified an important problem of secure data deduplication that has been overlooked in the prior approaches. Motivated by this problem, we propose a new primitive for oblivious pseudo-random function (OPRF) on committed vector inputs in the universal composability (UC) framework and give efficient constructions for OPRF. We believe this new primitive will find applications beyond secure data-deduplication. Improving the concrete efficiency of the OPRF protocol on committed vector inputs is an interesting direction to explore.

References

1. Algesheimer, J., Camenisch, J., Shoup, V.: Efficient computation modulo a shared secret with application to the generation of shared safe-prime products. In: Yung, M. (ed.) CRYPTO 2002. LNCS, vol. 2442, pp. 417–432. Springer, Heidelberg (2002). https://doi.org/10.1007/3-540-45708-9_27
2. Boneh, D., Boyen, X.: Short signatures without random oracles. In: Cachin, C., Camenisch, J.L. (eds.) EUROCRYPT 2004. LNCS, vol. 3027, pp. 56–73. Springer, Heidelberg (2004). https://doi.org/10.1007/978-3-540-24676-3_4
3. Boneh, D., Bünz, B., Fisch, B.: Batching techniques for accumulators with applications to IOPs and stateless blockchains. Cryptology ePrint Archive, Report 2018/1188 (2018)
4. Boneh, D., Corrigan-Gibbs, H.: Bivariate polynomials modulo composites and their applications. In: Sarkar, P., Iwata, T. (eds.) ASIACRYPT 2014. LNCS, vol. 8873, pp. 42–62. Springer, Heidelberg (2014). https://doi.org/10.1007/978-3-662-45611-8_3

5. Bootle, J., Cerulli, A., Chaidos, P., Groth, J.: Efficient zero-knowledge proof systems. In: Aldini, A., Lopez, J., Martinelli, F. (eds.) FOSAD 2015-2016. LNCS, vol. 9808, pp. 1–31. Springer, Cham (2016). https://doi.org/10.1007/978-3-319-43005-8_1

6. Camenisch, J., Caro, A.D., Ghosh, E., Sorniotti, A.: Oblivious PRF on committed vector inputs and application to deduplication of encrypted data. IACR Cryptology ePrint Archive 2019 (2019). https://eprint.iacr.org/2019

7. Camenisch, J., Dubovitskaya, M., Rial, A.: UC commitments for modular protocol design and applications to revocation and attribute tokens. In: Robshaw, M., Katz, J. (eds.) CRYPTO 2016. LNCS, vol. 9816, pp. 208–239. Springer, Heidelberg (2016). https://doi.org/10.1007/978-3-662-53015-3_8

8. Camenisch, J., Kiayias, A., Yung, M.: On the portability of Generalized Schnorr Proofs. In: Joux, A. (ed.) EUROCRYPT 2009. LNCS, vol. 5479, pp. 425–442. Springer, Heidelberg (2009). https://doi.org/10.1007/978-3-642-01001-9_25

9. Camenisch, J., Shoup, V.: Practical verifiable encryption and decryption of discrete logarithms. In: Boneh, D. (ed.) CRYPTO 2003. LNCS, vol. 2729, pp. 126–144. Springer, Heidelberg (2003). https://doi.org/10.1007/978-3-540-45146-4_8

10. Camenisch, J., Stadler, M.: Efficient group signature schemes for large groups. In: Kaliski, B.S. (ed.) CRYPTO 1997. LNCS, vol. 1294, pp. 410–424. Springer, Heidelberg (1997). https://doi.org/10.1007/BFb0052252

11. Canetti, R.: Universally composable security: a new paradigm for cryptographic protocols. In: 42nd FOCS, pp. 136–145. IEEE Computer Society Press (2001)

12. Canetti, R.: Universally composable signatures, certification and authentication. Cryptology ePrint Archive, Report 2003/239 (2003). http://eprint.iacr.org/2003/239

13. Catalano, D., Fiore, D.: Vector commitments and their applications. In: Kurosawa, K., Hanaoka, G. (eds.) PKC 2013. LNCS, vol. 7778, pp. 55–72. Springer, Heidelberg (2013). https://doi.org/10.1007/978-3-642-36362-7_5

14. Chase, M., Meiklejohn, S.: Déjà Q: using dual systems to revisit q-type assumptions. In: Nguyen, P.Q., Oswald, E. (eds.) EUROCRYPT 2014. LNCS, vol. 8441, pp. 622–639. Springer, Heidelberg (2014). https://doi.org/10.1007/978-3-642-55220-5_34

15. Damgård, I.: Efficient concurrent zero-knowledge in the auxiliary string model. In: Preneel, B. (ed.) EUROCRYPT 2000. LNCS, vol. 1807, pp. 418–430. Springer, Heidelberg (2000). https://doi.org/10.1007/3-540-45539-6_30

16. Dodis, Y., Shoup, V., Walfish, S.: Efficient constructions of composable commitments and zero-knowledge proofs. In: Wagner, D. (ed.) CRYPTO 2008. LNCS, vol. 5157, pp. 515–535. Springer, Heidelberg (2008). https://doi.org/10.1007/978-3-540-85174-5_29

17. Dodis, Y., Yampolskiy, A.: A verifiable random function with short proofs and keys. In: Vaudenay, S. (ed.) PKC 2005. LNCS, vol. 3386, pp. 416–431. Springer, Heidelberg (2005). https://doi.org/10.1007/978-3-540-30580-4_28

18. Freedman, M.J., Ishai, Y., Pinkas, B., Reingold, O.: Keyword search and oblivious pseudorandom functions. In: Kilian, J. (ed.) TCC 2005. LNCS, vol. 3378, pp. 303–324. Springer, Heidelberg (2005). https://doi.org/10.1007/978-3-540-30576-7_17

19. Halevi, S., Harnik, D., Pinkas, B., Shulman-Peleg, A.: Proofs of ownership in remote storage systems. In: Chen, Y., Danezis, G., Shmatikov, V. (eds.) ACM CCS 2011, pp. 491–500. ACM Press (2011)

20. Jarecki, S., Kiayias, A., Krawczyk, H., Xu, J.: Highly-efficient and composable password-protected secret sharing (or: How to protect your bitcoin wallet online). In: EuroS&P, pp. 276–291 (2016). https://doi.org/10.1109/EuroSP.2016.30

21. Jarecki, S., Liu, X.: Efficient oblivious pseudorandom function with applications to adaptive OT and secure computation of set intersection. In: Reingold, O. (ed.) TCC 2009. LNCS, vol. 5444, pp. 577–594. Springer, Heidelberg (2009). https://doi.org/10.1007/978-3-642-00457-5_34

22. Keelveedhi, S., Bellare, M., Ristenpart, T.: Dupless: server-aided encryption for deduplicated storage. In: USENIX Security 2013, pp. 179–194. USENIX (2013). https://www.usenix.org/conference/usenixsecurity13/technical-sessions/presentation/bellare

23. Liu, J., Asokan, N., Pinkas, B.: Secure deduplication of encrypted data without additional independent servers. In: Ray, I., Li, N., Kruegel, C. (eds.) ACM CCS 2015, pp. 874–885. ACM Press (2015)

24. Meyer, D.T., Bolosky, W.J.: A study of practical deduplication. Trans. Storage **7**(4), 14:1–14:20 (2012). https://doi.org/10.1145/2078861.2078864

25. Pedersen, T.P.: Non-interactive and information-theoretic secure verifiable secret sharing. In: Feigenbaum, J. (ed.) CRYPTO 1991. LNCS, vol. 576, pp. 129–140. Springer, Heidelberg (1992). https://doi.org/10.1007/3-540-46766-1_9

26. Shacham, H., Waters, B.: Compact proofs of retrievability. In: Pieprzyk, J. (ed.) ASIACRYPT 2008. LNCS, vol. 5350, pp. 90–107. Springer, Heidelberg (2008). https://doi.org/10.1007/978-3-540-89255-7_7

27. Visconti, I.: Efficient zero knowledge on the internet. In: Bugliesi, M., Preneel, B., Sassone, V., Wegener, I. (eds.) ICALP 2006. LNCS, vol. 4052, pp. 22–33. Springer, Heidelberg (2006). https://doi.org/10.1007/11787006_3

Adaptively Secure Constrained Pseudorandom Functions

Dennis Hofheinz[1], Akshay Kamath[2], Venkata Koppula[3(✉)], and Brent Waters[2]

[1] Karlsruhe Institute of Technology, Karlsruhe, Germany
dennis.hofheinz@kit.edu
[2] University of Texas at Austin, Austin, USA
{kamath,bwaters}@cs.utexas.edu
[3] Weizmann Institute of Science, Rehovot, Israel
venkata.koppula@weizmann.ac.il

Abstract. A constrained pseudo random function (PRF) behaves like a standard PRF, but with the added feature that the (master) secret key holder, having secret key K, can produce a constrained key, K_f, that allows for the evaluation of the PRF on a subset of the domain as determined by a predicate function f within some family $\mathcal{F}$. While previous constructions gave constrained PRFs for poly-sized circuits, all reductions for such functionality were based in the selective model of security where an attacker declares which point he is attacking before seeing any constrained keys.

In this paper we give new constrained PRF constructions for arbitrary circuits in the random oracle model based on indistinguishability obfuscation. Our solution is constructed from two recently emerged primitives: an adaptively secure Attribute-Based Encryption (ABE) for circuits and a Universal Sampler Scheme as introduced by Hofheinz et al. Both primitives are constructible from indistinguishability obfuscation ($i\mathcal{O}$) (and injective pseudorandom generators) with only polynomial loss.

1 Introduction

Constrained Pseudorandom Functions. The concept of constrained pseudorandom functions (constrained PRFs) was proposed independently by Boneh and Waters [5], Boyle, Goldwasser and Ivan [7] and Kiayias et al. [23]. A constrained PRF like a standard PRF [16], but with the added feature that the (master) secret key holder, having secret key K, can produce a constrained key, K_f, that allows for the evaluation of the PRF on a subset of the domain as determined by a predicate function f within some family $\mathcal{F}$. The security definition of a constrained PRF system allows for a poly-time attacker to query adaptively on several functions $f_1, \ldots, f_Q$ and receive constrained keys $K_{f_1}, \ldots, K_{f_Q}$. Later

Supported by NSF CNS-0952692, CNS-1228599 and CNS-1414082. DARPA through the U.S. Office of Naval Research under Contract N00014-11-1-0382, Google Faculty Research award, the Alfred P. Sloan Fellowship, Microsoft Faculty Fellowship, and Packard Foundation Fellowship.

I. Goldberg and T. Moore (Eds.): FC 2019, LNCS 11598, pp. 357–376, 2019.
https://doi.org/10.1007/978-3-030-32101-7_22

the attacker chooses a challenge point x^* such that $f_i(x^*) = 0$ $\forall i$. The attacker should not be able to distinguish between the output of the PRF $F(K, x^*)$ and a randomly chosen value with better than negligible probability.

Constrained PRFs can hence be seen as PRFs in which the ability to evaluate the PRF can be delegated, using a constrained key. This feature has proved useful in various applications, e.g., broadcast encryption [5], multiparty key exchange [6] and the development of "punctured programming" techniques using obfuscation [28].

Ideally, we would like to have constrained PRFs that are as universally useful as possible. In particular, they should support as expressive constraints, and thus delegation capabilities, as possible. In their initial work, Boneh and Waters [5] gave a construction for building constrained PRFs for polynomial sized circuits (with a priori fixed depth) based on multilinear encodings [11, 13]. Furthermore, they demonstrated the power of constrained PRFs with several motivating applications.

For instance, one application (detailed in [5]) is a (secret encryption key) broadcast key encapsulation mechanism with "optimal size ciphertexts", where the ciphertext consists solely of a header describing the recipient list S. The main idea is that the key assigned to a set S is simply the PRF evaluated on S as $F(K, S)$. A user i in the system is assigned a key for a function $f_i(\cdot)$, where $f_i(S) = 1$ if and only if $i \in S$. Other natural applications given include identity-based key exchange and a form of non-interactive policy-based key distribution. Later Sahai and Waters [28] showed the utility of (a limited form of) constrained PRFs in building cryptography from indistinguishability obfuscation and Boneh and Zhandry [6] used them (along with obfuscation) in constructing recipient private broadcast encryption.

Focus: Adaptive Security. While the functionality of the Boneh-Waters construction was expressive, their proof reduction was limited to selective security where the challenge point x^* is declared by the attacker before it makes any queries. For many applications of constrained PRFs, achieving adaptive security requires an underlying adaptively secure constrained PRF. In particular, this applies to the optimal size broadcast, policy-based encryption, non-interactive key exchange and recipient-private broadcast constructions mentioned above.

In this work we are interested in exploring adaptive security in constrained PRFs. Hence, we are interested in the question

Is there an adaptively secure constrained PRF for expressive families of constraints? Specifically, is there an adaptively secure constrained PRF for the family of poly-sized circuits?

Any selectively secure constrained PRF can be proven adaptively secure if one is willing to use a technique called complexity leveraging (as used, e.g., in the context of IBE schemes [4]). This technique, however, leads to a reduction with superpolynomial loss (which leads to a significant quantitative loss in security), and thus it can be desirable to look for alternative ways to achieve adaptive security. Hence, here we are interested in polynomial-time reductions, and thus in avoiding complexity leveraging.

Up until now, constrained PRF constructions that achieve adaptive security have relatively limited functionality. Hohenberger, Koppula, and Waters [21] show how to build adaptive security from indistinguishability obfuscation for a special type of constrained PRFs called puncturable PRF. In a puncturable PRF system the attacker is allowed to make several point queries adaptively, before choosing a challenge point x^* and receiving a key that allows for evaluation at all points $x \neq x^*$. While their work presents progress in this area, there is a large functionality gap between the family of all poly-sized circuits and puncturing-type functions. Fuchsbauer et al. [12] give a subexponential reduction to obfuscation for a larger class of "prefix-type" circuits, however, their reduction is still super polynomial. In addition, they give evidence that the problem of achieving full security with polynomial reductions might be difficult. They adapt the proof of [24] to show a black box impossibility result for a certain class of "fingerprinting" constructions that include the original Boneh-Waters [5] scheme.

The Difficulty of Achieving Adaptive Security (and Why We Utilize the Random Oracle Model). In order to describe the technical problem that arises with adaptively secure constrained PRFs, say that we want to construct a bit-fixing constrained PRF F, i.e., one that allows for constrained keys $K_{f_{\overline{x}}}$ for "bit-matching" predicates of the form $f_{\overline{x}}(x) = 1 \Leftrightarrow \forall i : x_i = \overline{x}_i \vee \overline{x}_i = \bot$ with $\overline{x} = (\overline{x}_i)_{i=1}^n \in (\{0,1\} \cup \{\bot\})^n$. An adversary A on F may first ask for polynomially many constrained keys $K_{f_{\overline{x}}}$, and then gets challenged on a preimage x^*. The goal of a successful simulation is to be able to prepare all $K_{f_{\overline{x}}}$, but *not* to be able to compute $F(K, x^*)$.

Now if $x^* = (x_i^*)_{i=1}^n$ is known in advance, then the simulation can set up the function $F(K, \cdot)$ in an "all-but-one" way, such that all images except $F(K, x^*)$ can be computed. For instance, the selective-security simulation from [5] sets up

$$F(K, x) = e(g, \ldots, g)^{\prod_{i=1}^n \alpha_{i,x_i}} \qquad (\text{for } K = (\alpha_{i,b})_{i,b}), \qquad (1)$$

where e is an $(n-1)$-linear map, and the simulation knows all $\alpha_{i,1-x_i^*}$ (while the α_{i,x_i^*} are only known "in the exponent," as $g^{\alpha_{i,x_i^*}}$). This setup not only allows to compute $F(K, x)$ as soon as there is an i with $x_i \neq x_i^*$ (such that the corresponding $\alpha_{i,x_i} = \alpha_{i,1-x_i^*}$ is known); also, assuming a graded multilinear map, evaluation can be *delegated*. (For instance, a constrained key that allows to evaluate all inputs with $x_1 = 1$ would contain $\alpha_{1,1}$ and $g^{\alpha_{i,b}}$ for all other i, b.)

However, observe now what happens when A chooses the challenge preimage x^* only *after* asking for constrained keys. Then, the simulation may be forced to commit to the full function $F(K, \cdot)$ (information-theoretically) before even knowing where "not to be able to evaluate." For instance, for the constrained PRF from [5] sketched above, already a few suitably chosen constrained keys (for predicates f_i) fully determine $F(K, \cdot)$, while the corresponding predicates f_i leave exponentially many potential challenge preimages x^* uncovered. If we assume that the simulation either can or cannot evaluate $F(K, x)$ on a given preimage x (at least once $F(K, \cdot)$ is fully determined), we have the following dilemma. Let $\mathcal{C}$ be set of preimages that the simulation *cannot* evaluate. If $\mathcal{C}$ is too small, then $x^* \in \mathcal{C}$ will not happen sufficiently often, so that the simulation cannot learn anything from A. But if $\mathcal{C}$ is too large, then the simulation will not be able to construct "sufficiently general" constrained keys for A (because the corresponding predicates f would evaluate to 1 on some elements of $\mathcal{C}$).[1]

This argument eliminates not only guessing x^* (at least when aiming at a polynomial reduction), but also the popular class of "partitioning arguments". (Namely, while guessing x^* corresponds to $|\mathcal{C}| = 1$ above, partitioning arguments consider larger sets $\mathcal{C}$. However, the argument above excludes sets $\mathcal{C}$ of *any* size for relevant classes of constraining predicates and superpolynomial preimage space.) In particular, since the selectively-secure constrained PRFs from [5,7,23] fulfill the assumptions of the argument, it seems hopeless to prove them fully secure, at least for standard preimage sizes.

Hence, to obtain adaptively secure constrained PRFs, we feel that leaving the standard model of computation is unavoidable, and so we utilize the random oracle for our security analysis.

The Random Oracle Model Versus the Random Oracle Heuristic. When attempting to instantiate a scheme described and proven in the random oracle model the most common method is to apply the heuristic [3] of replacing oracle calls with an evaluation of a hash function such as SHA-256. This heuristic has been (apparently) successful for a number of deployed cryptographic schemes (e.g., [22,29]), but on the other hand there are well documented [9] issues with this heuristic.

While the random oracle heuristic is tightly associated with the random oracle model, we wish to emphasize that there are potentially other avenues to instantiate the model. In particular, one could try to realize a random oracle like object via specialized and limited trusted hardware or a distributed consensus protocol such as a blockchain. It could even be the case that an existing blockchain could be obliviously leveraged for such a functionality in a similar vein to the work Goyal and Goyal [18] for one time programs.

Our Contributions. In this paper, we give an affirmative answer to the question above. That is, we present the first constrained PRF constructions for poly-sized circuits[2] that have polynomial reductions to indistinguishability obfuscation in the random oracle model. While our construction does use heavy tools such as indistinguishability obfuscation, and our proof involves the random oracle heuristic, we wish to emphasize that our solution is currently the only known one for this problem. Moreover, recent results [1] have shown that for certain

---

[1] In fact, for many classes of allowed constraining predicates, A can easily ask for constrained keys that, taken together, allow to evaluate $F(K, \cdot)$ *everywhere* except on x^*. For instance, in our case, A could ask for all keys K_{f_i} with $f_i(x) = 1 \Leftrightarrow x_i = 1 - x_i^*$. Hence, in this case, the simulation *must* fail already whenever $|\mathcal{C}| \geq 2$.

[2] More specifically, we present a construction for polynomial-sized circuits of any apriori bounded depth.

problems, it is impossible to get the desired security guarantees, even assuming the existence of indistinguishability obfuscation and the random oracle heuristic.

Ingredients Used in Our Construction. Our solution is constructed from two recently emerged primitives: an adaptively secure Attribute-Based Encryption (ABE) [27] for circuits and Universal Samplers as introduced by Hofheinz et al. [19]. Both primitives are constructible from indistinguishability obfuscation $(i\mathcal{O})$ (and injective pseudorandom generators) with only polynomial loss. Waters [30] recently gave an adaptively secure construction of ABE[3] based on indistinguishability obfuscation and Hofheinz et al. [19] showed how to build Universal Samplers from $i\mathcal{O}$ in the random oracle model—emphasizing that the random oracle heuristic is applied outside the obfuscated program.

Before we describe our construction we briefly overview the two underlying primitives. An ABE scheme (for circuits) has four algorithms. A setup algorithm $\mathsf{ABE.setup}(1^\lambda)$ that outputs public parameters $\mathsf{pk}_{\mathsf{ABE}}$, and a master secret key $\mathsf{msk}_{\mathsf{ABE}}$. The encryption algorithm $\mathsf{ABE.enc}(\mathsf{pk}_{\mathsf{ABE}}, t, x)$ takes in the public parameters, message t, and "attribute" string x and outputs a ciphertext c. A key generation algorithm $\mathsf{ABE.keygen}(\mathsf{msk}_{\mathsf{ABE}}, C)$ outputs a secret key given a boolean circuit C. Finally, the decryption algorithm $\mathsf{ABE.dec}(\mathsf{SK}, c)$ will decrypt an ABE ciphertext encrypted under attribute x iff $C(x) = 1$, where C is the circuit associated with the secret key.

The second primitive is a universal sampler scheme. Intuitively, a universal sampler scheme behaves somewhat like a random oracle except it can sample from arbitrary distributions as opposed to just uniformly random strings. More concretely, a universal sampler scheme consists of two algorithms, $\mathsf{US.setup}$ and $\mathsf{US.sample}$. In a set-up phase, $U \leftarrow \mathsf{US.setup}(1^\lambda)$ will take as input a security parameter and output "sampler parameters" U. We can use these parameters to "obliviously" sample from a distribution specified by a circuit d, in the following sense. If we call $\mathsf{US.sample}(U, d)$ the scheme will output $d(z)$ for hidden random coins z that are pseudorandomly derived from U and d.

Security requires that in the random oracle model, $\mathsf{US.setup}$ outputs images that look like independently and honestly generated d-samples, in the following sense. We require that an efficient simulator can simulate U and the random oracle such that the output of $\mathsf{US.sample}$ on arbitrarily many adversarially chosen inputs d_i coincides with independently and honestly chosen images $d_i(z_i)$ (for truly random z_i that are hidden even from the simulator). Of course, the simulated U and the programmed random oracle must be computationally indistinguishable from the real setting.

Our Solution in a Nutshell. We now describe our construction that shows how to build constrained PRFs from adaptively secure ABE and universal samplers. One remarkable feature is the simplicity of our construction once the underlying building blocks are in place.

The constrained PRF key is setup by first running $U \leftarrow \mathsf{US.setup}(1^\lambda)$ and $(\mathsf{pk}_{\mathsf{ABE}}, \mathsf{msk}_{\mathsf{ABE}}) \leftarrow \mathsf{ABE.setup}(1^\lambda)$. The master PRF key K is

---

[3] The construction is actually for Functional Encryption which implies ABE.

$(U, (\mathsf{pk}_{\mathsf{ABE}}, \mathsf{msk}_{\mathsf{ABE}}))$. To define the PRF evaluation on input x we let $d_{\mathsf{pk}_{\mathsf{ABE}}, x}(z = (t, r))$ be a circuit in some canonical form that takes as input random $z = (t, r)$ and computes $\mathsf{ABE.enc}(\mathsf{pk}_{\mathsf{ABE}}, t, x; r)$. Here we view $\mathsf{pk}_{\mathsf{ABE}}, x$ as constants hard-wired into the circuit d and t, r as the inputs, where we make the random coins of the encryption algorithm explicit. To evaluate the PRF $F(K, x)$ we first compute $c_x = \mathsf{US.sample}(U, d_{\mathsf{pk}_{\mathsf{ABE}}, x})$. Then we compute and output $\mathsf{ABE.dec}(\mathsf{msk}_{\mathsf{ABE}}, c_x)^4$. Essentially, the evaluation function on input x first uses the universal sampler to encrypt an ABE ciphertext under attribute x for a randomly chosen message t. Then it uses the master secret key to decrypt the ciphertext which gives t as the output.

To generate a constrained key for circuits C, the master key holder simply runs the ABE key generation to compute $\mathsf{sk}_C = \mathsf{ABE.keygen}(\mathsf{msk}_{\mathsf{ABE}}, C)$ and sets the constrained key to be $K\{C\} = (U, (\mathsf{pk}_{\mathsf{ABE}}, \mathsf{sk}_C))$. Evaluation can be done using $K\{C\}$ on input x where $C(x) = 1$. Simply compute c_x from the sampler parameters U as above, but then use sk_C to decrypt. The output will be consistent with the master key evaluation.

The security argument is organized as follows. We first introduce a hybrid game where the calls to the universal sampler scheme are answered by a sampling oracle that generates a fresh sample every time it is called. The security definition of universal samplers schemes argues (in the random oracle model) that the attacker's advantage in this game must be negligibly close to the original advantage. Furthermore, any polynomial time attacker will cause this samples oracle to be called at most some polynomial Q number of times. One of these calls must correspond to the eventual challenge input x^*.

We can now reduce to the security of the underlying ABE scheme. First the reduction guesses with $1/Q$ success probability which samples oracle call will correspond to x^* and embed an ABE challenge ciphertext here. An attacker on the constrained PRF scheme now maps straightforwardly to an ABE attacker.

Future Directions. A clear future direction is to attempt to achieve greater functionality in the standard model. There is a significant gap between our random oracle model results of constrained PRFs for all circuits and the standard model results of Hohenberger, Koppula, and Waters for puncturable PRFs [21]. It would be interesting to understand if there are fundamental limitations to achieving such results. Fuchsbauer et al. [12] give some initial steps to negative results, however, it is unclear if they generalize to larger classes of constructions.

Other Related Work. Attribute-Based Encryption for circuits was first achieved independently by Garg, Gentry, Halevi, Sahai and Waters [14] from multilinear maps and by Gorbunov, Vaikuntanathan and Wee [17] from the learning with errors [26] assumption. Both works were proven selectively secure; requiring complexity leveraging for adaptive security. In two recent works, Waters [30] and Garg, Gentry, Halevi and Zhandry [15] achieve adaptively secure ABE for

---

[4] We use the convention that the master secret key can decrypt all honestly generated ABE ciphertexts. Alternatively, one could just generate a secret key for a circuit that always outputs 1 and use this to decrypt.

circuits under different cryptographic assumptions. We also note that Boneh and Zhandry [6] show how to use indistinguishability obfuscation for circuits and punctured PRFs to create constrained PRFs for circuits. This construction is limited though to either selective security or utilizing complexity leveraging.

In a recent work, Brakerski and Vaikunthanathan [8] showed a constrained PRF construction that is secure against single query attackers based on the LWE assumption. However, our construction and motivating applications are concerned with the case of multiple queries or collusions.

1.1 Discussion of Our Assumptions

Our construction uses "heavyweight" tools (i.e., indistinguishability obfuscation and random oracles) for a problem that can also be solved in a much simpler way with complexity leveraging. In this section, we would like to argue the benefits of a "more structured" solution like ours. Specifically, while an ideal or "last word" solution would be given under better assumptions, we feel that our work makes interesting progress that sets a bar for the future work to try to overcome.

One obvious way to relax the required assumptions for our work would be to only build on *one* heavyweight assumption (instead of two, as we do). In other words, this would mean to remove the random oracle or work under standard assumptions with a random oracle. While we definitely agree this would be an improvement, either one of these appears to require completely new techniques. For instance, consider the task of achieving expressive constrained PRFs from standard assumptions (that is, assumptions not based on indistinguishability obfuscation/multilinear maps). Currently, there are no known collusion-resistant constrained PRFs from standard assumptions. Achieving such a constrained PRF would be highly surprising even if it were selectively (not adaptively secure), used subexponential assumptions and the random oracle model.

On the other hand, consider the problem of achieving adaptive security from indistinguishability obfuscation alone, avoiding random oracles. The most similar problem to this is achieving adaptive security in Attribute-Based Encryption schemes. All such solutions in this regime have used dual system encryption (or similar) techniques. With those techniques, the simulation maintains and manipulates a special relationship between the private keys and challenge ciphertext. This lets one circumvent impossibilities and lower bounds such as the ones from [10, 20, 24]. In constrained PRFs there are no challenge ciphertexts (only an input point) so the only techniques we know do not apply. Indeed, our contribution, which uses random oracles (in a rather nontrivial way), proposes some approach to this problem. We think our work helps make the challenge clear to the community.

A fine point here is that known approaches to proving indistinguishability obfuscation from non-interactive assumptions seem to already imply some form of complexity leveraging or sub-exponential hardness. So given that we can get adaptive security with sub-exponential hardness anyway, why should our approach help? While we understand this argument, we think it can be misleading. For example, [30] gave an adaptively secure functional encryption scheme from indistinguishability obfuscation where one could have given the exact same ratio-nale. In fact, later [2] built upon these ideas to give a generic selective to adaptive FE conversion where subexponential hardness is not inherent. For our case, we currently do not have such a next step, but it is well possible some future work could find it. As a starting point, [25, Section 1.5] provide an interesting dis-cussion about how in the future one might avoid the subexponential barrier in indistinguishability obfuscation for certain cases.

2   Preliminaries

2.1   Notations

Let $x \leftarrow \mathcal{X}$ denote a uniformly random element drawn from the set $\mathcal{X}$. Given integers $\ell_{ckt}, \ell_{inp}, \ell_{out}$, let $\mathcal{C}[\ell_{ckt}, \ell_{inp}, \ell_{out}]$ denote the set of circuits that can be represented using ℓ_{ckt} bits, take ℓ_{inp} bits input and output ℓ_{out} bits.

2.2   Constrained Pseudorandom Functions

The notion of constrained pseudorandom functions was introduced in the con-current works of [5,7,23]. Let $\mathcal{K}$ denote the key space, $\mathcal{X}$ the input domain and $\mathcal{Y}$ the range space. A PRF $F : \mathcal{K} \times \mathcal{X} \to \mathcal{Y}$ is said to be *constrained* with respect to a boolean circuit family $\mathcal{F}$ if there is an additional key space $\mathcal{K}_c$, and three algorithms F.setup, F.constrain and F.eval as follows:

- F.setup(1^λ) is a PPT algorithm that takes the security parameter λ as input and outputs a key $K \in \mathcal{K}$.
- F.constrain(K, C) is a PPT algorithm that takes as input a PRF key $K \in \mathcal{K}$ and a circuit $C \in \mathcal{F}$ and outputs a constrained key $K\{C\} \in \mathcal{K}_c$.
- F.eval($K\{C\}, x$) is a deterministic polynomial time algorithm that takes as input a constrained key $K\{C\} \in \mathcal{K}_c$ and $x \in \mathcal{X}$ and outputs an element $y \in \mathcal{Y}$. Let $K\{C\}$ be the output of F.constrain(K, C). For correctness, we require that for all security parameters $\lambda \in \mathbb{N}$, keys $K \leftarrow F$.setup(1^λ), circuit $C \in \mathcal{F}$, $K\{C\} \leftarrow F$.constrain(K, C) and $x \in \mathcal{X}$,

$$F.\text{eval}(K\{C\}, x) = F(K, x) \text{ if } C(x) = 1.$$

Security of Constrained Pseudorandom Functions. Intuitively, we require that even after obtaining several constrained keys, no polynomial time adversary can distinguish a truly random string from the PRF evaluation at a point not accepted by the queried circuits. This intuition can be formalized by the following security game between a challenger and an adversary Att.

Let $F : \mathcal{K} \times \mathcal{X} \to \mathcal{Y}$ be a constrained PRF with respect to a circuit family $\mathcal{F}$. The security game consists of three phases.

Setup Phase. The challenger chooses a random key $K \leftarrow \mathcal{K}$ and a random bit $b \leftarrow \{0, 1\}$.

Query Phase. In this phase, Att is allowed to ask for the following queries:

- **Evaluation Query.** Att sends $x \in \mathcal{X}$, and receives $F(K, x)$.
- **Key Query.** Att sends a circuit $C \in \mathcal{F}$, and receives $F.\mathsf{constrain}(K, C)$.
- **Challenge Query.** Att sends $x \in \mathcal{X}$ as a challenge query. If $b = 0$, the challenger outputs $F(K, x)$. Else, the challenger outputs a random element $y \leftarrow \mathcal{Y}$.

Guess. Att outputs a guess b' of b.

Let $E \subset \mathcal{X}$ be the set of evaluation queries, $L \subset \mathcal{F}$ be the set of constrained key queries and $Z \subset \mathcal{X}$ the set of challenge queries. The attacker Att wins if $b = b'$ and $E \cap Z = \phi$ and for all $C \in L, z \in Z, C(z) = 0$. The advantage of Att is defined to be $\mathsf{Adv}_{\mathsf{Att}}^{F}(\lambda) = \left| \Pr[\mathsf{Att\ wins}] - 1/2 \right|$.

Definition 1. *The PRF F is a secure constrained PRF with respect to $\mathcal{F}$ if for all PPT adversaries* Att, $\mathsf{Adv}_{\mathsf{Att}}^{F}(\lambda)$ *is negligible in λ.*

In the above definition the challenge query oracle may be queried multiple times on different points, and either all the challenge responses are correct PRF evaluations or they are all random points. As argued in [5], such a definition is equivalent (via a hybrid argument) to a definition where the adversary may only submit one challenge query. For our proofs, we will use the single challenge point security definition.

Another simplification that we will use in our proofs is with respect to the evaluation queries. Note that since we are considering constrained PRFs for circuits, without loss of generality, we can assume that the attacker queries for only constrained key queries. This is because any query for evaluation at input x can be replaced by a constrained key query for a circuit C_x that accepts only x.

2.3 Universal Samplers and Attribute Based Encryption

Due to space constraints, the definitions of universal samplers and attribute based encryption are given in Appendix A.

3 Adaptively Secure Constrained PRF

In this section, we will describe our constrained pseudorandom function scheme for circuit class $\mathcal{F}$. Let $n = n(\lambda), \ell_{\mathrm{rnd}} = \ell_{\mathrm{rnd}}(\lambda)$ be polynomials in λ, and let ℓ_{ckt} be a polynomial (to be defined in the construction below). We will use an adaptively secure ABE scheme (ABE.setup, ABE.keygen, ABE.enc, ABE.dec) for a circuit family $\mathcal{F}$ with message and attribute space $\{0, 1\}^n$. Let us assume the encryption algorithm ABE.enc uses ℓ_{rnd} bits of randomness to compute the ciphertext. We will also use an $(\ell_{\mathrm{ckt}}, \ell_{\mathrm{inp}} = n + \ell_{\mathrm{rnd}}, \ell_{\mathrm{out}} = n)$ universal sampler scheme $\mathcal{U} = (\mathsf{US.setup}, \mathsf{US.sample})$.

The PRF $F : \mathcal{K} \times \{0, 1\}^n \rightarrow \{0, 1\}^n$, along with algorithms $F.\mathsf{setup}$, $F.\mathsf{constrain}$ and $F.\mathsf{eval}$ are described as follows.

$F.\text{setup}(1^\lambda)$. The setup algorithm computes the sampler parameters $U \leftarrow$ US.setup(1^λ) and $(\text{pk}_{\text{ABE}}, \text{msk}_{\text{ABE}}) \leftarrow \text{ABE.setup}(1^\lambda)$. In order to define F, we will first define a program $\text{Prog}\{\text{pk}_{\text{ABE}}, x\}$ (see Fig. 1).

Prog

Input : $t \in \{0,1\}^n, r \in \{0,1\}^{\ell_{\text{rnd}}}$.

Constants : $\text{pk}_{\text{ABE}}, x \in \{0,1\}^n$.

Output $\text{ABE.enc}(\text{pk}_{\text{ABE}}, t, x; r)$.

Fig. 1. Program used by setup algorithm: Prog

Let $\mathcal{C}\text{-Prog}\{\text{pk}_{\text{ABE}}, x\}$ be an $\ell_{\text{ckt}} = \ell_{\text{ckt}}(\lambda)$ bit canonical description of $\text{Prog}\{\text{pk}_{\text{ABE}}, x\}$,[5] where the last n bits of the representation are x, and let $\mathcal{C}\text{-Prog}\{\text{pk}_{\text{ABE}}\}$ be $\mathcal{C}\text{-Prog}\{\text{pk}_{\text{ABE}}, x\}$ without the last n bits; that is, $\forall x \in \{0,1\}^n$, $\mathcal{C}\text{-Prog}\{\text{pk}_{\text{ABE}}\}\|x = \mathcal{C}\text{-Prog}\{\text{pk}_{\text{ABE}}, x\}$.

The PRF key K is set to be $(U, (\text{pk}_{\text{ABE}}, \text{msk}_{\text{ABE}}), \mathcal{C}\text{-Prog}\{\text{pk}_{\text{ABE}}\})$. To compute $F(K, x)$, the setup algorithm first 'samples' a ciphertext $c = \text{US.sample}(U, \mathcal{C}\text{-Prog}\{\text{pk}_{\text{ABE}}\}\|x)$ and output $\text{ABE.dec}(\text{msk}_{\text{ABE}}, c)$.

$F.\text{constrain}(K = (U, (\text{pk}_{\text{ABE}}, \text{msk}_{\text{ABE}}), \mathcal{C}\text{-Prog}\{\text{pk}_{\text{ABE}}\}), C)$: The constrain algorithm first computes an ABE secret key corresponding to circuit C. It computes an ABE secret key $\text{sk}_C = \text{ABE.keygen}(\text{msk}_{\text{ABE}}, C)$ and sets the constrained key to be $K\{C\} = (U, (\text{pk}_{\text{ABE}}, \text{sk}_C), \mathcal{C}\text{-Prog}\{\text{pk}_{\text{ABE}}\})$.

$F.\text{eval}(K\{C\} = (U, (\text{pk}_{\text{ABE}}, \text{sk}_C), \mathcal{C}\text{-Prog}\{\text{pk}_{\text{ABE}}\}), x)$: The evaluation algorithm first computes the canonical circuit $\mathcal{C}\text{-Prog}\{\text{pk}_{\text{ABE}}, x\} = \mathcal{C}\text{-Prog}\{\text{pk}_{\text{ABE}}\}\|x$. Next, it computes $c = \text{US.sample}(U, \mathcal{C}\text{-Prog}\{\text{pk}_{\text{ABE}}, x\})$. Finally, it outputs $\text{ABE.dec}(\text{sk}_C, c)$.

Correctness. Consider any key $K = (U, (\text{pk}_{\text{ABE}}, \text{msk}_{\text{ABE}}), \mathcal{C}\text{-Prog}\{\text{pk}_{\text{ABE}}\})$ output by $F.\text{setup}(1^\lambda)$. Let $C \in \mathcal{F}$ be any circuit, and let $\text{sk}_C \leftarrow \text{ABE.keygen}(\text{msk}_{\text{ABE}}, C)$, $K\{C\} = (U, (\text{pk}_{\text{ABE}}, \text{sk}_C), \mathcal{C}\text{-Prog}\{\text{pk}_{\text{ABE}}\})$. Let x be any input such that $C(x) = 1$. We require that $F.\text{eval}(K\{C\}, x) = F(K, x)$.[6]

$$F.\text{eval}(K\{C\}, x)$$
$$= \text{ABE.dec}(\text{sk}_C, \text{US.sample}(U, \mathcal{C}\text{-Prog}\{\text{pk}_{\text{ABE}}, x\}))$$
$$= \text{ABE.dec}(\text{msk}_{\text{ABE}}, \text{US.sample}(U, \mathcal{C}\text{-Prog}\{\text{pk}_{\text{ABE}}, x\}))$$
$$= F(K, x)$$

---

[5] Note that the value ℓ_{ckt} required by the universal sampler scheme is determined by the ABE scheme. It depends on the size of the encryption circuit ABE.enc and the length of pk_{ABE}.

[6] Recall $\text{ABE.dec}(\text{msk}_{\text{ABE}}, \text{ABE.enc}(\text{pk}_{\text{ABE}}, m, x))$ outputs m, and so does $\text{ABE.dec}(\text{sk}_C, \text{ABE.enc}(\text{pk}_{\text{ABE}}, m, x))$ if $C(x) = 1$.

4   Proof of Security

In this section, we will prove adaptive security for our constrained PRF in the random oracle model. We assume the random oracle outputs ℓ_{RO} bit strings as output. We will first define a sequence of hybrid experiments, and then show that if any PPT adversary Att has non-negligible advantage in one experiment, then it has non-negligible advantage in the next experiment. Game 0 is the constrained PRF adaptive security game in the random oracle model. In Game 1, the challenger simulates the sampler parameters and the random oracle queries. It also implements a Samples Oracle O which is used for this simulation. Let q_{par} denote the number of queries to O during the Setup, Pre-Challenge and Challenge phases. In the next game, the challenger guesses which samples oracle query corresponds to the challenge input. Finally, in the last game, it modifies the output of the samples oracle on challenge input.

4.1   Sequence of Games

Game 0. In this experiment, the challenger chooses PRF key K. It receives random oracle queries and constrained key queries from the adversary Att. On receiving the challenge input x^*, it outputs either $F(K, x^*)$ or a truly random string. The adversary then sends post-challenge random oracle/constrained key queries, and finally outputs a bit b'.

1. **Setup Phase.** Choose $U \leftarrow$ US.setup(1^λ), (pk$_{ABE}$, msk$_{ABE}$) $\leftarrow$ ABE.setup(1^λ).
   Let C-Prog$\{$pk$_{ABE}\}$ be the canonical circuit as defined in the construction.
2. **Pre Challenge Phase**
   - **Constrained Key Queries:** For every constrained key query C, compute sk$_C \leftarrow$ ABE.keygen(msk$_{ABE}$, C).
     Send $(U, ($pk$_{ABE}$, sk$_C), C$-Prog$\{$pk$_{ABE}\})$ to Att.
   - **Random Oracle Queries:** For each random oracle query y_i, check if y_i has already been queried.
     If yes, let (y_i, α_i) be the tuple corresponding to y_i. Send α_i to Att.
     If not, choose $\alpha_i \leftarrow \{0, 1\}^{\ell_{RO}}$, send α_i to Att and add (y_i, α_i) to table.
3. **Challenge Phase.** On receiving challenge input x^*, set $d^* = C$-Prog$\{$pk$_{ABE}\} \| x^*$.
   Compute $c =$ US.sample(U, d^*), $t_0 =$ ABE.dec(msk$_{ABE}$, c).
   Choose $b \leftarrow \{0, 1\}$. If $b = 0$, send t_0 to Att. Else send $t_1 \leftarrow \{0, 1\}^n$.
4. **Post Challenge Phase.** Respond to constrained key and random oracle queries as in pre-challenge phase.
5. **Guess.** Att outputs a bit b'.

Game 1. This game is similar to the previous one, except that the sampler parameters U and responses to random oracle queries are simulated. The challenger implements a Samples Oracle O, and O is used for simulating U and the random oracle. Also, instead of using US.sample to compute $F(K, x^*)$, the challenger uses the samples oracle O. Please note that even though O is defined during the Setup Phase, it is used in all the remaining phases.

1. **Setup Phase.** Choose $(\mathsf{pk}_{\mathsf{ABE}}, \mathsf{msk}_{\mathsf{ABE}}) \leftarrow \mathsf{ABE.setup}(1^\lambda)$. Let $\mathcal{C}\text{-Prog}\{\mathsf{pk}_{\mathsf{ABE}}\}$ be the canonical circuit as defined in the construction. Implement the Samples Oracle O as follows:
   - Implement a table T. Initially T is empty.
   - For each query $d \in \mathcal{C}[\ell_{\mathsf{ckt}}, \ell_{\mathsf{inp}}, \ell_{\mathsf{out}}]$ (recall $\mathcal{C}[\ell_{\mathsf{ckt}}, \ell_{\mathsf{inp}}, \ell_{\mathsf{out}}]$ is the family of circuits whose bit representation is of length ℓ_{ckt}, takes input of length ℓ_{inp} and provides output of length ℓ_{out}),
     - If $\exists$ an entry of the form (d, α, β), output α.
     - Else if d is of the form $\mathcal{C}\text{-Prog}\{\mathsf{pk}_{\mathsf{ABE}}\}\|x$,
       choose $t \leftarrow \{0,1\}^n$, $r \leftarrow \{0,1\}^{\ell_{\mathsf{rnd}}}$.
       Output $c = \mathsf{ABE.enc}(\mathsf{pk}_{\mathsf{ABE}}, t, x; r)$.
       Add (d, c, t) to T.
     - Else, choose $t \leftarrow \{0,1\}^{\ell_{\mathsf{inp}}}$, compute $\alpha = d(t)$.
       Add $(d, \alpha, \perp)$ to T and output α.
   Choose $U \leftarrow \mathsf{SimUGen}(1^\lambda)$.
2. **Pre Challenge Phase**
   - **Constrained Key Queries:** For every constrained key query C, compute $\mathsf{sk}_C \leftarrow \mathsf{ABE.keygen}(\mathsf{msk}_{\mathsf{ABE}}, C)$.
     Send $(U, (\mathsf{pk}_{\mathsf{ABE}}, \mathsf{sk}_C), \mathcal{C}\text{-Prog}\{\mathsf{pk}_{\mathsf{ABE}}\})$ to Att.
   - **Random Oracle Queries:** For each random oracle query y_i, output $\mathsf{SimRO}(y_i)$ (recall SimRO can make polynomially many calls to Samples Oracle O).
3. **Challenge Phase.** On receiving challenge input x^*, set $d^* = \mathcal{C}\text{-Prog}\{\mathsf{pk}_{\mathsf{ABE}}\}\|x^*$.
   If T does not contain an entry of the form (d^*, α, β),
   Query the Samples Oracle O with input d^*.
   Let (d^*, α, β) be the entry in T corresponding to d^*.
   Set $t_0 = \mathsf{ABE.dec}(\mathsf{msk}_{\mathsf{ABE}}, O(d^*)) = \beta$[7].
   Choose $b \leftarrow \{0,1\}$. If $b = 0$, send t_0 to Att. Else send $t_1 \leftarrow \{0,1\}^n$.
4. **Post Challenge Phase.** Respond to constrained key and random oracle queries as in pre-challenge phase.
5. **Guess.** Att outputs a bit b'.

Game 2. In this game, the challenger 'guesses' the samples oracle query which will correspond to the challenge input. The attacker wins if this guess is correct, or if the challenge input has not been queried before. Recall q_{par} denotes the number of calls to the Samples Oracle O during the Setup, Pre-Challenge and Challenge phases.

---

[7] Recall $O(d^*) = \alpha$, and $\mathsf{ABE.dec}(\mathsf{msk}_{\mathsf{ABE}}, \alpha) = \beta$.

1. **Setup Phase.** Choose $i^* \leftarrow [q_{par}]$. Remaining experiment is same as in Game 1.

Game 3. The only difference between this game and the previous one is in the behavior of the Sample Oracle on the $(i^*)^{th}$ query. Suppose the $(i^*)^{th}$ input is of the form $d^* = C\text{-Prog}\{pk_{ABE}\}||x^*$. In the previous game, the entry in table T corresponding to d^* is of the form (d^*, α^*, β^*) where α^* is an encryption of β^* for attribute x^* using public key pk_{ABE}. In this game, the entry corresponding to d^* is (d^*, α^*, β^*), where α^* is the encryption of a random message for attribute x^* using pk_{ABE}.

1. **Setup Phase.** Choose $i^* \leftarrow [q_{par}]$.
   Choose $(pk_{ABE}, msk_{ABE}) \leftarrow \text{ABE.setup}(1^\lambda)$. Let $C\text{-Prog}\{pk_{ABE}\}$ be the canonical circuit as defined in the construction. Implement the Samples Oracle O as follows:
   - Implement a table T. Initially T is empty.
   - For each query $d \in C[\ell_{ckt}, \ell_{inp}, \ell_{out}]$,
     - If there exists an entry of the form (d, α, β), output α.
     - Else if d is of the form $C\text{-Prog}\{pk_{ABE}\}||x$ for some x, choose $t, \tilde{t} \leftarrow \{0, 1\}^n$, $r \leftarrow \{0, 1\}^{\ell_{rnd}}$.
       If d is not the $(i^*)^{th}$ unique query,
       output $c \leftarrow \text{ABE.enc}(pk_{ABE}, t, x; r)$, add (d, c, t) to T.
       Else set $c \leftarrow \text{ABE.enc}(pk_{ABE}, \tilde{t}, x; r)$, add (d, c, t).
     - Else, choose $t \leftarrow \{0, 1\}^{\ell_{inp}}$, compute $\alpha = d(t)$. Add $(d, \alpha, \perp)$ to T and output α.
   Choose $U \leftarrow \text{SimUGen}(1^\lambda)$.
2. Remaining experiment is same as in Game 2.

4.2   Analysis

For any PPT adversary Att, let $\text{Adv}_{\text{Att}}^i$ denote the advantage of Att in Game i.

Claim 1. *Assuming* $\mathcal{U} = (\text{US.setup}, \text{US.sample})$ *is a secure* $(\ell_{ckt}, \ell_{inp}, \ell_{out})$ *universal sampler scheme, for any PPT adversary* Att,

$$\left| \text{Adv}_{\text{Att}}^0 - \text{Adv}_{\text{Att}}^1 \right| \leq negl(\lambda).$$

Proof. Suppose there exists a PPT adversary Att such that $\left| \text{Adv}_{\text{Att}}^0 - \text{Adv}_{\text{Att}}^1 \right| = \epsilon$. For any SimUGen, $SimRO$, we will construct a PPT algorithm $\mathcal{B}$ such that

$$\left| \Pr[\text{Real}^{\mathcal{B}}(1^\lambda) - 1] - \Pr[\text{Ideal}_{\text{SimUGen}, \text{SimRO}}^{\mathcal{B}}(1^\lambda) = 1] \right| = \epsilon.$$

$\mathcal{B}$ interacts with Att and participates in either the Real or Ideal game. It receives the sampler parameters U. It chooses $(pk_{ABE}, msk_{ABE}) \leftarrow \text{ABE.setup}(1^\lambda)$.

During the pre-challenge phase, $\mathcal{B}$ receives either secret key queries or random oracle queries. On receiving secret key query for circuit $\mathcal{C}$, it computes $\mathsf{sk}_C \leftarrow$ ABE.keygen($\mathsf{msk}_{\mathsf{ABE}}, C$) and sends $K\{C\} = (U, (\mathsf{pk}_{\mathsf{ABE}}, \mathsf{sk}_C), \mathcal{C}\text{-Prog}\{\mathsf{pk}_{\mathsf{ABE}}\})$ to Att. On receiving random oracle query y, it forwards it to the universal sampler challenger. It receives response α, which it forwards to Att.

On receiving the challenge message x^*, it sets d^* to be the circuit $\mathcal{C}\text{-Prog}\{\mathsf{pk}_{\mathsf{ABE}}\}||x^*$, computes $c = \mathsf{US.sample}(U, d^*)$, $t_0 = \mathsf{ABE.dec}(\mathsf{msk}_{\mathsf{ABE}}, c)$. It chooses $b \leftarrow \{0, 1\}$. If $b = 0$, it sends t_0, else it sends $t_1 \leftarrow \{0, 1\}$.

The post challenge queries are handled similar to the pre challenge queries. Finally, Att outputs b'. If $b = b'$, $\mathcal{B}$ send 0 to the universal sampler challenger, indicating Real experiment. Else it sends 1.

Note that due to the honest sample violation probability being 0, Att participates in either Game 0 or Game 1. This concludes our proof.

Observation 1. For any adversary Att, $\mathsf{Adv}_{\mathsf{Att}}^2 \geq \frac{\mathsf{Adv}_{\mathsf{Att}}^1}{q_{\mathrm{par}}}$.

Proof. Since the challenger's choice i^* is independent of Att, if $d = \mathcal{C}\text{-Prog}\{\mathsf{pk}_{\mathsf{ABE}}\}||x^*$ was queried before the challenge phase, then the challenger's guess is correct with probability $1/q_{\mathrm{par}}$.

Claim 2. *Assuming* ABE = *(*ABE.setup, ABE.keygen, ABE.enc, ABE.dec*) is an adaptively secure attribute based encryption scheme, for any PPT adversary* Att,

$$\left| \mathsf{Adv}_{\mathsf{Att}}^2 - \mathsf{Adv}_{\mathsf{Att}}^3 \right| \leq negl(\lambda).$$

Proof. Note that the only difference between Game 2 and Game 3 is in the implementation of Samples Oracle O. Suppose there exists a PPT adversary Att such that $\left| \mathsf{Adv}_{\mathsf{Att}}^2 - \mathsf{Adv}_{\mathsf{Att}}^3 \right| = \epsilon$. We will construct a PPT algorithm $\mathcal{B}$ that interacts with Att and breaks the adaptive security of ABE scheme with advantage ϵ.

$\mathcal{B}$ receives $\mathsf{pk}_{\mathsf{ABE}}$ from the ABE challenger. It chooses $i^* \leftarrow [q_{\mathrm{par}}]$ and computes $U \leftarrow \mathsf{SimUGen}(1^\lambda)$.

Implementing the Samples Oracle O : $\mathcal{B}$ must implement the Samples Oracle. It maintains a table T which is initially empty. On receiving a query d for O, if there exists an entry of the form (d, α, β) in T, it outputs α. Else, if d is a new query, and is not of the form $\mathcal{C}\text{-Prog}\{\mathsf{pk}_{\mathsf{ABE}}\}||x$ for some x, it chooses $t \leftarrow \{0, 1\}^{\ell_{\mathrm{inp}}}$, outputs $d(t)$ and stores $(d, d(t), \bot)$. Else, if $d = \mathcal{C}\text{-Prog}\{\mathsf{pk}_{\mathsf{ABE}}\}||x$, and d is not the $(i^*)^{\mathrm{th}}$ query, it chooses $t \in \{0, 1\}^n$, computes $c = \mathsf{ABE.enc}(\mathsf{pk}_{\mathsf{ABE}}, t, x)$ and stores (d, c, t) in T. Else, if $d^* = \mathcal{C}\text{-Prog}\{\mathsf{pk}_{\mathsf{ABE}}\}||x^*$ is the $(i^*)^{\mathrm{th}}$ query, $\mathcal{B}$ chooses $t, \tilde{t} \leftarrow \{0, 1\}^n$, sends $t, \tilde{t}$ as the challenge messages and x^* as the challenge attribute to the ABE challenger. It receives c in response. $\mathcal{B}$ stores (d^*, c, t) in T and outputs c.

The remaining parts are identical in both Game 2 and Game 3. During the pre-challenge query phase, $\mathcal{B}$ receives either constrained key queries or random oracle queries. On receiving constrained key query for circuit C, it sends C to the ABE challenger as a secret key query, and receives sk_C. It sends $(U, (\mathsf{pk}, \mathsf{sk}_C), \mathcal{C}\text{-Prog}\{\mathsf{pk}_{\mathsf{ABE}}\})$ to Att. On receiving a random oracle query y, it computes $\mathsf{SimRO}(y)$, where SimRO is allowed to query the Samples Oracle O. If $\mathcal{B}$ receives any constrained key query C such that $C(x^*) = 1$ (where $d^* = C\text{-Prog}\{\mathsf{pk_{ABE}}\}||x^*$ was the $(i^*)^{\text{th}}$ unique query to O), then B aborts.

In the challenge phase, $\mathcal{B}$ receives input x^*. If $d^* = C\text{-Prog}\{\mathsf{pk_{ABE}}\}||x^*$ was not the $(i^*)^{\text{th}}$ query to O, $\mathcal{B}$ aborts. Else, let (d^*, α^*, β^*) be the corresponding entry in T. It chooses $b \leftarrow \{0,1\}$. If $b = 0$, it outputs $t_0 = \beta^*$, else it outputs $t_1 \leftarrow \{0,1\}^n$.

The post challenge phase is handled similar to the pre-challenge phase. Finally, Att outputs b'. If $b = b'$, $\mathcal{B}$ outputs 0, indicating c is an encryption of t. Else it outputs 1.

We will now analyse $\mathcal{B}$'s winning probability. Let x^* be the challenge input sent by Att. Note that if $\mathcal{B}$ aborts, then the $(i^*)^{\text{th}}$ unique query to O was not $d^* = C\text{-Prog}\{\mathsf{pk_{ABE}}\}||x^*$, in which case, Att wins with probability exactly $1/2$.

If d^* was the $(i^*)^{\text{th}}$ query and c is an encryption of t, then this corresponds to Game 2. Else, it corresponds to Game 3. Note that $\Pr[\mathcal{B}$ outputs $0 - c \leftarrow \mathsf{ABE.enc}(\mathsf{pk_{ABE}}, t, x^*)] = \Pr[\mathsf{Att}$ wins in Game 2$]$ and similarly, $\Pr[\mathcal{B}$ outputs $0 - c \leftarrow \mathsf{ABE.enc}(\mathsf{pk_{ABE}}, \tilde{t}, x^*)] = \Pr[\mathsf{Att}$ wins in Game 3$]$. Therefore, $\mathsf{Adv}_{\mathcal{B}}^{\mathsf{ABE}} = \epsilon$.

Observation 2. For any adversary Att, $\mathsf{Adv}_{\mathsf{Att}}^3 = 0$.

Proof. Note that Att receives no information about t_0 in the pre-challenge and post challenge phases. As a result, t_0 and t_1 look identical to Att.

A Preliminaries Continued

A.1 Universal Samplers

In a recent work, Hofheinz et al. [19] introduced the notion of universal samplers. Intuitively, a universal sampler scheme provides a concise way to sample pseudorandomly from arbitrary distributions. More formally, a universal sampler scheme $\mathcal{U}$, parameterized by polynomials ℓ_{ckt}, ℓ_{inp} and ℓ_{out}, consists of algorithms $\mathsf{US.setup}$ and $\mathsf{US.sample}$ defined below.

- $\mathsf{US.setup}(1^\lambda)$ takes as input the security parameter λ and outputs the sampler parameters U.
- $\mathsf{US.sample}(U, d)$ is a deterministic algorithm that takes as input the sampler parameters U and a circuit d of size at most ℓ_{ckt} bits. The circuit d takes as input ℓ_{inp} bits and outputs ℓ_{out} bits. The output of $\mathsf{US.sample}$ also consists of ℓ_{out} bits.

Intuitively, $\mathsf{US.sample}$ is supposed to sample from d, in the sense that it outputs a value $d(z)$ for pseudorandom and hidden random coins z. However, it is nontrivial to define what it means that the random coins z are hidden, and that even multiple outputs (for adversarially and possibly even adaptively chosen circuits d) look pseudorandom.

Hofheinz et al. [19] formalize security by mandating that US.sample is programmable in the random oracle model. In particular, there should be an efficient way to simulate U and the random oracle, such that US.sample outputs an externally given value that is honestly sampled from d. This programming should work even for arbitrarily many US.sample outputs for adversarially chosen inputs d simultaneously, and it should be indistinguishable from a real execution of US.setup and US.sample.

In this work, we will be using a universal sampler scheme that is even adaptively secure. In order to formally define adaptive security for universal samplers, let us first define the notion of an admissible adversary $\mathcal{A}$.

An admissible adversary $\mathcal{A}$ is defined to be an efficient interactive Turing Machine that outputs one bit, with the following input/output behavior:

- $\mathcal{A}$ takes as input security parameter λ and sampler parameters U.
- $\mathcal{A}$ can send a random oracle query (RO, x), and receives the output of the random oracle on input x.
- $\mathcal{A}$ can send a message of the form (params, d) where $d \in \mathcal{C}[\ell_{\mathrm{ckt}}, \ell_{\mathrm{inp}}, \ell_{\mathrm{out}}]$. Upon sending this message, $\mathcal{A}$ is required to honestly compute $p_d = \mathsf{US.sample}(U, d)$, making use of any additional random oracle queries, and $\mathcal{A}$ appends (d, p_d) to an auxiliary tape (this is required to check for *Honest Sample Violation* in the Ideal experiment).

Let SimUGen and SimRO be PPT algorithms. Consider the following two experiments:

$\mathsf{Real}^{\mathcal{A}}(1^{\lambda})$:

1. The random oracle RO is implemented by assigning random outputs to each unique query made to RO.
2. $U \leftarrow \mathsf{US.setup}^{\mathsf{RO}}(1^{\lambda})$.
3. $\mathcal{A}(1^{\lambda}, U)$ is executed, where every random oracle query, represented by a message of the form (RO, x), receives the response $\mathsf{RO}(x)$.
4. Upon termination of $\mathcal{A}$, the output of the experiment is the final output of the execution of $\mathcal{A}$.

$\mathsf{Ideal}^{\mathcal{A}}_{\mathsf{SimUGen}, \mathsf{SimRO}}(1^{\lambda})$:

1. A truly random function F that maps ℓ_{ckt} bits to ℓ_{inp} bits is implemented by assigning random ℓ_{inp}-bit outputs to each unique query made to F. Throughout this experiment, a Samples Oracle O is implemented as follows: On input d, where $d \in \mathcal{C}[\ell_{\mathrm{ckt}}, \ell_{\mathrm{inp}}, \ell_{\mathrm{out}}]$, O outputs $d(F(d))$.
2. $(U, \tau) \leftarrow \mathsf{SimUGen}(1^{\lambda})$. Here, SimUGen can make arbitrary queries to the Samples Oracle O.
3. $\mathcal{A}(1^{\lambda}, U)$ and $\mathsf{SimRO}(\tau)$ begin simultaneous execution.
   - Whenever $\mathcal{A}$ sends a message of the form (RO, x), this is forwarded to SimRO, which produces a response to be sent back to $\mathcal{A}$.
   - SimRO can make any number of queries to the Samples Oracle O.

- Finally, after $\mathcal{A}$ sends any message of the form (params, d), the auxiliary tape of $\mathcal{A}$ is examined until an entry of the form (d, p_d) is added to it. At this point, if p_d is not equal to $d(F(d))$, then experiment aborts, resulting in an *Honest Sample Violation*.
4. Upon termination of $\mathcal{A}$, the output of the experiment is the final output of the execution of $\mathcal{A}$.

Definition 2. *A universal sampler scheme* $\mathcal{U} = ($US.setup, US.sample$)$, *parameterized by polynomials* $\ell_{\mathrm{ckt}}, \ell_{\mathrm{inp}}$ *and* ℓ_{out}, *is said to be adaptively secure in the random oracle model if there exist PPT algorithms* SimUGen *and* SimRO *such that for all admissible PPT adversaries* $\mathcal{A}$, *the following hold:*[8]

$$\Pr[\mathsf{Ideal}_{\mathsf{SimUGen},\mathsf{SimRO}}^{\mathcal{A}}(1^{\lambda}) \textit{ aborts }] = 0,$$

and

$$\left| \Pr[\mathsf{Real}^{\mathcal{A}}(1^{\lambda}) = 1] - \Pr[\mathsf{Ideal}_{\mathsf{SimUGen},\mathsf{SimRO}}^{\mathcal{A}}(1^{\lambda}) = 1] \right| \leq \mathit{negl}(\lambda)$$

Hofheinz et al. [19] construct a universal sampler scheme that is adaptively secure in the random oracle model, assuming a secure indistinguishability obfuscator, a selectively secure puncturable PRF and an injective pseudorandom generator.

A.2   Attribute Based Encryption

An attribute based encryption scheme ABE for a circuit family $\mathcal{F}$ with message space $\mathcal{M}$ and attribute space $\mathcal{X}$ consists of algorithms ABE.setup, ABE.keygen, ABE.enc and ABE.dec defined below.

- ABE.setup(1^{λ}) is a PPT algorithm that takes as input the security parameter and outputs the public key $\mathsf{pk}_{\mathsf{ABE}}$ and the master secret key $\mathsf{msk}_{\mathsf{ABE}}$.
- ABE.keygen$(\mathsf{msk}_{\mathsf{ABE}}, C)$ is a PPT algorithm that takes as input the master secret key $\mathsf{msk}_{\mathsf{ABE}}$, a circuit $C \in \mathcal{F}$ and outputs a secret key sk_C for circuit C.
- ABE.enc$(\mathsf{pk}_{\mathsf{ABE}}, m, x)$ takes as input a public key $\mathsf{pk}_{\mathsf{ABE}}$, message $m \in \mathcal{M}$, an attribute $x \in \mathcal{X}$ and outputs a ciphertext c. We will assume the encryption algorithm takes ℓ_{rnd} bits of randomness[9]. The notation ABE.enc$(\mathsf{pk}_{\mathsf{ABE}}, m, x; r)$ is used to represent the randomness r used by ABE.enc.
- ABE.dec(sk_C, c) takes as input secret key sk_C, ciphertext c and outputs $y \in \mathcal{M} \cup \{\bot\}$.

---

[8] The definition in [19] only requires this probability to be negligible in λ. However, the construction actually achieves zero probability of Honest Sample Violation. Hence, for the simplicity of our proof, we will use this definition.

[9] This assumption can be justified by the use of an appropriate pseudorandom generator that maps ℓ_{rnd} bits to the required length.

Correctness. For any circuit $C \in \mathcal{F}$, $(\mathsf{pk_{ABE}}, \mathsf{msk_{ABE}}) \leftarrow \mathsf{ABE.setup}(1^\lambda)$, message $m \in \mathcal{M}$, attribute $x \in \mathcal{X}$ such that $C(x) = 1$, we require the following:

$$\mathsf{ABE.dec}(\mathsf{ABE.keygen}(\mathsf{msk_{ABE}}, C), \mathsf{ABE.enc}(\mathsf{pk_{ABE}}, m, x)) = m.$$

For simplicity of notation, we will assume $\mathsf{ABE.dec}(\mathsf{msk_{ABE}}, \mathsf{ABE.enc}(\mathsf{pk_{ABE}}, m, x)) = m$ for all messages m, attributes x^{10}.

Security. Security for an ABE scheme is defined via the following adaptive security game between a challenger and adversary Att.

1. **Setup Phase.** The challenger chooses $(\mathsf{pk_{ABE}}, \mathsf{msk_{ABE}}) \leftarrow \mathsf{ABE.setup}(1^\lambda)$ and sends $\mathsf{pk_{ABE}}$ to Att.
2. **Pre-Challenge Phase.** The challenger receives multiple secret key queries. For each $C \in \mathcal{F}$ queried, it computes $\mathsf{sk}_C \leftarrow \mathsf{ABE.keygen}(\mathsf{msk_{ABE}}, C)$ and sends sk_C to Att.
3. **Challenge.** Att sends messages $m_0, m_1 \in \mathcal{M}$ and attribute $x \in \mathcal{X}$ such that $C(x) = 0$ for all circuits queried during the Pre-Challenge phase. The challenger chooses $b \leftarrow \{0, 1\}$, computes $c \leftarrow \mathsf{ABE.enc}(\mathsf{pk_{ABE}}, m_b, x)$ and sends c to Att.
4. **Post-Challenge Phase.** Att sends multiple secret key queries $C \in \mathcal{F}$ as in the Pre-Challenge phase, but with the added restriction that $C(x) = 0$. It receives $\mathsf{sk}_C \leftarrow \mathsf{ABE.keygen}(\mathsf{msk_{ABE}}, C)$.
5. **Guess.** Finally, Att outputs its guess b'.

Att wins the ABE security game for scheme ABE if $b = b'$. Let $\mathsf{Adv}^{\mathsf{ABE}}_{\mathsf{Att}} = \left| \Pr[\text{Att wins}] - 1/2 \right|$.

Definition 3. *An ABE scheme* $\mathsf{ABE} = (\mathsf{ABE.setup}, \mathsf{ABE.keygen}, \mathsf{ABE.enc}, \mathsf{ABE.dec})$ *is said to be adaptively secure if for all PPT adversaries* Att, $\mathsf{Adv}^{\mathsf{ABE}}_{\mathsf{Att}} \leq negl(\lambda)$.

In a recent work, Waters [30] showed a construction for an adaptively secure functional encryption scheme, using indistinguishability obfuscation. An adaptively secure functional encryption scheme implies an adaptively secure attribute based encryption scheme. Garg, Gentry, Halevi and Zhandry [15] showed a direct construction based on multilinear encodings. Ananth, Brakerski, Segev and Vaikuntanathan [2] showed how to transform any selectively secure FE scheme to achieve adaptive security.

---

[10] We can assume this holds true, since given $\mathsf{msk_{ABE}}$, one can compute a secret key sk for circuit C_{all} that accepts all inputs, and then use sk to decrypt $\mathsf{ABE.enc}(\mathsf{pk_{ABE}}, m, x)$.

References

1. Agrawal, S., Koppula, V., Waters, B.: Impossibility of simulation secure functional encryption even with random oracles. Cryptology ePrint Archive, Report 2016/959 (2016)
2. Ananth, P., Brakerski, Z., Segev, G., Vaikuntanathan, V.: From selective to adaptive security in functional encryption. In: Advances in Cryptology - CRYPTO 2015–35th Annual Cryptology Conference, Proceedings, Part II, Santa Barbara, CA, USA, 16–20 August 2015, pp. 657–677 (2015)
3. Bellare, M., Rogaway, P.: Random oracles are practical: A paradigm for designing efficient protocols. In: ACM Conference on Computer and Communications Security, pp. 62–73 (1993)
4. Boneh, D., Boyen, X.: Efficient selective-ID secure identity-based encryption without random oracles. In: Advances in Cryptology - EUROCRYPT 2004, International Conference on the Theory and Applications of Cryptographic Techniques, Interlaken, Switzerland, Proceedings, 2–6 May 2004, pp. 223–238 (2004)
5. Boneh, D., Waters, B.: Constrained pseudorandom functions and their applications. In: ASIACRYPT, pp. 280–300 (2013)
6. Boneh, D., Zhandry, M.: Multiparty key exchange, efficient traitor tracing, and more from indistinguishability obfuscation. In: Proceedings of CRYPTO 2014 (2014)
7. Boyle, E., Goldwasser, S., Ivan, I.: Functional signatures and pseudorandom functions. In: Public-Key Cryptography - PKC 2014–17th International Conference on Practice and Theory in Public-Key Cryptography, Buenos Aires, Proceedings, Argentina, 26–28 March 2014, pp. 501–519 (2014)
8. Brakerski, Z., Vaikuntanathan, V.: Constrained key-homomorphic PRFs from standard lattice assumptions - or: How to secretly embed a circuit in your PRF. In: Theory of Cryptography - 12th Theory of Cryptography Conference, TCC 2015, Warsaw, Poland, 23–25 March 2015, Proceedings, Part II, pp. 1–30 (2015)
9. Canetti, R., Goldreich, O., Halevi, S.: The random oracle methodology, revisited (preliminary version). In: STOC, pp. 209–218 (1998)
10. Coron, J.-S.: Optimal security proofs for PSS and other signature schemes. In: Knudsen, L.R. (ed.) EUROCRYPT 2002. LNCS, vol. 2332, pp. 272–287. Springer, Heidelberg (2002). https://doi.org/10.1007/3-540-46035-7_18
11. Coron, J., Lepoint, T., Tibouchi, M.: Practical multilinear maps over the integers. In: Advances in Cryptology - CRYPTO 2013–33rd Annual Cryptology Conference, Proceedings, Part I, Santa Barbara, CA, USA, 18–22 August 2013, pp. 476–493 (2013)
12. Fuchsbauer, G., Konstantinov, M., Pietrzak, K., Rao, V.: Adaptive security of constrained PRFs. In: Advances in Cryptology - ASIACRYPT 2014–20th International Conference on the Theory and Application of Cryptology and Information Security, Proceedings, Part II, Kaoshiung, Taiwan, R.O.C., 7–11 December 2014, pp. 82–101 (2014)
13. Garg, S., Gentry, C., Halevi, S.: Candidate multilinear maps from ideal lattices. In: Johansson, T., Nguyen, P.Q. (eds.) EUROCRYPT 2013. LNCS, vol. 7881, pp. 1–17. Springer, Heidelberg (2013). https://doi.org/10.1007/978-3-642-38348-9_1
14. Garg, S., Gentry, C., Halevi, S., Sahai, A., Waters, B.: Attribute-based encryption for circuits from multilinear maps. In: Advances in Cryptology - CRYPTO 2013–33rd Annual Cryptology Conference, Proceedings, Part II, Santa Barbara, CA, USA, 18–22 August 2013, pp. 479–499 (2013)

15. Garg, S., Gentry, C., Halevi, S., Zhandry, M.: Fully secure attribute based encryption from multilinear maps. Cryptology ePrint Archive, Report 2014/622 (2014). http://eprint.iacr.org/
16. Goldreich, O., Goldwasser, S., Micali, S.: How to construct random functions (extended abstract). In: FOCS, pp. 464–479 (1984)
17. Gorbunov, S., Vaikuntanathan, V., Wee, H.: Attribute-based encryption for circuits. In: STOC (2013)
18. Goyal, R., Goyal, V.: Overcoming cryptographic impossibility results using blockchains. In: Theory of Cryptography - 15th International Conference, TCC 2017, Proceedings, Part I, Baltimore, MD, USA, 12–15 November 2017, pp. 529–561 (2017)
19. Hofheinz, D., Jager, T., Khurana, D., Sahai, A., Waters, B., Zhandry, M.: How to generate and use universal parameters. In: ASIACRYPT (2016)
20. Hofheinz, D., Jager, T., Knapp, E.: Waters signatures with optimal security reduction. In: Fischlin, M., Buchmann, J., Manulis, M. (eds.) PKC 2012. LNCS, vol. 7293, pp. 66–83. Springer, Heidelberg (2012). https://doi.org/10.1007/978-3-642-30057-8_5
21. Hohenberger, S., Koppula, V., Waters, B.: Adaptively secure puncturable pseudorandom functions in the standard model. In: Advances in Cryptology - ASIACRYPT 2015–21st International Conference on the Theory and Application of Cryptology and Information Security, Proceedings, Part I, Auckland, New Zealand, 29 November–3 December 2015, pp. 79–102 (2015)
22. Kaliski, B., Staddon, J.: PKCS #1: RSA cryptography specifications version 2.0 (1998)
23. Kiayias, A., Papadopoulos, S., Triandopoulos, N., Zacharias, T.: Delegatable pseudorandom functions and applications. In: ACM Conference on Computer and Communications Security, pp. 669–684 (2013)
24. Lewko, A.B., Waters, B.: Why proving HIBE systems secure is difficult. In: Advances in Cryptology - EUROCRYPT 2014–33rd Annual International Conference on the Theory and Applications of Cryptographic Techniques, Proceedings, Copenhagen, Denmark, 11–15 May 2014, pp. 58–76 (2014)
25. Liu, Q., Zhandry, M.: Decomposable obfuscation: a framework for building applications of obfuscation from polynomial hardness. In: Kalai, Y., Reyzin, L. (eds.) TCC 2017. LNCS, vol. 10677, pp. 138–169. Springer, Cham (2017). https://doi.org/10.1007/978-3-319-70500-2_6
26. Regev, O.: On lattices, learning with errors, random linear codes, and cryptography. In: Proceedings of the 37th Annual ACM Symposium on Theory of Computing, Baltimore, MD, USA, 22–24 May 2005, pp. 84–93 (2005)
27. Sahai, A., Waters, B.: Fuzzy identity-based encryption. In: Cramer, R. (ed.) EUROCRYPT 2005. LNCS, vol. 3494, pp. 457–473. Springer, Heidelberg (2005). https://doi.org/10.1007/11426639_27
28. Sahai, A., Waters, B.: How to use indistinguishability obfuscation: deniable encryption, and more. In: STOC, pp. 475–484 (2014)
29. U.S. Department of Commerce/National Institute of Standards and Technology: Digital Signature Standards (DSS) (2013). Federal Information Processing Standards Publication 186-4
30. Waters, B.: A punctured programming approach to adaptively secure functional encryption. In: Advances in Cryptology - CRYPTO 2015–35th Annual Cryptology Conference, Proceedings, Part II, Santa Barbara, CA, USA, 16–20 August 2015, pp. 678–697 (2015)

LARA: A Design Concept for Lattice-Based Encryption

Rachid El Bansarkhani[(✉)]

QuantiCor Security GmbH, TU-Darmstadt, Darmstadt, Germany
ra.el@quanticor-security.de

Abstract. Lattice-based encryption schemes still suffer from a low message throughput per ciphertext and inefficient solutions towards realizing enhanced security properties such as CCA1- or CCA2-security. This is mainly due to the fact that the underlying schemes still follow a traditional design concept and do not tap the full potentials of LWE. Furthermore, the desired security features are also often achieved by costly approaches or less efficient generic transformations. Recently, a novel encryption scheme based on the A-LWE assumption (relying on the hardness of LWE) has been proposed, where data is embedded into the error term without changing its target distributions. By this novelty it is possible to encrypt much more data as compared to the classical approach. In this paper we revisit this approach and propose several techniques in order to improve the message throughput per ciphertext. Furthermore, we present a very efficient trapdoor construction of reduced storage size. More precisely, the secret and public key sizes are reduced to just 1 polynomial, as opposed to $O(\log q)$ polynomials following previous constructions. Finally, we give an efficient implementation of the scheme instantiated with the new trapdoor construction. In particular, we attest high message throughputs and low ciphertext expansion factors at efficient running times. Our scheme even ensures CCA (or RCCA) security, while entailing a great deal of flexibility to encrypt arbitrary large messages or signatures by use of the same secret key.

Keywords: Lattice-based encryption · Lattice-based assumptions

1 Introduction

In [EDB15], a novel lattice-based encryption scheme has been proposed that encrypts data in a way that differs from previous constructions [Reg05, GPV08, Pei09, Pei10, ABB10, LP11, SS11, MP12] following the one-time-pad approach. It is equipped with many features such as a high message throughput per ciphertext as compared to current state-of-the-art encryption schemes while simultaneously ensuring different security notions (e.g. CCA security) for many cryptographic applications, for instance utilized for sign-then-encrypt scenarios or to securely transmit bundles of keys as required for the provisioning of remote

© International Financial Cryptography Association 2019
I. Goldberg and T. Moore (Eds.): FC 2019, LNCS 11598, pp. 377–395, 2019.
https://doi.org/10.1007/978-3-030-32101-7_23

attestation keys during manufacturing. Public key encryption schemes also represent important building blocks of advanced primitives such as group signature and ABS schemes. In many application scenarios it is also desired to ensure CCA1- or CCA2-security. The Augmented Learning with Errors problem (A-LWE) [EDB15], a modified LWE variant, has been introduced that allows to inject auxiliary data into the error term without changing the target distributions. In fact, the A-LWE problem has been proven to be hard to solve in the random oracle model assuming the hardness of LWE. Using a suitable trapdoor function as a black-box such as [EB14, MP12], the owner of the trapdoor is empowered to recover the secret resp. error-term and hence reveal the injected data. By this novelty, it is possible to exploit the error term as a container for the message or further information such as lattice-based signatures following the distributions of the error-term. It further encompasses a great deal of flexibility and other important properties such as CCA-security.

1.1 Our Contributions

In this paper we revisit the A-LWE problem and the implied encryption schemes from [EDB15]. In particular, we provide several theoretical improvements, introduce new tools, and give an efficient software implementation of the scheme testifying its conjectured efficiency. Below, we give an overview of features that can be realized by our scheme LARA (LAttice-based encryption of data embedded in RAndomness):

1. *Flexibility.* The encryptor of the scheme can increase the amount of encrypted data without invoking the encryption engine several times. Since the message is embedded into the error term, increasing the error size (to at most $\|e_i\|_2 < q/4$ depending on the parameters) results in a higher message throughput. Thus, we achieve very low ciphertext expansion factors as compared to recent schemes. Furthermore, using a trapdoor allows to retrieve the secret and error polynomials for inspection. The retrieved secret polynomial could also play the role of a uniform random key for a symmetric key cipher.
2. *Signature embedding.* Due to the coinciding distributions of the error term and lattice-based signatures, the encryptor can exploit the signature as the error term. For instance, (c_2, c_3) contains the signature on the error or message encrypted in c_1. This offers an CCA2 like flavour as the decryptor can verify that the ciphertext has not been altered during transmission and the source of the data is authenticated via the signature. In case the size of the signature is too large, the encryptor can further exploit its flexibility.
3. *Security.* An increase of the error size already enhances the security of the scheme. However, it is also possible to further lift the security from CPA or CCA1 to RCCA or CCA2 almost for free via the transformations from [EDB15].
4. *Efficiency.* Due to the resemblance of ciphertexts to plain LWE samples, the efficiency of the scheme is very close to that required to generate ring-LWE samples, which intuitively seems to be a lower bound for many encryption schemes that are based on ring-LWE.

Improved Message Throughput. We introduce new techniques in order to increase the message throughput per ciphertext. In fact, we are able to exploit almost the full min-entropy of the error term to embed arbitrary messages. Previously, only one bit of the message was injected into a coefficient of the error term. By our new method, we are able to inject about $\log_2(\alpha q/\omega(\sqrt{\log n}))$ bits per entry for an error vector sampled according to the discrete Gaussian distribution with parameter αq. Encoding and decoding of the message requires only to reduce the coefficients modulo some integer.

$m = c \cdot n\bar{k}$ $k = \log q$	CCA **[MP12]**	CPA/CCA **[EDB15]**	CPA/CCA **This work**	CPA **[LP11], others**
Ciphertext size	$m \cdot k$	$m \cdot k$	$m \cdot k$	$m \cdot k$
Message size	$n\bar{k}$	$c \cdot n\bar{k}$	$c \log(\alpha q/4.7)n\bar{k}$	$cn\bar{k} - n$
Message Exp.	$c \cdot k$	k	$\frac{k}{\log(\alpha q/4.7)}$	$k + \frac{k}{ck-1}$

Following this approach we can revise the parameters from [EDB15] according to the table above (for a fixed ciphertext size). When comparing our approach with the CPA-secure encryption scheme from Lindner and Peikert [LP11] and other recently proposed schemes, we attest an improvement factor of at least $O(\log(\alpha q))$.

Improved Trapdoors, Scheme Instantiation and Security. We give an improved construction of trapdoors in the random oracle model, which allows to significantly reduce the number of ring elements in the public key by a factor $O(\log q)$, hence moving trapdoor constructions towards practicality. More precisely, we give an improved construction of trapdoor algorithms (TrapGen, LWEGen, LWEInv), in case the secret vector is sampled uniformly at random and can thus be selected $\mathbf{s} = F(\mathbf{r}, H(\mathbf{r}))$ involving a deterministic function F and a cryptographic hash function H modeled as a (quantum-) random oracle. This is a crucial ingredient of our construction and the resulting schemes. In particular, we achieve public and secret keys each consisting only of 1 polynomial. Hence, our construction improves upon previous proposals, where the public key contains at least $\lceil \log q \rceil$ polynomials (matrix dimension in [MP12] is $n \times n(1 + \lg q)$, see also [LPR13]), and is thus comparable with the public key size used in current state-of-the-art encryption schemes. This makes the usage of trapdoor based constructions more attractive for practice as it provides direct access to the secret and error vectors, which can be exploited in many different ways and at least for inspection.

Implementation and Analysis. In order to attest the conjectured efficiency of our scheme that we call LARA$_{CPA}$ or LARA$_{CCA}$, we implement the (quantum-) random oracle variants of our CPA- and CCA-secure schemes in software. This implementation is optimized with respect to the underlying architecture. To this end, we applied optimized techniques for discrete Gaussian sampling and FFT multiplication, the core elements governing the efficiency of the scheme. In particular, we adopt several optimizations for the polynomial representation and polynomial multiplication by use of efficient FFT/NTT operations. We implement our scheme and compare it with various schemes. For our reference implementation and $n = 1024$ (conservative parameters), we attest running times of 418 000 cycles for encryption and about 289 000 cycles for decryption in the CPA-secure setting. Thus, in comparison to the other schemes, we achieve by our improved trapdoor construction high message throughputs at low ciphertext expansion factors and at efficient running times and key sizes. The AVX-implementation is about twice as fast.

1.2   Organization

This paper is structured as follows. Section 2 provides the relevant background of our work. In Sect. 3 we introduce the A-LWE problem from [EDB15] and present our improvements to enhance the message throughput. In Sect. 4 a description of new trapdoor algorithms is proposed. The resulting encryption schemes are detailed in Sect. 5. In Sect. 6 we present our software implementation and experimental results.

2   Preliminaries

Notation. We will mainly focus on polynomial rings $\mathcal{R} = \mathbb{Z}[X]/\langle X^n + 1\rangle$ and $\mathcal{R}_q = \mathbb{Z}_q[X]/\langle X^n + 1\rangle$ for integers $q > 0$ and n being a power of two. We denote ring elements by boldface lower-case letters e.g. $\mathbf{p}$, whereas for vectors of ring elements we use $\hat{\mathbf{p}}$ and upper-case bold letters for matrices (e.g., $\mathbf{A}$). By $\oplus$ we denote the XOR operator.

Discrete Gaussian Distribution. We define by $\rho : \mathbb{R}^n \to (0, 1]$ the n-dimensional Gaussian function

$$\rho_{s,\mathbf{c}}(\mathbf{x}) = e^{-\pi \cdot \frac{\|\mathbf{x} - \mathbf{c}\|_2^2}{s^2}}, \ \forall \mathbf{x}, \mathbf{c} \in \mathbb{R}^n.$$

The discrete Gaussian distribution $\mathcal{D}_{\Lambda+\mathbf{c},s}$ is defined to have support $\Lambda + \mathbf{c}$, where $\mathbf{c} \in \mathbb{R}^n$ and $\Lambda \subset \mathbb{R}^n$ is a lattice. For $\mathbf{x} \in \Lambda + c$, it basically assigns the probability $\mathcal{D}_{\Lambda+\mathbf{c},s}(\mathbf{x}) = \rho_s(\mathbf{x})/\rho_s(\Lambda + c)$.

Lattices. Throughout this paper we are mostly concerned with q-ary lattices $\Lambda_q^\perp(\mathbf{A})$ and $\Lambda_q(\mathbf{A})$, where $q = poly(n)$ denotes a polynomially bounded modulus and $\mathbf{A} \in \mathbb{Z}_q^{n \times m}$ is an arbitrary matrix. $\Lambda_q^\perp(\mathbf{A})$ resp. $\Lambda_q(\mathbf{A})$ are defined by

$$\Lambda_q^\perp(\mathbf{A}) = \{\mathbf{x} \in \mathbb{Z}^m \mid \mathbf{A}\mathbf{x} \equiv \mathbf{0} \mod q\}$$
$$\Lambda_q(\mathbf{A}) = \{\mathbf{x} \in \mathbb{Z}^m \mid \exists \mathbf{s} \in \mathbb{Z}^m \text{ s.t. } \mathbf{x} = \mathbf{A}^\top \mathbf{s} \mod q\}.$$

Definition 1. *For any n-dimensional lattice Λ and positive real $\epsilon > 0$, the smoothing parameter $\eta_\epsilon(\Lambda)$ is the smallest real $s > 0$ such that $\rho_{1/s}(\Lambda^*\backslash\{0\}) \leq \epsilon$.*

Lemma 1 ([Ban95, Lemma 2.4]). *For any real $s > 0$ and $T > 0$, and any $\mathbf{x} \in \mathbb{R}^n$, we have*

$$P[|\langle \mathbf{x}, \mathcal{D}_{\mathbb{Z}^n, s} \rangle | \geq T \cdot s \, \|\mathbf{x}\|] < 2exp(-\pi \cdot T^2).$$

Lemma 2 ([GPV08, Theorem 3.1]). *Let $\Lambda \subset \mathbb{R}^n$ be a lattice with basis $\mathbf{S}$, and let $\epsilon > 0$. We have $\eta_\epsilon(\Lambda) \leq \| \tilde{\mathbf{S}} \| \cdot \sqrt{\ln\left(2n\left(1 + \frac{1}{\epsilon}\right)\right)/\pi}$. In particular, for any function $\omega(\sqrt{\log n})$, there is a negligible $\epsilon(n)$ for which $\eta_\epsilon(\Lambda) \leq \| \tilde{\mathbf{S}} \| \cdot \omega(\sqrt{\log n})$.*

Corollary 1 ([DM14, Corollary 4]). *Let $n \geq 4$ be a power of two, $q \geq 3$ a power of 3, and set $\mathcal{R}_q = \mathbb{Z}_q[x]/\langle x^n + 1 \rangle$, then any nonzero polynomial $\mathbf{t} \in \mathcal{R}_q$ of degree $d < n/2$ and coefficients in $\{0, \pm 1\}$ is invertible in $\mathcal{R}_q$.*

Definition 2 (LWE Distribution). *Let n, m, q be integers and χ_e be distribution over $\mathbb{Z}$. By $L_{n,m,\alpha q}^{\mathsf{LWE}}$ we denote the LWE distribution over $\mathbb{Z}_q^{n \times m} \times \mathbb{Z}_q^m$, which draws $\mathbf{A} \leftarrow_R \mathbb{Z}_q^{n \times m}$ uniformly at random, samples $\mathbf{e} \leftarrow_R \mathcal{D}_{\mathbb{Z}^m, \alpha q}$ and returns $(\mathbf{A}, \mathbf{b}^\top) \in \mathbb{Z}_q^{n \times m} \times \mathbb{Z}_q^m$ for $\mathbf{s} \in \mathbb{Z}_q^n$ and $\mathbf{b}^\top = \mathbf{s}^\top \mathbf{A} + \mathbf{e}^\top$.*

Definition 3 (LWE Problem). *Let $\mathbf{u} \in$ be uniformly sampled from $\mathbb{Z}_q^m$.*

- *The decision problem of LWE asks to distinguish between $(\mathbf{A}, \mathbf{b}^\top) \leftarrow L_{n,m,\alpha q}^{\mathsf{LWE}}$ and $(\mathbf{A}, \mathbf{u}^\top)$ for a uniformly sampled secret $\mathbf{s} \leftarrow_R \mathbb{Z}_q^n$.*
- *The search problem of LWE asks to return the secret vector $\mathbf{s} \in \mathbb{Z}_q^n$ given an LWE sample $(\mathbf{A}, \mathbf{b}) \leftarrow L_{n,m,\alpha q}^{\mathsf{LWE}}$ for a uniformly sampled secret $\mathbf{s} \leftarrow_R \mathbb{Z}_q^n$.*

3 Augmented Learning with Errors

In this section, we give a description of the message embedding approach as proposed in [EDB15] and how it is used in order to inject auxiliary data into the error term of LWE samples. This feature represents the main building block of the generic encryption scheme from [EDB15], which allows to encrypt huge amounts of data without increasing the ciphertext size. In fact, it is even possible to combine this concept with the traditional one-time-pad approach in order to take the best from both worlds and hence increase the message size per ciphertext at almost no cost.

Lemma 3 ([EDB15, Statistical]). *Let $\mathbf{B} \in \mathbb{Z}_p^{n \times m}$ be an arbitrary full-rank matrix and $\epsilon = \mathsf{negl}(n)$. The statistical distance $\Delta(\mathcal{D}_{\mathbb{Z}^m, r}, \mathcal{D}_{\Lambda_{\mathbf{v}}^\perp(\mathbf{B}), r})$ for uniform $\mathbf{v} \leftarrow_R \mathbb{Z}_p^n$ and $r \geq \eta_\epsilon(\Lambda^\perp(\mathbf{B}))$ is negligible.*

Lemma 4 ([EDB15, Computational]). *Let $\mathbf{B} \in \mathbb{Z}_p^{n \times m}$ be an arbitrary full-rank matrix. If the distribution of $\mathbf{v} \in \mathbb{Z}_p^n$ is computationally indistinguishable from the uniform distribution over $\mathbb{Z}_p^n$, then $\mathcal{D}_{\Lambda_{\mathbf{v}}^\perp(\mathbf{B}), r}$ is computationally indistinguishable from $\mathcal{D}_{\mathbb{Z}^m, r}$ for $r \geq \eta_\epsilon(\Lambda^\perp(\mathbf{B}))$.*

3.1 Message Embedding

The proposed technique aims at embedding auxiliary data into the error term $\mathbf{e}$ such that it still follows the required error distibution. In particular, Lemmas 3 and 4 are used, which essentially state that a discrete Gaussian over the integers can be sampled by first picking a coset $\Lambda_{\mathbf{c}}^{\perp}(\mathbf{B}) = \mathbf{c} + \Lambda_p^{\perp}(\mathbf{B})$ uniformly at random for any full-rank matrix $\mathbf{B} \in \mathbb{Z}_p^{n \times m}$ and then invoking a discrete Gaussian sampler outputting a preimage $\mathbf{x}$ for $\mathbf{c}$ such that $\mathbf{B} \cdot \mathbf{x} \equiv \mathbf{c} \bmod p$ However, this requires the knowledge of a suitable basis for $\Lambda_q^{\perp}(\mathbf{B})$. In fact, the random coset selection can be made deterministic by means of a random oracle H taking a random seed with enough entropy as input.

The fact that xoring a message $\mathbf{m}$ to the output of H does not change the distribution, allows to hide the message within the error vector without changing its target distribution. As a result, we obtain $\mathbf{e} \leftarrow D_{\Lambda_{H(\mu) \oplus \mathbf{m}}^{\perp}(\mathbf{B}), r}$, which is indistinguishable from $D_{\mathbb{Z}^m, r}$ for a random seed μ and properly chosen parameters (see Lemmas 3 and 4). Subsequently, based on the message embedding approach the Augmented LWE problem (A-LWE) has been introduced, where A-LWE samples resemble ordinary LWE instances except for the modified error vectors. In particular, the A-LWE problem is specified with respect to a specific matrix $\mathbf{G}$, which allows to efficiently sample very short vectors according to the discrete Gaussian distribution. We note that other choices are also possible as long as the parameter of the error vectors exceed the smoothing parameter of the associated lattice. We now give a generalized description of the A-LWE distribution using any preimage sampleable public matrix $\mathbf{B}$.

Definition 4 (Augmented LWE Distribution). *Let $n, n', m, m_1, m_2, k, q, p$ be integers with $m = m_1 + m_2$, where $\alpha q \geq \eta_\epsilon(\Lambda^{\perp}(\mathbf{B}))$. Let $H : \mathbb{Z}_q^n \times \mathbb{Z}^{m_1} \rightarrow \{0,1\}^{n' \cdot \log(p)}$ be a cryptographic hash function modeled as random oracle. Let $\mathbf{B} \in \mathbb{Z}_p^{n' \times m_2}$ be a preimage sampleable full-rank matrix (such as $\mathbf{B} = \mathbf{G}$ from [MP12]). For $\mathbf{s} \in \mathbb{Z}_q^n$, define the A-LWE distribution $L_{n, m_1, m_2, \alpha q}^{\text{A-LWE}}(\mathbf{m})$ with $\mathbf{m} \in \{0,1\}^{n' \log p}$ to be the distribution over $\mathbb{Z}_q^{n \times m} \times \mathbb{Z}_q^m$ obtained as follows:*

1. *Sample $\mathbf{A} \leftarrow_R \mathbb{Z}_q^{n \times m}$ and $\mathbf{e}_1 \leftarrow_R D_{\mathbb{Z}^{m_1}, \alpha q}$.*
2. *Set $\mathbf{v} = \mathsf{encode}(H(\mathbf{s}, \mathbf{e}_1) \oplus \mathbf{m}) \in \mathbb{Z}_p^{n'}$.*
3. *Sample $\mathbf{e}_2 \leftarrow_R D_{\Lambda_{\mathbf{v}}^{\perp}(\mathbf{B}), \alpha q}$.*
4. *Return $(\mathbf{A}, \mathbf{b}^{\top})$ where $\mathbf{b}^{\top} = \mathbf{s}^{\top} \mathbf{A} + \mathbf{e}^{\top}$ with $\mathbf{e} = (\mathbf{e}_1, \mathbf{e}_2)$.*

We note that the Step 3 returns a discrete Gaussian that is distributed as $D_{\mathbb{Z}^{m_2}, \alpha q}$ follwoing [EDB15, Computational]. In principal, for A-LWE one differentiates the decision problem decision A-LWE$_{n, m_1, m_2, \alpha q}$ from the corresponding search problem search-s A-LWE$_{n, m_1, m_2, \alpha q}$, as known from LWE. Furthermore, there exists a second search problem search-m A-LWE$_{n, m_1, m_2, \alpha q}$, where a challenger is asked upon polynomially many A-LWE samples to find in polynomial time the message $\mathbf{m}$ injected into the error vector. Note that the error distribution could also differ from the discrete Gaussian distribution. For instance, one could use the uniform distribution, for which one obtains similar results. All the proofs from [EDB15] go through without any modifications, since the security proofs are not based on the choice of $\mathbf{B}$.

Theorem 1 (adapted [EDB15]). *Let* n, n', m, m_1, m_2, q, p *be integers with* $m = m_1 + m_2$. *Let* H *be a random oracle. Let* $\alpha q \geq \eta_\epsilon(\Lambda_q^\perp(\mathbf{B}))$ *for a real* $\epsilon = \mathsf{negl}(\lambda) > 0$ *and preimage sampleable public matrix* $\mathbf{B} \in \mathbb{Z}_p^{n' \times m_2}$. *Furthermore, denote by* χ_s *and* χ_{e_1} *the distributions of the random vectors* $\mathbf{s}$ *and* $\mathbf{e}_1$ *involved in each A-LWE sample. If* $\mathbb{H}_\infty(\mathbf{s}, \mathbf{e}_1) > \lambda$, *then the following statements hold.*

1. *If* search $\mathsf{LWE}_{n,m,\alpha q}$ *is hard, then* search-s $\mathsf{A\text{-}LWE}_{n,m_1,m_2,\alpha q}$ *is hard.*
2. *If* decision $\mathsf{LWE}_{n,m,\alpha q}$ *is hard, then* decision $\mathsf{A\text{-}LWE}_{n,m_1,m_2,\alpha q}$ *is hard.*
3. *If* decision $\mathsf{LWE}_{n,m,\alpha q}$ *is hard, then* search-m $\mathsf{A\text{-}LWE}_{n,m_1,m_2,\alpha q}$ *is hard.*

One easily notes, that these hardness results also hold for the ring variant (see [ABBK17]). We remark that for encryption schemes the secret $\mathbf{s}$ is always resampled such that $H(\mathbf{s})$ suffices to output a random vector and the complete bandwidth of $\mathbf{e}$ is exploited for data to be encrypted.

3.2   Improved Message Embedding

For the sake of generality, we used in all our statements an abstract matrix $\mathbf{B} \in \mathbb{Z}_p^{n' \times m}$ for integers p, n', and m. This is used to embed a message into the error term via $\mathbf{e}_2 \leftarrow_R \mathcal{D}_{\Lambda_v^\perp(\mathbf{B}),\alpha q}$, where $\mathbf{v} = \mathsf{encode}(H(\mathsf{seed}) \oplus \mathbf{m}) \in \mathbb{Z}_p^{n'}$ is uniform random. However, we can specify concrete matrices that optimize the amount of information per entry with respect to the bound given in Lemma 2. We propose several techniques in order to enhance the message throughput per discrete Gaussian vector. These techniques could also be applied to the error vector involved in the A-LWE distribution. In other words, we aim at choosing an appropriate preimage sampleable full-rank matrix $\mathbf{B} \in \mathbb{Z}_p^{n' \times m}$ such that $n' \cdot \log p$ is maximized. For now, we will focus on how to apply this technique to the different encryption schemes and omit the term $\mathbf{e}_1$ when invoking the random oracle, since the secret $\mathbf{s} \in \mathbb{Z}_q^n$ is always resampled in encryption schemes and hence provides enough entropy for each fresh encryption query. The first approach is based on a method used to construct homomorphic signatures in [BF11]. We also propose a simpler approach that avoids such complex procedures while entailing the same message throughput.

Intersection Method. The intersection method as proposed in [BF11] considers two m-dimensional integer lattices Λ_1 and Λ_2 such that $\Lambda_1 + \Lambda_2 = \mathbb{Z}^m$, where addition is defined to be element-wise. Therefore, let $\mathbf{m}_1$ and $\mathbf{m}_2$ be two messages, where $\mathbf{m}_1$ and $\mathbf{m}_2$ define a coset of Λ_1 and Λ_2 in $\mathbb{Z}^m$, respectively. As a result, the vector $(\mathbf{m}_1, \mathbf{m}_2)$ defines a unique coset of the intersection set $\Lambda_1 \cap \Lambda_2$ in $\mathbb{Z}^m$. By the Chinese Remainder theorem one can compute a short vector $\mathbf{t}$ such that $\mathbf{t} = \mathbf{m}_1 \bmod \Lambda_1$ and $\mathbf{t} = \mathbf{m}_2 \bmod \Lambda_2$ using a short basis for $\Lambda_1 \cap \Lambda_2$. In fact, it is easy to compute any vector $\mathbf{t}$ that satisfies the congruence relations.

Subsequently, by invoking a preimage sampler one obtains a short vector from $\Lambda_1 \cap \Lambda_2 + \mathbf{t}$.

Lattices of the Form $p\mathbb{Z}^m$. One realizes that for a given parameter αq for the distribution of the error vector one can be much more efficient, if one considers only the lattice $\Lambda_p^\perp(\mathbf{I}) = p\mathbb{Z}^m$. In this case, the message space is simply defined by the set $\mathcal{M} = \mathbb{Z}^m/\Lambda_p^\perp(\mathbf{I}) \cong \mathbb{Z}_p^m$. When comparing with the previous approach, for instance, it is only required to increase p by a factor of 2 in order to obtain the same message throughput $m\log 2p = m \cdot (\log p + 1)$. Furthermore the decoding and encoding phase is much faster, since encoding requires only to sample $\mathbf{e} \leftarrow D_{\mathbf{b}+p\mathbb{Z}^m,\alpha q}$ for $\mathbf{b} = H(\mathbf{r}) \oplus \mathbf{m}$ using fast discrete Gaussian samplers such as the Knuth-Yao algorithm or efficient lookup tables. Decoding is performed via $H(\mathbf{r})\oplus(\mathbf{e} \bmod p)$. Optimizing the message throughput requires to increase p such that $\eta_\epsilon(\Lambda) \leq p \cdot \mathsf{const} \leq \alpha q$ still holds for $\mathsf{const} = \sqrt{\ln(2(1+1/\epsilon))/\pi}$. Doing this, one can embed approximately $m \cdot \log p$ bits of data, which almost coincides with the min-entropy of a discrete Gaussian with parameter αq, since $\mathsf{const} \approx 4.7$. Therefore, one prefers to choose a parameter $\alpha q = p \cdot \mathsf{const}$ with $p = 2^i$ and integer $i > 0$ in order to embed i bits of data into the error term.

Uniform Error. For uniformly distributed errors one can directly employ the output of the random function $H(\cdot)$ as the error term. More specifically, suppose $\mathbf{e} \in ([-p,p]\cap\mathbb{Z})^m$, then let $H(\cdot) : \{0,1\}^* \to ([-p,p]\cap\mathbb{Z})^m$ be a random function (e.g. RO) such that $\mathbf{e} \leftarrow \mathsf{encode}(H(\mathbf{r}) \oplus \mathbf{m})$ for $\mathbf{m} \in \{0,1\}^{m\log_2(2p)}$. As a result, one can use the full bandwidth of the error term and inject $m\log_2(2p)$ message bits.

4   New Trapdoor Algorithms for Ideal-Lattices

In [EB14] a generic approach of how to instantiate the trapdoor construction is given that allows to retrieve the error term and the secret vector from A-LWE instances. However, the number of public key polynomials is with $\bar{m} + k$ polynomials where $k = \lceil \log q \rceil$ rather large and hence not suitable for practice. In fact, the trapdoor constructions [EB14, MP12] require at least 2 public key polynomials in order to generate signatures. For encryption, one requires even more as the LWE inversion algorithm has to efficiently recover the correct secret. Thus, a new approach is needed in order to tackle this issue.

In this section, we give new trapdoor algorithms and show how to reduce the size of the public key to just 1 polynomial. This is due to the fact that we can select the secret vector in A-LWE instances to be of the form $\mathbf{s} = F(\mathbf{r}, H_1(\mathbf{r}))$ for a deterministic function $F(\cdot)$, where $\mathbf{r}$ is a random bit string and H_1 is a cryptographic hash function modeled as RO. Remarkably, the secret key consists only of 1 polynomial, which improves upon the construction from [MP12, EB14]. We start with a description of our new trapdoor algorithms in the ring setting $\mathcal{K} = (\mathsf{TrapGen}, \mathsf{LWEGen}, \mathsf{LWEInv})$. Lemma 5 shows that $\mathsf{TrapGen}$ outputs a public key that is computationally indistinguishable from uniform random. In order to use tags for CCA-secure constructions, we need to modify the way, in which tags are applied.

4.1 Construction of Efficient Trapdoors for A-LWE

We present new trapdoor algorithms for public key generation (TrapGen), ring-LWE generation (LWEGen) and inversion (LWEInv). These algorithms will serve to instantiate our new encryption scheme from ring A-LWE. For the sake of simplicity, we only consider the case where $q = p^k$, where p is any positive (prime) integer.

1. TrapGen(1^n) : Let $q = p^k$ for a prime integer $p > 0$. Let further $\mathbf{g} = p^{k-1}$. The system parameters are two uniform random polynomials $\mathbf{a}_1, \mathbf{a}_2 \in \mathcal{R}_q$ (e.g. sampled from a seed). Sample 2 random polynomials $\mathbf{r}_i$ according to $\mathcal{D}_{\mathbb{Z}^n, r_{sec}}$ for $i \in \{1, 2\}$. The public and secret keys are given by pk := $\mathbf{a}_3$, sk = $[\mathbf{r}_1, \mathbf{r}_2]$ with

$$\mathbf{A} = \left[\mathbf{a}_1, \mathbf{a}_2, \underbrace{\mathbf{g} - (\mathbf{a}_1 \cdot \mathbf{r}_1 + \mathbf{a}_2 \cdot \mathbf{r}_2)}_{\mathbf{a}_3} \right] \in \mathcal{R}_q^3.$$

   If a tag $\mathbf{t}_u$ is applied, we obtain $\mathbf{A}_u$ via $\mathbf{t}_u \cdot \mathbf{g}$ (see below).
2. LWEGen(1^n) : In order to generate an (A-)LWE instance, we let H_1 be a cryptographic hash function modeled as a random oracle. For $\mathbf{A}$ we generate ring-LWE instances

$$[\mathbf{b}_1, \ \mathbf{b}_2, \ \mathbf{b}_3] = [\mathbf{a}_1, \mathbf{a}_2, \mathbf{g} - (\mathbf{a}_1 \cdot \mathbf{r}_1 + \mathbf{a}_2 \cdot \mathbf{r}_2)] \cdot \mathbf{s} + \hat{\mathbf{e}} \in \mathcal{R}_q^3.$$

   Each coefficient of $\mathbf{s} \in \mathcal{R}_q$ is of the form

$$s_i = c_{i,0} + c_{i,1} \cdot p + \ldots + c_{i,k-1} \cdot p^{k-1}$$

   for $c_{i,j} \in \{0, \ldots, p-1\}$ and $i \in \{1, \ldots, n\}$, where $c_{i,0} \leftarrow_R \{0, \ldots, p-1\}$ is sampled uniformly at random. Then, invoke $\mathbf{d} = H(c_{1,0}, \ldots, c_{n,0}) \to \mathbb{Z}_{p^{k-1}}^n$ and set $s_i = c_{i,0} + p \cdot d_i$.
   - For the special case $\mathbf{q} = 2^\mathbf{k}$, the binary number $c_{i,0}$ corresponds to the least significant bit of the coefficient s_i. That is LSB(s_i) $\leftarrow_R \{0, 1\}$, where LSB denotes the least significant bit. Then, in order to set the remaining bits of s_i invoke $\mathbf{d} = H_1(\text{LSB}(s_1), \ldots, \text{LSB}(s_n)) \in \mathbb{Z}_{2^{k-1}}^n$. Finally, determine $s_i = \text{LSB}(s_i) + 2 \cdot d_i \in \mathbb{Z}_q$ by appending the bit $c_{i,0}$ to d_i.
   The error polynomials $\mathbf{e}_i$ can now be sampled from the discrete Gaussian distribution $\mathcal{D}_{\mathbb{Z}^n, \alpha q}$, where $1 \leq i \leq 3$ and $\alpha q > 0$.
3. LWEInv($\hat{\mathbf{b}}$, sk) : We first compute

$$\mathbf{v} = \mathbf{g} \cdot \mathbf{s} + \mathbf{t} = \mathbf{b}_0 + \mathbf{b}_1 \cdot \mathbf{r}_1 + \mathbf{b}_2 \cdot \mathbf{r}_2,$$

   where $\mathbf{t}$ is a some small error.
   The closest integer $c_{i,0} \cdot p^{k-1}$ to each coefficient v_i is recovered. This is possible if $|t_i| < p^{k-1}/2$. In particular, we recover $c_{i,0}$ via

$$c_{i,0} = \lfloor v_i / p^{k-1} \rceil \bmod p \text{ for } 0 \leq i < n$$

- For $q = 2^k$, we have $c_{i,0} = \mathsf{LSB}(s_i) = \lfloor v_i/2^{k-1} \rceil \bmod 2$.
  Once having recovered all $c_{i,0}$, the hash function is invoked $\mathbf{d} = H_1(c_{1,0}, \ldots, c_{n-1,0}) \in \mathbb{Z}_{p^{k-1}}^n$ such that $s_i = c_{i,0} + d_i \cdot p$. The error vector is subsequently retrieved via $\hat{\mathbf{e}} = \hat{\mathbf{b}} - \mathbf{A} \cdot \mathbf{s}$.

Remark 1. For odd q and small secrets, we can instead set $\mathbf{g} = (q-1)/2$. The most significant bits do not vanish but wrap around modulo q. We note, that the case $q = 2^k$ is very efficient due to cheap sampling and modulo operations.

Lemma 5. *Let* $\mathbf{a}_1, \mathbf{a}_2 \in \mathcal{R}_q$ *be uniform random polynomials and* $\mathbf{r}_1, \mathbf{r}_2$ *be sampled according to* $\mathcal{D}_{\mathcal{R},\alpha q} = \mathcal{D}_{\mathbb{Z}^n,\alpha q}$ *(via the coefficient embedding) for* $\alpha q > 2\sqrt{n}$. *The public key*

$$\mathbf{A} = [\mathbf{a}_1, \mathbf{a}_2, \mathbf{a}_1 \cdot \mathbf{r}_1 + \mathbf{a}_2 \cdot \mathbf{r}_2]$$

is computationally indistinguishable from uniform.

Proof. For simplicity, we can assume that $\mathbf{a}_1$ is a unit in $\mathcal{R}_q$, since the ring of units $\mathcal{R}_q^\times$ represents a non-negligible subset of $\mathcal{R}_q$ for the rings in consideration. Then

$$\mathbf{A} = \mathbf{a}_1 \cdot [1, \bar{\mathbf{a}}, \bar{\mathbf{a}} \cdot \mathbf{r}_2 + \mathbf{r}_1],$$

where $[\bar{\mathbf{a}}, \bar{\mathbf{a}} \cdot \mathbf{r}_2 + \mathbf{r}_1]$ is a ring-LWE instance with a uniform random polynomial $\bar{\mathbf{a}} = \mathbf{a}_1^{-1} \mathbf{a}_2$, since $\mathbf{a}_2$ is uniform random. As a result and due to the independence of $\mathbf{a}_1$ from $\mathbf{a}_2$ the claim follows. □

Lemma 6 (Correctness). *For* $q = p^k$, *error polynomials* $\mathbf{e}_i$ *and secret key polynomials* $\mathbf{r}_j$, *the algorithm* $\mathsf{LWEInv}(\hat{\mathbf{b}}, \mathsf{sk})$ *correctly inverts the (A-)LWE instance, if*

$$\|\mathbf{e}_3 + \mathbf{e}_1 \cdot \mathbf{r}_1 + \mathbf{e}_2 \cdot \mathbf{r}_2\|_\infty < p^{k-1}/2.$$

Proof. The inversion algorithm computes

$$\mathbf{b}_3 + \mathbf{b}_1 \cdot \mathbf{r}_1 + \mathbf{b}_2 \cdot \mathbf{r}_2 \bmod q = \mathbf{g} \cdot \mathbf{s} + \mathbf{e}_3 + \mathbf{e}_1 \cdot \mathbf{r}_1 + \mathbf{e}_2 \cdot \mathbf{r}_2 \bmod q$$

$$= p^{k-1} \cdot \mathbf{s} + \mathbf{e}_3 + \mathbf{e}_1 \cdot \mathbf{r}_1 + \mathbf{e}_2 \cdot \mathbf{r}_2 \bmod q$$

$$= p^{k-1} \cdot \begin{bmatrix} c_{1,0} \\ \vdots \\ c_{n,0} \end{bmatrix} + \mathbf{e}_3 + \mathbf{e}_1 \cdot \mathbf{r}_1 + \mathbf{e}_2 \cdot \mathbf{r}_2 \bmod q$$

So, if $\|\mathbf{e}_3 + \mathbf{e}_1 \cdot \mathbf{r}_1 + \mathbf{e}_2 \cdot \mathbf{r}_2\|_\infty < p^{k-1}/2$, then we cleary can recover $c_{i,0}$ of each coefficient. From the coefficients we can recover $\mathbf{s}$ and $\mathbf{e}_j$ and thus the message □

Tagging the public key (in order to achieve CCA security) in the ring setting is accomplished similar to [MP12, EDB15], but with some practical obstacles to be solved for decryption. This is due to the random oracle instantiation, which prevents from recovering the tag $\mathbf{t}_u$ in a straightforward way, because the inversion algorithm only recovers $c_{i,0}$ (for $q = p^k$) of the coefficients from $\mathbf{t}_u \cdot \mathbf{s}$. However, via a trick we can circumvent this obstacle in a computationally indistinguishable way. This is mainly possible, since $\mathbf{t}_u$ is a unit and multiplication with a uniform random polynomial is again uniform. Thus, we can instead generate $\mathbf{t}_u \cdot \mathbf{s} := c_{i,0} + p \cdot d_i$ in LWEGen and cancel out $\mathbf{t}_u$ from it via its inverse when $\mathbf{s}$ is required. Here, we denote $\mathbf{A}_u = [\mathbf{a}_1, \mathbf{a}_2, \mathbf{t}_u \cdot \mathbf{g} - (\mathbf{a}_1\mathbf{r}_1 + \mathbf{a}_2\mathbf{r}_2)]$ in accordance to Sect. 4.

5 Public Key Encryption

In order to build a public key encryption scheme we need to combine the trapdoor construction described in Sect. 4 with the message embedding approach from Sect. 3. The main idea is to inject data to be encrypted into the error polynomials from LWEGen. To this end, we need the error terms to be partially deterministic and simultaneously look random by use of a random oracle (Fig. 1).

LARA.KGen(1^λ)

1: $(\mathsf{sk}, \mathsf{pk}) \leftarrow \mathsf{TrapGen}(1^\lambda)$
2: We replace $\mathbf{a}_1, \mathbf{a}_2$ in the public key with the **seed** generating those elements, i.e. $\mathsf{pk} = (\mathsf{seed}, \mathbf{a}_3)$.

LARA.Enc($\mathsf{pk}, (\mathsf{m}_1, \mathsf{m}_2, \mathsf{m}_3) \in \{0,1\}^{3n \log w}$)

1: $\mathbf{a}_1, \mathbf{a}_2 \leftarrow \mathsf{G}(\mathsf{seed})$
2: $\mathbf{c}_0 = (c_{1,0}, \ldots, c_{n,0}) \leftarrow \mathbb{Z}_p^n$
3: $(\mathbf{v}_1, \mathbf{v}_2, \mathbf{v}_3), \mathbf{d} \leftarrow \mathsf{H}(\mathbf{c}_0) \in \mathbb{Z}_w^{3n} \times \mathbb{Z}_{p^k-1}^n$
4: $\mathbf{s} = \mathbf{c}_0 + p \cdot \mathbf{d}$
5: $\mathbf{t}_i = \mathsf{Encode}(\mathsf{m}_i) + \mathbf{v}_i \bmod w$ for $1 \leq i \leq 3$
6: $\mathbf{e}_i \leftarrow \mathcal{D}_{\mathbf{t}_i + w \cdot \mathbb{Z}^n, s}$ for $1 \leq i \leq 3$
7: Output $\mathbf{b}_i = \mathbf{a}_i \cdot \mathbf{s} + \mathbf{e}_i$ for $1 \leq i \leq 3$

LARA.Dec($\mathsf{sk}, \mathbf{b} \in \mathcal{R}_q^3$)

1: $\mathbf{a}_1, \mathbf{a}_2 \leftarrow \mathsf{G}(\mathsf{seed})$
2: $(\mathbf{s} := \mathbf{c}_0 + p \cdot \mathbf{d}, \mathbf{e}_1, \mathbf{e}_2, \mathbf{e}_3) \leftarrow \mathsf{LWEInv}(\mathsf{sk}, \mathbf{b})$
3: $(\mathbf{v}_1, \mathbf{v}_2, \mathbf{v}_3), \mathbf{d} \leftarrow \mathsf{H}(\mathbf{c}_0) \in \{0,1\}^{3n \log w} \times \mathbb{Z}_{p^k-1}^n$
4: $\mathbf{t}_i = \mathbf{e}_i \bmod w$ for $1 \leq i \leq 3$
5: $\mathsf{m}_i = \mathsf{Decode}(\mathbf{t}_i - \mathbf{v}_i \bmod w)$
6: Output $(\mathsf{m}_1, \mathsf{m}_2, \mathsf{m}_3)$

Fig. 1. Description of the CPA-secure encryption scheme.

We now give a description of our new CPA-secure public key encryption scheme. Thus, let $s = w \cdot \sqrt{\ln\left(2n\left(1 + \frac{1}{\epsilon}\right)\right)/\pi}$ for an integer $w > 2$. Hence, we embed the message into the cosets of the lattice $w \cdot \mathbb{Z}^n$ (see Sect. 3.2).

For key generation, the CPA-secure scheme just invokes TrapGen. For a compact scheme, we let the uniform random polynomials $\mathbf{a}_1, \mathbf{a}_2$ be generated from a large enough $\mathsf{seed} \in \{0,1\}^\lambda$ ensuring $\lambda(n)$ classical bits. Here G is instantiated as a random oracle, which in practice can be replaced by pseudorandom generators such as Shake.

The encryption function works similar to LWEGen with the main difference that H outputs the additional random vectors $\mathbf{v}_i$ used to mask the message and to generate the error polynomials via Lemma 3. The Encode and Decode routines are used to translate between bit strings and vectors/polynomials. The decryption routine invokes LWEInv to recover the error polynomials and the secret $\mathbf{s}$. Finally, all steps from the encryption function are reversed such that the message is unmasked again.

Remark 2. For $q = 2^k$, $\mathbf{t}_i = \mathsf{Encode}(m_i) + \mathbf{v}_i \bmod 2$ is equivalent to $\mathbf{t}_i = \mathsf{Encode}(m_i \oplus h_i)$, where $h_i := \mathsf{Decode}(\mathbf{v}_i)$. This complies with the representation of Sect. 3, when defining the ALWE problem. We can also directly generate $\mathbf{v}_i$ as a bit string during encryption without the need for conversion. In the standard IND-CPA security game the adversary is challenged to correctly guess the bit b with non-negligible advantage given two distinct messages of his/her choice.

Experiment $\mathbf{Exp}_{\mathcal{E},\mathcal{A}}^{\mathrm{ind-CPA}}(n)$

$(\mathsf{pk},\mathsf{sk}) \leftarrow \mathsf{KGen}(1^k)$

$(\mu_0, \mu_1) \leftarrow \mathcal{A}(\mathrm{CHOOSE},\mathsf{pk})$

$\mathbf{c}_b \leftarrow \mathsf{Enc}_{\mathsf{pk}}(\mu_b)$ for $b \leftarrow_R \{0,1\}$

$b' \leftarrow \mathcal{A}(\mathrm{GUESS}, \mathbf{c}_b)$

Output 1 iff

    1. $b' = b$

    2. $|\mu_0| = |\mu_1|$

We now state the main theorem of this section, which can easily be extended to the quantum random oracle case (adjustment of the guessing probability). By $\mathsf{lb - RLWE}$ we define the problem of finding low order bits in ring-LWE instances.

Theorem 2. *Let $\mathsf{lb - RLWE}$ be defined as in Lemma 7. In the random oracle model, assume that there exists a PPT-adversary $\mathcal{A}$ against the scheme with $s \geq \mathsf{w} \cdot \sqrt{\ln\left(2n\left(1 + \frac{1}{\epsilon}\right)\right)/\pi}$, then there exists a reduction $\mathcal{M}$ that breaks ring-LWE/ring-ALWE such that*

$$\mathsf{Adv}_{\mathsf{LARA}}^{\mathsf{CPA}}(\mathcal{A}) \leq 3\mathsf{Adv}_{n,3}^{\mathsf{dec-RLWE}}(\mathcal{M}) + \mathsf{Adv}_{n,3}^{\mathsf{lb-RLWE}}(\mathcal{M}) + q_{\mathsf{H}}/p^n.$$

Proof. We proceed via a sequence of hybrids and show that the ciphertext is pseudorandom under any of the computational assumptions, namely ring-LWE or ring-ALWE, where latter is itself based on ring-LWE. Let $\mathcal{H}_0$ be the real $\mathsf{IND - CPA}$ game. In the first hybrid $\mathcal{H}_1$, we replace $\mathbf{a}_3$ by a uniform random polynomial. If there exists a distinguisher that can distinguish $\mathcal{H}_0$ from $\mathcal{H}_1$, then there exists a reduction $\mathcal{M}_0$ that breaks decision ring-LWE ($\mathsf{dec - RLWE}$). Thus, $\mathsf{Adv}_{\mathcal{H}_0,\mathcal{H}_1}(\mathcal{A}) \leq \mathsf{Adv}_{n,1}^{\mathsf{dec-RLWE}}(\mathcal{M}_0)$. In the second hybrid $\mathcal{H}_2$, we change the random oracle output $(\mathbf{v}_1, \mathbf{v}_2, \mathbf{v}_3), \mathbf{d}$ of $\mathsf{H}(\mathbf{c}_0)$ by uniform random values and thus also $\mathbf{t}_i$ for $1 \leq i \leq 3$. A PPT adversary can only distinguish $\mathcal{H}_1$ from $\mathcal{H}_2$, if it queries H on $\mathbf{c}_0$ (see below). But then, a reduction $\mathcal{M}_1$ exists (Lemma 7) that breaks $\mathsf{lb} - \mathsf{RLWE}$. Thus, we have $\mathsf{Adv}_{\mathcal{H}_1,\mathcal{H}_2}(\mathcal{A}) \leq \mathsf{Adv}_{n,3}^{\mathsf{lb}-\mathsf{RLWE}}(\mathcal{M}_1)+\mathsf{q_H}/\mathsf{p}^n$. Latter term represents the probability of a correct guess with at most q_H queries to H. In the third hybrid $\mathcal{H}_3$, we replace $\mathbf{e}_i \leftarrow \mathcal{D}_{\mathbf{t}_i+p\mathbb{Z}^n,s}$ by $\mathbf{e}_i \leftarrow \mathcal{D}_{\mathbb{Z}^n,s}$ (coefficient embedding) via Lemma 3. Here, $\mathbf{e}_i$ is distributed statistically close to the discrete Gaussian distribution. Thus, $\mathsf{Adv}_{\mathcal{H}_2,\mathcal{H}_3}(\mathcal{A}) \leq \mathsf{Adv}_{n,3}^{\mathsf{dec}-\mathsf{RLWE}}(\mathcal{M}_2)$ for appropriate parameters. Note that $\mathsf{Adv}_{\mathcal{H}_2,\mathcal{H}_3}(\mathcal{A})$ is bounded by the statistical distance. We note that samples from $\mathcal{H}_2$ are ring-LWE instances (except with negligible statistical distance). In the last hybrid $\mathcal{H}_4$, we let the ciphertexts $\mathbf{b}_i$ for $1 \leq i \leq 3$ be generated uniformly at random rather than as ring-LWE instances. Thus, $\mathsf{Adv}_{\mathcal{H}_3,\mathcal{H}_4}(\mathcal{A}) \leq \mathsf{Adv}_{n,3}^{\mathsf{dec}-\mathsf{RLWE}}(\mathcal{M}_3)$. The claim follows from

$$\mathsf{Adv}_{\mathcal{H}_0,\mathcal{H}_4}(\mathcal{A}) \leq \mathsf{Adv}_{\mathcal{H}_0,\mathcal{H}_1}(\mathcal{A}) + \mathsf{Adv}_{\mathcal{H}_1,\mathcal{H}_2}(\mathcal{A}) + \mathsf{Adv}_{\mathcal{H}_2,\mathcal{H}_3}(\mathcal{A}) + \mathsf{Adv}_{\mathcal{H}_3,\mathcal{H}_4}(\mathcal{A})$$
$$\leq 3\mathsf{Adv}_{n,3}^{\mathsf{dec}-\mathsf{RLWE}}(\mathcal{M}) + \mathsf{Adv}_{n,3}^{\mathsf{lb}-\mathsf{RLWE}}(\mathcal{M}) + \mathsf{q_H}/\mathsf{p}^n,$$

We stress that the adversary cannot tell apart samples from $\mathcal{H}_1$ and $\mathcal{H}_2$ unless he queries the RO on $\mathbf{c}_0$, i.e., before querying the RO on $\mathbf{c}_0$ samples from $\mathcal{H}_1$ are indistinguishable from ones in $\mathcal{H}_2$ (ring-LWE samples) in the adversary's view. Thus, with the same probability as in $\mathcal{H}_1$ the adversary queries the RO on $\mathbf{c}_0$ when he is only given ring-LWE samples from $\mathcal{H}_2$. In $\mathcal{H}_2$ the only information the adversary gets about $\mathbf{c}_0$ is the ring-LWE instance with least significant bits $\mathbf{c}_0$ of the secret. Thus, if it queries H on $\mathbf{c}_0$ with non-negligible probability, it breaks ring-LWE as per Lemma 7. $\qquad\square$

Lemma 7. *Let $q = O(n)$ and ℓ the error size. Suppose there exists a PPT algorithm $\mathcal{S}$ that can output the low order bits of the secret in ring-LWE instances (lb − RLWE problem), then there exists a PPT algorithm $\mathcal{B}$ that breaks the search version of ring-LWE.*

Proof. Suppose there exists such an algorithm. For simplicity, let p be coprime to q. The ring-LWE samples $\{(\mathbf{a}_i, \mathbf{b}_i := \mathbf{a}_i \cdot \mathbf{s} + \mathbf{e}_i \bmod q)\}_i$ define the problem instance. $\mathcal{B}$ is challenged to find $\mathbf{s}$. With high probability, there exists an invertible element $\mathbf{a}_j \in \mathcal{R}_q$ (see e.g. [Pei15]). Taking any other sample, e.g. $(\mathbf{a}_1, \mathbf{b}_1 := \mathbf{a}_1 \cdot \mathbf{s} + \mathbf{e}_1 \bmod q)$, we can construct samples $\mathbf{b}_i^{(0)} := (\mathbf{a}_j^{-1}\mathbf{a}_i) \cdot (\mathbf{e}_j + \mathbf{d}) + \mathbf{e}_i = \mathbf{a}_j^{-1}\mathbf{a}_i \cdot (\mathbf{b}_j + \mathbf{d}) - \mathbf{b}_i \bmod q$ with $\mathbf{e}_j + \mathbf{d}$ as the secret and $i \neq j$ [ACPS09]. Here, the term $\mathbf{d}$ is filled with the tail bound at each coefficient such that all coefficients of $\mathbf{e}_j + \mathbf{d}$ are positive. Finding $\mathbf{s}$ is equivalent to recovering $(\mathbf{e}_j + \mathbf{d}) := \mathbf{e}_j^{(0)} = \mathbf{c}_0 + p \cdot \mathbf{c}_1 + \ldots + p^{\ell-1}\mathbf{c}_{\ell-1}$ with $\mathbf{c}_i \in \mathbb{Z}_p^n$ for some small $\ell < k$. The first input to $\mathcal{S}$ is therefore $(\mathbf{a}_i^{(0)} := \mathbf{a}_j^{-1}\mathbf{a}_i, \mathbf{b}_i^{(0)})$ which outputs $\mathbf{c}_0$ in polynomial time by assumption. In the second iteration the input is modified to $(\mathbf{a}_i^{(1)}, \mathbf{b}_i^{(1)})$ with $\mathbf{a}_i^{(1)} := p \cdot \mathbf{a}_i^{(0)}$,

$$\mathbf{b}_i^{(1)} := \mathbf{b}_i^{(0)} - \mathbf{a}_i^{(0)} \cdot \mathbf{c}^{(0)} \bmod q = \mathbf{a}_i^{(0)} \cdot (p \cdot \mathbf{c}_1 + \ldots + p^{\ell-1}\mathbf{c}_{\ell-1}) + \mathbf{e}_i \bmod q$$
$$= (p \cdot \mathbf{a}_i^{(0)}) \cdot (\mathbf{c}_1 + \ldots + p^{\ell-2}\mathbf{c}_{\ell-1}) + \mathbf{e}_i \bmod q = \mathbf{a}_i^{(1)} \cdot \mathbf{e}_j^{(1)} + \mathbf{e}_i \bmod q$$

and secret $\mathbf{e}_j^{(1)} := (\mathbf{c}_1 + \ldots + p^{\ell-2}\mathbf{c}_{\ell-1})$. Then, $\mathcal{S}$ outputs $\mathbf{c}_1$ by assumption. Analogously, via $(\mathbf{a}_i^{(t)} := p^t \cdot \mathbf{a}_i^{(0)}, \mathbf{b}_i^{(t)} := \mathbf{b}_i^{(t-1)} - \mathbf{a}_i^{(t-1)} \cdot \mathbf{c}^{(t-1)})$ as input instances to $\mathcal{S}$ the algorithm $\mathcal{B}$ obtains all $\mathbf{c}_t$ for $0 \leq t \leq \ell - 1$, recovers $\mathbf{e}_j + \mathbf{d} = \mathbf{c}_0 + p \cdot \mathbf{c}_1 + \ldots + p^{\ell-1}\mathbf{c}_{\ell-1}$ and thus $\mathbf{s}$ (after ℓ iterations) solving $\mathsf{search} - \mathsf{RLWE}$. Adding small errors to $\mathbf{a}_i^{(t)}$ generalizes the proof to all p, q.

5.1 CCA-secure Encryption

In order to obtain CCA-security, there exist 2 approaches. The first approach just requires to turn a CPA-secure public key encryption scheme via the Fujisako-Okamoto transform [FO99] into a CCA-secure hybrid encryption scheme. This can indeed be made very efficiently, where the symmetric key cipher could be instantiated by a random oracle or pseudorandom function (such as Shake). The other approach is realized based on the so-called tag approach, where a random tag [MP12, ABB10, PV08] is applied to the public key prior to encryption, i.e. we have $\mathbf{A}_u = [\mathbf{a}_1, \mathbf{a}_2, \mathbf{t}_u \cdot \mathbf{g} - (\mathbf{a}_1\mathbf{r}_1 + \mathbf{a}_2\mathbf{r}_2)]$. This has been realized in several works such as [MP12, EDB15]. To this end, a large tag space $\mathcal{T}$ has to be defined, out of which the tag is drawn uniformly at random. An element is called a tag, if it is a unit in the ring and satisfies the unit difference property. That is, for two units $\mathbf{u}, \mathbf{v} \in \mathcal{T}$ the difference $\mathbf{u} - \mathbf{v}$ is again a unit. Beside of these properties, a further objective is to specify efficient algorithms that allow to sample elements from $\mathcal{T}$ uniformly at random. In fact, for $q = 3^k$ the tag space may be defined to consist of binary polynomials of degree smaller than $n/2$ such that it satisfies the unit difference property as per Corollary 2. Thus, it suffices to sample binary strings of length $n/2$ bits and map them to the corresponding binary polynomial of degree smaller than $n/2$. In Sect. 4.1 we explained how to generate $\mathbf{t}_u \cdot \mathbf{s}$ such that we can recover $\mathbf{s}$. Using the framework from [EDB15] we give a CCA-secure scheme in Appendix A.

Corollary 2 (Unit Difference Property). *Let the tag space be defined as* $\mathcal{T} = \{a_0 + a_1 \cdot x + \ldots + a_{n/2-1} \cdot x^{n/2-1} \mid for\ a_i \in \{0,1\}\} \backslash \mathbf{0}$. *Then, any tag* $\mathbf{u} \in \mathcal{T}$ *satisfies the unit difference property.*

Proof. Any two elements $\mathbf{u}_1, \mathbf{u}_2 \in \mathcal{T}$ are invertible as per Corollary 1. Since both tags of degree at most $n/2 - 1$ have coefficients in $\{0,1\}$, the difference $\mathbf{u}_1 - \mathbf{u}_2$ has coefficients in $\{0, \pm 1\}$; thus invertible as per Corollary 1.   □

6   Software Implementation and Performance Analysis

At the implementation front we consider several optimizations and present an overview of the main ingredients. The error polynomials are generated as

$\mathbf{e}_i \leftarrow \mathcal{D}_{p\mathbb{Z}^n + \mathbf{v}_i, \alpha q}$ for uniform random cosets $\mathbf{v}_i$ following Lemma 3. This is realized with the aid of lookup tables, where almost 0.99 of the probability mass is concentrated on the 10 mid elements. Furthermore, we can use buckets for the 10 mid elements such that one call suffices to obtain a sample in 0.99 of all cases. In general, we find the right element after around 2 table lookups. By this technique we can build an efficient discrete Gaussian sampler. We instantiate the random oracle $H(\cdot)$, when encrypting messages, by an efficient and secure pseudo-random generator such as Salsa20 or Shake[1]. The secret key might consist of uniform random elements deduced from a seed and pk. We refer to the table below for a description parameters in use.

Parameter	Description
n	Dimension
q	Modulus
λ	Size of seed generating $\mathbf{a}_1, \mathbf{a}_2$
w	Message range
s	Error distribution $\mathcal{D}_{\mathbb{Z}^n, s}$
r_{sec}	Distribution of secret keys: $\mathcal{D}_{\mathbb{Z}^n, r_{sec}}$ or uniform with integer coefficients from $(-r_{sec}, r_{sec}]$
Message size	$3n \log_2 w$
Ciphertext size	$3n \log_2(q)$
Public key size	$\lambda + n \lceil \log_2(q) \rceil$
Secret key size	$2\lambda + n \lceil \log_2(q) \rceil$

6.1 Performance Analysis and Implementation Results

We implemented both our CPA/CCA secure schemes for $n = 1024$ on a machine that is specified by an Intel Core i5-6200U processor operating at 2.3 GHz and 8 GB of RAM. We used a gcc-5.4 compiler with compilation flags Ofast (Fig. 2). Figure 2 compares different schemes at a security level of 256 bits,

Scheme (Ref-Impl)	LARA$_{CPA}$ This work	LARA$_{CCA}$ This work	Kyber1024 − KEM [BDK+]	spLWE$_{CCA}$ [CHK+17]
q	2^{15}	3^9	7681	520
Enc (in cycles)	414 586	497 239	481 042	813 800
Dec (in cycles)	289 463	418 147	558 740	787 800
Message size (in bits)	6 144	6 144	256	256
Ciphertext exp	7.5	7.5	>33	25
PK size (in bytes)	1 984	1 984	1 081	-
SK size (in bytes)	2 048	2 048	2 400	-

Fig. 2. Experimental results from our reference implementation.

---

[1] KeccakCodeProject: https://github.com/gvanas/KeccakCodePackage/.

where $\mathsf{spLWE_{CCA}}$ provides only 128 bits of security. LARA has very small ciphertext expansion factors represented by a very low ratio of the ciphertext size per message bit. The number of cycles per encrypted message bit as well as its absolute performance and key sizes are very competitive for the CPA and CCA secure schemes. For instance, we are able to encrypt 2 bits per entry for $q = 2^{15}$ or $q = 2^{14}$ resulting in 414 586 cycles for encryption or 67 cycles per message bit. In order to estimate the security we used the LWE estimator[2].

Acknowledgements. The work presented in this paper was performed within the context of the project P1 within the CRC 1119 CROSSING. We thank Douglas Stebila for his useful comments.

A   CCA-secure Encryption with Tags

Let $q = 3^k$ and $\mathcal{T}$ define the tag space containing binary polynomials of degree less than $n/2$.

Remark 3. We note that in the encryption routine we have $(\mathbf{t}_u \cdot \mathbf{g} - \mathbf{a}_3) \cdot \mathbf{s} + \mathbf{e}_3 = \mathbf{t}_u \mathbf{s} \cdot \mathbf{g} - \mathbf{a}_3 \cdot \mathbf{s} + \mathbf{e}_3$. Furthermore, the trapdoor inversion algorithm LWEInv' computes the same quantities as LWEInv with the difference that it also deduces $\mathbf{t}_u$ from u via the coefficient embedding. Once $\mathbf{t}_u \cdot \mathbf{s}$ is recovered, one can compute $\mathbf{s}$ and thus $\hat{\mathbf{e}} = \hat{\mathbf{b}} - \mathbf{A}_u \cdot \mathbf{s}$ (see Sect. 4).

A.1   Chosen Ciphertext Security and Variants

We recall the definitions of (replayable) chosen ciphertext security of encryption schemes. Let $\mathcal{E} = (\mathsf{KGen}, \mathsf{Enc}, \mathsf{Dec})$ be a public key encryption scheme and consider the following experiments for $\mathsf{atk} \in \{\mathsf{cca1}, \mathsf{cca2}, \mathsf{rcca}\}$:

Experiment $\mathbf{Exp}_{\mathcal{E},\mathcal{A}}^{\mathsf{ind-atk}}(n)$

$(\mathsf{pk}, \mathsf{sk}) \leftarrow \mathsf{KGen}(1^k)$
$(\mu_0, \mu_1) \leftarrow \mathcal{A}^{\mathsf{Dec}(\cdot)}(\text{CHOOSE}, \mathsf{pk})$
$\mathbf{c}_b \leftarrow \mathsf{Enc}_{\mathsf{pk}}(\mu_b)$ for $b \leftarrow_R \{0,1\}$
$b' \leftarrow \mathcal{A}^{\mathcal{O}_2(\cdot)}(\text{GUESS}, \mathbf{c}_b)$
Output 1 iff
  1. $b' = b$
  2. $|\mu_0| = |\mu_1|$
  3. $\mathbf{c}_b$ was not queried to $\mathcal{O}_2$

If $\mathcal{A}$ queries $\mathcal{O}_2(\mathbf{c})$, and

- if $\mathsf{atk} = \mathsf{cca1}$, then return $\bot$.
- if $\mathsf{atk} = \mathsf{cca2}$, then return $\mathsf{Dec}(\mathsf{sk}, \mathbf{c})$.
- if $\mathsf{atk} = \mathsf{rcca}$ and $\mathsf{Dec}(\mathsf{sk}, \mathbf{c}) \notin \{\mu_0, \mu_1\}$,
     then return $\mathsf{Dec}(\mathsf{sk}, \mathbf{c})$.
- Otherwise, return $\bot$.

The security of the scheme directly follows from the framework as described in [EDB15] (Fig. 3).

---

[2] https://bitbucket.org/malb/lwe-estimator.

$\mathsf{LARA_{CCA}.KGen} : (1^{\ell})$

1: $(\mathsf{sk}, \mathsf{pk}) \leftarrow \mathsf{TrapGen}(1^n)$
2: We replace $\mathbf{a}_1, \mathbf{a}_2$ in the public key with the seed generating those elements, i.e. $\mathsf{pk} = (\mathsf{seed}, \mathbf{a}_3)$, where $\mathbf{a}_3 = (\mathbf{a}_1 \cdot \mathbf{r}_1 + \mathbf{a}_2 \cdot \mathbf{r}_2)$.

$\mathsf{LARA_{CCA}.Enc}(\mathsf{pk}, (\mathsf{m}_1, \mathsf{m}_2, \mathsf{m}_3) \in \{0,1\}^{3n \log w})$

1: $\mathbf{a}_1, \mathbf{a}_2 \leftarrow G(\mathsf{seed})$
2: $\mathbf{t}_u \in \mathcal{T}$
3: $\mathbf{c}_0 = (c_{1,0}, \ldots, c_{n-1,0}) \leftarrow \mathbb{Z}_p^n$
4: $(\mathbf{v}_1, \mathbf{v}_2, \mathbf{v}_3), \mathbf{d} \leftarrow H(\mathbf{c}_0) \in \mathbb{Z}_w^{3n} \times \mathbb{Z}_{p^{k-1}}^n$
5: $\mathbf{t}_u \cdot \mathbf{s} = \mathbf{c}_0 + p \cdot \mathbf{d}$
6: $\mathbf{s} := \mathbf{t}_u^{-1} \cdot (\mathbf{c}_0 + p \cdot \mathbf{d})$
7: $\mathbf{t}_i = \mathsf{Encode}(\mathsf{m}_i) + \mathbf{v}_i \bmod w$ for $1 \le i \le 3$
8: $\mathbf{e}_i \leftarrow \mathcal{D}_{\mathbf{t}_i + w \cdot \mathbb{Z}^n, s}$ for $1 \le i \le 3$
9: $\mathbf{b}_i = \mathbf{a}_i \cdot \mathbf{s} + \mathbf{e}_i$ for $i = 1, 2$
10: $\mathbf{b}_3 = \mathbf{t}_u \mathbf{s} \cdot \mathbf{g} - \mathbf{a}_3 \cdot \mathbf{s} + \mathbf{e}_3$
11: $\mathsf{h} = H(\mathbf{s}, \mathbf{t}_u, \hat{\mathbf{e}})$
12: Output $u, \mathsf{h}, \hat{\mathbf{b}} = (\mathbf{b}_1, \mathbf{b}_2, \mathbf{b}_3)$.

$\mathsf{LARA_{CCA}.Dec}(\mathsf{sk}, (u, \mathsf{h}, \hat{\mathbf{b}}) \in \{0,1\}^{n/2} \times \{0,1\}^{\lambda} \times \mathcal{R}_q^3)$

1: $\mathbf{a}_1, \mathbf{a}_2 \leftarrow G(\mathsf{seed})$
2: $(\mathbf{t}_u \mathbf{s} := \mathbf{c}_0 + p \cdot \mathbf{d}, \mathbf{e}_1, \mathbf{e}_2, \mathbf{e}_3) \leftarrow \mathsf{LWEInv}'(\mathsf{sk}, \hat{\mathbf{b}})$
3: $(\mathbf{v}_1, \mathbf{v}_2, \mathbf{v}_3), \mathbf{d} \leftarrow H(\mathbf{c}_0) \in \{0,1\}^{3n \log w} \times \mathbb{Z}_{p^{k-1}}^n$
4: if $\mathsf{h} = H(\mathbf{s}, \mathbf{t}_u, \hat{\mathbf{e}}) \wedge \| \hat{\mathbf{e}} \| \le \sqrt{3n} \cdot s$
5: $\quad \mathbf{t}_i = \mathbf{e}_i \bmod w$ for $1 \le i \le 3$
6: $\quad \mathsf{m}_i = \mathsf{Decode}(\mathbf{t}_i - \mathbf{v}_i \bmod w)$
7: $\quad$ Output $(\mathsf{m}_1, \mathsf{m}_2, \mathsf{m}_3)$

Fig. 3. Description of the CCA-secure encryption scheme.

References

[ABB10] Agrawal, S., Boneh, D., Boyen, X.: Efficient lattice (H)IBE in the standard model. In: Gilbert, H. (ed.) EUROCRYPT 2010. LNCS, vol. 6110, pp. 553–572. Springer, Heidelberg (2010). https://doi.org/10.1007/978-3-642-13190-5_28

[ABBK17] Alkadri, N.A., Buchmann, J., El Bansarkhani, R., Krämer, J.: A framework to select parameters for lattice-based cryptography. Cryptology ePrint Archive, Report 2017/615 (2017). http://eprint.iacr.org/2017/615

[ACPS09] Applebaum, B., Cash, D., Peikert, C., Sahai, A.: Fast cryptographic primitives and circular-secure encryption based on hard learning problems. In: Halevi, S. (ed.) CRYPTO 2009. LNCS, vol. 5677, pp. 595–618. Springer, Heidelberg (2009). https://doi.org/10.1007/978-3-642-03356-8_35

[Ban95] Banaszczyk, W.: Inequalities for convex bodies and polar reciprocal lattices in r^n. Discrete Comput. Geom. **13**(1), 217–231 (1995)

[BDK+] Bos, J.W., et al.: CRYSTALS kyber: a CCA-secure module-lattice-based KEM (2018)

[BF11]   Boneh, D., Freeman, D.M.: Homomorphic signatures for polynomial func-
          tions. In: Paterson, K.G. (ed.) EUROCRYPT 2011. LNCS, vol. 6632, pp.
          149–168. Springer, Heidelberg (2011). https://doi.org/10.1007/978-3-642-
          20465-4_10

[CHK+17] Cheon, J.H., Han, K., Kim, J., Lee, C., Son, Y.: A practical post-quantum
          public-key cryptosystem based on spLWE. In: Hong, S., Park, J.H. (eds.)
          ICISC 2016. LNCS, vol. 10157, pp. 51–74. Springer, Cham (2017). https://
          doi.org/10.1007/978-3-319-53177-9_3

[DM14]   Ducas, L., Micciancio, D.: Improved short lattice signatures in the standard
          model. In: Garay, J.A., Gennaro, R. (eds.) CRYPTO 2014. LNCS, vol. 8616,
          pp. 335–352. Springer, Heidelberg (2014). https://doi.org/10.1007/978-3-
          662-44371-2_19

[EB14]   El Bansarkhani, R., Buchmann, J.: Improvement and efficient implementa-
          tion of a lattice-based signature scheme. In: Lange, T., Lauter, K., Lisoněk,
          P. (eds.) SAC 2013. LNCS, vol. 8282, pp. 48–67. Springer, Heidelberg
          (2014). https://doi.org/10.1007/978-3-662-43414-7_3

[EDB15]   El Bansarkhani, R., Dagdelen, Ö., Buchmann, J.: Augmented learning with
          errors: the untapped potential of the error term. In: Böhme, R., Okamoto,
          T. (eds.) FC 2015. LNCS, vol. 8975, pp. 333–352. Springer, Heidelberg
          (2015). https://doi.org/10.1007/978-3-662-47854-7_20

[FO99]   Fujisaki, E., Okamoto, T.: Secure integration of asymmetric and symmetric
          encryption schemes. In: Wiener, M. (ed.) CRYPTO 1999. LNCS, vol. 1666,
          pp. 537–554. Springer, Heidelberg (1999). https://doi.org/10.1007/3-540-
          48405-1_34

[GPV08]   Gentry, C., Peikert, C., Vaikuntanathan, V.: Trapdoors for hard lattices
          and new cryptographic constructions. In: Ladner, R.E., Dwork, C. (eds.)
          40th Annual ACM Symposium on Theory of Computing, May 2008, pp.
          197–206. ACM Press (2008)

[LP11]   Lindner, R., Peikert, C.: Better key sizes (and attacks) for LWE-based
          encryption. In: Kiayias, A. (ed.) CT-RSA 2011. LNCS, vol. 6558, pp.
          319–339. Springer, Heidelberg (2011). https://doi.org/10.1007/978-3-642-
          19074-2_21

[LPR13]   Lyubashevsky, V., Peikert, C., Regev, O.: A toolkit for Ring-LWE cryptog-
          raphy. In: Johansson, T., Nguyen, P.Q. (eds.) EUROCRYPT 2013. LNCS,
          vol. 7881, pp. 35–54. Springer, Heidelberg (2013). https://doi.org/10.1007/
          978-3-642-38348-9_3

[MP12]   Micciancio, D., Peikert, C.: Trapdoors for lattices: simpler, tighter, faster,
          smaller. In: Pointcheval, D., Johansson, T. (eds.) EUROCRYPT 2012.
          LNCS, vol. 7237, pp. 700–718. Springer, Heidelberg (2012). https://doi.
          org/10.1007/978-3-642-29011-4_41

[Pei09]   Peikert, C.: Public-key cryptosystems from the worst-case shortest vector
          problem: extended abstract. In: Mitzenmacher, M. (ed) 41st Annual ACM
          Symposium on Theory of Computing, May–June 2009, pp. 333–342. ACM
          Press (2009)

[Pei10]   Peikert, C.: An efficient and parallel gaussian sampler for lattices. In: Rabin,
          T. (ed.) CRYPTO 2010. LNCS, vol. 6223, pp. 80–97. Springer, Heidelberg
          (2010). https://doi.org/10.1007/978-3-642-14623-7_5

[Pei15]   Peikert, C.: A decade of lattice cryptography. Cryptology ePrint Archive,
          Report 2015/939 (2015). https://eprint.iacr.org/2015/939

[PV08] Peikert, C., Vaikuntanathan, V.: Noninteractive statistical zero-knowledge proofs for lattice problems. In: Wagner, D. (ed.) CRYPTO 2008. LNCS, vol. 5157, pp. 536–553. Springer, Heidelberg (2008). https://doi.org/10.1007/978-3-540-85174-5_30

[Reg05] Regev, O.: On lattices, learning with errors, random linear codes, and cryptography. In: Gabow, H.N., Fagin, R. (eds.) 37th Annual ACM Symposium on Theory of Computing, May 2005, pp. 84–93. ACM Press (2005)

[SS11] Stehlé, D., Steinfeld, R.: Making NTRU as Secure as Worst-Case Problems over Ideal Lattices. In: Paterson, K.G. (ed.) EUROCRYPT 2011. LNCS, vol. 6632, pp. 27–47. Springer, Heidelberg (2011). https://doi.org/10.1007/978-3-642-20465-4_4

Short Paper: The Proof is in the Pudding
Proofs of Work for Solving Discrete Logarithms

Marcella Hastings[1]([⊠]), Nadia Heninger[2], and Eric Wustrow[3]

[1] University of Pennsylvania, Philadelphia, USA
mhast@cis.upenn.edu
[2] University of California, San Diego, San Diego, USA
[3] University of Colorado Boulder, Boulder, USA

Abstract. We propose a proof of work protocol that computes the discrete logarithm of an element in a cyclic group. Individual provers generating proofs of work perform a distributed version of the Pollard rho algorithm. Such a protocol could capture the computational power expended to construct proof-of-work-based blockchains for a more useful purpose, as well as incentivize advances in hardware, software, or algorithms for an important cryptographic problem. We describe our proposed construction and elaborate on challenges and potential trade-offs that arise in designing a practical proof of work.

Keywords: Proofs of work · Discrete log · Pollard rho

1 Introduction

We propose a proof of work scheme that is useful for cryptanalysis, in particular, solving discrete logarithms. The security of the ECDSA digital signature scheme is based on the hardness of the elliptic curve discrete log problem. Despite the problem's cryptographic importance, the open research community is small and has limited resources for the engineering and computation required to update cryptanalytic records; recent group sizes for elliptic curve discrete log records include 108 bits in 2002 [11], 112 bits in 2009 [10], and 113 bits in 2014 [30].

Our proposition aims to harness the gigawatts of energy spent on Bitcoin mining [29] to advance the state of the art in discrete log cryptanalysis. Jakobsson and Juels [16] call this a *bread pudding* proof of work. Just as stale bread becomes a delicious dessert, individual proofs of work combine to produce a useful computation. While memory-hard functions aim to discourage specialized hardware for cryptocurrency mining [21], we hope for the exact opposite effect. Just as Bitcoin has prompted significant engineering effort to develop efficient FPGAs and ASICs for SHA-256, we wish to use the lure of financial rewards from cryptocurrency mining to incentivize special-purpose hardware for cryptanalysis.

© International Financial Cryptography Association 2019
I. Goldberg and T. Moore (Eds.): FC 2019, LNCS 11598, pp. 396–404, 2019.
https://doi.org/10.1007/978-3-030-32101-7_24

2   Background

Let G be a cyclic group with generator g of order q. We represent the group operation as multiplication, but every algorithm in our paper applies to a generic group. Every element $h \in G$ can be represented as an integer power of g, $g^a = h$, $0 \le a < q$, and also has a unique representation as a sequence of bits. The discrete logarithm $log_g(h)$ is a, $0 \le a < q$ satisfying $g^a = h$. Computing discrete logs is believed to be difficult for certain groups, including multiplicative groups modulo primes and elliptic curve groups. The conjectured hardness of discrete log underlies the security of multiple important cryptographic algorithms, including the Diffie-Hellman key exchange [4,12] and the Digital Signature Algorithm [20]. Efficient computation of a discrete log for a group used for Diffie-Hellman key exchange would allow an adversary to compute the private key from the public key exchange messages; for DSA signatures, such an adversary could compute the private signing key from the public key and forge arbitrary signatures.

2.1   Discrete Log Cryptanalysis

There are two main families of algorithms for solving the discrete log problem. The first family works over any group, and includes Shanks's baby step giant step algorithm [24], and the Pollard rho and lambda algorithms [22]. These algorithms run in time $O(\sqrt{q})$ for any group of order q. It is this family of algorithms we target in this paper. A second family of algorithms is based on index calculus [3,15]; these algorithms have sub-exponential running times only over finite fields.

Current best practices for elliptic curves are to use 256-bit curves [4], although 160-bit curves remain supported in some implementations [27]. Bitcoin miners currently perform around 2^{90} hashes per year and consume 0.33% of the world's electricity [29]. If this effort were instead focused on discrete log, a 180-bit curve could be broken in around a year[1]. Scaling this to discrete logs in 224-bit groups would require all current electricity production on Earth for 10,000 years. Alternative cryptocurrencies such as Litecoin, Ethereum, and Dogecoin achieve lower hash rates of about 2^{72} hashes per year[2].

2.2   Pollard Rho with Distinguished Points

The protocols we study in this paper compute the discrete log of an element h by finding a collision $g^a h^b = g^{a'} h^{b'}$ with $b \not\equiv b'$ mod q. Given such an equivalence, the discrete log of h can be computed as $(a' - a)/(b - b')$ mod q.

Pollard's rho algorithm for discrete logarithms [22] works for any cyclic group G of order q. The main idea is to take a deterministic pseudorandom walk inside of the group until the same element is encountered twice along the walk. By

---

[1] Elliptic curve point multiplications take about 2^{10} times longer than SHA-256 on modern CPUs.

[2] Extrapolated from peak daily hash rates at bitinfocharts.com.

the birthday bound, such an element will be found with high probability after $\Theta(\sqrt{q})$ steps. The non-parallelized version of this algorithm uses a cycle-finding algorithm to discover this collision, and computes the log as above.

We base our proof of work on Van Oorschot and Wiener's [28] parallelized Pollard rho algorithm using the method of distinguished points. A distinguished point is an element whose bitwise representation matches some easily-identifiable condition, such as having d leading zeros. Each individual process j independently chooses a random starting point $g^{a_j} h^{b_j}$ and generates a psuedorandom walk sequence from this starting element. When the walk reaches a distinguished point, the point is saved to a central repository and the process starts over again from a new random starting point until a collision is found.

The number of steps required to compute the discrete log is independent of d, which we call the difficulty parameter below; d only determines the storage required. We expect to find a collision after $\Theta(\sqrt{q})$ steps by all processes. With m processes running in parallel, the calendar running time is $O(\sqrt{q}/m)$.

The pseudorandom walk produces a deterministic sequence within the group from some starting value. Given a group generator g and a target h, the walk generates a random starting point $x_0 = g^{a_0} h^{b_0}$ by choosing random exponents a_0, b_0. In practice, most implementations use the Teske pseudorandom walk [26]: given a disjoint partition of G with 20 sets of equal size $T_1, \ldots, T_{20}$ parameterized by the bitwise representation of an element, choose $m_s, n_s \in [1, q]$ at random and define $M_s = g^{m_s} h^{n_s}$ for $s \in [1, 20]$. Then we can define the walk $\mathcal{W}(x) = M_s * x$ for $x \in T_s$. In general, an effective pseudorandom walk updates the group representation of a point based on some property of the bitwise representation.

2.3   Proofs of Work

A proof of work [13,16] protocol allows a *prover* to demonstrate to a *verifier* that they have executed an amount of work. We use the definition from [2].

Definition 1. *A $(t(n), \delta(n))$-Proof of Work (PoW) consists of three algorithms* (Gen, Solve, Verify) *that satisfy the following properties:*

- **Efficiency:**
  - Gen(1^n) *runs in time* $\tilde{O}(n)$.
  - *For any* $c \leftarrow$ Gen(1^n), Solve(c) *runs in time* $\tilde{O}(t(n))$.
  - *For any* $c \leftarrow$ Gen(1^n) *and any* π, Verify(c, π) *runs in time* $\tilde{O}(n)$.
- **Completeness:** *For any* $c \leftarrow$ Gen(1^n) *and any* $\pi \leftarrow$ Solve(c),
  $\Pr[\text{Verify}(c, \pi) = accept] = 1$.
- **Hardness:** *For any polynomial* ℓ, *any constant* $\epsilon > 0$, *and any algorithm* Solve$_\ell^*$ *that runs in time* $\ell(n)t(n)^{1-\epsilon}$ *when given as input* $\ell(n)$ *challenges* $\{c_i \leftarrow$ Gen$(1^n)\}_{i \in [\ell(n)]}$,
  $\Pr\left[\forall i \, \text{Verify}(c_i, \pi_i) = accept \mid (\pi_1, \ldots, \pi_{\ell(n)}) \leftarrow \text{Solve}_\ell^*(c_1, \ldots, c_{\ell(n)})\right] < \delta(n)$

We can describe the hash puzzle proof of work [1] used by Bitcoin [19] in this framework as follows. The challenge generated by Gen is the hash of the previous block. Solve is parameterized by a difficulty d; individual miners search for a nonce n such that SHA-256$(c, n) \leq 2^{256-d}$ when mapped to an integer. Assuming that SHA-256 acts like a random function, miners must brute force search random values of n; the probability that a random fixed-length integer is below the difficulty threshold is 2^{-d}, so the conjectured running time for Solve is $t(n) = O(2^d)$. Verify runs in constant time and accepts if SHA-256$(c, n) \leq 2^{256-d}$.

Proposals for "Useful" Proofs of Work. Primecoin [17] proofs contain prime chains, which may be of scientific interest. DDoSCoin [31] proofs can cause a denial of service attack. TorPath [6] increases bandwidth on the Tor network. Ball et al. [2] describe theoretical proof-of-work schemes based on worst-case hardness assumptions from computational complexity theory. Lochter [18] independently outlines a similar discrete log proof of work.

3 Proof of Work for Discrete Log

The goal of this thought experiment is to develop a proof of work scheme that, if provided with mining power at Bitcoin's annual hash rate, can solve a discrete log in a 160-bit group. We outline our proposed scheme, explain limitations of the simple model, and describe possible avenues to fix the gap.

3.1 Strawman Pollard Rho Proof of Work Proposal

In our rho-inspired proof of work scheme, workers compute a pseudorandom walk from a starting point partially determined by the input challenge and produce a distinguished point. The parameters defining the group G, group generator g, discrete log target h, and deterministic pseudorandom walk function $\mathcal{W}$, are global for all workers and chosen prior to setup. A distinguished point x at difficulty d is defined as having d leading zeros in the bitwise representation, where d is a difficulty parameter provided by the challenge generator.

In the terminology of Definition 1, Gen produces a challenge bit string c; when used in a blockchain, c can be the hash of the previous block.

To execute the Solve function, miners generate a starting point for their walk, for example by generating a pair of integers $(a_0, b_0) = H(c||n)$ where n is a nonce chosen by a miner and H is a cryptographically secure hash function, and computing the starting point $P_0 = g^{a_0} h^{b_0}$. Workers then iteratively compute $P_i = \mathcal{W}(P_{i-1})$ until they encounter a distinguished point $P_D = g^{a_D} h^{b_D}$ of difficulty d, and output $\pi = (n, a_D, b_D, P_D)$. A single prover expects to take $O(2^d)$ steps before a distinguished point is encountered.

The Verify function can check that $P_D = g^{a_D} h^{b_D}$ and has d leading zeros. This confirms that P_D is distinguished, but does not verify that P_D lies on the random walk of length ℓ starting at the point determined by (a_0, b_0). Without this check, a miner can pre-mine a distinguished point and lie about its relationship to the starting point. A verifier can prevent this by verifying every step of the random walk, but this does not satisfy the efficiency constraints of Definition 1.

A discrete log in a group of order q takes $\sqrt{q}$ steps to compute (see Sect. 2.2). A set of m honest miners working in parallel expect to perform $O(2^d)$ work per proof. If all miners have equal computational power, the winning miner will find a distinguished point after expected $O(2^d/m)$ individual work. This construction expects to store $\sqrt{q}m/2^d$ distinguished points in a block chain before a collision is found; the total amount of work performed by all miners for all blocks to compute the discrete log is $\sqrt{q}m$. Each distinguished point wastes $(m-1)/m$ work performed by miners who do not find the "winning" point.

We next examine several modified proof-of-work schemes based on this idea that attempt to solve the problems of verification and wasted work.

3.2   Reducing the Cost of Wasted Work

To reduce wasted work, we can allow miners that do not achieve the first block to announce their blocks and receive a partial block reward. One technique is to use the Greedy Heaviest-Observed Sub-Tree method [25] to determine consensus, which has been adopted by Ethereum in the form of Uncle block rewards [14]. In this consensus method, the main (heaviest) chain is defined as the sub-tree of blocks containing the most work, rather than the longest chain. This allows stale blocks to contribute to the security of a single chain, and allocates rewards to their producers. In Ethereum, this supports faster block times and lowers orphan rates but we could use it to incentivize miners to publish their useful work rather than discard it when each new block is found.

3.3   Limiting the Length of the Pseudorandom Walk

We attempt to reduce the cost of the Verify function by limiting the length of the random walk in a proof to at most 2^ℓ steps for some integer ℓ. Individual miners derive a starting point from the challenge c and a random nonce n. They walk until they either find a distinguished point or pass 2^ℓ steps. In the latter case, the miner chooses another random nonce n and restarts the walk.

Solve requires miners to produce a proof $\pi = (n, \mathcal{L}, a_D, b_D)$ satisfying four criteria: (1) the walk begins at the point derived from a hash of the challenge and nonce values $((a_0, b_0) = H(c\|n))$, (2) walking from this initial point for $\mathcal{L}$ steps leads to the specified endpoint $(\mathcal{W}^\mathcal{L}(g^{a_0}h^{b_0}) = g^{a_D}h^{b_D})$, (3) the bitwise representation of the endpoint $g^{a_D}h^{b_D}$ is distinguished and (4) the walk does not exceed the maximum walk length $(\mathcal{L} < 2^\ell)$. Solve runs in expected time $O(2^d)$.

Verify retraces the short walk and runs in $O(2^\ell)$ steps. Overall, fixing a maximum walk length forces more total work to be done, since walks over 2^ℓ steps are never published. The probability that a length 2^ℓ random walk contains a distinguished point of difficulty d is $2^{\ell-d}$, so a prover expects to perform $2^{d-\ell}$ random walks before finding a distinguished point. An individual prover in a group of order q can expect to store $O(\sqrt{q}/2^\ell)$ distinguished points before a collision is found. With 2^d work performed per distinguished point stored, the total amount of work is $O(2^{d-\ell}\sqrt{q})$. For $m \ll 2^{d-\ell}$ miners working in parallel, the work wasted by parallel mining is subsumed by that of discarded long walks.

To target a 160-bit group with mining power of around 2^{90} hashes per year, the total amount of work performed by miners should not exceed $2^{90} \geq 2^{d-\ell}2^{80}$, or $10 \geq d-\ell$, with a total of $2^{80-\ell}$ distinguished points. If we allow 1 GB $= 8 \cdot 10^9$ storage, this allows up to 2^{25} 160-bit distinguished points, so we have $\ell = 55$, and thus we set the difficulty $d = 65$. This is feasible: as of Sep 2018, Bitcoin miners produce nearly 2^{75} hashes per block and the blockchain is ~183 GB.

3.4 Efficiently Verifying Pseudorandom Walks

In theory, a SNARK [7] solves the efficient verification problem for the proof of work. Provers compute the SNARK alongside the pseudorandom walk, and include the result with the proof of work. Verification executes in constant time. Unfortunately, generating a SNARK is thousands of times more expensive than performing the original computation. A STARK [5] takes much less work to solve but slightly longer to verify and comes with a non-negligible space trade-off. In our framework, Solve finds a distinguished point and build a STARK: this takes time $O(d^2 2^{2d})$ and space $O(d2^d)$ group elements. Verify executes the STARK verify function in time $O(d)$. Verifiable delay functions [9] could also be used to solve this problem, but existing solutions appear to take advantage of algebraic structure that we do not have in our pseudorandom walk.

We attempted to emulate a verifiable delay function by defining an alternate pseudorandom walk. We experimented with several possibilities, for example a "rotating" walk that performs a set of multiplications and exponentiations in sequence. A walk of this type has the convenient algebraic property that it is simple to verify for a given start point, end point, and length $\mathcal{L}$, that the end point is $\mathcal{L}$ steps from the start. Unfortunately, it has terrible pseudorandom properties: collisions are either trivial or occur after $O(q)$ steps. There appears to be a tension between the pseudorandomness properties required for the Pollard rho algorithm to achieve $O(\sqrt{q})$ running time and an algebraic structure allowing efficient verification of the walk. Effective random walks determine each step by the bitwise representation of a given element—independent of its group element representation $g^{a_i}h^{b_i}$—but this independence makes it difficult to reconstruct or efficiently summarize the group steps without repeating the entire computation. We leave the discovery of such a pseudorandom walk to future work.

3.5 Distributed Verification

An alternate block chain formulation has miners accept blocks unless they see a proof that it is invalid, and incentivizes other validators to produce such proofs. This technique has been proposed for verifying off-chain transactions in Ethereum Plasma [23]. We extend this idea to allow validators to prove a miner has submitted an invalid block and offer rewards for such discoveries.

In this scheme, the Verify function accompanies a *reject* decision with a proof of falsification f, and can take as long as mining: $\tilde{O}(t(n))$. We define a function

Check(c, f) to check whether this proof of falsification is accurate, which runs in time $\tilde{O}(n)$. In a block chain, miners Solve proofs of work and dedicated verifiers Verify. If a verifier produces a proof of falsification f (that is, finds an invalid block) it broadcasts (c, f) to all participants, who must Check the falsification.

To increase verification cost, there must be a matching increase in incentive. For example, a time-delayed bounty system requires a miner to provide a bounty with each new block, which is either collected by the miner with the block reward after a fixed amount of time, or partially poached by a verifier who produces a valid falsification. Such a scheme aims to prevent collusion between miners and verifiers to collect rewards and bounty for no useful work.

Walk Summaries. A first idea modifies the proof of work π to include intermediate points $s_0, s_1, \ldots$ spaced at regular intervals along the walk. The Verify function picks a random subset of the s_i and retraces the walks from s_i to s_{i+1}. An invalid proof has the property that at least one interval does not have a valid path between the endpoints. For a walk with I intervals of length ℓ, a verifier that checks k intervals has probability k/I of detecting an invalid proof with work kI. However, checking a claimed falsification f requires ℓ work. A malicious verifier can report incorrect falsifications and force other participants to perform arbitrary work. To fix this, we need more efficiently checkable falsifications.

Bloom Filters for Secondary Validation. One approach to efficiently checkable proof falsifications uses Bloom filters [8], a probabilistic data structure that tests set membership. It may return false positives, but never false negatives. We modify our walk summary proof of work π above to also include a Bloom filter containing every point on the walk. The Verify function chooses a random interval s_i and takes ℓ walk steps, which takes work ℓ. If an element e_i on the walk is absent from the filter, the verifier broadcasts the sequence of points $f = (e_{i-k}, \ldots, e_i)$. The Check function confirms that the points f are a correctly generated random walk and that all points except e_i are contained in the Bloom filter. This takes time k. The short sequence prevents a malicious verifier from invalidating a correct block by taking advantage of false positives in Bloom filters.

A Bloom filter containing every element in a random walk for a reasonable difficulty value will be too large (we estimate at least 150 TB for a walk of length 2^{60}). To shrink the filter, we could store hashes of short sub-walks of length ℓ', rather than every step. To Check, a participant must walk ℓ' steps for each of the k broadcast sub-walks. This increases the work to $k\ell'$, but decreases Bloom filter size by a factor of ℓ'.

Acknowledgement. Joseph Bonneau, Brett Hemenway, Michael Rudow, Terry Sun, and Luke Valenta contributed to early versions of this work. Nadia Heninger carried out this research while at the University of Pennsylvania. This work was supported by the National Science Foundation under grants no. CNS-1651344 and CNS-1513671 and by the Office of Naval Research under grant no. 568751.

References

1. Back, A.: Hashcash-a denial of service counter-measure (2002)
2. Ball, M., Rosen, A., Sabin, M., Vasudevan, P.N.: Proofs of work from worst-case assumptions. In: Shacham, H., Boldyreva, A. (eds.) CRYPTO 2018. LNCS, vol. 10991, pp. 789–819. Springer, Cham (2018). https://doi.org/10.1007/978-3-319-96884-1_26
3. Barbulescu, R., Gaudry, P., Joux, A., Thomé, E.: A heuristic quasi-polynomial algorithm for discrete logarithm in finite fields of small characteristic. In: Nguyen, P.Q., Oswald, E. (eds.) EUROCRYPT 2014. LNCS, vol. 8441, pp. 1–16. Springer, Heidelberg (2014). https://doi.org/10.1007/978-3-642-55220-5_1
4. Barker, E., Chen, L., Roginsky, A., Vassilev, A., Davis, R.: SP 800–56A Revision 3. Recommendation for pair-wise key establishment schemes using discrete logarithm cryptography. National Institute of Standards & Technology (2018)
5. Ben-Sasson, E., Bentov, I., Horesh, Y., Riabzev, M.: Scalable, transparent, and post-quantum secure computational integrity. Cryptology ePrint Archive (2018)
6. Biryukov, A., Pustogarov, I.: Proof-of-Work as anonymous micropayment: rewarding a tor relay. In: Böhme, R., Okamoto, T. (eds.) FC 2015. LNCS, vol. 8975, pp. 445–455. Springer, Heidelberg (2015). https://doi.org/10.1007/978-3-662-47854-7_27
7. Bitansky, N., et al.: The hunting of the SNARK. J. Cryptol. **30**(4) (2017)
8. Bloom, B.H.: Space/time trade-offs in hash coding with allowable errors. Commun. ACM **13**(7), 422–426 (1970). https://doi.org/10.1145/362686.362692
9. Boneh, D., Bonneau, J., Bünz, B., Fisch, B.: Verifiable delay functions. In: Shacham, H., Boldyreva, A. (eds.) CRYPTO 2018. LNCS, vol. 10991, pp. 757–788. Springer, Cham (2018). https://doi.org/10.1007/978-3-319-96884-1_25
10. Bos, J.W., Kaihara, M.E., Kleinjung, T., Lenstra, A.K., Montgomery, P.L.: Solving a 112-bit prime elliptic curve discrete logarithm problem on game consoles using sloppy reduction. Int. J. Appl. Crypt. **2**(3) (2012)
11. Certicom ECC challenge (1997). http://certicom.com/images/pdfs/challenge-2009.pdf. Accessed 10 Nov 2009
12. Diffie, W., Hellman, M.: New directions in cryptography. IEEE Trans. Inf. Theory **22**(6), 644–654 (1976)
13. Dwork, C., Naor, M.: Pricing via processing or combatting junk mail. In: Brickell, E.F. (ed.) CRYPTO 1992. LNCS, vol. 740, pp. 139–147. Springer, Heidelberg (1993). https://doi.org/10.1007/3-540-48071-4_10
14. Ethereum Project: Ethereum white paper. https://github.com/ethereum/wiki/wiki/White-Paper#modified-ghost-implementation
15. Gordon, D.M.: Discrete logarithms in GF(P) using the number field sieve. SIAM J. Discret. Math. **6**(1), 124–138 (1993). https://doi.org/10.1137/0406010
16. Jakobsson, M., Juels, A.: Proofs of work and bread pudding protocols (Extended Abstract). In: Preneel, B. (ed.) Secure Information Networks. ITIFIP, vol. 23, pp. 258–272. Springer, Boston, MA (1999). https://doi.org/10.1007/978-0-387-35568-9_18
17. King, S.: Primecoin: cryptocurrency with prime number proof-of-work (2013)
18. Lochter, M.: Blockchain as cryptanalytic tool. Cryptology ePrint Archive, Report 2018/893 (2018). https://eprint.iacr.org/2018/893.pdf
19. Nakamoto, S.: Bitcoin: A Peer-to-Peer Electronic Cash System. White paper (2008)
20. National Institute of Standards and Technology: FIPS PUB 186–4: Digital Signature Standard (DSS). National Institute of Standards and Technology, July 2013

21. Percival, C., Josefsson, S.: The scrypt password-based key derivation function. RFC 7914, RFC Editor, August 2016. http://rfc-editor.org/rfc/rfc7914.txt
22. Pollard, J.M.: Monte carlo methods for index computation (mod p). In: Mathematics of Computation, vol. 32 (1978)
23. Poon, J., Buterin, V.: Plasma: scalable autonomous smart contracts (2017)
24. Shanks, D.: Class number, a theory of factorization, and genera. In: Proceedings of Symposium Mathematical Society, vol. 20, pp. 41–440 (1971)
25. Sompolinsky, Y., Zohar, A.: Secure high-rate transaction processing in bitcoin. In: Böhme, R., Okamoto, T. (eds.) FC 2015. LNCS, vol. 8975, pp. 507–527. Springer, Heidelberg (2015). https://doi.org/10.1007/978-3-662-47854-7_32
26. Teske, E.: Speeding up Pollard's rho method for computing discrete logarithms. In: Buhler, J.P. (ed.) ANTS 1998. LNCS, vol. 1423, pp. 541–554. Springer, Heidelberg (1998). https://doi.org/10.1007/BFb0054891
27. Valenta, L., Sullivan, N., Sanso, A., Heninger, N.: In search of CurveSwap: measuring elliptic curve implementations in the wild. In: EuroS&P. IEEE (2018)
28. Van Oorschot, P.C., Wiener, M.J.: Parallel collision search with cryptanalytic applications. J. Cryptol. **12**(1), 1–28 (1999)
29. de Vries, A.: Bitcoin's growing energy problem. Joule **2**(5), 801–805 (2018)
30. Wenger, E., Wolfger, P.: Harder, better, faster, stronger: elliptic curve discrete logarithm computations on FPGAs. J. Crypt. Eng. (2016)
31. Wustrow, E., VanderSloot, B.: DDoSCoin: cryptocurrency with a malicious proof-of-work. In: WOOT (2016)

Getting Formal

Minimizing Trust in Hardware Wallets with Two Factor Signatures

Antonio Marcedone[1]([✉]), Rafael Pass[1], and Abhi Shelat[2]

[1] Cornell Tech, New York, USA
{marcedone,rafael}@cs.cornell.edu
[2] Northeastern University, Boston, USA
abhi@neu.edu

Abstract. We introduce the notion of *two-factor signatures (2FS)*, a generalization of a two-out-of-two threshold signature scheme in which one of the parties is a *hardware token* which can store a high-entropy secret, and the other party is a *human* who knows a low-entropy password. The security (unforgeability) property of 2FS requires that an external adversary corrupting either party (the token or the computer the human is using) cannot forge a signature.

This primitive is useful in contexts like hardware cryptocurrency wallets in which a signature conveys the authorization of a transaction. By the above security property, a hardware wallet implementing a two-factor signature scheme is secure against attacks mounted by a malicious hardware vendor; in contrast, all currently used wallet systems break under such an attack (and as such are not secure under our definition).

We construct efficient provably-secure 2FS schemes which produce either Schnorr signature (assuming the DLOG assumption), or EC-DSA signatures (assuming security of EC-DSA and the CDH assumption) in the Random Oracle Model, and evaluate the performance of implementations of them. Our EC-DSA based 2FS scheme can directly replace currently used hardware wallets for Bitcoin and other major cryptocurrencies to enable security against malicious hardware vendors.

1 Introduction

Cryptocurrency hardware wallets are increasingly popular among Bitcoin and Ethereum users as they offer seemingly stronger security guarantees over their software counterparts. A hardware wallet is typically a small electronic device (such as a USB device with an input button) that holds the secret key(s) to one or more cryptocurrency "accounts". It provides a simple interface that can be used by client software on a computer or smartphone to request a signature on a particular transaction; the wallet returns a signature to the client if the user

R. Pass—Supported in part by NSF Award CNS-1561209, NSF Award CNS-1217821, NSF Award CNS-1704788, AFOSR Award FA9550-15-1-0262, AFOSR Award FA9550-18-1-0267, a Microsoft Faculty Fellowship, and a Google Faculty Research Award.
A. Shelat—Supported in part by NSF grants 1664445 and 1646671.

ⓒ International Financial Cryptography Association 2019
I. Goldberg and T. Moore (Eds.): FC 2019, LNCS 11598, pp. 407–425, 2019.
https://doi.org/10.1007/978-3-030-32101-7_25

has authorized it by pressing the physical button[1]. Typically, the user also has to enter a pin or password, either on the device itself or through the client. Some hardware wallets like the Trezor include a screen that can be used by the user to confirm the details of the transaction before authorizing it.

Ideally, a hardware wallet runs a firmware that is smaller and simpler than the software running on a common laptop (and thus may be less vulnerable to bugs and exploits), is built using tamper proof hardware that makes it difficult to directly read its memory, and is designed to prevent the private keys it holds from ever leaving the device. Thus, stealing funds from an address controlled by a hardware wallet is considered to be harder than stealing from a software wallet installed on the user's laptop.

Can we trust the hardware manufacturer? However, most hardware wallets suffer from a serious issue: since the wallet generates and holds the secret keys for the user's account, a compromised wallet might be used to steal the entirety of the coins it controls. Consider, for instance, a malicious wallet manufacturer who introduces a backdoored pseudorandom generator (to be used, for example, to generate the signing keys) into a hardware wallet. Because of the tamperproof properties of the hardware, such a backdoor might be extremely hard to detect and go unnoticed even to a scrupulous user, especially if it only affects a small portion of the company's devices (perhaps those shipped to customers who hold large coin balances). Yet, without the need of ever communicating with the devices again, the manufacturer might suddenly steal all the money controlled by those addresses before anyone has time to react! This is also true in the case where the user picks a password to supplement the entropy generated by the backdoored PRG, since passwords have limited entropy which can be bruteforced and, as we detail later, the wallet can bias the randomness in the signatures to leak information about such password.

Even if the company producing the wallet is reputable and trusted, supply chain attacks by single employees or powerful adversaries are still hard to rule out for customers. For example, the NSA reportedly intercepts shipments of laptops purchased online in transit to install malware/backdoors [17]. Indeed, trust in a wallet manufacturer, its supply chain, and the delivery chain are a serious concern.

One possible solution is to store the funds in a multi-signature account controlled by a combination of hardware (and possibly software) wallets from different manufacturers. However, the above is inconvenient and limiting. It may also be possible for a single supplier to corrupt multiple manufacturers of hardware wallets.

A Formal Treatment of Hardware Wallets. In this paper, we initiate a formal study of the security of hardware wallets. As discussed above, completely relying on the token to perform key generation and signing operations requires a strong trust assumption on the hardware manufacturer. To avoid this, we focus

---

[1] The physical button prevents malware from abusing the wallet without cooperation from the user.

on a scenario in which the user has both a single *hardware token* and a (low-entropy) *password*, and formally define appropriate an appropriate cryptographic primitive, which we name *two factor signature scheme (2FS)*.

Roughly speaking, a 2FS scheme can be thought of a special type of two-out-of-two threshold signature scheme [4] but where one of the parties (the user) only has a (potentially low-entropy) password, whereas the other party (the hardware token) can generate and store high-entropy secrets. Even defining unforgeability properties of such 2FS schemes turns out to be a non-trivial task; we provide the first such definitions. Our notions of unforgeability consider both malicious clients, malicious tokens, and attackers that may have selective access to honestly implemented tokens.

As already mentioned, as far as we know, in all currently known/used schemes, unforgeability does not hold when the hardware token can be maliciously designed, and thus no currently known schemes satisfies even a subset of our unforgeability definitions. Our main contribution is next the design of 2FS that satisfy them. In fact, we present a general transformation from any two-out-of-two threshold signature scheme which satisfies some additional technical property—which we refer to as *statistical Non-Signalling*—into a 2FS in the random oracle model, which produces public keys and signatures of the same form as the underlying threshold signature scheme.

We note that it may be possible to generically modify any TS to become Non-Signalling by having the parties perform coin-tossing to generate the randomness, and then prove in zero knowledge that they executed the signing protocol consistently with the pre-determined (and uniform) randomness. Using such a method, however, would result in a (polynomial-time but) practically inefficient scheme. In contrast, in the full version of this work [13], we show how to adapt two existing threshold signature schemes to satisfy this new technical property with very little overhead. Using our transformation, this gives secure 2FS schemes which efficiently generate Schnorr and ECDSA signatures.

Theorem (Informal). Assuming the discrete logarithm assumption, there exists a secure 2FS scheme in the Random Oracle model which generates Schnorr Signatures.

Theorem (Informal). Assuming the DDH assumption holds and that EC-DSA is unforgeable, there exists a secure 2FS scheme in the Random Oracle model that generates EC-DSA signatures.

The first construction is based on the Schnorr TS signature scheme of Nicolosi *et al.* [15], while the second one is a slight modification of an EC-DSA threshold scheme of Lee *et al.* [5]. As EC-DSA signature are currently used in Bitcoin, Ethereum and most other major crypto currencies, our 2FS for EC-DSA can be directly used for hardware wallets supporting those crypto currencies. To demonstrate its practicality, we evaluate such scheme and estimate its performance on hardware tokens that are much less powerful than the CPUs on which we can benchmark the protocol. We confirm that running the protocol on two server-class CPUs (Intel) requires roughly 3ms to sign a message. When one of the parties is run on a weak computer (e.g., a Raspberry Pi 3b) and the other is run on a server, the protocol requires roughly 50 ms. Our estimates confirm that the bottleneck in our scheme will be the processing capacity of the hardware token. Using a very secure, but weak 8-bit 1Mhz ATECC family processor [14], we estimate that ECDSA keys can be produced in under a minute and signatures can be completed in 3 s. The entire signing process requires human input to complete (button press), and thus is likely to take seconds overall anyway.

1.1   Technical Overview

The Definition. At a high level, in a Two Factor Signature scheme the signatures are generated by two parties: a client C who receives a (typically low entropy) password as input from a user, and a token T, which can store and generate secrets of arbitrary length, can produce signatures for multiple public keys and as such keeps a state which can be modified to add the ability to sign for new public keys. It consists of a tuple of algorithms ($\mathbf{KeyGen_C}, \mathbf{KeyGen_T}, \mathbf{PK_C}, \mathbf{PK_T}, \mathbf{Sign_C}, \mathbf{Sign_T}, \mathbf{Ver}$), where $\mathbf{KeyGen_T}(1^\kappa, s_T)$ and $\mathbf{KeyGen_C}(pwd)$ are an interactive protocol used by the token and client respectively to produce a public key and to accordingly update the token state s_T by "adding a share of the corresponding secret key"; $\mathbf{PK_C}(pwd)$ and $\mathbf{PK_T}(s_T)$ are two algorithms used by the client and the token (on input the password and the current token state s_T respectively) interacting with each other to retrieve a public key pk which was previously generated using the first two algorithms; $\mathbf{Sign_C}(pwd, m)$ and $\mathbf{Sign_T}(s_T, m)$ are similarly used to produce signatures; $\mathbf{Ver}(pk, m, \sigma)$ is used to verify the signatures.

We proceed to outline the unforgeability properties we require from such Two Factor Signature scheme. We consider 4 different attack scenarios, and define "best-possible" unforgeability properties for each of them. The first two are simply analogs of the standard unforgeability (for "party 1" and "party 2") properties of two-out-of-two threshold signatures.

1. *For the Client*: The simplest and most natural attack scenario is when the user's laptop is compromised (i.e. by malware), even before the key generation phase. We require that, except with negligible probability, such an adversary cannot forge signatures on a message m with respect to a public key which the token outputs (and would typically show to the user on its local screen) unless it asked the token to sign m. This notion mirrors the classic one of unforgeability (for party 1) of threshold signature schemes.

2. *For the Token*: We next consider an attack scenario in which the adversary can fully control the token T. We let it interact arbitrarily with an honest client, and receive the signatures and public keys output by such client during these interactions. We require that the probability that such an adversary can produce a forgery on a message m that would verify with respect to one of the public keys output by the client (during a **KeyGen** execution) without asking the client to sign m, is bounded by the min-entropy of the user's password. Again, this notion mirrors the classic notion of unforgeability of

threshold signatures (for party 2), except that since the user only has a low-entropy password, we cannot require the probability of forging to be negligible; instead, we bound it by $q/2^m$ where q is the number of random oracle queries performed by the adversary, and m is the min-entropy of the password distribution.

Note that the unforgeability for the token security bound is rather weak (when the password has low entropy), but is necessarily so because the only secret held by the client is the password, and thus an attacker that "fully controls the token" (i.e., controls its input/outputs while at the same time participating in other outside interaction) and gets to see public keys, can simply emulate the client algorithm with a guessed password and attempt to create a forgery. Yet, note that to carry out this type of attack (which leads to the "unavoidable" security loss) and profit from it is quite non-trivial in practice as it requires the token to be able to somehow communicate with an attacker in the outside world (which is challenging given that a hardware wallet is a physically separate entity without a direct network connection).

Consequently, we consider two alternative attack scenarios that leverage the fact that often the token cannot communicate with the adversary and capture more plausible (i.e weaker) attack models. Yet, in these weaker attack models, we can now require the forging probability bounds to be significantly stronger.

3. *For the Token Manufacturer*: We consider an adversary who cannot fully control the T party, but can specify ahead of time a program Π which the T party runs. For example, this models the case of a malicious token manufacturer who embeds a PRG with a backdoor. Program Π can behave arbitrarily, but its answers to the interactions with any client have to satisfy the correctness properties of the scheme with overwhelming probability (if the token aborted or caused the client to return signatures which do not verify w.r.t. the expected public keys, the user could easily identify such token as faulty or malicious). The adversary can then have an honest client interact arbitrarily with Π ($\mathcal{A}$ is given the resulting public keys and signatures), and should not be able to produce a forgery on a message m that would verify with respect to one of the public keys output by the client (during a **KeyGen** execution) unless it received a signature on m as a result of such an interaction. We require the forging probability to be negligible (as opposed to bounded by $q/2^m$).

4. *With Access to the Token*: An alternative scenario is one where the token is not corrupted, but the attacker can get access to it (for example, in the case of a lost/stolen token, or a token shared between multiple users). More precisely, the adversary can interact with an honest T and may also interact with an honest client C (which itself interacts with T) and has to produce forgeries on a message m (which C did not sign, but on which T can be queried) w.r.t. a public key which C output during an interaction with T. Whereas unforgeability for the token implies that the above-mentioned adversary's forging probability is bounded by $q/2^m$ where q is the number of random oracle queries, we here sharpen the bound to $q'/2^m$ where q' is the number

of invocations of T. (As T could rate-limit its answers by e.g., 1 sec, q' will be significantly smaller than q in practice.)

As far as we know, no previously known scheme satisfies all of the the above properties; in fact, none satisfy even just (1) and (2), or (1) and (3).[2]

The Construction. The high-level idea behind our construction is natural (although the approach is very different from Trezor and other currently used hardware wallets). We would like to employ a two-out-of-two threshold signature (TS) scheme where the token is one of the parties and the client is the other. The problem is that the client only has a low-entropy password and cannot keep any persistent state. In fact, even if it had a high-entropy password, it wouldn't be clear how to directly use the threshold schemes as in general (and in particular for EC-DSA), secret key shares for threshold schemes are generated in a correlated way.

To overcome this issue, the key generation algorithm begins by running the key generation procedure for the TS: the token and the client each get a secret key share (which we denote sk_T and sk_C respectively), as well as the public key pk. Next, since the client cannot remember pk, sk_C, it encrypts pk, sk_C using a key that is derived—by using a random oracle (RO)—from its password; additionally, the client generates (deterministically) a random "handle" as a function of its password, again by applying the RO to the password. It then sends both the handle and the (password-encrypted) ciphertext to the token for storage.

Later on, when a client wants to get a signature on a message m, it first asks the token to retrieve its password-encrypted ciphertext: the token will only provide it if the client provides the correct handle (which the honest client having the actual password can provide). Next, the client decrypts the ciphertext (again using the password), and can recover its public and secret key. Finally, using its secret key, and interacting with the token the client can engage in the threshold signing process to obtain the desired signature on m.

The Analysis: Exploiting Non-Signalling and Exponential-Time Simulation. While we can show that the above construction satisfies properties 1,2 and 4 assuming the underlying threshold scheme is secure, demonstrating property 3—that is, security against malicious token manufacturers, which in our opinion is the most cruicial property—turns out to be non-trivial.

The issue is the following: as already mentioned, if the token is fully controlled by the attacker (which participates in outside interactions), then we can never hope to show that unforgeability happens with negligible probability as the attacker can always perform a brute-force attack on the password. In particular, in our scheme, the attacker can simply brute-force password guesses against the ciphertext c to recover the client's threshold secret key share. However, a malicious manufacturer which generates a malicious token but cannot directly communicate with it, would have more trouble doing so. Even if the malicious

---

[2] Although we are not aware of any formal analysis of Trezor, it would seem that it satisfies (1) and (4), but there are concrete attacks against the other properties.

token program can perform a brute-force attack, it cannot directly communicate the correct password (or the client key share) to the manufacturer! If the token could somehow signal these information to the manufacturer, then the manufacturer could again break the scheme. And in principle, with general threshold signatures, there is nothing that prevents such signalling. For example, if the token could cause the threshold signing algorithm to output signatures whose low-order bits leak different bits of c, after sufficiently many transactions that are posted on a blockchain, the adversary could recover c and brute force the password himself.

Towards addressing this issue, we define a notion of *Non-Signalling* for TS: roughly speaking, this notion says that even if one of the parties (the token) is malicious, as long as they produce accepting signatures (with overwhelming probability), they cannot bias the distribution of the signatures generated—i.e., such signatures will be indistinguishable from honestly generated ones. In fact, to enable our proof of security—which proceeds using a rather complex sequence of hybrid arguments relying on *exponential-time simulation*—we will require the TS scheme to satisfy a *statistical* notion of Non-Signalling which requires that the distribution of signatures generated interacting with the malicious party is statistically close to the honest distribution.

We next show that if the underlying TS indeed satisfies statistical Non-Signalling, then our 2FS also satisfies property 3. Towards doing this, we actually first show that our 2FS satisfies an analogous notion of Non-Signalling, and then show how to leverage this property to prove unforgeability for the token manufacturer. We mention that the notion of Non-Signalling for 2FS is interesting in its own right: it guarantees that a maliciously implemented token Π (whose answers are restricted to satisfy the correctness properties of the scheme with overwhelming probability) cannot leak (through the public keys and the signatures which it helps computing) to an attacker any information which an honestly implemented token would not leak. In particular, if the honest token algorithm generates independent public keys and uses stateless signing (as the ones we consider do), even a malicious token cannot leak correlations between which public keys it has been used to create, or what messages it has signed.

1.2 Related Work

Threshold Signatures. Threshold signatures [1,2,4,7,16] are signature schemes distributing the ability to generate a signature among a set of parties, so that cooperation among at least a threshold of them is required to produce a signature. Nicolosi *et al.* [15] present a threshold signature scheme for the Schnorr signature scheme. Particularly relevant to the cryptocurrency application are the works of Goldfeder *et al.* [6,8], Lindell [0,10], and Lee *et al.* [5] which propose a threshold signature scheme to produce ECDSA signatures, which is already compatible with Bitcoin and Ethereum.

Passwords + Threshold Signatures. MacKenzie and Reiter [11,12] and Camenish *et al.* [3] consider notions somewhat similar to the one of a password-based threshold signature scheme: as in our setting, signing requires knowledge of a password and access to an external party (in their case a server rather than a hardware token), but in contrast to our setting the signer may additionally hold some *high-entropy secret state* (and indeed, the schemes considered in those papers require such secret state). This rules out the usage of such schemes in our scenario, as we want the user to be able to operate his wallet from any client without relying on any external state beyond its password.

1.3   Organization of the Paper

After introducing some notation in Sect. 2, we recall the definition of Threshold Signature scheme and introduce the Non-Signalling property in Sect. 3. Section 4 defines Two Factor Signature schemes and Sect. 5 presents our main construction and a sketch for some of the security proofs.

Due to lack of space, some of the security definitions (introduced earlier in the introduction), the full proofs of security, as well as the two modified TS schemes (based on Schnorr and EC-DSA) are deferred to the full version of this paper [13]. There, we also discuss an additional useful *Unlinkability* property satisfied by our construction.

2   Notation

If X is a probability distribution, we denote with $x \leftarrow X$ the process of sampling x according to X. When, in a probabilistic experiment, we say that an adversary outputs a probability distribution, we mean that such a distribution is given as a poly-time randomized program such that running the program with no input (and uniform randomness) samples from such distribution. For two-party (randomized) algorithms we denote with $\langle \alpha; \beta \rangle \leftarrow \langle A(a); B(b) \rangle$ the process of running the algorithm A on input a (and uniform randomness as needed) interacting with algorithm B on input b (and uniform randomness), where α is the local output of A and β is the local output of B. Whenever an algorithm has more than one output, but we are interested in only a subset of such outputs, we will use $\cdot$ as a placeholder for the other outputs (for example we could write $(\cdot, pk) \leftarrow \textbf{KeyGen}(1^\kappa)$ to denote that pk is a public key output by the **KeyGen** algorithm of a signature scheme in a context where we are not interested in the corresponding secret key).

Token Oracles. In our definitions, we will often model a party/program implementing party T. We say that a Token Oracle is a stateful oracle which can answer **KeyGen, PK, Sign** queries. Initially, its state is set to $\bot$. To answer such queries, the oracle interacts with its caller by running the $\textbf{KeyGen}_T$, $\textbf{PK}_T$, $\textbf{Sign}_T$ algorithms respectively using its own inner state (and a message m supplied by the caller for **Sign** queries). As a result of $\textbf{KeyGen}_T$ queries, its state is also updated. Moreover, when explicitly specified, the oracle could also return to the caller the public keys pk which are part of its local output during $\textbf{KeyGen}_T$ and $\textbf{Sign}_T$ queries.

3   Threshold Signature Scheme

This section recalls the definition of a Threshold Signature scheme. The formalization presented here is for a 2-party setting (C and T) and the key shares are computed by the parties using a distributed key generation algorithm (as opposed to being provided by a trusted dealer).

Definition 1. *A (2-out-of-2) Threshold Signature scheme consists of a tuple of distributed PPT algorithms defined as follows:*

- $\langle \mathbf{TS.GC}(1^\kappa); \mathbf{TS.GT}(1^\kappa) \rangle \rightarrow \langle sk_C, pk; sk_T, pk \rangle$ *are two randomized algorithms which take as input the security parameter and, after interacting with each other, produce as output a public key pk (output by both parties) and a secret key share for each of them. We use $\mathbf{TS.Gen}(1^\kappa) \rightarrow (sk_C, sk_T, pk)$ as a compact expression for the above computation.*
- $\langle \mathbf{TS.SC}(sk_C, m); \mathbf{TS.ST}(sk_T, m) \rangle \rightarrow \langle \sigma; \bot \rangle$ *are two randomized algorithms interacting to produce as output a signature[3] σ. We use $\mathbf{TS.Sign}(sk_C, m, sk_T) \rightarrow \sigma$ as as a compact expression for the above computation.*
- $\mathbf{TS.Ver}(pk, m, \sigma) \rightarrow 0 \vee 1$ *is a deterministic algorithm. It takes as input a public key, a message and a signature and outputs 1 (accept) or 0 (reject).*

These algorithms have to satisfy the following correctness property: for all messages m

$$\Pr\left[\begin{array}{c} (sk_C, sk_T, pk) \leftarrow \mathbf{TS.Gen}(1^\kappa): \\ \mathbf{TS.Ver}(pk, m, \mathbf{TS.Sign}(sk_C, m, sk_T)) = 1 \end{array} \right] = 1$$

The definitions of Unforgeability for the two parties (T and C) we require are quite standard and are deferred to the full version [13]. In the following, we introduce a new security definition, which we call *Non-Signalling*. It consists of two properties. First, we require that a malicious token cannot bias the distribution of the public keys output by **TS.Gen** when interacting with an honest client (as long as such token does not make the **TS.Gen** execution abort). More in detail, we require that for any polynomial sized circuit Π (which does not make the execution of **TS.Gen** abort with more than negligible probability), the distribution of public keys output by an execution of the **TS.GC** interacting with Π in the role of T is statistically indistinguishable from the distribution obtained by running **TS.Gen** with both parties implemented honestly. This is formalized as an experiment where an adversary $\mathcal{A}$ (not necessarily running in polynomial time) outputs a PPT program Π and then has to distinguish whether it is given a public key generated by an honest client interacting with Π or by an honest client interacting with an honest token.

---

[3] This definition states that party T does not output the signature. However, in our construction we do not rely on σ being "hidden" from T, so threshold schemes where both parties learn the signature can also be used in our construction.

Analogously, the second property requires that a malicious token cannot bias the distribution of signatures output by the **TS.Sign** algorithm. An adversary $\mathcal{A}$ outputs a public key pk, a message m, a secret key for the client sk_C and a polynomial sized circuit Π which can interact with a client running **TS.SC**(sk_C, m), such that (with all but negligible probability) the output for the client interacting with Π is a valid signature on m w.r.t. pk. We require that $\mathcal{A}$ cannot distinguish between the output of such an interaction and a valid signature on m w.r.t. pk sampled uniformly at random.

Definition 2. *Let TS = (**TS.GC, TS.GT, TS.SC, TS.ST, TS.Ver**) be a Threshold Signature scheme. Consider the following two experiments between an adversary $\mathcal{A}$ and a challenger, each parameterized by a bit b:*
TS.NS1$_{\mathcal{A}}^{2FS,b}(1^{\kappa})$:

1. $\mathcal{A}(1^{\kappa})$ *outputs a polynomial size (in κ) circuit Π, such that $\Pr[\langle \cdot, pk; \cdot \rangle \leftarrow \langle$**TS.GC**$(1^{\kappa}); \Pi \rangle : pk \neq \bot] > 1 - \mu(\kappa)$ (i.e. running the circuit interacting with an honest **TS.GC** implementation results in such honest implementation outputting $\bot$ with at most negligible probability).*
2. *If $b = 0$, the challenger computes $\langle \cdot, pk; \cdot \rangle \leftarrow \langle$**TS.GC**$(1^{\kappa}); \Pi \rangle$; otherwise it computes $\langle \cdot, pk; \cdot \rangle \leftarrow \langle$**TS.GC**$(1^{\kappa}); $**TS.GT**$(1^{\kappa}) \rangle$. Then it returns pk to $\mathcal{A}$.*
3. $\mathcal{A}$ *outputs a bit b', which defines the output of the experiment.*

TS.NS2$_{\mathcal{A}}^{2FS,b}(1^{\kappa})$:

1. $\mathcal{A}(1^{\kappa})$ *outputs a polynomial size (in κ) circuit Π, a secret key share sk_C, a message m and a public key pk, such that $\Pr[\langle \sigma; \cdot \rangle \leftarrow \langle$**TS.SC**$(sk_C, m); \Pi \rangle : $**TS.Ver**$(pk, m, \sigma) = 1] > 1 - \mu(\kappa)$ (i.e. running the circuit interacting with an honest **TS.SC** implementation on input sk_C, m results in such honest implementation outputting a valid signature for m under pk with overwhelming probability).*
2. *If $b = 0$, the challenger computes $\langle \sigma; \cdot \rangle \leftarrow \langle$**TS.SC**$(1^{\kappa}); \Pi \rangle$; otherwise it samples a valid signature at random, i.e. it samples $\sigma \leftarrow_R \{\sigma : $**Ver**$(pk, m, \sigma) = 1\}$. Then it returns σ to $\mathcal{A}$.*
3. $\mathcal{A}$ *outputs a bit b', which defines the output of the experiment.*

*TS is said to be **Non-Signalling** if for all PPT adversaries $\mathcal{A}$ there exist a negligible function μ such that*

$$|\Pr[\mathbf{TS.NS1}_{\mathcal{A}}^{2FS,0}(1^{\kappa}) = 1] - \Pr[\mathbf{TS.NS1}_{\mathcal{A}}^{2FS,1}(1^{\kappa}) = 1]| < \mu(\kappa)$$
$$|\Pr[\mathbf{TS.NS2}_{\mathcal{A}}^{2FS,0}(1^{\kappa}) = 1] - \Pr[\mathbf{TS.NS2}_{\mathcal{A}}^{2FS,1}(1^{\kappa}) = 1]| < \mu(\kappa)$$

*If the above equations hold even for adversaries $\mathcal{A}$ which are not bounded to be PPT (but that output circuits Π which still have to be polynomially sized), the TS is said to be **Statistically Non-Signalling**.*

4   Two Factor Signature Schemes

A Two Factor Signature scheme is similar to a 2-out-of-2 threshold signature scheme, where signatures are generated by two parties: a client C whose only long term state is a (typically low entropy and independently generated) password, and a token T, who can store and generate secrets of arbitrary length. We envision the token party T to be implemented on a hardware token (which a user would carry around) with a dedicated screen and button which would ask the user for confirmation before producing signatures.

The semantics of the scheme are designed to capture the fact that a token party T has a single state s_T which can be used as input to produce signatures according to different public keys (for which an initialization phase was previously performed). This is useful, as typically a hardware wallet would offer support for multiple cryptocurrency accounts, and therefore such semantics allow us to design a scheme which natively supports multiple such accounts and reason about the security of the whole system.

More specifically, one can think of each public key that the scheme can produce signatures for as being associated with both a password and a (not necessarily private) mnemonic key identifier (or account identifier in the hardware wallets application) chosen by the user (i.e. "savings" or "vacation_fund"). In order to generate a new public key the client executes the **KeyGen** algorithm with a token T. The client's inputs are the key identifier and its password pwd, while the token updates its state s_T as a result of running this algorithm. Later, the client can produce signatures for that public key on a message m by running the **Sign** algorithm (interacting with the same token) on input m and the same password and key identifier. Additionally, the **PK** algorithm can be used to reconstruct a previously generated public key (both the password and the key identifier are required in this case as well). In our formal description, for the sake of simplicity and w.l.o.g., we consider such key identifier to be part of the password itself.

Definition 3. *A Two Factor Signature scheme (2FS) consists of a tuple of PPT algorithms:*

- $\langle \mathbf{KeyGen_C}(pwd); \mathbf{KeyGen_T}(s_T) \rangle \rightarrow \langle pk; pk, s'_T \rangle$ *are two randomized algorithms interacting with each other to produce as output a public key pk (output by both parties). s_T represents the state of party T before running the algorithm (which would be $\bot$ on the first invocation), and s'_T represents its new updated state. We use $\mathbf{KeyGen}(pwd, s_T) \rightarrow (pk, s'_T)$ as a compact expression for the above computation.*
- $\langle \mathbf{PK_C}(pwd); \mathbf{PK_T}(s_T) \rangle \rightarrow \langle pk; pk \rangle$ *are two algorithms interacting with each other to produce as output a public key. We use $\mathbf{PK}(pwd, sid, s_T) \rightarrow pk$ as a compact expression for the above computation.*
- $\langle \mathbf{Sign_C}(pwd, m); \mathbf{Sign_T}(s_T, m) \rangle \rightarrow \langle \sigma; \bot \rangle$ *are two randomized algorithms interacting with each other to produce as output a signature σ, output by the first party only. We use $\mathbf{Sign}(pwd, m, s_T) \rightarrow \sigma$ as as a compact expression for the above computation.*

– **Ver**$(pk, m, \sigma) \to 0 \vee 1$ *is a deterministic algorithm. It takes as input a public
key, a message and a signature and outputs 1 (accept) or 0 (reject).*

These algorithms have to satisfy the following correctness properties. Let s_T
be any valid token state (i.e. any state obtained by starting with $\perp$ as the initial state and then updating it through several executions of **KeyGen** on input
arbitrary passwords), pwd be any password which was used in at least one such
execution of **KeyGen**, pk be the output of the **KeyGen**$_C$ algorithm in the most
recent of the executions of **KeyGen** on input pwd. We require that both

$$\Pr[\mathbf{PK}(pwd, s_T) = pk] = 1, \ \Pr[\mathbf{Ver}(pk, m, \mathbf{Sign}(pwd, m, s_T)) = 1] = 1$$

Security Notions. We define five notions of security for a 2FS, all introduced in
the introduction. Unforgeability for the Token, and Unforgeability with access to
the Token are formalized in the full version [13]. Here, we define Unforgeability
for the Client, Unforgeability for the Token Manufacturer and Non-Signalling.

Definition 4 (Unforgeability for the Client). *Given a Two Factor Signa-
ture scheme 2FS =* (**KeyGen**$_C$, **KeyGen**$_T$, **PK**$_C$, **PK**$_T$, **Sign**$_C$, **Sign**$_T$, **Ver**),
consider the following experiment between an adversary $\mathcal{A}$ and a challenger:
ExpForgeC$_\mathcal{A}^{2FS}(1^\kappa)$:

1. *The challenger runs the adversary $\mathcal{A}$, giving it access to a token oracle* **T**
   ($\mathcal{A}$ is given the pk values output by such oracle during **KeyGen** *and* **PK**
   *queries). $\mathcal{A}$ can interact with the oracle arbitrarily. In addition, the challenger
   records the pk values locally output by the token oracle for* **KeyGen** *queries
   on an (initially empty) list g, and for* **PK** *queries on an (initially empty) list
   p.*
2. *$\mathcal{A}$ halts and outputs a message m and a list of forgeries $(pk_1, \sigma_1), \dots, (pk_n, \sigma_n)$.
   We define the output of the experiment as 1 if either there exists a pk that belongs
   to p but not to g, or if for all $i \in \{1, \dots, n\}$,* **Ver**$(pk_i, m, \sigma_i) = 1$, *all the pk_i are
   distinct and are in g, and $\mathcal{A}$ made at most $n - 1$* **Sign** *queries to the oracle* **T** *on
   input m.*

2FS is said to be **Unforgeable for the Client** *if for all PPT adversaries $\mathcal{A}$
there exist a negligible function μ such that for all κ*

$$\Pr[\mathbf{ExpForgeC}_\mathcal{A}^{2FS}(1^\kappa) = 1] \leq \mu(\kappa).$$

The purpose of the two lists g and p in the experiment above is to ensure
that either the adversary can cause the honest token to output a public key pk
during a **PK** query which it did not output during a **KeyGen** query, or that all
the forgeries returned by the adversary are w.r.t. public keys which were output
by the honest token oracle, that the number of forgeries on m is greater than
the number of signing queries which the challenger answered for m.

The next definition, Unforgeability for the Token Manufacturer, is formalized
as an experiment where the adversary first outputs a stateful program Π, and

then can ask an honest client (simulated by the challenger) to interact with such program in arbitrary **KeyGen**, **PK** and **Sign** queries (where the adversary can pick the *pwd* and *m* inputs for such client and receives its outputs). The definition requires that (except with negligible probability) the adversary cannot produce a forgery on a message *m* valid w.r.t. one of the public keys *pk* output by the client, unless it previously received a valid signature on *m* w.r.t. *pk* as the output of a **Sign** query.

We restrict such definition to adversaries which satisfy a *compliance* property. Informally, an adversary is compliant if during any execution of the unforgeability experiment, with overwhelming probability, it outputs programs Π such that the outputs of the honest client (simulated by the challenger) on the adversary's queries respect the same correctness conditions as if the simulated client was interacting with an honestly implemented token. In particular, running a **PK** query on input some password *pwd*, the client should obtain the same *pk* which it output during the most recent **KeyGen** query on input the same *pwd*; similarly, the output of a **Sign** query on input *m* and *pwd* should be a valid signature w.r.t. the public key *pk* which was output during the most recent **KeyGen** query for *pwd*.

Remark 1. Restricting to compliant adversaries is a reasonable limitation: if a user notices that her hardware token is not producing signatures or public keys correctly, for example by selectively aborting during signature generation or by returning invalid signatures or inconsistent public keys, such abnormal behavior would be easy to detect or even impossible to go unnoticed. For example, if a 2FS was used to sign a cryptocurrency transaction, but the client output an invalid signature for the user's expected public key/source address of the transaction, then even if the client side software did not check the signature and it got broadcasted to the network, the receiver of the funds would eventually complain that the funds were never transferred.

Definition 5. *Let* $2FS = ($**KeyGen**$_C,$ **KeyGen**$_T,$ **PK**$_C,$ **PK**$_T,$ **Sign**$_C,$ **Sign**$_T,$ **Ver**$)$ *be a Two Factor Signature scheme. Consider the following experiment between a PPT adversary* $\mathcal{A}$ *and a challenger, parameterized by a bit b:* $\mathbf{ExpForgeTokMan}_{\mathcal{A}}^{2FS}(1^{\kappa}):$

1. $\mathcal{A}(1^{\kappa})$ *outputs a polynomial size circuit* Π, *which implements the same interface as a Token Oracle. We stress that this program is not bound to implement the honest algorithms, but may deviate in arbitrary ways (subject to* $\mathcal{A}$ *being compliant as specified below).*
2. $\mathcal{A}$ *can now ask an arbitrary number of* **KeyGen**, **PK** *and* **Sign** *queries to the challenger. In each query, the challenger simulates an honest client* C *interacting with* Π *in the role of* T *on input a pwd and possibly a message m both arbitrarily chosen by the adversary (in the case of a* **Sign** *query,* Π *is also given as input m), and gives* $\mathcal{A}$ *such client's output.*

   In addition, for each **KeyGen** *query, the challenger records the simulated client's output pk in an (initially empty) list g, and for each* **Sign** *query on input some message m where the client's output is* σ, *the challenger adds* a record (pk, m) to an (initially empty) list s for any $pk \in g$ such that $\mathbf{Ver}(pk, m, \sigma) = 1$ (if such a pk exists).

3. $\mathcal{A}$ halts and outputs a triple (pk', m', σ'). The output of the experiment is 1 if $\mathbf{Ver}(pk', m', \sigma') = 1$, $pk' \in g$ and $(pk', m') \notin s$. Otherwise, the output is 0.

During an execution of $\mathbf{ExpForgeTokMan}^{2FS}$, we say that a query asked by $\mathcal{A}$ (i.e. an execution of either $\mathbf{KeyGen}$, $\mathbf{PK}$ or $\mathbf{Sign}$ where the challenger executes the algorithm for C interacting with Π in the role of T) is compliant if the output of the challenger in this interaction satisfies the same correctness conditions that interacting with an honest token implementation would. In more detail, the query is compliant (with respect to a specific execution of $\mathbf{ExpForgeTokMan}$) if:

- in the case of a $\mathbf{KeyGen}$ query, the output of the client (simulated by the challenger) is a $pk \neq \perp$ (which implies that Π did not abort or send an otherwise invalid message)
- in the case of a $\mathbf{PK}$ query on input some password pwd, the simulated client output the same pk which it output the most recent time it executed a $\mathbf{KeyGen}$ query on input the same pwd (or $\perp$ if the adversary never asked any $\mathbf{KeyGen}$ query on input pwd)
- in the case of a $\mathbf{Sign}$ query on input m and pwd, the simulated client outputs a valid signature w.r.t. the pk which was output during the most recently executed $\mathbf{KeyGen}$ query on input pwd (or $\perp$ if the adversary never asked any $\mathbf{KeyGen}$ query on input pwd).

We say that an execution of $\mathbf{ExpForgeTokMan}^{2FS}$ is compliant if all the queries in that execution are compliant. We say that an adversary $\mathcal{A}$ is compliant if, with all but negligible probability, any execution of $\mathbf{ExpForgeTokMan}_{\mathcal{A}}^{2FS}(1^\kappa)$ is compliant.

2FS is said to be **Unforgeable for the Token Manufacturer** if for all PPT compliant adversaries $\mathcal{A}$ there exist a negligible function μ such that for all κ

$$\Pr[\mathbf{ExpForgeTokMan}_{\mathcal{A}}^{2FS}(1^\kappa) = 1] < \mu(\kappa)$$

Towards proving unforgeability for the token manufacturer, it will be useful to first show that our scheme satisfies a notion of *Non-Signalling*, which is of independent interest. This property is formalized as an indistinguishability definition: the adversary outputs a circuit Π, and then asks the challenger to interact with such circuit on arbitrary $\mathbf{KeyGen}$, $\mathbf{PK}$ and $\mathbf{Sign}$ queries. The challenger either uses Π to answer all such queries, or an honest implementation of the token algorithms; we require that no adversary can notice this difference with better than negligible probability. As in the previous definition, we restrict our attention to *compliant* adversaries.

Definition 6. Let $2FS = (\mathbf{KeyGen_C}, \mathbf{KeyGen_T}, \mathbf{PK_C}, \mathbf{PK_T}, \mathbf{Sign_C}, \mathbf{Sign_T}, \mathbf{Ver})$ be a Two Factor Signature scheme. Consider the following experiment between an adversary $\mathcal{A}$ and a challenger, parameterized by a bit b:

ExpNonSignal$_{\mathcal{A}}^{2FS,b}(1^\kappa)$:

1. $\mathcal{A}(1^\kappa)$ *outputs a polynomial sized circuit* Π, *which implements the same interface as a Token Oracle. We stress that this program is not bound to implement the honest algorithms, but may deviate in arbitrary ways (subject to* $\mathcal{A}$ *being compliant as specified below).*
2. $\mathcal{A}$ *can now ask an arbitrary number of* **KeyGen**, **PK** *and* **Sign** *queries to the challenger. In each query, the adversary provides the inputs for* C *(i.e. pwd and possibly m). If* $b = 0$, *the challenger interacts with program* Π *using the appropriate algorithms for* C *and the inputs given by* $\mathcal{A}$ *(note that in the case of a* **Sign** *query,* Π *is also given the message m supplied by the adversary as an input), and gives* $\mathcal{A}$ *the local output of the* C *algorithm in such computation. If* $b = 1$, *instead, the challenger answers the queries by interacting with an honestly implemented Token Oracle.*
3. $\mathcal{A}$ *halts and outputs a bit* b', *which defines the output of the experiment.*

Note that in an execution of **ExpNonSignal**^{2FS,0}, $\mathcal{A}$*'s view has exactly the same distribution as in an execution of* **ExpForgeTokMan***. Thus, we can define a compliant query asked by* $\mathcal{A}$ *w.r.t. an* **ExpNonSignal**^{2FS,0} *execution, a compliant execution of* **ExpNonSignal**^{2FS,0} *and a compliant adversary as in Definition 5.*

2FS is said to be ***Non-Signalling*** *if for all compliant PPT adversaries* $\mathcal{A}$ *there exist a negligible function* μ *such that for all* κ

$$| \Pr[\mathbf{ExpNonSignal}_{\mathcal{A}}^{2FS,0}(1^\kappa) = 1] - \Pr[\mathbf{ExpNonSignal}_{\mathcal{A}}^{2FS,1}(1^\kappa) = 1]| < \mu(\kappa)$$

5 Constructing a Two Factor Signature Scheme

In this section, we show how to construct a secure Two Factor Signature scheme (in the random oracle model), by combining any IND-CPA and INT-CTXT secure Symmetric Encryption scheme, a hash function (modelled as a random oracle) and any Unforgeable and Statistically Non-Signalling Threshold Signature scheme.

Let TS = (**TS.GC**, **TS.GT**, **TS.SC**, **TS.ST**, **TS.Ver**) be a Threshold Signature scheme, SE = (**SE.G**, **SE.E**, **SE.D**) be a Symmetric Encryption scheme, and **RO**$_\kappa$ be hash function which maps strings of arbitrary length to $\{0,1\}^\kappa \times \{0,1\}^\kappa$. Our proposed construction depends on a security parameter κ, which is given as implicit input to all algorithms.

The token state s_T is structured as a key-value store (map), where the keys are strings in $\{0,1\}^\kappa$ called *handles* and the values are tuples of strings. Initially, the **KeyGen**$_T$ algorithm can be supplied $\bot$, which is treated as an empty store. We define $s_T.\mathbf{Add}(handle, y)$ as the map obtained from s_T by additionally associating the key *handle* with the value y (which overwrites any previous value associated with *handle*), and $s_T.\mathbf{Find}(handle)$ as the value associated to *handle* by s_T, or $\bot$ if no such pair exists.

All algorithms will abort (i.e. return $\bot$) if any of their sub-algorithms abort (for example if decrypting a ciphertext fails or the store s_T does not contain the expected value) or the other party aborts or sends a malformed message. Using these conventions, we can define a Two Factor Signature scheme as follows (the scheme is also illustrated in Fig. 1):

- **KeyGen$_C$**(*pwd*) → *pk*: Run **TS.GC**(1^κ) interacting with **KeyGen$_T$** and obtain (sk_C, pk) as the local output. Then, compute ($ek, handle$) ← **RO**$_\kappa$(*pwd*), c ← **SE.E**($ek, (sk_C, pk)$) and send ($handle, c$) to T. Output *pk*.
- **KeyGen$_T$**(s_T) → s'_T: Run **TS.GT**(1^κ) interacting with **KeyGen$_C$** and obtain sk_T, pk as the local output. Then, receive ($handle, c$) from **KeyGen$_C$**, set s'_T ← s_T.**Add**($handle, (c, sk_T, pk)$) and output (s'_T, pk).
- **PK$_C$**(*pwd*): Compute ($ek, handle$) ← **RO**$_\kappa$(*pwd*), send *handle* to **PK$_T$**. Upon receiving c in response, compute (sk_C, pk) ← **SE.D**(ek, c) and output *pk*.
- **PK$_T$**(s_T): Upon receiving *handle* from **PK$_C$**, retrieve c and pk from the state by computing (c, sk_C, pk) ← s_T.**Find**($handle$), send c to **PK$_C$** and output *pk*.
- **Sign$_C$**(*pwd, m*): Compute ($ek, handle$) ← **RO**$_\kappa$(*pwd*) and send *handle* to **Sign$_T$**. Upon receiving c in response, compute (sk_C, pk) ← **SE.D**(ek, c), then execute **TS.SC**(sk_C, m) (interacting with **Sign$_T$**) and output the resulting σ.
- **Sign$_T$**(s_T, m): Upon receiving *handle* from **PK$_C$**, compute (c, sk_C, pk) ← s_T.**Find**($handle$), send c to **Sign$_C$** and run **TS.ST**(sk_T, m).
- **Ver**(pk, m, σ): Output **TS.Ver**(pk, m, σ).

KeyGen$_C$(*pwd*) :		**KeyGen$_T$**(s_T) :
(sk_C, pk) ← **TS.GC**(1^κ)	↔	**TS.GT**(1^κ) → (sk_T, pk)
($ek, handle$) ← **RO**$_\kappa$(*pwd*)		
c ← **SE.E**($ek, (sk_C, pk)$)	$\xrightarrow{handle, c}$	s'_T ← s_T.**Add**($handle, (c, sk_T, pk)$)
Output *pk*		Output (s'_T, pk)
PK$_C$(*pwd*) :		**PK$_T$**(s_T) :
($ek, handle$) ← **RO**$_\kappa$(*pwd*)	$\xrightarrow{handle}$	(c, sk_T, pk) ← s_T.**Find**($handle$)
(sk_C, pk) ← **SE.D**(ek, c)	$\xleftarrow{c}$	
Output *pk*		Output *pk*
Sign$_C$(*pwd, m*) :		**Sign$_T$**(s_T, m) :
($ek, handle$) ← **RO**$_\kappa$(*pwd*)	$\xrightarrow{handle}$	(c, sk_T, pk) ← s_T.**Find**($handle$)
(sk_C, pk) ← **SE.D**(ek, c)	$\xleftarrow{c}$	
σ ← **TS.SC**(sk_C, m)	↔	**TS.ST**(sk_T, m)
Output σ		

Fig. 1. The Two Factor Signature scheme construction. The verification algorithm is the one of the underlying TS.

The security of the scheme is established by the following theorems. We provide a proof sketch for some of them, and defer the details to the full version [13].

Theorem 1. *If the underlying Threshold Signature scheme is Unforgeable for the Client, the Two Factor Signature scheme described above is Unforgeable for the Client.*

Proof Sketch. The proof of this theorem is essentially a reduction to the unforgeability for C of the Threshold Signature scheme. The adversary $\mathcal{B}$ (against the TS) simulates for any adversary $\mathcal{A}$ (against the 2FS) an execution of **ExpForgeC**; $\mathcal{B}$ guesses which of the **KeyGen** queries by $\mathcal{A}$ will produce a public key pk such that $\mathcal{A}$ outputs a forgery on m w.r.t. pk but $\mathcal{A}$ does not ask any **Sign** queries "with respect to pk" (see the full version for details). $\mathcal{B}$ makes $\mathcal{A}$ interact with its challenger for such **KeyGen** query (and the related **Sign** queries), so that if its guess is correct then the forgery produced by $\mathcal{A}$ can directly be used as a forgery to win **TS.ForgeC**. □

Theorem 2. *If TS is Unforgeable for the Token, and SE is both IND-CCA and INT-CTXT secure, the Two Factor Signature scheme described above is Unforgeable for the Token.*

Theorem 3. *If the underlying Threshold Signature scheme is Unforgeable for the Client, the Two Factor Signature scheme described above is Unforgeable with Access to the Token.*

Theorem 4. *Assuming the underlying Threshold Signature scheme is Statistically Non-Signalling, the Two Factor Signature scheme described above is Non-Signalling.*

Proof Sketch. The proof is structured as an hybrid argument on the number of queries made by the adversary. Starting from the experiment where the challenger always uses the circuit Π output by the adversary to answer all queries, we progressively substitute such answers one at a time, starting from the last query. Signing queries on a message m which should be produced w.r.t. a public key that the adversary has seen are substituted with a randomly sampled signature on m with respect to the same public key, while queries for new public keys are answered by running $(sk_C, sk_T, pk) \leftarrow$ **TS.Gen**(1^κ) (i.e. by running the threshold key generation algorithm honestly and without interacting with Π) and returning the resulting pk to $\mathcal{A}$. We prove that an adversary who can distinguish between two adjacent hybrids can contradict one of the two Non-Signalling property of the Threshold Signature scheme. Moreover, in the last hybrid the view of the adversary does not depend on the circuit Π, and so we can switch in an analogous way to an experiment where the challenger always uses an honest token oracle. Note that sampling signatures at random without knowing the corresponding secret key shares makes the reduction require exponential time, but this is not a problem because the Non-Signalling properties of the Threshold Signature scheme hold even against an exponential time adversary. □

Theorem 5. *Assuming the underlying Threshold Signature scheme is Statistically Non-Signalling and Unforgeable for the Client, the TFS described above is also Unforgeable for the Token Manufacturer.*

Proof Sketch. The proof is structured as an hybrid argument. First, instead of using the circuit Π output by the adversary, all queries by $\mathcal{A}$ are answered using an honestly implemented token oracle. Due to the Non-Signalling property of the 2FS, this cannot affect $\mathcal{A}$'s view and therefore its success probability. Given that $\mathcal{A}$ is now interacting with an honest token, we can prove that $\mathcal{A}$ cannot forge using a similar argument as in the proof of Unforgeability for the Client.   □

References

1. Almansa, J.F., Damgård, I., Nielsen, J.B.: Simplified threshold RSA with adaptive and proactive security. In: Vaudenay, S. (ed.) EUROCRYPT 2006. LNCS, vol. 4004, pp. 593–611. Springer, Heidelberg (2006). https://doi.org/10.1007/11761679_35
2. Boneh, D., Ding, X., Tsudik, G., Wong, C.-M.: A method for fast revocation of public key certificates and security capabilities. In: USENIX Security Symposium, p. 22 (2001)
3. Camenisch, J., Lehmann, A., Neven, G., Samelin, K.: Virtual smart cards: how to sign with a password and a server. In: Zikas, V., De Prisco, R. (eds.) SCN 2016. LNCS, vol. 9841, pp. 353–371. Springer, Cham (2016). https://doi.org/10.1007/978-3-319-44618-9_19
4. Desmedt, Y., Frankel, Y.: Threshold cryptosystems. In: Brassard, G. (ed.) CRYPTO 1989. LNCS, vol. 435, pp. 307–315. Springer, New York (1990). https://doi.org/10.1007/0-387-34805-0_28
5. Doerner, J., Kondi, Y., Lee, E., Shelat, A.: Secure two-party threshold ECDSA from ECDSA assumptions. In: 2018 IEEE Symposium on Security and Privacy (SP), pp. 595–612 (2018)
6. Gennaro, R., Goldfeder, S.: Fast multiparty threshold ECDSA with fast trustless setup. In: Proceedings of the 2018 ACM SIGSAC Conference on Computer and Communications Security, pp. 1179–1194. ACM (2018)
7. Gennaro, R., Jarecki, S., Krawczyk, H., Rabin, T.: Robust and efficient sharing of RSA functions. In: Koblitz, N. (ed.) CRYPTO 1996. LNCS, vol. 1109, pp. 157–172. Springer, Heidelberg (1996). https://doi.org/10.1007/3-540-68697-5_13
8. Goldfeder, S., et al.: Securing bitcoin wallets via a new DSA/ECDSA threshold signature scheme (2015)
9. Lindell, Y.: Fast secure two-party ECDSA signing. In: Katz, J., Shacham, H. (eds.) CRYPTO 2017. LNCS, vol. 10402, pp. 613–644. Springer, Cham (2017). https://doi.org/10.1007/978-3-319-63715-0_21
10. Lindell, Y., Nof, A.: Fast secure multiparty ECDSA with practical distributed key generation and applications to cryptocurrency custody. In: Proceedings of the 2018 ACM SIGSAC Conference on Computer and Communications Security, pp. 1837–1854. ACM (2018)
11. MacKenzie, P., Reiter, M.K.: Delegation of cryptographic servers for capture-resilient devices. Distrib. Comput. **16**(4), 307–327 (2003)
12. MacKenzie, P., Reiter, M.K.: Networked cryptographic devices resilient to capture. Int. J. Inf. Secur. **2**(1), 1–20 (2003)

13. Marcedone, A., Pass, R., Shelat, A.: Minimizing trust in hardware wallets with two factor signatures. Cryptology ePrint Archive, Report 2019/006 (2019)
14. Microchip. Atecc608a datasheet (2018)
15. Nicolosi, A., Krohn, M.N., Dodis, Y., Mazieres, D.: Proactive two-party signatures for user authentication. In: NDSS (2003)
16. Rabin, T.: A simplified approach to threshold and proactive RSA. In: Krawczyk, H. (ed.) CRYPTO 1998. LNCS, vol. 1462, pp. 89–104. Springer, Heidelberg (1998). https://doi.org/10.1007/BFb0055722
17. Sottek, T.C.: NSA reportedly intercepting laptops purchased online to install spy malware, December 2013. https://www.theverge.com/2013/12/29/5253226/nsa-cia-fbi-laptop-usb-plant-spy. Accessed 29 Dec 2013

A Formal Treatment of Hardware Wallets

Myrto Arapinis[1], Andriana Gkaniatsou[1], Dimitris Karakostas[1,2(✉)],
and Aggelos Kiayias[1,2]

[1] University of Edinburgh, Edinburgh, UK
marapini@inf.ed.ac.uk,
{agkaniat,dimitris.karakostas,aggelos.kiayias}@ed.ac.uk
[2] IOHK, Edinburgh, UK

Abstract. Bitcoin, being the most successful cryptocurrency, has been repeatedly attacked with many users losing their funds. The industry's response to securing the user's assets is to offer tamper-resistant hardware wallets. Although such wallets are considered to be the most secure means for managing an account, no formal attempt has been previously done to identify, model and formally verify their properties. This paper provides the first formal model of the Bitcoin hardware wallet operations. We identify the properties and security parameters of a Bitcoin wallet and formally define them in the Universal Composition (UC) Framework. We present a modular treatment of a hardware wallet ecosystem, by realizing the wallet functionality in a hybrid setting defined by a set of protocols. This approach allows us to capture in detail the wallet's components, their interaction and the potential threats. We deduce the wallet's security by proving that it is secure under common cryptographic assumptions, provided that there is no deviation in the protocol execution. Finally, we define the attacks that are successful under a protocol deviation, and analyze the security of commercially available wallets.

1 Introduction

Wallets are the only means to access and manage Bitcoin assets and, although they exist since Bitcoin's inception [19], little or no attention has been paid on formally verifying them. Access to the Bitcoin network, key management, cryptographic operations, and transaction processing are only a few cases of wallet operations. Up until now, there does not exist a specific model of the wallet, nor a thorough threat model, resulting in implementations based on common criteria and security assumptions (*e.g.*, secure key management, correct transaction processing *etc.*) without a complete security treatment. As a result, industry focuses more on securing the cryptographic primitives, and neglects the secure operation of the system as a whole.

The current industry state of the art for managing cryptocurrency assets is hardware wallets. They currently dominate the market as the most secure solution for account management. Although the demand, together with the number of commercially available products, keeps growing, their specifications and security goals remain unclear and understudied. Incorporating expensive hardware

© International Financial Cryptography Association 2019
I. Goldberg and T. Moore (Eds.): FC 2019, LNCS 11598, pp. 426–445, 2019.
https://doi.org/10.1007/978-3-030-32101-7_26

as a wallet is bound to bring some security guarantees; however, proprietary assumptions of the offered functionality and lack of a universal threat model frequently lead to implementations prone to attacks. In this work we formally define the characteristics, specifications and security requirements of hardware wallets in the Universal Composable (UC) Framework [9]; we identify all the potential attack vectors, and the conditions under which a wallet is secure. To that end, we manually inspect the KeepKey, Ledger and Trezor wallets and extract the implementations which we then map to our model. As we show, the wallets are prone to a set of attacks and are secure only under specific assumption. Therefore, our model not only proves the security of existing implementations, but also acts as a reference guide for future implementations.

As wallets are the only way for a user to access her funds, they are repeatedly targeted for attacks that aim to access the account's keys or redirect the payments, ranging from clipboard hijacking [20] and malware [28] to implementation bugs, *e.g.*, the Parity hack in Ethereum [4], and more specific attacks, *e.g.*, brain wallets [25]. In order to address such threats, different ways to harden the wallet's security have been proposed, with the most notable one being the utilization of cryptographic hardware. The module known as a *hardware wallet* is responsible for the account's key management and the execution of the required cryptographic operations. The remaining operations are completed by a dedicated software, either provided together with the hardware or by a third party, with which the hardware communicates. Although hardware wallets are becoming the de facto means of securely managing an account, they have not been formally studied before. Currently, the security of commercially available products can only be checked through manual inspection of their implementation; a process that requires a strong engineering and technical background, and a significant effort and time commitment. Our work aims at bridging the gap between formally modeling and verifying the wallet's properties and claimed specifications. We present a formal model of hardware wallets, which is built using cryptographic primitives and is proven secure under common assumptions. Instead of capturing a hardware wallet as a single module, we conceptualize it as a system of different modules that communicate with each other in order to complete the wallet's operations. This approach allows us to identify a greater set of potential attacks and the conditions for them to be successful. As we show, *perfect cryptographic components by themselves* cannot guarantee security; any module might be proved vulnerable, thus compromising the entire wallet.

Related Work. The importance of formal methods for the Bitcoin protocol is well understood, with existing literature showcasing different approaches. Garay *et al.* [12], after extracting and analyzing the core Bitcoin blockchain protocol, presented a formal abstraction to prove that Bitcoin satisfies a set of security and quality properties. Pass *et al.* [21] analyzed the consistency and liveness properties of the consensus protocol in an asynchronous setting, proving Bitcoin secure assuming an upper bound on the network delay. Badertscher *et al.* [6] suggested a universally composable treatment of the Bitcoin ledger, defining Bitcoin's goals and proving that their model is securely realized in the UC framework.

Transactions, being a core part of Bitcoin, have also attracted attention. Atzei *et al.* [5] proposed a formal model of Bitcoin transactions in order to prove security *e.g.*, against double-spending attacks, and other blockchain properties *e.g.*, blockchain's decreasing value.

Until now, Bitcoin wallets have only been empirically studied. Previous research on the topic focused on the integrity of transactions and suggested ways to enhance the security of the wallets. Gentilal *et al.* [13] stressed the necessity of separating the wallet into two environments, the trusted and the non-trusted, and proposed that a wallet remains secure against attacks by isolating the sensitive operations in the trusted environment. Similarly, Lim *et al.* [18] and Bamert *et al.* [7], argue that security in Bitcoin wallets equals with tamper-resistance and propose the use of cryptographic hardware. Hardware wallets have not yet been extensively studied, since no formal attempt to specify the functionalities and the security properties of such wallets exists so far. As of September 2018, research has only focused on attacking commercially available implementations. Gkaniatsou *et al.* [14] showed that the low-level communication between the hardware and its client is vulnerable to attacks which escalate to the account management. Their research concluded to a set of attacks on the Ledger wallets, which allowed to take control of the account's funds. Hardware wallets have also been studied against physical attacks. Volotikin [26] showed that specific parts of the Ledger's flash memory are accessible, exposing the private keys used for the second factor verification mechanism. Datko *et al.* presented fault injection, timing and power analysis attacks on KeepKey [1] and Trezor [3], which allowed them to extract the private key.

Our Contributions and Roadmap. This work provides a holistic treatment of hardware wallets: from identifying their core specifications and security properties to defining a formal model, which allows reasoning about the offered security of existing wallets and acts as the foundation for designing and implementing new ones. To the best of our knowledge our work is the first to (i) define the properties and requirements of hardware wallets, (ii) provide a formal model and security guarantees of such wallets, and (iii) evaluate the security of commercial products under a formal model.

In Sect. 2 we define the hardware wallet properties and their security specifications. Section 3.3 presents a formal model for the wallet in the UC framework. We define the ideal functionality of the wallet, which models the wallet's operations and the adversary's capabilities. Instead of conceptualizing the wallet as a single entity, in Sect. 3.4 we adopt a modular treatment in which the wallet becomes an ecosystem of different components, namely the human, the client and the hardware. Each component runs a protocol, which defines the operations that it carries out, so the wallet functionality is realized as a composition of these protocols. Section 4 addresses the wallet's security. We present the set of attacks that our ideal functionality identifies, including a novel family of attacks that has not been previously discussed. We then prove that the hybrid setting securely realizes the wallet ideal functionality, and showcase examples when perfect cryptography is inadequate for securing an account. Finally, we evaluate the security of three commercially available wallets: KeepKey, Ledger, and Trezor.

2   Hardware Wallets

Bitcoin relies on the Elliptic Curve Signature Scheme (ECDSA) for signing the transactions and proving ownership of the assets. An account is defined by a key pair (sk, vk): the public portion vk is hashed to create an address α for receiving assets, and the private portion sk is used to sign transactions that spend the assets that α received. Unauthorized access to sk results in loss of funds, thus raising the issue of securing the account's private keys. A wallet offers access to the Bitcoin network and management of an account, and is either based on software, *i.e.*, is hosted online by a third party or run locally, or hardware.

Threat Model. The usage of a broken cryptographic primitive may lead to loss of funds: a broken hash function means potential loss of the receiving funds, whereas a broken signature scheme may result in loss of the spending funds. Protecting against unauthorized access to the wallet's operations has been previously proven to be equally important as using secure cryptographic primitives [8,14]. Hardware wallets are tamper-resistant and offer an isolated environment for the cryptographic primitives. However, if they connect to a compromised client, then any inputs/outputs of the hardware can potentially be malicious. For example, consider Bob, whose account is defined by the key pair (sk, vk), and an adversary $\mathcal{A}$, who is able to forge Bob's signature. In this case any signature $s_{\mathcal{A}}$ of a message $m_{\mathcal{A}}$ chosen by $\mathcal{A}$ can be verified by vk; hence the adversary can spend all assets that Bob has previously received, *i.e.*, the assets sent to the hash of vk. Let us now assume that Bob's signature is unforgeable but $\mathcal{A}$ controls the signing algorithm inputs, such that for any message m that Bob wishes to sign, $\mathcal{A}$ substitutes it with $m_{\mathcal{A}}$. Even though the signature is unforgeable, the adversary can still spend Bob's assets by tampering with the message. Our model captures the family of such attacks, which result in loss of funds by tampering the inputs/outputs of the wallet operations. Thus, the security of a Bitcoin wallet is reduced to the security of the underlying cryptographic primitives *and* the honesty of the communicating parties.

The Wallet Setting. Software, not being tamper-resistant, cannot guarantee a secure environment for the wallet's operations. Instead, hardware wallets are designed to offer such an environment by separating the wallet's cryptographic primitives from the other operations *e.g.*, connection to the Bitcoin network. These devices do not offer network connectivity; instead they operate in an offline mode. Due to their limited memory capabilities and the absence of network access, they cannot keep track of the account's activities, *e.g.*, past transactions. Thus, they require connection with a dedicated software, *the client*, which keeps records of the account's actions and provides a usable interface with which the user can interact. Hardware wallets operate under the assumption of a malicious host, and they provide a trusted path with the user. Both the client and the hardware display transaction related data, which the user compares to decide on their validity. As such, the user becomes part of the system and is responsible for identifying potentially malicious actions of the client.

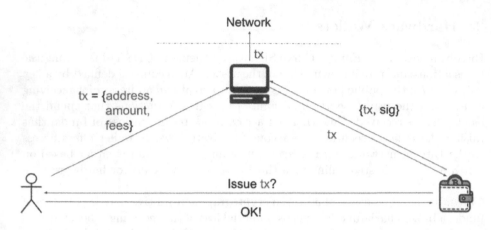

Fig. 1. Transaction issuing in the hardware wallet setting.

The wallet operations are initiated by the user, they are executed by the client, the hardware, or both, and are: (i) *Setup*: the hardware generates the master key pair (msk, mvk) and returns the private key msk, *i.e.*, the wallet's *seed*, to the user; currently all wallets are Hierarchical Deterministic, as defined by the BIP32 standard [27], so the keys are derived from a master key pair by the simplified functions $sk_i = msk + hash(i, mvk)(\mathrm{mod}\ n)$ and $vk_i = mvk + hash(i, mvk) \times N$, where i is the index of the key and n, N are public parameters of the used Elliptic Curve; (ii) *Session Initialization*: the hardware connects to the client and sends it the master public key mvk; (iii) *Generate Address*: both the client and the hardware generate a new address and return it to the user. The hardware derives from (msk, mvk) a new pair (sk_i, vk_i), generates a new address α_i and returns it to the user. The client may either generate vk_i using mvk or receive vk_i from the hardware, then generates and stores the corresponding address, and finally returns it to the user; (iv) *Calculate Balance*: given a list of the account's addresses, the client iterates over the ledger's transactions, calculates the account's available assets and returns this amount to the user; (v) *Transaction Issuing*: the user provides the payment data to the client, which then forwards them to the hardware together with the available inputs, *i.e.*, the account's addresses and balances, and requests its signature. The hardware checks whether the input addresses belong to the managed account and generates a *change address* upon demand, *i.e.*, if the balance is larger than the payable amount plus transaction fees. Then, it requests the user's approval of the payment data. If the user confirms the payment, then the hardware signs it and returns the signature together with the corresponding public key to the client in order to publish it. Figure 1 presents an abstraction of the transaction issuing process in the hardware-enhanced wallet setting.

In our model a wallet is not a single module, but rather an "ecosystem", which consists of different modules that communicate during an operation: the user, the client and the hardware. In order to treat it under the UC framework, we will describe an ideal functionality for it as well as its real world implementation.

In the ideal world the wallet is a single component (functionality) responsible for all the aforementioned operations while in reality the wallet is split into multiple modules which communicate during the execution of each operation. In the real world, the wallet emerges through the interaction of the human operator, the client (which is a device like a desktop computer or tablet/smartphone) and a tamper resistant hardware component.

Ideal World. The wallet functionality, $\mathcal{F}_w$, is responsible for the wallet's operations. $\mathcal{F}_w$ interacts with the global Bitcoin ledger functionality $\mathcal{G}_{LEDGER}$, as defined in [6], in order to execute operations requiring access to the decentralized system. $\mathcal{G}_{LEDGER}$ is the ideal functionality that models the Bitcoin ledger and allows a wallet to register itself, publish transactions and retrieve the state of the ledger, *i.e.*, all published transactions. $\mathcal{F}_w$ generates a unique address per public key and also incorporates a signature functionality, $\mathcal{F}_{SIG}$ as defined in [10] (for convenience we will treat $\mathcal{F}_{SIG}$ as a separate component in the ideal world). The wallet registers itself with $\mathcal{F}_{SIG}$ which creates fresh keys for the account upon request, *e.g.*, during address generation, and signs messages, *e.g.*, transactions. $\mathcal{F}_{SIG}$ is also accessed by the validation predicate of $\mathcal{G}_{LEDGER}$ in order to verify a transaction's signature during the validation stage.

Real World. The operations are executed by a set of communicating parties: the *hardware*, the *client* and the *user*. Thus the protocols of the hardware π_{hw}, the client π_{client}, and the human π_{human} define the actions of the corresponding parties. The hardware protocol π_{hw}, uses a signature scheme $\Sigma \equiv \langle \mathsf{KeyGen}, \mathsf{Verify}, \mathsf{Sign} \rangle$, a cryptographic hash function H and a pseudorandom key generation function $\mathsf{HierarchicalKeyGen}(msk, i)$, in order to derive children keys from the master key. A basic assumption of this setting is that π_{client} runs in an untrusted environment, *i.e.*, we do not consider the software to be secure. Thus, connection to a malicious client, in our model, is equivalent to corruption of the client by the adversary. The human communicates with the hardware and the client via a secure channel, *i.e.*, the user interacts directly with the device.

Figure 2 presents the ideal and the real world settings. In both worlds the environment Z interacts with the adversary, *i.e.*, in the ideal world it interacts with the simulator S, and in the real world with the adversary $\mathcal{A}$. In the ideal world the wallet consists of the ideal wallet functionality $\mathcal{F}_w$ and the signature functionality $\mathcal{F}_{SIG}$; in the real world it consists of the combination of the user, client and hardware wallet parties who execute the respective protocols $(\pi_{human}, \pi_{client}, \pi_{hw})$. The communication between the human, the client and the hardware is achieved over a *UC-secure channel protocol* as presented by Canetti [11]: the adversary is able to observe the encrypted communication between the honest parties and only retrieve the length of the exchanged messages. In practice, this can be achieved by establishing a secure channel between the client and the hardware module using standard key exchange techniques, while the human-hardware channel is assumed to be secure by default. In the absence of a secure channel, the adversary may tamper with the communication thus, in our model, an insecure channel is equivalent to the client being corrupted.

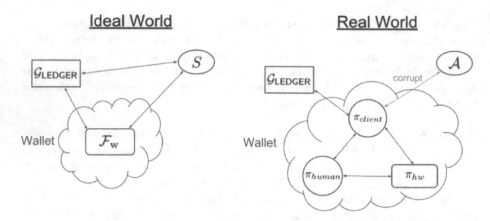

Fig. 2. A high-level comparison of the ideal and the real worlds.

3   Formal Model

This section defines a formal model of the hardware wallet ecosystem in the UC Framework, in which we compare the execution of a security definition, *i.e.*, the ideal setting, with a concrete protocol setting, *i.e.*, the real world. We first define a wrapper for the validation predicate which is used by the Bitcoin ledger functionality $\mathcal{G}_{\text{LEDGER}}$ and is accessed in both the ideal and the real worlds upon publishing a transaction. In the ideal world, a functionality defines the wallet operations. In the real world, the hardware wallet is defined as a hybrid setting which we prove to securely realize the ideal definition.

3.1   Notations

An address α is a unique string chosen from $\{0,1\}^{\ell}$, where ℓ is the length of α in bits, and is associated with a payment key pair (vk, sk), where vk is the public and sk the private key. The wallet's key pairs and, consequently, the addresses are generated using the master key pair (msk, mvk), which is randomly selected from the key domain $\mathbb{K}$ upon the wallet's setup. A transaction is defined as a tuple $tx := (\alpha_s, \alpha_r, \theta_{\text{pay}}, \alpha_c, \theta_{\text{change}})$, where α_s denotes the sender's address, α_r the receiver's address and α_c the change address; θ_{pay}, θ_{change} θ_{fee} are the payment, change and fee funds respectively, where θ_{change} equals to the account's balance minus the payment and the fee amounts, *i.e.*, $\theta_{\text{change}} := \text{balanceOf}(\alpha_s) - \theta_{\text{pay}} - \theta_{\text{fee}}$. A signed transaction is the tuple (tx, vk, σ), where σ is the signature of tx under the public key vk. We note that, for ease of notation, this is a simplified transaction model - adapting it for multiple inputs and outputs, *e.g.*, to properly model Bitcoin, should be straightforward though. The parties that execute an operation are the user $\mathcal{U}$ *i.e.*, the owner of the wallet, the client to which the hardware connects $\mathcal{C}$, and the hardware $\mathcal{H}$. Each message is associated with a session id $sid' = \mathcal{UCH}$, which defines the parties that the message is related with.

3.2 Validation Predicate

The Bitcoin Ledger functionality $\mathcal{G}_{\text{LEDGER}}$, as defined in [6], is parameterized with the validation predicate Validate. This predicate identifies whether a transaction can be added to the buffer, *i.e.*, whether it is valid for publishing to the ledger. Although a concrete instantiation is not provided, it is stated that it takes as input the candidate transaction, the buffer and the current state. The candidate transaction consists of the signed transaction $stx = (tx, vk, \sigma)$ and the ledger parameters, *e.g.*, the transaction id, which is a unique identifier of the transaction, and the timestamp, *i.e.*, the time which is defined by a global clock. Intuitively, in Bitcoin the state is the blockchain and the buffer is the mempool which contains the transactions that have not yet been included in a block. The validation predicate is used for the signature verification of a candidate transaction. This is formalized with a wrapper ValidateWrapper, which wraps all instantiations of the validation predicate. In the ideal world the wrapper accesses the signature functionality $\mathcal{F}_{\text{SIG}}$ to verify the transaction's signature: if the signature is not valid, then it directly outputs 0, otherwise it performs all additional checks, such as verifying the funds which are consumed and checking whether the amounts are valid. We refrain from constraining our setting to a specific Validate predicate, but rather describe it for all generic ledger settings. The ideal wrapper IdealValidateWrapper is described in Algorithm 1. The real world wrapper RealValidateWrapper uses a signature scheme instead of $\mathcal{F}_{\text{SIG}}$ and behaves similarly to Algorithm 1, *i.e.*, it first parses BTX and then performs the same branch checks on $\text{Verify}(tx, vk, \sigma)$ and returns the proper boolean value.

3.3 The Wallet Ideal Model

$\mathcal{F}_{\text{w}}$ incorporates $\mathcal{F}_{\text{SIG}}$ and runs in the $\mathcal{G}_{\text{LEDGER}}$-setting, interacting with the adversary $\mathcal{A}$, a set of parties $\mathbb{P}$ and the environment $\mathcal{Z}$, and keeps the initially empty items: (i) $A_{[]}$: a list of lists of addresses and the corresponding public keys, (α, vk), (ii) $B_{[]}$: a list of lists of the account's addresses and their corresponding balance, (α, θ), and (iii) $K_{[]}$: a list of master key pairs (mvk, msk). $\mathcal{F}_{\text{w}}$ realizes the following operations: (i) *Wallet setup*: Upon a setup request, it initializes the

---

Algorithm 1 The validation predicate wrapper, parameterized by Validate and $\mathcal{F}_{\text{SIG}}$. The input is a transaction BTX, the buffer buffer and the state state.

---
function IdealValidateWrapper(BTX, buffer, state)
    $(tx, vk, \sigma, \text{txid}, \tau_L, p_i) := \text{parse}(\text{BTX})$
    Send $(\text{VERIFY}, \text{sid}, tx, \sigma, vk)$ to $\mathcal{F}_{\text{SIG}}$ and receive $(\text{VERIFIED}, \text{sid}, tx, f)$
    if $f = 0$ **then**
        return 0
    else
        return Validate(BTX, buffer, state)
    end if
end function

---

list of addresses, generates the account's master key pair, registers to $\mathcal{G}_{\text{LEDGER}}$ and returns the master private key. (ii) *Client Corruption*: When $\mathcal{A}$ corrupts a client $\mathcal{C}$, $\mathcal{F}_{\text{w}}$ leaks the past public keys and addresses that $\mathcal{C}$ has obtained. (iii) *Client session initialization*: In order to start a new session, it identifies the $\mathcal{C}$ defined in sid' and and returns a new assigned pass phrase "pass"; in the real world, the pass phrase acts as the authentication mechanism between the parties. (iv) *Address generation*: It requests a new public key from $\mathcal{F}_{\text{SIG}}$ and picks an associated address at random. It then stores the new address in the corresponding list and also returns it to $\mathcal{Z}$. If the connected client is corrupted, then the functionality leaks the address and the public key to $\mathcal{A}$. (v) *Balance calculation*: If $\mathcal{C}$ is honest then it queries the ledger to retrieve the blockchain; if the connected client is corrupted, then it requests from $\mathcal{A}$ to provide the chain. Then, it calculates the amount of available assets and returns it to $\mathcal{Z}$. iv) *Transaction issuing*: Upon receiving a transaction request, if $\mathcal{C}$ is corrupted, then it leaks the transaction information to the adversary and retrieves a new transaction object from it. If $\mathcal{U}$ is also corrupted, then it discards the original request and keeps the adversarial transaction, otherwise it ignores the adversary's response. Finally, it requests a signature from $\mathcal{F}_{\text{SIG}}$ for the transaction which it then publishes to $\mathcal{G}_{\text{LEDGER}}$.

Functionality $\mathcal{F}_{\text{w}}$

All messages below contain a session id of the form $\text{sid} = (\mathbb{P}, \text{sid}')$.

- **Setup:** Upon receiving $(\text{SETUP}, \text{sid})$ from some party $\mathcal{U} \in \mathbb{P}$, forward it to $\mathcal{A}$. Then add the empty list $A_{\mathcal{U}}$ to $A_{[]}$, register with $\mathcal{G}_{\text{LEDGER}}$, pick the master key pair $(msk_{\mathcal{U}}, mvk_{\mathcal{U}}) \xleftarrow{\$} \mathbb{K}$ and add it to $K_{[]}$ and return $(\text{SETUPOK}, \text{sid})$ to $\mathcal{U}$.

- **Client Corruption:** When $\mathcal{A}$ corrupts a party $\mathcal{C}$, for every $\mathcal{U}$ such that a **Setup** session with $\mathcal{C}$ has been completed send $(\text{ADDRESSLIST}, \text{sid}, A_{\mathcal{U}})$ and $(\text{MASTERPUBKEY}, \text{sid}, mvk_{\mathcal{U}})$ to $\mathcal{A}$.

- **Initialize Client Session:** Upon receiving $(\text{INITSESSION}, \text{sid})$ from party $\mathcal{U}$, pick $pass_{client} \xleftarrow{\$} \{0,1\}^{\lambda}$ and send $(\text{INITSESSION}, \text{sid}, pass_{client})$ to $\mathcal{C}$. If $\mathcal{C}$ is corrupted, then send $(\text{INITSESSION}, \text{sid}, pass_{client})$ to $\mathcal{A}$ and wait for a response $(\text{INITSESSIONOK}, \text{sid}, pass_{client})$. Finally, send $(\text{SESSION}, \text{sid}, pass_{client})$ to $\mathcal{U}$.

- **Generate Address:** Upon receiving $(\text{GENADDR}, \text{sid})$ from $\mathcal{U}$, send $(\text{KEYGEN}, \text{sid})$ to $\mathcal{F}_{\text{SIG}}$. Upon receiving $(\text{VERIFICATION KEY}, \text{sid}, vk)$ from $\mathcal{F}_{\text{SIG}}$, pick an address $\alpha \xleftarrow{\$} \{0,1\}^{\ell}$ and add (α, vk) to $A_{\mathcal{U}}$. If $\mathcal{C}$ is corrupted then send $(\text{ADDRESS}, \text{sid}, (\alpha, vk))$ to $\mathcal{A}$ and wait for a response $(\text{ADDRESSOK}, \text{sid}, \alpha')$. If $\mathcal{U}$ is corrupted then set $a := \alpha'$, else set $a := \alpha$. Finally, return $(\text{ADDRESS}, \text{sid}, a)$ to $\mathcal{U}$.

- **Calculate Balance:** Upon receiving $(\text{GETBALANCE}, \text{sid})$ from $\mathcal{U}$, send $(\text{READ}, \text{sid})$ to $\mathcal{G}_{\text{LEDGER}}$ and wait for the response $(\text{READ}, \text{sid}, chain)$. If $\mathcal{C}$ is corrupted, then send $(\text{READ}, \text{sid})$ to $\mathcal{A}$ and, upon receiving the response $(\text{READ}, \text{sid}, chain')$, set $chain := chain'$. Then set $balance := 0$, initialize the list $B_\mathcal{U} \in B_{[]}$ which contains $(a, 0)$ for every address $(a, \cdot)$ in $A_\mathcal{U}$, and $\forall tx \in$ chain, *i.e.*, the ordered transactions in the ledger such that $tx = (\alpha_s, \alpha_r, \theta_{pay}, \alpha_c, \theta_{change})$, do:

- If $\exists (\alpha_s, \cdot) \in A_\mathcal{U}$, then update the entry $(\alpha_s, \theta_{past}) \in B_\mathcal{U}$ to $(\alpha_s, 0)$;
- If $\exists (\alpha_r, \cdot) \in A_\mathcal{U}$, then update the entry $(\alpha_r, \theta_{past}) \in B_\mathcal{U}$ to $(\alpha_r, \theta_{past} + \theta_{pay})$;
- If $\exists (\alpha_c, \cdot) \in A_\mathcal{U}$, then update the entry $(\alpha_c, \theta_{past}) \in B_\mathcal{U}$ to $(\alpha_c, \theta_{past} + \theta_{change})$;

Finally, for every $(\cdot, \theta) \in B_\mathcal{U}$ do balance $:=$ balance $+ \theta$ and send (BALANCE, sid, balance) to $\mathcal{U}$.

- **Issue Transaction:** Upon receiving (ISSUETX, sid, $(\alpha_r, \theta_{pay}, \theta_{fee})$) from $\mathcal{U}$, if $\mathcal{C}$ is corrupted then forward the message to $\mathcal{A}$ and wait for a response (ISSUETX, sid, $pass_{client}$, $(\alpha'_r, \theta'_{pay}, \theta'_{fee})$). If $\mathcal{U}$ is corrupted then set $(\alpha_r, \theta_{pay}, \theta_{fee}) := (\alpha'_r, \theta'_{pay}, \theta'_{fee})$. Then find $(\alpha_{in}, \theta_{in}) \in B_\mathcal{U} : \theta_{in} \geq \theta_{pay} + \theta_{fee}$. If such entry exists then compute an address α_c and its public key vk_c as per the *Generate Address* interface, set $\theta_{change} := \theta_{in} - \theta_{pay} - \theta_{fee}$ and $tx := (\alpha_{in}, \alpha_{out}, \theta_{pay}, \alpha_c, \theta_{change})$, send (SIGN, sid, tx) to $\mathcal{F}_{SIG}$ and wait for (SIGNATURE, sid, tx, σ). Then find $(\alpha_{in}, vk) \in A_\mathcal{U}$ and set $stx := (tx, vk, \sigma)$. If $\mathcal{C}$ is corrupted, send (ADDRESS, sid, α_c, vk_c) and (SUBMIT, sid, stx) to $\mathcal{A}$ and wait for the response (SUBMITOK, sid). Finally, send (SUBMIT, sid, stx) to $\mathcal{G}_{LEDGER}$.

3.4   The Hardware Wallet Hybrid Setting

The hybrid setting consists of the human π_{human}, client π_{client}, and hardware π_{hw} protocols, which define the set of operations run by the parties.

Human Protocol. π_{human} interacts with $\mathcal{C}$, $\mathcal{H}$, and the environment $\mathcal{Z}$, and defines the following, initially empty, items: (i) T: a list of transactions $tx = (\alpha_r, \theta_{pay}, \theta_{fee})$, and (ii) S: a list of client sessions sid. The model assumes that a session is initialized when $\mathcal{U}$ connects the hardware module to the client device and assigns a pass phrase $pass_{client} \in \{0, 1\}^\lambda$ to each client with which she interacts, which is chosen at random upon session initialization. Although it is assumed that the user samples an unguessable pass phrase, future work will explore functionalities that allow a malicious client to perform (dictionary) password attacks against it. Also $\mathcal{U}$ keeps track of the initiated sessions and pending transactions. The user does not perform complex computations, *e.g.*, verifying a signature, or maintain a large state, like the entire list of generated addresses. It is only assumed to have a memory T, only as large as the pending transactions it is processing, and also that it is capable of performing equality checks between strings.

Protocol π_{human}

- **Setup:** Upon receiving (SETUP, sid) from $\mathcal{Z}$, forward it to $\mathcal{H}$, and initialize T to empty. Then upon receiving (SETUPOK, sid) from $\mathcal{H}$ forward it to $\mathcal{Z}$.

- **Initialize Client Session:** Upon receiving (INITSESSION, sid) from $\mathcal{Z}$, pick $pass_{client} \xleftarrow{\$} \{0,1\}^\lambda$ and send (INITSESSION, sid, $pass_{client}$) to $\mathcal{C}$. Upon receiving (INITSESSION, sid, $pass'_{client}$) from $\mathcal{H}$, if $pass'_{client} = pass_{client}$ then add $pass_{client}$ to S and send (SESSION, sid, $pass'_{client}$) to $\mathcal{H}$ and to $\mathcal{Z}$.
- **Generate Address:** Upon receiving (GENADDR, sid) from $\mathcal{Z}$, forward it to $\mathcal{C}$ and wait for two messages, (ADDRESS, sid, α_{client}) from $\mathcal{C}$ and (ADDRESS, sid, α_{hw}) from $\mathcal{H}$. Upon receiving them, if $\alpha_{client} = \alpha_{hw}$ then send (ADDRESS, sid, α_{hw}) to $\mathcal{Z}$.
- **Calculate Balance:** Upon receiving (GETBALANCE, sid) from $\mathcal{Z}$, forward it to $\mathcal{C}$. Then upon receiving (BALANCE, sid, balance) from $\mathcal{C}$, forward it to $\mathcal{Z}$.
- **Issue Transaction:** Upon receiving (ISSUETX, sid, tx) from $\mathcal{Z}$, such that $tx = (\alpha_r, \theta_{pay}, \theta_{fee})$, add tx to T and forward the message to $\mathcal{C}$. Upon receiving (CHECKTX, sid, $pass_{client}, tx'$, balance$'$) from $\mathcal{H}$, if $pass_{client} \in S$, $tx' \in T$ and balance$' =$ balance $- \theta_{pay} - \theta_{fee}$ then remove tx' from T and send (ISSUETX, sid, $pass_{client}, tx$) to $\mathcal{H}$.

Client Protocol. The client $\mathcal{C}$ interacts with the user $\mathcal{U}$, the hardware wallet $\mathcal{H}$ and the environment $\mathcal{Z}$. The protocol π_{client} defines the following items: (i) mvk: the master public key of the wallet, (ii) i: the key derivation index, (iii) $pass$: the pass phrase that the user assigns to the client, (iv) A_{client}: a list of the account's addresses, and v) T_{utxo}: a list of unspent balances like $tx = (\alpha_{in}, \theta_{in})$, where $\alpha_{in} \in A_{client}$ and $\theta_{in} > 0$. $\mathcal{C}$ acts a proxy between $\mathcal{U}$ and $\mathcal{H}$, provides connectivity to the ledger and executes blockchain-related operations, *e.g.*, computing the account's balance. Although during the address generation, $\mathcal{C}$ retrieves the public key from $\mathcal{H}$, in practice this is optional and the client can generate the address independently via the derivation process of the hierarchical deterministic wallets.

Protocol π_{client}

- **Initialize Client Session:** Upon receiving (INITSESSION, sid, $pass_{client}$) · from $\mathcal{U}$, forward it to $\mathcal{H}$. Upon receiving (MASTERPUBKEY, sid, mvk) from $\mathcal{H}$, set $pass := pass_{client}$, mvk $:= mvk$ and $i := 1$.
- **Generate Address:** Upon receiving (GENADDR, sid) from $\mathcal{U}$, forward it to $\mathcal{H}$. Then upon receiving (PUBKEY, sid, vk_i) from $\mathcal{H}$, compute $\alpha_i := \mathsf{H}(vk_i)$, set $i := i + 1$ and add α_i to A_{client}. Finally, send (ADDRESS, sid, α_i) to $\mathcal{U}$.
- **Calculate Balance:** Upon receiving (GETBALANCE, sid) from $\mathcal{U}$, send (READ, sid) to $\mathcal{G}_{\mathsf{LEDGER}}$. Upon receiving (READ, sid, chain) from $\mathcal{G}_{\mathsf{LEDGER}}$, set balance $:= 0$ and T_{utxo} to the empty list and $\forall tx \in$ chain, *i.e.*, the ordered transactions in the ledger such that $tx = (\alpha_s, \alpha_r, \theta_{pay}, \alpha_c, \theta_{change})$, do:
  - If $\alpha_s \in A_{client}$ then update the entry $(\alpha_s, \theta_{past}) \in T_{utxo}$ to $(\alpha_s, 0)$;

- If $\alpha_r \in A_{client}$ then update the entry $(\alpha_r, \theta_{past}) \in T_{utxo}$ to $(\alpha_r, \theta_{past} + \theta_{pay})$;
- If $\alpha_c \in A_{client}$ then update the entry $(\alpha_c, \theta_{past}) \in T_{utxo}$ to $(\alpha_c, \theta_{past} + \theta_{change})$;

Finally, for every $(\cdot, \theta) \in T_{utxo}$ do balance := balance + θ and send (BALANCE, sid, balance) to $\mathcal{U}$.

- **Issue Transaction:** Upon receiving (ISSUETX, sid, tx) from $\mathcal{U}$, such that $tx = (\alpha_r, \theta_{pay}, \theta_{fee})$, send (SIGNTX, sid, $pass, tx, T_{utxo}$) to $\mathcal{H}$. Upon receiving (CHANGEINDEX, sid, idx), set $i := idx$ and compute and store the public key and the address for the change as in the *Generate Address* interface. Then upon receiving (SIGNTX, sid, stx) from $\mathcal{H}$, send (SUBMIT, sid, stx) to $\mathcal{G}_{\text{LEDGER}}$.

Hardware Wallet Protocol. The hardware $\mathcal{H}$ interacts with $\mathcal{C}$ and $\mathcal{U}$ and runs the protocol π_{hw}, which defines the following items: (i) i: the key derivation index, (ii) S: a list of the active client sessions, (iii) (msk, mvk): the master key pair of the wallet, and (iv) A: a list that contains tuples like $(i, \alpha_i, sk_i, vk_i)$ where i is an index, α_i a generated address and (sk_i, vk_i) the corresponding key pair.

Protocol π_{hw}

- **Setup:** Upon receiving (SETUP, sid) from $\mathcal{U}$, initialize S and A to empty lists. Then compute $(msk, mvk) \leftarrow \mathsf{KeyGen}(1^\lambda)$ and set $i := 1$. Finally, return (SETUP, sid, msk) to $\mathcal{U}$.
- **Initialize Client Session:** Upon receiving (INITSESSION, sid, $pass_{client}$) from $\mathcal{C}$, forward it to $\mathcal{U}$. Upon receiving (SESSION, sid, $pass'_{client}$) from $\mathcal{U}$ add $pass'_{client}$ to S and send (MASTERPUBKEY, sid, mvk) to $\mathcal{C}$.
- **Generate Address:** Upon receiving (GENADDR, sid) from $\mathcal{C}$, compute $(sk_i, vk_i) := \mathsf{HierarchicalKeyGen}(msk, i)$ and $\alpha_i := \mathsf{H}(vk_i)$. Then store $(i, \alpha_i, sk_i, vk_i)$ to A, set $i := i + 1$, and return (ADDRESS, sid, α_i) to $\mathcal{U}$ and (PUBKEY, sid, vk_i) to $\mathcal{C}$.
- **Issue Transaction:** Upon receiving (SIGNTX, sid, $pass_{client}, tx, T_{utxo}$) from $\mathcal{C}$, where $tx = (\alpha_r, \theta_{pay}, \theta_{fee})$, find an entry $(\alpha_{in}, \theta_{in}) \in T_{utxo}$: $\theta_{in} \geq \theta_{pay} + \theta_{fee}$. If such entry exists, then: (i) find $(\cdot, \alpha_{in}, sk_{in}, vk_{in}) \in A$, (ii) compute the remaining change $\theta_{change} := \theta_{in} - \theta_{pay} - \theta_{fee}$, (iii) create a change address α_c as in the *Generate Address* interface, and (iv) compute balance as the sum of θ for every $(\cdot, \theta) \in T_{utxo}$ and set balance' := balance $- \theta_{pay} - \theta_{fee}$. Then send (CHANGEINDEX, sid, i) to $\mathcal{C}$ and (CHECKTX, sid, $pass_{client}, tx'$, balance') to $\mathcal{U}$, where $tx' = (\alpha_r, \theta_{pay}, \theta_{fee})$. Upon receiving (ISSUETX, sid, $pass_{client}, tx$) from $\mathcal{U}$, set $tx := (\alpha_{in}, \alpha_r, \theta_{pay}, \alpha_c, \theta_{change})$, compute $stx := (tx, vk_{in}, \mathsf{Sign}(tx, sk_{in}))$ and send (SIGNTX, sid, stx) to $\mathcal{C}$.

4   Security in the Hybrid Setting

We now assess the security of our proposed model in order to prove the security of the hybrid setting with respect to the wallet ideal functionality. The attacks that our model considers are the following:

(1) *Privacy loss*: when the adversary corrupts a client, he accesses the account's public keys, addresses and their balance;
(2) *Payment attack*: during the transaction issuing operation, the adversary may tamper with the inputs to alter the payment amount, the receiving address, and/or the fee amount. This attack is successful if and only if the client is corrupted and the user deviates from her expected behavior, *i.e.*, does not reject the malicious transaction data;
(3) *Address generation attack*: the adversary may tamper with address generation on the client's side, so that the user acquires an address which is adversarially controlled. This attack will be successful if and only if the client is corrupted and the user deviates from her expected behavior, *i.e.*, does not cross-check the address that the client provides with the hardware one;
(4) *Chain attack*: the adversary may tamper with the balance calculation by providing to the wallet a malicious chain. This family of attacks is successful only if the client is corrupted, regardless if the user follows the protocol.

Chain Attacks. The attacks 1, 2 and 3 have been previously identified by empirical studies showcasing their applicability [2,14]. However, the *chain attack* has not been previously discussed, and is more nuanced compared to the others. Under our model, the client is the only party that connects to the network. Therefore, a corrupted client can mount any type of eclipse attack [15], including the chain attacks that we describe here. We showcase an example of these attacks.

Assume the honest chain $\mathsf{chain_w}$, and a transaction tx, which transfers θ_{in} funds to an address α and is published in the j-th block of $\mathsf{chain_w}$. Prior to block j, *i.e.*, blocks with indices in $[0, j-1]$, a number of transactions were published that sent an aggregated amount of θ_{past} funds to α. The adversary $\mathcal{A}$ substitutes $\mathsf{chain_w}$ with a chain $\mathsf{chain}_\mathcal{A}$, which is the prefix chain up to, but not including, the j-th block, *i.e.*, it consists of the blocks with indices $0 \ldots j-1$. Hence, during the balance calculation, the wallet assumes that α owns θ_{past} funds. When the user requests a transaction $tx = (\alpha_r, \theta_{pay}, \theta_{fee})$, where $\theta_{past} = \theta_{pay} + \theta_{fee}$ (same as $\theta_{past} > \theta_{pay} + \theta_{fee}$), the wallet computes the amount of change according to θ_{past}, and spends the rest as fees. The attack results in forcing the wallet to spend more funds than it would in an honest setting.

The Hybrid Setting Security Theorem. In order to prove the security of our model, we denote the hybrid setting described in Sect. 3.4 by π_{hybrid}. We show that π_{hybrid} securely realizes the wallet ideal functionality $\mathcal{F}_w$ defined in Sect. 3.3. In the ideal execution, $\mathcal{G}_{\text{LEDGER}}$ uses the ideal wrapper IdealValidateWrapper defined in Sect. 3.2, whereas in the real world it utilizes RealValidateWrapper. Theorem 1 restricts to environments that do not corrupt the hardware party $\mathcal{H}$, therefore it cannot cover attacks mounted by the hardware wallet's manufacturer or cases when the hardware wallet gets corrupted due to insecure hardware.

Theorem 1 (Hybrid Wallet). *Let the hybrid setting π_{hybrid}, which is parameterized by a signature scheme Σ and a hash function H and interacts with $\mathcal{G}_{LEDGER}$ parameterized by* RealValidateWrapper. *π_{hybrid} securely realizes the ideal functionality $\mathcal{F}_w$, which interacts with $\mathcal{G}_{LEDGER}$ parameterized by* IdealValidateWrapper, *if and only if Σ is EUF-CMA and H is an instantiation of the random oracle.*

Proof. **The "if" part** For this part of the theorem we assume that the environment $\mathcal{Z}$ can distinguish between the ideal and the real execution with non-negligible probability. We then describe a "generic" simulator S for each adversary $\mathcal{A}$, which emulates the interfaces defined by the functionality. S also runs an internal copy of $\mathcal{A}$ and forwards the outputs of its computations to $\mathcal{A}$. We then construct a forger G that runs an internal simulation of the environment $\mathcal{Z}$. Thus, for each property assumption, we show that there exists a "bad" event E such that, as long as E does not occur, the two executions are statistically close. However, when E occurs, the environment $\mathcal{Z}$ distinguishes between the executions. At this point, G uses $\mathcal{Z}$ and outputs the values that break the property under question. Therefore since, by assumption, E occurs with non-negligible probability, we show that G is also successful with non-negligible probability.

The Simulator. Let us now construct the generic simulator S. For every interface defined by the ideal functionality, S completes the operations in the manner defined by the protocols in the hybrid setting. It internally runs a copy of the adversary $\mathcal{A}$ and forwards the necessary messages to it as defined in the hybrid setting. So, the view of the $\mathcal{A}$ when it interacts with S is the same as in the case it operates in the real world setting. S performs as follows:

– Any inputs received from the environment $\mathcal{Z}$, forward them to the internal copy of $\mathcal{A}$. Moreover, forward any output from $\mathcal{A}$ to $\mathcal{Z}$;
– **Party Setup:** For every party P for which $\mathcal{F}_w$ sends messages, spawn an internal simulation of the parties for human $\mathcal{U}$, client $\mathcal{C}$ and hardware wallet $\mathcal{H}$, which also interact with $\mathcal{A}$ as needed and run the protocols π_{human}, π_{client} and π_{hw} respectively;
– **Party Corruption:** Whenever the adversary $\mathcal{A}$ corrupts a party, S corrupts it in the ideal process and hands to $\mathcal{A}$ its internal state;
– **(Setup, Initialize Session, Generate Address, Issue Transaction):** For any message for these interfaces, follow the protocols π_{human}, π_{client} and π_{hw} for the human, client and hardware parties.

In order to prove the theorem regarding the properties of the signature scheme we follow the reasoning of Canetti [10]. We will show the proof for the *unforgeability* property of the signature scheme, as the proofs for the other properties are similar to it.

Unforgeability: Assume that *consistency* and *completeness* hold for Σ and H instantiates the random oracle. In this case, the *Setup, Initialize Session* and *Generate Address* interfaces are the same in the both settings from the adversary's point of view. Since, by assumption, $\mathcal{Z}$ distinguishes between the two, this occurs during the *Issue Transaction* phase, *i.e.*, by observing a valid signature of a transaction which has not been issued by the hardware wallet.

We now construct a forger G that runs a simulated copy of $\mathcal{Z}$. G follows the generic simulator as above, except for the transaction issuing interface. Upon receiving (SUBMIT, sid, stx), where $stx = (tx, vk, \sigma)$, it checks if Verify$(tx, vk, \sigma) = True$. If so, it accesses the internal state of the hardware $\mathcal{H}$ and checks whether it has issued stx. If so, then it continues the simulation. Else G outputs stx as a forgery. Since, as long as this does not occur, the two executions are statistically close and, by assumption, $\mathcal{Z}$ is successful with non-negligible probability, then the probability that G is also successful is non-negligible.

The "Only if" Direction. We show that if one property does not hold, then the probability that the "bad" event E (as above) occurs is non-negligible, so that the environment $\mathcal{Z}$ can distinguish between the real and ideal executions.

Again we prove the theorem for the *unforgeability* property - the proofs for the other properties of Σ are constructed similarly.

Unforgeability: Assume that *unforgeability* does not hold for Σ, so there exists a forger G for Σ. When G wishes to obtain a signature for some message m, the environment sends the message (ISSUETX, sid, m) and forwards the response to G. When G outputs a forgery $stx = (tx, vk, \sigma)$, if tx has been previously signed then the environment halts. Else it sends stx to $\mathcal{G}_{\text{LEDGER}}$ and observes the ledger's updates. In the ideal setting the transaction will be rejected by the validation predicate and it will never be included in the ledger, whereas in the real world the probability that the transaction is accepted and eventually published in the ledger is non-negligible.

Finally, we show the proof for the *address randomness* property which accompanies the assumption that H instantiates a random oracle.

Address Randomness: Assume that all properties for Σ hold. Now the *Setup, Initialize Session* and *Issue Transaction* interfaces are similar in both settings. So if $\mathcal{Z}$ distinguishes between the two worlds, then this occurs during an address generation interaction. Specifically, it should observe addresses which are not uniformly distributed over the space of possible addresses. This is impossible in the ideal world by construction. However, if this was true for the real world, then H would not instantiate the random oracle, therefore by assumption it is impossible for $\mathcal{Z}$ to distinguish between the two worlds.   □

Theorem 1 can be used to prove the security of any wallet scheme that realizes the hybrid setting. To evaluate a wallet implementation, first it is identified whether it realizes the *human, client* and *hardware* protocols. Under the premise of a faithful realization of these protocols, *i.e.*, in terms of exchanged messages and internal operations, the security assumptions of its building components are evaluated. More precisely, the signature algorithm that the wallet uses must be

EUF-CMA, the hash function must act as a random oracle, and the communication channels between the parties must be secure. Typical examples of such components are the *ECDSA* [17] signature algorithm and a *SHA-2* [22] hash function. If these assumptions hold, then the wallet is secure under our model.

The Negligent User. In Sect. 3.4 we presented a well-defined protocol that the user should follow. As shown in Sect. 4, as long as the parties follow the defined protocols faithfully - and the cryptographic primitives used are strong enough - then the hardware wallet setting is secure. The integrity of the transaction issuing and the address generation operations are entirely based on the premise that the user will identify any malicious data, by comparing correctly the data shown by the client with the data shown by the hardware. However, even though this might be trivial for software, *e.g.*, for the client and the hardware wallet, people are prone to errors. Comparison of long hexadecimal strings has long been proved a challenging procedure, with many research outcomes suggesting that it is unrealistic to expect a perfect comparison of cryptographic hashes *e.g.*, [16,23,24], as humans find this process difficult and are prone to errors. In real world scenarios, the user aims at performing any operation quickly and being into a hurry often causes deviations from the expected behavior. Additionally, expecting the user to manually copy a Bitcoin address shown on the hardware's screen, defeats the usability purposes of the wallets. Thus, it is more than possible that the user will choose to simply copy the address directly from the client. However, such usability difficulties of the compare-and-confirm process open an attack vector for the payment and address generation attacks.

We model the probability of a user diverging from the human protocol π_{human} as a random variable $R_h \in [0,1]$, which equally denotes the probability of successful payment and address attacks. The distribution of R_h varies, depending both on the vigilance of the user and usability parameters. For example, a user allowing all requests to be completed without checking, *i.e.*, because the process takes too long and the data is difficult to read, would be identified by R_h close to 1. A user who carefully checks the data, *i.e.*, because there are no time restrictions or because the hardware presents it is such way that captures the user's attention, would be identified by R_h closer to 0. Another factor that may affect R_h is the length of the addresses: the longer the address, the more difficult to read and compare. However, the experimental evaluation of R_h through usability studies of Bitcoin addresses and the user's capability to compare-and-confirm them correctly is out of the scope of this work and is left as future research.

5   Product Evaluation

As of September 2018, the hardware wallets suggested by bitcoin.org are Digital Bitbox, KeepKey, Ledger, and Trezor. All, except Digital Bitbox, have an embedded screen to present information to the user, thus we focus on KeepKey, Trezor and Ledger. We manually inspected these wallets, extracted their protocols, and mapped them to our model. Our results show that the implementations bare significant similarities. Although the wallets do have different low-level implementations, the protocols that they execute are captured by the hybrid setting presented in Sect. 3.4. Instantiating our model to the actual implementations indicates the correctness of previous empirical studies, which suggest that the Ledger wallets are prone to the payment [14] and address generation [2] attacks. The wallets are subject to these attacks when the client is dishonest and are secure only if the cryptographic primitives are secure and the user does not deviate from the defined protocol, *i.e.*, successfully identifies any tampered data. Moreover, the instantiation of our model to the three implementations suggests that the wallets are prone to the chain attack, which has not been previously discussed. In this case, the attack cannot be blocked by the user, thus the wallets are secure against these attacks if and only if the underlying cryptographic mechanisms are secure *and* the client is honest.

In this section we use the model of Sect. 3.4 to evaluate these products. We identify whether such implementations are faithful to our protocols and, if not, identify the possible attacks that can be mounted against them. We expect this type of evaluation to become an industry standard for hardware wallets, so that vendors can improve the security and performance of their products by employing formal verification methods, instead of empirical techniques.

For each implementation we focus on the two core wallet operations: *address generation* and *transaction issuing*. Since all implementations are susceptible to chain attacks, we focus on the viability of payment and address attacks in each case. We show that Trezor and KeepKey are secure against payment and address attacks, as long as the user follows the protocol and verifies the data, whereas Ledger wallets are prone to address attacks, due to divergence from our model.

Trezor and KeepKey. We investigate the implementation of the Trezor Model T and KeepKey hardware wallets. Both products are implemented similarly, so we will focus Trezor, since our findings also apply to KeepKey. Trezor provides a touch screen for both displaying information and receiving input from the user. Based on the developer's guide[1], which is publicly accessible, we describe an abstraction of Trezor's behavior under our model.

During address generation, Trezor requires that the user connects the token to the client and unlocks it, *i.e.*, the user *initiates a session* similar to our model definition. The client then retrieves the address from the hardware token and displays it to the user. The hardware also displays the address, as long as the "Show on Trezor" option is enabled[2]. If this option is disabled, then the user cannot verify the client's address and is prone to an address attack, *i.e.*, the client might display a malicious address which the user cannot cross-check with the hardware wallet. However, the user manual does urge the user to always check the two addresses[3], in order to avoid such attack scenarios.

During transaction issuing, the user again connects the device to the client and unlocks it. Then she initiates a transaction by giving to the client the recip-

---

[1] Trezor developer's guide: https://wiki.trezor.io/Developers_guide.

[2] See: https://wiki.trezor.io/Developers_guide:Trezor_Connect_API_Methods.

[3] See: https://wiki.trezor.io/User_manual:Receiving_payments.

ient's address, and the payment and fee amounts, similarly to our hybrid model setting. The client initiates the transaction signing process with the hardware by providing this data, which the token then displays to the user for verification[4]. After the user has verified the transaction, the hardware communicates with the client and signs the needed data[5]. Again, given our high level investigation, this process matches the communication steps that our model describes.

Ledger. We investigate the implementation of Ledger Nano S according to the user manual[6] and our own analysis. Similarly to Trezor, before performing any operation the user is required to initiate a session by connecting the hardware to the client and unlocking it. The hardware provides a small screen for displaying information and a pair of two buttons for receiving commands from the user.

During the address generation, the client displays the newly generated address to the user. However, there is no option for the hardware wallet to also display the address[7], so that the user can cross-check and verify the two. This is a clear divergence from our model and allows for address attacks, *e.g.*, by a corrupted client that displays a malicious address to the user.

The transaction issuing process is also similar to Trezor and captured by our model: the user inputs to the client the transaction data, *i.e.*, the recipient's address, and the payment and the fee amounts. The client forwards this data to the hardware, which displays it to the user for verification. After receiving the user's confirmation, the hardware interacts with the client in order to sign and publish the transaction.

6 Conclusion

The presented work is the first effort to formally describe Bitcoin wallets. We focus on hardware wallets, as they are considered the most secure means of account management, while also being the least studied part of cryptocurrency ecosystems, and devise a model to formally prove their security specifications. We prove that their security is not one-dimensional and entirely based on secure primitives as expected; external factors such as the client to which the hardware connects and the user who operates the wallet play a major role in the overall wallet's security. Our model provides a guide for implementing and verifying existing or future wallets. Indeed, by evaluating the Keepkey, Ledger and Trezor wallets we show that security can only be guaranteed if the cryptographic primitives are secure *and* if each party executes their protocol correctly. However, since a user's deviation from the protocol is to be expected, due to human errors and usability problems of hash comparison techniques, future work will focus on evaluating this error probability and proposing techniques to reduce such risk.

---

[4] See: https://wiki.trezor.io/User_manual:Making_payments.

[5] See: https://wiki.trezor.io/Developers_guide:API_Workflows.

[6] See: https://support.ledgerwallet.com/hc/en-us/articles/360009676633.

[7] Ledger has issued firmware update to address this issue and allow both the client and the hardware to generate and display the address. However, the firmware needs to be updated manually, a process that is commonly neglected by common users.

Acknowledgements. This work was partially supported by the EPSRC grant EP/P002692/1. Research also partly supported by the H2020 project FENTEC, No. 780108.

References

1. KeepKey (2018). https://keepkey.com/. Accessed 1 Sept 2018
2. Ledger Receive Address Attack (2018). https://www.docdroid.net/Jug5LX3/ledger-receive-address-attack.pdf Accessed 19 Sept 2018
3. Trezor (2018). https://trezor.io/. Accessed 1 Sept 2018
4. Alois, J.: Ethereum parity hack may impact ETH 500.000 or 146 million (2017). https://www.crowdfundinsider.com/2017/11/124200-ethereum-parity-hack-may-impact-eth-500000-146-million/. Accessed 1 Sept 2018
5. Atzei, N., Bartoletti, M., Lande, S., Zunino, R.: A formal model of bitcoin transactions. Cryptology ePrint Archive, Report 2017/1124 (2017). https://eprint.iacr.org/2017/1124
6. Badertscher, C., Maurer, U., Tschudi, D., Zikas, V.: Bitcoin as a transaction ledger: a composable treatment. In: Katz, J., Shacham, H. (eds.) CRYPTO 2017. LNCS, vol. 10401, pp. 324–356. Springer, Cham (2017). https://doi.org/10.1007/978-3-319-63688-7_11
7. Bamert, T., Decker, C., Wattenhofer, R., Welten, S.: BlueWallet: the secure bitcoin wallet. In: Mauw, S., Jensen, C.D. (eds.) STM 2014. LNCS, vol. 8743, pp. 65–80. Springer, Cham (2014). https://doi.org/10.1007/978-3-319-11851-2_5
8. Bonneau, J., Miller, A., Clark, J., Narayanan, A., Kroll, J.A., Felten, E.W.: SoK: research perspectives and challenges for bitcoin and cryptocurrencies. In: 2015 IEEE Symposium on Security and Privacy (SP), pp. 104–121. IEEE (2015)
9. Canetti, R.: Universally composable security: a new paradigm for cryptographic protocols, pp. 136–145 (2001)
10. Canetti, R.: Universally composable signatures, certification and authentication. Cryptology ePrint Archive, Report 2003/239 (2003). http://eprint.iacr.org/2003/239
11. Canetti, R., Krawczyk, H.: Universally composable notions of key exchange and secure channels. Cryptology ePrint Archive, Report 2002/059 (2002). http://eprint.iacr.org/2002/059
12. Garay, J., Kiayias, A., Leonardos, N.: The bitcoin backbone protocol: analysis and applications. In: Oswald, E., Fischlin, M. (eds.) EUROCRYPT 2015. LNCS, vol. 9057, pp. 281–310. Springer, Heidelberg (2015). https://doi.org/10.1007/978-3-662-46803-6_10
13. Gentilal, M., Martins, P., Sousa, L.: Trustzone-backed bitcoin wallet. In: Proceedings of the Fourth Workshop on Cryptography and Security in Computing Systems, pp. 25–28. ACM (2017)
14. Gkaniatsou, A., Arapinis, M., Kiayias, A.: Low-level attacks in bitcoin wallets. In: Nguyen, P., Zhou, J. (eds.) ISC 2017. LNCS, vol. 10599. Springer, Cham (2017). https://doi.org/10.1007/978-3-319-69659-1_13
15. Heilman, E., Kendler, A., Zohar, A., Goldberg, S.: Eclipse attacks on bitcoin's peer-to-peer network. In: 24th USENIX Security Symposium (USENIX Security 15), pp. 129–144. USENIX Association, Washington, D.C. (2015). https://www.usenix.org/conference/usenixsecurity15/technical-sessions/presentation/heilman

16. Hsiao, H.C., et al.: A study of user-friendly hash comparison schemes. In: 2009 Annual Computer Security Applications Conference, ACSAC 2009, pp. 105–114. IEEE (2009)
17. Johnson, D., Menezes, A., Vanstone, S.: The elliptic curve digital signature algorithm (ECDSA). Int. J. Inf. Secur. 1(1), 36–63 (2001). https://doi.org/10.1007/s102070100002
18. Lim, I.-K., Kim, Y.-H., Lee, J.-G., Lee, J.-P., Nam-Gung, H., Lee, J.-K.: The analysis and countermeasures on security breach of bitcoin. In: Murgante, B., et al. (eds.) ICCSA 2014. LNCS, vol. 8582, pp. 720–732. Springer, Cham (2014). https://doi.org/10.1007/978-3-319-09147-1_52
19. Nakamoto, S.: Bitcoin: a peer-to-peer electronic cash system (2008)
20. Parker, L.: Bitcoin stealing malware evolves again (2016). https://bravenewcoin.com/news/bitcoin-stealing-malware-evolves-again/. Accessed 1 Sept 2018
21. Pass, R., Seeman, L., Shelat, A.: Analysis of the blockchain protocol in asynchronous networks. In: Coron, J.-S., Nielsen, J.B. (eds.) EUROCRYPT 2017. LNCS, vol. 10211, pp. 643–673. Springer, Cham (2017). https://doi.org/10.1007/978-3-319-56614-6_22
22. Penard, W., van Werkhoven, T.: On the secure hash algorithm family. In: Cryptography in Context, pp. 1–18 (2008)
23. Tan, J., Bauer, L., Bonneau, J., Cranor, L.F., Thomas, J., Ur, B.: Can unicorns help users compare crypto key fingerprints? In: Proceedings of the 2017 CHI Conference on Human Factors in Computing Systems, pp. 3787–3798. ACM (2017)
24. Uzun, E., Karvonen, K., Asokan, N.: Usability analysis of secure pairing methods. In: Dietrich, S., Dhamija, R. (eds.) FC 2007. LNCS, vol. 4886, pp. 307–324. Springer, Heidelberg (2007). https://doi.org/10.1007/978-3-540-77366-5_29
25. Vasek, M., Bonneau, J., Castellucci, R., Keith, C., Moore, T.: The bitcoin brain drain: examining the use and abuse of bitcoin brain wallets. In: Grossklags, J., Preneel, B. (eds.) FC 2016. LNCS, vol. 9603, pp. 609–618. Springer, Heidelberg (2017). https://doi.org/10.1007/978-3-662-54970-4_36
26. Volotikin, S.: Software attacks on hardware wallets. Black Hat USA 2018 (2018)
27. Wuille, P.: Hierarchical Deterministic Wallets (2018). https://en.bitcoin.it/wiki/BIP_0032. Accessed 1 Sept 2018
28. Huang, D.Y., et al.: Botcoin: monetizing stolen cycles (2014)

VeriSolid: Correct-by-Design Smart Contracts for Ethereum

Anastasia Mavridou[1], Aron Laszka[2(✉)], Emmanouela Stachtiari[3], and Abhishek Dubey[1]

[1] Vanderbilt University, Nashville, USA
[2] University of Houston, Houston, USA
alaszka@uh.edu
[3] Aristotle University of Thessaloniki, Thessaloniki, Greece

Abstract. The adoption of blockchain based distributed ledgers is growing fast due to their ability to provide reliability, integrity, and auditability without trusted entities. One of the key capabilities of these emerging platforms is the ability to create self-enforcing smart contracts. However, the development of smart contracts has proven to be error-prone in practice, and as a result, contracts deployed on public platforms are often riddled with security vulnerabilities. This issue is exacerbated by the design of these platforms, which forbids updating contract code and rolling back malicious transactions. In light of this, it is crucial to ensure that a smart contract is secure before deploying it and trusting it with significant amounts of cryptocurrency. To this end, we introduce the *VeriSolid* framework for the formal verification of contracts that are specified using a transition-system based model with rigorous operational semantics. Our model-based approach allows developers to reason about and verify contract behavior at a high level of abstraction. VeriSolid allows the generation of Solidity code from the verified models, which enables the *correct-by-design* development of smart contracts.

1 Introduction

The adoption of blockchain based platforms is rising rapidly. Their popularity is explained by their ability to maintain a *distributed public ledger*, providing reliability, integrity, and auditability *without a trusted entity*. Early blockchain platforms, e.g., Bitcoin, focused solely on creating cryptocurrencies and payment systems. However, more recent platforms, e.g., Ethereum, also act as distributed computing platforms [43,45] and enable the creation of *smart contracts*, i.e., software code that runs on the platform and automatically executes and enforces the terms of a contract [10]. Since smart contracts can perform any computation[1], they allow the development of decentralized applications, whose execution is safeguarded by the security properties of the underlying platform. Due to their

---

[1] While the virtual machine executing a contract may be Turing-complete, the amount of computation that it can perform is actually limited in practice.

I. Goldberg and T. Moore (Eds.): FC 2019, LNCS 11598, pp. 446–465, 2019.
https://doi.org/10.1007/978-3-030-32101-7_27

unique advantages, blockchain based platforms are envisioned to have a wide range of applications, ranging from financial to the Internet-of-Things [9].

However, the trustworthiness of the platform guarantees only that a smart contract is executed correctly, not that the code of the contract is correct. In fact, a large number of contracts deployed in practice suffer from software vulnerabilities, which are often introduced due to the semantic gap between the assumptions that contract writers make about the underlying execution semantics and the actual semantics of smart contracts [25]. A recent automated analysis of 19,336 contracts deployed on the public Ethereum blockchain found that 8,333 contracts suffered from at least one security issue [25]. While not all of these issues lead to security vulnerabilities, many of them enable stealing digital assets, such as cryptocurrencies. Smart-contract vulnerabilities have resulted in serious security incidents, such as the "DAO attack," in which $50 million worth of cryptocurrency was stolen [14], and the 2017 hack of the multisignature Parity Wallet library [32], which lost $280 million worth of cryptocurrency.

The risk posed by smart-contract vulnerabilities is exacerbated by the typical design of blockchain based platforms, which does not allow the code of a contract to be updated (e.g., to fix a vulnerability) or a malicious transaction to be reverted. Developers may circumvent the immutability of code by separating the "backend" code of a contract into a library contract that is referenced and used by a "frontend" contract, and updating the backend code by deploying a new instance of the library and updating the reference held by the frontend. However, the mutability of contract terms introduces security and trust issues (e.g., there might be no guarantee that a mutable contract will enforce any of its original terms). In extreme circumstances, it is also possible to revert a transaction by performing a hard fork of the blockchain. However, a hard fork requires consensus among the stakeholders of the entire platform, undermines the trustworthiness of the entire platform, and may introduce security issues (e.g., replay attacks between the original and forked chains).

In light of this, it is crucial to ensure that a smart contract is secure before deploying it and trusting it with significant amounts of cryptocurrency. Three main approaches have been considered for securing smart contracts, including secure programming practices and patterns (e.g., Checks–Effects–Interactions pattern [40]), automated vulnerability-discovery tools (e.g., OYENTE [25,42]), and formal verification of correctness (e.g., [17,21]). Following secure programming practices and using common patterns can decrease the occurrence of vulnerabilities. However, their effectiveness is limited for multiple reasons. First, they rely on a programmer following and implementing them, which is error prone due to human nature. Second, they can prevent a set of typical vulnerabilities, but they are not effective against vulnerabilities that are atypical or belong to types which have not been identified yet. Third, they cannot provide formal security and safety guarantees. Similarly, automated vulnerability-discovery tools consider generic properties that usually do not capture contract-specific requirements and thus, are effective in detecting typical errors but ineffective in detecting atypical vulnerabilities. These tools typically require security properties and patterns to be specified at a low level (usually bytecode) by security experts. Additionally, automated vulnerability-discovery tools are not precise; they often produce false positives.

On the contrary, formal verification tools are based on formal operational semantics and provide strong verification guarantees. They enable the formal specification and verification of properties and can detect both typical and atypical vulnerabilities that could lead to the violation of some security property. However, these tools are harder to automate.

Our approach falls in the category of formal verification tools, but it also provides an end-to-end design framework, which combined with a code generator, allows the *correctness-by-design* development of Ethereum smart contracts. We focus on providing usable tools for helping developers to eliminate errors early at design time by raising the abstraction level and employing graphical representations. Our approach does not produce false positives for safety properties and deadlock-freedom.

In principle, a contract vulnerability is a programming error that enables an attacker to use a contract in a way that was not intended by the developer. To detect vulnerabilities that do not fall into common types, developers must specify the intended behavior of a contract. Our framework enables developers to specify intended behavior in the form of liveness, deadlock-freedom, and safety properties, which capture important security concerns and vulnerabilities. One of the key advantages of our model-based verification approach is that it allows developers to specify desired properties with respect to high-level models instead of, e.g., bytecode. Our tool can then automatically verify whether the behavior of the contract satisfies these properties. If a contract does not satisfy some of these properties, our tool notifies the developers, explaining the execution sequence that leads to the property violation. The sequence can help the developer to identify and correct the design errors that lead to the erroneous behavior. Since the verification output provides guarantees to the developer regarding the actual execution semantics of the contract, it helps eliminating the semantic gap. Additionally, our verification and code generation approach fits smart contracts well because contract code cannot be updated after deployment. Thus, code generation needs to be performed only once before deployment.

Contributions. We build on the *FSolidM* [27, 28] framework, which provides a graphical editor for specifying Ethereum smart contracts as transitions systems and a *Solidity* code generator.[2] We present the *VeriSolid* framework, which introduces *formal verification capabilities*, thereby providing an approach for correct-by-design development of smart contracts. Our contributions are:

- We extend the syntax of FSolidM models (Definition 1), provide formal operational semantics (FSolidM has no formal operational semantics) for our model (Sect. 3.3) and for supported Solidity statements ([29, Appendix A.3]), and extend the Solidity code generator ([29, Appendix E]).

---

[2] Solidity is the high-level language for developing Ethereum contracts. Solidity code can be compiled into bytecode, which can be executed on the Ethereum platform.

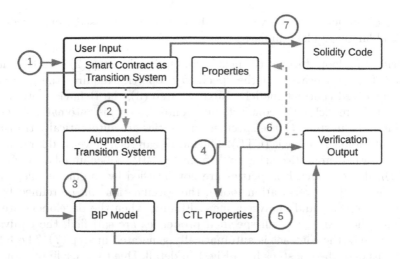

Fig. 1. Design and verification workflow.

- We design and implement developer-friendly natural-language like templates for specifying safety and liveness properties (Sect. 3.4).
- The developer input of VeriSolid is a transition system, in which each transition action is specified using Solidity code. We provide an automatic transformation from the initial system into an augmented transition system, which extends the initial system with the control flow of the Solidity action of each transition (Sect. 4). We prove that the initial and augmented transition systems are observationally equivalent (Sect. 4.1); thus, the verified properties of the augmented model are also guaranteed in the initial model.
- We use an overapproximation approach for the meaningful and efficient verification of smart-contract models (Sect. 5). We integrate verification tools (i.e., nuXmv and BIP) and present verification results.

2   VeriSolid: Design and Verification WorkFlow

VeriSolid is an open-source[3] and web-based framework that is built on top of WebGME [26] and FSolidM [27,28]. VeriSolid allows the collaborative development of Ethereum contracts with built-in version control, which enables branching, merging, and history viewing. Figure 1 shows the steps of the VeriSolid design flow. Mandatory steps are represented by solid arrows, while optional steps are represented by dashed arrows. In step ①, the developer input is given, which consists of:

- A contract specification containing (1) a graphically specified transition system and (2) variable declarations, actions, and guards specified in Solidity.

---

[3] https://github.com/anmavrid/smart-contracts.

– A list of properties to be verified, which can be expressed using predefined natural-language like templates.

The verification loop starts at the next step. Optionally, step ② is automatically executed if the verification of the specified properties requires the generation of an augmented contract model[4]. Next, in step ③, the Behavior-Interaction-Priority (BIP) model of the contract (augmented or not) is automatically generated. Similarly, in step ④, the specified properties are automatically translated to Computational Tree Logic (CTL). The model can then be verified for deadlock freedom or other properties using tools from the BIP tool-chain [5] or nuXmv [7] (step ⑤). If the required properties are not satisfied by the model (depending on the output of the verification tools), the specification can be refined by the developer (step ⑥) and analyzed anew. Finally, when the developers are satisfied with the design, i.e., all specified properties are satisfied, the equivalent Solidity code of the contract is automatically generated in step ⑦. The following sections describe the steps from Fig. 1 in detail. Due to space limitations, we present the Solidity code generation (step ⑦) in [29, Appendix E].

3   Developer Input: Transition Systems and Properties

3.1   Smart Contracts as Transition Systems

To illustrate how to represent smart contracts as transition systems, we use the *Blind Auction* example from prior work [27], which is based on an example from the Solidity documentation [38].

In a blind auction, each bidder first makes a deposit and submits a blinded bid, which is a hash of its actual bid, and then reveals its actual bid after all bidders have committed to their bids. After revealing, each bid is considered valid if it is higher than the accompanying deposit, and the bidder with the highest valid bid is declared winner. A blind auction contract has four main states:

1. `AcceptingBlindedBids`: bidders submit blinded bids and make deposits;
2. `RevealingBids`: bidders reveal their actual bids by submitting them to the contract, and the contract checks for each bid that its hash is equal to the blinded bid and that it is less than or equal to the deposit made earlier;
3. `Finished`: winning bidder (i.e., the bidder with the highest valid bid) withdraws the difference between her deposit and her bid; other bidders withdraw their entire deposits;
4. `Canceled`: all bidders withdraw their deposits (without declaring a winner).

This example illustrates that smart contracts have *states* (e.g., `Finished`). Further, contracts provide functions, which allow other entities (e.g., users or contracts) to invoke *actions* and change the states of the contracts. Hence, we can represent a smart contract naturally as a *transition system* [39], which comprises

---

[4] We give the definition of an augmented smart contract in Sect. 4.

a set of states and a set of transitions between those states. Invoking a transition forces the contract to execute the action of the transition if the *guard* condition of the transition is satisfied. Since such states and transitions have intuitive meanings for developers, representing contracts as transition systems provides an adequate level of abstraction for reasoning about their behavior.

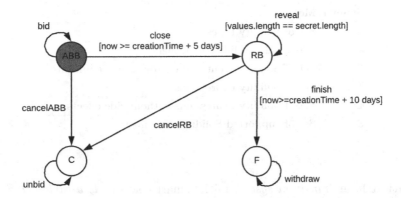

Fig. 2. Blind auction example as a transition system.

Figure 2 shows the blind auction example in the form of a transition system. For ease of presentation, we abbreviate `AcceptingBlindedBids`, `RevealingBids`, `Finished`, and `Canceled` to ABB, RB, F, and C, respectively. The initial state of the transition system is ABB. To differentiate between transition names and guards, we use square brackets for the latter. Each transition (e.g., `close`, `withdraw`) corresponds to an action that a user may perform during the auction. For example, a bidding user may execute transition `reveal` in state RB to reveal its blinded bid. As another example, a user may execute transition `finish` in state RB, which ends the revealing phase and declares the winner, if the guard condition `now >= creationTime + 10 days` is true. A user can submit a blinded bid using transition `bid`, close the bidding phase using transition `close`, and withdraw her deposit (minus her bid if she won) using transitions `unbid` and `withdraw`. Finally, the user who created the auction may cancel it using transitions `cancelABB` and `cancelRB`. For clarity of presentation, we omitted from Fig. 2 the specific actions that the transitions take (e.g., transition `bid` executes—among others—the following statement: `pendingReturns[msg.sender] += msg.value;`).

3.2   Formal Definition of a Smart Contract

We formally define a contract as a transition system. To do that, we consider a subset of Solidity statements, which are described in detail in [29, Appendix A.1]. We chose this subset of Solidity statements because it includes all the essential control structures: loops, selection, and **return** statements. Thus, it is a Turing-complete subset, and can be extended in a straightforward manner to capture all other Solidity statements. Our Solidity code notation is summarized in Table 1.

Table 1. Summary of notation for Solidity code

Symbol	Meaning
$\mathbb{T}$	Set of Solidity types
$\mathbb{I}$	Set of valid Solidity identifiers
$\mathbb{D}$	Set of Solidity event and custom-type definitions
$\mathbb{E}$	Set of Solidity expressions
$\mathbb{C}$	Set of Solidity expressions without side effects
$\mathbb{S}$	Set of supported Solidity statements

Definition 1. *A* transition-system *initial smart contract is a tuple* $(D, S, S_F, s_0, a_0, a_F, V, T)$, *where*

- $D \subset \mathbb{D}$ *is a set of custom event and type definitions;*
- $S \subset \mathbb{I}$ *is a finite set of states;*
- $S_F \subset S$ *is a set of final states;*
- $s_0 \in S$, $a_0 \in \mathbb{S}$ *are the initial state and action;*
- $a_F \in \mathbb{S}$ *is the fallback action;*
- $V \subset \mathbb{I} \times \mathbb{T}$ *contract variables (i.e., variable names and types);*
- $T \subset \mathbb{I} \times S \times 2^{\mathbb{I} \times \mathbb{T}} \times \mathbb{C} \times (\mathbb{T} \cup \emptyset) \times \mathbb{S} \times S$ *is a transition relation, where each transition* $\in T$ *includes: transition name* $t^{name} \in \mathbb{I}$; *source state* $t^{from} \in S$; *parameter variables (i.e., arguments)* $t^{input} \subseteq \mathbb{I} \times \mathbb{T}$; *transition guard* $g_t \in \mathbb{C}$; *return type* $t^{output} \in (\mathbb{T} \cup \emptyset)$; *action* $a_t \in \mathbb{S}$; *destination state* $t^{to} \in S$.

The initial action a_0 represents the constructor of the smart contract. A contract can have *at most one constructor*. In the case that the initial action a_0 is empty (i.e., there is no constructor), a_0 may be omitted from the transition system. A constructor is graphically represented in VeriSolid as an incoming arrow to the initial state. The fallback action a_F represents the fallback function of the contract. Similar to the constructor, a contract can have *at most one fallback* function. Solidity fallback functions are further discussed in [29, Appendix C.1].

Lack of the Re-entrancy Vulnerability. VeriSolid allows specifying contracts such that the re-entrancy vulnerability is prevented by design. In particular, after a transition begins but before the execution of the transition action, the contract changes its state to a temporary one (see [29, Appendix E]). This prevents re-entrancy since none of the contract functions[5] can be called in this state.

---

[5] Our framework implements transitions as functions, see [29, Appendix E].

One might question this design decision since re-entrancy is not always harmful. However, we consider that it can pose significant challenges for providing security. First, supporting re-entrancy substantially increases the complexity of verification. Our framework allows the efficient verification—within seconds—of a broad range of properties, which is essential for iterative development. Second, re-entrancy often leads to vulnerabilities since it significantly complicates contract behavior. We believe that prohibiting re-entrancy is a small price to pay for security.

3.3 Smart-Contract Operational Semantics

We define the operational semantics of our transition-system based smart contracts in the form of Structural Operational Semantics (SOS) rules [37]. We let Ψ denote the state of the ledger, which includes account balances, values of state variables in all contracts, number and timestamp of the last block, etc. During the execution of a transition, the execution state $\sigma = \{\Psi, M\}$ also includes the memory and stack state M. To handle return statements and exceptions, we also introduce an execution status, which is E when an exception has been raised, $R[v]$ when a return statement has been executed with value v (i.e., return v), and N otherwise. Finally, we let $\mathrm{Eval}(\sigma, \mathrm{Exp}) \rightarrow \langle(\hat{\sigma}, x), v\rangle$ signify that the evaluation of a Solidity expression Exp in execution state σ yields value v and—as a side effect—changes the execution state to $\hat{\sigma}$ and the execution status to x.[6]

A transition is triggered by providing a transition (i.e., function) $name \in \mathbb{I}$ and a list of parameter values $v_1, v_2, \ldots$. The normal execution of a transition without returning any value, which takes the ledger from state Ψ to Ψ' and the contract from state $s \in S$ to $s' \in S$, is captured by the TRANSITION rule:

$$\text{TRANSITION} \quad \frac{\begin{array}{c} t \in T, name = t^{name}, s = t^{from} \\ M = Params(t, v_1, v_2, \ldots), \sigma = (\Psi, M) \\ \mathrm{Eval}(\sigma, g_t) \rightarrow \langle(\hat{\sigma}, N), \mathbf{true}\rangle \\ \langle(\hat{\sigma}, N), a_t\rangle \rightarrow \langle(\hat{\sigma}', N), \cdot\rangle \\ \hat{\sigma}' = (\Psi', M'), s' = t^{to} \end{array}}{\langle(\Psi, s), name\,(v_1, v_2, \ldots)\rangle \rightarrow \langle(\Psi', s', \cdot)\rangle}$$

This rule is applied if there exists a transition t whose name t^{name} is $name$ and whose source state t^{from} is the current contract state s (first line). The execution state σ is initialized by taking the parameter values $Params(t, v_1, v_2, \ldots)$ and the current ledger state Ψ (second line). If the guard condition g_t evaluates $\mathrm{Eval}(\sigma, g_t)$ in the current state σ to $\mathbf{true}$ (third line), then the action statement a_t of the transition is executed (fourth line), which results in an updated execution state $\hat{\sigma}'$ (see statement rules in [29, Appendix A.3]). Finally, if the resulting execution status is normal N (i.e., no exception was thrown), then the updated ledger state Ψ' and updated contract state s' (fifth line) are made permanent.

We also define SOS rules for all cases of erroneous transition execution (e.g., exception is raised during guard evaluation, transition is reverted, etc.)

---

[6] Note that the correctness of our transformations does not depend on the exact semantics of Eval.

and for returning values. Due to space limitations, we include these rules in [29, Appendix A.2]. We also define SOS rules for supported statements in [29, Appendix A.3].

3.4 Safety, Liveness, and Deadlock Freedom

A VeriSolid model is automatically verified for deadlock freedom. A developer may additionally verify safety and liveness properties. To facilitate the specification of properties, VeriSolid offers a set of predefined natural-language like templates, which correspond to properties in CTL. Alternatively, properties can be specified directly in CTL. Let us go through some of these predefined templates. Due to space limitations, the full template list, as well as the CTL property correspondence is provided in [29, Appendix B].

```
uint amount = pendingReturns[msg.sender];
if (amount > 0) {
  if (msg.sender!= highestBidder)
    msg.sender.transfer(amount);
  else
    msg.sender.transfer(amount - highestBid);
  pendingReturns[msg.sender] = 0;
}
```

Fig. 3. Action of transition `withdraw` in Blind Auction, specified using Solidity.

$\langle$ *Transitions* $\cup$ *Statements* $\rangle$ cannot   happen   after
$\langle$ *Transitions* $\cup$ *Statements* $\rangle$.

The above template expresses a safety property type. **Transitions** is a subset of the transitions of the model (i.e., **Transitions** $\subseteq T$). A statement from **Statements** is a specific inner statement from the action of a specific transition (i.e., **Statements** $\subseteq T \times \mathbb{S}$). For instance, we can specify the following safety properties for the Blind Auction example:

– **bid** cannot happen after **close**.
– **cancelABB; cancelRB** cannot happen after **finish**,

where **cancelABB; cancelRB** means **cancelABB** $\cup$ **cancelRB**.

If $\langle$ *Transitions* $\cup$ *Statements* $\rangle$ happens, $\langle$ *Transitions* $\cup$ *Statements* $\rangle$ can happen only after $\langle$ *Transitions* $\cup$ *Statements* $\rangle$ happens.

The above template expresses a safety property type. A typical vulnerability is that currency withdrawal functions, e.g., `transfer`, allow an attacker to withdraw currency again before updating her balance (similar to "The DAO" attack). To check this vulnerability type for the Blind Auction example, we can specify the following property. The statements in the action of transition `withdraw` are shown in Fig. 3.

- if `withdraw.msg.sender.transfer(amount);` happens,
  `withdraw.msg.sender.transfer(amount);` can happen only after
  `withdraw.pendingReturns[msg.sender]=0;` happens.

As shown in the example above, a statement is written in the following form:
Transition.Statement to refer to a statement of a specific transition. If there
are multiple identical statements in the same transition, then all of them are
checked for the same property. To verify properties with statements, we need to
transform the input model into an augmented model, as presented in Sect. 4.

⟨***Transitions*** ∪ ***Statements***⟩   will   eventually   happen   after
⟨***Transitions*** ∪ ***Statements***⟩.

Finally, the above template expresses a liveness property type. For instance,
with this template we can write the following liveness property for the Blind Auction example to check the Denial-of-Service vulnerability ([29, Appendix C.2]):

- `withdraw.pendingReturns[msg.sender]=0;` will eventually happen after
  `withdraw.msg.sender.transfer(amount);`.

4   Augmented Transition System Transformation

To verify a model with Solidity actions, we transform it to a functionally equivalent model that can be input into our verification tools. We perform two transformations: First, we replace the initial action a_0 and the fallback action a_F
with transitions. Second, we replace transitions that have complex statements
as actions with a series of transitions that have only simple statements (i.e., variable declaration and expression statements). After these two transformations, the
entire behavior of the contract is captured using only transitions. The transformation algorithms are discussed in detail in [29, Appendices D.1 and D.2]. The
input of the transformation is a smart contract defined as a transition system (see
Definition 1). The output of the transformation is an *augmented smart contract*:

Definition 2. *An* augmented contract *is a tuple* (D, S, S_F, s_0, V, T), *where*

- $D \subset \mathbb{D}$ *is a set of custom event and type definitions;*
- $S \subset \mathbb{I}$ *is a finite set of states;*
- $S_F \subset S$ *is a set of final states;*
- $s_0 \in S$, *is the initial state;*
- $V \subset \mathbb{I} \times \mathbb{T}$ *contract variables (i.e., variable names and types);*
- $T \subset \mathbb{I} \times S \times 2^{\mathbb{I} \times \mathbb{T}} \times \mathbb{C} \times (\mathbb{T} \cup \emptyset) \times \mathbb{S} \times S$ *is a transition relation (i.e., transi-*
  tion name, source state, parameter variables, guard, return type, action, and
  destination state).

Figure 4 shows the augmented `withdraw` transition of the Blind Auction
model. We present the complete augmented model in [29, Appendix F]. The
action of the original `withdraw` transition is shown by Fig. 3. Notice the added
state `withdraw`, which avoids re-entrancy by design, as explained in Sect. 3.2.

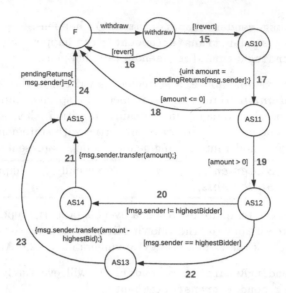

Fig. 4. Augmented model of transition `withdraw`.

4.1 Observational Equivalence

We study sufficient conditions for augmented models to be behaviorally equivalent to initial models. To do that, we use observational equivalence [30] by considering non-observable β−transitions. We denote by S_I and S_E the set of states of the smart contract transition system and its augmented derivative, respectively. We show that $R = \{(q, r) \in S_I \times S_E\}$ is a weak bi-simulation by considering as observable transitions A, those that affect the ledger state, while the remaining transitions B are considered non-observable transitions. According to this definition, the set of transitions in the smart contract system, which represent the execution semantics of a Solidity named function or the fallback, are all observable. On the other hand, the augmented system represents each Solidity function using paths of multiple transitions. We assume that final transition of each such path is an α transition, while the rest are β transitions. Our weak bi-simulation is based on the fact the effect of each $\alpha \in A$ on the ledger state is equal for the states of S_I and S_E. Therefore, if $\sigma_I = \sigma_E$ at the initial state of α, then $\sigma'_I = \sigma'_E$ at the resulting state.

A weak simulation over I and E is a relation $R \subseteq S_I \times S_E$ such that we have:

Property 1. For all $(q, r) \in R$ and for each $\alpha \in A$, such that $q \xrightarrow{\alpha} q'$, there is r' such that $r \xrightarrow{\beta^* \alpha \beta^*} r'$ where $(q', r') \in R$

For each observable transition α of a state in S_I, it should be proved that (i) a path that consists of α and other non-observable transitions exists in all its equivalent states in S_E, and (ii) the resulting states are equivalent.

Property 2. For all $(q, r) \in R$ and $\alpha \in A$, such that $r \xrightarrow{\alpha} r'$, there is q' such that $q \xrightarrow{\alpha} q'$ where $(q', r') \in R$.

For each observable outgoing transition in a state in S_E, it should be proved that (i) there is an outgoing observable transition in all its equivalent states in S_I, and (ii) the resulting states are equivalent.

Property 3. For all $(q, r) \in R$ and $\beta \in B$ such that $r \xrightarrow{\beta} r'$, $(q, r') \in R$

For each non observable transition, it should be proved that the the resulting state is equivalent with all the states that are equivalent with the initial state.

Theorem 1. *For each initial smart contract I and its corresponding augmented smart contract E, it holds that $I \sim E$.*

The proof of Theorem 1 is presented in the [29, Appendix D.3].

5   Verification Process

Our verification approach checks whether contract behavior satisfies properties that are required by the developer. To check this, we must take into account the effect of data and time. However, smart contracts use environmental input as control data, e.g., in guards. Such input data can be infinite, leading to infinitely many possible contract states. Exploring every such state is highly inefficient [11] and hence, appropriate data and time abstractions must be employed.

We apply data abstraction to ignore variables that depend on (e.g., are updated by) environmental input. Thus, an overapproximation of the contract behavior is caused by the fact that transition guards with such variables are not evaluated; instead, both their values are assumed possible and state space exploration includes execution traces with and without each guarded transition. In essence, we analyze a more abstract model of the contract, with a set of reachable states and traces that is a superset of the set of states (respectively, traces) of the actual contract. As an example, let us consider the function in Fig. 5.

```
void fn(int x) {
    if (x < 0) {
        ...        (1)
    }
    if (x > 0) {
        ...       (2)
    }
}
```

Fig. 5. Code example.

An overapproximation of the function's execution includes traces where both lines (1) and (2) are visited, even though they cannot both be satisfied by the same values of x. Note that abstraction is not necessary for variables that are independent of environment input (e.g. iteration counters of known range). These are updated in the model as they are calculated by contract statements.

We also apply abstraction to time variables (e.g. the now variable in the Blind Auction) using a slightly different approach. Although we need to know which transitions get invalidated as time increases, we do not represent the time spent in each state, as this time can be arbitrarily high. Therefore, for a time-guarded transition in the model, say from a state s_x, one of the following applies:

- if the guard is of type $t \leq t_{max}$, checking that a time variable does not exceed a threshold, a loop transition is added to s_x, with an action $t = t_{max} + 1$ that invalidates the guard. A deadlock may be found in traces where this invalidating loop is executed (e.g., if no other transitions are offered in s_x).
- if the guard is of type $t > t_{min}$, checking that a time variable exceeds a threshold, an action $t=t_{min}+1$ is added to the guarded transition. This sets the time to the earliest point that next state can be reached (e.g., useful for checking bounded liveness properties.)

This overapproximation has the following implications.

Safety Properties: *Safety properties that are fulfilled in the abstract model are also guaranteed in the actual system.* Each safety property checks the non-reachability of a set of erroneous states. If these states are unreachable in the abstract model, they will be unreachable in the concrete model, which contains a subset of the abstract model's states. This property type is useful for checking vulnerabilities in currency withdrawal functions (e.g., the "DAO attack").

Liveness Properties: *Liveness properties that are violated in the abstract model are also violated in the actual system.* Each liveness property checks that a set of states are reachable. If they are found unreachable (i.e., liveness violation) in the abstract model, they will also be unreachable in the concrete model. This property type is useful for "Denial-of-Service" vulnerabilities ([29, Appendix C.2]).

Deadlock Freedom: States without enabled outgoing transitions are identified as deadlock states. If no deadlock states are reachable in the abstract model, they will not be reachable in the actual system.

5.1   VeriSolid-to-BIP Mapping

Since both VeriSolid and BIP model contract behavior as transition systems, the transformation is a simple mapping between the transitions, states, guards, and actions of VeriSolid to the transitions, states, guards, and actions of BIP (see [29, Appendix C.3] for background on BIP). Because this is an one-to-one mapping, we do not provide a proof. Our translation algorithm performs a single-pass syntax-directed parsing of the user's VeriSolid input and collects values that are appended to the attributes list of the templates. Specifically, the following values are collected:

- variables $v \in V$, where $type(v)$ is the data type of v and $name(v)$ is the variable name (i.e., identifier);
- states $s \in S$;

– transitions $t \in T$, where t^{name} is the transition (and corresponding port) name, t^{from} and t^{to} are the outgoing and incoming states, a_t and g_t are invocations to functions that implement the associated actions and guards.

Figure 6 shows the BIP code template. We use fixed-width font for the generated output, and *italic* font for elements that are replaced with input.

$$
\begin{aligned}
&\texttt{atom type Contract()} \\
\forall v \in V: \quad &\texttt{data } type(v) \ name(v) \\
\forall t \in T: \quad &\texttt{export port synPort } t^{name}() \\
&\texttt{places } s_0, \ldots, s_{|S|-1} \\
&\texttt{initial to } s_0 \\
\forall t \in T: \quad &\texttt{on } t^{name} \texttt{ from } t^{from} \texttt{ to } t^{to} \\
&\texttt{provided } (g_t) \texttt{ do } \{a_t\} \\
&\texttt{end}
\end{aligned}
$$

Fig. 6. BIP code generation template.

Table 2. Analyzed properties and verification results for the case study models.

Case Study	Properties	Type	Result
BlindAuction (initial) states: 54	(i) **bid** cannot happen after **close**: $\texttt{AG}(close \rightarrow \texttt{AG}\neg bid)$	Safety	Verified
	(ii) **cancelABB** or **cancelRB** cannot happen after **finish**: $\texttt{AG}(finish \rightarrow \texttt{AG}\neg(cancelRB \lor cancelABB))$	Safety	Verified
	(iii) **withdraw** can happen only after **finish**: $\texttt{A}[\neg withdraw \text{ W } finish]$	Safety	Verified
	(iv) **finish** can happen only after **close**: $\texttt{A}[\neg finish \text{ W } close]$	Safety	Verified
BlindAuction (augmented) states: 161	(v) **23** cannot happen after **18**: $\texttt{AG}(18 \rightarrow \texttt{AG}\neg 23)$	Safety	Verified
	(vi) if **21** happens, **21** can happen only after **24**: $\texttt{AG}(21 \rightarrow \texttt{AX A}[\neg 21 \text{ W }(24)])$	Safety	Verified
DAO attack states: 9	if **call** happens, **call** can happen only after **subtract**: $\texttt{AG}(call \rightarrow \texttt{AX A}[\neg call \text{ W } subtract])$	Safety	Verified
King of Ether 1 states: 10	**7** will eventually happen after **4**: $\texttt{AG}(4 \rightarrow \texttt{AF } 7)$	Liveness	Violated
King of Ether 2 states: 10	**8** will eventually happen after **fallback**: $\texttt{AG}(fallback \rightarrow \texttt{AF } 8)$	Liveness	Violated

5.2   Verification Results

Table 2 summarizes the properties and verification results. For ease of presentation, when properties include statements, we replace statements with the augmented-transition numbers that we have added to [29, Figures 9, 10, and 12]. The number of states represents the reachable state space as evaluated by nuXmv.

Blind Auction. We analyzed both the initial and augmented models of the Blind Auction contract. On the initial model, we checked four safety properties (see Properties (i)–(iv) in Table 2). On the augmented model, which allows for more fine-grained analysis, we checked two additional safety properties. All properties were verified to hold. The models were found to be deadlock-free and their state space was evaluated to 54 and 161 states, respectively. The augmented model and generated code can be found in [29, Appendix F].

The DAO Attack. We modeled a simplified version of the DAO contract. Atzei et al. [2] discuss two different vulnerabilities exploited on DAO and present different attack scenarios. Our verified safety property (Table 2) excludes the possibility of both attacks. The augmented model can be found in [29, Appendix G.1].

King of the Ether Throne. For checking Denial-of-Service vulnerabilities, we created models of two versions of the King of the Ether contract [2], which are provided in [29, Appendix G.2]. On "King of Ether 1," we checked a liveness property stating that crowning (transition 7) will happen at some time after the compensation calculation (transition 4). The property is violated by the following counterexample: *fallback* → *4* → *5*. A second liveness property, which states that the crowning will happen at some time after fallback fails in "King of Ether 2." A counterexample of the property violation is the following: *fallback* → *4*. Note that usually many counterexamples may exist for the same violation.

Resource Allocation. We have additionally verified a larger smart contract that acts as the core of a blockchain-based platform for transactive energy systems. The reachable state space, as evaluated by nuXmv, is 3, 487. Properties were verified or shown to be violated within seconds. Due to space limitations, we present the verification results in [29, Appendix G.3].

6   Related Work

Here, we present a brief overview of related work. We provide a more detailed discussion in [29, Appendix H].

Motivated by the large number of smart-contract vulnerabilities in practice, researchers have investigated and established taxonomies for common types of contract vulnerabilities [2,25]. To find vulnerabilities in existing contracts, both verification and vulnerability discovery are considered in the literature [36]. In comparison, the main advantage of our model-based approach is that it allows developers to specify desired properties with respect to a high-level model instead of, e.g., EVM bytecode, and also provides verification results and counterexamples in a developer-friendly, easy to understand, high-level form. Further, our approach allows verifying whether a contract satisfies all desired security properties instead of detecting certain types of vulnerabilities; hence, it can detect atypical vulnerabilities.

Hirai performs a formal verification of a smart contract used by the Ethereum Name Service [20] and defines the complete instruction set of the Ethereum Virtual Machine (EVM) in Lem, a language that can be compiled for interactive theorem provers, which enables proving certain safety properties for existing contracts [21]. Bhargavan et al. outline a framework for verifying the safety and correctness of Ethereum contracts based on translating Solidity and EVM bytecode contracts into F^* [6]. Tsankov et al. introduce a security analyzer for Ethereum contracts, called SECURIFY, which symbolically encodes the dependence graph of a contract in stratified Datalog [23] and then uses off-the-shelf solvers to check the satisfaction of properties [42]. Atzei et al. prove the well-formedness properties of the Bitcoin blockchain have also been proven using a formal model [3]. Techniques from runtime verification are used to detect and recover from violations at runtime [12,13].

Luu et al. provide a tool called OYENTE, which can analyze contracts and detect certain typical security vulnerabilities [25]. Building on OYENTE, Albert et al. introduce the ETHIR framework, which can produce a rule-based representation of bytecode, enabling the application of existing analysis to infer properties of the EVM code [1]. Nikolic et al. present the MAIAN tool for detecting three types of vulnerable contracts, called prodigal, suicidal and greedy [33]. Fröwis and Böhme define a heuristic indicator of control flow immutability to quantify the prevalence of contractual loopholes based on modifying the control flow of Ethereum contracts [16]. Brent et al. introduce a security analysis framework for Ethereum contracts, called VANDAL, which converts EVM bytecode to semantic relations, which are then analyzed to detect vulnerabilities described in the Soufflé language [8]. Mueller presents MYTHRIL, a security analysis tool for Ethereum smart contracts with a symbolic execution backend [31]. Stortz introduces RATTLE, a static analysis framework for EVM bytecode [41].

Researchers also focus on providing formal operational semantics for EVM bytecode and Solidity language [17–19,24,46]. Common design patterns in Ethereum smart contracts are also identified and studied by multiple research efforts [4,44]. Finally, to facilitate development, researchers have also introduced a functional smart-contract language [35], an approach for semi-automated translation of human-readable contract representations into computational equivalents [15], a logic-based smart-contract model [22].

7 Conclusion

We presented an end-to-end framework that allows the generation of correct-by-design contracts by performing a set of equivalent transformations. First, we generate an augmented transition system from an initial transition system, based on the operational semantics of supported Solidity statements ([29, Appendix A.3]). We have proven that the two transition systems are observationally equivalent (Sect. 4.1). Second, we generate the BIP transition system from the augmented transition system through a direct one-to-one mapping. Third, we generate the NuSMV transition system from the BIP system (shown to be observationally equivalent in [34]). Finally, we generate functionally equivalent Solidity code, based on the operational semantics of the transition system ([29, Appendix A.2]).

To the best of our knowledge, VeriSolid is the first framework to promote a model-based, correctness-by-design approach for blockchain-based smart contracts. Properties established at any step of the VeriSolid design flow are preserved in the resulting smart contracts, guaranteeing their correctness. VeriSolid fully automates the process of verification and code generation, while enhancing usability by providing easy-to-use graphical editors for the specification of transition systems and natural-like language templates for the specification of formal properties. By performing verification early at design time, we provide a cost-effective approach; fixing bugs later in the development process can be very expensive. Our verification approach can detect typical vulnerabilities, but it may also detect any violation of required properties. Since our tool applies verification at a high-level, it can provide meaningful feedback to the developer when a property is not satisfied, which would be much harder to do at bytecode level. Future work includes extending the approach to model and generate correct-by-design *systems of interacting smart contracts*.

References

1. Albert, E., Gordillo, P., Livshits, B., Rubio, A., Sergey, I.: ETHIR: a framework for high-level analysis of Ethereum bytecode. In: Lahiri, S.K., Wang, C. (eds.) ATVA 2018. LNCS, vol. 11138, pp. 513–520. Springer, Cham (2018). https://doi.org/10.1007/978-3-030-01090-4_30

2. Atzei, N., Bartoletti, M., Cimoli, T.: A survey of attacks on Ethereum smart contracts (SoK). In: Maffei, M., Ryan, M. (eds.) POST 2017. LNCS, vol. 10204, pp. 164–186. Springer, Heidelberg (2017). https://doi.org/10.1007/978-3-662-54455-6_8

3. Atzei, N., Bartoletti, M., Lande, S., Zunino, R.: A formal model of Bitcoin transactions. In: Meiklejohn, S., Sako, K. (eds.) FC 2018. LNCS, vol. 10957. Springer, Berlin (2018). https://doi.org/10.1007/978-3-662-58387-6_29

4. Bartoletti, M., Pompianu, L.: An empirical analysis of smart contracts: platforms, applications, and design patterns. In: Brenner, M., et al. (eds.) FC 2017. LNCS, vol. 10323, pp. 494–509. Springer, Cham (2017). https://doi.org/10.1007/978-3-319-70278-0_31

5. Basu, A., et al.: Rigorous component-based system design using the BIP framework. IEEE Softw. **28**(3), 41–48 (2011)

6. Bhargavan, K., et al.: Short paper: formal verification of smart contracts. In: Proceedings of the 11th ACM Workshop on Programming Languages and Analysis for Security (PLAS), in Conjunction with ACM CCS 2016, pp. 91–96, October 2016

7. Bliudze, S., et al.: Formal verification of infinite-state BIP models. In: Finkbeiner, B., Pu, G., Zhang, L. (eds.) ATVA 2015. LNCS, vol. 9364, pp. 326–343. Springer, Cham (2015). https://doi.org/10.1007/978-3-319-24953-7_25

8. Brent, L., et al.: Vandal: a scalable security analysis framework for smart contracts. arXiv preprint arXiv:1809.03981 (2018)

9. Christidis, K., Devetsikiotis, M.: Blockchains and smart contracts for the Internet of Things. IEEE Access 4, 2292–2303 (2016)

10. Clack, C.D., Bakshi, V.A., Braine, L.: Smart contract templates: foundations, design landscape and research directions. arXiv preprint arXiv:1608.00771 (2016)

11. Clarke, E.M., Grumberg, O., Long, D.E.: Model checking and abstraction. ACM Trans. Program. Lang. Syst. 16(5), 1512–1542 (1994)

12. Colombo, C., Ellul, J., Pace, G.J.: Contracts over smart contracts: recovering from violations dynamically. In: Margaria, T., Steffen, B. (eds.) ISoLA 2018. LNCS, vol. 11247, pp. 300–315. Springer, Cham (2018). https://doi.org/10.1007/978-3-030-03427-6_23

13. Ellul, J., Pace, G.: Runtime verification of Ethereum smart contracts. In: Workshop on Blockchain Dependability (WBD), in Conjunction with 14th European Dependable Computing Conference (EDCC) (2018)

14. Finley, K.: A $50 million hack just showed that the DAO was all too human. Wired. https://www.wired.com/2016/06/50-million-hack-just-showed-dao-human/ (2016)

15. Frantz, C.K., Nowostawski, M.: From institutions to code: towards automated generation of smart contracts. In: 1st IEEE International Workshops on Foundations and Applications of Self* Systems (FAS*W), pp. 210–215. IEEE (2016)

16. Fröwis, M., Böhme, R.: In code we trust? In: Garcia-Alfaro, J., Navarro-Arribas, G., Hartenstein, H., Herrera-Joancomartí, J. (eds.) ESORICS/DPM/CBT -2017. LNCS, vol. 10436, pp. 357–372. Springer, Cham (2017). https://doi.org/10.1007/978-3-319-67816-0_20

17. Grishchenko, I., Maffei, M., Schneidewind, C.: A semantic framework for the security analysis of Ethereum smart contracts. In: Bauer, L., Küsters, R. (eds.) POST 2018. LNCS, vol. 10804, pp. 243–269. Springer, Cham (2018). https://doi.org/10.1007/978-3-319-89722-6_10

18. Grishchenko, I., Maffei, M., Schneidewind, C.: A semantic framework for the security analysis of Ethereum smart contracts. Technical report, TU Wien (2018)

19. Hildenbrandt, E., et al.: KEVM: a complete semantics of the Ethereum virtual machine. Technical report, UIUC (2017)

20. Hirai, Y.: Formal verification of deed contract in Ethereum name service, November 2016. https://yoichihirai.com/deed.pdf

21. Hirai, Y.: Defining the Ethereum virtual machine for interactive theorem provers. In: Brenner, M., et al. (eds.) FC 2017. LNCS, vol. 10323, pp. 520–535. Springer, Cham (2017). https://doi.org/10.1007/978-3-319-70278-0_33

22. Hu, J., Zhong, Y.: A method of logic-based smart contracts for blockchain system. In: Proceedings of the 4th International Conference on Data Processing and Applications (ICPDA), pp. 58–61. ACM (2018)

23. Jeffrey, D.U.: Principles of Database and Knowledge-base Systems. Computer Science Press, New york (1989)

24. Jiao, J., Kan, S., Lin, S.W., Sanan, D., Liu, Y., Sun, J.: Executable operational semantics of Solidity. arXiv preprint arXiv:1804.01295 (2018)

25. Luu, L., Chu, D.H., Olickel, H., Saxena, P., Hobor, A.: Making smart contracts smarter. In: Proceedings of the 23rd ACM SIGSAC Conference on Computer and Communications Security (CCS), pp. 254–269. ACM, October 2016
26. Maróti, M., et al.: Next generation (meta) modeling: web-and cloud-based collaborative tool infrastructure. In: Proceedings of the MPM@ MoDELS, pp. 41–60 (2014)
27. Mavridou, A., Laszka, A.: Designing secure Ethereum smart contracts: a finite state machine based approach. In: Meiklejohn, S., Sako, K. (eds.) FC 2018. LNCS, vol. 10957. Springer, Berlin (2018). https://doi.org/10.1007/978-3-662-58387-6_28
28. Mavridou, A., Laszka, A.: Tool demonstration: FSolidM for designing secure ethereum smart contracts. In: Bauer, L., Küsters, R. (eds.) POST 2018. LNCS, vol. 10804, pp. 270–277. Springer, Cham (2018). https://doi.org/10.1007/978-3-319-89722-6_11
29. Mavridou, A., Laszka, A., Stachtiari, E., Dubey, A.: Verisolid: correct-by-design smart contracts for Ethereum. arXiv preprint arXiv:1901.01292 (2019). https://arxiv.org/pdf/1901.01292.pdf
30. Milner, R.: Communication and Concurrency, vol. 84. Prentice Hall, New York (1989)
31. Mueller, B.: Smashing Ethereum smart contracts for fun and real profit. In: 9th Annual HITB Security Conference (HITBSecConf) (2018)
32. Newman, L.H.: Security news this week: $280m worth of Ethereum is trapped thanks to a dumb bug. Wired, November 2017. https://www.wired.com/story/280m-worth-of-ethereum-is-trapped-for-a-pretty-dumb-reason/
33. Nikolic, I., Kolluri, A., Sergey, I., Saxena, P., Hobor, A.: Finding the greedy, prodigal, and suicidal contracts at scale. In: 34th Annual Computer Security Applications Conference (ACSAC) (2018)
34. Noureddine, M., Jaber, M., Bliudze, S., Zaraket, F.A.: Reduction and abstraction techniques for BIP. In: Lanese, I., Madelaine, E. (eds.) FACS 2014. LNCS, vol. 8997, pp. 288–305. Springer, Cham (2015). https://doi.org/10.1007/978-3-319-15317-9_18
35. O'Connor, R.: Simplicity: a new language for blockchains. In: Proceedings of the 2017 Workshop on Programming Languages and Analysis for Security, PLAS 2017, pp. 107–120. ACM, New York (2017). https://doi.org/10.1145/3139337.3139340
36. Parizi, R.M., Dehghantanha, A., Choo, K.K.R., Singh, A.: Empirical vulnerability analysis of automated smart contracts security testing on blockchains. In: 28th Annual International Conference on Computer Science and Software Engineering (CASCON) (2018)
37. Plotkin, G.D.: A structural approach to operational semantics. Computer Science Department, Aarhus University, Denmark (1981)
38. Solidity by example: blind auction (2018). https://solidity.readthedocs.io/en/develop/solidity-by-example.html#blind-auction. Accessed 25 Sept 2018
39. Solidity documentation: common patterns (2018). http://solidity.readthedocs.io/en/develop/common-patterns.html#state-machine. Accessed 25 Sept 2018
40. Solidity documentation: security considerations - use the checks-effects-interactions pattern (2018). http://solidity.readthedocs.io/en/develop/security-considerations.html#use-the-checks-effects-interactions-pattern. Accessed 25 Sept 2018
41. Stortz, R.: Rattle - an Ethereum EVM binary analysis framework. In: REcon, Montreal (2018)
42. Tsankov, P., Dan, A., Cohen, D.D., Gervais, A., Buenzli, F., Vechev, M.: Securify: practical security analysis of smart contracts. In: 25th ACM Conference on Computer and Communications Security (CCS) (2018)

43. Underwood, S.: Blockchain beyond Bitcoin. Commun. ACM **59**(11), 15–17 (2016)
44. Wöhrer, M., Zdun, U.: Design patterns for smart contracts in the Ethereum ecosystem. In: Proceedings of the 2018 IEEE Conference on Blockchain, pp. 1513–1520 (2018)
45. Wood, G.: Ethereum: a secure decentralised generalised transaction ledger. Technical report, EIP-150, Ethereum Project - Yellow Paper, April 2014
46. Yang, Z., Lei, H.: Lolisa: formal syntax and semantics for a subset of the solidity programming language. arXiv preprint arXiv:1803.09885 (2018)

Bitcoin Security Under Temporary Dishonest Majority

Georgia Avarikioti[(✉)], Lukas Käppeli, Yuyi Wang, and Roger Wattenhofer

ETH Zurich, Zürich, Switzerland
{zetavar,yuwang,wattenhofer}@ethz.ch,
lukas.kaeppeli@hotmail.com

Abstract. We prove Bitcoin is secure under temporary dishonest majority. We assume the adversary can corrupt a specific fraction of parties and also introduce crash failures, i.e., some honest participants are offline during the execution of the protocol. We demand a majority of honest online participants on expectation. We explore three different models and present the requirements for proving Bitcoin's security in all of them: we first examine a synchronous model, then extend to a bounded delay model and last we consider a synchronous model that allows message losses.

Keywords: Bitcoin · Security · Dishonest majority · Offline players · Sleepy model

1 Introduction

Bitcoin [10] is the predominant cryptocurrency today. Nevertheless, our understanding of Bitcoin' s correctness is limited. Only relatively recently, there have been attempts to formally capture Bitcoin' s security properties. In a seminal work, Garay et al. [7] proposed a formal framework (the "backbone protocol") to describe the Bitcoin system. They defined security properties for the backbone protocol and proved these both in the synchronous and bounded-delay model.

Our work extends the work of Garay et al. [7] in several dimensions. First, in contrast to our model, [7] assumed a constant honest majority of the participants. However, the Bitcoin protocol has been proven to be more fault-tolerant and able to allow for a majority of dishonest players, as long as this dishonest majority is only temporary. Specifically, in 2014 there was a majority takeover (approximately 54% of the network) by the mining pool GHash.io. The cost to perform such attacks have been studied in [3] and https://www.crypto51.app/. In this work, we extend the original work of Garay et al. [7] to capture these attacks, by allowing a temporary dishonest majority. We provide a formal analysis and investigate under which circumstances Bitcoin is secure when the honest majority holds only on expectation.

Second, motivated by a model of Pass and Shi [12], we not only have honest ("alert") or dishonest ("corrupted") nodes. Instead, there is a third group of

© International Financial Cryptography Association 2019
I. Goldberg and T. Moore (Eds.): FC 2019, LNCS 11598, pp. 466–483, 2019.
https://doi.org/10.1007/978-3-030-32101-7_28

nodes that are currently not able to follow the protocol. We call them "sleepy", which really is a euphemism for nodes that are basically offline, eclipsed from the action, for instance by a denial of service attack. Understanding this trade-off between corrupted and sleepy nodes gives us a hint whether a dishonest attacker should rather invest in more mining power (to get more corrupted players) or in a distributed denial of service architecture (to get more sleepy players).

Third, we introduce a parameter c that upper bounds the mining power of the adversary over the mining power of "alert" nodes. This is not necessary for the security analysis. However, as showed in [13], if the adversary follows a selfish mining strategy, he can gain a higher fraction of blocks (rewards) compared to his fraction of the mining power. Hence, parameter c allows us to clearly capture the correlation between this parameter and the advantage of the adversary when he deviates from the honest protocol execution.

Fourth, we study network delays since they significantly affect the performance and security. By extending our synchronous model to the a semi-synchronous model, we show that the upper bound on sleepy parties heavily depends on the maximum allowed message delay.

Finally, we extend our analysis to a synchronous model, where we allow message losses. This is inspired by an idea described in [8], where the adversary may perform an eclipse attack [14,15] on some victims which enables the adversary to control their view of the blockchain. We show security under the assumption that the adversary can eclipse a certain number of players, depending on the number of corrupted players.

The omitted theorems, lemmas and proofs can be found in the full version of the paper [2].

2   The Model

We adapt the model originally introduced by Garay et al. [7] to prove the security of the Backbone protocol. We initially present all the components of a general model and then parametrize the model to capture the three different models under which we later prove that the backbone protocol is secure.

2.1   The Execution

We assume a fixed set of n parties, executing the Bitcoin backbone protocol. Each party can either be *corrupted, sleepy* or *alert*; *sleepy* is an offline honest node and *alert* an honest node that is actively participating in the protocol.

Involved Programs. All programs are modeled as polynomially-bounded interactive Turing machines (ITM) that have communication, input and output tapes. An ITM instance (ITI) is an instance of an ITM running a certain program or protocol. Let the ITM $\mathcal{Z}$ denote the environment program that leads the execution of the Backbone protocol. Therefore $\mathcal{Z}$ can spawn multiple ITI's running the protocol. These instances are a fixed set of n parties, denoted by $P_1, \ldots, P_n$. The control program C, which is also an ITM, controls the spawning of these new ITI's and the communication between them. Further, C forces the environment $\mathcal{Z}$ to initially spawn an adversary $\mathcal{A}$. The environment will then activate each party in a round-robin way, starting with P_1. This is done by writing to their input tape. Each time, a corrupted party gets activated, $\mathcal{A}$ is activated instead. The adversary may then send messages ($\texttt{Corrupt}, P_i$) to the control program and C will register the party P_i as corrupted, as long as there are less than $t < n$ parties corrupted. Further, the adversary can set each party asleep by sending a message ($\texttt{sleep}, P_i$) to the control program. The control program C will set the party P_i asleep for the next round with probability s, without informing $\mathcal{A}$ if the instruction was successful or not.

Each party P_i has access to two ideal functionalities, the "random oracle" and the "diffusion channel", which are also modelled as ITM's. These functionalities, defined below, are used as subroutines in the Backbone protocol.

Round. A round of the protocol execution is a sequence of actions, performed by the different ITI's. In our setting, a round starts with the activation of the party P_1, which then performs the protocol-specific steps. By calling the below defined diffuse functionality, P_1 has finished it's actions for the current round and $\mathcal{Z}$ will activate P_2. If the party P_i is corrupted, $\mathcal{A}$ will be activated and if P_i is asleep, P_{i+1} gets activated instead. The round ends after P_n has finished. Rounds are ordered and therefore enumerated, starting from 1.

Views. Let us formally define the view of a party P. The only "external" input to the protocol is the security parameter κ. Therefore, we can consider κ to be constant over all rounds of the execution and we can exclude it from the random variable describing the view of a party. We denote by the random variable $VIEW_{\mathcal{A},\mathcal{Z}}^{P,t,n}$ the view of a party P after the execution of the Bitcoin backbone protocol in an environment $\mathcal{Z}$ and with adversary $\mathcal{A}$. The complete view over all n parties is the concatenation of their views, denoted by the random variable $VIEW_{\mathcal{A},\mathcal{Z}}^{t,n}$.

Communication and "Hashing Power". The two ideal functionalities, which are accessible by the parties, model the communication between them and the way of calculating values of a hash function $H(\cdot) : \{0,1\}^* \rightarrow \{0,1\}^\kappa$ concurrently.

The Random Oracle Functionality. The random oracle (RO) provides two functions, a calculation and a verification function. Each party is given a number of q calculation queries and unlimited verification queries per round. Thus, an adversary with t corrupted parties may query the random oracle for $t \cdot q$ calculation queries per round. Upon receiving a calculation query with some value x by a party P_i, the random oracle checks, whether x was already queried before. If not, the RO selects randomly $y \in \{0,1\}^\kappa$ and returns it. Further, the RO maintains a table and adds the pair (x, y) into this table. If x was already queried before, the RO searches in the table for the corresponding pair and returns the value y from it. It's easy to see that a verification query now only returns true/valid, if such a pair exists in the table of the RO. Note that the RO can maintain tables for different hash functions and can be used for all hash functions we need.

The Diffuse Functionality. The diffuse functionality models the communication between the parties and thus maintains a $RECEIVE()$ string for each party P_i. Note that this is not the same as the previously mentioned input tape. Each party can read the content of its $RECEIVE()$ string at any time. The message delay is denoted by Δ, where $\Delta = 0$ corresponds to a synchronous setting.

The diffuse functionality has a *round* variable, which is initially set to 1. Each party P_i can send a message m, possibly empty, to the functionality, which then marks P_i as complete for the current round. We allow $\mathcal{A}$ to read all the messages that are sent by some P_i, without modifying, dropping or delaying it. When all parties and the adversary are marked as complete, the functionality writes all messages that are Δ rounds old to the $RECEIVE()$ strings of either only the alert or all parties. We denote by B a Boolean function that indicates exactly that; if $B = 0$ the diffuse functionality writes all messages to the $RECEIVE()$ strings of the alert parties, while if $B = 1$ the diffuse functionality writes all messages to the $RECEIVE()$ strings of all parties. Each party can read the received messages in the next round being alert. At the end, *round* is incremented.

Note that in the case where $B = 1$, if a party is asleep at a round, it automatically gets marked as complete for this round. Further, upon waking up, it can read all the messages that were written to its $RECEIVE()$ string while it was asleep.

Successful Queries. A query to the RO oracle is successful, if the returned value $y < T$, where T is the difficulty parameter for the PoW function. The party, which have issued the query will then create a new valid block and may distribute it by the diffuse functionality. We denote the success probability of a single query by $p = Pr[y < T] = \frac{T}{2^\kappa}$. Note that in Bitcoin, the difficulty parameter is adjusted such that the block generation time is approximately ten minutes.

2.2 Sleepy, Alert and Corrupted

For each round i, we have at most t corrupted and $n_{honest,i} = n - t$ honest parties. Furthermore, the number of honest parties are divided to alert and sleepy parties, $n_{honest,i} = n_{alert,i} + n_{sleepy,i}$. We assume without loss of generality that no corrupted party is asleep, since we only upper-bound the power of the adversary. Since $n_{alert,i}$ and $n_{sleepy,i}$ are random variables, we can also use their expected value. The expected value is constant over different rounds, thus we will refer to them as $E[n_{alert}]$ and $E[n_{sleepy}]$. Since each honest party is independently set to sleep with probability s and thus the random variable $n_{sleepy,i}$ is binomially distributed with parameters $(n-t)$ and s. Accordingly, $n_{alert,i}$ is also binomially distributed with parameters $(n-t)$ and $(1-s)$. Hence, $E[n_{sleepy}] = s \cdot (n-t)$ and $E[n_{alert}] = (1-s) \cdot (n-t)$.

2.3 Parametrized Model

Let $M(q, \Delta, B)$ be the model, defined in this section. In the following sections, we will look at three instantiations of this model. First of all, we are going to analyze the model $M(q, 0, 1)$, which corresponds to a synchronous setting, in which each party has the ability to make q queries to the random oracle and receives every message, even if the party is asleep. Then, we extend these results to the bounded delay model, which corresponds to $M(1, \Delta, 1)$. As before, every party will always receive messages, but we restrict q to be 1. In the last section, we analyze the model $M(q, 0, 0)$, which corresponds to the synchronous model, but we do not allow the diffuse functionality to write messages on the $RECEIVE()$ tapes of sleepy parties.

2.4 Properties

In order to prove the security of the Bitcoin backbone protocol, we are going to analyze three different properties, following the analysis of [7]. These properties are defined as predicates over $VIEW_{\mathcal{A},\mathcal{Z}}^{t,n}$, which will hold for all polynomially bounded environments $\mathcal{Z}$ and adversaries $\mathcal{A}$ with high probability.

Definition 1. *Given a predicate Q and a bound $q, t, n \in \mathbb{N}$ with $t < n$, we say that the Bitcoin backbone protocol satisfies the property Q in the model $M(q, \Delta, B)$ for n parties, assuming the number of corruptions is bounded by t, provided that for all polynomial-time $\mathcal{Z}, \mathcal{A}$, the probability that $Q(VIEW_{\mathcal{A},\mathcal{Z}}^{t,n})$ is false is negligible in κ.*

The following two Definitions concern the liveness and eventual consistency properties of the Backbone protocol. We are using the notation of [7]: We denote a chain C, where the last k blocks are removed, by $C^{\lceil k}$. Further, $C_1 \preceq C_2$ denotes that C_1 is a prefix of C_2.

Definition 2. *The chain growth property Q_{cg} with parameters $\tau \in \mathbb{R}$ and $s \in \mathbb{N}$ states that for any honest party P with chain C in $VIEW_{\mathcal{A},\mathcal{Z}}^{t,n}$, it holds that for any $s + 1$ rounds, there are at least $\tau \cdot s$ blocks added to the chain of P.*[1]

---

[1] The Chain-Growth Property in [7] is defined slightly different: ... *it holds that for any s rounds, there are at least $\tau \cdot s$ blocks added to the chain of P.* Considering the proof for Theorem 1 (of [2]), one can see, why we use $s + 1$ instead of s. It follows by the fact that the sum in Lemma 13 (of [2]) only goes from $i = r$ to $s - 1$ and not to s.

Definition 3. *The common-prefix property Q_{cp} with parameter $k \in \mathbb{N}$ states that for any pair of honest players P_1, P_2 adopting the chains C_1, C_2 at rounds $r_1 \leq r_2$ in $VIEW^{t,n}_{\mathcal{A},\mathcal{Z}}$ respectively, it holds that $C_1^{\lceil k} \preceq C_2$.*

In order to argue about the number of adversarial blocks in a chain, we will use the chain quality property, as defined below:

Definition 4. *The chain quality property Q_{cq} with parameters $\mu \in \mathbb{R}$ and $l \in \mathbb{N}$ states that for any honest party P with chain C in $VIEW^{t,n}_{\mathcal{A},\mathcal{Z}}$, it holds that for any ℓ consecutive blocks of C the ratio of adversarial blocks is at most μ.*

The following two definitions formalize typical executions of the Backbone protocol. Both of them are related to the hash functions, used for implementing the Backbone Protocol. Further, the parameters ϵ and η are introduced. Throughout the paper, $\epsilon \in (0, 1)$ refers to the quality of concentration of random variables in typical executions and η corresponds to the parameter, determining block to round translation.

Definition 5 ([7], **Definition 8**). *An insertion occurs when, given a chain C with two consecutive blocks B and B', a block B^* is such that B, B^*, B' form three consecutive blocks of a valid chain. A copy occurs if the same block exists in two different positions. A prediction occurs when a block extends one which was computed at a later round.*

Definition 6 ([7], **Definition 9**). *(Typical execution). An execution is (ϵ, η) − typical if, for any set S of consecutive rounds with $|S| \geq \eta\kappa$ and any random variable $X(S)$, the following holds:*

(a) $(1 - \epsilon)E[X(S)] < X(S) < (1 + \epsilon)E[X(S)]$
(b) No insertions, no copies and no predictions occurred.

Lemma 1. *An execution is typical with probability $1 - e^{-\Omega(\kappa)}$.*

Proof. To prove a), we can simply use a Chernoff bound by arguing that $E[X(S)]$ is in $\Omega(|S|)$. The proof for b) is equivalent to [7], by reducing these events to a collision in one of the hash functions of the Bitcoin backbone protocol. Such collisions only happen with probability $e^{-\Omega(\kappa)}$.   □

3   The q-bounded Synchronous Model Without Message Loss $M(q, 0, 1)$

In this section, we analyze the Bitcoin backbone protocol in the previously defined model, instantiated as $M(q, 0, 1)$. This corresponds to the q-bounded synchronous setting in [7]. First, we define the success probabilities for the alert and corrupted parties, which are used to prove the relations between them. At the end, we use these results to show the properties of chain growth, common prefix and chain quality.

Following the definition in [7], let a successful round be a round in which at least one honest party solves a PoW. The random variable X_i indicates successful rounds i by setting $X_i = 1$ and $X_i = 0$ otherwise. Further, we denote for a set of rounds S: $X(S) = \sum_{i \in S} X_i$. We note that if no party is asleep, we have $E[X_i] = Pr[X_i = 1] = 1 - (1 - p)^{q(n-t)}$.

Lemma 2. *It holds that* $\frac{pqE[n_{alert}]}{1 + pqE[n_{alert}]} \leq E[X_i] \leq pqE[n_{alert}]$.

Proof. By the definition of X_i, we know that $E[X_i] = E[1 - (1 - p)^{qn_{alert,i}}]$. Thus, the second inequality can easily be derived using Bernoulli. And for the first inequality holds:

$$E[X_i] = \sum_{k=0}^{n-t} E[X_i | n_{alert,i} = k] \cdot Pr[n_{alert,i} = k]$$

$$= \sum_{k=0}^{n-t} \left(1 - (1-p)^{qk}\right) \cdot \binom{n-t}{k} (1-s)^k s^{n-t-k}$$

$$= 1 - \left(s - (s-1)(1-p)^q\right)^{n-t} \geq 1 - \left(s - (s-1)(1-pq)\right)^{n-t}$$

$$\geq 1 - e^{-(1-s)(n-t)pq} = \frac{pqE[n_{alert}]}{1 + pqE[n_{alert}]}$$

$\square$

We also adapt the notation of a unique successful round from [7]. A round is called a unique successful round, if exactly one honest party obtains a PoW. Accordingly to the successful rounds, let the random variable Y_i indicates a unique successful round i with $Y_i = 1$ and $Y_i = 0$ otherwise. And for a set of rounds S, let $Y(S) = \sum_{i \in S} Y_i$.

Lemma 3. *It holds* $E[Y_i] = E[pqn_{alert,i}(1-p)^{q(n_{alert,i}-1)}] \geq E[X_i](1 - E[X_i])$.

Proof. To prove the required bounds, we need a few intermediary steps. Using Bernoulli, we can derive the following:

$$E[Y_i] = E[pqn_{alert,i}(1-p)^{q(n_{alert,i}-1)}] \geq E[pqn_{alert,i}(1 - pq(n_{alert,i} - 1))]$$

Then, we have to prove that $pqE[n_{alert}](1 - pqE[n_{alert}]) \geq E[X_i](1 - E[X_i])$. From the upper bound on $E[X_i]$, we can derive $E[X_i] = pqE[n_{alert}] - b$, for $b \geq 0$. Therefore:

$$E[X_i](1 - E[X_i]) = (pqE[n_{alert}] - b)(1 - pqE[n_{alert}] + b)$$

$$= pqE[n_{alert}](1 - pqE[n_{alert}]) - b^2 - b + 2pqE[n_{alert}]b$$

In order to prove the required bound, it must hold that $0 \geq -b^2 - b + 2pqE[n_{alert}]b$, which is equivalent to $1 \geq E[X_i] + pqE[n_{alert}]$ and holds by the fact that $2E[X_i] \leq 1$. This is also required by the proof in [7], but not stated explicitly. Since in Bitcoin, $E[X_i]$ is between $2\% - 3\%$, the inequality can be justified.

To conclude the proof, we just have to prove the following:

$$E[pqn_{alert,i}(1 - pq(n_{alert,i} - 1))] \geq pqE[n_{alert}] - (pq)^2 E[n_{alert}]^2$$
$$\Leftarrow E[n_{alert}^2] - E[n_{alert}] \leq E[n_{alert}]^2$$

Which is equivalent to $Var[n_{alert}] \leq E[n_{alert}]$ and holds for the binomial distribution. $\square$

Let the random variable $Z_{ijk} = 1$ if the adversary obtains a PoW at round i by the jth query of the kth corrupted party. Otherwise, we set $Z_{ijk} = 0$. Summing up, gives us $Z_i = \sum_{k=1}^{t} \sum_{j=1}^{q} Z_{ijk}$ and $Z(S) = \sum_{i \in S} Z_i$. Then, the expected number of blocks that the adversary can mine in one round i is:

$$E[Z_i] = qpt = \frac{t}{E[n_{alert}]} pqE[n_{alert}] \leq \frac{t}{E[n_{alert}]} \cdot \frac{E[X_i]}{1 - E[X_i]}$$

3.1 Temporary Dishonest Majority Assumption

We assume the honest majority assumption holds on expectation. In particular, for each round the following holds: $t \leq c \cdot (1 - \delta) \cdot E[n_{alert}]$, where $\delta \geq 2E[X_i] + 2\epsilon$ and $c \in [0, 1]$ is a constant. As in [7], δ refers to the advantage of the honest parties and ϵ is defined in Definition 6.

From the expected honest majority assumption, we can derive a possible upper bound for s, depending on t, δ and c. Formally,

$$s \leq \frac{n - t - \frac{t}{c(1-\delta)}}{n - t} = 1 - \frac{1}{c(1 - \delta)} \frac{t}{n - t}$$

3.2 Security Analysis

First of all, by Definition 6 the properties of the typical execution hold for the random variables $X(S), Y(S), Z(S)$, assuming $|S| \geq \eta\kappa$.

The following lemma shows the relations between the different expected values. The bounds are required in all proofs of the three properties and therefore essential.[2]

Lemma 4. *The following hold for any set S of at least $\eta\kappa$ consecutive rounds in a typical execution.*

(a) $(1 - \epsilon)E[X_i]|S| < X(S) < (1 + \epsilon)E[X_i]|S|$
(b) $(1 - \epsilon)E[X_i](1 - E[X_i])|S| < Y(S)$
(c) $Z(S) < (1 + \epsilon)\frac{t}{E[n_{alert}]} \frac{E[X_i]}{1 - E[X_i]}|S| \leq c(1 + \epsilon)(1 - \delta)\frac{E[X_i]}{1 - E[X_i]}|S|$

---

[2] The statement (d) uses different factors as [7]. The problem is, that it's even not possible to prove the bounds from [7] with their theorems, lemmas and assumptions.

(d) For $\sigma = (1 - \epsilon)(1 - E[X_i])$:

$$Z(S) < \left(1 + \frac{\delta}{\sigma}\right)\frac{t}{E[n_{alert}]}X(S) \le c\left(1 - \frac{\delta^2}{2\sigma}\right)X(S)$$

(e) $Z(S) < Y(S)$

Next, we prove Bitcoin is secure under temporary dishonest majority in the q-bounded synchronous setting by proving the three properties defined in [7]: *chain growth*, *common prefix* and *chain quality*. The proofs can be found in the full version.

4 The Semi-synchronous Model Without Message Loss $M(1, \Delta, 1)$

In this section, we extend the previously seen results to the semi-synchronous (bounded delay) model. This means, that we allow Δ^3 delays for the messages, as described in the Definition of our model. In order to realize the proofs, we have to restrict q to be 1. And as in the last section, we do not assume message losses.

Due the introduced network delays, we need to redefine unique successful rounds, because they do not provide the same guarantees in the this model. Especially, Lemma 15 (of [2]) will not hold in the new model. Therefore, we will introduce two new random variables, one for successful and one for unique successful rounds in the bounded delay model. Note, that the chances for the adversary do not change and we can use the bounds from the synchronous model.

Let the random variable X_i' be defined such that for each round i, $X_i' = 1$, if $X_i = 1$ and $X_j = 0$, $\forall j \in \{i - \Delta + 1, \ldots, i - 1\}$. A round i is called Δ-isolated successful round, if $X_i' = 1$. Further, let $X'(S) = \sum_{i \in S} X_i'$. Using Bernoulli, we can derive the following bound on $E[X_i']$:

$$E[X_i'] = E[X_i](1 - E[X_i])^{\Delta - 1} \ge E[X_i](1 - (\Delta - 1)E[X_i]).$$

In order to prove eventual consistency, we have to rely on stronger events than just uniquely successful rounds. In [7], this is achieved by defining the random variable Y_i' such that for each round i, $Y_i' = 1$, if $Y_i = 1$ and $X_j = 0$, $\forall j \in \{i - \Delta + 1, \ldots, i - 1, i + 1, \ldots, i + \Delta - 1\}$. Then, a round i is called Δ-isolated unique successful round, if $Y_i' = 1$. Further, let $Y'(S) = \sum_{i \in S} Y_i'$. As before, we can lower bound $E[Y_i']$ using Bernoulli:

$$E[Y_i'] = E[X_i](1 - E[X_i])^{2\Delta - 1} \ge E[X_i](1 - (2\Delta - 1)E[X_i]).$$

---

[3] According to Theorem 11 of [12], the parameter Δ has to be known by the honest parties to achieve state machine replication, e.g. achieving consensus.

4.1   Temporary Dishonest Majority Assumption

We assume again honest majority on expectation, such that for each round $t \leq c \cdot (1 - \delta) \cdot E[n_{alert}]$, where $\delta \geq 2\Delta E[X_i] + 4\epsilon + \frac{4\Delta}{\eta \kappa}$ and $c \in [0, 1]$ is a constant.[4] The reason for the higher value of δ (compared to the synchronous model) is that $E[Y_i'] \leq E[Y_i]$ and we need a way to compensate this difference.

4.2   Security Analysis

In this subsection, we prove Bitcoin is secure, i.e. the chain growth, common prefix and chain quality properties hold, for the semi-synchronous model without message loss. We note that the properties of the typical execution apply to the predefined random variables $(X'(S), Y'(S), Z(S))$, given that $|S| \geq \eta \kappa$.

The following lemma corresponds to the semi-synchronous version of Lemma 4. Most of the relations follow the same structure and are similar to prove as in the synchronous model.

Lemma 5. *The following hold for any set S of at least $\eta \kappa$ consecutive rounds in a typical execution.*

(a) $(1 - \epsilon)E[X_i](1 - E[X_i])^{\Delta-1}|S| < X'(S)$
(b) $(1 - \epsilon)E[X_i](1 - E[X_i])^{2\Delta-1}|S| < Y'(S)$
(c) $Z(S) < (1 + \epsilon)\frac{t}{E[n_{alert}]}\frac{E[X_i]}{1-E[X_i]}|S| \leq c(1 + \epsilon)(1 - \delta)\frac{E[X_i]}{1-E[X_i]}|S|$
(d) *Let* $S' = \{r, \ldots, r'\}$ *with* $|S'| \geq \eta \kappa$. *For* $S = \{r, \ldots, r' + \Delta\}$ *and* $\sigma' = (1 - \epsilon)(1 - E[X_i])^{\Delta}$:

$$Z(S) < \left(1 + \frac{\delta}{2\sigma'}\right)\frac{t}{E[n_{alert}]}X'(S')$$

(e) *Let* $S' = \{r, \ldots, r'\}$ *with* $|S'| \geq \eta \kappa$. *For* $S = \{r - \Delta, \ldots, r' + \Delta\}$:

$$Z(S) < Y'(S')$$

The proof of Lemma 5 as well as the proofs of the security properties can be found in the full version.

5   The q-bounded Synchronous Model with Message Loss $M(q, 0, 0)$

As in the synchronous case, we do not restrict the number of queries and assume no message delays. In the previous sections, we assumed that messages, sent from the diffusion functionality, will be written on the *RECEIVE*() string of each party. However, in this section, we assume that the messages only get

---

[4] One might notice that our lower bound of δ differs from the lower bound from [7]. First of all, they provided two different values for δ, where both of them are wrong in the sense that they are too small in order to prove the needed bounds.

written to the $RECEIVE()$ strings of alert parties, i.e. sleepy parties do not receive messages. This models the worst possible event of the reality, because in Bitcoin itself, parties that were offline will check on the currently longest chain, once they get back online. This model captures the effects if none of them receives one of the currently longest chains, thus are eventually a victim of an eclipse attack. This implies that it's not necessarily true that all parties' local chains have the same length.

This change to the model leads to major differences compared to the results from the previous sections. In this case, unique successful rounds doesn't provide the same guarantees as before, especially Lemma 15 (of [2]) doesn't hold any more.

In the following, we denote by C_i the set of chains containing all longest chains that exist at round i. Further, we refer to the local chain of player P_j at round i by L_i^j.

The following lemma shows the expected number of honest players, which have adopted one of the longest chains existing at the current round.

Lemma 6. *At every round i, there are expected $E[n_{alert}] = (1-s)(n-t)$ parties j, such that $L_i^j \in C_i$.*

Proof. We will prove the lemma by induction over all rounds of an execution. The base case is trivial, because at round 1, every party starts with the genesis block. Now for the step case, assume that the lemma holds at round i. Then we show that it holds at round $i+1$ too. In order to prove this, we perform a case distinction:

- Case $X_i = 0$: No new chains will be diffused, therefore no new chains can be adopted and we can apply the induction hypothesis.
- Case $Z_i = 0$: Analogue to the previous case.
- Case $X_i = 1$: (But $Y_i = 0$) Now we have to differentiate, if the new blocks extend some chain in C_i not:
  (a) Some longest chain is extended:
      Every party, which is not asleep at round i will adopt one of the possibly multiple resulting new longest chains. Thus, there are expected $E[n_{alert}]$ alert parties which will have adopted one of the longest chains at round $i+1$.
  (b) No longest chain is extended:
      No honest party, whose local chain is already one of the currently longest chain will adopt a new chain, since it's length will not be larger than the length of its local chain. Thus, we can apply the induction hypothesis.
- Case $Y_i = 1$: As in the case before, every party, which was alert at round i, will adopt the resulting chain, if its length is larger than the length of its local chain. As before, there are $E[n_{alert}]$ alert parties which will have adopted one of the longest chains at round $i+1$.
- Case $Z_i = 1$: Analogue to the previous case. But if the adversary withholds the found block, the case $Z_i = 0$ applies and at the round, where it diffuses this block, this case applies.   □

By the lemma above, at every round i only expected $(1 - s)(n - t)$ parties j have a local chain $L_i^j \in C_i$. And a fraction of $(1 - s)$ of them will again be sleepy in the following rounds. Therefore, let $n_{alert,i}^*$ denote the number of alert parties j at round i, where $L_i^j \in C_i$.

It's easy to see that $n_{alert,i}^*$ is binomially distributed with parameters $(n - t)$ and $(1 - s)^2$. Let $E[n_{alert}^*] = (1 - s)^2(n - t)$ denote the expected value of $n_{alert,i}^*$, omitting the round index i, since the expected value is equal for all rounds. We define the random variable X_i^* which indicates, if at least one of the $n_{alert,i}^*$ parties solves a PoW at round i. Thus, we set $X_i^* = 1$, if some honest party j with $L_i^j \in C_i$ solves a PoW at round i and $X_i^* = 0$ otherwise. Further, we define for a set of rounds S: $X^*(S) = \sum_{i \in S} X_i^*$.

Lemma 7. *It holds that* $\frac{pqE[n_{alert}^*]}{1+pqE[n_{alert}^*]} \leq E[X_i^*] \leq pqE[n_{alert}^*]$.

Proof. The lemma can be proven using the same argumentation as in the proof for the Lemma 2. □

Accordingly, let Y_i^* denote the random variable with $Y_i^* = 1$, if exactly one honest party j solves a PoW at round i and $L_i^j \in C_i$. Note that the resulting chain, will be the only longest chain. Further, for a set of rounds S let $Y^*(S) = \sum_{i \in S} Y_i^*$.

Lemma 8. *It holds* $E[Y_i^*] = E[pqn_{alert,i}^*(1-p)^{q(n_{alert,i}^*-1)}] \geq E[X_i^*](1-E[X_i^*])$.

Proof. The proof follows the exactly same steps as the proof for Lemma 3. □

5.1 Temporary Dishonest Majority Assumption

In this setting, the honest majority assumption changes slightly. We cannot simply assume that t is smaller than some fraction of $E[n_{alert}^*]$, because we have also to consider parties j with $L_i^j \notin C_i$. We assume that for each round holds $t + (1 - s)E[n_{sleepy}^*] \leq c \cdot (1 - \delta) \cdot E[n_{alert}^*]$, where $\delta \geq 3\epsilon + 2E[X_i^*]$ and some constant $c \in [0, 1]$. Note that $(1 - s)E[n_{sleepy}^*]$ is the fraction of alert parties, working on shorter chains.

In order to compute the upper bound for s, we reformulate the honest majority assumption. Using the quadratic formula, this results in the following:

$$s \leq \frac{2c(1 - \delta) - \sqrt{1 + 4(1 + c(1 - \delta))\frac{t}{n-t}}}{2(1 + c(1 - \delta))}$$

In the model description, we specified that the adversary is not informed if a party P_i is set to sleep, after sending an instruction (sleep, P_i) to the control program C. This assumption is realistic since the adversary can not be certain about the success of his attempt to create a crash-failure. Further, allowing the adversary to know when he successfully set to sleep a node makes him quite powerful. Specifically, in our model we have a fraction of $1 - s$ alert parties. Subtracting the parties, which are working on a longest chain, from the $(1 - s)(n - t)$ parties, leaves us an expected fraction of $s(1 - s)$ parties, which can be found on the left hand side of the honest majority assumption. If we would assume that the adversary knows, which parties are asleep at each round, we would have to change the temporary dishonest majority assumption to $t + E[n_{sleepy}] \leq c \cdot (1 - \delta) \cdot E[n^*_{alert}]$. Then, the adversary could exploit this knowledge to his advantage and send sleep instructions to the parties working on the longest chains. To capture this adversarial behavior a different model would be necessary (since s cannot be considered constant).

5.2   Security Analysis

For this section, we note that the properties of an typical execution apply for the random variables $X^*(S), Y^*(S)$ and $Z(S)$, given that $|S| \geq \eta\kappa$.

Lemma 9. *Suppose that at round r, the chains in C_i have size l. Then by round $s \geq r$, an expected number of $E[n_{alert}] = (1 - s)(n - t)$ parties will have adapted a chain of length at least $l + \sum_{i=r}^{s-1} X_i^*$.*

Proof. By Lemma 6, for every round i, the expected number of parties j with $L_i^j \in C_i$ is $E[n_{alert}]$. Therefore, we only have to count the number of times, when one of these longest chains gets extended. $\square$

In the following, we define a new variable ϕ and provide an upper bound for it. This is required for the proof of the common prefix property. Although the proven bound is not tight, it is sufficient for proving the desired properties.

Lemma 10. *The probability that the honest parties j with $L_i^j \notin C_i$ can create a new chain $C' \in C_r$ for some round $r \geq i$, before any chain from C_i gets extended is denoted by ϕ. It holds that:*

$$\phi \leq \frac{s}{1 - s}$$

Proof. Without loss of generality, we may assume that all parties j with $L_i^j \notin C_i$ have the same local chain. Further, we can assume that this chain is just one block shorter than the currently longest chain. Thus, we search an upper bound for the probability that the parties $\{P_j\}_{L_i^j \notin C_i}$ are faster in solving two PoW's than the parties $\{P_j\}_{L_i^j \in C_i}$ solving one PoW.

In order to prove that, we have to introduce a new random variable $\tilde{X}_i$, with $\tilde{X}_i = 1$ if some honest party j with $L_i^j \notin C_i$ solves a PoW. By the same argumentation as in Lemma 2, we can argue that $\frac{pq(1-s)E[n_{sleepy}]}{1+pq(1-s)E[n_{sleepy}]} \leq E[\tilde{X}_i] \leq pq(1 - s)E[n_{sleepy}]$. Therefore, the upper bound on the required probability is:

$$\sum_{k=2}^{\infty}(k-1)E[\tilde{X}_i]^2(1-E[\tilde{X}_i])^{k-2}(1-E[X_i^*])^k$$

$$=\frac{E[\tilde{X}_i]^2}{(1-E[\tilde{X}_i])^2}\cdot\sum_{k=2}^{\infty}(k-1)\big((1-E[\tilde{X}_i])(1-E[X_i^*])\big)^k$$

$$=\frac{E[\tilde{X}_i]^2(1-E[X_i^*])^2}{(E[\tilde{X}_i]+E[X_i^*]-E[\tilde{X}_i]E[X_i^*])^2}$$

Now, let $a := pq(1-s)^2(n-t) = pqE[n_{alert}^*]$ and $b := pqs(1-s)(n-t) = pq(1-s)E[n_{sleepy}]$. Then by the Definition of $E[\tilde{X}_i]$ and $E[X_i^*]$ holds:

$$\frac{E[\tilde{X}_i]^2(1-E[X_i^*])^2}{(E[\tilde{X}_i]+E[X_i^*]-E[\tilde{X}_i]E[X_i^*])^2}=\frac{b^2}{(1+a)^2(1-ab)^2(a+ab+b)^2}$$

Thus, $\phi \leq \frac{s}{1-s}$ is equivalent to:

$$\frac{b^2}{(1+a)^2(1-ab)^2(a+ab+b)^2}\leq\frac{s}{1-s}$$
$$\Leftrightarrow ab \leq (1+a)^2(1-ab)^2(a+ab+b)^2$$

The inequality holds, since $(1+a)^2(1-ab)^2 \geq 1$ and $ab \leq (a+ab+b)^2$.   □

The lemma below replaces Lemma 15 (of [2]). The possibility to have chains of different length at the same round offers various ways to replace a block from round i, where $Y_i^* = 1$. Thus, we cannot use the same arguments as in Lemma 15 (of [2]).

Lemma 11. *Suppose the kth block B of a chain C was computed at round i, where $Y_i^* = 1$. Then with probability at least $1 - \phi$, the kth block in a chain C' will be B or requires at least one adversarial block to replace B.*

As in the previous sections, the properties of the typical execution hold and executions are typical with high probability, by Lemma 1.

Since we allow message losses in this model, we require more unique successful rounds than in other models. This leads to a different bound in part (e) of the following lemma.

Lemma 12. *The following hold for any set S of at least $\eta\kappa$ consecutive rounds in a typical execution.*

(a) $(1-\epsilon)E[X_i^*]|S| < X^*(S)$
(b) $(1-\epsilon)E[X_i^*](1-E[X_i^*])|S| < Y^*(S)$
(c) $Z(S) < (1+\epsilon)\frac{t}{E[n_{alert}^*]}\frac{E[X_i^*]}{1-E[X_i^*]}|S| < (1+\epsilon)\big(c(1-\delta)-\frac{s}{1-s}\big)\frac{E[X_i^*]}{1-E[X_i^*]}|S|$

(d) For $\sigma^* = (1 - \epsilon)(1 - E[X_i^*])$:

$$Z(S) < \left(1 + \frac{\delta}{\sigma^*}\right)\frac{t}{E[n_{alert}^*]}X^*(S) \le c\left(1 - \frac{\delta^2}{2\sigma^*}\right)X^*(S)$$

(e)

$$Z(S) < Y^*(S)(1 - \epsilon)(1 - \phi)$$

Next, we prove Bitcoin is secure in the synchronous model with message loss. The proof can be found in the full version.

6   Security Analysis Results

As a result of the temporary dishonest majority assumptions, we have derived upper bounds for the probability s as shown in Fig. 1. Therefore, we fixed $c = 0.5$ to limit the advantage of an adversary, following a Selfish Mining strategy. Further, we have chosen for all three models $\epsilon = 0.005$. For the synchronous model without message losses, we set $E[X_i] = 0.03$, which results in $\delta = 0.07^5$. For the Semi-Synchronous model, we set also $E[X_i] = 0.03$, resulting in $E[X_i'] = 0.022$. For $\Delta = 10$, we then get $\delta = 0.46$. And for the synchronous model with message losses, we have chosen $E[X_i^*] = 0.03$, which results in $\delta = 0.075$.

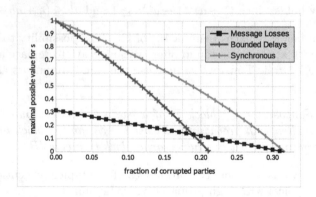

Fig. 1. This figure shows the upper bound on the fraction of sleepy parties, depending on the fraction of corrupted parties.

One might be wondering how we could allow such high values for s. We have fixed $E[X_i]$, respectively $E[X_i^*]$, for our calculations. We can do this without loss of generality, since these expected values are dependent on p, which depends on the difficulty parameter T. The adjustment of T, used to regulate the block

---

[5] Note that δ is dependent on $E[X_i]$, which is again dependent on s. If we would remove this dependency, the results would be at most 2% better than the actual results shown in Fig. 1.

generation rate, depends on the fraction of sleepy parties, because they do not provide computational power (e.g. new blocks) to the blockchain.

These results are also consistent with the results from [4], where the upper bound on the adversarial fraction is stated at 49.1%. If we set $c = 1$ and $s = 0$, due the value of δ, we get an maximal possible adversarial fraction of 48.5%.

7   Related Work

To model temporary dishonest majority in Bitcoin we used an idea, originally introduced by Pass and Shi [12]. In this work, they introduced the notion of sleepy nodes, i.e. nodes that go offline during the execution of the protocol, and presented a provably secure consensus protocol. In this paper, we model the dynamic nature of the system by additionally allowing the adversary to set parties to sleep, thus enabling temporary dishonest majority.

Bitcoin has been studied from various aspects and multiple attacks have been proposed, concerning the network layer [1,8,11] as well as the consensus algorithm (mining attacks) [5,6,9,13]. The most famous mining attack is selfish mining [6], where a selfish miner can withhold blocks and gain disproportionate revenue compared to his mining power. The chain quality property, originally introduced in [7], encapsulates this ratio between the mining power and the final percentage of blocks, and thus rewards, the adversary owns. On the other hand, Heilman et al. [8] examined eclipse attacks on the Bitcoin's peer-to-peer network. In turn, Nayak et al. [11] presented a novel attack combining selfish mining and eclipse attacks. They showed that in some adversarial strategies the victims of an eclipse attack can actually benefit from being eclipsed. Our last model, where offline parties do not get the update messages, captures this attack.

8   Conclusion and Future Work

In this paper, we prove Bitcoin is secure under temporary dishonest majority. Specifically, we extended the framework of Garay et al. [7] to incorporate offline nodes and allow the adversary to introduce crush failures. This way we can relax the honest majority assumption and allow temporary dishonest majority. We prove Bitcoin' s security by showing that under an expected honest majority assumption the following security properties hold: chain growth, common prefix and chain quality.

We examine three models: the synchronous model, the bounded delay model and the synchronous model with message loss. The first two models result in similar bounds regarding the fractions of corrupted and sleepy parties. In contrast, the last model that allows message losses when a party goes offline is less resilient to sleepy behavior. This is expected since this model captures the nature of eclipse attacks where the adversary can hide part of the network form an honest party and either waste or use to his advantage the honest party's mining power. We illustrate in Fig. 1 the upper bounds on the fraction of sleepy parties depending on the fraction of corrupted parties for all three models.

For future work, we did not consider the bounded delay with message loss model. We expect the difference on the results from synchronous to bounded delay model to be similar to the model without message loss. Another interesting future direction is to consider a more powerful adversary, who knows whether his attempt to set a party to sleep is successful or not.

Acknowledgments. We thank Dionysis Zindros for the helpful and productive discussions. Y. W. is partially supported by X-Order Lab.

References

1. Apostolaki, M., Zohar, A., Vanbever, L.: Hijacking bitcoin: routing attacks on cryptocurrencies. In: 2017 IEEE Symposium on Security and Privacy, SP 2017, San Jose, CA, USA, 22–26 May 2017, pp. 375–392 (2017)
2. Avarikioti, G., Käppeli, L., Wang, Y., Wattenhofer, R.: Bitcoin Security under Temporary Dishonest Majority (2019)
3. Bonneau, J.: Hostile blockchain takeovers (short paper). In: Bitcoin'18: Proceedings of the 5th Workshop on Bitcoin and Blockchain Research (2018)
4. Decker, C., Wattenhofer, R.: Information propagation in the bitcoin network. In: IEEE P2P 2013 Proceedings, September 2013
5. Eyal, I.: The miner's dilemma. In: 2015 IEEE Symposium on Security and Privacy, SP 2015, San Jose, CA, USA, 17–21 May 2015, pp. 89–103 (2015)
6. Eyal, I., Sirer, E.G.: Majority is not enough: bitcoin mining is vulnerable. Commun. ACM **61**(7), 95–102 (2013)
7. Garay, J., Kiayias, A., Leonardos, N.: The bitcoin backbone protocol: analysis and applications. In: Oswald, E., Fischlin, M. (eds.) EUROCRYPT 2015, Part II. LNCS, vol. 9057, pp. 281–310. Springer, Heidelberg (2015). https://doi.org/10.1007/978-3-662-46803-6_10
8. Heilman, E., Kendler, A., Zohar, A., Goldberg, S.: Eclipse attacks on bitcoin's peer-to-peer network. In: Proceedings of the 24th USENIX Conference on Security Symposium, SEC 2015, pp. 129–144. USENIX Association, Berkeley (2015)
9. Kwon, Y., Kim, D., Son, Y., Vasserman, E.Y., Kim, Y.: Be selfish and avoid dilemmas: fork after withholding (FAW) attacks on bitcoin. In: Proceedings of the 2017 ACM SIGSAC Conference on Computer and Communications Security, CCS 2017, Dallas, TX, USA, 30 October–03 November 2017, pp. 195–209 (2017)
10. Nakamoto, S.: Bitcoin: A peer-to-peer electronic cash system, October 2008. https://bitcoin.org/bitcoin.pdf
11. Nayak, K., Kumar, S., Miller, A., Shi, E.: Stubborn mining: generalizing selfish mining and combining with an eclipse attack. In: 2016 IEEE European Symposium on Security and Privacy (EuroS&P), pp. 305–320 (2015)
12. Pass, R., Shi, E.: The sleepy model of consensus. In: Takagi, T., Peyrin, T. (eds.) ASIACRYPT 2017. LNCS, vol. 10625, pp. 380–409. Springer, Cham (2017). https://doi.org/10.1007/978-3-319-70697-9_14
13. Sapirshtein, A., Sompolinsky, Y., Zohar, A.: Optimal selfish mining strategies in bitcoin. In: Grossklags, J., Preneel, B. (eds.) FC 2016. LNCS, vol. 9603, pp. 515–532. Springer, Heidelberg (2017). https://doi.org/10.1007/978-3-662-54970-4_30

14. Singh, A., Ngan, T.W.J., Druschel, P., Wallach, D.S.: Eclipse attacks on overlay networks: threats and defenses. In: IEEE INFOCOM 2006, April 2006
15. Sit, E., Morris, R.: Security considerations for peer-to-peer distributed hash tables. In: Druschel, P., Kaashoek, F., Rowstron, A. (eds.) IPTPS 2002. LNCS, vol. 2429, pp. 261–269. Springer, Heidelberg (2002). https://doi.org/10.1007/3-540-45748-8_25

Off-Chain Mechanisms and More Measurement

VAPOR: A Value-Centric Blockchain that is Scale-out, Decentralized, and Flexible by Design

Zhijie Ren and Zekeriya Erkin$^{(\boxtimes)}$

Department of Intelligent Systems, Delft University of Technology,
Delft, The Netherlands
renzhijie.max@gmail.com, z.erkin@tudelft.nl

Abstract. Blockchains is a special type of distributed systems that operates in unsafe networks. In most blockchains, all nodes should reach consensus on all state transitions with Byzantine fault tolerant algorithms, which creates bottlenecks in performance. In this paper, we propose a new type of blockchains, namely Value-Centric Blockchains (VCBs), in which the states are specified as values (or more comprehensively, coins) with owners and the state transition records are then specified as proofs of the ownerships of individual values. We then formalize the "rational" assumptions that have been used in most blockchains. We further propose a VCB, VAPOR, that guarantees secure value transfers if all nodes are rational and keep the proofs of the values they owned, which is merely parts of the whole state transition record. As a result, we show that VAPOR enjoys significant benefits in throughput, decentralization, and flexibility without compromising security.

Keywords: Blockchain · Distributed ledgers · Consensus algorithm · Scalability · Decentralization

1 Introduction

Blockchain technology, also referred as distributed ledger technology, considers a distributed system operating in a network with untrusted nodes. In blockchains, all nodes of the system apply the same rules to process consistent data, which mainly takes form of data blocks chained with unbreakable hash functions. We can categorize all existing blockchains into two categories by their data structures: one follows the idea of Bitcoin [22] and we call Transaction-Centric Blockchains (TCBs), and the other follows from Ethereum [32] and the classical state machine replication model, we call Account-Centric Blockchains (ACBs). The former is commonly referred as ledgers, since all data are transactions, i.e., value transfer records. The concepts of account and balance are not explicitly emphasized. The latter, on the other hand, the states of nodes like their balances and other variables are defined and the state transition records, e.g., the transactions, are put to the back-end of the system. In either case, all nodes in the

I. Goldberg and T. Moore (Eds.): FC 2019, LNCS 11598, pp. 487–507, 2019.
https://doi.org/10.1007/978-3-030-32101-7_29

blockchain system should essentially always keep a consistent state regardless of whether the concept of state is explicitly emphasized. Then, in blockchains, nodes should only pre-agree with the initial state, i.e., the genesis block, and then be able to use a consistent rule to independently validate each input and then perform their state transitions. As a result, both TCBs and ACBs require the complete state transition records to be acquired reliably and consistently by all nodes in the network, which causes a critical bottleneck in the performance of blockchain. In this paper, we use the term "traditional blockchains" to refer to all blockchains that all nodes need to acquire the whole state transition records.

A straightforward consequence of the bottleneck is the scalability issue which has been addressed in several other works [9, 31]. The throughput of blockchains does not grow with the number of nodes as the requirement of communication, computation, and storage grow at least proportionally to the number of nodes in the network. Hence, the throughput is limited to the capacity of the least capable node in the network and will not increase as the network grows.

Then, we also observe that centralization is an indirect consequence of the requirement for the whole state transition record. As novel blockchain systems are pursuing high throughput in terms of transaction per second (TPS), the requirement for communication, computation, and storage becomes a threshold too high for normal users to participate. Then, the *participation threshold* is a crucial factor in evaluating the decentralization of the blockchain, since a blockchain with a high participation threshold will be consequentially unfriendly to normal users and more centralized, regardless of whether a fully decentralized consensus algorithm is used.

The third problem we address in traditional blockchains is inflexibility. As blockchains are decentralized by their nature, an upgrade or change to the system is much more difficult than centralized systems as inconsistency might happen if nodes follow different rules. Some examples of such inconsistency are "forks" like Bitcoin Cash/Bitcoin and Ethereum Classic/Ethereum, which cause the system to split and degrade in security.

In this paper, we address the problem of "all nodes need to acquire and agree with all state transitions" which essentially causes all above mentioned problems. To solve this problem, we propose a new type of blockchains called Value-Centric Blockchains (VCBs) that are equally secure as traditional blockchains but requires each node to only acquire partial state transitions. More precisely:

- We formalize the rationality of nodes in value transfer system, we call Rationality of Value Owner (RVO), which has already been explicitly or implicitly used in almost all blockchains without specification.
- We propose a novel type of blockchains, called VCBs, which differ from traditional blockchains as the states are specified as the distribution for all values. A value can have an arbitrary amount and can be conceptually interpreted as

a banknote. Then, all state transitions are sorted into proofs for the ownership
of individual values.[1]

- We propose a VCB called VAPOR in which nodes only needs to hold the
  proof of their own values. We further prove that it guarantees secure and
  fully decentralized value-transfer under the RVO assumption. Moreover, with
  examples, we show that VAPOR can be easily extended with extra functionalities like fast payment channels.
- We show that VAPOR has significant advantages over traditional blockchains
  in throughput, decentralization, and flexibility.

This paper is organized as follows. In Sect. 2, we formally introduce the rationality of value owners in blockchains. Then, in Sect. 3, we introduce VCBs, their
features, and the conditions required for a valid VCB. In Sect. 4, we introduce
a VCB, called VAPOR, and prove that it guarantees reliable value transfer. We
show some examples of extension of VAPOR in Sect. 5 and show the advantages of VAPOR over traditional blockchains in Sect. 6. At last, we compare our
system to some related works in Sect. 7 and conclude in Sect. 8.

2   Rationality of Value Owner

Blockchain technology is no stranger to the notion of rationality as it was introduced as one of the fundamentals of Bitcoin. However, the rational behaviors
of nodes in blockchains, especially regarding the values they owned, are seldom
formalized. A commonly utilized rationality assumption is that rational transaction issuers are motivated to prove to the receivers that the transactions are
successful. It is mostly in the form of transaction fees, i.e., rational nodes would
like to pay reasonable transaction fees so that their transactions could be added
to the chains by the "miners", which is shown as the evidences that the transactions are successful. It has also been utilized in other forms, e.g., in the Tangle
[27], rational nodes will do a POW and validate two previous transactions to
make a transaction and in Omniledger [17], rational nodes will take initiative
in issuing their inter-shard transactions to all related shards and take effort in
completing the transactions.

There is another type of rationality, the rationality of receiving values, which
is mostly ignored in literature. In Bitcoin for instance, once a transaction is
issued, a rational receiver should observe the chain for the transaction and a
number of consecutive blocks to confirm the transaction. However, this is not
emphasized since in most blockchains, the receiver do not need to validate extra
information besides the blockchain itself. However, some off-chain solutions like
Lightning Network (LN) and Plasma [25, 26] introduce new requirements for the
rational receivers to validate some off-chain information to confirm a transaction.

Finally, we also specify a rationality, the rationality of holding values, which
is usually considered trivial. In the basic Bitcoin system, it is simply holding

---

[1] Similar ideas can be found in many classical digital cash systems, i.e., Ecash [7,8].
The relationship and difference between VCBs and early digital cash systems will
be discussed in Subsect. 7.1.

the private key and keeping it secret. However, in current Bitcoin system, there are some special transactions called Pay-to-Script-Hash (P2SH) transactions, in which the values are locked by scripts that the value owners should be able to provide. Then, in LN, rational nodes also need to keep certain "commitment transactions" secretly. Moreover, they should actively monitor the chain to check if some specific transactions appear and take certain responses. Otherwise, their received transactions could be canceled.

In this paper, we formally introduce the Rationality of the Value Owners (RVO), which is the combination of all three rationalities mentioned above. These rules are in fact no stronger than the common rationality assumptions made in existing blockchains. We say that if a rational node follow the RVO rules, then he (we use the pronouns "he" for a node throughout this paper) would use his communication, computation, and the storage resources to perform the following:

- **Rationality in Holding Value:** If he owns a value, he will make sure that he could prove the ownership.
- **Rationality in Sending Value:** If he sends a value, then he will take responsibility of proving to the receiver that (1), he owned this value; (2), the value is successfully transferred to the receiver.
- **Rationality in Receiving Value:** If he receives a value, then he will take responsibility of validating (1), the authenticity of that value; (2), the value transfer is successful.

3   Value Centric Blockchains

The data structure of VCBs is similar to many "off-chain" schemes like [19]. Each node individually puts its own transactions in off-chain transaction blocks and periodically sends an abstract of those blocks to a globally agreed main chain. Then, the key elements in VCBs are values and their ownership. A value can be conceptually interpreted as a banknote with arbitrary denomination. Virtually, there exists a list of all values in the system, their amount, and their owners which updates with the system states. Moreover, for each ownership, there is a proof and an verification algorithm that could be used to determine the ownership, which consists of a subset of all transaction blocks. In this section, we introduce the basic concepts in VCBs: the main chain, the values, the verification algorithm, and the conditions required for a valid VCB, i.e., a valid VCB should be able to guarantee secure value transfers between nodes.

3.1   Main Chain

For a VCB, we define the *main chain* as a sequence of data blocks chained with unbreakable hash function, denoted by $\mathcal{B} = \{B_1, B_2, \ldots\}$. The main chain should have the following property, which is essentially achieved by all traditional blockchains.

Property 1 (Consensus on the Main Chain).

- **Asynchronous Consistency:** In the situation where the message delay in the network is arbitrary, if an honest node agrees with a block B_i as the i-th block of the chain, then another honest node will not agree with $B'_i \neq B_i$ as the i-th block of the chain.
- **Synchronous Liveness:** In the situation where the message delay in the network could be bounded by a constant τ, if an honest node proposes a message m, then eventually an honest node will agree with a block B containing m.

The main chain has two functions. First, it serves as a global clock. Throughout this paper, we use the term "the system is at state B_i" to represent a state that the system has just reached consensus on B_i. Second, it is used to reach consensus on data that needs global agreements, e.g., the initial value distribution, the verification algorithm, and digital signatures of the transaction blocks of nodes, which we will specify later.

3.2 Value, Ownership, and Proof

We assume that there are N nodes in the network, denoted by $1, 2, \ldots, N$. We assume that there is a unique public key attached to each node and we can match the node and its public key when both are shown. In VCB, at each state of the system B_i, associated with a value $v_j, j = 1, 2, \ldots$, we have the amount of the value $\mathcal{Q}(B_1) = \{Q(v_1), Q(v_2), \ldots, \}$ and the owner of the value $O(v_j, B_i) \in \{NA, 1, 2, \ldots, N\}$. Here, $O(v_j, B_i) = NA$ suggests that this value is not owned by anyone at state B_i. We define value distribution of state B_i as $\mathcal{V}(B_i) = \{[v_j, O(v_j, B_i)] : \forall v_j\}$. The initial value distribution and the amount of each value, i.e., $\mathcal{V}(B_1)$ and $\mathcal{Q}(B_1)$, are contained in the first block of the main chain B_1. Then, for a transaction, or more specifically a transfer of the value v_j from owner x to y, denoted by $tx_m(v_j, x \rightarrow y)$, we will have $O(v_j, B_i) = x$ and $O(v_j, B_{i+1}) = y$ for a certain state B_i. Furthermore, we define a verification scheme, consists of an verification algorithm $\texttt{GetOwner}(v_j, B_i, p)$ and proofs $P(v_j, B_i)$ for all i, j, that satisfies that (1), $\texttt{GetOwner}(v_j, B_i, p)$ returns $O(v_j, B_i)$ if $p = P(v_j, B_i)$; (2), $\texttt{GetOwner}(v_j, B_i, p)$ returns "Fail" if $p \neq P(v_j, B_i)$. The algorithm $\texttt{GetOwner}(v_j, B_i, p)$ should also be agreed in B_1.

Now, we have all fundamental elements of VCBs: for a state B_i, there exists a set of values $v_j, \forall j$, their corresponding owners $O(v_j, B_i)$, their proofs of the ownership of the values $P(v_j, B_i)$, and an algorithm $\texttt{GetOwner}(v_j, B_i, p)$ that could determine the owner of a value when the proof is given.

Creating, Demolishing, Merging, and Dividing Values. The creation and demolition of values are crucial in many blockchains with Nakamoto-like consensus algorithms, since usually part of the incentives is given by creating new values. On the other hand, merging and dividing values are optional since the value exchange does not require the values to be divisible or mergeable, e.g., fiat currencies with banknotes and coins. Hence, we introduce how values could be created or demolished here, and the merging and dividing of values will be introduced in Sect. 5.1 as an additional functionality.

The creation and demolition of value should be agreed by all nodes, thus will be contained in the main chain. More precisely, to create a new value v_j : $[v_j, O(v_j, B_i)] \notin \mathcal{V}(B_i)$, a statement $[\texttt{Add} : v_j, Q(v_j), O(v_j, B_{i+1})]$ should be in block B_{i+1}. Similarly, to demolish value v_j, we put a statement $[\texttt{Delete} : v_j]$ in block B_{i+1}.

3.3   Validity of VCB

As far as we know, a rigorous definition of a valid value transfer system is still lacking, which remains a non-trivial and interesting topic for future research. In this work, we aim to propose a system that provides an equivalent value transfer functionality as other traditional blockchain systems, e.g., Bitcoin. Hence, we have the following definition for a valid VCB.

Definition 1 (Valid VCB). *Firstly, we give the following properties.*

- **Ownership:** *The owner of a value v_j is able to validate the value and prove it to others, i.e., if $O(v_j, B_i) = x$, then node x will eventually have $P(v_j, B_i)$. Moreover, the ownership can only be transferred by the owner.*
- **Liquidity:** *The owner of a value can transfer it to any other node within a certain period of time, i.e., if $O(v_j, B_i) = x$, then node x can make $O(v_j, B_{i+k}) = y$ for some $k, k \geq 1$.*
- **Authenticity:** *All values have at most one owner at each state, i.e., for all v_j, B_i, we have $O(v_j, B_i) \in \{NA, 1, 2, \ldots, N\}$.*

A VCB is valid if and only if Ownership and Authenticity are guaranteed under asynchronous network settings and Liquidity is guaranteed in synchronous network settings.

3.4   RVO Rules in VCBs

In a VCB, the RVO rules becomes:

- **Rationality in Holding Value:** At a state B_i, if node x is the owner of value v_j, he will always make sure that he has a proof p such that $\texttt{GetOwner}(v_j, B_i, p) = x$ unless he sends v_j at B_i.
- **Rationality in Sending Value:** At a state B_k, for a value v_j that $O(v_j, B_k) = x$, if node x would like to send this value, he will take responsibility of providing to the receiver y: (1), the time of the transaction $B_i, i > k$; (2), a proof p such that $\texttt{GetOwner}(v_j, B_{i-1}, p) = x$ and; (3), a proof p such that $\texttt{GetOwner}(v_j, B_i, p') = y$.
- **Rationality in Receiving Value:** For node y to receive this transaction, it will check (1), $\texttt{GetOwner}(v_j, B_{i-1}, p) = x$; and (2), $\texttt{GetOwner}(v_j, B_i, p') = y$.

4   VAPOR

In this section, we propose a VCB, namely VAPOR, which stands for the five basic elements of our system, Value, Agreement, Proof, Ownership, and Rationality. As introduced in Sect. 3, a valid VCB should have the following.

- A main chain that guarantees Property 1.
- The owner and proof of value $O(v_j, B_i)$, and a valid authenticating scheme including $P(v_j, B_i)$ for all i, j and a verification algorithm $\texttt{GetOwner}(v_j, B_i, p)$ as described in Subsect. 3.2.

Now we describe these two parts in VAPOR. Then, we prove its validity and state its features.

4.1   Main Chain and Its Consensus Algorithm

There are two major types of algorithms that could achieve Property 1: BFT algorithms and Nakamoto-like algorithms. The former includes [6,13,18,21] which explicitly requires the identity/public keys and the number of nodes to be predetermined and known by all nodes. The latter is inspired by Bitcoin and has been greatly developed in recent years. It contains a large number of algorithms such as Proof-of-Work based algorithms [10,16,24], Proof-of-Stake based algorithms [4,12,15], Directed Acyclic Graph based algorithms [27,29,30], etc. This type of algorithms do not require nodes to be predetermined. However, economical and game theoretical aspects have to be introduced to prevent Sybil attack as well as to encourage honest behaviors, and Property 1 is achieved with overwhelmingly high probability rather than absolute.

In VAPOR, any of the existing consensus algorithms that guarantee Property 1 (with a high probability) can be used for the main chain $\mathcal{B} = \{B_1, B_2, \ldots\}$. Then, VAPOR has the same requirements as the consensus algorithm and achieve the same level of security. For instance, if PBFT [6] is chosen, then VAPOR allows less than $1/3$ of the predetermined nodes to be malicious. Then, if Bitcoin POW is chosen, then VAPOR tolerates less than $1/4$ of the total mining power to be malicious [11] and the confirmation of the transactions is probabilistic.

4.2   Proofs and the Verification Algorithm

The main content of VAPOR is transactions. The proofs of the ownership of values are just different subsets of the whole transaction set. Here, we first introduce the data structure of the transactions, then introduce how the proof is chosen for each value.

Transaction Blocks. In VAPOR, each node independently makes transaction blocks with the transacitons sent by itself. A transaction $tx_m(v_j, x \rightarrow y)$ is defined as

$$tx_m(v_j, x \rightarrow y) = [v_j, y, sn],$$

in which sn is an internal serial number generated by node x to identify his transactions. Since transactions are then put in blocks with index of x, x is omitted in individual transactions. Note that here m is a virtual global transaction identifier we used in this paper and it does not actually acknowledged by any node. Periodically, a node puts transactions in a transaction block b and send an abstract,

$$a(x) = [x, H(pk_x), Sig_x(x|H(pk_x)|MR(b))],$$

to reach consensus on the main chain, where $H(pk_x)$ is the hash of the public key of x and $Sig_x(H(pk_x)|MR(b))$ is a digital signature made with $H(pk_x)$ concatenated with the Merkle root of b encrypted by the private key of x. In each round, at most one abstract from a node can be included in the main chain. If multiple different abstracts from the same node are received in the same round, then only one of them is considered valid. By the property of digital signature, the content of b is immutable once the abstract $a(x)$ is confirmed on the main chain. Hence, we denote the abstract $a(x)$ contained in block B_i by $a_i(x)$ and the block b by $b_i(x)$ and call it a confirmed block. Then, as $\mathcal{B}$ is agreed by all nodes, blocks $b_i(x), \forall x$ will also form a chain that as immutable as $\mathcal{B}$. Then, we define $\mathcal{CB} = \{b_i(x), \forall i, x\}$.

Transaction Fee for Abstracts. In our system, instead of individual transactions, the consensus is only reached on the abstracts. Then, for many consensus algorithms, a transaction fee should be provided to the block proposers, namely the miners, for them to include the abstract. The amount of the transaction fee should not be fixed so that a market can be created between the nodes and the miners. It can be achieved by introducing a new type of transactions in which the receiver is the miner, i.e., in a transaction block $b_i(x)$, node x could create transactions in form of $tx_m(v_j, x \rightarrow [\texttt{miner}]) = [v_j, x, [\texttt{miner}], sn]$, where $[\texttt{miner}]$ is a variable that equals to the proposer of the block B_i. A non-trivial problem for the transaction fee is that the sender of this transaction does not know the receiver in advance, which hinders him from sending the proof to the receiver. Hence, in the scope of this paper, the transaction fees are only feasible if the main chain uses BFT algorithms or algorithms that the block proposer is determined before the block, e.g., [10,12,15]. Then, the sender will give the proof of this transaction to the corresponding node so that the abstract would be included.

Value Ownership and Proof. Firstly, we define the ownership of values as the following.

Definition 2 (Value Ownership).

- *The initial value ownership is agreed on the main chain, either by the initial value distribution in B_1 or value creation in $B_k, k \geq 1$.*
- *We assume that node x started owning a value v_j at $B_{i'}$. Then, he will transit the ownership of this value to node y if he makes a transaction in a confirmed*

block $b_i(x)$ and has not make any transaction of this value in any confirmed blocks $b_k(x), k \in [i' + 1, i - 1]$.

- If there are more than one transaction of the same value in one transaction block, it is a clear sign of an attempt of double spending. Hence, we forbid this by stating that if a value is transacted more than once by its owner in a confirmed block, then the owner of that value is NA.

Then, we define the proof $P(v_j, B_i)$ as a subset of $\mathcal{CB}$, which is essentially all confirmed transaction blocks that are considered in the second item of Definition 2, as well as all necessary public keys to verify them. The algorithm $\texttt{Proof}(v_j, B_i, \mathcal{CB})$ can be used to get the proof $P(v_j, B_i)$, which is given in Appendix A.

Verification Algorithm. Further, as defined in Subsect. 3.2, a verification algorithm in a VCB should be able to determine the ownership when the proof is given and output "Fail" if any input other than the correct proof is given. In Algorithm 1, we propose $\texttt{GetOwner}(v_j, B_i, p)$ that outputs $O(v_j, B_i)$ if $p = P(v_j, B_i)$ and outputs 'Fail' for $p \neq P(v_j, B_i)$.

Algorithm 1. Verification Algorithm $\texttt{GetOwner}(v_j, B_i, p)$

Get the block of initial distribution (creation) of value v_j in the main chain: B_{index}
Set **owner** according to the initial distribution from the main chain.
index++;
while $a_{\text{index}}(\textbf{owner})$ exists in B_{index} **do**
    if $b_{\text{index}}(\textbf{owner})$ or the public key of **owner** does not exist in p **then return** Fail;
    if Merkle root and signature do not match **then return** Fail;
    count $\leftarrow$ number of transactions of v_j in $b_{\text{index}}(\textbf{owner})$;
    if count $= 0$ **then**
        index++;
    else if count $= 1$ **then**
        index++;
        owner $\leftarrow$ the receiver of the transaction of v_j;
    else return Fail;
    if index $> i$ **then**
        if All data in p are blocks and all blocks have been checked **then return** owner;
        else return Fail;

The validity of $\texttt{GetOwner}(v_j, B_i, p)$ as an verification algorithm could be easily shown. First, it uses the same method as the second item in Definition 1 to check whether p consists of the exact transaction blocks as $P(v_j, B_i)$ and any mismatch returns 'Fail'. Then, since the algorithm use exactly the same rules as the definition of ownership to determined the owner, it returns $O(v_j, B_i)$ if $p = P(v_j, B_i)$.

4.3   Validity of VAPOR

Here, we prove that VAPOR is a valid VCB under RVO rules and the consistency of the system is uncompromised even if RVO rules do not hold.

Theorem 1. *In VAPOR, the properties of a valid VCB will hold in the following conditions.*

Properties	Ownership	Liquidity	Authenticity
Conditions	RVO rules	Synchrony	—

Due to space limitation, we only give an outline of the proof and provide the full proof in Appendix B. The Ownership could be proved by induction: for each owner of the value, he is always able to receive the proof of the value from a rational previous owner. Moreover, only the owner can transfer the value since the transaction only happens when the block is confirmed. The Liquidity follows from the Synchronous Liveness property of the main chain. Then, the Authenticity follows from the Asynchronous Consistency of the main chain, which also guarantees the consistency of all confirmed transaction blocks. Then, Authenticity is proved as at each state, the values, owners, and proofs are based on the confirmed transactions blocks in a deterministic and one-to-one mapped fashion.

The holding condition of each property in Theorem 1 provides a good insight on VAPOR and its differences from traditional blockchains. First, even if RVO rules do not hold, e.g., a sender refuses to send the proof to the receiver, it only causes a fail to prove the ownership of this exact value. The Liquidity and Authenticity of the system are not violated and other values are not corrupted. Second, the Ownership does not depend on synchrony. Hence, if a value is transferred and the network lose synchrony for Liquidity, the proof of the value could still be delivered to the receiver if the sender is rational.

4.4   Features of VAPOR

The most distinctive feature of VAPOR is that each node only needs to acquire and keep the proofs of the values that it owns, i.e., at a state B_i, node x only needs to have $P(v_j, B_i), \forall O(v_j, B_i) = x$. To efficiently record the proofs, we propose the following implementation:

- The main chain is stored and updated according to the consensus algorithm.
- A node keeps a transaction block database of for all confirmed transaction blocks that he has.
- A node keeps a value ownership table that updates with the main chain and keeps track of the values, their owners, and the proofs that he knows, which includes his own values. The proofs are simply pointers to the transaction block database.

Comparing to TCBs and ACBs, a transaction of multiple values need to be recorded as multiple transactions in VAPOR. However, for all these transactions plus all transactions included in the same transaction block, only one signature is required in VAPOR, which is in fact more efficient in storage. The communication is also efficient as transaction blocks are acquired directly from the sender of the value with point-to-point communication and guaranteed security under the RVO rules. Moreover, the receivers could inform the sender about the transaction blocks that it already has to avoid overhead. Then, as a trade-off between storage and communication, a node can choose to not delete the proofs of the already spent values. This means that they do not need to re-acquire some transaction blocks for future received values.

5   Extending VAPOR by Modifying the Verification Algorithm

In Sect. 4, we introduced how transactions could be verified with the verification algorithm GetOwner with the proof $P(v_j, B_i)$. In this section, we show the flexibility of this framework by providing examples of extended functionalities. More precisely, we will show that the functionalities of value division, fast off-chain transactions, and value-related smart contracts can be easily achieved by simple modifications to the verification algorithms.

5.1   Value Division

The functionality of value division can be achieved with a new type of transactions called value division that has the form:

$$[\texttt{Divide} : v_{\text{source}} \rightarrow (v_{\text{source},1}, Q(v_{\text{source},1})), \ldots, (v_{\text{source},n}, Q(v_{\text{source},n})).$$

The index source forms a chain that can be traced back to the origin. Then, to validate a value divided from another value, we simply call GetOwner to check the owner of each value on the chain recursively from the origin. This new type of transactions can either be added by making modifications to GetOwner or defining another algorithm GetOwnerDV on the main chain that recursively calls GetOwner. We describe GetOwnerDV in Appendix C.

5.2   Fast Off-chain Payment

In VAPOR, the confirmation of the transaction is dependent on the main chain, thus it essentially has the same latency as traditional blockchains. However, a fast off-chain payment solution like LN or Plasma [25, 26] can also be deployed in VAPOR. Briefly speaking, an off-chain payment scheme works as follows. Firstly, some value is locked on the main chain as the deposit for the "fast payment channel" to a particular receiver. Then, transactions can be made to that receiver without confirmations on the main chain. The safety of the transactions are guaranteed by a mechanism for the receiver to take all deposit when the sender tries to cancel a transaction. However, this mechanism requires synchrony between the receiver and the main chain. Then, there is a mechanism allowing the sender to safely shut the off-chain payment channel at any time.

In VAPOR, similar ideas can be implemented under the same synchrony assumption. A node can independently lock its values for a receiver and then makes off-chain transactions by signing them and sending signed transactions to the receivers as proofs. Then, the verification scheme should be modified to be able to verify these proofs. The detail of this scheme will be given in Appendix D.

5.3 Smart Contracts

In the previous subsections, it is revealed that additional functionalities can be easily achieved by changing the rules for verification, which is merely a modification to GetOwner, or agreeing on new verification algorithms on the main chain. In fact, as long as values are transferred and there are interested parties following RVO rules, smart contracts can be written in VAPOR as new verification algorithms with one principle: only data that is against the value owners' interest is required to be put on the main chain and other data can be safely moved off-chain to the corresponding value owners. We give an example of such smart contracts, a betting game, in Appendix E.

6 Advantages of VAPOR

It has been shown that in VAPOR, nodes do not necessarily need to record the whole transaction set to allow secure value transfer. This fundamental difference from traditional blockchains leads to the advantageous in throughput, decentralization, and flexibility.

6.1 Throughput

The most straightforward advantage of VAPOR is the throughput because nodes only need to acquire the proofs of their own values instead of the whole transaction set, as stated in Subsect. 4.4. However, this improvement is not trivial to quantify as it depends heavily on the networks and the transaction patterns. Here, we theoretically analyze the throughput in terms of the transaction cost C, defined as a combination of the expected bandwidth, computation, and storage resources required to communicate, validate, and store a transaction in the whole network.

Unlike traditional blockchains, the cost of an individual transaction in VAPOR is determined by the proof size, which is situational. Hence, we calculate C by looking at the expected transaction blocks in a round that a node eventually needs to acquire, which we denote by b. Then, we have $C = O(b)$ since a transaction will be eventually acquired by b nodes on average. Let us consider a transaction block $b_i(x)$. It will eventually be acquired by node y if node x holds a value at state B_i and at a state $B_j, j > i$ node y receives that value. In other words, for the set of values $\mathcal{V}_i(x)$ holding by node x at state B_i, if all other nodes will receive a value from $\mathcal{V}_i(x)$ sometime in the future, then VAPOR have no throughput gain over traditional blockchains. In all other cases, as long as there exists some nodes that will never acquire any value in $\mathcal{V}_i(x)$, then we have $b < N$ and VAPOR has a throughput benefit.

In [28], a concept of spontaneous sharding is proposed, which roughly works as the following. When performing a transaction, a rational node will choose the value with the least transaction blocks to transmit among all values that he has. In other words, they tends to use the values for which the most part of the proof is already known and validated by the receiver, e.g., the value that once owned by the receiver. As a result, some values will only cycle in a part of the network, namely a shard, instead of the whole network. Then, a node holding g values is equivalent to participating in g shards and b will then equal to the expected size of the union of these shards. Then, it is shown in [28] that in many scenarios, we have $C = O(b) = o(N)$, i.e., the throughput will scale out. Note that any group of frequent transacting nodes can decide to perform this optimization at any time to gain the throughput benefit, regardless of the rest of the network. Hence, since spontaneous sharding gives direct benefit to individuals even if other nodes refuse to cooperate, the "the tragedy of the commons" [14] problem will not occur. We refer the readers to [28, Remark 2] for more discussion.

6.2 Decentralization

In Sect. 1, we address the centralization problem due to the high participation threshold. In VAPOR, this problem is significantly mitigated due to the value centric principle: nodes only transmit and store the data needed for validation of their own values, which is mostly not the whole transaction set. For example, in traditional blockchains, for nodes who only own a few coins in a blockchain, they still have to acquire and validate the whole chain to validate their own values and make transactions. In VAPOR, their cost of validating their own values and making transactions is $O(1)$.

6.3 Flexibility

As shown in Sect. 5, VAPOR enjoys benefits of easy modification, extension, and upgrading by simply agreeing on new verification algorithms on the main chain. However, this can be pushed one step further by allowing nodes to individually choose the algorithms that they like to use. Then, hard forks like Bitcoin/Bitcoin Cash or Ethereum/Ethereum Classic can be avoided. Instead, the forks will be "hidden" as some values might not be validated by some users as they disagree with a certain rules. However, they could still agree with the main chain and contribute to the security of the entire system. We consider this as an advantage of flexibility, as nodes are more freely to agree/disagree with each other, without destroying the consistency of the whole system as long as they have the basic agreement.

7 Related Works

This work is mainly inspired and developed from [28]. However, it does has similarities to other studies if we view VAPOR in different perspectives. We explain the similarities and relations of this work and other works in this section.

7.1 Value Centric Principle

The origin of describing value transfer systems by values (or alternatively called coins, notes, bills) can be dated back to some pioneering digital cash works like [7,8,23]. However, in these schemes, the notions of value and transaction are interchangeable as a central authority is required to validate each transaction. Hence, Bitcoin, as well as most of its successors known as alt-coins, use TCBs that focus on the validity of individual transactions rather than the value. The main difference from TCBs and VCBs can be clarified using the example of the Simple-Payment-Verification (SPV) nodes in Bitcoin. SPV nodes could verify whether all related transactions of a value are validated by the miners and are on-chain, but they could not validate the authenticity of this value, i.e., could not detect double-spending.

Chainspace [2] is a blockchain with sharding that uses a similar value-centric idea for inter-shard transactions, i.e., each transaction should include a "Trace" pointing back to the source of the value, so that the validators from the value-receiving shard only need to check the shards of the sources to prevent double spending. However, it has more redundancy as the value-centric idea is used in a shard level instead of the node level, and thus has less throughput improvement comparing to VAPOR.

7.2 Off-chain and DAG Techniques

In the perspective of data structure, VAPOR has its similarities to many off-chain systems like RSK [19] as data is stored off-chain and a main chain is used for the hash of the data. However, most off-chain systems compromise in decentralization as some trusted nodes are required to validate the contents of the off-chain data. Also, comparing to the off-chain payment schemes like LN and Plasma [25,26], VAPOR essentially moves all proofs for values off-chain. As a result, it is no longer necessary to use deposits to enforcing the consistency of the off-chain and on-chain values. Then, it is also similar to Hashgraph [3] in the sense that node individually create their own transactions. However, in Hashgraph, all nodes eventually need the whole transaction set.

7.3 Sharding

Recently, many sharding schemes have been proposed to divide the network into small shards. Then, the transactions in a shard do not need to be communicated outside the shard. However, a key problem is that the double spending prevention of inter-shard transactions relies on the security of shards instead of the whole network, which is a degradation in the security. Shards can be either determined artificially by the network topology [5] or at random [17,20], or determined based on applications or users [1,2], to reduce the number of inter-shard transactions as well as the probability of malicious shards. However, our system guarantees no degradation on security since essentially, the shards are spontaneously formed by the value transfer patterns. In other words, all shards are secure for their own intra-shard transactions and there will be no inter-shard transactions.

7.4   Performance Comparison

It is difficult to make fair throughput comparison between VAPOR and other systems using a uniform standard, e.g., transaction per second (TPS), as schemes have different security assumptions and the throughput also depends on the network settings. Therefore, we use a theoretical approach to analyze and compare the throughput and security of VAPOR with a typical system of each kind, i.e., LN for off-chain schemes, PHANTOM for DAG, and Omniledger for sharding schemes. We consider the transaction cost C (defined in Subsect. 6.1) and the security S of a transaction, which is defined as the amount of compromised nodes (corresponding resources for POW or POS) required to perform a double-spending attack. We present the results in Table 1.

Table 1. The cost and security of a transaction in VAPOR, LN, PHANTOM, and Omniledger for the whole network. Here b is the average transaction blocks of each state acquired by a node and d is size of the shard.

Schemes	VAPOR	LN	PHANTOM	Omniledger
C	$O(b)$	$O(1)$	$O(N)$	$O(d)$
S	$O(N)$	$O(1)$ or $O(N)$	$O(N)$	$o(N)$

The cost and security of VAPOR are given in Subsects. 6.1 and 4.3, respectively. For LN, note that this transaction is different from classical notion of transactions as it relies on a deposit and the value would be locked until the channel is shut down. The security relies on the synchrony between the receiver and the system (explained in Appendix D), thus would be compromised if either one is compromised. PHANTOM uses a block DAG structure to remove the dependency of security on the throughput of a chain-structure blockchain. However, all nodes still need to eventually acquire all transactions and the system will not scale out. Omniledger reduces the cost to $O(d)$ where d is the shard size and promises a throughput benefit that is proportional to N/d. However, as Omniledger yields a random approach to keep the malicious nodes within each shard to be below $1/3$, the security of the system becomes a non-trivial function of d and N, which is dominated by N but not explicitly stated in [17].

8   Conclusion

In this paper, we address and formalize the fundamentals of a value-transfer system and the rationality assumptions. The highlight of this work is that we clarify the redundancy in traditional blockchains for value-transfer and how this redundancy can be removed by using the rationality assumptions and VCBs. We hope that this work would set a theoretical framework for future blockchain designs and inspire many theoretical studies on other basic concepts in blockchains, e.g., the rational assumptions in non-value-transfer blockchains.

A   Algorithm $\texttt{Proof}(v_j, B_i, \mathcal{CB})$

We define the proof of the ownership $P(v_j, B_i)$ as a subset of $\mathcal{CB}$ that output by an algorithm $\texttt{Proof}(v_j, B_i, \mathcal{CB})$ shown in Algorithm 2.

Algorithm 2. $\texttt{Proof}(v_j, B_i, \mathcal{CB})$

Get the block of initial distribution (creation) of value v_j in the main chain: B_{index}
Set **owner** according to the initial distribution from the main chain.
index++
Proof={}
while $a_{\text{index}}(\text{owner})$ exists in B_{index} **do**
    if Merkle root and signature do not match **then return** Proof
    Add $b_{\text{index}}(\text{owner})$ and the public key of **owner** to Proof
    count $\leftarrow$ number of transactions of v_j in $b_{\text{index}}(\text{owner})$
    if count $= 0$ **then**
        index++
    else if count $= 1$ **then**
        index++
        owner $\leftarrow$ the receiver of the transaction of v_j.
    else return Proof
    if index $> i$ **then return** Proof

B   Proof for Theorem 1

Proof. Firstly, we prove Ownership by induction. It is clear that the first owner of any value v_j will have the proof of this value, which are basically all of his public key and his own confirmed transaction blocks until the block before the one that spends it. Then, assume that the t-th owner of v_j, denoted by o_t, has the proof $P(v_j, B_k)$ proving the ownership $O(v_j, B_k) = o_t$ at state B_k. Then, assume that the $t + 1$-th owner, o_{t+1} starts to own the value at state B_i, i.e., $O(v_j, B_{i-1}) = o_t, O(v_j, B_i) = o_{t+1}$. Then, by the definition of proof, there exists a transaction in $b_i(o_t)$ that send the value to o_{t+1}. By the Rationality of

Holding Value in RVO, o_t would not make this transaction unless he would like to send this value. Then, by the Rationality of Sending Value in RVO, o_t will take responsibility of giving proof $P(v_j, B_i)$ to o_{t+1}. Again, by the definition of proof, $P(v_j, B_i)$ is merely $P(v_j, B_k) \cup \{b_l(o_t) : k < l \leq i\} \cup \{\text{public key of } o_t\}$, which can be independently provided by o_t. Hence, we prove that in this case o_{t+1} will eventually has the proof $P(v_j, B_i)$. Furthermore, it is clear that only the owner of a value could transfer it as a transaction must be included in a block confirmed with the private key of the owner.

Then, we prove Liquidity. To transact a value, the owner simply needs to put a transaction in a confirmed transaction block. Then the property (Partial) Synchronous Liveness in Property 1 guarantees that the transaction block can be confirmed as the abstract will be included in the main chain.

At last, we prove Authenticity. This is actually guaranteed by the design of VAPOR. Firstly, the initial ownership of a value is unambiguous because it is on the main chain which has Asynchronous Consistency in Property 1. Then, the ownership transition is always determined by a confirmed block which is immutable. Then, there are three possibilities for the number of transactions of the same value in a confirmed block: (1) if there is no transactions of that value, then the ownership remains unchanged; (2) if there is one transaction of that value, then the ownership is changed to the receiver; (3) if there are more than one transactions of that value, then the ownership becomes NA. Since all three possibilities result in unambiguous ownership, we proved Authenticity. ∎

C   Verification Algorithm for Value Division GetOwnerDV

Here we introduce GetOwnerDV in Algorithm 3. Note that in here, a minor modification should be made on GetOwner so that the result will not be 'Fail' if redundant elements are detected in p.

Algorithm 3. Verification Algorithm for Divided Value GetOwnerDV($v_{[\text{seq}]}, B_i, p$)

Find all value division transactions and their corresponding states in p. Order the states by $[s_1, s_2, \ldots]$;

$j \leftarrow$ the first entry of [**seq**];

$t \leftarrow 1$;

while $t \leq$ the length of **seq. do**

    owner $=$ GetOwner(v_j, B_{s_1}, p);

    Check if the corresponding value division transaction is in $b_{s_t}(\text{owner})$ and the sum of the amount of the divided value equals to the amount of the source value. Return 'Fail' if the check fails.

    $t++, j = [j, \text{next element in } \textbf{seq}]$;

if All blocks in p are checked **then return owner**

else return Fail

D   Off-chain Payment Scheme

Our fast payment scheme contains two new type of transactions, two new types of message to the main chain, and a new verification algorithm `GetOwnerFP`. If node x wants to make fast payment to node y, he simply performs the following:

- Node x makes deposit transactions to lock up a number of values with indications that they could only be send to y, confirm the blocks, and send them to node y to initialize the fast payment.
- When a fast payment of value v_j is issued, node x sends a signed transaction of v_j to node y, denoted by tx. Then, node y can include this transaction in his own blocks at any time and confirm them to receive the value.
- When node x wants to end the fast payment and unlock a value v_k, he sends an unlock message to the main chain.
- The unlock will succeed in T rounds if no objection message shows in the main chain. An objection message can be made by any node by sending tx to the main chain.

Then, in `GetOwnerFP` we define three new rules on checking the proofs for ownership:

1. A value v_j locked by node x is no longer considered as owned by x, but NA indicating no owner. It will be reconsidered as owned by x if there is only one unlock message is on the main chain, assume that it is included in B_i, and there is no objection message included in $B_k, i+1 \leq k \leq i+T$.
2. A value v_j is transacted from node x to node y in state B_i if it is locked by node x to send to node y at a state $B_{i'}, i' < i$, and there is a signed transaction by x included in block $b_i(y)$. There should not be a unlocking message for this value on the main chain that is not responded for more than T blocks.

Note that although a fast transaction is only confirmed when the block is confirmed, the transaction itself is completed as soon as the signed transaction is received by node y, since node y can then independently make the proof of him owning this value.

Some drawbacks in existing off-chain payment schemes, e.g., LN, are: (1), the values in the transactions and deposit will be locked until the channel is closed. Hence, it is a different type of transaction and can only be considered as a supplement to the value transfer system. (2), the receiver should have a certain synchrony, i.e., the receiver should be able to issue a transaction to the chain to take the deposit before it is refunded to the sender when he catches the sender cheating. (3), the security of this scheme is not formally proved. A big advantage of the off-chain payment scheme in VAPOR is that node y can spend v_j as soon as he owns it, without requiring shutting down the whole channel, i.e., all deposit values been spend or unlocked. Moreover, we could use similar arguments as the proof in Subsect. 4.3 to prove the Ownership property holds when the network is synchronous and the RVO rules apply.

E   Betting Game

Here, we give a smart contract for on-chain betting. Node x and node y would like to bet even or odd on the hash of block B_i. Then, we simply add a new type of transaction which is $Bet : [v_j, x, y, B_i, sn]$. The bet transaction will lock the value v_j until B_i with one unlocking condition: another value with the same amount is bet by y before B_i with x and the ownership will depend on the hash of B_i. Then, the verification algorithm is simply checking the lock transaction, the ownership for both values, and the hash of B_i, i.e., if node x bet on even, then the ownership of both locked values will be node x at state B_i if the hash of B_i is even.

However, the difficulty is to make sure that both node x and node y could get the proofs of ownership and the locking message for both values. This is a problem since there is always one node in the betting would benefit from not sharing the proof and/or the locking message, which will cause a scenario similar to Two Generals Problem. As a result, the verification algorithm must also check for a confirmation send by one node on the main chain, which shows the agreement for both nodes that both proofs are acquired. Without such confirmation, the value will be unlocked at state B_i to its original owner.

References

1. Rchain. https://www.rchain.coop/platform
2. Al-Bassam, M., Sonnino, A., Bano, S., Hrycyszyn, D., Danezis, G.: Chainspace: a sharded smart contracts platform. CoRR abs/1708.03778 (2017). http://arxiv.org/abs/1708.03778
3. Baird, L.: The swirld hashgraph consensus algorithm: fair, fast, byzantine fault tolerance (2016). http://www.swirlds.com/downloads/SWIRLDS-TR-2016-01.pdf
4. Bentov, I., Pass, R., Shi, E.: Snow white: provably secure proofs of stake. IACR Cryptology ePrint Archive 2016, 919 (2016)
5. Buterin, V.: On sharding blockchains. Sharding FAQ (2017). https://github.com/ethereum/wiki/wiki/Sharding-FAQ
6. Castro, M., Liskov, B.: Practical byzantine fault tolerance. In: OSDI, vol. 99, pp. 173–186 (1999)
7. Chaum, D.: Blind signatures for untraceable payments. In: Chaum, D., Rivest, R.L., Sherman, A.T. (eds.) Advances in Cryptology, pp. 199–203. Springer, Boston, MA (1983). https://doi.org/10.1007/978-1-4757-0602-4_18
8. Chaum, D., Fiat, A., Naor, M.: Untraceable electronic cash. In: Goldwasser, S. (ed.) CRYPTO 1988. LNCS, vol. 403, pp. 319–327. Springer, New York (1990). https://doi.org/10.1007/0-387-34799-2_25
9. Croman, K., et al.: On scaling decentralized blockchains. In: Clark, J., Meiklejohn, S., Ryan, P.Y.A., Wallach, D., Brenner, M., Rohloff, K. (eds.) FC 2016. LNCS, vol. 9604, pp. 106–125. Springer, Heidelberg (2016). https://doi.org/10.1007/978-3-662-53357-4_8
10. Eyal, I., Gencer, A.E., Sirer, E.G., Van Renesse, R.: Bitcoin-NG: a scalable blockchain protocol. In: 13th USENIX Symposium on Networked Systems Design and Implementation (NSDI 2016), pp. 45–59. USENIX Association (2016)

11. Eyal, I., Sirer, E.G.: Majority is not enough: bitcoin mining is vulnerable. In: Christin, N., Safavi-Naini, R. (eds.) FC 2014. LNCS, vol. 8437, pp. 436–454. Springer, Heidelberg (2014). https://doi.org/10.1007/978-3-662-45472-5_28

12. Gilad, Y., Hemo, R., Micali, S., Vlachos, G., Zeldovich, N.: Algorand: scaling byzantine agreements for cryptocurrencies. In: Proceedings of the 26th Symposium on Operating Systems Principles, pp. 51–68. ACM (2017)

13. Guerraoui, R., Knežević, N., Quéma, V., Vukolić, M.: The next 700 BFT protocols. In: Proceedings of the 5th European conference on Computer systems. pp. 363–376. ACM (2010)

14. Hardin, G.: The tragedy of the commons. J. Nat. Resources Policy Res. 1(3), 243–253 (2009)

15. Kiayias, A., Russell, A., David, B., Oliynykov, R.: Ouroboros: a provably secure proof-of-stake blockchain protocol. In: Katz, J., Shacham, H. (eds.) CRYPTO 2017. LNCS, vol. 10401, pp. 357–388. Springer, Cham (2017). https://doi.org/10.1007/978-3-319-63688-7_12

16. Kokoris-Kogias, E., Jovanovic, P., Gailly, N., Khoffi, I., Gasser, L., Ford, B.: Enhancing bitcoin security and performance with strong consistency via collective signing. CoRR abs/1602.06997 (2016). http://arxiv.org/abs/1602.06997

17. Kokoris-Kogias, E., Jovanovic, P., Gasser, L., Gailly, N., Ford, B.: Omniledger: a secure, scale-out, decentralized ledger. IACR Cryptology ePrint Archive. https://eprint.iacr.org/2017/406.pdf

18. Kotla, R., Alvisi, L., Dahlin, M., Clement, A., Wong, E.: Zyzzyva: speculative byzantine fault tolerance. In: ACM SIGOPS Operating Systems Review, vol. 41, pp. 45–58. ACM (2007)

19. Lerner, S.D.: RSK: bitcoin powered smart contracts (2015). https://uploads.strikinglycdn.com/files/90847694-70f0-4668-ba7f-dd0c6b0b00a1/RootstockWhitePaperv9-Overview.pdf

20. Luu, L., Narayanan, V., Zheng, C., Baweja, K., Gilbert, S., Saxena, P.: A secure sharding protocol for open blockchains. In: Proceedings of the 2016 ACM SIGSAC Conference on Computer and Communications Security, CCS 2016, pp. 17–30. ACM, New York (2016). https://doi.org/10.1145/2976749.2978389

21. Miller, A., Xia, Y., Croman, K., Shi, E., Song, D.: The honey badger of BFT protocols. In: Proceedings of the 2016 ACM SIGSAC Conference on Computer and Communications Security, pp. 31–42. ACM (2016)

22. Nakamoto, S.: Bitcoin: A peer-to-peer electronic cash system (2008). https://bitcoin.org/bitcoin.pdf

23. Okamoto, T., Ohta, K.: Universal electronic cash. In: Feigenbaum, J. (ed.) CRYPTO 1991. LNCS, vol. 576, pp. 324–337. Springer, Heidelberg (1992). https://doi.org/10.1007/3-540-46766-1_27

24. Pass, R., Shi, E.: Hybrid consensus: efficient consensus in the permissionless model. IACR Cryptology ePrint Archive (2016). http://eprint.iacr.org/2016/917.pdf

25. Poon, J., Buterin, V.: Plasma: scalable autonomous smart contracts (2017). https://plasma.io/plasma.pdf

26. Poon, J., Dryja, T.: The bitcoin lightning network: Scalable off-chain instant payments. Technical Report (draft) (2015). https://lightning.network/lightning-network-paper.pdf

27. Popov, S.: The tangle (2014). https://iota.org/IOTA_Whitepaper.pdf

28. Ren, Z., Erkin, Z.: A scale-out blockchain for value transfer with spontaneous sharding. CoRR abs/1801.02531 (2018). http://arxiv.org/abs/1801.02531

29. Sompolinsky, Y., Zohar, A.: Phantom: A scalable blockdag protocol (2018)

30. Sompolinsky, Y., Zohar, A.: Secure high-rate transaction processing in bitcoin. In: Böhme, R., Okamoto, T. (eds.) FC 2015. LNCS, vol. 8975, pp. 507–527. Springer, Heidelberg (2015). https://doi.org/10.1007/978-3-662-47854-7_32

31. Vukolić, M.: The quest for scalable blockchain fabric: proof-of-work vs. BFT replication. In: Camenisch, J., Kesdoğan, D. (eds.) iNetSec 2015. LNCS, vol. 9591, pp. 112–125. Springer, Cham (2016). https://doi.org/10.1007/978-3-319-39028-4_9

32. Wood, G.: Ethereum: a secure decentralised generalised transaction ledger. Ethereum Project Yellow Paper 151 (2014). http://gavwood.com/paper.pdf

Sprites and State Channels: Payment Networks that Go Faster Than Lightning

Andrew Miller[1]($\boxtimes$), Iddo Bentov[2], Surya Bakshi[1], Ranjit Kumaresan[3],
and Patrick McCorry[4]

[1] University of Illinois at Urbana-Champaign, Urbana, IL, USA
soc1024@illinois.edu
[2] Cornell Tech, New York, NY, USA
[3] VISA Research, Palo Alto, CA, USA
[4] King's College London, London, UK

Abstract. Bitcoin, Ethereum and other blockchain-based cryptocurrencies, as deployed today, cannot support more than several transactions per second. Off-chain payment channels, a "layer 2" solution, are a leading approach for cryptocurrency scaling. They enable two mutually distrustful parties to rapidly send payments between each other and can be linked together to form a payment network, such that payments between any two parties can be routed through the network along a path that connects them.

We propose a novel payment channel protocol, called Sprites. The main advantage of Sprites compared with earlier protocols is a reduced "collateral cost," meaning the amount of *money* $\times$ *time* that must be locked up before disputes are settled. In the Lightning Network and Raiden, a payment across a path of ℓ channels requires locking up collateral for $\Theta(\ell\Delta)$ time, where Δ is the time to commit an on-chain transaction; every additional node on the path forces an increase in lock time. The Sprites construction provides a *constant* lock time, reducing the overall collateral cost to $\Theta(\ell + \Delta)$. Our presentation of the Sprites protocol is also modular, making use of a generic state channel abstraction. Finally, Sprites improves on prior payment channel constructions by supporting partial withdrawals and deposits without any on-chain transactions.

1 Introduction

Popular cryptocurrencies such as Bitcoin and Ethereum have at times reached their capacity limits, leading to transaction congestion and higher fees. A limit to scalability seems inherent in their model, since they are designed for security through replication, every node validates every transaction.

A leading proposal for improving the scalability of cryptocurrencies is to form a network of "off-chain" rapid payment channels. Payment channels require initial deposits of on-chain currency, but once established can support an unbounded number of payments in a session using only off-chain messages. Payments can be routed through a network of such channels, with changes in

© International Financial Cryptography Association 2019
I. Goldberg and T. Moore (Eds.): FC 2019, LNCS 11598, pp. 508–526, 2019.
https://doi.org/10.1007/978-3-030-32101-7_30

balance flowing from one intermediary to the next. Only when the channel must be settled is blockchain interaction required. The protocol is centered around a smart contract, which handles deposits and withdrawals and defines the rules for handling disputes.

In this paper we introduce the "collateral cost" of a payment channel, which roughly corresponds to the amount of time that an amount of money is locked up in the smart contract, ($money \times time$). The main result of our paper is a new payment channel protocol called Sprites that improves on the state-of-the-art in worst-case collateral cost.

Collateral Costs in Payment Channels. A chief concern for the feasibility of payment channel networks is whether or not enough collateral will be available for payments to be routed at high throughput. For every pending payment, some money in the channel must be reserved and held aside as collateral until the payment is completed, called the "locktime." Even though off-chain payments complete quickly in the typical case, if parties fail (or act to maliciously impose a delay), the collateral can be locked up for longer, until a dispute handler can be activated on-chain.

We characterize the performance of a payment channel protocol as its "collateral cost," which we think of as the lost time value of money held in reserve (i.e., in units of $money \times time$) during the locktime.[1] For a linked payment, the longer the payment path, the more total collateral must be reserved: for a payment of size $\$X$ across a path of ℓ channels, a total of $\theta(\ell \$X)$ money must be reserved. Payment channel protocols depend on a worst-case delay bound, Δ for the underlying blockchain. Essentially, Δ is a safe bound on how long it takes to observe a transaction committed on the blockchain and commit one new transaction in response, i.e., one blockchain round trip. In practical terms, Δ is roughly 1 day.

In the Lightning Network and in Raiden, the two most well-known payment networks, Δ is incorporated into the locktime parameter. However, a payment on a path of length ℓ requires an additional Δ delay added to the locktime for each link. Thus the worst-case total collateral cost of a $\$X$ payment over a path of length ℓ is $\Theta(\ell^2 \$X\Delta)$. The diameter of the Lightning network is 8, and with a payment of $10, the collateral costs for Lightning and Sprites are 360 dollar-days and 116 dollar-days, respectively. Therefore, Sprites has an approximately 3x collateral cost improvement over Lightning.

Sprites: Constant-Locktime Payment Channels. Sprites improves on Lightning and other linked-payments by avoiding the need to add an additional Δ delay for each payment on the path, reducing the collateral cost by a factor of ℓ with a constant locktime. The key insight behind this improvement is the use of a globally accessible smart contract that provides shared state between individual payment channels. As such, this is expressible in Ethereum, but does not appear possible in Bitcoin.

---

[1] The rational investor's preference is to obtain and use money now rather than later.

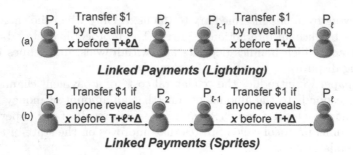

Fig. 1. The underlying currency serves as collateral for a payment network [4,19]. A payment channels allow rapid payment to another party, requiring on-chain transactions in case of disputes. Payments can be routed through multiple channels based on a condition (a). We improve the worse case delay for ℓ-hop payments, (b), to $\Theta(\ell + \Delta)$.

Although the Sprites protocol builds on prior payment channel designs, we present it from scratch in a simplified and modular way. Our presentation is based on a generic abstraction, the state channel, which serves two roles: First, it neatly encapsulates the necessary cryptography (mainly exchanging digital signatures), separating concerns in the protocol presentation. Second, it provides a flexible interface bridging the off-chain and on-chain worlds. Sprites makes use of this interface in several ways, both to define its constant-locktime dispute handler, but also to support incremental deposits and withdrawals without interruption. Our security and worst-case performance analysis ensures that intermediaries are never at risk of losing money, and that the protocol provides real time guarantees even in spite of Byzantine failures. Finally, we implemented a proof of concept of Sprites, and deployed it on the Ropsten Ethereum Testnet.[2] We found that the transaction fees required to resolve a dispute on-chain are around $\approx$\$0.20 USD as of November 2018, comparable to the Lightning Network.

2   Background and Preliminaries

2.1   Blockchains and Smart Contracts

At a high level, a blockchain is a distributed ledger of balances. The primary use of blockchains are as decentralized cryptocurrencies, which allow users to exchange a native token without trusted intermediaries. Transactions are made by users (addressed by pseudonyms) and published on the blockchain (on-chain transaction) to be confirmed by the rest of the network. Decentralized cryptocurrencies like Ethereum, however, require state replication across all nodes and can not support more than several transactions per second.

---

[2] The reference implementation can be found at https://github.com/amiller/sprites, Sprites: 0x85DF43619C04d2eFFD7e14AF643aef119E7c8414, Manager: 0x62E2D8cfE64a28584390B58C4aaF71b29D31F087.

Concretely, a blockchain ensures the following properties:

1. All parties can agree on a consistent log of committed transactions
2. All parties are guaranteed to be able to commit new transactions in a predictable amount of time, Δ.

The time delay, Δ, is meant to capture the worst-case bound on how long it takes to learn about a new transaction, then to publish a transaction in response. We say one unit of time is the maximum time needed to transmit a point-to-point message to any other party.

Modern cryptocurrencies, like Ethereum, also feature smart contracts. A smart contract is an autonomous piece of code that exists at an address in the Ethereum blockchain. It can hold funds like any other address and can act on those funds through its functionality. To execute a piece of code in the contract, a user account must submit a transaction to it specifying the method to be executed. The method's execution may change the state of the contract's balance or persistent storage, and the changes are eventually committed to the blockchain. The main benefits of contracts are that they are essentially autonomous machines that always execute their code correctly. Throughout this paper, we show smart contracts using pseudocode resembling reactive processes that respond to method invocations.

2.2   Blockchain Scaling

Proposed scalability improvements fall in roughly two complementary categories. The first, "on-chain scaling," aims to make the blockchain itself run faster [7,9,11,17]. A recurring theme is that the additional performance comes from introducing stronger trust assumptions about the nodes.

The second category of scaling approaches, which includes our work, is to develop "off-chain protocols" that minimize the use of the blockchain itself. Instead, parties transact primarily by exchanging off-chain messages (point-to-point messages), and interact with the blockchain only to settle disputes or withdraw funds.

2.3   Off-Chain Payment Channels

There have been many previous payment channel constructions prior to this work. However, for simplicity we present only the approach using signatures over round numbers [2,15,18]. We also make the assumption that transactions can depend on a "global" event recorded in the blockchain—and therefore Sprites cannot (we conjecture) be implemented in Bitcoin.

An off-chain payment channel protocol roughly comprises the following three phases:

Channel Opening. The channel is initially opened with an on-chain deposit transaction. This reserves a quantity of digital currency and binds it to the smart contract program.

Off-Chain Payments. To make an off-chain payment, the parties exchange signed messages, reflecting the updated balance. For example, the current state would be represented as a signed message $(\sigma_A, \sigma_R, i, \$A, \$B)$, where a pair of signatures σ_A and σ_B are valid for the message $(i, \$A, \$B)$, where $\$A$ (resp. $\$B$) is the balance of Alice (resp. Bob) at round number i. Each party locally keeps track of the current balance, corresponding to the most recent signed message.

Dispute Handling. The blockchain smart contract serves as a "dispute handler." It is activated when either party suspects a failure, or wishes to close the channel and withdraw the remaining balance. The dispute handler remains active for a fixed time during which either party can submit evidence (e.g., signed messages) of their last-known balance. The dispute handler accepts the evidence with the highest round number and disburses the money accordingly.

The security guarantees, roughly, are the following:

(Liveness): Either party can initiate a withdrawal, and the withdrawal is processed within a predictable amount of time. If both parties are honest, then payments are processed very rapidly (i.e., with only off-chain messages).

(No Counterparty Risk): The payment channel interface offers Bob a local estimate of his current balance (i.e., how many payments he has received). Alice, of course, knows how much she has sent. The "no counterparty risk" property guarantees that local views are accurate, in the sense that each party can actually withdraw (at least) the amount they expect.

2.4   Linked Payments and Payment Channel Networks

Duplex payment channels alone cannot solve the scalability problem; opening each channel requires an on-chain transaction before any payments can be made. To connect every pair of parties in the network by a direct channel would require $O(N^2)$ transactions.

Poon and Dryja [19] developed a method for linking payments across a path of channels where the capacity within each channel is sufficient to facilitate the transfer.

Linked payments are based on the "hashed timelock contract" (HTLC) for conditional payments that relies on a single hash $h = \mathcal{H}(x)$ to synchronize a payment across all channels. We denote an HTLC conditional payment from P_1 to P_2 by the following:

$$P_1 \xrightarrow[h,T]{\$X} P_2$$

which says that a payment of $\$X$ can be claimed by P_2 if the preimage of h is revealed via an on-chain transaction. In the optimistic case, the sender can create and send a new *unconditional* payment with a higher round number. Otherwise, the conditional payment can be canceled after a deadline T. Operationally, opening a conditional payment means signing a message that defines the deadline, the amount of money, and the hash of the secret $h = \mathcal{H}(x)$; and finally sending the signed message to the recipient.

Consider a path of parties, $P_1, ..., P_\ell$, where P_1 is the sender, P_ℓ is the recipient, and the rest are intermediaries. In a linked off-chain payment, Each node P_i opens a conditional payment to P_{i+1}, one after another.

$$P_1 \xrightarrow[h, T_1 = T_{\ell-1} + \Theta(\ell\Delta)]{\$X} P_2 \ldots P_{\ell-1} \xrightarrow[h, T_{\ell-1}]{\$X} P_\ell \qquad (\pounds)$$

Note that the hash condition h is the same for all channels. However, the deadlines may be different. In fact, Lightning requires that $T_1 = T_\ell + \Theta(\ell\Delta)$ as we explain shortly. The desired security properties of linked payments are the following (in addition to those for basic channels given above):

(Liveness): The entire chain of payments concludes (success or cancellation) within a bounded amount of on-chain cycles. If all parties on the path are honest, then the entire payment should complete successfully using only off-chain messages.

(No Counterparty Risk): A key desired property is that intermediaries should not be placed at risk of losing funds. During the linked payment protocol, a portion of the channel balance may be "locked" and held in reserve, but it must returned by the conclusion of the protocol.[3] This property poses a challenge that constrains the choice of deadlines $\{T_i\}$ in Lightning. Consider the following scenario from the point of view of party P_i.

$$\ldots P_{i-1} \xrightarrow[h, T_i]{\$X} P_i \xrightarrow[h, T_{i+1}]{\$X} P_{i+1} \ldots$$

We need to ensure that if the outgoing conditional payment to P_{i+1} completes, then the incoming payment from P_{i-1} also completes. In the worst case where P_{i+1} attempts to introduce the maximum delay for P_i (which we call the "petty" attacker), the party P_i only learns about x because x is published in the blockchain at the last possible instant, at time T_{i+1}. In order to complete the incoming payment, if P_{i-1} is also petty then P_i must publish x to the blockchain by time T_i. It must therefore be the case that $T_i \geq T_{i+1} + \Delta$, meaning P_i is given an additional grace period of time Δ (the worst-case bound on the time for one on-chain round).

We use the term "collateral cost" to denote the product of the amount of money $\$X$ multiplied by the locktime (i.e., from when the conditional payment is opened to the time it is completed or canceled). Since the payment can be claimed by time $T_\ell + \Theta(\ell\Delta)$ in the worst case, the overall collateral cost is $\Theta(\ell^2 \$X\Delta)$ for each party (see Fig. 1(a)). The worst-case collateral cost may occur because of failures or malicious attacks intended to slow the network. The main goal of our Sprites construction (Sect. 3) is to reduce this collateral cost.

---

[3] The intermediary nodes in a path can also be incentivized to participate in the route if the sender allocates an extra fee that will be shared among them.

3   Overview of the Sprites Construction

We first give a high-level overview of our construction, focusing on the main improvements versus Lightning [19]: constant locktimes and incremental withdrawals/deposits. We assume as a starting point the duplex payment channel construction described earlier in Sect. 2.3 and presented in related works [2,15,18]).

3.1   Constant Locktime Linked Payments

To support linked payments across multiple payment channels, we use a novel variation of the standard "hashed timelock contract" technique [1,10,16,19].

We start by defining a simple smart contract, called the PreimageManager (PM), which simply records assertions of the form "the preimage x of hash $h = \mathcal{H}(x)$ was published on the blockchain before time T_{Expiry}." This can be implemented in Ethereum as a smart contract with two methods, publish and published (see Fig. 5).

Next, we extend the duplex payment channel construction with a conditional payment feature, which can be linked across a path of channels as shown:

$$P_1 \xrightarrow[\mathsf{PM}[h,T_{\mathsf{Expiry}}]]{\$X} P_2 \dots P_{\ell-1} \xrightarrow[\mathsf{PM}[h,T_{\mathsf{Expiry}}]]{\$X} P_\ell \qquad (\star)$$

In the above, the conditional payment of $\$X$ from P_1 to P_2 can be completed by a command from P_1, canceled by a command from P_2, or in case of dispute, will complete if and only if the PM contract receives the value x prior to T_{Expiry}. As with the existing linked payments constructions [15,18], operationally this means extending the structure of the signed messages (i.e., the off-chain state) to include a hash h, a deadline T_{Expiry}, and an amount $\$X$. To execute the linked payment, each party first opens a conditional payment with the party to their right, each with the same conditional hash. Note that here the deadline T_{Expiry} is also a common value across all channels.

The difference between Sprites and Lightning is how Sprites handles disputes. Instead of locally enforcing the preimage x be revealed on time, in Sprites we delegate this to the global PM contract. In short, each Sprites contract defines a dispute handler that queries PM to check if x was revealed on time, guaranteeing that all channels (if disputed on-chain) will settle in a consistent way (either all completed or all canceled). It then suffices to use a single common expiry time T_{Expiry}, as indicated above $(\star)$.

The preimage x is initially known to the recipient; after the final conditional payment to the recipient is opened, the recipient publishes x, and each party completes their outgoing payment. Optimistically, (i.e., if no parties fail), the process finishes after only $\ell + 1$ off-chain rounds. Otherwise, in the worst case, any honest parties that complete their outgoing payment submit x to the PM contract, guaranteeing that their incoming payment will complete. This procedure ensures that each party's collateral is locked for a maximum of $O(\ell + \Delta)$ rounds.

The worst-case delay scenarios for both Lightning and Sprites are illustrated in Fig. 2. In the worst-case, the attacker publishes x at the latest possible time. However, the use of a global synchronizing gadget, the PM contract, ensures that all payments along the path are settled consistently. In contrast, Lightning [19] (and other prior payment channel networks [4,5,12,15]) require the preimage to be submitted to *each* payment channel contract separately, leading to longer locktimes.

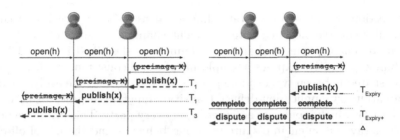

Fig. 2. The worst-case delay scenario, in Lightning (left) and in Sprites (right). The two parties shown are "petty," dropping off-chain messages (~~striken red~~) after the initial open, and sending on-chain transactions (blue) only at the last minute. Disputes in Lightning may cascade, whereas in Sprite they are handled simultaneously. (Color figure online)

3.2 Supporting Incremental Deposits and Withdrawals

A Lightning channel must be closed and re-opened in order for either party to withdraw or deposit currency. Furthermore, all pending conditions must be settled on-chain and no new off-chain transactions can occur for an on-chain round ($O(\Delta)$ time) until a new channel is opened on the blockchain. On the other hand, Sprites permits either party to deposit/withdraw a portion of currency without interrupting the channel.

To support incremental deposits, we extend the off-chain state to include local views, deposits$_{\{L,R\}}$, which reflect the total amount of deposits from each party. If one party proposes a view that is too stale (i.e., more than some bound $O(\Delta)$ behind), then the other party initiates an on-chain dispute. Of course, the on-chain dispute handler can read the current on-chain state directly.

To support incremental withdrawals, we implement the following. We extend the off-chain state with an optional withdrawal value wd$_i$, which can be set whenever either party wishes to make a withdrawal. The on-chain smart contract is then extended with an **update** method that either party can invoke to submit a signed message with a withdrawal value. Rather than close, the smart contract verifies the signatures, disburses the withdrawal, and advances the round number to prevent replay attacks. Further off-chain payments can continue, even while waiting for the blockchain to confirm the withdrawal.

Incremental withdrawals and deposits are also supported in another Ethereum payment network called Raiden [15]. Like Sprites, Raiden allows incremental deposits to be made at any time by any party *without* interrupting the channel. However, unlike Sprites, Raiden does not currently support partial withdrawals and forces a channel to close before any withdrawal is possible.

4   The State Channel Abstraction

In this section, we present the state channel abstraction, which is the key to our modular construction of Sprites payment channels. A state channel generalizes the off-chain payment channel mechanism as described in Sect. 2.3. The state channel primitive exposes a simple interface: a consistent replicated state machine shared between two or more parties. The state machine evolves according to an arbitrary, application-defined transition function. It proceeds in rounds, during each of which inputs are accepted from every party. This primitive neatly abstracts away the on-chain dispute handling behavior and the use of off-chain signed messages in the optimistic case.

Each time the parties provide input to the state channel, they exchange signed messages on the newly updated state, along with an increasing round number. If at any time a party aborts or responds with invalid data, remaining parties can raise a dispute by submitting the most recent agreed-upon state to the blockchain, along with inputs for the next round. Once activated, the dispute handler proceeds in two phases. First, the dispute handler waits for one on-chain round, during which any party can submit their evidence (i.e., the most recently signed agreed-upon state). The dispute handler checks the signatures on the submitted evidence, and ultimately commits the state with the highest round number. Finally, after committing the previous state, the dispute handler then allows parties to submit new inputs for the next round.

To summarize, the security guarantees of a state channel are:

(Liveness): Each party is able to provide input to each iteration of the state machine, and a corrupt party cannot stall.

(Safety): Each party's local view of the most recent state is finalized and consistent with every other party's view.

A novel feature of our model is a general way to express side effects between the state channel and the blockchain. Besides the inputs provided by parties, the application-specific transition function can also depend on auxiliary input from an external contract C on the blockchain (which, for example, can collect currency deposits submitted by either party). The transition function can also define an auxiliary output for each transition, which is translated to a method invocation on the external smart contract C (e.g., triggering a disbursement of **coins**). This feature generalizes the handling of withdrawals as transfers of on-chain currency.

4.1 Instantiating State Channels

We focus on explaining the behavior of the dispute handler smart contract, $\mathsf{Contract}_{\mathsf{State}}$, defined in Fig. 3; a detailed description of the local behavior for each party is deferred to the Appendix (A.4). At a high level, the off-chain state can be advanced by having parties exchange a signed message of the following form (for the party P_i):

$$\sigma_{r,i} := \mathsf{Sign}_{P_i}(r\|\mathsf{state}_r\|\mathsf{out}_r) \tag{1}$$

where r is the number of the current round, state_r is the result after applying the state transition function to every party's inputs, and out_r is the resulting blockchain output (or $\perp$ if this transition makes no output). In the appendix we describe a leader-based broadcast protocol used to help parties optimistically agree on a vector of inputs. We now explain how $\mathsf{Contract}_{\mathsf{State}}$ handles disputes.

Protocol $\varPi_{\mathsf{State}}(U, P_1, ... P_N)$

Contract $\mathsf{Contract}_{\mathsf{State}}$

Initialize bestRound $:= -1$
Initialize state $:= \emptyset$
Initialize flag $:= \mathsf{OK}$
Initialize deadline $:= \perp$
Initialize applied $:= \emptyset$
on **contract input** evidence(r, state$'$, out, $\{\sigma_{r,j}\}$):
  discard if $r \leq$ bestRound
  verify all signatures on the message ($r\|$state$'\|$out)
  if flag $==$ DISPUTE then
    flag $:= \mathsf{OK}$
    emit EventOffchain(bestRound $+ 1$)
  bestRound $:= r$
  state $:=$ state$'$
  invoke C.aux_output(out)
  applied $:=$ applied $\cup \{r\}$

on **contract input** dispute(r) at time T:
  discard if $r \neq$ bestRound $+ 1$
  discard if flag $\neq \mathsf{OK}$
  set flag $:= \mathsf{DISPUTE}$
  set deadline $:= T + \Delta$
  emit EventDispute(r, deadline)
on **contract input** input(r, $v_{r,j}$) from party P_j:
  if this is the first such activation, store $v_{r,j}$
on **contract input** resolve(r) at time T:
  discard if $r \neq$ bestRound $+ 1$
  discard if flag $\neq \mathsf{PENDING}$
  discard if $T <$ deadline
  apply the update function state $:=$ U(state, $\{v_{r,j}\}$, aux$_{in}$), where the default value is used for any $v_{r,j}$ such that party P_j has not provided input
  set flag $:= \mathsf{OK}$
  emit EventOnchain(r, state)
  bestRound $:=$ bestRound $+ 1$

Fig. 3. Contract portion of the protocol $\varPi_{\mathsf{State}}$ for implementing a general purpose state channel.

Raising a Dispute. Suppose in round r a party fails to receive off-chain signatures from all the other parties for some (state_r, out_r) before an $O(1)$ timeout. They then (1) invoke the **evidence** method to provide evidence that round $(r - 1)$ has already been agreed upon, and (2) invoke the **dispute**(r) method, which notifies all the other parties (EventDispute).

Resolving Disputes Off-Chain. Once raised, a dispute for round r will be resolved in one of two ways. First, another party may invoke the `evidence(r', ...)` method to provide evidence that an r or a later round $r' \geq r$ has already been agreed upon off-chain, clearing the dispute (`EventOffchain`). This occurs, for example, if a corrupted node attempts to dispute an earlier already-settled round.

Resolving Disputes On-Chain. Alternatively, if a party P_j has no more recent evidence than $(r - 1)$, they invoke the `input` method on-chain with their input $v_{r,j}$. After the deadline $T + \Delta$, any party can invoke the `resolve` method to apply the update function to the on-chain inputs (`EventOnchain`).

Avoiding On-Chain/Off-Chain Conflicts. We now explain how we avoid a subtle concurrency hazard. Suppose in round r, a party receives the `Dispute(r, T)` event, and shortly thereafter (say, $T + \epsilon$, for some $\epsilon > 0$), receives a final signature completing the off-chain evidence for round r. It would be incorrect for the party to then invoke `evidence(r, ...)`, since this invocation may not be confirmed until after $T + \Delta + \epsilon$. If a malicious adversary equivocates, providing $\text{input}(v'_{r,j})$ on-chain but $v_{r,j}$ off-chain, the off-chain evidence would arrive too late. Instead, upon receiving a `Dispute(r)` event, if the party does not already have evidence for round r, it pauses the off-chain routine until the dispute is resolved.

Update function U_{Pay}	**Auxiliary smart contract**
$U_{\text{Pay}}(\text{state}, (\text{input}_L, \text{input}_R), \text{aux}_{in})$:	$\text{Contract}_{\text{Pay}}(P_L, P_R)$
if state $= \bot$, set state $:= (0, \emptyset, 0, \emptyset)$	Initially, $\text{deposits}_L := 0, \text{deposits}_R := 0$
parse state as $(\text{cred}_L, \text{oldarr}_L, \text{cred}_R, \text{oldarr}_R)$	on **contract input** $\text{deposit}(\text{coins}(\$X))$ from
parse aux_{in} as $\{\text{deposits}_i\}_{i \in \{L,R\}}$	P_i :
for $i \in \{L, R\}$:	$\text{deposits}_i \mathrel{+}= \$X$
if $\text{input}_i = \bot$ then $\text{input}_i := (\emptyset, 0)$	$\text{aux}_{in}.\text{send}(\text{deposits}_L, \text{deposits}_R)$
parse each input_i as $(\text{arr}_i, \text{wd}_i)$	on **contract input** $\text{output}(\text{aux}_{out})$:
$\text{pay}_i := 0, \text{newarr}_i := \emptyset$	parse aux_{out} as $(\text{wd}_L, \text{wd}_R)$
while $\text{arr}_i \neq \emptyset$	for $i \in \{L, R\}$ send $\text{coins}(\text{wd}_i)$ to P_i
pop first element of arr_i into e	**Local protocol Π_{Pay} for party P_i**
if $e + \text{pay}_i \leq \text{deposits}_i + \text{cred}_i$:	initialize $\text{pay}_i := 0, \text{wd}_i := 0, \text{paid}_i = 0$
append e to newarr_i	on **receiving state** $(\text{cred}_L, \text{new}_L, \text{cred}_R, \text{new}_R)$
$\text{pay}_i \mathrel{+}= e$	from Π_{State},
if $\text{wd}_i > \text{deposits}_i + \text{cred}_i - \text{pay}_i$: $\text{wd}_i := 0$	foreach e in new_i: set $\text{paid}_i \mathrel{+}= e$
$\text{cred}_L \mathrel{+}= \text{pay}_R - \text{pay}_L - \text{wd}_L$	provide $(\text{arr}_i, \text{wd}_i)$ as input to Π_{State}
$\text{cred}_R \mathrel{+}= \text{pay}_L - \text{pay}_R - \text{wd}_R$	$\text{arr}_i := \emptyset$
if $\text{wd}_L \neq 0$ or $\text{wd}_R \neq 0$:	on **input** $\text{pay}(\$X)$ from $\text{Contract}_{\text{Pay}}$,
$\text{aux}_{out} := (\text{wd}_L, \text{wd}_R)$	if $\$X \leq \text{Contract}_{\text{Pay}}.\text{deposits}_i + \text{paid}_i - \text{pay}_i -$
otherwise $\text{aux}_{out} := \bot$	wd_i:
state $:= (\text{cred}_L, \text{newarr}_L, \text{cred}_R, \text{newarr}_R)$	append $\$X$ to arr_i
return $(\text{aux}_{out}, \text{state})$	$\text{pay}_i \mathrel{+}= \$X$
	on **input** $\text{withdraw}(\$X)$ from $\text{Contract}_{\text{Pay}}$,
	if $\$X \leq \text{Contract}_{\text{Pay}}.\text{deposits}_i + \text{paid}_i - \text{pay}_i -$
	wd_i then $\text{wd}_i \mathrel{+}= \$X$

Fig. 4. Implementation of a duplex payment channel with the Π_{State} primitive.

4.2   Modeling Payment Channels with State Channels

To demonstrate the use of the Π_{state} abstraction, we now construct a duplex payment channel (e.g., as in [2,15,18]). In Fig. 4, we give a construction that realizes Π_{Pay} given a state channel protocol Π_{State}. Our construction consists of (1) an update function, U_{Pay}, which defines the structure of the state and the inputs provided by the parties, (2) an auxiliary contract $\mathsf{Contract_{Pay}}$ that handles deposits and withdrawals and (3) local behavior for each party.

The update function U_{Pay} encodes the state with two fields, cred_i and $\mathsf{deposists}_i$, instead of a single "balance" field. This encoding is designed to cope with the fact that blockchain transactions are not synchronized with state updates and may arrive out of order. So when $\mathsf{Contract_{Pay}}$ receives a deposit of $\mathbf{coins}(x)$, we have it accumulate in a monotonically increasing value, $\mathsf{deposits}_i$, that can safely be passed to $\mathtt{aux\_input}$. The state then includes cred_i as a balance offset, such that the balance available is $\mathsf{deposits}_i + \mathsf{cred}_i$.

Since the state channel abstraction handles synchronization between the parties, when reasoning about the security of the payment channel we need only to consider the update function. Notice that each party's balance can only be lowered by a pay input provided by them, and the overall sum of balances, withdrawals, and deposits is maintained as an invariant.

As a consequence of our generic state channel, each payment requires two signatures and two rounds of communication, from the sender to the recipient (assuming the sender is the leader, see Appendix A.4) and back again. An optimization taken in Lightning and in Raiden is to omit the return trip if receipt of the payment is not necessary. The on-chain dispute resolution requires the same number of transactions as in Lightning: one transaction establishes the deadline ($\mathtt{dispute}$, $\mathtt{evidence}$, and $\mathtt{input}$ can be invoked simultaneously) and $\mathtt{resolve}$ applies the next update on-chain.

5   Linked Payments from State Channels

In this section we complete the Sprites construction, focusing on how we link payments together along a path of payment channels from a sender to receiver. The challenge is to ensure the collateral provided by intermediaries is returned to them within a bounded time.

Our construction for linked payment chains is modular, relying on multiple instances of duplex channels Π_{Pay}. Like Π_{Pay}, the definition for linked payments consists of an update function U_{Linked}, an auxiliary contract, and a local protocol for each party. Figure 5 defines the update function, the auxiliary contract and the preimage management contract, $\mathsf{Contract_{PM}}$ (a contract accessed through the auxiliary contract). The update function U_{Linked} is an outer layer around the U_{Pay} function (Fig. 4), but extends state with a status flag to include support for conditional payments.

To establish a path of linked payments off-chain, the initial sender P_1 first creates a secret x, shares it with the recipient P_ℓ, and creates an outgoing conditional payment to P_2 using $h = \mathcal{H}(x)$. Each subsequent party P_i in turn, upon receiving the incoming conditional payment, establishes an outgoing conditional payment to P_{i+1}. Once the recipient P_ℓ receives the final conditional payment, it multicasts x to every other party.

When a conditional payment is in-flight, all parties on the path must wait for the preimage to be revealed to them by the receiver, P_ℓ, before T_{Crit}; if it arrives on time P_i completes the outgoing payment off-chain. If the outgoing payment doesn't complete before T_{Crit}, but P_i has received the preimage, then P_i sends it to the preimage manager, $\mathsf{Contract}_{\mathsf{PM}}$. By T_{Expiry}, if the preimage was published the payment is completed; otherwise, it is canceled (by all P_i, because publishing the preimage is a global event). Finally, if after T_{Dispute} the payment has failed to complete or cancel, the party raises a dispute and forces the payment be completed or canceled on-chain.

Security Analysis of Linked Payments. Our model begins with parties P_i through P_ℓ that have established $\ell - 1$ payment channels, such that Π_{Pay}^i denotes the payment channel established between parties P_i and P_{i+1}. Given the state channel abstraction, it is easy to check that the desired properties described earlier (Sect. 2.3) are exhibited by this protocol:

(Liveness). If all parties P_1 through P_ℓ are honest, and if sufficient balance is available in each payment channel, then the chained payment completes successfully after $O(\ell)$ rounds. More specifically, for each channel Π_{Pay}, the outgoing balance $\Pi_{\mathsf{Pay}}^i.\mathsf{cred}_R$ is increased by \$$x$ and each incoming balance $\Pi_{\mathsf{Pay}}^i.\mathsf{cred}_L$ is decreased by \$$x$. If the sender and receiver, P_1 and P_ℓ, are both honest the payment either completes or cancels after $O(\ell + \Delta)$ rounds.

(No Counterparty Risk). Even if some parties are corrupt, no honest party on the path should lose any money. In the dispute case, the preimage manager, $\mathsf{Contract}_{\mathsf{PM}}$, acts like a global condition. If the preimage manager receives x before time T_{Expiry}, then *every* conditional payment that is disputed will complete. Otherwise they are canceled. Therefore, for an honest party that receives x before $T_{\mathsf{Expiry}} - \Delta$, it is safe to `complete` their outgoing payment. In the worst case then can use the preimage manager and claim their incoming payment.

Implementation and Performance Analysis. We created a proof-of-concept implementation using Solidity and pyethereum available online[4]. In the typical case, the off-chain communication pattern in Sprites is similar to that of Lightning. We need one round of communication between each adjacent pair of parties to open each conditional payment, and finally one round to complete all the payments.

In the worst-case scenario, each channel that must be resolved via the dispute handler requires one on-chain transaction to initiate the dispute and send the preimage to $\mathsf{Contract}_{\mathsf{PM}}$, and, later, a transaction to complete the dispute and

---

[4] https://github.com/amiller/sprites.

withdraw the balance (Section 4.1). Based on our implementation, the dispute process costs up to 137294 gas per disputed channel, or $\approx\$0.20$ in November 2018. For comparison, in the Lightning Network the typical cost of closing a channel is 0.00002025 BTC $(\approx\$0.072)$[5].

Protocol $\Pi_{\mathsf{Linked}}(\$X, T, P_1, ... P_\ell)$

Let $T_{\mathsf{Expiry}} := T + 6\ell + \Delta$.
Let $T_{\mathsf{Crit}} := T_{\mathsf{Expiry}} - \Delta$
Let $T_{\mathsf{Dispute}} := T_{\mathsf{Expiry}} + \Delta + 3$.

Update Function
$U_{\mathsf{Linked},\$X}(\mathsf{state}, \mathsf{in_L}, \mathsf{in_R}, \mathsf{aux}_{in})$

if $\mathsf{state} = \bot$, set $\mathsf{state} := (\mathsf{init}, \bot, (\mathbf{0,0}))$
parse state as $(\mathsf{flag}, h, (\mathsf{cred_L}, \mathsf{cred_R}))$
parse in_i as $(\mathsf{cmd}_i, \mathsf{in}_i^{\mathbf{Pay}})$, for $i \in \{\mathsf{L}, \mathsf{R}\}$
if $\mathsf{cmd_L} = \mathsf{open}(h')$ and $\mathsf{flag} = \mathsf{init}$, then
  set $\mathsf{cred_L} \mathrel{-}= \$X$, $\mathsf{flag} := \mathsf{inflight}$, and
  $h := h'$
else if $\mathsf{cmd_L} = \mathsf{complete}$ and $\mathsf{flag} = \mathsf{inflight}$,
  set $\mathsf{cred_L} \mathrel{+}= \$X$, and $\mathsf{flag} := \mathsf{complete}$
else if $\mathsf{cmd_R} = \mathsf{cancel}$ and $\mathsf{flag} = \mathsf{inflight}$,
  set $\mathsf{cred_L} \mathrel{+}= \$X$ and $\mathsf{flag} := \mathsf{cancel}$
else if $\mathsf{cmd_R} = \mathsf{dispute}$ or $\mathsf{cmd_L} = \mathsf{dispute}$,
and $\mathsf{flag} = \mathsf{inflight}$, and current time $>$
T_{Expiry}, then
  $\mathsf{aux_{out}} := (\mathsf{dispute}, h, \$X)$ and $\mathsf{flag} = \mathsf{dispute}$
let $\mathbf{state^{Pay}} := (\mathsf{cred_L}, \mathsf{cred_R})$
$(\mathbf{aux_{out}^{Pay}, state^{Pay}}) := U_{\mathsf{Pay}}(\mathbf{state^{Pay}}, \mathsf{in}_L^{\mathbf{Pay}}, \mathsf{in}_R^{\mathbf{Pay}},$
$\mathsf{aux_{in}})$
set $\mathsf{state} := (\mathsf{flag}, h, \mathbf{state^{Pay}})$
return $(\mathsf{state}, (\mathsf{aux_{out}}, \mathbf{aux_{out}^{Pay}}))$

Auxiliary contract $\mathsf{Contract_{Linked}}$

Copy the auxiliary contract from Figure 5, renaming the output handler to $\mathbf{output^{Pay}}$
on **contract input** $\mathsf{output}(\mathsf{aux_{out}^*})$:
  parse $\mathsf{aux_{out}}$ as $(\mathsf{aux_{out}}, \mathsf{aux_{out}^{Pay}})$
  if $\mathsf{aux_{out}^*}$ parses as $(\mathsf{dispute}, h, \$X)$ then
    if $\mathsf{PM.published}(T_{\mathsf{Expiry}}, h)$, then
      $\mathsf{deposits_R} \mathrel{+}= \$X$
    else
      $\mathsf{deposits_L} \mathrel{+}= \$X$
    $\mathsf{aux_{in}} := (\mathsf{deposits_L}, \mathsf{deposits_R})$
  invoke $\mathbf{output^{Pay}}(\mathsf{aux_{out}^{Pay}})$

Global Contract $\mathsf{Contract_{PM}}$

initially $\mathsf{timestamp}[]$ is an empty mapping
on **contract input** $\mathsf{publish}(x)$ at time T:
  if $\mathcal{H}(x) \notin \mathsf{timestamp}$: then set $\mathsf{timestamp}[\mathcal{H}(x)] := T$
constant function $\mathsf{published}(h, T')$:
  return True if $h \in \mathsf{timestamp}$ and $\mathsf{timestamp}[h] \leq T'$
  return False otherwise

Fig. 5. Smart contract for protocol Π_{Linked} that implements linked payments with the Π_{State} primitive. Parts of $U_{\mathsf{Linked},\$X}$ that are delegated to the underlying U_{Pay} are in **bold** to help readability. See Appendix (Fig. 6) for local behavior.

6   Related Works

The first off-chain protocols were Bitcoin payment channels, due to Spilman [23]. These channels, however, only allow for payments to be made in one direction— from Alice to Bob. Subsequent channel constructions by Decker and Wattenhofer [4] as well as Poon and Dryja [19] supported "duplex" payments back-and-forth from either part, however, they require an every growing list of keys to defend against malicious behavior.

---

[5] Representative Lightning transaction https://www.blockchain.com/btc/tx/ c9e6a9200607871e18fcfdd54dcb0da17ac8eca005101b82c8a807def9885d3e.

Improvements to Payment Channels. Gervais et al. [8] proposed a protocol for rebalancing payment channels entirely off-chain. Dziembowski et al. [5] developed a mechanism for virtual payment channel overlays, enabling two parties with a path to establish a rapid payment channel between them. A limitation of payment channels is that their security requires honest parties to be online at all times. McCorry et al. [13] discuss how channel participants can hire third parties to arbitrate channel disputes (see Sect. 2.3). These ideas are all complementary to our work and we think could be combined.

Routing in Payment Channels. While in our presentation we assume the payment path is given, in reality finding a route is a challenging problem. Sprites can be used with proposed routing protocols [20–22] which are complimentary. Although the T_{Expire} deadline is defined in terms of the path length, ℓ (see Fig. 5), to avoid revealing path length for privacy, we can pad the deadline to a conservative upper bound. Given that measurements of the Lightning Network [6] today show a diameter of 8, we suppose an upper bound of $\ell = 16$ is conservative. The expiration time is dominated by the block time Δ (1 day, if we follow Lightning and Raiden).

Malavolta et al. [12] identified a potential for deadlock when multiple concurrent payments need to use the same link. They propose a solution, Rayo, that guarantees non-blocking progress. Rayo assumes the existence of global identifiers for payments and a global payment ordering. We conjecture such a global identifier can be implemented on top of Sprites payment channels; for example, it can be derived from the channel address and hash of the proposed state.

Credit Networks. Malavolta et al. [14] developed a protocol for privacy-preserving credit networks. The main difference between a payment channel and a credit line is that payment channel balances are fully backed by on-chain deposits, and can be settled without any counterparty risk, where lines of credit seem inherently to expose counterparty risk.

7 Conclusion

Cryptocurrencies face several ongoing challenges: they must be scaled up beyond several transactions per second to accommodate increasing user demand and compete with centralized alternatives. Off-chain payment channel networks are currently a leading proposal to scale blockchain-based cryptocurrencies. However, the current state of the art payment network scaling solutions, like Lightning [19], require collateral to be locked up for a maximum period that scales linearly with the number of hops, $O(\ell\Delta)$. In this paper, we introduced a construction of payment channels and networks, Sprites, that drastically improves upon the current worst-case locktime—reducing it to a constant, $O(\ell + \Delta)$. We also introduce a modular construction for payment channels, building on top of a generalized state channel primitive. State channels abstract away all blockchain interaction, allow arbitrary off-chain protocols (e.g. channels and linked payments) to be more easily defined and analyzed.

Our constant locktime construction relies on a global contract mechanism, which is easily expressed in Ethereum, although it cannot (we conjecture) be emulated in Bitcoin without modification to its scripting system. We therefore pose the following question for future work: what minimal modifications to Bitcoin script would enable constant locktimes?

A   Appendix

A.1   Acknowledgements

This work is funded in part by NSF grants CNS-1801321 and CNS-1617676 and a gift from DTR Foundation.

A.2   Further Discussion

Supporting Fees. Participants who act as intermediaries in a payment path contribute their resources to provide a useful service to the sender and recipient. The intermediaries' collateral is tied up for the duration of the payment, but the sender and recipient would not be able to complete their payment otherwise. Therefore the sender may provide a fee along with the payment, which can be claimed by each intermediary upon completion of the payment. To achieve this, each conditional payment along the path should include a slightly less amount than the last; the difference can be pocketed by the intermediary upon completion. The following example provides a \$1 fee to each intermediary, P_2 and P_3.

$$P_1 \xrightarrow[\text{PM}[h,T_{\text{Expiry}}]]{\$X+2} P_2 \xrightarrow[\text{PM}[h,T_{\text{Expiry}}]]{\$X+1} P_3 \xrightarrow[\text{PM}[h,T_{\text{Expiry}}]]{\$X} P_4$$

A.3   Details of the Linked Payments Construction

In the body of the paper (Sect. 4) we presented the update function and auxiliary smart contracts (Figure 5) for the state channel protocol Π_{Linked}. In Fig. 6 we define the local behavior of the parties.

A.4   Local Protocol for the State Channel Construction

In the body of the paper (Figure 3) we presented the smart contract portion of the state channel protocol. In Fig. 7 we define the local behavior of the parties.

Reaching Agreement Off-Chain. The main role of the local portion of the protocol is to reach agreement on which inputs to process next. To facilitate this we have one party, P_1, act as the leader. The leader receives inputs from each party, batches them, and then requests signatures from each party on the entire batch. After receiving all such signatures, the leader sends a COMMIT message containing the signatures to each party. This resembles the "fast-path" case of a fault tolerant consensus protocol [3]; However, in our setting, there is no need for a view-change procedure to guarantee liveness when the leader fails; instead the fall-back option is to use the on-chain smart contract.

Protocol $\Pi_{\text{Linked}}(\$X, T, P_1, ... P_\ell)$

Local protocol for sender, P_1

on **input** pay from the environment:

$x \xleftarrow{\$} \{0,1\}^\lambda$, and $h \leftarrow \mathcal{H}(x)$

pass (open, h, $\$X$, T_{Expiry}) as input to Π^1_{State}

send (preimage, x) to P_ℓ

if (preimage, x) is received from P_2 before T_{Expiry}, then pass complete to Π^1_{State}

at time $T_{\text{Expiry}} + \Delta$, if PM.published($T_{\text{Expiry}}, h$), then

pass input complete to Π^1_{State}

at time T_{Dispute}, then pass input dispute to Π^1_{State}

Local protocol for party P_i, where $2 \leq i \leq \ell - 1$

on **receiving state** (inflight, h, _) from Π^{i-1}_{State}

store h

provide input (open, h, $\$X$, T_{Expiry}) to Π^i_{State}

on **receiving state** (cancel, _, _) from Π^i_{State},

provide input (cancel) to Π^{i-1}_{State}

on **receiving** (preimage, x) from P_ℓ before time T_{Crit}, where $\mathcal{H}(x) = h$,

pass complete to Π^i_{State}

at time T_{Crit}, if state (complete, _, _) has not been received from Π^i_{State}, then

pass contract input PM.publish(x)

at time $T_{\text{Expiry}} + \Delta$,

if PM.published(T_{Expiry}, h), pass complete to Π^i_{State}

otherwise, pass cancel to Π^{i-1}_{State}

at time T_{Dispute}, pass input dispute to Π^{i-1}_{State} and Π^i_{State}

Local protocol for recipient, P_ℓ

on **receiving** (preimage, x) from P_1, store x and $h := \mathcal{H}(x)$

on **receiving state** (inflight, h, _) from $\Pi^{\ell-1}_{\text{State}}$,

multicast (preimage, x) to each party

at time T_{Crit}, if state (complete, _, _) has not been received from Π^ℓ_{State}, then

pass contract input PM.publish(x)

at time T_{Dispute}, pass input dispute to $\Pi^{\ell-1}_{\text{State}}$

Fig. 6. Construction for Π_{Linked} with the Π_{State} primitive. (Local portion only. See Fig. 5 for the smart contract portion.) Portions of the update function $U_{\text{Linked},\$X}$ that are delegated to the underlying U_{Pay} update function (Fig. 5) are in bold to help readability.

Protocol $\Pi_{\mathsf{State}}(U, P_1, ...P_N)$

Local protocol for the leader, P_1

Proceed in consecutive virtual rounds numbered r:
  Wait to receive messages $\{\mathtt{INPUT}(v_{r,j}))\}_j$ from each party.
  Let in_r be the current state of aux_{in} field in the the contract.
  Multicast $\mathtt{BATCH}(r, \mathsf{in}_r, \{v_{r,j}\}_j)$ to each party.
  Wait to receive messages $\{(\mathtt{SIGN}, \sigma_{r,j})\}_j$ from each party.
  Multicast $\mathtt{COMMIT}(r, \{\sigma_{r,j}\}_j)$ to each party.

Local protocol for each party P_i (including the leader, L)

$\mathsf{flag} := \mathtt{OK} \in \{\mathtt{OK}, \mathtt{PENDING}\}$; $\mathsf{lastRound} := -1$; $\mathsf{lastCommit} := \bot$

Fast Path (while $\mathsf{flag} == \mathtt{OK}$): Proceed in rounds r, with $r := 0$

Wait input $v_{r,i}$ from environment. Send $\mathtt{INPUT}(v_{r,i})$ to L.
Wait $\mathtt{BATCH}(r, \mathsf{in}'_r, \{v'_{r,j}\}_j)$ from L. Discard if $v'_{r,i} \neq v_{r,i}$ OR in'_r not a *recent* aux_{in}.
$(\mathsf{state}, \mathsf{out}_r) := U(\mathsf{state}, \{v_{r,j}\}_j, \mathsf{in}'_r)$
Send $(\mathtt{SIGN}, \sigma_{r,i})$ to P_1, $\sigma_{r,i} := \mathsf{sign}_i(r\|\mathsf{out}_r\|\mathsf{state})$
Wait $\mathtt{COMMIT}(r, \{\sigma_{r,j}\}_j)$ from L. Discard if $!(\mathsf{verify}_j(\sigma_{r,j}\|\mathsf{out}_r\|\mathsf{state}))$ for each j.
$\mathsf{lastCommit} := (\mathsf{state}, \mathsf{out}_r, \{\sigma_{r,j}\}_j)$; $\mathsf{lastRound} := r$
If $\mathsf{out}_r \neq \bot$, invoke $\mathsf{evidence}(r, \mathsf{lastCommit})$.
If $\mathtt{COMMIT}$ not received within one time-step, then:
  if $\mathsf{lastCommit} \neq \bot$, invoke $\mathsf{evidence}(r - 1, \mathsf{lastCommit})$ and $\mathsf{dispute}(r)$

Handling on-chain events

On $\mathtt{EventDispute}(\mathtt{r}, \_)$, if $r \leq \mathsf{lastRound}$, invoke $\mathsf{evidence}(\mathsf{lastRound}, \mathsf{lastCommit})$.
Else if $r = \mathsf{lastRound} + 1$, then:
  Set $\mathsf{flag} := \mathtt{PENDING}$, buffer inputs of "waiting" until returning to fast path.
  Send $\mathsf{input}(r, v_{r,i})$ to the contract.
  Wait to receive $\mathtt{EventOffchain}(r)$ or $\mathtt{EventOnchain}(r)$ from the contract. Attempt
  to invoke $\mathsf{resolve}(r)$ if Δ elapses, then continue waiting. In either case:
    $\mathsf{state} := \mathsf{state}'$
    $\mathsf{flag} := \mathtt{OK}$
    Enter the fast path with $r := r + 1$

Fig. 7. Construction of a general purpose state channel parameterized by transition function U. (Local portion only, for the smart contract see Fig. 3.)

References

1. Bentov, I., Kumaresan, R.: How to use bitcoin to design fair protocols. In: Garay, J.A., Gennaro, R. (eds.) CRYPTO 2014. LNCS, vol. 8617, pp. 421–439. Springer, Heidelberg (2014). https://doi.org/10.1007/978-3-662-44381-1_24

2. Bentov, I., Kumaresan, R., Miller, A.: Instantaneous decentralized poker. In: Takagi, T., Peyrin, T. (eds.) ASIACRYPT 2017. LNCS, vol. 10625, pp. 410–440. Springer, Cham (2017). https://doi.org/10.1007/978-3-319-70697-9_15. https://arxiv.org/abs/1701.06726
3. Castro, M., Liskov, B.: Practical byzantine fault tolerance. In: OSDI (1999)
4. Decker, C., Wattenhofer, R.: A fast and scalable payment network with bitcoin duplex micropayment channels. In: Pelc, A., Schwarzmann, A.A. (eds.) SSS 2015. LNCS, vol. 9212, pp. 3–18. Springer, Cham (2015). https://doi.org/10.1007/978-3-319-21741-3_1
5. Dziembowski, S., Eckey, L., Faust, S., Malinowski, D.: PERUN: virtual payment channels over cryptographic currencies (2017)
6. hashxp: September 2018. https://hashxp.org/lightning
7. Eyal, I., Gencer, A.E., Sirer, E.G., van Renesse, R.: Bitcoin-NG: a scalable blockchain protocol. In: NSDI (2016)
8. Khalil, R., Gervais, A.: Revive: rebalancing off-blockchain payment networks. In: ACM CCS (2017). http://eprint.iacr.org/2017/823
9. Kokoris-Kogias, E., Jovanovic, P., Gailly, N., Khoffi, I., Gasser, L., Ford, B.: Enhancing bitcoin security and performance with strong consistency via collective signing. In: USENIX Security Symposium (2016)
10. Kumaresan, R., Bentov, I.: How to use bitcoin to incentivize correct computations. In: CCS (2014)
11. Luu, L., Narayanan, V., Baweja, K., Zheng, C., Gilbert, S., Saxena, P.: SCP: a computationally-scalable byzantine consensus protocol for blockchains. In: CCS (2016)
12. Malavolta, G., Moreno-Sanchez, P., Kate, A., Maffei, M., Ravi, S.: Concurrency and privacy with payment-channel networks (2017)
13. McCorry, P., Bakshi, S., Bentov, I., Meiklejohn, S., Miller, A.: Pisa: arbitration outsourcing for state channels (2018). https://www.cs.cornell.edu/~iddo/pisa.pdf
14. Moreno-Sanchez, P., Kate, A., Maffei, M.: Silentwhispers: enforcing security and privacy in decentralized credit networks (2016)
15. Network, R.: (2015). http://raiden.network/
16. Nolan, T.: Alt chains and atomic transfers, May 2013. bitcointalk.org
17. Pass, R., Shi, E.: Hybrid consensus: efficient consensus in the permissionless model. Cryptology ePrint Archive, Report 2016/917 (2016). http://eprint.iacr.org/2016/917
18. Peterson, D.: Sparky: a lightning network in two pages of solidity. http://www.blunderingcode.com/a-lightning-network-in-two-pages-of-solidity
19. Poon, J., Dryja, T.: The bitcoin lightning network: scalable off-chain instant payments (2016). https://lightning.network/lightning-network-paper.pdf
20. Prihodko, P., Zhigulin, S., Sahno, M., Ostrovskiy, A., Osuntokun, O.: Flare: an approach to routing in lightning network. Whitepaper (2016). http://bitfury.com/content/5-white-papers-research/whitepaper_flare_an_approach_to_routing_in_lightning_network_7_7_2016.pdf
21. Roos, S., Moreno-Sanchez, P., Kate, A., Goldberg, I.: Settling payments fast and private: efficient decentralized routing for path-based transactions. In: NDSS (2018)
22. Sivaraman, V., Venkatakrishnan, S.B., Alizadeh, M., Fanti, G., Viswanath, P.: Routing cryptocurrency with the spider network. arXiv preprint arXiv:1809.05088 (2018)
23. Spilman, J.: Anti DoS for tx replacement (2013). https://lists.linuxfoundation.org/pipermail/bitcoin-dev/2013-April/002433.html

Echoes of the Past: Recovering Blockchain Metrics from Merged Mining

Nicholas Stifter[1,3]($\boxtimes$), Philipp Schindler[1], Aljosha Judmayer[1],
Alexei Zamyatin[1,2], Andreas Kern[1], and Edgar Weippl[1,3]

[1] SBA Research, Vienna, Austria
{nstifter,pschindler,ajudmayer,azamyatin,
akern,eweippl}@sba-research.org
[2] Imperial College London, London, UK
[3] Christian Doppler Laboratory for Security and Quality Improvement
in the Production System Lifecycle (CDL-SQI),
Institute of Information Systems Engineering, TU Wien, Vienna, Austria

Abstract. So far, the topic of *merged mining* has mainly been considered in a security context, covering issues such as mining power centralization or cross-chain attack scenarios. In this work we show that key information for determining blockchain metrics such as the *fork rate* can be recovered through data extracted from merge mined cryptocurrencies. Specifically, we reconstruct a long-ranging view of forks and stale blocks in Bitcoin from its merge mined child chains, and compare our results to previous findings that were derived from live measurements. Thereby, we show that live monitoring alone is not sufficient to capture a large majority of these events, as we are able to identify a non-negligible portion of stale blocks that were previously unaccounted for. Their authenticity is ensured by cryptographic evidence regarding both, their position in the respective blockchain, as well as the Proof-of-Work difficulty.

Furthermore, by applying this new technique to Litecoin and its child cryptocurrencies, we are able to provide the first extensive view and lower bound on the stale block and fork rate in the Litecoin network. Finally, we outline that a recovery of other important metrics and blockchain characteristics through merged mining may also be possible.

1 Introduction

In blockchain-based cryptocurrencies the *fork rate* is considered to be an essential metric to better gauge the performance, capacity, and health of the respective communication network [1], and may also help in estimating other aspects such as their security [2] or degree of decentralization [3]. Furthermore, the fork rate can be indicative of adversarial behavior, such as *selfish mining* and its variants [2,4–6] and other attacks that induce a higher ratio of stale blocks [7–9], or highlight periods of contention over protocol rule changes [10]. Historic and long-ranging data on stale blocks and the fork rate could also help determine the effectiveness of improvement measures and also provide a vital empirical basis for both predicting and directing future development.

© International Financial Cryptography Association 2019
I. Goldberg and T. Moore (Eds.): FC 2019, LNCS 11598, pp. 527–549, 2019.
https://doi.org/10.1007/978-3-030-32101-7_31

However, for many cryptocurrencies such extensive data sets are not always readily available as a consequence of both design decisions, as well as the necessity to perform ongoing live monitoring to try and capture these events from gossip in the peer-to-peer (p2p) network. Moreover, while public sources of live monitoring data from popular cryptocurrencies, such as Bitcoin, do provide information on stale blocks [11–13], it is not clear how extensive and well-connected these monitoring efforts were for the data to be considered representative. Finally, some of the available information may lack the necessary data to perform verification, such as establishing the validity of the respective Proof-of-Work.

In this paper we present a novel reconstruction technique for stale blocks that can be applied to Bitcoin-like Proof-of-Work blockchains, which have served the role as a *parent* chain for merged mining. Specifically, we shine light on the aspect that the prevalent implementation of merged mining requires the *child* blockchain to include both, the full block header, as well as the Merkle branch and coinbase transaction, of a candidate parent block *every time* a child block is produced through merged mining, to be able to validate its correctness.

Using Bitcoin as an example parent, we extract and analyze the additional data embedded through merged mining from several of Bitcoin's child currencies, and compare our findings to those of Decker and Wattenhofer [1] and other stale block and fork rate data derived from live measurements [11–13]. Based on this analysis, we are not only able to show that our technique is successful in recovering stale blocks and forks, but also that our method uncovers a non-negligible portion of blocks that have otherwise not been captured by live monitoring. This raises interesting new questions on the accuracy of former fork rate estimates and shows that the ratio of stale blocks is higher than previously anticipated. The contributions of this paper can be summarized as follows:

- We outline how the process of merged mining provides an interesting, but generally overlooked side channel for gaining additional information about the involved *parent* cryptocurrencies.
- We show that the data from merged mining can be used to recover stale blocks and forks in the parent chain, and may also enable the inference of other key blockchain metrics.
- Our analysis reveals a sizable portion of forks and stale blocks that were not recognized through live monitoring activities, suggesting that this new approach serves as a complementary mechanism for determining the fork rate. Furthermore, our findings suggest that previous models and estimates on fork rates and stale blocks should be re-evaluated.
- We demonstrate that our approach can be readily applied to other merge mined parent cryptocurrencies by reconstructing (a lower bound of) the fork- and orphan-block rate in Litecoin [14].

2   Background

First, this section outlines the concept and relevance of forks and stale blocks to Bitcoin-like cryptocurrencies, and why they can be considered key metrics, after which the core ideas and primitives related to merged mining are presented.

2.1   Forks and Stale Blocks

Simplified, in Bitcoin and similar cryptocurrencies, the *heaviest chain rule*, i.e. the chain with the most consecutive Proof-of-Work (PoW), determines which sequence of blocks is considered canonical and defines the ledger's current valid state [15]. In this context, PoW puzzles that are based on blocks play a key role as part of the consensus mechanism through which Bitcoin achieves aspects of decentralization [16,17]. Because the discovery of puzzle solutions, referred to as mining, is probabilistic, and also because of propagation delays in the underlying peer-to-peer network [1], it is possible that more than one block with a solution can exist for a particular height of the chain at the same time, leading to a so called *fork* in the blockchain. In this case miners may choose to extend either one of these valid chain tips. Assuming an honest majority of computational power[1] follows the heaviest chain rule, it can nevertheless be shown that eventual agreement (and other desirable properties) over a distributed ledger can be achieved as miners converge on a single common chain [17,19].

Within this paper, we refer to any blocks which satisfy the prescribed PoW puzzle difficulty of the main chain at that time or height, but are not part of the canonical chain, as being *stale*. Further, we consider a *fork* to be a branch of stale blocks of length $n \geq 1$ that can be cryptographically linked to a block in the canonical main chain. On the other hand, blocks for which we cannot ascertain such a link are called *orphans*.

Blockchain metrics such as the *fork rate* and *ratio of stale blocks* can provide useful information about the health and current state of cryptocurrencies. A high stale block rate may be indicative of insufficient network or block validation capacities [1,20] and is detrimental to the overall security, as it can increase the likelihood of successful double-spending attacks [2]. Additionally, many described attacks, such as selfish mining and its variants, or attempts at double spending, have an impact on the stale block rate [2,5]. Finally, contentious or unsuccessful protocol changes may also manifest themselves in high stale block rates as a portion of the network may fall into disagreement and mine on different branches [10]. Here, it depends both on the protocol upgrade mechanism and rule set a node prescribes to if a block is only considered stale or deemed invalid and not considered at all.

However, the Bitcoin protocol and many of its direct derivatives do not provide mechanisms or incentives to include information on stale blocks and forks as part of the consensus layer, though it has been outlined that taking these aspects

---

[1] We exclude attacks such as *selfish mining* [4] and possible countermeasures [18] in this example to simplify the discussion.

into consideration could improve protocol characteristics [15,21] and would generally lead to underlying structures that form a directed acyclic graph instead of a chain [22,23].

Furthermore, while protocol implementations do serialize information on stale blocks observed through p2p gossiping locally[2], due to privacy concerns that arise from the ability to fingerprint [25] a node based on the set of stale blocks it knows, a limit of thirty days is imposed on how far back stale blocks will be served to peers [24]. Hence, up until now, the primary source for both historic and current data related to stale blocks and forks for Bitcoin and similar cryptocurrencies comes from dedicated monitoring operations that gather and provide this additional information [1,3,11–13,26].

2.2 Merged Mining

Merged mining is an approach, whereby miners can leverage on the same process for searching for a valid PoW solution in more than one cryptocurrency, without having to split their computational resources among them. The motivation behind merged mining originally stemmed from the problem of how to avoid that competing cryptocurrencies reduce each other's security by competing in hash rate, and has also been suggested as a suitable bootstrapping and hardening mechanism for fledgling cryptocurrencies [27,28]. The idea of repurposing or reusing the computational effort spent in computing Proofs-of-Work is not new, and was first systematically described by Jakobson and Juels as *bread pudding protocols* [29].

The prevalent mechanism among existing cryptocurrencies by which merged mining is implemented follows a *parent* and *child* relationship. Thereby, no substantial changes to the block header and verification logic of already deployed cryptocurrencies is required. The hash of a candidate block in the child cryptocurrency is to be embedded into the candidate block of the parent in a prescribed way, generally within the coinbase transaction [30] of the block. Then the search for a valid PoW is performed on the parent's block header as usual. While such an approach necessitates the explicit support of merged mining in the child cryptocurrency, the parent can be oblivious to any ongoing merged mining activity, relating this protocol change to the concept of a *velvet fork* [10,31].

This form of merged mining requires miners to additionally attach the block header and coinbase transaction (and its Merkle branch) of the parent to the block submitted to the child chain (see Fig. 1). These elements are necessary to validate the PoW performed on the header of the parent block, the so called Auxiliary PoW (*AuxPoW*). Thereby, merge mined blockchains contain additional information from their parents (see Fig. 3). The PoW difficulty for the child chain is usually lower than that of the parent chain [28] and is instead encoded and adjusted in the headers of the child chain blocks. Therefore, partial

---

[2] In Bitcoin core [24] the RPC command *getchaintips* can be used to list all forks and stale blocks the local node knows of.

(also called weak or near) PoW solutions for a parent blockchain may nevertheless be valid for one or more child chains. If more than one child blockchain is to be merge mined with the same parent chain, a Merkle tree root hash as well as a parameter defining its size is included by the miner. The leaves of the tree represent the hashes of the block headers of each child blockchain. If merged mining involves only one child blockchain, the hash of the block header of the child blockchain can be included directly in the coinbase of the parent.

When mining multiple child chains, it is vital to ensure that merged mining does not occur for multiple forks of the same child blockchain; this would compromise the security of the latter as two branches of a fork can be mined at the same time. To address this issue, each child blockchain has a fixed `chainID` that is defined by its developers. For example, the `chainID` for Namecoin is set [32] to the value `0x0001`. Every miner can choose freely for how many and for which PoW child blockchains they want to perform merged mining and, hence, maintain a different Merkle tree. The combination of `MerkleSize`, `MerkleNonce`, and `chainID` are fed to a linear congruential generator so as to produce the unique position of a child blockchain `chainID` on a Merkle tree of a given size [33].

Merged mining was first introduced in Namecoin at block height 19200 (2011-10-11) and the corresponding AuxPoW built upon the Bitcoin block at height 148553. Since then merged mining has been deployed in a variety of other cryptocurrencies [28].

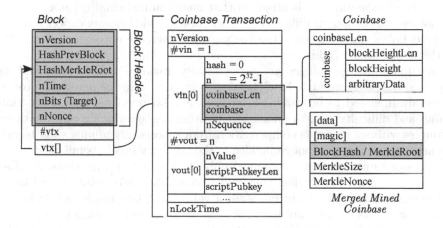

Fig. 1. Common Bitcoin block and merged mining data structures [30]

3 Merged Mining as a Side Channel

After having covered the principle mechanisms of merged mining, we first describe how the accrued data can serve as a side channel for gaining information about a parent chain, and then outline potential information that could leak this way.

3.1   Auxiliary Proofs-of-Work as Informants

The prevalent form of merged mining requires the child chain to include the block header, coinbase transaction and Merkle branch of the parent, otherwise it is not possible to verify the correctness of the Auxiliary Proof-of-Work. Hereby, the difficulty requirement for the child chain does not have to be equivalent to that of the parent, and other parametrizations, such as the target block interval, can also differ. For example, I0Coin [34], which can be merge mined with Bitcoin, has a target block interval of 90 s compared to the 600 s target of Bitcoin. This means that a valid AuxPoW for a child block may not necessarily be considered a valid PoW in the parent. In principle, the child cryptocurrency could even go as far as to change characteristics of the PoW itself while still retaining the ability for merged mining, such as reversing the final output bits of the utilized hash function, or additionally applying a bit mask before checking the output. For instance, Garay et al. [17] outlines how such *2-for-1 PoWs* can be achieved.

However, in practice the required PoW format is the same for child and parent, thereby encoding additional useful information regarding parent solution candidates because their discovery probability is no longer independent. An explanation for this behavior may be that the used mining hardware (ASICs) is not readily adaptable. If the difficulty requirement of the PoW for the parent, D_p, exceeds the difficulty for the child, D_c, i.e $D_p \geq D_c$, then finding a valid PoW in the parent will at the same render it a valid AuxPoW for the child. With few distinct exceptions, it is observed that merge mined child cryptocurrencies do not exceed the parent difficulty [28], and one would therefore expect a subset of valid PoWs that were mined in the parent to become encoded as AuxPoWs in the merge mined children.

Assuming merge miners are economically rational actors, it would be expected that the candidate block headers being mined in the parent cryptocurrency are intended to be valid, i.e., contain a valid previous block hash, time stamp and difficulty etc., as miners would otherwise be wasting computational resources without receiving compensation from successfully mining valid blocks. Because transactions are not embedded in the auxiliary PoW, its full validity can not be ascertained, unless it contained only the coinbase transactions. A miner does not, a priori, know when they will find a valid PoW solution and hence is incentivized to update and maintain a valid candidate block and its header while mining. As we later outline in the discussion of our findings in Sect. 6, we identified sporadic patterns in our data that are not easily explained under this assumption and may be indicative of software malfunction or misconfiguration.

3.2   Parent Block Information Leaking Potential

As previously outlined, the AuxPoW provides a snapshot of the particular miner's parent block header candidate at the time the child solution was found. Depending on both the block interval and difficulty requirement of the child chain, multiple such snapshots from different miners can exist between the discovery of blocks in the parent cryptocurrency, providing different vantage points of the network. Because the entire coinbase transaction is also available for each

AuxPoW, miner identification schemes such as the approach from Judmayer et al. [28] are also applicable. Additionally, most valid merge mined PoWs of the parent chain are likely to be recorded in the child chain because the child block would also meet its respective difficulty requirement.

Further, in the case of a fork event in the parent chain, there is a chance that one, or even both, of the parent block headers are captured through AuxPoWs if they were merge mined, and consecutive stale blocks from a prolonged fork may also be recorded in child cryptocurrencies in this fashion. In this respect, being able to draw information from multiple merge mined children with different block intervals may increase the likelihood that the block headers of competing forks are present in at least one of them.

Another interesting aspect is the additional, and possibly better, timing information that can be gained through both the child block(s) directly linked to an AuxPoW, as well as the additional time stamps from candidate parent block headers.

Categorization of Recoverable Blocks: Based on the information available within an AuxPoW, we categorize recoverable parent block headers and illustrate their relationship to the canonical parent chain in terms of difficulty requirements in Fig. 2.

- **Canonical Block:** If the block header belongs to a block that is part of the canonical main chain in the parent it is considered a canonical block.
- **Stale Block:** A block header that does not end up as part of the canonical parent chain but could have been a valid fork based on its (verifiable) difficulty and respective height or time stamp relative to the parent.
- **Near Block:** Parent block headers that do not meet the difficulty requirement of the canonical chain are referred to as near blocks. While near blocks are not valid in the parent chain, they may still provide useful information such as the particular miner's view of the longest chain at that time[3].
- **Orphan Block:** Blocks for which we are unable to establish a cryptographic link that eventually leads to a canonical block are considered orphan blocks. Orphan blocks have weaker guarantees as to their potential validity, as it is unclear if they were actually related to the parent chain being analyzed.
- **Shadow Block:** We refer to predecessors, where we can not obtain the full block header, e.g. only a hash, as shadow blocks. Even without the ability of cryptographic verification it can be possible to perform some basic validation, i.e, by checking if the hash itself could have met the required difficulty of the parent chain at the approximate time or height, which can be inferred from data in successors that build upon the shadow block.[4] Any parent headers that build upon a shadow block are implicitly *orphans* because they cannot be linked to the canonical chain.

---

[3] Assuming the miner follows the protocol rule of extending the longest chain it knows of.

[4] In Litecoin and its children this validation is not possible because a DSHA256 hash of the block header is used for linking, instead of the scrypt hash used for the PoW.

- **Invalid Block:** Based on the information available in the AuxPoW, some
  parent block headers may be identified as invalid because they do not follow
  the prescribed protocol rules of the parent chain. For instance, the encoded
  target difficulty may be too low or the time stamp outside of the permissible
  range.

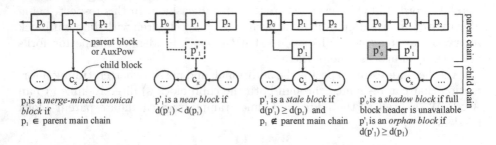

Fig. 2. Recoverable block categories and their relationship to the parent chain.

4   Data Sources and Processing

In this work, we primarily consider *Bitcoin* [35], as it not only has the longest
history of being a parent to merged mining, but also because there exists both live
monitoring services that provide information on forks and stale blocks [11–13], as
well as scientific literature that relates to forks and stale block rates [1,2,36,37].
Thereby, we gain access to necessary information for comparing and validating
our results, for instance through forming the intersection of block headers that
have been discovered by live monitoring and merged mining. Furthermore, we
also apply our approach to *Litecoin* [14] to determine if it is readily adaptable
to other merge mined cryptocurrencies.

Our raw blockchain data sources related to Bitcoin, Litecoin, and their merge
mined children herein considered, are listed in Table 1 in the appendix, and were
collected using fully validating clients. In total, we gathered data from 7 merge
mined children for Bitcoin, and 2 merge mined children for Litecoin. Furthermore, we also included data from the Bitcoin Cash fork to help identify orphan
blocks, because it has served as a parent for DSHA256 merge mined currencies.
The set of merge mined cryptocurrencies we selected is not exhaustive, and the
focus was placed on projects with a long history of merged mining in order to
gain as extensive of a view as possible. Relevant blockchain and AuxPoW data
was then extracted through the respective RPC interface of the cryptocurrency
client and aggregated in a graph database (Neo4J [38]), to aid in our exploratory
data analysis and simplify searching for interesting patterns.

To determine if the extracted AuxPoW block headers can be considered stale
block candidates for the target parent chain, several steps were followed:

1. The encoded difficulty target in the AuxPoW header was checked against the resulting block hash to determine if the parent header forms a valid PoW[5].
2. To establish a time frame for Bitcoin difficulty epochs (2016 blocks), we consider the time stamp of the first block in the epoch as the starting point and the time stamp of the first block in the *next* epoch as its end.
3. A link between the AuxPoW and a particular difficulty epoch in the parent was established to determine if the PoW difficulty is high enough to be considered valid. This was first attempted based on the block height, which can either be inferred if the block is linked to the canonical chain or, if the block is BIP34 compliant [39], determined from the height encoded in the coinbase transaction.
4. If the height could not be inferred in the previous step, the time stamp in the block header is used instead. For shadow blocks, the lowest time stamp of any AuxPoW that builds on top of it was used.

In respect to the live monitoring data that was used to compare and evaluate our results against, we rely on different sources. First, we gathered publicly available data on forks and stale blocks from block explorers [11–13, 26]. Second, we reached out to the authors of academic measurement studies related to Bitcoin's fork rate and inquired if they could provide us with the relevant monitoring data, and were kindly provided data from [1]. See Table 2 in the appendix for more details on live monitoring data.

5 Analysis

To analyze the feasibility and effectiveness of merged mining as a side channel, we focus on the recovery of information related to a key metric in the parent, namely the *stale block rate* and hereby resulting *forks*. This is of particular value, as long-ranging views that estimate stale block and fork rates are not readily retrievable from the data persisted in the respective blockchain for most cryptocurrencies, and require additional live monitoring efforts.

We subsequently first compare our findings on stale blocks and forks in Bitcoin to the measurement study conducted by Decker and Wattenhofer [1], as the authors have kindly provided us with raw data that was used in their work. Following this initial evaluation, we then extend our analysis over a wider time span and draw upon multiple live monitoring data sources for comparison.

5.1 Comparison to Decker and Wattenhofer Monitoring Data

The Bitcoin p2p measurement study of Decker and Wattenhofer (DW) has provided important insights on the blockchain fork rate and its dependency on propagation times, and serves as a critical reference point for Bitcoin's performance [20]. Therein, live monitoring data gathered over two 10000 block intervals, ranging from block height 180000 to 190000 and 200000 to 210000, was

---

[5] We also validated if the AuxPoW actually meets the difficulty encoded in the child.

analyzed and compared to a formal model for predicting the probability of a blockchain fork. In particular, while the first monitoring interval only involved passive observation, the second interval was actively influenced by relaying block information to as many peers as possible. Thereby, it was empirically shown that propagation delay, and consequently also block size, plays an important factor in the probability of forks, as the fork rate dropped from a measured 1.69% in the first interval to 0.78% in the second interval. Furthermore, at a 1.78% predicted fork rate, the presented formal model using propagation metrics from the live measurements was relatively close to the actual monitored fork rate of the first interval.

Because the commencement of merged mining in Bitcoin dates back far enough to cover both intervals, an obvious approach would be to compare the fork rate recoverable through merged mining with these results. Unfortunately, while we were able to obtain a large portion of the raw monitoring captures from the respective authors, it was reported to us that some of the data was rendered unrecoverable due to storage failure. Specifically, we were unable to obtain any data related to the second monitoring interval. Nevertheless, a comparison of our recovered stale blocks with live monitoring from the first interval already reveals interesting insights.

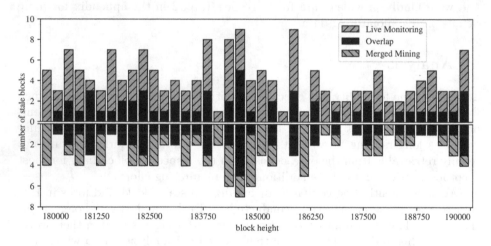

Fig. 3. Number of stale blocks observed by live monitoring (Decker and Wattenhofer) and merged mining; a single bar accounts for 250 blocks

Figure 3 shows our recovered stale blocks, the blocks captured by DW, as well as the overlap between the two data sets. All of the stale blocks we consider are linkable to the canonical parent chain and meet the correct difficulty requirement of the respective epoch, i.e. have a cryptographic link to Bitcoin. Surprisingly, our recovery technique is able to reveal 58 new stale blocks that were previously unaccounted for. The overlap in both data sets (54 blocks) further confirms that we are able to capture valid stale blocks observable through live monitoring.

Combining both data sources, we distinguish 227 forks, which corresponds to a total fork rate of 2.27% for the first monitoring interval.

5.2   Long Range Comparison of Stale Blocks and Forks

Based on the initial approach from the DW monitoring interval, we extend our analysis over a wider time frame that stretches over the entire set of complete difficulty epochs for which we can recover stale blocks through merged mining, starting at epoch 74 and ending with epoch 264. Hereby, we aggregate and filter duplicates from all considered live monitoring data sources and compare the results to the stale blocks we were able to recover. Analogous to the methodology previously used, we only include stale blocks from our data that we can directly link to Bitcoin, i.e. are *not orphans*, and for which we can ensure that the PoW meets the target requirement of the parent chain at that height.

The results are shown in Fig. 4, which contains some interesting patterns. First, an overall decline in the stale block rate as time progresses can be observed, which is to be expected as both, relay networks such as Falcon [3] (2016-06-8) and FIBRE [40] (2016-07-07), as well as and more efficient block announcement mechanisms, i.e. BIP130 [41] (2016-03-17), have come into play. Second, it appears that even though the overall stale block rate improves over time, blocks continue to be uncovered through merged mining which have otherwise not been observed.

In Figs. 5 and 6 we further visualize this aspect by plotting, on the one hand, the derived *fork rate* and on the other hand, the ratio of stale blocks that were exclusively identified through merged mining. The latter also includes the ratio if we were to additionally consider orphan and shadow blocks that we link to an appropriate difficulty epoch and which would meet the prescribed difficulty requirement.

We further derive two *average total fork rates* for the Bitcoin network, including both live monitoring and merged mining, for difficulty epochs 146 to 209 and 209 to 264. The first range is chosen such that it begins with several of our live monitoring data sets and avoids gaps, while the second interval begins roughly after the commencement of relay network activities. Our results show a total fork rate of 0.85% for the first range of epochs (approx. 03/2014–07/2016) and 0.24% for the second range of epochs (approx. 07/2016–07/2018).

Based on our data, one possible explanation for the more recent increase in exclusively observed stale blocks, while at the same time observing a decrease in the fork rate may be, that the technique of fork observation through merged mining captures blocks which are either never announced over the p2p network or are not propagated for other reasons. The occurrence of such blocks would hence not be readily affected by improvements in the communication infrastructure and may stay at a certain level, even if the remaining fork rate is lowered.

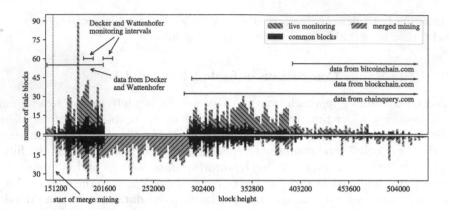

Fig. 4. Number of stale blocks observed by live monitoring (all considered data sources) and merged mining; a single bar accounts for a single difficulty period of 2016 blocks

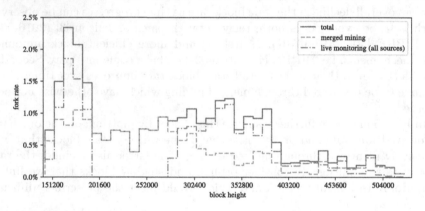

Fig. 5. Estimate of the fork rate in Bitcoin based on different data sources; 5 difficulty epochs grouped together

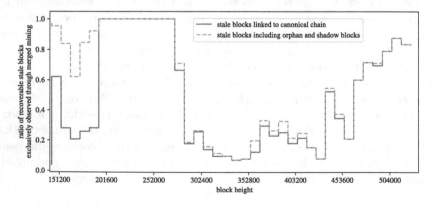

Fig. 6. Ratio of stale blocks exclusively identified through merged mining; 5 difficulty epochs grouped together

5.3 Stale Blocks and Forks in Litecoin

Through a stale block and fork rate recovery in Bitcoin we have shown the feasibility of our approach. By employing the same technique as before to Litecoin, we highlight that the same methodology can also be expanded to other merge mined blockchains. While we were able to obtain some live monitoring data [26] for Litecoin that includes forks, it is substantially less than what we were able to source for Bitcoin and not representative. We hence only show our recovered number of stale blocks as well as the fork rate, and point the interested reader to the appendix for further details (Appendix A.2). The methodology for deriving these values is analogous to the one previously used for Bitcoin (Figs. 7 and 8).

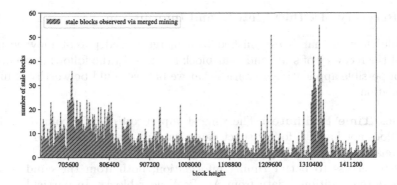

Fig. 7. Estimate of the stale block rate in Litecoin based only on merge mined data; 5 difficulty epochs grouped together

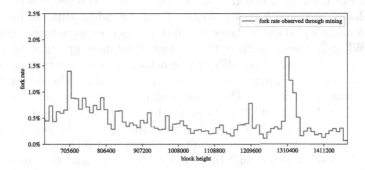

Fig. 8. Estimate of the fork rate in Litecoin based only on merge mined data; 5 difficulty epochs grouped together

6   Discussion

In Sect. 5 we show that the recovery of stale blocks and forks in merge mined parent cryptocurrencies is not only possible, but can also reveal new insights regarding their occurrence and the apparent inability to be fully captured by live monitoring alone. This raises the interesting question if other key metrics, such as the block propagation delay could, at least to some degree, be recovered in a similar fashion. Furthermore, it is important to acknowledge inherent limitations and necessary assumptions of this analysis method. Hereinafter, we address both of these points and additionally share some interesting anomalies and patterns that we discovered.

6.1   Recovery of Other Metrics and Information

The side channel that is established to a merge mined parent may be useful beyond the recovery of stale and near block headers. In the following we present a list of possible application scenarios that we believe could be worthy of further investigation.

- **Block Time Estimates:** The time stamp encoded in Bitcoin block headers does not have to follow strict clock synchronization rules and hence can be relatively unreliable [1,42]. Through merged mining, it may be possible to gain access to better timing information, both from the child block as well as the additional data from AuxPoW near blocks. In particular, merge mined cryptocurrencies with very short block intervals ranging in the order of seconds, such as GeistGeld [43], could prove helpful for improving timing estimates.
- **Information Propagation:** Also relating to better time estimates, near and stale blocks recovered from the AuxPoW can provide additional information about a miner's particular choice which chain tip they were extending at that time. While it seems unlikely that a high enough sampling rate and timing precision through AuxPoWs can be achieved to reconstruct propagation delays, anomalies or large discrepancies may nevertheless be detectable.
- **Hash Rate Estimates:** The additional PoW samples that are available through AuxPoWs could help improve the quality and granularity of hash rate estimates [44] and may also allow for better approximations of how much of the computational power was split-off during past fork events.
- **Miner Behavior Analysis:** In Sect. 3 we have outlined that miner identification schemes are also applicable to AuxPoWs, because the full coinbase transaction is included for verification purposes. Thereby, the additional data gained from merged mining allows for a more detailed analysis of miner behavior, and may even reveal suspicious or adversarial behavior of bad actors, such as block withholding, if they also engaged in merged mining at the time.

6.2   Limitations

While merged mining can be used to recover certain information related to the parent chain, several limiting factors apply that may diminish its effectiveness. First and foremost, the presented technique only applies to currencies that have served as the parent in a merge mined relationship. The merge mining landscape is currently not well documented and information pertaining to merged mining in general is not readily available. Previous literature has shed some light on this topic [27,28], however many details still remain relatively unknown outside of the specific mining communities. While we are aware of merge mining activities for cryptocurrencies that use Proofs-of-Work other than the herein considered DSHA256 and scrypt, such as X11 [45] or CryptoNote [46], we leave a detailed survey of potential merge mined parents to future work.

Furthermore, the effectiveness of merged mining as a side channel is dependent on a variety of factors, such as the degree of its adoption, the number and concrete parametrizations of the child chains, as well as the technique by which merged mining is achieved. In particular, the recovery of full block headers that meet the parent chain difficulty becomes increasingly unlikely, if only a small subset of the total hash rate is actively participating in merged mining. A similar situation can be observed for long consecutive forks, where linking may be prevented if only shadow blocks are registered.

Another important issue is the fact that merge mined cryptocurrencies may have more than one possible parent with which they can be merge mined. Without an explicit cryptographic link to the canonical parent chain, orphan stale blocks could therefore belong to a different parent. For instance, we have recovered close to 15000 AuxPoW block headers that meet the encoded parent difficulty in their header, but which actually belong to a different parent cryptocurrency than Bitcoin (see Appendix Table 1). Section 4 outlines how orphan stale blocks can be linked to a particular difficulty epoch in the analyzed parent, which discards these blocks as false positives as long as the difficulties of both parents are not the same. Nevertheless, certainty is only achieved when all orphan stale blocks are not taken into consideration. In our analysis in Sect. 5 we clearly state when such orphan stale blocks were included in figures or tables. Furthermore, we specifically decided not to rely on the additional data sources from live monitoring in our recovery process, which could have aided in bridging gaps between orphan stale blocks, to retain a clear picture of what is achievable solely through blockchain data and merged mining AuxPoWs.

6.3   Anomalies and Interesting Patterns

During the process of our analysis we were able to identify interesting patterns and anomalies that are not always readily explained by rational miner behavior. For instance, it is not widespread knowledge that several of the merge mined children to Bitcoin and Litecoin have, on occasion, also served the role as a *parent* for their siblings. This is possible because the requirements extended toward the AuxPoW do not include additional verification logic and only demand that the data structure and PoW follows an expected format. Because the child chains will generally also adhere to the same header format as the parent, it hence becomes possible to merge mine them interchangeably. As an example, the AuxPoW and parent block header of canonical Namecoin block "a10e863165101af92314..." at height 19236 actually stems from GeistGeld block "00000000000026c050e6..." at height 144590. We were further able to verify this insight through online references from respective mining communities [47,48].

Another highly interesting pattern emerges when searching for the most concurrent forks extending a single parent block. For Bitcoin, we were able to identify a maximum of 18 concurrent stale blocks, i.e. 19 forks, that meet the correct parent difficulty and extend block "0000000000000d331567..." at height 153210. By applying a miner identification scheme similar to [28], we believe that all of these stale blocks were possibly mined by the same entity, namely *BTC Guild*. A similar pattern can also be observed in Litecoin, where the number of concurrent forks extending a parent is even higher, at a staggering 47 potentially valid blocks. In this case we were unable to achieve a possible match with a mining entity. The occurrence of such large concurrent fork events however is very rare in our recovered data, and the total count of situations where forks with more than 2 children exist is only 14 for Bitcoin and 37 for Litecoin. We believe that the above pattern can be explained by considering software issues or misconfiguration in the merged mining setup of the respective miner.

When checking for monotonically increasing heights, we were able to identify one case in Bitcoin where the BIP34 encoded height was not properly incremented while the target difficulty of the canonical chain was met, rendering the block invalid. Overall, we discovered 55 blocks in Bitcoin and one block in Litecoin in our recovered data where the BIP34 encoded height did not correspond to the respective position to which the block could be linked in the parent chain and which are consequently invalid.

7   Related Work

In [1] Decker and Wattenhofer consider peer-to-peer network and information propagation characteristics of the Bitcoin network. Donet et al. [49] present an extensive survey of the Bitcoin p2p network and its topology, including block and transaction propagation delays, however information on stale blocks and forks is not included. Gervais et al. [2] presents a framework for quantifying and analyzing parametrizations of PoW blockchains. They include live measurements in Bitcoin, Litecoin, Dogecoin and Ethereum conducted in February 2016, from which a stale block rate of 0.41% for Bitcoin and 0.273% for Litecoin is derived. The presented simulation results predict a stale block rate of 0.14% (relay network and unsolicited block push) and 1.85% (standard propagation mechanism) for Bitcoin and 0.24% (standard propagation) for Litecoin. In Gencer et al. [3] a measurement study on decentralization metrics in Bitcoin and Ethereum is conducted, including aspects related to the peer-to-peer network such as provisioned bandwidth and latency. The work introduces a *fairness* property, which is defined as the ratio of a miner's share of pruned (stale) blocks to her mining power.

The encoding of additional data within the Bitcoin blockchain is addressed by Bartoletti and Pompianu [50], which analyze *OP_RETURN* metadata, and Matzutt et al. [51], which systematically analyzes and conducts an extensive quantitative and qualitative study of arbitrary encoded data within Bitcoin. Grundmann et al. [52] exploit characteristics of transaction processing and forwarding in the Bitcoin p2p network to infer its topology.

8   Conclusion

In this paper we outline and analyze a novel technique for recovering stale blocks through data that is accrued from merged mining. Thereby, we show that merged mining can act as a side channel for gaining information about the parent cryptocurrency, and that this data helps to infer key metrics such as the *fork rate*. Interestingly, a cryptocurrency is not trivially able to prevent another cryptocurrency from designating it as its parent in a merge mine relationship [28], and this fact has been identified as a potential attack vector in the context of hostile blockchain forks [53].

Our results indicate that live monitoring alone is not sufficient to capture all stale blocks and forking events in Bitcoin, as merged mining data is able to exclusively identify a majority of the stale blocks in more recent difficulty epochs. The authenticity of the recovered blocks and forks is hereby cryptographically ensured both, by the ability to link them to the canonical main chain, as well as the correct Proof-of-Work difficulty they satisfy. Important questions are therefore raised as to the nature of these newly identified stale blocks, to be addressed in future work.

Overall, we show that data embedded through merged mining can provide interesting new insights and may help augment and improve the fidelity and quality of empirical measurements to provide a more effective basis for future models, analysis, and simulations of Proof-of-Work cryptocurrencies.

Acknowledgments. We thank Georg Merzdovnik as well as the participants of Dagstuhl Seminar 18152 "Blockchains, Smart Contracts and Future Applications" for valuable discussions and insights. We thank Christian Decker, Roger Wattenhofer, Till Neudecker, Blockchain.com and chainz.cryptoid.info for the live monitoring data they kindly provided. This research was funded by Bridge Early Stage 846573 A2Bit, Bridge 1 858561 SESC, Bridge 1 864738 PR4DLT (all FFG), the Christian Doppler Laboratory for Security and Quality Improvement in the Production System Lifecycle (CDL-SQI), Institute of Information Systems Engineering, TU Wien, Blockchain.com and the competence center SBA-K1 funded by COMET. The financial support by the Christian Doppler Research Association, the Austrian Federal Ministry for Digital and Economic Affairs and the National Foundation for Research, Technology and Development is gratefully acknowledged.

A   Appendix

Table 1. Considered blockchain data of merge mined cryptocurrencies and their parents

Cryptocurrency	PoW	Merge M	Start of merge M	Considered block heights	Parent blocks	Child blocks
Bitcoin (BTC)	DSHA256	✗	–	0–532485	181658	0
Bitcoin Cash (BCH)	DSHA256	✗	–	478559–544355	12389	0
Namecoin (NMC)	DSHA256	✓	19200 (2011-10-08)	0–409629	0	390300
IXCoin (IXC)	DSHA256	✓	45001 (2011-12-31)	0–455051	861	409969
I0Coin (I0C)	DSHA256	✓	160045 (2011-12-20)	0–2556904	1620	2395170
GeistGeld (XGG)	DSHA256	✓	14092 (2011-09-16)	0–7309971	2	2493631
Devcoin (DVC)	DSHA256	✓	25000 (2012-01-07)	0–337624	135	312624
Groupcoin (GPC)	DSHA256	✓	17187 (2012-02-16)	0–235751	0	218494
Unobtanium (UNO)	DSHA256	✓	600135 (2015-05-08)	0–1163483	6	561355
Litecoin (LTC)	scrypt	✗	–	0–1477146	699714	0
Dogecoin (DOGE)	scrypt	✓	371337 (2014-09-11)	0–2357918	3	1983945
Viacoin (VIA)	scrypt	✓	551885 (2014-12-25)	0–5324736	973	4767508

Table 2. Considered live monitoring data for Bitcoin and Litecoin

Cryptocurrency	Source	First block height	Start time	Last block height	Stop time	Stale blocks
Bitcoin	Decker and Wattenhofer [1]	142258	2011-08-23	200206	2012-09-23	612
Bitcoin	blockchain.com	291123	2014-03-18	525890	2018-06-04	932
Bitcoin	chainquery.com	283421	2014-01-31	525890	2018-06-04	715
Bitcoin	bitcoinchain.com	395001	2016-01-25	525890	2018-06-04	51
Litecoin	chainz.cryptoid.info	1217073	2017-06-05	1472513	2018-08-11	223

A.1   Bitcoin Total Number of Stale Blocks for Different Data Sources

Table 3 shows both, the total number of unique stale blocks exclusive to the data source, as well as the overall number of (non-duplicate) stale blocks it contains.

Table 3. Comparison of total stale blocks in Bitcoin observed by different live monitoring sources and merged mining

	Unique stale blocks	Total stale blocks
Merged mining	1164	1678
Decker and Wattenhofer	410	612
blockchain.com	256	932
chainquery.com	113	715
bitcoinchain.com	4	51
	2863	3988

A.2   Litecoin Stale Block Rate Comparison

As we have previously outlined in Subsect. 5.3, the live monitoring data we were able to obtain for Litecoin was relatively limited and only contained 223 stale blocks/forks. Nevertheless, we plot this live monitoring data against the recovered stale blocks through merged mining in Fig. 9 and show that the data sets also contain some overlap. Again, our recovered data only contains stale blocks that can be cryptographically linked to the canonical Litecoin chain and which meet the prescribed difficulty target (Table 4).

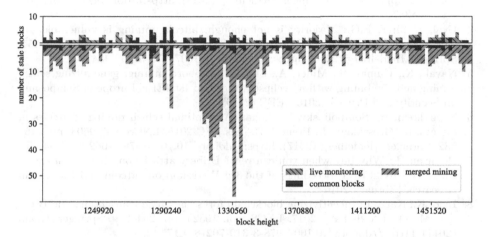

Fig. 9. Stale block rate recovered from merged mining in Litecoin compared to available live measurements [26]; 5 difficulty epochs grouped together

Table 4. Structure of the coinbase of a merge-mined block [30]

Field name		Type (size)	Description
coinbaseLen		VarInt (1–9 bytes)	Length of the coinbase field in bytes as a variable length integer. Maximum size is 100 bytes
coinb.	blockHeightLen	(1 bytes)	Length in bytes required to represent the current blockHeight
	blockHeight	(3 bytes)	Current block height
	[data]	char[] (0–52 bytes)	Optional: Arbitrary data that can be filled by the miner (e.g., identifying the block miner)
	[magic]	char[] (4 bytes)	Optional: If len(coinbase) ≥ 20, magic bytes indicate the start of the merged mining information, e.g., "\xfa\xbe\x6d\x6d"
	BlockHash or MerkleRoot	char[] (32 bytes)	Hash of the merge-mined block header. If more than one cryptocurrencies are merge-mined, this is the Merkle tree root hash of those cryptocurrencies
	MerkleSize	uint32_t (4 bytes)	Size of the Merkle tree, i.e., the maximum number of contained cryptocurrencies
	MerkleNonce	uint32_t (4 bytes)	Used to calculate indices of the mined cryptocurrencies in the Merkle tree. If no Merkle tree is used, set to 0

References

1. Decker, C., Wattenhofer, R.: Information propagation in the bitcoin network. In: Thirteenth International Conference on Peer-to-Peer Computing (P2P), pp. 1–10. IEEE (2013)
2. Gervais, A., Karame, O., Wüst, K., Glykantzis, V., Ritzdorf, H., Capkun, S.: On the security and performance of proof of work blockchains. In: Proceedings of the 2016 ACM SIGSAC, pp. 3–16. ACM (2016)
3. Gencer, A.E., Basu, S., Eyal, I., van Renesse, R., Sirer, E.G.: Decentralization in bitcoin and ethereum networks. In: Meiklejohn, S., Sako, K. (eds.) FC 2018. LNCS, vol. 10957, pp. 439–457. Springer, Heidelberg (2018). https://doi.org/10.1007/978-3-662-58387-6_24
4. Eyal, I., Sirer, E.G.: Majority is not enough: bitcoin mining is vulnerable. In: Christin, N., Safavi-Naini, R. (eds.) FC 2014. LNCS, vol. 8437, pp. 436–454. Springer, Heidelberg (2014). https://doi.org/10.1007/978-3-662-45472-5_28
5. Nayak, K., Kumar, S., Miller, A., Shi, E.: Stubborn mining: generalizing selfish mining and combining with an eclipse attack. In: 1st IEEE European Symposium on Security and Privacy, 2016. IEEE (2016)
6. Sapirshtein, A., Sompolinsky, Y., Zohar, A.: Optimal selfish mining strategies in bitcoin. In: Grossklags, J., Preneel, B. (eds.) FC 2016. LNCS, vol. 9603, pp. 515–532. Springer, Heidelberg (2017). https://doi.org/10.1007/978-3-662-54970-4_30
7. Bonneau, J.: Why buy when you can rent? Bribery attacks on bitcoin consensus. In: BITCOIN 2016: Proceedings of the 3rd Workshop on Bitcoin and Blockchain Research, February 2016
8. Liao, K., Katz, J.: Incentivizing blockchain forks via whale transactions. In: Brenner, M., et al. (eds.) FC 2017. LNCS, vol. 10323, pp. 264–279. Springer, Cham (2017). https://doi.org/10.1007/978-3-319-70278-0_17
9. McCorry, P., Hicks, A., Meiklejohn, S.: Smart contracts for bribing miners. In: Zohar, A., et al. (eds.) FC 2018. LNCS, vol. 10958, pp. 3–18. Springer, Heidelberg (2019). https://doi.org/10.1007/978-3-662-58820-8_1
10. Zamyatin, A., Stifter, N., Judmayer, A., Schindler, P., Weippl, E., Knottenbelt, W.J.: A wild velvet fork appears! Inclusive blockchain protocol changes in practice. In: Zohar, A., et al. (eds.) FC 2018. LNCS, vol. 10958, pp. 31–42. Springer, Heidelberg (2019). https://doi.org/10.1007/978-3-662-58820-8_3
11. Blockchain.com: Blockchain.com orphaned blocks. https://www.blockchain.com/btc/orphaned-blocks, Blockchain.com. Accessed 25 Sept 2018
12. BitcoinChain.com: Bitcoinchain bitcoin block explorer. https://bitcoinchain.com/block_explorer, BitcoinChain.com. Accessed 25 Sept 2018
13. ChainQuery.com: A web based interface to the bitcoin API JSON-RPC. http://chainquery.com/bitcoin-api, ChainQuery.com. Accessed 25 Sept 2018
14. Project, L.: Litecoin. https://litecoin.org/. Accessed 29 Mar 2016
15. Sompolinsky, Y., Zohar, A.: Accelerating bitcoin's transaction processing. fast money grows on trees, not chains (2013). http://eprint.iacr.org/2013/881.pdf
16. Miller, A., LaViola, J.J.: Anonymous Byzantine consensus from moderately-hard puzzles: a model for bitcoin (2014). https://socrates1024.s3.amazonaws.com/consensus.pdf. Accessed 09 Mar 2016
17. Garay, J., Kiayias, A., Leonardos, N.: The bitcoin backbone protocol: analysis and applications. In: Oswald, E., Fischlin, M. (eds.) EUROCRYPT 2015. LNCS, vol. 9057, pp. 281–310. Springer, Heidelberg (2015). https://doi.org/10.1007/978-3-662-46803-6_10

18. Pass, R., Shi, E.: FruitChains: a fair blockchain (2016). http://eprint.iacr.org/2016/916.pdf

19. Pass, R., Seeman, L., Shelat, A.: Analysis of the blockchain protocol in asynchronous networks. In: Coron, J.-S., Nielsen, J.B. (eds.) EUROCRYPT 2017. LNCS, vol. 10211, pp. 643–673. Springer, Cham (2017). https://doi.org/10.1007/978-3-319-56614-6_22

20. Croman, K., et al.: On scaling decentralized blockchains. In: Clark, J., Meiklejohn, S., Ryan, P.Y.A., Wallach, D., Brenner, M., Rohloff, K. (eds.) FC 2016. LNCS, vol. 9604, pp. 106–125. Springer, Heidelberg (2016). https://doi.org/10.1007/978-3-662-53357-4_8

21. Kiayias, A., Panagiotakos, G.: On trees, chains and fast transactions in the blockchain. In: Lange, T., Dunkelman, O. (eds.) LATINCRYPT 2017. LNCS, vol. 11368, pp. 327–351. Springer, Cham (2019). https://doi.org/10.1007/978-3-030-25283-0_18

22. Sompolinsky, Y., Lewenberg, Y., Zohar, A.: SPECTRE: a fast and scalable cryptocurrency protocol. Cryptology ePrint Archive, Report 2016/1159 (2016). http://eprint.iacr.org/2016/1159.pdf

23. Sompolinsky, Y., Zohar, A.: PHANTOM: a scalable blockdag protocol. Cryptology ePrint Archive, Report 2018/104 (2018). https://eprint.iacr.org/2018/104.pdf

24. Bitcoin community: Bitcoin-core source code. https://github.com/bitcoin/bitcoin. Accessed 25 Sept 2018

25. Miller, A., et al.: Discovering bitcoin's public topology and influential nodes, May 2015. http://cs.umd.edu/projects/coinscope/coinscope.pdf. Accessed 09 Mar 2016

26. Chainz.cryptoid.info: Chainz blockchain explorers. chainz.cryptoid.info/. Accessed 25 Sept 2018

27. Narayanan, A., Bonneau, J., Felten, E., Miller, A., Goldfeder, S.: Bitcoin and Cryptocurrency Technologies. Princeton University Press, Princeton (2016). Accessed 29 Mar 2016

28. Judmayer, A., Zamyatin, A., Stifter, N., Voyiatzis, A.G., Weippl, E.: Merged mining: curse or cure? In: Garcia-Alfaro, J., Navarro-Arribas, G., Hartenstein, H., Herrera-Joancomartí, J. (eds.) ESORICS/DPM/CBT -2017. LNCS, vol. 10436, pp. 316–333. Springer, Cham (2017). https://doi.org/10.1007/978-3-319-67816-0_18

29. Jakobsson, M., Juels, A.: Proofs of work and bread pudding protocols (extended abstract). In: Preneel, B. (ed.) Secure Information Networks. ITIFIP, vol. 23, pp. 258–272. Springer, Boston, MA (1999). https://doi.org/10.1007/978-0-387-35568-9_18

30. Judmayer, A., Stifter, N., Krombholz, K., Weippl, E.: Blocks and chains: introduction to bitcoin, cryptocurrencies, and their consensus mechanisms. Synth. Lect. Inf. Secur. Priv. Trust 9(1), 1–123 (2017)

31. Kiayias, A., Miller, A., Zindros, D.: Non-interactive proofs of proof-of-work. Cryptology ePrint Archive, Report 2017/963 (2017). https://eprint.iacr.org/2017/963.pdf

32. Namecoin community: Namecoin source code - chainparams.cpp. https://github.com/namecoin/namecoin-core/blob/fdfb20fc263a72acc2a3c460b56b64245c1bedcb/src/chainparams.cpp#L123. Accessed 25 Sept 2018

33. Namecoin community: Namecoin source code - auxpow.cpp. https://github.com/namecoin/namecoin-core/blob/fdfb20fc263a72acc2a3c460b56b64245c1bedcb/src/auxpow.cpp#L177-L200. Accessed 25 Sept 2018

34. I0Coin community: I0coin source code. https://github.com/domob1812/i0coin. Accessed 25 Sept 2018

35. Nakamoto, S.: Bitcoin: a peer-to-peer electronic cash system, December 2008. https://bitcoin.org/bitcoin.pdf. Accessed 01 Jul 2015

36. Courtois, N.T., Bahack, L.: On subversive miner strategies and block withholding attack in bitcoin digital currency. arXiv preprint arXiv:1402.1718 (2014). https://arxiv.org/pdf/1402.1718.pdf

37. Göbel, J., Keeler, H.P., Krzesinski, A.E., Taylor, P.G.: Bitcoin blockchain dynamics: the selfish-mine strategy in the presence of propagation delay. Perform. Eval. **104**, 23–41 (2016)

38. Neo4J Developers: Neo4j (2012). https://neo4j.com/

39. Andresen, G.: Bitcoin improvement proposal 34 (bip34): block v2, height in coinbase. https://github.com/bitcoin/bips/blob/master/bip-0034.mediawiki. Accessed 25 Sept 2018

40. Corello, M.: Fast internet bitcoin relay engine. http://bitcoinfibre.org/. Accessed 25 Sept 2018

41. Daftuar, S.: Sendheaders message. https://github.com/bitcoin/bips/wiki/Comments:BIP-0130. Accessed 25 Sept 2018

42. Bowden, R., Keeler, H.P., Krzesinski, A.E., Taylor, P.G.: Block arrivals in the bitcoin blockchain (2018). https://arxiv.org/pdf/1801.07447.pdf

43. GeistGeld community: Geistgeld source code. https://github.com/Lolcust/GeistGeld. Accessed 25 Sept 2018

44. Ozisik, A.P., Bissias, G., Levine, B.: Estimation of miner hash rates and consensus on blockchains. arXiv preprint arXiv:1707.00082 (2017). https://arxiv.org/pdf/1707.00082.pdf. Accessed 25 Sept 2017

45. Duffield, E., Diaz, D.: Dash: a payments-focused cryptocurrency, August 2013. https://github.com/dashpay/dash/wiki/Whitepaper. Accessed 25 Sept 2018

46. Van Saberhagen, N.: Cryptonote v 2.0, October 2013. https://cryptonote.org/whitepaper.pdf

47. Hall, G.: Guide: merge mining 6 scrypt coins at full hashpower, simultaneously, April 2014. https://www.ccn.com/guide-simultaneously-mining-5-scrypt-coins-full-hashpower/. Accessed 25 Sept 2018

48. United-scrypt coin: [ann][usc] first merged minable scryptcoin unitedscryptcoin, November 2013. https://bitcointalk.org/index.php?topic=353688.0. Accessed 25 Sept 2018

49. Donet Donet, J.A., Pérez-Solà, C., Herrera-Joancomartí, J.: The bitcoin P2P network. In: Böhme, R., Brenner, M., Moore, T., Smith, M. (eds.) FC 2014. LNCS, vol. 8438, pp. 87–102. Springer, Heidelberg (2014). https://doi.org/10.1007/978-3-662-44774-1_7

50. Bartoletti, M., Pompianu, L.: An analysis of bitcoin OP_RETURN metadata. In: Brenner, M., et al. (eds.) FC 2017. LNCS, vol. 10323, pp. 218–230. Springer, Cham (2017). https://doi.org/10.1007/978-3-319-70278-0_14

51. Matzutt, R., et al.: A quantitative analysis of the impact of arbitrary blockchain content on bitcoin. In: Meiklejohn, S., Sako, K. (eds.) FC 2018. LNCS, vol. 10957, pp. 420–438. Springer, Heidelberg (2018). https://doi.org/10.1007/978-3-662-58387-6_23

52. Grundmann, M., Neudecker, T., Hartenstein, H.: Exploiting transaction accumulation and double spends for topology inference in bitcoin. In: Zohar, A., et al. (eds.) FC 2018. LNCS, vol. 10958, pp. 113–126. Springer, Heidelberg (2019). https://doi.org/10.1007/978-3-662-58820-8_9

53. Judmayer, A., Stifter, N., Schindler, P., Weippl, E.: Pitchforks in cryptocurrencies: enforcing rule changes through offensive forking- and consensus techniques (short paper). In: Garcia-Alfaro, J., Herrera-Joancomartí, J., Livraga, G., Rios, R. (eds.) DPM/CBT -2018. LNCS, vol. 11025, pp. 197–206. Springer, Cham (2018). https://doi.org/10.1007/978-3-030-00305-0_15

TxProbe: Discovering Bitcoin's Network Topology Using Orphan Transactions

Sergi Delgado-Segura[1]([⊠]), Surya Bakshi[2], Cristina Pérez-Solà[3], James Litton[4], Andrew Pachulski[4], Andrew Miller[2]([⊠]), and Bobby Bhattacharjee[4]

[1] Universitat Autònoma de Barcelona, Bellaterra, Spain
s.delgado@ucl.ac.uk
[2] University of Illinois Urbana-Champaign, Urbana, USA
soc1024@illinois.edu
[3] Universitat Rovira i Virgili, Tarragona, Spain
[4] University of Maryland, College Park, USA

Abstract. Bitcoin relies on a peer-to-peer overlay network to broadcast transactions and blocks. From the viewpoint of network measurement, we would like to observe this topology so we can characterize its performance, fairness and robustness. However, this is difficult because Bitcoin is deliberately designed to hide its topology from onlookers. Knowledge of the topology is not in itself a vulnerability, although it could conceivably help an attacker performing targeted eclipse attacks or to deanonymize transaction senders.

In this paper we present TxProbe, a novel technique for reconstructing the Bitcoin network topology. TxProbe makes use of peculiarities in how Bitcoin processes out of order, or "orphaned" transactions. We conducted experiments on Bitcoin testnet that suggest our technique reconstructs topology with precision and recall surpassing 90%. We also used TxProbe to take a snapshot of the Bitcoin testnet in just a few hours. TxProbe may be useful for future measurement campaigns of Bitcoin or other cryptocurrency networks.

1 Introduction

Bitcoin builds on top of a peer-to-peer (P2P) network to relay transactions and blocks in a decentralized manner. Broadcast is the routing scheme chosen to propagate transactions and blocks over the network, in order to spread the information as quick as possible and facilitate agreement on a common state. The topology of the Bitcoin network is unknown by design and it is built to mimic a random network. While knowing the topology of the network does not pose a threat by itself, it eases the performance of several network based attacks, such as eclipse attacks [8,12], or attacks on users anonymity [2,10]. On top of that, a study of the network topology may reveal to what extent the network is really decentralized, whether there exist supernodes, bridge nodes, potential points of failure, etc.

© International Financial Cryptography Association 2019
I. Goldberg and T. Moore (Eds.): FC 2019, LNCS 11598, pp. 550–566, 2019.
https://doi.org/10.1007/978-3-030-32101-7_32

In this paper we present TxProbe, a technique to infer the topology of the publicly reachable Bitcoin network. Nodes of the non-reachable network, such as nodes behind NAT or firewalls, or nodes not accepting incoming connections will not be inferred with our technique. Our work builds on prior work in exploiting Bitcoin network side channels as measurement techniques, but exploits a new side channel involving the handling of orphan transactions (transactions that arrive out of order).

To validate our technique, we have conducted an experiment in which our custom node is connected to our own ground truth nodes (running Bitcoin Core software). We then check whether we were able to get the connections of such nodes. On top of that, a scan of the entire live network has been performed resulting on a snapshot of the Bitcoin testnet. Finally, a comparative analysis of the obtained testnet graph against similar random graphs is provided to quantify whether or not the network resembles a random network.

TxProbe is an active measurement technique, and we have not conclusively ruled out that it could interfere with ordinary transactions. We have therefore limited our measurement and validate activities to the Bitcoin testnet. The technique could be used in the future to infer the topology of Bitcoin or any alt-coin sharing its network protocol, including Bitcoin Cash, Litecoin or Dogecoin.

2   Related Work

Network topology inference is a topic that has been previously analysed in several other works. Biryukov et al. [2] showed how a node could be uniquely identified by a subset of its neighbourhood, and how the neighbourhood could be easily inferred by checking the address messages propagation throughout the network. Biryukov et al. [3] also showed how using Tor to guard against the aforementioned technique was not useful, and it could even ease the deanonymization process.

The use of address message propagation along with timestamp analysis was used by Miller et al. [11] to infer the topology of the Bitcoin network. The analysis highlighted how the network did not behave as a random graph but, instead, it was filled with several influential nodes representing a disproportionate amount of mining power. Their AddressProbe technique took advantage of the two-hour penalty applied to received address messages from connected peers. However, the two-hour penalty was removed from the Bitcoin Core nodes after 0.10.1 release [16,17], reducing the fingerprint left by address messages, and therefore, making AddressProbe no longer useful to infer the topology of the network.

Neudecker et al. [13] performed timing analyses of the transaction propagation to infer the topology of the Bitcoin network with a substantial precision and recall ($\sim$40%).

Network information from the P2P network has also been used, alongside with address clustering heuristics, to check whether such information could be useful in the deanonymization of Bitcoin users [14]. The study shows how while most of the network information cannot ease the address clustering process, a small number of users show correlations that may make them vulnerable to network based deanonymization attacks.

A recent proposal by Grundmann et al. [6] has shown how transaction accumulation of double-spending transactions can also be used to infer the neighbourhood of a targeted node with precision and recall as high as 95%.

Finally, Efe Gencer et al. [5] have presented a comparative analysis of the decentralization on two of the most popular cryptocurrencies to the date, Bitcoin and Ethereum, using application layer information obtained from the Falcon Network. Their results show how around 56% of Bitcoin nodes are run in datacenters. On top of that, their study highlights how the top four Bitcoin miners control more than the 54% of the mining power.

3 Background

In this section we give an overview of Bitcoin's transaction propagation behavior. Since our TxProbe technique relies on subtleties of this process, we go into detail on just the relevant parts.

3.1 Three-Round Transaction Propagation

Bitcoin nodes propagate transactions by flooding, such that each node relays data about each transaction to every one of its peers. However, to minimize network traffic, nodes follow a three-step protocol, first sending just the transaction hash (32 bytes) and only sending the entire transaction (range from a few hundred bytes up to tens of kilobytes) if it is requested. This protocol is depicted in Fig. 1. In more detail, the three steps are:

- **Inventory messages (inv)** are used to announce the knowledge of one or more transactions or blocks. When a node receives (or generates) a new transaction or block he announces it to his peers by creating an inv message containing the transaction hash. Those peers who do not know about the announced item will ask for it back using a getdata message. Furthermore, when a node receives an inv message asking for a certain item, and he requests it back using a getdata message, the requester will wait up to 2 min for the node offering the item to respond back with it. Any other request offering the same item will be queued and only responded, first in first out, if the first node fails to reply.
- **Get data messages (getdata)** are used by Bitcoin nodes to request transactions and blocks to their peers. Such messages are sent as a response to the aforementioned inv messages when the receiver of the latter is interested in any of the offered items.
- **Transaction messages (tx)** are used to send transactions between peers. They are usually sent as a response to a getdata message. In contrast to the previously introduced messages, tx messages always contain a single transaction.

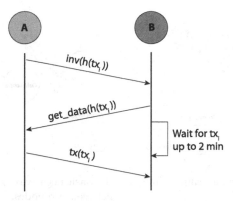

Fig. 1. Three-step protocol used to forward transactions in Bitcoin.

3.2 Mempool and Unspent Transaction Outputs (UTXOs)

A Bitcoin node validates each transaction it receives before relaying to its peers as described above. A valid transaction must have correct signatures, and must only spend existing and currently-unspent coins. Otherwise the transaction is discarded and not propagated further.

To aid in validation, each Bitcoin full node maintains a view of the current set of available coins (the `utxo set`). It also maintains a collection of pending transactions, called `mempool`, all of which have been validated against the `utxo set` and contain no double-spends amongst themselves.

Much of the complexity in the Bitcoin software, and the behavior we exploit in TxProbe, involves handling special cases during validation. Hence when a transaction is received, it is validated against the current `utxo set`. Since mempool is also kept free of double-spends, when a Bitcoin node receives a second transaction that spends the same coin as a transaction held in `mempool`, the second transaction is simply discarded.[1]

3.3 Handling Orphan Transactions

Sometimes a node receives transactions out of order. A transaction is considered an "orphan" if it is received prior to its direct ancestors, i.e. it spends a coin that is not yet part of the blockchain or in `mempool`. Since orphan transactions cannot be validated until the parent arrives, they are not immediately relayed to peers. Instead, orphan transactions are stored in a buffer, `MapOrphanTransactions` so that when the parent arrives it can be validated without re-requesting it from the network.

---

[1] There is a special case, called replace-by-fee (RBF) [7], in which a double-spending transaction replaces a previous transaction as long as the previous transaction is flagged to allow this and if the new transaction pays a larger fee. This does not affect the TxProbe technique.

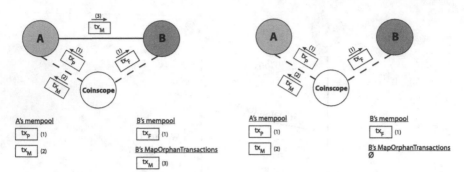

(a) Basic positive edge inferring technique between two nodes.   (b) Basic negative edge inferring technique between two nodes.

Fig. 2. Basic edge inferring technique.

To point out a detail relevant to our TxProbe technique: If a node receives a notice about a transaction from a peer (an `inv` message), but that transaction has already been stored as an orphan, then that transaction will be omitted from subsequent `get_data` messages. Looking ahead, this behavior enables our measurement node to probe whether an orphan transaction has already been received or not. We discuss other details about `MapOrphanTransactions`, such as eviction policies, later on when discussing optimizations to TxProbe.

4   Inferring the Bitcoin Network Topology

In this section we explain our technique for inferring the topology of Bitcoin's reachable peer-to-peer network, making use of the subtleties of transaction propagation in Bitcoin as described earlier, and in particular conflicting transactions and orphan transactions. We start by introducing a basic edge inference technique that tests for an edge between a single pair of peers. Later we discuss how to scale the technique up to take network-wide snapshots efficiently.

4.1   Basic Edge Inferring Technique

To explain the main idea behind our technique, we start by describing a scenario in which our Coinscope measurement node is connected to two nodes A and B, and we want to check if there exists an edge between them. Note that such a scenario is not realistic, but we will discuss real cases later on. First we create a pair of double spending transactions referred to as the parent (tx_P) and the flood (tx_F). We send tx_P to A and tx_F to B and assume that both transactions arrive to their destination at the same time, so A will reject tx_F if B sends it to him and vice versa. Now we create a third transaction, the marker (tx_M), that spends from tx_P and we send it to A. On receiving tx_M, A will forward it to all his peers. If the edge between the two nodes exists, as depicted in Fig. 2a, B will receive the transaction. It is worth noting that B does not know about tx_P, so tx_M will be flagged as orphan and not relayed any further. On the contrary, if the edge between nodes A and B does not exist, as depicted in Fig. 2b, tx_M will never be sent to B.

At this point we can check if the connection between the two nodes exists. To do so, we ask B about tx_M by sending him an inv message containing tx_M's hash. If the connection between the two nodes exists, B will have tx_M stored in his MapOrphanTransactions pool, so he will not request it back. On the other hand, if the edge does not exist, B will respond with a getdata message containing tx_M's hash.

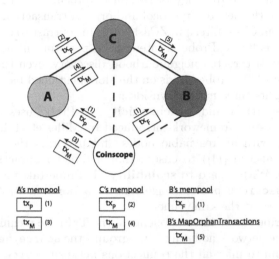

Fig. 3. Incorrect edge inferring with three nodes.

While this basic technique works in the most simple scenario, namely with two nodes potentially connected only between them, it can drastically fail if just one additional node is added to the picture. Let's see what happens if we connect one additional node C, as depicted in Fig. 3, and repeat the procedure. Since A is connected to C, tx_P and tx_M will be forwarded to him, C will treat both transactions as regular ones, and forward them to B, who will reject tx_P as double spending of tx_F, but accept tx_M as orphan. Ultimately, we will ask B about tx_M, and infer a non-existing edge between him and A.

Such a basic example highlights the first main issue of the basic approach: **isolation.** We need to ensure that tx_P remains only in the node we have sent it to. Otherwise, we may end up inferring non-existent edges. Moreover, this basic technique also builds on top of another fragile property: **synchronicity.** If node A receives tx_P before B receives tx_F, A can forward tx_P to B, and the latter will end up rejecting tx_F upon reception, making the technique to fail. Finally, the basic technique lacks **scalability.** Assuming we can sort out the two previous issues, for every three transactions created we will be able to infer at most the whole neighbourhood of a single node. Inferring the topology of the whole reachable network will require creating almost three transactions per node, namely $3 \cdot (n - 1)$ where n is the number of reachable nodes in the network. In order to solve the three aforementioned problems, we have created a technique called TxProbe.

4.2   TxProbe

TxProbe is a topology inference technique that uses double spending and orphan transactions to check the existence of edges between a pair of nodes. TxProbe can be used to infer the topology of several cryptocurrency P2P networks, as long as they share the network protocol and orphan transactions handling with Bitcoin (i.e. Bitcoin Cash, Litecoin, ZCash, etc). In contrast to recently proposed techniques, such as [6], TxProbe is intended to perform full network topology inference, instead of targeted neighbourhood discovery, even though the latter can be also achieved. TxProbe builds on the aforementioned basic edge inferring technique solving its three main downsides:

Regarding **isolation** and **synchronicity**, TxProbe uses Coinscope, the observation and testing framework introduced by Miller et al. in [11], to maintain connections with all reachable nodes and performs the invblock technique (proposed also in [11]) to ensure that a target transaction will remain in a target node. With regard to **scalability**, TxProbe takes advantage of the MapOrphanTransactions pool management to perform multiple nodes neighbourhood discovery at the same time.

We now describe the main components of the TxProbe technique. In a single trial, we break the network nodes into two groups, the source set and the sink set, where we aim to infer all the connections between source set nodes and sink set nodes. The source set will be usually smaller than the sink set, and should at least be less than the size of the mapOrphanTransactions pool.

Setup

Create Conflicting Transactions: First, we need to create the set of conflicting transactions, namely the parents, markers, and flood transactions. This time we are not targeting a single node to infer his peers (as we did with A in the basic inferring technique), but all the nodes in the source set. Therefore instead of creating a single parent and the flood transaction spending from the same utxo, we will create $n + 1$ distinct double spending transactions, n being the number of nodes in the source set: n of those transactions will be tagged as parents, while the remaining one will be the flood transaction. Finally we create a marker transaction from each of the parents, resulting in n parents, n markers, and the flood transaction. Figure 4 depicts a high level representation of the created transactions (spending from $UTXO_1$).

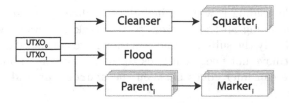

Fig. 4. High level representation of the transactions created in TxProbe

Invblock the Network: Once all the parents, markers and the flood transaction have been created, it is time to ensure that the **isolation** property will hold during the experiment. It is worth noting that for the isolation property to hold there are two things we need to ensure: First, that the flood transaction (tx_F) remains within the **sink set**. Secondly, that each parent (tx_{Pi}) remains only in the **source set** node (N_i) it will be sent to. To ensure so, we will perform an invblock of tx_F and every tx_P. invblock consists of sending inv messages to all the nodes in the network with the transaction hashes we want to block the propagation. Recall that a node requesting a transaction with a getdata message in response to a inv message will wait up to two minutes until requesting such transaction to any other peer offering it. By sending multiple inv messages containing the same transaction hashes to a node it can be blocked to request those transactions to any other node for an arbitrary number of minutes, which gives enough time to send all the transactions without having to worry about the isolation property being broken. It is also worth noting that the network will not be blocked with the markers hashes, since their propagation from the **source set** to the **sink set** is what will allow us to infer edges between nodes.

Main protocol

Once we have set the proper conditions for the experiment to be run, we can start sending the transactions we created earlier.

Send Transactions: First, the flood transaction is sent to all the nodes in the **sink set**. After waiting a few seconds for the flood transaction to propagate, we can send the proper transactions to the **source set**. We start by sending a different parent to each node in the set, wait a couple of seconds, and then send the corresponding marker to each node. Since we have invblocked the whole network with the flood and parents, at this point we are sure that, as long as the nodes behave properly, the flood transaction is only present in the **sink set** and each parent is only present in its respective node from the **source set**.

Requesting Markers Back: After waiting a few seconds for the propagation of the markers, we will request all of them back from every node in the **sink set**. Despite being orphans, markers are still considered known transactions by those **sink set** nodes. In that sense, as we have already seen in the basic inferring technique, when an orphan transaction is requested as part of a getdata message the node holding it will not include it in their response. By sending an inv message containing all the markers to the sink set nodes we will receive back a request of only the subset of markers they have not heard of.[2] By mapping the markers that have not been sent back to the source set node we originally sent them to, we can infer edges between the source set and the respondent sink set nodes.

Permuting the Sets: With all the aforementioned steps, we are able to infer the edges between a certain configuration of the network, that is, a specific set of nodes forming the source set and sink set. However, the technique cannot infer edges between nodes in the same set. In order to infer the whole topology, we need to run several rounds permuting the sets. Therefore, both the setup and the main protocol will be run until every pair of nodes have been in a different set at least once.

4.3   Making Room for Marker Transactions

The MapOrphanTransactions pool is not allowed to grow unbounded. In fact, it has a small default limit of only 100 transactions at a time. When this limit is exceeded, orphan transactions are evicted. The eviction mechanism works as follows: First, it generates a random hash *randomhash*. Next, it selects the transaction in the pool with the closest hash higher than *randomhash* and evicts it from the pool. The eviction mechanism repeats until the pool size is within limits.

Eviction poses a problem for scaling up the TxProbe technique. Marker transactions must not be evicted until they are read back at the end of a measurement trial. However, the eviction policy has a design flaw, which enables us to make preferential transactions that are hard to evict. By crafting transactions for which their hashes lay between a small fixed range (e.g: by re-signing the transaction), and since the *randomhash* hash used in the eviction mechanism picks values over an uniform distribution, we can bound the odds of our transaction being evicted depending on how small the range is set.

Cleansing the Orphan Pool: When we were performing the basic inferring technique there was no need to worry about transactions being evicted from the MapOrphanTransactions pool since we were only creating a single marker. However, now up to n markers would need to be stored by a single node. In order to ensure that there is enough space to store all the markers, we will empty the MapOrphanTransactions pool of all nodes in the sink set. We start by creating a transaction we call the cleanser, and spending from it we create 100 distinct double spending transactions we call the squatters. Next, we send all the squatters to every single node in the sink set aiming to full the orphan pool. Finally, we send the cleanser to every sink set node. Upon reception of the cleanser, all transactions in the orphan transactions pool will no longer be orphans. One of the squatters will be flagged as valid, whereas the rest will

---

[2] Notice that some times the subset will be the actual set.

be discarded as double-spending transactions. Regardless of which squatter is accepted by each node, the `MapOrphanTransactions` pool of each `sink set node` will be emptied. Figure 4 depicts a high level representation of the orphans and cleanser transaction creation (spending from $UTXO_0$).

5   Costs of Topology Inference

In this section we discuss the costs of running TxProbe both in terms of time and transaction fees.

5.1   Time Costs

How long it takes to infer the topology of a network using TxProbe directly depends on the number of reachable nodes r_n in the network. As we have already seen, the size of our `source sets` is bound by the `MapOrphanTransactions` pool size, which is 100 by default. Our set partitioning algorithm works as a grid, in order to separate nodes in two sets we create a grid of width $w = min(\lceil \sqrt{r_n} \rceil, 100)$ and length $h = \lceil \frac{r_n}{w} \rceil$, and we traverse the grid by rows and columns, being the selected row/column in iteration i our `source set` for the i-th round of the experiment, and the rest of nodes our `sink set`.[3] The total number of different `source sets`, and therefore, the total number of rounds required to run an experiment will then be:

$$t_r = \begin{cases} h + w - 2, \text{for } h \leq w \\ h - 1 + \lceil \frac{h}{w} \rceil \cdot w, \text{for } h > w \end{cases}$$

Each round of the TxProbe can be run in about 2.5 min, resulting in $2.5 \cdot t_r$ min to run TxProbe over a network of r_n nodes. Inferring the topology of a network like Bitcoin testnet (~1000 nodes) requires, therefore, about 2.6 h, whereas inferring the topology of Bitcoin mainnet (~10000 nodes) requires about 8.25 h. The partitioning algorithm can be found depicted in Fig. 5.

5.2   Transaction Fee Costs

The costs of running TxProbe directly depend on the number of rounds of the experiment t_r and the fee rate to be paid in order to get our transactions relayed by the network. For every round we will perform an orphan cleansing, resulting in two standard 1-1 P2PKH transactions (only the cleanser and one squatter will be accepted, the rest will be eventually flagged as double-spends). Moreover, at every round either the flood will be accepted (1-1 P2PKH transaction) or a parent-marker pair will be accepted (two 1-1 P2PKH transactions).

---

[3] Notice that when traversing columns the number of elements in the set can be higher than w, in which case the algorithm will create $\lceil h/w \rceil$ sets per column.

round 1 round 2 round 3   round w

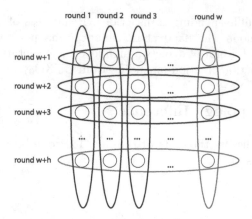

round w+1
round w+2
round w+3
round w+h

Fig. 5. Set-partitioning algorithm used in TxProbe. Sets corresponding to the last row and column (marked in red) can be skipped since they will be already counted by the rest of sets. (Color figure online)

The size of a 1-1 P2PKH transaction using compressed public keys and assuming a signature of maximum length (73-byte signature) is 193 bytes long. Putting all together, the cost of running TxProbe in a network of r_n nodes ranges between $3 \cdot 193 \cdot fee\_rate \cdot t_r$ and $4 \cdot 193 \cdot fee\_rate \cdot t_r$.

At a fee rate of 5 sat/byte[4], running the experiment in a network like Bitcoin mainnet will cost between 573210 and 764280 satoshi.

Impact of TxProbe Measurement. We say a few words about the feasibility of using TxProbe to do ethical measurement. The TxProbe measurement involves sending many kinds of abnormal transactions, and thus it can only be used ethically if we ensure it does not harm or burden the network we are measuring. To start with, although TxProbe transactions are unusual in that they are multi-way conflicting double-spends, they are not relayed and thus do not increase network or storage utilization compared to ordinary transactions.

The TxProbe experiment can have a destructive effect, however, on the `MapOrphanTransactions` data structure. As we discussed earlier, if the orphan transactions pool is full, then adding new orphan transactions (such as the marker transactions in TxProbe) can evict others. We could not rule out the potential that our measurement would add to this congestion (i.e., over an 8+ h for a scan of the entire network) and could adversely affect real transactions.

6   Experiments and Results

We conducted experiments using the Bitcoin testnet in order to evaluate our topology inference technique. We first conducted ground truth experiments to

---

[4] Fee to get transactions confirmed between 1–2 blocks on 27th August 2018 according to https://bitcoinfees.earn.com/.

quantify its precision and recall, and then took a snapshot measurement of test-net to demonstrate its usefulness for network-wide scans.

6.1   Validation

In order to validate our results we run 5 local Bitcoin nodes as ground truth. The ground truth nodes are included as part of the `source set` in each round of the experiment. This means that, if our results are correct, at the end of the experiment we would have inferred every edge between the ground truth nodes and the `sink set` nodes.

For every run of the experiment there are always nodes that do not behave according to the default client, for example by ignoring `invblock` and therefore, sending transactions without receiving `getdata` messages. In order to detect such nodes, an `invblock` test is performed before every experiment using two Coinscope instances: the first instance crafts a random 32-byte hash and offers it to the whole network using `inv` messages. The second instance offers the exact same hash within the next two minutes and collects all the `getdata` responses. All those nodes who responded the second instance are flagged as unblockable nodes and taken out of the experiment.

Transitory edges (i.e. edges that have been there for a short amount of time) are also removed from the inferred results, as well as nodes who know about transactions they are not supposed to (nodes who missed a parent/marker when it has been sent to them, nodes holding the flood transaction when they were supposed to hold a parent transactions, etc). Finally, disconnecting nodes (nodes that have disconnected from Coinscope while the experiment was running) are also removed, as well as all inferred edges referring them.

Our validation reported a precision of 100% and recall between 93.86% and 95.45% with a 95% confidence over 40 runs of the experiment.

6.2   Analysis of the Inferred Network

This section includes a description of a testnet network snapshot taken on 21st February, 2018, as obtained using our technique, which reported a precision of 100% with a recall of 97.40%.

The observed network has 733 nodes and 6090 edges, with an average degree of 16.6. The degree distribution of the network is far from uniform (Fig. 6a), with most of the nodes having between 7 and 14 neighbors. The most common degree observed in the network is 8 (shown by 12% of the nodes), a value that matches the default maximum number of outgoing nodes of the Bitcoin Core client.[5] The maximum degree is 59, less than half of the maximum number of default peer connections of Bitcoin Core.[6]

---

[5] https://github.com/bitcoin/bitcoin/blob/v0.16.2/src/net.h#L59.

[6] The maximum number of default connections is set to 125: https://github.com/bitcoin/bitcoin/blob/v0.16.2/src/net.h#L73.

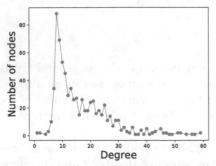

(a) Degree distribution of nodes in the testnet snapshot.

(b) Communities detected in the
testnet snapshot.

Table 1 provides a summary of basic properties of the network regarding clustering, distances, assortativity, and community structure, comparing the observed values with those obtained over random graphs with similar characteristics. That is, for each property, we create 100 random graphs that *resemble* the obtained testnet graph, compute the property over the random graphs, and provide both the average of the results over the random graphs and the percentage of times the value over the random graph is higher than the observed in the testnet snapshot. We have considered three different models for generating random graphs: Erdős-Rényi [4] (ER), configuration model [15] (CM), and Barabási-Albert [1] (BA). The Erdős-Rényi model generates graphs where each pair of nodes may have an edge with the same probability, and independently of the other edges of the network. ER generates graphs with a binomial degree distribution, and it is commonly used as baseline to analyse networks. However, the observed testnet graph does not seem to have an ER-like degree distribution (recall Fig. 6a). Therefore, we also create random graphs using the configuration model, that allows creating networks with a chosen degree distribution. Finally, since many real world computer networks have been reported to be preferential attachment networks, we also include Barabási-Albert model. BA generates scale-free networks, that have power-law degree distributions. The random graphs we create *resemble* the observed network: ER graphs are created with the same number of nodes and edges, CM graphs have the same degree distribution (and, therefore, they implicitly also have the same number of nodes and edges), BA graphs have the same number of nodes and a similar number of edges (by adjusting the number of new edges created at each step of the graph generation algorithm, the number of edges is adjusted to be as close as possible to the observed one).

Distances are the properties analyzed in the testnet graph that most approximate those obtained in random graphs. For instance, the radius of the testnet snapshot is 3, exactly the same value observed in all the generated random graphs. The diameter (the maximum distance between any pair of nodes) of the testnet graph is 5, which is higher than most of the random graphs, but

Table 1. Network properties. For random graphs, the 100-run average is provided, with the percentage of times the property over the random graph is higher than the observed in the testnet snapshot in parenthesis.

Metric	Testnet	ER		CM		BA	
Diameter	5	4	(0%)	4.93	(1%)	4	(0%)
Periphery size	6	612.9	(100%)	21.2	(80%)	379.6	(100%)
Radius	3	3	(0%)	3	(0%)	3	(0%)
Center size	45	120.7	(100%)	57.9	(70%)	362.9	(100%)
Eccentricity	3.946	3.827	(0%)	3.979	(70%)	3.528	(0%)
Clustering coefficient	0.052	0.023	(0%)	0.036	(0%)	0.066	(100%)
Transitivity	0.128	0.023	(0%)	0.036	(0%)	0.057	(0%)
Degree assortativity	0.291	−0.001	(0%)	−0.008	(0%)	−0.043	(0%)
Country assortativity	0.007	−0.001	(0%)	−0.001	(0%)	−0.002	(0%)
Clique number	24	3.73	(0%)	4.05	(0%)	6.58	(0%)
Modularity	0.270	0.220	(0%)	0.216	(0%)	0.214	(0%)

very close to their diameters. Moreover, by removing just 3 of the lowest degree nodes of the testnet graph, its diameter becomes 4 (removing the degrees from the sequence in the CM model has the same effect). On the contrary, the number of nodes in the center and in the periphery (i.e. nodes with eccentricity equal to the radius and the diameter, respectively) differs largely from random graphs.

With respect to clustering, the testnet graph exhibits a higher average clustering coefficient than ER and CM graphs, but less than BA graphs. However, observed transitivity is higher than any of the random graphs. Clustering coefficient analyses how well connected the neighborhood of a node is (taking into account the neighborhood regardless of its size), whereas transitivity is focused on studying 3-node substructures.

The testnet snapshot shows higher assortativity than the expected for random graphs, that is, nodes in the testnet tend to connect to other nodes that are similar to themselves more often than what ER, CM and BA random graphs exhibit. Specifically, nodes tend to connect to other nodes with the same degree and, to a less extent but also in a significant manner, to nodes in the same country.

Regarding community structure, we have computed the modularity over the best partition found using the Louvain method. The modularity of the testnet graph is higher than any of the random graphs, regardless of the chosen model. That is, the network shows more community structure than what should be expected for a random graph. Figure 6 depicts a visualization of the communities found in the testnet snapshot, with the color of the node denoting the community it belongs to. There are nine communities, with the biggest two (purple and green in the image) having 37% of the nodes of the network. Notably, there is one community (colored in pink) that contains only 7.5% of the nodes but

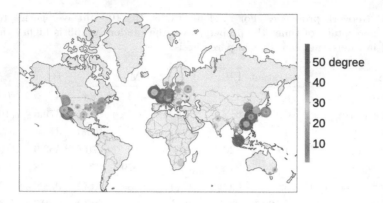

Fig. 6. Geographical location of nodes. (Color figure online)

includes the 25 highest degree nodes of the network. This is consistent with the high degree assortativity reported in the network. Remarkably, the testnet graph contains a clique (a fully connected graph) of 24 nodes. This clique is found inside the high-degree community (depicted in pink in the visualization). In contrast, the largest clique formed by nodes of any other community has a size of just 6 nodes.

We have also used an IP Geolocation API[7] to obtain the geographical location of the nodes in the testnet snapshot. Figure 6 shows a map with the node's locations, where both the size and color of the nodes are used to denote nodes' degree. Most nodes are located in the United States, Central Europe, and East Asia.

7   Conclusions

We set out to design an effective measurement technique that can reconstruct the Bitcoin network topology. We validated TxProbe to show that it is accurate and can indeed be scaled up to snapshot the entire network with reasonably low fees. However, we decided not to carry out a measurement of the main network because we could not rule out its potential to delay the propagation of real users' transactions. We consider it an open question whether this technique (or analysis thereof) can be improved so it can be used less invasively.

We did, however, take network measurement snapshots of the Bitcoin test network topology (over 700 nodes). Our analysis of the Bitcoin testnet reveals significant non-random structure, including several communities, as well as a clique of high-degree nodes. Although our findings over testnet cannot be applied to the mainnet, it demonstrates that the technique is viable not only in Bitcoin, but in any other cryptocurrency sharing the network protocol and orphan transaction handling with it.

---

[7] http://ip-api.com/.

Like other measurement techniques, TxProbe makes use of implementation-specific behaviors in the Bitcoin software. While cryptocurrencies have not made topology-hiding an explicit design requirement, in the past software changes that improve user anonymity have also had the effect of closing off measurement avenues. Viewed in this light, TxProbe is the next step in a tacit arms race between measurement efforts and privacy enhancing design. We make the following suggestions to the cryptocurrency community to avoid this cycle: First, determine whether network topology or other metrics should be an explicit design goal, in which case effort can be focused on achieving it robustly. Second, follow the Tor project [9] for example, in deploying measurement-supporting mechanisms into the software itself, that balances the positive goals of network measurement (such as quantifying decentralization, detecting weaknesses or attacks, etc.) with the privacy goals of users.

References

1. Albert, R., Barabási, A.: Statistical mechanics of complex networks. CoRR cond-mat/0106096 (2001)
2. Biryukov, A., Khovratovich, D., Pustogarov, I.: Deanonymisation of clients in bitcoin p2p network. In: Proceedings of the 2014 ACM SIGSAC Conference on Computer and Communications Security, CCS 2014, pp. 15–29. ACM, New York, NY, USA (2014)
3. Biryukov, A., Pustogarov, I.: Bitcoin over tor isn't a good idea. In: Proceedings of the 2015 IEEE Symposium on Security and Privacy, SP 2015, pp. 122–134. IEEE Computer Society, Washington, DC, USA (2015). https://doi.org/10.1109/SP.2015.15
4. Erdös, P., Rényi, A.: On the evolution of random graphs. Publ. Math. Inst. Hung. Acad. Sci. 5, 17–61 (1960)
5. Gencer, A.E., Basu, S., Eyal, I., van Renesse, R., Sirer, E.G.: Decentralization in bitcoin and ethereum networks. In: Meiklejohn, S., Sako, K. (eds.) FC 2018. LNCS, vol. 10957, pp. 439–457. Springer, Heidelberg (2018). https://doi.org/10.1007/978-3-662-58387-6_24
6. Grundmann, M., Neudecker, T., Hartenstein, H.: Exploiting transaction accumulation and double spends for topology inference in bitcoin. In: Zohar, A., et al. (eds.) FC 2018. LNCS, vol. 10958, pp. 113–126. Springer, Heidelberg (2019). https://doi.org/10.1007/978-3-662-58820-8_9
7. Harding, D.A., Todd, P.: Opt-in Full Replace-by-Fee Signaling (2015). https://github.com/bitcoin/bips/blob/master/bip-0125.mediawiki
8. Heilman, E., Kendler, A., Zohar, A., Goldberg, S.: Eclipse attacks on bitcoin's peer-to-peer network. In: 24th USENIX Security Symposium (USENIX Security 15), pp. 129–144. USENIX Association, Washington, D.C. (2015)
9. Jansen, R., Johnson, A.: Safely measuring tor. In: Proceedings of the 2016 ACM SIGSAC Conference on Computer and Communications Security, pp. 1553–1567. ACM (2016)
10. Koshy, P., Koshy, D., McDaniel, P.: An analysis of anonymity in bitcoin using P2P network traffic. In: Christin, N., Safavi-Naini, R. (eds.) FC 2014. LNCS, vol. 8437, pp. 469–485. Springer, Heidelberg (2014). https://doi.org/10.1007/978-3-662-45472-5_30

11. Miller, A., et al.: Discovering bitcoin's public topology and influential nodes (2015)
12. Nayak, K., Kumar, S., Miller, A., Shi, E.: Stubborn mining: generalizing selfish mining and combining with an eclipse attack. In: 2016 IEEE European Symposium on Security and Privacy (EuroS&P), pp. 305–320, March 2016
13. Neudecker, T., Andelfinger, P., Hartenstein, H.: Timing analysis for inferring the topology of the bitcoin peer-to-peer network. In: 2016 Intl IEEE Conferences on Ubiquitous Intelligence Computing, Advanced and Trusted Computing, Scalable Computing and Communications, Cloud and Big Data Computing, Internet of People, and Smart World Congress (UIC/ATC/ScalCom/CBDCom/IoP/SmartWorld), pp. 358–367, July 2016
14. Neudecker, T., Hartenstein, H.: Could network information facilitate address clustering in bitcoin? In: Brenner, M., et al. (eds.) FC 2017. LNCS, vol. 10323, pp. 155–169. Springer, Cham (2017). https://doi.org/10.1007/978-3-319-70278-0_9
15. Newman, M.E.: The structure and function of complex networks. SIAM Rev. **45**(2), 167–256 (2003)
16. Nick, J.: Guessing bitcoin's p2p connections (2015). https://jonasnick.github.io/blog/2015/03/06/guessing-bitcoins-p2p-connections/
17. The Bitcoin Core developers: Bitcoin core 0.10.1 release notes, April 2015. https://github.com/bitcoin/bitcoin/blob/v0.10.1/doc/release-notes.md

Fraud Detection and Game Theory

Forecasting Suspicious Account Activity at Large-Scale Online Service Providers

Hassan Halawa[1]([✉]), Konstantin Beznosov[1], Baris Coskun[2], Meizhu Liu[3], and Matei Ripeanu[1]

[1] University of British Columbia, Vancouver, Canada
{hhalawa,beznosov,matei}@ece.ubc.ca
[2] Amazon Web Services, New York, USA
barisco@amazon.com
[3] Yahoo! Research, New York, USA
meizhu@oath.com

Abstract. In the face of large-scale automated social engineering attacks to large online services, fast detection and remediation of compromised accounts are crucial to limit the spread of the attack and to mitigate the overall damage to users, companies, and the public at large. We advocate a fully automated approach based on machine learning: we develop an early warning system that harnesses account activity traces to predict which accounts are likely to be compromised in the future. We demonstrate the feasibility and applicability of the system through an experiment at a large-scale online service provider using four months of real-world production data encompassing hundreds of millions of users. We show that—even limiting ourselves to login data only in order to derive features with low computational cost, and a basic model selection approach—our classifier can be tuned to achieve good classification precision when used for forecasting. Our system correctly identifies *up to one month in advance* the accounts later flagged as suspicious with precision, recall, and false positive rates that indicate the mechanism is likely to prove valuable in operational settings to support additional layers of defense.

Keywords: Forecasting · Machine learning for security · Big data analytics for security · Large-scale cyberattacks · Cloud security

1 Introduction

Online services are an integral part of our personal and professional lives. To support widespread adoption and improve usability, large-scale online service providers (LSOSPs) have made it simple for users to access any of the provided services using a single credential. Such "single sign-on" systems make it much

---

This work was done when Baris Coskun was with Yahoo! Research.

I. Goldberg and T. Moore (Eds.): FC 2019, LNCS 11598, pp. 569–587, 2019.
https://doi.org/10.1007/978-3-030-32101-7_33

easier for users to manage their interactions through a single account and sign-in interface. As users become more invested in the platform, the single login credential becomes a valuable key to a whole set of services, as well as the 'key' to their digital identity and the personal information stored on the platform. As a consequence, these credentials are highly attractive targets to attackers.

As LSOSPs improve their defense systems to protect their user base, attackers have shifted their efforts to social engineering attacks: e.g, attacks that exploit incorrect decisions made by individual users to trick them into disclosing their login credentials [14]. Once an account is compromised, the attackers hijack the account from its legitimate owner and, typically, use it for their own purposes [19]: for example, to evade detection while perpetuating an attack (e.g., multi-stage phishing, or malware distribution campaigns) or to carry out other fraudulent activity (e.g., sending out spam email).

Thus, detecting compromised accounts early and giving back control to their legitimate owners quickly, as well as designing defense mechanisms that add additional layers of defense to protect users likely to fall prey to social engineering attacks, is crucial. Doing so can mitigate the damage an attacker can do while in control of a compromised account, protect the account owner's digital identity, and reduce the damage inflicted by an automated large-scale social-engineering attack to a LSOSP and its user community. It should be noted that, detecting compromised accounts is much more challenging than just identifying fake ones (i.e., those created by an attacker) since, in the former case, suspicious activity is typically interleaved with the account owner's legitimate activity [8].

This paper tests the hypothesis that it is feasible to identify likely future victims of mass-scale social-engineering attacks. In a nutshell, we postulate that the behavioral patterns of the users that have little incentives or low ability to fend off social-engineering attacks can be learned. To this end we propose an early warning system based on a completely automated pipeline using machine learning (ML) to identify the accounts with similar behavioral patterns to those that have been flagged as suspicious in the past.

Predicting accounts that are more likely to be compromised in the future can be used to develop new defenses, to fine-tune and better target existing defense mechanisms, as well as to better protect vulnerable users [10]. While we briefly discuss the intuition behind some of these defense mechanisms in the discussion section (Sect. 7), their design and evaluation, however, is beyond the scope of this paper and we focus here solely on evaluating our conjecture that predicting which accounts are more likely to be compromised is feasible.

We have tested our hypothesis using real-world data from a large LSOSP (i.e., at the scale of Amazon, Facebook, Google, or Yahoo). Throughout this paper we will refer to it as a *LSOSP* (in italics, the non-italicized LSOSP refers to a generic Large-Scale Online Service Provider). Our experiments were carried out over four months of production data covering hundreds of millions of users generating hundreds of billions of login events to *LSOSP*'s platform. Due to space constraints we omit some relevant in-depth descriptions from this paper, and we refer interested readers to our more exhaustive technical report [11] for more information.

This paper makes the following contributions:

- We formulate the hypothesis that it is feasible to identify the users more likely to fall prey to mass-scale social-engineering attacks (Sect. 2), propose an approach to identify their accounts, and design an early warning system (Sect. 3).
- We demonstrate the feasibility and applicability of the proposed approach on real-world production data (Sect. 5). We show that, even using low-cost features extracted from two basic datasets (Sect. 4) and a simple model selection approach (Sect. 3) leading to acceptable training runtime, the proposed classifier can be tuned to achieve good classification quality based on the recall, precision, and false positive rate metrics (Sect. 5). For example (CE_C in Sect. 5), using only *one week of login event history and predicting one month in advance*, our classifier predicts more than half of the accounts later flagged as having suspicious behaviour (i.e., achieves a recall of 50.62%) and, at the same time, around one in five of the predicted accounts is actually labeled as suspicious at *LSOSP* within a 30-day prediction horizon (i.e., precision of 18.33%, with a low false positive rate of 0.49%). While, overall, our results indicate that it is feasible to achieve good classification quality, we stress two important points: first, it is important to note that our results should be seen as a lower bound of the achievable classification performance: this can likely be further improved by using richer data or additional computational resources (e.g., to support more sophisticated learning methods). Second, efficient defense mechanisms can be developed based on future victim predictors as, for example, Boshmaf et al. [5] demonstrate in the context of a social-bot infiltration attack. We expand on these points in the discussion Sect. 7.

2 Problem Formulation

We present an overview of our problem (Sect. 2.1) by abstracting away from all company- and experiment-specific details which we describe in detail in Sects. 3, 4 and 5. Here, we go over the assumptions and objectives that influenced our approach, we elaborate on the datasets required to carry out the classification task (Sect. 2.2), and we introduce our *classification exercises (CEs)*, which are the means by which we organize our *experiments* (Sect. 2.3).

2.1 Overview

Our goal is to develop an early warning system that can be used by LSOSPs to harness observable user behavior to identify accounts likely to be compromised in the future. Our intuition is the following: over the course of everyday use, the history of user interactions encapsulates information from which one can infer whether an account is more likely to be compromised in the future (e.g., because the user does not have the interest or the ability to fend off social-engineering attacks); eventually (some of) these accounts are compromised, generate suspicious activity, and are later flagged. In other words, to forecast future suspicious activity, we aim for features that approximate user behavioral patterns to infer similarity to accounts that are later flagged as suspicious and develop a binary classifier to act as an *early warning system*. We chose a supervised learning app-roach as, over the past few years, it has been shown to achieve good performance for a variety of classification tasks [3,6,16,21,22].

2.2   Assumptions, Objectives, and Datasets

Assumptions. We treat the prediction of suspicious accounts as a binary clas-sification problem (suspicious vs. non-suspicious). We assume that only a small subset of the overall population is likely to exhibit suspicious activity. We believe that this is true for large providers that offer services to a large number of users around the world (up to billions of users) and dedicate resources to maintain a "healthy" user population. The direct implication is that the ML techniques used, the data selection for the training of the classifiers, and the success metrics used are all tuned for imbalanced data.

Objectives. We aim to meet the following objectives when designing and tuning the binary classifier. First, a low rate of false positives: accounts incorrectly predicted as suspicious (i.e., false positives) should be minimized even at the cost of decreasing the number of correctly predicted suspicious accounts (i.e., true positives). This trade-off can be controlled by tuning the classifier's prediction threshold when generating the final binary classification. We also discuss tuning for a low rate of false negatives in (Sect. 7).

Second, and crucially for deployment at a LSOSP, with hundreds of mil-lions of users and tens of billions of user activity events per day (or more!), the classifier should be optimized for runtime efficiency during both training (feature extraction and model building) and testing/use (prediction and clas-sification). This can be accomplished by employing features that can be easily extracted/computed from the raw data, and by choosing ML models that offer a good trade-off between the quality of prediction and performance. Balancing this trade-off is crucial for timely forecasting of suspicious activity and thus faster remediation (as well as adoption in realistic settings).

Required Datasets. We assume that the LSOSP has access to at least two types of data. First, data that can be mined to extract behavioral patterns. Second, a sample of accounts previously flagged as suspicious that can be used as ground truth. We detail the data we use from *LSOSP* in Sect. 4.

2.3   Experiment Organization

Here we establish the terminology we use for the rest of this paper. We define the means by which we organize our experiments (*Classification Exercises*), and we detail the categories of accounts that can be observed in the datasets and how we use them.

Classification Exercises (CEs). CEs are our way of grouping together all parameters of a binary classification experiment (e.g., training time interval, testing time interval, ML model hyperparameters) and the associated results. As with any typical supervised ML approach, a CE is divided into two distinct phases: *training* and *testing* (Figure. 1 provides an overview). During training, our goal is to fit a model that learns user behavioral patterns that can be used as early predictors of suspicious account activity. During testing, the fitted model is applied to new data *not seen during training* and the classifier's performance is evaluated against a labeled ground truth.

Categories of Accounts. We consider U as the set of all accounts registered with the LSOSP. Depending on the scale and popularity of the LSOSP, U can be extremely large potentially exceeding a billion users. We use days as a coarse-grain measure of time. We consider L_d as the set of users with login activity on day d. For the set L_d, we extract easy-to-compute low-cost features representing the users' login behavior on day d. We aim to learn the behavioral patterns of legitimate accounts prior to them being flagged as suspicious. We denote with S_d the set of user accounts flagged as suspicious on day d. Existence of an account in set S_d on day d is a clear indication that the account exhibited some suspicious activity prior to or on day d. However, it is important to note that the opposite is not true: if an account is absent from the set S_d on day d that does not imply that it did not exhibit any irregular activity prior to or on day d. The reason for this is that the pipeline used for detecting suspicious accounts at the LSOSP is expected to have some lag. In other words, it takes time for an account to be flagged as suspicious after it first starts exhibiting irregular behavior.

Avoiding Attacker-Controlled Accounts. The set L_d contains not only legitimate user accounts but also those that are under the control of an attacker (the set A_d). These include fake as well as compromised accounts (considered as sets F_d and C_d respectively). *We implement several heuristics to prune such accounts and avoid learning user behavioral patterns from accounts that may be under attacker control.* Thus, we do not use the sets L_d and S_d directly. Instead, to avoid learning the behavior of accounts under attacker control (A_d), we prune both L_d and S_d in order to eliminate accounts that may be under attacker control. We discuss this preprocessing step in detail in Sect. 3.3.

3   Proposed Approach

This section outlines our proposed approach: the details of our classification exercises (Sect. 3.1), the proposed supervised ML pipeline (Sect. 3.2), and the heuristics we implement to avoid learning from accounts under the control of an attacker and to reduce bias when evaluating our approach (Sect. 3.3). The following sections describe our datasets (Sect. 4) and the evaluation results (Sect. 5).

3.1   Classification Exercise Composition

We organize our classification exercises (CEs) as outlined in Fig. 1. During *training*, we attempt to fit a model (M) that learns which behavioral patterns during the training Data Window (training-DW[1]) correlated to the account being labeled as suspicious later in the Label Window (LW). We introduce a Buffer Window (BW) between the DW and LW, to account for any lag (delay) in the suspicious account flagging pipeline used to generate the ground truth of suspicious accounts. The reason is that, in the absence of the BW, a lag in the pipeline will cause the fitted model to learn user behavioral patterns from accounts that are already under the control of an attacker. In Sect. 3.3, we present our heuristics to estimate the width of the Buffer Window (BW).

During *testing*, the fitted model (M) obtained during training, is applied during the *testing-DW* to forecast the set of accounts that are likely to have suspicious behaviour (P_{CE}). The quality of those predictions is then evaluated against the ground truth of labeled suspicious accounts extracted from the *testing-LW*.

Training Interval			Testing Interval	
Data Window (DW)	Buffer Window (BW)	Label Window (LW)	Data Window (DW)	Label Window (LW)

Time →

Fig. 1. Overview of a Classification Exercise (CE). Each exercise is divided into two broad phases: *training*, during which the classifier is fitted, and *testing*, during which the classifier predictions are evaluated. Each phase is subdivided into smaller non-overlapping time windows: *Data Window* (DW), *Buffer Window* (BW) and *Label Window* (LW). The DW is the period of time over which behavioural features are mined. The BW is a period of time introduced to avoid learning from accounts that may already be compromised but not yet labeled as such. The LW is the period over which labels are extracted.

3.2   The Early Warning Pipeline

Our system is composed of a pipeline that can be easily integrated into existing systems. We note that our pipeline design stresses efficiency, scalability, and, ultimately, achieving a practical training runtime sometimes even to the detriment of the learned classifiers (e.g., using simple low-cost features as opposed to sophisticated feature extraction). With production data, similar in scale to what we have access to at *LSOSP*, our pipeline is designed to extract behavioral patterns and to train in reasonable time on log traces from hundreds of millions of accounts leading to hundreds of billions of log entries over the duration of each CE. We developed our pipeline in Scala 2.11, employed SparkML for all our developed classifiers, and ran our CEs on Spark 2.0.2 [28].

Data Preprocessing. We preprocess the datasets from which we extract the user behavioral patterns (e.g., login activity dataset) as well as the ground truth (e.g., accounts flagged as suspicious). Importantly, *we also carry out a series of*

---

[1] Where the context makes the notation unambiguous, we skip the prefix and use *DW* only for *training-DW* or *testing-DW*. Similarly for *LW*.

pruning operations in order to exclude accounts that may bias either learning or evaluation as discussed in Sect. 3.3. During this stage, for each account, we extract features at the day level and aggregate them for the intervals associated with the classification exercise. There is an inherent trade-off here: extracting and computing a large number of features over a long duration of time could potentially include more behavioral information thereby increasing the prediction accuracy. However, this comes at the cost of longer runtime and might affect prediction timeliness. At *LSOSP*, we find that extracting only a relatively small set of low-cost features that are both simple and quick enough to compute is both sufficient and also more practical from a performance perspective in a production environment (details in Sect. 4).

Preprocessing Imbalanced Data. Typically at LSOSPs, suspicious accounts (the positive class) are a minority compared to the overall population. Naively training an ML classifier on such imbalanced data will typically result in a classifier that always predicts the dominant class (the negative class in our case) to achieve the highest accuracy [20]. Approaches to mitigate this problem include simple preprocessing techniques such as undersampling the majority class or oversampling the minority class [12], or Cost-Sensitive Learning [17] that attempts to minimize the cost of misclassifications by assigning asymmetrical costs during the training process. At LSOSP, given the scale of the data and our focus on building a practical pipeline with good balance between runtime and classification performance, we use undersampling during training (however, we test on the whole set of labeled data in the test set).

Classifier Tuning. Second, during the hyperparameter optimization stage, model selection is carried out in order to find the best model (or set of parameters) for the classification task. This only needs to be done once during training (or periodically, with low frequency and offline, to learn new user behavioral patterns) and is not carried out during inference using the fitted model in production. We use a Random Forest (RF) classifier considering the good trade-off it offers between runtime and classification accuracy [9]. We carry out the hyperparameter optimization on an independent dataset extracted from the available history and specifically reserved for this purpose (CE_A in Sect. 5). The extracted model parameters are then fixed for all the subsequent CEs.

Model Fitting and Inference. Third, after data preprocessing and hyperparameter tuning, a ML model M is fitted and later applied to make predictions on new data (i.e., inference). On the one hand, this data could be one for which there already exists labeled ground truth. In that case, the goal is to evaluate the performance of the developed classifier. On the other hand, this could be new data from production for which no ground truth exists (i.e., during the real-world deployment) and in this case, the goal is to put the classifier into practice to predict accounts likely to generate suspicious activity in the future based on their recent behavioral patterns.

Model Evaluation. Finally, we obtain the confusion matrix based on the resulting predictions and collect statistical measures of the classifier's performance.

3.3   Heuristics

Our goal is to learn behaviour from legitimate accounts (i.e., that are not attacker-controlled: fake and compromised accounts—$A_d\{d|d \in$ *Training Interval*$\}$) and predict which legitimate accounts may later get compromised and get labeled as suspicious. To this end we use a number of heuristics. We also implement additional heuristics to increase the confidence in our evaluation.

Heuristics to increase the chance that we capture only the behaviour of accounts under the control of legitimate users. During training, we attempt to exclude all accounts that are potentially under the control of an attacker. In practice the set of accounts A_d is unknown, even for historical data for which there is collected ground truth, as this set may include not-yet-detected fakes and compromised accounts. We take advantage of having an extremely large dataset to carry out aggressive exclusions that reduce the chance that we capture behaviour from attacker-controlled accounts. We use three heuristics:

- First, we exclude any account flagged as suspicious during the training DW or at a later point of time within the Buffer Window (BW). By excluding these accounts, we reduce the likelihood that our classifier learns behavioral patterns stemming from detected compromised accounts.
- Second, to the same end, for the classification exercises where there is available data before the start of the training interval (CE_C in Sect. 5), we exclude accounts flagged as suspicious before the start of training (as they are more likely to be compromised in the future).
- Finally, to eliminate fakes, one of our classification exercises (CE_C in Sect. 5) attempts to eliminate all recently-created or dormant fakes by selecting for training only accounts that are older than two months and have at least one month of activity (our assumption is that once fakes generate enough activity the LSOSP can detect them through existing techniques [25, 27] as detecting fakes is easier than detecting compromised accounts [8]).

Heuristics to Reduce Bias During Classifier Evaluation. Our preliminary experiments suggest that user accounts that have been flagged as suspicious in the past are more likely to be flagged again in the future (a possible indication that their users are more vulnerable to attacks than the general user population). To provide a conservative (lower-bound) evaluation of the developed classifier's performance, we exclude all accounts that have been previously labeled as suspicious during training (i.e., flagged at any point during the training-LW or before). Moreover, one of our classification exercises (CE_C in Sect. 5), also excludes any accounts flagged as suspicious during the first month of the data collection. As a result, the classifier is evaluated on never seen before true positives.

Heuristics to Size the Buffer Window (BW). It is expected that, at any LSOSP, detection of suspicious activity is not instantaneous, thus accounts may be under the control of an attacker for a while before they are flagged. We developed an experiment to estimate how aggressive is *LSOSP*'s suspicious activity flagging pipeline. For this experiment, we only rely on two types of events: flagging events for accounts marked as suspicious on day d (extracted from set S_d) and login events for these accounts (extracted from set L_d). We include only user accounts that have at least one login event and at least one flagging event within the period of time over which we run the experiment. We define the *lag* per flagged user as the number of days between the first time that account is flagged and the most recent previous login event. Over a period of 30 days, the results showed that 90% of accounts flagged within that period have a lag of at most one week and 98.6% have a lag of less than three weeks. As such, we decided on a 1-week buffer window (BW) for most of our CEs, yet we also experimented with a 3-week BW (CE_D in Sect. 5).

Table 1. Summary of low-cost features. (from login traces)

Brief description	Type
# Login Attempts	Numeric
# Unique Login Sources (e.g., Web Login, Mobile Login, etc.)	
# Unique Login Types (e.g., Password Login, Account Switch, etc.)	
# Unique Login Statuses (e.g., Success, Session Extension, etc.)	
# Unique Password Login Statuses (e.g., Success, Invalid Password, etc.)	
# Unique Actions (e.g., Login/Logout, Device Authentication, etc.)	
# Unique Login Geographical Locations	
# Unique Login Geographical Location Statuses (e.g., Neutral Location, White-listed Location, etc.)	
# Unique Login Autonomous Systems (ASNs)	
# Unique Login User Agents (e.g., Browser, Mobile App, etc.)	
# Successful Logins	
# Unsuccessful Logins	
User has a "verified" mobile number	2-Categorical

4   Datasets

Overall, we had access to 118 days ($\approx$4 months or $\approx$16 weeks) worth of production data collected from September 1st, 2016 to the December 27th, 2016 across two datasets which were updated daily. Overall, these datasets are representative of any LSOSP with a global user base, an extensive set of offered online services, as well as the latest techniques to identify potentially compromised accounts.

4.1   Extracting Features

The first dataset includes features associated with all login events. Whenever a user logs-in to a service offered by *LSOSP* or has their session re-authenticated, a login event is recorded into this dataset with all relevant features that can be associated with the event at that time. We use this dataset to extract a minimal set of 13 basic and easy to compute features that reflect users' login behavioral patterns (summarized in Table 1) from login traces at a day-level granularity, and then aggregate them for each user account as a way of characterizing its behavioral pattern over the DW. It is important to note that we do not have access to any fine-grained account features such as account/user details. Importantly, we do not have access to any personally identifiable information. Moreover, given the diversity of the login methods as well as the services offered at *LSOSP*, the features extracted for each login event are not uniform and the set of features extracted for each user is sparse.

4.2 Groundtruth: Suspicious Account Flagging

The second dataset includes events from which we extract our groundtruth. At *LSOSP*, a list of accounts flagged as suspicious is generated daily by combining information from various sources that include human content moderators, manual reports from internal teams, user reporting, in addition to automated systems employing heuristics (which include clustering techniques to identify anomalies, and regression models to identify spammers). We used this daily list of accounts flagged as suspicious as our ground truth.

For this study, we had access to this daily list of accounts flagged as suspicious and a high-level description of the system. The detailed internals of the flagging pipeline were not available. As a consequence, we are neither able to distinguish between the different classes of suspicious accounts nor to identify the reason why a particular account had been flagged. We believe that, the lack of such fine-grained information poses only limited threats to the validity of our findings: on the one side we have developed heuristics to exclude attacker-controlled accounts from training (see Sect. 3.3), and, on the other side, at this point our machine learning model aims to provide only predictive power (will an account be flagged as suspicious?) rather than explanatory power (why will the account be flagged?). We extend this discussion in Sect. 7.

5   Evaluation Results

The Objectives of our Classification Exercises. We present four of the classification exercises (CEs) carried out at *LSOSP* labeled CE_A, CE_B, CE_C, and CE_D in Table 2. The table outlines the Training and Testing intervals assigned to each CE and their respective Data Window (DW), Buffer Window (BW), and Label Window (LW). For each CE, we have a specific objective:

- CE_A: evaluating the feasibility of our proposed pipeline, its applicability at *LSOSP*, and optimizing hyperparameters.
- CE_B: testing the tuned model on new data to ensure that no overfitting occurred in CE_A.
- CE_C: investigating how the performance of our classifier changes when excluding accounts previously flagged as suspicious (higher chance to be flagged again) or accounts that have little previous activity (lower chance to include fakes).

■ CE_D: evaluating the impact of more training data (longer data and label windows) and more aggressive exclusion of potentially not-yet-flagged attacker-controlled accounts (longer buffer window).

Summary of Results. Tables 3 and 4 summarize the results for all CEs carried out (their setup is outlined in Table 2). For conciseness, we focus here only on the most relevant metrics we collected. The two tables highlight how several metrics are impacted by the selected operating threshold T of the classifier as well as by the duration of the prediction horizon (presented as Test-LW and Extended-Test-LW in Table 2 and whose combined size in days is denoted as *the prediction horizon*: H). The tables present results for operating thresholds of $T = 0.5$ and $T = 0.9$ and prediction horizons of $H = 7, 21, 30, 34,$ *and* 90 *days*, in separate columns. Note that the minimum and maximum values of H depend on the CE.

In summary, these results show:

■ High accuracy (ACC) ≈99.9% and low false positive rate (FPR) <0.01% for an operating threshold $T = 0.9$,
■ Good evidence for the absence of overfitting (CE_B),
■ Good balance between precision (PRE) and recall (REC): ≈18.33% and ≈50.62% respectively, when forecasting with a Horizon H = 30 days and Operating Threshold T = 0.5 (CE_C),
■ A small improvement after excluding recent/no activity accounts (more likely to be fakes) and those flagged as suspicious before training (Comparing CE_B and CE_C),
■ As the Horizon (H) increases, precision increases while recall stays roughly constant (We expand on this in Sect. 5.1),
■ High AUC as shown in Fig. 2 (≈0.947 for CE_D), and
■ More training data and a more aggressive exclusion of not-yet-flagged attacker-controlled accounts do not significantly impact classification performance (CE_D).

5.1 The Impact of the Prediction Horizon

Our classifier's precision markedly improves with the depth of the prediction horizon H (Fig. 3). Some of the accounts that are false positives for a small precision window then become true positives as the prediction window increases. We speculate that those accounts are owned by users that do not have the ability or the interest to fend off social engineering attacks, and thus a longer horizon increases the chance that they fall victim to an attack, and then generate suspicious activity which gets them flagged during the longer prediction horizon.

6   Related Work

Statistical methods (including ML) have achieved widespread adoption within LSOSPs not only to provide rich business features (e.g., product recommendations) but also for cybersecurity purposes. For instance, such approaches have

Table 2. Timeline of the four classification exercises (CEs) Performed CE_A, CE_B, CE_C, and CE_D. Notation: DW - Data Window, BW - Buffer Window, LW - Label Window, H - Prediction Horizon.

CE	Week															
	1	2	3	4	5	6	7	8	9	10	11	12	13	14	15	16
A	Train			Test					Extended Test							
	DW	BW	LW	DW	LW				Extended LW $(H = [7, 90]$ days$)$							
B	Unused								Train			Test		Extended Test		
	Unused								DW	BW	LW	DW	LW	Extended LW		
C	Preprocess			Unused					Train			Test		Extended Test		
	Preprocess			Unused					DW	BW	LW	DW	LW	Extended LW		
D	Train									Test						Ext. Test
	DW		BW			LW			DW				LW			Ext. LW

Table 3. Summary of results using an operating threshold (T) = 0.5 for different prediction horizons (H days). Notation used: AUC-Area Under Receiver Operating Characteristic Curve, BTR-%-tile better than a random classifier, PRE-Precision, REC-Recall, ACC-Accuracy, FPR-False Positive Rate. Values in bold represent the best result for that performance metric.

CE	H_{Min}	H_{Max}	Performance Evaluation Metrics											
			H=H_{Min}		H=7				H=21		H=30		H=H_{Max}	
			AUC	BTR	PRE	REC	ACC	FPR	PRE	REC	PRE	REC	PRE	REC
A	7	90	0.928	85.61%	**6.38%**	**46.87%**	99.43%	0.52%	**19.79%**	45.81%	**20.14%**	43.81%	**24.99%**	31.02%
B	7	30	0.910	82.14%	3.78%	41.26%	**99.50%**	**0.46%**	18.18%	46.82%	19.98%	42.28%	19.98%	42.28%
C	7	30	0.922	84.42%	3.18%	42.96%	99.38%	0.58%	16.58%	57.32%	18.33%	**50.62%**	18.33%	**50.62%**
D	21	34	**0.947**	**89.41%**	H < H_{Min}				10.64%	**57.42%**	11.68%	48.96%	12.34%	48.13%

Table 4. Summary of results using an operating threshold (T) = 0.9 for different prediction horizons (H days). Notation used: AUC-Area Under Receiver Operating Characteristic Curve, BTR-%-tile better than a random classifier, PRE-Precision, REC-Recall, ACC-Accuracy, FPR-False Positive Rate. Values in bold represent the best result for that performance metric.

CE	H_{Min}	H_{Max}	Performance Evaluation Metrics									
			H=H_{Min}		H=H_{Min}				H=H_{Max}			
			AUC	BTR	PRE	REC	ACC	FPR	PRE	REC	ACC	FPR
A	7	90	0.928	85.61%	12.92%	0.47%	**99.92%**	**0.0024%**	33.99%	0.20%	99.54%	**0.0018%**
B	7	30	0.910	82.14%	7.11%	13.15%	99.88%	0.0760%	**35.96%**	12.90%	99.74%	0.0520%
C	7	30	0.922	84.42%	6.91%	**15.57%**	99.86%	0.0940%	35.33%	**16.29%**	99.75%	0.0650%
D	21	34	**0.947**	**89.41%**	**26.19%**	14.45%	99.86%	0.0430%	28.47%	11.36%	**99.82%**	0.0420%

been used for detecting compromised accounts, fake accounts, spam, and phishing. None of these approaches has focused on evaluating the feasibility of predicting which legitimate accounts are more vulnerable and likely to be compromised in the future (our long term aim). In this section each paragraph focuses on a specific area, surveys related approaches, and outlines the statistical methods and features used.

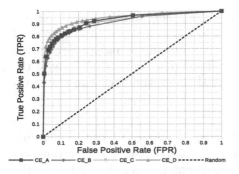

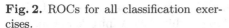

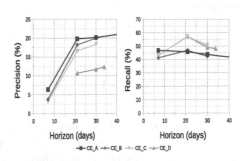

Fig. 2. ROCs for all classification exercises.

Fig. 3. Impact of the prediction horizon on precision (left) and recall (right) at operating threshold $T = 0.5$

Compromised Accounts. Egele et al. [8] combined statistical modeling and anomaly detection techniques in order to detect compromised accounts on Online Social Networks (OSNs). Their approach was based on identifying sudden changes in user behavioral patterns in addition to observing whether those changes are common to a large group of accounts therefore potentially a result of a malicious campaign. Thomas et al. [24] employed clustering and classification (via logistic regression) in order to detect account hijacking on Twitter. Their approach was based on the observation that legitimate account owners frequently delete tweets posted via their accounts after recognizing the compromise. Those deletions are thus used as a feature to retroactively identify hijacked accounts and clustering is then used to detect similarly compromised accounts. Zhang et al. [29] made use of a ML-based approach to automatically detect compromised accounts at a large academic institution. Their approach employed logistic regression on features extracted from web login and VPN authentication logs.

Fake Accounts. Yang et al. [27] proposed approaches to identify Sybil (i.e., fake) accounts on the Renren OSN. One approach was based on ML and employed Support Vector Machines (SVMs) on basic user-level features (e.g., the frequency of friendship requests and the fraction of accepted incoming friendship requests). Wang el al. [25] instead used clustering to identify fake accounts on Renren. Their approach clustered users with similar behavior based on features extracted from their clickstreams (e.g., the average session length, the average number of clicks per session).

Spam. Benevenuto et al. [2] developed an ML-based approach to identify spammers on Twitter. Their approach was based on a non-linear Support Vector Machine (SVM) classifier with the Radial Basis Function (RBF) kernel and made use of both content- and user-level features (e.g., the age of the user account, the number of followers, the average number of URLs per tweet). Castillo et al. [7] developed a ML-based approach using cost-sensitive decision trees to detect spam pages on the Web. Their approach makes use of content- and link-based features extracted from the Web graph (e.g., the ratio between the average degree of a page and that of its neighbours, number of words in the page/title). In the context of email spam, Blanzieri et al. [4] carried out a survey of many of the approaches to detect email spam proposed in the literature based on statistical methods (including ML).

Phishing. Ludl et al. [18] developed a ML-based approach to identify phishing web pages. Their approach was based on the C4.5 decision tree algorithm and made use of features extracted from a page's content as well as its URL (e.g., the number of forms/fields tags on the page, whether the page is served over HTTPS, whether the URL's domain appears on a Google whitelist). Whittaker et al. [26] developed a scalable ML-based approach to detect phishing websites that is used to maintain Google's phishing blacklist automatically. Their approach is based on a Random Forest (RF) classifier and employed both content-, host- and URL-based features (e.g., PageRank, the host geolocation/ASN).

7   Summary and Discussion

Summary. We explore the feasibility of predicting the legitimate (i.e., not attacker-controlled) accounts more likely to generate suspicious activity in the future, a likely indication that they have fallen for a mass-scale social engineering attack. To this end, we propose an early warning system that employs supervised machine learning to identify the accounts whose behavioral patterns indicate that they are similar to other accounts that have been eventually labeled as suspicious in the past. We implement this early warning system at a Large-Scale Online Service Platform (LSOSP) and evaluate it on four months of real-world production data covering hundreds of millions of users. Our evaluation demonstrates that our approach is not only feasible but that it also offers promising classification performance based on which further defense mechanisms can be developed as we discuss below.

Discussion. We continue by exploring several interrelated topics:
How can a defense system use information about which users are likely to be compromised in the future, and thus more "vulnerable", to enhance its robustness? User vulnerability can be thought of as an additional "signal" that can inform a number of defense mechanisms. For example, it can: *(i)* serve as an indicator to prioritize the allocation of limited defense resources (e.g., use of human analyst time [13], or compute-intensive filters [23]), *(ii)* support differentiated defenses that take into account user vulnerability (e.g., additional CAPTCHAs [1] on login attempts into vulnerable accounts, or imposing rate limits on the outbound messages of vulnerable users to slow-down the spread of multi-stage—and potentially epidemic—phishing attacks), *(iii)* enable faster remediation of compromised accounts (e.g., by enabling more efficient inspection campaigns that focus on the accounts of vulnerable users instead of the entire

user population [15]), *(iv)* facilitate the detection of the origin of an attack (as, in effect, the differentiated response between vulnerable and robust users to similar interactions initiated by the same source can be used as a weak yet effective signal [5]); and *(v)* even facilitate the detection of new attacks (as, in effect, the differentiated response between vulnerable and robust—yet otherwise similar—user groups to the same "stimuli" is an indication of an attack). We explore the use of such information for several cybersecurity domains in [10].

Is the prediction quality good enough? Even if defense mechanisms based on vulnerability predictions can be imagined, an immediate subsequent question is whether the classification quality implied by our results (e.g., $PRE \approx 15$–25%, $REC \approx 40$–50%, and $FPR \approx 0.1$–0.5%) is good enough to support such mechanisms. While we have not yet extensively studied such mechanisms, our intuition is that this signal, although noisy, is useful. Consider, for example, defense resource prioritization - it is evident that a heuristic that uses this signal, as weak as it is, to prioritize those resources is better than randomly allocating them (the only alternative when capacity is constrained). Others have also experimented with a heuristic that harnesses the different responses to similar requests between vulnerable and robust users [5] to infer attack source(s) (although in the context of a social network). In this case, even a vulnerability predictor significantly weaker than the one we have obtained here has proven useful, leading to a technique that improves over the state-of-the-art. While the above indicates that even low quality predictions can still be used to improve defenses, we believe that the prediction quality threshold above which these mechanisms become valuable is context specific and we are studying this issue in a related project [10].

Why do we focus on minimizing the false positive rate (FPR)? What if the focus were on maximizing recall instead? We envisage that the predictions made by our early warning system will be used to better target existing defenses. As many of these defenses are not lightweight and may lead to increased friction for users (e.g., rate-limiting outbound emails of vulnerable users to prevent an attack outbreak, delaying incoming suspicious email addressed to vulnerable users to give enough time for more robust users to report mass-phishing emails), or allocating costly resources (e.g., human analyst time), the resulting cost of false positives is high: thus, we have focused on minimizing the FPR at the expense of lower recall. Other situations, however, offer a different cost/benefit balance between the false positive rate and recall. For these situations, our classifier can be tuned by either using lower threshold values (T as highlighted by the ROC across all CEs available in Fig. 2), or by specifically optimizing for recall.

What are the threats to validity? Our study indicates that it is feasible to harness account behaviour to predict the accounts that are more likely to generate suspicious traffic in the future (an indicator that they may be compromised). There are two main concerns regarding the validity of our conclusions. The first one relates to the quality of the ground truth we use—this is a threat to validity common to any study using a methodology based on machine learning.

The second one relates to the accuracy of the heuristics used to avoid learning behavioural patterns from accounts that may be controlled by an attacker (i.e., compromised or fake accounts) detailed in Sect. 3.3. We prune: *(i)* all accounts flagged for suspicious activity in the data window (DW) - as they are highly likely to be compromised, *(ii)* all accounts flagged as suspicious in the buffer window (BW) - as these accounts are more likely to have been compromised but not yet flagged as such (thus contaminating our training data), *(iii)* all accounts which have been labeled as suspicious at any point *before* the training data window - as our experience shows that these accounts are more likely to be compromised again (in experiment CE_C); and, finally *(iv)* new/low activity accounts (for which the system may not have enough history to determine whether the accounts are fakes). We run various experiments that compare the impact of these heuristics - even the most conservative experiments appear to support our conclusions.

It is worth discussing, however, the alternative: assume that our heuristics fail to eliminate a large portion of attacker controlled accounts. Even in this case, we believe that our pipeline provides value through forecasting. Assume, for example, that these accounts are predominantly (dormant) fakes that mimic legitimate user behaviour. In this case, our pipeline predicts the fakes that will likely be "awakened" by the attacker and start generating suspicious activity. Assume, on the other side, that these are compromised accounts not yet exploited by the attacker, then our pipeline predicts which compromised accounts are under the control of the attacker but not yet exploited. In this case as well the forecasting pipeline can give an early sign of the attacker resources and strategy.

A final concern may be that our proposed approach may be learning the heuristics by which some accounts are flagged as suspicious in the ground truth (other accounts in the ground truth are flagged by humans). We believe that this represents a limited threat due to the way we formulated our forecasting problem (i.e., making future predictions) as opposed to the underlying heuristics which operate in real-time by design.

Why are the presented results positioned as lower-bounds? Our goal was to test the feasibility of our proposed approach within constraints related to:

- *Access to Data (i.e., login traces only).* Datasets with additional information that characterizes user behaviour (e.g., email or browsing traces) would likely improve classification performance.
- *Limited Computational Resources (i.e, runtime feasibility for processing billions of events).* More resources enabling additional data preprocessing (e.g., to extract complex aggregate features), model optimization, or sophisticated learning methods (e.g., deep neural networks) would likely improve classification performance.
- *Imperfect Ground Truth (i.e., detection lag as well as the presence of false positives and false negatives).* This impairs the learned models during training, and impacts the evaluation during testing.

■ *Aggressive Pruning Heuristics (i.e., extensive pruning of accounts during training as described in* Sect. 3.3*).* This reduces bias during the evaluation of the classifier but leads to more conservative results.

References

1. von Ahn, L., Blum, M., Hopper, N.J., Langford, J.: CAPTCHA: using hard AI problems for security. In: Biham, E. (ed.) EUROCRYPT 2003. LNCS, vol. 2656, pp. 294–311. Springer, Heidelberg (2003). https://doi.org/10.1007/3-540-39200-9_18
2. Benevenuto, F., Magno, G., Rodrigues, T., Almeida, V.: Detecting spammers on twitter. In: Collaboration, Electronic Messaging, Anti-Abuse and Spam Conference (CEAS), vol. 6, p. 12 (2010)
3. Bilge, L., Han, Y., Dell'Amico, M.: Riskteller: predicting the risk of cyber incidents. In: Proceedings of the 2017 ACM SIGSAC Conference on Computer and Communications Security, CCS 2017, pp. 1299–1311. ACM, New York, NY, USA (2017). https://doi.org/10.1145/3133956.3134022, https://doi.acm.org/10.1145/3133956.3134022
4. Blanzieri, E., Bryl, A.: A survey of learning-based techniques of email spam filtering. Artif. Intell. Rev. **29**(1), 63–92 (2008). https://doi.org/10.1007/s10462-009-9109-6. https://dx.doi.org/10.1007/s10462-009-9109-6
5. Boshmaf, Y., et al.: Integro: leveraging victim prediction for robust fake account detection in OSNs. In: 22nd Annual Network and Distributed System Security Symposium (NDSS), San Diego, California, USA, 8–11 February 2015, pp. 1–15. http://www.internetsociety.org/doc/integro-leveraging-victim-prediction-robust-fake-account-detection-osns
6. Canali, D., Bilge, L., Balzarotti, D.: On the effectiveness of risk prediction based on users browsing behavior. In: Proceedings of the 9th ACM Symposium on Information, Computer and Communications Security, ASIA CCS 2014, pp. 171–182. ACM, New York, NY, USA (2014). https://doi.org/10.1145/2590296.2590347, https://doi.acm.org/10.1145/2590296.2590347
7. Castillo, C., Donato, D., Gionis, A., Murdock, V., Silvestri, F.: Know your neighbors: web spam detection using the web topology. In: Proceedings of the 30th Annual International ACM SIGIR Conference on Research and Development in Information Retrieval, SIGIR 2007, pp. 423–430. ACM, New York, NY, USA (2007). https://doi.org/10.1145/1277741.1277814, https://doi.acm.org/10.1145/1277741.1277814
8. Egele, M., Stringhini, G., Kruegel, C., Vigna, G.: COMPA: detecting compromised accounts on social networks. In: Proceedings of the Network & Distributed System Security Symposium, NDSS 2013, ISOC, February 2013
9. Fernández-Delgado, M., Cernadas, E., Barro, S., Amorim, D.: Do we need hundreds of classifiers to solve real world classification problems? J. Mach. Learn. Res. **15**(1), 3133–3181 (2014). http://dl.acm.org/citation.cfm?id=2627435.2697065
10. Halawa, H., Beznosov, K., Boshmaf, Y., Coskun, B., Ripeanu, M., Santos-Neto, E.: Harvesting the low-hanging fruits: defending against automated large-scale cyber-intrusions by focusing on the vulnerable population. In: Proceedings of the 2016 New Security Paradigms Workshop, NSPW 2016, pp. 11–22. ACM, New York, NY, USA (2016). https://doi.org/10.1145/3011883.3011885, https://doi.acm.org/10.1145/3011883.3011885

11. Halawa, H., Ripeanu, M., Beznosov, K., Coskun, B., Liu, M.: Forecasting suspicious account activity at large-scale online service providers. CoRR abs/1801.08629 (2018). http://arxiv.org/abs/1801.08629

12. He, H., Garcia, E.A.: Learning from imbalanced data. IEEE Trans. Knowl. Data Eng. **21**(9), 1263–1284 (2009). https://doi.org/10.1109/TKDE.2008.239

13. Ho, G., Javed, A.S.M., Paxson, V., Wagner, D.: Detecting credential spearphishing attacks in enterprise settings. In: Proceedings of the 26rd USENIX Security Symposium, USENIX Security 2017, pp. 469–485 (2017)

14. Jagatic, T.N., Johnson, N.A., Jakobsson, M., Menczer, F.: Social phishing. Commun. ACM **50**(10), 94–100 (2007)

15. Liu, G., Xiang, G., Pendleton, B.A., Hong, J.I., Liu, W.: Smartening the crowds: computational techniques for improving human verification to fight phishing scams. In: Proceedings of the Seventh Symposium on Usable Privacy and Security, SOUPS 2011, pp. 8:1–8:13. ACM, New York, NY, USA (2011). https://doi.org/10.1145/2078827.2078838, https://doi.acm.org/10.1145/2078827.2078838

16. Liu, Y., et al.: Cloudy with a chance of breach: forecasting cyber security incidents. In: Proceedings of the 24th USENIX Security Symposium, USENIX Security 2015, pp. 1009–1024 (2015)

17. Lomax, S., Vadera, S.: A survey of cost-sensitive decision tree induction algorithms. ACM Comput. Surv. **45**(2), 16:1–16:35 (2013). https://doi.org/10.1145/2431211.2431215. https://doi.acm.org/10.1145/2431211.2431215

18. Ludl, C., McAllister, S., Kirda, E., Kruegel, C.: On the effectiveness of techniques to detect phishing sites. In: M. Hämmerli, B., Sommer, R. (eds.) DIMVA 2007. LNCS, vol. 4579, pp. 20–39. Springer, Heidelberg (2007). https://doi.org/10.1007/978-3-540-73614-1_2

19. Moore, T., Clayton, R., Anderson, R.: The economics of online crime. J. Econ. Perspect. **23**(3), 3–20 (2009). https://doi.org/10.1257/jep.23.3.3. https://www.aeaweb.org/articles/?doi=10.1257/jep.23.3.3

20. Provost, F., Fawcett, T.: Robust classification for imprecise environments. Mach. Learn. **42**(3), 203–231 (2001). https://doi.org/10.1023/A:1007601015854. https://dx.doi.org/10.1023/A:1007601015854

21. Shon, T., Moon, J.: A hybrid machine learning approach to network anomaly detection. Inf. Sci. **177**(18), 3799–3821 (2007)

22. Soska, K., Christin, N.: Automatically detecting vulnerable websites before they turn malicious. In: Proceedings of the 23rd USENIX Security Symposium, USENIX Security 2014, pp. 625–640 (2014)

23. Stein, T., Chen, E., Mangla, K.: Facebook immune system. In: Proceedings of the 4th Workshop on Social Network Systems, SNS 2011, pp. 8:1–8:8. ACM, New York, NY, USA (2011). https://doi.org/10.1145/1989656.1989664. https://doi.acm.org/10.1145/1989656.1989664

24. Thomas, K., Li, F., Grier, C., Paxson, V.: Consequences of connectivity: characterizing account hijacking on twitter. In: Proceedings of the 2014 ACM SIGSAC Conference on Computer and Communications Security, CCS 2014, pp. 489–500. ACM, New York, NY, USA (2014). https://doi.org/10.1145/2660267.2660282. https://doi.acm.org/10.1145/2660267.2660282

25. Wang, G., Konolige, T., Wilson, C., Wang, X., Zheng, H., Zhao, B.Y.: You are how you click: clickstream analysis for sybil detection. In: Proceedings of the 22Nd USENIX Conference on Security, SEC 2013, pp. 241–256. USENIX Association, Berkeley, CA, USA (2013). http://dl.acm.org/citation.cfm?id=2534766.2534788

26. Whittaker, C., Ryner, B., Nazif, M.: Large-scale automatic classification of phishing pages. In: Proceedings of the 17th Annual Network and Distributed System Security Symposium, NDSS Symposium 2010, San Diego, CA, USA (2010)
27. Yang, Z., Wilson, C., Wang, X., Gao, T., Zhao, B.Y., Dai, Y.: Uncovering social network sybils in the wild. In: Proceedings of the 2011 ACM SIGCOMM Conference on Internet Measurement Conference, IMC 2011, pp. 259–268. ACM, New York, NY, USA (2011). https://doi.org/10.1145/2068816.2068841. https://doi.acm.org/10.1145/2068816.2068841
28. Zaharia, M., Chowdhury, M., Franklin, M.J., Shenker, S., Stoica, I.: Spark: cluster computing with working sets. In: Proceedings of the 2Nd USENIX Conference on Hot Topics in Cloud Computing, HotCloud 2010, p. 10. USENIX Association, Berkeley, CA, USA (2010). http://dl.acm.org/citation.cfm?id=1863103.1863113
29. Zhang, J., et al.: Safeguarding academic accounts and resources with the university credential abuse auditing system. In: IEEE/IFIP International Conference on Dependable Systems and Networks (DSN 2012), pp. 1–8, June 2012. https://doi.org/10.1109/DSN.2012.6263961

Thinking Like a Fraudster: Detecting Fraudulent Transactions via Statistical Sequential Features

Chen Jing[1,2,3(✉)], Cheng Wang[1,2,3(✉)], and Chungang Yan[1,2,3(✉)]

[1] Department of Computer Science and Technology, Tongji University,
Shanghai, China
{jingchen23,cwang}@tongji.edu.cn, cgyan2@163.com
[2] Key Laboratory of Embedded System and Service Computing,
Ministry of Education, Shanghai, China
[3] Shanghai Electronic Transactions and Information Service Collaborative
Innovation Center, Shanghai, China

Abstract. Aiming at the increasing threat of fraud in electronic transactions, so far researchers have already proposed many different models. However, few previous studies take advantage of the sequential characteristics of fraudulent transactions. In this paper, by statistical analysis on a real dataset, we discover that partial-order sequential features are able to reflect the intrinsic motivation of fraudsters, e.g., stealing the money as quickly as possible before being intercepted. Based on the sequential features, we propose a novel model, *SeqFD (Sequential feature boosting Fraud Detector)*, to detect fraudulent transactions real-timely. *SeqFD* applies a sliding time window strategy to aggregate the historical transactions. In specific, statistical sequential features are computed based on the transactions within the time window. Thus, the raw dataset can be transformed into a feature set. Several classification models are evaluated on the feature set, and finally, XGBoost is validated to be a fast, accurate and robust classifier which fits well with *SeqFD*. The experiments on real dataset show that the proposed model reaches a 97.2% *TPR (True Positive Rate)* when *FPR (False Positive Rate)* is less than 1%. Furthermore, the average time for giving a prediction is 1.5 ms, which meets the real-time requirement in the industry.

Keywords: Fraudulent transaction detection · Statistical sequential features · Sliding time window · Machine learning

This work was supported in part by the National Natural Science Foundation of China under Grant 61332008, in part by the National Key Research and Development Program of China under Grant 2018YFC0831403.

I. Goldberg and T. Moore (Eds.): FC 2019, LNCS 11598, pp. 588–604, 2019.
https://doi.org/10.1007/978-3-030-32101-7_34

1   Introduction

1.1   Background

Recent years, the huge development in e-commerce makes more and more people shop online. The amount of money people spend online is also increasing. In China's 2017 Double Eleven shopping festival, the total sales on Tmall[1] reached 168.2 billion yuan [1]. However, this prosperity gives criminals chances to steal money. According to the Nilson Report in October 2016, worldwide losses from credit card fraud rose to 21 billion dollars in 2015, and will possibly reach 31 billion dollars by 2020 [13]. There is no doubt that it is meaningful to prevent people's properties from being stolen by fraudsters.

Although the criminals have various tricks, such as telephone fraud, Trojan and pseudo base station [7], their unchanged goal is to steal money from people's bank accounts. It is spontaneous to think about how to prevent fraud when fraud is presenting as fraudulent transactions. In the literature, fraud detection methodologies using behavioral models are proposed [2,5]. Behavioral models mainly fall into two categories: individual behavioral models and crowd behavioral models. For the individual models, concept drift [17] and lack-of-history are the two main tough challenges faced by individual behavioral models. Basically, concept drift means that a change in behavior may not be due to fraud [10]. The lack-of-history problem is that a portion of customers do not have sufficient historical records to depict their behavioral patterns. To handle concept drift, one common solution is using the time window strategy [11] to neglect the old transaction and keep the model updated. This strategy will make the lack of history problem severer, but if we set a larger time window to contain more records, it contradicts the original intention to solve the problem of concept drift.

As a result, researchers are trying to build models based on crowd behavior. In general, their models extract normal and fraud behavioral patterns from a large number of customers. By measuring the differences between the two patterns, effective features can be designed, then a classifier or an anomaly detector can be trained. Crowd behavioral models alleviate the lack of history problem because the history of active customers can be used to make up for that of inactive customers. In the literature, many crowd behavioral models have been proposed for e-transaction fraud detection. However, most of the previous studies have one or more of the three problems below.

Lack of Sequential Features. In order to build a behavioral model, sequences of transactions are supposed to be taken into consideration rather than isolated transactions. In order to avoid dimension disaster, transaction aggregation strategies are applied to build the behavioral models [18]. A common way for transaction aggregation is to set up several time spans, and calculate the statistical values of spending for each time span, such as average and variance, as aggregated features [6,7]. However, in previous studies, the aggregated features

---

[1] Tmall is a Chinese-language website for business-to-consumer (B2C) online retail.

do not contain information about the partial-order relationship between consecutive transactions. Thus they are not sequential features. By real data analysis, we find out that the sequential features are strongly correlated with fraud. In Sect. 2 this will be explained in detail.

Lack of Efficiency Tests. Recent studies also tried to implement more complex models, such as deep learning models, to detect fraudulent transactions. For example, CNN (Convolutional Neural Network) is used for credit card fraud detection in recent studies [6,12]. However, most of them ignored the efficiency test. Deep learning models are probably not fast enough to meet the requirement of efficiency, because nowadays a deep learning model usually contains at least hundreds of thousands of units [8], needs GPUs and parallelized clusters to compute. As a result, both the training and predicting process could take a long time. On the contrary, banks usually require their fraud detection systems to give a response in a couple of milliseconds, and the training time should also be as short as possible.

Lack of Real Dataset. Banks are usually very sensitive to the confidentiality of their data, this makes the publication of a real electronic transaction dataset nearly impossible [16]. Therefore, some previous studies used simulated datasets to train and test their models. Nevertheless, the results obtained from simulated datasets might be inconvincible. In addition, some of the previous studies which used simulated dataset employed *Accuracy* as a performance indicator [4]. However, *Accuracy* is an unsuitable indicator in the area of fraud detection, because real datasets are highly unbalanced [15]. This paper applies *TPR (True Positive Rate)* and *FPR (False Positive Rate)* as the indicators.

1.2 Our Work

In this paper, by statistical analysis, we discover that sequential features are a reflection of the intrinsic motivation of the fraudsters. We apply a sliding time window to aggregate the simple sequential features into statistical sequential features. Based on These features, we propose a real-time fraudulent transaction detection model, *SeqFD (Sequential feature boosting Fraud Detector)*. By experiments on a real dataset, we validate that *SeqFD* can detect more than 97% fraudulent transactions but only disturb less than 1% normal transactions, and it can give a prediction in 1.5 ms on average. To choose a suitable classifier, we conduct experiments on six machine learning models. Finally, XGBoost is validated to be a suitable classifier for *SeqFD*. Moreover, experiments are also conducted to choose a feasible window size, and to test the influence of under-sampling.

At the same time of presenting *SeqFD* in detail, a practical workflow for fraudulent transaction detection is presented. After *SeqFD* gives a prediction, staffs of banks can check the suspicious transactions by phone call, so the confirmed fraudulent transactions can be labeled. With continuously new-coming labeled instances, *SeqFD* can be trained periodically to be kept updating. Our contributions are summarized as follows:

- We design novel statistical sequential features which are effective for fraudulent transaction detection, and which can reflect the intrinsic motivation of fraudsters.
- We propose and implement *SeqFD*. By comprehensive experimental evaluation, we prove the effectiveness and the usability of *SeqFD*.
- Based on real data, we present our statistical discoveries and learned lessons of fraudulent transactions, which are valuable for future studies.

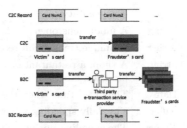

Fig. 1. The difference between fraudulent transactions in B2C and C2C scenarios.

The rest of this paper is organized as follows: Sect. 2 offers the statistical analysis and the learned lessons of the dataset. In Sect. 3, the mechanism of *SeqFD* is demonstrated. In Sect. 4, the results of the experiments are shown. Section 5 gives a complimentary discussion on *SeqFD* and Sect. 6 draws a conclusion for this paper.

2   Real Data Analysis

In this section, the dataset we study is introduced in detail first. Afterward, the statistical characteristics of the fraudulent transactions are shown graphically. Based on the abnormal patterns we observe from the fraudulent transactions, we explore the possible motivations behind their fraudulent behaviors.

2.1   Dataset Description

We study a real electronic transaction dataset provided by a real commercial bank. The dataset totally contains 3502048 B2C transaction records made by 92133 customers in 3 months (from April 1, 2017, to June 30, 2017). Among all the transaction records, 65291 are labeled fraudulent manually by staffs of the bank. Although this dataset only covers a small portion of all the customers of the bank, it covers all the customers who were defrauded in the 3-month time span. Among the 92133 customers, 8238 are victims, and all of their transactions in the time span are extracted into our dataset. The other normal customers are picked out randomly, and all of their transaction records in the time span are extracted. These two parties form the whole dataset.

Although the original dataset has more than 20 attributes, some of the attribute values are missing in many instances, and some of the attributes have the same value for all the instances. We omit those helpless attributes. After data preprocessing, for each transaction record, we preserve 8 attributes. Their explanations are listed in Table 1. Note that Customer ID and Vendor ID do not have the same format.

Table 1. Attributes explanation

Attribute Name	Type	Representation
Customer ID	String	A unique customer.
Transaction ID	String	A unique transaction record.
Vendor ID	String	A shop, a restaurant or a third-party payment provider, etc.
Transaction Time	Date	The exact time when the transaction occurred.
Daily Limit	Numeric	The daily spending upper limit of an account.
Single Limit	Numeric	The spending upper limit for one transaction.
Transaction Amount	Numeric	The amount of money that the customer pay.
Frequently-Used IP Address	Boolean	If the transaction comes from an IP address which is frequently used by the customer

2.2 Learned Lessons

Why B2C Other Than C2C. Besides the B2C transaction records, actually we are also provided the C2C transaction records of those 92133 customers in the three months, but the number of fraudulent instances in those C2C transactions is only 1. Why criminals steal money mainly by B2C transactions instead of C2C transactions? Regarding the difference of their procedures shown in Fig. 1, the explanation is as follows: If a fraudster transfers the money into his/her own card directly by a C2C transaction, it will be too risky because his/her card number can be seen in the C2C transaction record. But in a B2C scenario, B can be a non-bank e-transaction service provider, such as PayPal. For example, a fraudster can transfer money from the stolen card to a PayPal account for the first step and then transfer the money from the PayPal account to multiple fraudulent cards. In the B2C scenario, the PayPal account and the fraudulent cards are untraceable in the transaction record, because in a B2C transaction record, the Vendor Id field only contains a String that stands for the PayPal company, not the specific PayPal account. By stealing money via B2C transactions, a fraudster can keep himself/herself invisible in the transaction records. This is probably the reason why fraudsters usually commit crimes through B2C other than C2C transactions.

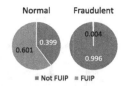

Fig. 2. Distribution of the transaction records when they are divided by the frequently-use IP address attribute.

Statistical Discoveries. We conduct statistical analysis on a month of transactions. We find out that 99.6% of the fraudulent transactions did not use a frequently-used IP address (FUIP), as shown in Fig. 2. This means that these transactions are highly possible to be made by the criminals after they have stolen the accounts, instead of being made by the deceived victims themselves. We also discover that more than 96% of the fraudulent B2C transactions are not the first transaction made by the customer in the month (without the influence of data boundary, this ratio could be higher). Furthermore, we discover that the time intervals between each two consecutive fraudulent transactions of a customer are often abnormally short, and the amounts of the two transactions are often close. We name these two quantities *TTD* (Transaction Time Difference) and *TAD* (Transaction Amount Difference), so the graph of the joint cumulative density function is drawn in Fig. 3. It is obvious that fraudulent transactions usually have smaller *TTD* and *TAD* than normal transactions. In another word, fraudsters usually steal the money with multiple consecutive quick transfers. Another abnormal phenomenon about the fraudulent transactions we find out is shown in Fig. 4. The amounts of normal transactions present a power-law distribution, by contrast, the amounts of fraudulent transactions present a quite different distribution which has several isolated peaks. The two dominating peaks are 1000 and 2000.

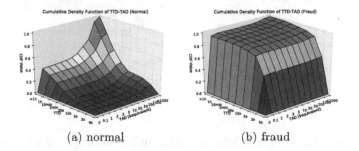

(a) normal   (b) fraud

Fig. 3. The TTD-TAD distribution.

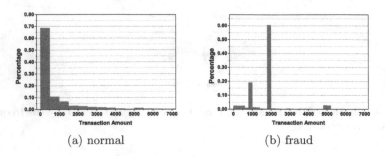

(a) normal   (b) fraud

Fig. 4. The difference between fraudulent and normal transactions in amount distribution.

Explore Fraudsters' Motivation. So far we have presented the observations and discoveries we obtained from the statistical results. In this part, we want to explore the reasons behind the abnormal fraudulent behavioral patterns.

Let's start with the abnormally small TTD. Consider such a scenario: When a fraudster has just stolen an account, his goal is to take more money away. However, in most instances, as soon as a transfer occurs, the customer will be informed by the bank immediately probably by phone message. Then the customer will immediately inform the bank to freeze the account. This leads to the abnormal small TTD, because if the fraudsters want to steal more money, they have to do it quickly. They don't even have time to camouflage the TTD. But why the fraudsters do not steal money in a single transaction? Why the fraudulent transactions often present in sequences?

Table 2. Frequencies of different daily spending upper limits.

Daily spending upper limit	Frequency
1000	1.65%
2000	10.80%
5000	80.60%
10000	1.40%
20000	5.54%
50000 or more	0.07%

Usually, a bank will set a daily spending upper limit for each customer. We make statistics for all the upper limits on a month of transaction records, which is shown in Table 2. It shows that over 80% of the customers have a daily upper limit of 5000. This fact can explain the two peaks (1000 and 2000) in Fig. 4(b): Consider a criminal has stolen a bank account and does not know whether or not the card has been used for shopping on the very day. In such a situation, $1000+2000+2000$ could be one good combination of transfer amounts because of three advantages: First, compared to a single transfer with larger amount, such as 5000, 1000+2000+2000 is more likely to succeed, at least partially, because more than 93% of the customers have a daily spending limit equal to or less than 5000. Once the customers have used their card for shopping today, a transfer request of 5000 will fail, because it exceeds the daily spending upper limit. Second, once the card is not used yet on the very day, then this combination can take as much money as possible without any remnant. Third, compared to transfer amount less than 1000, this combination needs fewer transaction requests, which leads to fewer risk of being intercepted by fraud detection systems.

To summarize, fraudsters are willing to steal the money in smaller amounts by multiple quick transfers, because this way has a higher profit expectation and fewer risks. As a result, the fraudulent transactions present a sequential form for most of the time, and the time intervals between every two consecutive transactions are often small.

3   Proposed Model

In response to the threat of fraudulent B2C transactions, we propose a novel model, *SeqFD*, for real-time fraudulent transaction detection. The innovation of *SeqFD* lies in the statistical sequential features. In this section, we first overview the mechanism and deployment scenario of *SeqFD*. Then, we elaborate on how to compute the statistical sequential features by using the sliding time window. Finally, we list all the 9 features applied by *SeqFD*.

3.1   Overview

The workflow of *SeqFD* is depicted in Fig. 5. Within the dashed line in the right part, the mechanism of *SeqFD* is demonstrated in detail. In the left part, a possible deployment scenario is shown.

The Mechanism of SeqFD. *SeqFD* has two stages: the training stage and the classification stage. At the training stage, the labeled transaction records will be sampled to form a raw dataset. The reasons for sampling are two-fold: First, the volume of the whole dataset is very large, using the whole dataset to train the classifier is quite time-consuming. Second, in reality, fraudulent instances are often far less than normal instances so the dataset is extremely skewed. One feasible sampling strategy is just like how the dataset is extracted for our study: Obtain all the victims in a time span first (we use three months in this work), then query for all the transactions these customers have made within the time span. After that, randomly pick out some normal customers and retrieve their transaction records in the same time span. Finally, combine these two parts to form a labeled training set, which is not that large or skewed.

Through the sliding time window strategy for transaction aggregation, a raw instance can be turned into a feature vector which includes sequential features. Feed the feature set to a machine learning model for training, and after that, a trained classifier will be ready to give a prediction. At the classification stage, streaming transaction requests will be sent to *SeqFD*, and *SeqFD* will give a real-time response. In specific, *SeqFD* will first turn the raw request into a feature vector composed of the same features as above, and then the feature vector will be sent to the classifier. Finally, the classifier gives the prediction.

Deployment Scenario of *SeqFD*. The left part of Fig. 5 shows how to put *SeqFD* into a real application. When *SeqFD* receives a transaction request, it gives a prediction. If *SeqFD* judges a transaction request suspicious, people of the bank could give a phone call to the customer to figure out if the transaction is truly fraudulent. Then the transaction can be labeled and be added into the database of labeled transaction records. Another source of labeled instances is police reports. *SeqFD* cannot catch all the fraudulent transactions, and some of the missing fraudulent instances might be obtained from the police. With these two sources of labeled transactions, *SeqFD* can be retrained periodically to make the model updated. Therefore, *SeqFD* is able to adjust itself in accordance with the change in crowd behavior patterns. No matter how the normal crowd behavior change, as long as it is different from the fraudulent crowd behavior, then *SeqFD* is able to work effectively.

3.2   Sliding Time Window

This subsection introduces the detailed design of the transaction aggregation technique based on sliding time window strategy. In the database of historical behavior which is in the middle of Fig. 5, an independent list of historical transactions is kept individually for every customer. An example of such a list of a certain customer is shown in Fig. 6. In this simple example, the size of the time window is set to 1 minute, which means that the list will only contain the newest transaction records that happened within 1 minute ago. Every time a new-coming transaction is added into the list, the time window slides forward, then the obsolete transactions will be thrown out of the time window. Sliding time window ensures that the features computed by aggregated transactions can precisely depict the recent behavior pattern of a customer.

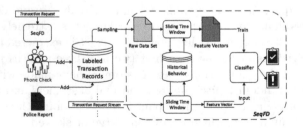

Fig. 5. *SeqFD* overview.

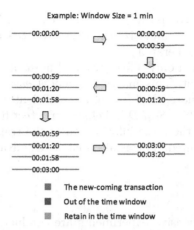

Fig. 6. An exemplary illustration of how the time window slides on the historical transactions of a certain customer.

3.3 Feature Engineering

The features and their explanations are shown in Table 3.

As mentioned in Sect. 2.2, *TTD* and *TAD* are two typical sequential features, but they only include information on two consecutive transactions. What we need are features that can summarize a bunch of transactions, so the sequential features should be aggregated. In specific, within the time window, the *TTD*s and

Table 3. Selected features

Name	Type	Explanation	Sequential?	Original?
Amount	Numeric	The amount of the transaction	No	Yes
FUIP	Boolean	If this transaction is made from a frequently used IP address	No	Yes
OverLim	Boolean	If this transaction is over the spending limitation	No	No
AmtAvg	Numeric	The average of the transaction amounts in the time window	No	No
Times	Numeric	The number of transactions within the time window	No	No
TDAvg	Numeric	The average of all the TTDs within the time window	Yes	No
TDVar	Numeric	The variance of all the TTDs within the time window	Yes	No
ADAvg	Numeric	The average of all the TADs within the time window	Yes	No
ADVar	Numeric	The variance of all the TADs within the time window	Yes	No

*TAD*s are aggregated by computing their average and variance. Thus, statistical sequential features which summarize the characteristics of all the transactions in the time window are generated.

In this work, we design only 9 features, and most of them can be computed just by time and amount. This makes our model easy to be transplanted to other datasets. Furthermore, *SeqFD* can also sufficiently protect the privacy of customers. If a bank deploys *SeqFD* to help them detect fraudulent transactions, *SeqFD* will only gather the basic information of the transactions. No personal information will be gathered. This is also one of the advantages of *SeqFD*.

4   Evaluations

In this section, comprehensive experiments are conducted to evaluate *SeqFD*. The questions for which we want to find out answers are as follows:

(1) Which machine learning model performs best on the features?
(2) What size is appropriate for the sliding time window?
(3) Are the statistical sequential features really important?
(4) Are there any possible negative influences when the under-sampling is applied to solve the skewed-data problem?

4.1   Experimental Setup

We use the dataset of April and May as the training set and the dataset of June as the test set. *Cross-validation* is not adopted in the experiment because it will cause the *time travel problem*, e.g., using the data from future to train a model and using the data from past to test. The training set contains 2393817 normal instances and 40393 fraudulent instances, and the testing set contains 1003539 normal instances and 24898 fraudulent instances. The ratio of the two classes seem approximately 59 : 1, but it is not the true ratio because 2393817 is just a portion of the normal instances. Actually, the number of transactions in a month is nearly 14 million, so the actual ratio is nearly 693 : 1. As the two classes are highly unbalanced, we sample 10% of the normal instances.

Note that we do the sampling process after the raw dataset have been transformed to feature set so that the statistical sequential features are kept lossless. The instances of the test set are sent to the classifier in the right temporal order to simulate the transaction stream.

Window Size Candidates. We prepare six candidate window sizes on different scales: 1 minute, 10 minutes, 1 hour, 1 day, 1 week and 1 month. Our goal is to figure out which one can lead to the best performance of classification. The window size will be referred to as *WS* for short afterward. A *WS* larger than 1 month is not taken into account since the intervals of the adopted dataset for training is only two months.

Machine Learning Model Candidates. For classification, the candidate machine learning models we choose are the Random Forest [9], XGBoost [3], Decision Tree, Naive Bayes, 2-hidden-layer Neural Network, and Logistic Regression. For Neural Network, we set 10 perceptrons to each hidden-layer. For other models, we use the default hyper-parameters preset in Scikit-Learn [14].

Assessment Criteria. We use three assessment criteria to evaluate the *WS* and choose a suitable classifier.

AUC (Area Under ROC Curve): For each window size, we take the *AUC* of the machine learning models as a performance indicator.

The highest *TPR* when *FPR* is less than 0.01: According to our dataset provider, in the industry 1% is the tolerance upper limit for *FPR*. As a result, a *TPR* reached with a *FPR* higher than 1% is regarded as meaningless in this work.

The time for generating features: For a practical model, the efficiency, e.g., the time of generating features, is a necessary factor.

4.2   Evaluation Results

Figue 7 shows that XGBoost has the highest AUC for all the six candidate window sizes, it performs robustly and stably. Random Forest is able to take the second place except when *WS* is 1 minute. The performances of the other four machine learning models fall behind.

Figure 8 presents the highest *TPR* reached by each machine learning model when *FPR* is controlled under 0.01 by tuning the classification threshold. The best record is 97.2%, which is achieved by XGBoost when *WS* is set to be 1 month. Random Forest performs better than XGBoost when the *WS* is smaller, except for 1 minute. And the other four models still fall behind.

In common sense, a larger window size could lead to more cost for efficiency, because for the customers who make transactions frequently and continuously, a larger window size will contain more transactions to compute. Thus we test the average time it costs to transform a raw transaction into a feature vector on a

Table 4. The training and predicting time (seconds) of the candidate ML models.

Model	Training time	Predicting time
Random forest	7.18	1.79
Naive Bayes	0.94	0.83
Decision tree	6.38	0.62
Logistic Regression	7.05	0.67
XGBoost	9.44	1.09
Neural Network	32.96	0.78

server with a dual-core 2.40 GHz CPU and 32 GB RAM, and the result is shown in Fig. 9. Surprisingly, it shows that when the *WS* is 1 month, the average time is only about 1.5 ms, which is not far more than the average time when the *WS* is smaller. Therefore, 1 month is adopted as the appropriate *WS*.

Furthermore, we also test the training time and the predicting time of each machine learning model. These two indicators are not influenced by the *WS*, because the number of instances and the number of features remain unchanged when *WS* is changed. Therefore, we set the *WS* to be 1 month and test the training and test efficiency for each classifier. The result is shown in Table 4. For the training stage, the time cost of XGBoost is 9.44 s. For the test stage, the test set contains 1028437 instances, so the average predicting time of XGBoost for one instance is less than 2 μ. Therefore, the total time cost for the predicting stage is 1.5 ms+2μs $\approx$ 1.5 ms. According to our experience of the industry, this time cost is far below the tolerance upper bound. XGBoost is nearly 40% faster than Random Forest. In addition, XGBoost has the best performance when the *WS* is 1 month. Therefore, it should be applied by *SeqFD*.

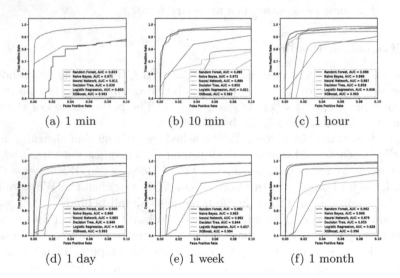

Fig. 7. The ROC curves of the candidate machine learning models under different window sizes.

4.3   Feature Importance

As XGBoost and Random Forest are both capable to output the importance of the features, we use them to evaluate the importance of the features. The result is shown in Fig. 10(a).

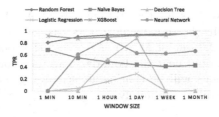

Fig. 8. The highest TPR reached by the candidate machine learning models when FPR is less than 0.01.

Figure 10(a) shows that all of the 4 statistical sequential features play indispensable roles in $SeqFD$, especially $TDAvg$. The other two features generated by the sliding time window, $Times$ and $AmtAvg$, are also quite important. For the original features, $Amount$ plays an important role in both models. $FUIP$ is quite important in Random Forest but seems useless in XGBoost. We also conduct a comparative experiment with different features. For the first set, all the nine features are included; For the second set, the four statistical sequential features are eliminated; For the third set, transaction aggregation is not used and only two original features, $Amount$ and $FUIP$, are included. The result in Fig. 10(b) shows that the statistical sequential features truly boost the performance of $SeqFD$.

4.4   Effects of Under-Sampling

In the evaluations above, we use a training set composed of 10% normal instances (about 100000) and all fraudulent instances (24898). Actually, 10% is out of intuition. Therefore, we want to figure out if different sampling ratios will lead to fluctuations in performance. We use the ROC of XGBoost to represent the classification performance. The WS is set to be 1 month. The candidate sampling ratios for the normal instances are 5%, 10%, 20%, 50% and non-sampling, respectively. The result is shown in Fig. 11.

Figure 11 shows that all of the candidate sampling ratios have an AUC larger than 0.995, which means that $SeqFD$ performs robustly without a large fluctuation under different sampling ratios. Surprisingly, when the sampling ratio is set to be 5%, XGBoost performs the best. Although this result may be due to fortuitous, the rationality of under-sampling for solving the skewed-data problem is proved.

5   Discussion

Although $TPR = 97.2\%$ with $FPR < 1\%$ is the highest performance we get from the experiment, actually the performance can be improved further in practice because our dataset has a boundary. Some of the seemingly first transactions in sequences are actually not the first ones, because those plausible headers could have precedents in the data outside the boundary. For example, when we compute the feature vectors for the transactions in April, the transactions of March should be within the time window if *WS* is set to be 1 month. But we are not provided the dataset of March. As a result, a portion of the feature vectors, especially the ones near the boundary, are not computed precisely. In practice, the transactions will be continuous streaming data. The problem of data boundary can be diluted infinitely.

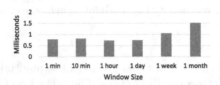

Fig. 9. The average time it costs to transform a raw transaction to a feature vector.

Another issue is about the test set. As mentioned before, the test set contains a sampled portion of the normal transactions. However, as the normal transactions are picked randomly, they are supposed to have the same distribution as the whole transaction dataset. Thus, there is no straightforward reason for the *FPR* to rise if the whole transaction dataset is used to test *SeqFD*, because with the rise of the numerator (the number of error-alarmed transactions), the denominator (the number of all the normal transactions) is also rising. In addition, as our test set contains all the fraudulent transactions in the time span, the *TPR* has absolutely no reason to decrease when using the whole dataset to test *SeqFD*. Thus the performances of *SeqFD* in the evaluations are reliable indeed.

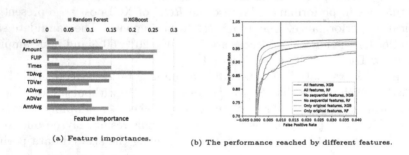

(a) Feature importances.

(b) The performance reached by different features.

Fig. 10. Evaluations of the feature importance. In common sense, when the performance gets higher, it will be harder to get improved.

The third point we want to discuss is the scalability of *SeqFD*. For the classification process of *SeqFD*, the top two classifiers, Random Forest and XGBoost, are both scalable models [3,9]. For the feature generation process of *SeqFD*, the historical records retained by the sliding time window of two customers have no coupling, so transactions of different customers can also be transformed into feature vectors in parallel. We use Redis to implement the data warehouse of the historical records. The Redis data warehouse can be distributed in multiple servers in cluster mode, and it has high efficiency for both reading and writing. As a result, *SeqFD* is scalable and is possible to be applied to real bank systems with a huge volume of data.

Our work in progress is to deploy *SeqFD* in a distributed structure for real banking transaction systems with high concurrency and burst network traffic, and to test the performance of *SeqFD* in real streaming data.

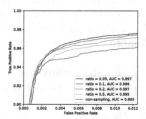

Fig. 11. The ROC curves of XGBoost when the *WS* is 1 month under different sampling ratios of normal instances.

6   Conclusion

To reach the goal of detecting effectively fraudulent transactions, we propose a novel model, *SeqFD*. The main innovation of *SeqFD* is a new-designed set of statistical sequential features. Instead of intuition, the sequential features come from statistical analysis of a real dataset. By observing the difference between normal and fraudulent transactions, we discover several typical abnormal patterns of the fraudulent transactions which can be distinguished by sequential features. We explore the reasons behind the observations, and find out that the fraudulent behavior patterns are possibly caused by the fraudsters' intrinsic motivation: They always want to steal more money as quickly as possible. Accordingly, we apply a sliding time window strategy to aggregate the sequential features into statistical sequential features, and we present the mechanism and deployment scenario of *SeqFD* in detail.

Through experimental evaluations, among the six representative machine learning models, we find that XGBoost is the classifier which fits the best with *SeqFD*. In specific, when the window size is set to be 1 month, XGBoost reaches an *AUC* of 0.996, and a *TPR* of 97.2% when *FPR* is less than 1%. In *SeqFD*, the problem of concept drift is alleviated by the sliding time window, and the problem of class-imbalanced data is solved by the under-sampling. The experiment shows that no observable negative influence emerges when the sampling ratio is smaller. Furthermore, the result of the efficiency test is also given. On a server with dual-core 2.40 GHz CPU and 32 GB RAM, the trained *SeqFD* can give a response to a transaction request in about 1.5 ms, which can competently meet the requirement of real-time. This makes *SeqFD* a practical model for fraudulent transaction detection in real-world applications.

References

1. China double 11 shopping festival sales statistics 2017 (2017). https://www.chinainternetwatch.com/22791/double-11-2017/
2. Bolton, R.J., Hand, D.J.: Statistical fraud detection: a review. Stat. Sci. **17**(3), 235–249 (2002)
3. Chen, T., Guestrin, C.: Xgboost: a scalable tree boosting system. In: Proceedings of the 22nd ACM SIGKDD International Conference on Knowledge Discovery and Data Mining, pp. 785–794. ACM (2016)
4. Duman, E., Elikucuk, I.: Solving credit card fraud detection problem by the new metaheuristics migrating birds optimization. In: International Conference on Artificial Neural Networks: Advences in Computational Intelligence, pp. 62–71 (2013)
5. Fawcett, T., Provost, F.: Adaptive fraud detection. Data Min. Knowl. Disc. **1**(3), 291–316 (1997)
6. Fu, K., Cheng, D., Tu, Y., Zhang, L.: Credit card fraud detection using convolutional neural networks. In: International Conference on Neural Information Processing, pp. 483–490 (2016)
7. Jiang, C., Song, J., Liu, G., Zheng, L., Luan, W.: Credit card fraud detection: a novel approach using aggregation strategy and feedback mechanism. IEEE Internet Things J. **5**(5), 3637–3647 (2018)
8. LeCun, Y., Bengio, Y., Hinton, G.: Deep learning. Nature **521**(7553), 436 (2015)
9. Liaw, A., Wiener, M., et al.: Classification and regression by randomforest. R news **2**(3), 18–22 (2002)
10. Malekian, D., Hashemi, M.R.: An adaptive profile based fraud detection framework for handling concept drift. In: 2013 10th International ISC Conference on Information Security and Cryptology (ISCISC), pp. 1–6. IEEE (2013)
11. Masud, M., Gao, J., Khan, L., Han, J., Thuraisingham, B.M.: Classification and novel class detection in concept-drifting data streams under time constraints. IEEE Trans. Knowl. Data Eng. **23**(6), 859–874 (2011)
12. Modi, K.: Fraud detection technique in credit card transactions using convolutional neural network (2017)
13. NilsonReport: The nilson report, October 2016. https://www.nilsonreport.com/upload/content_promo/The_Nilson_Report_10-17-2016.pdf
14. Pedregosa, F., et al.: Scikit-learn: machine learning in Python. J. Mach. Learn. Res. **12**, 2825–2830 (2011)
15. Pozzolo, A.D., Caelen, O., Borgne, Y.A.L., Waterschoot, S., Bontempi, G.: Learned lessons in credit card fraud detection from a practitioner perspective. Expert Syst. Appl. **41**(10), 4915–4928 (2014)
16. Srivastava, A., Kundu, A., Sural, S., Majumdar, A.: Credit card fraud detection using hidden Markov model. IEEE Trans. Dependable Secure Comput. **5**(1), 37–48 (2008)
17. Wang, P., Zhang, P., Guo, L.: Mining multi-label data streams using ensemble-based active learning. In: Proceedings of the 2012 SIAM International Conference on Data Mining, pp. 1131–1140. SIAM (2012)
18. Whitrow, C., Hand, D.J., Juszczak, P., Weston, D., Adams, N.M.: Transaction aggregation as a strategy for credit card fraud detection. Data Min. Knowl. Disc. **18**(1), 30–55 (2009)

Secure Multiparty PageRank Algorithm for Collaborative Fraud Detection

Alex Sangers[1(✉)], Maran van Heesch[1], Thomas Attema[1,5], Thijs Veugen[1,5], Mark Wiggerman[2], Jan Veldsink[3], Oscar Bloemen[4], and Daniël Worm[1]

[1] Netherlands Organisation for Applied Scientific Research (TNO),
The Hague, The Netherlands
`alex.sangers@tno.nl`
[2] ABN AMRO, Amsterdam, The Netherlands
[3] Rabobank, Utrecht, The Netherlands
[4] ING, Amsterdam, The Netherlands
[5] CWI, Amsterdam, The Netherlands

Abstract. Collaboration between financial institutions helps to improve detection of fraud. However, exchange of relevant data between these institutions is often not possible due to privacy constraints and data confidentiality. An important example of relevant data for fraud detection is given by a transaction graph, where the nodes represent bank accounts and the links consist of the transactions between these accounts. Previous works show that features derived from such graphs, like PageRank, can be used to improve fraud detection. However, each institution can only see a part of the whole transaction graph, corresponding to the accounts of its own customers. In this research a new method is described, making use of secure multiparty computation (MPC) techniques, allowing multiple parties to jointly compute the PageRank values of their combined transaction graphs securely, while guaranteeing that each party only learns the PageRank values of its own accounts and nothing about the other transaction graphs. In our experiments this method is applied to graphs containing up to tens of thousands of nodes. The execution time scales linearly with the number of nodes, and the method is highly parallelizable. Secure multiparty PageRank is feasible in a realistic setting with millions of nodes per party by extrapolating the results from our experiments.

Keywords: Multiparty computation · PageRank · Fraud detection · Collaborative computation

1 Introduction

Cyber security, anti-fraud and other anti-crime activities benefit from cooperation amongst involved parties like financial institutions, governments and law enforcement agencies. The public and private sectors are actually stimulated by regulators to perform joint activities and share threat intelligence and other

© International Financial Cryptography Association 2019
I. Goldberg and T. Moore (Eds.): FC 2019, LNCS 11598, pp. 605–623, 2019.
https://doi.org/10.1007/978-3-030-32101-7_35

data as they have a common goal to battle this type of crime. Examples of such data are lists of known criminals, confirmed money mules and known malicious IP addresses. Sharing benign operational data on customers, transactions and events between different organizations would be beneficial as well. However, sharing benign data between organizations has always been strongly limited due to competition and privacy regulations, especially if it concerns personal data of customers and employees. The risks of sharing data for companies as well as public services are loss of trust in services, integrity, financial losses, societal damage and damaged reputation.

1.1   The Financial Sector

The financial sector continuously fights the misuse of the financial infrastructure for criminal activities like fraud and money laundering. An example of such a criminal activity is the following.

Example 1 ('Carousel'). *Loan applications are based on income of the client that requests the loan. A criminal may try to feign income by creating repeated transactions to his account, or node, coming from another node pretending to be a company - just as legitimate salary payments. To keep the needed funds for a criminal low, the money is often drained from the account and placed back on the node of the fake company where the process is repeated.*

By looking at the whole network, we may quickly realize that while the feigned salary payments look similar to other salary payments, the node pretending to be a company lacks the structure we see of nodes known to be companies.

Protected by privacy regulations such as the recent GDPR, these bank-transcending fraud and money laundering cases can be challenging to detect. In fact, even malign transaction sequences moving through different departments or channels within a bank may be troublesome to detect, due to the confidentiality of the involved data.

Financial crime detection is an example of a situation in which different parties share a common interest, but confidentiality and privacy regulations prevent collaboration. In a payment transaction a financial institution typically only knows one of the parties involved in the payment. Financial institutions would greatly benefit from accessing information from other organizations.

1.2   Secure Multiparty Computation

Secure multiparty computation (MPC) provides a cryptographic solution to the described dilemma above. MPC protocols are cryptographic techniques that allow multiple parties to collaboratively evaluate a function on private input data in such a way that only the output of the function is revealed, i.e. private input remains private. MPC could be explained as the implementation of a trusted third party that collects all relevant input data, evaluates the desired function and reveals its output. However, using an actual trusted third party, such as a consultancy agency, to collect and analyse all private information is often not allowed by regulations and usually expensive.

Already in the 1980s it was shown that any computable function can be evaluated securely, i.e. in an MPC fashion [3,9,14,27,28]. However, early MPC protocols came at a cost as they introduced a significant computation and/or communication overhead. Over the years progress has been made and research interests have shifted towards practical applicability making MPC ready for deployment [4,12,17,19,22].

MPC has been applied to various use cases ranging from sugar-beet auctions [5] to key-management systems [25]. Moreover, applications in the financial domain include confidential benchmarking [10] and off-exchange trading [24]. All these use cases fall under the MPC paradigm in which multiple parties aim to collaboratively evaluate some function without revealing its private input values.

Secure graph algorithmic has been another particular area of interest. Shortest path and max-flow algorithms, for example, find their applicability in many situations and a natural question to ask is whether these algorithms can be evaluated in a privacy-preserving manner. In [8], a secure shortest path algorithm is constructed for the 2-party setting. In [1], the shortest path and max-flow algorithm are considered in the general multi-party setting. However, the complexity of these algorithms renders them only applicable to small graphs.

In 2015, Nayak et al. [21] developed a framework for securely computing graph algorithms like PageRank. The main difference is that they outsource the secure graph algorithm to two parties, who execute a garbled circuit. In our solution, the partial graph owners jointly perform the algorithm by means of additively homomorphic encryption. Their solution has complexity $\mathcal{O}(M \log M)$, where $M = |V| + |E|$, because edges and nodes need to be obliviously sorted. We exploit the fact that in our setting each party knows its own transaction graph, because then additively homomorphic encryption allows for local computations with private values, and sorting is not necessary, which leads to an overall $\mathcal{O}(M)$ complexity. Both solutions can easily be parallellised.

MPC delivers the mechanisms needed to collaborate and safeguard data security and privacy without the need for a trusted third party, which would be highly beneficial for the financial industry.

The rest of this paper is structured as follows. The PageRank algorithm is explained in Sect. 2. Secure multiparty PageRank is described in Sect. 3. In Sect. 4 the performance results are presented and the conclusions are presented in Sect. 5.

2   PageRank for Fraud Detection

In a transaction graph, nodes represent bank accounts, and edges consist of the unique transactions between accounts. Several graph-based features can be used in machine-learning algorithms to improve existing fraud detection algorithms, by reducing the false positives of existing techniques [20]. Namely, after the graph-based features are computed, new transactions that are classified as fraudulent by an existing fraud-detection technique can be re-evaluated by an algorithm that uses these features.

One of these graph-based features is *PageRank*, developed by Google to return a ranking of websites when searching on the web. In essence, PageRank is a centrality measure for all nodes in the directed graph, and can be used for other purposes as well. Together with other features, PageRank and reverse PageRank (PageRank on the reversed directed graph) have shown their value in discriminating between fraudulent and non-fraudulent transactions [20].

2.1   Requirements for PageRank Application for Fraud Detection

Financial institutions could compute the PageRank values of bank accounts with their observation of the transaction graph. However, in that case they would use only a part of the whole transaction graph. The PageRank values would be much more accurate if the PageRank algorithm were securely applied on transaction data of multiple financial institutions.

In order to apply secure multiparty PageRank in the fraud detection of a bank, the PageRank values need to be available as a feature for machine learning models that use PageRank as input feature. They need to be calculated based on the transaction graph for a predefined period, which is typically one or two months, and need to be updated regularly, e.g. on a monthly basis.

This requires the PageRank and the reverse PageRank computations to take place within $\sim$15 days each. For practical application, however, it would be preferable to compute the PageRank values within $\sim$1 day. This process spans from the starting point where all participants have their graph for the given period ready, to the moment when the PageRank values for all nodes of the participants have been computed and can be used. Furthermore, a reasonable bandwidth for each participant is required, e.g., 100 Mbit/s.

In terms of information, it is not allowed for any participant to learn anything about the graph of another participant, other than what can be learned from the final private PageRank values.

2.2   PageRank and the Power Method

The original goal of the PageRank algorithm is to compute a scalable centrality measure for websites using the hyperlink structure of the web. Intuitively, imagine an Internet user that randomly follows hyperlinks on websites, goes to the next website, etc. As soon as it encounters a website without hyperlinks (a so-called *dangling* website), a new website is chosen at random. In addition to this behavior of following hyperlinks, the Internet user will 'teleport' to any random website with a known probability $1 - p$. The resulting probability distribution of visiting frequencies of the Internet user on the websites represents the PageRank value of each website.

Inspired by [20], this idea can easily be translated to transaction graphs. Similarly as with the websites, as soon as a dangling node is encountered, a new node is chosen at random, and there is a teleport probability $1 - p$. The PageRank values of the transaction graph is the probability distribution based on the visiting frequency of an imaginary coin on the bank accounts.

A commonly used iterative solution method to compute the PageRank is the so-called *power method*. A useful variant thereof has been presented in [18], where only the PageRank values of non-dangling nodes have to be computed during the power method iterations, while correcting for the contribution of dangling nodes. Moreover, this variant has the added benefit of closely matching the intuition given at the beginning of this subsection. The set of dangling nodes is denoted by D and the set of non-dangling nodes is denoted by U. The PageRank value of node j at the k-th iteration is denoted as x_k^j. Equation (1) describes the initialization and iterations of the power method variant of [18] to compute the PageRank values of the non-dangling nodes.

$$x_0^j = \frac{1}{n}, \quad \forall j \in U.$$

$$x_{k+1}^j = \frac{1-p}{n} + p \cdot \sum_{i \in S(j)} \frac{x_k^i}{c_i} + \frac{p}{n}(1 - \sum_{i \in U} x_k^i), \quad \forall j \in U,$$

$$= \frac{1}{n} + p \cdot \sum_{i \in S(j)} \frac{x_k^i}{c_i} - \frac{p}{n}\sum_{i \in U} x_k^i, \quad \forall j \in U, \tag{1}$$

where p is a fixed probability, n the total number of nodes, c_i the out-degree of node i, $S(j)$ is the set of incoming edges of node j intersected with U. Note that $c_i \geq 1$ for $\forall i \in S(j)$. Equation (2) describes how the PageRank values of the dangling nodes can be computed after convergence of the power method iterations in Eq. (1).

$$x^j = \frac{1}{n} + p \cdot \sum_{i \in S(j)} \frac{x^i}{c_i} - \frac{p}{n}\sum_{i \in U} x^i, \quad \forall j \in D. \tag{2}$$

Under mild conditions that are satisfied by transaction graphs, the convergence rate of the power method equals p [15] (and is thus independent of the size of the graph). For the commonly used $p = 0.85$, the power method converges within 50 to 100 iterations.

3 A Secure Multiparty PageRank Algorithm

Several factors make securely implementing an algorithm a non-trivial task. The overhead introduced by MPC is significant, requiring a careful analysis of the PageRank algorithm in order to select the optimal MPC protocol. Moreover, most cryptographic protocols work over finite groups, rings or fields and not over the real or complex numbers. This requires a specific representation of the PageRank algorithm, which is originally defined over the real numbers.

3.1 Additively Homomorphic Encryption

A key observation is that the PageRank algorithm consists of mainly linear operations, i.e. additions and multiplications by constants. It is assumed that the total number of nodes n (bank accounts) and the PageRank probability p are publicly known constants, and therefore the only non-linearity in Eq. (1) is division by the private value c_i. The variable c_i represents the number of outgoing edges of node $i \in V$, is fixed throughout the algorithm and is known by the associated party, for which this division can thus be seen as a linear operation.

A crucial observation is that all nodes i are owned by one of the parties participating in the protocol. In practice, this does not have to be the case as there might be transactions to accounts owned by other banks. To take into account these nodes, other approaches, that are out-of-scope for this paper, are required.

An approach to utilize the linear properties of the PageRank algorithm is additively homomorphic encryption. A homomorphic encryption scheme allows the evaluation of certain functions on encrypted input values while remaining oblivious to the actual input values.

Any of the parties could play the evaluator role and perform the computations, as long as the other parties deliver their encrypted input values. The computations can also be distributed amongst the parties so that they share the computational effort. By distributing the computations in such a way that the division by the private value c_i is executed by the party that knows this value, all computations become linear, i.e. ciphertexts do not have to be multiplied by other ciphertexts. Because of this linearity the encryption scheme only has to be additively homomorphic and there is no need to use the more sophisticated but far less efficient fully homomorphic encryption (FHE) schemes. For this reason, the additively homomorphic Damgård-Jurik encryption scheme [11], which is a generalization of the Paillier encryption scheme [23], has been adapted.

Damgård-Jurik is a public-key encryption scheme that takes plaintexts from $\mathbb{Z}_{N^s}$ and maps them to ciphertexts in $\mathbb{Z}^*_{N^{s+1}}$, for some $s \in \mathbb{Z}_{>0}$,

$$\mathrm{Enc}_{pk} : \mathbb{Z}_{N^s} \to \mathbb{Z}^*_{N^{s+1}},$$

where N is an RSA-modulus and pk is the public key with the associated private key sk. The Damgård-Jurik encryption function is probabilistic; it takes as additional input a random argument $r \in_R \mathbb{Z}_{N^{s+1}} \backslash \{0\}$ for each invocation, which we omit in our notation. The additive homomorphic property means that for all $a, b \in \mathbb{Z}_N$,

$$\mathrm{Dec}_{sk}\left(\mathrm{Enc}_{pk}(a) \cdot \mathrm{Enc}_{pk}(b)\right) = \mathrm{Dec}_{sk}\left(\mathrm{Enc}_{pk}(a+b)\right) = a + b \quad \mathrm{mod}\ N^s,$$

and, as a consequence, for all $c \in \mathbb{Z}$,

$$\mathrm{Dec}_{sk}\left(\mathrm{Enc}_{pk}(a)^c\right) = \mathrm{Dec}_{sk}\left(\mathrm{Enc}_{pk}(c \cdot a)\right) = c \cdot a \quad \mathrm{mod}\ N^s.$$

The parameter s influences the size of the plaintexts, the size of the ciphertexts and the ratio of the former two. In Sect. 3.6 we will see that, in our case, $s = 1$

results in a sufficiently large plaintext space. For this reason we will fix $s = 1$ from now on.

It must also be noted that this approach of distributing the computations does introduce a communication overhead in contrast to using, for example, a fully homomorphic encryption scheme. This trade-off between computation and communication complexity is typical for applying MPC. As we will see later in Sect. 4, the communication overhead of our solution is acceptable.

3.2 PageRank Algorithm over $\mathbb{Z}_N$

The PageRank algorithm is defined over the real numbers, whereas the Damgård-Jurik encryption scheme assumes plaintexts in the finite ring $\mathbb{Z}_N$. To solve this discordance the PageRank algorithm has to be defined over $\mathbb{Z}_N$ such that the outcome (approximately) coincides with the outcome of the original PageRank algorithm.

An integer representative y of the real number x can be found by applying a scaling factor $f_x \in \mathbb{Z}_+$,

$$y = \lfloor f_x \cdot x \rceil \in \mathbb{Z}.$$

The fixed scaling factor f_x determines the precision of the computations, in fact, the real number x can be approximated by $\frac{y}{f_x}$ and

$$\left| x - \frac{y}{f_x} \right| \le \frac{1}{2 f_x}.$$

The scaling factor f_c is applied to find an integer representation of the fraction $\frac{p}{c_i}$. Multiplying both sides of Eq. (1) with the factor $(f_c)^{k+1} f_x$ then results in the following recurrence relation:

$$(f_c)^{k+1} f_x x_{k+1}^j = \frac{(f_c)^{k+1} f_x}{n} + \sum_{i \in S(j)} \frac{p f_c}{c_i} (f_c)^k f_x x_k^i - \frac{p f_c}{n} \sum_{i \in U} (f_c)^k f_x x_k^i.$$

Defining $\tilde{y}_k^j := \left\lfloor (f_c)^k f_x x_k^j \right\rceil$, $\phi_k := \left\lfloor \frac{(f_c)^{k+1} f_x}{n} \right\rceil$, $\rho_i := \left\lfloor \frac{p f_c}{c_i} \right\rceil$ and $\psi := \left\lfloor \frac{p f_c}{n} \right\rceil$ for all nodes i and iterations k yields the following approximation:

$$\tilde{y}_{k+1}^j \approx \phi_k + \sum_{i \in S(j)} \rho_i \tilde{y}_k^i - \psi \sum_{i \in U} \tilde{y}_k^i.$$

From this the recurrence relation of Eq. (3) is deduced, which is defined over the integers and can be used to approximate the PageRank values of the non-dangling nodes.

$$y_{k+1}^j = \phi_k + \sum_{i \in S(j)} \rho_i y_k^i - \psi \sum_{i \in U} y_k^i \quad \text{with} \quad y_0^j = \left\lfloor f_x x_0^j \right\rceil, \quad \forall j \in V. \quad (3)$$

The same scaling approach is applied to Eq. (2) in which the PageRank values for the dangling nodes are computed. The PageRank values x_k^i can be approximated by $y_k^i/((f_c)^k f_x)$ with a precision that can be modified by changing the scaling factors f_x and f_c.

It is now straightforward to define the PageRank algorithm over $\mathbb{Z}_N$, where the RSA-modulus N should be chosen such that we avoid modular reductions (or overflows) during the evaluation of the PageRank algorithm. It is easy to see that more precision, or larger scaling factors, requires N to be larger as well. In Sect. 3.6 the exact parameter choices will be presented.

3.3   PageRank Algorithm in the Encrypted Domain

The encryption function Enc_{pk} maps Eq. (3) to the following recursive relation over $\mathbb{Z}_{N^2}^*$,

$$z_{k+1}^j = \Phi_k \cdot \prod_{i \in S(j)} \left(z_k^i\right)^{\rho_i} \cdot \left(\prod_{i \in U} z_k^i\right)^{-\psi} \quad \text{mod } N^2 \quad \forall k,$$

$$z_0^j = \text{Enc}_{pk}\left(y_0^j\right) \quad \forall j \in V.$$

Here $\rho_i, \psi \in \mathbb{Z}$ are as in Sect. 3.2, $\Phi_k := \text{Enc}_{pk}(\phi_k) \in \mathbb{Z}_{N^2}^*$ and $z_k^j \in \mathbb{Z}_{N^2}^*$ for all j, k. Since the encryption scheme is additively homomorphic it follows that $\text{Dec}_{sk}\left(z_k^j\right) = y_k^j$ for all j, k.

Note that the value ρ_i is derived from the out-degree of node $i \in V$, and therefore contains private information. For this reason, the terms $\left(z_k^i\right)^{\rho_i}$ should be computed by the party owning node i. Similarly, the sets $S(j)$ and U contain private information, hence summing over these sets can only be done collaboratively. More precisely, the product $\prod_{i \in S(j)} \left(z_k^i\right)^{\rho_i}$ should be computed by the party owning node j, and the product $\prod_{i \in U} z_k^i$ should be computed as the product of all privately computed products $\prod_{i \in U^P} z_k^i$, for all parties $P \in \mathcal{P}$. Here U^P is the set of non-dangling nodes belonging to party P and $\mathcal{P}$ is the set of all parties.

Algorithm 1 describes the computations that have to be performed by party P, assuming that the encryption key has already been generated. Except for the initialization phase all computations take place in $\mathbb{Z}_{N^2}^*$, hence modular reductions are implicit. Each party executes this algorithm and it is evident that it can only be performed collaboratively.

All values that are broadcast are ciphertexts, hence they do not leak private information. However, together multiple ciphertexts might leak information. In particular, we see that ρ_j could be derived from the two ciphertexts Z_k^j and z_k^j. For this reason, every ciphertext is rerandomized before it is broadcast. By rerandomization we obtain another unlinkable ciphertext that decrypts to the same value. We therefore maintain the required functionality without leaking private information. Rerandomization is a standard technique and, in our case, comes down to multiplying the ciphertext with a fresh encryption of 0.

Furthermore, the broadcasting introduces unnecessary communication and even leaks some private information, namely the set U^P. Both can be avoided by only sending the ciphertexts to the parties that require them.

Algorithm 1. Secure PageRank algorithm for party P

Public inputs: pk, n, p, f_x, f_c
Private input: $U^P, D^P, (c_j)_{j \in V^P}, (S(j))_{j \in V^P}$
Output: Encrypted and scaled PageRank values $\left(z_K^j\right)_{j \in V^P}$

1:   $\psi \leftarrow \left\lfloor \frac{pf_c}{n} \right\rceil$ ▷ Initialization
2:   **for** $j \in U^P$ **do**
3:      $z_0^j \leftarrow \mathrm{Enc}_{pk}\left(\left\lfloor \frac{f_x}{n} \right\rceil\right)$
4:      $\rho_j \leftarrow \left\lfloor \frac{pf_c}{c_j} \right\rceil$
5:   **for** $k = 0$ **to** $K - 1$ **do**   ▷ Non-dangling nodes
6:      $\Phi_k \leftarrow \mathrm{Enc}_{pk}\left(\left\lfloor \frac{(f_c)^{k+1}f_x}{n} \right\rceil\right)$
7:      $s_k^P \leftarrow \left(\prod_{i \in U^P} z_k^i\right)^{-\psi}$
8:      Rerandomize and broadcast s_k^P
9:      **Upon receiving** s_k^Q for all $Q \in \mathcal{P}$ **do**
10:        $S_k \leftarrow \prod_{Q \in \mathcal{P}} s_k^Q$
11:      **for** $j \in U^P$ **do**
12:        $Z_k^j \leftarrow \left(z_k^j\right)^{\rho_j}$
13:        Rerandomize and broadcast $\left(j, Z_k^j\right)$
14:      **for** $j \in U^P$ **do**
15:        **Upon receiving** Z_k^i for all $i \in S(j)$ **do**
16:          $z_{k+1}^j \leftarrow \Phi_k \cdot S_k \cdot \prod_{i \in S(j)} Z_k^i$
17:   **for** $j \in D^P$ **do**   ▷ Dangling nodes
18:      $z_K^j \leftarrow \Phi_{K-1} \cdot S_{K-1} \cdot \prod_{i \in S(j)} Z_{K-1}^i$

3.4 Key Generation and Decryption

In conventional deployments of public key cryptosystems (e.g. securing communication channels) both the public pk and private key sk are generated by one of the parties. In our setting, however, giving one of the parties complete knowledge of the private key would undermine our privacy requirements. For this reason, our solution requires a distributed implementation of the key generation and decryption algorithm, ensuring that ciphertexts can only be decrypted collaboratively, while individually no information can be deduced. Solutions for distributed key-generation and decryption, allowing up to $|\mathcal{P}| - 1$ passive corruptions, are readily available for some cryptosystems [11, 16], including, in particular, the DJ scheme of our choice.

3.5   Security Model

The implementation achieves computational security in the semi-honest model (passive security), i.e. assuming that all parties follow the prescribed protocol. The number of passive corruptions that can be tolerated is $|\mathcal{P}| - 1$.

It is assumed that the number of nodes n in the entire graph is publicly known. This can be achieved by each party P sharing their number of nodes n^P, or by again applying an MPC solution to avoid leaking n^P, and only revealing n. In our solution the values are n^P are made public.

3.6   Parameters

An overview of all public parameters and private parameters can be found in Tables 3 and 4 of Appendix A.

As discussed in Sect. 2, the parameter p and the number of iterations K are set to 0.85 and 50 respectively. The size of the RSA-modulus N is set to 2048 bit, as is recommended for 112-bit computational security [2], hence $N > 2^{2047}$. Moreover, the scaling parameters f_x and f_c are both chosen to be equal to $2^7 n$, where n is the total number of nodes in the graph. In Sect. 4 we will show that these scaling factors achieve a desirable level of precision.

Each PageRank value x_k^i is upper bounded by 1, and the total scaling factor after 50 iterations equals $(f_c)^{50} f_x = 2^{357} n^{51}$; the following condition will therefore guarantee that we do not encounter overflows:

$$n < 2^{33} \implies 2^{357} n^{51} < N.$$

In other words, the chosen parameter set returns approximated PageRank values for all graphs with less than 2^{33} nodes and there is no need to initialize the Damgård-Jurik cryptosystem with parameter $s > 1$.

For larger graphs a larger RSA-modulus N can be chosen or the Damgård-Jurik cryptosystem can be initialized with a larger exponent s. Another approach is the implementation of a secure division protocol, see for example [26], by which the size of the accumulated scaling factor, $(f_c)^k f_x$, can be reduced after some iterations.

4   Results

In this section, our secure multiparty PageRank solution is evaluated, both in terms of accuracy and in terms of computational and communication complexity. Firstly, the securely-computed PageRank values are compared to the standard PageRank values. Secondly, the running time of the algorithm is evaluated for various randomly-generated transaction graphs. Thirdly, the communication complexity of the protocol is analyzed, and finally, the results of the experiment are extrapolated to large-scale transaction graphs.

Our solution has been implemented in Python 3.5 using the General Multi-Precision library *gmpy2* and the Partially Homomorphic Encryption library *phe*.

All experiments were run in a single virtual machine with 48 CPU cores (2.4 GHz Intel Xeon E5-2680v4) and 16 GB RAM. The multiparty setting is emulated by assigning every core to exactly one party. The parties communicate by reading and writing data in a given folder on the virtual machine, which means the communication between the parties is performed instantly in this experimental set-up.

4.1 Accuracy of the Secure Multiparty PageRank Algorithm

According to Sect. 3.2 the results of the secure multiparty PageRank algorithm should be approximations of the standard PageRank values. For $i \in V$ let $s(i)$ be the standard PageRank value of node i and let $x(i)$ be the associated approximation computed by the secure multiparty PageRank algorithm. The accuracy of our solution can be quantified by various metrics. For the application in fraud detection, we are interested in point-wise comparison on the accuracy of secure PageRank. The maximum relative error satisfies this requirement and is computed as follows:

$$\max_{i \in V} \frac{|s(i) - x(i)|}{|s(i)|}.$$

To evaluate the accuracy of our algorithm, we randomly sampled directed graphs G, with n nodes and average out-degree d. To be more precise, for distinct nodes $i, j \in V$ we draw an edge from i to j with probability d/n. The nodes of this graph are distributed equally amongst 3 parties to represent the multiparty setting. Figure 1 displays the maximum relative error for randomly generated graphs with n ranging from 3×256 to 3×4096 and d ranging from 10 to 160.

The values $x(i)$ are computed by our implementation of the secure multiparty PageRank algorithm and the values $s(i)$ are computed with the PageRank functionality of the Python3 package NetworkX. These results show that the maximum relative error is between 0.0057 and 0.0064, meaning that our implementation indeed gives an accurate approximation of the standard PageRank values. For realistic graphs, it is more likely that large transaction graphs will approximate a scale-free graph [6]. Experiments on more realistic scale-free large graphs, with resulting PageRank values ranging from 10^{-6} to 10^{-2}, show that the maximum relative error stays under 0.006.

The accuracy of our algorithm is actually independent of the number of parties. To further increase it, the number of iterations K and/or the scaling factors f_x and f_c could be increased.

4.2 Performance of the Secure Multiparty PageRank Algorithm

To benchmark the computational complexity of our algorithm, we again consider randomly generated graphs with a total number of nodes n ranging from $|\mathcal{P}| \times 256$ to $|\mathcal{P}| \times 4096$ and an average out-degree d ranging from 10 to 160. Recall that $\mathcal{P}$ is the set of parties. In our first experiment, we fixed the number of parties to 3 and consider the computation time for various graph sizes. In our second experiment, we fix the average out-degree to 80 and vary the number of parties.

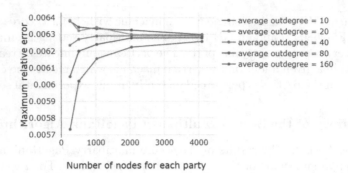

Fig. 1. Maximum relative error with increasing number of nodes and edges.

Note that the final step of our protocol, the decryption, is executed collaboratively, and therefore the computation times for each party are approximately equal. For this reason, only the computation time for party 1 is considered.

Graph Size. Figure 2 shows the results of our first experiment, in which the number of parties is fixed at 3 and each party runs their part of the protocol on a single core of the virtual machine. The computation time of the algorithm scales linearly in the number of nodes and in the average out-degree.

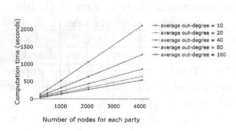
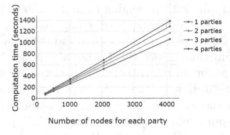

Fig. 2. Computation time for increasing numbers of nodes and edges.

Fig. 3. Computation time for increasing numbers of parties.

Number of Parties. Figure 3 shows the results of our second experiment, in which the average out-degree is fixed to 80 and the number of parties is varied between 1 and 4. In the setting of our instantiations, each party is assigned the same number of nodes. Hence, the size of the total graph increases with the number of parties. The results show that increasing the number of parties only has a minor effect on the computational complexity of the protocol.

4.3   Parallelization

The secure multiparty PageRank algorithm is well-suited for distributed computing, an effect that we already observed when varying the number of parties. In our third experiment, the number of parties is fixed to 3 and each party owns 4096 nodes of a randomly-generated graph with an average out-degree of 80. Figure 4 shows the computation time of our algorithm when increasing the number of CPU cores per party. For this relatively small graph, a speed-up of factor 3.4 can be achieved by using 12 cores per party (instead of 1). By inspecting our algorithm, it is easily seen that larger graphs will benefit even more from distributing the computations over several CPU cores. Note that the upload respectively download communication times are excluded from this experiment (using 1 machine), but are expected to be within 5 respectively 9 s based on Table 1.

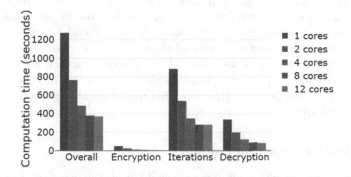

Fig. 4. Computation time for increasing numbers of cores.

4.4   Communication

The experiments of the above section were all run on a single machine, and the communication between the parties thus amounted to reading and writing data in a given folder. In real-life scenarios, the parties would be physically separated, and this data has to be communicated over some network. It is therefore important to measure the communication complexity of the protocol, both in terms of communication rounds and in terms of communicated data.

The number of communication rounds of our secure multiparty PageRank algorithm, excluding the key generation phase, equals $K + 1$, where K is the number of PageRank iterations. Table 1 displays the number of ciphertexts that have to be communicated in our protocol, under the assumption that the graph is randomly generated with average out-degree $d \gg |\mathcal{P}|$. Recall that $|\mathcal{P}|$ is the number of parties, n is the total number of nodes and n^P is the number of nodes of party P.

Table 1. The number of cipher texts that each party P uploads and downloads during the secure multiparty PageRank algorithm.

Phase	Number of uploaded cipher texts	Number of downloaded cipher texts
PageRank computation	$K(n^P + 1)$	$K(|\mathcal{P}| + n - n^P - 1)$
Decryption	n	$n - 2n^P + n^P|\mathcal{P}|$

Thus for a realistic-size 3-party setting with 10 million nodes per party and 50 PageRank iterations, Table 1 amounts to 530 million and 1040 million 2048-bit cipher texts that have to be uploaded and downloaded, respectively. Assuming a bandwidth of 100 Mbit/s, this results in 2.8 h upload time and 5.5 h download time.

The communication complexity is thus significant. However, it is currently not the main bottleneck as our experiments have shown that the required computation times are even larger. For this reason, we have not focused on improving the communication complexity. A first improvement could be made by noting that parties are not required to download the encrypted PageRank contributions of the entire graph for every iteration. Alternatively, another MPC paradigm with a much smaller communication complexity, such as fully homomorphic encryption [13], could be used. However, this would negatively impact the computation complexity.

4.5   Realistic Transaction Graphs

Based on experiments with scale-free graphs [6], it was shown that the maximum relative error of secure PageRank stays under 0.006.

The performance of our solution was evaluated on relatively small graphs, while in practice, transaction graphs contain millions of nodes. The first column of Table 2 shows the expected computation time for a 3-party setting in which each party has 10 million bank accounts with 80 transaction per bank account on average. Moreover, we assume a very conservative performance gain of a factor 3.4 by distributing the computation over 12 cores instead of using a single core per party; in practice, this gain will likely be much closer to a factor 12 for large graphs.

A significant improvement can be expected by judiciously implementing the algorithm in C++. In particular, 2048-bit modular multiplications have been reported to take only 3.012 ms on a Xeon X64 processor [7]. Modular multiplications take up a significant part of the computation time and can be accelerated up to a factor 17 compared to our Python implementation. The estimates in the second column of Table 2 show such an implementation would enable a running time of less than 1 day for a large-scale graph as described above.

Table 2. The estimated runtime for the application of the secure multiparty PageRank algorithm to a graph with 30 million nodes and average out-degree 80 in the 3-party setting.

	Python implementation	C++ implementation
Computation time (days)	10.62	~0.62
Communication time (days)	0.35	0.35
Total time (days)	10.97	~0.97

5 Conclusions and Future Research

Existing techniques for fraud detection would highly benefit from collaboration between financial institutes. However, the exchange of relevant information is often limited, or not even possible, due to privacy restrictions or commercial confidentiality. This paper illustrated that secure multiparty computation can help tackle this challenge.

It was previously shown that fraud detection techniques can be improved by taking into account features, such as PageRank values, derived from transaction graphs [20]. Transaction graphs of multiple financial institutes are coupled through interbank transactions and analyzing a combined transaction graph leads to a more complete picture and, possibly, to more effective fraud detection.

An innovative solution has been described for multiple financial institutes to securely and collaboratively compute the PageRank values of a combined transaction graph without revealing private and/or confidential information to each other or to any other party. Each financial institute learns the PageRank values of its own bank accounts that are derived from the joint network. To achieve the desired security properties an additively homomorphic encryption scheme has been used.

The feasibility of this secure multiparty PageRank algorithm has been shown by implementing it in Python and applying it successfully on randomly generated test networks while simulating up to four different parties. Furthermore, the results show that the secure multiparty PageRank algorithm is scalable and can handle transaction graphs of realistic size in reasonable time, while remaining sufficiently accurate. In particular, this allows financial institutes to update PageRank scores at reasonable intervals, e.g. over a month, and use these as features for their own fraud detection methods.

Planned future work includes developing, in contrast to the current passively secure protocol, an actively secure solution. In addition, other homomorphic encryption schemes, in particular ones that can withstand the attack of a quantum computer, will be considered.

Moreover, our MPC solution is tailor made to evaluate the PageRank algorithm securely as it specifically utilizes the linearity of this algorithm. However, this linearity applies to many other algorithms and an analysis of the broader applicability of this MPC approach would be of interest. In particular since

PageRank is only one of many graph-based features that may be extracted from transaction graphs as input for fraud detection methods. In addition, there are other application domains in the financial sector that could benefit from the secure analysis of transaction graphs, such as commercial banking and anti-money laundering. Further important future work is testing the algorithm on actual combined transaction graphs and analyzing its effect on the resulting PageRank values and its effectiveness in improving fraud detection.

In conclusion, the feasibility of securely analyzing features of a large-scale network that is distributed over multiple parties has been demonstrated, thus paving the way for several collaboration initiatives that were previously not possible.

Acknowledgments. The research activities that have led to this paper were funded by the Shared Research Program Cyber Security; a research collaboration between TNO, ABN AMRO, Rabobank, ING, Achmea and Volksbank. The authors would also like to thank Gabriele Spini for his valuable feedback and his help in improving the paper.

A   Parameters

The following public and private parameters are considered in the secure PageRank algorithm, Algorithm 1.

Table 3. Public parameters of the secure multiparty PageRank algorithm

Parameter	Description
$\mathcal{P}$	Set of parties
n	Number of nodes
N	RSA modulus
K	Number of PageRank iterations
p	PageRank probability
f_c	Scaling factor for all $\frac{p}{c_i}$
f_x	Scaling factor for all x_k^i
ϕ_k	Integer PageRank constant of iteration k
Φ_k	Encrypted PageRank constant of iteration k
ψ	Integer PageRank constant
pk	Public Damgård-Jurik encryption key
z_k^i	Encrypted and scaled PageRank value of node i at iteration k

Table 4. Private parameters of the secure multiparty PageRank algorithm

Parameter	Description
V^P	Set of all nodes belonging to party P
U^P	Set of non-dangling nodes belonging to party P
D^P	Set of dangling nodes belonging to party P
$S(i)$	Set of incoming nodes at node $i \in V$
c_i	The out-degree of node $i \in V$

References

1. Aly, A., Cuvelier, E., Mawet, S., Pereira, O., Van Vyve, M.: Securely solving simple combinatorial graph problems. In: Sadeghi, A.-R. (ed.) FC 2013. LNCS, vol. 7859, pp. 239–257. Springer, Heidelberg (2013). https://doi.org/10.1007/978-3-642-39884-1_21

2. Barker, E., Barker, W., Burr, W., Polk, W., Smid, M., Zieglar, L.: Recommendation for key management - part 1: General (revision 4). National Institute of Standards and Technology - Special Publication **800**(57), 1–156 (2015)

3. Ben-Or, M., Goldwasser, S., Wigderson, A.: Completeness theorems for non-cryptographic fault-tolerant distributed computation (extended abstract). In: Simon, J. (ed.) Proceedings of the 20th Annual ACM Symposium on Theory of Computing, 2–4 May 1988, Chicago, Illinois, USA, pp. 1–10. ACM (1988). https://doi.org/10.1145/62212.62213

4. Bogdanov, D., Laur, S., Willemson, J.: Sharemind: a framework for fast privacy-preserving computations. In: Jajodia, S., Lopez, J. (eds.) ESORICS 2008. LNCS, vol. 5283, pp. 192–206. Springer, Heidelberg (2008). https://doi.org/10.1007/978-3-540-88313-5_13

5. Bogetoft, P., et al.: Secure multiparty computation goes live. In: Dingledine, R., Golle, P. (eds.) FC 2009. LNCS, vol. 5628, pp. 325–343. Springer, Heidelberg (2009). https://doi.org/10.1007/978-3-642-03549-4_20

6. Bollobás, B., Borgs, C., Chayes, J., Riordan, O.: Directed scale-free graphs. In: Proceedings of the Fourteenth Annual ACM-SIAM Symposium on Discrete Algorithms, SODA 2003, Society for Industrial and Applied Mathematics, Philadelphia, PA, USA, pp. 132–139 (2003). http://dl.acm.org/citation.cfm?id=644108.644133

7. Bos, J.W., Montgomery, P.L., Shumow, D., Zaverucha, G.M.: Montgomery multiplication using vector instructions. IACR Cryptology ePrint Archive, vol. 2013, p. 519 (2013). http://eprint.iacr.org/2013/519

8. Brickell, J., Shmatikov, V.: Privacy-preserving graph algorithms in the semi-honest model. In: Roy, B. (ed.) ASIACRYPT 2005. LNCS, vol. 3788, pp. 236–252. Springer, Heidelberg (2005). https://doi.org/10.1007/11593447_13

9. Chaum, D., Crépeau, C., Damgård, I.: Multiparty unconditionally secure protocols (extended abstract). In: Simon, J. (ed.) Proceedings of the 20th Annual ACM Symposium on Theory of Computing, 2–4 May 1988, Chicago, Illinois, USA, pp. 11–19. ACM (1988). https://doi.org/10.1145/62212.62214

10. Damgård, I., Damgård, K., Nielsen, K., Nordholt, P.S., Toft, T.: Confidential benchmarking based on multiparty computation. In: Grossklags, J., Preneel, B. (eds.) FC 2016. LNCS, vol. 9603, pp. 169–187. Springer, Heidelberg (2017). https://doi.org/10.1007/978-3-662-54970-4_10

11. Damgård, I., Jurik, M.: A generalisation, a simplification and some applications of Paillier's probabilistic public-key system. In: Kim, K. (ed.) PKC 2001. LNCS, vol. 1992, pp. 119–136. Springer, Heidelberg (2001). https://doi.org/10.1007/3-540-44586-2_9
12. Damgård, I., Pastro, V., Smart, N.P., Zakarias, S.: Multiparty computation from somewhat homomorphic encryption. In: Proceedings of Advances in Cryptology - CRYPTO 2012 - 32nd Annual Cryptology Conference, Santa Barbara, CA, USA, 19–23 August 2012, pp. 643–662 (2012). https://doi.org/10.1007/978-3-642-32009-5_38
13. Gentry, C.: Fully homomorphic encryption using ideal lattices. In: Mitzenmacher, M. (ed.) Proceedings of the 41st Annual ACM Symposium on Theory of Computing, STOC 2009, Bethesda, MD, USA, 31 May – 2 June 2009, pp. 169–178. ACM (2009). https://doi.org/10.1145/1536414.1536440
14. Goldreich, O., Micali, S., Wigderson, A.: How to play any mental game or a completeness theorem for protocols with honest majority. In: Proceedings of the 19th Annual ACM Symposium on Theory of Computing 1987, New York, USA, pp. 218–229 (1987). https://doi.org/10.1145/28395.28420
15. Haveliwala, T., Kamvar, S.: The second eigenvalue of the google matrix. Tech. rep. 2003–20, Stanford InfoLab (2003). http://ilpubs.stanford.edu:8090/582/
16. Hazay, C., Mikkelsen, G.L., Rabin, T., Toft, T.: Efficient RSA key generation and threshold Paillier in the two-party setting. In: Dunkelman, O. (ed.) CT-RSA 2012. LNCS, vol. 7178, pp. 313–331. Springer, Heidelberg (2012). https://doi.org/10.1007/978-3-642-27954-6_20
17. Henecka, W., Kögl, S., Sadeghi, A., Schneider, T., Wehrenberg, I.: TASTY: tool for automating secure two-party computations. In: Al-Shaer, E., Keromytis, A.D., Shmatikov, V. (eds.) Proceedings of the 17th ACM Conference on Computer and Communications Security, CCS 2010, Chicago, Illinois, USA, 4–8 October 2010, pp. 451–462. ACM (2010). https://doi.org/10.1145/1866307.1866358
18. Ipsen, I.C.F., Selee, T.M.: Pagerank computation, with special attention to dangling nodes. SIAM J. Matrix Anal. Appl. **29**(4), 1281–1296 (2007). https://doi.org/10.1137/060664331
19. Malkhi, D., Nisan, N., Pinkas, B., Sella, Y.: Fairplay - secure two-party computation system. In: Blaze, M. (ed.) Proceedings of the 13th USENIX Security Symposium, 9–13 August 2004, San Diego, CA, USA, pp. 287–302. USENIX (2004). http://www.usenix.org/publications/library/proceedings/sec04/tech/malkhi.html
20. Molloy, I., et al.: Graph analytics for real-time scoring of cross-channel transactional fraud. In: Grossklags, J., Preneel, B. (eds.) FC 2016. LNCS, vol. 9603, pp. 22–40. Springer, Heidelberg (2017). https://doi.org/10.1007/978-3-662-54970-4_2
21. Nayak, K., Wang, X.S., Ioannidis, S., Weinsberg, U., Taft, N., Shi, E.: GraphSC: parallel secure computation made easy. In: 2015 IEEE Symposium on Security and Privacy (SP), pp. 377–394. IEEE (2015)
22. Nielsen, J.B., Nordholt, P.S., Orlandi, C., Burra, S.S.: A new approach to practical active-secure two-party computation. In: Safavi-Naini, R., Canetti, R. (eds.) CRYPTO 2012. LNCS, vol. 7417, pp. 681–700. Springer, Heidelberg (2012). https://doi.org/10.1007/978-3-642-32009-5_40
23. Paillier, P.: Public-key cryptosystems based on composite degree residuosity classes. In: Stern, J. (ed.) EUROCRYPT 1999. LNCS, vol. 1592, pp. 223–238. Springer, Heidelberg (1999). https://doi.org/10.1007/3-540-48910-X_16
24. Partisia: Secure order matching (2018). https://partisia.com/order-matching/. Accessed 31 July 2018

25. Unbound: Hybrid cloud key management for any key, any cloud (2018). https://www.unboundtech.com/usecase/hybrid-it-key-management-any-key-any-cloud/. Accessed 31 Jul 2018
26. Veugen, T.: Encrypted integer division and secure comparison. IJACT **3**(2), 166–180 (2014). https://doi.org/10.1504/IJACT.2014.062738
27. Yao, A.C.: Protocols for secure computations (extended abstract). In: 23rd Annual Symposium on Foundations of Computer Science, Chicago, Illinois, USA, 3–5 November 1982, pp. 160–164. IEEE Computer Society (1982). https://doi.org/10.1109/SFCS.1982.38
28. Yao, A.C.: How to generate and exchange secrets (extended abstract). In: 27th Annual Symposium on Foundations of Computer Science, Toronto, Canada, 27–29 October 1986, pp. 162–167. IEEE Computer Society (1986). https://doi.org/10.1109/SFCS.1986.25

IoT Security, and Crypto Still Means Cryptography

HEALED: HEaling & Attestation
for Low-End Embedded Devices

Ahmad Ibrahim[1]($\boxtimes$), Ahmad-Reza Sadeghi[1], and Gene Tsudik[2]

[1] Technische Universität Darmstadt, Darmstadt, Germany
{ahmad.ibrahim,ahmad.sadeghi}@trust.tu-darmstadt.de
[2] University of California, Irvine, CA, USA
gts@ics.uci.edu

Abstract. We are increasingly surrounded by numerous embedded systems which collect, exchange, and process sensitive and safety-critical information. The Internet of Things (IoT) allows a large number of interconnected devices to be accessed and controlled remotely, across existing network infrastructure. Consequently, a remote attacker can exploit security vulnerabilities and compromise these systems. In this context, remote attestation is a very useful security service that allows to remotely and securely verify the integrity of devices' software state, thus allowing the detection of potential malware on the device. However, current attestation schemes focus on detecting whether a device is infected by malware but not on disinfecting it and restoring its software to a benign state.

In this paper we present HEALED – the first remote attestation scheme for embedded devices that allows both detection of software compromise and disinfection of compromised devices. HEALED uses Merkle Hash Trees (MHTs) for measurement of software state, which allows restoring a device to a benign state in a secure and efficient manner.

1 Introduction

Embedded devices are being increasingly deployed in various settings providing distributed sensing and actuation, and enabling a broad range of applications. This proliferation of computing power into every aspect of our daily lives is referred to as the Internet of Things (IoT). Examples of IoT settings range from small deployments such as smart homes and building automation, to very large installations, e.g., smart factories. Similarly, an embedded or (IoT device) may constitute a low-end smart bulb in a smart home or a sophisticated high-end Cyber-Physical System (CPS) in a smart factory.

Increasing deployment and connectivity combined with the collection of sensitive information and execution of safety-critical (physical) operations has made embedded devices an attractive target for attacks. Prominent examples include: the Stuxnet worm [36], the Mirai botnet [10], the HVAC attack [1] and the Jeep hack [2]. One common feature of such attacks is that they usually involve modifying the software state of target devices. This is referred to as malware infestation.

© International Financial Cryptography Association 2019
I. Goldberg and T. Moore (Eds.): FC 2019, LNCS 11598, pp. 627–645, 2019.
https://doi.org/10.1007/978-3-030-32101-7_36

Remote attestation has evolved as a security service for detecting malware infestation on remote devices. It typically involves a standalone (or network of) *prover* device(s) securely reporting its software state to a trusted party denoted by *verifier*. Several attestation protocols have been proposed based on trusted software for securing the measurement and reporting of a prover's software state [14,17,20,32–34], on trusted hardware [19,21,22,27,29,31,35], or on software/hardware co-design [12,13,18]. In the recent years, several collective attestation schemes have been proposed that enable efficient attestation of large networks of devices [5,8,15,16].

While prior remote attestation schemes focus on detection of malware infestation on prover devices, the problem of disinfecting a prover, i.e., restoring its software to a benign state, has been totally overlooked. Prior remote attestation schemes usually focus on malware presence detection and consider the reaction policy to their presence to be out of scope. In this paper we present HEALED – HEaling & Attestation for Low-end Embedded Devices – which is the first attestation scheme that provides both detection and *healing* of compromised embedded devices. HEALED is applicable in both standalone and network settings. It allows measuring the software state of a device based on a novel Merkle Hash Tree (MHT) construction.

Main contributions of this paper are:

- Software Measurement: HEALED presents a novel measurement of prover's software state based on MHT which allows the verifier to pinpoint the exact software blocks that were modified.
- Device Healing: HEALED enables disinfecting compromised provers by restoring their software to a genuine benign state.
- Proof-of-concept Implementation: We implemented HEALED on two recent security architectures for low-end embedded devices as well as on our small network testbed composed of 6 Raspberry Pi-based drones.
- Performance Evaluation: We provide a thorough performance and security evaluation of HEALED based on our implementations and on network simulations.

2   HEALED

In this section, we present the system model, protocol goals, and a high-level overview of HEALED.

2.1   System Model

Our system model involves a group of two or more devices with a communication path between any two of them. A *device class* refers to the set of devices with the same software configuration. We denote by s be the number of devices in the smallest class. A device (regardless of its class) is denoted by D_i. Whenever a device D_v wants to attest another device D_p, we refer to the former as *prover*, and to the latter as *verifier*. As common to all current attestation schemes, we assume that D_v has prior knowledge of the expected benign software configuration of D_p. We also assume that D_v and D_p share a unique symmetric key k_{vp}.[1] Devices can be heterogeneous, i.e., have different software and hardware. However, all devices satisfy the minimal hardware requirements for secure remote attestation (see Sect. 2.2). Moreover, each device D_c can always find a *similar* device D_h with the same software/hardware configuration.

The goal of HEALED is to detect and eliminate malware on a device. HEALED consists of two protocols: (1) an attestation protocol between D_v and D_p, through which a verifier device D_v assesses the software state of a prover device D_p, and (2) a healing protocol between two similar devices D_h and D_c, through which a healing device D_h restores the software of a compromised device D_c to a benign state. Software state of a device refers to its static memory contents and excludes memory locations holding program variables.

2.2   Requirements Analysis

Threat Model. Based on a recent classification [4], we consider two types of adversaries:

1. *Local communication adversary:* has full control over all communication channels, i.e., it can inject, modify, eavesdrop on, and delay all packets exchanged between any two devices.
2. *Remote (software) adversary:* exploits software bugs to infect devices, read their unprotected memory regions, and manipulate their software state (e.g., by injecting malware).

We assume that every device is equipped with minimal hardware required for secure remote attestation, i.e., a read only memory (ROM) and a simple Memory Protection Unit (MPU) [12]. A remote software adversary cannot alter code protected by hardware (e.g., modifying code stored in ROM), or extract secrets from memory regions protected by special rules in the MPU. These memory regions are used to store cryptographic secrets and protocol intermediate variables.

Key Observation. Let $\mathtt{Benign}(\mathtt{t_a}, D_x, D_y)$ denote "device D_x believes that device D_y is not compromised at $\mathtt{t_a}$, $\mathtt{Equal}(\mathtt{t_a}, D_x, D_y)$ denote "device D_x and device D_y have the same software state at time $\mathtt{t_a}$. We make the following key observation:

- Healing: If two devices D_x and D_y have the same software state, then either both are benign or both are compromised.

---

[1] In the case of networks of embedded devices, we rely on the initialization protocol of existing collective attestation schemes for sharing software configurations and symmetric keys between devices [8].

$$\forall x \, \forall y \, \forall y \, \forall t_a \, \texttt{Equal}(t_a, D_y, D_z)$$
$$\wedge \, \texttt{Benign}(t_a, D_x, D_y) \rightarrow \texttt{Benign}(t_a, D_x, D_z)$$

Consequently, healing can be supported by letting similar devices (i.e., devices having the same software configuration) attest and recover each other.

Objectives. A remote attestation protocol should not only detect presence of malware on a compromised devices, it should also identify exact regions in memory, where the malware resides in order to eliminate it. Consequently, a remote attestation protocol should have the following properties:

- Exact measurements: The measurement process on the prover should be capable of detecting software compromise and determining exact memory regions that have been manipulated.
- Healing: The protocol should allow secure and efficient disinfection of compromised devices, i.e., enable restoring the software of a compromised device to a benign state with low overhead.

Requirements. A verifier device D_v shares a symmetric key k_{vp} with every prover device D_p that it needs to attest. Similarly, every healer device D_h shares a symmetric key k_{hc} with every compromised device D_c that it heals, i.e., every device D_i shares a key with some (or all) similar devices. For brevity we assume that all devices in the group share pairwise symmetric keys. This assumption applies to small groups of device and is indeed not scalable. To achieve better scalability, keys and software configurations management might follow the design of collective attestation [8,16]. Every device that is involved in one of the protocols, i.e., D_v, D_p, D_h, and D_c supports a lightweight trust anchor for attestation, e.g., devices are equipped with a small amount of ROM and a simple MPU. During the execution of the attestation and healing protocols there should exist a communication path (or logical link) between D_v and D_p and between D_h and D_c respectively.

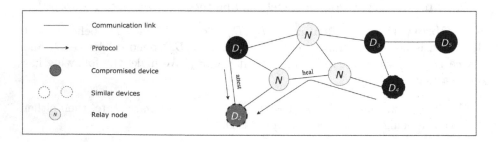

Fig. 1. HEALED in a group of 5 devices.

2.3   High Level Protocol Description

We now present a high level description of HEALED based on the example scenario shown in Fig. 1. The figure shows a group of five devices D_1–D_5, in addition to 3 communication nodes that are responsible for relaying messages between devices, e.g., routers. HEALED incorporates two protocols:

- **attest:** At predefined intervals, each device (e.g., D_1 in Fig. 1) acts as a verifier device and attests a random prover device (e.g., D_2). The prover uses a MHT-based measurement to report its software state. If a software compromise is detected by the verifier it initiates the healing protocol heal for the prover. The output of attest is a bit b_1 indicating whether attestation of D_p was successful.
- **heal:** When a compromised prover device (e.g., D_2) is detected, a benign healer device (e.g., D_4), which is similar to the prover, is identified. The healer uses the MHT-based measurement to pinpoint corrupted memory regions on the prover and restore them to their original state. The result of heal is a bit b_2 indicating whether healing by D_h was successful.

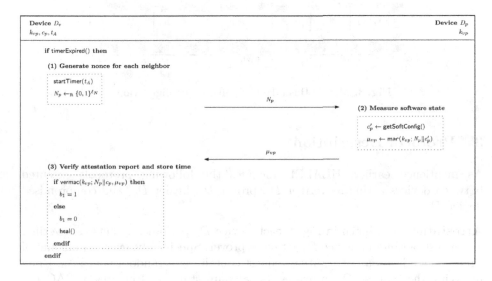

Fig. 2. Protocol attest

2.4   Limitations

HEALED has some limitations in terms of system model, adversary, and application that we briefly described below:

- System model: HEALED is applicable to a set of devices under the same administrative control, e.g., devices in a smart home. Extending it to a more generic model, e.g., across multiple IoT environments, might require involving public key cryptography and using device manufacturers as certification authorities. Moreover, gateways between multiple networks would need to be configured to exchange protocol messages.

- Adversary model: HEALED assumes that, at all times, at least one device of each class is not compromised, i.e., at most $s-1$ devices can be compromised at the same time.
- Application: HEALED provides secure and efficient detection and disinfection of compromised devices. However, it neither *guarantees* successful disinfection, nor does it prevent subsequent compromise of these devices.

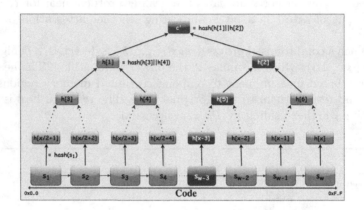

Fig. 3. Merkle Hash Tree of software configurations

3   Protocol Description

As mentioned earlier, HEALED includes the following protocols executed between devices acting as verifier D_v, prover D_p, healer D_h, and compromised device D_c.

Attestation. As shown in Fig. 2, each device D_v periodically acts as a verifier and attests a random device D_p acting as prover. Specifically, every t_A amount of time, D_v sends D_p an attestation request containing a random nonce N_p. Upon receiving the request D_p measures its software state, and creates a MAC μ_{vp} over the generated measurement c'_p and the received nonce based on the key k_{vp} shared with D_v. The MAC μ_{vp} is then sent back to D_v. Having the reference benign software configuration c_p of D_p and the shared key k_{vp}, D_v can verify μ_{vp}. Successful verification of μ_{vp} by D_v implies that D_p is in a benign software state. In this case attest returns $b_1 = 1$. On the contrary, if μ_{vp}'s verification failed, D_v deduce that D_p is compromised and initiates the healing protocol for D_p. In this case attest returns $b_1 = 0$.

The measurement of software state on D_p is created as a root of a Merkle Hash Tree (MHT) [23], as shown in Fig. 3. In particular, D_p divides the code to be attested into w segments: $s_1, \ldots, s_w$ of equal length, and computes hashes:

$h_p[\frac{x}{2}+1], \ldots, h_p[x]$ of each segment. A MHT is then constructed, with $h_p[\frac{x}{2}+1]$, $\ldots, h_p[x]$ as leaves and c'_p as the root, where x denotes the number of nodes in the MHT excluding the root node. Note that, a malware-infected code segment (e.g., s_{w-3}), leads to generation of false hash values along the path to the root. attest is formally:

$$\mathsf{attest}\begin{bmatrix} D_v &:& k_{vp}, c_p, t_A; D_p &:& k_{vp}; * &:& - \end{bmatrix} \rightarrow \begin{bmatrix} D_v &:& b_1; D_p &:& N_p \end{bmatrix}.$$

Based on attest the compromise of any device will be detected.

Healing. Whenever a device D_v detects a compromised device D_c through attest, it searches for a healer device D_h, whose reference software configuration c_h is identical to that of D_c, i.e., a D_h that has the same version of the same software of D_c. Note that, if D_v and D_c are similar D_v directly initiates heal with D_c acting as healer device. Otherwise, D_v broadcasts the reference software configuration c_c of D_c along with a constant (protocol specific) Time-to-Live (TTL), and a random nonce N. Every device D_i that receives this tuple (1) checks TTL, and (2) compares c_c to its reference software configuration c_i. If c_c and c_i do not match, and TTL is not equal to zero, D_i re-broadcasts the tuple after TTL is decremented. Consequently, this tuple is flooded across devices until TTL is exceeded or a healer device D_h is found.

When a device D_h, whose reference software configuration c_h matches c_c, receives the tuple it sends a reply to D_v, which includes its *current* software configuration c'_h, authenticated along with the received nonce N, using a MAC based on the key k_{vh} shared with D_v.

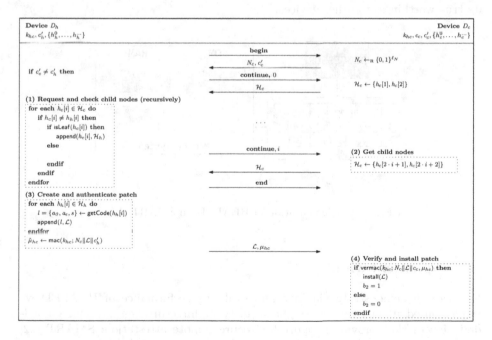

Fig. 4. Protocol heal

After proving its software trustworthiness, D_h initiates heal with D_c (as shown in Fig. 4). Note that, messages between D_h and D_c may go through D_v using the newly established route between D_h and D_v. D_h may also exploit an existing routing protocol to find a shorter path to D_c.

In details, D_h sends a protocol message **begin** to D_c. Upon receiving **begin**, D_c sends its software configuration c'_c and a fresh nonce N_c to D_h. D_h compares c'_c to its own software configuration c'_h. If the two configurations did not match, D_h replies requesting children $h_c[0]$ and $h_c[1]$ of c'_c in the Merkle Hash Tree (MHT) rooted at c'_c (protocol message **continue**). D_h continues recursively requesting child nodes of every hash that does not match its reference value (i.e., the value at the same position in D_h's tree) until leaf nodes are reached. Next, D_h sends a protocol message **end** indicating that it has reached leaf nodes. Finally, D_h adds a code segment l, for each modified leaf node, to the *patch* $\mathcal{L}$, authenticates $\mathcal{L}$ with a MAC based on k_{hc} and sends it back to D_c. A code segment $l = \{a_0, a_\epsilon, s\}$ is identified by its starting address a_0, its end address a_ϵ, and its code s. D_c, in turn verifies $\mathcal{L}$. If the verification was successful, it installs the patch, i.e., replaces segments indicated by $\mathcal{L}$ with the code in $\mathcal{L}$, and outputs $b_2 = 1$. Otherwise, D_c outputs $b_2 = 0$. heal is formally:

$$\mathsf{heal}\left[D_h : k_{hc}, c'_h, \{h_h[0], \ldots, h_h[x]\};\right.$$
$$\left. D_c : k_{hc}, c_c, c'_c, \{h_c[0], \ldots, h_c[x]\}; * : -\right] \to \left[D_h : N_c; D_c : \mathcal{L}, b_2\right].$$

Device healing allows devices that have the same software configuration to recover from malware. By refusing to participate in the healing process (e.g., not installing the patch), D_c remains malicious and would not be able to prove its trustworthiness to other devices.

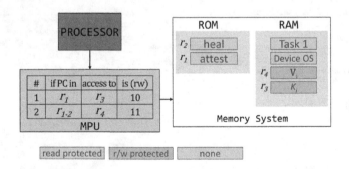

Fig. 5. Implementation of HEALED on SMART [12]

4   Implementation

In order to demonstrate viability and evaluate performance of HEALED we implemented it on two lightweight security architectures for low-end embedded devices that provide support for secure remote attestation: SMART [12] and TrustLite [18]. We also implemented HEALED on a testbed formed of six autonomous drones in order to demonstrate its practicality. In this section we present the details of these implementations.

4.1 Security Architectures

SMART [12] and TrustLite [18] are two lightweight security architectures for low-end embedded devices that enable secure remote attestation based on minimal hardware requirements. These two architectures mainly require: (1) A Read-Only Memory (ROM), which provides emutability and ensures integrity of the code it stores; and (2) A simple Memory Protection Unit (MPU), which controls access to a small region in memory where secret data is stored. Memory access control rules of MPU are based on the value of the program counter.

In SMART, the ROM code stores the attestation code and an attestation key, and the MPU ensures that the attestation code has exclusive access to the attestation key. As a consequence, only unmodified attestation code can generate an authentic attestation report. TrustLite exploits ROM and MPU to provide isolation of critical software components. In particular, ROM is used to ensure the integrity of a secure boot code which has exclusive access to a securely stored platform key. TrustLite enables isolation by initiating critical components via secure boot, which sets up appropriate memory access rules for each component in the MPU. We implemented HEALED on SMART replacing the attestation code in ROM, and on TrustLite as two isolated critical components. Our prototype implementations for SMART and TrustLite are shown in Figs. 5 and 6 respectively.

4.2 Implementation Details

Let $\mathcal{K}_i$ denote the set of all symmetric keys shared between a device D_i and any other device, and V_i denote the protocol variables processed and stored by HEALED. These include all nodes in the Merkle Hash Tree (MHT), including the root c_i. Integrity of HEALED code is protected through ROM of SMART (see Fig. 5), or secure boot of TrustLite (see Fig. 6). The secrecy of the set $\mathcal{K}_i$ of D_i is protected by the MPU of SMART and TrustLite (rule #1 in Fig. 5 and rule #2 in Fig. 6 respectively). Further, rules #2 in SMART and #3 in TrustLite ensure that variables processed and produced by HEALED are exclusively read- and write-accessible to HEALED's code.

4.3 Autonomous Testbed

In order to test and demonstrate the practicality of HEALED, we implemented and tested it on our autonomous drones testbed. The testbed is formed of six Raspberry Pi-based drones forming an ad-hoc network, where four of the drones are involved in HEALED while the remaining two drones act as relay drones. The Pi-s are equipped with a 1.2 GHz Quad-core 64-bit CPU and they are connected through a 150 MBit/s WiFi link. Our setup is shown in Fig. 7. Our implementation uses C programming language and is based on mbed TLS [6] cryptographic library.

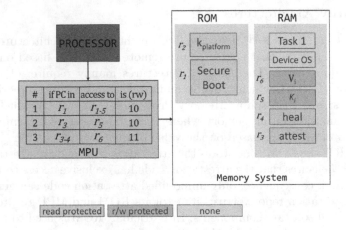

Fig. 6. Implementation of HEALED on TrustLite [18]

5   Performance Evaluation

HEALED was evaluated on SMART [12], TrustLite [18], and on the drones testbed. The results of evaluation on TrustLite and the runtimes on our drones testbed are presented in this section. Results for SMART are very similar to those of TrustLite and will therefore be omitted.

Hardware Costs. A comparison between the hardware costs of our implementation of HEALED and that of the existing implementation of TrustLite [18] is shown in Table 1. As shown in the table, HEALED requires 15324 LUTs and 6154 registers in comparison to 15142 LUTs and 6038 registers required by TrustLite. In other words, HEALED incurs a negligible additional increase of 1.20% and

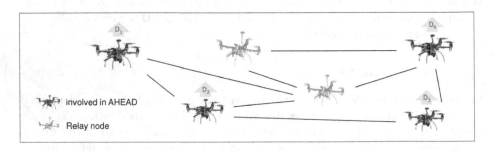

Fig. 7. Testbed setup

1.92% on the original hardware costs of TrustLite in terms of number of LUTs and registers respectively.

Memory Requirements. TrustLite already includes all the cryptographic operation that are involved in HEALED. Implementing HEALED on TrustLite required incorporating the code that is responsible for handling protocol messages and generating the Merkle Hash Tree (MHT). Further, every device D_i needs to securely store g_i symmetric keys (20 bytes each), where g_i corresponds to the number of devices D_i is expected to attest or heal. For every device D_i, g_i is upper bounded by the total number n of devices involved in HEALED. Furthermore, D_i should store the entire MHT that represents its benign software configuration. MHT size depends on the size of the code and the number of code segments. Each hash value is represented by 20 bytes.

Table 1. Hardware cost of HEALED

	Look-up Tables	Registers
TrustLite	15142	6038
HEALED	15324	6154
% of increase	1.20%	1.92%

Energy Costs. We estimated the energy consumption of HEALED based on reported energy consumption for MICAz and TelosB sensor nodes [24].[2] Note that, SMART [12] and TrustLite [18] support the same class of low-end devices that these sensor nodes belong to. Figure 8 shows the estimated energy consumption of attest and heal as function of the number of attested and healed devices respectively. We assume 100 KB of code divided into 128 segments.

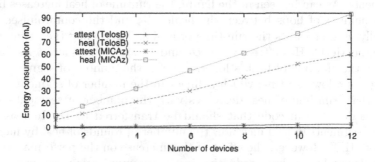

Fig. 8. Energy consumption of HEALED

---

[2] It is not possible to provide accurate measurements of the energy consumption of HEALED since our FPGA implementations of SMART and TrustLite tend to consume considerably more energy than manufactured chips.

Energy consumption of both the healing and attestation protocols increases linearly with the number of attested/healed devices. Moreover, this consumption can be as low as 21 mJ for attesting then healing 4 devices.

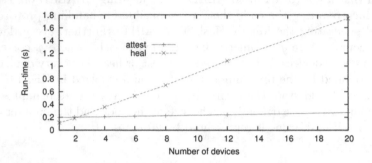

Fig. 9. Runtime of HEALED

Simulation Results. In order to measure the runtime of HEALED we used network simulation. We based our simulation on OMNeT++ [25] network simulator, where we emulated cryptographic operations as delays based on measurements we made for these operations on SMART [12] and TrustLite [18]. We measured the runtime of attest and heal for different number of attested/healed devices. We also varied the number of hops between the compromised device and the healer, as well as the number w of segments the attested code is divided into. The results of our simulation are shown in Figs. 9, 10, and 11.

As shown in Fig. 9 runtimes of attest and heal increase linearly with the number of attested and healed devices respectively. Further, these runtimes can be as low as 0.6 s for attesting then healing 4 devices.

Figure 10 shows the runtime of heal when the attested code is divided into 128 segments. As can be seen in the figure, the runtime of heal increases linearly with the number of hops between the healer D_h and the compromised device D_c. Finally, Fig. 11 shows the run-time of heal and getConfig (i.e., time needed to create the Merkle Hash Tree) when D_h and D_c are 10 hops away. As shown in the figure, the runtime of heal is logarithmic in the number of segments, while getConfig has a low run-time which is linear in the number of segments.

Note that, runtime of heal decreases with the number of segments, due to consequent decrease in code that should be transferred to D_c. Increasing the number of segments indeed increases the number of rounds of heal by increasing the size of MHT. However, the effect of this increase on the performance of heal is overshadowed by the huge reduction in the communication overhead.

Our simulation results also show that the runtimes of heal and attest are constant in the size of the network. These results are omitted due to space constraints. On the other hand, increasing the size of the network while keeping the number of similar devices constant could increase the expected number of hops between a healer D_h and a compromised device D_c. This would indeed lead to an increase in the runtime of heal (see Fig. 10).

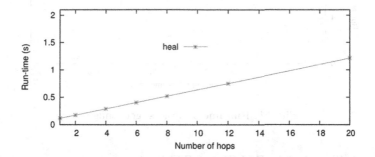

Fig. 10. Runtime of heal as function of number of hops

Drones Testbed. We also measured the runtime of HEALED on our drones testbed shown in Fig. 7. These runtimes are smaller than those of TrustLite since our Raspberry Pi-s utilize a much more powerful processor. The runtime of attest on drone D_2 attesting drones D_1 and D_3 is 11 ms, and the runtime of heal on drone D_1 healing drone D_4 through one relay node is 34 ms. Note that, the attested code is 100 KB in size and is divided into 128 segments. Further, these runtimes are averaged over 100 executions.

6   Security Consideration

Recall that the goal of HEALED is to allow secure detection and disinfection of compromised devices. We formalize this goal as a security experiment $\mathbf{Exp}_\mathcal{A}$, where the adversary $\mathcal{A}$ interacts with involved devices. In this experiment $\mathcal{A}$ compromises the software of two similar devices D_c and D_h. Then, after a polynomial number (in ℓ_{mac}, ℓ_{hash}, and ℓ_N) of steps by $\mathcal{A}$, one verifier device D_v outputs its decision b_1 signifying whether D_c is benign. The compromised device D_h executes heal with D_c which outputs b_2 signifying whether healing was successful. The result of the experiment is defined as the OR of outputs b_1 and b_2 of D_v and D_c respectively, i.e., $\mathbf{Exp}_\mathcal{A} = b \mid b = b_1 \vee b_2$. A secure attestation & healing scheme is defined as follows:

Definition 1 (Secure attestation & healing). *An attestation & healing scheme is secure if* $\Pr\left[b = 1 | \mathbf{Exp}_\mathcal{A}(1^\ell) = b\right]$ *is negligible in* $\ell = f(\ell_{mac}, \ell_{hash}, \ell_N)$, *where function f is polynomial in* ℓ_{mac}, ℓ_{hash}, *and* ℓ_N.

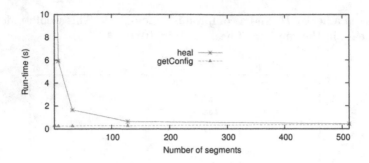

Fig. 11. Runtime of heal vs. getConfig

Theorem 1 (Security of HEALED). *HEALED is a secure attestation & healing scheme* (Definition 1) if the underlying MAC scheme is selective forgery resistant, and the underlying hash function is collision resistant.

Proof sketch of Theorem 1. $\mathcal{A}$ can undermine the security HEALED by either tricking D_v into returning $b_1 = 1$ or tricking D_c into returning $b_2 = 1$ We distinguish among the following two cases:

- $\mathcal{A}$ *attacks* attest: In order for D_v to return $b_1 = 1$ it should receive an attestation report containing a MAC $\mu_{vc} = \mathsf{mac}(k_{vc}; N_c \| c_c)$, where k_{vc} is the symmetric key shared between D_v and D_c, N_c is the fresh random nonce sent from D_v to D_c, and c_c is a benign software configuration of D_c. Consequently, $\mathcal{A}$ can try to: (1) extract the symmetric k_{vc} and generate such a MAC, (2) modify the measurement process on D_c to return a MAC over benign software configuration regardless of the software state on D_c, (3) replay an old attestation report containing a MAC $\mu_{old} = \mathsf{mac}(k_{vc}; N_{old} \| c_c)$ over a benign software configuration c_c and an old nonce N_{old}, (4) forge a MAC $\mu_{vc} = \mathsf{mac}(k_{vc}; N_c \| c_c)$ over a benign software configuration c_c and the current nonce N_c, or (5) modify the code on D_c in a way that is not detectable by the measurement process. However, the adversary is not capable of performing (1) and (2) since the secrecy of the key k_{vc} and the integrity of the measurement code are protected by the hardware of the underlying lightweight security architecture. Moreover, since D_v is always sending a fresh random nonce, the probability of success of (3) is negligible in ℓ_N. Furthermore, the probability of $\mathcal{A}$ being able to forge a MAC as in (4) is negligible in ℓ_{mac}. Finally, modifying the value of one bit of D_c's code would change the hash value of the segment containing this bit. This will change the hash value on the higher level in the Merkle Hash Tree and so on leading to a different root value, i.e., a different software configuration. Consequently, in order to perform (5) $\mathcal{A}$ should find at least on collision of the hash function that is used for constructing the MHT which is negligible in ℓ_{hash}.
- $\mathcal{A}$ *attacks* heal: In order for D_c to return $b_2 = 1$ it should receive a healing message containing a patch $\mathcal{L}$ and a MAC $\mu_{hc} = \mathsf{mac}(k_{hc}; N_c \| \mathcal{L} \| c_c)$, where k_{hc}

is the symmetric key shared between D_h and D_c, N_c is the fresh random nonce sent from D_c to D_h, and c_c is a benign software configuration of D_c. Similar to attest $\mathcal{A}$ may try to extract k_{hc}, modify the code responsible for generating the healing message, replay an old healing message, forge μ_{hc}, or compromise D_h in a way that is not detectable by the measurement process. However, because of the security of the underlying hardware and cryptographic primitives the success probabilities of these attacks are negligible in ℓ_{mac}, ℓ_{hash}, and ℓ_N. Indeed D_c may refuse to execute the healing protocol or install the patch, thus remaining compromised. However, the compromise of D_c will be detected by any subsequent attestation. One remedy for this problem could incorporate performing a subsequent attestation for healed devices and reporting devices that do not comply to the healing protocol.

This means that the probability of $\mathcal{A}$ bypassing the attestation protocol or infecting a benign device through the healing protocol is negligible in ℓ_{mac}, ℓ_{hash}, and ℓ_N. Consequently, HEALED is capable of securely detecting and disinfecting compromised devices.   □

7   Related Work

Attestation. Attestation is a security service that aims at the detection of (malicious) unintended modifications to the software state of a device. Attestation is typically realized as an interactive protocol involving two entities: a verifier and a prover. Through this protocol the prover sends the verifier an attestation report indicating its current software state. Existing attestation schemes can be categorized into their main classes: (1) software-based attestation [14,17,20,32–34] which does not requires hardware support, but is based on strong assumptions and provides weak security guarantees; (2) hardware-based attestation [19,21,22,27,29,31,35] which provides stronger security guarantees based on complex and expensive security hardware; and (3) hybrid attestation [12,13,18] which aims at providing strong security guarantees while imposing minimal hardware costs. Additionally, recent advances have lead to the development of attestation schemes for verifying the intergrity of networks of embedded devices – collective attestation [5,8,15], and for detecting runtime attacks – control-flow attestation [3,11,37]. All existing attestation schemes, regardless of the type, aim at the detection of software compromise and overlook the problem of disinfecting compromised devices. These schemes usually consider the reaction policy to malware detection to be out of scope. HEALED is, to the best of our knowledge, the first attestation scheme that allows the detection and elimination of software compromise in both single-device and group settings.

Software Update and Healing. There is not much of prior work on attestation that allows the disinfection of compromised devices. SCUBA [33] leverages verifiable code execution based on software-based attestation to guarantee an untampered execution of a software update protocol. While SCUBA is built on top of a software-based attestation scheme that is based on unrealistic assumptions [7] to perform software update, HEALED leverages a lightweight security architecture to provide security guarantees regarding efficient disinfection of compromised devices. POSH [28] is a self-healing protocol for sensor networks which enables collective recovery of sensor nodes from compromise. The core idea of POSH is to enable sensor nodes to continuously compute new keys that are unknown to the adversary based on randomness provided by other sensors. Consequently, an adversary that compromises a device and extracts its current key would not be capable of extracting its future keys. TUF [30] is a software update for embedded systems that aims at reducing the impact of key compromise on the security of software update. TUF is based on role separation and multisignatures, where particular signatures using distinct private keys ensure different properties of the software update, e.g., timeliness or authenticity. ASSURED [9] enables applying secure update techniques, such as TUF, to the IoT setting while providing end-to-end security and allowing the verification of successful updates. In HEALED, we rely on a lightweight security architecture for protecting the secrecy of the keys and leverage MHT to restore the software state of compromised devices. Finally, PoSE [26] presents a secure remote software update for embedded devices via proof of secure erasure. The protocol allows restoring a device to its benign software state by ensuring the erasure of all code on that device. However, PoSE imposes a high communication overhead which is linear in the size of the genuine software. Moreover, similar to all existing software-based attestation protocols, PoSE assumes adversarial silence during the execution of the update protocol.

8   Conclusion

Most of the prominent attacks on embedded devices are at least started through malware infestation [1,2,10,36]. Remote attestation aims at tackling the problem of malware infestation by detecting device software compromise. However, current attestation schemes focus on the detection of malware, and ignore the problem of malware removal. These schemes usually consider the reaction to software compromise to be an orthogonal problem. In this paper, we present HEALED – the first attestation scheme for embedded devices which is capable of disinfecting compromised devices in a secure and efficient manner. The core of HEALED is a software measurement process based on Merkle Hash Tree (MHT) which allows identifying infected memory regions, and a healing protocol that efficiently restores these regions to their benign state. We implemented HEALED on two lightweight security architectures that support remote attestation and on an autonomous drones testbed. Moreover, we evaluated the energy, runtime, and hardware costs of HEALED based on measurements of real execution and on network simulation.

Acknowledgements. We thank the anonymous reviewers and, in particular, Alvaro Cardenas for his constructive feedback. This research was co-funded by the German

Science Foundation, as part of project S2 within CRC 1119 CROSSING, HWSec, and Intel Collaborative Research Institute for Collaborative Autonomous & Resilient Systems (ICRI-CARS). Gene Tsudik was supported in part by: (1) DHS under subcontract from HRL Laboratories, (2) ARO under contract W911NF-16-1-0536, and (3) NSF WiFiUS Program Award 1702911.

References

1. Target attack shows danger of remotely accessible HVAC systems (2014). http://www.computerworld.com/article/2487452/cybercrime-hacking/target-attack-shows-danger-of-remotely-accessible-hvac-systems.html
2. Jeep Hacking 101 (2015). http://spectrum.ieee.org/cars-that-think/transportation/systems/jeep-hacking-101
3. Abera, T., et al.: C-FLAT: control-flow attestation for embedded systems software. In: Proceedings of the 2016 ACM SIGSAC Conference on Computer and Communications Security, CCS 2016, pp. 743–754. ACM, New York (2016), https://doi.org/10.1145/2976749.2978358
4. Abera, T., et al.: Invited - things, trouble, trust: On building trust in iot systems. In: Proceedings of the 53rd Annual Design Automation Conference, DAC 2016, pp. 121:1–121:6. ACM, New York (2016). https://doi.org/10.1145/2897937.2905020
5. Ambrosin, M., Conti, M., Ibrahim, A., Neven, G., Sadeghi, A.R., Schunter, M.: SANA: secure and scalable aggregate network attestation. In: Proceedings of the 23rd ACM Conference on Computer & Communications Security, CCS 2016 (2016)
6. ARM Limited: SSL library mbed TLS/polarssl (2016). https://tls.mbed.org/
7. Armknecht, F., Sadeghi, A.R., Schulz, S., Wachsmann, C.: A security framework for the analysis and design of software attestation. In: ACM Conference on Computer and Communications Security (2013)
8. Asokan, N., et al.: SEDA: scalable embedded device attestation. In: Proceedings of the 22nd ACM Conference on Computer & Communications Security, CCS 2015, pp. 964–975 (2015)
9. Asokan, N., Nyman, T., Rattanavipanon, N., Sadeghi, A., Tsudik, G.: Assured: architecture for secure software update of realistic embedded devices. IEEE Trans. Comput. Aided Des. Integr. Circuits Syst. **37**(11), 2290–2300 (2018)
10. Botnet, M.: Website (2016). https://www.incapsula.com/blog/malware-analysis-mirai-ddos-botnet.html
11. Dessouky, G., et al.: LO-FAT: low-overhead control flow attestation in hardware. In: 54th Design Automation Conference (DAC 2017), June 2017
12. Eldefrawy, K., Tsudik, G., Francillon, A., Perito, D.: SMART: secure and minimal architecture for (establishing a dynamic) root of trust. In: Network and Distributed System Security Symposium (2012)
13. Francillon, A., Nguyen, Q., Rasmussen, K.B., Tsudik, G.: A minimalist approach to remote attestation. In: Design, Automation & Test in Europe (2014)
14. Gardner, R., Garera, S., Rubin, A.: Detecting code alteration by creating a temporary memory bottleneck. IEEE Trans. Inf. Forensics Secur. **4**(4), 638–650 (2009)
15. Ibrahim, A., Sadeghi, A.R., Tsudik, G.: DARPA: device attestation resilient against physical attacks. In: Proceedings of the 9th ACM Conference on Security and Privacy in Wireless and Mobile Networks. WiSec 2016 (2016)
16. Ibrahim, A., Sadeghi, A.R., Tsudik, G.: US-AID: unattended scalable attestation of IOT devices. In: Proceedings of the 37th IEEE International Symposium on Reliable Distributed Systems, SRDS 2018 (2018)

17. Kennell, R., Jamieson, L.H.: Establishing the genuinity of remote computer systems. In: USENIX Security Symposium (2003)
18. Koeberl, P., Schulz, S., Sadeghi, A.R., Varadharajan, V.: TrustLite: a security architecture for tiny embedded devices. In: European Conference on Computer Systems (2014)
19. Kovah, X., Kallenberg, C., Weathers, C., Herzog, A., Albin, M., Butterworth, J.: New results for timing-based attestation. In: IEEE Symposium on Security and Privacy, pp. 239–253 (2012)
20. Li, Y., McCune, J.M., Perrig, A.: VIPER: verifying the integrity of peripherals' firmware. In: ACM Conference on Computer and Communications Security (2011)
21. McCune, J.M., et al.: TrustVisor: efficient TCB reduction and attestation. In: Proceedings of the 2010 IEEE Symposium on Security & Privacy, S&P 2010, pp. 143–158 (2010)
22. McCune, J.M., Parno, B.J., Perrig, A., Reiter, M.K., Isozaki, H.: Flicker: an execution infrastructure for TCB minimization. SIGOPS Operating Syst. Rev. **42**(4), 315–328 (2008)
23. Merkle, R.C.: Protocols for public key cryptosystems. In: IEEE Symposium on Security and Privacy, pp. 122–134. IEEE Computer Society (1980). http://dblp.uni-trier.de/db/conf/sp/sp1980.html#Merkle80
24. de Meulenaer, G., Gosset, F., Standaert, O.X., Pereira, O.: On the energy cost of communication and cryptography in wireless sensor networks. In: IEEE International Conference on Wireless and Mobile Computing (2008)
25. OpenSim Ltd.: OMNeT++ discrete event simulator. http://omnetpp.org/ (2015)
26. Perito, D., Tsudik, G.: Secure code update for embedded devices via proofs of secure erasure. In: Gritzalis, D., Preneel, B., Theoharidou, M. (eds.) ESORICS 2010. LNCS, vol. 6345, pp. 643–662. Springer, Heidelberg (2010). https://doi.org/10.1007/978-3-642-15497-3_39
27. Petroni, Jr., N.L., Fraser, T., Molina, J., Arbaugh, W.A.: Copilot – a coprocessor-based Kernel runtime integrity monitor. In: USENIX Security Symposium, pp. 13–13. USENIX Association (2004)
28. Pietro, R.D., Ma, D., Soriente, C., Tsudik, G.: POSH: proactive co-operative self-healing in unattended wireless sensor networks. In: 2008 Symposium on Reliable Distributed Systems, October 2008, pp. 185–194 (2008)
29. Sailer, R., Zhang, X., Jaeger, T., Van Doorn, L.: Design and implementation of a TCG-based integrity measurement architecture. In: Proceedings of the 13th USENIX Security Symposium, pp. 223–238 (2004)
30. Samuel, J., Mathewson, N., Cappos, J., Dingledine, R.: Survivable key compromise in software update systems. In: Proceedings of the 17th ACM Conference on Computer and Communications Security, pp. 61–72. CCS 2010. ACM, New York (2010). https://doi.org/10.1145/1866307.1866315
31. Schellekens, D., Wyseur, B., Preneel, B.: Remote attestation on legacy operating systems with trusted platform modules. Sci. Comput. Program. **74**(1), 13–22 (2008)
32. Seshadri, A., Perrig, A., van Doorn, L., Khosla, P.: SWATT: software-based attestation for embedded devices. In: IEEE Symposium on Security and Privacy (2004)
33. Seshadri, A., Luk, M., Perrig, A., van Doorn, L., Khosla, P.: SCUBA: secure code update by attestation in sensor networks. In: ACM Workshop on Wireless Security (2006)
34. Seshadri, A., Luk, M., Shi, E., Perrig, A., van Doorn, L., Khosla, P.: Pioneer: verifying code integrity and enforcing untampered code execution on legacy systems. In: ACM Symposium on Operating Systems Principles (2005)

35. Trusted Computing Group (TCG): Website. http://www.trustedcomputinggroup. org (2015)

36. Vijayan, J.: Stuxnet renews power grid security concerns, June 2010. http:// www.computerworld.com/article/2519574/security0/stuxnet-renews-power-grid-security-concerns.html

37. Zeitouni, S., et al.: ATRIUM: runtime attestation resilient under memory attacks. In: 2017 International Conference on Computer Aided Design, ICCAD 2017, November 2017

One-Time Programs Made Practical

Lianying Zhao[1](✉), Joseph I. Choi[2], Didem Demirag[3], Kevin R. B. Butler[2],
Mohammad Mannan[3], Erman Ayday[4], and Jeremy Clark[3]

[1] University of Toronto, Toronto, ON, Canada
lianying.zhao@utoronto.ca
[2] University of Florida, Gainesville, FL, USA
[3] Concordia University, Montreal, QC, Canada
[4] Case Western Reserve University, Cleveland, OH, USA

Abstract. A one-time program (OTP) works as follows: Alice provides Bob with the implementation of some function. Bob can have the function evaluated exclusively on a single input of his choosing. Once executed, the program will fail to evaluate on any other input. State-of-the-art one-time programs have remained theoretical, requiring custom hardware that is cost-ineffective/unavailable, or confined to ad-hoc/unrealistic assumptions. To bridge this gap, we explore how the Trusted Execution Environment (TEE) of modern CPUs can realize the OTP functionality. Specifically, we build two flavours of such a system: in the first, the TEE directly enforces the one-timeness of the program; in the second, the program is represented with a garbled circuit and the TEE ensures Bob's input can only be wired into the circuit once, equivalent to a smaller cryptographic primitive called one-time memory. These have different performance profiles: the first is best when Alice's input is small and Bob's is large, and the second for the converse.

1 Introduction

Consider the well-studied scenario of secure two-party computation: Alice and Bob want to compute a function on their inputs, but they do not want to disclose these inputs to each other (beyond what can be inferred from the output of the computation). This is traditionally handled by an interactive protocol between Alice and Bob.[1] In this paper, we instead study a non-interactive protocol as follows: Alice prepares a device for Bob with the function and her input included; once Bob receives this device from Alice, he supplies his input and learns the outcome of the computation. The device will not reveal the outcome for any additional inputs (thus, a one-time program [12]). Alice might be a company selling the device in a retail store, and Bob the customer; the two never interact directly. By using the device offline, Bob is assured that his input remains private.

To build a one-time program (OTP), we use the Trusted Execution Environment (TEE), a hardware-assisted secure mode on modern processors, where

---

[1] Hazay and Lindell [19] give a thorough treatment of interactive two-party protocols.

© International Financial Cryptography Association 2019
I. Goldberg and T. Moore (Eds.): FC 2019, LNCS 11598, pp. 646–666, 2019.
https://doi.org/10.1007/978-3-030-32101-7_37

execution integrity and secrecy are ensured [31], with qualities that include platform state binding and protection of succinct secrets. TEEs may appear to offer a trivial solution to OTPs; however, complexities arise due to Bob's physical possession of the device and, more importantly, performance issues. We propose two configurations for one-time programs built on TEEs: (1) deployed directly in the TEE, and (2) deployed indirectly via TEE-backed one-time memory (OTM) [12] and garbled circuits [50] outside of the TEE. OTMs hold two keys, only one of which gets revealed (dependent on its input); the other is effectively destroyed.

Contributions. Our system, built using Intel Trusted Execution Technology (TXT) [13] and Trusted Platform Module (TPM) [45] as the TEE, is available today (as opposed to custom OTP/OTM implementations using FPGA [21], PUF [24], quantum mechanisms [5], or online services [25]) and could be built for less than \$500.[2]

We propose and implement the following OTP variants, considering that TPM-sealing[3] or encrypting data is time-consuming.

- *TXT-only* seals/unseals Alice's input directly, and performance is thus sensitive to Alice's input size. Bob's input is entered in plaintext and processed in TXT after he has received the device.
- *GC-based* converts the logic into garbled circuit, where number of key pairs is determined by Bob's input size. Key pairs are encrypted/decrypted with a master key (MK). This way, the performance is largely determined by Bob's input size. Upon receiving the device, he does the one-time selection of key pairs in TXT to reflect his input. Thereafter, evaluation of the garbled circuit can be done on any machine with the selected keys.

To illustrate the generality of our solution, we also map the following application into our proposed OTP paradigm: a company selling devices that will perform a private genomic test on the customer's sequenced genome. For this use case, in one of our two variants (TXT-only), a company can initialize the device in 5.6 s and a customer can perform a test in 34 s.

2 Preliminaries

2.1 One-Time Program Background

A one-time program can be conceived of as a non-interactive version of a two party computation: $y = f(a, b)$ where a is Alice's private input, b is Bob's, f is a public function (or program), and y is the output. Alice hands to Bob an implementation of $f_a(\cdot)$ which Bob can evaluate on any input of his choosing: $y_b = f_a(b)$. Once he executes on b, he cannot compute $f_a(\cdot)$ again on a different input. For our practical use-case, we conceive of OTPs with less generality

---

[2] As an example, Intel STK2mv64CC, a Compute Stick that supports both TXT and TPM, was priced at \$499.95 USD on Amazon.com (as of September 2018).

[3] A state-bound cryptographic operation performed by the TPM chip, like encryption.

as originally proposed by Goldwasser et al. [12]; essentially we treat them as one-time, non-interactive programs that hide Alice and Bob's private inputs from each other without any strong guarantees on f itself. Note with a general compiler for f (which we have for both flavours of our system), it is easy but inefficient to keep f private.[4]

2.2   Threat Model and Requirements

We informally consider an OTP to be secure if the following properties are achieved: (1) Alice's input a is confidential from Bob; (2) Bob's input b is confidential from Alice, and (3) no more than one b can be executed in $f(a,b)$ per device. We argue the security of our two systems in Sect. 8 but provide a synopsis here first. Property 3 is enforced through a trusted execution environment, either directly (TXT-only variant in Sect. 4) or indirectly via a one-time memory device (GC-based TXT in Sect. 5) as per the Goldwasser et al. construction. Given Property 3, we consider Property 1 to be satisfied if an adversary learns at most negligible information about a when they choose b and observe $\langle OTP, f(a,b), b \rangle$ as opposed to simply $\langle f(a,b), b \rangle$, where OTP is the entire instantiation of the system, including the TPM-sealed memory and system details (and for the GC-variant: the garbled circuit and keys revealed through specifying b). Property 2 is achieved by being provisioned an offline device that can compute $f_a(b)$ without any interaction with Alice. There is a possibility that the device surreptitiously stores Bob's input and tries to leak it back to Alice. We discuss this systems-level attack in Sect. 8. We also address a subtle adaptive security attack in the full version of our paper.

The selection of TEE has to reflect the aforementioned Properties 1 and 3. Property 3 is achieved by stateful (recording the one-time state) and integrity-protected (enforcing one-timeness) execution, which is the fundamental purpose of all today's TEEs. Moreover, both Properties 1 and 3 mandate no information leakage, which can occur through either software or physical side-channels. We choose Intel TXT, primarily because of its *exclusiveness*, which means: TXT occupies the entire system when secure execution is started and no other code can run in parallel. This naturally avoids all software side-channels, an advantage over non-exclusive TEEs. We do consider using non-exclusive TEEs as future exploration when the challenge of software side-channels has been overcome, e.g., for Intel SGX, the (recent) continually identified side-channel attacks, such as Foreshadow [6], branch shadowing [29], cache attacks [4], and more; for ARM TrustZone, there have been TruSpy [51], Cachegrab [36], etc. They all point to the situation when trusted and untrusted code run on shared hardware.

The known physical side-channels can also be mitigated in the setting of our OTP, i.e., DMA attacks are impossible if I/O protection is enable

---

[4] Essentially, one would define a very general function we might call Apply that will execute the first input variable on the second: $y = \mathsf{Apply}(f, b) = f(b)$. Since f is now Alice's private input, it is hidden. The implementation of Apply might be a universal circuit where f defines the gates' logic—in this case Apply would leak (an upper-bound on) the circuit size of f but otherwise keep f private.

(by the chipset), and the cold-boot attack [17] can be avoided if we choose computers with RAM soldered on the motherboard (cannot be removed to be mounted on another machine, see Sect. 8).

We strive for a reasonable, real-world threat model where we mitigate attacks introduced by our system but do not necessarily resolve attacks that apply broadly to practical security systems. Specifically, we assume:

- Alice is monetarily driven or at least curious to learn Bob's input, while Bob is similarly curious to learn the algorithm of the circuit and/or re-evaluate it on multiple inputs of his choice.
- We assume Alice produces a device that can be reasonably assured to execute as promised (disclosed source, attestation quotes over an integral channel, and no network capabilities).
- We assume that Alice's circuit (including the function and her input) actually constitutes the promised functionality (e.g., is a legitimate genomic test).
- We assume the sound delivery of the device to Bob. We do not consider devices potentially subverted in transit which applies to all electronics [40].
- Both Alice and Bob have to trust the hardware manufacturer (in our case, Intel and the TPM vendor) for their own purposes. Alice trusts that the circuit can only be evaluated once on a given input from Bob, while Bob trusts that the received circuit is genuine and the output results are trustworthy.
- Bob has only bounded computational power, and may go to some lab effort, such as tapping pins on the motherboard and cloning a hard drive, but not efforts as complicated as imaging a chip [27,28,43].
- Components on the motherboard cannot be manipulated easily (e.g., forwarding TPM traffic from a forged chip to a genuine one by desoldering).

2.3   Intel TXT and TPM

Intel Trusted Execution Technology (TXT) is also known as "late launch", for its capability to launch secure execution at any point, occupying the entire system. When the CPU enters the special mode of TXT, all current machine state is discarded/suspended and a fresh secure session is started, hence its exclusiveness, as opposed to sharing hardware with untrusted code.

Components. TXT relies on three mandatory hardware components to function: (a) CPU. The instruction set is extended with a few new instructions for the management of TXT execution. (b) Chipset. The chipset (on the motherboard) is responsible for enforcing I/O protection such that the specified range of I/O space is only accessible by the protected code in TXT; and (c) TPM. Trusted Platform Module [45] is a microchip, serving as the secure storage (termed Secure Element). Its *PCR* (Platform Configuration Register) is volatile storage containing the machine state, in the form of concatenated hash values. There are also multiple PCRs for different purposes. On the TPM, there is also non-volatile storage (termed *NVRAM*), allocated in the unit of *index* of various sizes. Multiple indices can be defined depending on the capacity of a specific TPM model.

Measured Launch. A provisioning stage is always involved where the platform is assumed trusted and uncompromised. A piece of code is measured (similar to hashing) and the measurements are stored in certain TPM NVRAM indices as policies. Thereafter (in our case in the normal execution mode with Bob), the program being loaded is measured and compared with the policies stored in TPM. The system may then abort execution if mismatch is detected, or otherwise proceed. This process is enforced by the CPU.

Machine State Binding. As run-time secrecy (secret in use) is ensured by measured launch and I/O isolation, we also need secrecy for stored data (secret at rest). Alice's input should not be learned by Bob when the device is shipped to him. From the start of TXT execution, each stage measures the next stage's code and *extends* the hash values as measurement to the PCR (concatenated and hashed with the existing value). This way, the measurements are chained, and at a specific time the PCR value reflects what has been loaded before. The root of this chained trust is the measured launch.

Such chained measurements (in PCRs) can be used to derive the key for data encryption, so that only when a desired software stack is running can the protected data be decrypted. This cryptographic operation performed by the TPM is termed *sealing*. A piece of data sealed under certain PCRs can only be unsealed under the same PCRs, hence bound to a specific machine state. The sealed data (ciphertext) can be stored anywhere depending on its size. It is noteworthy to mention that there exists a distinct equivalent of sealing which, instead of just encryption, stores data in a TPM NVRAM index and binds its access to a set of PCRs. As a result, without the correct machine state, the NVRAM index is completely inaccessible (read/write) and thus replaying the ciphertext is prevented. We term it *PCR-bound NVRAM sealing* in this paper and use it for our OTP prototype implementation.

3   Related Work

In the original one-time program paper by Goldwasser et al. [12], OTM is left as a theoretical device. In the ensuing years, there have been some design suggestions based on quantum mechanisms [5], physically unclonable functions [24], and FPGA circuits [21]. (a) Järvinen et al. [21] provide an FPGA-based implementation for GC/OTP, with a GC evaluation of AES, as an example of a complex OTP application. They conclude that although GC/OTP can be realized, their solution should be used only for "truly security-critical applications" due to high deployment and operational costs. They also provide a cryptographic mechanism for protecting against a certain adaptive attack with one-time programs; it is tailored for situations where the function's output size is larger than the length of a special holdoff string stored at each OTM. (b) Kitamura et al. [25] realize OTP without OTM by proposing a distributed protocol, based on secret sharing, between non-colluding entities to realize the 'select one key; delete the other key' functionality. This introduces further interaction and entities. Our approach is in the opposite direction: removing all interaction (other than transfer of the device) from the protocol. (c) Prior to OTP being proposed, Gunupudi and Tate [16] proposed count-limited private key usage for realizing non-interactive oblivious transfer using a TPM. Their solution requires changes in the TPM design (due to lack of a TEE). In contrast, we utilize unmodified TPM 1.2. (d) In a more generalized setting, ICE [41] and Ariadne [42] consider the state continuity of any stateful program (including N-timeness) in the face of unexpected interruption, and propose mechanisms to ensure both rollback protection and usability (i.e., liveness). We solve the specific problem of one-timeness/N-timeness, focusing more on how to deal with input/output and its implication on performance. We do sacrifice liveness (i.e., we flip the one-timeness flag upon entry and thus the program might run zero time if crashed halfway). We believe their approaches can be applied in conjunction with ours.

4   System 1: TXT-Only

Overview. In the first system, we propose to achieve one-timeness by running the protected program in TEE only once (relying on logic integrity) and storing its persistent state (e.g., the one-time indicator) in a way that it is only accessible from within the TEE. To eliminate information leakage from software side-channels, we have chosen Intel TXT for its exclusiveness (i.e., no other software in parallel).[5] We hence name this design *TXT-only*.

To achieve minimal TCB (Trusted Computing Base) and simplicity, we choose native C programming in TXT (as opposed to running an OS/VM). Therefore, for one-time programs that have an existing implementation in other languages, per-application adaptation is required (cf. similar porting effort is needed for the GC-based variant in Sect. 5). New programs may not require extra effort.

Design. We briefly describe the components and workflow of the TXT-only system as follows. A one-time indicator (flag) is sealed into the PCR-bound TPM NVRAM to prevent replay attacks. The indicator is checked and then flipped upon entry of the OTP. Without network connection, the device shipped to the client can no longer leak any of the client's secrets to the vendor. Therefore, only the vendor's secret input has to be protected. We TPM-seal the vendor input on hard drive for better scalability, and there is no need to address replay attacks for vendor input as one-timeness is already enforced with the flag.

The OTP program is loaded by the Intel official project *tboot* [20] and GRUB. It complies with the Multiboot specification [11], and for accessing TPM, we reuse part of the code from tboot, and develop our own functions for commands that are unavailable elsewhere, e.g., reading/writing indices with PCR-bound NVRAM sealing. Since we do not load a whole OS into TXT with tboot, we cannot use OS services for disk I/O access; instead, we implement raw PATA (Parallel ATA, a legacy interface to the hard drive, compatible mode with SATA) logic and directly access disk sectors with DMA (Direct Memory Access).

---

[5] We consider various TEEs and justify this choice in the full version of our paper.

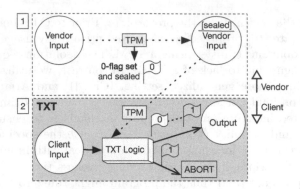

Fig. 1. Our realization of OTPs spans two phases when relying on TXT alone for the entire computation. Alice is active only during phase 1; Bob only during phase 2.

In the *provisioning mode*, the OTP program performs a one-time setup, such as initiating the flag in NVRAM, sealing (overwriting) Alice's secret, etc. Once the *normal execution mode* is entered, the program will refuse to run a second time.

Memory Exposure. As an optional feature for certain computers with swappable RAM, we expose the unsealed vendor input in very small chunks during execution. For example, if the vendor input has 100 records, we would unseal one record into RAM each iteration for processing the whole user input. This way, in case of the destructive cold boot attack, the adversary only learns one-hundredth of the vendor's secret, and no more attempts are possible (the indicator is already updated).

4.1   TXT-Only Provisioning/Evaluation.

Figure 1 gives an overview of *TXT-only*, illustrating the initial provisioning by Alice and evaluation of the function upon delivery to Bob. Note that what is delivered to Bob is the entire computer in our prototype (laptop or barebone like Intel NUC).

Provisioning at Alice's Site. At first, Alice is tasked with setting up the box, which will be delivered to Bob. Alice performs the following: (1) Write the integrity-protected payload/logic in C adapted to the native TXT environment, e.g., static-linking any external libraries and reading input data in small chunks. We may refer to it as the TXT program thereinafter. (2) In the provisioning mode, initialize the flag to 0 and seal.[6] The one-timeness flag is stored with the PCR-bound NVRAM sealing. Instead of depending on a password and regular sealing, this is like stronger access-controlled ciphertext. (3) Seal Alice's input onto the hard drive.

---

[6] A flag is more straightforward to implement than a TPM monotonic counter, thanks to the PCR-bound NVRAM sealing, whereas a counter would involve extra steps (such as attesting to the counterAuth password).

Evaluation at Bob's Site. After receiving the computation box from Alice, Bob performs the following: (1) Place the file with Bob's input on the hard drive. (2) Load the TXT program in normal execution mode, which will read in Bob's input and unseal Alice's input to compute on. (3) Receive the evaluation result (e.g., from the screen or hard drive). As long as it is Bob's first attempt to run the TXT program, the computation will be permitted and the result will be returned to Bob. Otherwise, the TXT program will abort upon loading in step (2), as shown in Fig. 1.

5   System 2: GC-Based

As seen in our TXT-only approach to OTP (System 1) the data processing for protection is only applied to Alice's input (with either sealing/unsealing or encryption/decryption), and Bob's input is always exposed in plaintext due to the machine's physical possession by Bob. Intuitively, we may think that it is a good choice when Alice's input is relatively small regardless of Bob's input size. However, there might be other applications where Alice's input is substantially larger and become the performance bottleneck. Is there a construction that complements TXT-only and is less sensitive to Alice's input size? The answer may lie in garbled circuits. During garbled circuit execution, randomly generated strings (or keys) are used to iteratively unlock each gate until arriving at the final output. Alice's input (size) is only "reflected" in the garbled circuit (assumed not trivially invertible [12]), and the key pairs (whose number is determined by Bob's input size, not to do with Alice's) are sealed/encrypted, hence insensitive to Alice's input size.

To adapt garbled circuits for OTP, key generation and key selection steps are separated. As long as we limit key selection to occur a single time, and the unchosen key of each key pair is never revealed, we can prevent running a particular circuit on a different input. To prevent keys from being selected more than once, we need to instantiate a one-time memory (OTM), which reveals the key corresponding to each input bit and effectively destroys (or its equivalent) the unchosen key in the key pair. OTM is left as a theoretical device in the original OTP paper [12]. We realize it using Intel TXT and the TPM. As in System 1, we seal a one-time flag into the PCR-bound TPM NVRAM, and minimize the TXT logic to just handle key selection, in preparation for GC execution. Alice will seal (in advance) key pairs for garbling Bob's inputs. Bob may then boot into TXT to receive the keys corresponding to his input. When Bob reads a key off the device (say for input bit 0), the corresponding key (for input bit 1) is erased.[7] By instantiating an OTM in this manner, we can replace interactive oblivious transfer (OT) and perform the rest of the garbled circuit execution offline, passing key output from trusted selection. By combining TXT and garbled circuits in this way, sealing complexity is now tied to Bob's inputs. We name this alternate construction *GC-based* (System 2).

---

[7] Unselected keys remain sealed, if never unsealed it serves as cryptographic deletion.

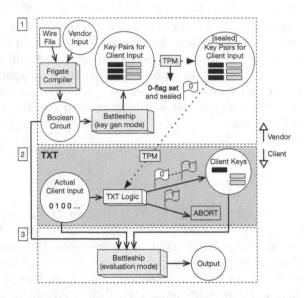

Fig. 2. In our GC-based approach to OTP, Alice generates key pairs and seals them. Bob unseals the keys that correspond to his input and locally evaluates the function.

Performance Overhead with TPM Sealing. According to our measurement, each TPM sealing/unsealing operation takes about 500 ms, and therefore 1 GB of key pairs would need about 1000 h, which is infeasible. Instead, we generate a random number as an encryption key (MK) at provisioning time and the GC key pairs are encrypted with MK. We only seal MK. This way, MK becomes per-deployment, and reprovisioning the system will not make the sealed key pairs reusable due to the change of MK (i.e., the old MK is replaced by the new key). Note that we could also apply the same approach to TXT-only (i.e., encrypting Alice's input with MK and sealing only MK), if needed by the application.

Memory Exposure. Similarly to the TXT-only OTP, our GC-based approach can also optionally adapt to address the cold-boot attack. MK becomes a single point of failure if exposed in such memory attacks, i.e., all key pairs can be decrypted and one-timeness is lost. As with TXT-only, for smaller-sized client input, we can seal the key pairs directly and only unseal into RAM in small chunks.

5.1   Implementation

We use the Boolean circuit compiler *Frigate* [32] to implement the garbled circuit components of *GC-based*. We choose the Frigate compiler for the following reasons: Frigate outperforms several other garbled-circuit compilers; it is also extensively validated and found to produce correct and functioning circuits where other compilers fail [32]. The interpreter and execution functionalities of *Frigate* are separately referred to as *Battleship*. For our purposes, we split *Battleship* execution into two standalone phases: a key pair generation phase (gen) and a function evaluation phase (evl). Our specific modifications to *Battleship* that make split-phase execution possible are detailed in the full version of our paper.

Our GC-based approach to OTP relies on TXT for trusted key selection and leaves the computation for garbled circuits, as shown in Fig. 2. In our setting, Alice represents the vendor and Bob represents the client.

Provisioning at Alice's Site. Alice sets up the OTP box by doing the following: (1) Initialize flag to 0 and seal in the TXT program's provisioning mode. (2) Write and compile, using *Frigate*, the wire program (.wir), together with Alice's input, into the circuit.[8] (3) Load the compiled .mfrig and .ffrig files, vendor's input, and the *Battleship* executable onto the box. (4) Write the TXT program (for key selection) in the same way as in TXT-only. (5) Run *Battleship* in key-generation mode to generate the k_i^0 and k_i^1 key-pairs corresponding to each of the i bits of Bob's input. These are saved to file. (6) Seal the newly generated key pairs onto the hard-drive in provisioning mode of the TXT program. Alice is able to generate the correct number of key pairs, since garbled circuit programs take inputs of a predetermined size, meaning Alice knows the size of Bob's input. Costly sealing of all key pairs could be switched out for sealing of the master key (MK) used to encrypt the key pairs.

Evaluation at Bob's Site. Bob, upon receiving the OTP box from Alice, performs the following steps to evaluate the function on his input: (1) Place the file with Bob's input bits on the hard drive. (2) Load the TXT program in normal (non-provisioning) mode for key selection. (3) Receive selected keys corresponding to Bob's input bits; these are output to disk in plaintext. As long as it is Bob's first attempt to select keys, the TXT program will return the keys corresponding to Bob's input. Otherwise, the TXT program will abort upon loading in step (2), as shown in Fig. 2. After Bob's inputs have been successfully garbled (or converted into keys) and saved on the disk, Bob can continue with the evaluation properly. TXT is no longer required. (4) Reboot the system into the OS (e.g., Ubuntu). (5) Launch *Battleship* in circuit-evaluation mode. (6) Receive the evaluation result from *Battleship*. When *Battleship* is launched in circuit-evaluation mode, the saved keys corresponding to Bob's input are read in. *Battleship* also takes vendor input (if not compiled into the circuit) before processing the garbled circuit. The Boolean circuit is read in from the .mfrig and .ffrig files produced by *Frigate*. Evaluation is non-interactive and offline. The evaluation result is available only to Bob.

6   Case Study

We apply our proposed systems on a concrete use case based on genomic testing as a prototype. Single nucleotide polymorphism (SNP) is a common form

---

[8] The wire program may be written and compiled on a separate machine from that which will be shipped to Bob. If Alice chooses to use the same machine, the (no longer needed) raw wire code and *Frigate* executable should be removed from the box before provisioning continues.

of mutation in human DNA. Certain sets of SNPs determine the susceptibility of an individual to specific diseases. Analyzing an individual's set of SNPs may reveal what kind of diseases a person may have. More generally, genomic data can uniquely identify a person, as it not only gives information about a person's association with diseases, but also about the individual's relatives [35]. Indeed, advancements in genomics research have given rise to concerns about individual privacy and led to a number of related work in this space. For instance, Canim et al. [7] and Fisch et al. [10] utilize tamper-resistant hardware to analyze/store health records. Other works [2,49] investigate efficient, privacy-preserving analysis of health data.

While a number of different techniques have been proposed for privacy-preserving genomic testing, ours is the first work to address this using one-time programs grounded in secure hardware. Other than providing one-timeness, the proposed scheme also provides (i) *non-interactivity*, in which the user does not need to interact with the vendor during the protocol, and (ii) *pattern-hiding*, which ensures that the patterns used in vendor's test are kept private from the user. On the other hand, homomorphic encryption-based schemes [1] lack non-interactivity and functional encryption-based schemes [34] lack non-interactivity and pattern-hiding. We did not specifically implement these other techniques and compare our solution with them. However, from the performance results that are reported in the original papers, we can argue that our proposed scheme provides comparable (if not better) efficiency compared to these techniques.

Our aim is to prevent the adversary (the client/Bob), who uses the device for genomic testing, from learning which positions of his genome are checked and how they are checked, specifically for the genomic testing of the breast cancer (BRCA) gene. BRCA1 and BRCA2 are tumor suppressor genes. If certain mutations are observed in these genes, the person will have an increased probability of having breast and/or ovarian cancer [48]. Hence, genomic testing for BRCA1 and BRCA2 mutations is highly indicative of individuals' predisposition to develop breast and/or ovarian cancer.

We aim also to protect the privacy of the vendor (the company/Alice) that provides the genomic testing and prevent the case where the adversary extracts the test, learns how it works, and consequently, tests other people without having to purchase the test. We aim to protect both the locations that are checked on the genome and the magnitude of the risk factor corresponding to that position. Note that client's input is secure, as Bob is provided the device and he does not have to interact with Alice to perform the genomic test.

6.1   Genomic Test

In order to perform our genomic testing, we obtained the SNPs related with BRCA1[9] along with their risk factors from SNPedia [8], an open source wiki site

---

[9] Similarly, we can also list the SNPs for BRCA2 and determine the contribution of the observed SNPs to the total risk factor.

that provides the list of these SNPs. The SNPs that are observed on BRCA1 and their corresponding risk factors for breast cancer are omitted here for brevity.

We obtain genotype files of different people from the openSNP website [14]. The genotype files contain the extracted SNPs from a person's genome. At a high level, for each SNP of the patient that is linked to BRCA1, we add the corresponding risk factor to the overall risk.

If a BRCA1-associated SNP is observed in the patient's SNP file, we check the allele combination and add the corresponding risk factor to the total. In order to prevent a malicious client from discovering which SNPs are checked, we check every line in the patient's SNP file. If an SNP related to breast cancer is not observed at a certain position, we add zero to the risk factor rather than skipping that SNP to prevent inference of checked SNPs using side channels.

Let i denote the reference number of an SNP and s_i^j be the allele combination of SNP i for individual j. Also, S_i and C_i are two vectors keeping all observed allele combinations of SNP i and the corresponding risk factors, respectively. Then, the equation to calculate the total risk factor for individual j can be shown as $RF_j = \sum_i f(s_i^j)$ where

$$f(s_i^j) = \begin{cases} C_i(\ell) & \text{if } s_i^j = S_i(\ell) \text{ for } \ell = 0, 1, \ldots, |S_i| \\ 0 & \text{otherwise} \end{cases}$$

For instance, for the SNP with ID $i = $ rs28897696, $S_i = <AA, AC>$ and $C_i = <7, 6>$. If the allele combination of SNP rs28897696 for individual j corresponds to one of the elements in S_i, we add the corresponding value from C_i to the total risk factor.

6.2 Construction for GC-Based

The garbled circuit version of the genomic test presented in Sect. 6.1 is written as wire (.wir) code accepted by the *Frigate* garbled circuit compiler. The code follows the test description in Sect. 6.1, adjusting overall risk factor upon comparing allele-pairs of matching SNPs and explicitly adding zero when needed.

We choose Bob's input from AncestryDNA files available on the openSNP website [14]. We perform preprocessing on these to obtain a compact representation of the data. Alice's input is hard-coded into the circuit at compile-time, by initializing an **unsigned int** of vendor input size and assigning each bit's value using *Frigate*'s wire operator.

Final Input Representation. Following the original design of *Battleship*, inputs are accepted as a single string of hex digits (each 4 bits). Each digit is treated separately, and input is parsed byte-by-byte (e.g., 41_{16} is represented as 10000010_2).

We use 7 hex digits (28 unsigned bits) for the SNP reference number and a single hex digit (4 unsigned bits) to represent the allele pair out of 16 possible combinations of A/T/C/G. Alice's input contains 2 more hex digits (8 signed bits) for risk factor, supporting individual risk factor values ranging from -128 to 127. We keep risk factor a signed value, since some genetic mutations lower the risk of disease. Although we did not observe any such mutations pertaining to BRCA1, our representation gives extensibility to tests for other diseases.

Output Representation. The program outputs a signed 16-bit value, allowing us to support cumulative risk factor ranging from $-32,768$ to $32,767$.[10]

6.3   Construction for TXT-only

In TXT-only, the genomic test logic of Sect. 6.1 is ported in pure C but largely keeps the representation used by the GC program (Sect. 6.2). Alice's input is in the form of 7 hex digits for the SNP ID, 1 hex digit for the allele pair and 2 digits for the risk factor. Bob's input is 2 digits shorter without the risk factor.

We pay special attention to minimizing exposure of Alice's input in RAM to defend against potential cold-boot attack. We achieve this by processing one record at a time performing all operations on and deleting it before moving on to the next record. We also seal each record (10 bytes) into one sealed chunk (322 bytes), which consumes more space. In each iteration, we unseal one of Alice's records and compare with all of Bob's records. For certain laptops and other computers with RAM soldered on the motherboard, this is optional.

Table 1. TXT-only results with vendor input fixed at 880 bits and varying client input size, averaged over 10 runs. Prov./Exec. refers to the provisioning mode and execution mode respectively.

Client input (bits)	Prov. (ms)	Exec. (ms)
224	5640.17	9394.58
2K	5640.17	9393.88
22K	5640.17	9388.27
224K	5640.17	9426.56
2M	5640.17	11078.19
22M	5640.17	33427.50

Table 2. TXT-only results with client input fixed at 224k bits and varying vendor input size, averaged over 10 runs. Performance of TXT-only is linear and time taken is proportional to vendor input size.

Vendor input (bits)	Prov. (ms)	Exec. (ms)
880	5640.17	9426.56
8800	53515.75	92551.43
88000	527026.89	921338.53

7   Performance Evaluation

In this section, we evaluate the two OTP systems' performance/scalability, with varying client and vendor inputs, and try to statistically verify the suitability of the two intuitive designs in different usage scenarios. We perform our evaluation

---

[10] This can easily be adjusted, but is accompanied by substantial changes in the resulting circuit size. For example, an 11 GB circuit that outputs 16 bits grows to 18 GB by doubling the output size to 32 bits. We conservatively choose 16 bits for demonstration purposes, but the output size may be reduced as appropriate.

on a machine with a 3.50 GHz i7-4771 CPU, Infineon TPM 1.2, 8 GB RAM, 320 GB primary hard-disk, additional 1 TB hard-disk[11] functioning as a one-time memory (dedicated to storing garbled circuit, and client and vendor input), running Ubuntu 14.04.5 LTS. In one case, we required an alternate testing environment: a server-class machine with a 40 core 2.20 GHz Intel Xeon CPU and 128 GB of RAM.[12]

We perform experiments to determine the effects of varying either client or vendor input size. Based on the case study, the vendor has 880 bits and the client has 22.4M bits of input, so we use 224 and 880 as the base numbers for our evaluation. We multiply by multiples of 10 to show the effect of order-of-magnitude changes on inputs. We start with 224 for client and 880 for vendor inputs. When varying client input, we fix vendor input at 880 bits. When varying vendor input, we fix client input at 224K bits.

7.1 Benchmarking TXT-only

Varying Client Input. Table 1 shows the timing results for TXT-only provisioning and execution with fixed vendor input and varying client input size. During provisioning, only the vendor input is sealed, so the provisioning time is constant in all cases. As client input size increases, so does execution time, but moderately. Performance is insensitive to client input size up through the 224K case. Even for the largest (22M) test case, increasing the client input size by two orders of magnitude results only in a slowdown by a factor of 3.5x.

Varying Vendor Input. Table 2 shows the timing results with fixed client input and varying vendor input size. Although we only tested against three configurations, we see an order-of-magnitude increase in vendor input size is accompanied by an order-of-magnitude increase in both provisioning and execution times.

7.2 Benchmarking GC-Based

We use the same experimental setup as used in TXT-only, but with additional time taken by the GC portion. Vendor and client each incur runtime costs from a GC (gen/evl) and a sealing-based (Prov./Sel.) phase.

Table 3. GC-based results with client input fixed at 224k bits, varying vendor input size, and encryption of keys by a sealed master key, averaged over 10 runs.

Vendor input (bits)	gen (ms)	Prov. (ms)	Sel. (ms)	evl (ms)
880	2323.7	4244.03	2508.73	31815.4
8800	3198.7	4244.03	2508.73	32200.4
88000	3286.9	4244.03	2508.73	32000.9

---

[11] We use a second disk to simulate what is shipped to the client (with all test data consolidated), separate from our primary disk for development.

[12] Another option would have been to upgrade the memory of the initial evaluation machine, but we chose to forgo this, as a test run on the server-class machine revealed that upwards of 60 GB would be required (not supportable by the motherboard).

Varying Vendor Input. We are interested in whether *GC-based* is less sensitive to the size of Alice's input than *TXT-only*; see Table 3. Since provisioning (Prov.) involves sealing a constant number of key pairs, and selection (Sel.) is dependent on the unsealing of these key pairs to output one key from each, there is no change. Both *Battleship* gen and evl mode timing is largely invariant, as well. Whereas System 1 performance was linearly dependent on vendor input size, we observe that *GC-based* (System 2) is indeed not sensitive to vendor input.

Table 4. GC-based results with vendor input fixed at 880 bits, varying client input size, and encryption of keys by a sealed master key, averaged over 10 runs. Provisioning- and execution-mode times were measured separately. *s indicate tests run in an alternate environment, due to insufficient memory on our primary setup.

Client input (bits)	gen (ms)	Prov. (ms)	Sel. (ms)	evl (ms)
224	1503.7	843.64	600.55	1350.8
2K	1318.9	906.70	688.62	1631.8
22K	1659.7	991.91	724.24	3643.7
224K	2323.7	4244.03	2508.73	31815.4
2M	16842.8	33934.54	19188.31	305362.8
22M	148387.9*	346606.87	283704.57	3108271*

Varying Client Input. For completeness, we also examine the effects of varying client input size on runtime; see Table 4. Prov. and Sel. stages are both slow as client input size increases, since more key pairs must be sealed/unsealed. gen and evl times are also affected by an increase in client input bits. Most notably, evl demonstrates a near order-of-magnitude slowdown from the 224K case to the 2M case, and the slowdown trend continues into the 22M case (despite using the better-provisioned machine to

Table 5. Performance for TXT-only and GC-based OTP implementations of the BRCA1 genomic test, averaged over 10 runs. Vendor input is 880 bits. Client input is 22,447,296 bits. *s indicate tests run in an alternate environment, due to insufficient memory on our primary testing setup.

OTP type	Mode	Timing (ms)
TXT-only	Prov.	5640.17
	Exec.	33427.50
GC-based	gen	148387.9*
	Prov.	346606.87
	Sel.	283704.57
	evl	3108271*

evaluate the 22M case). We indeed find that TXT-only OTP is complemented by GC-based OTP, where performance is sensitive to client input.

7.3   Analysis

Onto our real-world genomic test (among other padded data sets for the evaluation purpose), Alice's input comprises the 22 SNPs associated with BRCA1. Each SNP entry takes up 40 bits, so Alice's input takes up 880 bits. Bob's input comprises the 701,478 SNPs drawn from his AncestryDNA file, each of which is represented with 32 bits, adding up to a total size of 22,447,296 bits. This genomic test corresponds to our earlier experiment with vendor input size of 880 bits and client input size of 22M bits.

Table 5 puts together the results for both OTP systems. Even at first glance, we see that TXT-only OTP vastly outperforms the GC-based OTP. Provisioning is two orders of magnitude slower in GC-based OTP, and trusted selection itself is an order of magnitude slower than the entire execution mode of TXT-only OTP. gen and evl further introduce a performance hit to GC-based OTP (again, despite the fact that we evaluated this case on a better-provisioned machine). TXT-only is the superior option for our genomic application.

Choosing One OTP. We already saw in Sect. 7.1 that TXT-only OTP is less sensitive to client input, whereas we saw in Sect. 7.2 that GC-based OTP is less sensitive to vendor input. We illustrate the four cases in Table 6.

In this specific use-case of genomic testing, we are in the upper-right quadrant and thus the TXT-only OTP dominates. However, other use cases (considered in the full version of our paper) might occupy the lower-left quadrant; if so, GC-based will outperform the TXT-only OTP. What should we do if both inputs are of similar size (i.e., equally "small" or "large")? A safe bet is to stick with the TXT-only OTP. Even though GC technology continues to improve, garbled circuits will always be less efficient than running the code natively.

Table 6. Depending on the input sizes of vendor and client, one system may be preferred to the other. GC-based OTP is favorable when large vendor input is paired with small client input; TXT-only OTP otherwise.

Small vendor + Small client **TXT-only**	Small vendor + Large client **TXT-only**
Large vendor + Small client **GC-based**	Large vendor + Large client **TXT-only**

7.4   Another Use Case: Database Queries

To give an example where the vendor input can be significantly large, we may consider another potential and feasible application of our proposed OTP designs, where GC-based can outperform TXT-only. It is also in a medical setting where the protocol is between two parties, namely a company that owns a database consisting of patient data and a research center that wants to utilize patient data. The patient data held at the company contains both phenotypical and genotypical properties. The research center wants to perform a test to determine the relationship of a certain mutation (e.g., a SNP) with a given phenotype. There may be three approaches for this scenario:

1. **Private information retrieval** [9]: PIR allows a user to retrieve data from a database without revealing what is retrieved. Moreover, the user also does not learn about the rest of the data in the database (i.e., symmetric PIR [37]). However, it does not let the user compute over the database (such as calculating the relationship of a certain genetic variant with a phenotype among the people in the database).
2. **Database is public, query is private:** The company can keep its database public and the research center can query the database as much as it wants. However, with this approach the privacy of the database is not preserved. Moreover, there is no limit to the queries that the research center does.

As an alternative to this, database may be kept encrypted and the research center can run its queries on the encrypted database (e.g., homomorphic encryption). The result of the query would then be decrypted by the data owner at the end of the computation [23]. However, this scheme introduces high computational overhead.

3. **Database is not public, query is exposed:** In this approach, the company keeps its database secret and the research center sends the query to the company. This time the query of the research center is revealed to the company and the privacy of the research center is compromised.

In the case of GC-based, the company stores its database into the device (in the form of garbled circuit) and the research center purchases the device to run its query (in TXT) on it. This system enables both parties' privacy. The device does not leak any information about the database and also the company does not learn about the query of the research center, as the research center purchases the device and gives the query as an input to it. In order to determine the relationship of a certain mutation to a phenotype, chi-squared test can be used to determine the p-value, that helps the research center to determine whether a mutation has a significant relation to a phenotype. We leave this to future work.

8   Security Analysis

(a) **Replay attacks.** The adversary may try to trick the OTP into executing multiple times by replaying a previous state, even without compromising the TEE, or the one-time logic therein. The secrets (e.g., MK) only have per-deployment freshness (fixed at Alice's site). Nevertheless, in our implementation, the TPM NVRAM indices where the one-timeness flag and MK are stored are configured with PCR-bound protection, i.e., outside the correct environment, they are even inaccessible for read/write, let alone to replay.

(b) **Memory side-channel attacks.** Despite the hardware-aided protection from TEE, sensitive plaintext data must be exposed at certain points. For instance, MK is needed for encrypting/decrypting key pairs, and the key pairs when being selected must also be in plaintext. Software memory attacks [6,26,30] do not apply to our OTP systems, as the selected TEE (TXT) is exclusive. In our design, the code running in TEE does not even involve an OS, driver, hypervisor, or any software run-time. There are generally two categories of physical memory attacks: non-destructive ones that can be repeated (e.g., DMA attacks [38]); and the destructive (only one attempt) physical cold-boot attack [17]. All I/O access (especially DMA) is disabled for the TEE-protected regions and thus DMA attacks no longer pose a threat.

The effective cold-boot attack requires that the RAM modules are swappable and plaintext content is in RAM. For certain laptops or barebone computers [22], their RAM is soldered on the motherboard and completely unmountable (and thus immune). To ensure warm-boot attacks [47] (e.g., reading RAM content on the same computer by rebooting it with a USB stick) are also prevented, we can set the Memory Overwrite Request (MOR) bit to signal the UEFI/BIOS to wipe RAM on the next reboot before loading any system (cf. the official TCG mitigation [44]). We do take into account the regular desktops/laptops vulnerable to the cold-boot attack: For small-sized secrets like MK, existing solutions [15,33,39,46] can be used, where CPU/GPU registers or cache memory are used to store secrets. For larger secrets, like the key pairs/vendor input, we perform block-wise processing so that at any time during the execution, only a very small fraction is exposed. Also, as cold-boot attack is destructive, the adversary will not learn enough to reveal the algorithm or reuse the key pairs. At least, the vendor can always choose computers with soldered-down RAM.

(c) **Attack cost.** Bob may try to infer the protected function and vendor inputs by trying different inputs in multiple instances. This attack may incur a high cost as Bob will need to order the OTP from Alice several times. This is a limitation of any offline OTP solution, which can only guarantee one query per box.

(d) **Cryptographic attacks.** The security of one-time programs (and garbled circuits) is proven in the original paper [12] (updated after caveat [3]), so we do not repeat the proofs here.

(e) **Clonability.** Silicon attacks on TPM can reveal secrets (including the Endorsement Key), but chip imaging/decapping requires high-tech equipment. Thus, cloning a TPM or extracting an original TPM's identity/data to populate a virtual TPM (vTPM) is considered unfeasible. Sealing achieves platform-state-binding without attestation, so non-genuine environments (including vTPM) will fail to unseal. We discuss TPM relay and SMM attacks in the full version of our paper. Furthermore, there has been a recent software attack [18] that resets and forges PCR values during S3 processing exploiting a TPM 2.0 flaw (SRTM) and a software bug in tboot (DRTM). They (allegedly patched) do not pose a threat to our OTP design, as neither SRTM nor any OS software (e.g., Linux) is involved, not to mention our OTP does not support/involve any power management.

9 Concluding Remarks

Until now, one-time programs have been theoretical or required highly customized/expensive hardware. We shift away from crypto-intensive approaches to the emerging but time-tested trusted computing technologies, for a practical and affordable realization of OTPs. With our proposed techniques, which we will release publicly, anyone can build a one-time program today with off-the-shelf devices that will execute quickly at a moderate cost. The cost of our proposed hardware-based solution for a single genomic test can be further diluted by extension to support multiple tests and multiple clients on a single device (which our current construction already does). The general methodology we provide can be adapted to other trusted execution environments to satisfy various application scenarios and optimize the performance/suitability for existing applications.

A   Appendix

For space considerations, we also publish a full version [52] of this paper that provides additional information as follows:

- More background helpful for understanding on one-time programs, garbled circuits, and one-time memories;
- Discussion of an adaptive security attack on OTP systems;
- Detailed modifications we make to *Battleship*;
- Preprocessing steps for our case study application;
- Additional one-time program use cases;
- A list of the SNPs associated with BRCA1;
- Details of our genomic algorithm;
- Comments on porting efforts required for OTP; and
- Discussion of more attacks (e.g., SMM and TPM relay attacks).

References

1. Ayday, E., Raisaro, J.L., Laren, M., Jack, P., Fellay, J., Hubaux, J.P.: Privacy-preserving computation of disease risk by using genomic, clinical, and environmental data. In: Proceedings of USENIX Security Workshop on Health Information Technologies (HealthTech 2013). No. EPFL-CONF-187118 (2013)
2. Baldi, P., Baronio, R., De Cristofaro, E., Gasti, P., Tsudik, G.: Countering gattaca: efficient and secure testing of fully-sequenced human genomes. In: Proceedings of the 18th ACM CCS 2011, pp. 691–702 (2011)
3. Bellare, M., Hoang, V.T., Rogaway, P.: Adaptively secure garbling with applications to one-time programs and secure outsourcing. In: Wang, X., Sako, K. (eds.) ASIACRYPT 2012. LNCS, vol. 7658, pp. 134–153. Springer, Heidelberg (2012). https://doi.org/10.1007/978-3-642-34961-4_10
4. Brasser, F., Müller, U., Dmitrienko, A., Kostiainen, K., Capkun, S., Sadeghi, A.R.: Software grand exposure: SGX cache attacks are practical. In: 11th USENIX Workshop on Offensive Technologies (WOOT 2017), Vancouver, BC (2017)
5. Broadbent, A., Gutoski, G., Stebila, D.: Quantum one-time programs. In: Canetti, R., Garay, J.A. (eds.) CRYPTO 2013. LNCS, vol. 8043, pp. 344–360. Springer, Heidelberg (2013). https://doi.org/10.1007/978-3-642-40084-1_20
6. Bulck, J.V., et al.: Foreshadow: extracting the keys to the Intel SGX kingdom with transient out-of-order execution. In: USENIX Security Symposium, Baltimore, MD, USA, pp. 991–1008 (2018)
7. Canim, M., Kantarcioglu, M., Malin, B.: Secure management of biomedical data with cryptographic hardware. IEEE Trans. Inf Technol. Biomed. **16**(1), 166–175 (2012)
8. Cariaso, M., Lennon, G.: SNPedia: a wiki supporting personal genome annotation, interpretation and analysis (2010). http://www.SNPedia.com
9. Chor, B., Goldreich, O., Kushilevitz, E., Sudan, M.: Private information retrieval. In: Proceedings of the 36th Annual Symposium on Foundations of Computer Science, pp. 41–50. IEEE (1995)
10. Fisch, B.A., Vinayagamurthy, D., Boneh, D., Gorbunov, S.: Iron: functional encryption using Intel SGX. Technical report, IACR eprint (2016)
11. Gnu.org: The multiboot specification (2009). http://www.gnu.org/software/grub/manual/multiboot/multiboot.html

12. Goldwasser, S., Kalai, Y.T., Rothblum, G.N.: One-time programs. In: Wagner, D. (ed.) CRYPTO 2008. LNCS, vol. 5157, pp. 39–56. Springer, Heidelberg (2008). https://doi.org/10.1007/978-3-540-85174-5_3

13. Greene, J.: Intel® trusted execution technology. Technical report (2012)

14. Greshake, B., Bayer, P.E., Rausch, H., Reda, J.: Opensnp-a crowdsourced web resource for personal genomics. PLoS ONE **9**(3), 1–9 (2014)

15. Guan, L., Lin, J., Luo, B., Jing, J.: Copker: computing with private keys without RAM. In: NDSS, San Diego, CA, USA, February 2014

16. Gunupudi, V., Tate, S.R.: Generalized non-interactive oblivious transfer using count-limited objects with applications to secure mobile agents. In: Tsudik, G. (ed.) FC 2008. LNCS, vol. 5143, pp. 98–112. Springer, Heidelberg (2008). https://doi.org/10.1007/978-3-540-85230-8_8

17. Halderman, J.A., et al.: Lest we remember: cold boot attacks on encryption keys. In: USENIX Sec 2008, San Jose, CA, USA (2008)

18. Han, S., Shin, W., Park, J.H., Kim, H.: A bad dream: subverting trusted platform module while you are sleeping. In: 27th USENIX Security Symposium (USENIX Security 2018), Baltimore, MD, USA, pp. 1229–1246 (2018)

19. Hazay, C., Lindell, Y.: Efficient Secure Two-Party Protocols. ISC. Springer, Heidelberg (2010). https://doi.org/10.1007/978-3-642-14303-8

20. Intel Corporation: Trusted boot (tboot), version: 1.8.0 (2017). http://tboot.sourceforge.net/

21. Järvinen, K., Kolesnikov, V., Sadeghi, A.-R., Schneider, T.: Garbled circuits for leakage-resilience: hardware implementation and evaluation of one-time programs. In: Mangard, S., Standaert, F.-X. (eds.) CHES 2010. LNCS, vol. 6225, pp. 383–397. Springer, Heidelberg (2010). https://doi.org/10.1007/978-3-642-15031-9_26

22. Jefferies, C.P.: How to identify user-upgradeable notebooks, June 2017. http://www.notebookreview.com/feature/identify-user-upgradeable-notebooks/

23. Kantarcioglu, M., Jiang, W., Liu, Y., Malin, B.: A cryptographic approach to securely share and query genomic sequences. IEEE Trans. Inf Technol. Biomed. **12**(5), 606–617 (2008)

24. Kirkpatrick, M.S., Kerr, S., Bertino, E.: PUF ROKs: a hardware approach to read-once keys. In: Proceedings of the 6th ACM Symposium on Information, Computer and Communications Security, AsiaCCS 2011, Hong Kong, China, pp. 155–164 (2011)

25. Kitamura, T., Shinagawa, K., Nishide, T., Okamoto, E.: One-time programs with cloud storage and its application to electronic money. In: APKC (2017)

26. Kocher, P., et al.: Spectre attacks: exploiting speculative execution. CoRR (2018)

27. Kollenda, B., Koppe, P., Fyrbiak, M., Kison, C., Paar, C., Holz, T.: An exploratory analysis of microcode as a building block for system defenses. In: Proceedings of the 2018 ACM SIGSAC Conference on Computer and Communications Security, CCS 2018, Toronto, ON, Canada, 15–19 October 2018, pp. 1649–1666 (2018)

28. Koppe, P., et al.: Reverse engineering x86 processor microcode. In: 26th USENIX Security Symposium (USENIX Security 2017), Vancouver, BC, pp. 1163–1180 (2017)

29. Lee, S., Shih, M.W., Gera, P., Kim, T., Kim, H., Peinado, M.: Inferring fine-grained control flow inside SGX enclaves with branch shadowing. In: 26th USENIX Security Symposium (USENIX Security 2017), Vancouver, BC, pp. 557–574 (2017)

30. Lipp, M., et al.: Meltdown. CoRR (2018)

31. McCune, J.M.: Reducing the trusted computing base for applications on commodity systems. Ph.D. thesis, Carnegie Mellon University (2009)

32. Mood, B., Gupta, D., Carter, H., Butler, K., Traynor, P.: Frigate: a validated, extensible, and efficient compiler and interpreter for secure computation. In: Euro-SP (2016)
33. Müller, T., Freiling, F.C., Dewald, A.: TRESOR runs encryption securely outside RAM. In: USENIX Security Symposium, San Francisco, CA, USA, August 2011
34. Naveed, M., et al.: Controlled functional encryption. In: CCS 2014, pp. 1280–1291. ACM (2014)
35. Naveed, M., et al.: Privacy and security in the genomic era. In: CCS 2014 (2014)
36. nccgroup: Cachegrab, December 2017. https://github.com/nccgroup/cachegrab
37. Saint-Jean, F.: Java implementation of a single-database computationally symmetric private information retrieval (cSPIR) protocol. Technical report, Yale University Department of Computer Science (2005)
38. Sevinsky, R.: Funderbolt: Adventures in Thunderbolt DMA Attacks. Black Hat USA (2013)
39. Simmons, P.: Security through Amnesia: a software-based solution to the cold boot attack on disk encryption. In: ACSAC (2011)
40. Sottek, T.: NSA reportedly intercepting laptops purchased online to install spy malware, December 2013. https://www.theverge.com/2013/12/29/5253226/nsa-cia-fbi-laptop-usb-plant-spy
41. Strackx, R., Jacobs, B., Piessens, F.: ICE: a passive, high-speed, state-continuity scheme. In: Proceedings of the 30th Annual Computer Security Applications Conference, ACSAC 2014, New Orleans, Louisiana, USA, pp. 106–115 (2014)
42. Strackx, R., Piessens, F.: Ariadne: a minimal approach to state continuity. In: 25th USENIX Security Symposium (USENIX Sec 2016), Austin, TX, pp. 875–892 (2016)
43. Tarnovsky, C.: Attacking TPM part 2: a look at the ST19WP18 TPM device, July 2012. dEFCON presentation. https://www.defcon.org/html/links/dc-archives/dc-20-archive.html
44. Trusted Computing Group: TCG Platform Reset Attack Mitigation Specification, May 2008
45. Trusted Computing Group: Trusted Platform Module Main Specification, version 1.2, revision 116 (2011). https://trustedcomputinggroup.org/tpm-main-specification/
46. Vasiliadis, G., Athanasopoulos, E., Polychronakis, M., Ioannidis, S.: PixelVault: using GPUs for securing cryptographic operations. In: CCS 2014, Scottsdale, AZ, USA, November 2014
47. Vidas, T.: Volatile memory acquisition via warm boot memory survivability. In: 43rd Hawaii International Conference on System Sciences, pp. 1–6, January 2010
48. Walsh, T., et al.: Detection of inherited mutations for breast and ovarian cancer using genomic capture and massively parallel sequencing. Natl Acad. Sci. **107**(28), 12629–12633 (2010)
49. Wang, X.S., Huang, Y., Zhao, Y., Tang, H., Wang, X., Bu, D.: Efficient genome-wide, privacy-preserving similar patient query based on private edit distance. In: CCS, pp. 492–503. ACM (2015)
50. Yao, A.C.: Protocols for secure computations. In: FOCS (1982)
51. Zhang, N., Sun, K., Shands, D., Lou, W., Hou, Y.T.: Truspy: cache side-channel information leakage from the secure world on ARM devices. IACR Cryptology ePrint Archive 2016, 980 (2016)
52. Zhao, L., et al.: One-time programs made practical (2019). http://arxiv.org/abs/1907.00935

Statement Voting

Bingsheng Zhang[1]($\boxtimes$) and Hong-Sheng Zhou[2]

[1] Lancaster University, Bailrigg, UK
`b.zhang2@lancaster.ac.uk`
[2] Virginia Commonwealth University, Richmond, USA
`hszhou@vcu.edu`

Abstract. The conventional (election) voting systems, e.g., representative democracy, have many limitations and often fail to serve the best interest of the people in a collective decision-making process. To address this issue, the concept of liquid democracy has been emerging as an alternative decision-making model to make better use of "the wisdom of crowds". However, there is no known cryptographically secure e-voting implementation that supports liquid democracy.

In this work, we propose a new voting concept called *statement voting*, which can be viewed as a natural extension of the conventional voting approaches. In the statement voting, instead of defining a concrete election candidate, each voter can define a statement in his/her ballot but leave the vote "undefined" during the voting phase. During the tally phase, the (conditional) actions expressed in the statement will be carried out to determine the final vote. We initiate the study of statement voting under the Universal Composability (UC) framework, and propose several construction frameworks together with their instantiations. As an application, we show how statement voting can be used to realize a UC-secure liquid democracy voting system. We remark that our statement voting can be extended to enable more complex voting and generic ledger-based non-interactive multi-party computation. We believe that the statement voting concept opens a door for constructing a new class of e-voting schemes.

1 Introduction

Elections provide people with the opportunity to express their opinions in the collective decision making process. The existing election/voting systems can be mainly divided into two categories: direct democracy and representative democracy. Unfortunately, either approach has many limitations, and it often fails to serve the best interest of the people. For example, to make correct decisions, the voters have to invest tremendous effort to analyze the issues. The cost of identifying the best voting strategy is high, even if we assume that the voter has collected all the necessary information accurately. In addition, misinformation campaigns often influence the voters to select certain candidates which could be against the voters' true interests. We here ask the following challenging question:

© International Financial Cryptography Association 2019
I. Goldberg and T. Moore (Eds.): FC 2019, LNCS 11598, pp. 667–685, 2019.
https://doi.org/10.1007/978-3-030-32101-7_38

Is it possible to introduce new technologies to circumvent the implementation barriers so that more effective democracy can be enabled?

A New Concept. We could approach the above problem via multiple angles. In this paper, we propose a new powerful concept: *statement voting*. Statement voting can be viewed as a natural extension of traditional candidate voting. Instead of defining a fixed election candidate, each voter can define a statement in his/her ballot but leave the vote "undefined" during the voting phase. During the tally phase, the (conditional) actions expressed in the statement will be carried out to determine the final vote. More specifically, in a statement voting, the ballots typically contain a conditional statement that requires external inputs (a.k.a. parameters and/or arguments) to be executed. For simplicity of illustration, here we consider (nested) if-statements or switch-statements: If A and B then C_1 else C_2, where A, B are conditions and C_1, C_2 are election candidates. We emphasize that A and B are usually not defined yet at the time this ballot is created; In the case that, A and B are defined, i.e., all the necessary information is readily collected during the voting phase, the voter can evaluate such a statement himself, and statement voting boils down to conventional voting. Thus, statement voting can be viewed as a non-trivial extension of conventional voting. We note that statement voting can be very flexible. For instance, a ballot statement could be "if tomorrow is rainy, I vote for 'staying at home'; otherwise, I vote for 'hiking'." Note that the ballot can be cast today without even being aware of tomorrow's weather.

Single Transferable Vote (STV) is a special case of statement voting, where the voters rank the election candidates instead of naming only one candidate in their ballots. The ranked candidate list together with the STV tally rule can be viewed as an outcome-dependent statement. Roughly speaking, the statement declares that if my favorite candidate has already won or has no chance to win, then I would like to vote for my second favorite candidate, and so on[1].

Modeling Statement Voting. We provide a rigorous modeling for statement voting. More concretely, we model statement voting in the well-known Universal Composability (UC) framework, via an ideal functionality $\mathcal{F}_{SV}$. The functionality interacts with voters and trustees, where trustees are the set of voting committee members who prepare the election and calculate the tally result. In our formulation, we introduce a *family of functionalities* to facilitate various realizations. In practice, there is a trade-off between efficiency and privacy guarantees; typically, more efficient constructions yield more privacy leakage. To capture various leakage scenarios, in our ideal functionality, a working table $\mathbb{W}$ is introduced to trace the election transcripts. Depending on which parties are corrupted (and which scheme is considered), some part of the working table will be leaked to the adversary.

Realizing Statement Voting. In this work, we provide several methods to implement statement voting. Similar to most conventional e-voting systems, we

---

[1] Note that this is not a complete description of STV. For those readers who are unfamiliar with STV, please see its full definition to avoid misunderstanding.

assume a trusted *Registration Authority* (RA) to ensure voter eligibility and a consistent *Bulletin Board* (BB) where the voting transactions and result will be posted. The protocol involves a set of voters and a set of trustees, where the trustees are the set of voting committee members who prepare the election and compute the tally.

A Fully Homomorphic Encryption (FHE) Based Scheme. Intuitively, in this scheme, the trustees first run a distributed key generation protocol to setup the voting public key PK. Each voter V_i then encrypts, signs and submits their *voting statements*, x_i (in forms of $(\mathsf{PID}_i, \mathsf{Enc}_{\mathsf{PK}}(x_i))$) to the BB. To prevent re-play attacks, non-interactive zero-knowledge (NIZK) proofs are necessary to ensure the voter knows the plaintext included in his/her submitted ciphertext. After that, the tally processing circuit is evaluated over $\{(\mathsf{PID}_i, \mathsf{Enc}_{\mathsf{PK}}(x_i))\}_{i \in [n]}$ by every trustee. The final tally ciphertext is then decrypted by the trustees and the result will be announced on the BB.

A Publicly Auditable MPC Based Scheme. Intuitively, we can adopt BDO-type of publicly auditable MPC [4], where the trustees form the MPC system. During the preparation phase, they pre-compute sufficiently many correlated randomness (e.g., Beaver triples), and also set up a voting public key. Each voter V_i then encrypts, signs and submits their *voting statements*, x_i (in forms of $(\mathsf{PID}_i, \mathsf{Enc}_{\mathsf{PK}}(x_i))$) together with necessary NIZK proofs to the BB. After that, the trustees perform MPC online computation to first decrypt those encrypted ballots and then evaluate the tally processing circuit over the secretly shared ballots. Finally, the tally result will be posted on the BB. Note that during the online phase, the BDO MPC scheme also posts audit information on the BB to enable public verifiability.

Application: Liquid Democracy. In the past decades, the concept of liquid democracy [16] has been emerging as an alternative decision making model to make better use of collective intelligence. Liquid democracy is a hybrid of direct democracy and representative democracy, where the voters can either vote directly on issues, or they can delegate their votes to representatives who vote on their behalf. Due to its advantages, liquid democracy has received high attentions since the spread of its concept; however, there is no provably secure solution in the form of either paper-voting or e-voting yet. Liquid democracy can be viewed as a special case of statement voting. The vote delegation can be expressed as a target-dependent statement, where a voter can define that his/her ballot is the same as the target voter's ballot. Therefore, we can have an immediate construction for liquid democracy based on the above FHE based and MPC-based schemes. In addition to those "generic" constructions, we also show how to realize liquid democracy with a more efficient construction. In Sect. 3.1, we first define an ideal functionality for liquid democracy, and we then provide a mix-net based construction. Note that the tally processing function must be symmetric, otherwise we cannot use mix-net.

Further Remarks. In this work, we initiate the study of statement voting and liquid democracy. Our statement voting concept can be significantly extended to support much richer ballot statements. It opens a door for constructing a new class of e-voting schemes. This area of research is far from being completed, and our design and modeling ideas can be further improved. For example, if there is a delegation loop in which a set of voters delegate their votes to each other while no one votes, then what should be the "right" policy? One possible approach is to extend the delegation statement to include a default vote. When a delegation loop exists, the involved ballots could be counted as their default votes. On the other hand, if we don't allow delegation loop in a liquid democracy voting, to what extend can we guarantee voter privacy? How to refine the conventional e-voting privacy to fit liquid democracy is still an open problem. We emphasize that, voting policies can be heavily influenced by local legal and societal conditions. How to define "right" voting policy itself is a very interesting question. We believe our techniques have the potential to help people to identify suitable voting policies which can further eliminate the barriers to democracy. Finally, we note that several important security requirements, e.g., coercion resilience, have not been investigated in this work. See more details in Sect. 4.

Related Work. To our best knowledge, Ford [16] first officially summarized the main characteristics of liquid democracy and brought it to the vision of computer science community. However, in terms of implementation/prototyping, there was no system that can enable liquid democracy until very recently. All the existing liquid democracy voting systems only focus on the functionality aspect of liquid democracy, and no privacy or some other advanced security properties were considered. For instance, Google Votes [20] is a decision-making system that can support liquid democracy, and it is built on top of social networks, e.g., the internal corporate Google+ network. Similarly, systems such as LiquidFeedback [26], Adhocracy [1], GetOpinionated, [15] also fail to offer provable security guarantees. It is worth mentioning that Sovereign [29] is a blockchain-based voting protocol for liquid democracy; therefore, its privacy is inherited from the underlying blockchain. As a special case of liquid democracy, Kulyk *et al.* proposed several proxy voting schemes [23–25]. In terms of UC modeling on e-voting. Groth [18] gave the first UC definition for an e-voting system, and he proposed a protocol using (threshold) homomorphic encryption. Moran and Naor [27] later studied the privacy and receipt-freeness of an e-voting system in the stand-alone setting. Unruh and Muller-Quade [30] gave a formal study of e-voting coerciability in the UC framework. Alwen *et al.* [3] considered stronger versions of coerciability in the MPC setting under UC framework. Almost all the end-to-end verifiable e-voting systems [2,13,21,22] requires a consistent bulletin board. Finally, our temporary ID matching technique is closely related to the queried term matching technique used in UnLynx[17] and the anonymous ID linking technique used in [31].

2   Modeling

The parties involved in a statement voting system are a set of trustees $\mathbb{T} := \{T_1, \ldots, T_k\}$, and a set of voters $\mathbb{V} := \{V_1, \ldots, V_n\}$.

Functionality $\mathcal{F}_{SV}$

The functionality $\mathcal{F}_{SV}$ interacts with voters V, trustees T, and the adversary $\mathcal{S}$. It is parameterized by an algorithm TallyProcess (see Fig. 2), a working table W, and variables *result*, T_1, T_2, and B_i for all $i \in [n]$. Let V_{honest}, $V_{corrupt}$ and $\mathbb{T}_{honest}$, $\mathbb{T}_{corrupt}$ denote the set of honest/corrupt voters and trustees, respectively.

Initially, set *result* := $\emptyset$, T_1 := $\emptyset$, T_2 := $\emptyset$; for $i \in [n]$, set B_i := $\emptyset$. Table W consists of n entries, and each entry consists of voter's real ID, voter's alternative ID, and the statement that the voter submitted; for all $i \in [n]$, the ith entry $W[i]$:= $(V_i, w_i, statement_i)$, where $w_i \leftarrow \{0,1\}^\lambda$, $statement_i$:= $\emptyset$.

Preparation:

1. Upon receiving input (INITIALTRUSTEE, sid) from the trustee $T_j \in T$, set T_1 := $T_1 \cup \{T_j\}$, and send (INITIALTRUSTEENOTIFY, sid, T_j) to $\mathcal{S}$.

Ballot Casting:

1. Upon receiving input (CAST, sid, (s_i, w_i^*)) from $V_i \in V$, if $|T_1| < k$, ignore it. Otherwise,
   - if V_i is honest (w_i^* := $\bot$), update $W[i]$:= (V_i, w_i, s_i); send (CASTNOTIFY, sid, V_i) to $\mathcal{S}$.
   - if V_i is corrupt, then update $W[i]$:= (V_i, w_i^*, s_i).
   If $|\mathbb{T}_{corrupt}| = k$, then additionally send a message (LEAK, sid, $W[i]$) to $\mathcal{S}$.

Tally:

1. Upon receiving input (TALLY, sid) from the trustee $T_j \in T$, set T_2 := $T_2 \cup \{T_j\}$ and
   - set U := W; then eliminate all V_i's in U; sort the entries in U lexicographically.
   - define L. For example, set L := TallyProcess(U) or L := U or L := W.
   Send a notification message (TALLYNOTIFY, sid, T_j) to $\mathcal{S}$.
   If $|T_2 \cap \mathbb{T}_{honest}| + |\mathbb{T}_{corrupt}| = k$, send a leakage message (LEAK, sid, L) to $\mathcal{S}$.
   If $|T_2| = k$, compute *result* $\leftarrow$ TallyProcess(U).
2. Upon receiving input (READRESULT, sid) from a voter $V_i \in V$, if *result* = $\emptyset$, ignore the input. Otherwise, return (RESULTRETURN, sid, *result*) to V_i.

Fig. 1. The voting functionality $\mathcal{F}_{SV}$.

The Statement Voting Functionality. The ideal functionality for statement voting, denoted as $\mathcal{F}_{SV}$, is formally described in Fig. 1. Let V_{honest}, $V_{corrupt}$ and $\mathbb{T}_{honest}$, $\mathbb{T}_{corrupt}$ denote the set of honest/corrupt voters and trustees, respectively. $\mathcal{F}_{SV}$ consists of three phases—Preparation, Ballot Casting, and Tally. The functionality uses a working table W to track the voters' behavior during the entire ideal execution. The working table W stores each voter's information including the voter's original ID, his alternative/temporary ID, and the voting statement that he submitted.

Preparation Phase. During the preparation phase, the trustees needs to indicate their presence to $\mathcal{F}_{SV}$ by sending (INITIALTRUSTEE, sid) to it. The election will not start until all the trustees have participated in the preparation.

Ballot Casting Phase. During the ballot casting phase, each voter can submit his voting statement, and this voting statement will be recorded in the corresponding entry. If a voter is corrupt, then he is also allowed to revise his own alternative/temporary ID in the working table. More concretely, based on the input (CAST, sid, (s_i, w_i^*)) from voter V_i, the corresponding entry will be

┌─ TallyProcess ───┐

Input: a set of ballots $\mathcal{B} := (B_1, \ldots, B_n)$

Output: the tally result *result*

Statement interpretation:

- Compute $(v_1, \ldots, v_n) \leftarrow \mathsf{StatementProcess}(B_1, \ldots, B_n)$, where StatementProcess takes input as the set of statements and outputs the voters' final votes.

Tally computation:

- Compute *result* $\leftarrow \mathsf{TallyAlg}(v_1, \ldots, v_n)$, where $\mathsf{TallyAlg}(\cdot)$ is the tally algorithm that takes input as the votes and outputs the tally result.
- Return *result*.

└──┘

Fig. 2. The extended tally processing algorithm.

updated, i.e., $\mathbb{W}[i] := (\mathsf{V}_i, w_i, s_i)$ if the voter is honest, and $\mathbb{W}[i] := (\mathsf{V}_i, w_i^*, s_i)$ if V_i is corrupt. When all the trustees are corrupted, the functionality $\mathcal{F}_{\mathrm{SV}}$ leaks the entire working tape of the election transcript (i.e., $\mathbb{W}$), to the adversary.

Tally Phase. Voters' information in the working table $\mathbb{W}$ will be used in the tally phase to define the privacy leakage as well as the final result. More concretely, we compute a new table $\mathbb{U}$ by first eliminating all V_i's in $\mathbb{W}$, and then sorting all the entries lexicographically. This carefully sanitised table $\mathbb{U}$ can now be used to define (1) the final result via applying a circuit TallyProcess on $\mathbb{U}$, and (2) certain level of privacy leakage L. This formulation allows us to define a *class* of statement voting functionalities. For instance, to define a functionality with full privacy guarantees, we can set $L := \mathsf{TallyProcess}(\mathbb{U})$; we can also set $L := \mathbb{U}$ to define a functionality with relatively weaker privacy guarantees, or set $L := \mathbb{W}$ to define a functionality without privacy guarantees.

The Liquid Democracy Ideal Functionality. Given that liquid democracy is the special case of statement voting, we can easily derive an ideal functionality for liquid democracy from $\mathcal{F}_{\mathrm{SV}}$. The full description of the concrete functionality for liquid democracy, $\mathcal{F}_{\mathrm{LIQUID}}$, can be found in the full version. At a high level, $\mathcal{F}_{\mathrm{LIQUID}}$ uses the following statement interpretation step in the TallyProcess. Each ballot is in form of either $B_i = (w_i, u_i, \bot)$ or $B_i = (w_i, \bot, x_i)$, where w_i and u_i are temporary ID's, and x_i is a vote. To resolve the delegation, the algorithm needs to follow the "chain of delegation", i.e., for each ballot B_i:

- If B_i is in form of $(w_i, u_i, \bot)$, try to locate a ballot B_j in form of (u_i, X, Y). If founded, replace $B_i := (w_i, X, Y)$.
- Repeat the above step, until B_i is in form of $(w_i, \bot, Z)$. If there is a delegation loop, define $B_i := (w_i, \bot, \bot)$.

In case of delegation loop, we set the ballot to blank ballot. Of course, we can enrich the statement by adding another variable to indicate whether a voter wants to be delegated. When the "chain of delegation" breaks by V_i wants to delegate his vote to V_j, while V_j does not want to be delegated. In this case,

V_i's ballot will be re-set to a blank ballot. The most preferable statement for liquid democracy in practice shall be determined by computational social choice theory, which is outside the scope of this paper.

3   Constructions

Due to space limitation, we present the two generic constructions – (i) FHE-based construction and (ii) MPC-based construction, in the full version. In the former one, the voters use FHE to encrypt and upload their statements to the BB. The tally evaluation circuit can be then publicly evaluated over the encrypted statements by any party. After that the trustees will jointly decrypt the final ciphertext(s). In the latter one, any public key encryption scheme can be adopted, so it is more efficient. Similarly, during the voting, the voters encrypt their statements and post them on the BB. The trustees will then participate the MPC evaluation to jointly decrypt the submitted statements and then compute the tally algorithm in the shared format with privacy assurance.

3.1   A Practical Construction for Liquid Democracy

The construction is based on mix-net, and the privacy that it achieves is known as pseudonymity. We emphasize that this level of privacy has been widely accepted and is consistent with the existing paper-based voting systems.

As mentioned before, *liquid democracy* is an emerging type of voting system that receives high attentions since the spread of its concept; however, there is no provably secure solution in the form of either paper-voting or e-voting yet.[2] We now show that how to define a simple statement to enable liquid democracy.

In a generic statement voting, the ballot can be defined in the following form: (ID, targets, statement), where ID is the voter's ID, targets is a set of target voters' IDs which will be referenced in the statement, and statement is the (conditional) statement. To realize liquid democracy voting, we can define the following simple statement: (i) if voter V_i wants to delegate his vote to V_j, then the ballot is $B := (V_i, \{V_j\}, \texttt{delegate})$; (ii) if voter V_i wants to vote directly for election option x, then the ballot is $B := (V_i, \bot, \texttt{vote } x)$; and (iii) if the voter does not want to be delegated, then he can set his own ID to $\bot$. To obtain the basic intuition, let's first leave privacy aside and consider the following toy example.

Toy Example. Take the Yes/No election as an example. Suppose there are 7 ballots: $B_1 := (V_1, V_7, \texttt{delegate})$, $B_2 := (V_2, \bot, \texttt{vote Yes})$, $B_3 := (V_3, \bot, \texttt{vote No})$,

---

[2] All the existing liquid democracy implementations do not consider privacy/anonymity. This drawback prevents them from being used in serious elections. Here, we note that straightforward blockchain-based solutions cannot provide good privacy in practice. Although some blockchains (e.g., Zerocash [5]) can be viewed as a global mixer, they implicitly require anonymous channels. In practice, all the implementations of anonymous channels suffer from time leakage, i.e., the user's ID is only hidden among the other users who are also using the system at the same time. Subsequently, the adversary may easily identify the users during quiet hours.

$B_4 := (\perp, \perp, \text{vote Yes})$, $B_5 := (V_5, V_4, \text{delegate})$, $B_6 := (\perp, V_3, \text{delegate})$ and $B_7 := (V_7, V_3, \text{delegate})$. Here, the effective vote of B_1 is defined by B_7, which is further defined by B_3; note that B_3 votes for No; that means, B_1 and B_7 vote for No by following B_3. Now let's consider B_6: B_6 follows B_3; however, B_6 is not willing to be followed by anyone; as a result, B_6 also votes for No. Finally, let's consider B_5: B_5 follows B_4; however, B_4 is not willing to be followed by anyone; as a consequence, B_5 is re-defined as blank ballot, $\perp$. After interpreting the delegation statements, the final votes are $(\text{No}, \text{Yes}, \text{No}, \text{Yes}, \perp, \text{No}, \text{No})$.

Intuition. At the beginning of each election, the voters V_i, $i \in [n]$, are assigned with a temporary random ID, denoted as ID_i. Let $\mathcal{I} := \{\text{ID}_1, \ldots, \text{ID}_n\}$ be the set of all the voter's random IDs. The voter's statement takes the input as an ID in $\mathcal{I}$, and use it as a reference to point to the corresponding ballot that will be involved in the statement execution, i.e., the potential vote delegation of liquid democracy. To ensure privacy, the voters cannot post their temporary IDs publicly on the bulletin board $\bar{\mathcal{G}}_{\text{BB}}$; however, the voters should be allowed to freely refer to any voter's ID.

To address this challenge, we introduce the following technique. Before the ballot casting phase, each voter picks a random ID and posts the (re-randomizable) encryption of the ID on the $\bar{\mathcal{G}}_{\text{BB}}$. If a voter wants to refer to another voter in the statement, he/she simply copies and re-randomizes the ciphertext of the corresponding voter's ID. At the tally phase, all the ballots are passing through re-encryption based mix-net, and then are decrypted to calculate the statements and tally result. We remark that in practice the mix-net servers can be different from talliers (a.k.a. decrypters). As such, they could have different threshold.

Building Blocks. Our protocol utilises a bulletin board functionality, a certificate functionality, a threshold re-randomizable encryption scheme, and the corresponding non-interactive zero-knowledge proofs. Their formal descriptions and defintions can be found in the full version.

Bulletin Board Functionality. The public bulletin board (BB) is modeled as a global functionality $\bar{\mathcal{G}}_{\text{BB}}$. The functionality is parameterized with a predicate Validate that ensures all the newly posted messages are consistent with the existing BB content w.r.t. Validate. Any party can use (SUBMIT, sid, msg) and (READ, sid) to write/read the BB.

Certificate Functionality. We adopt the multi-session version of certificate functionality following the modeling of [7]. The multi-session certificate functionality $\widehat{\mathcal{F}}_{\text{CERT}}$ can provide direct binding between a signature for a message and the identity of the corresponding signer. This corresponds to providing signatures accompanied by "certificates" that bind the verification to the signers' identities.

Threshold Re-randomizable Encryption. A threshold re-randomizable encryption scheme TRE consists of a tuple of algorithms: (Setup, Keygen, Enc, Dec, CombinePK, CombineSK, ShareDec, ShareCombine, ReRand) as follows.

- param $\leftarrow$ Setup(1^λ). The algorithm Setup takes input as the security parameter λ, and outputs public parameters param. All the other algorithms implicitly take param as input.
- (pk, sk) $\leftarrow$ Keygen(param). The algorithm Keygen takes input as the public parameter param, and outputs a public key pk, a secret key sk.
- $c \leftarrow$ Enc(pk, m). The algorithm Enc takes input as the public key pk and the message m, and outputs the ciphertext c.
- $c' \leftarrow$ ReRand(pk, c). The algorithm ReRand takes input as the public key pk and a ciphertext c, and outputs a re-randomized ciphertext c'.
- $m \leftarrow$ Dec(sk, c). The algorithm Dec takes input as the secret key sk and a ciphertext c, and outputs the decrypted plaintext m.
- pk := CombinePK(pk$_1$,..., pk$_k$). The algorithm CombinePK takes input as a set of public keys (pk$_1$,..., pk$_k$), and outputs a combined public key pk.
- sk $\leftarrow$ CombineSK(sk$_1$,..., sk$_k$). The algorithm CombineSK takes input as a set of secret key (sk$_1$,..., sk$_k$), and outputs combined secret key sk.
- $\mu_i \leftarrow$ ShareDec(sk$_i$, c). The algorithm ShareDec takes input as the secret key sk$_i$ and a ciphertext c, and outputs a decryption share μ_i.
- $m \leftarrow$ ShareCombine($c, \mu_1, \ldots, \mu_k$). The algorithm ShareCombine takes input as a ciphertext c and k decryption shares ($\mu_1, \ldots, \mu_k$), and outputs a plaintext m.
- $c' \leftarrow$ Trans($c, \{sk_i\}_{i \in [k] \setminus \{j\}}$). The algorithm Trans takes input as a ciphertext $c \leftarrow$ TRE.Enc(pk$_j$, m) and a set of secret keys $\{sk_i\}_{i \in [k] \setminus \{j\}}$, and outputs a ciphertext c'.
- $\{\mu_j\}_{j \in [k] \setminus \mathcal{I}} \leftarrow$ SimShareDec($c, m, \{\mu_i\}_{i \in \mathcal{I}}$). The algorithm SimShareDec takes as input a ciphertext c, a plaintext m, and a set of decryption shares $\{\mu_i\}_{i \in \mathcal{I}}$ and outputs a set of decryption shares $\{\mu_j\}_{j \in [k] \setminus \mathcal{I}}$. Here $\mathcal{I} \subsetneq [k]$.

In Appendix A, we provide the corresponding TRE security definitions.

Non-interactive Zero-Knowledge Proofs/Arguments. Here we briefly introduce non-interactive zero-knowledge (NIZK) schemes in the Random Oracle (RO) model. Let $\mathcal{R}$ be an efficiently computable binary relation. For pairs $(x, w) \in \mathcal{R}$ we call x the statement and w the witness. Let $\mathcal{L}_\mathcal{R}$ be the language consisting of statements in $\mathcal{R}$, i.e. $\mathcal{L}_\mathcal{R} = \{x | \exists w \text{ s.t. } (x, w) \in \mathcal{R}\}$. An NIZK scheme includes following algorithms: a PPT algorithm Prov that takes as input $(x, w) \in \mathcal{R}$ and outputs a proof π; a polynomial time algorithm Verify takes as input (x, π) and outputs 1 if the proof is valid and 0 otherwise.

Definition 1 (NIZK Proof in the RO Model). NIZK$_\mathcal{R}^{RO}$.{Prov, Verify, Sim, Ext} *is an NIZK Proof of Membership scheme for the relation $\mathcal{R}$ if the following holds:*

- *Completeness: For any $(x, w) \in \mathcal{R}$,*

$$\Pr\left[\zeta \leftarrow \{0, 1\}^\lambda; \pi \leftarrow \text{Prov}^{RO}(x, w; \zeta) : \text{Verify}^{RO}(x, \pi) = 0\right] \leq \text{negl}(\lambda).$$

- *Zero-knowledge: If for any PPT distinguisher $\mathcal{A}$ we have*

$$\left| \Pr[\mathcal{A}^{RO, \mathcal{O}_1}(1^\lambda) = 1] - \Pr[\mathcal{A}^{RO, \mathcal{O}_2}(1^\lambda) = 1] \right| \leq \text{negl}(\lambda).$$

Preparation

Upon receiving (INITIALTRUSTEE, sid) from the environment $\mathcal{Z}$, the trustee T_j, $j \in [k]$, operates as the follows:

— Generate $(\overline{\mathrm{pk}}_j, \overline{\mathrm{sk}}_j) \leftarrow$ TRE.Keygen(param; α_j) where α_j is the fresh randomness, and then compute

$$\pi_j^{(1)} \leftarrow \mathsf{NIZK}_{\mathcal{R}_4} \left\{ (\overline{\mathrm{pk}}_j), (\alpha_j, \overline{\mathrm{sk}}_j) : (\overline{\mathrm{pk}}_j, \overline{\mathrm{sk}}_j) = \mathsf{TRE.Keygen(param; \alpha_j)} \right\}$$

— Send (SIGN, sid, ssid, $(\overline{\mathrm{pk}}_j, \pi_j^{(1)})$) to $\widehat{\mathcal{F}}_{\mathrm{CERT}}$ and receives

(SIGNATURE, sid, ssid, $(\overline{\mathrm{pk}}_j, \pi_j^{(1)}), \sigma_j^{(1)}$) from $\widehat{\mathcal{F}}_{\mathrm{CERT}}$, where ssid $= (\mathsf{T}_j, \mathrm{ssid}')$ for some ssid$'$.

— Send (SUBMIT, sid, $\langle \mathrm{ssid}, (\overline{\mathrm{pk}}_j, \pi_j^{(1)}), \sigma_j^{(1)} \rangle$) to $\bar{\mathcal{G}}_{\mathrm{BB}}$.

Fig. 3. Mix-net based liquid democracy scheme $\Pi_{\mathrm{MIX\text{-}LIQUID}}$ in $\{\bar{\mathcal{G}}_{\mathrm{BB}}, \widehat{\mathcal{F}}_{\mathrm{CERT}}\}$-hybrid world (Part I)

The oracles are defined as follows: $\mathcal{O}_1$ on query $(x, w) \in \mathcal{R}$ returns π, where $(\pi, aux) \leftarrow \mathsf{Sim}^{\mathrm{RO}}(x)$; $\mathcal{O}_2$ on query $(x, w) \in \mathcal{R}$ returns π, where $\pi \leftarrow \mathsf{Prov}^{\mathrm{RO}}(x, w; \zeta)$ and $\zeta \leftarrow \{0,1\}^\lambda$.
- *Soundness: For all PPT adversary $\mathcal{A}$,*

$$\Pr\left[(x, \pi) \leftarrow \mathcal{A}^{\mathrm{RO}}(1^\lambda) : x \notin \mathcal{L}_R \wedge \mathsf{Verify}^{\mathrm{RO}}(x, \pi) = 1 \right] \leq \mathsf{negl}(\lambda).$$

Definition 2 (NIZK PoK in the RO Model). $\mathsf{NIZK}_{\mathcal{R}}^{\mathrm{RO}}.\{\mathsf{Prov}, \mathsf{Verify}, \mathsf{Sim}, \mathsf{Ext}\}$ *is an NIZK Proof of Knowledge scheme for the relation $\mathcal{R}$ if the completeness, zero-knowledge, and extraction properties hold, where the extraction is defined as follows. For all PPT adversary $\mathcal{A}$, the following is $1 - \mathsf{negl}(\lambda)$.*

$$\Pr\left[(x, \pi) \leftarrow \mathcal{A}^{\mathrm{RO}}(1^\lambda); w \leftarrow \mathsf{Ext}^{\mathrm{RO}}(x, \pi) : (x, w) \in \mathcal{R} \text{ if } \mathsf{Verify}^{\mathrm{RO}}(x, \pi) = 1 \right]$$

Protocol Description. The protocol is designed in the $\{\bar{\mathcal{G}}_{\mathrm{BB}}, \widehat{\mathcal{F}}_{\mathrm{CERT}}\}$-hybrid world and it consists of three phases: preparation, ballot casting, and tally. For the sake of notation simplicity, we omit the processes of filtering invalid messages on $\bar{\mathcal{G}}_{\mathrm{BB}}$. In practice, $\bar{\mathcal{G}}_{\mathrm{BB}}$ contains many messages with invalid signatures, and all those messages should be ignored. We will use threshold re-randomizable encryption (TRE) as a building block.

Preparation Phase. As depicted in Fig. 3, in the preparation phase, each trustee T_j, $j \in [k]$ first picks a randomness generates α_j and generates a partial public key using $(\overline{\mathrm{pk}}_j, \overline{\mathrm{sk}}_j) \leftarrow$ TRE.Keygen(param; α_j). It then generates an NIZK proof

$$\pi_j^{(1)} \leftarrow \mathsf{NIZK}_{\mathcal{R}_4} \left\{ (\overline{\mathrm{pk}}_j), (\alpha_j, \overline{\mathrm{sk}}_j) : (\overline{\mathrm{pk}}_j, \overline{\mathrm{sk}}_j) = \mathsf{TRE.Keygen(param; \alpha_j)} \right\}$$

to show that this process is executed correctly; namely, it shows knowledge of $(\alpha_j, \overline{\mathrm{sk}}_j)$ w.r.t. to the generated partial public key $\overline{\mathrm{pk}}_j$. It then signs and posts $(\overline{\mathrm{pk}}_j, \pi_j^{(1)})$ to $\bar{\mathcal{G}}_{\mathrm{BB}}$.

Ballot Casting

Upon receiving $(\text{CAST}, \text{sid}, (s_i, \bot))$ from the environment $\mathcal{Z}$, the voter V_i does:

o Round 1:
— Send $(\text{READ}, \text{sid})$ to $\bar{\mathcal{G}}_{\text{BB}}$, and obtain $(\text{READ}, \text{sid}, state)$ from $\bar{\mathcal{G}}_{\text{BB}}$. If
$\left\{ \langle \text{ssid}, (\overline{\text{pk}}_j, \pi_j^{(1)}), \sigma_j^{(1)} \rangle \right\}_{j \in [k]}$ is contained in $state$, then for $j \in [k]$, send
$(\text{VERIFY}, \text{sid}, \text{ssid}, (\overline{\text{pk}}_j, \pi_j^{(1)}), \sigma_j^{(1)})$ to $\widehat{\mathcal{F}}_{\text{CERT}}$, and receive
$(\text{VERIFIED}, \text{sid}, \text{ssid}, (\overline{\text{pk}}_j, \pi_j^{(1)}), b_j^{(1)})$ from $\widehat{\mathcal{F}}_{\text{CERT}}$; If $\prod_{j=1}^k b_j^{(1)} = 1$, check
$\text{NIZK}_{\mathcal{R}_4}.\text{Verify}(\overline{\text{pk}}_j, \pi_j^{(1)}) = 1$ for $j \in [k]$.
— Compute and store $\text{pk} \leftarrow \text{TRE.CombinePK}(\{\overline{\text{pk}}_j\}_{j=1}^k)$.
— Randomly selects $w_i \leftarrow \{0,1\}^\lambda$ and compute $W_i \leftarrow \text{TRE.Enc}(\text{pk}, w_i; \beta_i)$ with fresh
randomness β_i together with

$$\pi_i^{(2)} \leftarrow \text{NIZK}_{\mathcal{R}_5} \left\{ (\text{pk}, W_i), (\beta_i, w_i) : W_i = \text{TRE.Enc}(\text{pk}, w_i; \beta_i) \right\} \ .$$

— Send $(\text{SIGN}, \text{sid}, \text{ssid}, (W_i, \pi_i^{(2)}))$ to $\widehat{\mathcal{F}}_{\text{CERT}}$, and receive
$(\text{SIGNATURE}, \text{sid}, \text{ssid}, (W_i, \pi_i^{(2)}), \sigma_i^{(2)})$ from $\widehat{\mathcal{F}}_{\text{CERT}}$, where $\text{ssid} = (V_i, \text{ssid}')$ for some
ssid'.
— Send $(\text{SUBMIT}, \text{sid}, \langle \text{ssid}, (W_i, \pi_i^{(2)}), \sigma_i^{(2)} \rangle)$ to $\bar{\mathcal{G}}_{\text{BB}}$.

o Round 2:
— Send $(\text{READ}, \text{sid})$ to $\bar{\mathcal{G}}_{\text{BB}}$, and obtain $(\text{READ}, \text{sid}, state)$ from $\bar{\mathcal{G}}_{\text{BB}}$. For $\ell \in [n]$, if
$\langle \text{ssid}, (W_\ell, \pi_\ell^{(2)}), \sigma_\ell^{(2)} \rangle$ is contained in $state$, then send
$(\text{VERIFY}, \text{sid}, \text{ssid}, (W_\ell, \pi_\ell^{(2)}), \sigma_\ell^{(2)})$ to $\widehat{\mathcal{F}}_{\text{CERT}}$, and receive
$(\text{VERIFIED}, \text{sid}, \text{ssid}, (W_\ell, \pi_\ell^{(2)}), b_\ell^{(2)})$ from $\widehat{\mathcal{F}}_{\text{CERT}}$; For $\ell \in [n]$, set
$W_\ell \leftarrow \text{TRE.Enc}(\text{pk}, \bot; 0)$ if W_ℓ is missing or $b_\ell^{(2)} = 0$ or
$\text{NIZK}_{\mathcal{R}_5}.\text{Verify}((\text{pk}, W_\ell), \pi_\ell^{(2)}) = 0$.
— (i) If $s_i = (\bot, v_i)$: compute
  – $V_i \leftarrow \text{TRE.ReRand}(\text{pk}, W_0; \gamma_i)$ and
    $\pi_i^{(3)} \leftarrow \text{NIZK}_{\mathcal{R}_6} \left\{ (\text{pk}, (W_0, \ldots, W_n), V_i), (\gamma_i, 0) : V_i = \text{TRE.ReRand}(\text{pk}, W_\ell; \gamma_i) \right\}$.
  – $U_i \leftarrow \text{TRE.Enc}(\text{pk}, v_i; \delta_i)$ and
    $\pi_i^{(4)} \leftarrow \text{NIZK}_{\mathcal{R}_5} \left\{ (\text{pk}, U_i), (\delta_i, v_i) : U_i = \text{TRE.Enc}(\text{pk}, v_i; \delta_i) \right\}$.
— (ii) If $s_i = (V_j, \bot)$: compute
  – $V_i \leftarrow \text{TRE.ReRand}(\text{pk}, W_j; \gamma_i)$ and
    $\pi_i^{(3)} \leftarrow \text{NIZK}_{\mathcal{R}_6} \left\{ (\text{pk}, (W_0, \ldots, W_n), V_i), (\gamma_i, j) : V_i = \text{TRE.ReRand}(\text{pk}, W_\ell; \gamma_i) \right\}$.
  – $U_i \leftarrow \text{TRE.Enc}(\text{pk}, \bot; \delta_i)$ and
    $\pi_i^{(4)} \leftarrow \text{NIZK}_{\mathcal{R}_5} \left\{ (\text{pk}, U_i), (\delta_i, \bot) : U_i = \text{TRE.Enc}(\text{pk}, \bot; \delta_i) \right\}$.
— Send $(\text{SIGN}, \text{sid}, \text{ssid}, (U_i, V_i, \pi_i^{(3)}, \pi_i^{(4)}))$ to $\widehat{\mathcal{F}}_{\text{CERT}}$ and receive
$(\text{SIGNATURE}, \text{sid}, \text{ssid}, (U_i, V_i, \pi_i^{(3)}, \pi_i^{(4)}), \sigma_i^{(3)})$ from $\widehat{\mathcal{F}}_{\text{CERT}}$, where $\text{ssid} = (V_i, \text{ssid}')$ for
some ssid'.
— Send $(\text{SUBMIT}, \text{sid}, \langle \text{ssid}, (U_i, V_i, \pi_i^{(3)}, \pi_i^{(4)}), \sigma_i^{(3)} \rangle)$ to $\bar{\mathcal{G}}_{\text{BB}}$.

Fig. 4. Mix-net based liquid democracy scheme $\Pi_{\text{MIX-LIQUID}}$ in $\{\bar{\mathcal{G}}_{\text{BB}}, \widehat{\mathcal{F}}_{\text{CERT}}\}$-hybrid world
(Part II)

Ballot Casting Phase. As depicted in Fig. 4, the ballot casting phase consists of
two rounds. In the first round, each voter V_i, $i \in [n]$ first fetches the trustees'
partial public keys $\{\overline{\text{pk}}_j\}_{j=1}^k$ from $\bar{\mathcal{G}}_{\text{BB}}$. She then checks the validity of their
attached NIZK proofs. If all the NIZK proofs are verified, she computes and
stores the election public key as $\text{pk} \leftarrow \text{TRE.CombinePK}(\{\overline{\text{pk}}_j\}_{j=1}^k)$. In addition,
the voter V_i picks a random temporary ID $w_i \leftarrow \{0,1\}^\lambda$. She then uses the

---

Tally (Part I)

Upon receiving (TALLY, sid) from the environment $\mathcal{Z}$, the trustee T_j, where $j \in [k]$, operates as the follows:

o Round 1 to k:
- If $j = 1$, send (READ, sid) to $\bar{\mathcal{G}}_{BB}$, and obtain (READ, sid, $state$) from $\bar{\mathcal{G}}_{BB}$. For $\ell \in [n]$:
    - If $\langle$ssid, $(W_\ell, \pi_\ell^{(2)}), \sigma_\ell^{(2)}\rangle$ is contained in $state$, then send
      (VERIFY, sid, ssid, $(W_\ell, \pi_\ell^{(2)}), \sigma_\ell^{(2)})$ to $\widehat{\mathcal{F}}_{CERT}$, and receive
      (VERIFIED, sid, ssid, $(W_\ell, \pi_\ell^{(2)}), b_j^{(2)})$ from $\widehat{\mathcal{F}}_{CERT}$;
    - If $\langle$ssid, $(U_\ell, V_\ell, \pi_\ell^{(3)}, \pi_\ell^{(4)}), \sigma_\ell^{(3)}\rangle$, is contained in $state$, then send
      (VERIFY, sid, ssid, $(U_\ell, V_\ell, \pi_\ell^{(3)}, \pi_\ell^{(4)}), \sigma_\ell^{(3)})$ to $\widehat{\mathcal{F}}_{CERT}$, receive
      (VERIFIED, sid, ssid, $(U_\ell, V_\ell, \pi_\ell^{(3)}, \pi_\ell^{(4)}), b_j^{(3)})$ from $\widehat{\mathcal{F}}_{CERT}$;

    Set $i = 0$. For $\ell \in [n]$, define $e_i^{(0)} := (W_\ell, U_\ell, V_\ell)$ and $i = i + 1$ if the following holds:
    - W_ℓ, U_ℓ, V_ℓ exist in $state$ and $b_\ell^{(2)} \cdot b_\ell^{(3)} = 1$;
    - $\mathsf{NIZK}_{\mathcal{R}_5}.\mathsf{Verify}((pk, W_\ell), \pi_\ell^{(2)}) = 1$;
    - $\mathsf{NIZK}_{\mathcal{R}_6}.\mathsf{Verify}((pk, (W_0, \ldots, W_n), V_\ell), \pi_\ell^{(3)}) = 1$;
    - $\mathsf{NIZK}_{\mathcal{R}_5}.\mathsf{Verify}((pk, U_\ell), \pi_\ell^{(4)}) = 1$;
      (Set $n' := i$ after the above process.)
- (If $j > 1$, T_j sends (READ, sid) to $\bar{\mathcal{G}}_{BB}$, and obtain (READ, sid, $state$) from $\bar{\mathcal{G}}_{BB}$; T_j
  then fetches $(e_{i,t}^{(j-2)})_{i=1}^{n'}, (e_{i,t}^{(j-1)})_{i=1}^{n'}, \pi_{j-1}^{(5)}$ from $state$ and check
  $\mathsf{NIZK}_{\mathcal{R}_7}.\mathsf{Verify}((pk, (e_{1,t}^{(j-1)}, \ldots, e_{n',t}^{(j-1)}), (e_{1,t}^{(j)}, \ldots, e_{n',t}^{(j)})), \pi_j^{(5)}) = 1$, for $t \in [3]$.)
  T_j randomly picks a permutation Π_j over [n']; For $i \in [n']$, set
  $e_{i,1}^{(j)} \leftarrow \mathsf{TRE.ReRand}(pk, e_{\Pi_j(i),1}^{(j-1)}; r_{i,1}^{(j)})$, $e_{i,2}^{(j)} \leftarrow \mathsf{TRE.ReRand}(pk, e_{\Pi_j(i),2}^{(j-1)}; r_{i,2}^{(j)})$, and
  $e_{i,3}^{(j)} \leftarrow \mathsf{TRE.ReRand}(pk, e_{\Pi_j(i),3}^{(j-1)}; r_{i,3}^{(j)})$, where $r_{i,1}^{(j)}, r_{i,2}^{(j)}, r_{i,3}^{(j)}$ are fresh randomness.
  Compute

$$
\pi_j^{(5)} \leftarrow \mathsf{NIZK}_{\mathcal{R}_7}
\left\{
\begin{array}{c}
\left(pk, (e_1^{(j-1)}, \ldots, e_{n'}^{(j-1)}), (e_1^{(j)}, \ldots, e_{n'}^{(j)})\right), \\
\left(\Pi_j, (r_{i,1}^{(j)}, r_{i,2}^{(j)}, r_{i,3}^{(j)})_{i \in [n']}\right) : \\
\forall i \in [n'] : \quad e_{i,1}^{(j)} = \mathsf{TRE.ReRand}\left(pk, e_{\Pi_j(i),1}^{(j-1)}; r_{i,1}^{(j)}\right) \\
\wedge \ e_{i,2}^{(j)} = \mathsf{TRE.ReRand}\left(pk, e_{\Pi_j(i),2}^{(j-1)}; r_{i,2}^{(j)}\right) \\
\wedge \ e_{i,3}^{(j)} = \mathsf{TRE.ReRand}\left(pk, e_{\Pi_j(i),3}^{(j-1)}; r_{i,3}^{(j)}\right)
\end{array}
\right\}
$$

- Send (SIGN, sid, ssid, $(e_{i,1}^{(j)}, e_{i,2}^{(j)}, e_{i,3}^{(j)})_{i=1}^{n'}, \pi_j^{(5)})$) to $\widehat{\mathcal{F}}_{CERT}$ and receive
  (SIGNATURE, sid, ssid, $(e_{i,1}^{(j)}, e_{i,2}^{(j)}, e_{i,3}^{(j)})_{i=1}^{n'}, \pi_j^{(5)}), \sigma_j^{(4)})$ from $\widehat{\mathcal{F}}_{CERT}$, where
  ssid = (T_j, ssid') for some ssid'.
- Send (SUBMIT, sid, $\langle$ssid, $(e_{i,1}^{(j)}, e_{i,2}^{(j)}, e_{i,3}^{(j)})_{i=1}^{n'}, \pi_j^{(5)}, \sigma_j^{(4)}\rangle$) to $\bar{\mathcal{G}}_{BB}$.

Fig. 5. Mix-net based liquid democracy scheme $\Pi_{\text{MIX-LIQUID}}$ in $\{\bar{\mathcal{G}}_{BB}, \widehat{\mathcal{F}}_{CERT}\}$-hybrid world (Part III)

election public key pk to encrypt w_i as $W_i \leftarrow \mathsf{TRE.Enc}(pk, w_i; \beta_i)$ with fresh randomness β_i. She also computes the corresponding NIZK

$$
\pi_i^{(2)} \leftarrow \mathsf{NIZK}_{\mathcal{R}_5}\left\{(pk, W_i), (\beta_i, w_i) : W_i = \mathsf{TRE.Enc}(pk, w_i; \beta_i)\right\}
$$

┌─ **Tally (Part II)** ───

○ Round $k + 1$:

— Send (READ, sid) to $\bar{\mathcal{G}}_{BB}$, and obtain (READ, sid, $state$) from $\bar{\mathcal{G}}_{BB}$. For $j \in [k]$, if $\langle$ssid, $(e_{i,1}^{(j)}, e_{i,2}^{(j)}, e_{i,3}^{(j)})_{i=1}^{n'}, \pi_j^{(5)}, \sigma_j^{(4)}\rangle$ is contained in $state$, then send (VERIFY, sid, ssid, $(e_{i,1}^{(j)}, e_{i,2}^{(j)}, e_{i,3}^{(j)})_{i=1}^{n'}, \pi_j^{(5)}), \sigma_\ell^{(4)})$ to $\widehat{\mathcal{F}}_{CERT}$, and receive (VERIFIED, sid, ssid, $(e_{i,1}^{(j)}, e_{i,2}^{(j)}, e_{i,3}^{(j)})_{i=1}^{n'}, \pi_j^{(5)}), b_j^{(4)})$ from $\widehat{\mathcal{F}}_{CERT}$; if $b_j^{(4)} = 1$, check $\mathsf{NIZK}_{\mathcal{R}_7}.\mathsf{Verify}((\mathsf{pk}, (e_{1,t}^{(j-1)}, \ldots, e_{n',t}^{(j-1)}), (e_{1,t}^{(j)}, \ldots, e_{n',t}^{(j)})), \pi_j^{(5)}) = 1$, for $t \in [3]$. If any of the above checks is invalid, halt.

— For $i \in [n']$, $t \in [3]$ compute $\overline{m}_{i,t}^{(j)} \leftarrow \mathsf{TRE.ShareDec}(\mathsf{pk}, \overline{\mathsf{sk}}_j, e_{i,t}^{(k)})$. and

$$\pi_{j,i,t}^{(6)} \leftarrow \mathsf{NIZK}_{\mathcal{R}_8} \left\{ \begin{array}{l} (\overline{\mathsf{pk}}_j, e_{i,t}^{(k)}, \overline{m}_{i,t}^{(j)}), (\alpha_j, \overline{\mathsf{sk}}_j) : \\ \overline{m}_{i,t}^{(j)} \leftarrow \mathsf{TRE.ShareDec}(\overline{\mathsf{sk}}, e_{i,t}^{(k)}) \\ \wedge (\overline{\mathsf{pk}}_j, \overline{\mathsf{sk}}_j) \leftarrow \mathsf{TRE.Keygen}(\alpha_j) \end{array} \right\}$$

— Send (SIGN, sid, ssid, $(\overline{m}_{i,t}^{(j)}, \pi_{j,i,t}^{(6)})_{i \in [n'], t \in [3]})$ to $\widehat{\mathcal{F}}_{CERT}$ and receives (SIGNATURE, sid, ssid, $(\overline{m}_{i,t}^{(j)}, \pi_{j,i,t}^{(6)})_{i \in [n'], t \in [3]}, \sigma_j^{(5)})$ from $\widehat{\mathcal{F}}_{CERT}$, where ssid = $(\mathsf{T}_j, \text{ssid}')$ for some ssid'.

— Send (SUBMIT, sid, $\langle$ssid, $(\overline{m}_{i,t}^{(j)}, \pi_{j,i,t}^{(6)})_{i \in [n'], t \in [3]}, \sigma_j^{(5)})\rangle$) to $\bar{\mathcal{G}}_{BB}$.

Upon receiving (READRESULT, sid) from the environment $\mathcal{Z}$, the voter V_i, where $i \in [n]$, operates as follows:

— Send (READ, sid) to $\bar{\mathcal{G}}_{BB}$, and and obtain (READ, sid, $state$) from $\bar{\mathcal{G}}_{BB}$.

  For $j \in [k]$, if $\langle$ssid, $(\overline{m}_{i,t}^{(j)}, \pi_{j,i,t}^{(6)})_{i \in [n'], t \in [3]}, \sigma_j^{(5)}\rangle$ is contained in $state$, send (VERIFY, sid, ssid, $(\overline{m}_{i,t}^{(j)}, \pi_{j,i,t}^{(6)})_{i \in [n'], t \in [3]}, \sigma_j^{(5)})$ to $\widehat{\mathcal{F}}_{CERT}$, and receive (VERIFIED, sid, ssid, $(\overline{m}_{i,t}^{(j)}, \pi_{j,i,t}^{(6)})_{i \in [n'], t \in [3]}, b_j^{(5)})$ from $\widehat{\mathcal{F}}_{CERT}$. If $\prod_{j=1}^k b_j^{(5)} = 1$, for all $j \in [k], i \in [n'], t \in [3]$, check $\mathsf{NIZK}_{\mathcal{R}_8}.\mathsf{Verify}((e_{i,t}^{(k)}, \overline{m}_{i,t}^{(j)}, \overline{\mathsf{pk}}_i), \pi_{i,j,t}^{(6)}) = 1$. If any of the above checks is invalid, return (ERROR, sid) to the environment $\mathcal{Z}$ and halt.

— For $i \in [n']$: compute $m_{i,t} \leftarrow \mathsf{TRE.ShareCombine}((k, k), e_{i,t}^{(k)}, \{\overline{m}_{i,t}^{(j)}\}_{j=1}^k)$, $t \in [3]$; define $B_i := (m_{i,1}, m_{i,2}, m_{i,3})$.

— Calculate election result $result \leftarrow \mathsf{TallyProcess}(\{B_i\}_{i \in [n']})$, and return (READRESULTRETURN, sid, $result$) to $\mathcal{Z}$.

───

Fig. 6. Mix-net based liquid democracy scheme $\Pi_{\text{MIX-LIQUID}}$ in $\{\bar{\mathcal{G}}_{BB}, \widehat{\mathcal{F}}_{CERT}\}$-hybrid world (Part IV)

to show she is the creator of this ciphertext. Voter V_i then signs and posts $(W_i, \pi_i^{(2)})$ to $\bar{\mathcal{G}}_{BB}$. In the second round, each voter V_i, $i \in [n]$ first fetches all the posted encrypted temporary IDs from $\bar{\mathcal{G}}_{BB}$, and checks their attached NIZK proofs. For any missing or invalid (encrypted) temporary IDs, the voters replace them with $\mathsf{TRE.Enc}(\mathsf{pk}, \bot; 0)$, which is the encryption of $\bot$ with trivial randomness. Moreover, the voters also defines $W_0 \leftarrow \mathsf{TRE.Enc}(\mathsf{pk}, \bot; 0)$. The statement for liquid democracy, s_i, can be parsed as either (i) $(\mathsf{V}_j, \bot)$ or (ii) $(\bot, v_i)$.

In Case (i) $(\mathsf{V}_j, \bot)$, i.e. delegating to voter V_j, the voter produces V_i as a re-randomized W_j and U_i as encryption of $\bot$. She then gives a NIZK proof showing that V_i is re-randomized from one of the ciphertexts in $(W_0, \ldots, W_n)$ and another NIZK proof showing U_i is created by her. Denote the corresponding proofs as $\pi_i^{(3)}$ and $\pi_i^{(4)}$, respectively. V_i signs and posts $(U_i, V_i, \pi_i^{(3)}, \pi_i^{(4)})$ to $\bar{\mathcal{G}}_{BB}$.

In Case (ii) $(\perp, v_i)$, i.e. voting directly v_i, analogous to Case (ii), the voter produces V_i as a re-randomized W_0 and U_i as encryption of v_i. Meanwhile, she also gives a NIZK proof showing that V_i is re-randomized from one of the ciphertexts in $(W_0, \ldots, W_n)$ and another NIZK proof showing U_i is created by her. Denote the corresponding proofs as $\pi_i^{(3)}$ and $\pi_i^{(4)}$, respectively. V_i signs and posts $(U_i, V_i, \pi_i^{(3)}, \pi_i^{(4)})$ to $\bar{\mathcal{G}}_{BB}$.

Tally Phase. The tally phase is depicted in Figs. 5 and 6. The trustees first fetches (W_i, V_i, U_i) (which is viewed as the submitted ballot for voter V_i) from $\bar{\mathcal{G}}_{BB}$ and check their attached NIZK proofs. All the invalid ballots will be discard. Let n' be the number of valid ballots. All the trustees then jointly shuffle the ballots via a re-encryption mix-net. More specifically, each trustee sequentially permutes (W_i, V_i, U_i) as a bundle using shuffle re-encryption. To ensure correctness, the trustee also produces a NIZK proof showing the correctness of the shuffle re-encryption process. After that, upon receiving (TALLY, sid) from the environment, all the trustees T_j check the correctness of the entire mix-net and then jointly decrypt the mixed ballots using TRE.ShareDec. More specifically, each trustee will sign and post its decryption shares to $\bar{\mathcal{G}}_{BB}$.

Each voter can then compute the tally result as follows. The voter first fetches all the decryption shares and checks their validity using $\mathsf{NIZK}_{\mathcal{R}_8}$.Verify. Upon success, the voter uses TRE.ShareCombine to reconstruct the messages. She then use TallyProcess as described in Fig. 2 to calculate the final tally.

Remark 1. The re-randmonizable encryption (TRE) scheme used in this protocol can be replaced by a re-randomizable RCCA encryption scheme. Here RCCA is the short name for *replayable CCA* defined by Canetti, Krawczyk, and Nielsen [9]. Several RCCA constructions can be found in literature [11,12,19,28]. In our construction, it is possible to distribute a publicly verifiable RCCA encryption scheme, e.g. [12] and then use it as an enhanced version of TRE. Subsequently, $\mathsf{NIZK}_{\mathcal{R}_6}$ can be removed. Since the running time of proving/verifying $\mathsf{NIZK}_{\mathcal{R}_6}$ is linear in the number of voters n, it is more efficient to use RCCA instead of TRE for large n in practice.

Theorem 1. *Protocol $\Pi_{\text{MIX-LIQUID}}$ described in Figs. 3, 4, 5 and 6 UC-realizes $\mathcal{F}_{\text{LIQUID}}$ in the $\{\bar{\mathcal{G}}_{BB}, \widehat{\mathcal{F}}_{\text{CERT}}\}$-hybrid world against static corruption.*

4   Further Discussions

Statement Policy. We initiate the study of statement voting and liquid democracy in this work. Our statement voting concept can be significantly extended to support much richer ballot statements, which opens a door for designing a new class of e-voting schemes. A natural question to ask is what type of statements are allowed. For correctness, the (deterministic) TallyProcess function should be a symmetric function in the sense that its output does not depend on the order of the ballots to be counted. Moreover, the voting statement has a maximum running time restriction to prevent DoS, and it should not depend on partial tally result. This is known as fairness. Namely, the statement execution cannot be conditional on the partial tally result at the moment when the ballot is counted. On the other hand, the statement can take input as external information oracles, such as News, Stock market, etc. When statement voting is integrated with a blockchain infrastructure, our scheme can be used to enable *offline voting* or *smart voting*. In particular, the voters may submit their statement ballot any time before the election on the blockchain; during the tally phase, the voter's ballots will be decrypted, and their statements will define their final votes based on the latest information provided by News oracles on the blockchain.

This line of research is far from being completed. We also remark that, voting policies can be heavily influenced by local legal and societal conditions. How to define "right" voting policy itself is a very interesting question. We believe our techniques here have the potential to help people to identify suitable voting policies which can further eliminate the barriers to democracy.

Trusted Setup. Typically, trusted setup assumptions[3] are required for constructing UC-secure e-voting systems. Common Reference String (CRS) and Random Oracle (RO) are two popular choices in practice. If an e-voting system uses CRS, then we need to trust the party who generates the CRS, which, in our opinion, is a stronger assumption than believing no adversary can break a secure hash function, e.g., SHA3. Therefore, in this work, we realize our liquid democracy voting system in the RO model. As a future direction, we will construct more solutions to liquid democracy. For example, an alternative approach is as follows: we first use MPC to generate a CRS; then we construct liquid democracy voting system by using the CRS. As argued above, we need to trust the parties who generate the CRS; e.g., at least one honest MPC player.

Privacy and Coercion Resilience. Both statement voting and liquid democracy voting extend (deviate) from the conventional e-voting; therefore, the conventional privacy definitions are no longer suitable for these new types of voting schemes. For instance, if delegation loop is not allowed in the liquid democracy, how much voter privacy can be possibly achieved? We will investigate the privacy of statement voting and liquid democracy in depth in our future work.

Finally, we note that coercion resilience is critical in many scenarios. We will investigate this strong security requirement in our future work, too. Recently, Daian *et al.* [14] discussed the difficulty to achieve coercion resilience in the on-chain voting. We remark that Daian *et al.* only excluded a special class of voting protocols that "users can generate their own keys outside of a trusted environment". A potential approach is to follow our preliminary result [3]; there, very different technique has been explored for achieving coercion resilience: voters' keys and correlated secret information are generated *inside* a trusted hardware which cannot be obtained by the coercer.

Voter's Complexity. In our FHE-based and MPC-based solutions, the voter's complexity is constant in the number of ballots; the voting tally members have

---

[3] Most non-trivial functionalities (including the e-voting functionality) cannot be UC-realized in the plain model [6,8,10].

linear (or superlinear) complexity with respect to the number of voters, which is asymptotically the same as many existing voting schemes. In our mix-net based protocol, the voter's complexity is linear in the number of ballots; we remark that, this is our implementation choice for small scale, statement voting. As already discussed in Remark 1 in previous section, we can replace the TRE encryption with an RCCA encryption [11,12,19,28] to achieve better (i.e., constant) voter's complexity in the mix-net based protocol.

Acknowledgement. We thank Jeremy Clark and the anonymous reviewers for their constructive comments. The first author was partially supported by EPSRC grant EP/P034578/1. The second author was partially supported by NSF award #1801470. This work is also supported by Ergo platform, Fractal Platform, and Blockchain institute.

A   Security Definition for TRE

Definition 3. *We say* TRE = {Setup, Keygen, Enc, Dec, CombinePK, CombineSK, ShareDec, ShareCombine, ReRand} *is a secure threshold re-randomizable public key encryption if the following properties hold:*

Key combination correctness: *If* $\{(\mathrm{pk}_i, \mathrm{sk}_i)\}_{i \in [k]}$ *are all valid key pairs,*
   $\mathrm{pk} := \mathsf{TRE.CombinePK}(\{\mathrm{pk}_i\}_{i \in [k]})$ *and* $\mathrm{sk} := \mathsf{TRE.CombineSK}(\{\mathrm{sk}_i\}_{i \in [k]})$,
   then $(\mathrm{pk}, \mathrm{sk})$ *is also a valid key pair. For all ciphertext* $c \in \mathcal{C}_{\mathrm{pk}}$, *where* $\mathcal{C}_{\mathrm{pk}}$ *is the ciphertext-space defined by* pk, *we have*

$$\mathsf{TRE.Dec}(\mathrm{sk}, c) = \mathsf{TRE.ShareCombine}(c, \mathsf{TRE.ShareDec}(\mathrm{sk}_1, c), \dots, \mathsf{TRE.ShareDec}(\mathrm{sk}_k, c))$$

Ciphertext transformative indistinguishability:
   There exists a PPT *algorithm* Trans *such that if* $\{(\mathrm{pk}_i, \mathrm{sk}_i)\}_{i \in [k]}$ *are all valid key pairs,* $\mathrm{pk} := \mathsf{TRE.CombinePK}(\{\mathrm{pk}_i\}_{i \in [k]})$ *and* $\mathrm{sk} := \mathsf{TRE.CombineSK}(\{\mathrm{sk}_i\}_{i \in [k]})$, *then for all message* m, *for any* $j \in [k]$, *the following holds.*

$$\left(\mathsf{param}, \mathsf{TRE.Trans}(c, \{\mathrm{sk}_i\}_{i \in [k] \setminus \{j\}})\right) \approx \left(\mathsf{param}, \mathsf{TRE.Enc}(\mathrm{pk}, m)\right)$$

IND-CPA security: *We say that a* TRE *scheme achieves* indistinguishability *under plaintext attacks (IND-CPA) if for any* PPT *adversary* $\mathcal{A}$ *the following advantage* AdvCPA *is negligible.*

   EXPERIMENT$^{\mathsf{CPA}}(1^\lambda)$
   ———————————————————
   1. Run param $\leftarrow$ TRE.Setup(1^λ).
   2. Run $(\mathrm{pk}, \mathrm{sk}) \leftarrow$ TRE.Keygen(param);
   4. $\mathcal{A}(\mathrm{pk})$ *outputs* m_0, m_1 *of equal length;*
   5. Pick $b \leftarrow \{0,1\}$; *Run* $c \leftarrow$ TRE.Enc(pk, m_b);
   6. $\mathcal{A}(c)$ *outputs* b^*; *It returns* 1 *if* $b = b^*$; *else, returns* 0.
   We define the advantage of $\mathcal{A}$ *as*

$$\mathsf{AdvCPA}_{\mathcal{A}}(1^\lambda) = \left| \Pr[\text{EXPERIMENT}^{\mathsf{CPA}}(1^\lambda) = 1] - \frac{1}{2} \right|.$$

Unlinkability: *We say a* TRE *scheme is* unlinkable *if for any* PPT *adversary* $\mathcal{A}$ *the following advantage* AdvUnlink *is negligible.*

$\text{EXPERIMENT}^{\text{Unlink}}(1^\lambda)$

   1. $\mathcal{A}$ outputs a set $\mathcal{I} \subset \{1,\dots,k\}$ of up to $k-1$ corrupted indices.

   2. For $i = [n]$, run $(\overline{pk}_i, \overline{sk}_i) \leftarrow$ TRE.Keygen$(1^\lambda; \omega_i)$;

   3. $\mathcal{A}(\{pk_j\}_{j \in [k] \setminus \mathcal{I}})$ outputs c_0, c_1;

   4. $b \leftarrow \{0,1\}$; $c' \leftarrow$ TRE.ReRand$(pk, c_b; \omega)$;

   5. $\mathcal{A}(c')$ outputs b^*; It returns 1 if $b = b^*$; else, returns 0.

We define the advantage of $\mathcal{A}$ as

$$\text{AdvUnlink}_{\mathcal{A}}(1^\lambda) = \left| \Pr[\text{EXPERIMENT}^{\text{Unlink}}(1^\lambda) = 1] - \frac{1}{2} \right|.$$

Share-simulation indistinguishability: *We say* TRE *scheme achieves* share-simulation indistinguishability *if there exists a* PPT *simulator* SimShareDec *such that for all valid key pairs $\{(pk_i, sk_i)\}_{i \in [k]}$, all subsets $\mathcal{I} \subsetneq [k]$, all message m, the following two distributions are computationally indistinguishable:*

$$(\text{param}, c, \text{SimShareDec}(c, m, \{\mu_i\}_{i \in \mathcal{I}})) \approx (\text{param}, c, \{\mu_j\}_{j \in [k] \setminus \mathcal{I}})$$

where param $\leftarrow$ TRE.Setup(1^λ), $c \leftarrow$ TRE.Enc(pk, m) *and* $\mu_j \leftarrow$ TRE.ShareDec(sk_j, c) *for* $j \in [k] \setminus \mathcal{I}$.

References

1. Adhocracy. Adhocracy official website. Accessed 21 Oct 2017
2. Adida, B.: Helios: web-based open-audit voting. In: USENIX Security (2008)
3. Alwen, J., Ostrovsky, R., Zhou, H.-S., Zikas, V.: Incoercible multi-party computation and universally composable receipt-free voting. In: Gennaro, R., Robshaw, M. (eds.) CRYPTO 2015, Part II. LNCS, vol. 9216, pp. 763–780. Springer, Heidelberg (2015). https://doi.org/10.1007/978-3-662-48000-7_37
4. Baum, C., Damgård, I., Orlandi, C.: Publicly auditable secure multi-party computation. In: Abdalla, M., De Prisco, R. (eds.) SCN 2014. LNCS, vol. 8642, pp. 175–196. Springer, Cham (2014). https://doi.org/10.1007/978-3-319-10879-7_11
5. Ben-Sasson, E., et al.: Zerocash: decentralized anonymous payments from bitcoin. In: 2014 IEEE Symposium on Security and Privacy, pp. 459–474. IEEE Computer Society Press, May 2014
6. Canetti, R.: Universally composable security: a new paradigm for cryptographic protocols. In: 42nd FOCS, pp. 136–145. IEEE Computer Society Press, October 2001
7. Canetti, R.: Universally composable signatures, certification and authentication. Cryptology ePrint Archive, Report 2003/239 (2003). http://eprint.iacr.org/2003/239
8. Canetti, R., Fischlin, M.: Universally composable commitments. In: Kilian, J. (ed.) CRYPTO 2001. LNCS, vol. 2139, pp. 19–40. Springer, Heidelberg (2001). https://doi.org/10.1007/3-540-44647-8_2

9. Canetti, R., Krawczyk, H., Nielsen, J.B.: Relaxing chosen-ciphertext security. In: Boneh, D. (ed.) CRYPTO 2003. LNCS, vol. 2729, pp. 565–582. Springer, Heidelberg (2003). https://doi.org/10.1007/978-3-540-45146-4_33

10. Canetti, R., Kushilevitz, E., Lindell, Y.: On the limitations of universally composable two-party computation without set-up assumptions. In: Biham, E. (ed.) EUROCRYPT 2003. LNCS, vol. 2656, pp. 68–86. Springer, Heidelberg (2003). https://doi.org/10.1007/3-540-39200-9_5

11. Chaidos, P., Cortier, V., Fuchsbauer, G., Galindo, D.: Beleniosrf: a non-interactive receipt-free electronic voting scheme. In: CCS 2016, pp. 1614–1625. ACM, New York (2016)

12. Chase, M., Kohlweiss, M., Lysyanskaya, A., Meiklejohn, S.: Malleable proof systems and applications. In: Pointcheval, D., Johansson, T. (eds.) EUROCRYPT 2012. LNCS, vol. 7237, pp. 281–300. Springer, Heidelberg (2012). https://doi.org/10.1007/978-3-642-29011-4_18

13. Chaum, D., Ryan, P.Y.A., Schneider, S.: A practical voter-verifiable election scheme. In: di Vimercati, S.C., Syverson, P., Gollmann, D. (eds.) ESORICS 2005. LNCS, vol. 3679, pp. 118–139. Springer, Heidelberg (2005). https://doi.org/10.1007/11555827_8

14. Daian, P., Kell, T., Miers, I., Juels, A.: On-Chain Vote Buying and the Rise of Dark DAOs (2018). http://hackingdistributed.com/2018/07/02/on-chain-vote-buying/

15. Degrave, J.: Getopinionated. GitHub repository. Accessed 21 Oct 2017

16. Ford, B.: Delegative democracy (2002). http://www.brynosaurus.com/deleg/deleg.pdf

17. Froelicher, D., et al.: Unlynx: a decentralized system for privacy-conscious data sharing. Proc. Privacy Enhancing Technol. **4**, 152–170 (2017)

18. Groth, J.: Evaluating security of voting schemes in the universal composability framework. In: Jakobsson, M., Yung, M., Zhou, J. (eds.) ACNS 2004. LNCS, vol. 3089, pp. 46–60. Springer, Heidelberg (2004). https://doi.org/10.1007/978-3-540-24852-1_4

19. Groth, J.: Rerandomizable and replayable adaptive chosen ciphertext attack secure cryptosystems. In: Naor, M. (ed.) TCC 2004. LNCS, vol. 2951, pp. 152–170. Springer, Heidelberg (2004). https://doi.org/10.1007/978-3-540-24638-1_9

20. Hardt, S., Lopes, L.: Google votes: a liquid democracy experiment on a corporate social network. Technical Disclosure Commons (2015). http://www.tdcommons.org/dpubs_series/79

21. Kiayias, A., Zacharias, T., Zhang, B.: DEMOS-2: scalable E2E verifiable elections without random oracles. In: Ray, I., Li, N., Kruegel, C. (eds.) ACM CCS 2015, pp. 352–363. ACM Press, October 2015

22. Kiayias, A., Zacharias, T., Zhang, B.: End-to-end verifiable elections in the standard model. In: Oswald, E., Fischlin, M. (eds.) EUROCRYPT 2015, Part II. LNCS, vol. 9057, pp. 468–498. Springer, Heidelberg (2015). https://doi.org/10.1007/978-3-662-46803-6_16

23. Kulyk, O., Marky, K., Neumann, S., Volkamer, M.: Introducing proxy voting to helios. In: ARES, pp. 98–106. IEEE Computer Society (2016)

24. Kulyk, O., Neumann, S., Marky, K., Budurushi, J., Volkamer, M.: Coercion-resistant proxy voting. In: ICT Systems Security and Privacy Protection (2016)

25. Kulyk, O., Neumann, S., Marky, K., Volkamer, M.: Enabling vote delegation for boardroom voting. In: Brenner, M., et al. (eds.) FC 2017. LNCS, vol. 10323, pp. 419–433. Springer, Cham (2017). https://doi.org/10.1007/978-3-319-70278-0_26

26. LiquidFeedback. LiquidFeedback official website. Accessed 21 Oct 2017

27. Moran, T., Naor, M.: Receipt-free universally-verifiable voting with everlasting privacy. In: Dwork, C. (ed.) CRYPTO 2006. LNCS, vol. 4117, pp. 373–392. Springer, Heidelberg (2006). https://doi.org/10.1007/11818175_22
28. Prabhakaran, M., Rosulek, M.: Rerandomizable RCCA encryption. In: Menezes, A. (ed.) CRYPTO 2007. LNCS, vol. 4622, pp. 517–534. Springer, Heidelberg (2007). https://doi.org/10.1007/978-3-540-74143-5_29
29. Democracy Earth. The social smart contract. An open source white paper, 1 September 2017. Accessed 21 Oct 2017
30. Unruh, D., Müller-Quade, J.: Universally composable incoercibility. In: Rabin, T. (ed.) CRYPTO 2010. LNCS, vol. 6223, pp. 411–428. Springer, Heidelberg (2010). https://doi.org/10.1007/978-3-642-14623-7_22
31. Zhai, E., Wolinsky, D.I., Chen, R., Syta, E., Teng, C., Ford, B.: Anonrep: towards tracking-resistant anonymous reputation. In: NSDI 2016, pp. 583–596 (2016)

Fast Authentication from Aggregate Signatures with Improved Security

Muslum Ozgur Ozmen[1][(✉)], Rouzbeh Behnia[1], and Attila A. Yavuz[2]

[1] Oregon State University, Corvallis, USA
{ozmenmu,behniar}@oregonstate.edu
[2] University of South Florida, Tampa, USA
attilaayavuz@usf.edu

Abstract. An attempt to derive signer-efficient digital signatures from aggregate signatures was made in a signature scheme referred to as Structure-free Compact Rapid Authentication (SCRA) (IEEE TIFS 2017). In this paper, we first mount a practical universal forgery attack against the NTRU instantiation of SCRA by observing only 8161 signatures. Second, we propose a new signature scheme (**FAAS**), which transforms any single-signer aggregate signature scheme into a signer-efficient scheme. We show two efficient instantiations of **FAAS**, namely, **FAAS-NTRU** and **FAAS-RSA**, both of which achieve high computational efficiency. Our experiments confirmed that **FAAS** schemes achieve up to 100× faster signature generation compared to their underlying schemes. Moreover, **FAAS** schemes eliminate some of the costly operations such as Gaussian sampling, rejection sampling, and exponentiation at the signature generation that are shown to be susceptible to side-channel attacks. This enables **FAAS** schemes to enhance the security and efficiency of their underlying schemes. Finally, we prove that **FAAS** schemes are secure (in random oracle model), and open-source both our attack and **FAAS** implementations for public testing purposes.

Keywords: Authentication · Digital signatures · Universal forgery · NTRU-based signatures

1 Introduction

Efficient authentication is critical for applications that need to generate a large throughput of authenticated data in a short amount of time. For instance, in smart grids [23,42], vehicular [1,24] and commercial drone networks [38,43], a large number of messages should be authenticated and transmitted to ensure reliable service and safe operation. While conventional digital signatures (e.g., RSA [36], ECDSA [5]) are deemed as an ideal mean to provide authentication, they might not offer the computational efficiency required by such applications.

Work done in part while Attila A. Yavuz was at Oregon State University.

© International Financial Cryptography Association 2019
I. Goldberg and T. Moore (Eds.): FC 2019, LNCS 11598, pp. 686–705, 2019.
https://doi.org/10.1007/978-3-030-32101-7_39

It is essential to propose fast digital signature schemes that can meet with the stringent requirements of such applications.

Achieving this computational efficiency becomes even harder when considering security in the post-quantum era [2,28]. While efficient and easy-to-implement one-time/multiple-time signatures exist (e.g., [26]), the case for polynomially-unbounded signatures seems to be more difficult. The proposal of such schemes is also necessary to support post-quantum key encapsulation schemes [11]. In this direction, the Department of Energy (DOE) and the Department of Homeland Security (DHS) have shown increased interest in proposals on post-quantum secure authentication schemes [3] for smart grids. To ensure a smooth and timely transition, National Institute of Standards and Technology (NIST) has started the initial rounds of accepting proposals for PQ secure constructions [4].

Aggregate digital signature schemes allow multiple signatures to be aggregated into a single one [10]. They are used to achieve efficient signature generation as shown in [44] with Rapid Authentication (RA) scheme. In RA, the signer precomputes a set of individual signatures in the key generation algorithm, and aggregates a subset of them to efficiently compute signatures. However, RA requires messages to be in a predefined (fixed-length) format.

It is very desirable to develop fast digital signature schemes that can avoid both the storage/re-generation of one-time signatures and the need of a predefined message format. Such schemes can potentially support the legacy systems (aggregate RSA-based signatures [31]) and be secure against quantum computers, with the advent of post-quantum aggregate signature schemes [25]. One recent attempt to address these issues was proposed in *Structure-free Compact and Rapid Authentication (SCRA)* [45]. In this paper, we show that, it is a challenging and yet feasible task to create such fast signatures by first mounting an attack to SCRA [45], and then constructing a new generic scheme that can address the aforementioned limitations.

1.1 Our Contributions

Our contributions are two-fold: (i) We identify a weakness in SCRA which leads to a universal forgery attack on its lattice-based instantiations. (ii) We then present a new scheme called *Fast Authentication from Aggregate Signatures* (FAAS) which achieves significant performance gains on the signer's side along with an improved security in terms of side-channel resiliency.

Attack on Lattice-Based Instantiation of SCRA [45]: We identified a flaw in generic SCRA where each signature leaks the aggregation of a subset of the private key, along with their corresponding indexes. In the lattice-based instantiation of SCRA, we show how the adversary can form a set of linear equations, and forge signatures on any message only after observing 8161 signatures. We have fully implemented our attack and forged signatures in a few milliseconds after a one-time 2.5-hour learning phase.

Table 1. Experimental performance comparison and analysis.

Schemes	Sign	Verify	Delay	Sig size	SK size	PK size	Online phase		
							Gauss	Exp	RS
RSA [36]	8.08	0.05	8.13	372	768	386	✗	✓	✗
ECDSA [5]	0.73	0.93	1.66	64	32	32	✗	✓	✗
Ed25519 [9]	0.13	0.33	0.46	64	32	32	✗	✓	✗
SPHINCS [8]	13.46	0.37	13.83	41000	1088	1056	✗	✗	✗
pqNTRUsign [25]	14.52	0.30	14.82	576	1024	1024	✓	✗	✓
FAAS-RSA	**0.19**	0.06	**0.25**	768	197408	1024	✗	✗	✗
FAAS-NTRU	**0.49**	0.71	**1.20**	3072	525328	1024	✗	✗	✗
FAAS-NTRU'	**0.14**	0.71	**0.85**	3072	1049600	1024	✗	✗	✗

FAAS schemes do not require any Gaussian sampling (Gauss), exponentiation (Exp) or rejection sampling (RS) at its online calculations. Therefore, they have an improved side-channel resiliency and better performance that is further explained in Sect. 5.1.

All sizes are in *Bytes (B)*. All times are in *milliseconds (ms)*. The results are obtained on a laptop equipped with an Intel i7 6th generation CPU operating at 2.6 GHz. All parameter sizes are selected to provide $\kappa = 128$-bit security level (except for SPHINCS [8], that provides $\kappa = 256$-bit security). A detailed performance analysis and comparison are given in Sect. 6.

Fast Authentication from Aggregate Signatures (FAAS): We present our new signature scheme **FAAS** that can be instantiated from any aggregate signature scheme. We prove the security of **FAAS** in the random oracle model (ROM) under the hardness of breaking the underlying aggregate signature scheme. We propose two efficient instantiations of **FAAS**: (i) An instantiation with *pqNTRUsign* [25] called **FAAS-NTRU** (ii) and an instantiation with *Condensed-RSA* [31] called **FAAS-RSA**. The desired properties of **FAAS** are as follows:

(i) Improved Side-Channel Resiliency: The signature generation of **FAAS** only relies on signature aggregation, and therefore improves the side-channel resiliency of its base schemes (i.e., [25,31]). For instance, **FAAS-NTRU** does not require any Gaussian sampling algorithm (in its signature generation) which is known to be susceptible to a number of side-channel attacks (e.g., [18,22]). Besides, **FAAS-NTRU** offers a fixed-time sign algorithm (as opposed to its underlying scheme [25]) since it does not require any rejection sampling. Moreover, **FAAS** instantiations offer deterministic signing and therefore immune to side-channel attacks targeting weak pseudorandom number generators (PRNGs). Lastly, **FAAS-RSA** is not susceptible to the attacks targeting the square-and-multiply method on traditional RSA signatures [20,34].

(ii) High Computational Efficiency: We instantiate **FAAS** with verification-efficient digital signature schemes to complement the benefits of the improved signature generation, and therefore achieving a low delay[1] for **FAAS** instantiations.

---

[1] Delay is defined as the aggregated time required to compute and verify a signature.

For instance, FAAS-RSA and FAAS-NTRU' improve the delay of their base schemes by $32\times$ and $17\times$, respectively.

(iii) Generic Design: FAAS can be instantiated with any aggregate signature. For example, several lattice-based post-quantum signature schemes (which require Gaussian and/or rejection sampling) have been proposed to the NIST post-quantum competition (e.g., Dilithium [16]). FAAS can be used to enhance the security (from side-channel perspective) and performance of these schemes provided that they offer a secure signature aggregation capability.

Limitations: FAAS has an increased private key size due to the storage of precomputed signatures. FAAS-RSA and FAAS-NTRU require 193 KB and 511 KB private keys, respectively, with $\kappa = 128$-bit security (see Table 1). This increased private key size; however, translates into $30\times$ and $42\times$ faster signing with an improved side-channel resiliency, for FAAS-RSA and FAAS-NTRU, respectively.

2   Preliminaries

Notation. $|a|$ denotes the bit length of variable a. $\mathcal{M}$ denotes the message space. $a \xleftarrow{\$} S$ denotes that a is selected from set S at random. In $x||y$, $||$ denotes the concatenation of bit strings of x and y. We represent vectors as bold letters (i.e., $\mathbf{a}$), and matrices are defined by bold capital letters (i.e., $\mathbf{A}$), while scalars are represented as non-bold letters (i.e., a). $||\mathbf{a}||_2$ and $||\mathbf{a}||_\infty$ denote the Euclidean norm and infinity norm of vector $\mathbf{a}$, respectively. We define hash functions $H_0 : \{0,1\}^* \to \{0,1\}^{l_0}$, $H_1 : \{0,1\}^* \to \{0,1\}^{l_1}$ and $H_2 : \{0,1\}^* \to \{0,1\}^{l_2}$ for some integers l_0, l_1 and l_2, to be defined in Sect. 6.2. $\mathcal{A}^{\mathcal{O}_1,\dots,\mathcal{O}_i}$ denotes that algorithm $\mathcal{A}$ is provided with access to oracles $\mathcal{O}_1, \dots, \mathcal{O}_i$.

Definition 1. *A digital signature* SGN = (Kg, Sig, Ver) *is defined as follows.*

- $(sk, PK) \leftarrow$ SGN.Kg(1^κ): Given the security parameter κ, it outputs the public/private key pair (sk, PK).
- $\sigma \leftarrow$ SGN.Sig(m, sk): Given a message m and sk, it outputs the signature σ.
- $\{0,1\} \leftarrow$ SGN.Ver(m, σ, PK): Given a message-signature pair (m, σ), and PK, it outputs $b \in \{0,1\}$.

We say that SGN *is correct if* $1 \leftarrow$ *SGN.Ver*($m,$ *SGN.Sig*(m, sk), PK).

Definition 2. *Existential Unforgeability under Chosen Message Attack (EU-CMA) [27] experiment* $Expl_{SGN,\mathcal{A}}^{EU-CMA}$ *against an adversary* $\mathcal{A}$ *is as follows.*

$L_m \leftarrow \emptyset$	$\mathrm{Sign}_{sk}(m_i)$
$(sk, PK) \leftarrow$ SGN.Kg(1^κ)	$\quad \sigma_i \leftarrow$ SGN.Sig(m_i, sk)
$(m^*, \sigma^*) \leftarrow \mathcal{A}^{\mathrm{Sign}_{sk}(\cdot)}(PK)$	$\quad L_m \leftarrow L_m \cup m_i$

We say $\mathcal{A}$ *wins in time* t, *and after making* q_S *signatures and* q_h *queries to random oracles* $(H_1, H_2,$ *and* $H_3)$, *if* $((\mathrm{SGN.Ver}(m^*, \sigma^*, PK) \wedge (m \cap L_m = \emptyset))$. *The advantage of* $\mathcal{A}$ *is defined as* $Adv_{SGN,\mathcal{A}}^{EU-CMA}(t, q_S, q_h) = \Pr[Exp_{SGN,\mathcal{A}}^{EU-CMA} = 1]$.

We define the notion of EU-CMA for aggregate signatures (A-EU-CMA) in Appendix A.

Definition 3. *A single-signer aggregate signature* ASig = (Kg,Sig,Agg,Ver) *is defined as follows.*

- *(sk, PK)* ← Asig.Kg(1$^\kappa$): *Given the security parameter κ as the input, it returns a private/public key pair (sk, PK).*
- *σ* ← Asig.Sig(m, sk): *Given a message $m \in \{0,1\}^*$ and sk as the input, it returns a signature γ of the message under sk.*
- *s* ← Asig.Agg($\sigma_1, \ldots, \sigma_L$): *Given a set of signatures ($\sigma_1, \ldots, \sigma_L$) as the input, it returns a single-compact signature s .*
- *$\{0,1\}$* ← Asig.Ver($\vec{m}, s, PK$): *Given messages $\vec{m} = (m_1, \ldots, m_L)$, s and PK as the input, it returns a bit: 1 means valid and 0 means invalid.*

Definition 4. *Agg function, that is used to aggregate multiple messages to a single message, is defined as follows.*

- *m* ← Agg($m_1, \ldots, m_L$): *Given a set of messages ($m_1, \ldots, m_L$) as the input,* Agg *function returns a single message m as the output.*

Agg function is also a part of the Asig.Ver algorithm that allows the batch verification of multiple messages. This function can be instantiated as modular multiplication in RSA [31] or vector addition in pqNTRUsign [25].

2.1 Lattice-Based Tools

We work over a polynomial ring $\mathcal{R}_q = \mathbb{Z}_q[x]/(x^N+1)$ for a prime q and a positive integer N [25]. For FAAS-NTRU, we model a hash function $H_N : \{0,1\}^* \to \mathbb{Z}_q^N$. This enables generating random elements $\mathbf{m_p} = (\mathbf{u_p}, \mathbf{v_p})$ with $\mathbf{u_p} \in \mathbb{Z}_p^{N_1}$ and $\mathbf{v_p} \in \mathbb{Z}_p^{N_2}$ for a prime p and $N = N_1 + N_2$.

NTRU Lattice: Following the work in [25], we work over a NTRU lattice as an $\mathcal{R}_q$ module of rank 2. We let $f(x), g(x), h(x) \in \mathcal{R}_q$ where $f(x)$ and $g(x)$ have small coefficients and $h(x) = p^{-1}g(x)f^{-1}(x)$.

The NTRU lattice associated with $\mathbf{h}$ is defined as $\mathcal{L} = \{(\hat{\mathbf{u}}, \hat{\mathbf{v}}) \in \mathcal{R}_q^2 : \hat{\mathbf{u}}\mathbf{h} = \hat{\mathbf{v}}\}$. A vector in NTRU lattice can be written as $\mathbf{v} = \langle \hat{\mathbf{s}}, \hat{\mathbf{t}} \rangle$ where $\hat{\mathbf{s}}, \hat{\mathbf{t}} \in \mathcal{R}_q$, following [25], we refer to $\hat{\mathbf{s}}$ as the s-side and $\hat{\mathbf{t}}$ as the t-side of the vector.

Definition 5. *An N-dimensional Gaussian function $\rho_{\tilde{\sigma},c} : \mathbb{R} \to (0,1])$ is defined as $\rho_{\tilde{\sigma},c}(x) \triangleq \exp(-\frac{\|x-c\|^2}{2\tilde{\sigma}^2})$. Given a lattice $\Lambda \subset \mathbb{R}^n$, the discrete Gaussian distribution over Λ is $D_{\Lambda,s,c}(\mathbf{x}) = \frac{\rho_{\tilde{\sigma},c}(\mathbf{x})}{\rho_{\tilde{\sigma},c}(\Lambda)}$ for all $\mathbf{x} \in \Lambda$.*

Hoffstein et al. uses a Bimodal Gaussian distribution $\chi_{\tilde{\sigma}}^N$ [15] with standard deviation $\tilde{\sigma}$ to sample an N-dimension random vector $\mathbf{r}$. Hoffstein et al. also uses rejection sampling to ensure that the signature components do not leak any information about the private keys by checking if its norm is in $(-\frac{q}{2} +$

Algorithm 1. pqNTRUsign Signature Generation [25]

$(\mathbf{v}') \leftarrow$ pqNTRUsign.Sig$(m, sk', \mathbf{h})$:

1: Compute $(\mathbf{u_p}, \mathbf{v_p}) = H_N(m\|\mathbf{h})$ and sample $\mathbf{r} \leftarrow \chi_{\tilde{\sigma}}^N$ and $b \xleftarrow{\$} \{0, 1\}$
2: Compute $\mathbf{u_1} \leftarrow \mathbf{pr} + \mathbf{u_p}$, $\mathbf{v_1} \leftarrow \mathbf{u_1 h} \mod q$ and $\mathbf{a} \leftarrow (\mathbf{v_p} - \mathbf{v_1})/\mathbf{g} \mod p$
3: if $\|\mathbf{af}\|_2 > \nu_s$ or $\|\mathbf{ag}\|_\infty > \nu_t$ then go to Step 1
4: $\mathbf{v}' = \mathbf{v_1} + (-1)^b \mathbf{ag}$
5: if $\|\mathbf{v}'\|_\infty > q/2 - B_t$ then go to Step 1
6: Calculate $\mathbf{b} = (\mathbf{r} + (-1)^b \mathbf{af})$ with probability $1/\big(M_s \exp\big(-\frac{\|\mathbf{af}\|}{2\tilde{\sigma}^2}\big)\cosh\big(\frac{\langle \mathbf{b},\mathbf{af}\rangle}{\tilde{\sigma}^2}\big)\big)$, else go to Step 1
7: Return $\mathbf{v}'$

Algorithm 2. SCRA - pqNTRUsign Instantiation

$(sk, PK) \leftarrow$ SCRA-NTRU.Kg(1^κ):

1: Generate secrets $\mathbf{f}, \mathbf{g} \in \mathcal{R}_q$ such that $h(x) = p^{-1}g(x)f^{-1}(x)$
2: If $\mathbf{f}$ and $\mathbf{g}$ are not invertible mod q, go to Step 1
3: $sk' \leftarrow (\mathbf{f}, \mathbf{g})$, $PK' \leftarrow \mathbf{h}$ and $P \xleftarrow{\$} \{0, 1\}^{l_0}$ and
4: Select integers (b, L) such that $b \cdot L = l_0$
5: $\tilde{m}_{i,j} \leftarrow (i\|j\|P)$, $\gamma_{i,j} \leftarrow$ pqNTRUsign.Sig$(\tilde{m}_{i,j}, sk', PK')$, $i = 1, \ldots, L$ and $j = 0, \ldots, 2^b - 1$
6: $sk \leftarrow (sk', \boldsymbol{\Gamma})$ and $PK \leftarrow (PK', P)$, where $\boldsymbol{\Gamma} \leftarrow \{\gamma_{i,j}\}_{i=1,j=0}^{L, 2^b-1}$

$\sigma \leftarrow$ SCRA-NTRU.Sig(m, sk):

1: $(M_1^*, \ldots M_L^*) \leftarrow H_0(m\|r)$ where $r \xleftarrow{\$} \{0, 1\}^\kappa$ and $M_i^* \in [0, 2^b - 1]$, $i = 1, \ldots, L$.
2: $\mathbf{s} \leftarrow \sum_{i=1}^{L} \gamma_{i, M_i^*}$ and $\sigma \leftarrow (r, \mathbf{s})$

$\{0, 1\} \leftarrow$ SCRA-NTRU.Ver(m, σ, PK):

1: $(M_1^*, \ldots M_L^*) \leftarrow H_0(m\|r)$
2: $\hat{\mathbf{u}} = \mathbf{sh}^{-1} \mod q$
3: if $\|\hat{\mathbf{u}}\|_\infty > \sqrt{(k+L)}\tau p \tilde{\sigma}$ then return 0
4: $(\mathbf{u_{p_i}}, \mathbf{v_{p_i}}) \leftarrow H_N(i\|M_i^*\|P\|\mathbf{h})$ where $i = 1, \ldots, L$
5: if $(\hat{\mathbf{u}}, \mathbf{s}) = \sum_{i=1}^{L}(\mathbf{u_{p_i}}, \mathbf{v_{p_i}})$ then return 1, else return 0

$\nu_y, \frac{q}{2} - \nu_y)$ for some public parameter ν where $y \in \{s\text{-side}, t\text{-side}\}$. This is done as in the Step 3 of Algorithm 1. We also note that $\tilde{\sigma}$ in Algorithm 1 is a Gaussian distribution parameter which ensures a bound on the value of the sampled vector's coordinates. In Step 6, $b \leftarrow \{0, 1\}$ is a random bit related to bimodal Gaussian distribution [15]. M_s as defined in [25], is the repetition rate which determines the rate of rejection.

3   On the Security of SCRA-NTRU

We first recall SCRA signature scheme and also present its lattice-based instantiation. We then describe the idea behind our attack, followed by its detailed description and implementation.

3.1   SCRA Signature Scheme

SCRA was proposed as a generic scheme that transforms a single-signer aggregate signature scheme into a fast signature scheme. Before we highlight the weakness that leads to our attack, we briefly recall the generic SCRA signature scheme below. For a detailed description, we refer the interested reader to [45].

Key Generation: A set of signatures are precomputed for each b-bit L fields of the hash output, where $l_0 = b \cdot L$, and l_0 is the bit length of the hash output. These signatures are stored in a precomputed table containing $2^b \cdot L$ signatures. This table and the public key of the underlying aggregate signature are the private and public keys, respectively.

Signature Generation: The message is hashed with a randomness, and for each of L fields of the hash output, their corresponding precomputed signatures (retrieved from the private key of the signer) are aggregated. The randomness is sent along with the aggregated signature to enable signature verification.

Signature Verification: Individual indexes are recovered and their batch verification is performed under the signer's public key.

SCRA Lattice-Based Instantiations: SCRA was instantiated with lattice-based aggregate signatures in [17]. Recently, Hoffstein et al. [25] proposed an NTRU-based signature scheme called pqNTRUsign which offers *provably secure* single-signer secure aggregation [25]. Therefore, we instantiate SCRA with the scheme in [25]. We present this instantiation in Algorithm 2 with a reference to the signature generation of pqNTRUsign in Algorithm 1. We remark that given the similarity of pqNTRUsign with the schemes used in the instantiations of SCRA (e.g., [17]), our attack can be directly applied to the lattice-based instantiations originally proposed in SCRA.

3.2   Our Attack

In generic SCRA, the signature generation algorithm releases an aggregation of a subset of the precomputed signature components without any masking. Furthermore, to enable signature verification, the message fields (i.e., indexes), dictating the selected precomputed components, are publicly released. These leakages can be observed in all instantiations of SCRA and they permit an adversary $\mathcal{A}$ to learn which private key components are aggregated to form the signature for a given message. In this paper, we leverage such leakages to mount a universal forgery attack on the lattice-based instantiations of SCRA.

Algorithm 3. Attack on SCRA Lattice-Based Instantiation

Setup:
1: $(sk, PK) \leftarrow$ SCRA-NTRU.Kg(1^κ) and $L_m \leftarrow \emptyset$

Learning:
2: Query $\sigma_i \leftarrow$ SCRA-NTRU.Sig(m_i, sk) and $L_m = L_m \cup m_i$ for $i = 1, \dots, (2^b - 1) \cdot L + 1$
3: Parse $(\mathbf{s}_i, r_i) \leftarrow \sigma_i$ and form $\mathbf{B} = [\mathbf{B}|\mathbf{s}_i]$ for $i = 1, \dots, (2^b - 1) \cdot L + 1$
4: $L_i = (M^*_{1,i}, \dots, M^*_{L,i}) \leftarrow H_0(m || r_i)$ for $i = 1, \dots, (2^b - 1) \cdot L + 1$
5: Set $\mathbf{A}$ s.t. $A[i, j] = 1$ if $j \in L_i$, for $i = 1, \dots, (2^b - 1) \cdot L + 1$, $j = 1, \dots, 2^b \cdot L$, otherwise, $A[i, j] = 0$.
6: $\mathbf{C} \leftarrow [\mathbf{A}|\mathbf{B}]$ and $\mathbf{C}' \leftarrow$ echelon$(\mathbf{C})$

Forgery:
7: $m' \xleftarrow{\$} \mathcal{M}$ where $m' \notin L_m$
8: $r' \xleftarrow{\$} \{0,1\}^\kappa$, and $L = (M^*_1, \dots M^*_L) \leftarrow H_0(m' || r')$.
9: Linearly combine rows of $\mathbf{C}'$ to generate a row, such that for $i = 1 \dots 2^b \cdot L$, $\mathbf{a}[i] = 1$ if $i \in L$ and 0 otherwise.
10: The right side of the new row $\mathbf{a}$ gives a valid signature over m'.

Attack Algorithm: Since one can compute the indexes used to form the signature, each signature leaks the aggregation of L private keys. For lattice-based instantiations, these are vector additions of individual private key components.

In our first attempt, our goal was to observe enough signatures to perform a key recovery attack. Since there are $2^b \cdot L$ private key components, we have $2^b \cdot L$ variables in our linear equations, and $\mathcal{A}$ needs the observe the same number of equations/signatures. However, to solve this equation system, each equation $\mathcal{A}$ observes must be *linearly independent*. However, due to the selection of private keys in signature generation (i.e., one private key component from each L fields), the adversary can only observe $(2^b - 1) \cdot L + 1$ linearly independent equations. While one can use methods such as least mean squares to estimate the private key components, it is not possible to fully recover them with this many equations. However, we observed that $(2^b - 1) \cdot L + 1$ linearly independent equations are enough for $\mathcal{A}$ to generate signatures on any message (i.e., universal forgery). The details of this attack are given in Algorithm 3, and further explained below.

The function $\mathbf{Y} \leftarrow$ echelon$(\mathbf{X})$ computes the row echelon form of matrix $\mathbf{X}$. Following the definition of *EU-CMA* in Definition 2, our attack takes place in two phases, namely the learning phase and the forgery phase.

In the attack, $\mathcal{A}$ first observes enough signatures to construct the linear equations. In Step 3, $\mathcal{A}$ parses signatures $(\mathbf{s}_i, r_i) \leftarrow \sigma_i$ and extracts $\mathbf{s}_i$'s to form the matrix $\mathbf{B}$. This matrix represents *the solutions of each linear equation, since they are derived by vector addition in SCRA.Sig*. In Step 4, $\mathcal{A}$ derives all the indexes from the messages as in the signature verification. Using these indexes, $\mathcal{A}$ forms a matrix $\mathbf{A}$, that represents which private key components are aggregated to derive the signature $\mathbf{s}_i$. $\mathcal{A}$ then concatenates these two matrices (as in Step 6) and calculates the *row echelon form* of the new matrix. This enables the adversary to easily form the linear combinations of these vectors to generate new signatures. Therefore, after this point, $\mathcal{A}$ selects *any message* that was not queried before, get the indexes with a simple hash function, and forms a new row from the row echelon matrix, based on the indexes of the target message. Since this matrix includes the signature components observed $(\mathbf{C} \leftarrow \mathbf{A}|\mathbf{B})$, the right side of this vector gives the signature for the selected message.

Attack Implementation: We have fully implemented our attack[2] and forged a signature over the message *"May the force be with you"*. We used C for the hash operations and computing SCRA signatures and Matlab for the matrix operations. Specifically, we used the predefined `rref` function in Matlab to generate the row echelon form of the matrix and then used this matrix to forge signatures. With the suggested parameters of SCRA ($b = 8, L = 32$), `rref` function of Matlab took around 2.5 h (executed only once). After that, each forgery only took a few milliseconds. Therefore, we were able to forge signatures on any message, by observing only 8161 signatures. Note that, although SCRA can be instantiated with different (b, L) parameters, since the storage overhead is $2^b \cdot L$, increasing parameters to make our attack impractical would also make the signature scheme impractical for the signer.

4   The Proposed Scheme

Main Idea: Following the works in [44,45], we capitalize on the observations that signature aggregation of some signature schemes is significantly faster than their signature generation. FAAS differs from the previous constructions in the way that messages and randomness are encoded and computed: (i) FAAS has significantly shorter private keys since we only rely on sampling L-out-of-2^b different combinations (as in [12]) rather than encoding the message as L b-bit structures as in SCRA. (ii) Most importantly, FAAS masks the aggregation of private key components (i.e., individual signatures) via an aggregate one-time masking technique (elaborated below) to address the vulnerability identified in SCRA [45] (see Sect. 3 for our attack).

Aggregate One-time Masking of Signatures: The security flaw in SCRA stems from disclosing the aggregation of private key components. To efficiently overcome this, we (deterministically) generate *random* message components u_i and their corresponding signatures β_i in the key generation phase (Step 3 in FAAS.Kg of Algorithm 4) and then aggregate a subset of them to generate a random message-signature pair (u, σ_U) as in Step 3–4 of FAAS.Sig (Algorithm 4). We then use this one-time randomness σ_U to hide the aggregation of private keys at Step 6 of FAAS.Sig. Although the aggregated message u is released with the signature, computing the individual message components or the selected indexes is as hard as breaking the underlying signature scheme.

---

[2] www.github.com/ozgurozmen/SCRA-NTRU_ATTACK.

Algorithm 4. Generic FAAS Scheme

$(sk, PK) \leftarrow$ FAAS.Kg(1^κ):

1: Select integers (k, t) such that $k \cdot |t| = l_2$ and (b, L) such that $b \cdot L = l_0$
2: $(sk', PK') \leftarrow$ ASig.Kg(1^κ) and $z \leftarrow \{0, 1\}^\kappa$
3: $u_i \leftarrow H_1(i||z)$ and $\beta_i \leftarrow$ ASig.Sig(u_i, sk') for $i = 0, \ldots, t-1$
4: Set precomputed signature table $B \leftarrow \{\beta_i\}_{i=0}^{t-1}$
5: $\gamma_i \leftarrow$ ASig.Sig(i, sk') for $i = 0, \ldots, 2^b - 1$
6: Set precomputed signature table $\Gamma \leftarrow \{\gamma_i\}_{i=0}^{2^b-1}$
7: $sk \leftarrow (z, B, \Gamma)$ and $PK \leftarrow PK'$

$\sigma \leftarrow$ FAAS.Sig(m, sk):

1: $(j_1, \ldots, j_k) \leftarrow H_2(m||z)$, where each $\{j_i\}_{i=1}^k$ is interpreted as a $|t|$-bit integer.
2: $u_{j_i} \leftarrow H_1(j_i||z)$ for $i = 1, \ldots, k$
3: $u \leftarrow Agg(u_{j_1}, \ldots, u_{j_k})$
4: $\sigma_U \leftarrow$ ASig.Agg($\beta_{j_1}, \ldots, \beta_{j_k}$)
5: $(j_1^*, \ldots, j_L^*) \leftarrow H_0(m||u)$, where each $\{j_i\}_{i=1}^L$ is interpreted as a b-bit integer.
6: $s \leftarrow$ ASig.Agg($\sigma_U, \gamma_{j_1^*}, \ldots, \gamma_{j_L^*}$) and set $\sigma \leftarrow (u, s)$

$\{0, 1\} \leftarrow$ FAAS.Ver(m, σ, PK):

1: $(j_1^*, \ldots, j_L^*) \leftarrow H_0(m||u)$
2: $\{0, 1\} \leftarrow$ ASig.Ver($\langle u, j_1^*, \ldots, j_L^* \rangle, s, PK'$)

4.1 Generic FAAS

Generic FAAS is presented in Algorithm 4, and is further elaborated as follows.

Key Generation: In Step 1–2, first, parameters (k, t) and (b, L) are generated. We then create the private/public key pair of the underlying aggregate signature and a random seed z, which are used to generate two precomputed signature tables: (i) In Step 3–4, we deterministically derive t random numbers u_i with a keyed hash and compute their corresponding individual signatures β_i to be stored in table B. (ii) In Step 5–6, we generate 2^b signatures, from which L of them will be selected to encode the message in signature generation (FAAS.Sig Step 5–6). Finally, the tables (B, Γ) and z constitute FAAS private key, while the public key of the underlying aggregate signature scheme is used as FAAS public key.

Signature Generation: In Step 1–2, we derive *the secret indexes* $(j_1, \ldots, j_k)$ from the message m and compute their corresponding random numbers $(u_{j_1}, \ldots, u_{j_k})$ via a keyed hash. In Step 3–4, we set u as the aggregation of the random $(u_{j_1}, \ldots, u_{j_k})$ and aggregate their corresponding signatures $(\beta_{j_1}, \ldots, \beta_{j_k})$ fetched from table B, as σ_U. In Step 5–6, we first encode the message and u to get indexes $(j_1^*, \ldots, j_L^*)$, and then mask the aggregation of $(\gamma_{j_1^*}, \ldots, \gamma_{j_1^*})$ with σ_U as $s \leftarrow$ ASig.Agg($\sigma_U, \gamma_{j_1^*}, \ldots, \gamma_{j_1^*}$). We set FAAS signature as $\sigma = (u, s)$.

Signature Verification: This algorithm checks if the aggregated random number u and indexes $(j_1^*, \ldots, j_L^*) \leftarrow H_0(m||u)$ are verified with s under PK'.

Algorithm 5. FAAS pqNTRUsign instantiation

$(sk, PK) \leftarrow$ FAAS-NTRU.Kg(1^κ):

1: Generate secrets $\mathbf{f}, \mathbf{g} \in \mathcal{R}_q$ such that $h(x) = p^{-1}g(x)f^{-1}(x)$
2: If $\mathbf{f}$ and $\mathbf{g}$ are not invertible mod q, go to Step 1
3: $sk' \leftarrow (\mathbf{f}, \mathbf{g})$, $PK' \leftarrow \mathbf{h}$ and $z \leftarrow \{0,1\}^\kappa$
4: Select integers (k, t, b, L) as in generic FAAS.Kg Step 1
5: $u_i \leftarrow H_1(i\|z)$, $\beta_i \leftarrow$ pqNTRUsign.Sig(u_i, sk', PK'), where $|u_i| = \kappa$ for $i = 0, \dots, t-1$
6: Set precomputed signature table $\mathbf{B} \leftarrow \{\beta_i\}_{i=0}^{t-1}$
7: $\gamma_i \leftarrow$ pqNTRUsign.Sig(i, sk'), for $i = 0, \dots, 2^b - 1$
8: Set precomputed signature table $\boldsymbol{\Gamma} \leftarrow \{\gamma_i\}_{i=0}^{2^b-1}$
9: $sk \leftarrow (z, \mathbf{B}, \boldsymbol{\Gamma})$ and $PK \leftarrow PK'$

$\sigma \leftarrow$ FAAS-NTRU.Sig(m, sk):

1: $(j_1, \dots, j_k) \leftarrow H_2(m\|z)$, where each $\{j_i\}_{i=1}^k$ is interpreted as a $|t|$-bit integer.
2: $u_{j_i} \leftarrow H_1(j_i\|z)$ and $(\mathbf{u_{p_{j_i}}}, \mathbf{v_{p_{j_i}}}) \leftarrow H_N(u_{j_i}\|h)$ where $i = 1, \dots, k$
3: $(\mathbf{u_p}, \mathbf{v_p}) \leftarrow \sum_{i=1}^k (\mathbf{u_{p_{j_i}}}, \mathbf{v_{p_{j_i}}})$, and $\sigma_U \leftarrow \sum_{i=1}^k \beta_i$
4: $(j_1^*, \dots, j_L^*) \leftarrow H_0(m\|\mathbf{u_p}\|\mathbf{v_p})$, where each $\{j_i\}_{i=1}^L$ is interpreted as a b-bit integer.
5: $\mathbf{s} \leftarrow \sigma_U + \sum_{i=1}^L \gamma_{j_i^*}$ and $\sigma \leftarrow (\mathbf{u_p}, \mathbf{v_p}, \mathbf{s})$

$\{0,1\} \leftarrow$ FAAS-NTRU.Ver(m, σ, PK):

1: $(j_1^*, \dots, j_L^*) \leftarrow H_0(m\|u)$
2: $\hat{\mathbf{u}} = \mathbf{s}h^{-1} \bmod \hat{q}$
3: **if** $\|\hat{\mathbf{u}}\|_\infty > \sqrt{(k+L)}\tau p\tilde{\sigma}$ **then** return 0
4: $(\mathbf{u_{p_i}}, \mathbf{v_{p_i}}) \leftarrow H_N(j_i^*\|\mathbf{h})$ where $i = 1, \dots, L$
5: **if** $(\hat{\mathbf{u}}, \mathbf{s}) = (\mathbf{u_p}, \mathbf{v_p}) + \sum_{i=1}^L (\mathbf{u_{p_i}}, \mathbf{v_{p_i}})$ **then** return 1, **else** return 0

Remark 1. It is essential to keep individual random messages and their indexes as secrets. We do this with an aggregation function $u \leftarrow Agg(u_{j_1^*}, \dots, u_{j_k^*})$ as in Step 4 for random message components. The aggregation function $Agg(.)$ is instantiated as modular multiplication and vector addition in Condensed RSA (C-RSA) [31] and pqNTRUSign [25], respectively. We derive indexes $(j_1, \dots, j_k)$, which select random numbers to be aggregated, via the private key z. Therefore, unlike public indexes $(j_1^*, \dots, j_L^*)$ that are used to encode the message, secret indexes $(j_1, \dots, j_k)$ are only known to the signer.

4.2 FAAS Instantiations

FAAS can be instantiated with any single-signer aggregate signature scheme. We propose two efficient instantiations of FAAS as below.

Lattice-Based Instantiation (FAAS-NTRU): Lattice-based signature schemes provide a viable post-quantum security promise [16]. Among the identified lattice-based signature schemes with secure aggregation [17,25], pqN-TRUsign [25] offers fast verification with a slow signature generation that

---

Algorithm 6. Instantiation of FAAS with $C\text{-}RSA$

$(sk, PK) \leftarrow$ FAAS-C-RSA.Kg(1^κ):

1: Generate two large primes (p, q) and $n \leftarrow p \cdot q$. Compute (e, d) such that $e \cdot d \equiv 1 \bmod \phi(n)$, where $\phi(n) \leftarrow (p - 1)(q - 1)$
2: $sk' \leftarrow (n, d)$, $PK' \leftarrow (n, e)$ and $z \leftarrow \{0, 1\}^\kappa$
3: Select integers (k, t, b, L) as in generic FAAS.Kg Step 1
4: $u_i \leftarrow H_1(i\|z)$ and $\beta_i \leftarrow u_i{}^d \bmod n$, where $|u_i| = |n|$ for $i = 0, \ldots, t - 1$
5: Set precomputed signature table $B \leftarrow \{\beta_i\}_{i=0}^{t-1}$
6: $\gamma_i \leftarrow H_F(i)^d \bmod n$, for $i = 0, \ldots, 2^b - 1$, where $H_F : \{0, 1\}^* \rightarrow Z_n^*$
7: Set precomputed signature table $\Gamma \leftarrow \{\gamma_i\}_{i=0}^{2^b - 1}$
8: $sk \leftarrow (z, B, \Gamma)$ and $PK \leftarrow PK'$

$\sigma \leftarrow$ FAAS-C-RSA.Sig(m, sk):

1: $(j_1, \ldots, j_k) \leftarrow H_2(m\|z)$, where each $\{j_i\}_{i=1}^k$ is interpreted as a $|t|$-bit integer.
2: $u_{j_i} \leftarrow H_1(j_i\|z)$ for $i = 1, \ldots, k$
3: $u \leftarrow \prod_{i=1}^k u_{j_i} \bmod n$ and $\sigma_U \leftarrow \prod_{i=1}^k \beta_{j_i} \bmod n$
4: $(j_1^*, \ldots, j_L^*) \leftarrow H_0(m\|u)$, where each $\{j_i\}_{i=1}^L$ is interpreted as a b-bit integer.
5: $s \leftarrow \sigma_U \cdot \prod_{i=1}^L \gamma_{j_i^*} \bmod n$ and set $\sigma \leftarrow (u, s)$

$\{0, 1\} \leftarrow$ FAAS-C-RSA.Ver(m, σ, PK):

1: $(j_1^*, \ldots, j_L^*) \leftarrow H_0(m\|u)$
2: **if** $s^e = u \cdot \prod_{i=1}^L H_F(j_i^*) \bmod n$ **then** return 1, **else** return 0

---

requires Gaussian sampling. Thus, FAAS-NTRU improves the security and signing efficiency of pqNTRUsign by eliminating the Gaussian sampling and rejection sampling from the online signature generation phase. The detailed description of FAAS-NTRU is presented in Algorithm 5, that refers to pqNTRUsign signature generation algorithm defined in Algorithm 1, to refrain from repetitions in the algorithm description. Notice that expensive calculations such as Gaussian sampling and polynomial multiplication are done in the key generation algorithm (once and offline). At the signing phase, only polynomial additions are performed.

RSA-Based Instantiation (FAAS-RSA): We instantiate FAAS with Condensed RSA (C-RSA) [31], which is secure under the RSA assumption in the ROM [7]. The signature generation of C-RSA requires an exponentiation over a large modulus, whereas its verification only requires an exponentiation over a small modulus (e.g., 65537). Therefore, FAAS-RSA, given in Algorithm 6, gains significant improvements over C-RSA in terms of signature generation.

5 Security Analysis

Theorem 1. $Adv_{FAAS,\mathcal{A}}^{EU\text{-}CMA}(t, q_S, q_h) \leq Adv_{Asig,\mathcal{B}}^{A\text{-}EU\text{-}CMA}(t', q_S', q_h')$ where $t' = O(t) + 2q_S(t_{RNG} + t_{Sig} + t_{Agg})$, $q_S' \geq 2q_S$ and $q_H = q_H'$.

Proof. Please refer to the appendix in the full version of the paper in [35].

5.1   Security and Performance of Online Operations

Side-channel attacks pose a serious threat to cryptographic implementations. Some critical operations that are prone to side-channel attacks are given below.

Gaussian Sampling: Lattice-based cryptography offers efficient solutions with post-quantum security promise. However, most of the efficient lattice-based signature schemes require a (high precision) sampling from a distribution, mostly a Gaussian, which not only degrades their performance on the signer's side but also is highly prone to side-channel attacks. For instance, BLISS [15], as one of the most efficient instances of such schemes, has been targeted with a number of side-channel attacks [18,22]. Secure implementation approaches might mitigate some of these side-channel attacks; however, they are deemed to be a highly challenging and error-prone task [16].

Rejection Sampling: This operation is required in lattice-based signatures to ensure signatures do not leak information about the private key. The number of rejections can significantly decrease the performance of a scheme. For instance, in pqNTRUsign [25], the probability that the signature lies in a desired range is only 6%. Aside from the performance burdens, an efficient variant of this algorithm is shown to be prone to side-channel attacks [18,22]. These attacks showed the vulnerability of the Bernoulli-based algorithm for rejection sampling in BLISS signature.

Exponentiation and PRNG: There has been many attacks on the efficient exponentiations and elliptic curve scalar multiplications [13,20,29]. While countermeasures were proposed in [37], similar to the blinding technique, they incur performance sacrifice. The security of PRNGs is highly dependent on the hardware. Although one can find secure PRNGs in well-developed CPUs, the PRNG implementations in low-end IoT processors are prone to attacks. Therefore, it is a desirable property for a signature scheme to be deterministic (i.e., do not require any fresh randomness in signature generation phase) [9].

FAAS instantiations do not require any of the above operations in their signing algorithm. Therefore, we believe FAAS instantiations can offer improved side-channel resiliency and easy implementation as compared to some of their underlying schemes.

6   Performance Evaluation and Comparison

We first give the analytical costs of FAAS instantiations and their counterparts in terms of computational overhead and key/signature sizes. We then outline our experimental setup, parameters and provide a detailed experimental comparison.

6.1 Analytical Performance Analysis

Key Generation: Key generation of FAAS instantiations require the computation of two tables, and therefore, it is more expensive than their base schemes. Specifically, to generate the two tables, $2^b + t$ signatures of the underlying aggregate signature schemes should be computed.

Signature Generation: FAAS signature generation requires signature aggregations $(k + L) \cdot \mathtt{ASig.Agg}(\cdot)$, message aggregations $k \cdot \mathtt{Agg}(\cdot)$ and hash calls $k \cdot H(\cdot)$.

pqNTRUsign [25] requires Gaussian sampling and polynomial multiplication to generate a signature. This is reduced to polynomial additions and mapping functions H_N in FAAS-NTRU. We present a variant of FAAS-NTRU (referred to as FAAS-NTRU$'$) to improve the efficiency of signature generation with the cost of an increased private key size. Our implementation (see Sect. 6.2) showed that the mapping function in FAAS-NTRU takes a significant time. FAAS-NTRU$'$ stores the results of the mappings as the private key to eliminate this overhead. Aside from the Gaussian sampling, pqNTRUsign also requires a rejection sampling to ensure that signatures do not leak information about the private key distribution. Due to rejection sampling, the signature generation of this scheme does not have a constant time, whereas FAAS instantiations do not require any rejection sampling during signature generation.

FAAS-RSA signing only requires a few hash calls and modular multiplications over n, while RSA takes an exponentiation with a large exponent d.

Signature Verification and Delay: FAAS instantiations add a slight overhead to the verification of their base schemes, which is equal to L message aggregations. However, since message aggregation is efficient, this only incurs a slight overhead, especially considering the overall gain in terms of the total delay due to the highly improved signature generation.

Storage and Transmission Overhead: FAAS requires two tables to be stored at the signer's side, with the size of $(2^b + t + 1) \cdot |\sigma_i| + \kappa$ where $\sigma_i \leftarrow \mathtt{ASig.Sig}(\cdot)$. Moreover, in addition to their base scheme, FAAS requires an aggregated randomness which makes the total signature size $|s| + |u|$. Note that, in FAAS-NTRU, the signature size changes from $|s|$ bits to $|v'|$ bits, since the 't-side' of the vector should be transmitted for aggregate verification in pqNTRUsign [25]. Therefore, the signature size of FAAS-NTRU increases slightly more. The public key size of FAAS instantiations is the same with that of their base signature schemes.

6.2 Performance Evaluation

Experimental Setup: We implemented FAAS instantiations on a laptop equipped with Intel i7 Skylake 2.6 GHz processor and 12 GB RAM. Our operating system was Ubuntu 16.04 with gcc version 5.4.0.

Software Libraries and Implementation: We developed FAAS instantiations[3] in C. We implemented FAAS-RSA with GMP due to its optimized modular

---

[3] www.github.com/ozgurozmen/FAAS.

arithmetic operations [21]. We used the open-source pqNTRUsign implementation available in NTRU open-source project [25] to develop FAAS-NTRU. We used Blake2 as our hash function (as in SPHINCS [8]), due to its high efficiency [6].

We ran the open-source implementations of our state-of-the-art counterparts in our experimental setup, to draw a fair comparison. We benchmarked the ECDSA in MIRACL library [40] and RSA in GMP library [21]. We benchmarked Ed25519 and SPHINCS using their Supercop implementations. Lastly, we used the open-source implementation of pqNTRUsign [25].

Parameters. We selected parameters to achieve $\kappa = 128$-bit security.

PQ Secure Schemes: We used the suggested parameters providing $\kappa \approx 128$-bit security for pqNTRUsign [25]. More specifically, $\tilde{\sigma} = 107$, $N = 512$, and $q = 2^{16} + 1$ and $d = 77$ to achieve $\kappa = 128$. For SPHINCS, we refer the reader for the suggested parameters to [8].

Traditional Schemes: We selected $|n| = 3072$ bit, $|e| = 17$ bit and $|d| \approx 3072$ bit for RSA-based schemes. We chose $|p'| = |q'| = 256$ bit for ECC-based schemes.

FAAS Parameters: FAAS parameters are selected as $(b, L) = (8, 32)$ and $(k, t) = (32, 256)$ for $l_0 = l_2 = 256$. The security of these parameters depend on how many different combinations one can derive with k-out-of-t precomputed components, that is $\binom{t}{k} = \binom{2^b}{L}$. With current parameters, there are 2^{141} different combinations that can be created. Another important aspect is to keep the indexes secret. As discussed in Sect. 4, this ensures that presented attack cannot be applied to FAAS. Since we are concatenating a secret (z) in the hash call (H_1), the indexes will remain as secret. On the other hand, one can attack H_0 and try to obtain an m^* such that $H_0(m||u)$ corresponds to the same indexes as $H_0(m^*||u)$. However, since u is a random value derived based on secret indexes, the attacker must conduct a *target collision attack* to find such m^*. Since, any permutation of the indexes would correspond to a collision on H_0, there are $k!$ different possible index permutations. Thus, the probability to find such an m^* is $\frac{L!}{2^{2^b}}$. With the current parameter selection, the probability for this is 2^{-138}. Since the underlying signature schemes' parameters are selected to provide $\kappa = 128$-bit security, all in all, FAAS instantiations offer $\kappa = 128$-bit security.

Experimental Comparison: Table 1 shows numerical evaluation and comparison of FAAS instantiations and their counterparts.

FAAS instantiations offer notably faster signing over their base schemes with a slightly slower verification. (i) FAAS-NTRU and FAAS-NTRU' improve pqNTRUsign [25] signature generation by 29.67× and 105.29×, respectively. (ii) For FAAS-RSA, signature generation is over 40× faster than traditional RSA.

However, FAAS instantiations require storing a private key up to 1 MB (Table 1). With their improved side-channel resiliency and fast signature generation, FAAS instantiations can be preferred for delay-aware applications where the signer can tolerate storing up to 1MB of private key. We observed that the signing cost of FAAS-NTRU was dominated by the mapping functions, which map messages to vectors. We also noticed that these vectors can be stored as a private key component, instead of being deterministically generated during signing. This resulted in a trade-off between the signing time and private key size, where signing speeds up 3.55× with a 2× increased private key size (Table 1).

Recall that, SCRA [45] does not use a masking strategy, and therefore, leaks its private key (as shown in Sect. 3). Since FAAS uses an efficient and constant-size aggregate masking strategy, its signature generation requires only twice as much signature aggregations and k message aggregations compared to insecure SCRA. This results in an approximately three times slower signature generation. The signature verification times of the both schemes are highly similar. Moreover, since FAAS relies on an efficient message encoding (see Sect. 4), the private key of FAAS is $L×$ smaller than that of SCRA. In practice, since L is selected as 32, this results in a significant improvement in terms of private key size. Therefore, FAAS addresses the flaws of SCRA with a small computation overhead and a more compact private key size.

7   Related Work

Online/offline signatures [19,33,39,44] offer fast signing since they precompute tokens for each message to be signed in the offline phase. In the online phase, these precomputed tokens are used to provide efficient signature generation. However, such methods incur linear storage with respect to the number of messages to be signed. Moreover, as tokens are depleted, they should be renewed that might introduce further overhead. Therefore, we believe they may not be practical for real-time networks that require continuous signature generation.

There are many schemes that leverage signature aggregation to ensure authentication and integrity in outsourced databases (e.g., [31,32,41]). In such applications, the signatures of a small set of messages with well-defined indexes (e.g., signatures belonging to some row elements in a database table) are aggregated to obtain compact signatures for the response of database queries [32]. Despite their merits, potential security issues that stem from the homomorphic properties of these signatures were pointed out [30,32]. Specifically, it has been shown that since aggregate signatures are mutable, one can create "new signatures" on data items that have not been explicitly queried by combining previously obtained aggregate signatures. To prevent this, immutable signatures (e.g., [30,32]) have been developed, which generally rely on one-time masking and/or sentinel signatures. Recently, signature schemes that depend on secure aggregation (e.g. RA [44] and SCRA [45]) have been proposed. However, as discussed, RA [44] is an online/offline signature with a dependency on predefined structures in messages. In this paper, we showed that an adversary can forge signatures on any message in SCRA by observing a small number of signatures.

8   Conclusion

We first presented an attack to SCRA signature scheme that can forge signatures over any message by observing only 8161 signatures. We fully implemented our attack and forged signatures in only a few milliseconds after a one-time 2.5-h preparation phase. We then proposed a new generic signature scheme (i.e., FAAS) that can transform any secure single-signer aggregate signature into a signer efficient signature scheme. We proposed two instantiations of FAAS called FAAS-RSA and FAAS-NTRU that can offer up to 42× and 105× faster signature generation as compared to their base signature schemes, respectively. Moreover, FAAS instantiations do not require some operations that are vulnerable to side-channel attacks, and therefore, they provide an improved side-channel resiliency, where FAAS-NTRU also provides a post-quantum promise.

Acknowledgments. We would like to thank Zhenfei Zhang and the anonymous reviewers for their insightful comments and suggestions. This work is supported by the Department of Energy Award DE-OE0000780 and NSF Award #1652389.

Appendix A   Security Definitions

Definition 6. *Aggregate Existential Unforgeability under Chosen Message Attack (A-EU-CMA) for a single user aggregate signature is as follows.*

$Exp_{Asig,\mathcal{A}}^{A\text{-}EU\text{-}CMA}(1^\kappa):$

$\quad L_m \leftarrow \emptyset \qquad\qquad\qquad\qquad\quad \left| \mathrm{SigA}_{sk}(\overrightarrow{m}) \right.$

$\quad (sk, PK) \leftarrow \mathrm{Asig.Kg}(1^\kappa) \qquad \left| \quad \gamma_i \leftarrow \mathrm{Asig.Sig}(m_i, sk) \text{ for } i = 1, \ldots, j \right.$

$\quad (\overrightarrow{m}^*, \sigma^*) \leftarrow \mathcal{A}^{\mathrm{SigA}_{sk}(\cdot),RO(\cdot)}(PK) \quad \left| \quad \sigma \leftarrow \mathrm{Asig.Agg}(\gamma_1, \ldots, \gamma_j) \right.$

$\qquad\qquad\qquad\qquad\qquad\qquad\qquad\quad \left| \quad L_m \leftarrow L_m \cup \overrightarrow{m} \right.$

We say $\mathcal{A}$ wins in time t, and after q_S and q_h queries if $((\mathrm{Asig.Ver}(\overrightarrow{m}^*, \sigma^*, PK) \wedge (\overrightarrow{m}^* \cap L_m = \emptyset))$. The   *A-EU-CMA*   advantage of $\mathcal{A}$ is defined as $Adv_{Asig,\mathcal{A}}^{A\text{-}EU\text{-}CMA}(t, q_S, q_h) = \Pr[Exp_{Asig,\mathcal{A}}^{A\text{-}EU\text{-}CMA} = 1].$

FAAS requires that the underlying aggregate signature achieves *k-element Aggregate Extraction (AE)* property [10,14], which is defined in the following.

Definition 7. *For a given aggregate signature* $s \leftarrow SigA_{sk}(\overrightarrow{m})$ *computed on* k *individual data items* $\overrightarrow{m} = (m_1, \ldots, m_k)$, *it is difficult to extract the individual signatures* $(\gamma_1, \ldots, \gamma_k)$ *of* $(m_1, \ldots, m_k)$ *provided that only* s *is known to the extractor.*

Initially, Boneh et al. [10] assumed that it is a hard problem to extract individual BLS signatures given an aggregate BLS signature, which was then proven to hold in [14] under the Computational Diffie-Hellmann assumption. We note that C-RSA [31] and pqNTRUsign [25], which are used in FAAS instantiations, achieve this property.

References

1. IEEE guide for wireless access in vehicular environments (wave) - architecture. IEEE Std 1609.0-2013, pp. 1–78, March 2014
2. D-Wave Systems Previews 2000-Qubit Quantum System (2016). https://www.dwavesys.com/press-releases/d-wave-systems-previews-2000-qubit-quantum-system
3. The cyber resilient energy delivery consortium (CREDC) (2018). https://cred-c.org/
4. Post-quantum cryptography standardization conference (2018). https://csrc.nist.gov/Projects/Post-Quantum-Cryptography
5. American Bankers Association: ANSI X9.62-1998: Public Key Cryptography for the Financial Services Industry: The Elliptic Curve Digital Signature Algorithm (ECDSA) (1999)
6. Aumasson, J.P., Henzen, L., Meier, W., Phan, R.C.W.: SHA-3 proposal blake. Submission to NIST (Round 3) (2010). http://131002.net/blake/blake.pdf
7. Bellare, M., Garay, J.A., Rabin, T.: Fast batch verification for modular exponentiation and digital signatures. In: Nyberg, K. (ed.) EUROCRYPT 1998. LNCS, vol. 1403, pp. 236–250. Springer, Heidelberg (1998). https://doi.org/10.1007/BFb0054130
8. Bernstein, D.J., et al.: SPHINCS: practical stateless hash-based signatures. In: Oswald, E., Fischlin, M. (eds.) EUROCRYPT 2015. LNCS, vol. 9056, pp. 368–397. Springer, Heidelberg (2015). https://doi.org/10.1007/978-3-662-46800-5_15
9. Bernstein, D., Duif, N., Lange, T., Schwabe, P., Yang, B.Y.: High-speed high-security signatures. J. Cryptogr. Eng. 2(2), 77–89 (2012)
10. Boneh, D., Gentry, C., Lynn, B., Shacham, H.: Aggregate and verifiably encrypted signatures from bilinear maps. In: Biham, E. (ed.) EUROCRYPT 2003. LNCS, vol. 2656, pp. 416–432. Springer, Heidelberg (2003). https://doi.org/10.1007/3-540-39200-9_26
11. Bos, J., et al.: Frodo: take off the ring! practical, quantum-secure key exchange from LWE. In: Proceedings of the 2016 ACM SIGSAC Conference on Computer and Communications Security, CCS 2016, pp. 1006–1018. ACM, New York (2016). https://doi.org/10.1145/2976749.2978425
12. Bos, J.N.E., Chaum, D.: Provably unforgeable signatures. In: Brickell, E.F. (ed.) CRYPTO 1992. LNCS, vol. 740, pp. 1–14. Springer, Heidelberg (1993). https://doi.org/10.1007/3-540-48071-4_1
13. Brier, É., Joye, M.: Weierstraß elliptic curves and side-channel attacks. In: Naccache, D., Paillier, P. (eds.) PKC 2002. LNCS, vol. 2274, pp. 335–345. Springer, Heidelberg (2002). https://doi.org/10.1007/3-540-45664-3_24
14. Coron, J.-S., Naccache, D.: Boneh et al.'s k-element aggregate extraction assumption is equivalent to the diffie-hellman assumption. In: Laih, C.-S. (ed.) ASIACRYPT 2003. LNCS, vol. 2894, pp. 392–397. Springer, Heidelberg (2003). https://doi.org/10.1007/978-3-540-40061-5_25
15. Ducas, L., Durmus, A., Lepoint, T., Lyubashevsky, V.: Lattice signatures and bimodal gaussians. In: Canetti, R., Garay, J.A. (eds.) CRYPTO 2013. LNCS, vol. 8042, pp. 40–56. Springer, Heidelberg (2013). https://doi.org/10.1007/978-3-642-40041-4_3
16. Ducas, L., Lepoint, T., Lyubashevsky, V., Schwabe, P., Seiler, G., Stehle, D.: Crystals - dilithium: digital signatures from module lattices. Cryptology ePrint Archive, Report 2017/633 (2017). https://eprint.iacr.org/2017/633

17. El Bansarkhani, R., Buchmann, J.: Towards lattice based aggregate signatures. In: Pointcheval, D., Vergnaud, D. (eds.) AFRICACRYPT 2014. LNCS, vol. 8469, pp. 336–355. Springer, Cham (2014). https://doi.org/10.1007/978-3-319-06734-6_21

18. Espitau, T., Fouque, P., Gérard, B., Tibouchi, M.: Side-channel attacks on BLISS lattice-based signatures: exploiting branch tracing against strongswan and electromagnetic emanations in microcontrollers. In: Proceedings of the 2017 ACM SIGSAC Conference on Computer and Communications Security, CCS 2017, pp. 1857–1874 (2017)

19. Even, S., Goldreich, O., Micali, S.: On-line/off-line digital signatures. In: Brassard, G. (ed.) CRYPTO 1989. LNCS, vol. 435, pp. 263–275. Springer, New York (1990). https://doi.org/10.1007/0-387-34805-0_24

20. Genkin, D., Valenta, L., Yarom, Y.: May the fourth be with you: a microarchitectural side channel attack on several real-world applications of curve25519. In: Proceedings of the 2017 ACM SIGSAC Conference on Computer and Communications Security, CCS 2017, pp. 845–858. ACM, New York (2017). https://doi.org/10.1145/3133956.3134029

21. Granlund, T.: GNU multiple precision arithmetic library 6.1.2. https://gmplib.org/

22. Groot Bruinderink, L., Hülsing, A., Lange, T., Yarom, Y.: Flush, gauss, and reload – a cache attack on the BLISS lattice-based signature scheme. In: Gierlichs, B., Poschmann, A.Y. (eds.) CHES 2016. LNCS, vol. 9813, pp. 323–345. Springer, Heidelberg (2016). https://doi.org/10.1007/978-3-662-53140-2_16

23. Gungor, V.C., et al.: Smart grid technologies: communication technologies and standards. IEEE Trans. Industr. Inf. **7**(4), 529–539 (2011)

24. Harding, J., et al.: Vehicle-to-Vehicle Communications: Readiness of V2V Technology for Application. U.S, Department of Transportation National Highway Traffic Safety Administration (NHTSA), August 2014

25. Hoffstein, J., Pipher, J., Whyte, W., Zhang, Z.: A signature scheme from learning with truncation. Cryptology ePrint Archive, Report 2017/995 (2017). https://eprint.iacr.org/2017/995

26. Kalach, K., Safavi-Naini, R.: An efficient post-quantum one-time signature scheme. In: Dunkelman, O., Keliher, L. (eds.) SAC 2015. LNCS, vol. 9566, pp. 331–351. Springer, Cham (2016). https://doi.org/10.1007/978-3-319-31301-6_20

27. Katz, J., Lindell, Y.: Introduction to Modern Cryptography (Chapman & Hall/CRC Cryptography and Network Security Series). Chapman & Hall/CRC (2007)

28. Kelly, J.: A preview of bristlecone, Google's new quantum processor (2018). https://ai.googleblog.com/2018/03/a-preview-of-bristlecone-googles-new.html

29. Kocher, P.C.: Timing attacks on implementations of diffie-hellman, RSA, DSS, and other systems. In: Koblitz, N. (ed.) CRYPTO 1996. LNCS, vol. 1109, pp. 104–113. Springer, Heidelberg (1996). https://doi.org/10.1007/3-540-68697-5_9

30. Ma, D., Tsudik, G.: A new approach to secure logging. ACM Trans. Storage (TOS) **5**(1), 1–21 (2009)

31. Mykletun, E., Narasimha, M., Tsudik, G.: Signature bouquets: immutability for aggregated/condensed signatures. In: Samarati, P., Ryan, P., Gollmann, D., Molva, R. (eds.) ESORICS 2004. LNCS, vol. 3193, pp. 160–176. Springer, Heidelberg (2004). https://doi.org/10.1007/978-3-540-30108-0_10

32. Mykletun, E., Tsudik, G.: Aggregation queries in the database-as-a-service model. In: Damiani, E., Liu, P. (eds.) DBSec 2006. LNCS, vol. 4127, pp. 89–103. Springer, Heidelberg (2006). https://doi.org/10.1007/11805588_7

33. Naccache, D., M'Raïhi, D., Vaudenay, S., Raphaeli, D.: Can D.S.A. be improved?—complexity trade-offs with the digital signature standard. In: De Santis, A. (ed.) EUROCRYPT 1994. LNCS, pp. 77–85. Springer, Heidelberg. https://doi.org/10.1007/BFb0053426

34. Nguyen, P.Q., Shparlinski, I.E.: The insecurity of the elliptic curve digital signature algorithm with partially known nonces. Des. Codes Crypt. **30**(2), 201–217 (2003)

35. Ozmen, M.O., Behnia, R., Yavuz, A.A.: Fast authentication from aggregate signatures with improved security. Cryptology ePrint Archive, Report 2018/1141 (2018). https://eprint.iacr.org/2018/1141

36. Rivest, R., Shamir, A., Adleman, L.: A method for obtaining digital signatures and public-key cryptosystems. Commun. ACM **21**(2), 120–126 (1978)

37. Schindler, W.: Exclusive exponent blinding may not suffice to prevent timing attacks on RSA. In: Güneysu, T., Handschuh, H. (eds.) CHES 2015. LNCS, vol. 9293, pp. 229–247. Springer, Heidelberg (2015). https://doi.org/10.1007/978-3-662-48324-4_12

38. Seo, S.H., Won, J., Bertino, E., Kang, Y., Choi, D.: A security framework for a drone delivery service. In: Proceedings of the 2nd Workshop on Micro Aerial Vehicle Networks, Systems, and Applications for Civilian Use, DroNet 2016, pp. 29–34. ACM (2016)

39. Shamir, A., Tauman, Y.: Improved online/offline signature schemes. In: Kilian, J. (ed.) CRYPTO 2001. LNCS, vol. 2139, pp. 355–367. Springer, Heidelberg (2001). https://doi.org/10.1007/3-540-44647-8_21

40. Shamus: Multiprecision integer and rational arithmetic C/C++ library (MIRACL). https://github.com/miracl/MIRACL. Accessed 30 Jan 2018

41. Song, W., Wang, B., Wang, Q., Peng, Z., Lou, W.: Tell me the truth: practically public authentication for outsourced databases with multi-user modification. Inf. Sci. **387**, 221–237 (2017)

42. Tesfay, T., Boudec, J.Y.L.: Experimental comparison of multicast authentication for wide area monitoring systems. IEEE Trans. Smart Grid **9**(5), 4394–4404 (2017)

43. Won, J., Seo, S.H., Bertino, E.: A secure communication protocol for drones and smart objects. In: Proceedings of the 10th ACM Symposium on Information, Computer and Communications Security, ASIA CCS 2015, pp. 249–260. ACM (2015)

44. Yavuz, A.A.: An efficient real-time broadcast authentication scheme for command and control messages. IEEE Trans. Inf. Forensics Secur. **9**(10), 1733–1742 (2014)

45. Yavuz, A.A., Mudgerikar, A., Singla, A., Papapanagiotou, I., Bertino, E.: Real-time digital signatures for time-critical networks. IEEE Trans. Inf. Forensics Secur. **12**(11), 2627–2639 (2017)

Author Index

Printed in the United States
By Bookmasters